Frommer's®

Cruises
& Ports of Call

7th Edition

by Heidi Sarna & Matt Hannafin

WILEY

Wiley Publishing, Inc.

Published by:

Wiley Publishing, Inc.

111 River St.
Hoboken, NJ 07030-5774

ISBN 978-0-470-63613-8 (paper); ISBN 978-0-470-91083-2 (ebk);
ISBN 978-0-470-40657-1 (ebk)

Editors: Shelley Bance and Naomi P. Kraus
Production Editor: Lindsay Conner
Cartographer: Anton Crane
Photo Editor: Richard Fox
Production by Wiley Indianapolis Composition Services

Front cover photo: *Carnival Glory* in the Havensight port in Charlotte Amalie, St. Thomas, U.S. Virgin Islands. © D. Hurst / Alamy Images
Back cover photo: © Fyne Photos / eStock Photo

For information on our other products and services or to obtain technical support, please contact our Customer Care Department within the U.S. at 877/762-2974, outside the U.S. at 317/572-3993 or fax 317/572-4002.

Wiley also publishes its books in a variety of electronic formats. Some content that appears in print may not be available in electronic formats.

Manufactured in the United States of America

5 4 3 2 1

Contents

Part 1: Planning, Booking & Preparing for Your Cruise

3 Things to Know Before You Go — 47

4 The Cruise Experience — 57

Part 2: The Cruise Lines & Their Ships

5 The Ratings & How to Read Them — 71

6 The Mainstream Lines — 84

Part 3: The Ports

10 The Caribbean, The Bahamas & the Panama Canal   490

11 Alaska & British Columbia   584

12 The Mexican Riviera & Baja   612

List of Maps

About the Authors

Matt Hannafin is a freelance writer, editor, and musician based physically in Portland, Oregon, and spiritually in his hometown of New York, New York. Author of *Frommer's Day by Day Vancouver & Whistler,* he also writes the daily Cruise Blog and biweekly travel features for Frommers.com and freelances for various newspapers, magazines, and websites. He's written on topics ranging from speed traps and genealogical travel to minimalist art and the 2008–09 world financial crisis; provided writing and editing services for congressional candidates, global consulting firms, and UN agencies; and performed concerts of Persian classical music, Ukrainian and Sephardic folk music, and contemporary improvisation for audiences of 2 to 2,000. He's married to do-gooder lawyer and pianist Rebecca, is the father of ridiculously handsome and talented 2-year-old Malcolm, is best friends with an Irish terrier named Rooster, and is also good buds with mother-and-son felines Musetta and Puccini.

Heidi Sarna is not a cat person, but loves dogs and people, especially her adorable twin sons and cute husband. She's a freelance writer who has sailed the oceans blue for more than a decade in ships of all sizes all over the world. Author of *Frommer's Day by Day Singapore,* and a contributor to several other guidebooks, she also writes regular travel columns for Frommers.com and *Porthole* magazine. She's written for countless magazines, newspapers, and websites on travel and cruising, but also covers diverse topics from relationships to charities, furniture, nutrition, and interesting people. Go figure.

Acknowledgments

A select group of travel writers and experts contributed to this book. Mike Driscoll, editor of the probing industry newsletter *Cruise Week,* provided insights into current booking trends. Industry expert and traveler extraordinaire Art Sbarsky updated our Cunard, MSC, Regent, Crystal, Princess, and Bermuda sections; guidebook guru/biologist Dr. Christina Colón updated our Caribbean coverage; and our Frommer's editor, Naomi Kraus, who updated our coverage of Orlando.

Matt would like to thank not only his wife and son, Rebecca and Malcolm, who keep him on his toes, but also the many travel writers, travel experts, cruise line PR people, and others who've helped us update this guide since 1997. He'd also like to give a big intercontinental hug to his co-author, Heidi, with whom he's collaborated on cruise books and stories for nearly a third of his life, and counting. Yo, Heidi: It's still fun!

Heidi totally agrees with Matt (hug hug) and also thanks her best shipmates, twin sons Kavi and Tejas, for being such good sailors over the past decade (they've racked up 23 cruises and counting), and toasts hubby Arun for going along with the crazy cruising life all these years.

How to Contact Us

In researching this book, we discovered many wonderful places—hotels, restaurants, shops, and more. We're sure you'll find others. Please tell us about them, so we can share the information with your fellow travelers in upcoming editions. If you were disappointed with a recommendation, we'd love to know that, too. Please write to:

Frommer's Cruises & Ports of Call, 7th Edition
Wiley Publishing, Inc. • 111 River St. • Hoboken, NJ 07030-5774
frommersfeedback@wiley.com

An Additional Note

Please be advised that travel information is subject to change at any time—and this is especially true of prices. We therefore suggest that you write or call ahead for confirmation when making your travel plans. The authors, editors, and publisher cannot be held responsible for the experiences of readers while traveling. Your safety is important to us, however, so we encourage you to stay alert and be aware of your surroundings. Keep a close eye on cameras, purses, and wallets, all favorite targets of thieves and pickpockets.

Travel Resources at Frommers.com

Frommer's travel resources don't end with this guide. **Frommers.com** has travel information on more than 4,000 destinations. We update features regularly, giving you access to the most current trip-planning information and the best airfare, lodging, and car-rental bargains. You can also listen to podcasts, connect with other Frommers.com members through our active-reader forums, share your travel photos, read blogs from guidebook editors and fellow travelers, and much more.

Cruising 2011–12: From Super-big to Super-small, More Options Than Ever

If you've picked up this book, it's unlikely we'll have to talk you into a cruise—that idea is probably already in your head. Besides, it's not our job to talk you into anything. We know some people just love traveling by ship and others just hate it. We also know that some people just *assume* they'd hate it, without having the full story.

The fact is, it's a pretty big story, and new chapters are being added every year. At one time, the typical cruise passenger profile was totally predictable: mostly older folks plus a smattering of honeymooners and party-makers who hit the high seas. They're all still there, but today, so is everyone else: young families, young professionals, middle-aged couples in Harley shirts, skinny-jeans teens, 50-something gym rats, multigenerational family groups, Democrats, Republicans, Rastafarians, eggheads, dingbats, and a corps of Canadians, Brits, and some "others" to help us all get along.

In a certain sense, it's an old-fashioned kind of vacation, a throwback to the classic European Grand Tours, with travelers hitting a region's high points in quick succession—bam, bam, bam—then getting back aboard ship to socialize with people who were strangers until circumstance pushed them together. In another sense, though, today's cruise lines could hardly be more modern, their newest ships packed with every possible widget to win new customers and turn them into regulars. We'll be honest, though. It's not that stuff that grabs us—not the surfing simulators or sushi bars, not the rock-climbing walls or theme-park water slides. It's simply being at sea on a ship. It's the teak decks, the thick steel hull, the smell of the sea, and that distant rumble of the engines way down below. It's the feeling that you've been untethered from the world, as you stand on deck at night, lean over the rail, and watch the waves break around your ship's bow as it heads . . . somewhere. The sea: It's a powerful thing.

Big & Brimming with Out-of-the-Box Features

Despite the ups and downs of the world economy and the fickle nature of cruise fares, cruise ship size is trending only one way: bigger. Sure there are niche lines with small ships (we love small ships!), but in terms of new construction, even the high-end luxury lines, à la Seabourn and Silversea, have been building new ships that are much larger than their older vessels. The *average* newly built vessel will carry literally twice the number of passengers as the average ship built a decade ago, but several of the biggest will be literally three times the size of a 1990s cruise ship, and more than five times the size of the legendary *Titanic*.

Along with their enormous size, cruise ships have features no one could have imagined just a decade or two ago. Certain standard amenities have come to be expected from cruise lines that now take great pleasure in one-upping each other. From theme-park-style twisty water slides, carousels, boxing rings, bowling alleys, water parks, movie-theater-size outdoor video screens and surfing simulators to real grass lawns and parks with live trees, the days of ships offering nothing more titillating than comfy deck chairs, shuffleboard, and bingo are long gone and downright quaint.

In 2010, six major new vessels launched, including the second of Royal Caribbean's enormous **Oasis** class, *Allure of the Seas,* a 220,000-ton, 5,400-passenger behemoth that's a full 25% larger than Royal's next largest Freedom class. *Allure* and sister ship *Oasis,* which debuted in 2009, boast distinct "neighborhoods" of public rooms and attractions with everything from an onboard carousel to a zipline and bona fide park with real trees and foliage.

Norwegian Cruise Line's **Norwegian Epic,** a 153,000-ton, 4,200-passenger monster, debuted in mid-2010 with cool features like hip studio-style budget cabins with mood lighting, a giant water slide, a bowling alley and rock-climbing wall, the cruise world's first ice bar, and an entertainment repertoire including the Blue Man Group's funky fusion of comedy, theatrics, and paint.

The third beauty in Celebrity's **Solstice** class, the 122,000-ton, 2,850-passenger **Celebrity Eclipse,** also debuted in 2010, with a starkly modern, supercool, downtown boutique-hotel ethos. Along with some of the most well-thought-out staterooms at sea, the three sisters boast entertainment innovations ranging from glass-blowing shows to a real half-acre outdoor lawn for picnics and lawn games.

At Holland America, the 2,044-passenger, 86,000-ton **Nieuw Amsterdam** launched in 2010 as the second vessel in the line's elegant **Signature** class, with spa staterooms, graceful poolside cabanas, and the new pan-Asian Tamarind and Italian Canaletto alternative restaurants.

The 92,000-ton, 2,092-passenger **Queen Elizabeth** debuted in 2010 as Cunard's newest tribute to traditional cruising, with her classic grandeur and Art Deco flavor setting the backdrop for modern entertainment, dining, and recreational diversions.

At the other end of the size spectrum, in 2010, ultraluxury line Seabourn introduced **Seabourn Sojourn,** a 32,000-ton, 450-passenger sister ship to 2009's *Seabourn Odyssey.* Though twice as big as the line's older vessels, *Sojourn* and *Odyssey* maintain Seabourn's intimate aesthetic and enormous passenger-space ratio.

At press time, 2011 was on target to welcome six more major ships, with the most notable being the new 128,000-ton, 2,500-passenger (double occupancy) **Disney Dream** in January, primed to impress with an exciting water flume ride, expanded kids' offerings, a new adult restaurant, and lots of high-tech fun. Carnival will roll out the 130,000-ton, 3,652-passenger **Carnival Magic,** sister to *Dream;* Costa will debut the 114,000-ton, 3,012-passenger **Costa Favolosa;** Celebrity will show off its fourth Solstice-class ship, the 122,000-ton, 2,850-passenger **Celebrity Silhouette;** Seabourn will launch the 32,000-ton, 450-passenger **Seabourn Quest;** and Oceania Cruises will introduce the 65,000-ton, 1,260-passenger **Marina.**

At this writing, another five megaships were in the pipeline for 2012, coming from Carnival, Costa, Disney, Celebrity, and Oceania cruise lines.

Check Out the Frommers.com Cruise Blog & Newsletter!

For daily coverage of the cruise world, with news, commentary, and occasional snark, click over to Matt Hannafin's **Frommers.com Cruise Blog,** at www.frommers.com/community/blogs/cruise.html. The **Frommer's Cruise Newsletter,** meanwhile, is authored by both Matt and co-writer Heidi Sarna, and delivers feature stories with an edge, ship reviews, and the best current cruise deals direct to your e-mail inbox twice a month, no charge. Just go to **www.frommers.com,** look for the "Preview Newsletters" box, select "Cruise News," and then subscribe. Newsletters are also available for deals and news about general travel, family travel, national parks, and winter sports.

Finding a Ship Is Easy, But Will You Click?

Comparing cruise ships and lines is like scanning an online dating site: "Attractive young cruise ship with nice body and good personality seeks friend for dating, possible relationship." The ship looks good, but we all know how photos can lie. Ditto for the descriptions.

Just like in dating, there are ships that you'll get along with and ships that you won't. It's all a matter of personality. Your dream ship is probably out there, somewhere—you just need to figure out what you want. If those huge Vegas-style floating resorts advertised on TV aren't your cup of tea, there are also quiet, refined ships where you're left to do your own thing, with outstanding service staff standing by in case you need anything—anything at all. Other ships are more like intimate B&Bs, where the vibe is casual, the cabins are cozy, and the focus is all on history, culture, and the outdoors. A few are honest-to-God sailing ships that afford nostalgic adventure.

Chances are, there's a ship out there with your name on it, and as your cruise matchmakers, we're here to help you wade through the different options and experiences and meet the cruise of your dreams. To do this, we've divided the cruise lines into three main categories—**mainstream lines** (chapter 6), **ultraluxury lines** (chapter 7), and **small ships, sailing ships, and adventure cruises** (chapter 8)—and developed a rating system that judges them only against other ships in the same category: megaship against megaship, luxe against luxe, small ship against small ship.

The Real Scoop on Cruise Prices

Cruise pricing has always been a game of smoke and mirrors. Once upon a time, cruise lines would print brochures listing wildly inflated rates—on the off-chance, we suppose, that somebody would be sucker enough to pay them. Today, though, the Internet has made comparison shopping so easy that nobody falls for that old game—not you, and certainly not us. For this book, we've actually partnered with the mega-agency Just Cruisin' Plus (www.justcruisinplus.com) to provide you with the actual prices consumers were paying at press time for cruises aboard all the ships reviewed in this book. In each review, you'll see a range of typical per diems that show you what people were paying, per day, for the most popular cabin categories, from the cheapest windowless staterooms up through standard balcony staterooms. Just multiply that figure by the number of days on the cruise you're contemplating, and you'll probably get a fairly good idea of what you'll have to pay.

The Best of Cruising

People are always asking us about our favorite ships, and we always say, "Well, what do you like to do when you're *not* on a ship?" In this section, we've broken out different kinds of cruises, interests, and destinations to help you find a ship that best matches what you're looking for. You'll find complete information on each pick in Part 2, "The Cruise Lines & Their Ships," and Part 3, "The Ports."

1 Best Mainstream Megaships

Mainstream megaships are the big boys of the industry, carrying the most passengers and providing the most diverse cruise experiences for those with many different tastes, from luxury-loving wine drinkers to the sports-bar-and-beer set.

- **Royal Caribbean's Oasis class:** The biggest cruise ships ever, by far, Royal Caribbean's 5,400-passenger *Oasis* and *Allure of the Seas* transcend their enormity through a layout that bunches experiences in "neighborhoods" around the vessel. It allows many of the ships' restaurants and entertainment spaces to be surprisingly intimate. The biggest innovation is the vessels' split superstructures, with the top eight decks bisected lengthwise by a long canyon that contains an open-air garden and a boardwalklike entertainment zone. Besides letting light and air into the center of the ship, this makes the whole vessel feel more 3-D—like you're walking around a city, not shuffling from one horizontal deck to another. See p. 246.

- **Celebrity's Solstice class:** Introduced in 2008, 2009, and 2010, the 122,00-ton 2,850-passenger *Celebrity Solstice, Equinox,* and *Eclipse* are the most flagrantly beautiful megaships ever built. Outside, their form is both massive and sleek, while inside a unifying high-end aesthetic ties the many moods and experiences of their public rooms into a satisfying whole. Mirroring all that's great about Celebrity's older Millennium-class and Century-class ships—their elegance, their remarkable modern art collections, and so on—the Solstice class also outshines them all, with a more contemporary look and a far wider range of dining and activity choices—and they have a half-acre of real grass lawn growing on the top deck, too. See p. 123.

- **NCL's Jewel class and *Norwegian Epic.*** Megaships for Generations X and Y, the 93,000-ton, 2,390-passenger siblings *Jewel, Pearl, Jade,* and *Gem* might be the most fun big ships at sea today. Designed with a mix of class and fantasy, they have a super-social atmosphere, creative decor, 10 different restaurants (from teppanyaki to Tex-Mex), and music and pop culture references tailored to a surprisingly youngish demographic—think 20-something to 50-something. They have the best beer-and-whiskey bars at sea and some of the best entertainment, and *Pearl* and *Gem* even have onboard bowling alleys. NCL's newest ship, the giant, 153,000-ton, 4,200-passenger **Norwegian Epic,** doesn't really make our list of favorite ships (see review), but two main things get her onto this list: (a) She's probably the best ship at sea today for entertainment, featuring performances by the Blue Man Group, several innovative shows, and fantastic music, and (b) she's also the best ship today for solo travelers, with 128 funky little studio cabins designed for one. See p. 197 and 204.

• **Princess's Diamond class and Grand class:** Princess's huge but cozy *Diamond Princess* and *Sapphire Princess* are its most beautiful ships to date, combining gorgeous exterior lines with wood-heavy, old-world

lounges and a great covered promenade that lets you stand right in the ship's prow. Big kudos also go to the line's very similar Grand-class ships, especially those launched since 2004: *Caribbean Princess, Crown Princess, Emerald Princess,* and *Ruby Princess.* See p. 231 and 227.

• **Cunard** *Queen Mary 2:* QM2 has her very own niche in the cruise world. She's the only true, super-tough ocean liner at sea, built for hard sailing on the Atlantic, not tooling around the Caribbean. Plus, with two classes on board—the hoity-toity luxury Grill Class with its special suites, restaurants, and lounges, and the normal areas for everybody else—this ship gives you a pretty good idea of life aboard the old-time ocean liners. And she even looks like one, at least on the inside. See p. 149.

2 Best Midsize Ships

Carrying between 500 and 1,800 passengers, today's midsize cruise ships are about the size all cruise ships were before the late 1980s, when Royal Caribbean's *Sovereign of the Seas* inaugurated the megaship era. Perfect for people who can do without the megaships' marquee attractions but want more variety than you get on a true small ship, the midsize vessels offer perhaps the most classic cruise experience out there. This list includes ships in both the luxury and mainstream segments of the cruise biz.

• **Silversea** *Silver Spirit:* The largest vessel ever from ultraluxe Silversea, the stylish, 540-passenger *Spirit* has one of the highest passenger-space ratios in the cruise biz, plus several features not available on the line's older vessels—including six restaurants and a huge, 8,300-square-foot spa. See p. 311.

• **Crystal** *Symphony* **and** *Serenity:* Carrying 922 to 1,070 passengers, these are some of the best midsize ships out there, big enough to provide lots of dining, entertainment, and fitness options, and small enough to bathe passengers in luxury. See p. 279 and 277.

• **Regent Seven Seas** *Navigator* **and** *Voyager:* Not only are cabins aboard these midsize 490- and 700-passenger, all-suite ships roomy, but their huge bathrooms are also fabulous. To top it off, food and service on both are among the very best at sea. See p. 288 and 286.

• **Holland America** *Volendam, Zaandam, Rotterdam,* **and** *Amsterdam:* The 1,316-passenger *Rotterdam* and 1,380-passenger *Amsterdam* are two of the classiest mainstream ships in the biz, modern throwbacks to the great ocean liners of the 1950s and 1960s. The 1,440-passenger twins *Volendam* and *Zaandam* merge Holland America's traditional elegance with a slightly younger (if still baby boomer) vibe. See p. 180 and 177.

• **Oceania *Regatta*, *Insignia*, and *Nautica*:** Built originally for defunct Renaissance Cruises, these 684-passenger gems are more boutique hotel than cruise ship, with a simultaneously stylish, casual, and comfortable vibe. See p. 218 and 219.

• **Azamara *Journey* and *Quest*:** Like Oceania's triplets (above), *Journey* and *Quest* are ex-Renaissance vessels enjoying a second life. Nearly identical in look and style to Oceania's ships, they're big enough to be interesting but small enough that you never feel overwhelmed by crowds or activities. See p. 90.

3 Best Luxury Cruises

Here's the very best for the cruise passenger who's used to traveling deluxe and doesn't mind paying for the privilege. These ships have the best cuisine, service, and accommodations at sea.

• **Silversea (whole fleet):** Silversea is the best of the highbrow small- and midsize-ship luxury lines, with its exquisite cuisine, roomy suites, over-the-top service, and niceties such as complimentary free-flowing champagne. See p. 307.

• **SeaDream Yacht Club (whole fleet):** What's not to love? The cool 110-passenger *SeaDream I* and *SeaDream II* are elegant but casual, and carry along jet skis, mountain bikes, and kayaks for jaunts around such ports as St. Barts and Jost Van Dyke. See p. 300.

• **Seabourn *Odyssey* and *Sojourn*:** Seabourn's first new ships in nearly 2 decades are simply stunning. Carrying 450 passengers apiece, they're much larger than the line's earlier ships but even more luxurious, with a very high passenger-space ratio and several wonderful restaurants. See p. 295.

4 Best Small-Ship Adventure Cruises

Among the small-ship lines, some afford great opportunities for real adventure, whether it's getting out into the wilderness, interacting with wind and wildlife, or just sailing to places you never imagined you'd go.

• **Lindblad Expeditions (Alaska and Baja):** Lindblad is the most adventure- and learning-oriented of the small-ship lines, with itineraries that stay far away from the big ports, concentrating instead on wilderness, wildlife, and history. Your time is spent learning about the outdoors from high-caliber expedition leaders and guest scientists, some of them aboard as part of Lindblad's alliance with the National Geographic Society. Try them in Alaska or in Mexico's Sea of Cortez for whale-watching and exploring starkly beautiful, uninhabited islands. See p. 340.

• **The Maine Windjammers (Maine Coast):** You get a fairly relaxing adventure on these owner-operated vessels, but it's an adventure nonetheless because these are real sailing ships, relying on the coastal winds for propulsion. If you like, you're welcome to learn the ropes of sailing while aboard, as you sail to small islands around Penobscot Bay. See p. 344.

5 The Most Romantic Cruises

Of course, all cruises are romantic when you consider the props they have to work with—the sea all around, moonlit nights on deck, cozy dining and cocktails, cozy cabins—but some are better than others for getting you in the mood.

- **Star Clippers (whole fleet, but especially *Royal Clipper*):** With the wind in your hair and sails fluttering overhead, the top decks of the tall-masted *Royal Clipper* provide a most romantic setting. Below decks, the comfy cabins, lounge, and dining room make these ships the most comfortable adventure on the sea. See p. 356.

- **Cunard *Queen Mary 2:*** Like real royalty, *QM2* was born with certain duties attendant to her station, and one of the biggest is to embody the romance of transatlantic travel and bring it into the new century. Take a stroll around that promenade deck, dine in that fabulous dining room, and thrill to be out in the middle of the ocean on nearly a billion dollars' worth of Atlantic thoroughbred. See p. 149.

- **SeaDream Yacht Club *SeaDream I* and *II:*** With comfy Balinese daybeds lining the teak decks, champagne flowing freely, and toys like MP3 players and high-powered binoculars at your fingertips, these 110-passenger playboy yachts spell romance for the spoiled sailing set. See p. 305.

- **Windstar Cruises (whole fleet):** Windstar's tall-masted *Wind Surf* and *Wind Spirit* offer a truly unique cruise experience, giving passengers the delicious illusion of adventure and the ever-pleasant reality of great cuisine, service, and itineraries. See p. 365.

- **Sea Cloud Cruises (whole fleet, but especially *Sea Cloud*):** Really, when it comes right down to it, what setting is more movie-star romantic than a zillionaire's sailing yacht? That's what you get with *Sea Cloud,* once owned by Edward F. Hutton and Marjorie Merriweather Post, with some cabins retaining their original grandeur. See p. 354.

6 Best Cruises for Families with Kids

The kids are boss—or so you'd think, the way cruise lines cater to families these days. All the lines mentioned here have supervised activities for three to five different age groups between ages 2 or 3 and 17, plus well-stocked playrooms, group and/or private babysitting, wading pools, kids' menus, and cabins that can accommodate three to five people. The section, "Cruises for Families," in chapter 1, has more info.

- **Disney Cruise Line:** This family magnet provides the most sophisticated, flexible, and well-thought-out kids' program in the cruise world, bar none. From the huge play areas and family-friendly cabins (the majority have two bathrooms—a sink and toilet in one and a shower/tub combo

and sink in the other) to the baby nursery and the ubiquitous Mickey, it all spells success. Plus, the 3- and 4-night cruises to The Bahamas aboard the *Disney Wonder* are marketed in tandem with stays at Walt Disney World, so you can have your ocean voyage and your Cinderella Castle, too. See p. 153.

- **Royal Caribbean:** The biggest-in-history *Oasis* and *Allure of the Seas* also have Royal Caribbean's biggest and best kids' facilities. They include a 28,700-square-foot Youth Zone full of themed play areas, learning spaces, an arcade, a workshop, a science lab, a theater, a huge teen center, and one of the cruise world's very few onboard nurseries, accepting infants and toddlers 6 months and older. All this (but especially the nursery) puts *Oasis* and *Allure* in the rarified company of the Disney ships when it comes to family travel. Families also can't really go wrong with Royal's Voyager- and Freedom-class ships, which are like theme parks at sea. See p. 239.

- **Carnival Cruise Lines:** While Carnival's loose-and-fun attitude appeals to adults, the line also does a particularly fine job with kids. Several hundred kids per cruise is pretty normal, with as many as 800 to 1,000 on Christmas and New Year's cruises. You'll find the biggest and brightest playrooms in the fleet on *Carnival Dream* and aboard the newer models in the line's Conquest class. The playrooms have computer stations, a climbing maze, a video wall showing movies and cartoons, arts and crafts, oodles of toys and games, plus great water slides out on the main pool deck. See p. 92.

- **Princess Cruises:** The Grand-, Diamond-, and Coral-class ships each have a spacious children's playroom, a sizable and fenced-in outside deck for toddlers, and another for older kids, with a wading pool. Teen centers have computers, video games, and a sound system, and the ones on the Grand-class ships even have teen hot tubs and private sunbathing decks. See p. 221.

- **Norwegian Cruise Line:** The kids' facilities on *Norwegian Dawn, Star,* and *Spirit* are fantastic, with a huge, brightly colored crafts/play area, a TV corner full of beanbag chairs, an enormous ball-jump/play-gym, a teen center, and a huge outdoor play/pool area. Parents will appreciate the many restaurant options on board, while kids can dine in tiny chairs at a kid-size buffet of their own. The new *Norwegian Epic* has the same kind of great playrooms, as well as three amazing water slides and a kids' splash park on the Pool Deck. *Norwegian Jewel, Pearl, Jade, Gem,* and *Pride of America* have good indoor playrooms, but their tiny outdoor play areas are a disappointment. See p. 192.

- **Cunard:** Though you'd hardly expect it from such a seriously prestigious line, the *QM2* has a great program and facilities for kids, starting at age 1. Aside from Disney's ships and Royal Caribbean's Oasis-class ships, no other vessel provides such extensive care for children so young. There's even a special daily children's teatime that's perfect as an early dinner, and the children's programming is free of charge until midnight daily. See p. 140.

7 Best Cruises for the Party Set

Whether you're traveling solo or with your significant other, these ships can keep you in a party mood all day and night.

- **Costa Cruises:** Imagine a Carnival ship hijacked by an Italian circus troupe: That's Costa. More than anything else, the line is known for its lineup of exuberant and often Italian-inspired games and other participatory activities, and it attracts passengers who love to jump in and have fun.

The words of the day are festive and international. See p. 134.

- **Carnival Cruise Lines:** Lots of men and women in their 20s, 30s, and 40s seek out Carnival's "Fun Ships" for their nutty decor and around-the-clock excitement. The Pool Deck is always bustling (especially on the short 3- and 4-nighters), with music playing so loudly you have to go back to your cabin to think, and the discos and nightspots hop until the early morning hours. See p. 92.

- **Royal Caribbean:** This line draws a good cross-section of men and women from all walks of life. As with Carnival, a decent number of passengers are singles in their 20s, 30s, and 40s, especially on the short 3- and 4-night weekend cruises. For an exciting Saturday-night-out-on-the-town barhopping kind of thing, the Oasis-, Freedom-, and Voyager-class ships feature multideck, boulevard-like indoor promenades lined with bars, restaurants, shops, and entertainment outlets. See p. 239.

- **Norwegian Cruise Line:** At some point, NCL just decided to go with "sexy" as a leitmotif for at least some of its onboard spaces—most particularly the Bliss Ultra Lounge on *Norwegian Pearl* and *Norwegian Gem.* Decorated with a kind of fashion-world-meets-bordello ambience, the room's softly lit nooks are separated by thick red-velvet curtains and outfitted with large, pillow-strewn daybeds. And for a retro-hip touch, there are also four 10-pin, Day-Glo bowling lanes. That's an example of the onboard vibe NCL has chosen of late—hip, young, and definitely not your grandma's cruise. The new *Norwegian Epic* takes the idea even further, though many of the young and hip onboard will also have their kids with them. See p. 192.

8 Best Onboard Dining

Here's where you'll find the finest restaurants afloat, with food rivaling that in the world's major cities.

- **Silversea Cruises:** The candlelit La Terrazza restaurant is home for some of the best Italian cuisine at sea. Excellent wines accompany dinner and are included in the cruise rates. A second alternative eatery pairs fine wines with a multicourse tasting menu based on cuisine in the sailing region. See p. 308.

- **Crystal Cruises:** While all the food on Crystal's ships is first-class, their sleek, reservations-only Asian specialty restaurants overseen by master chef Nobuyuki "Nobu" Matsuhisa are the best at sea. An Asian-themed buffet lunch, served at least once per cruise, gives passengers an awesome spread, from jumbo shrimp to chicken and beef satays to stir-fry dishes. See p. 273.

- **Regent Seven Seas Cruises:** The award-winning chefs aboard this line's ships produce artful culinary presentations that compare favorably to those of New York's or San Francisco's top restaurants, and the waiters are some of the industry's best. See p. 284.

- **Seabourn Cruise Line:** There's nothing quite like dining at Restaurant 2, which offers five- to six-course tasting menus with fine wine pairings, for only about 70 guests a night. Aboard *Pride, Legend,* and *Spirit,* the restaurant is an evening re-use of the daytime cafe, but aboard the newer *Odyssey* and *Sojourn,* it has a stylish space all its own. See p. 292.

- **Celebrity Cruise Line:** It doesn't get much better than the alternative restaurants on the Millennium-class ships, all of them designed to mimic dining experiences aboard the golden-age ocean liners of yesteryear. *Millennium's* Olympic restaurant, for instance, boasts hand-carved French walnut wood paneling from White Star Line's 1911 *Olympic,* sister ship to *Titanic.* A highly trained staff dotes on diners with table-side cooking, musicians play elegant period pieces, and the entire decadent experience takes about 3 hours. See p. 119.

- **Oceania Cruises:** Oceania's dining experience is near the top in the mainstream category, with menus created by renowned chef Jacques Pepin and passengers able to choose between four different restaurants, all of them excellent. Service is doting and fine-tuned, even at the casual semibuffet dinner on an outdoor terrace—an elegant and totally romantic spot at sunset. See p. 215.

- **Norwegian Cruise Line:** NCL gets onto this list by sheer weight of numbers. The line's megaships each have between 8 and 20 different dining spots, including multiple main dining rooms, many specialty restaurants, teppanyaki rooms, and casual eateries. While the fare in the main dining rooms is average, it's quite good in some of the alternative places, including the sushi bar and the elegant French/Continental Le Bistro. See p. 193.

9 Best Onboard Spas

One company, Steiner Leisure, runs the vast majority of cruise ship spas, but facilities vary.

- **Cunard:** *QM2*'s two-story, 20,000-square-foot spa was designed and is operated by Canyon Ranch, one of the most famous spas in North America. Done up in a vaguely Art Deco and nautical motif, the place looks as good as it feels. More than 50 therapists dole out the latest treatments, and you can finish off your spa time with a dip in the ultrarelaxing aquatherapy pool. See p. 144.

- **Celebrity Cruises:** Celebrity's Solstice- and Millennium-class ships are at the top of the mainstream spa heap. Their roomy and attractive AquaSpas combine a huge repertoire of the latest wraps, packs, soaks, and massages with striking aesthetics inspired by Japanese gardens and bathhouses and Moorish and Turkish spas. Facilities include saunas, mud baths, massage rooms, Turkish baths, and thalassotherapy pools (a sort of giant New Age hot tub). See p. 121.

- **Royal Caribbean:** The two-level spa complexes aboard the line's Oasis-, Voyager-, and Freedom-class ships are among the largest and best equipped out there. A peaceful waiting area has New Age tropical bird-song music piped in. *Ahhhh,* relaxation—until you get your bill. The Radiance-class ships and especially the Oasis-class ships have huge, relaxing solariums. See p. 243.

- **Regent Seven Seas:** Regent's spas are some of the few not run by the ubiquitous Steiner. Instead, the French spa company Carita imports its staff and hairdressers from Parisian salons, and offers company specialties such as the Rénovateur exfoliating process, as well as such cruise spa standards as hydrotherapy, reflexology, aromatherapy, body wraps, facials, manicures/pedicures, and anti-stress, therapeutic, and hot-rock massages. See p. 285.

- **Windstar Cruises:** The intimate, 308-passenger *Wind Surf* has extensive spa facilities for a ship her size, with prebookable spa packages combining six or more treatments tailored to both men and women. See p. 371.

10 Best Onboard Fitness & Sports Facilities

Gone are the days when no one did anything more active at sea than play shuffleboard and perambulate the deck. In fact, we've heard of people who actually *lost* weight on their cruise by taking advantage of all the activity options. Here are some of the best.

- **Best Cruises for Onboard Sports:** Royal Caribbean wins hands down. Its five Voyager-class ships have huge gyms, full-size basketball courts, rock-climbing walls, miniature golf courses, in-line skating tracks, and ice-skating rinks. Their larger Freedom-class sisters go them one better by adding a surfing simulator, and the new *Oasis* and *Allure of the Seas* offer even more of all that, plus a zipline ride, a dedicated sports pool, and the longest jogging track at sea: nearly ½ mile! See p. 243.

- **Best Onboard Gyms:** The best gyms at sea are aboard Royal Caribbean's Oasis- and Freedom-class ships: huge spaces that include a Pilates studio and a full-size boxing ring, with boxing training available throughout the cruise. The Oasis ships also have a Kinesis wall (a system of cantilevered pulleys and weights that, in the right hands, can provide a total body workout). Gyms aboard Royal's Voyager-class ships are pretty spiffy, too, as are

those aboard Carnival's Destiny-class ships; NCL's *Pearl, Gem, Jewel,* and *Jade;* and the majority of Holland America's ships, sans the old Statendam class. See p. 252, 256, 260, 113, 208, and 167.

- **Best Golf Cruises:** While practically all the major cruise lines offer golf excursions and some level of golf instruction (usually at an outdoor driving net), several lines go the extra mile. Carnival, Princess, and Silversea all have programs created by Florida's Elite Golf Cruises, which provide comprehensive golf-cruise vacations, with onboard instruction, high-tech computer simulators, and golf excursions to major courses. See p. 97, 224, and 310.

- **Best Snorkeling and Scuba Cruises:** In the Caribbean, islands with particularly good waters for snorkeling and diving include Bonaire, Grand Cayman, Curaçao, and the U.S. Virgin Islands (at Buck Island Reef). In Central America, the waters off Belize (especially its famous Blue Hole) and Honduras's Roatan Island have great waters, and Hawaii is known as one of the best dive destinations in the world. See chapters 10 and 14 for more information on these destinations.

Part 1

Planning, Booking & Preparing for Your Cruise

With advice on choosing and booking your ideal cruise and tips on getting ready for the cruise experience.

1

Choosing Your Ideal Cruise

The common wisdom says that all cruises are the same: big, flashy ships carrying old, overfed passengers to touristy ports, then setting them free to shop. Like all clichés, this one has a grain (or maybe a boulder) of truth, but it's hardly the whole story. For that reason, we prefer to call what we write about "travel by ship" rather than "cruising"—a more comprehensive description for a travel segment that gets increasingly diverse almost every year. Sure, you can still do the standard Caribbean cruise on a big white megaship, but consider this: From a variety of U.S. ports, you can also sail a small ship to visit the reefs and indigenous cultures of Central America; take a floating boutique hotel to little yachting islands in the Caribbean; bop from port to port in Hawaii; take an expedition from Alaska to Siberia; take the *Queen Mary 2* across the pond to England; sail a century-old schooner off the Maine coast; or take a small ship along one of America's great rivers. Specialized cruises are also an option, geared to activities like kayaking and hiking, or interests such as fine food and wine, photography, history, art, and other themes. In this chapter, we'll introduce you to the lot of 'em.

1 Cruising from the U.S. & Canada: The Sailing Regions

Whether because of convenience or an aversion to flying (that is, the cost of flying or the fear of it), the idea of cruising from a port within driving distance holds a lot of appeal for a lot of folks. And anytime a lot of folks want to do something, you can be sure the cruise lines will be right there, ready to hand them an umbrella drink. Today, you can cruise to the Caribbean from close-in ports like Miami or more distant ones like New York, New Orleans, Charleston, and Houston. You can visit Bermuda on ships that depart from Boston, New York, and Baltimore. Alaska, western Mexico, and Hawaii are now accessible from half a dozen embarkation ports along the West Coast of the U.S. and Canada. With all of these choices, there's a good chance you can drive right up to the gangway. In this section, we'll introduce all the regions (detailed in chapters 10 through 16) to which you can cruise from 19 U.S. and Canadian home ports (all of which are discussed in chapter 9).

The Caribbean/The Bahamas/Central America

When most of us think of a cruise, we think of the islands. We imagine pulling up in our big white ship to a patch of sand and palm-tree paradise, a steel band serenading us as we step into the warm sun and stroll down the gangway in our shorts and flip-flops. The good news is that this image is a pretty accurate depiction of many islands in the Caribbean and The Bahamas (a group of islands that lie outside the Caribbean basin), as well as some coastal ports in Mexico and Central America. Sure, some are jampacked with cruise ship passengers, and many are pretty weak in the palm-tree department; however, you're guaranteed nearly **constant sunshine** and plenty of beaches. On some you'll find lush rainforests, volcanic peaks, Maya ruins, winding mountain roads, and beautiful tropical flowers. And all of them have **great beaches** and that laid-back, don't-hurry-me seaside pace.

Most Caribbean cruises are a week long, though you'll also find sailings as short as 5 nights and as long as 14 nights. Cruises that visit The Bahamas exclusively are usually 3 or 4 nights, though many longer Caribbean cruises also include a stop in Nassau or one of the cruise lines' **private Bahamian islands.** On Caribbean cruises, itineraries usually stick to one region, either the **eastern Caribbean** (typically calling on some combination of the U.S. Virgin Islands, Puerto Rico, St. Martin, and The Bahamas), the **western Caribbean** (usually Grand Cayman, Jamaica, Key West, Cozumel or one of the other Mexican ports, and sometimes ports in Belize or Honduras), or the **southern Caribbean** (less defined, but often departing from San Juan and including Aruba, Bonaire, Curaçao, Barbados, St. Lucia, Antigua, and/or Grenada). Small-ship cruises frequently visit the less developed islands, mostly in the eastern and southern Caribbean, including the beautiful British Virgin Islands and ports such as St. Barts, Dominica, Nevis, and the tiny islands of the Grenadines. **Season:** Year-round, with the greatest number of ships cruising between October and April.

The Panama Canal

Imagine the particularly 19th-century kind of hubris it took to say, "Let's dig a huge canal all the way across a country, linking two oceans." Imagine, too, the thousands of workers who pulled it off. That's on the minds of many people today as they sail through the Panama Canal, one of the greatest engineering achievements of all time. Many ships offer only two Panama Canal cruises annually, when repositioning between their summer season in Alaska and the fall/winter season in the Caribbean. However, many cruise lines also include **partial Canal crossings** as part of extended western Caribbean itineraries from Florida, sailing through the Canal's locks westbound to Gatun Lake, docking for a day of excursions that explore the Canal's history and Central America's rich culture, and then sailing back out in the evening. Others do **full crossings,** generally sailing between Miami or Fort Lauderdale and a port in California or the Mexican Riviera. The big draw of both full and partial crossings is the pure kick of sailing through the Canal, whose walls pinch today's megaships so tightly that there may be only a few feet of clearance on either side. The Canal's width and the length of its locks are so much on shipbuilders' minds that they coined the term *panamax* to describe the largest ships that are able to transit its length—as well as *post-panamax* to describe those that can't. Those distinctions will soon be changing, though, because in September 2007 Panama began digging a new, 60% wider channel to parallel the existing canal along its narrowest sections, thus allowing transit by larger ships. The larger channel is scheduled to be completed sometime around 2014. **Season:** Roughly November through April.

Alaska & British Columbia

Alaska is America's frontier, a land of mountains, forests, and tundra just remote enough and harsh enough that it remains mythic, even if some of its "frontier" towns have been infiltrated by Starbucks. The main draws here are all things grand: huge glaciers flowing down from the mountains, enormous humpback whales leaping from the sea, eagles soaring overhead, and forests that seem to go on forever. Alaska Native culture figures in, too, with the Tlingit, Haida, and Tsimshian tribes all holding a considerable place in everyday life, from the arts to the business world. Most cruises concentrate on the **Southeast Alaska panhandle** (the ancestral home of those three tribes), which stretches from Ketchikan in the south to Yakutat in the north, with British Columbia to the east and the vast reaches of interior Alaska and Canada's Yukon Territory to the north. Typical cruises sail either round-trip from Seattle or the nearby Canadian port of Vancouver, or north- or southbound between Vancouver and one of Anchorage's two main port towns, Seward and Whittier. Both options concentrate on ports and natural areas along the Southeast's **Inside Passage,** the intricate web of waterways that link the region's thousands of forested islands. Highlights of most itineraries include glaciers (those in famous Glacier Bay and/or several others), the old prospector town of Skagway, state capital Juneau, and boardwalked Ketchikan in the south. Cruises between Vancouver and Anchorage may also visit natural areas along the **Gulf of Alaska,** such as College Fjord and Hubbard Glacier. Small-ship cruises frequently visit much smaller towns and wilderness areas on the Inside Passage. Some avoid civilization almost entirely, sticking to wilderness areas for the entire voyage. **Season:** Roughly mid-May through mid-September, although some smaller ships start up in late April.

The Mexican Riviera & Baja

The so-called Mexican Riviera is the West Coast's version of the Caribbean: a string of sunny ports within proximate sailing distance of San Diego, Los Angeles, and San Francisco. The first stop geographically is **Cabo San Lucas,** a party-oriented town at the southern tip of the Baja Peninsula, with the Pacific Ocean on one side and the Sea of Cortés on the other. Think beaches, beer, and bikinis, with thatched palapa bars providing some regional character. From there, cruises head southeast to such ports as **Puerto Vallarta, Mazatlán, Acapulco,** and **Ixtapa/Zihuatanejo,** famed for their white-sand beaches, watersports, deep-sea fishing, and golf, with some history thrown in for good measure. Hernán Cortés blew through the region in the 1520s looking for treasure, and Hollywood did the same in the 1950s and 1960s, mining the area both for locations and off-camera relaxation. Small-ship lines tend to stick to **Baja and the Sea of Cortés,** concentrating on the peninsula's small towns, natural areas, and remarkable whale-watching. These cruises typically sail from Cabo San Lucas or the state capital, La Paz. **Season:** The heaviest traffic is October through April, though some ships sail year-round—especially short 3- and 4-night cruises that stop in Cabo San Lucas or Ensenada, just south of the U.S./Mexico border. Small ships typically cruise Baja in the winter months only.

Bermuda

Perhaps the one place in the world where you'll have a chance to see hundreds of British men's knees, Bermuda is a beautiful island chain known for its powdery pink-sand beaches (a mix of shells and coral pulverized over the eons), its golf courses, and its sane and friendly manner. The locals really do wear brightly colored Bermuda shorts with jackets, ties, and knee-highs, but don't feel obligated to join them. The largest ships dock in the west end at the **Royal Naval Dockyard,** while some smaller vessels call at **Hamilton** (the capital city) and **St. George's** (Bermuda's quaint former capital). Ships pull alongside piers at all three places, and it only takes minutes to walk into town. There's plenty to do, too, from shopping in Hamilton for English wool and Irish linens to checking out the many historical sites, which range from the 300-year-old St. Peter's Church to the impressive nautical exhibits at the Dockyard's Maritime Museum. Most people, though, head for Bermuda's many dreamy beaches, which are easily accessible by bus, taxi, or rented motor scooter. To keep things from getting too chaotic, Bermuda has always kept tight control over the number and size of ships allowed to dock in the country, but a new deal that took effect in 2009 now allows megaships to visit the island regularly, typically from New York and Boston, though ships sail occasionally too from Baltimore, Norfolk, and the Florida ports. **Season:** Late April through early October.

Hawaii

If a place can simultaneously be the number-one honeymoon destination in America *and* one of the few places to which the Brady Bunch schlepped Alice and the kids, it must have something going for it, right? Think gorgeousness, with an almost embarrassing richness of stunning beaches, hula girls, and hunky Polynesian men—plus perfect weather almost all the time, so both locals and visitors stay in a friendly, mellow mood. Learn to surf, go to a luau, snooze on the sand, enjoy the local coffee, or check out the native Hawaiian culture, of which the locals are fiercely proud. The past survives alongside the modern world in a vibrant arts scene, from traditional Polynesian dance and music to painting, sculpture, and crafts. Each island is different, whether it's all about fuming volcanoes or lush jungles and tropical flowers, but crashing surf and serene beaches are everywhere. The four main port calls are to **Oahu,** with its famous Waikiki beach; **Maui,** home of historic Lahaina town; the **Big Island,** where the state's famous volcanoes reside (including Mauna Kea and the still-active Kilauea); and **Kauai,** the most natural and undeveloped of the four. **Season:** Norwegian Cruise Line offers year-round inter-island cruises aboard *Pride of America.* Other lines typically visit the islands in April, May, September, and October, on their way between seasons in Alaska and the Caribbean.

New England & Eastern Canada

Lobster pots, Victorian mansions, lighthouses on windswept bluffs, and whales and fishermen out on the cold, choppy water—where else but New England, right? And what a place to visit by boat: In sailing-ship days, New England was the undisputed capital of U.S. shipbuilding, and the nearby Canadian provinces are known as the Maritimes. This is a seriously coastal place.

Both America and Canada were born in these parts, so you'll be in for lots of **historical sites** along the way, from Boston's Paul Revere House to Halifax, which received (and in many cases buried) victims of the *Titanic* disaster in 1912. Itineraries may include passing through **Nantucket Sound,** around **Cape Cod,** and into the **Bay of Fundy** or **Gulf of St. Lawrence.** Some ships traverse the St. Lawrence Seaway or the smaller Saguenay River. Big 2,000-passenger-plus ships cruise here, as well as much smaller vessels carrying 100 passengers or less. Most sail round-trip from New York or Boston, or one-way between those cities and Montréal. **Season:** The classic time to cruise here is in autumn (Sept–Oct), when a brilliant sea of **fall foliage** blankets the region, but cruise lines also run 4- to 12-night trips in spring and summer.

U.S. River Cruises

So who needs the ocean? If your interests run toward history, nature, and U.S. regional culture, a river cruise is a fantastic option. River cruises generally operate seasonally, following Lewis and Clark down the Pacific Northwest's **Columbia and Snake rivers,** or following the fall foliage up the **Hudson River** and **Erie Canal,** or heading down the **Mississippi River** and its tributaries to see the central United States the way travelers saw it in centuries past. **Season:** Columbia–Snake and Hudson/Erie Canal cruises usually run September to November.

2 Itineraries: The Long & the Short of It

Once you've decided where you want to go, you have to examine the available itineraries. Do you just want to get away for a few days or a few weeks? Do you want an itinerary that assigns a different stop to each day, or are you looking forward to just relaxing on the ship? And, if you're flying or driving a long way to your ship's home port, do you want to spend a few days seeing that part of the country before or after your cruise? Options are what you have; choices are what you need to make.

Long Cruise or Short?

The majority of cruises to the Caribbean, Alaska, Hawaii, and Mexico are **7 nights** long and depart on a Saturday or Sunday. Many of us like the weeklong vacation concept, but if you're looking to spend less money or you're a first-time cruiser who wants to test the waters, there are 2-, 3-, 4-, and 5-night cruises. Many of the **3- and 4-night cruises** sail from Florida to The Bahamas, or from California to Baja (Mexico). You can also find a lot of **4- and 5-night cruises** to the Caribbean and The Bahamas, as well as to New England/Canada in the summer and fall. Naturally, these depart on different days of the week, with some timed to sail over the weekend.

On the one hand, shorter cruises make sense if you're not sure you'll like the cruise experience. On the other hand, they also tend to be the rowdiest cruises, geared to people who want to pack a lot of partying into a short time frame. This is especially true of the 3-night weekend cruises offered by Carnival and Royal Caribbean. Also, be aware that cruise lines tend to put their oldest, most well-worn ships on short-cruise schedules, saving their new ships for their bread-and-butter weeklong itineraries.

Longer cruises, ranging from **9, 10, and 12 nights** to multiweek voyages, provide the chance to really get away and settle into the community aboard your ship. Longer cruises tend to be relaxed and steady, and are popular with older folks who have the time and money to travel. You'll find longer sailings in Alaska, the Caribbean, New England/Canada, and the Panama Canal, and also many long **repositioning cruises** when ships leave one cruise region and sail to another (for instance, heading from Alaska to the Caribbean in stages). These are often deeply discounted and sometimes visit unusual ports, but they also tend to spend more days at sea than they do in port—a plus or a minus, depending on your perspective.

Days at Sea vs. Days in Port

When evaluating an itinerary, take a look at its **day-by-day schedule.** A few ships will visit a different port every day, but it's much more typical for them to include 1, 2, or even 3 days at sea—either because they have to sail a long way between ports, and/or because days at sea (a) are relaxing, (b) give passengers more chance to explore their ship's onboard attractions, and (c) cruise lines make a lot of money when passengers are onboard and need distraction. If your main vacation goal is to decompress, days at sea can be fantastic; if your goal is to see a lot of different ports, go for an itinerary that includes the minimum of sea days. Ditto if you think you'll get that "are we there yet?" feeling between ports.

Cruisetours & Add-Ons

Cruise lines offer various options for extending your vacation on land, either before or after your cruise. These range from simple 1- and 2-night add-on **hotel packages** to longer resort stays and full-blown land tours of a week or longer. The latter, known as **cruisetours,** are offered mostly in Alaska, where Holland America, Princess, Royal

Caribbean, and Celebrity all have elaborate hotel and transportation infrastructure. Many parts of inland Alaska can be accessed this way, including Denali National Park, Fairbanks, Wrangell–St. Elias National Park, and the Kenai Peninsula. If you're so inclined, you can even go all the way to the oil fields of the North Slope of Prudhoe Bay, hundreds of miles north of the Arctic Circle. Many tours also head east into Canada, spending time in the starkly beautiful Yukon Territory or heading to Banff, Lake Louise, and Jasper National Park in the Canadian Rockies.

Caribbean-bound ships originating in Florida frequently offer extensions to **Orlando's theme parks.** Disney, naturally, is tops in this regard, offering seamless 1-week land/sea vacations, with 3 days in the park and 4 aboard *Disney Wonder,* or vice versa. Other regions have their own specialties: Small-ship cruises in Baja, for example, typically allow an extension to the amazing **Copper Canyon,** larger than the U.S. Grand Canyon.

3 Different Boats for Different Folks

Different cruise lines present different kinds of experiences, but physical factors—most notably the size of the ship—also play a part when choosing your ideal cruise. What size ship floats your boat?

Megaships (1,800–3,600 Passengers)

For the past dozen years, the so-called "megaships" have dominated the market, carrying upward of 1,800 passengers and providing an onboard experience any big-city dweller will recognize: food and drink available at any hour, entertainment districts filled with neon and twinkling lights, monumental architecture, big crowds, and a definite buzz. You often won't see the same faces twice from day to day, and, in fact, if you don't plan specific times and places to meet up with your spouse, squeeze, or friend(s), you may roam the decks for hours looking for them. (Luckily, most megaships are wired for cellphone service now, so you can call your travel companion if you can't find him or her.) The megas typically have more than a dozen passenger decks full of restaurants, bars, lounges, and shops, plus cabins of all shapes and sizes. Most have a grand atrium lobby, three or four swimming pools and hot tubs, theaters, a pizzeria, a specialty coffee shop, and one or more reservations-only restaurants. Mammoth gyms and spas boast dozens of exercise machines and treatment rooms, and vast children's areas include splash pools, playrooms, computer rooms, and video arcades. Activities go on all day, including wine tastings, fashion shows, dance lessons, aerobics classes, bingo, bridge, lectures, cooking demonstrations, pool games, computer classes, and trivia contests. And at night you have a choice of piano bars, discos, martini and champagne bars, sports bars, casinos, theaters, and big glitzy showrooms that put on big glitzy shows.

But even the megas aren't all alike. **Carnival**'s and **Costa**'s ships are the most theme-park-like, with their over-the-top decor and ambience. **NCL**'s are probably the most whimsical, with an overall design sense tuned to "fun," and a dollop of elegance in some rooms. **Royal Caribbean**'s megas blend a lot of flash with some elegant areas; **Princess** goes for a sort of Pottery Barn design sense and fun but not-too-daring activities and shows; **Holland America** and **Disney** blend tradition with some bright, modern spaces; and **Celebrity** is all about chic modernity.

As a general rule, these ships are so large that they're limited as to where they can go. Some ports lack large enough docking facilities, meaning you either won't visit them at all or you'll have to be tendered ashore in shuttle boats. Ships in the 100,000-ton range are also currently too big to fit through the Panama Canal, and so tend to operate in one or another sea year-round—with ships in the Pacific sailing Mexico itineraries in winter and Alaska in summer, say (or heading to the South Pacific or Asia), and ships on the Atlantic side sailing in the Caribbean year-round or spending the summers sailing in Europe or New England/Canada. Note that this may all change in 2014, when the Panama Canal's ongoing expansion allows larger ships to squeeze through.

Super-megaships (3,600–5,400 Passengers)

As if megaships weren't big enough, over the past half-dozen years cruise lines have been introducing vessels so large that they need their own supersize category. The trend sort of began with the introduction of **Queen Mary 2** in 2004, though that enormous vessel—at 150,000 gross tons and 1,132 feet in length—actually carries "only" 2,592 passengers, double occupancy (about the same number Carnival crams into vessels only two-thirds its size). The real monsters first hit the seas in 2006, when Royal Caribbean introduced the 160,000-ton, 3,634-passenger **Freedom of the Seas** (and later, sister ships *Liberty* and *Independence*). In *Freedom*'s wake, Royal Caribbean upped itself with the 220,000-ton, 5,400-passenger **Oasis** and **Allure of the Seas,** and Norwegian Cruise Line began building the 153,000-ton, 4,200-passenger **Norwegian Epic.** All these ships offer everything you find on a normal megaship and then some, with innovations only their enormous size makes possible. See individual ship reviews in chapter 6 for details.

Midsize Ships (500–1,800 Passengers)

For a while it looked as if midsize vessels were going the way of the dodo, but the past few years have seen a small resurgence in their fortunes.

The term *midsize* is, of course, relative. Weighing in at between 20,000 and 60,000 gross tons, most of these ships are still larger than some of the great old ocean liners. (*Titanic,* for instance, was only 46,000 tons.) They're plenty big and spacious enough to provide a diverse cruise experience, though you won't find the range of activities and attractions you do on the megaships. Consider that a good thing: For some people, a more toned-down, lower-key cruise is just what the doctor ordered. **Oceania** and **Azamara** both operate vessels that carry some 700 passengers apiece and have a country-club-type setting. Though somewhat larger, most of **Holland America**'s fleet also fits the midsize description, with a generally classic onboard vibe.

Among the true ultraluxury lines, midsize is about as big as it gets. **Crystal** and **Regent Seven Seas** both operate ships in the 50,000-ton range, carrying 700 to 900 passengers—a telling figure when you consider that HAL's similar-size ships carry almost 1,300. Along with high-toned service, cuisine, and amenities, personal space is a major difference between the mainstream and luxe lines.

Small Ships (12–500 Passengers)

If the thought of sailing with thousands of other people makes you want to jump overboard, a smaller ship may be more up your alley. Small ships are ideal for those who crave a calm, intimate experience where conversation is king. As in a small town, you'll quickly get to know your neighbors, because you'll see the same faces at meals and on deck throughout the week.

The small ships in this book can be broken down into four groups: sailing ships, coastal and river cruisers, expedition ships, and small luxury ships.

SHIP SIZE COMPARISONS

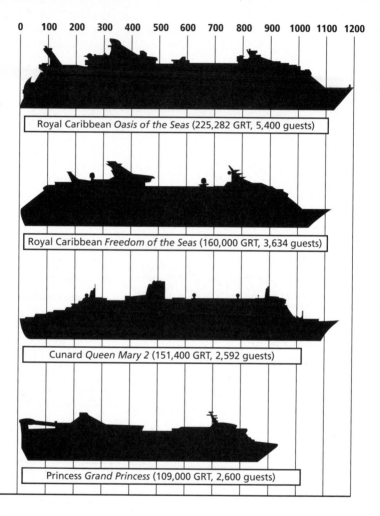

| 0 | 100 | 200 | 300 | 400 | 500 | 600 | 700 | 800 | 900 | 1000 | 1100 | 1200 |

Royal Caribbean *Oasis of the Seas* (225,282 GRT, 5,400 guests)

Royal Caribbean *Freedom of the Seas* (160,000 GRT, 3,634 guests)

Cunard *Queen Mary 2* (151,400 GRT, 2,592 guests)

Princess *Grand Princess* (109,000 GRT, 2,600 guests)

Ships in this chart represent the range of sizes in the current cruise market. See reviews in chapters 6 through 8 for sizes of ships not shown here, then compare. Note that GRT = gross register tons, the standard measure of vessel size. Rather than representing weight, it indicates the amount of interior, revenue-producing space on a vessel. One GRT = 100 cubic feet of enclosed, revenue-generating space.

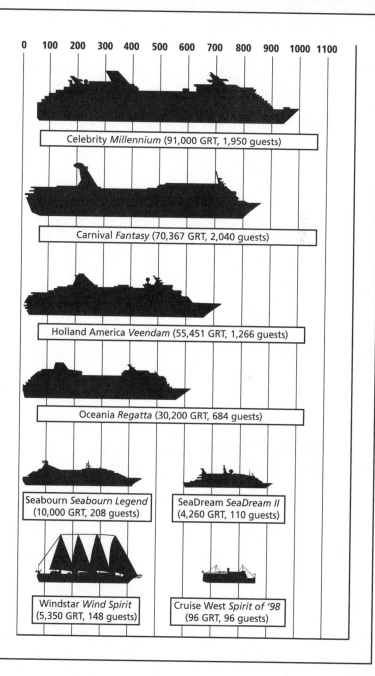

0   100   200   300   400   500   600   700   800   900   1000   1100

Celebrity *Millennium* (91,000 GRT, 1,950 guests)

Carnival *Fantasy* (70,367 GRT, 2,040 guests)

Holland America *Veendam* (55,451 GRT, 1,266 guests)

Oceania *Regatta* (30,200 GRT, 684 guests)

Seabourn *Seabourn Legend* (10,000 GRT, 208 guests)

SeaDream *SeaDream II* (4,260 GRT, 110 guests)

Windstar *Wind Spirit* (5,350 GRT, 148 guests)

Cruise West *Spirit of '98* (96 GRT, 96 guests)

Homeboat Security

For better or worse, we live in a security-obsessed world. People have to show ID to get into office buildings and take off their shoes to go through airport X-rays, so you'd better believe security measures are in place on cruise ships, too.

All the major cruise lines have their own **dedicated onboard security forces** who monitor people coming aboard (passengers, crew, delivery people, and contractors) and keep an eye out during the cruise, and we're not just talking about the kind of rent-a-cops you see at your local convenience store. Some lines have even hired former Navy SEALs as top-level security consultants and Nepalese Gurkha fighters as onboard security personnel, and trained their deck officers in how to react to takeover attempts. Other security measures are also in place, but the cruise lines prefer to keep them under their hats.

On a day-to-day basis, passengers will mostly notice ship security when boarding, both initially and at the ports of call. Most cruise lines photograph passengers digitally at embarkation, keying the photos to passengers' onboard IDs so that they can match face to picture every time they get back aboard thereafter. The system also allows the ship's staff to tell instantly who's aboard at any given time. Other security processes include **screening and X-raying of all hand-carried and checked bags,** the use of sniffer dogs in port, and maintenance of a security zone around docked vessels. Ships must also submit a complete list of passengers and crew to the Coast Guard 96 hours before arriving at a U.S. port. Internationally, regulations issued by the International Maritime Organization (IMO) in 2004 require all ports around the world to operate within a consistent framework to address security issues.

Sailing ships, obviously, have sails. But what's not necessarily obvious is how much—or how little—those sails are used to actually propel the ship. On Maine's coast, the independently owned schooners of the **Maine Windjammer Association** are honest-to-God sail-powered vessels, most without engines of any kind. If the wind stops blowing, their only option is to let down their motorized yawl boats and push the ship until it catches a breeze. The ships of **Star Clippers, Sea Cloud, Island Windjammers,** and **Windstar,** on the other hand, usually operate under wind power for a part of each cruise, but they have engines to do much or most of the pushing. All these vessels tend to attract as many passengers in their 30s as in their 70s, all of them looking for something a little different from a regular cruise.

Most of the other small ships in this book are **coastal and river cruisers**—small vessels designed to sail in protected coastal waters and rivers. Very casual (and for the most part relatively plain), these ships provide cruises oriented heavily toward nature, wildlife-watching, culture, and/or history, with onboard naturalists to help interpret what you see. In addition to coastal cruisers, **Cruise West** and **Lindblad** also operate tougher **expedition ships** able to sail in the open ocean.

See "Active Travel & Adventure Cruises," later in this chapter, and chapter 8, "Small Ships, Sailing Ships & Adventure Cruises," for more details on all these options.

The **small luxury ships** of high-end lines **Seabourn, Silversea,** and **SeaDream** have a refined, ultra-elegant ambience. Cabins are spacious, service is gracious, gourmet meals are served on fine china, and guests dress the part. These ships have few activities besides watersports, putting more emphasis on quiet relaxation and visits to high-end ports such as St. Barts. Somewhat straddling the luxe and outdoorsy categories, **American Safari Cruises** operates truly tiny 12- and 22-passenger yachts that are service-oriented like the luxe ships, but also provide lots of built-in active excursions.

4 Cruises for Families

If you've got kids, preserving your sanity and getting your rest are priorities, and that's why cruises are such a good family vacation choice: They're easy, safe, fun for the kids, and relaxing for Mom and Dad. Cruise lines go to great lengths to please parents and kids alike, as families become an ever larger and more influential segment of the cruising public. In fact, since 2000, the very family-friendly Royal Caribbean has seen a more than 50% increase in the number of families cruising with kids under the age of 3. Same story with Carnival, which now carries some 300% more children ages 17 and under than it did in 1995. During school holidays, there can be so many kids on board that playrooms get jampacked and you'll have to wait in line to sign in. Toddlers and teens are taken care of, too (Royal Caribbean, for instance, has daily play groups for parents and kids ages 6 months to 3 years), while elaborate teen facilities are all the rage across the industry.

Megaships cater most to families and attract the largest numbers of them, with playrooms, video arcades, and complimentary **supervised activities** usually provided for children ages 2 or 3 to 17 (generally, young children must be potty-trained to participate), and programs broken down into several age categories. Some lines set a **minimum age** for children to sail aboard (usually 6–12 months), but Disney provides a supervised **nursery** for ages 3 months and up; Royal Caribbean's *Oasis* and *Allure of the Seas* have a nursery for kids ages 6 to 17 months; and Carnival accepts kids as young as 4 months in its group babysitting program. See the individual cruise line reviews for details.

Disney has the most family-friendly ships at sea today, followed by **Royal Caribbean,** whose ships (especially *Oasis* and *Allure,* but also the Freedom-, Voyager-, and Radiance-class vessels) have huge play areas. The **Carnival** ships do a pretty good job, too (especially the Conquest class), as do the **Norwegian, Princess,** and **Celebrity** megaships, and the kids' facilities and programs on **Cunard**'s *QM2* are surprisingly phenomenal for such a high-toned vessel.

See the section "Best Cruises for Families with Kids," on p. 7, for more info.

BABYSITTING   After the complimentary daylong roster of supervised activities wraps up between about 7 and 10pm, most mainstream lines provide slumber-party-style **group babysitting** in the playroom. Services are usually from about 10pm until 1 to 3am and are for ages 3 to 12, costing about $4 to $8 per hour per child. Some lines do accommodate younger kids, with toys, cribs, and nap areas geared to infants and toddlers: Disney's nurseries take children as young as 3 months, Royal Caribbean's *Oasis* and *Allure* have a nursery for kids ages 6 to 17 months, and Carnival caters to kids as young as 4 months. The counselors will even change diapers. **Private in-cabin**

Family Cruising Tips

Here are some suggestions for better sailing and smoother seas on your family cruise.

- **Reserve a crib.** If you'll need a crib in your cabin, request one when booking your cruise.
- **Bring baby food and diapers.** If your infant is still on jar food, you'll have to bring your own. You can store milk and snacks in your cabin's minifridge/minibar, which is standard on most new ships. (Ships more than 5 or 10 years old may provide them only in suites.) If yours is pre-stocked with beer and peanuts, you can ask your steward to clear it out.
- **Keep a tote with you on embarkation day.** After boarding a big ship, it may take a few hours before your luggage gets delivered to your cabin, so be sure to hand-carry a tote filled with whatever you'll need for the afternoon: diapers, baby food, a change of clothes, bathing suits, and so on.
- **Pack some basic first-aid supplies, and even a thermometer.** Cruise lines have limited supplies of these items, and charge for them, too. If an accident should happen on board, virtually every ship (except the smallest ones) has its own infirmary staffed by doctors or nurses. Keep in mind that first aid can usually be summoned more readily aboard ship than in port.
- **Warn younger children about the danger of falling overboard,** and make sure they know not to play on the railings.
- **Make sure your kids know their cabin number** and what deck it's on. The endless corridors and doors on the megaships often look exactly alike, though some are color-coded.
- **Prepare kids for TV letdown.** Though many ships today receive satellite TV programming, you won't get the range of options you have at home.

babysitting by a crewmember is also available aboard Celebrity, Royal Caribbean, and most high-end lines at a steeper $8 to $10 per hour (and sometimes a few bucks more for additional siblings). Using a private babysitter every night isn't cheap, but this book's coauthor Heidi went this route when her boys were babies and swears by it—how else to dine and have cocktails in peace after a long, kid-centric day? Try to get them tucked in and asleep before the sitter arrives so that they won't have to deal with a new face just before bedtime.

FAMILY-FRIENDLY CABINS   If your travel budget is tight, a family of four can share a cabin and get a good deal in return for all that togetherness: The rates for third and fourth persons sharing a cabin with two full-fare (or even heavily discounted) passengers are usually about half of the lowest regular rates. Norwegian Cruise Line allows children ages 1 and under to sail free with two full-fare passengers (though you must pay port charges and government taxes for the kids, which run about $100–$200 per person) and MSC Cruises often has a "kids sail free" promotion for the under-17 set if occupying the same cabin as two parents or adults. *Note:* Because prices are based on double adult occupancy of cabins, single parents sailing with children usually have to pay adult prices for their kids, though deals for single parents are available every once in awhile.

As for how you'll all fit, think **bunk-style third and fourth berths** that fold out of the walls just above the regular beds. A few lines, such as Carnival and NCL, will even accommodate a fifth person on a rollaway bed on certain ships, if space permits, and a **baby crib** can be brought in if requested in advance. There are no two ways about it, though: A standard cabin with four people in it will be cramped, and with one bathroom . . . well, you can imagine. However, when you consider how little time you'll spend in the cabin, it's doable, and many families do take this option. The line that offers the best digs for families is definitely **Disney,** where the majority of cabins aboard *Magic* and *Wonder* boast two bathrooms (one with a bathtub, which is a real rarity), a minifridge, and a sitting area with a sofa bed. The cabins are almost as big as most ships' minisuites and comfortably sleep families of three or four—but, of course, Disney's rates are generally higher than those of its mainstream competitors. The ships' bona fide suites accommodate families of five to seven.

In general, whatever line you choose, families who can afford it should **consider booking a suite or junior suite.** Many have a pullout couch in the living room (or, better yet, two separate bedrooms) and can accommodate up to three or four children. If you have older kids, it may just be cheaper to book **connecting cabins**—two separate standard cabins with interconnecting doors. Almost every mid- and megasize ship reviewed in this book provides connecting cabins.

TAKING THE KIDS ON SMALL SHIPS   For the most part, small-ship cruises are not kid-friendly, because usually there are no kids' facilities or other kids on board, the pace is slow, and the clientele is older. Some possible exceptions include sailing ships like Star Clippers' *Royal Clipper* and some of the Maine Windjammer vessels, which make great ersatz pirate ships (though your kids will still have to be well behaved, since the ships are so cozy).

5 Cruises for Honeymooners & Anniversary Couples

Practically all cruises have what it takes to make your honeymoon or anniversary memorable: moonlight and stars, the undulating sea all around, dimly lit restaurants, and the pure romance of travel. Of course, different ships are romantic to different kinds of people. The megaships present a big, flashy experience, like a trip to Vegas without the dry heat. The ultraluxury lines are more like a trip to Paris, with gourmet cuisine, fine wine, perfect service, and the finest bed linens. And some of the small-ship lines are like staying at a Vermont B&B (though others are more like a Motel 6 with a view). Beyond the ships themselves are the ports of call, providing experiences that are variously exotic, charming, exciting, and sybaritic.

Honeymoon & Anniversary Packages

Besides their inherent romantic qualities, cruises are a practical honeymoon choice because many depart on Sundays, and couples who marry on Saturday can leave the next day. Some lines provide honeymooner freebies, such as a special cake in the dining room one night, or an invitation to a private cocktail party. Couples celebrating anniversaries are often invited as well. To get your share of freebies, be sure to tell your travel agent or the cruise line reservation agent that you'll be celebrating on the cruise. Beyond the freebies, the mainstream cruise lines aren't shy about selling a variety of **honeymoon/anniversary packages.** You'll get a pamphlet describing the available packages when you receive your cruise tickets in the mail. NCL's $135 Honeymoon Package is about average for its price range, and includes champagne and strawberries

Getting Married on Board or in Port

If you'd like to have your marriage and honeymoon all in one, you can legally get hitched on many cruises, either aboard ship or at one of your ports of call.

Practically all the mainstream lines have wedding packages, with Carnival, Princess, and Royal Caribbean being the romance leaders, followed by NCL, Celebrity, Disney, Holland America, and Costa. In almost all cases, a local justice of the peace, notary, or minister must officiate; so even if you choose to hold your ceremony aboard ship, it will have to take place while the ship is in port, not at sea. Princess's Grand-, Diamond-, and Coral-class ships have **wedding chapels** on board, as do Royal Caribbean's Freedom-, Voyager-, and Oasis-class ships, Carnival's Spirit-class ships, and NCL's *Norwegian Sun, Star, Dawn, Jewel, Pearl, Gem, Jade,* and *Pride of America*. Other ships hold ceremonies in lounges that are decorated for the occasion.

If you want nonsailing family and friends to attend, you can hold the ceremony and reception at your port of embarkation, before the ship leaves. Guests will be on a special list with port security, and they'll have to bring the requisite ID to board. Ceremonies can also be arranged at various ports of call. On Caribbean routes, you can tie the knot in ports such as Aruba, Barbados, Grand Cayman, St. Thomas, Sint Maarten, San Juan (Puerto Rico), Ocho Rios and Montego Bay (Jamaica), Cozumel (Mexico), Nassau (The Bahamas), and Key West (Florida). Other options include Bermuda and the Alaskan ports of Ketchikan and Juneau (at the latter, you can get married atop Mendenhall Glacier, flying in by helicopter). If contemplating marriage in a port of call, remember that your cruise itinerary limits how far afield you can go, because ships generally stay in port only a limited number of hours.

Wedding packages generally start in the $1,000 range for intimate shipboard ceremonies for the bride and groom only. That price usually includes the services of an officiant (though you can bring your own if you prefer), a bouquet and boutonniere, champagne and keepsake glasses, a wedding cake, and the services of a photographer, but not the photos themselves—those will cost extra, should you choose to buy them. Adding a reception for

at embarkation, a dinner for two with complimentary wine at the ship's specialty restaurant, an invitation to a cocktail party, a keepsake photo, and canapés in your cabin one evening. The $229 Deluxe Package adds breakfast in bed one day and two 25-minute massages at the spa. All the mainstream lines have similar deals, with packages in the $300 to $500 range generally piling on more spa treatments, champagne, shore excursions, canapés, chocolate-covered strawberries, and the like. These packages must be ordered before the cruise.

Ultraluxe lines such as Silversea, Seabourn, Regent Seven Seas, SeaDream, and Crystal are less involved in these kinds of promotions, but that's because, for them, free champagne and canapés, whirlpool bathtubs, and five-course dinners served in your cabin are all a matter of course.

eight guests will bring the price up. The basic wedding/reception package offered by Carnival is $1,195. Prices go up from there based on the complexity and size of your reception (from a simple open bar and hors d'oeuvres to a formal meal in the ship's restaurant) and by port. Additional guests can be accommodated for an additional per-person charge. Ceremonies can also be performed off-ship in port, at higher prices.

THE LEGAL DETAILS   No matter where you choose to wed, you must arrange for a marriage license from the U.S. or foreign port far in advance of your cruise. Policies vary from country to country, so you'll save a lot of headaches by having the cruise line's wedding department or consultant help you with the details. Be sure to check with these folks before booking your cruise to confirm that wedding space is available on the date you have in mind.

HAVING THE CAPTAIN OFFICIATE   Among all the lines in this book, only Princess, Celebrity, and Azamara give you the option of being married by the captain. At **Princess,** the Grand-, Diamond-, and Coral-class ships all have charming wedding chapels that seat about three dozen and are adorned with stained glass and fresh flower arrangements. Assistant pursers in dress-blue uniforms are available to escort a bride down the short aisle. Three different ceremony packages are offered, starting at $1,800 per couple (plus $450 for licensing fees). Depending on which you choose, they can include photography, video, music, and salon treatments for the bride. Onboard receptions can be custom-tailored with various options—hors d'oeuvres, champagne, wedding cake, and so on. Friends and relatives who aren't sailing can even monitor the wedding courtesy of the ships' chapel Web cams, which broadcast an updated photo every minute or so. (Look at the very bottom of the Princess website home page for "Bridge Cams." Pick a ship from the "Wedding Cams" drop-down menu.) At **Celebrity** and **Azamara,** weddings are performed in one of the ship's public rooms. A variety of packages are available that mix and match everything from cake and champagne to private receptions in the ship's specialty restaurant. Basic captain-performed wedding packages at both lines start at about $2,500.

Vow-Renewal & "Romance" Packages

Some lines have vow-renewal packages for couples who'd like to celebrate their marriage all over again, or packages that simply add romance to a vacation. On Holland America, for example, couples can renew their vows at a special group ceremony at sea, catered with drinks and cold hors d'oeuvres; the $114 package includes the vow-renewal ceremony (with hors d'oeuvres and beverages), a floral arrangement in your cabin, a certificate presented by the captain, and dinner for two at the Pinnacle alternative restaurant. Visitors can attend the ceremony, but they have to pay: $13 per adult, $6.25 for kids ages 2 to 12. Princess has souped-up vow-renewal packages for $205 and $485 per couple. The former includes the ceremony, an orchid bouquet and boutonniere, a bottle of champagne and souvenir champagne glasses, a framed formal portrait of the ceremony, and a commemorative certificate signed by the captain; the latter adds a champagne breakfast in bed, two terry-cloth robes, a visit to the spa for half-hour massages or facials, canapés or petits fours in your stateroom every evening, and a personalized invitation from the captain to visit the bridge while in port. These packages are fairly representative of what's provided by the other mainstream lines.

6 Cruises for Gay Men & Lesbians

A number of specialized travel agencies have cruises for gay men and/or lesbians, either chartering a full ship outright or reserving blocks of cabins aboard one ship or another. Full charters typically bring aboard their own entertainers (as well as the ship's usual entertainment staff) and program many of their own activities. Hosted group trips typically have cocktail parties for group members and specially programmed activities on board and in port.

- **Atlantis Events Inc.,** 9200 Sunset Blvd., Ste. 500, West Hollywood, CA 90069 (© **800/628-5268** or 310/859-8800; www.atlantisevents.com), provides all-gay charters with lines such as Celebrity, Azamara, Holland America, and Royal Caribbean. In addition to the lines' own entertainment, Atlantis brings aboard its own featured performers. Past guests have included Patti LuPone, Cybill Shepherd, and Chaka Khan.
- **Friends of Dorothy Travel,** 1177 California St., Ste. B, San Francisco, CA 94108-2231 (© **800/640-4918** or 415/864-1600; www.fodtravel.com), offers many full-gay charters with lines such as Celebrity, NCL, and the ultraluxe SeaDream yachts, as well as hosted tours on *Queen Mary 2* and other ships.
- **Olivia Cruises and Resorts,** 434 Brannan St., San Francisco, CA 94107 (© **800/631-6277** or 415/962-5700; www.olivia.com), provides full-ship charters targeted specifically to the lesbian community, mostly aboard Holland America's and NCL's ships. Guest performers over the years have included k.d. lang, Margaret Cho, Heart, the Indigo Girls, Wynonna Judd, Shawn Colvin, and Melissa Etheridge.
- **Pied Piper Travel,** 330 W. 42nd St., Ste. 1804, New York, NY 10036 (© **800/874-7312** or 212/239-2412; www.piedpipertravel.com), offers hosted gay cruises aboard lines like Cunard, Celebrity, Royal Caribbean, and Princess, with various onboard parties and activities.
- **R Family Vacations,** 1500 Broadway, Ste. 1710, New York, NY 10036 (© **866/732-6822;** www.rfamilyvacations.com), was founded by Rosie O'Donnell's former partner, Kelli O'Donnell, along with gay travel veteran Gregg Kaminsky. Trips to (so far) the Caribbean, Alaska, Canada/New England, Hawaii, and Europe are targeted to the gay and lesbian family market.
- **RSVP Vacations,** 2535 25th Ave. S., Minneapolis, MN 55406 (© **800/328-7787** or 612/729-1113; www.rsvpvacations.com), provides full-ship charters on lines such as NCL and Holland America. All sailings are targeted to both gay men and lesbians, and bring aboard their own guest performers. RSVP works through more than 10,000 different travel agencies; locate one by calling the 800 number or checking the website above.

7 Active Travel & Adventure Cruises

Several years ago, we met this great Australian couple in Alaska. They'd wanted to see the state for years, to really get into its forests and see its wildlife, but they didn't have time for a 3-week wilderness trek. Their solution? They booked a small-ship cruise that split its sailing week between exploring wilderness areas and visiting tiny fishing towns. It was a perfect choice.

These types of trips, offered by most of the cruise lines in chapter 8 (and in locales like Alaska, Baja, Central America, the Pacific Northwest, and elsewhere), include few of the usual activity options, but that's by design: Their focus is on what's outside the vessel, not inside, and some are more active than others. Lindblad Expeditions, for instance, builds activities such as hiking, kayaking, and exploring by inflatable launch into its adventure itineraries. On Star Clippers' sailing ships, those inflatable launches might be used to take passengers water-skiing or on banana-boat rides. Passengers aboard even smaller small ships, like the 12-passenger *Columbia III* of British Columbia–based Mothership Adventures or the six-passenger *David B* of Washington's Northwest Navigation Company, might spend every day of their cruises out sea kayaking, only returning to the vessel to eat and recuperate.

Active Shore Excursions

On shore, even the megaships offer a healthy number of active excursions in the Caribbean, Alaska, Mexico, Central America, Hawaii, and elsewhere, including snorkeling and diving, biking, hiking, kayaking, horseback riding, zipline canopy tours, and river rafting. For more details, see the port reviews in Part 3, "The Ports."

8 Cruises for the Young & Old

"So which are the ships for young people?" We get this question all the time, and the answer is, there aren't any. That is, there aren't any that attract *only* young people, just like there aren't many hotels or resorts that do. Most ships appeal to a mixed bag of ages, with couples in their 40s, 50s, and 60-plus making up the majority, along with a growing percentage of younger couples, often with kids. Destination plays into the balance, with the Caribbean and Mexican Riviera attracting a sizable young crowd as well as lots of retirees. Alaska, Europe, New England/Canada, and Asia itineraries, on the other hand, draw mostly an older, 50-plus crowd, though you will see families with young kids in Alaska (and Europe for that matter) during the summer. All that said, here are some general guidelines about ships and the ages of the people you'll find on them.

The **youngest crowds,** in the 20s-to-40s range, are typically found on 2-, 3-, and 4-night warm-weather cruises (and next on the 7-night cruises) offered by mainstream lines such as Carnival, Royal Caribbean, and NCL. Young-at-heart types, who may be 54 or 72, but wear bikinis and short-shorts and drink piña coladas for lunch, will also be attracted to those lines. **Young families** make up the majority of passengers on Disney Cruise Line.

The **oldest folks,** upward of 60, will be the vast majority on luxury lines such as Seabourn, Silversea, and Regent. Cunard and Holland America have also traditionally attracted a mature crowd, though both are trying hard to broaden their demographic. The high prices at many of the **small-ship lines** tend to keep the demographic older, but that's particularly true aboard Blount Small Ship Adventures, American Cruise Lines, and Cruise West.

9 Ships for Nonsmokers & Smokers

Once upon a time, all the cool kids smoked—Sinatra . . . JFK . . . Joe DiMaggio . . . Don Draper. It was an era when life was seen through a swirling bluish haze and, at least in the movies, nobody ever coughed. Today? Not so much. Around the world, cities, states, and even whole countries are banning smoking in many public places, even bars. It's enough to make a smoker want to run away to sea—except that doesn't really work anymore either.

As goes public opinion, so go the cruise lines, which generally prohibit smoking now in all restaurants, theaters, corridors, elevators, and many other public areas, too. Policies vary by line, with most allowing smoking in designated smoking sections of bars and lounges and on most open decks. Lines vary as to whether they allow smoking in

Norovirus: Montezuma's Revenge at Sea

Unless you've been living under a rock, you've seen, heard, or read news reports over the past few years detailing outbreaks of norovirus (aka Norwalk-like virus) aboard cruise ships. But what is it exactly, and how worried should you be?

Answer: It's a stomach bug that causes nausea, vomiting, and diarrhea. And really, there's not much to worry about. Norovirus is an extremely common bug that hits some 23 million Americans a year, mostly on land—and the reason you don't hear about those cases is they don't happen in a confined (and newsworthy) environment like a cruise ship. A hundred people might pick up a bug at the local mall, but what's the chance they'd all remember they caught it at the food court?

What makes Norovirus such a pain for cruise ships is that it's incredibly contagious: According to the Centers for Disease Control (CDC), people infected with the virus can pass it on from the moment they begin feeling ill to between 3 days and 2 weeks after they recover—meaning that cruise ship outbreaks are almost certainly the result of contagious passengers bringing the infection aboard, rather than of unsanitary practices on the ships themselves. Face it, cruise ships are a lot like kindergarten: When one kid shows up sick, everybody gets sick.

In any case, don't worry too much. It's no fun to have your vacation spoiled by rampant puking, but norovirus causes no long-term health effects for most people. Persons unable to replace liquids quickly enough—generally the very young, the elderly, and people with weakened immune systems—may become dehydrated and require special medical attention, but that's about the worst of it. More good news: Outbreaks have been on the downswing since they were first reported. Cruise lines are keeping a close eye on boarding passengers for signs of illness, and have further stepped up their already vigilant sanitation routines to reduce the chance of transmission. A small outbreak on one of our recent cruises was contained immediately after the first sick passengers were identified, and it did not spread any further among passengers and crew.

cabins. Among those that do, none has specifically designated smoking and nonsmoking cabins—you just get what you get, though the cruise lines do scrub their cabins well between cruises, if necessary by shampooing the rug and using air purifiers. In our hundreds of cruises, we've never found a cabin that reeked from last week's Marlboro Man.

The **best lines for nonsmokers** are Azamara Club Cruises, Oceania Cruises, and small-ship line American Cruise Lines. Both Azamara and Oceania allow smoking only in two small areas: one indoors, in a small section of one top-deck lounge, and the other outdoors, in a corner of the Pool Deck. Azamara also follows a no-smoking policy on all land components of its cruisetours. American Cruise Lines is the most stringent of all, operating entirely smoke-free vessels. Many of the Maine Windjammer schooners are also smoke-free, though some allow smoking in a small section of the outside deck.

Lines that prohibit smoking in staterooms, private balconies, and most public areas include Celebrity, MSC, and Regent Seven Seas. On Disney and Royal Caribbean, smoking on sea-facing private balconies is allowed.

Lines that allow smoking only on designated outside decks include Blount Small Ship Adventures, American Safari, Cruise West, Lindblad, Sea Cloud, SeaDream Yacht Club, Star Clippers, and Windstar.

For a detailed, **line-by-line summary of smoking regulations** on these and all other lines in this book, click over to www.frommers.com/articles/5872.html.

10 Cruises for People with Disabilities & Health Issues

Though most of the cruise industry's ships are foreign-flagged and are not required to comply with the **Americans with Disabilities Act,** ships built over the past 15 years are almost universally accessible, and some older ships have been retrofitted to offer access. Most ships that can accommodate wheelchair-bound passengers require that they be accompanied by a fully mobile companion. The ship reviews in chapters 6 through 8 include information about access and facilities in the "Cabins" sections, but be sure to discuss your needs fully with your travel agent prior to booking. Generally speaking, **service animals** are welcomed aboard cruise ships, though regulations at some ports may prohibit them from going ashore there, or at the least may require you to present health/vaccination records.

See the "Onboard Medical Care" box below for information on medical facilities aboard ship.

ACCESSIBLE CABINS & PUBLIC ROOMS   Most ships have a handful of cabins specifically designed for travelers with disabilities, with extra-wide doorways, large bathrooms with grab bars and roll-in showers, closets with pull-down racks, and furniture built to a lower height. The "Ships at a Glance" chart beginning on p. 74 identifies ships with accessible cabins, and the "Cabins" section in each of the ship reviews in chapters 6 through 8 indicates how many. The vast majority of the ships reviewed in the **mainstream** and **luxury** categories (chapters 6 and 7) have accessible cabins, but of the **adventure ships** in chapter 8, only the American Cruise Lines ships and Cruise West's *Spirit of '98* and *Spirit of Oceanus* are either fully or partially wheelchair-friendly. Most public rooms on newer vessels have ramps, and some also have lifts to help passengers with disabilities into the pools.

ELEVATORS   Most shipboard elevators (particularly aboard today's megaships) are wide enough to accommodate wheelchairs, but make sure before booking. Due to the

Onboard Medical Care

The vast majority of ships have a nurse and sometimes a doctor aboard to provide medical services for a fee. Most of their cases involve seasickness, sunburn, and the like, but they may also be required to stabilize a patient with a more serious ailment until he or she can be brought to a hospital at the next port of call or, in extreme cases, be evacuated by helicopter. If they're very unlucky, the medical staff may also have to deal with an outbreak of **norovirus,** the flulike gastrointestinal bug that strikes a ship every once in awhile (see "Norovirus: Montezuma's Revenge at Sea," above).

All large ships have **staffed infirmaries,** but if you have special needs, check with the line to find out exactly what medical services are provided. The quality of ships' staffs and facilities can definitely vary. Generally, big ships have the best-equipped facilities and largest staff because they deal with such a huge number of passengers and crew. A few years ago, the author of an extensive *New York Times* article concluded that **Holland America** and **Princess** had the best onboard medical facilities, as well as the most generous pay packages for their doctors. Note that shipboard doctors are not necessarily certified in the United States, and aren't always experts in important areas such as cardiology.

Small ships (those discussed in chapter 8) generally don't carry onboard medical staff because they sail close to shore and can evacuate sick passengers quickly. Usually, some crewmembers have nursing or first-aid experience. Small ships always carry doctors when sailing more far-flung international itineraries.

size of the megaships (where it can sometimes be a long way from place to place), cabins designed for wheelchair users are intentionally located near elevators. If you don't use a wheelchair but have trouble walking, you'll also want to choose a cabin close to an elevator to avoid a long hike. The vast majority of small vessels and sailing ships do not have elevators.

TENDERING INTO PORT   If your ship is too large to dock or if a port's docks are already reserved by other vessels, your ship may anchor offshore and shuttle passengers to land via small boats known as tenders. Some tenders are large and stable and others are not, but the choppiness of the water can be a factor when boarding either way. If you use a wheelchair or have trouble walking, it may be difficult or impossible to get aboard. Holland America has a wheelchair-to-tender transport system aboard all of its ships (except *Prinsendam*) that locks your wheelchair on a lift and transports it safely between the gangway and the tender.

Check with your travel agent to find out if itineraries you're interested in allow your ship to dock at a pier. Note that weather conditions and heavy traffic may occasionally affect the way your ship reaches a port.

2

Booking Your Cruise & Getting the Best Price

Like everything else in the world, cruise prices fluctuate based on supply and demand. Economic slumps, geopolitical crises, and too many ships deployed in a given region drive rates down, while prosperous times and stiff competition push them up. What does remain steady year after year is the great overall value and convenience of a cruise. Read on to learn how to find the best cruises at the best fares. In this chapter, we've laid out smart booking strategies, along with other money-saving suggestions and booking tips.

1 Doing the Math: Cruise Pricing 101

It's simple. When the lines have more ships than they can fill, prices are low. They're higher when people are clamoring to cruise. Given the shaky but recovering economy in 2010, at press time, many ships weren't sailing full, so cruise lines eager to fill cabins are offering fares as low as $499 and $599 for weeklong Caribbean cruises or 14-night transatlantic crossing, and not too much more for a week in Alaska. Expect prices to be higher during holiday periods (such as spring break and Christmas), but overall, if you can spare the dough, now's the time to go. "Consumers are definitely in the driver's seat these days," says Mike Driscoll, editor of industry bible *Cruise Week.*

As for the actual booking process, cruise lines still tend to do what they've been doing for years, relying on traditional **travel agents** and **websites** to sell their product, rather than retaining huge in-house reservations departments.

Generally, travel agents have less leeway in discounting than previously, as the cruise lines have taken more control of their pricing. This means you're less likely than in the past to find rates dramatically different from one travel agent to another.

For tips on using both online and brick-and-mortar agencies to the best advantage, see "Agents & the Web: Finding the Best Deals," later in this chapter.

2 The Prices in This Guide

Just like the airbrushed models dancing and lounging throughout cruise lines' brochures and across their websites, the prices printed in many of them are inflated. So remember that **you'll always pay less,** except aboard some of the specialized small-ship lines.

Many cruise guides and magazines print these brochure rates despite knowing how useless they are in the real world, but not us. Working with Nashville-based **Just Cruisin' Plus** (© **800/888-0922;** www.justcruisinplus.com), we've determined the **actual prices** people are paying for cruises aboard all the ships in this book. The difference can be startling, with the actual prices sometimes coming in $1,000 less than what's listed in the cruise lines' brochures. A few lines have recognized the ludicrousness of this situation and simply stopped printing brochure rates—and we have, too. In our ship-review chapters, we've opted to only print the sample actual pricing that we received from Just Cruisin' Plus, broken down to the approximate per-day cost for the lowest-priced **inside cabins** (ones without windows), lowest-priced **outside cabins** (with windows), and lowest-prices **suites** aboard each ship. Remember that cruise ships generally have many different categories of cabins within the basic divisions of inside, outside, and suite, all priced differently. The rates we've listed represent the *lowest priced* (which usually equates to smallest) in each division. If you're interested in booking a roomier, fancier cabin or suite, the price will be higher, with rates for high-end inside cabins being close to those for low-end outsides, and rates for high-end outsides being close to those for low-end suites.

Remember that rates are always subject to the basic principles of supply and demand, so those listed here are meant as a guide only and are in no way etched in stone—the price you pay may be higher or lower, depending on when you book, when you choose to travel, whether any special discounts are being offered by the cruise lines, and a slew of other factors. All rates are cruise only, per person, based on double occupancy, and, unless otherwise noted, include **port charges** (the per-passenger fee each island charges the cruise line for entry). Government fees and taxes are additional.

3 The Cost: What's Included & What's Not

Overall, a cruise is superconvenient and adds up to a pretty good deal when you consider that your main vacation ingredients—accommodations; meals and most snacks; stops at ports of call; a packed schedule of activities; use of gyms, pools, and other facilities; and shows, cabaret, jazz performances, and more—are covered in the cruise price. Just don't think it's *all* free. To beef up their bottom lines as much as possible, cruise lines are pushing a slew of **added-cost onboard extras,** and pushing them more aggressively than ever, we might add. You can always just say no, but if you're like most of us, you'll have an "oh, what the heck" attitude once you step across that gangway. So, when figuring out your budget, be sure to figure in the additional costs you'll incur for shore excursions (which can run from $50 up to $500, with many in the neighborhood of $75 to $100 a pop), bar drinks and specialty coffees, pricey spa treatments ($40–$500, plus tip, though $110–$150 is about average for a 50-min. massage), souvenirs, and even fresh flowers and fancy cakes if your self-restraint is really low. **Gratuities** are also typically charged to guests' accounts at the end of the cruise; the cruise lines pay their service staff minimal salaries on the assumption that they'll make most of their pay in tips. Generally, you can expect to tip about $70 per person during a weeklong cruise. (For more about tipping, see chapter 3, "Things to Know Before You Go.") If you're the gambling type, you're a prime candidate for increasing your ship's revenue stream, whether your game is craps, bingo, scratch-off cards, or Caribbean stud poker.

Some of the most luxurious and expensive lines—Silversea, Seabourn, Regent Seven Seas, and SeaDream Yacht Club—come closest to being truly all-inclusive by including all alcoholic beverages and gratuities in their cruise rates. Aside from these aberrations, though, you can expect to shell out at least another $250 to $500 per person for an average 7-night cruise. You can easily double or triple that if, for instance, you have a bottle of wine with dinner every night, a couple of cocktails after dinner, go on three $100 shore excursions, hit the ship's $30-per-person alternative restaurants a few times, try your luck at bingo, and buy some trinkets in the onboard shops or at ports of call. Of course, just as at a hotel, you'll also pay extra for items such as ship-to-shore phone calls and e-mails, massages, manicures, facials, haircuts, fancy coffees, and medical treatments in the ship's infirmary. If you're not cruising from a port you can drive to, then you'll have to figure in **airfare to the ship,** which is rarely included in cruise prices.

4 Money-Saving Strategies

From early-booking discounts and last-minute deals to sharing cabins and senior and frequent-cruiser discounts, there are a lot of ways to save money on your cruise.

As they have for years, cruise lines continue to offer **early-booking discounts,** though when times are tough, many of these discounts will be offered up until departure, so there's much less incentive to book early. Price aside, when booking early you naturally are more assured of getting exactly what you want in terms of cruise line, ship, and everything else.

If you're in the habit of traveling at the last minute, you can snag good deals for Caribbean cruises this way, even more so during **slow periods** such as September, October, and nonholiday weeks in November and December. The main thing you may sacrifice when booking late is a measure of choice: You'll have to take the ship,

Average Cost of Onboard Extras

Just so you're not shocked when your shipboard account is settled at the end of your trip, here are some average prices for onboard extras.

Laundry	$1–$7 per item
Self-service laundry	$1–$3 per load
Pressing	$1–$4 per item
5×7-inch photo from ship photographer	$7–$12
Scotch and soda at an onboard bar	$4–$7
Bottle of beer (domestic/imported)	$3.50/$6
Bottle of wine to accompany dinner	$25–$300
Glass of wine	$6–$18
Bottle of Evian water (.5 liter/1.5 liters)	$1.50/$4
Can of Coca-Cola	$1.50–$2
Ship-to-shore phone call or fax	$4–$15 per minute
Cellphone calls at sea	Approx. $2–$3 per minute
Sending e-mails	50¢–$1 per minute
50-minute massage	$110–$150
Sunscreen, 6-ounce bottle	$12
Disposable camera	$15–$25

itinerary, and cabin category that's available, whether it's the one you wanted or not. Getting airfare at the last minute may be tough, too. Plus, most last-minute deals are completely nonrefundable; if you book a week before the cruise, for example, the full fare is due upfront and you get zip back if you change your mind a few days later.

You'll find **last-minute deals** advertised online (for instance, on Frommers.com), but the best route is checking with travel agents who specialize in cruises, and getting on their e-mail blast lists that alert you to special promotions and discounts. See "Agents & the Web: Finding the Best Deals," later in this chapter.

From time to time, some cruise lines offer discounts to **seniors** (usually defined as anyone 55 years or older), so don't keep your age a secret, and always ask your travel agent about these discounts when you're booking. For discounts in general, the best organization to join is **AARP,** 601 E St. NW, Washington, DC 20049 (© **888/687-2277;** www.aarp.org), the biggest outfit in the United States for people age 50 and over.

If you've cruised with a particular cruise line before, you're considered a valued **repeat passenger,** and are usually rewarded with 5% to 10% discounts (sometimes higher) on future cruises. Depending on how many times you've sailed, you may also get cabin upgrades, invitations to private cocktail parties, priority check-in at the terminal, casino vouchers, logo souvenirs, a special newsletter, and a bottle of wine or a fruit basket in your cabin on embarkation days. The catch to all of this is that repeat-passenger discounts often cannot be combined with other pricing deals, particularly in the case of the mainstream lines.

If you're a serious repeater, though, the generous booty you get on the small upscale ships can add up to something substantial. Upscale lines like Seabourn and Silverseas will actually reward you with a free cruise after you rack up several hundred cruise days with them.

Some cruise lines offer reduced **group rates** to folks booking at least eight or more cabins, but this is really based on supply and demand. If a ship is selling well, group deals may not be available, but if it isn't, the cruise line has a lot more incentive to wheel and deal. Groups may be family reunions and the like, but travel agents may also create their own "groups" whose members don't even know they're part of one. Quick explanation: The travel agent reserves a block of cabins on a given ship and the cruise line in turn assigns it a discounted group rate that agents can pass on to their clients. The cruise line benefits because they're potentially selling a lot of cabins through agency X, and the agency benefits because it can offer its clients a good price. So, always ask your travel agent if you can be piggybacked onto some group space.

Very small groups—three or four people max in most cases—can share one cabin if it's equipped with **third or fourth berths** (sofa beds or bunk-style berths that pull down from the ceiling or wall). This route isn't recommended for anyone who suffers from claustrophobia. Disney, Carnival, and NCL go one better by offering standard cabins geared to families, which can accommodate five people—Disney's even have 1½ bathrooms. The rates for third, fourth, and fifth passengers in a cabin, whether adults or children, are typically 30% to 60% or more off the normal adult fare—and these days sometimes they're free. You can also look into **sharing a suite.** Many can accommodate five to seven people, and some are outlandishly roomy.

If cruising solo, you'll generally be charged something called the **single supplement,** which adds 50% to 100% to the standard per-person cruise fare—a consequence of cruise lines basing their revenue expectations on two people sharing every cabin, though the tide is turning for singles (NCL, for instance, now offers a bunch of small 100-foot studio cabins geared to singles aboard the *Norwegian Epic*). HAL offers another alternative for singles: a **cabin-share service** that will try to match you with a same-gender roommate; if they can't find a roommate, you may get the cabin at the regular double occupancy rate anyway.

5 Agents & the Web: Finding the Best Deals

Today, practically everybody has a website, and the difference between so-called **Web-based cruise sellers** and more **traditional travel agencies** is that the former rely on their sites for actual bookings, while the latter use theirs as glorified advertising space to promote their offerings, doing all actual business in person or over the phone. With a few exceptions, the cruise lines also have **direct-booking engines** on their own sites, but we don't recommend using them. Why? Because agents and Web-based sellers may have negotiated group rates with the lines, be part of a consortium with whom a line is doing an upgrade promotion, or have other deals going that enable them to offer you lower rates. Though it may sound peculiar, the cruise lines actually prefer that you book through third parties because having agents and websites do the grunt work allows the lines to maintain small reservations staffs and, simultaneously, maintain goodwill in a system that works—something they have to consider because the vast majority of cruises are booked through agencies of one type or another. Typically, mainstream cruise lines report that about 70% of their bookings come from traditional travel agencies (for the luxury lines, about 98% use travel agents). "The more you pay, the more likely you are to need or want a travel agent," says Mike Driscoll.

Which Offers Better Prices?

As far as cruise prices go, there's no absolutely quantifiable difference between the real-live travel agents (whether your hometown brick-and-mortar mom-and-pop agency or a big anonymous mega-agency) and Internet-based cruise sellers. For some years now, the major lines have been offering all agencies, large or small, the same basic rates, give or take. What may separate one agency from another are the extras that may be thrown in, from free bottles of wine to onboard spending credits.

Which Provides Better Service?

Because pricing is closer to being equitable across all types of cruise agencies than ever before, it's really service that distinguishes one agency from another. Most websites give you only a menu of ships and itineraries to select from, plus a basic search capability that takes into account only destination, price, length of trip, and date, without consideration of the type of cruise experience each line offers. That's fine if you know exactly what you want, and are comfortable on the computer. If, on the other hand, you have limited experience with cruising and with booking on the Web, it may be better to see a traditional agent, who can help you wade through the choices and answer your questions. For instance, a good agent can tell you which cabins have their views obstructed by lifeboats; which are near loud areas such as discos and the engine room; which ships and itineraries you should avoid if you're not looking for a party vibe; and, in general, what the major differences are between cabin categories. A lot of this kind of detailed information won't be found on the Web—you need to hear it from a person. To be better prepared before you call an agent, it's a good idea to do some research on the Web first.

Keep in mind, though, that you need to find an agent who really knows the business—and this applies to every type of agent: those who work out of their home or an agency office, those who work for large conglomerates and deal mostly over the

Be Savvy & Beware of Scams

With the number of offers seen by a potential cruise buyer, it can be difficult to know if an agency is or isn't reliable, legitimate, or, for that matter, stable. It pays to be on your guard against fly-by-night operators and agents who may lead you astray.

- **Get a referral.** A recommendation from a trusted friend or colleague (or from this guidebook) is one of the best ways to hook up with a reputable agent.
- **Use the cruise lines' agent lists.** Many cruise line websites include agency locator lists, naming agencies around the country with which they do business. These are by no means comprehensive lists of all good or bad agencies, but an agent's presence on these lists is usually another good sign of experience.
- **Beware of snap recommendations.** If an agent suggests a cruise line without asking you a single question first about your tastes, beware. Because agents work on commissions from the lines, some may try to shanghai you into cruising with a company that pays them the highest rates, even though that line may not be right for you.
- **Always use a credit card to pay for your cruise.** It gives you more protection in the event the agency or cruise line fails. When your credit card statement arrives, make sure the payment was made to the cruise line, not the travel agency. If you find that payment was actually made to the agency, it's a big red flag that something's wrong. If you insist on paying by check, you'll be making it out to the agency, so it may be wise to ask if the agency has default protection. Many do. (*Note:* The only exception to this is when an agency is running a charter cruise—for example, a music cruise with special entertainment.)
- **Always follow the cruise line's payment schedule.** Never agree to a different schedule the travel agency comes up with. The lines' terms are always clearly printed in their brochures and websites and usually require an initial deposit, with the balance due no later than 75 to 45 days before departure. If you're booking 2 months or less before departure, full payment is usually required at the time of booking.
- **Keep on top of your booking.** If you ever fail to receive a document or ticket on the date it's been promised, inquire about it immediately. If you're told that your cruise reservation was canceled because of overbooking and that you must pay extra for a confirmed and rescheduled sailing, demand a full refund and/or contact your credit card company to stop payment.

phone, and those who staff toll-free numbers associated with Web-based sellers. Some are little more than order takers: They may not know much more than pricing, and may never even have been on a cruise themselves. This system works okay for selling air travel, where the big question is coach or first class, case closed; however, a lot more variables are associated with booking a cruise. An experienced cruise agent—someone who has sailed on or inspected a variety of ships and booked many customers aboard in the past—will be able to tell you about special promotions (such as cabin upgrades), act as an intermediary should any problems arise with your booking, order special extras such as a bottle of champagne in your cabin when you arrive, and in general make your planning easy.

So how do you know if an agent is any good? The best way, of course, is to use one who has been referred to you by a reliable friend or acquaintance. This is particularly valuable these days, when agents are being pressed to squeeze more profit from every sale, making them less likely to take the time to discuss options. When you're searching for a good agent, it doesn't hurt if an agent is an **Accredited Cruise Counselor (ACC), Master Cruise Counselor (MCC), or Elite Cruise Counselor (ECC),** designations doled out by the Cruise Lines International Association (CLIA), an industry trade organization, after agents take classes and inspect a number of ships. Many of the cruise lines' websites list **preferred agencies** (generally broken down or searchable by city or state), as does the CLIA site (**www.cruising.org**). Many of the most reliable agencies are also members of **agent groups,** such as Virtuoso, Signature Travel Network, and Vacation.com. In the sections below, we list some of the best agencies and the major cruise-selling websites.

6 Agencies & Websites

Of the approximately 17,000 U.S. travel agencies (including home-based), 15% sell 90% of all cruise travel in North America. Agencies come in all shapes and sizes, from small neighborhood stores to huge chain operations. Like banking, telecommunications, and media, the travel industry has been rife with consolidation over the past decade, so even that mom-and-pop travel agency on Main Street may turn out to be an affiliate of a larger agency. When it comes to home-based agents, they may or may not be affiliated with a national group such as CruiseOne or SeaMaster Cruises. It's better if they are, so they have access to more resources and competitive rates. Use a home-based agent only if he or she has been doing this for a long time.

Even though you'll get similarly low rates from both traditional and Web-based agencies these days, we can't stress enough that service counts for something, too. There's value in using a travel agent you've worked with in the past or one who comes highly recommended by someone you trust. A good agent will be there for you if problems arise.

Finding a Good Travel Agent

To find a reputable cruise-only or full-service travel agency in your town, contact one of a handful of **agency groups** or **consortiums,** which screen their members. The three following groups, whose members specialize in mainstream cruises, maintain websites that allow you to search for local agencies with your postal code or city: **TravelSavers** (© 800/366-9895; www.travelsavers.com) and **Ensemble Travel Group** (© 866/350-7460;** www.ensembletravel.com) are both networks of more than 1,000 travel agencies; and **Vacation.com** (© 800/843-0733; www.vacation.com) is the largest group in the U.S., with some 6,000 members.

If you're looking for a top-of-the-line cruise, definitely use an agency that's a member of one of the following agency groups whose members specialize in luxury cruises. Agency members can pass on lots of great extras to clients, from cabin upgrades to private cocktail parties. Members are extremely knowledgeable and it's not unusual for someone from the agency to sail on board the cruise to assist clients. **Virtuoso** (© **866/ 401-7974;** www.virtuoso.com) is a consortium of more than 300 member agencies nationwide, including some on the list above. To find an agency in your area, call the toll-free number, or e-mail **travel@virtuoso.com**. Another group is **Signature Travel Network** (© **800/339-0868;** www.signaturetravelnetwork.com), with about 200 member agencies across the country. Call to find an agency in your area, or e-mail.

7 Choosing Your Cabin

When it comes right down to it, choosing a cabin is really a question of money. From a windowless lower-deck cabin with upper and lower bunks to a 1,400-square-foot suite with a butler and mile-long private veranda, cruise ships can present a dozen or more stateroom categories that differ by size, location in the ship, amenities, and, of course, price. To see what we mean, go to the Cruises Only website (**www. cruisesonly.com**); it presents 360-degree tours and photos of most ships in "About Your Ship" pages throughout the site.

Traditionally, the rule of thumb is that the higher up your cabin sits in a ship and the more daylight it has, the more you pay; the lower you go into the bowels of the ship, the cheaper the fare. On some of the more modern ships, however, that old rule doesn't always ring true. On ships launched recently by Carnival, for instance, designers have scattered their most desirable suites on midlevel decks as well as top decks, thereby diminishing the prestige of an upper-deck cabin. For the most part, though, and especially on small ships, where cabins are virtually identical, cabins on higher decks are still more expensive, and outside cabins (with windows or balconies) are more expensive than inside cabins (those without). Outside cabins whose windows are obstructed by lifeboats will be cheaper than ones with good views.

Evaluating Cabin Size

Inch for inch, cruise ship cabins are smaller than hotel rooms. Of course, having a private balcony attached to your cabin, as many do, makes your living space that much bigger.

A roomy **standard cabin** is about 170 to 190 square feet, although some of the smallest are about 85 to 100 square feet. Disney has some of the more spacious standard cabins at sea, at 226 square feet. Celebrity's standards are spacious enough at around 170 to 175 square feet, with those on its Millennium-class ships sometimes as big as 190 square feet. Carnival's and Holland America's are about 185 square feet or more. By way of comparison, equivalent standard cabins on a good number of ships in the Norwegian and Royal Caribbean lines are quite a bit smaller—try 120 to 160 square feet—and can be cramped. Cabins on the small-ship lines such as Blount Small Ship Adventures can be very snug—on the order of 70 to 100 square feet.

All the standard cabins on the high-end lines are roomy—in fact, many of the high-end ships are "suite only." For example, on Silversea's *Silver Shadow* and *Silver Whisper,* cabins are 287 square feet, plus a 58-square-foot balcony. Across the board, from mainstream to luxe, **suites and penthouses** are obviously the most spacious, measuring from about 250 square feet to more than 1,400 square feet, plus private verandas.

Most cruise lines publish schematic drawings in their brochures, with square footage and, in some cases, measurements of length and width, which should give you some idea of what to expect. (We also include square footage ranges for inside cabins, outside cabins, and suites in the cruise ship descriptions in chapters 6 to 8.) Consider measuring off the dimensions on your bedroom floor and imagine your temporary oceangoing home, being sure to block out part of that space for the bathroom and closet. As a rough guideline, within a cabin of around 100 square feet, about a third of the floor space is gobbled up by those functional necessities.

Now, while you may be thinking, "Gee, that's really not a lot of space," remember that, like a bedroom in a large house, your cabin will likely be a place you use only for sleeping, showering, and changing clothes.

The Scoop on Inside Cabins vs. Outside Cabins

Whether you really plan to spend time in your cabin is a question that should be taken into account when deciding whether to book an inside cabin or an outside cabin (that is, one without windows or one with windows or a balcony). If you plan to get up bright and early, hit the buffet breakfast, and not stop till the cows come home, you can probably get away with booking an inside cabin and save yourself a bundle. Inside cabins are generally neither as bad nor as claustrophobic as they sound. Many, in fact—such as those aboard most of the Carnival and Celebrity fleets—are the same size as the outside cabins, and most cruise lines design and decorate them to provide an illusion of light and space.

If, on the other hand, you want to lounge around and take it easy in your cabin, maybe ordering breakfast from room service and eating while the sun streams in—or, better yet, eating out *in* the sun, on your private veranda—then an outside cabin is definitely a worthwhile investment. They're also vital for smokers (though some lines prohibit smoking on cabin balconies). Remember, though, that if it's a view of the sea you want, be sure when booking that your window or balcony doesn't just give you a good view of a lifeboat or some other obstruction (and remember, there are likely to be balconies on the deck right above your balcony, so they're more like porches than actual verandas). Some cruise line brochures tell you which cabins are obstructed, and a good travel agent or a cruise line's reservation agent can tell you which cabins on a particular ship might have this problem.

Other Cabin Matters to Consider

Unless you're booking at the last minute (a few weeks or less before sailing), as part of a group, or in a cabin-share or cabin-guarantee program (which means you agree to a price, and find out your exact cabin at the last minute), you can work with your agent to choose a particular cabin. If possible, try to have some idea of what cabin category you'd like, or at least have a list of must-haves or must-avoids. Need a **bathtub** rather than just a shower? That narrows your choices on most ships. Want **connecting cabins** so you and your kids, friends, or relatives can share space? Most ships have 'em, but they sometimes book up early, as do cabins with **third or fourth berths** (usually pull-down bunks or a sofa bed). Almost all ships have cabin TVs these days, but a few don't. Want an **elevator** close by to make it easy to get between decks? Is the view out the cabin's windows obstructed by lifeboats or other ship equipment? Most important, **keep cabin position in mind if you suffer from seasickness.** A midships location on a middle deck is best because it's a kind of fulcrum point, the area least affected by the vessel's rocking and rolling in rough seas.

8 Booking Your Air Travel

Except during special promotions, airfare is rarely included in cruise rates for Caribbean, Alaska, Mexico, and New England/Canada cruises, though it often is for Europe and Asia itineraries. So if you can't drive to your port of embarkation and need to fly to get to Miami, New York, San Juan, New Orleans, or one of the other 20-plus home ports, you'll have to either purchase airfare on your own through an agent or online, or buy it as a package with your cruise. The latter is often referred to as an **air add-on** or **air/sea package.** You can usually find information on these programs in the back of cruise line brochures and on their websites, along with prices on flights from more than 100 U.S. and Canadian cities to the port of embarkation. Here are the pros and cons to booking your airfare through the cruise line.

- **Pros:** When you book through the cruise line, they'll know your airline schedule and, in the event of delayed flights and other unavoidable snafus, will do what they can to make sure you get to the ship.
- **Cons:** Odds are it'll be more expensive to book through the cruise line than on your own. Also, if you book through the lines, you probably won't be able to use any frequent-flier miles you've accumulated, and the air add-on could require a circuitous routing—with indirect legs and layovers—before you finally arrive at your port of embarkation. Sources tell us only about 10% of passengers book airfare through the cruise lines.

If you choose to arrange your own air transportation, make absolutely sure that airfare is not included as part of your cruise contract. It rarely is with the exception of Europe and Asia cruises, but if it is, you're often granted a deduction (usually around $250 per person) off the cruise fare. If you purchase your own airfare, you can buy **bus transfers from the airport to the ship** through the cruise line (if you buy the cruise line airfare, transfers are often included in the price), but it's often cheaper to take a taxi, as is the case in Miami and Fort Lauderdale.

9 Prebooking Your Dinner Table & Arranging Special Diets

In addition to choosing your cabin when booking your cruise, on most ships you can also choose an **early or late seating** for dinner in the main restaurant (the buffet restaurants on most ships are always open seating), and sometimes even put in a request for a particular size table (tables for 2, 4, 8, 10, and so on). Assignments for breakfast and lunch are rarely required, as dining rooms operate with open seating during these meals. At night, though, early seatings allow you to get first dibs on shipboard nightlife (or, conversely, promptly hit the sack), while late seatings allow you to linger a bit longer over your meal. In the past few years, more lines—especially Norwegian and, to a slightly lesser extent, Royal Caribbean and Princess—have junked this traditional early-late paradigm (in at least some of their restaurants) in favor of **open-seating dining** in which you simply show up when hunger pangs strike. For a more detailed discussion, see section 6, "Onboard Dining Options," in chapter 4.

If you follow a **special diet**—whether vegetarian, low salt, low fat, heart healthy, kosher, halal, or any other, or if you have certain food allergies—make this known to your travel agent when you book, or at least 30 or more days before the cruise, and make sure your diet can be accommodated at all three meals (sometimes special meal plans will cover only breakfast and dinner). The vast majority of ships provide vegetarian meals and health-conscious choices on their daily menus nowadays (Crystal even offers kosher food daily), but it can't hurt to arrange things ahead of time. A cruise is not the place to go on an involuntary starvation diet.

10 Booking Pre- & Post-Cruise Hotel Stays

Cruise lines often provide hotel stays in the cities of embarkation and debarkation, and most of them are tourist attractions in their own right. You may want to spend some time in New York, Oahu, or Vancouver before sailing, or drive to Disney World from Port Canaveral. The cruise lines' package deals usually include hotel stays and transportation from the hotel to the ship (before the cruise) or from the docks to the hotel (after the cruise). Inquire with your travel agent, and compare what the line is offering with what you may be able to arrange independently. Nowadays, you might get a hotel stay much cheaper on your own.

11 Cancellations & Insurance

Hey, stuff happens. Given today's unpredictable geopolitical situation, economic woes, and extreme weather conditions, you just never know what might occur. A cruise could be canceled, for example, because of shipyard delays (if you've booked an inaugural cruise), the outbreak of an infectious disease, mechanical breakdowns (such as nonfunctioning air-conditioning or an engine fire), the cruise line going out of business, an act of war, or a major flood. Some people feel more comfortable buying cancellation protection and insurance just in case, to the tune of typically several hundred dollars (on average, about 6% to 7% of the total cruise cost).

"It depends on the individual. For example, insurance makes much more sense if you're a senior citizen or are responsible for someone with health problems," says *Cruise Week* editor Mike Driscoll.

That said, in today's competitive market, cruise lines have been making extraordinary efforts to appease disappointed passengers, whether they bought insurance or not. Typically, a line will reschedule the canceled cruise and give passengers big discounts on future cruises—after all, they don't want bad press from cheating hundreds or thousands of people. There are, however, no set rules on how a line will compensate you, over and above a refund, in the event of a cancellation.

Now, if the shoe is on the other foot and you need to cancel your own cruise, you'll generally get a refund—most lines give you every cent back if you cancel at least 2 to 3 months before your departure date, although details vary from line to line. If you cancel closer to departure, you'll usually get at least a partial refund up until about 15 to 30 days before the cruise if you haven't yet made the final payment.

"You buy insurance if you're concerned about medical issues or work commitments possibly preventing you from taking a cruise at the last minute," adds Driscoll. For all of these reasons—worries about travel, worries about cruise lines canceling or going belly up, sudden illness or other emergencies, missed flights that cause you to miss the ship, or even if you just change your mind—you may want to think about purchasing **travel insurance.** Charlie Funk, co-owner of Just Cruisin' Plus in Nashville, points out that if your primary health insurance is Medicare, you should *not* travel abroad without trip insurance as Medicare covers zero medical costs if you're outside the U.S. (and few, if any, Medicare supplement providers offer coverage either). Remember, almost all cruise ships are foreign-flagged, which means they're considered international destinations, even if the cruise originates and/or ends in a U.S. port. Now, if you're *just* worried about missing the ship, go a day early and spend your money on a hotel and nice dinner instead. If you're worried about medical problems occurring during your trip, on the other hand, travel insurance may be more vital. Except for the small coastal cruisers described in chapter 8, most cruise ships have an infirmary staffed by a doctor and a nurse or two; but in the event of a dire illness, the ship's medical staff can only do so much. Therefore, you may want a policy that covers **emergency medical evacuation** (having a helicopter pick up a sick person on board a ship will cost a bundle without insurance) and, if your regular insurance doesn't cover it, the potential cost of major medical treatment while away from home. There are policies sold through the cruise lines (with details varying from line to line) and others sold independently, and both have pros and cons.

Cruise Line Policies vs. Third-Party Insurers

A good travel agent can tell you about policies sold through the cruise lines and ones sold independently of the lines. No matter which you choose, it's absolutely crucial to read the fine print because terms vary from policy to policy.

Both kinds typically reimburse you in some way when your trip is affected by unexpected events (such as flights canceled due to bad weather, plane crashes, dockworkers' strikes, or the illness or death of a loved one, as late as the day before or day of departure), but not by "acts of God," such as hurricanes and earthquakes (the exception being if your home is made uninhabitable, putting you in no mood to continue with your cruise plans). Both also typically cover **cancellation of the cruise** for medical reasons (yours or a family member's, whether they were a part of your traveling party or not); **medical emergencies** during the cruise, including evacuation from the ship; lost or damaged luggage; and a cruise missed due to weather-related airline delays (though some only cover if the delay is more than 3 hr.). Neither kind of policy will reimburse you if your travel agent didn't send in your payment and goes bankrupt, so using a travel agent you're very familiar with or one who's recommended is the safest precaution you can take. (And, of course, *always use a credit card,* never a check. If a corrupt travel agent cashes it, or a decent one just goes out of business, then you could get screwed.) Most cancellation policies also do not cover cancellations due to work requirements.

THIRD-PARTY COVERAGE   Even though agents get a commission for selling both cruise line policies and independent policies, most agents and industry insiders believe that non-cruise-line policies are the best bet. That's because many, such as Access America (see below), will issue insurance to cover those with **preexisting medical conditions** if the condition is stable when you purchase the insurance (a doctor would have to verify this if you ever made a claim) and if you purchase the policy within some specified time, usually within 14 days of your initial deposit on the cruise. They also offer **supplier-default coverage** that kicks in if a cruise line goes bankrupt, as a handful did between 2000 and 2003.

Still, you shouldn't be afraid to book a cruise. A well-connected travel agent should see the writing on the wall months before a cruise line fails—commissions will slow or stop being paid, phone calls won't be returned, and industry trade publications will report on any problems. The less customer-service-driven cruise sellers may not stop pushing a troubled cruise line, however, and may continue selling it up to the very last minute.

According to the Fair Credit Billing Act, if you paid by credit card (and again, you should *always* pay with a credit card), you'll generally get your money back if you dispute the charge within 60 days of the date the charge first appears. If you paid in full 4 months before the cruise, you'll likely be out of luck going the credit-reimbursement route and may have to resort to litigation. Also, while many lines post a multimillion-dollar bond with the Federal Maritime Commission, creating a fund from which they can reimburse creditors should they fail financially, it's no guarantee you'll get all or any of your money back. Technically, the bond covers cruise payments for all passengers embarking from U.S. ports, but because the line would have banks or other vendors to pay off first, you'd likely get only pennies on the dollar, if that. Still, it's better that a cruise line have a bond than not—and if you learn that a line is having trouble making bond payments, it may be a sign of serious financial woes.

Policies are available from reputable insurers such as **Access America,** P.O. Box 71533, Richmond, VA 23286 (© **800/284-8300;** www.accessamerica.com), and **Travel Guard International,** 1145 Clark St., Stevens Point, WI 54481 (© **800/826-4919;** www.travelguard.com), whose websites maintain lists of the lines they cover (or no longer cover); these are helpful in figuring out which lines may be financially shaky. **Travel Insured International,** 52-S Oakland Ave., P.O. Box 280568, East Hartford, CT 06128 (© **800/243-3174;** www.travelinsured.com), offers policies ranging from "Cancel for Work Reasons" to "Cancel for Any Reason" (up to 48 hr. before departure, and receive up to 75% of the nonrefundable trip cost), though restrictions apply (for instance, the coverage isn't offered to residents of New York, Oregon, and Washington State).

CRUISE LINE COVERAGE Cruise lines have their own policies, many of them administered by New York–based **BerkelyCare** (© **800/797-4514;** www.berkely.com), and they are considered secondary coverage. If you opt for this type of policy out of sheer convenience (the cost is added right onto your cruise fare), keep in mind they do not cover you in the event of a cruise line bankruptcy (though using a credit card can save you here; see above) or for cancellation of your cruise due to a preexisting medical condition, usually defined as an unstable condition existing within 60 days of your buying the insurance. Nor will their policy provide protection for airline tickets purchased on your own. Some lines' policies are cancellation *waivers* rather than insurance policies and will issue a cruise credit for the penalty amount if a medical claim is deemed preexisting, and issue cash if you cancel for a covered reason. Generally, the cancellation penalty imposed by the cruise line would be 100% of the cruise fare—for example, if you cancel a few days before the cruise (assuming you've paid in full)—or it could be just $300 if you cancel right after making the initial cruise deposit. Be sure the coverage offered is truly an insurance policy. In some cases, the coverage is really a cancellation waiver that provides credit for a future cruise under limited conditions. Even if you buy cruise line insurance, it's always a good idea to carry a credit card with a lot of available credit to ensure prompt emergency care in a foreign port, as you'll have to wait until you get home to file for a reimbursement.

Sounds like the third-party policies win hands down, right? Well, to make it just a little more complicated, a handful of cruise line policies are actually better in some areas than outside policies. For example, **Princess Cruises** has an insurance policy that allows you to cancel for all the reasons that an outside policy would (illness, injury) and get cash reimbursement, or it will let you cancel for any reason whatsoever (from fear of flying to a bad hair day) up until the day of departure and have 75% to 90% of the normal penalty for canceling your cruise applied toward a future trip. **Norwegian, Celebrity,** and **Royal Caribbean** have similar "any reason" policies, which provide a cruise credit for up to 75%.

For an extra 3% of your total Silversea vacation cost when purchased with a travel insurance product that contains trip cancellation benefits (or 8% of vacation cost if purchased alone), high-end Silversea allows you to cancel cruises for any reason 1 to 90 days before sailing and get a credit for 100% of the penalty amount (including airfare, if booked through Silversea), applicable toward any cruise during the following 12 months.

Many other lines have similar cancellation plans. The cruise lines using the Berkely-Care policies (see above) also reimburse passengers for days missed on a cruise—say, if you missed your flight and had to join up with the cruise 2 days later—covering hotel costs during the missed days and transportation to the ship (though typically only to a max of $500), as do third-party policies. Keep in mind, cruise line policies do change, so before purchasing insurance, be sure you understand exactly what you're getting.

12 Putting Down a Deposit & Reviewing Tickets

If you're booking several months or more ahead of time, then you have to leave a deposit to secure the booking; if you're booking at the last minute, the full fare will be due when you make the reservation. Depending on the policy of the line you selected, the deposit will either be fixed at a predetermined amount or represent a percentage of the ticket's total cost. The length of time that cruise lines will hold a cabin without a deposit is getting shorter by the minute. It seems pretty clear, in this age of near-obsessive "shopping around," that the cruise lines are doing their part to discourage it. It used to be that a cruise could be held for a week before you had to plunk down cash; most lines have now shortened this window to 1 to 3 days (exceptions include exotic itineraries that aren't ultracompetitive). Carnival, for instance, requires a deposit within 24 hours. Last-minute bookings may even have a window of a few hours or less.

The balance of the cruise price is due anywhere from 60 to 90 days before you depart; holiday cruises and longer sailings may require final payments earlier, perhaps 90 days before departure. The payment schedule for deposits on groups is often more liberal. Booking at the last minute usually requires payment in full at the time of booking.

Credit card payments are made directly to the cruise line, but payments by check are made out to the agency, which then passes payment on to the cruise line. As we've said repeatedly, it's preferable to pay by credit card, for the added protection.

"Except in certain circumstances, if the travel agency asks, prefers, or insists on running your credit card through the agency processing terminal, it is a *major* red flag that most often should send you running from the building," says Charlie Funk, co-owner of Just Cruisin' Plus in Nashville. The only exception to this is when an agency is doing a charter or group with special entertainment or features, and the cruise is offered only through the agency.

Carefully review your ticket, invoice, itinerary, and/or vouchers to confirm that they accurately reflect the departure date, ship, and cabin category you booked. The print-out usually lists a specific cabin number; if it doesn't, it designates a cabin category. Your exact cabin location may sometimes not be assigned to you until you board the ship.

If you need to cancel your cruise after putting down a deposit, you'll get all or most of your money back, depending on how close you are to departure. With Royal Caribbean, for instance, customers get a 100% refund if they cancel more than 70 days ahead. Less than 30 days from the cruise, the refund drops to 50%, and within the last week, it's your loss. Note that some travel agencies charge an administrative fee for cancellation, regardless of whether the cruise line does or does not. More service-oriented agencies tend not to charge these fees in most cases. Always ask *before* handing over your credit card number.

3

Things to Know Before You Go

You've bought your ticket and you're getting ready to cruise. Here are a few details you need to consider before setting sail.

1 Passports & Visas

Got a passport? If your ship docks at a foreign port—even a blatantly nonforeign foreign port like Vancouver, Canada—you'll probably need one. We say probably because there are loopholes: Technically speaking, U.S. citizens traveling on cruises that begin and end at the same U.S. port (which generally means cruises to the Caribbean, The Bahamas, Canada, and Mexico) can get away with presenting a birth certificate (original or copy) and a government-issued photo ID. **Children under age 16** can also cross U.S. land/sea borders using only a U.S. birth certificate. If you ask us, though, it's always a good idea to have a passport when traveling abroad—and it's an absolute necessity if traveling involves flying across the border, taking an open-jaw cruise, and so on.

If you don't have a passport or you need to replace an expired one, the **U.S. State Department website** (http://travel.state.gov) provides information. You can also inquire at your local passport acceptance facility, or call the **National Passport Information Center** (© 877/487-2778). Fees for new passports are $135 adults, $105 children ages 15 and under. Renewals cost $110. If you're in a hurry, you can pay an additional $60 fee to have your passport expedited for delivery within 2 weeks.

As you would before any trip abroad, make two photocopies of your documents and ID. Take one copy with you as a backup (keeping it in a different piece of luggage from the one holding your originals) and keep one copy at home.

After accepting your passport to board ship at the beginning of your cruise, the cruise line might hang onto it for the duration of your cruise, thus allowing the line to facilitate clearance procedures quickly at each port. Don't worry, this is normal. Your documents will be returned after the ship has departed its last foreign port of call, en route back to your home port.

Non–U.S./Canadian citizens departing from and/or returning to the U.S./Canada should check with their travel agent or cruise line to determine the required paperwork. Generally, you'll need a valid passport, alien-registration card as applicable, and occasionally a visa, as required by the individual countries you're visiting.

2 Money Matters

Know how they say cruises are all-inclusive vacations? They're lying. True, the bulk of your vacation expense is covered in the fare, but there are plenty of extras. We detail

Vaccinations Required?

Travel to the Caribbean, Mexico, and Central America does not generally warrant inoculations against tropical diseases, though the Centers for Disease Control (CDC) sometimes recommends prescription antimalarial drugs if conditions in certain destinations warrant. CDC recommendations and warnings can be viewed at **wwwn.cdc.gov/travel/default.aspx.**

the specifics in "The Cost: What's Included & What's Not" in chapter 2. In this section, we examine the way monetary transactions are handled on board and in port.

Onboard Charge Cards

Cruise ships operate on a cashless basis. Basically, this means you have a running tab and simply sign for what you buy on board during your cruise (bar drinks, meals at specialty restaurants, spa treatments, shore excursions, gift-shop purchases, and so on) and then pay up at the end. Very convenient, yes—and also very, very easy to forget your limits and spend more than you had intended.

Shortly before or after embarkation, a purser or check-in clerk will take an imprint of your credit card and issue you an **onboard charge card.** On the vast majority of ships, it also serves as both your room key and cruise ID, which you swipe through a scanner every time you leave or return to the ship. Small-ship lines that carry 100 or fewer passengers often forgo this kind of ID, and just ask for your cabin number when you're making onboard purchases.

On the last night of your cruise, an **itemized account** of all your charges will be slipped beneath your cabin door. If you agree with the charges, they'll automatically be billed to your credit card. If you'd rather pay in cash or if you dispute any charge, you'll need to stop by the office of the ship's cashier or purser. There may be a long waiting line, so don't go unless you have to.

Bringing Cash Ashore

The cashless system works just fine aboard ship, but remember, **you'll need cash in port.** Many people get so accustomed to not carrying their wallets aboard ship that they get off in port and find themselves without any money in their pockets. This is a minor inconvenience if your ship is docked and you have to trudge back aboard for cash, but a major annoyance if it's anchored offshore and you spend an hour ferrying back and forth by boat.

Credit cards are accepted at most port shops, but we recommend having some cash, ideally in small denominations, to cover the cost of taxi rides, tips for tour leaders, or purchases you make from crafts markets and street vendors. Information on local currency is included in chapters 9 through 16, but for the most part you don't have to worry about exchanging money at all. In the Caribbean, the U.S. dollar is the legal currency of the U.S. Virgin Islands, Puerto Rico, and (oddly enough) the British Virgin Islands, but vendors on islands that have their own currency almost always accept U.S. dollars too. Mexican, Central American, and Canadian ports are similarly dollar-friendly.

If you're running low on cash, **ATMs** are easy to find in every cruise port covered in this guide, often right at the cruise terminal. Remember that you'll get local currency from machines where the dollar isn't the legal tender, so don't withdraw more than you need. Many megaships also have ATMs (usually near the casino—surprise, surprise), but you can expect to be charged a hefty fee for using them—up to $5 in addition to what your bank charges you.

Many lines will cash **traveler's checks** at the purser's desk, and sometimes **personal checks** of up to about $200 to $250 (but sometimes only when accompanied by an American Express card, for guarantee). You can also often get a cash advance through your Visa, MasterCard, or Discover card.

Except aboard some of the ultraluxury lines, **gratuities for the crew** are not normally included in the cruise rates, though many lines these days either automatically add a suggested gratuity to your end-of-cruise bill or give you the option of charging gratuities. Where this is not the case, you should reserve some cash so that you won't feel like Scrooge at the end of the cruise. See "Tipping, Customs & Other End-of-Cruise Concerns," later in this chapter, for more about the subject.

3 Keeping in Touch While at Sea

Some people take a cruise to get away from it all, but others are communication addicts. For them, today's mainstream and luxury vessels (and some small ships) provide a spectrum of ways to keep in touch.

Cellphones & SAT Phones

All of the mainstream and most of the luxury lines in this book are wired with technology that enables cellphone users to make and receive calls aboard ship, even when far out at sea. The small ships in chapter 8 (and SeaDream's two luxury small ships in chapter 7) do not offer this service.

Cellphone service is enabled once a ship sails beyond the range of shore-side towers, typically at about 12 miles. Calls are billed through your regular carrier according to its usual roaming rates, which can vary depending on the provider and sometimes on where in the world you're calling from. Rates typically range between $2 and $3 per minute, with some going as high as $5. That's not cheap, but it's nowhere near the average $8 or $9 per minute (and sometimes up to $15 per min.) that cruise lines typically charge for **in-cabin satellite-phone service.** Text messages from cellphones and e-mails sent from PDAs are more affordable, sometimes costing only a few cents, making them a great idea for couples and families trying to find each other aboard very large megaships.

In addition to cell service and in-cabin SAT phones, each ship has a **central phone number, fax number, and e-mail address,** which are sometimes in the cruise line's brochure and usually in the documents you'll get with your tickets. Distribute these to family members or friends in case they have to contact you in an emergency. It's also a good idea to leave behind the numbers of the cruise line's headquarters and/or reservations department, both of which will be able to put people in touch with you.

Internet & E-Mail at Sea

Aside from some of the small, adventure-oriented ships in chapter 8, pretty much every cruise ship has an Internet center where passengers can send and receive e-mail and browse the Internet. Most are open around the clock, and many offer basic classes for computer novices. **E-mail access** is usually available through the Web via your personal account, with charges calculated on a per-minute basis (usually 50¢–$1) or in prepurchased blocks (say, $40 for a 3- or 4-night cruise or $90 for a 7-night cruise).

A few ships still provide e-mail through temporary accounts you set up once aboard ship, with rates averaging roughly $1 to $4 per message.

Wireless Internet (Wi-Fi) is available aboard all the mainstream and luxury ships in this book, excepting those in the SeaDream fleet. It's generally usable in designated areas such as the atrium and some public rooms, and sometimes in cabins, and an increasing number of ships—including almost the entire Carnival fleet, Royal Caribbean's Oasis- and Freedom-class ships, Celebrity's Solstice-class ships, the three Regent Seven Seas vessels, and the small luxury ships of Seabourn and Silversea—have wireless access pretty much everywhere on board. Among the small ships in chapter 8, only the Lindblad Expeditions and Windstar vessels offer Wi-Fi.

To take advantage of Wi-Fi service, you must have a wireless card for your laptop, rent a card, or rent a laptop, then purchase minutes on the basis of actual use or in packages. Some ships also offer hard-wired **dataports** in all, most, or some cabins and suites.

Keeping on Top of the News

Most ships have CNN or other news stations as part of their regular TV lineup. Some ships also maintain the old tradition of reprinting headline news stories pulled off the wire and slipping them under passengers' doors each morning.

4 Packing for the Different Cruise Climates

One of the great things about cruising is that even though you'll be visiting several countries (or at least several ports) on a typical weeklong itinerary, you won't be living out of your suitcase: You just check into your cabin on day one, put your clothes in the closet, and settle in. The destinations come to you. But what exactly do you need to pack? Evening wear aboard ship is about the same wherever you go, but your destination definitely affects what you'll need during the day.

Shipboard Dress Codes (or Lack Thereof)

Ever since Norwegian Cruise Line started the casual trend back at the turn of the millennium, cruise lines have been toning down or turning off their dress codes. During the day, no matter what the itinerary, you'll find T-shirts, polo shirts, and shorts or khakis predominating, plus casual dresses for women and sweatshirts or light sweaters to compensate for the air-conditioning. The vibe is about the same on the luxury lines, where polos and khakis probably sport fancier labels.

Evening wear aboard ship used to be a lot more complicated than it is today. On most contemporary lines, **formal nights** have either melted away entirely or slid closer to what used to be considered semiformal. When Oceania Cruises started up in 2003, for example, its dress code was set as "country club casual" every single night, on every voyage. NCL has also basically ditched formal nights, though its "optional formal" captain's cocktail night accommodates those who choose to dress up. Disney Cruise Line has toned formality down to the point where a sports jacket is considered dressy enough. Most other mainstream lines still have two traditional formal nights during any 7-night itinerary (usually the second and next-to-last nights of the cruise, the former for the captain's cocktail party). For these, imagine what you'd wear to a nice wedding: Men are encouraged to wear tuxedos or dark suits; women cocktail dresses, sequined jackets, gowns, or other fancy attire. If you just hate dressing up, women can get away with a blouse and skirt or pants—and, of course, jewelry, scarves, and other accessories can dress up an otherwise nondescript outfit. (Most cabins have personal safes where you can keep your good jewelry when you're not wearing it.) Men can get away with a blue blazer and tie.

Casual nights (sometimes called "smart casual" or something similar) make up the rest of the week, though some cruise lines still cling to an old distinction between full casual (decent pants and collared shirts for men, and maybe a sports jacket; dresses, skirts, or pantsuits for women) and informal or semiformal (suits or sports jackets; stylish dresses or pantsuits). Suggested dress for the evening is usually printed in the ship's daily schedule. Cruise lines also typically describe dress codes in their brochures and websites.

Most of the **ultraluxury lines** maintain the same ratio of formal, semiformal, and casual nights, with passengers tending to dress on the high end of all those categories. Tuxedos are very common. That said, even the luxe lines are relaxing their dress standards. Seabourn doesn't request ties for men anymore except on formal nights, and Windstar and SeaDream have a casual "no jackets required" policy every day, though dinners usually have some men in sports jackets and women in nice dresses.

Aboard all the **small-ship lines** covered in this book, it's very rare to see anything dressier than a sports jacket at any time, and even those are rare. Most of these lines are 100% casual 100% of the time, with passengers sometimes changing into clean shirts, trousers, and dresses for dinner.

Dressing for Your Destination

The cruise destinations covered in this book divide easily into warm-weather regions (Caribbean, The Bahamas, Central America, Mexican Riviera, Hawaii, and Bermuda) and the cooler northern regions of Alaska nd its milder neighbor on the other side of the continent, New England/Canada.

Average Temperatures in the Cruise Regions*

Destination	Jan	Feb	Mar	Apr	May	June	July	Aug	Sept	Oct	Nov	Dec
Eastern Caribbean	70/83	70/84	71/85	73/86	74/87	76/87	76/88	76/89	76/89	75/88	74/86	72/84
Western Caribbean	65/82	66/84	72/86	73/90	75/90	75/90	75/90	75/91	75/90	73/86	72/84	70/82
Southern Caribbean	73/82	73/82	73/84	75/88	76/88	76/88	77/88	77/88	77/88	76/87	77/84	74/83
Panama Canal/ Central America	76/84	76/84	76/85	77/86	76/87	75/86	75/85	75/85	75/87	74/86	74/84	75/84
Southeast Alaska	19/29	23/34	27/39	32/47	39/55	45/61	48/64	47/63	43/56	37/47	27/37	23/32
Mexican Riviera	72/87	72/87	72/87	72/87	76/89	77/89	77/89	77/89	77/88	77/88	75/88	73/88
Bermuda	61/69	60/68	60/69	63/71	68/75	73/81	77/85	78/86	76/84	72/80	67/75	63/70
Hawaii	65/78	65/78	66/78	68/79	70/81	72/83	73/84	74/85	73/85	72/83	70/81	67/79
Canada/New England*	19/30	19/30	25/40	34/48	41/57	50/66	57/73	57/73	54/68	45/57	36/48	25/37

*Temperatures are in degrees Fahrenheit, representing average lows and highs. Canada/New England temperatures represent Halifax, Nova Scotia; temperatures farther south along the coast will be on the high side of the temperature range. **Note:** Humidity can make summer temperatures in warm-weather destinations seem hotter, while Alaska's damp climate can make its summer temperatures seem colder.

Warm-Weather Itineraries

In the **Caribbean** and **The Bahamas,** the temperature stays within a fairly narrow range year-round, averaging between 75° and 85°F (24°–29°C), though in summer the combination of sun and humidity can get very intense, especially at midafternoon. Trade winds help cool things off on many of the islands, as does rainfall, which differs from island to island—Aruba, for instance, is very dry, while it seems to rain briefly every time we're in Nassau. Winter is generally the driest season throughout the

Tuxedo Rentals

Despite the casual trend, there's usually a contingent of folks on board who like to get all decked out. If you don't own a tuxedo or don't want to bother lugging one along, you can often arrange a rental through the cruise line or your travel agent for about $85 to $160 (the higher prices for packages with shirts and both black tuxedo jackets and white dinner jackets). Shoes can be rented for an additional $15 or so. In some cases, a rental offer arrives with your cruise tickets; if not, a call to your travel agent or the cruise line can facilitate a rental. If you choose this option, your suit will be waiting in your cabin upon arrival.

---

region; but even then, it can be wet in mountainous areas, and afternoon showers often give the shores a good soaking, sometimes just for a few minutes, sometimes for hours. Temperatures on Mexico's Yucatán Peninsula and in **Central America** can feel much hotter, especially on shore excursions to the humid interior regions. **Hurricane season** lasts officially from June 1 to November 30, traditionally the low cruise season.

The **Mexican Riviera** is traditionally sunny, with average daytime temperatures in the mid-80s. Showers are brief and usually occur at night, when the temperature drops by about 10 degrees. Humidity is moderate during the November to April dry season and higher from May to October.

Hawaii is, of course, paradise. Along the coast, daytime temperatures are usually between the mid-70s and mid-80s, while the mountains can be quite a bit cooler, with summer daytime temperatures in the 60s. On the leeward side of the islands, away from the wind, temperatures occasionally get into the low 90s, while the high slopes of Mauna Kea, the state's highest volcanic peak, are regularly covered with snow in the winter.

Bermuda, too, enjoys a wonderfully temperate climate due to the proximity of the Gulf Stream, which flows between the island and North America. There's no rainy season and no typical month of excess rain. Showers may be heavy at times, but the skies usually clear quickly. During the April-to-October cruise season, temperatures stay in the mid-70s to mid-80s, and even in summer the temperature rarely rises above 85°F (29°C), with a breeze cooling things down at night.

WHAT TO PACK   No matter which warm-weather region you visit, casual daytime wear aboard ship means shorts, T-shirts or polos, sundresses, and bathing suits (plus coverups and sandals if you go right from your deck chair to one of the restaurants or public rooms). The same dress code works in port too, but in many places it's best to cover that skimpy bikini top if straying from the beach area. Bring a good pair of **walking shoes** or sandals if you intend to do more than lie on the beach. A pair of cheap **aqua-socks** might also be a good idea if you plan to snorkel, take inflatable launches to shore, participate in watersports, or do any shore excursions that traverse wet, rocky terrain. A folding umbrella or lightweight raincoat or poncho is a good idea for destinations that have regular tropical showers.

Last, remember to pack sunglasses, a hat, and **sunscreen.** All are available aboard ship and in the ports, but sunscreen in particular will be a lot cheaper at your local market than in a gift shop. You might also consider bringing a **plastic water bottle** that you can refill aboard ship, rather than buying overpriced bottled water in port. And if you plan on hitting the gym aboard ship, don't forget your **workout clothes and sneakers.**

Alaska Itineraries

Southeast Alaska, where most cruises sail, has more temperate year-round weather than the rest of the state, but summers there are still unpredictable. In May, when the cruise season gets going, we've experienced icy rain at the waterline and hiked in new snow at the top of Juneau's Mount Roberts—but we've also seen a lot of beautiful, crisp, sunny days. June is the driest of the true summer months, July the warmest (and also the busiest), and August the month with the most rain. Rainy weather usually continues into September, though we've sailed here as the season wrapped up and had sunny days all week long. Some towns are rainier than others no matter what time you sail—Ketchikan, for instance, gets about 150 inches of precipitation annually, more than three times Juneau's total. In general, daytime summer temperatures are usually in the 50s and 60s, though the damp climate can make it seem colder (as can wind, proximity to glaciers, and excursions to higher elevations). Some days can also be nicely warm, getting up into the 70s or occasionally into the 80s. The all-time high temperature in Juneau was 90°F (32°C) in July 1975—a rarity.

This far south, you won't experience the famed **Midnight Sun,** though days still seem to go on forever. In June, Juneau gets about 18 hours of sunlight—sometimes at 10pm there's still enough to read by. Farther north, in Anchorage, Denali, and Fairbanks, the sun dips below the horizon for only a little more than 4 hours on some June days. Summer temperatures here are roughly comparable to those in Southeast Alaska.

WHAT TO PACK   The rule for Alaska is layering. In addition to some lightweight clothing to wear aboard ship (including a bathing suit, as most megaships have covered pool areas), you'll want to bring some variation of the following items for daytime use:

- A lightweight, waterproof jacket
- Two sweaters or fleece pullovers, or substitute a warm vest for one
- Two to four pairs of pants or jeans
- Two pairs of walking shoes (preferably waterproof)
- A warm hat and gloves
- Long underwear if you're on a May/September shoulder-season cruise
- A folding umbrella

Despite the cool temperatures and sometimes overcast conditions, you'll still want to pack **sunglasses and sunscreen,** especially if you'll be doing a lot of active shore excursions or spending a lot of time on deck whale-watching. That's also the reason you'll want to bring **binoculars** and/or a good **camera,** preferably with a telephoto or zoom lens and with lots of digital memory or film. Regarding binoculars, many of the small-ship adventure lines have enough aboard for all passengers, but it can't hurt to bring your own if you have them. Because whales, eagles, and bears aren't the only wildlife in Alaska, you'll also do well to pack some **mosquito repellent.** Bugs aren't as big a problem in Southeast Alaska as in the more central parts of the state, but if you get into the forest on shore excursions, they can still be annoying.

Eastern Canada/New England Itineraries

Temperatures on summer cruises in Canada/New England are usually very pleasant, averaging in the 60s and 70s. Temperatures in Nova Scotia will be on the low end of that scale, often dipping into the 50s at night, while you can expect hot temperatures if you're sailing from New York, where summer days are often in the 80s or 90s. Temperatures in Boston are usually in the 70s in summer. On September/October fall-foliage cruises, expect temperatures in Canada to range from the low 40s to the low 60s. Rain-wise, the situation is unpredictable. We've experienced bright, crisp, sunny days, then immediately have been socked with a full 24-hour storm. Fog is also common, especially on New Brunswick's Fundy Coast and the Atlantic Coast of Nova Scotia.

WHAT TO PACK   A lighter version of layering is called for here, with a long-sleeved shirt or light sweater over your T-shirts, polos, and dresses. Pack a combination of shorts and long casual pants as well, plus good walking shoes and a light jacket for the evenings. Fall cruises call for slightly heavier clothing, but you'll rarely experience bone-chilling cold. As always, remember your sunblock, sunglasses, hat, and folding umbrella.

Sundries

Except on the small ships, most vessels have **laundry service** on board and some dry cleaning, too, with about 24-hour turnaround; a price list will be in your cabin. Cleaning services tend not to be cheap—$1 or $1.50 per pair of socks, $2.25 to $3 for a T-shirt, and $7 to $10 to dry-clean a suit—so if you plan to pack light and wear the same outfit several times, consider the self-service laundry rooms aboard some ships (Carnival, Crystal, Princess, and Holland America, among others). The small-ship lines rarely provide laundry services.

Like hotel rooms, most cabins (especially those aboard the newest and the most high-end ships) come with **toiletries** such as soap, shampoo, conditioner, and lotion, but their quality varies. Bring your own products if you prefer them. If you forget something, all but a few of the smallest ships in this book have at least one shop on board, selling razor blades, toothbrushes, sunscreen, film, and other sundries, usually at inflated prices.

Most cabins also have **hair dryers,** but they tend to be weak, so don't expect miracles—if you have a lot of hair, bring your own. All ships reviewed in this book run on **110 AC current** (both 110 and 220 on many), so North Americans won't need an electrical adapter.

You don't need to pack a **beach towel,** as they're almost always supplied on board (again, except aboard some small-ship lines). Bird-watchers and whale-watchers will want their **binoculars** and manuals, golfers their clubs (unless they intend to rent), and snorkelers their gear (which can also be rented, usually through the cruise lines).

If you like to read but don't want to lug hefty novels on board, most ships of all sizes have **libraries** stocked with books and magazines. Some (such as the one on Cunard's *QM2*) are fantastic, while others are pretty bad. Most ships also stock paperback best-sellers in their shops.

5 Tipping, Customs & Other End-of-Cruise Concerns

We know you don't want to hear about the end of your cruise before you've even started it, but we had to fit this information somewhere.

Tipping

Most cruise lines pay their service staffs low base wages with the understanding that the bulk of the staff's income will come from tips. Each line has clear guidelines for gratuities, which are usually printed in their brochures and on their websites, on your cruise documents, and in the daily schedule toward the end of your trip. The **traditional** way of tipping was to simply hand your waiter, assistant waiter, and cabin steward cash in a little envelope, but these days many lines add an **automatic gratuity** (sometimes called a "service charge") to a passenger's onboard account—generally between $8.50 and $12 per person, per day total, with the amount adjustable up or down if requested at the purser's desk before the end of the cruise. Other lines give you the option of paying cash directly to staff or adding the gratuities onto your account. Some small-ship lines pool the tips and divide them equitably among all crew. The ultraluxury lines tend to include tips in their cruise rates.

Among lines that don't add an automatic charge, **suggested tipping amounts** vary slightly with the line and its degree of luxury, from about $8 to $14 total per passenger, per day. As a rule of thumb, each passenger (not each couple) should expect to tip at least $3.50 per day for the cabin steward, $3.50 for the dining room waiter, and about $2 for the assistant waiter, and sometimes 75¢ for the headwaiter. Some lines suggest you tip the maitre d' about $5 per person for the week and slip another couple of bucks to the chief housekeeper, but it's your choice. If you've never even met these people, don't bother. Guests staying in suites with butler service should also send $3.50 per day to the butler. A 15% gratuity is usually included on every **bar bill** to cover gratuities to bartenders and wine stewards. The captain and other professional officers do not accept tips.

Higher suggested gratuities sometimes apply to guests booked in **suites.** Those folks sometimes have a butler to tip as well, which increases the total amount. Automatic gratuities are sometimes waived for young children.

On lines that follow traditional person-to-person gratuity policies, tip your waiter and assistant waiter during the cruise's final dinner, and leave your cabin steward his or her tip on the final night or morning, just before you debark. Tip **spa personnel** immediately after they work on you, but note that on some ships, the spa will automatically add a tip to your account unless you indicate otherwise, so inquire before adding one yourself.

Information on how each cruise line deals with gratuities is included in the "Service" section of the reviews in chapters 6 through 8.

Debarkation

It's a good idea to begin packing before dinner on your final night aboard. Be sure to fill out the **luggage tags** given to you and attach them securely to each piece. Most ships ask that you leave your luggage outside your cabin door by midnight or so, after which service staff will pick it up and spirit it away. Two points here: (1) First-time cruisers always worry about leaving their bags out in public, but we've never heard an instance of anything being stolen; and (2) because ship's personnel have to get thousands of pieces of luggage into bins and off the ship, don't expect your luggage to be treated gently. Never pack bottles of duty-free liquor or other breakables. Instead, carry them off the ship yourself.

Once you debark, you'll find the bags waiting in the terminal, organized by the colored or numbered tags you attached. Attendants stand by to help if your baggage is not where it's supposed to be.

Ships normally arrive in port on the final day between 6 and 8am, and need at least 90 minutes to unload baggage and complete docking formalities. Debarkation rarely begins much before 9am, and sometimes it may be 10am before you're allowed to leave the ship, usually via debarkation numbers assigned based on flight times. (Not surprisingly, suite passengers get expedited debarkation.) Have breakfast. Have coffee. Have patience.

In the cruise ship terminal, claim your luggage and then pass through **Customs** before exiting. This normally entails handing the officer your filled-out declaration form as you breeze past, but occasionally the officers will ask to look in your bags. There are generally porters available in the terminals (to whom it's traditional to pay about $2 per bag carried), but you'll have to haul your luggage through Customs before you can get to them.

U.S. Customs

Except for some small-ship itineraries in Alaska and along U.S. rivers and coasts, and NCL's cruises in Hawaii, all the other ships in this book will visit at least one foreign port on their itinerary, meaning you'll have to go through Customs and be subject to duty-free purchase allowances when you return. We've found clearing Customs at U.S. cruise ports usually painless and speedy, with officials rarely asking for anything more than your filled-out declaration form as they nod you through. Better safe than sorry, though, so keep receipts for all purchases you make abroad. If you use any medication containing controlled substances or requiring injection, carry an original prescription or note from your doctor.

The standard personal duty-free allowance for U.S. citizens is $800, an amount that applies to **Mexico, Canada,** and most of the **Caribbean** islands. There are also limits on the amount of alcoholic beverages (usually 1 liter), cigarettes (1 carton), cigars (100 total, and no Cubans), and other tobacco products you may include in your personal duty-free exemption. If returning directly from the **U.S. Virgin Islands,** you may bring in $1,600 worth of merchandise duty-free, including 5 liters of alcohol, of which at least 1 liter should be a product of those islands.

As you may be visiting both foreign and U.S.-territory ports, things get more complicated; if, for instance, your cruise stops in the U.S. Virgin Islands and The Bahamas, your total limit is $1,600, of which no more than $800 can be from The Bahamas.

Joint Customs declarations are possible for family members traveling together. For instance, for a husband and wife with two children, the total duty-free exemption from most destinations would be $3,200.

Note that most meat or meat products, fruit, plants, vegetables, or plant-derived products will be seized by U.S. Customs agents unless they're accompanied by an import license from a U.S. government agency. The same import rules apply even if you are returning from Puerto Rico, Hawaii, and the U.S. Virgin Islands.

For more specifics, visit the **U.S. Customs Service** website at **www.customs.gov**. Canadian citizens should look at the **Canada Border Services Agency** site (**www.cbsa.gc.ca**), and citizens of the U.K. should visit the **U.K. Customs and Excise** site (**www.hmce.gov.uk**).

4

The Cruise Experience

Cruise ships evolved from ocean liners, which were once the only way of getting across from point A to point B, assuming there was an ocean in between. This was often no easy matter, entailing a real journey of several weeks, often in harsh weather. Competition quickly came down to two elements over which the shipping lines had some control: speed ("Get me off this damn ship as fast as possible") and comfort ("Don't rush on my account; I'm having a great time"). While the former was great for businessmen in a rush, the latter had more intriguing possibilities. It wasn't long before ship owners began offering pleasure cruises around scenic parts of the world, lavishing their passengers with shipboard comforts between ports of call—and thus the cruise industry was born.

Today, though the cruise experience varies from ship to ship, the common denominator is choice. On most of the big ships, you can run from an aerobics class to ballroom dancing, then to a computer class or informal lecture, then to a wine-tasting session or goofy poolside contest—all before lunch. On warm-weather itineraries, you can do nothing more than sunbathe in a quiet corner of the deck all day. In Alaska, you can camp out on deck with your binoculars, scanning for whales. Your cruise is what you make of it. In the pages that follow, we'll give you a taste of life at sea in 2011–12.

1 Checking In, Boarding & Settling into Your Cabin

It's cruise day. If you've flown to your city of embarkation, uniformed attendants will be waiting at the airport baggage claim, holding signs bearing your cruise line's or ship's name and ready to direct you to buses bound for the terminal. You've probably already paid for these **transfers** when you bought your ticket. If not, you can arrange them now, or take a taxi to the ship. If you've driven to the port, it's just a matter of parking and trundling your luggage into the terminal. If it's still morning or early afternoon, don't feel rushed: Remember, another shipload of passengers is just getting off, and ship personnel still need to clean the cabins, load supplies, and complete paperwork and Customs documents before you can board. Even if your ship has been berthed since 6am, new passengers are often not allowed on board until about 1pm, though lines are increasingly offering **preboarding**—which means you can get on at 11am or noon, have lunch, and start checking out the ship (though your cabin probably won't be ready till early afternoon). Due to U.S. Customs and Border Protection requirements, passengers must be checked in and on board at least an hour prior to sailing, though each line has its own rules, with most asking all passengers to be aboard at least 2 hours ahead of time.

Chapter 9, "The Ports of Embarkation," has more information about flying, driving, and parking at each embarkation port.

When you arrive at the port, you'll find an army of **porters** to help transport your luggage into the terminal (for which you should pay them about $2 per bag) and another army of cruise line employees waiting to direct you to the check-in desks. Once inside, your tagged luggage will be taken, scanned, and delivered to your cabin, sometimes arriving not long after you check in, but more often showing up a few hours later. For this reason, it's a good idea to pack a small **essentials bag** you can carry on board, containing a change of clothes and maybe a swimsuit, plus a pair of sunglasses and any toiletries, medications, or other essentials you may need immediately.

Once in the terminal, you hand over your cruise tickets, show your **passport,** and give an imprint of your credit card to establish your **onboard account** (see "Passports & Visas" and "Money Matters" in chapter 3 for more about these). Depending upon when you arrive and how large the crowd is, you may find yourself waiting in line for an hour or more, but usually it's less. Many lines nowadays are also offering **online registration** that allows you to take care of a lot of these matters before your cruise, which speeds things up some.

Once on board, a steward may lead you to your **cabin** (you don't need to tip him, though we usually do if he's carried our bags), but in many cases you'll have to find it on your own. Your **cabin steward** will probably stop by shortly to introduce himself or herself, inquire if the configuration of beds is appropriate (that is, whether you want separate twin beds or a pushed-together double), and give you his or her phone extension so that you can call if you need anything. If your steward doesn't put in an appearance, feel free to call housekeeping to request anything you need. The brochures and **daily programs** in your cabin will answer many questions about the day's activities, the dress code for dinner that night, and the ship's safety procedures. There may also be a **deck plan** that will help you find your way around. If not, you can pick one up at the guest services desk. Signs near the staircases and elevators should be able to guide you there.

With very few exceptions, cruise ships have **direct-dial telephones** in cabins, along with instructions on how to use them and a directory of phone numbers for the departments or services on board. You can call anywhere in the world from most cabins' phones via satellite, but you'll break the bank to do it, with charges ranging from between $3 and $15 a minute (with $8 or $9 being about average). It's cheaper to call home from your **cellphone** if your ship is appropriately wired, or from a public telephone in port, or to send **e-mail** from the ship or, cheaper yet, from an Internet cafe in port. (See "Keeping in Touch While at Sea" in chapter 3 for more info.)

All ships reviewed in this book have North American–style **electrical outlets** (twin flat prongs, 110 AC), and some have outlets for both European current (220 AC) and North American. Keep in mind, there's often only one outlet for your curling iron or hair dryer, and it's usually above the desk or dresser rather than in the bathroom.

Most ships also have **in-cabin safes** for storing your valuables, usually operated via a self-set combination. On ships that don't provide them, you can usually check valuable items at the purser's desk.

A **lifeboat safety drill** will be held either just before or after sailing. It's required by the Coast Guard, and attendance is mandatory. Check to make sure your cabin has enough life preservers for everyone in your party, because you'll probably have to wear them to the drill (but only "probably" since some lines are experimenting with not requiring this). If you need extra life preservers—or for that matter, additional blankets or pillows—let your steward know ASAP.

2 Exploring the Ports of Call: Shore Excursions vs. Going It on Your Own

How you spend your time in port can make the difference between a great cruise experience and a big fat disappointment. The ports covered in this guide vary greatly, from quiet **untouristed ports** such as Jost Van Dyke, where your ship will likely be the only one in sight, to **bustling tourist towns** such as Ketchikan, Alaska, which is almost always jampacked with other ships. Due to factors such as accessibility of local transportation, condition of roads, terrain, and the amount of time your ship is in port (which can range from 4 or 5 hr. to 10 or more), some ports are easy to **explore independently,** others less so. In the port chapters later in this guide (chapters 10–15), we advise you about which ports of call are good for solo exploration (and whether you should go it on foot or by taxi, motor scooter, ferry, or otherwise) and which ones are better experienced via **organized shore excursions.**

Sometimes a port's real attractions may be miles (sometimes a lot of miles) from where your ship is docked—a common enough occurrence in Hawaii, Alaska, and Mexico's Yucatán Peninsula, among other places. In such cases, touring on your own could be an inefficient use of your time, entailing lots of hassles and planning, and possibly costing more. In these places, the shore excursions offered by the cruise lines are a good way to go. In other places, exploring on your own may be easier, cheaper, more rewarding, and more fun than taking the excursions. You may miss out on the kind of **narrative** you get from a tour guide (though sometimes that's a good thing) but, on the other hand, you'll almost certainly have a more personal experience of your destination, and may find little nuances that organized tours ignore or downplay.

Note: If you do decide to go the solo route, be sure you know exactly when your ship departs, because the captain won't wait forever if you're late, and could leave you on your own to get to the next port of call.

Shore excursions run the gamut, from snoresville bus tours and booze cruises to more stimulating options such as snorkeling, jungle walks, whale-watching, and glacier helicopter treks. For those who like a little sweat in their port visits, there are **physically challenging options** such as kayaking, horseback riding, mountain biking, ziplining, dog sledding, and river rafting. There's a decent selection of tours in all the regions covered in this guide (generally at least 10 to 20 per port), with the greatest number in Alaska, Hawaii, and the Caribbean.

Some things to keep in mind:

- In almost every case, the cruise lines themselves do not operate the excursions; instead, they contract them out to operators in each individual port. That's why most lines seem to offer the same tours, though prices often vary slightly.
- Excursion prices are often (but not always) lower for kids.
- Excursions can often fill up fast, especially on the megaships, so don't dawdle in signing up. If your cruise line is set up for prebooking before your trip, that's a good option. If not, sign up on the first day of your cruise.

Most lines list their shore excursions on their websites, and allow you to **prebook or prereserve them,** either online or through a reservation form that comes with your cruise documents.

If a tour offered by your ship is booked up, you can try to **book it independently** once you get to port. The popular *Atlantis* submarine tour, for example—offered at Grand Cayman, Nassau, and St. Thomas, among other places—usually has an office/agent in the cruise terminals or nearby. In Alaska, as another example, Juneau's popular Mount Roberts Tramway is located just a few meters from the cruise dock, so it's easy enough to just walk over and buy a ticket yourself.

3 A Typical Day at Sea: Onboard Activities

Most of the mainstream lines and the larger luxury ships provide an extensive schedule of activities throughout each day, especially during days when the ship isn't visiting a port. To keep track of the games, lessons, contests, classes, and so on, ships print a **daily program,** which is placed in your cabin while you're at dinner and applies to the next day. A cruise director and his or her staff are in charge of the action and do their best to make sure passengers are having a good time. As a general rule, the smaller the ship, the fewer the diversions.

Onboard Learning Opportunities

For years, lists of shipboard classes read as if they were lifted straight out of the Eisenhower-era home-entertainment playbook: napkin folding, vegetable carving, scarf tying, mixology, and the like. Old habits die hard, so you'll still find these kinds of things aboard many ships; however, over the past decade the cruise lines have finally started catching up to the modern world. Today, most megaships and midsize ships also offer **informal lectures** on subjects such as digital photography, website design, history, music, astronomy, health and wellness, personal investing, word processing, and other topics. Don't expect to earn credits toward your college degree—these are mostly hourlong sessions, and tend to be pretty basic—but they make a nice addition to the day.

Many lines also feature **cooking demonstrations** and **wine-tasting seminars,** the former often resembling the kind you see on TV, complete with model kitchen and video monitors for an up-close view of the preparations. Wine tastings are usually conducted by the ship's sommeliers, though some lines bring aboard guest experts. There's usually a charge of between $5 and $20 for wine tastings, with selections coming from the dining room's wine list. Participants may be offered special prices if they care to order wine in advance for dinner.

Dance classes (most frequently salsa, country, and ballroom) are usually held several times a week, taught by one of the onboard entertainers. Staff from the gym, spa, and salon hold frequent seminars on **health, beauty, and fitness,** with topics including skin and hair care, detox for weight loss, and wrinkle reduction. These seminars are free, but they have an ulterior motive: getting you to sign up for not-so-cheap spa treatments or buy expensive beauty products. Just remember: *You don't have to buy anything.*

In general, the ultraluxury lines have more refined and interesting enrichment programs. **Crystal**'s Creative Learning Institute (CLI), for example, includes some programs run in collaboration with well-known organizations, schools, and brands—Berlitz for language classes, the Cleveland Clinic for health topics, and Yamaha for music classes, to name a few. Otherwise, lectures and classes focus on topics such as wine and food (for example, wine appreciation, spa cuisine), arts and entertainment (fashion design, language instruction), lifestyle (interior design, book clubs), wellness (CPR, tai chi), and business and technology. **Cunard**'s *Queen Mary 2* offers a similar program on its transatlantic crossings, developed in association with Oxford University and featuring talks on history, global politics, cultural trends, theater, science, music, literature, and more.

Shipboard Casinos & Games of Chance

As a general rule, the bigger the ship, the bigger and flashier its **casino,** with literally hundreds of slot machines and dozens of roulette, blackjack, poker, and craps tables. Luxury lines such as Regent and Seabourn have scaled-down versions. Stakes aboard most ships are relatively low, with maximum bets rarely exceeding $200. Average minimum bets at blackjack and poker tables are generally $5 or $10; the minimum at roulette is typically 50¢ or $1.

Most ships also have a **card room,** which is occasionally supervised by a full-time instructor. Most ships furnish cards for free, although some charge $1 or so per deck. Another time-honored shipboard tradition is **horse racing,** a very goofy activity in which toy horses mounted on poles are moved around a track by hand, based on rolls of the dice. Passengers bet on the outcome, and the end of the cruise features an "owner's cup" race and best-dressed-horse show.

Ships are free to allow gambling in international waters, but local laws almost always require ships to close their onboard casinos when in or close to port. Big gamblers should keep this in mind when cruising to Bermuda, where ships stay in port for 3 whole days, with no gambling whatsoever during that period. Also, Hawaiian law prohibits casino gambling on ships sailing round-trip from the state, so there's no casino on NCL's *Pride of America.* In Alaska, where ships sail mostly in the protected waters of the Inside Passage, a dispensation allows their casinos to stay open except when they're within 3 miles of a port.

Children are not permitted to enter onboard casinos; the minimum age is generally 18 or 21.

Disney's two ships lack casinos due to Disney's essentially puritan nature. Most of the small ships in chapter 8 lack casinos because their passengers are too busy looking for whales.

Art Auctions

You'll find shipboard art auctions either a fun way to buy pictures for your living room or a **seriously dubious** and **blatantly tacky** way for the cruise lines to make more money by selling overpriced, marginally interesting, or just plain awful prints, lithographs, and animation cels to unsuspecting passengers—not that we're taking sides, of course. The auctions are big business on the mainstream lines, held three or four times a week in one of the ship's lounges, for an hour or two at a time. The auctioneer (a salesman for an outside company that arranges the shows) begins with a talk about the hundreds of pieces spread around the room, and usually seems (to us at least) to give the impression these are rare and important works of original art—which, of course, they're not. Generally they're **prints,** which is a fancy way of saying *copies.* Bid if you feel compelled, but we wouldn't—ever. Happily, some cruise lines (like Royal Caribbean and Celebrity) are moving away from these kinds of godawful art auctions and offering more honest and interesting art programs instead.

The only caveat to our criticism of the tacky auctions? **Free champagne.** Just sign up and look interested, and they'll keep bringing it whether you bid or not.

4 Keeping Fit: Gyms, Spas & Sports

The well-equipped **fitness centers** on today's megaships may feature 20 or more treadmills and just as many stationary bikes (many with virtual reality screens), step machines, upper- and lower-body machines, free weights, and aerobics rooms. Expect great gym facilities on Royal Caribbean's Oasis-, Freedom-, Radiance-, and Voyager-class ships; Carnival's Conquest, Spirit, and Destiny classes; Princess's Grand and Coral classes; all of NCL's modern megaships; Holland America's Signature- and Vista-class ships; and Celebrity's Solstice and Millennium classes. Working out on your own is free, as are many basic aerobics and stretching classes, but if you want to take a trendier class such as boxing, spinning, Pilates, yoga, or tai chi, it'll usually cost you $10 or more. **Personal training sessions** are usually available for $75 to $100 a pop. Royal Caribbean's Oasis- and Freedom-class ships, currently the biggest cruise ships on earth, have absolutely gigantic gyms, boasting everything from a full-size Everlast boxing ring to lots of trendy classes, machines, and training accouterments.

Sports-wise, today's megaships offer jogging tracks; outdoor volleyball, basketball, and paddle-tennis courts; plus several pools for water polo, volleyball, aqua-aerobics, and swimming. The most mega of the megas—Royal Caribbean's enormous Oasis-, Freedom-, and Voyager-class ships—pack a bona fide ice-skating rink, an outdoor rock-climbing wall, an in-line skating track (on the Voyager ships), surfing simulators, a full-size basketball court, miniature golf, and—drum roll please—a sky-high zipline above bustling public areas (Oasis ships).

Onboard Spas: Taking Relaxation One Step Further

If your idea of a heavenly vacation is stripping down to a towel and having someone rub mystery oil over your body, choose a cruise ship with a well-stocked spa—it won't be hard. For the past 15 years, spas have been big business on cruise ships, and have gotten progressively more amazing as the years pass. Most are perched on top decks and boast views from as many as 20 or so treatment rooms, where you can choose from dozens of massages, mud packs, facials, and even teeth whitening, acupuncture, and other esoteric treatments.

If you've taken a few cruises and noticed that the spas on different lines look suspiciously alike, that's because almost all of them (as well as the ships' salons) are staffed and operated by the London-based firm **Steiner Leisure.** NCL's spas are operated by a company called **Mandara,** but (surprise) it's owned by Steiner, too. Companies bucking the Steiner hegemony include Regent Seven Seas (whose spas are run by **Carita**), Cunard (whose *QM2* spa is run by **Canyon Ranch**), and SeaDream and Star Clipper, both of which have in-house spa operations.

The young, mostly female Steiner employees are professional and charming for the most part, but we've found their abilities to be inconsistent, with some definitely more talented than others. Overall, **massages** are a pretty safe bet, whether you choose a standard neck massage, a full-body shiatsu massage, or a deep-tissue sports massage (which can verge on painful but gives you the most bang, wallop, and burn for your buck). The highest profile massage today is the **hot stone massage,** in which the therapist rubs you down with heated river rocks and oil—think soothing rather than invigorating. Trendy treatments include teeth whitening and, yes, Botox injections.

We've found other treatments often to be disappointing and not worth the money, unless you live in a place where access to unusual spa and beauty treatments is limited.

For the same 50 bucks you spend on a pedicure aboard ship, you could get two much better ones in New York, but if you live in, say, rural North Dakota? Well, it's your vacation, so live it up.

Prices for identical treatments can vary widely from ship to ship, but tend to range from about $25 to $55 for a manicure, $40 to $75 for a pedicure, $80 to $100 for a 25-minute Swedish massage, $110 to $160 for a 50-minute full-body massage, and $175 to $225 for a 75-minute hot stone massage. Treatments are charged to your onboard account. Usually they do not include a **gratuity,** but on a few lines Steiner does add it directly to your bill—so ask your therapist or the desk attendant whether a tip is included, before you write one in.

It's almost guaranteed that at the end of your session, just as you're coming out of a semiconscious trance, your Steiner or Mandara therapist will give you an itemized list of expensive **creams, exfoliants, moisturizers, toners,** and **masks** that will help you get the spa effect at home—all for just a couple of hundred bucks. In fact, on a *Norwegian Dawn* cruise, coauthor Heidi's massage therapist spent a whopping 15 minutes telling her how Gwyneth Paltrow and other stars swore by the $125 Elemis face cream she was pushing. Enough already!

Tip: Make your spa appointments on the first day out to snag the best times.

5 Programs for Kids & Teens

With the cruise lines falling all over themselves to cater to kids these days, amenities and services for children rival those offered for adults. The cruise execs know that if the kiddos are happy, mom and dad will be too (and will hopefully want to book more cruises). Dedicated playrooms, camplike counselors (some who are wonderful, others morose and tired—it's hit or miss), computers, state-of-the-art video arcades, pools, and new teen centers have most kids so gaga for cruising, you'll have to drag them away kicking and screaming at the end of the week. Even if your kids are too young to join the programming (which typically starts at ages 2 or 3), there are more options than ever. In this age of play dates, it's no surprise that a line, Royal Caribbean, has daily 45-minute **play groups** for infants, toddlers, and parents. Disney and Royal Caribbean's *Oasis* and *Allure of the Seas* also have drop-off nurseries for the baby set.

The youngest kids frolic in toy- and game-stocked **playrooms,** listen to stories, go on treasure hunts, play dodge ball, and do arts and crafts; older kids keep busy with **computer games,** lip-sync competitions, pool games, volleyball, and now vaguely educational-oriented activities focused on art, science, music, and exercise. There's usually a TV showing movies at times throughout the day, and, for the younger ones, there might be ball bins and plastic jungle gyms to crawl around in. Many megaships have shallow kiddie pools for diaper-trained young'uns, sometimes sequestered on an isolated patch of deck.

The newest ships of the mainstream lines invite hard-to-please **teens** to hang out in their very own space, complete with a dance floor, bar (nonalcoholic, of course), video wall for movie watching, video arcade, and sometimes their own Internet cafe. Some of the best facilities are found on the *Carnival Dream, Splendor, Freedom, Liberty, Valor, Glory,* and *Conquest; Disney Wonder, Magic,* and upcoming *Dream;* Royal Caribbean's Oasis, Allure, Freedom, Voyager, and Radiance classes; *Norwegian Epic, Dawn, Star,* and *Spirit;* and the *Grand, Golden, Star,* and *Caribbean Princess.* Many ships are now offering spa treatments for teens and special kid-only shore excursions, too.

See section 4, "Cruises for Families," in chapter 1, for more details, including information on **babysitting.**

6 Onboard Dining Options

Across the board, the evolution of onboard dining has probably been the single biggest change in the cruise biz over the past decade. When we started covering ships in the mid-1990s, almost all served traditional five-course, assigned-seating dinners in formal dining rooms, with an optional buffet for breakfast and lunch and a grill out on deck. Now it's a free-for-all, with numerous **casual dining options** that allow passengers not only to dress down, but also to dine with complete flexibility, choosing when, where, and with whom they want to eat. In mid-2000, **Norwegian Cruise Line** got the ball rolling with its Freestyle Dining concept, which lets passengers grab dinner anytime between 5:30pm and midnight in any of several venues, with the last seating at 10pm. **Azamara**'s and **Oceania**'s much smaller ships have essentially the same system, and **Carnival, Celebrity, Holland America, Princess,** and **Royal Caribbean** allow passengers the option of choosing either flexible or traditional dining. **Disney** puts a unique spin on things by having passengers and their servers rotate through three main themed dining rooms over the course of the cruise, in early or late seatings.

Formal or casual aside, the bottom line is that cruise lines are willing to feed you till you pop, and these days are providing more cuisine options, too. On the megaships, you can get elegant **multicourse meals** served in grand two- and three-story dining rooms; make reservations at an intimate specialty restaurant for Asian, Italian, French, Tex-Mex, or Pacific Northwest cuisine; drop in at the ship's buffet restaurant or cafe for an ultracasual meal; take in some **24-hour pizza** or other late-night option; grab a **snack** (ice cream, cookies, pastries, specialty coffees, and more); and maybe have some **sushi** to top it all off. Carnival has pizza, Caesar salad, and garlic rolls 24 hours a day; many lines now deliver pizza to your cabin; and Royal Caribbean's Oasis-, Freedom-, and Voyager-class ships have entire 1950s-style diners out on deck. The midsize ships generally have fewer choices, though Oceania's and Azamara's vessels, which carry only about 700 passengers apiece, have four different venues at dinner, including Mediterranean and steakhouse specialty restaurants and a casual option with table service.

All the cruise lines in this book will attempt to satisfy reasonable culinary requests, so if you follow a **special diet,** inform your line as early as possible (preferably when booking your cruise) to make sure it'll be able to satisfy your needs at all three meals. **Vegetarian dishes** and a selection of **healthier, lighter meals** (usually called "spa cuisine" or "light and healthy options") are available as a matter of course on just about every mainstream and luxury ship at breakfast, lunch, and dinner. Some of the small-ship lines need advance notice for any special requests. Most large ships will provide kosher and halal meals if requested in advance, but expect them to be prepackaged.

Traditional Dining

Though casual and specialty dining are all the rage, most ships still continue to offer formal, **traditional dinners** in at least one restaurant, generally from about 6:30 to 10pm. Ships carrying fewer than 400 passengers usually have one **open-seating dinner,** where guests can stroll in when they want and sit with whomever they choose. Those carrying more than 400 passengers typically have early and late **assigned seatings** in one or more main dining rooms.

If you opt for traditional dining (or if that's all your ship offers), you'll be asked to reserve the early or late seating when you book your cruise. Elderly passengers and families with children tend to choose the **early seating** (served at around 6 or 6:30pm), though you have to be ready to leave the table once the dishes are cleared. If you choose **late seating** (served around 8 or 8:30pm), you won't have to rush through pre-dinner showering and dressing after an active day in port, and the meal tends to be more leisurely, allowing you to linger over coffee and after-dinner drinks.

If you change your mind about your seating after you're aboard, see the maitre d' staff to make a change. They'll typically have a table set up in the dining room during embarkation for this purpose. Most can accommodate your wishes, if not on the first night of sailing, then on the second. Ditto if you find that you don't get along with your assigned tablemates. At most assigned dinners, you'll be seated at a table with 4 to 10 people. If you want privacy, you can request a table for two, but unless you're sailing aboard one of the smaller, more upscale ships, don't get your hopes up, as couples' tables are usually few and far between.

Seven-night cruises with traditional dining generally have 2 **formal nights** per week, when the dress code in the main dining room may call for dark suits or tuxedos for men and cocktail dresses or fancy pantsuits for women. Other nights in the main dining rooms will probably be designated informal and/or casual. The 10- to 14-night cruises usually have three formal nights. (See section 4, "Packing for the Different Cruise Climates," in chapter 3, for more information.) If you want to skip formality altogether, most ships have casual dining in the buffet restaurant every evening and/or other casual alternative options (see below).

Though some ships still have early and late seatings for breakfast and lunch (served around 7 and 8:30am and noon and 1:30pm, respectively), most ships are now operating on an open-seating basis for these meals, within certain hours.

Smoking is prohibited in all ships' dining rooms, specialty restaurants, and other food-service venues. There's even a no-smoking buffer zone around on-deck grills.

Specialty Dining

Variety + intimacy = specialty dining. Over the past decade, all the mainstream lines and most of the luxe lines have retooled their ships' layouts to make room for more small, alternative dining venues, where 100 or so guests can sample various international cuisine with sometimes elaborate presentation. Of course, you often have to pay for the treat, with most specialty restaurants charging between $10 and $30 per person, per meal (except on the luxury lines, where there's no extra charge). Sometimes the food and service are exceptional and sometimes they aren't any better than in the main dining rooms, but the venues are at least quieter and more intimate.

See the "Dining Options" section of each ship review in chapters 6, 7, and 8 to learn who's got what.

Casual Dining

If you'd rather skip the formality and hubbub of the main dining room, all but the tiniest ships serve breakfast, lunch, and often dinner in a **casual, buffet-style restaurant.** Usually located on the pool deck, with indoor and outdoor seating, these restaurants serve a spread of both hot and cold items. On the megaships, a grill may be nearby, serving burgers, hot dogs, and often chicken and veggie burgers at lunch. Increasingly, you can also find specialty stations with taco fixings, deli sandwiches, pasta specialties, Chinese food, and more. On most ships, breakfast and lunch buffets are generally served for a 3- to 4-hour period, so guests can stroll in and out whenever they want; but many of the mainstream lines also keep portions of their buffets open almost round-the-clock. Most lines serve nightly buffet-style dinners here as well, some providing a combination of sit-down service and buffet.

Increasingly, newer ships are also offering dedicated **casual specialty restaurants,** providing a middle-ground option between formal dining and the buffet model.

Between-Meal Snacking

"Between-meal snacking" is the cruise industry's middle name. Almost all the mega-ships and midsize vessels have complimentary **pizzerias** (some open 24 hr. a day) and **self-serve frozen yogurt and ice-cream machines,** as well as cafes or coffee shops where you can grab a snack, sandwich, or specialty coffee, the latter for an extra charge. The upscale lines and some of the mainstreamers (such as Azamara, Celebrity, Princess, Oceania, and Holland America) have **afternoon tea service,** serving finger sandwiches, pastries, and cookies along with tea and coffee. Carnival and several others do their own, less fancy versions. Most of the small-ship lines serve **pre-dinner snacks and hors d'oeuvres** on deck or in the main lounge or bar area, plus **late-night snacks** at the buffet or elsewhere around the ship.

If you'd rather not leave your cabin, most ships provide **24-hour room service** with menus that vary from limited to lush. Passengers on luxury ships (and suite guests on all ships) can usually have the same meals being served in the dining room delivered to their suites course by course.

7 Onboard Entertainment

Entertainment is a big part of the cruise experience on almost all ships, but especially on the megaships of Carnival, Royal Caribbean, Celebrity, Costa, Princess, NCL, and Holland America, which all present an extensive variety throughout the day. We have noticed, though, the number of live musicians definitely seems to be smaller the last few years, due to, we presume, lines cutting back to save money. Afternoons, you can dance on deck with the **live dance band** (which will likely be comprised of one or two musicians instead of four), which we'll bet 10-to-1 will be jamming calypso music or tunes by Bob Marley and Jimmy Buffett. Or put on your waltzing shoes and head inside to one of the lounges for some **swing dancing.** Lines such as Holland America, Crystal, NCL, Cunard, Oceania, and Royal Caribbean often feature a 1940s-style big band playing dance tunes. Some of the most pleasant concerts we've heard at sea were aboard the Royal Caribbean Voyager ships. On one, a trio was so inspiring that two passengers joined in, belting out Italian opera songs like real pros. At another, the ship's big band set up just outside the pub, among the crowd, and played a relaxed set of standards.

Pre-dinner entertainment starts to heat up around 5pm, and continues all night to accommodate passengers dining early and late. Head to the **piano bar** for a cocktail or do some pre-dinner dancing to small-group jazz.

Usually two or three times in any weeklong cruise, there are apt to be **Vegas-style musical revues** performed early and late in the main show lounge, with a flamboyant troupe of anywhere from 6 to 16 feather-boa-and-sequin-clad male and female dancers sliding, kicking, and lip-synching as a soloist or two belt out show tunes and pop favorites; the latest trend includes a ballroom dance couple in the mix. Expect a lot of Andrew Lloyd Webber; "YMCA"; at least one tune each from *Grease, Footloose,* and *A Chorus Line;* and maybe a few Richard Rodgers tunes. A live orchestra accompanies most of these productions, though not all (and overall, orchestras seem smaller than they were in the past). While the quality of shows industrywide is inconsistent, opinion here at Casa Frommer's is divided on the whole revue format: Heidi enjoys the medleys "if the singing's good—which, granted, it isn't always," and Matt thinks most of them are "all flash and no substance." Two cruise lines we can agree on, though, are Disney and NCL. Disney has absolutely the best shows at sea, with characters and stories based on its parent company's classic films. Recent shows on NCL are also standouts, with strong soloists and really original staging, choreography, and choice of material.

On nights when the shows aren't scheduled, there may be a **magic show** complete with a scantily clad assistant being sawed in half and rabbits pulled from a hat; **acrobatic acts** and **aerialists** (always a big hit); **headline soloists,** some of them quite good (such as singer Jane L. Powell, a perennial NCL favorite whose amazing range takes her from Louis Armstrong to Bette Midler); and **guest comedians** or **specialty acts,** such as Costa's regular operatic recitals, Oceania's pianists, and Royal Caribbean's and Crystal's a cappella singing groups. **Comedians** frequently perform in the main theater or a second performance space, sometimes doing PG- and R-rated material at an early show and then running the X up the mast at an adults-only midnight performance (now, surprisingly, Carnival offers this). Raising the humor bar, Norwegian Cruise Line has hysterical shows by the famed Second City improv comedy group on *Dawn, Spirit, Star, Jewel, Pearl, Gem,* and *Epic.* On its new *Norwegian Epic,* NCL is even featuring a show by the **Blue Man Group.** Royal Caribbean's newest ships feature full-scale, big name musicals: **Hairspray** aboard *Oasis of the Seas* and **Chicago** aboard *Allure of the Seas.*

The **disco** gets going on most ships around 9 or 10pm and works it until 2 or 3am, sometimes later. Occasionally a live band plays until about midnight, when a DJ takes over until the wee hours, spinning tunes from the 1970s through the present; sometimes there's only a DJ. A **karaoke session** may also be thrown in for an hour or two in the afternoon or evening. Riding the coattails of the ballroom dance craze, some lines like Royal Caribbean and Regent Seven Seas are holding **ballroom dance performances** led by the entertainers and sometimes incorporating passengers who are especially talented.

An alternative to the disco or the main show may be a pianist or jazz trio in one of the ship's romantic nightspots, or a **themed party,** sometimes on deck—NCL, Royal Caribbean, Costa, and Disney especially excel at after-dinner parties (often up on deck) complete with special effects and funky lighting. For a quiet evening, many lines show **recent-release movies** in a theater, a dedicated cinema, or up on deck on a giant LED screen.

To prove not all innovative entertainment has to be big, Crystal has **strolling vocal quartets** roaming around its ships in the evening, performing wherever people are gathered. On Royal Caribbean's Freedom-class ships, a troupe of **clowns** performs impromptu juggling, acrobatic, and comedy routines in various public areas. At different points of the cruise, they also give juggling lessons and might give a little talk about technique. Big thumbs up! Along similar lines, Carnival also features acrobats in the atria from time to time to liven things up.

Ships carrying 100 to 400 passengers have fewer entertainment options and a more mellow evening ambience overall. The high-end lines may feature a quartet or pianist performing before dinner and maybe a small-scale song-and-dance revue afterward, plus dancing in a quiet lounge. The small adventure-oriented ships may at most have a solo performer before and after dinner, or **local musicians** and/or **dancers** aboard for an afternoon or evening.

8 Shopping Opportunities on Ship & Shore

Even the smallest ships have at least a small shop on board selling T-shirts, sweatshirts, and baseball caps bearing the cruise line logo. The big new megaships, though, are like minimalls, with as many as 10 (or more) different stores selling items from toiletries and sundries to high-end china. All merchandise sold on board while a ship is at sea is **tax-free** (though you must declare it at Customs when returning to the U.S.); to maintain that tax-free status, the shops are closed whenever a ship is in port. Prices can vary, though, and just like at a resort, items such as disposable cameras, sunscreen, candy, and snack foods will cost substantially more than you'd pay at home. On the other hand, by mid-cruise there are often decent sales on things like T-shirts, tote bags, jewelry, and booze—but all and all, don't expect amazing bargains in the ship boutiques.

Before each port of call, the cruise director or shore-excursion manager gives a port talk about that place's attractions and shopping. Now, it's no secret that many cruise lines have mutually beneficial deals with certain shops in every port (generally of the touristy chain variety), so on the big, mass-market ships especially, the vast majority of the port info disseminated will be about shopping. Better bring along your own guidebook (this one!) if you want information on history or culture.

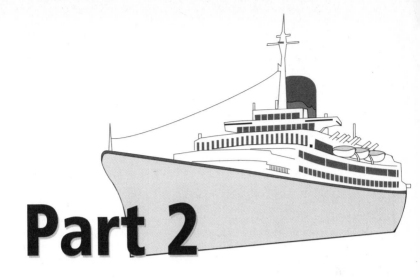

Part 2

The Cruise Lines & Their Ships

With advice on choosing and booking your ideal cruise and tips on getting ready for the cruise experience.

5

The Ratings & How to Read Them

The following three chapters are the heart and soul of this book, our expert reviews and ratings of the cruise lines and ships operating in the American market. This chapter is your instruction manual, with hints on how to use the reviews to compare the lines and find the one that's right for you.

1 Cruise Line Categories

To make your selection easier (and to make sure you're not comparing apples and oranges), we've divided the cruise lines into three distinct categories, given each category a chapter of its own, and rated each line only in comparison with the other lines in its category (see more about this in "How to Read the Ratings," below). The categories are as follows:

THE MAINSTREAM LINES (chapter 6)   This category includes the most prominent players in the industry, the jack-of-all-trades lines with the biggest ships, carrying the most passengers and providing the most diverse cruise experiences to suit many different tastes, from party-hearty to elegant and refined. With all the competition in the industry today, these lines tend to have good prices, too.

THE ULTRALUXURY LINES (chapter 7)   These are the Dom Perignon of cruises, providing elegant, refined, and doting service, extraordinary dining, spacious cabins, and high-toned entertainment aboard intimate, finely appointed, small and midsize vessels—and at a high price.

SMALL SHIPS, SAILING SHIPS & ADVENTURE CRUISES (chapter 8)   If you don't like crowds; want an experience that revolves around nature, history, or culture; want to visit out-of-the-way ports; and/or prefer quiet conversation to a large ship's constant activity, these small, casual ships may be your cup of tea.

2 Reading the Reviews & Ratings

Each cruise line's review begins with **"The Line in a Nutshell"** (a quick word about the line in general) and **"The Experience,"** which is just what it says: a short summation of the kind of cruise experience you can expect to have aboard that line, followed by a few major **pros and cons.** The **ratings table** judges the individual elements of the line's cruise experience compared with the other lines in the same category (see below for ratings details). The text that follows fleshes out these summations, providing all the details you need to get a feel for what kind of vacation the cruise line will give you.

The individual **ship reviews** give you details on each vessel's physical characteristics: accommodations, facilities, amenities, comfort level, upkeep, and vital statistics (size, passenger capacity, year launched and most recently upgraded, number of cabins, number of crew, and so on). Size is described in terms of **gross register tonnage (GRT),** which is a measure not of actual weight, but of the interior space (or volume) used to produce revenue on a ship: 1 GRT equals 100 cubic feet of enclosed, revenue-generating space. By dividing the GRTs by the number of passengers aboard, we arrive at the **passenger/space ratio,** which gives you some idea of how much elbowroom you'll have on each ship. To compare the amount of personalized service you can expect, we have the **passenger/crew ratio,** which tells you approximately how many passengers each crewmember is expected to serve—though this doesn't literally mean a waiter for every two or three passengers, because "crew" includes everyone from officers to deckhands to shop clerks.

Note that when several vessels are members of a class—built on the same design, with usually only minor variations in decor and attractions—we've grouped the ships together into one **class review.**

How to Read the Ratings

To make things easier on everyone, we've developed a simple ratings system based on the classic customer-satisfaction survey, rating both the cruise line as a whole and the individual ships as poor, fair, good, excellent, or outstanding on a number of important qualities. The **cruise line ratings** cover all the elements that are usually consistent from ship to ship within the line (overall enjoyability of the experience, quality of the dining experience, activities, children's program, entertainment, service, and value), while the **individual ship ratings** cover those things that vary from vessel to vessel—quality and size of the cabins and public spaces, comfort, appearance and upkeep, decor, number and attractiveness of dining options, gyms/spas (or, for the small-ship lines that don't have gyms and spas, "Adventure & Fitness Options"), and children's facilities—plus a rating for the overall enjoyability of the onboard experience. To provide an **overall score,** we've given each ship a star rating (for example, ★★★½) based on the combined total of our poor-to-outstanding ratings, translated into a 1-to-5 scale:

1	=	**Poor**	4	=	**Excellent**
2	=	**Fair**	5	=	**Outstanding**
3	=	**Good**			

In instances where the category doesn't apply to a particular ship (for example, none of the adventure ships has children's facilities), we've simply noted "not applicable" (N/A) and absented the category from the total combined score, as these unavailable amenities usually are not what people are looking for in that type of ship anyway.

Now for a bit of philosophy: The cruise biz today offers a profusion of experiences so different that comparing all lines and ships by the same set of criteria would be like comparing a luxury Manhattan hotel to a rural B&B. That's why, to rate the cruise lines and their ships, we grade on a curve that compares them only with others in their category—mainstream with mainstream, luxe with luxe, adventure with adventure. Once you've determined what kind of experience is right for you, look for the best ships in that category based on your particular needs. For example, if you see in the "Small Ships, Sailing Ships & Adventure Cruises" chapter that Windstar achieves an "outstanding" rating for dining, it means among the lines in that category/chapter,

Windstar has the best cuisine. It may not be up to the level of, say, the ultraluxurious Silversea (it's not), but if you're looking for a sailing-ship cruise that also has terrific food, this line would be a great bet.

3 Evaluating & Comparing the Listed Cruise Prices

As we explain in detail in chapter 2, the cruise lines' brochure prices are almost always wildly inflated—they're the "sticker prices" cruise line execs would love to get in an ideal world. In reality, passengers typically pay anywhere from 10% to 50% less. Instead of publishing these inflated brochure rates, then, we've worked with Nashville's **Just Cruisin' Plus** (© **800/888-0922;** www.justcruisinplus.com) to provide you with samples of the **actual prices** customers were paying at press time. Other travel agencies and online sites will generally offer similar rates. Each ship review includes a **typical per diem price range** (the total cruise price divided by the number of days) that encompasses everything from the ship's lowest-priced inside (windowless) cabin to its standard balcony cabin.

This represents the range of cabins that the vast majority of cruisers will book, and encompasses all the ship's inside cabins, all its oceanview cabins with windows, and obviously its standard balcony accommodations. Above this range are all the fancier balcony cabins and suites, some of which will cost only a few hundred dollars more per cruise, some of which will be way up in the thousands.

Keep in mind that because this book covers cruises in several different regions, the sample prices listed are not applicable to all sailings—cruises in Alaska and Hawaii, for instance, are almost always more expensive than comparable cruises in the Caribbean and The Bahamas. These prices are meant as a guide only and are in no way etched in stone—the price you pay may be higher or even lower, depending on when you choose to travel, when you book, what specials the lines are offering, and a slew of other factors. Prices listed include **port charges** (the per-passenger fee that ports charge for ships to dock), but do not include taxes.

See chapter 2, "Booking Your Cruise & Getting the Best Price," for more details on pricing.

Ships at a Glance

Cruise Line	Ship	Frommer's Star Rating	Year Built
American Cruise Lines (sm. ship): Part cruise, part Rotary Club meeting, part historical tour, this Connecticut-based line offers a comfortable, reserved, and hassle-free cruise experience.	American Glory	★★★½	2002
	American Spirit	★★★½	2005
	American Star	★★★½	2007
	Independence	★★★½	2010
	Queen of the West	★★★★	1995
American Safari Cruises (sm. ship): The most luxurious of the small-ship soft-adventure lines.	Safari Explorer	★★★★	1998
	Safari Quest	★★★★	1992
	Safari Spirit	★★★★	1981
Azamara (mainstream): Comfy exploration, country-club comfort.	Azamara Journey	★★★★	2000
	Azamara Quest	★★★★	2000
Blount Small Ship Adventures (formerly ACCL) (sm. ship): A family-owned New England line operating tiny, no-frills ships that travel to offbeat places, carrying casual, down-to-earth, older passengers.	Grande Caribe	★★★	1997
	Grande Mariner	★★★	1998
	Niagara Prince	★★★	1994
Carnival (mainstream): When you're hankering for an utterly unpretentious and totally laid-back cruise, Carnival's colorful, jumbo-size resort ships deliver plenty of bang for the buck. If you like the flash of Vegas and a serious party vibe, you'll love Carnival's brand of flamboyant fun.	Carnival Conquest	★★★★½	2002
	Carnival Destiny	★★★★½	1996
	Carnival Dream	★★★★½	2009
	Carnival Ecstasy	★★★½	1991
	Carnival Elation	★★★½	1998
	Carnival Fantasy	★★★½	1990
	Carnival Fascination	★★★½	1994
	Carnival Freedom	★★★★½	2007
	Carnival Glory	★★★★½	2003
	Carnival Imagination	★★★½	1995
	Carnival Inspiration	★★★½	1996
	Carnival Legend	★★★★	2002
	Carnival Liberty	★★★★½	2005
	Carnival Miracle	★★★★	2004
	Carnival Paradise	★★★½	1998
	Carnival Pride	★★★★	2001
	Carnival Sensation	★★★½	1993
	Carnival Spirit	★★★★	2001
	Carnival Splendor	★★★★½	2008
	Carnival Triumph	★★★★½	1999
	Carnival Valor	★★★★½	2004
	Carnival Victory	★★★★½	2000

Gross Tonnage	Passenger Capacity (Double Occupancy)	Passenger/Space Ratio	Passenger/Crew Ratio	Wheelchair Access	Full Review on Page
86*	49	N/A*	2.7 to 1	yes	322
97*	100	N/A*	3.8 to 1	yes	322
97*	100	N/A*	3.8 to 1	yes	322
1,200*	102	N/A*	3.8 to 1	yes	322
1,308	120	9.6	2.7 to 1	yes	324
N/A*	36	N/A*	2.25 to 1	no	326
99*	22	N/A*	2 to 1	no	326
N/A*	12	N/A*	1.7 to 1	no	326
30,277	710	42.6	1.8 to 1	yes	90
30,277	710	42.6	1.8 to 1	yes	90
99*	100	N/A*	5.5 to 1	no	327
99*	100	N/A*	5.5 to 1	no	327
99*	84	N/A*	5 to 1	no	327
110,000	2,974	37	2.5 to 1	yes	103
101,353	2,642	38.4	2.6 to 1	yes	111
130,000	3,646	35.7	2.7 to 1	yes	100
70,367	2,040	34.5	2.2 to 1	yes	114
70,367	2,040	34.5	2.2 to 1	yes	114
70,367	2,040	34.5	2.2 to 1	yes	114
70,367	2,040	34.5	2.2 to 1	yes	114
110,000	2,974	37	2.5 to 1	yes	103
110,000	2,974	37	2.5 to 1	yes	103
70,367	2,040	34.5	2.2 to 1	yes	114
70,367	2,040	34.5	2.2 to 1	yes	114
88,500	2,124	41.7	2.3 to 1	yes	108
110,000	2,974	37	2.5 to 1	yes	103
88,500	2,124	41.7	2.3 to 1	yes	108
70,367	2,040	34.5	2.2 to 1	yes	114
88,500	2,124	41.7	2.3 to 1	yes	108
70,367	2,040	34.5	2.2 to 1	yes	114
88,500	2,124	41.7	2.3 to 1	yes	108
113,300	3,006	37.7	2.6 to 1	yes	103
102,000	2,758	37	2.6 to 1	yes	111
110,000	2,974	37	2.5 to 1	yes	103
102,000	2,758	37	2.6 to 1	yes	111

Ships at a Glance *(continued)*

Cruise Line	Ship	Frommer's Star Rating	Year Built
Celebrity (mainstream): Celebrity offers an elegant and refined cruise experience, yet one that's fun, active, and doesn't cost a bundle. Each ship is spacious, glamorous, and comfortable, mixing sleekly modern and Art Deco styles and throwing in cutting-edge art collections to boot.	Celebrity Century	★★★★½	1995
	Celebrity Constellation	★★★★★	2002
	Celebrity Eclipse	★★★★★	2010
	Celebrity Equinox	★★★★★	2009
	Celebrity Infinity	★★★★★	2001
	Celebrity Mercury	★★★★½	1997
	Celebrity Millennium	★★★★★	2000
	Celebrity Silhouette	Not yet rated	2011
	Celebrity Solstice	★★★★★	2008
	Celebrity Summit	★★★★★	2001
Costa (mainstream): Fun, festive, international megaships.	Costa Atlantica	★★★½	2000
	Costa Mediterranea	★★★½	2003
Cruise West (sm. ship): Family-owned Cruise West is the preeminent small-ship line in Alaska, and over the past decade it's branched out to include trips in warmer destinations, too. Most of its itineraries are port-to-port and geared to older, well-traveled, intellectually curious passengers.	Pacific Explorer	★★★½	1995
	Spirit of Adventure	★★★½	1984
	Spirit of Alaska	★★★½	1980
	Spirit of Columbia	★★★½	1979
	Spirit of Discovery	★★★½	1976
	Spirit of Endeavour	★★★½	1983
	Spirit of '98	★★★★	1984
	Spirit of Oceanus	★★★★★	1991
	Spirit of Yorktown	★★★½	1988
Crystal (luxury): Fine-tuned and fashionable, with great service, cuisine, and so on.	Crystal Serenity	★★★★½	2003
	Crystal Symphony	★★★★½	1995
Cunard (mainstream): A legendary line with a nearly legendary vessel—the largest ocean liner in the world.	Queen Mary 2	★★★★★	2004
	Queen Victoria	★★★★★	2007
Disney (mainstream): Family ships where both kids and adults are catered to equally, and with style.	Disney Dream	Not yet rated	2011
	Disney Fantasy	Not yet rated	2011
	Disney Magic	★★★★½	1998
	Disney Wonder	★★★★½	1999

Gross Tonnage	Passenger Capacity (Double Occupancy)	Passenger/Space Ratio	Passenger/Crew Ratio	Wheelchair Access	Full Review on Page
70,606	1,750	41	2 to 1	yes	131
91,000	1,950	46.7	2 to 1	yes	127
122,000	2,850	42.8	2.3 to 1	yes	123
122,000	2,850	42.8	2.3 to 1	yes	123
91,000	1,950	46.7	2 to 1	yes	127
77,713	1,896	41	2 to 1	yes	131
91,000	1,950	46.7	2 to 1	yes	127
122,000	2,850	42.8	2.3 to 1	yes	123
122,000	2,850	42.8	2.3 to 1	yes	123
91,000	1,950	46.7	2 to 1	yes	127
85,000	2,114	40	2.3 to 1	yes	138
85,000	2,114	40	2.3 to 1	yes	138
1,716	100	17	3 to 1	no	334
1,471	102	14.2	3.2 to 1	no	334
97*	78	N/A	3.7 to 1	no	336
97*	78	N/A	3.7 to 1	no	336
94*	84	N/A	4 to 1	no	336
1,471	102	14.7	3.6 to 1	no	334
96*	96	N/A	4.2 to 1	partial	333
4,500	114	39.5	2 to 1	partial	332
2,354	138	17	3.5 to 1	no	334
68,870	1,070	64.1	1.6 to 1	yes	277
51,044	922	55.4	1.7 to 1	yes	279
151,400	2,592	58.4	2.1 to 1	yes	149
90,049	2,014	45	2.2 to 1	yes	146
128,000	2,500	51.2	1.7 to 1	yes	156
128,000	2,500	51.2	1.7 to 1	yes	156
83,000	1,754	47.3	1.8 to 1	yes	160
83,000	1,754	47.3	1.8 to 1	yes	160

Ships at a Glance *(continued)*

Cruise Line	Ship	Frommer's Star Rating	Year Built
Holland America (mainstream): Holland America has been in business since 1873, and has managed to hang on to more of its seafaring history and tradition than any line today, except Cunard. It offers a moderately priced, classic, and casual yet refined cruise experience.	Amsterdam	★★★★ ½	2000
	Eurodam	★★★★ ½	2008
	Maasdam	★★★★	1993
	Nieuw Amsterdam	★★★★ ½	2010
	Noordam	★★★★	2006
	Oosterdam	★★★★	2003
	Rotterdam	★★★★ ½	1997
	Ryndam	★★★★	1994
	Statendam	★★★★	1993
	Veendam	★★★★	1996
	Volendam	★★★★ ½	1999
	Westerdam	★★★★	2004
	Zaandam	★★★★ ½	2000
	Zuiderdam	★★★★	2002
InnerSea Discoveries (sm. ship): Active adventure sailings at a fair price.	Wilderness Adventurer	Not yet rated	1984
	Wilderness Discoverer	Not yet rated	1992
Island Windjammers (sm. ship): Ultracasual sailing adventure.	Diamant	★★★★	1978
Lindblad Expeditions (sm. ship): One of the most adventure-oriented small-ship lines, concentrating on wilderness and wildlife.	National Geographic Sea Bird	★★★ ½	1982
	National Geographic Sea Lion	★★★ ½	1981
MSC Cruises (mainstream): Italian line offers midsize ships and gadget-free fun.	MSC Poesia	★★★★ ½	2007
Norwegian (mainstream): NCL may be the most mainstream of the mainstream lines these days—and we mean that in a good way, hewing to the center with always casual dining (and lots of it); bright, cheerful decor; and fun innovations like gourmet beer bars and onboard bowling alleys. Its newest ships are real standouts, and it's the go-to line for Hawaii cruises.	Norwegian Dawn	★★★★ ½	2002
	Norwegian Epic	★★★★ ½	2010
	Norwegian Gem	★★★★★	2007
	Norwegian Jade	★★★★★	2007
	Norwegian Jewel	★★★★★	2005
	Norwegian Pearl	★★★★★	2006
	Norwegian Sky	★★★★	1999
	Norwegian Spirit	★★★★ ½	1999
	Norwegian Star	★★★★ ½	2001
	Norwegian Sun	★★★★	2001
	Pride of America	★★★★	2005

Gross Tonnage	Passenger Capacity (Double Occupancy)	Passenger/Space Ratio	Passenger/Crew Ratio	Wheelchair Access	Full Review on Page
61,000	1,380	44.2	2.1 to 1	yes	177
86,000	2,104	41.2	2.3 to 1	yes	170
55,451	1,266	43.8	2.1 to 1	yes	182
86,000	2,104	41.2	2.3 to 1	yes	170
85,000	1,848	46	2.3 to 1	yes	173
85,000	1,848	46	2.3 to 1	yes	173
56,652	1,316	43	2.2 to 1	yes	177
55,451	1,266	43.8	2.1 to 1	yes	182
55,451	1,266	43.8	2.1 to 1	yes	182
55,451	1,266	43.8	2.1 to 1	yes	182
63,000	1,440	43.7	2.2 to 1	yes	180
85,000	1,848	46	2.3 to 1	yes	173
63,000	1,440	43.7	2.2 to 1	yes	180
85,000	1,848	46	2.3 to 1	yes	173
89*	72	N/A*	N/A	no	338
95*	88	N/A*	N/A	no	338
57*	12	N/A*	6	no	339
100*	62	N/A	2.6 to 1	no	343
100*	62	N/A	2.6 to 1	no	343
89,600	2,550	35.1	2.6 to 1	yes	190
91,740	2,224	41.2	2 to 1	yes	204
155,873	4,100	35.7	2.4 to 1	yes	197
93,558	2,380	39.3	2 to 1	yes	204
93,558	2,380	39.3	2 to 1	yes	204
92,000	2,376	38.7	2 to 1	yes	204
93,502	2,394	39.3	2 to 1	yes	204
77,104	2,002	38.5	2 to 1	yes	211
77,000	1,966	39.1	2 to 1	yes	204
91,000	2,240	40.6	2 to 1	yes	204
78,509	1,936	40.6	2 to 1	yes	211
81,000	2,146	37.7	2.1 to 1	yes	208

Ships at a Glance (continued)

Cruise Line	Ship	Frommer's Star Rating	Year Built
Oceania (mainstream): Casual premium line.	Marina	Not yet rated	2011
	Regatta	★★★★	1998
Princess (mainstream): With a fleet of mostly large and extralarge megaships, including some of the biggest at sea, L.A.-based Princess offers a quality mainstream cruise experience with a nice balance of tradition and innovation, relaxation and excitement, casualness and glamour.	Caribbean Princess	★★★★ ½	2004
	Coral Princess	★★★★ ½	2003
	Crown Princess	★★★★ ½	2006
	Diamond Princess	★★★★ ½	2004
	Emerald Princess	★★★★ ½	2007
	Golden Princess	★★★★ ½	2001
	Grand Princess	★★★★ ½	1998
	Island Princess	★★★★ ½	2003
	Ruby Princess	★★★★ ½	2008
	Sapphire Princess	★★★★ ½	2004
	Sea Princess	★★★★	1998
	Star Princess	★★★★ ½	2002
Regent Seven Seas (luxury): Formerly known as Radisson Seven Seas, this line carries passengers in style and extreme comfort. Its brand of cruising is casually elegant and subtle, and its cuisine is near the top.	Seven Seas Mariner	★★★★ ½	2001
	Seven Seas Navigator	★★★★	1999
	Seven Seas Voyager	★★★★ ½	2003
Royal Caribbean (mainstream): Royal Caribbean offers some of the best-looking, best-designed, most activity-packed, and just plain fun megaships in the biz. Along with NCL, it's also out in the forefront of innovation, always challenging the status quo regarding what can and can't be done aboard ships.	Adventure of the Seas	★★★★ ½	2001
	Allure of the Seas	Not yet rated	2010
	Brilliance of the Seas	★★★★ ½	2002
	Enchantment of the Seas	★★★ ½	1997
	Explorer of the Seas	★★★★ ½	2000
	Freedom of the Seas	★★★★ ½	2006
	Grandeur of the Seas	★★★ ½	1996
	Independence of the Seas	★★★★ ½	2008
	Jewel of the Seas	★★★★ ½	2004
	Legend of the Seas	★★★ ½	1995
	Liberty of the Seas	★★★★ ½	2007
	Majesty of the Seas	★★★	1992
	Mariner of the Seas	★★★★ ½	2003

Gross Tonnage	Passenger Capacity (Double Occupancy)	Passenger/Space Ratio	Passenger/Crew Ratio	Wheelchair Access	Full Review on Page
65,000	1,258	51.7	1.6 to 1	yes	217
30,200	684	44.2	1.7 to 1	yes	218
113,000	3,100	36.8	2.6 to 1	yes	227
91,627	1,970	46.5	2 to 1	yes	234
113,000	3,070	36.8	2.6 to 1	yes	227
116,000	2,670	42.3	2.4 to 1	yes	231
113,000	3,070	36.8	2.6 to 1	yes	227
109,000	2,600	41.9	2.4 to 1	yes	227
109,000	2,600	41.9	2.4 to 1	yes	227
91,627	1,970	46.5	2 to 1	yes	234
113,000	3,070	36.8	2.6 to 1	yes	227
116,000	2,670	42.3	2.4 to 1	yes	231
77,000	1,950	39.5	2.2 to 1	yes	238
109,000	2,600	41.9	2.4 to 1	yes	227
50,000	708	71.4	1.6 to 1	yes	286
28,550	490	58.3	1.4 to 1	yes	288
46,000	708	65.7	1.6 to 1	yes	286
142,000	3,114	45.6	2.7 to 1	yes	257
225,282	5,400	41.7	2.3 to 1	yes	246
90,090	2,100	42.9	2.5 to 1	yes	261
80,700	2,252	35.8	2.7 to 1	yes	264
142,000	3,114	45.6	2.7 to 1	yes	257
160,000	3,634	44	2.7 to 1	yes	254
74,140	1,950	38	2.5 to 1	yes	264
160,000	3,634	44	2.7 to 1	yes	254
90,090	2,100	42.9	2.5 to 1	yes	261
69,130	1,804	38.3	2.5 to 1	yes	264
160,000	3,634	44	2.7 to 1	yes	254
73,941	2,390	30.9	2.9 to 1	yes	267
142,000	3,114	45.6	2.7 to 1	yes	257

Ships at a Glance *(continued)*

Cruise Line	Ship	Frommer's Star Rating	Year Built
Royal Caribbean *(continued)*	Monarch of the Seas	★★★	1991
	Navigator of the Seas	★★★★ ½	2002
	Oasis of the Seas	★★★★★	2009
	Radiance of the Seas	★★★★ ½	2001
	Rhapsody of the Seas	★★★ ½	1997
	Serenade of the Seas	★★★★ ½	2003
	Splendor of the Seas	★★★ ½	1996
	Vision of the Seas	★★★ ½	1998
	Voyager of the Seas	★★★★ ½	1999
Seabourn (luxury): Seabourn's ships are floating pleasure palaces, giving passengers doting service and some of the finest cuisine at sea.	Seabourn Legend	★★★★	1992
	Seabourn Odyssey	★★★★★	2009
	Seabourn Sojourn	★★★★★	2010
	Seabourn Spirit	★★★★	1989
Sea Cloud Cruises (sailing ships): Classic luxe.	Sea Cloud	★★★★★	1931
	Sea Cloud II	★★★★★	2001
SeaDream (luxury): An upscale yet casual line without the traditional regimentation.	SeaDream I	★★★★ ½	1984
	SeaDream II	★★★★ ½	1985
Silversea (luxury): Silversea caters to guests who won't settle for anything but the best, with free-flowing champagne and exceptional service.	Silver Cloud	★★★★	1994
	Silver Shadow	★★★★★	2000
	Silver Spirit	★★★★	2009
	Silver Whisper	★★★★★	2001
	Silver Wind	★★★★	1995
Star Clippers (sailing ships): Classic clipper ships with all the amenities.	Royal Clipper	★★★★	2000
	Star Clipper	★★★ ½	1992
	Star Flyer	★★★ ½	1991
Windstar (sailing ships): The no-jackets-required policy aboard Windstar sums up the line's casually elegant attitude. The ships feel like private yachts—they're down to earth, yet service and cuisine are first class.	Wind Spirit	★★★ ½	1988
	Wind Star	★★★ ½	1986
	Wind Surf	★★★★	1990

* *Tonnage figures for small ships are often calculated differently than those of larger ships, making comparisons and passenger/space figures difficult to gauge.*

Gross Tonnage	Passenger Capacity (Double Occupancy)	Passenger/Space Ratio	Passenger/Crew Ratio	Wheelchair Access	Full Review on Page
73,941	2,390	30.9	2.9 to 1	yes	267
142,000	3,114	45.6	2.7 to 1	yes	257
225,282	5,400	41.7	2.3 to 1	yes	246
90,090	2,100	42.9	2.5 to 1	yes	261
78,491	2,000	39.2	2.5 to 1	yes	264
90,090	2,100	42.9	2.5 to 1	yes	261
69,130	1,804	38.3	2.5 to 1	yes	264
78,491	2,000	39.2	2.5 to 1	yes	264
142,000	3,114	45.6	2.7 to 1	yes	257
10,000	208	48.1	1.5 to 1	yes	297
32,000	450	71	1.4 to 1	yes	295
32,000	450	71	1.4 to 1	yes	295
10,000	208	48.1	1.5 to 1	yes	297
2,532	64	39.6	1 to 1	no	354
3,849	94	41	1.6 to 1	no	354
4,260	112	38.7	1.2 to 1	no	305
4,260	112	38.7	1.2 to 1	no	305
16,800	296	57	1.4 to 1	yes	315
28,258	388	74	1.3 to 1	yes	313
36,000	540	67	1.4 to 1	yes	311
28,258	388	74	1.3 to 1	yes	313
17,400	296	57	1.4 to 1	yes	315
5,000	227	22	2.2 to 1	no	360
2,298	170	13.5	2.5 to 1	no	363
2,298	170	13.5	2.5 to 1	no	363
5,350	148	36	1.6 to 1	no	371
5,350	148	36	1.6 to 1	no	371
14,745	312	48	1.6 to 1	no	369

6

The Mainstream Lines

These are the cruise lines you know even if you've never set foot on one. They're the ones with the catchy TV spots, glossy magazine spreads, and omnipresent website banner ads that make cruises seem like sheer paradise—and for many people, they really are.

Today's mainstream ships are part theme park, part shopping mall, part gym, and part faux downtown entertainment and dining district, all packaged in a sleek hull with an oceanview resort perched on top. The biggest are *really* big: 14 stories tall, 1,000 feet long, with cabin space for between 2,000 and 5,000-plus passengers and a couple of thousand crewmembers. Most of the mainstream lines have spent the past 10 years pumping billions into ever-newer, bigger, and fancier ships, and the intense competition means they're constantly trying to outdo each other with entertainment and activities. The newer the ship, the more whoopee you can expect: open-air boardwalk districts, bowling alleys, water parks, ice-skating rinks, outdoor movie theaters, surfing machines, giant spas, rock-climbing walls, full-size basketball courts, and virtual-reality golf, plus classics like hot tubs, theaters, water slides, and bars, bars, bars. The action is just outside your cabin door, though if you crave some downtime, there's always your private balcony or some quiet lounge that's deserted while everybody else is living it up.

Overall the atmosphere is very social and active, especially on warm-weather cruises in the Caribbean, The Bahamas, Bermuda, and Mexico, which tend to draw the youngest mix of fun-loving, like-to-party passengers (lots of 20s, 30s, and 40s). Itineraries in Alaska and New England tend to draw a mellower crowd, mostly in their 50s and up.

The more elegant and refined of the lines are commonly referred to as **premium**, a notch up in the sophistication department from others that are described as **mass-market**. Quality-wise, they're all more similar than they are different, especially in regard to dining and entertainment. Ditto for lines such as Azamara and Oceania (and half the Holland America fleet), whose **midsize ships** are almost a throwback to the days before supersizing. Though these lines' vessels are tiny compared with the Royal Caribbeans, Carnivals, and Princesses of the world, they're in this chapter because they offer well-rounded cruises for a diverse mix of passengers.

DRESS CODES Aboard most lines in this chapter, most nights are designated as casual, "dressy casual," or semiformal, with one or two being formal or "formal optional." But, these days, those are more suggestions than rules, and in any case, most ships these days have at least one casual dining venue open every night in case you just can't face dressing up at all. (See chapter 3 for more about dress codes.)

Frommer's Ratings at a Glance: The Mainstream Lines

1 = poor   **2** = fair   **3** = good   **4** = excellent   **5** = outstanding

	Enjoyment Factor	Dining	Activities	Children's Program	Entertainment	Service	Worth the Money
Azamara	5	4	4	N/A	4	5	5
Carnival	4	3	3	4	3	3	4
Celebrity	5	4	4	3	3	5	5
Costa	3	2	4	2	3	2	3
Cunard	5	4	5	5	4	4	5
Disney	4	3	3	5	5	3	4
Holland America	4	4	3	2	4	5	5
MSC Cruises	3	3	3	3	3	2	4
Norwegian	5	4	4	4	5	4	5
Oceania	4	4	2	N/A	3	4	4
Princess	4	4	4	4	4	4	4
Royal Caribbean	5	4	5	4	5	4	5

Note: Cruise lines have been graded on a curve that compares them only with the other mainstream lines. See "How to Read the Ratings," in chapter 5, for a detailed explanation of the ratings methodology.

1 Azamara Club Cruises

1050 Caribbean Way, Miami, FL 33132. ℂ **877/999-9553.** www.azamaracruises.com.

THE LINE IN A NUTSHELL   Launched in mid-2007, Azamara Club Cruises is a more high-end and adult-oriented sister brand to Celebrity and Royal Caribbean, offering more out-of-the-way itineraries, better service and cuisine, more enrichment opportunities, and lots of little extras that make the experience extra-special. The line's two ships are midsize gems that were originally built for now-defunct Renaissance Cruises. **Sails to:** Caribbean, Panama Canal, Baja/Sea of Cortez (plus Europe, Asia, transatlantic).

THE EXPERIENCE   The idea behind Azamara is pretty much the same idea that animates all the other former Renaissance vessels (some of which are also operated by Oceania and Princess): smaller, more intimate ships sailing longer itineraries, visiting out-of-the-ordinary ports, and offering a casual yet country-clubbish experience, with great service. That's not to call Azamara a copycat, though. Fact is, there are only so many different kinds of cruise experiences that can be offered, and this is the kind for which these ships were made. In an age dominated by bigger and bigger megaships, we welcome the return of midsize vessels with open arms. Kudos to Celebrity/Azamara for putting the resources into keeping this kind of cruise option alive.

Overall (and like Oceania), Azamara provides an experience that straddles the mainstream and luxury segments of the cruise biz—somewhere between Celebrity and Crystal or Regent, though new **luxury initiatives** (complimentary house wines at lunch and dinner, free gratuities, free specialty coffees and bottled wines, more overnights in port and high-end excursions) are trying to nudge the line closer to the high end. Not that it was all that mainstream to begin with. On the Pool Deck, a quiet jazz trio replaces the kind of loud pop/reggae band found on most mainstream ships, and in the cafe you'll often find a harpist plucking out traditional and classical tunes, spiced with pop standards. Service is exceptional, from the butlers who attend to all cabins to little touches such as the cold towels offered at the gangway after a hot day in port. At dinner, things are entirely flexible—just show up when you like, either at the main restaurant, at two reservations-only alternatives, or at a casual but still waiter-serviced buffet restaurant. Onboard activities run from the usual (bingo, napkin folding, team trivia) to the unusual, including poetry reading/writing get-togethers and seminars on etiquette and art. At night you can take in a floor show at the theater, catch a performance by a guest magician or comedian, do the karaoke thing, watch a late-night movie, or take in music in several of the public rooms.

Pros

- **Perfect-size ships:** *Azamara Journey* and *Azamara Quest* are just the right size—large enough to keep things interesting over a long itinerary, but small enough to be cozy, comfortable, and easy to navigate.
- **Most all-inclusive of the mainstream lines:** In addition to free house wines with lunch and dinner, Azamara also includes gratuities, specialty coffees and teas, bottled water, free shuttles in many ports, and free self-service laundry in its rates. Suite guests can also dine free all week in the ships' specialty restaurants.
- **Long, interesting itineraries:** On their 12-night Caribbean itineraries, Azamara's ships concentrate on smaller, more interesting ports such as Virgin Gorda, Dominica, and Bequia.
- **Grace notes:** At breakfast, passengers can get fresh fruit or vegetable juice or a smoothie at a bar in the buffet. At the pool grill, there are hot pretzels available all day. Public areas are dotted with ornate fresh flower displays. In the public bathrooms, real rolled towels replace the cheesy paper kind.
- **Nonsmoking policy:** Smoking is permitted only in one corner of the Pool Deck and one corner of the nightclub. (Of course, this is a "con" for smokers.)

Cons

- **Crowded pool deck on sunny days:** On warm sea days, the smallish Pool Deck can get packed to the gills. Compensating factor? The wonderful, thickly cushioned wooden deck chairs.
- **No children's program:** The lack of any kind of kids' programs or playrooms discourages families from bringing kids on board—which may be the point, actually.

AZAMARA: MICROCHIC

When Renaissance Cruises folded in 2001, its beautiful fleet of eight identical and almost brand-new midsize ships was disbursed to the four winds. Oceania got two (and later a third), Princess got two (and later a third, which now sails for sister-line P&O), and two ended up being operated by Pullmantur S.A., Spain's largest cruise line. In late 2006, **Celebrity Cruises**' parent company, Royal Caribbean, purchased Pullmantur and soon pulled the old switcheroo, sending Celebrity's elderly *Zenith* to Spain and claiming the two ex-Renaissance ships in her place. Around them, Celebrity created an entirely new cruise, thus was born Azamara Cruises. The addition of "Club" as its middle name came later, after the line hired longtime cruise exec Larry

Compared with the other mainstream lines, here's how Azamara rates:

	Poor	Fair	Good	Excellent	Outstanding
Enjoyment Factor					✓
Dining				✓	
Activities				✓	
Children's Program	N/A				
Entertainment				✓	
Service					✓
Worth the Money					✓

Pimentel (ex-head of Cunard, Seabourn, and SeaDream Yacht Club) to be its president and CEO, and to take the experience to the next luxe level. Today, rather than being a sub-brand of Celebrity, Azamara has emerged as a stand-alone cruise line in its own right.

PASSENGER PROFILE

The line draws from the typical cruise demographic, roughly **ages 45 and up.** The relatively long and unusual itineraries and the quiet onboard atmosphere appeal to a more cultured, accomplished crowd, while the higher-than-mass-market prices and the length of the itineraries favor retirees. The majority of passengers on Caribbean, Mexico, and Panama Canal sailings are Americans, along with a smattering from Canada, Europe, Asia, and South America.

The lack of children's programming limits the number of families with kids who book this line, while the **stringent smoking regulations** mean few smokers sail Azamara. (Smoking is prohibited everywhere on board except in the aft port-side section of the Looking Glass Lounge and in the starboard forward section of the Pool Deck.)

DINING

Dining on Azamara is a step up from Celebrity in both cuisine and presentation. Dining service—which is excellent on Celebrity—is at least as good here, and probably a little better. At mealtimes, passengers have full flexibility in terms of where, when, and with whom they dine. Dinner is available in four restaurants: one traditional, two specialty, and one casual. House wines are complimentary with lunch and dinner in all restaurants, and more expensive vintages (including selections from boutique wineries around the world) are available for purchase.

TRADITIONAL   The main dining room aboard each ship is a one-level space with tables for 2, 4, 6, 8, and 10, serving breakfast, lunch, and dinner, the latter within a 3½-hour window. Menus run to five courses, with passengers able to choose from among five appetizers, three soups, two salads, and five main courses. Appetizer selections may include dishes such as marinated and cured salmon in cucumber dill cream; beef, Gruyère, and caramelized onion turnover; wild mushroom and chicken quiche; and scallops with Thai curry sauce and coconut rice cake. Soups might include oven-roasted tomato and garlic soup with goat cheese crostini; Louisiana gumbo with andouille sausage and okra; and rustic cannellini bean soup with beef, basil, roasted tomato, and olive oil. For main courses, expect the likes of herb-crusted South African white fish with toasted quinoa; sesame seared yellow-fin tuna steak with tamarind stir-fried Asian vegetables; filet mignon with black truffle sauce; penne pasta tossed with four cheeses; and beef short ribs braised in red Burgundy wine with creamy polenta, carrots, and turnips. In addition, you can always choose from an assortment of **classic favorites** (grilled filet of salmon with herb butter, lemon-marinated roasted chicken, and so on) and **vegetarian options** (we had some wonderful vegetarian curries while aboard *Journey*).

SPECIALTY Each ship has two specialty, reservations-only restaurants. Passengers in regular staterooms get one free specialty dinner per cruise and are free to make as many additional reservations as they like, paying the regular per-person cost. Suite guests can dine in both restaurants free throughout their cruise.

Set in the stern on Deck 10, **Prime C** is a classic steakhouse with a hardwood floor and dark wall paneling, a chunky wooden bar, a mix of modern art and classic Hollywood photos, and wraparound windows. The per-person cost is $15. Appetizers here include chilled jumbo shrimp cocktail, beef carpaccio, crispy popcorn rock shrimp, and lump crab cake. There's also a selection of soups and salads. Main courses run just like you'd figure, with a choice of steaks (16-oz. cowboy bone-in rib-eye, 12-oz. New York strip, 8-oz. filet mignon, or 8-oz. Kobe-style flat-iron), chops (double-cut Colorado lamb chop, 14-oz. veal chop, or 12-oz. Berkshire pork chop), and "other" (including oven-roasted sea bass, sesame grilled tuna, roasted organic chicken, surf 'n' turf, or seafood *pappardelle*). At the entrance to the restaurant, a raised table for 14 is set up in front of a glass-fronted wine locker and is used for **wine-appreciation seminars.**

Right next door, **Aqualina** is a Mediterranean/American restaurant adorned with white faux pillars, a rich sea-blue carpet, and a bright, sunny vibe that contrasts with Prime C's manly woodiness. Appetizers include pan-seared diver scallops and brie in crisp phyllo dough with candied pecans and cranberry compote. There's also a selection of soups and salads. Main courses include sautéed Chilean sea bass, rock lobster thermidor and lobster pot pie, and veal *osso bucco* with a butternut-squash ragout. Passengers can dine off the regular menu (at $15 per person) or choose the $50 **food-and-wine pairing menu.**

CASUAL Each ship has a traditional buffet restaurant with seating inside or on a nice stern-facing outdoor deck. In the morning, the restaurant has all the standards (eggs, bacon and sausage, made-to-order omelets, Virginia ham, cheese blintzes, a fruit selection, breads, a cold cereal bar, and so on), plus two nice extra touches: a separate window for **waffles and pancakes,** and a **juice bar** where attendants will whip you up a fresh carrot-apple, tomato, or carrot-ginger juice (or whatever combination you like), or a fresh smoothie. At lunch, the buffet serves an adventurous spread of salads, meats, pastas, and other dishes. At dinner, the restaurant offers a fixed casual menu as well as a buffet of fresh sushi, made-to-order pasta, and other choices.

Out on deck, the **poolside grill** has the usual burgers, hot dogs, veggie burgers, and pizza, plus a salad bar and fun oddities such as seafood-and-veggie shish kabobs, gyros, hot pretzels, and nachos. Toppings such as grilled onions and mushrooms are available for the burgers.

SNACKS & EXTRAS On each ship, an **Italian-style coffee shop** serves specialized coffee drinks and fine teas at extra cost, plus a cart of free tea sandwiches, cookies, and desserts that's kept stocked from about 7am to 1am. A similar traditional **tea time** spread is put out daily between 4 and 5pm at each ship's combo lounge/library/piano club. **Room service** is available 24 hours a day.

ACTIVITIES

A full roster of onboard activities identifies Azamara's roots in the mainstream, though the way it's spiced with unusual touches shows that the line is going for more depth.

For those who like to stick to cruise ship tradition, there are pool games, team trivia contests, quizzes, darts and Ping-Pong tournaments, shuffleboard, chess, bridge, and bingo. There are also computer classes, digital photography seminars, golf clinics, wine-appreciation seminars (some at extra cost), and destination lectures, plus culinary demonstrations, mixology clinics, and beauty and fitness clinics offered by the spa staff. Both ships also have relatively large **casinos.**

The ships' spas provide the usual array of massages, facials, manicures, pedicures, body-cleansing treatments, and wraps, as well as several expensive **spa packages** that bundle a number of treatments into a themed package.

CHILDREN'S PROGRAM

None. These ships have no children's facilities or programs.

ENTERTAINMENT

Azamara offers a mixed bag of entertainment, with evenings in the show lounges rotating between musical production shows and guest comedians, magicians, and musical acts. The smaller host quality musical acts.

During our last sailing, **production shows** featured five singers/dancers backed up by a live band, with the musical selections tilted toward American standards. While production shows aren't necessarily our cup of tea, these got extra points for their intimacy (the ships' show lounges have no stage, so the performers are down at floor level, just steps from the audience), for the energy of their performers, and for being 100% live, with no prerecorded backing tracks or lip-synching involved. Other shows on our trip included an improv comedian, a Bermudian steel-pan player, a cabaret entertainer, and the very talented magician Carl Andrews, a regular on such lines as Celebrity, Crystal, HAL, NCL, Princess, and Regent.

Musicians perform daily in various parts of the ship. In the cafe, each cruise features a harpist/vocalist who performs three hour-long sets per day, mixing classical, traditional, and popular melodies. A pianist performs after hours, and a jazz ensemble occasionally shows up to do a set of standards and classic jazz tunes. On the Pool Deck, Azamara replaces the usual thumping dance band with a quiet, subtle jazz trio of guitar, bass, and drums. Around the ship, even the piped-in background music is of a higher quality than you hear aboard most ships, mixing jazz, standards, New Agey selections, a few pop songs, and the occasional novelty number to get your attention.

For those who like to entertain themselves, there's also **karaoke** some evenings, as well as dancing in the disco "till late."

SERVICE

Service is one of the high points at Azamara, as it is aboard sister line Celebrity. In cabins, butlers do the usual cabin steward job but also help with packing/unpacking, making restaurant and spa reservations, serving full breakfasts en suite, delivering daily canapes, shining shoes, and so on. Service is unobtrusive but very personal when it does obtrude: Butlers know your name from day one and will go out of their way to greet you in the corridors. Dining service is good in the main restaurant and excellent in the specialty restaurants.

Gratuities for restaurant, housekeeping, and bar staff are included in the line's base rates, so no additional tipping for these staffmembers is necessary. Spa services have a gratuity added automatically to your bill, so don't tip more unless you really want to.

Regular send-out **laundry and dry cleaning** services are available at cost, and each ship also has a **free self-service laundry** located midship on Deck 7.

Azamara Journey • Azamara Quest

The Verdict

We wish more ships were like *Journey* and *Quest:* large enough to be interesting during long itineraries, but small enough to keep things cozy, comfortable, and convenient. These are some of our favorite mainstream cruise ships.

Azamara Journey *(photo: Azamara Club Cruises)*

Specifications   Typical Per Diems: $165–$255

Size (in tons)	30,277	Crew	390
Passengers (double occ.)	710	Passenger/Crew Ratio	1.8 to 1
Passenger/Space Ratio	42.6	Year Launched	2000
Total Cabins/Veranda Cabins	355/241	Last Major Upgrade	2007

Frommer's Ratings (Scale of 1–5)   ★★★★

Cabin Comfort & Amenities	4	Dining Options	4
Appearance & Upkeep	4	Gym, Spa & Sports Facilities	4
Public Comfort/Space	4.5	Children's Facilities	N/A
Decor	4	Enjoyment Factor	4

Sailing Regions, Seasons & Home Ports

Journey	**Mexico Sea of Cortez,** from San Diego (Jan 2011). **Panama Canal,** from San Diego (Jan 2011). **Caribbean,** from Miami (Feb–Mar 2011), from San Juan (Nov 2011–Mar 2012).
Quest	Not sailing from North America in 2011–12.

Journey and *Quest* are exactly the kind of cruise ships we love: small in scale, cozy, and traditionally decorated, with an onboard vibe that's all about passengers' personal interaction rather than eye-catching gimmicks. Like all the vessels that were originally built for Renaissance Cruises, they're more boutique hotel than Vegas resort, with a decor that hearkens back to the golden age of ocean liners—all warm woods, rich fabrics, and clubbily intimate public areas. When Celebrity and Royal Caribbean took over the ships, they put nearly $40 million into major refurbishments, moving the walls around on some cabin decks to create 32 new suites on each vessel; designing new specialty restaurants; expanding the spa; adding a cafe; and installing a new art collection, decking, carpets, paint schemes, bedding, cushions, drapes, table linens, and other soft goods. The result is a pair of lovely, practically new-looking ships, with only a few dents in cabin corridors (courtesy of luggage carts) betraying the fact that they've already been in service for more than a decade.

CABINS   Cabins on *Journey* and *Quest* are divided into just six configurations. Standard inside (158 sq. ft.), oceanview (143–170 sq. ft.), and oceanview Club Veranda cabins (175 sq. ft., plus balcony) are all almost identical in amenities. Each has a sitting area with a sofa bed and small table, a flatscreen TV, a minifridge, and a writing desk. Closet space is only just adequate for the long itineraries these vessels sail, though an abundance of drawers and storage space under the bed helps matters some. Bathrooms are on the tight side, with a small shower stall and awkwardly angled toilet, and are stocked with Elemis bath products. Cabin decor is nicely understated, with off-white walls, wood-tone furnishings and headboard, and upholstery and carpeting done in easy-on-the-eyes blues and golds. More than half the accommodations on board are oceanview Club Veranda cabins, each with a 40-square-foot balcony. Sunset Veranda cabins all face the bow or stern.

Club Continent suites (266 sq. ft., plus balcony) add considerably to your elbow-room and have such amenities as a 60-square-foot balcony, a bathroom tub, and a DVD/CD player. Club Ocean suites (430–508 sq. ft., plus balcony) and Club World owners' suites (560 sq. ft., plus balcony) have separate bedrooms and living rooms, master baths with a whirlpool tub and shower, a guest bathroom, huge 220-foot-plus balconies, and, in the owners' suites, a dressing room with vanity.

Four cabins on each ship are wheelchair accessible.

PUBLIC AREAS   Public rooms on these ships are clustered on Decks 5, 9, and 10. On Deck 5 forward, the Cabaret has space to seat about half the passengers on board. It has no raised stage, so productions are, by definition, floor shows. Aside from the semicircular banquettes that divide the room's slightly elevated perimeter from the main floor, all seating is in comfortable chairs interspersed with cocktail tables. The best seat in the house is a high table at the center of the rear bar area, between and slightly behind the two spotlights. In addition to production shows, the room is used for late-night movies, bingo, and other activities. Moving toward midships, there's a relatively large casino with a big-screen TV in one corner for sports events; the ship's two understated retail shops; and the cafe, a warm, inviting space that provides snacks 18 hours a day, along with complimentary specialty coffees and teas. A harpist and pianist perform here frequently throughout the day.

Deck 9 is primarily given over to the buffet restaurant, pool, and spa (see below), but tucked inside one corner are an Internet center and a small conference room.

On Deck 10 forward, the Looking Glass disco/observation lounge has wraparound floor-to-ceiling windows, a dance floor, and cocktail tables for two and four set in a large but still comfortably intimate space. Toward midships, the combo library and piano lounge maintains a generally quiet, gentlemen's club feel, with dark-wood bookcases and wall paneling, velvety couches, leather armchairs, oriental-patterned rugs, a chessboard, and a couple of globes showing the world that was. A faux fireplace, racing-dog ceramics, and a *trompe l'oeil* conservatory ceiling complete the picture. Afternoon tea is served here daily.

DINING OPTIONS   An evening in *Journey's* and *Quest's* main dining room is ideally a two-step process. First, you set a time to meet your friends at the clubby, wood-paneled bar located just outside the maitre d's station. Set below Sistine Chapel–esque ceiling murals, there's a chunky semicircular bar, couches, and comfy armchairs, with a faux fireplace and curio cabinets separating the bar area from the dining room itself. Next, get a table for dinner, preferably in the central portion of the room, where they seem to be more widely spaced than those along the periphery. Decor-wise, the room continues the ship's overall country-club feel, with Romanesque paintings, dark-wood paneling, decorative pillars, and understated upholstery. Tables are available for 2, 4, 6, 8, and 10 people.

At the stern on Deck 10, each ship's two specialty restaurants sit side by side, allowing views from practically every table. Aqualina is decorated with a Mediterranean sensibility to match its menu, with a polished black tile floor and a color scheme that favors white and blue. Next door, Prime C is a thoroughgoing steakhouse. At the entrance, a wood-floored bar area is dominated by a high table for 14 at which wine-tasting seminars are given. Tables for four dominate the rest of the C-shaped restaurant.

On Deck 9, Windows Cafe is a standard buffet restaurant with a few nonstandard features. At breakfast, you can get freshly made vegetable/fruit juices or a complicated smoothie from the Health Nut juice bar, and fresh pancakes and waffles from a dedicated window to the side of the buffet lines. At dinner, the space serves sushi and custom-made pasta dishes, along with a spread of favorites. Seating is available inside and out. On the Pool Deck, the grill spices up the usual burger-and-dogs menu with salad, seafood shish kabobs, gyros, hot pretzels, and nachos.

POOL, FITNESS, SPA & SPORTS FACILITIES   The Pool Deck has one smallish pool, two hot tubs, a small performance stage, and a bar, along with some of the best deck chairs we've ever seen—heavy, wooden, and dressed in thick navy-blue cushions with flip-back pillows. On the rear port side, a covered seating area has double-width deck lounges for couples. On warm days at sea, the Pool Deck can get very crowded, but a little walking (not much—these are small ships) will net you much less crowded lounging spots on the Sun Deck, two levels up. There's also a lovely little half-moon of sunning space and a hot tub just forward of the gym and spa. Shade worshipers can head to the Promenade Deck, which is filled with those same great deck chairs, set under an overhang in an area that gets little traffic.

The gym, located just forward of the Pool Deck, has treadmills, stationary bikes, elliptical trainers, dumbbells, weight machines, and a large aerobics floor. Though the space is not huge, it's adequate for the relatively small number of passengers on board. It got crowded only once during our last cruise. Pilates, spinning, stretch, abs, and yoga classes are given throughout the cruise at no extra charge. Next door there's a salon; a spa providing treatments in several pleasant rooms; and a separate suite for acupuncture, laser hair removal, and microdermabrasion.

A corner of the Pool Deck has Ping-Pong tables, and shuffleboard and a small golf-putting green are found on the Sun Deck.

2 Carnival Cruise Lines

3655 NW 87th Ave., Miami, FL 33178-2428. ⒸⒸ **800/227-6482** or 305/599-2200. Fax 305/405-4855. www.carnival.com.

THE LINE IN A NUTSHELL   When you're hankering for an utterly unpretentious and totally laid-back cruise, Carnival's colorful, jumbo-size resort ships deliver plenty of bang for the buck. If you like the flash of Vegas and a serious party vibe, you'll love Carnival's brand of flamboyant fun. **Sails to:** Caribbean, Mexican Riviera, Alaska, Canada/New England, Hawaii (plus Europe, transatlantic).

THE EXPERIENCE   The McDonald's of cruising, Carnival's got the most recognized name in the biz and serves up a very casual, down-to-earth, middle-American

Caribbean vacation. Food and service are pretty decent considering the huge numbers served, and Carnival gets points for trying to offer a higher-quality vacation than in years past, with upgraded cabin bedding, classier dishware in the buffet restaurants, and Wi-Fi access throughout each ship.

On most ships in the fleet, you'll find a sushi bar, supper club, wine bar, coffee bar, and great amenities for children. Like the frat boy who graduated to a button-down shirt and an office job, Carnival has definitely moved up and on to some extent. But like that reformed frat boy who still likes to meet his old pals for happy hour every week, Carnival hasn't lost touch with its past. Sure, the line's decor, like its clientele, has mellowed to some degree since its riotous, party-hearty beginnings, but each ship is still an exciting, bordering-on-nutty collage of textures, shapes, and images. Where else but on these floating playlands would you find a giant octopus-like chandelier with lights that change color, bar stools designed to look like baseball bats, or real oyster-shell wallpaper? The outrageousness of the decor is part of the fun. Evolved, yes; dull, no.

Pros

- **Fun, theme-park ambience:** The fanciful, sometimes wacko, decor on these vessels is unmatched.
- **Large standard cabins:** At 185 square feet or larger, Carnival's standard inside and outside cabins are among the roomiest in the mainstream category.
- **Melting pot at sea:** You name 'em, they'll be on a Carnival cruise, from rowdy, pierced 20-something singles and honeymooners, to *Leave It to Beaver* families with young kids, to grandparents along for the show.
- **An insomniac's delight:** When passengers on most ships are calling it a night, Carnival's guests are just getting busy with diversions such as midnight adult comedy shows, raging discos, and 24-hour pizza parlors.

Cons

- **You're never alone:** Not in the hot tubs, on shore excursions, in the pool, while sunbathing, at the gym, at the pizza counter . . .
- **Get in line:** At breakfast and lunch, the buffet restaurants are jammed; expect a 20- to 30-minute slow shuffle through the line to get your bowl of oatmeal and scrambled eggs . . . along with a few thousand other passengers.
- **No enrichment:** Activities are pretty much confined to fun and games on the pool deck; no guest speakers and classes like most other mainstream lines offer.

Compared with the other mainstream lines, here's how Carnival rates:

	Poor	Fair	Good	Excellent	Outstanding
Enjoyment Factor				✓	
Dining			✓		
Activities			✓		
Children's Program				✓	
Entertainment			✓		
Service			✓		
Worth the Money				✓	

CARNIVAL: BIG LINE, BIG FUN

Carnival has enjoyed an extended run as big cheese of the cruise world. The assets of its parent company, Carnival Corporation & plc are enormous and growing: In addition to the 22 ships of its Carnival brand, Carnival Corporation also owns Princess, Holland America, Costa, Cunard, and Seabourn, as well as several European and Australian lines. In total, Carnival Corporation operates a combined fleet of 93 ships, with another 13 scheduled for delivery through June 2012.

The origins of the Miami-based company were as precarious as they were accidental. Company patriarch Ted Arison, a somewhat reclusive billionaire who passed away in 1999, had sold an airfreight business in New York in 1966 and intended to retire to his native Israel to enjoy the fruits of his labor—after a few more little ventures. After he negotiated terms for chartering a ship, he assembled a group of paying passengers and then discovered that the ship's owner could no longer guarantee the vessel's availability. According to latter-day legend, a deal was hastily struck whereby Arison's passengers would be carried aboard a laid-up ship owned by Knut Kloster, a prominent Norwegian shipping magnate. The ship was brought to Miami from Europe, and the combination of Arison's marketing skill and Kloster's hardware created an all-new entity that, in 1966, became the corporate forerunner of Norwegian Cruise Line.

After a bitter parting of ways with Kloster, Carnival got its start in 1972 when Arison bought *Empress of Canada,* known for its formal and somewhat stuffy administration, and reconfigured it into Carnival's first ship, the anything-but-stuffy *Mardi Gras.* After a shaky start—the brightly painted ship, carrying hundreds of travel agents, ran aground just off the coast of Miami on her first cruise—Arison managed to pick up the pieces and create a company that, under the guidance of astute and tough-as-nails company president Bob Dickinson (now retired) and chairman Micky Arison (Ted's son), eventually evolved into the most influential trendsetter in the cruise ship industry. The rest is history, as they say.

Today, Carnival's fleet includes 22 ships, most of which cruise the Caribbean and The Bahamas year-round. The 110,000-ton, 2,974-passenger *Carnival Freedom,* sister to *Liberty, Valor, Conquest,* and *Glory,* is among Carnival's newest, having debuted in March 2007. In summer 2008, a new class of ship debuted. Based on the Conquest-class ships, the 113,000-ton, 3,006-passenger *Carnival Splendor* sports some new features, including a water park and the line's largest and most elaborate spa and kids' facilities to date . . . that is, until the 130,000-ton *Carnival Dream* was introduced in September 2009. They are both Carnival's largest vessels so far. The *Carnival Magic* will follow in 2011 and a third unnamed sibling in 2012.

PASSENGER PROFILE

In the old days, Carnival was basically a floating college frat house: our coauthor Heidi sailed in 1996 when more than 500 graduating high-school seniors practically took over (and ruined) a cruise on the old *Celebration.* She still gets nightmares. However, guidelines implemented in early 1997 put a stop to all of that, mandating that no one age 20 and under can sail unless sharing a cabin with an adult 26 and over, with exceptions made for married couples and young people traveling with their parents in separate cabins. So, while you'll still find teen groups on board (especially Mar–June), things are not what they were.

A Carnival cruise is a huge melting pot—couples, singles, and families; young, old, and lots in between. We've met doctors on Carnival cruises as well as truck drivers. And no matter what their profession, you'll see people wearing everything from Ralph

Carnival's Vacation Guarantee

Unhappy with your Carnival cruise? Dissatisfied guests may debark at their first non-U.S. port of call and, subject to some restrictions, get a refund for the unused portion of their cruise and reimbursement for coach-class airfare back to their ship's home port. To qualify, passengers must inform the ship's purser before their first port of call.

Lauren shirts and Gucci sunglasses to Harley-Davidson tank tops and eyebrow studs. Carnival estimates about 30% of passengers are under age 35, another 40% are between 35 and 55, and 30% are over age 55. A high percentage of all passengers are first-time cruisers. Although it's one of the best lines to choose if you're single, Carnival's ships certainly aren't overrun by singles—families and couples are definitely in the majority. The line's 3-, 4-, and 5-night cruises tend to attract the most families with kids and the highest number of 20- and 30-something single friends traveling together in groups.

Regardless of their age, passengers tend to be young at heart, ready to party, and keyed up for nonstop fun and games. Many have visited the casinos of Las Vegas and Atlantic City and the resorts of Cancún and Jamaica, and are no strangers to soaking in sardine-can hot tubs, sunbathing, hitting the piña coladas and beer before lunch, and dancing late into the night.

The typical Carnival passenger likes to dress casual, even at dinner, with sweat suits, jeans, and T-shirts just as prevalent as Dockers, sundresses, and Hush Puppies on all but formal nights—and even on formal nights, it's not uncommon for some passengers to run back to their cabins to change out of their dressier duds and put on shorts or jeans before heading out to the discos and bars. Tuxedos are in the minority here. A few don't even bother with dressing up at all, even on formal nights. A hotel director on the *Carnival Liberty* told Heidi about the restaurant dress codes. "We're very flexible on this," he said, adding that they draw the line only at bathing suits, and T-shirts or hats with "bad words." Otherwise, just about anything goes.

DINING

Carnival's newest Dream-, Conquest-, and Spirit-class ships offer about as many dining venues as you'll really need, and the rest of the fleet only has two choices: a buffet venue and a main dining room.

TRADITIONAL   In its two-story "formal" dining rooms (and take *formal* with a grain of salt—some Carnival passengers don't seem to think it means anything but T-shirts and jeans), Carnival's food quality and presentation, plus its wine selection, are much improved from its early days, and for the most part on par with Royal Caribbean, Princess, and NCL. You'll find more exotic options such as chicken satay with peanut sauce and Indian-themed meals that include lamb chops, basmati rice, lentils *(dal),* and potatoes *(aloo);* as well as all-American favorites such as lobster and prime rib, plus pasta dishes, grilled salmon, and Thanksgiving-style turkey served with all the trimmings. Unfortunately, the preparation is uneven (as is true on many of the mainstream lines); one night your entree is great, the other it's blah. On a recent *Victory* cruise, top tastes included a yummy roasted pumpkin soup and a New England lobster-and-crab-cake dish. There are some 50 healthier **Spa Carnival** dishes (which include calorie, fat, sodium, and cholesterol stats), and **vegetarian** options are also on each menu.

Despite the hectic pace and ambience, dining service is usually friendly if not always the most efficient, and is somewhat classier than in earlier years (to a point; Carnival still has its waiters handle all wine service, rather than employing sommeliers). The staff still presents dessert-time song-and-dance routines, at times quite elaborate, and passengers seem to love it.

In summer 2010, the entire Carnival fleet started offering a new flexible **anytime dining** option in the main restaurants, enabling guests to dine anytime between 5:45pm and 9:30pm nightly. More tradition-minded guests can still opt for the old-fashioned early (6pm) and late (8:15pm) assigned seatings.

SPECIALTY   *Carnival Spirit,* which debuted in spring 2001, was the line's first ship to have a reservations-only restaurant, a two-level steakhouse serving entrees for a $30-per-person cover charge (plus tip and not including wine). Subsequent Spirit-class and Conquest-class ships—and all future Carnival ships—have this intimate alternative venue. Here, service is more gracious, and dedicated sommeliers are on hand to take your wine order. Menus are leather-bound, and elegant table settings feature beautiful Versace show plates and Rosenthal, Fortessa, and Revol china. Tables for two and four are available. Like in a traditional steakhouse, the menu includes starters, salads, and side dishes such as creamed spinach and mashed potatoes. The steaks range from New York strip to porterhouse and filet mignon, and other options include grilled lamb chops, as well as fish and chicken dishes. The experience is intentionally designed to be slow and lingering, so don't go if you're looking for a fast meal. The food and service are the most doting you'll find on Carnival.

CASUAL   At the opposite end of the alternative-dining spectrum, guests aboard all Carnival ships can opt to have any meal in the buffet-style Lido restaurants at no extra charge. For an unstructured and casual dinner, walk in anytime between about 6 and 9:30pm for serve-yourself entrees such as chicken, pasta, stir-fry, and carved meats. At lunch, buffets in the Lido feature the usual suspects—salads, meats, cheeses, pastas, grilled burgers, and chicken filets, and several hot choices such as fish and chips, roast turkey, and stir-fry. The lunchtime buffets also feature specialty stations, serving up things such as pasta or Chinese food, fish and chips, and rotisserie meat. All ships have a deli station for sandwiches; a pizza station open 24 hours, where you can also get a Caesar salad; and an outlet for grilled chicken sandwiches, burgers, hot dogs, and fries—just be prepared for a *l-o-o-o-o-o-o-ong* line at lunchtime, as the Carnival crowd loves burgers and fries. In general, the various buffet sections can get very backed up at times as passengers wait for bins to be restocked and servers scramble to fill them. Though the food is not memorable, upgrades to tableware are: Kudos to Carnival for bringing in colorful ceramic sugar bowls, salt and pepper shakers, and dinnerware in place of the old white plastic stuff.

SNACKS & EXTRAS   But wait, there's more: Carnival ships give you 24-hour pizza (with as many as 500 pies flipped a day!), calzones that are surprisingly tasty, Caesar salad with or without chicken, and self-serve soft ice cream and frozen yogurt, as well as a complimentary **sushi bar** along the promenade and a deli on all ships. There are late-night eats in the buffet restaurant daily and there are also specialty (read: not free) coffee and pastry bars, some with milkshakes and banana splits, too.

All ships provide **24-hour room service,** with a menu including such items as panini and a focaccia sandwich with grilled zucchini, fresh mozzarella, and portobello mushrooms, plus the standard tuna salad, cookies, fruit, and so on. Kids can select

from **hildren's** m in the main dining rooms. Kids and adults can buy the Fun-ship Fountain C l is ally part of the deal.
tic cup with a lid

ACTIVITIES

Carnival is all ab out l unging by the pool, drink in hand (or bucket of beers at foot), and soaking up t e sun and some loud music or whatever **goofy contests** may be taking place. On sea days, you can get a hoot out of watching (or joining, if you're not the wallflower typ e) the men's hairy chest contest or similar tomfoolery, participate in a trivia contest, or sign up for some group dancing lessons. A blaring band will play a few sets by the p ol, and on nearly half the fleet (including all newbuilds going forward), a **giant vic** d eo screen smack-dab in the center of the pool area broadcasts various shipboard activities at eardrum-shattering decibels (and movies, concerts, a don't expect to have a conversation without shouting). Currently, do we mean loud— there's one on the Ca rnival Dream, Splendor, Liberty, Freedom, Conquest, Glory, Valor, Victory, Destiny, and T riumph.

There's a quieter poo l and sunbathing area at the stern called Serenity; the adults-only retreat is found abo ard all eight Fantasy-class ships as well as the Carnival Dream, Splendor, and Glory. Spirit -class vessels have a second midships pool separated from the main action by a bar and so lid dividers that keep most of the noise out and provide a more serene lounging space; one of the four pools on the Conquest-class ships is quieter and covered by a retractal le glass roof.

Slot machines begin clanging by 8 or 9am in the **casinos** when the ships are at sea (tables open at 11am), and server s start tempting passengers with trays of fruity theme cocktails long before the lunch ho ur. Expect to hear the ubiquitous art auctioneer shouting into a microphone about som e Peter Max masterpiece. There are **line-dancing and ballroom classes,** trivia contests, fac ial and hairdo demonstrations (intended to entice passengers to sign up for expensive tr eatments), singles and newlywed parties, game shows, shuffleboard, bingo, art auctions, and movies. Overall, though, there's not as much variety of activities as aboard lines such as Norwegian, Holland America, and Celebrity (read: absolutely no enrichment lectures on history or other cerebral topics).

You can spend some time in the roomy gyms on the Fantasy-, Destiny-, Spirit-, and Conquest-class ships (and take the handful of **free aerobics classes** or the ones that cost $10, such as Pilates, yoga, and spinning) or playing volleyball on the top deck, or treat yourself to one of dozens of relaxing (and expensive) treatments in the Steiner-managed **spas.** All ships have covered and lighted golf driving nets, with **golf pros** sailing on board to give lessons with video analysis starting at $25 for a 15-minute session and $80 for an hour. Pros also accompany guests on golf excursions on shore, and clubs, golf shoes, balls, gloves, and other paraphernalia are available for rent.

If you want to escape it all and find a truly quiet nook for awhile, retire to the subdued libraries/card/game rooms and 24-hour Internet centers on each ship; you'll find Wi-Fi service fleetwide as well. You can also now use your cellphone while at sea or in port. The Funhub on the Carnival Dream is the fleet's updated version of an Internet center. It's got a funky decor and Internet access, and passengers can also surf for shore-excursion information and ship announcements, news and weather, as well as view all the ship's daily activities.

CHILDREN'S PROGRAM

Carnival is right up there with the best ships for families—the li[ne] he estimates that about 625,000 kids sail aboard its ships annually. Some 600 to 800 c[hildren] children per cruise is pretty normal, and there can be in the neighborhood of 1,000 c[hildren] on holiday cruises and during the summer months, when it'll be difficult to find a kid-free hot tub. The **child facilities** are fairly extensive, with the newest and biggest D[ream]- Dream- and Conquest-class ships boasting the biggest and brightest playrooms in t[he] fleet, with arts and crafts, oodles of toys and games, video screens and televisions sh[owing] movies and cartoons, and computer stations loaded with the latest educational and entertainment software.

The **Camp Carnival program** has complimentary supervised ki[ds'] activities on sea days nearly nonstop from 9am to 10pm, and on port days, fro[m] 8am (or earlier, if there are shore excursions departing earlier) for ages 2 through 1[4] in four age groups: toddlers 2 to 5, juniors 6 to 8, intermediates 9 to 11, and teen[s] 12 to 14. The latter are part of a teen program called Circle C. The 10 to 16 coun[s]elors (all of whom are trained in CPR and first aid) organize the fun and games on e[a]ch ship, which include face painting, computer games, puzzles, fun with Play-Doh, picture bingo, pirate hat making, and pizza parties for toddlers. For juniors, there are PlayStation and computer games, ice-cream parties, story time and library visits, T-sh[i]rt coloring, and swimming. For intermediates, there are scavenger hunts, trivia and b[i]ngo, Ping-Pong, video-game competitions, arts and crafts, computer games, dance classes, and talent shows.

Across all age groups, activities with a somewhat educational bent may include art projects with papier-mâché, oil paintings, and wate[r]colors; music appreciation, which gets kids acquainted with different musical instru[m]ents; science projects where kids can make their own ice cream and create mini-[h]elicopters; and a fitness program that encourages today's couch-potato compu[t]er-head kids to actually get up and run around. Club 02 teen centers are geare[d] to the 15- to 17-year-old set and are quite elaborate on the newest ships. Besides karaoke parties, computer games, scavenger hunts, talent shows, card and trivia games, and Ping-Pong, teens can watch movies at the centers and go to dance parties. Some ships are also equipped with iMacs, but there is no Internet center specifically for teens as on some other ships. Of course, teens can also hang out in the video arcades—the newest ships have virtual-reality games and air-hockey tables. For something more refined, Carnival now provides a collection of spa treatments geared to teens (along with their parents).

The *Carnival Dream* has the line's most impressive water features, with her Water-Works aqua-park comprising a pair of twin 80-foot-long racing slides; a 104-foot-long enclosed spiral slide called the DrainPipe; and squirting fountains, splash zones, and dump buckets. *Carnival Splendor, Fantasy, Imagination, Inspiration, Sensation, Ecstasy,* and *Fascination* also have the WaterWorks aqua-park (sans the *Dream*'s DrainPipe). The rest of the Carnival ships all have two- or three-deck-high Twister slides adjacent to the main Lido Deck pools or aft of the funnel, ranging in length from 72 feet on the Spirit class to 214 feet on the Conquest-class ships.

Parents desiring a kid-free evening can make use of the supervised children's activities, offered from 7 to 10pm nightly free of charge, after which time group **slumber-party-style babysitting** kicks in for ages 6 months through 11 years until 3am in the playroom, at $6 per hour for the first child, $4 per hour for each additional child. No private babysitting is available. Infants between 6 and 23 months can also be cared for on port days between 8am and noon, but it's considered babysitting and the hourly fee mentioned above will apply. On sea days between noon and 2pm, you can also drop off children ages 1 and under at the rate above, or parents may use the playroom with their babies for these 2 hours at no charge. And, yes, counselors will change diapers (though parents are asked to provide them, along with wipes)! Parents with kids ages 8 and under who are checked into the children's program get free use of cellphones on most ships, in case their kids need to contact them. A handful of strollers are available for rent fleetwide for $25 for 7- and 8-night cruises (less for shorter cruises), and a limited number of bouncy seats, travel swings, and Game Boys are for rent.

Mom and Dad can get an earlier start on their kid-free evening, when the counselors supervise **kids' mealtime** in the Lido restaurant between about 6 and 7pm in a special section reserved for kids; it's offered nightly except the first night of the cruise. The children's dining room menu, printed on the back of a fun coloring/activity book (crayons are provided), has the usual favorites—hot dogs, hamburgers, french fries, chicken nuggets, pepperoni pizza, peanut-butter-and-jelly sandwiches, banana splits, Jell-O, and a daily special.

Cribs are available if you request them when making your reservations. When you first board, head for the kids' playroom to get a schedule for the week and to sign up your child for the program. Children must be at least 6 months old to sail on board.

ENTERTAINMENT

Aboard its newer megaships, Carnival has spent millions on stage sets, choreography, and sound equipment. The theaters on the Conquest-class, Spirit-class, and Destiny-class ships are spectacular three-deck extravaganzas, and the casinos are so large that you'll think you've died and gone to Vegas; but even aboard its smaller, older ships, Carnival consistently has some of the most lavish entertainment extravaganzas afloat.

Carnival megaships each carry about 8 to 16 flamboyantly costumed dancers (fewer on *Celebration* and *Holiday*) for twice- or thrice-weekly **Vegas-style musicals.** One or two live soloists carry the musical part of the show, while dancers lip-sync the chorus. A 5- to 10-piece orchestra of traditional and digital instruments deftly accompanies the acts each night, sometimes enhanced by synchronized recorded music. You'll also find comedians, jugglers, acrobats, rock-'n'-roll bands, country-and-western bands, classical string trios, pianists, and Tommy Dorsey– or Glenn Miller–style big bands, all performing during the same cruise, and sometimes on the same night. Special entertainment may include a local mariachi band when a ship's in port late in Cozumel.

Besides the main theater, most entertainment happens somewhere along the indoor Main Street–like promenade (except on the Spirit-class ships, which are more spread out). Many are called the "Something-or-other Boulevard" or "Something-or-other Way." This area stretches along one entire side of each ship and is lined with just about the entire repertoire of the ship's nightclubs, bars, lounges, and patisseries, as well as its disco and casino. One bar on all the Fantasy-, Destiny-, Spirit-, and Conquest-class ships welcomes cigar smoking, and fleetwide, cigars are sold at the pool bar and during midnight buffets.

By day, entertainment includes an ultraloud Caribbean-style calypso or steel-drum band performing Bob Marley tunes and other pop songs on a deck poolside, and a pianist, guitarist, or string trio playing in the atria of the line's newest ships. The *Dream, Splendor, Liberty, Freedom, Conquest, Glory, Valor, Victory, Destiny,* and *Triumph* all sport a giant video screen up on the Pool Deck (and all newbuilds will get one) and it tends to monopolize much of the day by loudly (and we mean loudly) broadcasting concerts, movies, and shipboard activities. Personally, we don't like 'em.

Sure, a couple of movies in the late afternoon and evening are nice, but who needs the thing screeching away all day long?

SERVICE

All in all, a Carnival ship is a well-oiled machine, and you'll certainly get what you need—but not much more. When you board, for instance, you're welcomed by polite and well-meaning staff at the gangway, given a diagram of the ship's layout, and then pointed in the right direction to find your cabin on your own, carry-on luggage in tow. Chalk it all up to the size of the line's ships. It's a fact of life that service aboard all megaliners is simply not as attentive as that aboard smaller vessels—with thousands of guests to help, your dining-room waiter and cabin steward have a lot of work ahead of them and little time for chitchat. Lines can get long at the breakfast and lunch buffets and, at certain times, at the pizza counter, though there always seem to be plenty of drink servers roaming the Pool Decks, looking to score drink orders.

Service certainly doesn't benefit from Carnival's **automatic tipping policy.** Like most of the major lines these days, gratuities for the crew are automatically added to your account at the end of your cruise to the tune of $10 per person per day fleetwide, and they're divvied up among the staff automatically. You can adjust the amount—or eliminate it completely and hand out cash in envelopes—by visiting the purser's desk. On Carnival and the other lines with automatic tipping policies, we've found waiters and cabin stewards don't seem as eager to please as they did when the tip carrot was hanging directly over them.

There is a **laundry service** aboard each ship for washing and pressing only (with per-piece charges), as well as a handful of **self-service laundry rooms** with irons and coin-operated washers and dryers. There's a pleasant-smelling liquid soap and shampoo dispenser in cabin bathrooms fleetwide, plus a small basket of trial-size toiletries (refilled only upon request).

Spa treatments can now be prebooked online at www.carnival.com, assuming your cruise booking is paid in full.

Carnival Dream *(photo: Carnival Cruise Lines)*

Carnival Dream

The Verdict

The largest ship in the Carnival fleet, *Dream* puts her extra space to extremely good use, mostly by expanding Carnival's signature attractions and adding new public rooms, most of which seem to have more legroom and elbowroom.

Specifications

Typical Per Diems: $60–$95

Size (in tons)	130,000	Crew	1,367
Passengers (double occ.)	3,646	Passenger/Crew Ratio	2.7 to 1
Passenger/Space Ratio	35.7	Year Launched	2009
Total Cabins/Veranda Cabins	1,823/887	Last Major Upgrade	N/A

Frommer's Ratings (Scale of 1–5)

Cabin Comfort & Amenities	4.5	Dining Options	4.5
Appearance & Upkeep	5	Gym, Spa & Sports Facilities	4.5
Public Comfort/Space	4.5	Children's Facilities	4.5
Decor	4	Enjoyment Factor	4.5

Sailing Regions, Seasons & Home Ports

Carnival Dream	Caribbean, from Port Canaveral (year-round).

At 139,000 gross tons, *Carnival Dream* represents an all-new class of ships for Carnival, offering a number of new features while retaining the overall look and feel that's come to define the line over the past decade. All in all, this vessel is about 15% larger than any other one in the Carnival fleet, and inches into the supermegaship territory dominated by Royal Caribbean—though she's still miles behind the enormous *Oasis of the Seas,* which debuted in the U.S. just a few weeks after *Dream,* squashing any hopes Carnival may have had for a big media splash.

Though this ship is a bit toned down from Carnival's over-the-top design past, and seems to have higher quality furnishings and fittings than previous Carnival ships, *Dream* still remains consistent with the line's "Fun" philosophy, with all the brightness and busyness that entails. Among the more interesting features developed for the ship is the Lanai, an indoor-outdoor area that runs clear through from one side of the ship to the other on Deck 5 (Promenade Deck), creating a social outdoor gathering spot in a space that gets short shrift on most vessels. Social networking of another kind (think Facebook, MySpace, and so on) goes on at the ship's virtual Fun Hub, an intranet site that allows guests to create a personal profile, meet and interact with others on board, send and receive private messages, create groups based on interests, and invite friends to attend shows or participate in onboard events. The Fun Hub also includes information on *Dream's* entertainment options, daily events, youth programs, and restaurant menus, plus weather updates, news and sports scores, shipboard announcements, ship maps, and more. Guests can access the Hub either via their personal computers, netbooks, smartphones, or other Wi-Fi devices, or via 36 stations located on Decks 3, 4, and 5. Other highlights of *Dream* include the largest spa in the Carnival fleet, a water park with one of the longest water slides at sea, and an unusual number of bars and small dining spots.

A twin sister ship, *Carnival Magic,* is scheduled to debut in 2011.

CABINS   Standard inside (185 sq. ft.) and outside staterooms (220 sq. ft.) are plain but pleasant, and are outfitted with a TV, safe, minibar, hair dryer, small sitting area, and bathroom with shower. Outside staterooms have either a picture window or (in category-5 rooms only) two nice old-fashioned portholes. Most have twin beds that push together into a king, but entry-level category-1A cabins (160 sq. ft.) have bunk beds.

Ideal for families are the new Deluxe Ocean View staterooms (185–230 sq. ft.), which feature all the above plus a full bathroom with shower and a separate washroom with a sink and junior tub. Another fun new option: the Cove Balcony cabins. Of average size (185 sq. ft.), the Cove cabins' distinguishing feature is their location way down near the waterline. Each cabin also has a 35-square-foot balcony that's literally carved like an alcove out of the ship's hull. The arrangement is very old-fashioned and ocean-liner-like, and being so close to the water gives you the feeling of being on a much smaller ship.

Probably the best among the balcony rooms are the Aft-View Extended Balcony staterooms (185 sq. ft.), located on four different decks. Their main features are the bigger 60-square-foot balconies and the wake views. Of course, there's an upcharge for them. Cloud 9 spa accommodations, available at several stateroom levels, allow private access, special amenities, and priority reservations at the Cloud 9 Spa. All accommodations, from small inside rooms to the largest Penthouse Suites, are appointed with Carnival Comfort Collection bedding, which includes comfy mattresses, high-thread-count linens, duvets, and custom pillows.

There are 35 wheelchair-accessible staterooms, spread across all cabin categories.

PUBLIC AREAS   From end to end, Decks 4 and 5 have an array of rooms for shows, dancing, drinking, eating, and—happily for those wanting to take a break—a small library and quiet room. The main show lounge, taking up the forward section of Decks 3, 4, and 5, is home to large-scale production shows. Extra legroom in the center part of the lower level makes that section very comfortable, while nicely tiered seating along the lower level's sides and the upper two decks means there's not really a bad view anywhere. At the opposite end of the ship on Deck 5 is the Burgundy Lounge, which offers up comedy and a variety of other acts. On a recent 7-night Caribbean voyage, six different comedians performed, doing prime-time shows as well as late-night adults-only sets.

On Deck 5, the Lanai straddles the line between indoor entertainment space and outdoor hot-tubbing, and is one of the best uses of a Promenade Deck we've seen in years. Located slightly aft of midships, the area has two semicircular, partially covered outdoor seating areas indented into the vessel at port and starboard from the ship's half-mile-long wraparound Promenade Deck. Tables and chairs are set up in each area, both outside and inside, and they face two large hot tubs that are cantilevered out over the ship's rail, with the sea bubbling below and 180-degree views over the horizon. (Two additional cantilevered hot tubs are located a bit farther forward along the Promenade.) Connecting the two Lanai areas is an indoor entertainment space called the Ocean Plaza, which has its own bar, dance floor, and cafe.

The ship's lobby area is also particularly nice, with not only the shore excursion and purser's desks but also a nice seating area and a bar. A piano stage cantilevered out over the space provides live music throughout the day.

For kids, *Dream* provides a huge Camp Carnival play area on Deck 11 for ages 2 to 11, while tweens (ages 12–14) and teens (ages 15–17) get their own spaces a full seven decks below, each with movie setups, dance floors, a soda bar, and Wii video games. There's also a full-on video arcade attached.

DINING OPTIONS   *Carnival Dream* has two main dining rooms, the two-deck-high Scarlet Restaurant and Crimson Restaurant, both done up in bright but comfortable red and serving all three meals, with two sittings at dinner. Scarlet offers up aft views in addition to side views for those lucky enough to get window tables. The upper level of Crimson has no external views; the windows look out on a ship hallway. On Deck 11, the Gathering is the two-deck casual restaurant for buffet meals and a whole lot more. On embarkation, for example, there's a customized pasta bar with three types of pasta, four sauces, and 12 toppings, including really nice size garlic shrimp. There's also a Mongolian Wok for stir-fry options, a deli-bar for custom-made sandwiches, a station for fresh-cut meats and poultry, and a vast array of salads. Pizza and ice cream are also available.

Aft on Deck 12, the Chef's Art steakhouse seats 122 for an outstanding menu heavy on meats and shellfish, at a cost of $20 per person. Special chef's dinners are also scheduled here. On Deck 5, the new Plaza Café (and accompanying bar) serves snacks in an indoor/outdoor setting called the Lanai. This is a new and welcome addition on what is usually a deck with no outside space.

POOL, FITNESS, SPA & SPORTS FACILITIES   The 23,750-square-foot Cloud 9 Spa, which takes up the forward section of Decks 12, 14, and 15 (there is no Deck 13!), is the largest in the Carnival fleet. The top portion, Serenity, is for adults only, and is appointed with really comfy deck furniture. The gym area on Deck 14 is a nice size, with 15 treadmills and dozens of other aerobics and weight machines. The spa has 10 treatment rooms with the usual range of offerings. There are several different thermal suites, some free and some that guests can use once they book a spa treatment. Guests staying in special spa cabins also get access.

The Deck 10 pool area is large and quite busy, with hundreds of deck chairs, a bandstand, and a grill. Up on Deck 12, Carnival's Seaside Theatre is an outdoor setup that screens movies, has concerts and shipboard activities, and is also home to the U.S. cruise industry's first outdoor laser shows—by which we mean LASER ROCK! The 15-minute shows choreograph patterns of blue, red, and green laser light to music by Pink Floyd, Van Halen, Styx, Rush, Boston, and others in the classic rock pantheon, all pumped through a 70,000-watt sound system and accompanied by the de rigueur smoke machines. The colorful paper-flower pots all around the area are a nice touch. Just forward are the termini of four different water slides, all of which have their jumping-off spots on Deck 15. Two go round and round, and two are set up side by side for racing.

Walkers, strollers, and sea-gazers take note: *Carnival Dream* has Carnival's only complete promenade, wrapping all the way around Deck 5.

The Conquest Class: Carnival Conquest • Glory • Valor • Liberty • Freedom • Splendor

The Verdict

The best of the Carnival bunch to be sure, the Conquest class has the fleet's largest children's and teen's facilities, a giant video screen on the Pool Deck, and plenty of bars and lounges—all packaged in a pastiche of both pleasing and jarring colors and design themes.

Carnival Splendor *(photo: Carnival Cruise Lines)*

Specifications

Typical Per Diems: $55–$100

Size (in tons)		*Splendor*	1,160
Conquest/Glory/Valor/Liberty/Freedom	110,000	Passenger/Crew Ratio	
Splendor	113,300	*Conquest/Glory/Valor/Liberty/Freedom*	2.5 to 1
Passengers (double occ.)		*Splendor*	2.6 to 1
Conquest/Glory/Valor/Liberty/Freedom	2,974	Year Launched	
Splendor	3,006	*Conquest*	2002
Passenger/Space Ratio		*Glory*	2003
Conquest/Glory/Valor/Liberty/Freedom	37	*Valor*	2004
Splendor	37.7	*Liberty*	2005
Total Cabins/Veranda Cabins		*Freedom*	2007
Conquest/Glory/Valor/Liberty/Freedom	1,487/556	*Splendor*	2008
Splendor	1,503/589	Last Major Upgrade	
Crew		*Conquest/Glory/Valor/Liberty/Freedom*	2008/2009
Conquest/Glory/Valor/Liberty/Freedom	1,160	*Splendor*	N/A

Frommer's Ratings (Scale of 1–5)

★★★★ ½

Cabin Comfort & Amenities	4.5	Dining Options	4
Appearance & Upkeep	5	Gym, Spa & Sports Facilities	5
Public Comfort/Space	4.5	Children's Facilities	4.5
Decor	4	Enjoyment Factor	4

Sailing Regions, Seasons & Home Ports

Conquest	**Caribbean,** from Galveston (year-round).
Freedom	**Caribbean,** from Fort Lauderdale (year-round).
Glory	**Caribbean,** from Miami (year-round).
Liberty	**Caribbean,** from Miami (year-round).
Splendor	**Mexican Riviera,** from Long Beach, CA (year-round).
Valor	**Caribbean,** from Miami (year-round).

The five 110,000-ton 2,974-passenger sisters were Carnival's largest vessels until the slightly larger *Carnival Splendor* was launched in mid-2008. *Splendor,* an evolutionary step beyond the previous five, is still very much the same overall but with, of course, certain changes. The $500-million Conquest-class ships closely resemble the Destiny series, though they stretch about 60 feet longer and add Spirit-class features such as steakhouse-style restaurants. If all berths are occupied, each Conquest liner can carry an eyebrow-raising 3,700-plus passengers (that's not counting the more than 1,000 crewmembers). These mondo megas boast more than 20 bars and lounges, a giant video screen on deck, Carnival's largest children's facilities, and an entire, separate zone dedicated to teens and tweens. Each has a state-of-the-art "teleradiology" system that enables the ship's doctors to digitally transmit X-rays and other patient information to medical facilities onshore for consultation on a broad range of medical situations.

CABINS Standard outside cabins measure a roomy 185 to 220 square feet. These categories (6A and 6B) take up most of the Riviera and Main decks. Of the ships' outside cabins, over 60% (556 of 917; 589 of 926 on *Splendor*) have balconies. The standard balcony cabins (categories 8A–8E) measure a still-ample 185 square feet and have a 35-square-foot balcony. For those who simply must have a bigger balcony, a little extra dough buys an "extended balcony" (60 sq. ft.) or "wraparound large balcony." There are only a handful of these category-9A accommodations, and they're tucked all the way aft on the Upper, Empress, and Verandah decks. The 42 suites are a full 275 square feet, plus a 65-square-foot balcony, and bigger still are the 10 Penthouse Suites at 345 square feet, plus an 85-square-foot balcony. Most of the suites are sandwiched in the middle of the ship on the Empress Deck and between two other accommodations decks, eliminating the danger of noisy public rooms above or below.

All categories of cabins come with a TV, safe, hand-held hair dryer (not the wall-mounted, wimpy variety), stocked minifridge (items consumed are charged to your onboard account), desk/dresser, chair and stool, and bathroom with a shower and handy makeup/shaving mirror. But the best part about Carnival's cabins these days is the beds. Called the Carnival Comfort Bed sleep system, they're darn comfortable. Mattresses, duvets, linens, and pillows are superthick and ultracomfy. The towels and bathrobes in each cabin are pretty luxurious, too.

Carnival Splendor is the first Carnival ship to have spa staterooms and suites. The 68 specially enhanced rooms with their Asian decor and private elevator access to the spa have Cloud 9 Spa logo items such as bathrobes, towels, and slippers, plus in-room amenity kits with brand-name samples for both men and women. Pre-cruise concierge consultation is available, as well as personal fitness bands and yoga mats.

There are 28 cabins for passengers with disabilities.

PUBLIC AREAS   The Conquest ships are bright and playful—a sort of Mardi Gras feel instead of the dark and glittery Las Vegas look sported by some of the older ships in the fleet. Architect Joe Farcus was inspired by the great Impressionist and post-Impressionist artists—not only their paintings, but also their color palette—so *Conquest* bursts with sunny yellows and oranges, and vivid blues and greens. Maybe Farcus is running a little low on inspiration these days, as the *Glory's* theme also revolves around "color," with public rooms bearing names such as the White Heat Dance Club, the Amber Palace (show lounge), and On the Green (golf-themed sports bar). On the *Valor*, a liberally applied "heroism" theme connects everything from the Bronx Bar, a Yankee-themed sports bar with white leather bar stools and banquettes designed to look like baseballs, to the One Small Step disco, a tribute to Neil Armstrong's walk on the moon a la weird little volcano-like craters that stand several feet tall and glow with LED lighting.

On the *Liberty*, "artisans and their crafts" is how Farcus describes the motif. In some places it works better than others. The Paparazzi wine bar is a cool place that's all about photography. A huge 3-D collage of celebrity photographs covers the walls, while images of cameras make up the ceiling and bar front. The floral laminate walls overlaid with wrought-iron-like curlicues in *Liberty's* atrium, stair landings, and elevators, on the other hand, may be a bit much. As might be imagined, Farcus has come up with a whole new look for the public rooms on *Carnival Splendor,* including the pink look and the pearls in the main dining rooms and elevator areas; the very stylish El Mojito with its Havana look; El Morocco, a cabaret lounge evoking memories of the famous 1930s New York club; and the Cool Lounge, a jazz bar paying homage to the great Miles Davis.

The general arrangement of public areas on these ships closely resembles that of the Destiny class, with a pair of two-story main dining rooms (one midships, one aft), a three-deck-high showroom within the bow, and a secondary lounge in the stern.

As on the Destiny-class ships, passengers step across the gangway and onto the base of a soaring nine-deck-high atrium, dressed to the nines in each ship's respective theme. On the *Conquest,* for example, it's a mural collage of works by masters such as Claude Monet, Paul Gauguin, and Edgar Degas, with backlit flowers of Murano glass popping up from the granite-topped atrium bar. On the *Liberty,* a giant octopus-like black wrought-iron-style chandelier is the focal point, and its many "arms" support light bulbs that continually change color. On *Splendor,* the walls are covered with a composite material made of stainless steel and 4-inch circular cut-outs backed by pink-stained wood with black pigment rubbed into the grain, along with gold-leaf beams and arches illuminated with hundreds of sparkling lights; it's an amazing look. Each vessel sports 22 bars and lounges, many of these rooms clustered on the Atlantic and Promenade decks.

The 1,400-seat Show Lounge stages Carnival's big production shows. On the *Valor,* it's called Ivanhoe and it comes complete with knights in shining armor a la Sir Walter Scott's classic tale. *Splendor*'s Vrooom pays tribute to rock-'n'-roll greats such as Elvis, Bob Seger, and Huey Lewis and the News, as well as the British invasion and Motown. There's also a secondary entertainment spot for dance bands and late-night comedians, as well as a piano bar, wine bar (the best place for people-watching, as it's open to the main promenade), and another live-music venue where combos belt out oldies, country-and-western songs, and requests.

Nobody does disco better than Carnival. You can groove on an enormous floor (on the *Conquest,* it's a jungle ambience straight from the exotic paintings of Henri Rousseau; on the *Valor,* it's all about the moon; and on *Liberty,* the theme is tattoos), or just perch with a drink on funky bar stools (lotus-shaped on the *Conquest,* and hand-shaped on the *Liberty,* for example). One deck down is the ships' most elegant lounge, done in wood paneling and dark, rich colors. The Internet cafe is tucked away off a back corner of the room; it's a real quiet retreat, if you can find it.

The casinos sprawl across 8,500 square feet, packing in almost 300 slot machines and about two dozen gaming tables. To one side is the sports bar; on the *Liberty,* the theme of boxing is worked into the furniture and decor.

After the *Dream,* these ships boast by far the biggest children's facilities in the fleet: At 4,200 square feet, Children's World, and the separate 1,800-square-foot teen center and Circle "C" facilities for tweens, have more than triple the space for kids and teens available on Destiny-class ships. Children's World sits atop the spa (instead of sharing the same deck, as on the Destiny vessels) and holds an arts-and-crafts station, video wall, computer lab, PlayStation game units, and lots of fun toys for younger children, from play kitchens to push toys, mini-sliding boards, farm sets, and more. The enclosed adjacent deck has a dipping pool that's oddly industrial-looking when compared to the kids' pools on many NCL, Celebrity, Disney, and Royal Caribbean ships.

The ships' nod to teenagers is a big one. Teen facilities on earlier ships were, at most, a room, but here's a space so large that it forms its own secondary promenade, branching off the main one. The teen area has a soda bar and separate dance floor flowing into a huge video games area with air-hockey tables which is open to all passengers. An inflatable laser tag arena is getting raves; for $5 all ages can have a go of it. The children's play area on *Carnival Splendor* is 5,500 square feet and includes a delightfully refreshing water-spray park (parents seem to enjoy this as well). *Splendor*'s water park concept was expanded even more so aboard the *Carnival Dream,* which features a 303-foot-long Twister water slide, the longest at sea, along with racing slides and a splash zone.

DINING OPTIONS   Each ship has a pair of two-story main restaurants, styled in keeping with each ship's theme. On the *Conquest,* a monumental sunflower marking the entrance to the Monet Restaurant is by the Murano glass artist Luciano Vistosi, while the artwork in the Renoir Restaurant is inspired by the cafe scene in the painting *Lunch at the Restaurant Fournaise.* On the *Valor,* the Washington and Lincoln dining rooms won't win any design awards; described by the line as "contemporary colonial," what oddly dominates the decor are bright peach-colored walls . . . hmmm. As coauthor Heidi's husband is fond of saying, "You can't eat ambience." Well, then, bring out the lobster. You'll see broiled lobster tail on the menu once during a cruise, and there are six desserts nightly. Low-fat, low-calorie, low-salt Spa Carnival Fare, vegetarian dishes, and children's selections are available.

The Conquest-class ships borrow the by-reservation steakhouse from the Spirit-class ships. The venue serves USDA prime aged steaks, seafood, and other deluxe items for a $30-per-person cover charge. On the Spirit ships, the restaurant is under a glass portion of the ship's funnel for a more dramatic setting, but the Conquest-class ships' restaurant has low ceilings and a more intimate feel. The best food and most refined service on board are here, where dinner is meant to stretch over several hours and several bottles of wine (for which there's an extra charge). Breakfast, lunch, and dinner are served in the two-story restaurant on the Lido Deck, where you'll also find a 24-hour pizza counter (the mushroom-and-goat-cheese pies are scrumptious). Separate buffet lines (more than on the Destiny ships, to alleviate crowding) are devoted to Asian and American dishes, deli sandwiches, salads, and desserts. A new concept (on the upper level) on select Conquest-class ships is Sur Mer: Carnival modestly describes this as a fish and chips shop, but the choices include such goodies as calamari, lobster salad, and bouillabaisse (other ships feature a rotisserie with broiled meats and traditional side dishes). There's no charge here or for the stand-up sushi bar down on the main promenade, but the pastries, cakes, and specialty coffees at the patisserie cost a couple of bucks each.

There's also 24-hour room service with new menus that include items such as a chicken fajita with greens and guacamole in a jalapeño-and-tomato wrap, plus the standard tuna salad, cookies, fruit, and so on.

POOL, FITNESS, SPA & SPORTS FACILITIES   The ships' four swimming pools include the main pool, with its two huge hot tubs, a stage for live (and really loud) reggae and calypso music, and a giant movie screen for blaring videos and ship events. This space is where all the action (and noise) of pool games occurs, plus the occasional outbreak of line dancing. (Anyone for the Electric Slide?) Carnival's trademark twisty slide shoots into a pool one deck up. The aft pool, covered by a retractable glass dome, usually provides a more restful setting, although the pizzeria and burger grill are here (along with two more oversize hot tubs). The fourth pool is a really basic one for kiddies outside the playroom. A new feature on *Carnival Splendor* is the retractable dome over the midships pool, which is open or shut depending on the weather.

The ships' 14,500-square-foot health club and salon, with neat his-and-hers ocean-view steam and sauna rooms, perches high on Deck 11. Though the decor is a real yawner—it's as though Farcus simply forgot about the waiting area and locker room—you'll find today's latest treatments available, from hot stone massages to hair and scalp massages. The spa is run by Steiner, the company that controls most cruise ship spas, so expect a superhard sell for products right after your treatment. One more pet peeve: You won't find a hair dryer, Q-tips, cotton balls, or any other amenities in the locker room—it's unabashedly no frills. On the fitness side, you'll find the nontrendy aerobics classes offered for free (such as stretching and step), and the cool stuff everyone wants to do, such as Pilates and spinning, going for $10 a class. There's a hot tub that sits in a glass-enclosed space jutting into the fitness room.

The Cloud 9 Spa on *Carnival Splendor* is huge by comparison, measuring 21,000 square feet. With 17 private rooms, there are all sorts of "European-style" treatments offered, plus an elaborate thermal suite and thalassotherapy pool. Right next to the spa aboard *Glory* and *Splendor* is Serenity, an adults-only getaway with two very large whirlpools, oversize umbrellas, and lots of comfy chaise longues and sofas. *Carnival Dream* takes the spa concept a step further with a 23,750-square-foot Cloud 9 Spa, the largest in the fleet.

The jogging track loops above an open deck so that no cabins underneath get pounded.

The Spirit Class: Carnival Spirit • Pride •Legend • Miracle

Carnival Spirit *(photo: Gero Mylius, Indav Ltd.)*

The Verdict

Bright and fun with multistory dining and entertainment rooms and a reservations-only restaurant, the Spirit-class ships offer everything you'll need, but packaged in a more sane size than the larger Destiny- and Conquest-class ships.

Specifications

Typical Per Diems: $60–$85

Size (in tons)	88,500	Year Launched	
Passengers (double occ.)	2,124	*Spirit*	2001
Passenger/Space Ratio	41.7	*Pride*	2001
Total Cabins/Veranda Cabins	1,062/682	*Legend*	2002
Crew	930	*Miracle*	2004
Passenger/Crew Ratio	2.3 to 1	Last Major Upgrade	2008

Frommer's Ratings (Scale of 1–5)

★★★★

Cabin Comfort & Amenities	5	Dining Options	4
Appearance & Upkeep	4	Gym, Spa & Sports Facilities	4
Public Comfort/Space	4	Children's Facilities	4
Decor	4	Enjoyment Factor	4

Sailing Regions, Seasons & Home Ports

Legend	**Caribbean,** from Tampa (year-round).
Miracle	**Caribbean,** from Fort Lauderdale (year-round).
Pride	**The Bahamas & Florida,** from Baltimore (year-round).
Spirit	**Mexican Riviera & Baja,** from San Diego (fall/winter). **Hawaii,** from Ensenada, Mexico, and Honolulu (repositioning, spring & fall). **Alaska,** from Seattle (summer).

When the $375-million Carnival *Spirit* debuted in April 2001, it ushered in a new class for the Fun Ship line. Bigger than Carnival's eight Fantasy-class ships and smaller than its three Destiny-class vessels, the 2,124-passenger, 88,500-ton, 960-foot *Spirit, Pride, Legend,* and *Miracle* update Carnival's rubber-stamp style with a handful of innovations and more elegance, placing them closer to the newest Royal Caribbean and Princess vessels than to Carnival's earlier Fun Ships. The Spirit-class ships eliminate the cluster of nightclubs in favor of stretching the music venues from bow to stern on Decks 2 and 3, and there's an appealing supper club, which the subsequent Conquest class has also adopted. A state-of-the-art "teleradiology" system enables the ship's doctors to digitally transmit X-rays and other patient information to medical facilities onshore for consultation on a broad range of medical situations.

Interestingly, the Spirit-class ships bear more than a little resemblance to Costa's *Costa Atlantica* and sister *Mediterranea:* Their hull and superstructure were built from identical plans, and Carnival design guru Joe Farcus did the decor for them all.

CABINS The Spirit-class ships have verandas on more than 60% of their cabins, though most are pretty small, with a wood-tone plastic chair, a small table, and a deck chair. (Cabins with larger balconies are amidships and aft on Decks 6, 7, and 8.) Their 213 inside cabins and outside cabins without balconies are a roomy 185 square feet (standard outsides with balconies are the same size plus a 40-sq.-ft. balcony). Of the 44 category-11 suites, most measure 275 square feet, plus an 85-square-foot balcony, while 10 located at the stern of Decks 4 through 8 measure 245 square feet, plus a jumbo wraparound 220-square-foot balcony. The six category-12 suites measure 300 square feet, plus a 115-square-foot balcony. On Deck 4, all category-5A cabins have lifeboats obstructing the view, though they do have sliding-glass doors that allow you to lean out into the fresh air.

In a subtle departure from the minimalist, somewhat cold cabin decor of the rest of Carnival's older ships, the *Spirit*'s cabins are warmer and more sophisticated, with toasted-caramel wood-tone furniture and mango- and coral-hued upholstery, drapes, and bedspreads. The pointy lighting fixtures are more stylish but don't throw a lot of light on the desk mirror. Also, there are none of those great little reading lights over the beds like the rest of the fleet provides, just lamps on the night tables.

All cabins, even the least expensive inside ones, have a decent amount of storage space in both closets and drawers (with small leather handles that some people find difficult to grab hold of), plus a safe, TV, desk and stool, chair, well-designed bathroom with a shower stall that is a tad larger than on other ships, and glass shelves on either side of the large mirror to stash your toiletries. Just about all cabins have a small sitting area with a sofa and coffee table (some inside cabins have only a chair and table), and all have a real hair dryer (stored in the desk/vanity drawer). Like the rest of the fleet, all beds are outfitted with extrathick and comfy mattresses, duvets, linens, and pillows, and you'll enjoy the thick and fluffy towels and bathrobes, too.

There are 16 cabins for passengers with disabilities.

PUBLIC AREAS   Carnival designer Joe Farcus works his whimsy once again aboard the Spirit-class ships, blending marble, wood-veneer walls, tile mosaic work, buttery leathers, rich fabrics, copper and bronze, Art Nouveau and Art Deco themes, and all manner of glass lighting fixtures. Though a relatively subdued bronze color scheme defines many public areas, these ships still are glitzy and blinding in the same fun Vegas way as the rest of the Carnival fleet.

A string trio or pianist performs throughout the day at the lower-level lobby bar that anchors each ship's spectacular, jaw-dropping, nine-deck atrium, even more of a central hub than aboard earlier Carnival ships owing to its placement amidships. Just about all the indoor action is on Decks 2 and 3, where you'll find the piano bar (on *Spirit*, it's a neat Oriental-style spot with carved rosewood detailing, paper-lantern lighting fixtures, a red lacquer piano, and rich Chinese silk walls; on *Legend*, it's an understated tribute to Billie Holiday in stainless steel), a large sports bar, disco, jazz nightclub (where karaoke and other contests are held), cafe (where you can purchase specialty coffees and pastries), combination library and Internet center (with a ridiculously spare book collection), an elegant string of shops, a modern-style wedding chapel, and a sprawling photo gallery. The low-ceilinged lounge tucked into the bow on Deck 1, at the end of a corridor of cabins, is so well hidden that it's often empty.

The three-level showrooms are something to see; on *Spirit*, Farcus had Verdi's Egypt-themed opera *Aida* in mind when he covered it head to toe in brightly painted gold-and-blue King Tut–style sarcophagi and hieroglyphics (on the *Legend*, it's a flashy Mediterranean-style movie palace). Sightlines are severely limited from parts of the Deck 2 and Deck 3 level, so arrive early if you want a decent view. The disco is a two-story barrel-shaped place with a giant video wall; on *Spirit*, the funky spot has a Jackson Pollock–inspired splatter-painted design. On the *Miracle*, the disco was made to look like a Gothic castle in ruins with faux stone walls.

The ships' broad outdoor promenade is wonderfully nostalgic (almost), but unfortunately does not wrap around the entire ship; near the bow you are channeled through a door and the promenade suddenly (and oddly) becomes enclosed and narrower, turning into a cute but kind of odd jungle-themed area lined with comfy chairs and small tables with views through jumbo-size portholes. The kids' playroom and a video arcade are tucked away in the far forward reaches of the bow on Decks 4 and 5. Playrooms are divided into three sections connected via tunnels and kids can enjoy sand art, a candy-making machine, a computer lab with a handful of iMacs and PlayStations, and other diversions. The playrooms are of decent size, but nowhere near the size and scope of what you'll find on the Splendor- and Conquest-class fleetmates or on Royal Caribbean's Oasis-, Freedom-, Voyager-, and Radiance-class ships and Disney's *Magic* and *Wonder*. The video arcade is huge, with 30-plus machines, including air hockey and foosball.

DINING OPTIONS   Unlike most of the fleet, the Spirit ships have one sprawling, two-story, 1,300-seat formal dining room (with traditional early and late seating, along with an open-seating option so guests can dine anytime between 5:45 and 9:30pm). It's a pleasant places to dine, especially if you can snag an intimate booth or a table along the glass railing on the second level, with views of the scene below. The Spirit ships were the first in the Carnival fleet to also have an alternative reservations-only restaurant for more intimate and elegant dining from a menu of mostly steaks and seafood, for a cover charge of $30 per person. The newer Conquest-class ships also have these restaurants. The main drawback on the Spirit class: Rowdy crowd noise sometimes filters up from the atrium bar below. In the huge, well-laid-out indoor/outdoor casual buffet restaurant, menu items range from standard American to French, Italian, and Asian dishes; sushi is served in the buffet restaurant at lunch. The food is fine, but don't expect anything resembling gourmet.

As aboard the rest of the fleet, 24-hour pizza and Caesar salad are available from a counter in the buffet restaurant. You can get a tasty deli sandwich from the New York Deli all day long, and self-serve frozen yogurt and soft ice cream are also on hand.

POOL, FITNESS, SPA & SPORTS FACILITIES The Spirit-class spas are the only ones in the fleet to have any real decor; the rest have had a bland, institutional look, as though Farcus forgot to design them. The *Spirit*, for instance, sports a Greek-inspired motif of white fluted columns and images of Greek gods on the walls. The multilevel gyms are based loosely on a Greek amphitheater, and though they're more than adequate, with dozens of machines, they're a bit more cramped than the huge spaces on the Conquest- and Destiny-class ships.

In general, there are lots of places for sunbathing across the three topmost decks, including the area around the two main pools amidships on the Lido Deck, as well as around a third pool on the aft end of this deck. All told, there are four hot tubs (including one in the gym), plus a jogging track, combination volleyball/basketball court, and shuffleboard. A fun, snaking water slide for kids and adults is sequestered high up and aft on a top deck, and adjacent is a small, sort of forlorn, fenced-in kids' wading pool. With no shade up on this part of the ship, don't forget to put sunscreen on your kids' delicate skin—and your own, for that matter.

The Destiny Class: Carnival Destiny • Triumph • Victory

The Verdict

These three behemoths capture the classic Carnival whimsy, though with a somewhat mellower color scheme than the line's older ships—but let's not split hairs, they're still bright.

Carnival Destiny *(photo: Carnival Cruise Lines)*

Specifications

Typical Per Diems: $55–$95

Size (in tons)		*Destiny*	1,321/480
Destiny	101,353	*Triumph/Victory*	1,379/508
Triumph/Victory	102,000	Crew	1,000
Passengers (double occ.)		Passenger/Crew Ratio	2.6 to 1
Destiny	2,642	Year Launched	
Triumph/Victory	2,758	*Destiny*	1996
Passenger/Space Ratio		*Triumph*	1999
Destiny	38.4	*Victory*	2000
Triumph/Victory	37	Last Major Upgrade	
Total Cabins/Veranda Cabins		*Destiny/Triumph/Victory*	2008

Frommer's Ratings (Scale of 1–5)   ★★★★ ½

Cabin Comfort & Amenities	5	Dining Options	3.5
Appearance & Upkeep	4	Gym, Spa & Sports Facilities	5
Public Comfort/Space	4.5	Children's Facilities	4
Decor	4	Enjoyment Factor	4.5

Sailing Regions, Seasons & Home Ports

Destiny	**Caribbean,** from Miami (year-round).
Triumph	**Caribbean,** from New Orleans (year-round).
Victory	**Caribbean,** from San Juan (year-round).

Taller than the Statue of Liberty, these 13-deck ships cost $400 million to $440 million apiece and carry 2,642 passengers based on double occupancy and 3,400-plus with every additional berth filled (and some cruises do indeed carry a full load). All three are nearly identical, though *Triumph* and *Victory* are a tad larger than *Destiny* (having an additional deck at top) and are reconfigured in a few minor ways. *Destiny* was the first cruise ship ever built to exceed 100,000 tons, and her sheer size and spaciousness inspired the cruise industry to build more in this league. In late 2005, the *Destiny* received a healthy multimillion-dollar face-lift that took 3 weeks and included the addition of a new teen club, renovated Lido buffet restaurant, vamped-up children's pool, redesigned casino, and spruced-up suites. All three ships now sport a giant video screen up on the pool deck.

CABINS   The Destiny-class sisters, along with the new Conquest-class ships, have the line's biggest standard outside cabins, with the category-6A and -6B cabins (which take up most of the Riviera and Main decks) measuring 220 square feet (and that's not including the balcony); the rest of the fleet's standard outside cabins measure 185 square feet—still very roomy. If that's not enough, more than 60% of the *Destiny* sisters' outside cabins (480–508 of them) have sitting areas and private balconies. That's compared to a paltry 54 private verandas out of 618 outside cabins on Carnival's Fantasy-class ships. In 2008, outside cabins on the *Destiny* and *Triumph* were retrofitted with private balconies, creating a total of 48 additional 230-square-foot veranda staterooms on both these ships.

There are two categories of suites: Veranda Suites measuring 275 square feet, plus a 65-square-foot balcony; and Penthouse Suites, where you can live like a king with 345 square feet, plus an 85-square-foot balcony. Both are located on Deck 7, smack-dab in the middle of the ship; both kinds of suites were upgraded in late 2005 with updated bathrooms, carpeting, and wall coverings. All cabins have new bed sarongs (replacing quilts), curtains, and fabrics. Specially designed family staterooms, at a comfortable but not roomy 230 square feet, are located convenient to children's facilities, and many of them can be connected to the stateroom next door. All standard cabins have a TV, safe, hair dryer, desk, dresser, chair and stool, bathroom with shower, and Carnival's great bedding system, featuring extrathick mattresses, duvets, linens, and pillows, along with fluffy towels and bathrobes. Only the suites have minifridges.

A total of 25 cabins on *Destiny,* 27 on *Triumph,* and 30 on *Victory* are wheelchair accessible.

PUBLIC AREAS   At the time these ships were designed, Carnival interior designer Joe Farcus never had so much public space to play with, and he took full advantage. The ships are dominated by staggering nine-deck atria with casual bars on the ground level, and the three-deck-high showrooms are a sight—*Destiny*'s was the first of this magnitude on any cruise ship, and subsequent models tread a fine line between outrageous and relatively tasteful: for example, *Triumph*'s wacko chandelier, which looks like DNA strands made from crystal golf balls, topped with little Alice-in-Wonderland candleholders. The ships' mondo casinos span some 9,000 square feet and feature more than 300 slot machines and about two dozen gaming tables.

Many of the ships' 18-plus bars and entertainment venues are located along the bustling main drag of the Promenade Deck. The Sports Bar on each ship boasts multiple TV monitors projecting different sporting events. Each ship has a wine bar, a cappuccino cafe, and a piano bar, which aboard *Triumph* is a bizarre New Orleans–themed place called the Big Easy, sporting thousands of real oyster shells covering its walls (collected from New Orleans' famous Acme Oyster House—only on Carnival!). Each also has a sprawling disco with a wild decor: On *Victory*, an Arctic motif features black faux-fur bar stools, while *Triumph*'s decor is a little more reserved, with goofy little Barney-purple chairs, and glass panels and tubes filled with bubbling water throughout. One deck below is an elegant lounge for a drink or a cigar: On *Triumph*, it's a clubby place called the Oxford Bar, with dark-wood paneling, leather furniture, and gilded picture frames (too bad you can hear the disco music pounding above late at night). The ships' Internet centers are adjacent to this lounge.

Each ship has several shopping boutiques, a spacious beauty salon, a library, a card room, and a fairly large children's playroom and video arcade. The *Destiny* has a teen club and it comes decked out with a dance floor, a high-tech sound/light system, three large-screen plasma TVs, music listening stations, video game pods, and a soft-drink bar.

DINING OPTIONS   Each ship has a pair of two-level dining rooms with ocean views from both the main floor and the mezzanine level, as well as a two-story indoor/outdoor casual buffet restaurant that includes two specialty food stations that make Asian stir-fry and deli-style sandwiches to order; sushi is also served in the buffet restaurant at lunch. There's also a grill section for burgers, fries, and kielbasa-size hot dogs, a salad bar, and a dessert island. Specialty coffee bars and patiseries sell gourmet goodies for a few bucks a pop.

POOL, FITNESS, SPA & SPORTS FACILITIES   Along with the Conquest-class ships, the Destiny-class facilities are the most generous among the Carnival vessels, with four pools (including a kids' wading pool); seven hot tubs; and a 214-foot, two-deck-high, corkscrew-shaped water slide.

The tiered, arena-style decks of the sprawling midships Lido Deck pool area provide optimal viewing of the band and stage, pool games, and all the hubbub that happens in this frenetically busy part of the ship. All three ships now also have a giant video screen up on deck. All thee ships have twisty slides and the aft pool area features two hot tubs and a retractable roof that covers all, enabling deck activities and entertainment to continue even in rainy weather. On *Triumph* and *Victory*, the big stage adjacent to the Main Continent pool is even bigger than the one on *Destiny*, and it has been reconfigured to provide more space for guests at deck parties, and to make the Pool Deck more open and visually appealing. Another modification is the placement of a small performance stage aft on the Lido Deck near the New World pool.

Even though the ships' huge gyms aren't as large as those on Royal Caribbean's Voyager class, Carnival's are much roomier and actually feel bigger. The two-deck-high spa and fitness centers have more than 30 state-of-the-art exercise machines, including virtual-reality stationary bikes. There are men's and women's saunas and steam rooms, and a pair of hot tubs. Spas have all the latest treatments (at the latest high prices), but as on all Carnival ships (except for the newer Spirit class), they're surprisingly drab, and the only place to wait for your masseuse is on a cold, high-school-locker-room bench, wrapped in a towel—no robes are provided (unless, supposedly, you ask for one). So much for ambience. There are separate aerobics rooms (though they're smaller than they used to be, as half the space was snapped up to create a teen room a few years back).

The well-stocked 1,300-square-foot indoor/outdoor children's play center has its own pool and is nicely sequestered on a top deck, out of the fray of the main Pool Deck areas. The ships also have video arcades that promise hours of fun.

The Fantasy Class: Carnival Fantasy • Ecstasy • Sensation • Fascination • Imagination • Inspiration • Elation • Paradise

Carnival Fantasy *(photo: Carnival Cruise Lines)*

The Verdict

These time-tested favorites are the line's original megas, and their whimsical decor and endless entertainment and activities spell excitement from the get-go—though they do feel outdated compared to Carnival's newer classes.

Specifications

Typical Per Diems: $50–$110

Size (in tons)	70,367	*Inspiration*	1996
Passengers (double occ.)	2,040	*Elation*	1998
Passenger/Space Ratio	34.5	*Paradise*	1998
Total Cabins/Veranda Cabins	1,020/54	Last Major Upgrade	
Crew	920	*Fantasy*	2008
Passenger/Crew Ratio	2.2 to 1	*Sensation*	2008
Year Launched		*Ecstasy*	2007
Fantasy	1990	*Inspiration*	2008
Ecstasy	1991	*Imagination*	2008
Sensation	1993	*Fascination*	2007
Fascination	1994	*Elation*	2006
Imagination	1995	*Paradise*	2008/09

Frommer's Ratings (Scale of 1–5)

Cabin Comfort & Amenities	4	Dining Options	3
Appearance & Upkeep	4	Gym, Spa & Sports Facilities	3.5
Public Comfort/Space	4	Children's Facilities	4
Decor	3.5	Enjoyment Factor	4

Sailing Regions, Seasons & Home Ports

Ecstasy	**Caribbean,** from Galveston (year-round).
Elation	**Caribbean,** from Mobile, AL (year-round).
Fantasy	**The Bahamas & Key West,** from Charleston (year-round).
Fascination	**The Bahamas & Key West,** from Jacksonville, FL (year-round).
Imagination	**Caribbean,** from Miami (year-round).
Inspiration	**Caribbean,** from Tampa (year-round).
Paradise	**Ensenada, Mexico & Catalina Island,** from Long Beach, CA (year-round).
Sensation	**The Bahamas,** from Port Canaveral (year-round).

These Fun Ships and their risqué names offer a successful combination of hands-on fun and a glamorous, fantasyland decor, with acres of teak decking plus all the diversions and entertainment choices for which Carnival is famous. They really are fun! (Or are they cheesy? It's such a fine line.) Each was built on the same cookie-cutter design at Finland's Kvaerner Masa shipyard (at a cost of $225 million–$300 million each . . . a bargain compared to the $600-million-plus price tag of a new ship today), and they are nearly identical in size, profile, and onboard amenities, with different decorative themes. These ships have been run hard and they look a bit worn out compared to their newer fleetmates, but you won't notice a thing after a couple of Carnival Fun Ship drink specials!

From the first ship of the series *(Fantasy)* to the last *(Paradise),* the ships' decor evolved toward a relatively mellow state (note: *relatively). Fantasy* features a Roman-themed entertainment promenade inspired (loosely, of course) by the ancient city of Pompeii, with a faux-stone floor, terra-cotta urns, Doric columns, and electric torches—but where's the flowing lava? In late 2003, the ship underwent her first major refurbishment, which included a brand-new atrium bar (like the ones on the *Elation* and all newer ships), completely overhauled cabins, a redesigned promenade, and new carpeting and wall coverings throughout much of the other areas.

Ecstasy follows a city-at-sea theme, with no shortage of neon-metallic skyscraper imagery. *Fascination* is big on flashy fantasy, with a retina-shattering chrome atrium and a heavy Broadway and Hollywood theme, while *Sensation* avoids obvious razzle-dazzle in favor of artwork enhanced with ultraviolet lighting, sound, and color. Aboard *Imagination,* miles of fiber-optic cable make the mythical and classical artwork glow in ways the Greek, Roman, and Assyrian designers of the originals never would have imagined. *Inspiration* was reportedly inspired by artists such as Toulouse-Lautrec and Fabergé, and architects such as Frank Lloyd Wright—though in a . . . brighter style. You'll find a Greek mythology theme on the *Elation* that's all about Carnival-style "classic" columns, flutes, and harps, while the *Paradise* pays tribute to classic ocean liners. The newest of the Fantasy-class ships—the *Paradise* and the *Elation*—sport a few improvements over their sisters, including an expanded kids' playroom and the hublike atrium bar. Atrium bars are now standard features on Fantasy-class ships.

By the way, the *Paradise,* touted as the line's only completely nonsmoking ship when she debuted in 1998, changed its policies in late 2004; you can now light up in designated areas, just like on the rest of the fleet.

The Fantasy-class ships are in the midst of a multimillion-dollar face-lift that has added, or will soon add, an expanded children's water park, the creation of the Serenity adults-only deck area, flatscreen televisions in staterooms, 98 more cabin balconies, a new Circle C facility for the 12- to 14-year-olds, a new atrium lobby bar and a new coffee bar, and a 9-hole miniature golf course. By early 2010, *Sensation, Imagination, Inspiration, Fantasy, Ecstasy,* and *Fascination* had received the upgrades, while *Elation* and *Paradise* both have many of the new features except for the water park and redesigned main pool.

CABINS   Accommodations range from lower-deck inside cabins with upper and lower berths to large suites with verandas, king-size beds, sitting areas, and balconies. Standard cabins are roomy (at least 185 sq. ft.) and minimalist in design, with stained-oak trim accents and conventional, monochromatic colors such as salmon red—subdued compared to the flamboyance of the public areas. The cabins are not big on personality, but are functional and well laid out. There are 26 demisuites and 28 suites, all with private verandas. Each of the 28 330-square-foot suites has a whirlpool tub and shower, an L-shaped sofa that converts into a foldaway bed, a safe, a minibar, a walk-in closet, and sliding-glass doors leading to a 70-square-foot private balcony; they are positioned midway between stern and bow, on a middle deck subject to the least tossing and rocking during rough weather.

All cabins, even the least expensive inside ones, have enough storage space to accommodate a reasonably diverse wardrobe, and feature a safe, TV, desk and stool, chair, reading lights for each bed, and a bathroom with a roomy shower and generous-size mirrored cabinet to store your toiletries (only suites have hair dryers and minifridges). Over the past few years, all cabins were spruced up and given new extrathick mattresses, duvets, linens, and pillows, along with fluffy towels and bathrobes.

About 20 cabins on each ship are suitable for passengers with disabilities.

DINING OPTIONS   In addition to a pair of big one-story dining rooms with windows, there's a large indoor/outdoor casual buffet restaurant (which was recently spruced up on the *Ecstasy*). You'll also find specialty coffee bars and patisseries selling gourmet goodies for a couple of bucks a pop. There's a complimentary sushi bar serving fresh, tasty sushi in late afternoons on all ships, with sake available for an extra charge.

PUBLIC AREAS   Each ship boasts the same configuration of decks, public lounges, and entertainment venues, including a six-story atrium flanked by glass-sided elevators, casinos, Internet centers, and at least eight bars, plus several (usually packed) hot tubs. The cluster of disappointing shops on each ship is surprisingly cramped and won't be winning any design awards; it's much better on the newer ships.

All Fantasy ships have new 9-hole miniature golf courses and new children's play areas for all ages through teens.

POOL, FITNESS, SPA & SPORTS FACILITIES   Although totally blah in the decor department, the 12,000-square-foot spas and fitness areas are well-enough equipped. Each has a roomy, mirrored aerobics room and a large, windowed gym with more than a dozen workout machines plus free weights. Each has men's and women's locker rooms and massage rooms (both areas surprisingly drab and institutional feeling), as well as a sauna and steam room, whirlpools, and two or three swimming pools, one of which has either a three-deck-high spiraling water slide or an even more elaborate Waterworks slide and splash zone. The Sun Deck of each ship has an unobstructed ⅛-mile jogging track covered with a rubberized surface. Both the spas and the gyms aboard the *Imagination, Inspiration,* and *Sensation* were updated in the last 5 or 6 years.

3 Celebrity Cruises

1050 Caribbean Way, Miami, FL 33132. ℂ **800/437-3111** or 305/539-6000. Fax 800/722-5329. www.celebrity cruises.com.

THE LINE IN A NUTSHELL Celebrity is the most stylish of the mainstream lines, operating big megaships spiced up with above-average service and a cutting-edge sense of design and style. **Sails to:** Alaska, Caribbean, The Bahamas, Bermuda, Canada/New England, the Pacific Northwest, Panama Canal (plus Europe, South America, Galapagos, transatlantic).

THE EXPERIENCE Celebrity juices up the mainstream cruise experience with a touch of refinement and a dash of class, all the while keeping things fun, active, and within the price range of Joe and Sally Cruiser. Each ship is glamorous, exciting, and comfortable, offering sleek modern styles accented with cutting-edge art collections. The new Solstice-class ships are, bar none, the most elegant megaships in the cruise world.

An exceedingly polite and professional staff contributes greatly to the overall mood. Dining-wise, the dashing alternative restaurants on the line's Millennium-class ships outclass all other mainstream ship restaurants for presentation and gorgeous decor, and match the best for cuisine.

Like all the big-ship lines, Celebrity provides lots for its passengers to do, from enrichment lectures to shows, sports, talent shows, and pool games. The line's spas are among the most attractive at sea, decor shipwide is the most original, and the art collections are the most compelling you'll find on any cruise ships, anywhere.

Pros

- **Elegance, style, and comfort:** The line's Solstice-class ships win every award for gorgeousness in the mainstream category, and throw in lots of restaurants and beautifully designed cabins to boot. The ships have been so successful that Celebrity has been retrofitting its older ships to make them more Solstice-like.
- **Best mainstream alternative restaurants at sea:** The Millennium-class ships have remarkable service, food, and wine in their classy alternative venues, whose elegant decor incorporates artifacts from cherished old ocean liners like the *Olympic, Normandie,* and SS *United States.*
- **Spectacular spas:** Beautiful and well equipped, the line's spas are some of the best at sea.
- **Contemporary art:** Celebrity's ships are the only ones in the cruise biz that can really be said to have world-class, museum-quality art collections, concentrating on modern and contemporary works. (See "The Best Art at Sea," below.)

Cons

- **Nickel-and-diming:** Though almost all cruise lines now supplement their income by offering extracharge alternative restaurants, fancy coffee drinks, specialty ice creams, and the like, Celebrity's high-toned image means the line's passengers get more ticked off by this kind of nickel-and-diming. For instance, passengers we polled on one recent Caribbean cruise were uniformly outraged by the $30 bingo charge.

CELEBRITY: MEGACHIC

Celebrity's roots go back to the powerful Greek shipping family Chandris, whose patriarch founded a cargo shipping company in 1915. The family expanded into the cruise business in the late 1960s and by 1976 had the largest cruise fleet in the world. In the late 1970s, they introduced the down-market Chandris-Fantasy Cruises, which served a mostly European clientele. In 1989, the Chandris family dissolved Fantasy and created Celebrity Cruises, building beautiful, innovative ships that were immediately recognizable by their crisp navy-blue-and-white hulls and their rakishly angled funnels decorated with a giant *X*—which was really the Greek letter *chi,* for Chandris. The company's rise to prominence was so rapid and so successful that in 1997 it was courted and acquired by the larger and wealthier Royal Caribbean Cruises, Ltd., which now operates Celebrity as a sister line to Royal Caribbean International and newer brand **Azamara Club Cruises,** which Celebrity launched before turning it loose as a stand-alone company.

In 2008, Celebrity introduced the first of its new generation of 118,000-ton, 2,850-passenger megaships: *Solstice*—the loveliest new ship to debut in years. Sister ships *Equinox* and *Eclipse* followed in summer 2009 and winter 2010, and two more sisters are scheduled to follow in fall 2011 and 2012.

PASSENGER PROFILE

Celebrity tries to focus on middle- to upper-middle-income cruisers and even wealthy patrons who want a great megaship experience (especially while nestled in one of the line's amazing upper-end suites), but its generally low prices—more or less comparable to those of sister-line Royal Caribbean—ensure the demographic stays democratically wider. For clients who choose their cruise based on more than just price, Celebrity is appealing because it offers a well-balanced cruise, with lots of activities and a glamorous, exciting atmosphere that's both refined and fun.

Most passengers are couples ages 35 and up. Many have cruised before and want something a little more hip and stylish than the cruise norm. That said, you'll still see passengers of all ages, with a decent number of honeymooners and couples celebrating anniversaries, as well as families with children in summer and during the holidays.

Compared with the other mainstream lines, here's how Celebrity rates:

	Poor	Fair	Good	Excellent	Outstanding
Enjoyment Factor					✓
Dining			✓		
Activities			✓		
Children's Program			✓		
Entertainment			✓		
Service				✓	
Worth the Money					✓

DINING

TRADITIONAL Though Celebrity started out with a reputation for truly exceptional cuisine, today the dishes served in its main dining rooms are really more on par with mainstream peers Princess, Royal Caribbean, NCL, and Holland America. **Dining service,** however, remains excellent. Dinner menus are likely to feature entrees such as veal shank cooked in an aromatic tomato velouté with orange zest, served with risotto; broiled sliced tenderloin with béarnaise and Madeira sauces; and boneless chicken breast with bananas and ham, coated with coconut flakes and served with curry peanut sauce. At every meal, Celebrity also serves lighter "spa" fare with calorie, fat, cholesterol, and sodium breakdowns listed on the back of the menu. **Vegetarian options** are available at every meal. There's also a good wine list that includes a line of proprietary wines called Celebrity Cruises Cellarmaster Selection.

In 2009, Celebrity joined the **flexible dining** club by launching Celebrity Select Dining, a program that allows guests to choose when they'd like to dine in the line's main dining rooms. It works like this: When you book your cruise, you'll decide whether you want to stick with traditional fixed-time dining or go with the Select option. If the latter, you can choose to dine either with just your travel companion(s) or with other guests on your cruise (for instance, family or friends who've booked the same sailing). You can also go online anytime up to 4 days before your cruise and make reservations for specific dining hours on a day-by-day basis—6pm one day, 7pm the next, 8pm the night after that, or any combination that suits your schedule. Reservations can also be made during your cruise with the main dining room's maitre d'. Note that if you do choose Celebrity Select, you're required to prepay gratuities before your cruise.

SPECIALTY Though its Millennium-class ships have long been known for their single specialty restaurants (see below), the new Solstice class is where Celebrity really went whole-hog into alternative dining. Each of the Solstice ships has four specialty restaurants in addition to the main restaurant and buffet. The **Tuscan Grille** serves specialty steaks and pastas in a high-style atmosphere—sort of Napa Valley meets Tuscany. The European-themed **Murano** serves elaborate, multicourse meals in the style of the Millennium-class specialty restaurants, featuring table-side cooking, carving, and flambé. **Blu,** a restaurant for the exclusive use of passengers booked in the ships' AquaClass staterooms (plus suite guests based on availability), serves cuisine that emphasizes healthful ingredients and preparation without sacrificing taste. On *Solstice* and *Equinox,* the Asian **Silk Harvest** restaurant serves a mix of Thai, Vietnamese, Japanese, and Chinese dishes. On *Eclipse,* Silk Harvest is replaced by **Qsine,** a playful, imaginatively designed space serving food from an eclectic international menu.

On the Millennium-class ships, cuisine, service, and ambience are the draw at Celebrity's original alternative restaurants, each of which carries a $30-per-person cover charge and seats just over 100 passengers. Presentation is paramount: Decor is centered around artifacts from the historic passenger vessels that give the restaurants their names; there often seems to be more waitstaff than diners; Caesar salads and zabaglione are prepared table-side; maitre d's carve passengers' meat dishes with the finesse of a concert pianist; and a selection of excellent French cheeses arrives at the end of the meal. In addition to these restaurants, each of the Millennium-class ships also has a **Tuscan Grille** in the style of the Solstice class. The older *Century,* meanwhile, has her own version of the Murano restaurant.

Reservations for Celebrity's specialty restaurants can be made online up to 4 days before your cruise.

CASUAL Breakfast and lunch in the buffet restaurants are on par with those of lines such as Royal Caribbean and Princess, and include such features as a **made-to-order pasta bar** and a **pizza station** serving very tasty pies. On most nights, the buffet space is transformed into the **Casual Dining Boulevard,** with waiters serving entrees such as pasta, gourmet pizzas, and chicken between about 6 and 9:30pm. Reservations are recommended, though if there's space, walk-ins are accepted, too. During dinnertime, Celebrity also has a **sushi bar** in one section of the buffet restaurant, serving both appetizer-size portions and full meals.

The Solstice-class ships also feature **Bistro on Five,** a chic-casual restaurant with a menu of specialty crepes, sandwiches, soups, salads, and comfort-food entrees like baked ziti, quiche, and chicken pot pie. (Look for these, too, on the Millennium-class ships once their next refurbishments are completed, scheduled in 2011 and 2012.) There's also the **AquaSpa Café,** where you can get low-cal treats for lunch or dinner from noon to 8pm, including raw veggie platters, poached salmon with asparagus tips, vegetarian sushi, and pretty salads with tuna or chicken. Spa breakfasts include items such as bagels and lox, fresh fruit, cereal, and boiled eggs. For the opposite of spa cuisine, outdoor grills on all ships serve burgers and the like.

SNACKS & EXTRAS For coffee-and-pastry breaks, the Solstice-class ships (and the Millennium-class ships once they're renovated in 2011–12) have **Café al Bacio & Gelateria,** an upscale coffeehouse serving specialty coffees, teas, fresh-baked pastries, traditional gelatos and Italian ices, and other desserts. The Century-class ships have the **Cova Café,** serving incredibly good croissants (for free) and specialty lattes and cappuccinos (not for free), plus other items. An "after-theater" menu at each of these coffee bars lists sandwiches, savories, tartlets, hot brochettes, canapes, artisan cheeses, fresh fruit, crackers, petit fours, and napoleons from 11pm to closing.

The line also has **afternoon tea** at least once per cruise fleetwide, with white-gloved waiters serving tea, finger sandwiches, scones, and desserts from rolling carts. There's also an elaborate **brunch** in the main dining room once per cruise, with the kind of over-the-top spreads and ice, fruit, and vegetable carvings that used to be featured at midnight buffets. **Room service** allows passengers to order off a limited menu 24 hours a day and also from the lunch and dinner menus during set meal hours. You can get tasty **pizza** delivered right to your cabin between 3 and 7pm and 10pm and 1am daily, in a box and pouch just like the ones used by your local pizzeria.

ACTIVITIES

Celebrity provides lots of options for those who want to stay active, but it also caters to those who want to vegetate.

In 2009, Celebrity repackaged its enrichment activities under the banner of **Celebrity Life,** a series of what the line calls "palate-pleasing, intellectually enriching, and life-enhancing programs." Basically, Celebrity Life takes three of the things Celebrity has always built its brand around—dining, enrichment, and spa/wellness— and expands them into categories of activities called **Savor, Discover,** and **Renew.** Savor activities include several different wine-tasting and education events, mixology classes, whiskey tastings, and interactive culinary demos and talks. Discover activities include computer classes, art tours, dance and language classes, basic astronomy lessons, and talks by guest speakers, who may include naturalists (on Alaska, South

The Best Art at Sea

Celebrity has been known from the beginning for its art collections, which are so far beyond the cruise ship norm that they're in an entirely different league—truly museum quality when other lines' collections are mostly decorative at best, with a few standout pieces that provide marquee value.

The older Century-class ships were personally curated by a member of the Chandris family, and have modern collections heavy on names from minimalism, pop art, and other movements from the '60s, '70s, and '80s. *Mercury* alone features works by Richard Serra, Dan Flavin, Richard Long, Roy Lichtenstein, and Robert Rauschenberg, plus an entire wall mural created for the ship by Sol LeWitt. The new Solstice-class ships feature exceedingly contemporary pieces from both up-and-coming and established artists, the latter including Damien Hirst, Ross Bleckner, John Baldessari, Robert Rauschenberg, and Alexander Calder. There's even a Picasso on *Solstice. Equinox's* collection takes its curatorial concept from the ship's name (think balance, harmony), and mixes new works with many rescued from Celebrity's old *Galaxy* before she left the fleet to serve with German line TUI Cruises.

Free handheld **audio art tours** are available on the line's Century-class and Millennium-class ships.

America, and Galapagos sailings), caricature artists (on weeklong Caribbean and Bermuda sailings), and occasionally actors, politicians, journalists, historians, and authors. Renew activities encompass exercise classes (including free step, abs, and tai chi classes, plus yoga, spinning, Pilates, and other fashionable workouts at additional charge, usually $12 per class) and seminars on health and wellness, some of which touch on topics like Chinese herbal medicine and acupuncture. No surprise there, because Celebrity's **spa program** has long been among the best in the business, with beautifully appointed spas and a nice raft of treatments, from the exotic to the everyday-but-it-still-feels-good. In addition to the talks, the spas offer actual **acupuncture** fleetwide on all cruises, with professionals targeting their treatments toward pain management, smoking cessation, weight loss, stress management, and other ailments.

Other activities include horse racing, bingo, bridge, art auctions, trivia games, game shows, and arts and crafts lessons.

All the ships have a well-equipped Internet center and Wi-Fi capability in various public areas as well as the majority of cabins and suites for guests who bring their laptops. The line's newest ship, *Eclipse,* has a souped-up Internet cafe called the iLounge, created in collaboration with Apple and offering classes and a retail component as well as the usual online access. In cabins and suites, interactive TVs allow guests to order room service from on-screen menus, select the evening's wine in advance of dinner, play casino-style games, browse in virtual shops, and order pay-per-view movies.

CHILDREN'S PROGRAM

Celebrity pampers kids as well as adults, especially during the summer months and holidays when its Caribbean- and Bermuda-bound ships typically carry 400-plus children. Each ship has a dedicated youth staff of six or more supervising playroom activities practically all day long, and private and group babysitting is available in the evenings.

During kid-intensive seasons, **supervised activities** are geared toward four age groups within ages 3 to 17. Kids ages 3 to 5, dubbed Ship Mates, can enjoy treasure hunts, clown parties, T-shirt painting, dancing, movies, ship tours, and ice-cream-sundae-making parties. Celebrity Cadets, ages 6 to 8, have T-shirt painting, scavenger hunts, board games, arts and crafts, ship tours, and computer games. Your 9- to 11-year-old may want to join the Ensign activities, such as karaoke, computer games, board games, trivia contests, arts and crafts, movies, and pizza parties. In summer, these three age groups put on summer-stock theater shows, with Ship Mates and Cadets singing, dancing, and acting, and Ensigns directing and producing. There are also masquerade parties where Ship Mates and Cadets make their own masks and then parade around the ship, and Junior Olympics where the whole family is encouraged to cheer on the kids who compete in relay races, diving, and basketball free throws. Various activities and tours give kids a behind-the-scenes look at the ship's entertainment, food and beverage, and hotel departments.

Toddlers ages 2 and under can participate in activities and use the playroom if accompanied by a parent.

For **teens** ages 12 to 17 (subdivided into two groups, 12–14 and 15–17, during peak season, but all mashed together off-peak), the Celebrity ships have attractive teen discos/hangout rooms with Xbox, Nintendo Wii, and PlayStation games, and activities such as talent shows, karaoke, pool games, and trivia contests.

Group babysitting in the playroom ($6 per child, per hour) is available for ages 3 to 11 between noon and 2pm on port days, and every evening from 10pm to 1am. Kids can dine with the counselors most nights between 5 and 7pm (free on sea days; $6 per child, per hour, on port days). A **V.I.P. Party Pass** covers all group babysitting for your cruise at a 40% discount, and kids get to attend one big-screen movie, with free popcorn and refreshments, behind-the-scenes tours, and souvenirs. Prices vary by itinerary. On the last night of the cruise, a complimentary **Parents' Night Out party** is held between 5pm and 1am, and includes pizza and fun activities for kids while their parents step out. Female crewmembers provide evening **private in-cabin babysitting** on a limited basis, for $8 per hour for up to two children. Kids must be at least 12 months old, and the service must be requested 24 hours in advance.

The **minimum age** for kids sailing on Celebrity's ships is 6 months.

ENTERTAINMENT

Celebrity offers all the popular cruise favorites, such as magicians, comedians, cabaret acts, passenger talent shows, and Vegas-style musical revues. The overall quality of music and comedy acts is good, but on our last sailing the musical revues were poor. For something a little different, the line provides some nice, understated entertainment touches such as **harpists, string quartets,** and **roving a cappella groups** performing in various lounges. You'll also find **karaoke,** recent-release movies, active casinos, and late-night disco dancing, usually until about 3am.

All the ships also have cozy lounges and bars where you can retreat for a romantic nightcap and some music, from laid-back jazz to music from the big-band era, spiced with interpretations of contemporary hits. The elegant and plush **Michael's Club** piano lounges, with their gentlemen's club style, serve several functions. Each day from 8 to 10am and 4 to 6pm, the rooms are reserved for "Elite" members of the line's loyalty program (folks who have taken 10 or more Celebrity cruises), with complimentary espresso, tea, and other items in the morning and drinks and wine-tasting events in the evening. Though the piano lounges are little used in between those events, they're a great place to snuggle up with a good book. At night, they're an excellent place for an after-dinner drink.

SERVICE

Along with sheer style, service is Celebrity's strongest suit, with staff uniformly polite, attentive, cheerful, knowledgeable, and professional. Stewards wear white gloves at embarkation as they escort passengers to their cabins. Waiters have a poised, upscale-hotel air about them, and their manner does much to create an elegant mood. There are very professional **sommeliers** in the dining room, and waiters are on hand in the Lido breakfast and lunch buffet restaurants to carry passengers' trays from the buffet line to a table of their choice. If you occupy a suite, you'll get a **tuxedo-clad personal butler** who serves afternoon tea, complimentary cappuccino and espresso, and complimentary pre-dinner hors d'oeuvres. If you ask, he'll also handle your laundry, shine your shoes, make sewing repairs, deliver messages, and even serve a full five-course dinner en suite or help you organize a cocktail party. (You foot the bill for food and drinks, of course.) Other hedonistic treats bestowed upon suite guests include a bottle of champagne on arrival, personalized stationery, terry robes, oversize bath towels, priority check-in and debarkation, express luggage delivery at embarkation, and so on. **ConciergeClass staterooms**—a middle zone between regular cabins and suites—provide some of the same perks but without the high price of actual suites (but no butler, sorry).

When it comes to **tipping,** Celebrity has gone the automatic route, adding a fee of $11.50 per person, per day to the accounts of guests in normal staterooms, with the figure going up to $12 per day for guests in ConciergeClass and AquaClass staterooms and $15 per day for guests in suites.

Laundry and dry-cleaning services are available fleetwide for a nominal fee, but there are no self-service laundry facilities.

The Solstice Class: Celebrity Solstice • Equinox • Eclipse • Silhouette (preview)

The Verdict

The most beautiful megaships at sea today, Celebrity's four (and soon five) Solstice-class sisters manage to simultaneously encapsulate all that was great about Celebrity's older vessels while also moving logically and stylistically into the future.

Celebrity Solstice *(photo: Celebrity Cruises)*

Specifications   Typical Per Diems: $85–$110

Size (in tons)	122,000	Year Launched	
Passengers (double occ.)	2,850	*Solstice*	2008
Passenger/Space Ratio	42.8	*Equinox*	2009
Total Cabins/Veranda Cabins	1,426/1,216	*Eclipse*	2010
Crew	1,246	*Silhouette*	2011
Passenger/Crew Ratio	2.3 to 1	Last Major Upgrade	N/A

Frommer's Ratings (Scale of 1–5)   ★★★★★

Cabin Comfort & Amenities	5	Dining Options	5
Appearance & Upkeep	5	Gym, Spa & Sports Facilities	5
Public Comfort/Space	5	Children's Facilities	4
Decor	5	Enjoyment Factor	5

Sailing Regions, Seasons & Home Ports

Eclipse	**Caribbean,** from Miami (winter).
Equinox	**Caribbean,** from Fort Lauderdale (winter).
Silhouette	**Caribbean,** from Cape Liberty, NJ (winter).
Solstice	**Caribbean,** from Fort Lauderdale (winter).

Since introducing its very first newbuild in 1990, Celebrity has consistently had the most stylish megaships in the cruise biz, so it's gratifying to be able to say that the line's new Solstice-class ships are an absolute knockout. On the outside, their form is both massive and sleek, while inside a unifying aesthetic ties the many moods and experiences of their public rooms into a satisfying whole. The ships' overall look is an extension of that employed on Celebrity's older Century- and Millennium-class ships, with their neo-deco lines, minimalist art, and rich, quality textures and surfaces. In the atrium, translucent backlit onyx panels and white drapes recall similar materials used in the Millennium atriums, while the dreamy white interiors of each ship's main restaurant and observation lounge evoke both the past and the future—hinting at elements of the Century class while taking a stylistic swipe at both *2001: A Space Odyssey* and 1930s Hollywood movies. Balancing the "wow" is a wealth of subtle details, evident in everything from the ship's art collection—a world-class assemblage that amplifies the ship's mood with textural, minimalist, and nature-evoking pieces from big names and emerging talents—to its cabins, which could win awards for innovation all by themselves.

Because *Silhouette* hadn't yet debuted at press time, all details in this review refer to *Solstice, Equinox,* and *Eclipse,* all of which are essentially identical, with only a few minor differences. A fifth, as yet unnamed sister will debut in 2012.

CABINS   When was the last time you got to your cabin, looked around, and thought, "Huh, why haven't other ships done that before?" It's the same-old same-old syndrome, created by one essential fact: There are only so many different ways to arrange things in rectangular boxes, and that's exactly what most cruise ship cabins are—premade modular units assembled in one place, trucked to the shipyard, and slotted into the new vessel like drawers in a dresser.

To break the mold, Celebrity broke the mold, changing the basic shape of its cabins so that one wall of each bulges slightly, interlocking with the cabin next door in a sort of squared-off yin-yang format. That simple change gives passengers more maneuvering room around the foot of the bed, but was accomplished without also having to increase the width of the cabin's open area—sizable enough as is due to Celebrity's decision to make *Solstice*'s and *Equinox*'s cabins about 15% larger than those on its older ships.

Standard inside (183–200 sq. ft.) and outside (176–192 sq. ft.) cabins have an open and airy feeling, an ergonomic design, and a modern, modular look. Beds have rounded corners, allowing for better flow, and are higher than normal to give more storage space underneath. At the wall, the beds are surrounded by a tall headboard topped with a narrow, completely unobtrusive storage unit perfect for handbags, shopping bags, and other small items. Some couches offer trundle beds for kids and other additional guests, while closet doors slide shut automatically—which isn't so unusual on land, but is a hard thing to accomplish on a moving ship. Cabin bathrooms and showers are substantially larger and roomier than aboard most other megaships; showers are equipped with a foot rail that makes it easier for women to shave their legs; and there's an ingenious collection of small drawers, nooks, and cabinets for storing toiletries and other necessities. All cabins have flatscreen TVs, sitting areas with sofas, minifridges, and hair dryers. Outside, cabin balconies are large and deep, with plenty of room for two reclining deck chairs and a table.

In addition to the usual range of inside, outside, balcony cabins, and suites (300–1,291 sq. ft.), *Solstice* and *Equinox* both have 130 adults-only AquaClass staterooms, where the cabin experience is tied to an overall wellness aesthetic. Grouped together on the Penthouse Deck, each AquaClass cabin has niceties such as large balconies, pillow menus, jetted body-wash showers, and special music/sound and aromatherapy options tied to specific vacation goals (relaxation, invigoration, and so on). AquaClass guests also get special perks around the ship, including unlimited access to the spa's Persian Garden aromatherapy steam room and relaxation room, special wellness classes and invitations to VIP events, and the option of dining at a 130-seat specialty restaurant called Blu (see below).

Each ship has 30 wheelchair-accessible staterooms, spread among the different types of accommodations onboard, from inside cabins to sky suites.

PUBLIC AREAS   The Solstice-class ships have one of the most logical arrangements of public rooms we've seen in a decade and a half of reviewing ships. Most are clustered on the Entertainment and Promenade decks, and rooms were consciously grouped by the designers so that different types are in different areas of the ship. Evening entertainment outlets, for instance (the Equinox Theatre and the several venues of the Entertainment Court), are all located forward and linked directly to the Sky Observation Lounge by elevator. Pre- and post-dinner entertainment (the Ensemble Lounge for predinner cocktails and after-dinner jazz; Michael's Club for more intimate piano music and libations) is located immediately adjacent to the ships' specialty restaurants.

The 1,115-guest main theater is particularly innovative, its rounded stage and a complex ceiling rigging allowing aerialist entertainers to fly right over audience members' heads. Down the corridor, Celebrity Central is a 200-seat, multifunction venue that presents late-night comedy shows, films, and other shows and events. Across the hall, the Quasar nightclub has a streamlined, space-age look, with clear plastic "bubble chairs" suspended from the ceiling and huge LED screens curving from the walls into the ceiling, their lights synched with the music's beat. Between these two venues, an Entertainment Court is the venue for vocal quartets and other small-scale entertainment designed to keep passengers' interest as they move between other nightlife options. Other diversions on these decks include Cellar Masters, a Napa-inspired space for formal wine tastings and informal sipping; the Martini Bar with its cool color palate and a perpetually frosted bar; and Crush, a tasting room where guests sit around an ice-filled table to sample pairings of vodka and caviar.

But the Solstice-class ships' most distinctive and innovative features are out on deck—most visibly way up on the top deck, where the Lawn Club has a half-acre of real grass growing 15 decks above the sea. A first for cruise ships, the area provides a country-club ambience: quiet, refined, and calming. In the central lawn, passengers can play croquet or putt some golf balls around, either in individual play or during scheduled tournaments, while two courts along the sides of the ship have space for bocce and other lawn games. Passengers can also picnic on the main lawn, relax at the shaded patio at its aft end (dotted with potted greenery and comfortable lounge chairs and couches), or grab a drink at the aft-facing Sunset Bar, with its views of the ship's wake.

At the forward end of the club is another of the Solstice-class signature features: the Hot Glass Show. Developed by the world-famous Corning Museum of Glass, it provides daily (and surprisingly high-energy) programs in which master artisans explain and demonstrate the art of glass-blowing. Presented in an open-air studio designed specifically for these ships, the shows give the audience a sort of "glassmaking 101" experience, taking them through the process of creating a piece from start to finish—from an undifferentiated blob of glass to bowls, vases, and more complex forms like glass conch shells.

For kids, there's a large, light-filled, multiroom children's center near the very top of the ship, on the same deck as the Lawn Club. A teen center is adjacent, along with a video arcade. One unusual activity for kids is the chance to draw items they'd like to see artisans at the ship's Hot Glass Studio create in glass. Once per cruise, one of the show's gaffers selects a design and creates it, and the kid gets to take the piece home.

DINING OPTIONS   The Solstice-class ships are the first in which Celebrity has really diversified its dining program, offering a grand main restaurant, a buffet, four specialty restaurants, and three light and casual eateries on each vessel. Four specialty restaurants are clustered aft on the Entertainment Deck, opening off the Ensemble Lounge. The Tuscan Grille is a high-style spot in the ship's stern, with a menu heavy on steaks and pastas. Murano blends classic and modern Continental cuisine in an elegant, romantic setting inspired by Venice's famous Murano glassmakers. Blu is reserved exclusively for passengers booked into the AquaClass staterooms (plus suite guests based on availability). It serves a healthy menu of savory appetizers (along the lines of roasted beet salad with goat cheese or Mediterranean chopped salad with pita chips and pomegranate vinaigrette) and entrees like blackened ahi tuna, pan-seared filet mignon, and herb-crusted rack of lamb. Aboard *Solstice* and *Equinox,* Silk Harvest offers a mix of Thai, Vietnamese, Japanese, and Chinese selections, complemented by a variety of sakes, Asian-influenced martinis, and cocktails created with ginger root and acai berries. In its place, *Eclipse* has the high-style Qsine, serving eclectic international cuisine with a theatrical twist. (Also of note: Menus in general aboard *Eclipse* include an unusual number of British favorites and Indian dishes—a nod to the fact that *Eclipse* is homeporting in the U.K. in the summer.)

Several other eateries are scattered around each ship. Forward of the Ensemble Lounge, the centrally located Bistro on Five is a casual, chic restaurant with a menu of specialty crepes, sandwiches, soups, salads, and entrees including quiche, fish and chips, baked ziti, and chicken potpie. Right across the corridor, Café al Bacio & Gelateria is an upscale coffeehouse serving specialty coffees, teas, fresh-baked pastries, traditional gelatos and Italian ices, and other desserts. In the Solarium, the AquaSpa Café serves spa cuisine, including salads, lean meats, seafood, and fresh fruit smoothies.

POOL, FITNESS, SPA & SPORTS FACILITIES   The Solstice-class Pool Deck is one of the most serene in the cruise biz, owing to the decision to place the ship's buffet restaurant and grill on a separate deck, one level up. That decision automatically changed the pool deck from a busy, multipurpose space into one whose sole purpose is serene, resortlike relaxation. Surrounding two pools (one for "sports," one for families) and four hot tubs are 12 white, 25-foot, A-frame canopies supporting cantilevered awnings and providing shade for chaise longues on both the Resort Deck (the ships' pool deck) and the Lido Deck above. A dancing fountain occupies a central position at the aft of the pool area, ringed with deck chairs. Forward of the pools, the glass-ceilinged Solarium is a peaceful enclave for adults only, with a lap pool, cushioned teak lounge chairs, views all around, and the AquaSpa Café.

The AquaSpa itself is done up in a soothing sea of white and Aegean blue, its colonnade and domed rotunda reception area designed as a contemporary interpretation of the architecture found on Greek Islands such as Santorini and Mykonos. Besides massages, facials, and other favorites, the treatment menu includes acupuncture, Botox wrinkle treatments, teeth whitening, and cosmetic dermal fillers to smooth smile lines. The Persian Garden is a steam room in the old style (think Ottoman Empire), glossed with a contemporary, New Agey vibe. It's complimentary for guests booked into AquaSpa staterooms and suites; everybody else has to pay. The ships' gyms are large and extremely well equipped.

The Millennium Class: Celebrity Millennium • Infinity • Summit • Constellation

Celebrity Millennium *(photo: Celebrity Cruises)*

The Verdict

Among the classiest big ships at sea, the Millennium ships offer all the leisure, sports, and entertainment options of a megaship and an atmosphere that combines old-world elegance and modern casual style.

Specifications

Typical Per Diems: $80–$150

Size (in tons)	91,000	Year Launched	
Passengers (double occ.)	1,950	*Millennium*	2000
Passenger/Space Ratio	46.7	*Infinity*	2001
Total Cabins/Veranda Cabins	975/590	*Summit*	2001
Crew	999	*Constellation*	2002
Passenger/Crew Ratio	2 to 1	Last Major Upgrade	2010–12

Frommer's Ratings (Scale of 1–5)

★★★★★

Cabin Comfort & Amenities	5	Dining Options	5
Appearance & Upkeep	5	Gym, Spa & Sports Facilities	5
Public Comfort/Space	5	Children's Facilities	4
Decor	5	Enjoyment Factor	5

Sailing Regions, Seasons & Home Ports

Constellation	**Caribbean,** from Fort Lauderdale (winter).
Infinity	**Alaska,** from Seattle (summer). **Panama Canal,** from Fort Lauderdale & San Diego (spring & fall).
Millennium	**Caribbean,** from Miami (fall & winter), from San Juan (winter). **Alaska,** from Vancouver & Seward (summer). **Panama Canal,** from San Juan (spring), from San Diego (fall).
Summit	**Caribbean,** from San Juan (winter). **Bermuda,** from Cape Liberty, NJ (summer). **New England/Canada,** from Cape Liberty, NJ (fall).

Time was, these ships were *it:* bigger than the line's first generation of megaships (the Century class), with bigger spas and theaters, more veranda cabins, more dining options, more shopping, more lounges, and more sports and exercise facilities—plus more of the same great service, cuisine, and high-style onboard art. Then *Celebrity Solstice* happened, and the bar got a lot higher—but don't count these ships out yet. Already very lovely and full of onboard options, they are, at this writing, about to be "Solstice-ized," receiving multimillion-dollar refurbishments designed to add some of the most attractive features of the Solstice class. When all's said and done, each ship will have a new Tuscan Grille steakhouse restaurant, a new Bistro on Five casual creperie and comfort food eatery, a new Martini Bar with permafrost bar top, a new vodka-and-caviar tasting bar, and a new Café al Bacio & Gelateria, replacing the Millennium ships' Cova Café. Additionally, staterooms and public areas will be restyled to reflect the Solstice class's more sleek lines and understated color palate. *Constellation* should already have received her Solstice-izing by the time you read this. *Infinity* and *Summit* are scheduled to get theirs in 2011, with *Millennium* finishing out the process in 2012. We've included the new features in the write-up below based on our experience of them on the Solstice-class ships, but note that they might not all be installed yet when you sail.

CABINS Standard inside (170 sq. ft.) and outside (170–191 sq. ft.) cabins are roomy and come with a small sitting area, stocked minifridge, TV, safe, ample storage space, cotton robes, a hair dryer, and shower-mounted shampoo dispensers. Only thing missing? Individual reading lights above the beds, though there are table lamps on the nightstands.

Premium and Deluxe staterooms have slightly larger sitting areas and approximately 40-square-foot verandas. The 12 Family Ocean View staterooms in the stern on Panorama, Sky, and Vista decks measure in at a very large 271 square feet and have two entertainment centers with TVs/VCRs, a partitioned sitting area with two convertible sofa beds, and very, very, very large 242-square-foot verandas facing the ship's wake.

Passengers booking the ConciergeClass staterooms on Sky Deck get a bunch of cushy extras, from a bottle of champagne to a choice of pillows, upgraded bedding, oversize towels, double-thick Frette bathrobes, priority for just about everything (dining, shore excursions, luggage delivery, embarkation, and debarkation), and cushioned chairs and high-powered binoculars on their 41-square-foot balconies. Unfortunately, many of those balconies (as well as those attached to several Deluxe Ocean View cabins at Sky Deck midships) catch a little shadow from the overhanging deck above. *Hint:* Several ConciergeClass cabins on the Sky Deck (9038 and 9043) and Panorama Deck (8045 and 8046) have extralarge verandas at no extra cost. Ask your travel agent.

Suites provide 24-hour butler service and come in four levels, from the 251-square-foot Sky Suites with balconies to the eight 467-square-foot Celebrity Suites (with a dining area, separate bedroom, two TV/VCR combos, and a whirlpool bathtub, but no verandas) and the 538-square-foot Royal Suites (also with a separate living/dining room, two TV/VCR combos, a standing shower and whirlpool bathtub, and a huge 195-sq.-ft. veranda with whirlpool tub). At the top of the food chain, the massive Penthouse Suites measure 1,432 square feet and have herringbone wood floors, a marble foyer, a computer station, a Yamaha piano, and a simply amazing bathroom with ocean views and a full-size hot tub. And did we mention a 1,098-square-foot veranda that wraps around the stern of the ship and features a whirlpool tub and full bar?

Passengers requiring use of a wheelchair have a choice of 26 cabins in several categories, from Sky Suites to balcony cabins to inside staterooms.

PUBLIC AREAS   There's simply nothing else at sea like the Grand Foyer atrium, the stunning hub of all four ships. Each rectangular, three-deck area features a translucent, inner-illuminated onyx staircase that glows beneath your feet, plus giant silk flower arrangements and topiaries, oceanview elevators, and an attractive Internet center.

In each ship's bow is an elegant three-deck theater with a warm glow provided by faux torches spaced all around. Seating on all three levels is unobstructed except in the far reaches of the balconies. You'll also find elegant martini, champagne, and caviar bars, as well as brighter, busier lounges for live music. For the real dancing, head up to the stunning observation lounge/disco on the Sunrise Deck. Other rooms include a two-deck library; a large casino; an oceanview florist/conservatory (filled mostly with silk flowers and trees, some of which are for sale); and the huge, high-tech conference center and cinema. Celebrity's signature Michael's Club is a quiet, dignified piano bar replete with a fake fireplace and comfy leather club chairs.

The ships' Emporium Shops have a nice variety of high-end name brands as well as cheap souvenirs.

For kids, the Fun Factory has both indoor and outdoor soft-surface jungle gyms, a wading pool, a ball bin, a computer room, a movie room, an arts-and-crafts area, a video arcade, a teen center, and more. There is no dedicated lounge for teens, though the youth staff does program teen activities at different venues onboard.

DINING OPTIONS   The main dining rooms are beautiful two-level spaces with huge stern-facing windows, oversize round windows to port and starboard, and a dramatic central double staircase. *Summit's* dining room boasts a 7-foot Art Deco bronze of the goddess Athena, which once overlooked the grand staircase on the legendary SS *Normandie* ocean liner. (She resided for years near the pool at Miami's Fontainebleau Hotel before Celebrity bought her and returned her to sea.)

The real *pièce de résistance* on these ships, however, is their alternative, reservations-only restaurants, which provide dining experiences unmatched on any other ship today. *Millennium's* is the Edwardian-style Olympic restaurant, whose decor features several dozen handcarved French walnut wall panels made by Palestinian craftsmen for the A La Carte restaurant on *Titanic*'s sister ship *Olympic,* which sailed from 1911 to 1935. *Infinity*'s SS United States restaurant has etched-glass panels from the 1950s liner of the same name, which still holds the transatlantic speed record for a liner. *Summit*'s Normandie restaurant has original gold-lacquered panels from the smoking room of the legendary *Normandie.* The *Constellation*'s Ocean Liners restaurant has artifacts from a variety of luxury liners, including sets of original red-and-black lacquered panels from the 1920s *Ile de France,* which add a whimsical Parisian air. Dining here is a 2- to 3-hour commitment, with some 100 guests served by a gracious staff of more than 20, including eight dedicated chefs, six waiters, five maitre d's, and four sommeliers. Waiters remove domed silver dish covers with a flourish, exceptional cheeses are offered postmeal, and a pianist or a piano/violin duo performs period music.

Cuisine here is a combination of Continental specialties mixed with original recipes from the ships the restaurants are named after—the original Waldorf Pudding recipe from the White Star Liner *Olympic,* for instance, served in *Millennium*'s Edwardian-style Olympic restaurant, or the Long Island duckling featured on the original SS *United States.* Appetizers include creamy lobster broth, tartare of salmon garnished with quail eggs, and goat cheese soufflé with tomato coulis, followed by entrees such as sea bass brushed with tapenade, scampi flambéed in Armagnac, and rack of lamb coated with mushroom duxelles and wrapped in a puff pastry. Some flambéed dishes are cooked table side. For dessert, you can't go wrong with a chocolate soufflé or a plate of bite-size desserts. You can order a la carte or opt for a set multicourse tasting menu (for $30), with an optional $28 slate of wine pairings. Wines are also available by the glass or bottle.

A second specialty restaurant, the Tuscan Grille, is being added to each ship as part of an ongoing upgrade. Very high style, it offers a menu heavy on steaks and pastas. For something more casual, Bistro on Five serves a menu of specialty crepes, sandwiches, soups, salads, and comfort food entrees.

The huge buffet restaurant on each ship is open for breakfast, lunch, and dinner, with regular buffet selections plus pizza, pasta, and ice-cream specialty stations. Depending on how busy the restaurant is, waiters may carry passengers' trays to their tables and fetch coffee. For fancy snacks, visit Café al Bacio & Gelateria, which serves specialty coffees, teas, fresh-baked pastries, traditional gelatos and Italian ices, and other desserts.

POOL, FITNESS, SPA & SPORTS FACILITIES The spas on the Millennium-class ships are gorgeous and sprawling, their 25,000 square feet taken up with hydrotherapy treatment rooms; New Agey Persian Garden steam suites whose nooks have showers that simulate a tropical rainforest, heated tiled couches, and the aromas of chamomile, eucalyptus, and mint; and large, bubbling thalassotherapy pools with soothing pressure jets in a solarium-like setting under a glass roof. The pool is free to all adult guests, and you can stretch out the experience by grabbing a casual breakfast or lunch at the AquaSpa Café, set back by the seaview windows.

Next door to the spa, there's a very large gym with dozens of the latest machines and free weights, and a large aerobics floor.

Up top, the Sports Deck has facilities for basketball, volleyball, quoits, and paddle tennis. Just below, on the Sunrise Deck, is the ship's jogging track. Below that is the well-laid-out Pool Deck, where you'll find two pools, four hot tubs, a couple of bars, and a sunning area. Head up to the balcony level above the pool, at both the bow and the stern, for quieter sunbathing spots.

The Century Class: Celebrity Century • Celebrity Mercury

Celebrity Mercury *(photo: Matt Hannafin)*

The Verdict

Now more than a decade old, Celebrity's Century-class ships still shine, with classic modernist style and Celebrity's elegant yet casual vibe.

Specifications   Typical Per Diems: $65–$110

Size (in tons)		Crew	
Century	70,606	*Century*	843
Mercury	77,713	*Mercury*	900
Passengers (double occ.)		Passenger/Crew Ratio	2 to 1
Century	1,750	Year Launched	
Mercury	1,896	*Century*	1995
Passenger/Space Ratio	41	*Mercury*	1997
Total Cabins/Veranda Cabins		Last Major Upgrade	
Century	875/375	*Century*	2006
Mercury	948/220	*Mercury*	2007

Frommer's Ratings (Scale of 1–5)   ★★★★ ½

Cabin Comfort & Amenities	5	Dining Options	4
Appearance & Upkeep	4	Gym, Spa & Sports Facilities	5
Public Comfort/Space	5	Children's Facilities	4
Decor	5	Enjoyment Factor	5

Sailing Regions, Seasons & Home Ports

Century	**Caribbean,** from Miami (winter/spring 2011), from Baltimore (winter 2012). **Panama Canal,** from Miami (spring), from San Diego (fall). **Alaska,** from Vancouver (summer). **Hawaii,** from San Diego (spring & fall).
Mercury	**Caribbean & The Bahamas,** from Baltimore & Charleston (winter, through Feb. 2011).

These are the ships that ushered Celebrity into the megaship world and also sealed the line's reputation for elegant, gorgeously designed vessels with a truly modern flair. It's difficult to say what's most striking: The elegant spas and their 15,000-gallon thalassotherapy pools? The distinguished Michael's Club piano lounges with their leather wingbacks and velvet couches? The two-story old-world dining rooms set back in the stern, with grand floor-to-ceiling windows allowing diners to spy the ship's wake glowing under moonlight? A modern-art collection unmatched in the industry? Take your pick—you won't go wrong.

In part through regular refurbishment and in part because they were ahead of their time to begin with, *Century* and *Mercury* have held up remarkably well in their decade and a half at sea, both in practical and aesthetic terms. That said, they aren't immune to the passage of time, and as this book was going to press we learned that *Mercury* is about to endure the fate of many aging cruise ships: In February 2011 she'll leave the Celebrity fleet to join TUI Cruises, a German company owned in part by Celebrity's parent company, Royal Caribbean Cruises Ltd. Sad news! Particularly since we, your humble authors, first met aboard *Mercury*, just before her launch, way back in 1997. Talk about the passage of time . . . .

CABINS   Simple yet pleasing decor is cheerful and based on light-colored furniture and muted color themes. Standard inside and outside cabins are larger than the norm, and suites, which come in four categories, are particularly spacious, with marble vanity/desk tops, Art Deco–style sconces, and rich inlaid wood floors. Some, such as the Penthouse Suite, have more living space than you find in many private homes (1,219 sq. ft., expandable to 1,433 sq. ft. on special request), plus such wonderful touches as a private whirlpool bath on the veranda. Royal Suites run about half that size (plus 100-ft. balconies) but offer touches such as French doors between the bedroom and seating area, both bathtub and shower in the bathroom, and TVs in each room. *Mercury*'s 246-square-foot Sky Suites have verandas that, at 179 square feet, are among the biggest aboard any ship—bigger, in fact, than those in the more expensive Penthouse and Royal suites on these ships (you may want to keep your robe on, though, as people on the deck above can see down onto part of the Sky Suite verandas). All suite bathrooms have bathtubs with whirlpools and magnified makeup mirrors. Like the Solstice- and Millennium-class ships, the Century-class ships also have Concierge-Class staterooms, which are located mostly on the Sky and Penthouse decks. Though a tad less cushy and amenities-filled than regular suites, they provide a lot of extras without the full-suite price.

All regular inside and outside cabins (170–175 sq. ft.) are outfitted with built-in vanities/desks, stocked minifridges (accounts are billed for any snacks or drinks consumed), hair dryers, cotton robes, and safes. Closets and drawer space are roomy and well designed, as are the bathrooms. Cabin TVs are wired with an interactive system that allows guests to order room service from on-screen menus, select wine for dinner, play casino-style games, or go shopping.

Eight cabins aboard each ship (one inside and seven outside) are specifically designed for passengers with disabilities.

PUBLIC AREAS   Both ships are designed so well that it's never hard to find a quiet retreat when you want to feel secluded but don't want to be confined in your cabin.

Each vessel boasts a cozy Michael's Club piano bar, decorated like the parlor of a London men's club. It's a great spot for a fine cognac or a good single-malt Scotch while enjoying soft music. On *Century*, Michael's Club piano bar maintains its wood-paneled clubby ambience somewhat better than aboard the *Mercury*, where it wraps around the main atrium and looks onto a very uncozy view of the shops below. Still, you can't beat the high-backed, buttery-leather chairs and dark setting.

For those who don't find that clubby ambience appealing, the Cova Café is an alternative, with specialized upscale java at extra cost. There's also the popular Rendez-Vous Square, arranged so that even large groups can achieve a level of privacy and couples can find a nook of their own. On *Mercury*, it's a gorgeous, two-level space defined by rounded wooden walls, champagne-bubble carpeting and glass panels, and a two-story Sol LeWitt mural created specifically for the ship. One level features a champagne bar, the other a martini bar. Various other bars, both indoor and outdoor, are tucked into nooks and crannies throughout both ships.

The multistoried, glass-walled nightclubs/discos are spacious and cleanly, modernly elegant, designed with lots of cozy nooks for romantic conversation over champagne. Both ships have double-decker theaters with unobstructed views from almost every seat (though avoid those at the cocktail tables at the back of the rear balcony boxes, unless you have a really long neck).

DINING OPTIONS   The two-story formal dining rooms on *Century* and *Mercury* are truly stunning spaces reminiscent of the grand liners of yesteryear, with wide, dramatic staircases joining the two levels and floor-to-ceiling walls of glass facing astern to a view of the ship's wake. If you lean toward the dramatic, don a gown or tux and slink down the stairs nice and slow like a 1930s Hollywood starlet. There aren't many places you can do that these days.

Century provides a dinner alternative at the Murano restaurant, named for the Venetian island famous for its glass blowing and decorated with Murano chandeliers. The restaurant's decor also includes a floor designed to resemble medieval European paving stones; a hand-painted mural themed on travel and adventure; and glass-fronted, polished-nickel wine armoires displaying backlit bottles. Elaborate, multi-course meals follow the style of Celebrity's Millennium-class specialty restaurants, with their table-side cooking, carving, and flambé.

Each ship also has an indoor/outdoor buffet restaurant open for breakfast, lunch, and dinner, as well as pizza and ice-cream stations.

POOL, FITNESS, SPA & SPORTS FACILITIES   Pool decks aboard these vessels feature a pair of good-size swimming areas rimmed with teak benches for sunning and relaxation. Even when the ships are full, these areas don't seem particularly crowded. Aboard *Mercury*, a retractable dome covers one of the swimming pools during inclement weather.

The ships' excellent 10,000-square-foot AquaSpa and fitness facilities are as aesthetically pleasing as they are functional. The gym wraps around the starboard side of an upper forward deck like a hook, the large spa straddles the middle, and a very modern and elegant beauty salon faces the ocean on the port side. On *Mercury*, the focal point of the spas is a 115,000-gallon thalassotherapy pool, a bubbling cauldron of warm, soothing seawater. After a relaxing 15- or 20-minute dip, choose a massage, a facial, or something more exotic, such as a Rasul treatment (a mudpack and steam bath for couples) or herbal steam bath. A day pass to the thalassotherapy pool is $20, a weeklong pass is $99, and you get use of the pool free if you book any spa package. Unfortunately, *Century*'s thalassotherapy pool was removed during her 2006 renovation. Both ships also have saunas and steam rooms.

The gyms are a generous size, with aerobics classes in a separate room. Standard classes are free, but trendy ones such as Pilates and spinning are $10 a pop. There is also an outdoor jogging track on an upper deck and one deck that's specifically designed for sports.

4 Costa Cruises

200 S. Park Rd., Ste. 200, Hollywood, FL 33021-8541. © 800/462-6782 or 954/266-5600. Fax 954/266-2100. www. costacruises.com.

THE LINE IN A NUTSHELL   Imagine a Carnival megaship hijacked by an Italian circus troupe: That's Costa. The words of the day are fun, festive, and international, with big, bright new megaships providing the venue. Expect a really good time, but don't set your sights too high for cuisine, with the exception of pasta and pizza. **Sails to:** Caribbean (plus Europe, Asia).

THE EXPERIENCE   For years, Costa has played up its Italian heritage as the main factor that distinguishes it from Carnival, Royal Caribbean, and the rest—even though the line is part of the Carnival Corporation empire, and many members of the service staff are as Italian as Chico Marx. Still, there's an Italianate essence here, with more pasta dishes on the menu than on any other line; more classical Italian music among the entertainment offerings; Italian-flavored activities facilitated by a young, often Italian, and ridiculously attractive "animation staff"; and a huge number of Italian Americans among the passengers. The interiors of the line's newest ships are by Carnival's designer-in-chief Joe Farcus, who took inspiration from Italy's traditions of painting and architecture but still stuck close to his signature "more is more" style— think Venice a la Vegas.

Pros
- **Italian flavor:** Entertainment, activities, and cuisine are presented with European (mostly Italian) carnival flair. Plus, most of the officers are Italians, too.
- **Very active, very fun:** There are a lot of activities, and Costa passengers love to participate, creating a festive and social environment morning to night (could be all those espressos that keep the andrenaline up!).

Cons
- **Average dining:** While the pizza and bread are excellent and some of the pasta dishes work well, overall the cuisine isn't memorable.

COSTA: CONTINENTAL FLAVOR IN THE CARIBBEAN

Costa's origins are as Italian as could be. In 1860, Giacomo Costa established an olive-oil refinery and packaging plant in Genoa. After his death, his sons bought a ship called *Ravenna* to transport raw materials and finished products from Sardinia through Genoa to the rest of Europe, thereby marking the founding of Costa Line in

Compared with the other mainstream lines, here's how Costa rates:

	Poor	Fair	Good	Excellent	Outstanding
Enjoyment Factor			✓		
Dining		✓			
Activities				✓	
Children's Program		✓			
Entertainment			✓		
Service		✓			
Worth the Money			✓		

1924. Between 1997 and 2000, Carnival Corporation bought up shares in Costa until it became sole owner. Today, Costa's Italianism is as much a marketing tool as anything else, but it must be working: The line's presence in Europe is huge—and it's even got a foothold in the Far East, too—and in the past decade it's introduced eight new megaships: *Costa Mediterranea* and *Costa Fortuna* in 2003; *Costa Magica* in 2004; *Costa Concordia* in 2006; and *Costa Serena,* which debuted in Europe in spring 2007; *Costa Luminosa* and *Costa Pacifica* in spring 2009; and *Costa Deliziosa* in early 2010.

With its main presence cruising in Europe, at press time only one ship, *Costa Atlantica,* offered itineraries in the Caribbean, so the review here covers that ship and sister *Mediterranea.*

PASSENGER PROFILE

Most of Costa's ships sail in Europe, where 80% to 85% of its passengers are Europeans. In the Caribbean, it's about the same ratio aboard the **Costa Atlantica.** But no matter the nationality or itinerary, Costa attracts passengers of all ages who want lots of fun and action, and like the idea of cruising on an Italian ship. In general, Costa passengers are big on participation, the goofier the better. We've never seen as many guests crowding the dance floor, participating in contests, or joining arts and crafts projects as aboard Costa's ships.

In the Caribbean, Costa appeals to retirees and young couples alike, although there are more passengers over age 45 than under. Typically you won't see more than 40 or 50 kids on any one cruise, except during holidays such as Christmas and spring break, when there may be as many as 500 children on board. Because of the international mix, public announcements, lifeboat drills, and some entertainment are given in English, Italian, and often German, French, and Spanish if there is a large number of guests on board from countries where those languages are spoken. The cruise director and most officers are typically Italian and much of the activities staff is composed of multilingual Italians.

DINING

Though it varies from ship to ship, Costa's cuisine has definitely improved over the years. Pastas are totally authentic and are often very good, and the Sicilian-style pizza is fantastic. On a recent cruise, the crusty Italian rolls baked from scratch were addictive, and it was difficult to sample the parmigiano cheese wheel and prosciutto ham at the lunch buffet in moderation. The *millefoglie,* a flaky puff pastry cake layered with cream or chocolate, is one of the best cruise ship desserts coauthor Heidi has ever eaten.

TRADITIONAL   Each dinner menu features five courses from a different region of Italy—Liguria one night, Sicily the next, and so on—plus several alternatives for each course, including the traditional pasta course. Most of the pastas, from fettuccine to spaghetti and ravioli, are shipped in direct from Italy. Many of these dishes are heavy on the cream and oil, and so are richer than some Americans are used to, but they're definitely the dining highlight. If you feel like a change from the pasta course, try one of the interesting risottos—the crabmeat-and-champagne selection on our last cruise was fantastic. Otherwise, expect cruise staples such as poached salmon, lobster tail, grilled lamb chops, roast duck, and beef tenderloin, plus classic selections such as Caesar salad and baked or grilled fish or chicken. **Vegetarian options** are available at each meal, and **Health and Wellness menu** selections are listed with their calorie, fat, and carbohydrate breakdowns. On the second formal night, flaming baked Alaska is paraded through the dining room and complimentary champagne is poured. Other desserts include tiramisu, gelato, and zabaglione (meringue pie).

SPECIALTY The ships have a reservations-only alternative Tuscan steakhouse restaurant ($23 per person) serving tenderloins, T-bones and other cuts, seafood, and a few pasta dishes like fettuccine Alfredo and *spaghetti ai gamberi* (prawns). The ambience is considerably quieter and more romantic than in the main dining room, with pleasant piano music and a small dance floor if you feel like a waltz between courses. The main caveat is the vibrations that can often be felt from the nearby funnels (but after a few glasses of wine, you won't notice anymore).

CASUAL There's a large buffet restaurant with multiple serving areas. Breakfast is a standard mix of eggs, meats, fruits, cereals, and cheeses. At lunch, several of the stations will serve standard dishes while others will be given over to a different national or regional cuisine (Spanish, Greek, Italian, Asian, and so forth). Casual dining is also available nightly until 9:30pm. The line's **fresh-baked pizza** (served in one section of the buffet noon–2am) looks a little weird, but trust us, it's fantastic—one of the highlights of the food on board. It's real Italian pizza (very thin, without excess cheese and sauce) and the homemade crust is so much better than the rubbery, doughy stuff most cruise lines use. Out on deck, there's a **grill** serving burgers and hot dogs, as well as a **taco bar** at lunch. If you're looking for another afternoon snack, head over to the ice-cream station in the buffet area, with daily special such as fresh banana or coconut, along with traditional flavors.

SNACKS & EXTRAS Most cruise lines have scrapped their **midnight buffets,** but Costa still offers them a few nights per cruise, often focusing on a theme taken from that evening's activity, whether it's Spain, Germany, France, or Asia. On another night, the guests may head below to the ship's massive galley for the buffet. **Room service** is available 24 hours a day.

ACTIVITIES

More than anything else, Costa is known for its lineup of exuberant activities, and passengers on these ships love to participate. In keeping with a European sensibility that appreciates visual **slapstick humor** and **musical acts,** and to offer a repertoire that speakers of many languages could appreciate, the entertainment ranges from a ventriloquist act to musical performances (Latin, Jazz, classical, and pop), ballroom dancing, crew talent shows, and standard Vegas-style productions. At dinnertime, one of the bustling lounges off the atrium might be the venue for the goofy comedic antics of several Carol Burnette–esque cruise staffmembers dressed up in frumpy cleaning lady garb and crazy wigs, mopping, dusting, and sweeping their way over people's shoes, shoulders, and bald heads. Late-night (11:30pm) entertainment is well attended, with **theme parties** typically ranging from the likes of a Mr. Costa Atlantica competition to a passenger talent show and a hilarious "sexy games night" that pits four couples against each other in silly pseudo-erotic dance moves and skits. The disco gets going around 1am, in keeping with the typically late-night European nightclub ethos.

During the day, activities include **arts and crafts projects** (from paper flower making to origami and T-shirt painting) and **cooking classes,** as well as traditional cruise staples such as jackpot bingo, dance classes, art auctions, horse racing, bridge, Ping-Pong, and fun poolside competitions in which teams have to put on Roman-style costumes or don silly hats. The ship has a combo library and Internet center, as well as a large card room. **Aerobics and stretch classes** are usually held on the covered pool area's dance floor, which also sees live steel-drum music throughout the rest of the day. Luckily, there's lots of deck space across several levels for sunbathing, so you can escape the noise if you want to. In the stern, a fun all-ages water slide operates a couple of hours per day.

A **Catholic Mass** and a nondenominational church service are held almost every day in each ship's small chapel.

CHILDREN'S PROGRAM

Costa's kids' programs aren't nearly as extensive as those on Disney or Royal Caribbean (or Carnival's Conquest-class and Spirit-class ships), but then, there are usually far fewer children on board. At least two full-time youth counselors sail aboard, with additional staff whenever more than a dozen or so kids are on the passenger list. **Supervised activities** are offered for kids ages 3 to 18, divided into two age groups unless enough children are aboard to divide them into three (3–6, 7–12, and 13–18 years) or four (3–6, 7–10, 11–14, and 15–18 years). The **Costa Kids Club,** for ages 3 to 12, includes such activities as arts and crafts, scavenger hunts, Italian-language lessons, bingo, board games, face painting, movies, kids' karaoke, and pizza and ice-cream-sundae parties. The ships each have a pleasant children's playroom and a teen disco. If there are enough teens on board, the **Costa Teens Club** for ages 13 to 18 has foosball and darts competitions, karaoke, and other activities.

When ships are at sea in the Caribbean, supervised Kids Club hours are typically from 9am to noon, 3 to 6pm, and 9 to 11:30pm. The program also operates during port days, but on a more limited basis.

On Gala nights, there's a great complimentary **Parents' Night Out program** from 6 to 11:30pm during which kids ages 3 and older (they must be out of diapers) are entertained and given a special buffet or pizza party while Mom and Dad get a night out alone. All other times, **group babysitting** for ages 3 and up is available every night from 9 to 11:30pm at no cost, and from 11:30pm to 1:30am if you make arrangements in advance. No private, in-cabin babysitting is available.

Children must be at least 6 months old to sail with Costa, and kids between ages 6 months and 2 years sail free.

ENTERTAINMENT

To entertain the mix of nationalities on board a typical Costa cruise, even in the Caribbean, expect concerts, operatic soloists, Broadway-style productions, talent shows, mimes, acrobats, and cabaret—no language skills required. On a recent cruise, one of the shows had a unicycle-riding, ball-balancing, flame-juggling, plate-spinning entertainer—the kind you used to see on *The Ed Sullivan Show.* Other featured performers included an operatic tenor singing a program of high-note crowd pleasers and a classical pianist performing Beethoven and Gershwin. The line's production shows mostly follow the typical song-and-dance revue formula; on recent sailings, creative costumes and choreography got big points, and so did the enthusiasm and versatility of the dance troupe. Participatory shows are much more fun overall, and more in tune with what Costa passengers seem to want. The Election of the Ideal Couple and a *Newlywed Game* takeoff, for instance, both clip along at a frantic pace, with the cruise staff helping and hindering as appropriate to get the most laughs. Who knew the criterion for being an ideal couple was the ability to burst a balloon with your butt? On a recent cruise, a hilarious "sexy games night" had four couples pitted against each other in silly pseudo-erotic dance moves and skits, and it was hilarious.

Both ships have glitzy casinos as well as hopping discos, which often get going only after 1am.

SERVICE

Waiters and servers are on par with the professionalism of the other big-ship lines, and many are hard-working, efficient, and friendly. On coauthor Heidi's last *Atlantica* cruise, her waiters and the bar staff were excellent, real pros.

For **tipping,** like many other lines, Costa adds an automatic gratuity of $10 per person per day to passengers' onboard accounts.

There are no self-service laundry facilities on any of the Costa ships.

Costa Atlantica •
Costa Mediterranea

Costa Atlantica *(photo: Costa Cruises)*

The Verdict

Is it Carnival or is it Carnivale? Decorated in a Europe-meets-Vegas style, these ships are eye candy for the ADD set.

Specifications

Typical Per Diems: $70–$110

Size (in tons)	85,000	Year Launched	
Passengers (double occ.)	2,114	*Atlantica*	2000
Passenger/Space Ratio	40	*Mediterranea*	2003
Total Cabins/Veranda Cabins	1,056/678	Last Major Upgrade	
Crew	920	*Atlantica*	2008
Passenger/Crew Ratio	2.3 to 1	*Mediterranea*	2007

Frommer's Ratings (Scale of 1–5)

★★★½

Cabin Comfort & Amenities	4	Dining Options	3
Appearance & Upkeep	4	Gym, Spa & Sports Facilities	4
Public Comfort/Space	4	Children's Facilities	3
Decor	4	Enjoyment Factor	4

Sailing Regions, Seasons & Home Ports

Atlantica	**Caribbean,** from Fort Lauderdale (winter). **New England/Canada,** from New York & Quebec City (spring).
Mediterranea	**New England/Canada,** from New York & Quebec City (fall).

Atlantica, and sister *Mediterranea,* ushered in the future for Costa, being a kind of European version of the Fun Ships operated by sister company Carnival. *Atlantica* was the first of the Farcus-designed Costa ships, and you'll recognize the designer's touch in the flashing lights along the elevators and also in the many mosaics and frescoes throughout and the tons of Carrara marble that would have driven a Renaissance sculptor crazy. The *Atlantica*'s Fellini theme and the *Mediterranea*'s 17th- and 18th-century Italian *palazzi* motif work particularly well to combine Italian flavor and Farcus's fantasy. Cruising on these ships is like being in an Escher painting: fantastic detail and endless illusion.

Built along the same lines as Carnival's Spirit-class ships, at nearly 1,000 feet long, the ships cut a sleek profile, and their bright yellow, barrel-like smokestacks, emblazoned with a big blue Costa *C,* distinguishes them from their Carnival cousins.

Despite the obvious success of the Spirit-class design (six Carnival and Costa ships are based on it, and Holland America has adapted it for its Vista-class vessels), there are some odd bits. The main public decks have a zigzagging layout that lacks the easy flow of some competitors, and some areas in the bow are downright bizarre: For instance, the wide outdoor promenade on Deck 3 ducks indoors as it goes forward, becoming a long, strange, marble-floored lounge with some small tables and chairs. Is it a place to sit? Is it a place to walk? No one seems to know, so it gets hardly any use.

CABINS   The cherry woods and jewel-tone fabrics in the cabins create a pleasant environment, and well over half of the cabins on each ship have private balconies. Inside cabins are a snug 160 square feet, while outside cabins are 175 square feet. All cabins have a stocked, pay-as-you-go minifridge, a hair dryer, a personal safe, and more than adequate storage space; all outside cabins have sitting areas with couches. The views from all category-4 cabins on Deck 4 are completely obstructed by lifeboats, and the category-6 balcony cabins directly above, on Deck 5, are partially obstructed as well. Bathrooms have good storage space.

The 32 Panorama Suites on Decks 5 and 6 are great for families, measuring 272 square feet with 90-square-foot balconies. They have attractive granite coffee tables and countertops, wooden chairs, and desks. Suites have large couches that can double as a bed, two separate floor-to-ceiling closets, lots of drawer space, and large bathrooms with whirlpool bathtubs, marble counters, and double sinks. Adjacent is a dressing room (on a recent *Atlantica* cruise with her family, coauthor Heidi loved hiding from her kids in it!) with a vanity table, drawers, and a closet. The Grand Suites are the largest accommodations aboard. Six are located amidships on Deck 7 and measure 372 square feet, plus 118-square-foot balconies; the other eight are aft on Decks 4, 6, 7, and 8 and measure 367 square feet, plus 282-square-foot balconies.

Both ships have new spa "wellness" cabins and suites that have direct access to the spa via elevator and stairs; perks include a personalized wellness consultation, three free spa treatments, two fitness or meditation classes, and cabin extras that range from special shower and air filters to a minibar stocked with healthy food and drinks.

Eight cabins are wheelchair accessible.

PUBLIC AREAS   *Atlantica*'s theme is taken from Fellini's movies with huge stills from his classics and blown-up paparazzi photos of stars. Each deck is named for a Fellini film—*La Dolce Vita, La Strada,* and so on—and the eighth deck is dubbed 8½. Playful fantasy permeates the ship, from the lipstick-red leather chairs to the suspended glass staircase connecting the two levels of Club Atlantica, the alternative restaurant/nightclub. *Mediterranea*'s decor is inspired by noble 17th- and 18th-century Italian *palazzi,* and it's heavy on dance and theater imagery. When you first lay eyes on the *Alice in Wonderland*–like fantasyland atrium, for instance, it's a bit jarring—all bright colors, glowing light panels, textured and sculpted metal surfaces, Roman-style ceiling murals, and fiber-optic squid swarming up eight decks. On both ships, warm wood tones, lots of art, and Italian marble everywhere create rooms that are über-rich and entertaining. These ships are destinations in and of themselves.

The discos are a darkish, two-story, cavelike space with video-screen walls, fog machines, and translucent dance floors. The three-level theater on each ship has velvety high-backed seating and very high-tech and elaborate stages. Downstairs, on the lowest passenger deck is a smaller show lounge used for late-night comedy acts, karaoke, and cocktail parties, but don't worry, you're still above the waterline (just barely). There's also a big glitzy casino with a festive Vegas-style mood, several large lounges that feature musical entertainment in the evenings, a smallish but pleasant library/Internet center, and a roomy, elegant card room. A kids' playroom, teen center, large video arcade, and chapel (these are not all alike) are all squirreled away in the bow on Decks 4 and 5.

DINING OPTIONS Aside from an elegant two-story dining room, there's a two-story alternative, reservations-only restaurant high up on Deck 10, charging guests $23 per person for the privilege of dining (suite guests can go free of charge once per cruise). With a quieter and more romantic mood, its atmosphere is its best feature, with dim lights, candlelight, fresh flowers, soft live music, and lots of space between tables (thought the vibrations from the funnel are distracting).

For casual breakfast, lunch, and dinner, head to the sprawling indoor/outdoor buffet restaurant. Soft ice cream and pizza made with herbs and fresh mozzarella are served from stations here. On a recent sailing, we were impressed by the variety of items at lunch, from a range of seafood to the beloved parmigiano cheese wheel and prosciutto ham (imported from Italy, of course), cold cuts and salami, daily hand-tossed pasta of the day, and cruise staples such as stir fries and burgers. The thin-crust pizza was delicious and featured toppings from salmon to Gorgonzola cheese.

One of *Atlantica*'s most delightful spaces is a faithful copy of Venice's Caffe Florian, a great choice for a glass of wine or a specialty coffee, complete with an old-world decor of dark red velvet upholstery and classical art (unfortunately, the *Mediterranea* does not have a Caffe Florian).

POOL, FITNESS, SPA & SPORTS FACILITIES The oceanview gym is a pleasant, two-tiered affair with machines on many different levels and a large hot tub in the center.

The spa provides your typical menu of treatments, including 50-minute massages, facials, and reflexology. There are three pools on each ship, two of them in the loud, active main pool area and another in the stern. Above the latter is a neat water slide for all ages. Other sports and relaxation amenities include four hot tubs, a golf driving net, and a combo volleyball, basketball, and tennis court. If you explore, you'll find lots of deck space for sunbathing and hiding away with a deck chair and a page turner.

5 Cunard

24303 Town Center Dr., Ste. 200, Valencia, CA 91355-0908. ℂ 800/7-CUNARD [728-6273]. www.cunard.com.

THE LINE IN A NUTSHELL The most venerable line in the cruise industry, Cunard is a classic, providing a link to the golden age of passenger ships. **Sails to:** Caribbean, New England/Canada, transatlantic (plus Europe, Africa, Asia, South America, world cruise).

THE EXPERIENCE The Cunard of today is not the Cunard of yesterday, but then again, it is. Formed in 1840 by Sir Samuel Cunard, the line provided the first regular steamship service between Europe and North America, and was one of the dominant players during the great years of steamship travel, which lasted roughly from 1905 to the mid-1960s. In 1969, long after it was clear that jet travel had replaced the liners, the company made what some considered a foolhardy move, launching *Queen Elizabeth 2* and setting her on a mixed schedule, half-crossing, half-cruising. Through sheer persistence, the ship proved the critics wrong, and thrived throughout 40 years of Cunard service, even if the company endured some rough times.

Today *QE2* has been retired from the Cunard fleet, departing in late 2008. Her replacement, the 151,400-ton *Queen Mary 2 (QM2)*, is as modern as ships get, and was bigger than all the others until Royal Caribbean's giant ships came along. *QM2* also pays homage to all that went before, designed with oversize grandeur and old-world formality in mind, and even a dose of blatant class structure: Some restaurants and outdoor decks are set aside specifically for suite guests only, if you please. Same story for the *Queen Victoria,* which is essentially a sister ship to the new *Queen Elizabeth*—both are in the 90,000-ton-plus category, carrying just over 2,000 passengers. And, unlike *QM2,* they can transit the Panama Canal. ***Note:*** *QE* was still being built at press time and will be fully reviewed in future editions.

Pros

- **Classic ambience:** Despite a few chintzy touches, these ships—especially *QM2*—are as close as you'll get to a 1940s liner.
- **Pure prestige:** There used to be ships that everyone in the world knew—"Oh, you're sailing on the *Queen Mary,*" they'd say. "That's the ship Marlene Dietrich took on her last crossing." *QM2* and her newer sisters are the only ships launched in more than a quarter-century with that kind of broad public cachet.
- **Special experiences:** Dancing in the bustling ballroom on formal evenings, dozing in one of the hundreds of teak deck chairs on the Promenade, or watching the ship's hull slice through Atlantic swells are intangible though immensely pleasurable experiences.

Cons

- **Not *quite* luxe:** Despite their grandeur, the Cunard dames carry too many passengers to provide the kind of intimacy and personal feel you get on the other luxe lines—especially those operating small ships (Silversea, SeaDream, and Seabourn), but also on the larger vessels such as *Crystal Serenity* and Regent's larger ships.

Compared with the other mainstream lines, here's how Cunard rates:

	Poor	Fair	Good	Excellent	Outstanding
Enjoyment Factor					✓
Dining				✓	
Activities					✓
Children's Program					✓
Entertainment				✓	
Service				✓	
Worth the Money					✓

CUNARD: GETTING THERE IS HALF THE FUN

Once upon a time, Cunard ruled the waves. Its ships—first *Mauretania* and *Lusitania,* later *Queen Mary* and *Queen Elizabeth*—were the fastest and most reliable at sea. Then somebody invented the jet airliner and the whole passenger-shipping business went to hell. Numbers dropped. Ships went cruising for their bread. Cunard stuck to its guns, though, keeping *QE2* on the Atlantic until sheer doggedness gave her a certain cachet as the last of the old breed. Fleetmates came and went, including the little *Sea Goddess* yachts (now with SeaDream) and a number of midsize ships acquired from other lines, but *QE2* soldiered on and managed to carry the company, and its reputation, through some rough times.

An almost 3-decade-long period of corporate troubles and shuffling ownership ended in April 1998, when Carnival Corporation acquired Cunard from the Norwegian company Kvaerner Group. To some it seemed a comedown for the venerable line, but Commodore Ronald Warwick and other Cunard employees saw it as an unqualified boon. "To my mind," Warwick told a group of journalists, "Carnival Corporation were the white knights that saved us from demise, and when the planning of the *Queen Mary 2* was announced, I experienced a feeling of pleasure and relief."

Today, Cunard is again very famous indeed after all the media attention that accompanied *QM2*'s launch in 2004, but it's hardly the old British brand that its advertising might lead you to believe. In late 2004, for instance, the company was swallowed whole by Carnival Corporation subsidiary Princess Cruises. Its operations and staff were absorbed into Princess's at the latter's suburban Los Angeles headquarters, which meant crewmembers and officers would be rotated between the two lines—a move considered blasphemous by many hard-core Cunard fans—but frankly, something that the average passenger won't realize or even mind.

Cunard's newest liner, the *Queen Victoria,* debuted in December 2007 and a third fleetmate, the new *Queen Elizabeth* was set to debut in mid-2010 just before this book went to press. (The *QE2* was retired in 2008.)

PASSENGER PROFILE

In general, Cunard attracts a well-traveled crowd of passengers mostly in their 50s and up, many of them repeaters who appreciate the line's old-timey virtues and are more the 4-o'clock-tea crowd than the hot-tub-and-umbrella-drink set. That said, the hoopla that surrounded, and still surrounds, the *QM2* (and to a lesser degree the *QV* and *QE*) is attracting a much wider demographic, especially on summer Atlantic crossings when families travel together and about 50% of passengers might be from the U.S. British passengers make up the next largest percentage, and usually several hundred passengers hail from various other nations, making Cunard one of the few truly international cruise lines.

DINING

TRADITIONAL   Cunard is the last bastion of the old steamship tradition of segregating passengers according to category of accommodations, though for the most part, the practice is limited to dining hours. This means that passengers are assigned to one of the three reserved-seating restaurants according to the level of cabin accommodations they've booked: Suite-and-above passengers dine in the **Queen's Grill;** passengers in the next levels of accommodations dine in the **Princess Grill;** and everyone else dines in the **Brittania Restaurant**—decor-wise, the most beautiful of the three and a fitting heir to the grand restaurants of the past. The two Grills are always single seating at an assigned table, while the Britannia has early and late seatings for dinner and open seating for breakfast and lunch.

To make matters a bit more confusing, in spring 2007 aboard the *QM2*, Cunard introduced the **Britannia Club,** an intimate section of the Britannia Restaurant seating around 100 passengers who are booked in the deluxe balcony cabins. Thanks to the Club's single-seating dining, and more table-side preparation and enhanced menu choices, those dining here won't have to pay the significant fare hike to dine in the Grills, while still having a more personalized and leisurely dining experience. Overall, the ships' cuisine sticks close to tradition, with entrees that might include pheasant with southern haggis and port-wine sauce, roasted prime rib, grilled lobster with garden pea risotto, and scallion wild-rice crepes with mushroom filling and red-pepper sauce. On our recent Cunard cruises, food and service were very good, roughly on par with what you might experience in the main dining rooms of the Celebrity ships. The Grill restaurants also allow the option of requesting whatever dish comes into your head—if they have the ingredients aboard, someone in the galley will whip it up for you (caviar is available on request). Otherwise, it's the intimacy and cachet of the Grill restaurants that set them apart more than the food does, as many of the same dishes are served in the Britannia as well. At all three restaurants, **special diets** can be accommodated, and **vegetarian** dishes and health-conscious **Canyon Ranch SpaClub dishes** are available as a matter of course.

SPECIALTY   Both *QM2* and *QV* have a **Todd English restaurant,** a small Mediterranean dining spot that echoes the original *Queen Mary's* Verandah Grill, one of that ship's most legendary spaces. Created by celebrity chef Todd English, the restaurant serves elaborate and often very rich lunches ($20 per person) and dinners ($30 per person), with some truly amazing desserts. On coauthor Heidi's *QM2* crossing, she enjoyed her best meal at Todd English.

One deck down on the *QM2*, adjacent to the buffet restaurant, is the contemporary **Chef's Galley,** which serves only two dozen guests (no cover charge) who get to watch the chef prepare their meal via an open galley and several large monitor screens. Just don't expect to be dazzled by the decor—it's minimalist.

CASUAL   Almost a third of *QM2's* Deck 7 is given over to the massive **King's Court,** a large buffet restaurant that stretches out for nearly half a deck along both sides of the ship. The somewhat overwhelming cluster of food stations runs down the center of the area, with many small, cozy areas along the sides; there is no outdoor seating. At night, the space is partitioned off into three separate casual restaurants for round-the-clock noshing: the **Carvery,** serving carved beef, pork, lamb, and poultry, along with gourmet English favorites; **La Piazza,** serving pizza, pasta, and other Italian specialties; and **Lotus,** a Pan-Asian restaurant blending Chinese, Japanese, Thai, and Indian influences. All are free, but reservations are recommended at dinner. The causal restaurant on *QV* is fittingly smaller and has a more typical location, up on Deck 11. Though its food items are not as extensive as *QM2's*, the *QV's* buffet venue is way more expansive than the industry's usual "lido" cafe.

SNACKS & EXTRAS   On both ships, the **Golden Lion Pub** serves English pub grub, while *w-a-a-a-ay* up on *QM2's* Deck 12, you can get standard burgers and hot dogs at the outdoor **Boardwalk Café,** weather permitting. Traditional **afternoon tea,**

usually accompanied by a string quartet, is served in the **Queen's Room,** the most classic, traditional space aboard both ships. The selection of more than 20 teas includes Darjeeling, jasmine, and Japanese green tea. The elegant room hearkens back to the dramatic ballrooms of yesteryear, with a high arched ceiling and crystal chandeliers. **Room service** is available 24 hours a day.

ACTIVITIES

As you would expect, Cunard ships have a more distinguished variety of activities than most other big liners, especially its Fun Ship cousins at Carnival. Rather than "woo-hoo" good times, Cunard concentrates on **learning experiences** and **the arts,** with a healthy dollop of pampering to keep things light.

Central to the onboard experience is *Cunard Insights,* the line's lecture program: Instructors, celebrities, and other learned authors and super-accomplished authorities present talks on literature, political history, marine science, ocean-liner history, music and pop culture, modern art, Shakespeare on film, architectural history, cooking, computer applications, languages, and many other topics. On crossings, there are so many worthwhile lectures that you may find yourself sitting in the theater all morning long. Cunard has even managed to attract a handful of stars, with Uma Thurman, Rod Stewart, Lenny Kravitz, Richard Dreyfuss, John Cleese, and others having sailed, and some lectured, in the last few years. On our last crossing, we had no problem filling up the 5 days at sea with "highbrow" things to do.

QM2 passengers who prefer book learning can take advantage of the largest and by far the most impressive **library** at sea: a huge, beautifully designed space that actually looks like a library, unlike the typical rooms-with-a-few-bookshelves on most megaships. Next door on *QM2,* a **bookshop** sells volumes on passenger-ship history, as well as Cunard memorabilia. The library on *QV* is smaller, but still carries an impressive 6,000 books and is staffed by two librarians. Other shops aboard the ships sell everything from high-end Hermès to low-end souvenirs and jewelry, some of it sold in a rather undignified way from long tables set up in the public corridors. Continuing the marine history topic, both ships offer museum-quality memorabilia from Cunard's 170-year-history. It's called **Maritime Quest** on the *QM2* and it's a history trail with a timeline set up in various places throughout the ship; on *QV,* it's called **Cunardia,** and it's more like a mini-museum exhibiting Cunard artifacts and vintage souvenirs.

A visit to *QM2*'s attractive **Canyon Ranch SpaClub** is another popular activity. The pleasant decor combines nautical undertones with a modern minimalist motif to create a most relaxing space that includes a thermal suite, a salon with wonderful ocean views, and more than 20 treatment rooms clustered around a coed thalassotherapy pool and hot tub reserved for spa-goers. The spa is a refreshing break from the Steiner-run spas on most ships; it offers some truly different therapies—for example, the Ashiatus massage incorporates the therapist's feet—and far less of Steiner's pushiness to sell skin-care products. The *QM2*'s gym, which wraps around the bow on Deck 7, is surprisingly small and uninspired for a ship this large and well conceived, but it does what it needs to do and has treadmills and stationary bikes with flatscreen TV monitors. Classes include Pilates and yoga. On *QV,* the **Cunard Royal Health Club** has all of the usual spa, salon, and gym facilities, but perhaps the most enjoyable and unusual is the Turkish Rasul chamber for a traditional hammam steam/mud bath.

Aside from all these interesting options, you'll find a number of less cerebral pursuits as well, from wine tastings to art auctions to scarf-tying seminars.

CHILDREN'S PROGRAM

A Cunard cruise is more than high tea and stiff upper lips. Finger paints and cartoons are just as much a part of the ship's activities as ballroom dancing and quoits. Though you might not expect it from a grand liner that (one imagines) is filled with sophisticated seniors, QM2 especially has great digs for kids; the QV also has a decent kids' program, though not quite as impressive as the QM2's. Called the **Zone** on both ships, it's open to kids ages 1 and up—an extraordinarily young minimum age shared only by Disney's ships. (Most ships with kids' programming welcome kids ages 3 and up, a few ages 2 and up.) The ages 1-to-6 set occupies half of a bright, cheery, and roomy area with lots of toys, arts and crafts, a play gym and ball pit, and big-screen TVs (and the staff do change diapers). On the QM2, there's also a separate **nursery** with 10 crib/toddler-bed combos for napping tots. Bring a stroller if your kids are young: Remember, the QM2 is really long, so getting from one end of a deck to the other is a hike.

Both ships also have an outdoor play area just outside the playroom, along with a wading pool and a regular pool. The other half of the play area is reserved for kids ages 7 to 17, with the ages 7-to-12 crowd usually occupying a play area with beanbag chairs, lots of board games, TVs, and a number of Xbox video-game systems. **Activities for teens**—including ship tours, movies and production shows in the theaters, and pizza parties—are usually held elsewhere.

The kids' program is staffed by certified British nannies, plus a handful of other qualified activity counselors. The best part? Aside from 2 hours at lunchtime and an hour or two in the afternoon, the playrooms provide complimentary supervised activities and care from 9am to midnight, so you have ample time to enjoy adult company and know that your offspring are being well cared for (on other lines, you must generally pay an hourly fee after 10pm). On Queen Mary 2, you can take your kids to eat earlier in the Chef's Galley, a special section of the King's Court buffet-style restaurant, reserved for a **children's tea** daily from 5 to 6pm (of course, it's not really tea that's served, but the standard kiddie favorites of pasta, chicken fingers, and the like).

Though the ships' kids' program is awesome, there are rarely more than 250 kids aboard any given sailing and usually fewer (compared to the 800–1,200 kids and teens typically aboard similar-size ships). This is a plus: Fewer kids means more attention and space for the ones who are there. Keep in mind, though, if a sailing is especially full, the counselors reserve the right to limit participation and will ask parents to choose either the morning or the afternoon session; everyone can be accommodated during evenings.

On top of everything else, the ships have impressive medical centers, which came in handy when Heidi's son got an ear infection on a QM2 crossing.

ENTERTAINMENT

Entertainment runs the gamut from plays featuring graduates of Britain's Royal Academy of Dramatic Art (RADA) to some pretty run-of-the-mill song-and-dance revues. The former perform generally from April to November as part of a partnership between Cunard and the school, with RADA graduates and students also giving a variety of readings and workshops, including acting classes. Besides **theater,** a wide variety of **music** is heard throughout the ships' many lounges, from string quartets and harpists to jazz groups and high-toned dance music in the gorgeous **Queen's Ballroom** (with gentleman hosts on hand to partner with single ladies). Both ships have a disco and a casino, which are more Monte Carlo than Vegas, with refined art and furnishings rather than the usual clangor of an arcade. Aboard the QV, there's an

Preview: *Queen Elizabeth*

The 92,000-ton, 2,092-passenger *Queen Elizabeth* is the second-largest ship Cunard has ever built, just slightly larger than *Queen Victoria* but essentially her sister. The first *Queen Elizabeth,* which sailed from 1940 to 1968, was one of Cunard's greatest ships, and the legendary *Queen Elizabeth 2* was no slacker either, so it follows that Cunard has designed the new one to reflect a similar traditional grandeur, decor, and style, but with a modern take on dining, entertainment, and activities. The QE's exterior will boast the classic black-and-red livery that differentiates a Cunard liner from a modern-day cruise ship, while inside, grand and elegant double- and triple-height public rooms with an Art Deco flavor will be outfitted with rich wood paneling, intricate mosaics, hand-woven carpets, and gleaming chandeliers. As the namesake of her two illustrious ancestors, she'll also have a permanent exhibit of photography, memorabilia, and exhibits about Cunard's storied maritime history and royal connections.

Though positioned as an ocean liner, the *QE,* like *QM2* and *Queen Victoria,* will do regular cruise itineraries as well as ocean crossings.

---

unusual show lounge arrangement where the best box seats can be reserved in advance for special performances and are first-come, first-seated for other shows.

Whereas most ships have one theater, *QM2*'s **lecture program** is so busy that there are two. As the secondary theater, **Illuminations** is smaller than the **Royal Court Theatre,** but is probably the most used room on the ship. It serves triple duty as a lecture hall, a movie theater, and also the world's only oceangoing planetarium that shows 3-D films, some of them created in conjunction with noted institutions such as the American Museum of Natural History and the Smithsonian's National Air and Space Museum.

See the ship reviews below for a discussion of the ships' other theaters and lounges.

SERVICE

With their classy uniforms and cordial, gracious efficiency, crewmembers exhibit a polished sort of British demeanor—even when they're actually from the Philippines. That said, they do their share of rushing around and keeping up, just as aboard all the other huge cruise ships today.

The line's automatic gratuity policy adds a fee of $11 per person, per day to the accounts of guests in standard cabins, and $13 per day for suite guests.

Queen Victoria

The Verdict

The *Queen Victoria* is far more than a smaller version of the *Queen Mary 2.* The classy *QV* has her own style, personality, and decor while maintaining much of the line's heritage.

Queen Victoria *(photo: Cunard)*

Specifications

Typical Per Diems: $175–$230

Size (in tons)	90,049	Crew	900
Passengers (double occ.)	2014	Passenger/Crew Ratio	2.2 to 1
Passenger/Space Ratio	45	Year Launched	2007
Total Cabins/Veranda Cabins	1007/591	Last Major Upgrade	N/A

Frommer's Ratings (Scale of 1–5)

★★★★★

Cabin Comfort & Amenities	4	Dining Options	4
Ship Cleanliness & Maintenance	5	Gym, Spa & Sports Facilities	4.5
Public Comfort/Space	5	Children's Facilities	3
Decor	5	Enjoyment Factor	4.5

Sailing Regions, Seasons & Home Ports

Queen Elizabeth	New England/Canada, from New York (fall).

Queen Victoria has traditional Cunard style, with the line's classic black-and-red hull on the outside and grand public spaces on the inside. At 90,049 gross tons, she was the second-largest Cunard ship ever (until the new and slightly bigger *QE* comes along, that is). Since she was built to cater to both the North American and British markets, there is lots of British flavor on board—from the pub to the lovely Chart Room and class structure of the cabins—though still, the official currency on board is the U.S. dollar.

A sleek, smooth-running modern ship that hasn't lost sight of her line's history, *Queen Victory* has many of Cunard's signature elements along with some very new ones. Fans of class division appreciate that the Queens Grill and Princess Grill diners have an exclusive centralized lounge for their use only (the *QM2* has two separate lounges for each of the Grills, on the *QV* they're combined), plus outside dining and sunning areas reserved only for Grill-class guests. The *QV*'s spa is not the huge grandiose area that *QM2* has; it feels more casual yet it has all sorts of treatment rooms. And this seems to be a trend as one navigates through all of the different public areas. There are no over-the-top huge spaces (or "wow" features such as *QM2*'s planetarium), which makes the ship feel relatively cozy throughout. Still, *QV* looks and feels like a very modern ocean liner.

CABINS   As might be expected on a ship that has a definite class structure, there is quite a range of accommodations, all of which are sleek and contemporary with some traditional touches. In fact, the non-Grill-class cabins are much nicer than they are on *QM2*. The inside rooms range from 152 to 207 square feet (try and get one of the bigger ones if you can, even if there's a slight increase in price) and all come with two beds (twin or combinable to a queen) and a shower; there are no single rooms. Outside rooms range from 180 to 197 square feet for those without balconies; rooms with balconies are all 249 square feet. There are 20 different categories of inside and outside rooms (not including suites and penthouses) spread out over five different decks, and all of them have TVs with multilanguage films and music channels, a refrigerator, safe, hair dryer, bathrobe, slippers, nightly turndown service, 24-hour room service, a daily shipboard paper, American and British electrical outlets, a direct-dial telephone, and a dataport outlet. There's also a half-bottle of sparkling wine upon embarkation for everyone (class be gone!).

As for the suites and penthouses, there are 11 different categories (127 rooms in all), with the four categories of Princess Suites all running 367 square feet including their balconies (the difference is only in the cruise fare and it's based on location/deck). Other amenities include upgraded linens, bathrobes and toiletries, plus there's a pillow menu, concierge service, shoe shine service, a separate bath and shower, a larger sitting area, and a full bottle of sparkling wine upon embarkation. Higher up on the accommodations spectrum are the seven categories of Queen's Grill Suites and Penthouses, ranging from 536 to 2,097 square feet, including their balconies. A higher level of amenities includes complimentary canapés, a fruit basket and bud vase, butler service, and sugar-iced strawberries to go along with a bottle of champagne upon embarkation. There are 20 wheelchair-accessible cabins total in various categories.

PUBLIC AREAS   There's a lot happening on Deck 2, where you'll find the first level of the extremely attractive Britannia Restaurant (where most guests are assigned their dining tables), as well as a series of bars all along one side of the ship: Chart Room, Café Carinthia, Midships Lounge, Champagne Bar, and the Golden Lion Pub. Each of the bars has its own personality, ranging from the nautical decor of the Chart Room to the pubby feel of the Golden Lion, especially great in daytime for casual pub food and nighttime for the lively piano player (and convenient access to the casino across the hall). There's also the Queen's Room ballroom with its gorgeous, 1,000-square-foot inlaid wood floor for dancing to a live orchestra (it's also the home of the Royal Nights–themed balls). Deck 2 also harbors the lower level of the library and the eponymous Todd English restaurant (available to all guests for lunch and dinner, but not as stunning as the version on *QM2*). Deck 3 has the upper level of the main restaurant, the many shopping areas, the Cunardia Museum (great to spend some time reading the quotes and history and enjoying the historical photos), and the upper level of the impressive library. Also on Deck 3 is access to the upper level of the theater with its 15 private boxes and lounge area; there's a charge for the boxes for special performances, but no charge for regular ones. While the sight lines to the stage are fine from all of the boxes, the ones more centrally located are by far the best.

The upper set of public decks, running from Decks 9 to 12, includes the forward-facing Cunard Royal Spa and Fitness Centre. Midships on Deck 10 is the indoor/outdoor space for kids, with separate spots for teens and younger kids. At the forward end of Deck 10 is the lovely Commodore Club lounge, probably the best place for that relaxing drink in the evening or quiet time during the day, and the 270-degree view Hemispheres, which by night becomes the disco. Adjacent is the cigar bar; it's named after Churchill, of course. Up above on Decks 11 and 12 are the exclusive areas for Grill-class guests: sunning/lounging areas with really nice cushions on the loungers, the Tuscan-themed courtyards, and a Grill Lounge serving both Grill restaurants. For anyone lost, a sign in the stairwell and restricted elevator access keep non-Grill guests at bay in these areas.

DINING OPTIONS   All guests are assigned a table in one of three restaurants: the gorgeous, two-level Britannia Restaurant (which is actually nicer looking than the Grill-class restaurants) for all non-Grill guests or, for Grill guests, either the Queens or Princess Grill depending on one's cabin category. There are two seatings for dinner in the Britannia Restaurant and it's single seating in the Grill Restaurants. Guests in the latter may also have the occasion to dine alfresco in the Tuscan-styled courtyard. One outstanding feature of the Britannia Restaurant, either upper or lower level, is the space between the tables. There's plenty of room for spreading out and to allow the waitstaff to comfortably serve all guests. Colors are muted with lots of golds and beiges and such. The Grill restaurants are shaped with a curve along the window side, allowing for even better views. Visually, there's little difference between the Grill classes (leather instead of fabric seats for the banquettes being an example).

The most casual of restaurants aboard *Queen Victoria* is the Lido Café; it's mostly buffet style with some custom-made areas for breakfast and lunch (it's open 24 hr. with dinner and late-night buffets). Other dining outlets available to all guests include the outstanding Todd English restaurant (English, by the way, is actually an American), $20 for lunch and $30 for dinner; the Golden Lion Pub; Lido Grill (casual poolside fare); and Café Carinthia, one of the bars on Deck 2, open for morning coffees and pastries.

POOL, FITNESS, SPA & SPORTS FACILITIES   Pools are located both midships and at the aft end of Deck 9, with two whirlpools adjacent to each. Though the main pool area isn't huge, at one end is the attractive Winter Garden, with its rattan furniture, ceiling fans, central fountain, movable glass wall, and sliding roof. The spa and fitness center, at the forward end of Deck 9, is terrific and there's even a 40-page guide describing the extensive services. There are facials, oxygen treatments, "aromasoul" massages and scrubs, all sorts of other massages, the regular nail and hair services, a Pilates institute, something described as "Kerastase style spa" (the Kerastase ambassador is apparently a highly educated scalp and hair professional), and a whole lot more. The gym sports 15 treadmills and dozens of other pieces of workout equipment and plenty of free weights. In addition, guests can stay fit by walking and jogging on several different decks, play paddle tennis or quoits (that quintessentially British game), and practice their golf swing.

Queen Mary 2

Queen Mary 2 *(photo: Cunard)*

The Verdict

QM2 is literally in a class by herself: a modern reinterpretation of the golden age luxury liner that's built to sail hard seas well into the 21st century. Though she's lost her place as the world's largest ship, she's an enormous vessel with a huge amount of elbowroom for everyone on board.

Specifications   Typical Per Diems: $135–$165

Size (in tons)	151,400	Crew	1,253
Passengers (double occ.)	2,592	Passenger/Crew Ratio	2.1 to 1
Passenger/Space Ratio	58.4	Year Launched	2004
Total Cabins/Veranda Cabins	1,296/783	Last Major Upgrade	2008

Frommer's Ratings (Scale of 1–5)

✦✦✦✦

Cabin Comfort & Amenities	4	Dining Options	4.5
Appearance & Upkeep	5	Gym, Spa & Sports Facilities	4.5
Public Comfort/Space	5	Children's Facilities	5
Decor	4.5	Enjoyment Factor	5

Sailing Regions, Seasons & Home Ports

Queen Mary 2	**Transatlantic,** from New York (spring, summer, fall). **New England/Canada,** from New York (fall). **Caribbean,** from New York (winter).

Before her launch, we often heard *QM2* referred to by industry types as "Micky's White Elephant"—Micky being Micky Arison, chairman of Carnival Corporation; the criticism referred to the fact that *QM2*'s design and construction sucked up about $1 billion and 5 years of labor, a record expenditure to match her record-breaking size.

But that was before her launch. That was before the Queen of England did the honors at the naming ceremony. That was before the fireworks and traffic jams that attended her first arrival into every port, and amazingly enough, still continue to this day in many ports. When all is said and done, *QM2* is a really remarkable ship: classic yet contemporary, refined yet fun, huge yet homey, and grand, grand, grand. The longest passenger ship at sea (when Royal Caribbean's *Freedom of the Seas* was launched in spring 2006, she snatched the title as biggest in terms of tonnage), she's also the only real ocean liner built since her older sister hit the water in 1969.

As a modern-day ocean liner, the *QM2* had a hull that had to be more knife-prowed than a normal cruise ship's, due to the need for speed. The need for strength meant her steel plating had to be uncommonly thick and her skeleton unusually dense and superreinforced. The need to battle high waves meant her superstructure had to be set much farther back on her hull than is common on today's cruise ships. The list goes on and on.

Inside, *QM2* is laid out in such a way that, even after a weeklong crossing, you might still find new places to explore on board. And it's very unlikely you'll feel hemmed in or claustrophobic, as Heidi feared before she made her first crossing. She never once felt antsy in the spacious and gracious ship, and, in fact, wished the crossing were a few days longer! Our favorite rooms? The Queen's Room ballroom on formal night; the classic Chart Room for drinks before dinner; the forward-facing Commodore Club with its clubby atmosphere; and the forward observation deck on Deck 11, just below the bridge—probably the best spot aboard when sailing out of New York harbor. Throughout, artwork functions both as decoration and for mood enhancement, with iconography that recalls the ocean liner's golden age. The most evocative art of all, though, may be a sound: Way up on *QM2*'s funnel, on the starboard side, is one of the original Tyfon steam whistles from the first *Queen Mary*—the same whistle that sounded when the *Mary* made her first crossing in 1936, now on permanent loan from the city of Long Beach, California.

In reality, *QM2* is really two ships in one. The top categories, the Grill classes, are very luxurious and come with their own dining rooms, lounge, and private deck space. Guests in these categories also enjoy all of the rest of the ship along with everyone else booked in non-Grill class accommodations. For the purposes of the ratings in this guide, they are based on the largest part of the ship, the non-Grill categories. It is very safe to presume that the accommodations and dining ratings for the Grill classes would be higher.

And, let's be realistic: Without *QM2,* it's doubtful Royal Caribbean would have spawned *Oasis of the Seas,* in the corporate battle of "can you top this."

CABINS   All of *QM2*'s cabins, from the smallest inside to the largest outside, are decorated in a smooth, contemporary style, with light-blond woods, simple lines, and a clean, uncluttered look. They range from 162-square-foot inside cabins; to roomy, 194-square-foot outside cabins with portholes, minifridges, and large showers; to the truly over-the-top Grand Duplex Suites. Each of the latter is 1,500 to 2,200 square feet and has views of the stern through two-story walls of glass. Our coauthor Heidi is living proof that a family of four can do fine in a standard cabin without a balcony (there are no standard balcony cabins that accommodate families of four), but if you've got a larger budget, the Junior Suites (aka Princess Grill suites) are ideal. They're almost twice as big as a standard and have a huge bathroom with tub, a walk-in closet, sitting area, and an oversize balcony. Even standard inside and outside cabins, though by no means huge, have a simple elegance and a nice helping of amenities, including robes and slippers, a fridge, safe, dataport, and TV with e-mail capability. The vast majority of cabins are outside ones with balconies, but to ensure they stay dry in even the roughest seas, many of them are recessed back into the hull with steel bulkheads that block ocean views when seated. All Queens Grill and Princess Grill suites feature Frette linens, dedicated concierge service, a full bottle of champagne or sparkling wine on embarkation, and access to the Queens Grill Lounge and a large private deck overlooking the stern (which is actually also open to Princess Grill guests as well, despite the signage). Queens Grill Suites also get fully stocked bars, daily canapés, flatscreen TVs, and personalized stationery.

There are 30 wheelchair-accessible cabins total in various cabin grades.

PUBLIC AREAS   Because *QM2* was designed for comfortable sailing in rough seas, most of the public areas are clustered unusually low, down on Decks 2 and 3. At midships, the relatively restrained (except what's with those jarring white pillars?) Grand Lobby atrium opens onto two central promenades, decorated with huge Art Deco wall panels. Some are stunning and recall decorated glass panels from the opulent liner *Normandie,* while others are a bit chintzy (they look like they're plastic) and miss the mark.

Getting beyond that one flaw, Deck 2's promenade leads down to the elegant Empire Casino and the too-big-to-be-cozy Golden Lion pub. Up one deck, the very attractive Veuve Clicquot Champagne Bar (serving a variety of champagnes, as well as caviar and foie gras) is decorated with slightly abstracted images of mid-20th-century movie stars and leads into one of the most beautiful rooms on board: the Chart Room, a high-ceilinged space with green-glass deco maps on one wall and the feel of a great ocean liner. You expect David Niven to come strolling through any minute. By day, both of these rooms are popular hangouts for book readers, letter writers, and daydreamers. Across, on the ship's port side, Sir Samuel's Wine Bar serves coffee, sandwiches, and cakes in the morning and afternoon. Forward, the Royal Court Theatre is a two-deck grand showroom and the principal theatrical venue on board, seconded by the striking Illuminations planetarium farther forward.

In the stern on Deck 3, the Queen's Room ballroom perfectly captures the essence of Cunard style, running the full width of the ship and boasting a high arched ceiling, the largest ballroom dance floor at sea, crystal chandeliers, and a truly royal quality.

The G32 nightclub, almost hidden behind silver doors at the head of the Queen's Room, is decorated in industrial style to match its name—"G32" was the number by which *QM2*'s hull was known at the shipyard, before Cunard decided what she would be called.

Other notable spaces include the Winter Garden on Deck 7, designed to provide an outdoor garden feel on long transatlantic crossings, which somehow misses the mark; and the Commodore Club bar/observation lounge on Deck 9, with its wonderful white-leather chairs, dramatic bow views, and attached Churchill's cigar room. There's also a card room hidden away on Deck 11, just behind the Observation Deck, as well as the remarkable library and bookshop forward on Deck 8 (see "Activities," above).

DINING OPTIONS   Decor-wise, the Queens Grill and Princess Grill restaurants that serve suite passengers exclusively are the very models of restrained good taste, with a series of elegant blown-glass vases as their one bold touch. The Britannia Restaurant, on the other hand, is a large dramatic space, intended to recall *Queen Mary*'s magnificent first-class restaurant and featuring a vaulted, Tiffany-style glass ceiling, a curved balcony that echoes the shape of the *QM*'s famous bridge, candlelit tables, soaring pillars, and the largest art tapestry at sea, depicting a liner against the New York skyline. Although it's large, the space is exceedingly glamorous, and designed to feel grand but not overwhelming. The new Britannia Club area has literally been carved out of a corner of the restaurant, but misses out on the full dramatic height of the room. Still, the 100-seat area succeeds in providing an exclusive, old-world dining experience, just as the suite guests have in the Grill restaurants. All guests can dine in the cozy and elegant Todd English restaurant for a $30 cover charge for dinner (it's $20 at lunch). King's Court is the ship's casual buffet option, and it becomes separate (complimentary) specialty restaurants each evening.

See "Dining," p. 142, for more details on the ship's dining experience.

POOL FITNESS, SPA & SPORTS FACILITIES   The Canyon Ranch Spa is a two-story complex occupying some 20,000 square feet. At the center of its treatment rooms is a coed 15×30-foot aqua-therapy pool whose relaxation gizmos include airbed recliner lounges, neck fountains, a deluge waterfall, an air tub, and body-massage jet benches. There's a hot tub adjacent, and nearby is a thermal suite composed of aromatic steam rooms and an herbal sauna. A salon occupies the top level of the complex, affording tremendous views from its lofty perch. The gym, one deck down, is sort of drab and chopped up, but is perfectly well equipped to make people sweat, with free weights and the latest digitally enhanced climbers, steppers, runners, and rowers.

A more classic exercise is a walk or jog around the wide outdoor Promenade Deck, which encircles the *l-o-o-o-o-o-ong* ship on Deck 7 and allows for beautiful sea views; three times around equals 1 mile. For some shoulder work, there's a pair of golf simulators adjacent to the covered pool solarium on Deck 12. Other dips include a splash pool and hot tubs way up on Deck 13, and several in the tiered stern, including a wading pool, family pool, and play fountain on Deck 6, outside of the children's playrooms. Rounding out the sports options are Ping-Pong, an outdoor golf driving net, basketball, quoits, a paddle-tennis court, and, of course, shuffleboard—this is a transatlantic liner, after all.

6 Disney Cruise Line

P.O. Box 10210, Lake Buena Vista, FL 32830. © **800/951-3532** or 888/325-2500. Fax 407/566-3541. www.disney cruise.com.

THE LINE IN A NUTSHELL   Hands down, Disney is at the top of the heap when it comes to family fun, and its cruises overall are among the very best in the mainstream category in terms of service, cabins, entertainment, and food. Though Royal Caribbean, Carnival, Celebrity, NCL, and Princess all devote significant attention to kids, it took Disney to create vessels in which both kids and adults are really catered to equally, and with style and elegance. If you love Disney, you'll love these two floating theme parks. **Sails to:** Caribbean, The Bahamas, Mexican Riviera, Alaska, and Europe.

THE EXPERIENCE   Both classic and ultramodern, the line's ships are like no others in the industry, designed to evoke the grand transatlantic liners but also boasting a handful of truly innovative, always-improving features. These include extralarge cabins for families, several restaurants through which passengers rotate on every cruise, fantastic Disney-inspired entertainment, separate adult pools and lounges, and the biggest kids' facilities at sea. In many ways, the experience is more Disney than it is cruise (for instance, there's no casino); but on the other hand, the ships are surprisingly elegant and well laid out, with the Disney-isms sprinkled around subtly, like fairy dust, amid the Art Deco and Art Nouveau design motifs. Head to toe, inside and out, they're a class act.

Disney is nothing if not organized, so its 3- and 4-night cruises are designed to be combined with a Disney theme park and hotel package to create a weeklong land/sea vacation. You can also book these shorter cruises (as well as longer cruises) separately.

Pros

- **Kids' program:** In both the size of the facilities and range of activities, it's the most extensive at sea.
- **Entertainment:** The line's family-oriented musicals are some of the best onboard entertainment today.
- **Family-style cabins:** All have sofa beds to sleep families of at least three, and the majority have one and a half bathrooms.
- **Innovative dining:** No other ships have diners rotating among three different but equally appealing sit-down restaurants.

Cons

- **No casinos:** If you're a gambler, you're out of luck.
- **Packed pools:** Though there are three pools on the *Wonder* and *Magic*, they're packed like sardine cans on sunny days, especially the kids' pools.
- **Expensive:** Compared to peers Royal Caribbean, Celebrity, Carnival, and Princess, Disney cruises tend to run a few hundred dollars more.

DISNEY: THE OLD MOUSE & THE SEA

For at least half a century now, Disney has been in the business of merging modern-day expectations and cutting-edge technology with a nostalgic sense of American culture: for childhood innocence, for the frontier, for an idealized turn-of-the-20th-century past, for our mythic heroes. And whether you're a fan or a critic, it's indisputable that at this point the company itself has become a part of our culture. There are probably few people alive—and certainly few Americans—who could fail to recognize Disney's

Compared with the other mainstream lines, here's how Disney rates:

	Poor	Fair	Good	Excellent	Outstanding
Enjoyment Factor				✓	
Dining			✓		
Activities			✓		
Children's Program					✓
Entertainment					✓
Service			✓		
Worth the Money				✓	

more high-profile creations: Mickey, Donald Duck, Sleeping Beauty, "When You Wish Upon a Star." They've become part of our national identity. And that's why *Disney Magic* and *Disney Wonder,* and new *Dream* and *Fantasy* work so well. In nearly every aspect of the onboard experience, they have what most other ships lack: a cultural frame of reference that's recognized by almost everyone.

Though 7- to 14-night cruise itineraries are available in the Caribbean, Mexico, Alaska, and Europe, many Disney passengers purchase their cruises as part of 7-night seamless land/sea packages that combine 3- or 4-night cruises out of Florida with 4- or 3-night pre-cruise park stays. Disney buses shuttle passengers between Orlando and the ship—about an hour's drive, during which an orientation video imparts some info about the cruise experience. At Disney's swank cruise terminal at Port Canaveral, check-in is usually made easier and faster because guests who have come from the resorts already have their all-purpose, computerized Key to the World cards, which identify them at boarding, get them into their cabins, and serve as their onboard charge cards. (If you're doing just the cruise, you get your Key to the World card when you arrive at the terminal.) You don't have to worry about your luggage, either: It's picked up at the resort and delivered to your cabin soon after you board.

PASSENGER PROFILE

Disney's ships attract a wide mix of passengers, from honeymooners to seniors, but naturally a large percentage is made up of young American families with children (with a smallish number of foreign passengers as well). Because of this, the overall age demographic tends to be younger than that aboard many of the other mainstream ships, with many passengers in their 30s and early to mid-40s. The bulk of the line's passengers are first-time cruisers and many (duh) are families, sometimes extended ones spread across several cabins.

DINING

While Disney's food is average cruise fare, its dining concept sets it apart from the big-ship crowd.

TRADITIONAL   The neat catch with Disney's version of set dining is that there are three restaurants among which passengers (and their servers) rotate for dinner over the course of the cruise. On one night, passengers dine on dishes such as roasted duck, garlic-roasted beef tenderloin in a green-peppercorn sauce, or herb-crusted Atlantic cod in *Magic*'s elegant 1930s-era **Lumiere's** restaurant or *Wonder*'s equally elegant nautical-themed **Triton's.** On another night, they enjoy the likes of potato-crusted grouper, baby back pork ribs, or mixed grill in the tropical **Parrot Cay** restaurant. And on the third, they nosh on maple-glazed salmon, pan-fried veal chop, or roasted chicken breast with mashed potatoes at **Animator's Palate,** a bustling eatery with a gimmick: It's a sort of living animation cel, its walls decorated with black-and-white sketches of Disney characters that over the course of the meal gradually become filled in with color. Video screens add to the illusion, and the waiters even disappear at some point to change from black-and-white to full-color vests. It's kinda corny, but fun.

Each restaurant has an early and a late seating, and similar groups are scheduled to rotate together as much as possible (for example, families with young children, adults alone, and families with teens). **Vegetarian options** are offered at all meals, and kosher, halal, low-salt, low-fat, and other **special diets** can be accommodated if you request them when you book your cruise, or soon thereafter; once you're aboard, a chef and head server will meet with you to determine your exact needs. Kids' menus start with appetizers such as fruit cocktail and chicken soup before heading on to such familiar entree items as spaghetti with meat sauce, pizza, hot dogs, hamburger, Jell-O, and mac-and-cheese. The wine list is fair, and includes bottles by Silverado Vineyards, owned by members of the Disney family (namely Walt Disney's daughter, Diane Disney Miller).

The 7-night itineraries have 1 formal night and 1 semiformal night (there are 2 formal nights on cruises of more than a week). The rest of the evenings are casual (no jackets or ties necessary for men). The shorter 3- and 4-night itineraries are casual throughout the cruise, though on all itineraries sports jackets are recommended for men dining in Palo, but not in Lumière's/Triton's. Overall, on Heidi's last cruise, many went ultracasual: You could always count on a number of people in shorts and flip-flops at dinner (except at Palo).

SPECIALTY   Both ships also have a romantic adults-only restaurant called **Palo,** serving Italian specialties such as tortellini stuffed with crabmeat, grilled salmon with risotto, and excellent gourmet pizzas, such as one topped with barbecued chicken, black olives, and spinach. A decent selection of Italian wines is available, and the dessert menu includes a fine chocolate soufflé and a weird-but-tasty dessert pizza. The restaurant itself is horseshoe-shaped and perched way up on a top deck to allow a 270-degree view. Service is attentive but not overly formal, and you don't have to dress up, though a jacket for men may be nice. Reservations are essential, and should be made immediately after you board, as the docket fills up fast ($15 per-person cover charge). Palos also serves a great champagne brunch for adults; for $15 enjoy bubbly with an extensive buffet that includes seafood, high-end cheese, fancy pastries, gourmet pizzas (the Gorgonzola with grapes pie is excellent), and more.

CASUAL   Breakfast and lunch are served in several restaurants, both sit-down and buffet. Casual dinners are served on most nights at the indoor/outdoor buffet. The chunky wood tables add a nice nautical touch and the food is impressive (from Mickey-shaped waffles at breakfast to shrimp cocktail at lunch), but overall, during rush hour, the restaurants on *Magic* and *Wonder* get too packed; considering the size of the ships, the space should be larger.

SNACKS & EXTRAS   A boon for families with fussy kids, **Pluto's Dog House,** on the main Pool Deck, is always bustling because of its complimentary chicken tenders, fries, burgers, nachos, bratwurst, and other quick snacks served from lunch through the dinner hour. Nearby, **Goofy's Galley** serves up wraps, panini, fresh fruit, and ice

Preview: *Disney Dream*

The first of Disney's greatly anticipated pair of newbuilds, the 128,000-ton, 2,500-passenger (double occupancy) *Disney Dream* was slated at press time to debut in January 2011 and sister *Disney Fantasy* by mid-2012. Both are being built at Germany's Meyer Werft shipyard, the newbuilds are 50% larger than the *Magic* and *Wonder,* have 1,250 cabins, and will likely be deployed closer to home while the older ships are sent abroad.

Highlights include a 765-foot-long, four-deck-high flume ride called the **AquaDuck** (guests board a two-person inflatable raft and get swept away on a high-speed ride around the perimeter of the ship's top deck, including a thrilling turn that takes you 13 ft. out over the ocean inside a transparent acrylic flume, 150 ft. above the sea). **Goofy's Sports Deck** will offer miniature golf, a full-size basketball court that doubles for volleyball and soccer, a pair of miniature sports courts for kids, a walking track, and two digital sports simulators that will let you play soccer, tennis, basketball, golf, and other sports. The focal point of the **Donald Pool** area is an enormous 30×18-foot LED movie screen that will show Disney films and other stuff. A separate **Mickey Pool** for kids only will resemble those on sisters *Disney Magic* and *Disney Wonder,* with an oversize yellow Mickey hand supporting a water slide. There will be a sprawling **Nemo's Reef water play area** with water jets and bubblers mounted on full-size re-creations of characters from the Disney film *Finding Nemo,* and for adults over age 18, there's the **Quiet Cover Pool and Cove Bar.** Taking up **nearly a full deck,** the impressive kids and teens areas include the multiple rooms of the Disney Oceaneer Club, featuring characters from *Toy Story* and *Monsters, Inc.,* as well as Tinker

cream with lots of toppings, and there's brick oven pizza at **Pinocchio's Pizzeria.** More highbrow options include champagne brunch (for $15 per person) on all sailings with sea days and an afternoon tea on itineraries a week and longer ($5 per person). On longer cruises, themed dining opportunities include breakfast with the Disney characters (for picture taking and posing) and afternoon iced tea and cookies with Peter Pan's pal Wendy. The 7-night and longer itineraries have the Pirates in the Caribbean dinner and deck party (the shorter cruises do only the deck party). It starts as a themed dinner in the restaurants, with waiters and passengers in pirate garb, and entree choices such as Black Beard's jumbo crab cakes, then moves up on deck for a party with music and lots of special effects, from black lighting to pirates rappelling from the funnel.

If you, or your kids, are soda junkies, Disney is the only mainstream line that dispenses the stuff for free, and it provides free milk, coffee, and tea 24 hours a day as well! You can pour yourself a fountain soda (and then another and another) from a poolside station 24-7 on both ships, which can add up to a substantial savings for you by the end of the cruise (though your teeth might not be better for it). There's also the **Cove Café,** serving gourmet coffees (at an extra cost) and light fare for adults (for free!).

The **24-hour room service** menu includes kid favorites such as pizza and cookies.

Bell's fairy forest. The Disney Oceaneer Lab is filled with maps, maritime instruments, and piratical gimcracks, and lets kids try their hand at animation, navigate ships through digital seas, and so on. Both playrooms will have an interactive play floor that kids can control with their movements and the playrooms will also boast an interactive 103-inch screen that allows kids to chat, play, and joke with Crush, the animated sea turtle from the Disney/Pixar motion picture *Finding Nemo,* and the mischievous animated alien Stitch. For tweens (ages 11–13), the Edge lounge is located within a false funnel atop the ship, and has a video karaoke system that uses green-screen technology. Teens have their own 9,000-square-foot club, called Vibe, an indoor/outdoor space where they can create and edit videos, play computer games, access an onboard social media application, or spin and mix their own dance tracks. Outdoors, there's a private deck with lounge chairs, two wading pools, misters and pop jets for cooling off, and deck games like Ping-Pong and foosball.

Other notable features aboard the *Dream* will include virtual porthole "windows" for inside cabins that feature real live footage of the sea; a spa with 17 treatment rooms including "spa villas" that come with their own private verandas; an adults-only entertainment area; three main restaurants, including the popular, digitally inspired, surface-changing Animator's Palate; and an adults-only French-inspired restaurant with a lavish tasting menu, a collaboration between Michelin two-star chef Arnaud Lallement of Reims's and chef Scott Hunnel from the AAA Five-Diamond restaurant at Disney World's Grand Floridian Resort & Spa.

ACTIVITIES

Unlike most other cruise ships, there's no casino of any kind on board, not even a card room. These are family ships. Activities on both vessels include basketball, Ping-Pong, and shuffleboard tournaments; sports trivia contests; weight-loss, health, and beauty seminars; bingo, Pictionary, and other games; wine tastings; and singles mixers (though these family-focused ships aren't great choices for singles). Each ship also has a spa and a gym. There are enrichment activities on all itineraries—though more of them are offered on the longer 7-night-plus routes—including galley tours, backstage theater tours, informal lectures on nautical themes and Disney history as well as current Disney productions, animation and drawing classes, Q & A sessions with the captain, and home entertaining and cooking demos. All these activities are complimentary except wine tasting, which costs a hefty $12 per person. There are also dance classes, movies, and that cruise stalwart, the Not-So-Newlywed Game, which Disney calls Match Your Mate. All itineraries have a captain's cocktail party with complimentary drinks once per cruise, where the master of the ship (and a bunch of Disney characters) makes an appearance. Sports fanatics can watch "the game" in the **Diversions** sports pub.

CHILDREN'S PROGRAM

Not surprisingly, with potentially hundreds of kids on any given sailing (1,000 is typical), Disney's kids' facilities are the most extensive at sea, with at least 50 counselors supervising the fun for ages 3 to 17 between 9am and midnight daily. Nearly half a deck (comprising two huge play spaces and a nursery) is dedicated to kids. The **Oceaneer Club** is a kid-proportioned playroom with a Neverland theme and activities revolving around Disney/Pixar's *Toy Story*. Kids can climb and crawl on the bridge, ropes, and rails of a giant pirate ship, as well as on jumbo-size animals, barrels, and a sliding board; get dressed up from a trunk full of costumes; dance with Snow White and listen to stories by other Disney characters; or play in the kiddie computer room on PlayStations. The interactive **Oceaneer Lab** allows kids a chance to work on computers, learn fun science with microscopes, build from an enormous vat of K'nex (they're like fancy Legos), do arts and crafts, hear how animation works, and direct their own TV commercial. A new scavenger hunt is based on the superpopular *High School Musical* movies.

Disney recently started customizing its children's activities, meaning activities in the Oceaneer Club and Lab are open to all kids between ages 3 and 12 (to age 10 on *Disney Magic*), so children and parents can choose programs based on interest, not just age. Now, your youngsters can join siblings or friends in activities from Cinderella's Royal Ball (for princess wannabes) and So You Want to be a Pirate (billed as pirate training for young buccaneers), to Ratatouille Cooking School (where children bake chocolate chip cookies together), Animal Tracking Series (conservation education), and Flubber (where kids create magical green goo and other interesting concoctions). The newest kids' space aboard the *Magic* is called **Ocean Quest** (it's called Edge on the *Dream*) and the hangout space is geared to tweens ages 11 to 13 and features a replica of the ship's bridge, with real live footage of the real thing upstairs. Kids can sit in a traditional captain's chair and play a simulation game in which they can pretend to steer the ship in and out of port. A computer simulator like this was added to the Oceaneer Lab on the *Wonder*. Both ships also have computer and video games, arts and crafts, and movies. Overall, new activities are being introduced all the time to keep the program fresh for the ages 8-to-17 set. There's also a video arcade, though it's really cramped compared to most on Royal Caribbean, Princess, and the newest Carnival ships. Kids can eat lunch and dinner with counselors in the Topsider and Beach Blanket buffet restaurants, or one of the other dining outlets, on all evenings but the first one of the cruise.

For teens (ages 13–17), there's a teen hangout called the **Stack** on the *Magic* and **Aloft** on the *Wonder*. Isolated from Mom and Dad, the teen centers have two separate rooms, one large living-room-like space with video screens for movies and the other a teen disco with a handful of computers with Internet access as well as the popular Guitar Hero music video game. Dance parties, karaoke, trivia games, improv comedy lessons, and workshops on photography are offered for teens on all cruises. There are even more options on 7-night sailings, including learning how to DJ!

Neither ship has private babysitting services. Instead, the **Flounder's Reef Nursery** for kids ages 3 months to 3 years operates from 6pm to midnight daily, and also for a few hours during the morning and afternoon (hours vary according to the day's port schedule). No other line provides such extensive care for babies. Stocked with toys and decorated with *Little Mermaid*–themed bubble murals and lighting that gives an "under the sea" look, the area also has one-way portholes that allow parents to check on their kids without the little ones seeing them. The space has cribs, and counselors do change diapers (though you should bring your own). The price is $6 per child per hour, and $5 for each additional child in a family (with a 2-hr. minimum). Parents get a tuned beeper when they first check into the nursery, or the kids' program, so that counselors can contact them anywhere on the ship if their child needs them. To avoid suitcases bulging with diapers, a new service allows you to preorder diapers, wipes, and other baby supplies and have them delivered to your cabin on the first day of the cruise.

When the ship calls on **Castaway Cay,** Disney's private island in The Bahamas, kids can head for the new **Pelican Plunge** floating platform of fun just offshore, with its two slides and other water features, or to the **Spring-a-Leak** water park onshore. Scuttle's Cove is also a veritable paradise for the ages 12-and-under set, with barrels to crawl through, a giant whale-dig site to explore, and a new water play area with jets and geysers. Kids' counselors are on hand to supervise the fun if Mom and Dad want to head to **Serenity Bay,** the adults-only beach. For families who want to play together, there are bike rentals and lots more. There's also a secluded teen hangout spot called **Hide Out.** For details, see section 1, "The Cruise Lines' Private Islands," in chapter 10.

Upon request, at the guest services desk, Disney provides the complimentary use of Diaper Genie units (for soiled diapers), cribs and playpens, bottle sterilizers, and strollers.

ENTERTAINMENT

Disney's fresh, family-oriented entertainment is some of the very best at sea. On both ships, performances by Broadway-caliber entertainers in the nostalgic Walt Disney Theatre include the Cirque du Soleil–style *Disney Dreams,* a musical medley of Disney classics, taking the audience from *Peter Pan* to *The Lion King;* the new *Villains Tonight* full-scale musical production featuring the likes of Hades, Captain Hook, Scar (of *The Lion King*), and the Evil Queen (of *Snow White* fame); and the *Golden Mickeys,* a tribute to Disney films through the years that combines song and dance, animated film, and special effects. Depending on the ship and length of the cruise, there's also *Toy Story—The Musical,* based on the original *Toy Story* animated film; *Twice Charmed—An Original Twist on the Cinderella Story; All Aboard: Let the Magic Begin Variety Show;* and the *Remember the Magic* show. On both ships, the stage design allows for lots of magic, with actors flying above the boards and disappearing in and out of trap doors, but the most refreshing thing about these shows is that they have story lines—rare almost to the point of extinction in the cruise world, which mostly presents musical revues. Besides the stage shows, there's also a wild deck party called Pirates in the Caribbean, with Captain Hook and Captain Mickey playing chase and rappelling from funnels and generally wowing the audience with stunts; the party ends with fireworks fired from the ship.

Family game shows (including a game show called On the Nose, a trivia contest called Mickey Mania, and Who Wants to Be a Mouseketeer, another trivia contest in the spirit of the millionaire quiz show) and karaoke take place in the **Studio Sea family nightclub.** Adults (18 and older) can take advantage of the **adults-only entertainment area** in the forward part of Deck 3, with its three themed nightclubs: one quiet, with piano music or soft jazz; the second a dance club; and the third, **Diversions,** a combination pub and sports bar, that won't win any design awards (it looks a lot like a T.G.I. Friday's or Houlihan's—yawn). Another nightspot is the **Promenade**

Lounge, where live music is featured daily. The **Buena Vista Theatre** shows movies day and evening, and since early 2009, **3-D movies** are shown here and in the Walt Disney Theatre throughout the cruise. There is one pull-out-the-stops 3-D film with special effects like lasers, fog, streamers, and lighting effects shown once a cruise in the Walt Disney Theatre.

SERVICE

Just like at the parks, Disney staffmembers hail from some 60 countries, including the United States. Service in the dining rooms is efficient and precise, but leans toward friendly rather than formal. The crew keeps the ship exceptionally clean and well maintained. Overall, things run very smoothly.

Though the ships typically sail full and are bustling, the crewmembers seem to remain perpetually good natured and smiley. The "happy to serve" mentality trickles right on up to the officer level, too: The captain personally autographs guests' scrapbooks, photographs, and mementos in a public area at least once per cruise, while top officers participate in the beloved Disney "pin-trading" sessions. So, what makes everyone work so dang hard? Hotel Director Mike Mahendran told our coauthor Heidi that performance expectations are high, but that it certainly doesn't hurt that crewmembers earn 10% to 30% more than the industry standard, and enjoy other perks that foster productivity.

It's no great surprise that travel agents tell us many guests rate service as one of the top features of a Disney Cruise.

Services include **laundry** and **dry cleaning** (the ships also have self-service laundry rooms) and 1-hour photo processing. Tips can be charged to your onboard account, which most passengers opt for ($12 per day is suggested), or you can give them out in the traditional method: cash.

Disney Magic • Disney Wonder

The Verdict

The only ships on the planet that successfully re-create the grandeur of the classic transatlantic liners, albeit in a modern, Disney-fied way.

Disney Magic *(photo: Disney Cruise Line)*

Specifications

Typical Per Diems: $115–$175

		Year Launched	
Size (in tons)	83,000		
Passengers (double occ.)	1,754*	*Magic*	1998
Passenger/Space Ratio	47.3	*Wonder*	1999
Total Cabins/Veranda Cabins	877/378	Last Major Upgrade	
Crew	950	*Magic*	2008
Passenger/Crew Ratio	1.8 to 1	*Wonder*	2006

** **Note:** With children's berths filled, capacity can go as high as 3,325.*

Frommer's Ratings (Scale of 1–5)

Cabin Comfort & Amenities	5	Dining Options	4.5
Appearance & Upkeep	5	Gym, Spa & Sports Facilities	3
Public Comfort/Space	4	Children's Facilities	5
Decor	5	Enjoyment Factor	5

Sailing Regions, Seasons & Home Ports

Magic	**Caribbean,** from Port Canaveral (fall, winter).
Wonder	**Mexican Riviera,** from Los Angeles (fall, winter).

These long, proud-looking ships carry 1,754 passengers at the rate of two per cabin, but because Disney is a family company and its ships were built expressly to carry three, four, and five people in virtually every cabin, the ship could theoretically carry a whopping 3,325 passengers. Although numbers rarely reach that high, Hotel Director Mike Mahendran told Heidi they rarely carry fewer than 2,500 passengers. Though service is a high point of a Disney cruise, these high numbers mean certain areas of the ship will feel crowded at times, namely the kids' pool area, the buffet restaurants, and the photo gallery and shops after dinner. Overall, though, the ships are well laid out and frequently updated and upgraded.

CABINS   The Disney ships have the most family-friendly cabins at sea, with standard accommodations equivalent to the suites or demisuites on most ships—they're about 25% larger than the industry standard (insides 184–214 sq. ft., outsides a roomy 226–268 sq. ft.). All of the 877 cabins have at least a sitting area with a sofa bed to sleep families of three (or four if you put two small children on the sofa bed). Some cabins also have one or two pull-down bunks to sleep families of four or five. Nearly half have private verandas. One-bedroom suites have private verandas and sleep four or five comfortably; two-bedroom suites sleep seven. Outside cabins that don't have verandas have jumbo-size porthole windows. *Note:* Due to the beds being lower to the ground than on most other ships, you may not be able to stow your suitcases underneath and will have to resort to taking up precious closet space with luggage.

The decor is virtually identical from cabin to cabin, combining modern design with nostalgic ocean-liner elements such as a steamer-trunk armoire for kids, globe- and telescope-shaped lamps, map designs on the bedspreads, and a framed black-and-white 1930s shot of Mr. and Mrs. Walt Disney aboard the fabled ocean liner *Rex.* Warm wood tones predominate, with Art Deco touches in the metal and glass fittings and light fixtures. The majority of cabins have two bathrooms—a sink and toilet in one and a shower/tub combo and a sink in the other (both of them compact, though with ample shelf space). This is something you won't find in any other standard cabin industrywide, and it's a great boon for families. All cabins have a minifridge (empty), hair dryer, safe, TV, tub/shower combo, sitting area, and lots of storage space. The high-quality H2O bathroom toiletries are a perk, especially the thick and creamy moisturizer and the tingly shower gel.

One-bedroom suites are done up with wood veneer in a definite deco mood. Sliding frosted-glass French doors divide the living room from the bedroom, which has a large-screen TV, queen-size bed (which can be split to make two twins), chair and ottoman, dressing room, makeup table, and whirlpool tub in the bathroom. A second guest bathroom is located off the living room, which also has a bar and a queen-size sofa bed. The veranda extends the length of both rooms. Two-bedroom and Royal suites are also available.

Sixteen cabins are fitted for wheelchair users.

PUBLIC AREAS Both ships have several theaters and lounges, including an adults-only area with three separate venues: a piano/jazz lounge, disco, and sports-pub-cum-karaoke bar. There's also a family-oriented entertainment lounge called Studio Sea for game shows, karaoke, and dancing; the Promenade Lounge for classic pop music in the evenings; and a 24-hour Internet cafe. The Cove Café is a comfy place for gourmet coffees (for a price) or cocktails in a relaxed setting with books, magazines, Internet stations, Wi-Fi access, and TVs. A 270-seat cinema shows mostly recent-release Disney movies; both ships have a jumbo 336-square-foot screen attached to the forward funnel outside on Deck 9, which shows classic Disney animated films and other stuff. The children's facilities, as you'd expect, are the largest of any ship at sea (see "Children's Program," above, for details).

Throughout, both ships have some of the best artwork at sea, owing to Disney's vast archive of animation cels, production sketches, costume studies, and inspirational artwork, featuring characters we've all grown up with. Other art—notably the *Disney Cruise Line Seaworthy Facts* near the photo shop and A-to-Z of seagoing terms near the theater—was created specifically for the ships and gets a big, big thumbs-up. Canned music pumped into the public areas and corridors tends toward big-band music and crooner tunes or surf-type pop.

DINING OPTIONS Disney's unique rotation dining setup has guests sampling three different restaurants at dinner over the course of their cruise, with an adults-only specialty restaurant also available, by reservation only (see "Dining," earlier in this section). At breakfast and lunch, the buffet-style spread in *Magic's* Topsider and *Wonder's* Beach Blanket restaurants has deli meats, cheeses, and rice and vegetable dishes, as well as a carving station, a salad bar, and a dessert table with yummy chocolate chip cookies. Though the culinary offerings are fine, the layout and tiny size of the place are not. During the morning rush, for example, it's tough to squeeze through the place, let alone with kids and a tray full of breakfast. Be prepared to dine elsewhere if the place is packed.

Options for afternoon noshing poolside include Pinocchio's Pizzeria; Pluto's Dog House for hot dogs, hamburgers, chicken tenders, fries, and more; and Goofy's Galley for wraps, fruit, and ice cream. There's 24-hour room service from a limited menu, but no midnight buffet unless you count the spread at the evening deck party held once per cruise and the dessert buffet presented once on 7-night itineraries. Instead, hors d'oeuvres are served to passengers in and around the bars at about midnight.

POOL, FITNESS, SPA & SPORTS FACILITIES The Pool Deck of each ship has three pools: Mickey's Kids' Pool, shaped like the mouse's big-eared head, with a great big, white-gloved Mickey hand holding up a snaking yellow slide (this pool can get *cr-o-o-o-w-ded!*); Goofy's Family Pool, where adults and children can mingle; and the Quiet Cove Adult Pool, with whirlpools, gurgling waterfalls, a teak deck and lounge chairs with plush cushions, a poolside bar, and a coffee spot called Cove Café. On sunny days, the kids' pool will feel like a sardine can—watch those cannon balls! A consolation prize for families with young children, adjacent is a splash pool with circulating water for diaper-wearing babies and toddlers. It's the only one at sea, as the official party line across the board is no diaper-wearing children (and that includes pull-ups and swim diapers) are allowed in any pool, wading or adult, for hygiene reasons. On both ships, there is now a new larger toddler pool that sports interactive fountains and splash zones.

Just beyond the adult pool area at the stern is a spa and gym. The Steiner-managed Vista Spa & Salon is impressive, with attractive tiled treatment rooms and a thermal suite with a sauna, steam room, misting shower, and heated contoured tile chaise longues. Among the many treatments is a selection geared to teens. Both ships' spas have been remodeled and three spa villas were added. Each one is an indoor treatment suite that's connected to a private outdoor veranda with a personal hot tub, an open-air shower, and a chaise longue. Sounds great, yes, but renting one isn't cheap! They can be reserved for one person or couples. A 50-minute massage for one in a spa villa, for example, is $199 and it includes 55 more minutes in the villa to enjoy tea, a soak in the hot tub, and what Disney calls a "foot bathing ceremony." (The couples' version of this villa treatment is $449 per couple and includes a pair of 50-min. massages and 70 min. to loll about the villa afterward.) Both ships have an outdoor Sports Deck with basketball and paddle tennis. There is also shuffleboard and Ping-Pong, and joggers and walkers can circuit the Promenade Deck, which is generally unobstructed (though the forward, enclosed section may be closed off when the ship is arriving and departing port because it's adjacent to the anchor mechanisms).

7 Holland America Line

300 Elliott Ave. W., Seattle, WA 98119. © **877/724-5425** or 206/281-3535. Fax 800/628-4855. www.hollandamerica.com.

THE LINE IN A NUTSHELL   In business since 1873, Holland America Line (HAL) has managed to hang on to more of its seafaring history and tradition than any line today except Cunard. It offers a moderately priced, classic, and casual yet refined cruise experience. **Sails to:** Caribbean, Panama Canal, Alaska, Mexico, Hawaii, Canada/New England (plus Asia, Australia/New Zealand, Europe, South America, Africa).

THE EXPERIENCE   Holland America is a classy operation, providing all-around appealing cruises with a touch of old-world elegance and such cushy amenities as plush bedding and flat-panel TVs with DVD players in all cabins. Though the line has been retooling itself to attract younger passengers and families, it still caters mostly to older folks, and so generally offers a more sedate and stately experience than other mainstream lines, plus excellent service for the money. Its fleet, which until a few years ago consisted of midsize, classically styled ships, is in the process of becoming supersize (relatively speaking), and the new *Eurodam* and recent Vista-class megaships are a bit bolder in their color palettes. New or old, the vessels are all well maintained and have excellent (and remarkably similar) layouts that ease passenger movement. Throughout the ships' public areas, you'll see flowers that testify to Holland's place in the floral trade, Indonesian touches that evoke Holland's relationship with its former colony, and seafaring memorabilia that often hearkens back to HAL's own history.

Pros

- **Great service:** HAL's primarily Indonesian and Filipino staff is exceptionally gracious and friendly.

- **Traditional classic ambience:** Overall, the line's ships are classy, with impressive art collections and a touch of traditional ocean-liner ambience. The new Signature-class *Eurodam* and *Niuew Amsterdam* retain most of the line's traditional features while introducing a very modern Northern European design sense.
- **Chocolate:** The once-per-cruise dessert extravaganzas and the occasional spreads of sweets guarantee you'll gain a few pounds.

Cons

- **Sleepy nightlife:** While there are always a few stalwarts and a couple of busy nights, these aren't party ships. If you're big on late-night dancing and barhopping, you may find yourself partying mostly with the entertainment staff.
- **Fairly homogenous passenger profile:** Although younger faces are starting to pepper the mix (especially on 7-night cruises to warm-weather destinations), most HAL passengers still tend to be low-key, fairly sedentary 55-plus North American couples.

HOLLAND AMERICA: GOING DUTCH

One of the most famous shipping companies in the world, Holland America Line was founded in 1873 as the Nederlandsch-Amerikaansche Stoomvaart Maatschappij (Netherlands-American Steamship Company). Its first ocean liner, the original *Rotterdam*, took her maiden, 15-day voyage from the Netherlands to New York City in 1872. By the early 1900s, the company had been renamed Holland America and was one of the major lines transporting immigrants from Europe to the United States, as well as providing passenger/cargo service between Holland and the Dutch East Indies via the Suez Canal. During World War II, the company's headquarters moved from Nazi-occupied Holland to Dutch-owned Curaçao, then the site of a strategic oil refinery, and after the war the company forged strong links with North American interests. The line continued regular transatlantic crossings up until 1971, and then turned to offering cruises full time. In 1989, it was acquired by Carnival Corporation, which improved the line's entertainment and cuisine while maintaining its overall character and sense of history. Today, most of HAL's vessels are named for other classic vessels in the line's history—*Rotterdam,* for example, is the sixth HAL ship to bear that name—and striking paintings of classic HAL ships by maritime artist Stephen Card appear in the stairways on every ship. But HAL isn't just about history: Over the past few years, it's upgraded its ships with what it called the Signature of Excellence initiative. All staterooms now have DVD players and flat-panel plasma TVs, extrafluffy

Compared with the other mainstream lines, here's how HAL rates:

	Poor	Fair	Good	Excellent	Outstanding
Enjoyment Factor				✓	
Dining				✓	
Activities			✓		
Children's Program		✓			
Entertainment				✓	
Service					✓
Worth the Money					✓

towels, terry-cloth bathrobes, massage shower heads, lighted magnifying makeup mirrors, salon-quality hair dryers, triple-sheeted mattresses, and 100% Egyptian cotton bed linens. Each ship also got a demonstration kitchen for interactive programs about food and wine; a combo lounge, library, coffee shop, and Internet cafe called the Explorations Café; and enhanced spa and kids' facilities.

Though Holland America offers cruises in every major region covered in this book, it's particularly strong in **Alaska,** where it operates one of the state's most extensive land-tour operations.

Holland America's 2,104-passenger, 86,000-ton *Eurodam* launched in July 2008 as the first vessel in the line's new **Signature class.** *Nieuw Amsterdam,* a second Signature-class sister, was built at Italy's Fincantieri shipyards and was set to launch in July 2010 just as this book went to press.

PASSENGER PROFILE

For years, HAL was known for catering to an almost exclusively older crowd, with most passengers in their 70s on up. Today, following intense efforts to attract younger passengers, about 25% of the line's guests are under age 55 (with the average age being 57), with a few young families peppering the mix, especially in summers and during holiday weeks. While the average age skews a bit lower on the newer Signature-class and Vista-class ships, HAL just isn't Carnival or Disney, and its older ships especially were designed with older folks in mind. On cruises longer than a week, there's no shortage of canes, walkers, and wheelchairs.

Passengers tend to be amiable, low key, and amenable to dressing up—you'll see lots of tuxedos and evening gowns on formal nights. Though you'll see some people walking laps on the Promenade Deck, others taking advantage of the ships' gyms, and some taking athletic or semiadventurous shore excursions, these aren't terribly active cruises, and passengers overall tend to be sedentary. HAL has a very high repeat-passenger rate, so many of the people you'll see aboard will have sailed with the line before.

Parties for solo travelers (only 30–40 of whom tend to be on any particular cruise) encourage mixing, and you can ask to be seated with other solo passengers at dinner. On cruises of 10 nights or longer, gentlemen hosts sail aboard to provide company for single women, joining them at dinner as well as serving as dance partners.

DINING

Much improved over the years, Holland America's cuisine is fine, but hardly memorable. On a recent cruise, meals in the main restaurant were hit-and-miss, ranging from so-so to pretty good. The line is making a push to serve more regional dishes to match the area where a given ship is sailing: salmon and other wild local seafood on Alaska cruises; chicken mole or guava-stuffed chicken on Mexico cruises; and jerk chicken or West Indian *lassi* soup in the Caribbean, plus local produce like chayote, breadfruit, and guava. The nonadventurous can still order menu standards such as New York strip steak and Caesar salad.

TRADITIONAL   In the line's lovely formal restaurants, appetizers may include prawns in spicy wasabi cocktail sauce, deep-fried hazelnut brie, and escargot; the soup-and-salad course always involves several options, from a plain house salad and minestrone to a chilled raspberry bisque and spicy two-bean soup; and main courses are heavy on **traditional favorites** such as broiled lobster tail, grilled salmon, beef tenderloin, roast turkey, seared tuna steak, grilled pork chop, and filet mignon, along with a **regional specialty** or two.

Those wanting something less substantial can opt for lighter dishes such as grilled fish or chicken, and fresh fruit medley. A few entrees on most dinner menus are marked as signature dishes recommended by master chef Rudi Sodamin, and include the likes of a salmon tartare with avocado appetizer and, as a main course, chicken *cordon bleu*. Some vegetarian entrees are available on the main menu, but you can also ask for a **full vegetarian menu,** with a half-dozen entrees and an equal number of appetizers, soups, and salads. (Don't miss the tofu Stroganoff and celery-and-Stilton soup if they're offered—yum.) Children can enjoy tried-and-true staples such as pizza, hot dogs, burgers with fries, chicken fingers, and tacos, plus chef's specials such as pasta and fish and chips.

A few years back, Holland America introduced its **As You Wish Dining** program, similar to Princess's Personal Choice program. At booking, passengers are asked to choose either traditional early- or late-seating dining (at the same table nightly, served on one level of the ship's main restaurant) or a completely flexible schedule (offered from 5:15 to 9pm nightly on the restaurant's other level). Guests opting for flexible dining can make reservations during the day or just show up whenever they like.

SPECIALTY   Aboard every vessel, the intimate **Pinnacle Grill** restaurant offers a menu of mostly steaks, chops, and fish. Options may include such dishes as Dungeness crab cakes, pan-seared rosemary chicken with cranberry chutney, wild-mushroom ravioli with pesto cream sauce, or lamb rack chops with drizzled mint sauce, plus premium beef cuts. All entrees are complemented with regional wines from Château Ste. Michelle, Canoe Ridge, Willamette Valley Vineyards, and others. The cover charge is $20 per person for dinner and $15 for lunch. On a recent *Statendam* outing, the service was top-rate and the food exceeded our expectations. Don't miss the opportunity to dine here at least once per cruise. Make reservations as early as possible when you come aboard. In addition to dinners, alternative restaurants may be open for lunch on sea days.

The new *Eurodam* and *Niuew Amsterdam* have further opened up the dining choices, with the really outstanding Pan-Asian **Tamarind** ($15 at dinner; no charge for dim sum at lunch) and Italian **Canaletto** (no extra cost), which takes over a portion of the buffet each evening and is also being added to the rest of the fleet. **Slice,** the pair's 24-hour pizzeria, makes custom pizzas with toppings ranging from mussels to eggplant, on standard or whole-wheat crust. The ships also offer **flexible cross-ordering;** for example, guests dining in the buffet can order selections from the dining room during dinner service. In addition, the new spa staterooms come with special **healthy room service menus** and the new cabanas with light breakfast and lunch selections.

CASUAL   As has become industry standard, **casual dining** is available each night in the ships' buffet-style Lido restaurants, which also serve breakfast and lunch. Fleetwide, a casual Italian restaurant called Canaletto has been carved out of part of the Lido buffet. There's also a new upscale pizzeria called Slice near the aft Pool Deck aboard *Eurodam, Nieuw Amsterdam, Veendam,* and *Rotterdam;* on the *Veendam* and *Rotterdam,* Slice is adjacent to a large new LED movie screen as well. Overall, Holland American has some of the best-laid-out buffets at sea, with separate stations for salads, desserts, drinks, and so on, keeping lines and crowding to a minimum. Diners here enjoy open seating from about 6 to 8pm. Tables are set with linens and a pianist may provide background music, but service is buffet-style, with waiters on hand to serve beverages. Most main dishes are similar to what you'll find in the main restaurant that evening. At lunch, the buffet restaurants offer pasta, salads, stir-fry, burgers, and usually an ethnic option, such as an Indian shrimp curry, sushi, or Dutch crepes. Pizza and ice-cream stations are open until late afternoon. Out on the Lido Deck, by the pool, a **grill** serves hamburgers, hot dogs, veggie and turkey burgers, and pizza, between about 11:30am and 6pm. A **taco bar** nearby has all the fixings for tacos or nachos, and it's generally open about the same hours. Once a week, the Lido also hosts a **barbecue buffet dinner.**

SNACKS & EXTRAS   Once per cruise, a special **Royal Dutch High Tea** features teatime snacks and music provided by the ships' string trio, making it one of the most truly "high" among the generally pretty low teas served on mainstream lines. A new **Indonesian Tea and Coffee Ceremony** is also being held once per cruise and features such goodies as spring rolls, sweet rice balls, and coconut. There's also a new **Cupcake Tea** that's especially popular with families with kids, which includes plates of delicious mini-cupcakes with your tea. On other days, a more standard **afternoon tea** has white-gloved waiters passing around teeny sandwiches, scones, and cookies in the dining room or one of the main lounges. Pizza, soft ice cream, and frozen yogurt round out the afternoon snacks.

Free hot canapés are served in some of the bars/lounges during the cocktail hour, and free iced tea is served on deck, one of many thoughtful touches provided at frequent intervals by the well-trained staff. The **Explorations Café** has a specialty coffee bar.

Each evening around midnight, a spread of snacks is available in the Lido restaurant, and at least once during each cruise, the dessert chefs go wild with a midnight **Dessert Extravaganza.** Cakes are decorated with humorous themes, marzipan animals guard towering chocolate castles, and trays are heavy with chocolate-covered strawberries, truffles, cream puffs, and other sinful treats.

Room service is available 24 hours a day and is typically efficient and gracious. As a plus, the breakfast options include eggs and meats, not just pastries and cereals as on most mainstream ships. You can also order room service on the final morning of the cruise, another rarity.

ACTIVITIES

Though varied and fun, HAL's onboard activities tend to be low-key. You can take ballroom dance lessons; take an informal class in photography; play bingo or bridge; sit in on a trivia game or Pictionary tournament; participate in Ping-Pong, golf-putting, basketball free-throw, or volleyball tournaments; take a gaming lesson in the casino or an aerobics class at the gym; take a self-guided iPod tour of the ship's art collection or a backstage theater tour; go high-toned at a wine tasting; or go low-toned at the goofy games poolside or in a lounge. During the Seaquest game on a 14-night cruise, we watched as a group of mostly senior passengers enthusiastically slipped off their bras and dropped their drawers in the name of friendly competition—the team that deposited more undergarments on the show lounge stage won. The place was a sea of geriatric goofballs tottering around in their boxers and briefs, crumbled trousers in hand. Some cruises also feature model shipbuilding contests in which you can use only junk you find around the ship, with seaworthiness tested in one of the ship's hot tubs.

Each ship has a great **Explorations Café,** which is a combo Internet center, coffee bar, and library. Comfy lounge chairs come equipped with music stations and headphones.

Generous shelves of books (Holland American has the most extensive libraries after Cunard), DVDs, and games line the walls, and a magazine stand holds current issues of popular magazines, plus the latest editions of various newspapers, when the ship can get them. If you're a crossword buff, you can tackle the *New York Times* crossword puzzles embedded under glass in the room's cafe tables (wax pencils are provided). Explorations also functions as the Internet cafe, but passengers toting their Wi-Fi–enabled laptops can take advantage of wireless hotspots here and throughout the ship. The ships' **Culinary Arts Centers** give free cooking demos and more intimate, hands-on cooking classes (available for a charge). The center is also used for other demos, such as flower arranging. Cooking demos usually happen twice per 7-day cruise; go early to get a front-row seat, or sit in the back and watch the food preparation on the flat-panel TVs around the room.

On 7-night Alaska cruises, Native artists demonstrate traditional arts such as ivory and soapstone carving, basket weaving, and mask making as part of the line's **Artists in Residence Program,** created under the auspices of Anchorage's Alaska Native Heritage Center. For another program during visits to Glacier Bay, a member of the Huna tribe comes aboard to talk about the land the Huna have called home for centuries. In Hawaii and Mexico, cultural dancers perform for passengers.

CHILDREN'S PROGRAM

Holland America isn't Disney, but the line is trying harder to cater to families with children. If there are more than about 30 kids aboard, activities are programmed for three age brackets (3–7, 8–12, and 13–17), and there's always at least one counselor on board every sailing, and more when demand warrants. You'll find the most children on cruises during summers and holiday weeks. At these times, there may be as many as 300 to 400 kids aboard the line's newer ships, especially in the Caribbean, though around 100 to 200 is typical overall. When there are fewer than 20 or 30 kids, a two-tiered Club HAL program is offered—children ages 3 to 12 in one group, teens in another—on a limited basis, generally about 6 hours on sea days and even fewer hours on port days. On cruises with more children, activities are offered for three or more age groupings and for much longer hours. Typically, each evening kids receive a program detailing the next day's activities, which may include arts and crafts, cooking classes, youth sports tournaments, movies and videos, scavenger hunts, PlayStations, disco for teens, storytelling for younger kids, miniature golf, charades, bingo, Ping-Pong, and pizza, ice-cream, and pajama parties. The playrooms typically operate on a limited schedule on port days, and in the Caribbean, the line offers kids' activities on its private beach, Half Moon Cay (see section 1, "The Cruise Lines' Private Islands," in chapter 10).

All the ships have **dedicated playrooms** with toys, games, arts and crafts, foosball, air hockey, PlayStations, and more. Fleetwide, you'll find a **separate teen center** called the Loft with video screens and a dance floor; most ships also have a totally cool outdoor space sequestered away on a top deck for teens called the Oasis, a beachlike setting complete with a waterfall and chaise longues. Otherwise, the playrooms are bright and cheerful, though they lack the ball jumps, padded climbing and crawling areas, and fanciful decor that make kids' facilities aboard Disney, Royal Caribbean, Princess, NCL, and Celebrity so compelling.

Families traveling with HAL tend to be multigenerational, and the line emphasizes activities for the whole family rather than kids only. Many onboard activities are geared for family fun or competition, especially in the Caribbean.

Group babysitting in the playroom is offered between 10pm and midnight for $5 per hour per child for kids ages 3 to 12. In-cabin babysitting is also offered, assuming a crewmember is available. The cost is $8 an hour for the first child (minimum age 12 weeks), and $5 per hour for additional kids. Inquire at the guest services desk.

Children must be 12 weeks or older to sail aboard.

ENTERTAINMENT

Don't expect HAL's shows to knock your socks off, but hey, at least they're trying. Each ship features small-scale **Vegas-style shows,** with laser lights and lots of glimmer and shimmer. Overall, though, you'll find better-quality entertainment from the soloists, trios, and quartets playing jazz, pop, and light-classical standards around the ship.

Recent-release movies are shown an average of twice a day in an onboard cinema and also up on deck via a new, large LED screen on the ships' aft deck (part of a new concept at the ships' stern called the Retreat which also includes a new pool bar and pizzeria). There's free popcorn available for the full movie effect. There's also a **crew talent show** once a week in which crewmembers (Indonesians one week, Filipinos the next) present songs and dances from their home countries. **Passenger-participation shows** are a different animal, with the crowd-pleasing *American Idol*–style contest called Superstar featuring passenger crooners being critiqued by a staff of judges.

Aboard each ship, one of the lounges becomes a disco in the evening, with a small live band generally playing before dinner and a DJ taking over for after-dinner dancing. The new Signature-class and Vista-class ships have dedicated discos; on the other ships, the Crow's Nest lounge goes disco in the evenings.

SERVICE

Holland America is one of the few cruise lines that maintains a real training school (a land-based school in Indonesia known in HAL circles as "ms Nieuw Jakarta") for the selection and training of staffers, resulting in service that's efficient, attentive, and genteel. The soft-spoken, primarily Indonesian and Filipino staffers smile more often than not and will frequently remember your name after only one introduction, though they struggle occasionally with their English. (Be cool about it: Remember, you probably can't speak even a word of Bahasa Indonesia or Tagalog.) During lunch, a uniformed employee may hold open the door of a buffet, and at dinnertime, stewards who look like vintage hotel pages walk through the public rooms ringing a chime to formally announce the dinner seatings.

Like many other lines these days, HAL now automatically adds **gratuities** to passengers' shipboard accounts, at the rate of $11 per day, adjustable up or down at your discretion. A 15% service charge is automatically added to bar bills and dining room wine accounts.

Only the Vista-class ships (and the *Prinsendam*) come with minifridges in standard cabins. On the other vessels, they can be rented for a few bucks a day (inquire before your cruise if you're interested) if staying in a standard cabin; suites do have fridges. All cabins have complimentary fruit baskets on embarkation day. An early-boarding program allows guests to get aboard in the port of embarkation as early as 11:30am, when some lounges and facilities will be open for their use, although cabins generally won't be ready until 1pm. All suite guests have access to a one-touch **24-hour concierge service** and concierge lounge.

Onboard services on every ship in the fleet include **laundry** and **dry cleaning.** Each ship—except the new Signature- and Vista-class ships, oddly enough—also maintains several self-service laundry rooms with irons.

The Signature Class: Eurodam • Nieuw Amsterdam

Eurodam *(photo: Holland America Line)*

The Verdict

More modern European and less Holland America—royal in feeling, these sleek ships are for all nations. Their logical evolution integrates HAL's traditionalism with new, sophisticated elements.

Specifications

Typical Per Diems: $85–$115

Size (in tons)	86,000	Crew	929
Passengers (double occ.)	2,104	Passenger/Crew Ratio	2.3 to 1
Passenger/Space Ratio	41.2	Year Launched	
Eurodam	2008		
Nieuw Amsterdam	2010		
Total Cabins/Veranda Cabins	1,052/708	Last Major Upgrade	N/A

Frommer's Ratings (Scale of 1–5)

★★★★ ½

Cabin Comfort & Amenities	5	Dining Options	5
Appearance & Upkeep	5	Gym, Spa & Sports Facilities	4
Public Comfort/Space	4	Children's Facilities	3
Decor	4	Enjoyment Factor	4.5

Sailing Regions, Seasons & Home Ports

Eurodam	**Caribbean,** from Fort Lauderdale (winter, spring). **New England/Canada,** from New York & Quebec (fall).
Nieuw Amsterdam	**Caribbean,** from Fort Lauderdale (winter, spring).

Holland America's largest ships to date, *Eurodam* and *Nieuw Amsterdam* have a stylish, tailored Northern European decor that updates the old HAL aesthetic while keeping many of its signature features in place. Artwork, as throughout the fleet, reflects the Dutch Golden Age or, aboard *Nieuw Amsterdam,* the Dutch connections to New York. A bit larger than HAL's earlier Vista-class ships, the pair includes a number of currently in-vogue features, including spa staterooms with special amenities, special room service, and a dedicated concierge; the graceful, tent-like cabanas by the Lido pool and in the Retreat; and three specialty restaurants: Pan-Asian Tamarind, Italian Canaletto, and the Pacific Northwest-y Pinnacle Grill.

Trivia for ship history buffs: *Nieuw Amsterdam* is the fourth Holland America ship to bear that name, going back to 1906 and including the *Nieuw Amsterdam* of 1938, generally regarded as one of the greatest of the great old ocean liners.

CABINS   With these ships, HAL's British country house style moves to sophisticated modern Northern Europe, with a more tailored look and rich, understated olives and golds, woods that run the gamut from blond to cherry, and more nickel and stainless steel than brass. Standard staterooms are very much like those on Vista-class ships, rated among the best in the industry, and start at a roomy 185 square feet for outside cabins and between 170 and 200 square feet for inside rooms. All categories have Signature of Excellence features, from Euro-top beds to Egyptian cotton towels, flatscreen TVs and DVD players (more than 1,000 DVDs are available free to all passengers in all cabin categories on these ships), massaging shower heads, and Elemis toiletries, plus minifridges and hair dryers. Closets are sufficient and well planned, but drawer space seems rather scarce until you realize that there are drawers under the beds. *Tip:* The veranda staterooms on Deck 4 have a bit more outside space than others.

Suites range in size from 389 to 1,138 square feet and passengers have perks including the private Neptune Lounge with its personal concierge, large-screen TV, library, sofas, Wi-Fi, minibar, and refreshments. Deluxe and Superior Verandah Suites have sitting and dressing areas, double sinks, whirlpool tubs, and separate showers.

The 56 spa staterooms and suites have different decor, soothing earth tones accented with fresh green and fernlike tracings on the linens. The 10 Deluxe Verandah OceanView rooms on the Observation Deck have scalloped balconies and floor-to-ceiling windows, but these are essentially French balconies and have no outdoor furniture.

All spa staterooms have a Greenhouse Spa concierge, although there is not a spa package or special discount that goes with these accommodations. They also have a direct connection to the spa, special bath amenities including aromatherapy bath salts and a luffa, and organic linens. Each is also equipped with a fitness DVD, a yoga mat, and pedometers, along with a water feature to generate soothing sounds. At turndown, the spa staterooms receive herb-infused organic chocolates. They also have a special healthy room-service menu with fresh squeezed fruit and vegetable juices, egg white omelets, turkey bacon, and soy patties among the options.

Thirty cabins, across the categories, offer wheelchair access.

PUBLIC AREAS   On *Eurodam,* the three-deck 890-seat Mainstage showroom, with a descending orchestra pit and revolving stage to showcase Vegas-style shows, is flanked by a number of bars and lounges. The Northern Lights disco and bar are also to one side of the casino; however, the nightly piano bar seems more popular with HAL guests, as are the blackjack tables in the casino, which benefits from the addition of a small adjoining bar. The dedicated movie theater, complete with popcorn and very cushy leather seats, also sees good use.

The three-deck atrium on both ships is really spectacular; on the *Eurodam,* it's a central backlit fiber-optic sculpture that changes color and a gorgeous green glass staircase; three sides reach into the top level of the Ocean Bar.

One of the nicest features of Holland America ships is their nooks and crannies, little private spaces and tables where peace and privacy are easy to find, and *Eurodam* and *Niuew Amsterdam* are no exceptions. There are comfortable corners in the Explorer's Lounge, with its excellent after-dinner libations, specialty coffees, and hand-dipped chocolates. The library also has some relaxing retreats, along with 1,000 novels and a nice supply of nonfiction.

Less quiet but also delightful, the Sports Bar departs from the European decor to give a very amusing salute to American baseball along with microbrews and the requisite huge flatscreen TV.

The shopping area has been expanded by about 1,000 square feet, with elegant wares including Versace jewelry, Omar Torres, and XOXO. Merabella, the upscale jewelry store introduced to several ships in the fleet, is showcased in the line's newest cruisers as well, and Fine Watches does a brisk business in Fendi, Tissot, Tag Heuer, and other designer timepieces.

On these two ships, HAL has positioned its Explorations Café within the Crow's Nest, bringing much more activity to this beautiful vantage point on top of the ship. The views from the Internet stations are gorgeous enough to distract anyone, and the usual specialty coffees and pastries have been augmented with treats like tiny cupcakes. At night, a live band and soloists take over, and the Internet cafe portion is screened off with a separate entrance.

Those who want to put their cameras or computers to better use will be very pleased with the beautifully designed HAL Digital Workshop powered by Microsoft Windows. Free workshops led by Microsoft techies somehow simultaneously work for complete beginners and still deliver an impressive amount of training in blogging, digital imagery, making movies, editing, and creating scrapbooks.

Club HAL has an expanded presence on *Eurodam* and *Niuew Amsterdam;* the clubs are very colorful and Euro-minimal for the most part, with a computer room, games arcade, craft room, small stage, and the teens-only Loft. The age groups are a little larger than on most family-oriented ships, with three ranges (3–7, 8–12, and 13–17). Families on board also have a tendency to take over the poolside cabanas, where they can lounge, eat, and nap in semiprivacy. The beautiful Culinary Arts Center has programs for children as well as adults.

DINING OPTIONS   There are eight different dining venues with HAL's choice of As You Wish or traditional dining, including three new ones: the Pan-Asian Tamarind, the family Italian Canaletto (dinner only), and Slice, a 24-hour pizzeria.

The star is unquestionably Tamarind and its adjacent companion, the very charming and intimate Silk Den, decorated in pale purple and yellow and serving signature "saketinis." Tamarind diners devoured chef Rudi Sodamin's wasabi-soy-crusted beef tenderloin, sea bass with hoisin-lime glaze, and roasted Peking duck, enjoying the exquisite presentation and the ladder of orchids at the door. The $15 fee for evening meals wouldn't even cover the tips for cuisine at this level in a major city, and dim sum is served at lunchtime without charge.

Canaletto takes over a portion of the Lido at night, turning into a 72-seat family-style Italian restaurant without a fee. It's popular enough that reservations are a very good idea. The extensive menu rotates with three entrees each evening, which brings back diners repeatedly. Table-side antipasto and signature dishes are served, such as chicken marsala scaloppini and penne alla vodka.

The new 24-hour pizzeria Slice does serve slices, but also 12-inch hand-tossed pizzas with whole wheat or regular crusts and toppings from eggplant and pesto to pineapple and mussels.

The ships' 1,114-seat dining rooms provide menu choices from steak and lobster to unusually imaginative vegetarian dishes, all served in quietly rich surroundings with a wave effect on the ceiling. The new Pinnacle Grill fare introduces dishes such as Colorado lamb chops and lobster macaroni and cheese, along with a new martini menu; the fee is $20 for dinner, $15 at lunch.

There are plenty of options for lunch and dinner. The Terrace Grill is a French twist on its former incarnation. At dinnertime, the Lido offers table service, and you can select dishes from the main dining room menu or the Lido's own menu. At breakfast and lunch, you do feel the increased number of passengers on board, with long lines and difficulty finding tables at hours of peak use.

Among the various bars and lounges are new additions, including the Explorer's Lounge bar and the new Pinnacle Bar, a modern wine bar with an industrial design aesthetic, next to the Pinnacle Grill.

POOL, FITNESS, SPA & SPORTS FACILITIES   The aptly named Retreat sunning and relaxation section, located a deck above the activity of the main pool area, is a new move for HAL, and it's been very well received. The biggest attraction is the set of 14 cabanas—tented, airy private worlds, very well furnished; eight cabanas are also positioned by the Lido pool. Both sets tend to be very popular, so it's important to arrange rentals as quickly as possible, whether for a day or for the cruise. The cabanas come with loaded iPods, Evian water, chilled grapes, fruit trays, champagne, and chocolate. Rentals for cabanas in the Retreat is $45 on port days and $75 on sea days; Lido cabanas are $30 on port days and $50 on sea days. Retreat cabana guests are offered light breakfasts and lunches, while Lido cabana guests can request selections from the Terrace Grill or Lido restaurants. The only drawback is space: The cabanas have significantly reduced the amount of sunning space in the Lido area, which could prove to be a problem in the Caribbean.

The Lido pools amidships are covered with a retractable Magrodome and have an 8-foot waterfall feature; the *Eurodam*'s is etched with the word "water" in 100 languages. Three poolside hot tubs are kept at different temperature levels for different tastes, and the surrounding lounges and sheltered tables and chairs are very comfortable. The smaller Sea View pool aft of the Lido has its own bar and the Slice pizzeria is adjacent.

The ship's Greenhouse Spa offers a full menu of spa treatments and salon services for men, women, and teens, with a particularly attractive central hydrotherapy pool and thermal suite and an aromatherapy steam room. The fitness center is well equipped with treadmills, bicycles, and elliptical machines, and it has a great ocean view. Resistance equipment, free weights, and aerobics classes round out the offerings, and for those who prefer to do their walking or jogging outside, one circuit of the Promenade Deck is ⅓ mile. Also outdoors on Deck 12 is the net-enclosed Sports Court, set up for basketball, volleyball, and the like.

The Vista Class: Zuiderdam • Oosterdam • Westerdam • Noordam

The Verdict

These ships were Holland America's first foray into mega-size vessels, and they marry traditional HAL style with a partying Caribbean feel—a weird fit that is toned back somewhat in each successive sister ship.

Zuiderdam *(photo: Holland America Line)*

Specifications

Typical Per Diems: $85–$150

Size (in tons)	85,000	*Oosterdam*	2003
Passengers (double occ.)	1,848	*Westerdam*	2004
Passenger/Space Ratio	46	*Noordam*	2006
Total Cabins/Veranda Cabins	924/623	Last Major Upgrade	
Crew	800	*Zuiderdam*	2005
Passenger/Crew Ratio	2.3 to 1	*Oosterdam*	2006
Year Launched		*Westerdam*	2006
Zuiderdam	2002	*Noordam*	N/A

Frommer's Ratings (Scale of 1–5)

★★★★

Cabin Comfort & Amenities	4.5	Dining Options	4
Appearance & Upkeep	4	Gym, Spa & Sports Facilities	4.5
Public Comfort/Space	4	Children's Facilities	3
Decor	3.5	Enjoyment Factor	4

Sailing Regions, Seasons & Home Ports

Noordam	**Caribbean,** from Fort Lauderdale (winter, spring).
Oosterdam	**Mexican Riviera,** from San Diego (winter, spring). **Alaska,** from Seattle (summer). **Hawaii,** from San Diego (fall 2011, winter/spring 2012).
Westerdam	**Caribbean,** from Fort Lauderdale (winter, spring), from San Francisco (fall). **Panama Canal,** from Fort Lauderdale (winter, spring). **Alaska,** from Seattle (summer).
Zuiderdam	**Caribbean,** from Fort Lauderdale (winter, spring). **Panama Canal,** from Fort Lauderdale (winter, spring), from San Diego (fall).

Built in a design similar to Carnival's Spirit-class ships, *Zuiderdam* (named for the southern point of the Dutch compass, and with a first syllable that rhymes with "eye"), *Oosterdam* (eastern, and with a first syllable like the letter O), *Westerdam,* and *Noordam* (northern compass point) were technically Holland America's first megaships, though they're downright cozy compared to the behemoths other lines are churning out these days.

Designed to help HAL shed its image as your grandmother's cruise line and attract baby boomers, the first of these vessels—2002's *Zuiderdam*—came off totally unnatural, mixing ultrabright Carnival-esque colors, stark W Hotel modernism, and the traditional style for which HAL was previously known. That mistake was toned down some for sister ship *Oosterdam,* and by the time *Westerdam* came on the scene in 2004, the new look had been refined. The fourth and final sister, *Noordam* (which replaced the previous *Noordam,* which left the fleet in Nov. 2004), seems to do it just right, mixing classic wine reds, dark blues, and earth tones with just a hint of zany, such as the silver-framed benches on the elevator landings and in the Pinnacle Grill and Pinnacle Bar.

In the spirit of learning from their mistakes, HAL has gone back and tweaked parts of the *Zuiderdam,* replacing some of the loudest carpeting with darker shades, for example, and removing some jarring "art" pieces like the giant-red-lips bench that graced one corridor. All four sisters are extraordinarily spacious, with large standard cabins, truly glamorous two-level dining rooms, and distinctive specialty restaurants.

CABINS Cabins in all categories are comfortable and, as aboard every HAL ship, are among the industry's largest, with insides and outsides ranging from 185 to 200 square feet. The simple decor of light woods, clean lines, and subtle floral bedding is very appealing. Overall, more than two-thirds of them have verandas, with the deluxe veranda suites and staterooms in the stern notable for their deep balconies, nearly twice the size of those to port and starboard. You get a romantic view of the ship's wake, too, but because the decks are tiered back here, residents of the cabins above you can see right down.

Standard outside and veranda cabins all have a small sitting area and a tub in the bathroom—a relatively rare thing in standard cabins these days. Closet space in all categories is more than adequate for 7-night cruises, with nicely designed fold-down shelves and a tie rack. Each has a flatscreen TV and DVD player, makeup mirror, real hair dryer, massage shower head, bathrobes, and extrathick, supercomfortable bedding. Dataports allow passengers to access e-mail and the Internet from every cabin via their own laptops.

Suites run from the comfortably spacious 298-square-foot Superior Verandah Suites (with wide verandas, a large sofa bed, walk-in closet, separate shower and bathroom, and extra windows) to the 1,000-square-foot Penthouse Verandah Suites—extremely large multiroom apartments with a flowing layout, a pantry, palatial bathrooms with oversize whirlpool baths, and ridiculously large private verandas with a second, outdoor whirlpool. Their decor is reminiscent of 1930s moderne style. Guests in every suite category have use of a concierge lounge whose staff will take care of shore-excursion reservations and any matters about which you'd normally have to wait in line at the front desk. The lounge is stocked with reading material, coffee, and juice, and a continental breakfast is served daily.

Twenty-eight cabins are wheelchair accessible.

PUBLIC AREAS Public rooms on the Vista-class ships run the gamut from the traditional to the modern, and from the lovely to the weird (again, we're talking mostly the *Zuiderdam* and *Oosterdam,* which still have some of their original ill-conceived public rooms). The more traditional spaces, done mostly in blues, teals, burgundies, and deep metallics, include the signature Explorer's Lounge, a venue for quiet musical performances and high tea. The top-of-the-ship Crow's Nest lounge, an observation lounge during the day and nightclub/disco at night, has wide-open views, comfortable leather recliners toward the bow (a perfect reading perch during days at sea), and even a few rococo thrones on the starboard side, good for "wish you were here" cruise photos. The rear port corner of the Crow's Nest is the most truly elegant lounge area aboard, with high-style, striking, and comfortable furniture; it's also one of the ships' Wi-Fi hot zones.

The Lower Promenade Deck is the hub of indoor activity on these ships. In the bow, the three-deck Vista Lounge is the venue for large-scale production shows, while the Queen's Lounge/Culinary Arts Center at midships hosts chef demos by day and comedians and other cabaret-style acts in the evening. Between the two, there's a piano bar and a casino, the latter really flashy on all but the *Noordam.* You'll also find HAL's first-ever dedicated discos, but they're uninspired at best (and, on *Zuiderdam,* just butt-ugly). Our favorite room, the Sports Bar, is as far from the standard rah-rah sports-hero-and-pennants sports bar as you can imagine, with comfortable free-form leather seating and table lamps. *Très* chic. Only the multiple TVs give away the place's true identity.

One deck up, the traditional Ocean Bar—with bay windows to port and starboard—wraps around the understated three-deck atrium, with its Waterford crystal chandelier centerpiece. Moving forward, you pass through the drab shopping arcade, whose displays spill right into the central corridor, courtesy of retractable walls, forcing you to browse as you walk from stem to stern. A lot of lines are doing this and it's a pretty crass sales pitch; it gets a big thumbs-down from us. Once you get through, you come to Explorations Café, the ships' hub, and a combination specialty coffee shop/Internet center/library, with HAL's signature inlaid marble tables.

Other public rooms include the Main Deck's Atrium Bar, a very comfortable, small-scale nook vaguely reminiscent of a 1930s nightclub; the wicker-furniture outdoor Lido Bar on the Lido Deck (which unfortunately lacks the charm of similar spaces on the line's older ships); and the KidZone and WaveRunner children/teen centers, which are a bit bare, though roomy and sunny. Art in the public areas of the ships includes maritime artwork by Stephen Card, replica 18th-century Dutch engravings, ship models, and on the *Zuiderdam,* some nice humorous paintings by Hans Leijerzapf, Commedia dell'Arte statues, and jazz sketches and paintings by Wil van der Laan. *Oosterdam*'s Java Corner has several sketches of landmark designs by Frank Lloyd Wright.

Oceanview elevators at port and starboard midships are a little boxy, closing off some of the intended inspiring views. Much better views are to be had from outdoor areas forward on Decks 5, 6, and 7, and from an area just forward of the gym, above the bridge. You can even check a ship's compass here.

DINING OPTIONS   The main Vista Dining Room is a two-deck affair, decorated traditionally but with nice touches of modernism—for instance, in *Zuiderdam*'s black, high-backed wooden chairs—which are very sharp. On *Noordam,* the elegant space is a throwback with wine-red fabrics, darkish woods, and a cozy living-room-like feeling. It's a lovely dining room. The ship's alternative Pacific Northwest restaurant, the 130-seat Pinnacle Grill, wraps partially around the three-deck atrium—ask for a table by the windows or in the aft corner for the coziest experience. The design is appealing, with marble floors, bright white linens, gorgeous Bulgari place settings, and ornate, organically sculpted chairs by Gilbert Lebirge, who also created the ships' beautiful, batik-patterned elevator doors.

Diners wanting something more casual can opt for the well-laid-out and attractive Lido buffet restaurant (and its new Italian section called Canaletto); the outdoor Grill for burgers, dogs, and the like; or, on all but the *Noordam,* the Windstar Café, serving specialty coffees (for a price), snacks, and light meals in a tall-ship atmosphere.

POOL, FITNESS, SPA & SPORTS FACILITIES   Gyms are well equipped with a full complement of cardio equipment and weight machines arranged in tiers around the cardio floor; the space is attached to another room where you'll find chaise longues and a large dipping pool. There's also a basketball/volleyball court on the Sports Deck. The Greenhouse Spa is fully 50% larger than any other in the HAL fleet, and besides offering the usual massage, mud, and exotic treatments, it has a couple of HAL firsts: a thermal suite (a series of saunas and other heat-therapy rooms) and a hydrotherapy pool, which uses heated seawater and high-pressure jets to alleviate muscle tension. Oddly, there's no compelling design motif like you'd find in other signature spas. Around the pool, extraheavy wooden lounge chairs are thickly padded and nap-worthy. The pool area doesn't quite work on *Zuiderdam,* where the colors are jarring and the materials cheap-looking. However, as in many other areas aboard, the colors on *Oosterdam, Westerdam,* and *Noordam* are a vast improvement, very pleasant all around.

Outdoors, the wraparound Promenade Deck is lined with classy wooden deck chairs—a nice touch of classic ocean-liner style—and is popular with walkers and joggers. The main Pool Deck is the hub of outdoor activity on sea days, with hot tubs, music, and pool games, and can be covered with a sliding roof in inclement weather. The hallmarks of the pool area on both ships are giant bronze animal statues—from a polar bear to a penguin and dolphin. Another pool, in the stern on Lido Deck, is a lovely spot for sunbathing and open views of the sea, and it's also the venue for outdoor movies and videos on a large LED screen.

Rotterdam • Amsterdam

The Verdict

Modern throwbacks to the glory days of transatlantic travel without the stuffiness or class separation, these attractive, gloriously midsize sisters have great features, from classic art to rich mahogany woodwork and elegant yet understated public rooms.

Amsterdam *(photo: Holland America Line)*

Specifications

Typical Per Diems: $95–$210

Size (in tons)		Crew	
Rotterdam	56,652	*Rotterdam*	593
Amsterdam	61,000	*Amsterdam*	647
Passengers (double occ.)		Passenger/Crew Ratio	
Rotterdam	1,316	*Rotterdam*	2.2 to 1
Amsterdam	1,380	*Amsterdam*	2.1 to 1
Passenger/Space Ratio		Year Launched	
Rotterdam	43	*Rotterdam*	1997
Amsterdam	44.2	*Amsterdam*	2000
Total Cabins/Veranda Cabins		Last Major Upgrade	
Rotterdam	658/161	*Rotterdam*	2009
Amsterdam	690/172	*Amsterdam*	2005

Frommer's Ratings (Scale of 1–5)

★★★★ ½

Cabin Comfort & Amenities	4.5	Dining Options	4
Appearance & Upkeep	4	Gym, Spa & Sports Facilities	4.5
Public Comfort/Space	5	Children's Facilities	3
Decor	5	Enjoyment Factor	4.5

Sailing Regions, Seasons & Home Ports

Amsterdam	**Panama Canal,** from Fort Lauderdale (winter, spring) & Los Angeles (winter). **Alaska,** from Seattle (summer).
Rotterdam	**Panama Canal,** from San Diego (winter, spring).

With 3 years separating them, near-twins *Rotterdam* and *Amsterdam* combine classic elegance with contemporary amenities and provide a very comfortable cruise, especially on itineraries of 10 nights and longer. Carrying just over 1,300 passengers at double occupancy, they're a breath of fresh air in the sea of supermegaships that ply the oceans these days. *Rotterdam* is the sixth HAL ship to bear that name, following the legendary *Rotterdam V,* which was sold in 1997.

Like the rest of the fleet, the ships were recently upgraded to feature HAL's Signature of Excellence enhancements, including the Explorations Café Internet center and coffee shop, beefed-up kids' facilities, a culinary-arts demonstration kitchen, and upgraded cabin amenities.

CABINS Unlike the beige color schemes of the older Statendam-class ships, the decor here is livelier, with coral and mango colors, and blues and whites brightening things up. At 182 to 197 square feet, the standard cabins are among the most spacious at sea and have enough hanging and drawer space for 10-night-plus cruises. Bathrooms are generous as well, with bathtubs in all but the standard inside cabins (and, on *Amsterdam,* in a handful of outsides as well). Each cabin has a sitting area, a desk, a safe, two lower beds convertible to a queen, and great reading lights above each bed, in addition to the line's recently added amenities: flat-panel plasma TVs and DVD players, terry-cloth bathrobes, massage shower heads, lighted magnifying makeup mirrors, and salon-quality hair dryers. Beds now have plush, amazingly comfy, triple-sheeted mattresses and 100% Egyptian cotton bed linens. Both ships now also have a handful of spa staterooms for convenient access to the spa and health club.

Verandah Suites are 225 square feet and have a 59-square-foot private veranda; Deluxe Verandah Suites measure 374 square feet and have a 189-square-foot veranda and a dressing room. Both have sitting areas, whirlpool tubs, and stocked minibars, and are kept stocked with fresh fruit. Penthouse Suites measure 937 square feet and have a 189-square-foot veranda, living room, dining room, guest bathroom, and an oversize whirlpool tub. All suite guests have use of a concierge lounge whose staff will take care of shore-excursion reservations and any matters about which you'd normally have to wait in line at the front desk. The lounge is stocked with reading material, and a continental breakfast is served daily.

Twenty-one cabins are wheelchair accessible.

PUBLIC AREAS Both ships have great, easy-to-navigate layouts that allow passengers to move easily among public rooms. Most of the inside public areas are concentrated on two decks; ditto for the pools, sunning areas, spa, sports facilities, and buffet restaurant, which are all on the Lido and Sports decks.

Overall, the ships give you the feeling of an elegant old hotel, with dark red and blue upholstery and leathers, damask fabrics, mahogany tones, and gold accents. Artwork is everywhere, from the stairwells to the walkways on the Promenade and Upper Promenade decks. Aboard *Amsterdam,* the theme is Dutch and nautical; aboard *Rotterdam,* it's Continental and Asian. In *Amsterdam*'s atrium, a clock tower combines an astrolabe, a world clock, a planetary clock, and an astrological clock. You can't miss it; it's been wedged into the space with barely an inch to spare. *Rotterdam*'s passengers are greeted in the atrium by a large reproduction Flemish clock.

The Explorations Café is a main hub on the ships and the place to check your e-mail or surf the Web while enjoying a cappuccino.

The Ocean Bar serves complimentary hot hors d'oeuvres before dinner nightly, and passengers pack into the bar to listen and dance to a lively trio. More elegant is the Explorer's Lounge, whose string ensemble performs a classical repertoire. Nearby is the open-sided piano bar, featuring a red lacquered baby grand piano on the *Amsterdam.*

The Crow's Nest observation lounge/disco gets fairly little use during the day unless there's a special event being held (such as line-dance classes), but it's a popular spot for predinner cocktails and after-dinner dancing. Near the room's entrance on *Amsterdam,* you'll see the *Four Seasons* sculptures originally created for the old *Nieuw Amsterdam* in 1938, and purchased back by the line from a private collector. On *Rotterdam,* a highlight of the Crow's Nest is the life-size terra-cotta human and horse figures, copies of ancient statues discovered in Xian, China.

The *Amsterdam's* main showroom, perhaps the brightest of the rooms, is done in red and gold and is more a nightclub than a theater. Sit on the banquettes for the best sightlines, as alternating rows of individual chairs sit lower and don't permit most passengers to see over the heads of those in front of them. The balcony has decent sightlines.

Other public rooms include a large casino, library, card room, and the Wajang Theatre—the spot for movie viewing as well as HAL's Culinary Arts Center demonstration kitchen.

DINING OPTIONS   Aboard both ships, the attractive two-level formal dining rooms have floor-to-ceiling windows and an elegant, nostalgic feel, and never seem crowded. The Pinnacle Grill seats fewer than 100 diners and offers romantic, intimate Pacific Northwest cuisine in an elegant setting. The only downside here: no windows. And be careful of those funky chairs; they tip forward if you lean too far toward your soup. Aboard *Amsterdam,* make a point of looking at the paintings, all of which have a joke hidden somewhere on the canvas—look for the RCA "his master's voice" dog on the Italian rooftop, and for Marilyn Monroe by the lily pond.

As in the rest of the fleet, a casual buffet-style breakfast, lunch, and dinner are served in the Lido restaurant, a bright, cheerful place done in corals and blues. It's a well-laid-out space, with separate salad, drink, deli, dessert, and stir-fry stations. There's a taco bar poolside at lunchtime and a new Italian section in the Lido as well as an upscale pizzeria called Slice.

POOL, FITNESS, SPA & SPORTS FACILITIES   *Amsterdam* and *Rotterdam* have spacious, well-equipped gyms with a very large separate aerobics area, floor-to-ceiling ocean views, plenty of elbowroom, and a nice spa. There's a pair of swimming pools: one amidships on the Lido Deck, with a retractable glass roof and a pair of hot tubs; and another smaller, less trafficked, and thus more relaxing one in the stern, which was renamed the Retreat because of a new pool bar, pizzeria, and giant LED movie screen. Both ships have great wraparound Promenade Decks lined with wooden deck chairs, a quiet and nostalgic spot for reading, snoozing, or scoping the scenery.

There's a combo volleyball and tennis court on the Sports Deck, and Ping-Pong tables are on the Lower Promenade in the sheltered bow.

Volendam • Zaandam

The Verdict

These handsome ships represent a successful marriage of HAL's usual elegance and gentility with a well-done dose of classy modern pizazz. And they're an ideal size, too: big enough to offer lots of amenities and small enough to be much more intimate than today's jumbo megaships.

Volendam *(photo: Holland America Line)*

Specifications

Typical Per Diems: $100–$205

Size (in tons)	63,000	Year Launched	
Passengers (double occ.)	1,440	*Volendam*	1999
Passenger/Space Ratio	43.7	*Zaandam*	2000
Total Cabins/Veranda Cabins	720/197	Last Major Upgrade	
Crew	647	*Volendam*	2005
Passenger/Crew Ratio	2.2 to 1	*Zaandam*	2005

Frommer's Ratings (Scale of 1–5)

★★★★ ½

Cabin Comfort & Amenities	4.5	Dining Options	4
Appearance & Upkeep	4	Gym, Spa & Sports Facilities	4.5
Public Comfort/Space	5	Children's Facilities	3
Decor	5	Enjoyment Factor	4.5

Sailing Regions, Seasons & Home Ports

Volendam	**Alaska,** from Vancouver & Skagway (summer).
Zaandam	**Mexican Riviera,** from San Diego (winter, spring). **Hawaii,** from San Diego (winter, spring). **Alaska,** from Vancouver & Seward (summer). **Hawaii,** from Vancouver (fall).

Introduced at the turn of this century, *Volendam* and *Zaandam* marked Holland America's first steps into a more diverse, mainstream future, offering an experience designed to attract the vital 40-something boomers while still keeping the line's core older passengers happy. The ships have alternative restaurants, Internet centers, and huge gyms that can't be matched by many lines attracting younger crowds, but their overall vibe is more traditional than Carnival, Princess, and Royal Caribbean—and, for that matter, than the line's newer and much more glitzy Vista-class vessels. These are classy, classic ships, but with just a touch of funk to keep things from seeming too old-fashioned—note the autographed Bill Clinton saxophone and Iggy Pop guitar in *Zaandam*'s elegant Sea View Lounge.

These ships, along with the rest of the HAL fleet, were upgraded over the past few years with the line's Signature of Excellence enhancements, including the Explorations Café Internet center, beefed-up kids' facilities, a Culinary Arts Center demonstration kitchen, and upgraded cabin amenities.

CABINS   In a word: roomy. These standard 186- to 196-square-foot cabins are among the largest in the industry, and with a much more modern, daring look than on the line's older ships. Fabrics are done in salmon red, burgundy, gold, and bronze, and the walls in a striped pale-gold fabric, hung with gilt-framed prints. Bathrooms are roomy and well designed, with adequate storage shelves and counter space. All outside cabins have shower/tub combos (short tubs, but tubs nonetheless), while inside cabins have only showers. Cabin drawer space is plentiful, and closets are roomy, with great shelves that fold down if you want to adjust the configuration of space. There's a storage drawer under each bed.

All cabins have sitting areas, plus Holland America's Signature of Excellence enhancements, from flat-panel TVs and DVD players, to terry-cloth bathrobes, massage shower heads, lighted magnifying makeup mirrors, and salon-quality hair dryers. Beds are supercomfy with plush triple-sheeted mattresses and 100% Egyptian cotton bed linens.

On the Verandah and Navigation decks, 197 suites and minisuites have balconies. The single gorgeous Penthouse Suite measures 1,126 square feet, including veranda, and is adorned with one-of-a-kind pieces such as 19th-century Portuguese porcelain vases and Louis XVI marble table lamps.

Twenty-one cabins are wheelchair accessible.

PUBLIC AREAS   *Volendam*'s public areas are floral-themed; *Zaandam*'s sport musical motifs. Aboard *Volendam,* each aft staircase landing has a still-life painting of flowers, and a spot outside the library has a collection of elaborate Delft tulip vases (ironically, with fake silk tulips). You could even call the gorgeous graduated colors in the show lounge seating floral-themed, with colors from magenta to marigold creating a virtual garden in bloom. *Zaandam*'s theme is exemplified by one of the more bizarre and inspired atrium decorations we know of—a huge, mostly ornamental baroque pipe organ decorated with figures of musicians and dancers—as well as by numerous musical instruments scattered around the ship in display cases, from a classic Ornette Coleman–style plastic Grafton sax in the Sea View Lounge to the elaborate Mozart harpsichord display (with busts and a candelabra) outside the card room. The display of electric guitars in the atrium stair tower, signed by Queen, Eric Clapton, and the Rolling Stones, says something about HAL's drive to attract younger passengers—even if "younger" means 50-somethings.

In general, as aboard almost the entire HAL fleet, public areas are very easy to navigate. Corridors are broad, and there's little chance of getting lost or disoriented. Surfaces and fabrics overall are an attractive medley of subtle textures and materials, from tapestry walls and ceilings to velveteen chairs, marble tabletops, and smoky glass. *Volendam* even has a red-lacquer piano and suede walls woven to resemble rattan. *Zaandam*'s pianos are all funky: The one in the piano bar is painted to look as though it's made of scrap lumber and rusty nails; the one in the Lido restaurant is downright psychedelic.

The main hub of the ship for many is the Explorations Café, a combination Internet center and coffee bar, with plenty of comfy seating and magazines to read.

The warm and almost glowingly cozy Explorer's Lounge is another favorite area, along with the nearby Sea View Lounge and the adjacent piano bar, with its round, pill-like leather bar stools and plush sofas. On busy nights, the Ocean Bar can get crowded by the bar, but there's usually plenty of space across the room or near the dance floor, where a live jazz band plays danceable music before and after dinner.

The ever-popular Crow's Nest nightclub has been redesigned and now has features such as banquettes in bright, modern colors and translucent white floor-to-ceiling curtains that function both as decor and movable enclosures for private events. Cocktail mixology classes and other events are held here during the day; after dinner, it becomes the ship's disco and nightclub. The Culinary Arts Center demo kitchen shares space with the Wajang Theatre, and is the venue for at least two cooking demonstrations per cruise that are hosted by well-regarded chefs. As on other HAL vessels, the ships' main showrooms are two-story affairs with movable clusters of single seats and banquettes on the ground level in front of the stage so that passengers can get comfortable.

Both vessels have impressive art and antiques throughout their public areas. The booty on *Volendam* includes an authentic Renaissance fountain outside the casino (the ship's most pricey piece), an inlaid marble table in the library (a HAL signature), and a small earthenware mask dating from 1200 B.C. that's kept in a display case near the Explorer's Lounge. On *Zaandam,* an area outside the library features reproductions of Egyptian jewelry and a huge repro Egyptian statue fragment.

DINING OPTIONS   The two-story main dining rooms are truly glamorous, framed with floor-to-ceiling windows and punctuated by dramatic staircases. A classical trio serenades guests from a perch on the top level. Just outside the second level of the dining room is a place that women won't want to miss: a wonderful powder room with ocean views and lots of elbowroom for primping, with vanity tables and stools in one room, and the toilets and sinks adjacent. Both ships also feature HAL's fleetwide Pacific Northwest specialty restaurant, the intimate Pinnacle Grill (see "Dining," on p. 165).

The Lido buffet restaurants are attractive and efficiently constructed, with separate stations for salads, desserts, and beverages, cutting down on the chance of monstrously long lines. A sandwich station serves its creations on delicious fresh-baked breads.

POOL, FITNESS, SPA & SPORTS FACILITIES   The gyms on these ships are attractive and roomy, with floor-to-ceiling windows surrounding dozens of state-of-the-art machines. The ship's spa has been upgraded and you won't be disappointed with the treatments.

Three pools are on the Lido Deck: a small and quiet aft pool (behind the Lido buffet restaurant, which now features a new bar, pizzeria, and large LED movie screen) and the main pool and wading pool, located under a retractable glass roof in a sprawling area that includes the pleasant, cafelike Dolphin Bar, with rattan chairs and shade umbrellas. There are more isolated areas for sunbathing above the aft pool on a patch of the Sports Deck and in little slivers of open space aft on most of the cabin decks. The Sports Deck also has a pair of practice tennis courts, as well as shuffleboard. Joggers can use the uninterrupted Lower Promenade Deck to get their workouts.

The Statendam Class: Statendam • Maasdam • Ryndam • Veendam

The Verdict

These ships are well made and designed, and for some, a perfect midsize in this age of gigantic circuslike megas. Public areas are functional and appealing, with just a dash of glitz and plenty of classic European and Indonesian art.

Veendam *(photo: Holland America Line)*

Specifications

Typical Per Diems: $90–$195

Size (in tons)	55,451	Maasdam	1993
Passengers (double occ.)	1,266	Ryndam	1994
Passenger/Space Ratio	43.8	Veendam	1996
Total Cabins/Veranda Cabins	633/149	Last Major Upgrade	
Crew	602	Statendam	2010
Passenger/Crew Ratio	2.1 to 1	Maasdam	2011
Year Launched		Ryndam	2010
Statendam	1993	Veendam	2009

Frommer's Ratings (Scale of 1–5)

★★★★

Cabin Comfort & Amenities	4	Dining Options	4
Appearance & Upkeep	4	Gym, Spa & Sports Facilities	4
Public Comfort/Space	5	Children's Facilities	3
Decor	4	Enjoyment Factor	4.5

Sailing Regions, Seasons & Home Ports

Maasdam	**Caribbean,** from Fort Lauderdale (winter, spring). **New England/Canada,** from Fort Lauderdale, Boston & Montreal (summer, fall).
Ryndam	**Caribbean,** from Tampa (winter, spring).
Statendam	**Panama Canal,** from Fort Lauderdale & San Diego (winter, spring, fall). **Alaska,** from Vancouver & Seward (summer). **Coastal,** from Vancouver (fall).
Veendam	**Bermuda,** from New York (summer, fall).

Refreshingly intimate, agile, and handsome looking, these four vessels are, like all the HAL ships, extremely well laid out and easy to navigate. Holland America's 55,451-ton Statendam-class ships are cozy at one-third the size of today's biggest megas and, relatively speaking, are classics at ages from 12 to 15 years. Decor is a subdued scheme of earthy tones and traditional artwork. Touches of marble, teak, polished brass, and multimillion-dollar collections of art and maritime artifacts lend a classic ambience, and many decorative themes emphasize the Netherlands' seafaring traditions. The onboard mood is low-key (though things get dressy at night), the cabins are large and comfortable, and there are dozens of comfortable nooks all over the ships in which you can curl up and relax. And, there's hardly anything more appealing about a ship than a sleek hull with a dark paint job, tiered aft decks, and a long sweeping foredeck—these are covered in teak, offering passengers a great place to view the passing scenery.

The Statendam-class ships have been upgraded recently and now feature HAL's Signature of Excellence enhancements, most notably an Explorations Café Internet center, improved kids' facilities, a Culinary Arts Center demonstration kitchen, upgraded cabin amenities, a pizzeria and large LED movie screen at the pool area, new bars, and a nightclub.

CABINS   Cabins are roomy at 186 to 197 square feet, unfussy, and comfortable, with light-grained furniture and fabrics in safe shades of blue, beige, and burgundy. All cabins have twin beds that can be converted to a queen and, in some cases, a king, all with plush triple-sheeted mattresses and 100% Egyptian cotton bed linens—the most comfortable cruise ship beds that our coauthor Heidi has ever slept on. About 200 cabins can accommodate a third and fourth passenger on a foldaway sofa bed and/or an upper berth. Closets and storage space are larger than the norm, and bathrooms are well designed and well lit, with bathtubs in all but the lowest category. All cabins have personal safes and music channels, plus flat-panel TVs and DVD players, terry-cloth bathrobes, massage shower heads, lighted magnifying makeup mirrors, and salon-quality hair dryers. There's also a handful of new spa cabins.

Outside cabins have picture windows and views of the sea, though those on the Lower Promenade Deck have pedestrian walkways (and, occasionally, pedestrians) between you and the ocean. Special reflective glass prevents outsiders from spying in during daylight hours. To guarantee privacy at nighttime, you have to close the curtains. No cabin views are blocked by dangling lifeboats or other equipment.

Minisuites are larger than those aboard some of the most expensive lines, such as SeaDream. Full suites are 563 square feet, and the Penthouse Suite sprawls across a full 1,126 square feet. Suite passengers have the choice of three pillow types.

Six cabins are outfitted for passengers with disabilities, and public areas are also wheelchair friendly, with spacious corridors, wide elevators, and wheelchair-accessible public toilets.

PUBLIC AREAS   For the most part, public areas are subdued, consciously tasteful, and soothing. The Sky Deck affords an almost 360-degree panorama where the only drawback is the roaring wind. One deck below, almost equivalent views are available from the ever-popular Crow's Nest nightclub, which offers a subtly glowing bar; banquettes in bright, modern colors; and translucent white floor-to-ceiling curtains that function as both decor and movable enclosures for private events. Cocktail mixology classes and other events are held here during the day; after dinner, it becomes the ship's disco and nightclub where theme parties and dancing take place. The ships' small, three-story atria are pleasant enough and refreshingly unglitzy, housing the passenger-services and shore-excursions desks as well as officers' offices.

The ships' two-story showrooms are modern and stylish, but not overdone. On the *Statendam,* for instance, muted gold columns blend elegantly with lovely tile mosaic work in shades of blue and green. Unlike most ships, which have rows of theater-like seats or couches, the lower levels are configured with cozy groupings of cushy banquettes and chairs that can be moved. The balcony, however, has bench seating, with low backs that make it impossible to lean back without slouching.

The trendiest spot is the Explorations Café, a well-stocked library and Internet center with a coffee bar and ocean views. A buzzing hub of activity, there are 12 computer stations and several plug points for those going wireless with laptops. Five leather chaise longues partnered with CD players and headphone stations face the sea through floor-to-ceiling windows, while other clusters of couches and chairs are set among the generous shelves of periodicals and books, which include everything from travel to fiction, science, history, gardening, and reference titles. A magazine rack holds current issues of popular magazines and newspapers, when the ship can get them. If you're a crossword buff, you can tackle the *New York Times* puzzles embedded under glass in the room's cafe tables (wax pencils are provided).

There's a dark and cozy piano bar, where requests are taken, and a new combo lounge called Mix, which feature three separate bars: one for martinis, another for champagne, and the third for spirits and ales. A live band plays for dancers before dinner in the very popular and refurbished Ocean Bar, and the casinos are a nice size and spacious, though not as pleasingly designed as aboard the line's newer ships. A small movie theater shows films a few times a day, and this space also houses the Culinary Arts Center demonstration kitchen—the movie screen descends in front of the kitchen during showtimes.

For children, the youngest play in a bright but smallish room decorated like a giant paint box, and preteens have a karaoke machine and video games. Lucky teens, however, get the Oasis, a top-deck Sun Deck with a wading pool with a waterfall, teak deck chairs, hammocks, colorful Astroturf, and lamps designed as metal palm trees, all enclosed by a bamboo fence. This would be a great space for group events on sailings with few kids aboard.

DINING OPTIONS   These ships have elegant, two-story main dining rooms at the stern, with dual staircases swooping down to the lower level for grand entrances and a music balcony at the top where a duo or trio serenades diners. Ceilings are glamorous with their lotus-flower glass fixtures, and two smaller attached dining rooms are available for groups. HAL's specialty restaurant, the Pinnacle Grill (see "Dining," p. 165), has a classy, more modern feel to it.

The casual indoor/outdoor buffet restaurant is well laid out, with separate stations for salads, desserts, and drinks, which helps keep lines to a minimum, and a new Italian section called Canaletto. The restaurant serves breakfast, lunch, and dinner daily, and its pizza and ice-cream stations are open until just before dinner. An outdoor grill on the Lido Deck serves burgers and other sandwich items throughout the afternoon, and a nearby station allows you to make your own tacos or nachos at lunch.

POOL, FITNESS, SPA & SPORTS FACILITIES   Each ship has a sprawling expanse of teak-covered aft deck surrounding a swimming pool, and now a pizzeria, bar, and large LED movie screen, too. One deck above and centrally located is a second swimming pool, plus a wading pool, hot tubs, and a spacious deck—all under a sliding glass roof to allow use in Alaska, or in inclement weather elsewhere. Imaginative, colorful tile designs and a dolphin sculpture add spice, and the attractive Dolphin Bar, with umbrellas and wicker chairs, is the perfect spot for a drink and snack in the late afternoon after a shore excursion.

The Sports Deck on each ship has combo basketball/tennis/volleyball courts, and the lovely Lower Promenade Deck allows an unobstructed circuit of the ship for walking, jogging, or just lounging in the snazzy, traditional-looking wooden deck chairs. The ships' windowed Ocean Spa gyms have a couple dozen exercise machines, a large aerobics area, steam rooms, and saunas. The redesigned Greenhouse Spas are an improvement, each including thermal suites with a hydrotherapy whirlpool and heated tile loungers.

The Forward Observation Deck, a huge expanse of open teak deck, is accessible only via two stairways hidden away in the forward (covered) portion of the Promenade Deck, and so gets little use. But don't miss going there. There's no deck furniture here, but standing in the very bow as the ship plows through the ocean is a wonderful, wonderful experience.

8 MSC Cruises

6750 N. Andrews Ave., Fort Lauderdale, FL 33309. ℂ **800/666-9333**. www.msccruises.com.

THE LINE IN A NUTSHELL   MSC is "the other Italian cruise line" (after more established Costa) that would really, really like to join the front ranks of the cruise business. Toward that end, it's invested gazillions in a new megaship fleet that's the youngest in the cruise biz, affording a European-style cruise experience and good prices to boot. All it needs to do is polish up its delivery and it'll be good to go. **Sails to:** Caribbean, New England/Canada (plus Europe, South America).

THE EXPERIENCE   Based in Italy, where it was born as an adjunct of Mediterranean Shipping Company (the world's second-largest container-shipping operation), MSC is all about "Italian style": Italian menus, lots of Italians (and other Europeans) on board, European-style entertainment, and a laid-back, nearly laissez-faire attitude. Its large, modern ships leaven their generally contemporary cruise experience with elements of what cruising was like in the distant and not-so-distant past, when it was more about interacting with other passengers than riding a surfing simulator or playing glorified video games. The line attempts to cater to a mostly American audience when it operates in the North American market, and primarily to Europeans when it's in Europe—a balancing act that its staff hasn't really mastered yet.

Pros

- **Fun activities:** As at Costa, the European entertainment staff knows how to get people in the mood for fun.
- **Italian cuisine:** MSC's distinctive regional dishes and pastas may be among the best at sea, and the evening pizza is superb. Ditto for the Italian wine list: excellent and quite reasonable.
- **Unusual entertainment touches:** While the line's internationalized production shows can lapse into the usual song and dance, novelties such as jugglers, magicians, classical pianists, and opera singers add a really nice touch.
- **Low prices:** Despite some negatives, this is still a line on which you can get good bang for your buck—especially true for families because kids up to age 17 traveling in third and fourth berths sail essentially for free.

Cons

- **Inconsistent service:** Staff ranges from superb to surprisingly inattentive, the latter (most evident among the Italian staff) provoking one guest we met to comment, "You get the feeling that everyone has something more important to do than focus on you."

MSC: ITALIAN LINE GOES BEYOND THE BOOT

MSC Cruises came into being in 1990 as the cruise wing of Mediterranean Shipping Company, one of the world's largest container-shipping operations. Originally concentrating on the European market, the line began making overtures to U.S. passengers after buying the "Big Red Boat" *Atlantic* from defunct Premier Cruises in 1998 and setting her off on 11-night Caribbean cruises. It was in 2003, however, that the line really began its hard sell to the English-speaking world, and it's been in the midst of a massive, sustained building program ever since, introducing so many new ships in recent years that, by fall 2008, it could boast the youngest fleet at sea.

Compared with the other mainstream lines, here's how MSC rates:

	Poor	Fair	Good	Excellent	Outstanding
Enjoyment Factor			✓		
Dining			✓		
Activities			✓		
Children's Program			✓		
Entertainment			✓		
Service		✓			
Worth the Money				✓	

MSC still concentrates on the European market but dips its toes into the U.S. market each winter, sailing one or two ships on Caribbean routes out of South Florida. Beginning in late 2010, it also offers a series of New England/Canada cruises from New York.

PASSENGER PROFILE

The typical age range is mid-40s and up, and while MSC's European itineraries tend to carry 85% European and 15% "other" (including North Americans), Caribbean itineraries are almost exactly reversed, with Americans dominating. Though the line doesn't currently carry as many kids in the Caribbean as it does in Europe, expect that to change as their "kids travel free" policy becomes better known in the U.S. To accommodate the cultural mix, announcements in the Caribbean are made in English and Italian (in that order) and sometimes Spanish, French, and German as well, though they attempt to keep to a "quiet ship" policy as much as possible.

DINING

In keeping with the line's intention of providing an international cruise experience, dining is generally traditional. Dining service has been MSC's main problem for years, and still needs to improve if the line ever expects to compete effectively with the American mainstream lines (see "Service," below).

The tug of war between Italian, American, and "other" traditions plays itself out in both positive and negative ways. On the positive (and surprising) side, MSC is the only line on which we've noticed a kosher category on the wine list—and the only line we've been on where poppy-seed bagels are a staple at the buffet. (On every other line, it's plain bagels, period.) On the annoying side, you may have to specially request coffee in the dining room after meals (only Americans do this, several Italian staffmembers told us), and you may be asked to order your dessert selection at the same time you make your full meal request (just tell them you haven't decided yet, if you haven't).

TRADITIONAL   All of the line's modern midsize and mega-size ships have two formal dining rooms apiece, serving open-seating breakfast and lunch. Dinner is served in two fixed seatings, with an emphasis on Italian cuisine. Six-course lunches include appetizers such as smoked salmon tartare, tomatoes stuffed with tuna mousse, and barbecued chicken wings; a soup of the day; a choice of salads; pasta selections such as ravioli, risotto with pears and Bel Paese cheese, and traditional spaghetti; and main courses that might include pan-roasted chicken breast in a Riesling wine sauce, sliced sirloin, Caribbean red snapper filet, frittata with zucchini and Swiss cheese, or a plain old turkey sandwich. A selection of vegetables, cheeses, and desserts round out the offerings, along with made-to-order burgers, a special **vegetarian menu,** and **healthy-choice options.**

Expect about the same for dinner, with appetizers such as lamb-and-mushroom quiche, avocado boat with seafood salad, and crispy fried spring rolls; a salad of the day; three soup selections, such as Trieste-style red bean soup, oxtail broth with sherry, and chilled orange and tomato cream soup. Pasta selections include risotto with artichokes and fresh mint leaves, and *pappardelle* pasta with white veal ragout. Choose one of the main courses such as rock Cornish hen with mushrooms and crispy bacon, prime rib, grilled mahimahi filet, and vegetable couscous with raisins and cashews. As at lunch, dinner offers a vegetarian menu, a healthy menu, and a selection of cheeses and desserts (including sugar-free desserts), plus a bread of the day. The daily **Italian regional specialties** tend to be the highlight of the menu, while other dishes can be inconsistent. On our last sailing, for example, the *chimichurri* minute steak came without the *chimichurri* sauce, and the crispy potato pancakes were delicious but not at all crispy. On the other hand, the Bolognese sauce was simply sublime.

An **always-available** list rounds out the menu with steak, chicken, salmon filets, Caesar salad (prepared with a little romaine and a dollop of sauce on top), baked potato, and corn on the cob.

SPECIALTY   *Poesia* has the stylish and delicious **Kaito Sushi Bar,** serving sushi, sashimi, tempura, and noodle dishes. It's open for lunch and dinner daily, and pricing is on an a la carte basis. In the evenings, the aft part of the buffet restaurant is sectioned off to create a second specialty venue, **L'Obelisco,** serving a more refined version of Italian cuisine than in the main restaurants, with waiter service and a la carte pricing. In addition, **La Piazzetta Pizzeria** is opened in the evening for custom-made and absolutely sensational Neapolitan-style pizzas, along with a variety of Greek sandwiches and yummy desserts such as tiramisu. There's a small per-item charge but it's well, well, well worth it.

CASUAL   A **buffet restaurant** serves all three meals, with dinner available from 6 to 8pm. To best avoid lines, guests should head to the back serving sections during breakfast and lunch.

SNACKS & EXTRAS   In true Italian style, every bar on these ships is also a **coffee bar,** so guests can enjoy a well-made espresso or macchiato virtually anytime, anywhere. In the late evening hours, waiters bring snacks around to prepublicized locations, and once per cruise there's a not-to-be-missed midnight buffet—an increasingly rare happening in the cruise world.

Room service is available 24 hours a day from two different menus: a very limited menu of complimentary items and a fancier menu with items at extra cost.

ACTIVITIES

Activities on MSC tend toward cruise traditions, many of them with a European sense of fun. Some of the entertainment and activities may not be highbrow, but they sure are enjoyable for those who want to cut loose. Outside, expect **goofy pool games,** including water polo, relay races, dance lessons, and various team games, plus darts and **golf**

tournaments, the latter on a miniature golf course. Goofiness continues in the evenings, with the kind of **participatory games** for which Italian ships are known. Leave your self-consciousness at home. Flamenco and tango **dance lessons** might be held in one of the lounges. Other classes may include Italian language lessons and wine talks, and other activities include cards and bingo, gambling in the **casino,** arts and crafts, and various meet-and-greet events such as singles and honeymooners cocktail parties.

CHILDREN'S PROGRAM

Poesia has an indoor/outdoor kids' complex of four rooms plus a wading pool on Deck 14, with activities broken down into three groups: Mini-Club (ages 3–8), Junior Club (9–13), and Teens (14–17). Activities include supervised circuses, disco, water yoga, shows, basketball, volleyball, pajama parties, treasure hunts, Olympic pool games, quizzes, and more. The indoor/outdoor jungle-gym complex is very appealing—even to smaller adults before and after hours.

ENTERTAINMENT

Evening entertainment is centered around each ship's main theater. On our most recent cruise, the internationally themed production shows were mostly well received. By design, they feature very little singing or talking in English, which distinguishes them from the usual shows you find at sea. Some shows draw on European circus traditions, featuring jugglers, magicians, opera singers, and classical musicians. It's that European influence—also evident in shows by opera singers and other guest performers, at **audience-participation shows,** at the lively disco, and in **karaoke** sessions—that distinguishes MSC's entertainment from the American cruise lines. In the evening, there's live music in multiple lounges, ranging from a pianist to a combo, from a Mexican trio to a string quartet. Strangely for ships with so much live music, there's no live orchestra for the shows: Even background music for the classical pianists and opera singers is prerecorded.

SERVICE

Service is the number-one downside that MSC must address if it wants to reach a wider audience. While the line touts its Italian officers and crew—a distinction that hearkens back to the Golden Age of ocean travel, which was dominated by European lines—it's actually those staffmembers who tend to have the most lackadaisical attitude. Their surprising inattentiveness—whether at the front desk or in the dining rooms—is a major deviation from the sophisticated ambience promised by the line's advertising. It's the inconsistency that's most frustrating: When the service is good, it's great; when it isn't, it can feel downright unfriendly.

Note that the line has, in fact, blurred its Italianism in recent years by recruiting service staff from Indonesia and other Asian nations. As on other lines, the Asian crew distinguishes itself with its attentiveness and professionalism, though occasional language barriers can pop up from time to time.

Tipping is handled on an automatic basis, with $12 per adult, per day ($6 per day for kids under 18) added to your onboard account. The amount can be adjusted up or down by contacting the Reception Desk.

Laundry service is also available, though there are no self-serve laundromats.

MSC Poesia

The Verdict

Poesia has exceptional styling and a full range of activities and amenities, all in the line's typically international and very social setting.

MSC Poesia *(photo: MSC)*

Specifications

Typical Per Diems: $75–$120

Size (in tons)	89,600	Crew	987
Passengers (double occ.)	2,550	Passenger/Crew Ratio	2.6 to 1
Passenger/Space Ratio	35.1	Year Launched	2007
Total Cabins/Veranda Cabins	1,275/827	Last Major Upgrade	N/A

Frommer's Ratings (Scale of 1–5)

⭑⭑⭑⭑½

Cabin Comfort & Amenities	4	Dining Options	4.5
Appearance & Upkeep	4.5	Gym, Spa & Sports Facilities	4.5
Public Comfort/Space	4	Children's Facilities	4
Decor	4.5	Enjoyment Factor	4.5

Sailing Regions, Seasons & Home Ports

Poesia	**Caribbean,** from Fort Lauderdale (winter). **New England/Canada,** from New York & Quebec City (fall).

Poesia and her sister ships *Musica, Orchestra,* and *Magnifica* represent an evolutionary leap for MSC Cruises, which had previously concentrated on midsize vessels that get the job done but are a little short on pizazz. These four, on the other hand, are truly modern megaships, with high-style decor, multiple dining options, elaborate spas, wine-tasting bars, a multistory theater, and many appealing lounges and other features. *Poesia* has been the line's Caribbean/Canada/New England ship for the past couple of years, and will be back again for 2011 and (we'd bet) 2012. So, all details in this review deal with *Poesia* only.

CABINS   The majority of accommodations on *Poesia* (some 65% of them) are 166-square-foot outside cabins with balconies. Each is done up in a clean, pleasingly modern style, with lovely jewel-toned upholstery patterns (mostly subdued reds and blues) and light-wood accents, though they're sized a bit smaller than cabins on many competing megaships. Standard inside (152 sq. ft.) and outside cabins have flatscreen TVs, minifridges, private safes, vanity/writing desks, a bathroom with shower, and Wi-Fi access. Outside cabins also have a small sitting area and hair dryer. Closet and storage space are adequate, and the bathrooms are efficiently designed, with adequate amounts of shelf space, though for toiletries you get only the basics. The 18 suites (269 sq. ft, including the large balcony) add a larger sitting area, a king-size bed, a tub/shower combo, upgraded toiletries, bathrobes, and more closet space.

Seventeen cabins are wheelchair accessible—12 insides, two outsides with windows, and three outsides with a balcony.

PUBLIC AREAS   Public areas on *Poesia* are done in an eclectic style that mixes the clean lines of Princess, the modernism of Celebrity, the flashy ornateness of Costa and Carnival, and the fun of NCL, yet manages to pull them all together into a unified whole.

In the bow, the three-deck Teatro Carlo Felice is an explosion of lights and color, looking like fireworks caught in midburst. At midships, the three-deck atrium has a curvaceous, aquiline look, with a baby grand on a glass platform and stairways sweeping between the decks. Lounges, bars, shops, an Internet center, a card room, a small library, and an art gallery all radiate out from the atrium on various levels.

Most public rooms are clustered on the two upper atrium decks, including a show-room, a large casino, a cigar lounge with comfy leather armchairs, and a bright wine bar lit by faux skylights and serving vintages from all over Italy (with complimentary cheeses and meats to match). At the top of the ship, the disco mixes touches of deco styling with a futuristic dance-floor vibe.

For kids, there's an indoor play area with PlayStations, games, arts and crafts supplies, and more. There's also an enclosed outdoor area with a play structure, tube slide, wading pool, and other amenities.

DINING OPTIONS   *Poesia* has two main dining rooms, a buffet restaurant, an evening pizzeria, and a terrific a la carte Chinese restaurant. The main dining rooms are both single-level spaces, one decorated in traditional fashion, the other more sleekly modern. Ceilings in these restaurants are a bit too low, resulting in loud rooms during meals. Breakfast and lunch are served in the spacious buffet restaurant, with multiple lines for different specialties, and dishes labeled in both Italian and English. At night, part of the buffet restaurant is partitioned off to create **L'Obelisco,** serving more high-end Italian cuisine at a la carte prices.

POOL, FITNESS, SPA & SPORTS FACILITIES   The main Pool Deck is an expansive space with a Mediterranean vibe and two separate pool areas linked by a pair of deck bars and elevated seating areas for those who want to see or be seen. There are two pools and four Jacuzzis in all, plus a movie screen above the forward pool area. A separate small Sun Deck immediately under the screen is removed from the busier main deck below. Like those aboard all MSC ships, lounge chairs on *Poesia* have their own attached sun canopies—a very neat and unusual feature. The jogging track wraps around one deck above the pool (though don't try running during pool times, as the deck chairs take over), while a miniature golf course, quoits, shuffleboard, and sports court are located on Deck 15 aft.

Indoors, the ship's stunning Balinese-themed spa, operated by Italy's OceanView, offers the usual range of massage, wellness, and beauty treatments, all in a lovely, relaxing atmosphere with hints of exotica, including two Turkish baths (one for women, one for men) with beautiful decorative tiles. The 12 massage rooms are gorgeous, each having its own theme and aroma. A pre- or post-treatment relaxation room provides views, lounge chairs, and hydromassage pools (plus a thalassotherapy pool in an adjacent room); it's open for free to all guests for an hour at a time, by reservation. The juice bar has a menu of energy drinks and fresh fruit cocktails, usually from noon to 8pm. Nearby, the ship's gym is pretty small for a vessel this size, but it has a great forward view through floor-to-ceiling windows. The treadmills, aerobics machines, and weights get a lot of use, and there aren't really enough of them.

9 Norwegian Cruise Line

7665 Corporate Center Dr., Miami, FL 33126. ℭ **866/234-0292** or 305/436-4000. Fax 305/436-4126. www.ncl.com.

THE LINE IN A NUTSHELL Norwegian Cruise Line (NCL) may be the most mainstream of the mainstream lines these days—and we mean that in a good way. At a time when every cruise line seems to be pushing the quote/unquote "luxury" elements of their onboard programs, NCL hews to the upper center, with always-casual dining (and lots of it), cheerful and creative decor, and hip innovations like onboard bowling alleys, outdoor nightclubs, gourmet beer bars, and inside cabins with adjustable mood lighting. Its newest vessels are the most fun megaships at sea, and it's the go-to line for inter-island Hawaii cruises. Nutshell? NCL's the kind of cruise line you want to sit down and have a beer with. **Sails to:** Caribbean, The Bahamas, Panama Canal, Alaska, Mexican Riviera, Bermuda, Hawaii, Canada/New England, Pacific Coast (plus South America, Europe).

THE EXPERIENCE Back in the mid- to late '90s, NCL operated a mixed-bag fleet of older ships whose onboard vibe was only a couple of steps above budget. Fast-forward a dozen years and presto-chango: NCL is now one of the top players in the industry, with innovative itineraries, a fleet of new megaships, a casual onboard atmosphere, top-drawer entertainment, and a staggering number of dining choices. The line was the first to dump the old system of formal/informal/casual nights, going totally casual and starting a trend across the industry. The new program also did away with fixed dining times and seating assignments, leaving passengers free to choose when and where they want to dine among a variety of venues. Traditional tipping also went away, replaced by a system where gratuities are added directly to passenger accounts. Busy, busy, busy they've been, and it shows.

Pros

- **Fun:** There's no pretension at NCL. Their ships are designed to be fun and they really *are* fun, designed like bright, interactive playrooms for adults.
- **Flexible dining:** NCL's Freestyle Cruising policy lets you dine when and where you want, dressed "however."
- **Restaurants galore:** With between 6 and 20 places to grab a meal, your taste buds won't be bored.
- **Above-average entertainment:** In addition to quality musical groups and Vegas-style shows that are actually *good* (a rarity in the cruise biz), NCL also has comedy shows by the Second City comedy troupe aboard its newer ships, and performances by the Blue Man Group aboard its newest, *Norwegian Epic.*
- **Hawaii-centricity:** If you want to sail the islands, NCL's U.S.-flagged sub-brand, NCL America, offers the only big-ship cruises that never leave state waters.

Cons

- **Small cabins:** Though they seem to get a little bigger with each new ship, NCL's standard inside and low-end outside cabins are still a tighter squeeze than you find at most of the competition.

NCL: SAY HELLO TO INNOVATION

Talk about pulling yourself up by your bootstraps. Though Norwegian was one of the pioneers of North American cruising (begun in 1966 as an alliance btw. Norwegian

Compared with the other mainstream lines, here's how NCL rates:

	Poor	Fair	Good	Excellent	Outstanding
Enjoyment Factor					✓
Dining				✓	
Activities				✓	
Children's Program				✓	
Entertainment					✓
Service				✓	
Worth the Money					✓

ship owner Knut Kloster and Israeli marketing genius Ted Arison, who later started Carnival), it spent many years relegated to the industry's back seat behind biggies Carnival and Royal Caribbean. In 1997, though, it began a sequence of moves that transformed it into a true leader and innovator.

First it went casual, knocking the whole industry on its ear and prompting many other lines to revamp their dining policies and dress codes. Then it took over the Hawaii market by launching the first U.S.-flagged cruise ships in decades (a legal requirement for operating ships entirely within U.S. waters). After that, it went modern: As part of an ongoing upgrade, the line has sold off all of its older vessels, with the last of them, 1992's *Norwegian Majesty,* going to Cyprus-based Louis Cruises in November 2009. That leaves NCL with an extremely up-to-date fleet whose oldest vessel, *Norwegian Sky,* only dates to 1999. The most modern of all is the 150,000-ton, 4,200-passenger **Norwegian Epic,** which is scheduled to debut just as this book goes to press—a bit of bad timing that prevented us from being able to include a full review here. As such, most details in this section refer to the rest of NCL's fleet, unless noted otherwise. Once *Epic* has launched, you'll be able to find a full review online in the cruise section of Frommers.com.

PASSENGER PROFILE

In general, NCL passengers are younger and more active than those aboard lines such as HAL, Celebrity, and Princess. Typical NCL passengers are couples ages 25 to 60, and include a fair number of honeymooners and families with kids during summers and holidays. Kids under age 2 travel at a substantially reduced fare. The atmosphere aboard all NCL vessels is informal and well suited to casual types, party-makers, and both first-time and experienced cruisers.

DINING

All the restaurants on all NCL ships follow an open-seating policy each and every evening, allowing you to dine whenever you like within the 5:30 to 10pm window, sit with whomever you want (rather than having a table pre-assigned), and dress however you like: Management says anything goes except jeans, shorts, and tank tops, but we've seen those in the restaurants, too. This flexible setup really works for families, groups, and anyone else who doesn't want to be tied down to fixed mealtimes and tables, and who hates the idea of having to chat up the same bunch of dinner companions all week. If you end up sitting with people you do like, you can always make plans to dine with them again.

The night of the captain's cocktail party is officially an **"optional formal" night,** meaning you can wear a suit, tie, or fancy dress if you like, but no one will complain if you don't. That said, we've been surprised on recent cruises at just how many people do dress up.

TRADITIONAL   The main dining rooms, like the rest of the ships' eating venues, operate with open seating and casual dress codes, so the only really "traditional" thing about them is their size and a touch of old ocean-liner elegance. For cuisine, you can usually count on such choices as beef Wellington, broiled lobster tail, chicken Parmesan, fettuccine Alfredo, grilled swordfish with lemon-caper sauce, salmon or poached sea bass, or perhaps a Jamaican jerk pork roast, Wiener schnitzel, or roast prime rib. And lobster fans take note: Your favorite crustacean is available in the main restaurant on multiple days and in one or another of the specialty restaurants every night of the cruise.

The NCL wine lists appeal to standard mid-American tastes, and prices aren't offensively high.

A **light choice** (prepared with recipes from NCL partner *Cooking Light* magazine) and a **vegetarian entree** are available at all lunches and dinners. **Children's menus** feature the popular standards (burgers, hot dogs, grilled cheese sandwiches and french fries, spaghetti and meatballs, ice-cream sundaes, and so on), plus unexpected dishes like vegetable crudités and cheese dip.

SPECIALTY   In addition to one or two main dining rooms, all the NCL ships have at least six alternative specialty restaurants serving food that's on a par with all but the very best of the competition. Each ship has a French/Continental restaurant called **Le Bistro** plus choices such as Pan-Asian, Italian, Japanese, Pacific Rim, and Tex-Mex tapas (see the individual ship reviews for which ship has what). The food in Le Bistro is better than that in the main dining rooms, and includes items such as Caesar salad made right at your table and a marvelously decadent chocolate fondue served with fresh fruit (both by request only). Tables are sometimes available for walk-ins, but make your reservations as early as possible to be on the safe side.

Most of the specialty restaurants carry a cover charge, which ranges from $10 to $20 per person. Even with a reservations system, it inevitably happens that you'll sometimes have to wait for a table, but NCL is working on that, too. At this writing, nearly every ship in the fleet is outfitted with large **computerized billboard screens** placed outside restaurants and in various public areas on board. Each displays a listing of every restaurant on board (with photos and a description of the cuisine), along with the restaurant's status (open/closed), how busy it is at that moment, how close it is to filling up, and how long a wait there will be if it *is* filled up. For those who don't like to plan too far ahead, it's a great boon: You can head out for the evening and just decide where to dine on the fly. Maitre d's at every restaurant can take reservations at any of the other restaurants, too, so if one looks like it's filling up, you won't have to sprint to catch that last table—just amble to the nearest restaurant and have them call ahead for you. The system will eventually be available fleetwide through an interactive TV system. To get a taste of what each restaurant serves, take a walk around on embarkation day, when each one offers food samples.

One or two alternative restaurants are open for **lunch** as well as dinner on every sea day.

CASUAL   In addition to the numerous sit-down venues highlighted above (all of them casual in their own way), all NCL ships also have a buffet restaurant with indoor/outdoor seating, which is open for breakfast, lunch, and dinner. In addition to the usual meats, salads, pastas, and desserts, NCL buffets often include stations serving stir-fry dishes and all-vegetarian Indian spreads. See the ship reviews for more details.

SNACKS & EXTRAS Snacking opportunities include pizza and ice cream throughout the day at the buffet restaurant, a coffee bar serving specialty java and other beverages, and 24-hour room service for pizza, sandwiches, and other munchies. Food is also available 24 hours a day from at least one restaurant on each ship. One night a week (on all but the Hawaii ship), you can also drool over the popular **Chocoholic Extravaganza** buffet, serving everything from tortes to brownies.

ACTIVITIES

NCL has all the usual cruise activities, plus some unusual ones to spice things up, including workshops on **improv comedy,** organic cooking, and bartending. You can also take cha-cha lessons; play bingo, shuffleboard, or basketball; attend an art auction or spa or beauty demonstration; and, on some cruises, sit in on enrichment lectures about classic ocean liners, nutrition, personal investing, or other topics. There are snorkeling demonstrations in the pool, makeovers, talent shows, wine tastings (for $15 per person), and trivia contests, plus your classic cruise ship "silly poolside games." In Hawaii, *Pride of America* has many activities themed on **Hawaiian arts and culture,** while *Norwegian Pearl, Gem,* and *Epic* have onboard **bowling alleys.**

Internet cafes allow e-mail and Internet access fleetwide. For those wanting flexibility in their Web surfing, a Wi-Fi wireless system lets you log on from various places on board using your own or a rented laptop and an NCL network card. You can also use your **cellphone** through an onboard relay system (see chapter 3 for more about cellphone usage). In Hawaii, *Pride of America* sails close enough to shore that signals get picked up by regular land towers.

Gyms fleetwide are open 24 hours and have free stretching, step, aerobics, and other traditional classes. Spinning, kickboxing, Pilates, yoga, and other trendy choices cost an extra $10. All ships have golf driving cages where guests can practice at their leisure. In port, NCL's **Dive-In program** provides at least one snorkeling and one scuba excursion at almost every Caribbean port, escorted by the ship's certified instructors. In Hawaii and Bermuda, the line offers a comprehensive program of **golf excursions** to some of the islands' best courses, including Puakea, Poipu Bay, Princeville, and Kaua'i Lagoons (Kauai); Mauna Lani Resort, Hapuna, and Big Island Country Club (Hawaii); Makena, Wailea, and the Dunes at Maui Lani (Maui); Ko'olau Golf Club (Oahu); and the Ocean View, Belmont Hills, Mid Ocean, Port Royal, Tucker's Point, St. George's, and Riddell's Bay courses (Bermuda). *Pride of America,* the line's full-time Hawaii ship, also has an onboard pro shop.

CHILDREN'S PROGRAM

NCL's Kids Crew program has year-round **supervised activities** for children ages 2 to 17, divided into four age groups: Junior Sailors, ages 2 to 5; First Mates, ages 6 to 9; Navigators, ages 10 to 12; and teens, ages 13 to 17. Activities include sports competitions, dances, face painting, treasure hunts, magic shows, arts and crafts, cooking classes, T-shirt painting, and the Officer Snook Water Pollution Program, which uses games, crafts, storytelling, and other activities to educate young people about the effects of marine pollution and ways to prevent it. **Family events** such as pizza-making parties and scavenger hunts are also on the schedule, and kids get their own daily program detailing the day's events.

All the most recent NCL ships have huge **kids' facilities** that include a separate teen center and a wading pool, as well as a large, well-stocked playroom. Those on *Dawn, Star,* and *Spirit* are especially wonderful, with a huge combo climbing maze and ball bin indoors, and an outdoor kids' pool and hot tub area themed on dinosaurs *(Dawn),* rockets *(Star),* and pirates *(Spirit). Jewel, Gem, Jade,* and *Pride of America* have a much smaller kids' pool. On sea days, youth programs are held from 9am to noon, 2 to 5pm, and then 7 to 10pm; on port days, the complimentary hours are from 7 to 10pm. Port program times can also be adjusted to accommodate parents on shore excursions.

Once per cruise, the ships have a **Mom and Dad's Night Out,** when kids dine with counselors. Otherwise, **group babysitting** for kids ages 2 to 12 is provided nightly between 10pm and 1am (and 9am–5pm on port days) for $5 per child per hour, plus $3 an hour for each additional sibling. Counselors do not do diapers; parents are given beepers so that they can be alerted when it's time for the dirty work. Private babysitting is not available.

Unlimited soda packages are $4 per day for kids ages 12 and under. For anyone ages 13 or older, the same deal costs $6.25 per day.

ENTERTAINMENT

NCL has some of the best entertainment of all the mainstream lines, including, aboard many of its ships, sketch comedy shows by members of the famed **Second City comedy troupe,** which launched the careers of such legends as Bill Murray, John Belushi, and Gilda Radner. **Production shows** are way above average, too, with talented performers and good choreography, costumes, and set design. A show called *Tubez,* offered aboard *Pearl* in 2007, was one of the few truly contemporary shows we've ever seen at sea, with a mix of older and recent pop hits, hip-hop-inflected choreography and ballet, a rapper as the lead male vocalist, and bizarro elements like BMX bicycle acrobatics. Bollywood– and South Beach–inspired shows in recent years have also been standouts. Ditto for most of the other performers, including the musicians and comedians who play the ships' lounge circuit. On *Pride of America*'s Hawaii itineraries, 1 night a week is devoted to **Polynesian music and dance,** while another features an extra-cost production of the interactive off-Broadway hit *Tony n' Tina's Wedding.* The new *Norwegian Epic* features performances by the **Blue Man Group,** as well as an interactive, 2-hour dinner theater show staged by **Cirque du Soleil.**

For closet entertainers, the line puts on an *American Idol* kind of talent program called **Star Seeker,** which gives adults and kids the chance to prove themselves onstage. Videos of the performances serve as audition tapes for NCL's shore-side entertainment department, which sometimes hires the winners for one-time performances aboard a future (free) NCL cruise.

Big gamblers should avoid *Pride of America,* as Hawaiian law prohibits all gambling onboard.

SERVICE

Fleetwide, cabin service, room service, bar service, and dining service tend to be speedy and efficient.

In Hawaii, *Pride of America* **has an all-American service staff**—it's the only ship of this size that does, anywhere. On the plus side, staffmembers are almost uniformly friendly and helpful, and there are no English-as-a-second-language problems to deal with. On the downside, some can be just a touch too casual. What are you gonna do? American 20-somethings aren't generally known for their formality and refinement.

Fleetwide, tipping is done automatically, with a $12-per-day **service charge** added to each passenger's onboard account ($5 for kids 3–12). Though officially nonrefundable, the charge can be adjusted if you've experienced serious problems that the customer-service staff was unable to remedy.

NCL ships provide **laundry** and **dry-cleaning service.** *Norwegian Dawn, Jewel, Pearl, Jade,* and *Gem* all have self-service launderettes and ironing facilities for guests, and all ships have ironing boards and irons available from housekeeping upon request.

Passengers booked in balcony cabins, minisuites, and suites can access the services of a dedicated **concierge hot line** to make restaurant reservations, and so on.

Norwegian Epic

The Verdict

One of the biggest cruise ships at sea, *Norwegian Epic* is busy, bustling, showy, and fun. She's the best ship at sea for entertainment, with an amazing lineup from big shows to small, and she's also a winner for families, with great kids' facilities and water slides. Downsides? Her cabins, though chic, aren't the most functional, and she can sometimes feel a bit too busy and crowded.

Norwegian Epic *(photo: NCL)*

Specifications

Typical Per Diems: $85–$135

Size (in tons)	155,873	Crew	1,730
Passengers (double occ.)	4,100	Passenger/Crew Ratio	2.4 to 1
Passenger/Space Ratio	38	Year Launched	2010
Total Cabins/Veranda Cabins	2,114/1,351	Last Major Upgrade	N/A

Frommer's Ratings (Scale of 1–5)

★★★★ ½

Cabin Comfort & Amenities	4	Dining Options	5
Appearance & Upkeep	4	Gym, Spa & Sports Facilities	5
Public Comfort/Space	4	Children's Facilities	5
Decor	4	Enjoyment Factor	4

Sailing Regions, Seasons & Home Ports

Norwegian Epic	**Caribbean,** from Miami (spring/winter).

Big ships, like big mountains, tend to create their own weather. There they sit, looming above everything else in the landscape, while around them swirl great clouds of hype and expectation. Will they live up to it all, or will they (metaphorically) sink like a stone? Will they be Chris Daughtry or Sanjaya Malakar? Prius or Yugo? *Avatar* or *Ishtar*?

NCL's new *Norwegian Epic* has an extra-tough row to hoe, debuting after a tumultuous building process and in the shadow of Royal Caribbean's own, almost universally well-received giant, the 225,282-ton, 5,400-passenger heavyweight champ *Oasis of the Seas.*

So how does she stack up? Let us tell you: She has greatness in her, but she's not all great. She has charm, but she's not all charming. She has va-va-voom like an old-time vaudeville revue, but some acts you just want to pull offstage with a long cane. She's not a true game-changer like *Oasis,* but she has some attributes that we'd love to see become industry standard.

Originally designed to be the first of three identical super-megaships that, NCL hoped, would usher its casual "Freestyle cruising" concept into a new era, *Epic* almost ended up not being launched at all due to disputes with the shipyard regarding design changes and cost overruns. In the end, a compromise led to her completion, but the orders for her sister-ships were cancelled, leaving *Epic* as the sole vessel in her class and sibling to none. In a sense, we think that's probably a good thing, because many of *Epic's* failures (none huge, but a few annoying) are in her hardware, while most of her great successes are in her software: innovations that could very well be implemented aboard other vessels in the NCL fleet, whether the wonderful Jewel- and Dawn-class ships or some new, as-yet-unknown new NCL vessels of the future.

Our major complaint is that her layout can feel choppy and unintuitive, and when indoors it's very easy to forget that you're at sea. Decks 5, 6, and 7, the main interior public decks, often force people to walk through public rooms (the casino, shopping) to get from one end to another, and the placement of furniture and other impediments leads to bottlenecks. The Pool Deck is also choppy and full of odd angles, and when crowded can be very difficult to cross. On cabin decks, some staterooms are hidden away down corridors you can only access once you find the unmarked doors that lead to them. Now, granted, *Epic* is no more guilty in this regard than most other megaships launched over the past dozen years, and some of these things (the bottleneck issue, for instance) can probably be alleviated by just moving things around or adding additional signage—all things we suspect will happen over the next few months. But the point is, *Epic* could have been done better. Rather than simply building a larger version of a standard megaship, NCL should have taken things to the next step, as Royal Caribbean did with *Oasis* and *Allure* and Celebrity did with *Solstice, Equinox,* and *Eclipse*: Made a ship of the future, not just a larger ship of the past or present.

Regarding the lack of "at sea" feel we noted, that's both a minus and a plus. On the minus side, public rooms are laid out in such a way that you're rarely reminded you're in the middle of the ocean. On the plus side, *Epic* appears to be remarkably stable. Our recent sailing was on smooth seas out of New York, but at no time (and we mean no time) did we feel the movement of the ocean at all.

When all is said and done, and we've aired all our complaints about *Epic* being not exactly epic, but more, y'know, the same but bigger, we're happy to report that she's fun—fun the way NCL ships usually are: casual, social, completely un-stuffy, and with a nice, friendly feel. At night, she really hops. Between the entertainment and the multitude of bars and lounges, fun-loving passengers won't ever get bored. But the ship isn't just for the party crowd. Very obviously, NCL has set her up as a family-oriented vessel, with a great kids' playroom, hideaway teen center, three huge water slides, several climbing features, and a partnership that brings characters like SpongeBob Squarepants and Dora the Explorer from Nickelodeon onboard for various kids' activities.

Epic is, really, a sort of huge, busy experiment that, we hope and expect, NCL will continue to experiment with over time, tweaking her until she really shines. She's got a lot going for her as is, so it's just a matter of learning from mistakes and finding ways to work around them. In this, we wish NCL good luck, because it's no secret: We have a real soft spot for the line.

CABINS Let's get our complaints out of the way first and talk about the cabins' one major, weird, and annoying failure: their bathrooms. Really, what was NCL thinking?

Here's the concept: In each stateroom on board, the traditional bathroom—a separate, space with a door and containing all the necessaries—has been deconstructed. As you enter a cabin, you'll see immediately to one side a shower or bathtub with a sliding glass door. To the other side, you'll find the toilet in its own little booth, also with a sliding glass door, and there's a curtain you can pull across the whole entryway/bathroom area for privacy. The sink and medicine cabinet are in the cabin space itself, just beyond the toilet and shower booths. The idea seems to have been that this arrangement would allow two or more people to use the bathroom facilities simultaneously, without having to crowd into a tiny space. The reality, though, is that it all just doesn't work.

The most egregious failure is with the sinks, which combine a tiny, tiny bowl with a foot-tall, gooseneck faucet that, when turned on full, nearly shoots right out of the bowl and *always* splashes over the edge, no matter how careful you are. Since counters are also tiny (and often placed right next to the cabin's sitting area), water often shoots out onto the floor and furniture. NCL executives acknowledged this problem soon after the ship's launch and noted that they planned to replace the faucets and then evaluate whether replacing the sinks would also be necessary, so future cruisers may not have to deal with this particular issue. Until that happens, *Epic* cruisers can expect to do a lot of mopping and sopping.

Beyond the sink debacle, though, the "in-cabin" arrangement of shower and toilet present other problems: steam, for one. We noted that after a normal shower, cabin ceilings are often covered in condensation—unpleasant at best, and at worst a recipe for mold (or at least a major pain for the stewards who have to clean up). It's also very difficult to keep the floor of your entryway dry, so you have to remember to put on shoes when getting ready for dinner or you may end up with soaked socks. In short, we'd bet pretty good money that this bathroom arrangement won't be repeated on future NCL ships.

Bathrooms aside, *Epic's* staterooms have a lot of interesting features. Her balcony staterooms—which means *every* outside stateroom, since all outsides have balconies on this ship—are a big departure from cruise tradition, featuring free-form, curving walls rather than the oblong boxes typical on every other ship today. Walls sort of undulate from front to back, meaning some parts—for instance, where the bed is located—are wider than others. The effect is very pleasant, accented by other cabin features like concealed contour LED lighting, large back-lit round ceiling fixtures over the beds (which, combined with rounded-edge beds, give the sleeping area a "domed" effect), dark wood trim, and an earth-tone color palate. Each balcony cabin has a sitting area, a flatscreen TV, minibar, and a tea- and coffee-maker. Balcony cabins measure between 216 and 245 square feet and vary in the amount of closet and drawer space provided—some have a ton, others not so much.

Standard inside cabins (128 sq. ft.) lack the balcony staterooms' wavy walls, but unfortunately mimic their bathroom arrangement. All in all, they're pleasantly if simply styled, and have a flatscreen TV, a minibar, and a tea- and coffee-maker.

Also inside, but of a completely different character, are *Epic's* major accommodations innovations: her 128 Studio cabins. Years ago, many cruise ships (the old *QE2* comes to mind) were built with a number of small staterooms designed specifically for people traveling on their own. That idea died out over the past 3 decades, but *Epic* brings it back with a vengeance, creating a whole separate "wing" of the ship for solo travelers, who in addition to their staterooms also get private keycard access to the Living Room. This modern, double-height space is just for Studio guests, with its own bar, quiet reading area, TV screens, and concierge area. You can think of it as a swinging singles hangout, but that all depends on what kind of singles end up signing on. The Studios themselves were designed by a different creative team than the rest of the staterooms onboard, and you can tell: Where the standard staterooms are woody and calming, the Studios are all neon and bold angles, and pack a lot into their modest 100 square feet of space. Each has a padded white wall surrounding the bed, a large one-way "port-hole" window that looks out into the corridor, ingenious small storage nooks, and neon-esque lighting that you can adjust according to your mood. Glowing track lights also line the corridors outside. All Studios come with a flatscreen TV and tiny desk area, but not much else. Priced for the solo traveler (at about $150 per stateroom more than the per-person price of a double-occupancy inside), they can actually accommodate two hipsters, so long as you like togetherness.

In terms of suites, the big draw on *Epic*, as aboard NCL's other recent ships, is its Courtyard Villas, a separate "ship within a ship" area perched way up on Decks 16 and 17. Each villa combines spacious suite accommodations with access to a villa-guests-only courtyard whose pool is surrounded by plush daybeds and deck chairs, private cabanas, and tables for alfresco dining. The complex also features two hot tubs; a steam room; a private bar; a concierge lounge; a sun deck; a private gym overlooking the pool; and two private dining spots just for suite guests, one casual, one formal. The suites themselves are knockouts, with separate bedrooms and living/dining rooms; huge, gorgeously appointed bathrooms with an oceanview, whirlpool tubs and showers; large private balconies; and floor space that ranges from 506 to 852 square feet. Smaller courtyard penthouses lack separate living and bedroom spaces, but their design is pretty cool, with an oval bed in the center of the room and elaborate bathroom spaces behind it, separated by a curving partition curtain.

A total of 42 staterooms and suites across a range of categories are wheelchair accessible.

PUBLIC AREAS   Public areas aboard *Epic* are clustered on Decks 5, 6, and 7, essentially bow to stern. In the bow on Decks 5 and 6, the main Epic Theater is home to two of the ship's main entertainment offerings: the *Blue Man Group* and *Legends in Concert.* Blue Man, for those who haven't seen it in Vegas, New York, or elsewhere, is an ever-evolving piece of performance art in which three . . . aliens, essentially, dressed in black coveralls and wearing blue body paint, run though a program of surrealistic gags and set pieces based around half-willing audience participation, edgy humor, drums (big ones), videography, unexpected detours, improvisation, and paint, lots and lots of paint—so much that audience members in the first rows are all given plastic ponchos to wear over their clothes. The Blue Men maintain a stony, Buster Keatonesque silence, communicating with the audience only through intense eye contact and gestures, but they set up such a great sense of play that sometimes a participatory routine will go on and on, just because no one in the audience is willing to stop having fun. Short story? They put on the best show at sea today, partly through pure quality (we laughed our butts off), party because they're essentially the anti-cruise-ship-show: quirky and renegade instead of staid and predictable. Big kudos to NCL for getting them aboard ship. The Epic Theater's other show, *Legends in Concert,* presents performances by celebrity-impersonators including faux Elvis, Madonna, Tina Turner, Britney Spears, Diana Ross, and others.

The remainder of Deck 5 comprises the ship's art gallery (pretty much a yawner), its Internet center (there's also Wi-Fi all around the ship, if you have your own computer or smartphone with you), and its photo gallery, which uses facial recognition technology so you can easily find all photos of you shot by the ship's photographers. Toward midships, a two-story atrium houses the ship's reception decks, a cafe, and a two-story video screen that's used for Wii video games, sports events, filmed concerts, and other specials. The screen is visible from the atrium floor and also from O'Sheehan's bar on Deck 6. One of our favorite spots onboard, O'Sheehan's Neighborhood Bar & Grill (named for NCL's CEO, Kevin Sheehan) is a multipurpose kind of bar, with three bowling lanes to one side, pool tables to the other, a Bennigan's-looking dining section on its port side, and a nice bar area to starboard, serving a decent if not applause-inducing selection of domestic and international beers and liquors. We found this to be the best meeting spot on board, but somehow we always ended up staying for awhile rather than going to do the work that we'd planned. Guess that means it's a good bar.

Just forward on Deck 6 is the hub of *Epic's* entertainment district, with access to three separate theaters and showrooms: the Epic Theater, the Spiegel Tent, and Headliners Comedy Club. The Spiegel Tent is a new kind of entertainment venue for a cruise ship, offering a dinner-theater-in-the-round experience, with seating around the main space and on a surrounding balcony. Unfortunately, the show to which it's normally dedicated, *Cirque Dreams and Dinner,* was for us a major disappointment. The concept: A troupe of allegedly penniless circus performers put on a show using whatever they can find at hand, which mostly means the audience. Doesn't sound bad so far, but it gets there. First problem: The audience is trapped. An actor announces at the beginning that there will be no bathroom breaks; audience members/diners are required to stay in their seats for the entire 2-hour performance. Second problem: Much of the performance is shrill, manic, and in-your-face—not what we enjoy while eating. Now, let us qualify by saying it's not all bad: The concept of a dinner-theater-in-the-round aboard ship has a lot of promise. Secondly, several vignettes throughout the show feature talented acrobats, including three musclemen who hoist each other into impossible positions, and trapeze artists and aerialists who do remarkable things in a confined space. If they put the emphasis more on the acrobatics and de-emphasized the silly accents and shrill speeches, they might have something. (And that's the beauty of live theater: If something isn't working, you can always change it.) The Spiegel Tent is also home to a special murder mystery show called *Presumed Murdered,* presented once per cruise by the Second City comedy troupe. Second City also provides great sketch and improv comedy acts throughout the cruise at Headliners, where you can also see a dueling-pianos-and-comedy show by a group called Howl at the Moon.

Heading sternward from O'Sheehan's on Deck 6, *Epic* funnels guests through a long expanse of casino before you reach Fat Cats Jazz & Blues Club. This was a big highlight of our recent cruise, made great by the fact that the musicians here play the way they would in a land-based club—no holding back for the little old ladies (or at least, not holding back much). Our first night aboard, the Slam Allen Blues Band kicked through a wide range of material, from Albert King to Otis Redding to George Benson, and also included passages of inspired improvisation. The show is also participatory: Both nights we ducked in, Allen invited any musicians who happened to be in the audience to come up and sit in, taking over for one of the band members—and some did, adding a dose of spontaneity to the usually well-planned cruise entertainment line-up.

One deck up from Fat Cats, *Epic* offers a "Bar Central" cluster of nightlife venues, similar to those on its recent Jewel-class ships. There's Maltings Whiskey Bar, Shakers Martini Bar, and, most interesting of all, the Svedka Ice Bar, a frozen locker kept at 17 degrees Fahrenheit, where the furniture and artwork are all made of ice, specialty vodka drinks are served in ice goblets, and guests have to wear parkas. Nearby, a small barbershop offers shaving services and other beauty touchups for men. Best touch here? The absolutely godawful haircut model pix from the 70s that adorn the walls. Moving forward, the remainder of Deck 7 is taken up with shops—a lot of shops, offering the usual range from logo-wear to dutyfree booze to high-end watches and jewelry. In the bow, the Bliss Ultra Lounge continues a concept inaugurated aboard *Norwegian Star* some years ago, with its velvety, bordello-meets-nightclub decor and (yo, hipsters!) a few bowling lanes and video games off to the sides. Up on Deck 15, the stern-facing Spice H2O is an outdoor nightclub with a dance floor and bar.

For kids, *Epic* has an extensive children's center on Deck 14, with Wii and Playstation 3 games, a dance floor, a movie room stuffed with beanbag chairs, a climbing maze and ball-jump pit, and more. Teens get their own space, a hangout and nightclub called Entourage, located up a hideaway staircase on Deck 16.

DINING OPTIONS   You can't argue with the numbers: In total, *Norwegian Epic* has 21 dining choices, some complimentary, some entailing an extra charge, and a few exclusively for guests in the ship's suites or Studio cabins. Taste, one of the two main restaurants, is set in a cool space at the bottom of the ship's main atrium, while restaurant no. 2, the Manhattan Room, is an Art Deco space with a two-deck window overlooking the ship's wake, and a bandstand and dance floor. Both serve contemporary menus that mix favorites with various daily specials. In the Manhattan room, musical acts mix it up on the stage with impersonators from the *Legends in Concert* show, and Manhattan cocktails are prepared tableside.

Specialty restaurants (all of which charge a per-person cover or price a la carte) include Cagney's Steakhouse, a classic dark, woody meatery ($25 per person); Moderno Churrascaria, a South American–style steakhouse where servers keep bringing slices of grilled meats to you until you pop or tell them to stop ($18 per person); La Cucina, a casual, family-style Italian restaurant hidden away in the stern and accessed via a stairway from the Garden Cafe ($10 per person); Le Bistro, the ship's fancy French eatery, serving suitably rich cuisine in an intimate, high-end space ($20 per person); Shanghai's, a classic Chinese restaurant ($15 per person); the Noodle Bar, attached to Shanghai's, serving a variety of casual noodle dishes (a la carte pricing); Teppanyaki, where knife-wielding chefs slice, dice, and grill your Asian specialties right in front of you on hot grills, sliding each order right onto your plate ($25 per person); and Wasabi, which serves lovely orders of sushi and sashimi accompanied by a selection of sakes (a la carte pricing). The *Cirque Dreams & Dinner* shows in the Spiegel Tent are accompanied with a straightforward menu of favorites accented by a chocolate decadence dessert ($15–$20 per person).

On the casual side, the Garden Cafe on Deck 15 has multiple stations serving different cuisine, including meats, pastas, salads, Indian (vegetarian and meat), sandwiches, and so on. Indoor tables surround the space, and there are also tables outside, facing the Great Outdoors grill, pizza, salad (and more) area. Down on Deck 6, O'Sheehan's Bar & Grill serves as an adjunct casual option at lower midships, serving comfort foods throughout the day, including breakfast. The Atrium Cafe and Wine Bar also serves desserts and specialty coffees throughout the day.

A nice touch: Pizza delivery is available 24 hours a day, and you can get it delivered anywhere on the ship—to your cabin, to a bar or nightclub, or elsewhere. Delivery costs $5.

POOL, FITNESS, SPA & SPORTS FACILITIES *Epic* has one of the busiest, most activity-packed Pool Decks we've ever seen—and whether that's a good thing or not depends on your taste.

The biggest standout feature is the deck's three giant water slides, which take off from a platform several decks up. Two allow for dark bodysurfing rides through long, twisting tubes, while the Epic Plunge involves riding an inner tube through a snaking, 200-foot pipe before being flung out into a large open-top bowl, where your momentum flings you into a few fast spins before you're flushed down a final short tube and into the deceleration zone. A great ride! But the water slides take up a lot of real estate—so much so that the actual pool area of the ship seems remarkably small and constrained, considering the number of people onboard. The area includes two main pools (with water jets that are illuminated at night for a little water-show fun), a wading pool and kids' pool, and five hot tubs. Behind and below the water slides, the kids' Splash and Play Zone has water-spouting sculptures and water sprays, along with a kiddie slide. Nearby, the ship's 33-foot-high, 64-foot-wide rock-climbing and rappelling wall has approaches at varying degrees of difficulty. Two decks up, on Deck 17, a sports and play area includes a full-size basketball court (which doubles for volleyball and soccer), a batting cage, a bungee trampoline, and the 24-foot-tall Spider Web, an enclosed cage laced with giant rubber bands that one has to climb on and through to get to the top.

Epic's fitness center and spa are located on Deck 14 in the stern. The giant Mandara Spa—allegedly the largest spa at sea, though we didn't get out our tape measure to check—has 24 treatment rooms, a relaxing thermal suite (offered for a fee and including a therapeutic plunge pool and heated tiled loungers), and a sprawling lobby stocked with expensive creams, lotions, and quick fixes. Our coauthor Heidi got a great massage here from a skilled South African therapist, though she could have done without the sales pitch for creams and elixirs at the end.

The ship's well-stocked fitness center has dozens of treadmills, cross-trainers, and exercise bikes; free weights and kettlebells (the first of the latter we've seen on a ship); and four different aerobics studios. Group classes include TRX suspension training, kettlebell training, yoga, Pilates, and group cycling.

A jogging track runs up and down the Promenade on the starboard side of Deck 7—you run one way, make a very tight loop, then run right back.

Dawn & Jewel Classes: Norwegian Spirit • Star • Dawn • Jewel • Jade • Pearl • Gem

The Verdict

With a mix of classy and fun spaces, a lively atmosphere, awesome kids' facilities, and an amazing number of restaurants, these are some of the most original mainstream megaships to come along in years.

Norwegian Pearl *(photo: NCL)*

Specifications

Typical Per Diems: $70–$115

Size (in tons)		Total Cabins/Veranda Cabins	
Spirit	77,000	*Spirit*	983/390
Star	91,000	*Star*	1,120/515
Dawn	91,740	*Dawn*	1,112/509
Jewel	92,000	*Jewel*	1,188/510
Pearl	93,502	*Pearl*	1,197/538
Jade/Gem	93,558	*Jade/Gem*	1,190/542
Passengers (double occ.)		Crew	
Spirit	1,966	*Spirit*	965
Star	2,240	*Star*	1,100
Dawn	2,224	*Dawn*	1,126
Jewel	2,376	*Jewel/Pearl/Jade/Gem*	1,150
Pearl	2,394	Passenger/Crew Ratio	2 to 1
Jade/Gem	2,380	Year Launched	
Passenger/Space Ratio		*Spirit*	1999
Spirit	39.1	*Star*	2001
Star	40.6	*Dawn*	2002
Dawn	41.2	*Jewel*	2005
Jewel	38.7	*Pearl*	2006
Pearl/Jade/Gem	39.3	*Jade/Gem*	2007
		Last Major Upgrade	
		Spirit	2004

Frommer's Ratings (Scale of 1–5)

★★★★ ¹/₂–★★★★★

Cabin Comfort & Amenities	4	Dining Options	5
Appearance & Upkeep	5	Gym, Spa & Sports Facilities	4
Public Comfort/Space	5	Children's Facilities	5
Decor	4.5	Enjoyment Factor	4.5

* More fully realized than their sister ships, Norwegian Jewel, Pearl, Jade, and Gem earn a five-star rating.

Sailing Regions, Seasons & Home Ports

Norwegian Dawn	**Caribbean,** from Miami (spring/winter). **Bermuda,** from New York (summer/fall).
Norwegian Gem	**The Bahamas & Florida,** from New York (spring/winter). **Bermuda,** from New York (summer/fall).
Norwegian Jade	**Europe** (year-round).
Norwegian Jewel	**Caribbean,** from Miami (winter). **The Bahamas & Florida,** from New York (spring/summer/fall).
Norwegian Pearl	**Caribbean,** from Miami (spring/winter). **Alaska,** from Vancouver (summer/fall).
Norwegian Spirit	**Caribbean,** from New Orleans (year-round).
Norwegian Star	**Mexican Riviera,** from Los Angeles (spring 2011). **Alaska,** from Seattle (summer/fall). **Caribbean,** from Tampa (winter, spring 2012).

These sexy sisters are (along with *Norwegian Epic*) the most fun megaships at sea today. Each has a supersocial atmosphere, creative decor, and onboard music and pop culture references tailored to a surprisingly young demographic—generally, from folks in their 20s to folks in their 50s. Are these the Generations X and Y megaships? Could be.

The word of the day is "options." Want fun? How about *Spirit*'s Maharini's Lounge, with its bordello-like, velvet-draped seating nooks (with beds even!), or the Bliss Ultra Lounge on *Pearl* and *Gem,* which juxtaposes the same bordello decor with a four-lane, Day-Glo bowling alley. Want food? Each of these ships has 8 to 10 different restaurants, from fancy steakhouses and teppanyaki restaurants to casual Tex-Mex and burger joints. Want fantasy? The nightclubs and atriums feature furniture right out of *Alice in Wonderland.* Want high style? Check out *Dawn*'s and *Star*'s Gatsby's Champagne Bar, and *Jewel, Pearl,* and *Gem*'s Bar Central on Deck 6.

Want extravagance? These ships' Garden Villas spread out to an astonishing 5,350 square feet, making them the largest suites at sea today. Each features private gardens, multiple bedrooms with mind-blowing bathrooms, separate living rooms, full kitchens, and private butler service. Zowie! Zowie, too, on their price: about $13,750 per person, per week, for the first two guests, and $499 for each additional guest (up to a maximum of six people). Normal cabins, on the other hand, come at normal prices.

NCL divides these ships into three classes: *Dawn* and *Star* in the Dawn class; *Jewel, Pearl, Jade,* and *Gem* in the Jewel Class; and *Spirit* all by herself, with no class name at all. Overall, though, these ships are vastly more similar than different, with all but *Spirit* (the oldest of the bunch, and which came to NCL from the Star Cruises fleet) sharing a nearly identical layout. The Jewel-class ships, though, are more fully realized vessels, with a number of additional attractions.

CABINS   Standard inside (142 sq. ft.) and outside (158–205 sq. ft.) cabins, though not overly large compared to some in the industry (particularly those of Carnival's and Holland America's ships), are larger than aboard NCL's older ships. Decor is a mix, with stylish elements (such as cherrywood wall paneling and snazzy rounded lights), kitschy elements (such as bright island-colored carpeting), and cheap touches (such as some spindly chairs and end tables, and wall-mounted soap dispensers in the bathrooms). Each comes with a small TV and minifridge, a tea/coffeemaker, a private safe, and cool, retro-looking hair dryers. Closets and drawer space are more than ample for weeklong sailings, and bathrooms in all categories are well designed, with large sinks whose faucets swing out of the way, a magnifying mirror inset in the regular mirror, adequate though not exceptional counter/shelf space, and (in all but inside cabins) separate shower and toilet compartments. Balconies in standard cabins accommodate two metal chairs and a small table, but aren't terribly roomy.

Minisuites (229 sq. ft.) provide about 60 more feet of floor space than standard cabins, with a large foldout couch, a curtain between the bed and the sitting area, and a bathtub. The so-called Romance Suites really are romantic, with 288 square feet of space, a stereo with CD/DVD library, a bathroom with separate shower and tub, and nice wooden deck chairs on the balcony. Penthouse Suites offer the same, plus gorgeous bathrooms with a whirlpool tub and tiled, seaview shower stall, a larger balcony, and a walk-in closet. Some suites have a separate kids' room and bathroom. Those facing the bow on Decks 9 and 10 have large windows and deep balconies, but safety requirements mandate that instead of a nice glass door, their balconies are accessed via honest-to-God steel bulkheads marked FOR YOUR OWN SAFETY, OPEN ONLY WHEN THE VESSEL IS IN PORT.

The ships' Owner's Suites are huge, with two balconies, living and dining areas, a powder room, a guest bathroom, and 750 square feet of space. Compared to the two Garden Villas up on Deck 14, though, these suites are peasant's quarters. The Garden Villas are, in a word, H-U-G-E, the biggest at sea today at 5,350 sq. ft., comprising an enormous living room with a grand piano, dining room, three bedrooms with their own extravagant seaview bathrooms with whirlpool tubs, private Italian garden (with pool, hot tub, and sun deck), panoramic views all around, and private butler service. They're priced beyond the range of . . . well, pretty much everybody, but on the other hand, they do sleep six adults and there's room for two rollaway beds and three cribs, so if you share with your whole clan, who knows?

Norwegian Jewel, Pearl, Jade, and *Gem* have an intermediate level of smaller Courtyard Villas on the same top-of-the-ship deck as the Garden Villa. They offer spacious suite accommodations coupled with access to a villa-guests-only courtyard, a private sun deck, and a staffed concierge lounge. The courtyard is a stunner, with a small private swimming pool, hot tub, and several plush, shaded sun beds. The suites (which open to a hallway around the courtyard rather than right into it) are also knockouts, with a separate bedroom and living/dining room; a huge, gorgeously appointed bathroom with an oceanview whirlpool tub and shower; a large private balcony; and floor space that ranges from 440 to 572 square feet. The larger Courtyard Penthouses also have a separate children's room with a foldout couch bed and a second bathroom. Prices for Courtyard Villas tend to hover in the $5,000 range for weeklong itineraries.

Four cabins are wheelchair accessible aboard *Spirit,* as are 20 on *Star,* 24 on *Dawn,* and 27 on *Jewel, Pearl,* and *Gem.*

PUBLIC AREAS You'll be in a party mood from the moment you step aboard into the ships' large, broad atrium lobbies. Public areas throughout the vessels are fanciful and extremely spacious, done in a mix of bright, Caribbean- and Miami-themed decor and high-style Art Deco, with lots of nooks and some downright wonderful lounges and bars mixed in among all the restaurants.

On the main entertainment deck, a multideck theater has 1,000 seats sloping down to a large stage. There's also a nightclub for smaller-scale cabaret entertainment and dancing. Deck 12 features a complex of "sit-down" rooms, including a comfortable cinema with traditional theater seats, a library, a card room, a reading room, a "lifestyles" room (used for classes, private functions, and so on), several meeting rooms, and a small wedding chapel. Forward of these is an observation lounge/disco with some fanciful *Alice in Wonderland* seating. Up top, on Deck 13, there's a nice bar/lounge with piano entertainment in the evening. *Dawn, Spirit,* and *Star* have a British-themed pub with piano entertainment, a big-screen TV for sports, and tasty fish and chips; and *Spirit* and *Star* also have a covered outdoor Bier Garten stocked with German pilsner, *hefeweizen,* and wheat beers. *Jewel, Pearl, Jade,* and *Gem* instead have three themed bars clustered together in a Bar Central arrangement on Deck 6. Their beer and whiskey bars are the best at sea, with about 45 beers and 65 whiskeys to choose from. Next door is a martini/cocktail bar and a champagne/wine bar.

Aboard *Spirit,* Maharini's combines Bollywood Indian themes with a kind of fashion-world ambience, its mood-lit nooks separated by thick red-velvet curtains and outfitted with large, comfortable daybeds strewn with pillows. Sexy! The similarly decorated Bliss Ultra Lounges on *Pearl* and *Gem* add four 10-pin bowling lanes to the bordello vibe, gaining NCL points for retro-chic credibility.

Other rooms include a spacious casino, an Internet center, several shops, and a coffee bar.

For kids, these ships have some of the better facilities at sea, with a huge, brightly colored crafts/play area, a big-screen TV room stuffed full of beanbag chairs, a huge ball jump/crawling maze play-gym, and a computer room. Outside, the pool areas on *Dawn, Star,* and *Spirit* are fantastic. On *Dawn,* it's right out of *The Flintstones,* with giant polka-dotted dinosaurs hovering around faux rock walls, slides, a paddling pool, and even a kids' Jacuzzi. *Star's* has a space-age rocket theme. *Norwegian Jewel, Pearl, Jade,* and *Gem* have much smaller outdoor play areas. There are video arcades and teen centers on all six ships, with computers, a dance floor equipped with a sound/video system, and a soda bar.

DINING OPTIONS These ships are all about their restaurants, with between 8 and 10 on each ship—two or three main formal restaurants plus a buffet, at least one casual diner/cafe, and several alternative specialty restaurants serving Italian, steakhouse, French/Continental, and Asian cuisine. The Asian restaurants provide three separate experiences: a main Asian-fusion restaurant, a sushi and sake bar, and an intimate Japanese teppanyaki room where meals are prepared from the center of the table as guests look on. The high-end French/Continental restaurant, Le Bistro, serves classic and nouvelle cuisine in an atmosphere of floral tapestry upholstery and fine place settings. On *Dawn,* Le Bistro is adorned with original Impressionist paintings by Matisse and Monet, while *Pearl* has paintings by Van Gogh and Renoir, all lent from the private collection of Tan Sri Lim Kok Thay, chairman and CEO of NCL's parent company, Star Cruises. All the ships but *Spirit* also have a casual Tex-Mex/tapas eatery. *Star* has a restaurant serving Pacific Rim cuisine. Specialty restaurants cost between $10 and $20 per person.

Out on deck, each ship has a casual grill serving up burgers, dogs, and fries during the day.

POOL, FITNESS, SPA & SPORTS FACILITIES   Main pool areas have the feel of a resort, ringed by flower-shaped "streetlamps," deck chairs arrayed around the central pool and hot tubs, and (on *Star, Jewel, Pearl, Jade,* and *Gem*) a large corkscrew water slide. At a huge bar, running almost the width of the ship, ice cream is served on one side, drinks on the other. Nice space, but the real plaudits go to the stylish spas, with the one aboard *Dawn* taking the prize. At the entrance, its sunlit foyer rises three decks high and is decorated with plants and Maya reliefs, with a juice bar on the side. Inside, the spa is centered on a kind of "aqua suite" with a large lap pool, hot tub, jet-massage pool, and sunny seating areas with windows and furnished with wooden deck chairs, all of it hearkening back to the indoor pools on the classic transatlantic liners. *Spirit* also has Aqua Swim, a room with two stationary lap pools. *Jewel, Pearl, Jade,* and *Gem* have four of the better onboard gyms of recent years—large and extremely well appointed, with dozens of fitness machines and a large aerobics/spinning room.

Outside there's an extralong jogging track, a sports court for basketball and volleyball, golf-driving nets, and facilities for shuffleboard and deck chess, plus acres of open deck space for sunning. *Dawn* and *Star* provide a nice spot on the tiered Sun Deck, where a lone hot tub looks out over the bow. *Spirit,* on the other hand, has a beautiful tiered, amphitheater-like stern looking down to a pirate-themed kids' pool.

Pride of America

The Verdict

Sailing from Honolulu, concentrating solely on the islands, and carrying an American crew, this vessel is literally in a class by herself.

Pride of America *(photo: NCL)*

Specifications   Typical Per Diems: $130–$165

Size (in tons)	81,000	Crew	1,000
Passengers (double occ.)	2,146	Passenger/Crew Ratio	2.1 to 1
Passenger/Space Ratio	37.7	Year Launched	2005
Total Cabins/Veranda Cabins	1,073/665	Last Major Upgrade	N/A

Frommer's Ratings (Scale of 1–5)   ★★★★

Cabin Comfort & Amenities	4	Dining Options	5
Appearance & Upkeep	4	Gym, Spa & Sports Facilities	4
Public Comfort/Space	4	Children's Facilities	4
Decor	4	Enjoyment Factor	5

Sailing Regions, Seasons & Home Ports

Pride of America	**Hawaii,** from Honolulu (year-round).

Because *Pride of America* is U.S.-flagged and U.S.-crewed, she's in compliance with U.S. cabotage laws, and that means she is legally permitted to sail entirely within U.S. waters, visiting only U.S. ports—and that makes her quite literally unique: There is no other large cruise ship in the world that can claim that distinction. Because of this, she's the only big ship with cruises that operate entirely within Hawaiian waters, sailing round-trip from Honolulu. Because Hawaii's islands are all relatively close together, that means she's able to visit a Hawaiian port every single day, and even do overnights in Kauai and Maui, giving you an opportunity to sample nightlife ashore and get a better feel for both of these beautiful islands. During the week, you get to choose from some 150 excursions, creating a Hawaii itinerary to suit your preferences.

On the downside, because these cruises put so much emphasis on the port experience, with many excursions starting in early morning and taking up most of the day, passengers tend to come back to the ship, eat an early dinner, and crash from exhaustion. Translation: If you want a cruise with lots of onboard activities and a heavy nightlife, this isn't the one for you. Lastly, although prices for the cruises themselves are relatively low, expect lots of extra costs, from the $12-a-day automatic gratuity to expensive drinks, pricey Internet access, and the bundle you're bound to spend on shore excursions or renting cars in port. (Because most of the islands' real attractions aren't near the port facilities, you have to take an excursion or rent a car if you want to see anything worth seeing.)

CABINS Cabins on *Pride* are pretty—with most sporting wood-grain walls, and carpets, upholstery, and bedspreads done in vibrant, Hawaiian-accented pinks, blues, oranges, purples, and greens—but they tend to be small, with the vast majority of standard inside (121–147 sq. ft.) and outside cabins (149–243 sq. ft.) being about 20% smaller than similar cabins aboard Carnival. Storage space is fairly limited. All staterooms have a small sitting area or desk, a minifridge, a hair dryer, TVs, coffee- and tea-making equipment, plus a dataport to accommodate laptop users. Bathrooms are adequate size. Balcony cabins particularly come in handy on the nighttime run between Kona and Hilo, since you can watch the lava flowing from Kilauea Volcano without changing out of your pajamas. The captain turns the ship 360 degrees at the optimum viewing point, so cabins on both sides get a view. The majority of outside cabins have balconies, including cabins located almost all the way forward (some to port and starboard, some facing front with recessed balconies).

There are 23 cabins equipped for wheelchairs. The ship has laundry and dry-cleaning service, but does not have self-serve launderettes.

PUBLIC AREAS *Pride of America's* decor matches her name, with public rooms throughout decorated to celebrate aspects of American culture and geography. Giant photographs of the Grand Canyon, Monument Valley, Mount Rainier, the Golden Gate Bridge, the Chicago skyline, and other sites adorn the stair towers, and U.S. themes dominate the decor of many restaurants (see below). *America,* the ship—that is, the old United States Line's vessel SS *America*—is the motif of the SS *America* Library, which holds memorabilia and artifacts from the vessel as well as a scale model built specifically for the room. Despite her year-round Hawaiian itineraries, *Pride's* actually employs relatively little Hawaiian imagery beyond some art, some carpeting and upholstery, and the small Hawaiian cultural display in the atrium. If you like, you can enjoy Hawaii's own Kona Beer on tap in the (hmmm . . .) Gold Rush Saloon, with its prospector decor. For a more elegant drinking experience, head to the Napa Wine Bar, with decor of stone-pattern walls, box-shaped light fixtures, and light woods and upholsteries, which straddles the line between Napa Valley casual and hip 1950s lounge. In a nice touch, a door opens to outdoor seating on the Promenade Deck. Nearby, Pink's Champagne and Cigar Bar spans the width of the ship, with bright Hawaii-patterned carpeting and a contrasting 19th-century-casino-style chandelier hovering above its piano-bar piano. Way up on Deck 13, the small, intimate, and beautifully designed Lanai Bar & Lounge is located next to one of the largest dedicated meeting spaces at sea, with auditoriums and facilities for up to 550 participants. For kids, the Rascal's Kids Club has an elaborate indoor jungle gym, a movie room full of beanbag chairs, computer terminals, a large play space, and a protected outdoor splash pool with tube slide. Next door, the teen center is designed like an adult lounge, with a "bar," dance floor, and games.

Because of Hawaiian law, there's no casino or any other gambling on board. If you've got a craving to gamble, head to the card room, where you might find a secret game of Texas Hold 'Em in progress. The password is *swordfish.*

DINING OPTIONS   *Pride of America's* two main restaurants are the Skyline Restaurant, with its Art Deco decor and skyscraper motifs, and the mucho Americano Liberty Restaurant, with its greeting statues of George Washington and Abe Lincoln, stars-and-ribbons carpeting, soaring-eagle-motif glass ceiling and glass Mount Rushmore, and bunting-style curtains that give it the look of an old-time political rally. Passengers can also choose from several intimate, extra-cost options: the Lazy J Texas Steakhouse, where waiters serve in cowboy hats; Jefferson's Bistro, an elegant eatery modeled after the president's home and serving French cuisine; the Little Italy Italian restaurant; and East Meets West, a Pan-Asian restaurant with attached sushi/sashimi bar and teppanyaki room. Alternative, reservations-only restaurants carry a charge of $10 to $20 per person. For late-night cravings, the Cadillac Diner serves burgers, shakes, and other diner fare 24 hours, with additional seating outside on the Promenade Deck. On Deck 11, the Aloha Cafe buffet is designed with multiple serving islands both inside and out.

Because of the ship's emphasis on port calls, restaurants tend to be busiest early, with long lines often forming right at 5:30pm. The later you dine, the less the wait and the better the service, as the staff won't be as rushed. *Tip:* It's easier to get reservations at alternative restaurants for the first couple of nights and on luau night in Maui, when most passengers stay ashore.

POOL, FITNESS, SPA & SPORTS FACILITIES   *Pride's* well-stocked oceanview gym is open 24 hours a day, and the adjacent aerobics room has floor-to-ceiling windows and a great selection of stretching, step, and other traditional classes at no extra charge, plus spinning, kickboxing, and other trendy choices for $10 per class. Nearby, the spa and salon afford ocean views as well, plus the small outdoor Oasis Pool. *Pride of America's* Pool Deck, its central outdoor space, is a bit underwhelming. Look to the deck above, however, for a couple of fun toys: a trampoline with bungee harness to keep you from flying over the side, and a "spaceball challenger" gyroscope in which passengers, suitably strapped in, can revolve 360 degrees in any direction, like astronauts in outer space.

A wraparound Promenade Deck allows for a great stroll.

Norwegian Sky •
Norwegian Sun

Norwegian Sun *(photo: Matt Hannafin)*

The Verdict

The older (but still not very old) *Sun* and *Sky* have a cozier feel than NCL's bigger, newer ships, yet still feature multiple restaurants and lots of cabins with balconies.

Specifications

Typical Per Diems: $60–$105

Size (in tons)		*Sun*	1,001/432
Sky	77,104	Crew	
Sun	78,509	*Sky*	1,000
Passengers (double occ.)		*Sun*	968
Sky	2,002	Passenger/Crew Ratio	2 to 1
Sun	1,936	Year Launched	
Passenger/Space Ratio		*Sky*	1999
Sky	38.5	*Sun*	2001
Sun	40.6	Last Major Upgrade	
Total Cabins/Veranda Cabins		*Sky*	2009
Sky	1,001/257	*Sun*	N/A

Frommer's Ratings (Scale of 1–5)

★★★★

Cabin Comfort & Amenities	4	Dining Options	4.5
Appearance & Upkeep	4	Gym, Spa & Sports Facilities	4
Public Comfort/Space	4	Children's Facilities	3.5
Decor	4	Enjoyment Factor	4

Sailing Regions, Seasons & Home Ports

Sky	**The Bahamas,** from Miami (year-round).
Sun	**Caribbean,** from Port Canaveral (spring/winter).

Norwegian Sky and *Sun* were the first two megaships built for NCL's modern era, and blazed the trail that all the later ships followed, with multiple restaurants and everything designed with casual cruising in mind. *Sky* spent 4 years sailing as *Pride of Aloha* for NCL's Hawaii operation, but is now sailing The Bahamas itineraries under her original name.

CABINS *Sky's* cabins are done up in fun, lively island colors, but they're quite small and have limited closet and storage space—just a two-panel closet and a small bureau with four slim drawers—so be prepared to use your suitcase to store whatever. Oh, and watch out for those reading lamps above the beds: Their protruding shades make sitting up impossible. The vast majority of standard inside cabins (118–191 sq. ft.) and outside and balcony cabins (147–173 sq. ft.) run smaller than similar cabins at a lot of competing lines. Bathrooms are also compact, with tubular shower stalls and slivers of shelving.

It's worth noting that *Sky*'s hull was originally built by Costa, which planned for the cabins to have portholes and no balconies. Costa sold the hull to NCL after the shipyard went bust, and, unwilling to bring out a megaship without balconies, NCL compromised, working around the existing portholes and adding balconies, resulting in an odd door-and-porthole combo (most ships have sliding-glass doors) between cabin and balcony.

Norwegian Sun is heavy on suites and minisuites, the latter of which measure a roomy 264 to 301 square feet (plus 68- to 86-sq.-ft. balconies) and have walk-in closets, sitting areas, and bathtubs. Twenty 355- to 570-square-foot Penthouse and Owner's suites (with 119- to 258-sq.-ft. balconies) include the services of a butler and concierge who will get you on the first tender to port, make dinner reservations, and generally try to please your every whim. The pair of penthouses also has a separate living room and dining area. Among the regular balcony cabins, categories BA, BB, and BC (which take up most of Decks 8–10) are laid out awkwardly, with the twin beds and the closet-dresser unit positioned too close together. A person dragging a suitcase has to twist up like a pretzel to squeeze by. Other than that, the decor is pleasant with caramel-wood veneers; attractive gilt-framed artwork; and navy, gold, and Kelly green fabrics and carpeting. Storage space is plentiful, so much so that on a recent cruise, we couldn't even manage to fill up all the shelves. The bathrooms have a pair of shelves above the counter and a really useful one in the shower, though otherwise the skinny shower stalls can be a tight squeeze. Cabins at the forward end of Deck 6 have large portholes that look out on the ship's wraparound Promenade Deck (which is popular with walkers and runners, so you'll probably want to have your curtains closed most of the time). Every cabin has a small sitting area, a minifridge (not stocked), a hair dryer, TV, desk and chair, and a coffee/tea-maker.

Six cabins on *Sky* and 20 cabins aboard *Sun* are equipped for wheelchairs.

PUBLIC AREAS   Even though *Norwegian Sky* is the older of these two vessels, refurbishments in 2008 and 2009 made her decor much fresher and more fun; *Sun* is still done up in a pleasing but not too jarring pastiche of mostly cool blues, sages, deep reds, and soft golds blended with marble, burled-wood veneers, and brass and chrome detailing.

Both ships are bright and sun-filled due to an abundance of floor-to-ceiling windows. Surrounding the understated three-level atrium on several levels is a bar, some clusters of chairs creating relaxing pockets, and an area where a pianist performs. Each ship has nearly a dozen bars, including a sports bar, wine bar, nightclub/disco, two large poolside bars, a coffee bar, an Internet cafe, and a dark and cozy cigar club with the most comfortable, thick, buttery leather chairs and couches around. With soft ballads coming from the adjacent piano bar as background music, the cigar bar is the most appealing place on the ship for quiet conversation (unless, of course, you can't stand smoke). Many of the balcony seats in the two-story show lounge have obstructed views of the stage, and decor-wise, this isn't one of the ships' most impressive spaces. Still, the lights are low most of the time, and the focus is on the stage, where it should be. There's a large, attractive observation lounge wrapped in windows on one of the top two decks; at night, it's a venue for live music. The casinos are large and flashy enough, though not as over the top as those on Carnival's and Royal

Caribbean's ships. The layout of the shops is attractive, with a wide streetlike corridor cutting between the main boutiques and a long, elegant jewelry counter.

For kids, the ships' huge children's area includes a sprawling playroom with ridiculously high ceilings, a teen center with a large movie screen and foosball games, and a video arcade. Each ship also has a wading pool.

DINING OPTIONS   Like the rest of the NCL fleet, *Sun* and *Sky* excel in the restaurant department. For breakfast, lunch, and dinner, there are two elegant dining rooms with lots of tables for two and four. A large, well-organized indoor/outdoor casual buffet restaurant serves all three meals, plus snacks (such as pizza and cookies) in between. For dinner, you can also choose from eight alternative restaurants on *Sun* and three on *Sky*. Both have **Le Bistro,** an elegant space with lots of windows and several comfy round booths mixed among the regular tables ($10 cover charge). Both ships also have a long, narrow restaurant that stretches between the two main restaurants. On *Sun,* it's **Il Adagio,** an Italian eatery where Caesar salads are prepared from scratch table-side and the warm chocolate hazelnut cake is to die for ($10 cover charge). On *Sky,* the space houses **Cagney's,** an elegant steakhouse. *Sky's* version of Il Adagio is located on the Pool Deck, where it mixes healthy cuisine with gourmet pizza and low-cal desserts. *Sun* also has a **sushi bar,** serving expertly prepared, fresh-tasting maki and California rolls ($15 cover); the adjacent teppanyaki venue, where a chef theatrically cuts and flings shrimp, chicken, beef, and other ingredients at a center table ($20 cover); the **East Meets West Steakhouse,** where $20 per person will buy you some mighty slabs of meat; **Pacific Heights,** a health-oriented dinner venue (no charge); the **Tex-Mex/tapas restaurant,** serving an assortment of finger food (no charge), along with sangria and a selection of Mexican beer; and the **Ginza Japanese Restaurant.**

POOL, FITNESS, SPA & SPORTS FACILITIES   The well-stocked oceanview gyms on these ships are open 24 hours a day, and the adjacent aerobics room has floor-to-ceiling windows and a great selection of classes, from spinning to kickboxing. Nearby, the Balinese-inspired spa and salon affords ocean views as well. On *Sun,* while you wait to be led to your treatment room, you can relax in a serene sitting area with a wall of glass facing the sea.

Out on deck, there's a pair of pools with a cluster of four hot tubs between them. One deck up, you'll find a combo basketball/volleyball court, a pair of golf driving nets, and shuffleboard. On *Sun,* the kids' wading pool and some cute mini-chaise-longues are conveniently tucked along the starboard side of the Sports Deck (near a door to the interior of the ship); on *Sky,* it's in a more desolate spot far forward on the Sports Deck, where there's also a fifth hot tub.

10 Oceania Cruises

8300 NW 33rd St., Ste. 308, Miami, FL 33122. ℂ **800/531-5619** or 305/514-2300. www.oceaniacruises.com.

THE LINE IN A NUTSHELL   Oceania is the phoenix that rose from the ashes after Renaissance Cruises went belly up in September 2001. The line operates three of Renaissance's lovely midsize ships and mimics some attributes of much pricier lines, with excellent service and cuisine and a quiet, refined onboard feel. It's also set to launch its first purpose-built newbuild ever, not long after this book hits the shelves. **Sails to:** Caribbean, Panama Canal (plus Europe, South America, Asia, Africa).

THE EXPERIENCE Oceania is positioned as an "upper premium" line intended to fill the service and ambience gap between big-ship premium lines such as Celebrity and Holland America and real luxe lines such as Crystal and Regent Seven Seas. It goes for a kind of floating country club feel, with a low-key ambience, few organized activities, small-scale entertainment, a casually sporty dress code, an emphasis on cabin comfort, and long itineraries that favor smaller, less visited ports. Prices are higher than premium competitors Azamara, Celebrity, Holland America, and Princess, though they often include airfare to the port of embarkation.

Pros

- **Excellent cuisine:** In both the main dining room and specialty restaurants, Oceania is near the top among mainstream lines.
- **Excellent, personal service:** The ships' international crews are extremely friendly and eager to please.
- **Intimate size:** Oceania's original three ships carry only 684 passengers apiece, making for a much more human-scale feel than you get aboard a megaship. Their much larger newbuilds still only carry 1,258, less than half the complement of the average new megaship.
- **Nonsmoking policy:** On these ships, smoking is permitted only in two small areas of the Pool Deck and nightclub. (Of course, this is a con for smokers.)

Cons

- **Few outside decks:** On the line's three 684-passenger ships, there's only a Pool Deck, a Sun Deck, and the deserted Promenade/Boat Deck, which is never used because it has no deck chairs or other furniture. Aside from the many private cabin balconies, you'd have a hard time finding a quiet little outdoor nook.
- **Few activities:** By design, Oceania generally leaves passengers to their own devices. This is a con only if you need constant stimulation.

OCEANIA: CLASS ACT, COZY SHIPS

Remember Renaissance Cruises? Founded in 1988, it made news in the '90s by building a large fleet of identical medium-size ships and going directly to consumers rather than working with travel agents. Both of these were fairly revolutionary moves back then, and, as often happens with revolutions, this one fizzled. Already in bad financial shape when 9/11 hit, the line was forced into bankruptcy during the resultant travel downturn. Left high and dry, its eight ships were put up for auction to the highest bidder. Oceania, founded by former Renaissance CEO Frank Del Rio, started up in 2003 with two of them (the former *R1* and *R2*, renamed *Regatta* and *Insignia*) and added a third, *Nautica,* in late 2005. The remaining Renaissance vessels are now owned by Princess (*Pacific Princess* and *Ocean Princess*), and Azamara (*Azamara Journey* and *Azamara Quest*), and P&O Cruises *(Adonia).* In 2007, Oceania was effectively bought by Apollo Management, an investment group that also owns Regent Seven Seas Cruises and has a 50% stake in NCL. The infusion of cash allowed Oceania to plan two new 1,260-passenger, 65,000-ton ships, which are being built at Italy's Fincantieri shipyards. The first, named *Marina,* will debut in January 2011. The second, named *Riviera,* will debut in April 2012. Because the new ships are appearing after this book goes to press, most details in this review refer to its original three 684-passenger vessels, unless otherwise noted.

Compared with the other mainstream lines, here's how Oceania rates:

	Poor	Fair	Good	Excellent	Outstanding
Enjoyment Factor				✓	
Dining				✓	
Activities		✓			
Children's Program	N/A				
Entertainment			✓		
Service				✓	
Worth the Money				✓	

PASSENGER PROFILE

Due partially to the length of these cruises (mostly 10, 12, and 14 days, with some monthlong sailings spicing up the mix) and partially to the low-key onboard atmosphere, Oceania tends to attract older passengers who prefer to entertain themselves and enjoy the destination-heavy itineraries. Most are Americans, and many have sailed previously with Oceania (or even with Renaissance back in the old days). A sprinkling of younger couples usually find themselves on board as well, though children are rare enough to be surprising. Whatever their age, passengers tend to be drawn by the line's 100% casual dress code and ambience.

Because of Oceania's stringent **nonsmoking rules,** most passengers are nonsmokers. Aside from one corner of the Pool Deck and one corner of the Horizons nightclub, smoking is not permitted anywhere on board—even in your cabin or private balcony.

DINING

Oceania's dining experience is one of its strongest suits, with menus created by renowned chef Jacques Pépin (one-time personal chef to Charles de Gaulle and, more recently, one of America's best-known chefs and food writers). Passengers are able to choose among four different restaurants for dinner: the main Grand Dining Room, the Mediterranean-style Toscana restaurant, the Polo Grill steakhouse, and the Tapas on the Terrace casual outdoor option. All four venues work on an open-seating basis (dine when you want, with whom you want), with meals usually served in a 3-hour window from 6:30 to 9:30pm. The new *Marina* and *Riviera* will have nine different dining options, including a main dining room and four specialty restaurants.

TRADITIONAL   The **Grand Dining Room,** the main restaurant aboard each ship, features French-inspired Continental cuisine in five courses, with a string quartet providing music at dinner. Appetizers might include grilled marinated prawns, frog-leg mousse, and crushed new potatoes with chives and Malossol caviar, while soups might be as traditional as beef oxtail consommé or as unusual as Moroccan harira chicken soup. There are always several salads and a pasta of the day, and entrees are elaborate, well-presented versions of the big favorites (lobster tail butterfly, beef Wellington, steamed Alaskan king crab legs), plus some uncommon dishes: sautéed sea bream filet and pheasant breast *ballotine* stuffed with morel mushrooms. There's always a tasty **vegetarian option,** plus an alternative selection of basics: grilled sirloin, broiled chicken, salmon filet, and the like, and a selection of **spa cuisine** created in conjunction with the Canyon Ranch Spa Club (available in the buffet restaurant as well).

SPECIALTY Two specialty restaurants—the Italian **Toscana** and the **Polo Grill** steakhouse—appear aboard every Oceania ship, both their original fleet and their two newbuilds. Toscana is sinfully overwhelming, serving half a dozen antipasti and an equal number of pasta dishes, soups, salads, and main courses such as medallions of filet mignon topped with sautéed artichoke and smoked mozzarella; swordfish steak sautéed in garlic, parsley, Tuscan olives, capers, and Orvieto wine; and braised double-cut lamb chops in a sun-dried tomato, olive, and roasted garlic sauce. Polo Grill serves chops, seafood, and cuts of slow-aged beef, with all the substantial trimmings: seafood appetizers, soups such as New England clam chowder and lobster bisque, straight-up salads such as Caesar and iceberg wedge with blue cheese and crumbled bacon, and side dishes such as a baked potato, wild mushroom ragout, and creamed spinach. Passengers can make reservations for either restaurant during breakfast or lunch hours at the Terrace Cafe. There's no extra charge, but there's an initial two-reservation limit to ensure that all guests get a chance. If you'd like to dine here more than twice, add your name to the waiting list and you'll be contacted if there's space (which there usually is).

The new *Marina* (the only one of the two new vessels for which details were known at press time) will have two additional specialty restaurants, as well as two even more intimate dining spots. **Jacques,** created by and named for Jacques Pépin, is intended to mimic the cozy bistros of Paris and of Pépin's hometown, Lyon. Meals will proceed at a relaxed, friendly pace, beginning with a basket of three different freshly baked baguettes served with pâté, gherkins, and pâté-like salmon and chicken *rillettes.* Menu highlights will include an appetizer of homemade pumpkin soup *à l'Anglaise* served in a pumpkin shell, fresh mussels *marinière,* freshly roasted free range chicken, duck, and lamb. There will also be daily chef's specials prepared from goods purchased in local markets at the ship's ports of call. Meals end with a choice of nine French desserts and a cheese tray. **Red Ginger** will be an Asian restaurant serving contemporary interpretations of Asian classics. The ships' **La Reserve wine bar** will also serve special wine-pairing dinners limited to 24 guests, while a little room called **Privée** will offer seven-course degustation menus for private groups limited to 10 passengers.

CASUAL On the casual side, the **Terrace Cafe** is a standard cruise ship buffet serving a range of sides, salads, main courses, and desserts. An attached pizzeria serves very tasty thin-crust pies. At lunch, the Pool Deck's grill is also fired up, serving burgers, hot dogs, and specialty sandwiches. In the evening, the outdoor portion of the Terrace is transformed into **Tapas on the Terrace,** a romantic eatery with regional Spanish and Mediterranean specialties, other ethnic dishes, and home-style favorites served from a buffet. Waiters are on hand to serve drinks and generally be charming.

SNACKS & EXTRAS **High tea** is served daily at 4pm in the Horizons Lounge, with a good spread of pastries, tea sandwiches, and scones. **Room service** is available 24 hours. Guests in Owners, Vista, and Penthouse suites can have full meals served course by course in their rooms.

ACTIVITIES

By design, activities are not a high priority for Oceania. Expect **enrichment lectures** themed around the region being visited; fitness, photography, and computer classes; informal health and beauty seminars by the spa and salon staff; and a handful of old cruise standards such as bingo and shuffleboard. For people who are self-motivated and/or prefer to spend their time aboard reading on deck or in one of the library's overstuffed leather armchairs, the sparse activities schedule is ideal. If you like a lot of

Preview: Oceania's *Marina & Riviera*

In late March 2007, Oceania announced plans to build a pair of 1,258-passenger, 65,000-ton vessels dubbed the Oceania class, a nod to the fact that they're the first new vessels built for the line. (*Regatta, Insignia,* and *Nautica* were all built originally for Renaissance Cruises.) Unfortunately for us, the first of the pair, *Marina,* was slated to debut just after this book hit the shelves, so we're unable to provide you with a firsthand look. However, we do know some details.

Both inside and out, the new ships will be an extension of the line's current Regatta-class vessels, retaining the same boutique-hotel feel while adding new amenities and a little extra engine punch that will allow them to travel 20% faster (and thus, sail farther on each itinerary). Also, 96% of all staterooms will have private teak verandas, and Owners Suites will be decorated with furniture, fabrics, bedding, and other accouterments from the Ralph Lauren Home collection. The ships will have four alternative restaurants (steakhouse, Mediterranean, Pan-Asian, and French bistro, the latter created by Jacques Pépin), they'll have spas operated by Canyon Ranch, and they'll have activities like cooking and art classes taught by visiting experts. According to the line, the ships will also employ the most advanced systems and technologies for minimizing their environmental impact.

Both vessels are being built by Italian shipbuilder Fincantieri, while their interiors are designed by Yran & Storbraaten, the architects behind the decor of Disney's *Magic* and *Wonder,* Silversea's *Silver Whisper* and *Silver Shadow,* and Regent's *Seven Seas Mariner* and *Seven Seas Navigator.*

At press time, *Marina* was set to debut for the line in January 2011, and *Riviera* was to follow in April 2012. More details about the ships' programs and features are sprinkled elsewhere throughout this review.

organized activities, though, this is not the line for you. Oceania's three original ships have smallish, 19th-century-style casinos that see a fair amount of action.

The newer *Marina* will have a few more options. The **Bon Appétit Culinary Center,** operated through a deal with *Bon Apétit* magazine, will offer hands-on cooking classes taught by guest chefs from around the world. At the **Artist Loft,** meanwhile, rotating artists-in-residence will give short courses in disciplines ranging from watercolors to needlepoint.

Spas aboard all the line's ships, old and new, are run by **Canyon Ranch,** which made its name with celebrated resort spas in Arizona and Massachusetts and later opened them at sea aboard *QM2* and the Regent Seven Seas ships. **Internet access** is available in each ship's Oceania@Sea Internet center, at terminals in the library, and via full-vessel Wi-Fi service. All cabins on all ships include a **wireless laptop** to allow Internet access, though you have to pay to use them.

CHILDREN'S PROGRAM

There are no special facilities on these ships, and the line typically carries very few children.

ENTERTAINMENT

The good news: You won't be assailed by steel-drum bands doing bad Bob Marley covers. Instead, you'll get a jazz band on deck in the afternoon and in the club at night; pianists performing Cole Porter, Hoagy Carmichael, and other standards at the martini bar before dinner; and an occasional string quartet.

The bad news: That's the high point of the onboard entertainment. Each night, the main show lounge presents a comedian, solo musician, folkloric act, or other guest headliner, but the shows don't have the breadth you'll find on larger vessels. Of course, there also aren't any big, bad Vegas-style song-and-dance revues, and for that we whisper a prayer of thanks.

Other entertainment includes the occasional karaoke session or movies.

SERVICE

The staff in the restaurants are crack troops, delivering each course promptly but without any sense that they're hurrying passengers through meals. Service balances precision with friendliness, skewing close to the kind of understated professionalism you see on the real luxury lines. The relatively small number of passengers aboard also means service is more personal than you find aboard the megaships. In the bars, staff tend to remember your drink order by the second day, and cabin stewardesses greet their passengers by name in the corridors. Like many other lines, Oceania adds an **automatic gratuity** to your shipboard account ($12.50 per person, per day, which may be adjusted up or down at your discretion). For guests occupying Owner's, Vista, and Penthouse suites, there's an additional $4-per-day gratuity for butler service.

There's a **self-service laundry** and ironing room on Deck 7, in addition to standard laundry, dry cleaning, and pressing service provided by the ship's laundry.

Regatta

Regatta *(photo: Oceania)*

The Verdict

With her smallish size, understated decor, and serene atmosphere, this mostly non-smoking ship is more like a quiet boutique hotel than a cruise vessel, providing a comfortable, laid-back, yet stylish way to experience the Caribbean.

Specifications

Typical Per Diems: $305+

Size (in tons)	30,200	Crew	400
Passengers (double occ.)	684	Passenger/Crew Ratio	1.7 to 1
Passenger/Space Ratio	44.2	Year Launched	1998
Total Cabins/Veranda Cabins	343/232	Last Major Upgrade	2005

Frommer's Ratings (Scale of 1–5)

★★★★

Cabin Comfort & Amenities	4	Dining Options	4
Appearance & Upkeep	4	Gym, Spa & Sports Facilities	4
Public Comfort/Space	4.5	Children's Facilities	N/A
Decor	4	Enjoyment Factor	4

Sailing Regions, Seasons & Home Ports

Regatta	**Caribbean,** from Miami (winter). **Panama Canal,** from Miami (spring), from San Francisco (fall). **Alaska,** from Vancouver, Anchorage & San Francisco (summer). **New England/Canada,** from New York & Montreal (fall).

Imagine a cozy, classically styled boutique hotel in the shape of a cruise ship and you've pretty much got the idea. Like all of the former Renaissance vessels, *Regatta* is comfortable and spacious, decorated mostly in warm, dark woods and rich fabrics. She's traditional and sedate, with an emphasis on intimate spaces rather than the kind of grand, splashy ones you'll find on most megaships. Of course, her small size means there'd be no *room* for grand spaces, even if they'd been desired: Carrying only 684 passengers, *Regatta's* intimacy is one of her main selling points. The atmosphere is relaxed and clubby, with no formal nights that demand tuxedos and gowns.

Since the beginning of its existence, Oceania has concentrated on worldwide itineraries, typically positioning just one of its ships—always *Regatta*—in the Caribbean for the winter season while sister ships *Insignia* and *Nautica* sail elsewhere. For 2011, *Regatta* will be joined on Panama Canal and Caribbean sailings by her newer, larger fleetmate *Marina*.

CABINS Staterooms aboard *Regatta* are straightforward, no-nonsense spaces with a hint of European city hotel: plain off-white walls, dark-wood trim and furniture, and rich carpeting. The highlight of each, though, is its Tranquility Bed, an oasis of 350-thread-count Egyptian cotton sheets and duvet covers, down duvets and pillows, custom-designed extrathick mattresses, and a mound of throw pillows to prop you up during the late-late show. Spacious balconies have teak decking for a classic nautical look, and all cabins have televisions, safes, vanities with mirrors, hair dryers, phones, sitting areas, and full-length mirrors. Closet space is a little skimpy considering the lengthy itineraries these ships sail, but drawer space scattered around the cabin, and space under the beds, make up for this a bit. Almost all cabins measure in the 165-square-foot range, with some measuring 216 square feet, including balcony—not tiny, but not exceptionally large, either. There are also some bizarre little quirks. Light switches, for instance, can be mystifying: There doesn't seem to be any way to turn off the bedside lights until you discover the tiny, almost hidden buttons up near their shades. There are also switches for the overheads right in the headboard, which makes it very easy to switch them on accidentally in your sleep.

Suites (322–982 sq. ft., including balcony) include minibars, bathtubs, and a small area with a cocktail table for intimate in-room dining. Ten Owner's Suites measure 786 to 982 square feet and are located at the ship's bow and stern, featuring wraparound balconies, queen-size beds, whirlpool bathtubs, minibars, living rooms, and guest bathrooms. Owners Suites, Vista Suites, and Penthouse Suites feature butler service. Concierge-class staterooms (in btw. regular cabins and suites) add some warm-and-fuzzy to the amenities, including a welcome bottle of champagne, complimentary shoeshine service, and a DVD player; priority embarkation, check-in, luggage delivery, and restaurant reservations; and additional bathroom amenities, such as massaging shower heads and luxury toiletries.

Three cabins are wheelchair accessible.

PUBLIC AREAS Overall, *Regatta* presents an elegant yet homey appearance, with dark-wood paneling, fluted columns, ornate faux-iron railings, gilt-framed classical paintings, Oriental-style carpets, frilly moldings, marble and brass accents, and deep-hued upholstery, all contributing to a kind of "English inn at sea" look. In the bow, the spacious, woodsy Horizons lounge has floor-to-ceiling windows and brass telescopes on three sides. It's used for dancing in the evenings and for various activities during the day. The 345-seat show lounge has cabaret and variety acts, musical recitals, magic shows, and comedy, and the smallish but comfortable casino allows for blackjack, poker tables, roulette, and slots. The attached Martini Bar has a ridiculously long martini list (some 30 recipes and an equal number of vodka choices) and is a very relaxing space in the pre-dinner hours, when a pianist plays standards. A jazz band performs here in the evenings.

Another notable space is the comfortable library, decorated in a traditional English style with warm red upholstery, mahogany paneling, a *trompe l'oeil* garden "skylight," and marble faux fireplace.

DINING OPTIONS The main dining room is an elegant single-level space surrounded on three sides by windows. It's spacious and understated, with simple wood-veneer wall panels, wall sconces, and teal carpeting. Tables seating between two and eight are available, though the smaller arrangements go fast. Just outside the maitre d' station is a cozy bar area where you can have a pre-dinner cocktail while waiting for your dinner companions. The ship's two specialty restaurants, the Polo Grill and Toscana, are both located in the stern on Deck 10, and are decorated to match their cuisine: woodsy, old-Hollywood decor in Polo and a bright white Mediterranean feel with Roman urns and reliefs in Toscana. The restaurants serve 96 and 90 guests, respectively. On Deck 9, the Terrace serves buffet breakfast, lunch, and dinner, the latter out under the stars, with drink service, Spanish cuisine, and candles flickering in lovely hurricane lamps. It's a very romantic spot if you can time your meal to the sunset.

POOL, FITNESS, SPA & SPORTS FACILITIES The attractive teak Pool Deck, dotted with canvas umbrellas, has a pair of hot tubs plus a slew of deck chairs and large daybeds for sunbathing. The Patio, a shaded outdoor lounge located in the aft port corner of the Pool Deck, is furnished with thickly cushioned sofas, chairs, and daybeds. Drapes and general ambience add a hint of partition from the pool goings-on (not to mention shade), but you still feel like you're in the action. For more privacy, passengers can rent one of eight private cabanas on Deck 11, each with privacy partitions and white drapes that can be drawn or left open, plus great sea views, a retractable shade roof, and a plush daybed built for two. They're available either daily ($50 on port days, $100 on sea days) or for the entirety of your cruise, and come with the services of an attendant who provides food and beverage service, chilled towels, and water spritzes. Guests can also arrange to get massages and other spa treatments in their cabanas.

A small jogging track wraps around the deck immediately above the Pool Deck, while the fully equipped Canyon Ranch spa on Deck 9 offers a variety of treatments, including aromatherapy massages, hot-stone treatments, and various wraps and facials. Just forward of the spa there's an outdoor hydrotherapy whirlpool overlooking the bow. A decent-size oceanview gym and beauty salon are attached.

11 Princess Cruises

24305 Town Center Dr., Santa Clarita, CA 91355. ℰ **800/PRINCESS** [774-6237] or 661/753-0000. Fax 661/259-3108. www.princess.com.

THE LINE IN A NUTSHELL   With a fleet of mostly large and extralarge megaships, L.A.-based Princess offers a quality mainstream cruise experience with a nice balance of tradition and innovation, relaxation and excitement, casualness and glamour. **Sails to:** Caribbean, Alaska, Mexican Riviera, Hawaii, Canada/New England, Panama Canal (plus Europe, Asia, Australia/New Zealand, South America, South Pacific, transatlantic).

THE EXPERIENCE   If you were to put Celebrity, Holland America, and Royal Caribbean in a blender and mix them together, then add a pinch of both British maritime tradition and California style, you'd come up with Princess. Dining, entertainment, and activities are geared to a wide cross section of cruisers. The more traditional minded can spend some time in the library, join a bridge tournament, enjoy a formal dinner in a grand dining room, and then take in a show. Those seeking something different can paint their own pottery, dine in an intimate Italian or steakhouse restaurant, then take in a set of small-group jazz or an outdoor big-screen movie afterward. The majority of the line's largest vessels are very large, yet still manage to have intimate spaces for quiet times. And they're good lookin', too.

Pros

- **Lovely ships:** All in all, Princess's Diamond-, Grand-, and Coral-class ships are among the best-looking megaships in the market, with good exterior lines and spacious, pleasant interiors.
- **Lots of dining choices and flexibility:** Each ship has multiple main dining rooms, plus an intimate alternative restaurant or two and a 24-hour buffet. You can dine at a fixed time and place or wing it as you go along.
- **Excellent lounge entertainment:** Princess books top-quality entertainers for its piano lounges and smaller showrooms.

Cons

- **Pottery Barn decor:** More of a qualifier than a con: Princess's ships are very pleasant, yes, but the sea of beiges and blues is so safe that it can be a bit of a yawn. Artwork in public areas and staterooms tends toward bland.
- **Small gyms:** For such large vessels, the gyms are surprisingly small and can even feel cramped.

PRINCESS: SMART CASUAL

The Princess story goes back to 1962, when company founder Stanley McDonald chartered a vessel called the *Yarmouth* to use as a floating hotel at the Seattle World's Fair. In 1965, he officially started Princess Cruises, naming the company after another chartered vessel, the *Princess Patricia,* which took cruises between Los Angeles, Alaska, and Mexico's Pacific coast. In 1974, Princess was snapped up by British shipping giant P&O, and later that decade got a big boost by having its ships featured on the TV series *The Love Boat*. To this day, Gavin "Captain Stubing" MacLeod acts as occasional pitchman for the line. (*Pacific Princess* and *Island Princess,* the twin 640-passenger vessels used in the series, left the fleet a decade ago, but their names have since been recycled on new vessels.) In 2003, P&O Princess was purchased by Carnival Corporation, the 500-pound gorilla of the cruise world.

Compared with the other mainstream lines, here's how Princess rates:

	Poor	Fair	Good	Excellent	Outstanding
Enjoyment Factor				✓	
Dining				✓	
Activities				✓	
Children's Program				✓	
Entertainment				✓	
Service				✓	
Worth the Money				✓	

Although its ships sail to nearly every destination covered in this book, Princess is particularly strong in **Alaska,** where it offers more than 20 different cruisetour itineraries in conjunction with its Gulf of Alaska and Inside Passage voyages, visiting Denali National Park, Fairbanks, the Kenai Peninsula, Wrangell–St. Elias National Park, Canada's Yukon Territory, and distant Prudhoe Bay on Alaska's north coast. Guests on these land tours stay in five Princess-owned wilderness lodges and travel via motorcoach and the line's domed train cars. A new **a la carte cruisetour option** introduced in 2010 bundles transportation and accommodations into relatively low-priced packages, then leaves you free to explore the destinations on your own rather than taking part in the line's organized tours.

PASSENGER PROFILE

The majority of Princess's guests are in their 40s, 50s, 60s, and older, though more and more 30-somethings (and their families) are sailing these days, particularly during summer school holidays. Overall, Princess passengers are less boisterous than those aboard Carnival and not quite as staid as those aboard Holland America. Its ships all have extensive kids' facilities and activities, making them suitable for families, while their balance of formal and informal makes them a good bet for a romantic vacation, too, with opportunities for doing your own thing mixed in among more traditional cruise experiences.

DINING

Princess has done a superb job in upgrading the quality of all its dining options in recent years, whether it be the main restaurants, the alternative restaurants, or the buffets. Only the pizza hasn't been upgraded, but that's because it's always been terrific.

TRADITIONAL   Princess's Personal Choice Dining program allows guests two options: dining at a set time with set dining companions in one of the ship's two or three main restaurants—that is, "traditional" cruise dining—or just showing up anytime during a 4½-hour window and being seated by the maitre d'. If you're not sure which option you'll prefer once you're on board, sign up for traditional since it's easier to switch to anytime dining than it is to go the other way 'round. Passengers choosing the flexible option, but wishing to be served by the same waiter nightly, can usually be seated in his or her section if they make a special request.

Whether you choose traditional or flexible dining, your menu in the main dining room will be the same, offering several appetizers, soup and salad, freshly made pastas, and a choice of five to eight dinner entrees that may include slow-roasted prime rib, surf and turf, rack of lamb with Dijon sauce, port wine–glazed pork, halibut in

Still the Love Boat

Ever the romantic, Princess has things covered from proposal through "I do." On most Princess ships, prospective fiancés can propose to their future mates via video on the ship's giant movie screens. Called **Engagement Under the Stars,** the $695 package includes the creation of a personalized proposal video with the ship's videographer as well as champagne and chocolates, an engagement portrait session, candid photos of the proposal, an in-cabin breakfast, dinner for two at one of the ship's specialty restaurants, a couple's massage in the Lotus Spa, and other extras. Meanwhile, the Grand-, Diamond-, and Coral-class ships are all outfitted with **wedding chapels.** Grand Princess was the first cruise ship to have one, and now a string of other ships have followed suit. Princess was also the first modern line to offer **weddings at sea performed by the captain,** though now Celebrity and Azamara provide that option as well.

Romantics sailing aboard any Princess ship can have a four-course **champagne balcony breakfast for two** ($32) or **dinner** served by a dedicated waiter on their private balcony, at a table set with a tablecloth, hurricane candle lamp, and champagne. While the waiter is setting everything up, you and your significant other can have a complimentary cocktail in one of the ship's bars. The dinner costs $50 per person.

creamy dill sauce, filet mignon with Madeira-truffle demi-glace, and duck a l'orange. There are always **healthy choices** and **vegetarian options,** too, plus staples such as broiled Atlantic salmon, grilled chicken, and grilled New York sirloin steak.

Unlike the "no dress code" that's part of NCL's Freestyle dining plan, Princess maintains the tradition of holding 2 formal nights per week, with the other nights designated smart casual (defined as "an open-neck shirt and slacks for gentlemen and a dress, skirt and blouse, or trouser suit outfit for ladies"). Men, however, should take our advice and pack at least a jacket. Otherwise, you may find yourself down in the gift shop buying one after you realize everyone on the ship except you decided to dress for dinner. We speak from experience on this one.

All of the restaurants have a **kids' menu,** which includes goodies such as burgers, hot dogs, fish sticks, chicken fingers, and, of course, PB&J sandwiches; this menu is also offered in the Horizon Court during its sit-down bistro hours from 11pm to 4am nightly.

For foodies, the line offers a **Chef's Table** experience that starts with cocktails and hors d'oeuvres in the ship's galley, where the executive chef previews the menu he has created for that evening. From there, participants move to a dedicated table in the dining room for a special multicourse tasting dinner with wine pairings. During dessert, the chef rejoins the group for a discussion of the evening's meal. The experience costs $75 per person and is available on all the line's megaships.

SPECIALTY   All Princess ships that sail from the U.S. feature alternative restaurants: an Italian trattoria and steakhouse on the Grand- and Diamond-class ships, trattoria and

New Orleans–style restaurants on *Coral* and *Island Princess,* and a steakhouse and free sit-down pizzeria on the Sun-class ships.

Sabatini's Trattoria ($20 per person) is a traditional Italian restaurant with an airy decor, an open kitchen, balloon-back chairs, and Italian scenes in faux tile work. Dinners here are eight-course extravaganzas emphasizing seafood, with most dishes brought automatically—you just select your main course.

The **Sterling Steakhouse** ($15 per person) has a dark and woodsy ambience. Guests can choose their favorite cut of beef—rib-eye, New York strip, porterhouse, and filet mignon—and have it cooked to order, with starters such as chili, blooming onion, jalapeño poppers, and fresh Caesar salad, plus the usual sides of baked potato or fries, sautéed mushrooms, creamed spinach, and corn on the cob.

Crown, Caribbean, Golden, Emerald, and *Ruby Princess* also have the **Crown Grill** steak and seafood restaurant ($25 per person).

Reservations are recommended for all alternative restaurants as seating is limited. See the individual ship reviews below for more details.

CASUAL   Fleetwide, passengers can choose casual dining at breakfast, lunch, and dinner in the 24-hour, buffet-style Horizon Court restaurant. At breakfast, you'll find the usual: fresh fruit, cold cuts, cereal, steam-table scrambled eggs, cooked-to-order fried eggs, a waffle station, meats, and fish. At lunch, you'll find several salads, fruits, hot and cold dishes, roasts, vegetarian choices, and sometimes sushi. Evenings (until 10pm), the space serves a casual buffet dinner that usually has many of the same dishes as in the main dining room. From 11pm to 4am every night, it serves a late-night menu of pastas, seafood, poultry, and red meats, along with a chef's special of the day. The atmosphere is strictly casual. *Crown, Emerald, Caribbean, Star, Golden,* and *Ruby Princess* have two casual dining venues in the piazza-style atrium: an International Café serving a rotating menu throughout the day, and a wine, cheese, and seafood bar (a la carte pricing at both).

SNACKS & EXTRAS   Poolside grills serve burgers, hot dogs, and pizza; a patisserie has coffee and pastries; and an ice-cream bar dispenses free soft-serve. There's 24-hour room service available in the staterooms. Guests will also find crewmembers passing out fresh-baked cookies and milk in the afternoons on deck and in the atrium.

ACTIVITIES

Like the other big mainstream lines, Princess has onboard activities designed to appeal to a wide range of ages and tastes. For active types, all the ships have traditional shipboard sports such as Ping-Pong and shuffleboard; more athletic activities such as aerobics classes and water volleyball; and virtual-reality golf simulators. The Grand-, Coral-, and Diamond-class ships all have basketball/volleyball courts and 9-hole miniature-golf courses, and the latter are also available on the Sun-class ships.

For something more cerebral, the line's **ScholarShip@Sea** enrichment program (one of the very best activity programs at sea) offers classes in cooking, computer skills (such as basic Web design, Photoshop, and Excel), finance, photography, scrapbooking, and even ceramics. Large-group seminars are free, while small-group and individual classes carry a charge of around $20 to $25 per person. Charges for paint-your-own ceramics are calculated based on the piece you create.

Sit-down activities include bingo, cards, trivia games, dance lessons, and recent-release big-screen movies on the ships' giant outdoor **Movies Under the Stars** movie screens, available on all the line's megaships. A related program, the **Leonard Maltin Movie Club,** presents films specially chosen by (and with a special video introduction by) the noted film critic and historian. Showings take place at the Movies Under the Stars venue or in the theater, and are followed by an hour-long group discussion hosted by the cruise staff. The "Leonard Maltin Movie Channel" is another option, showing specially chosen films on your stateroom TV.

Activities designed to part you from your cash include art auctions and beauty and spa demonstrations. Others designed to part you from your dignity include belly-flop contests, the perennial Newlywed/Not-So-Newlywed game, an *American Idol*–style Princess Pop Star competition, and a reality-TV style makeover show called If They Could Sea Me Now. In Alaska, rangers, naturalists, and guest lecturers present talks and slide shows on such topics as the Iditarod sled-dog race, the wildlife and ecology of Glacier Bay and the Tongass National Forest, oceanography and marine life, glaciers, Native Alaskan cultures, and Alaskan history. For folks interested in how ships work, the **Ultimate Ship Tour** takes a small group of guests behind the scenes, taking in the engine control room, the laundry room, the galley, the bridge, and more. Along the way, they get to meet various crewmembers and get a series of small gifts. The price is $150 per person, and the tour is available on all ships except *Sea Princess* and *Tahitian Princess.*

All Princess ships have well-stocked libraries, 24-hour Internet centers (moderate prices, slow service), in-stateroom Wi-Fi and cellphone service, and Wi-Fi hot spots in various parts of the ship.

CHILDREN'S PROGRAM

Princess has great facilities and amenities for kids and their parents, but it's not a line that's completely gung-ho about *only* catering to families—and therein lies a big advantage: Princess ships aren't overrun with children, typically carrying 20% to 50% fewer than you'll often see on the biggest Carnival, NCL, and Royal Caribbean ships, and way less than Disney.

Princess's Princess Kids program has activities year-round for three age groups: **Princess Pelicans** (ages 3–7), **Shockwaves** (8–12), and **Remix** (13–17), supervised by a counseling staff whose size varies depending upon the number of children aboard. Each ship has a spacious indoor/outdoor **children's playroom** with a splash pool, an arts-and-crafts corner, game tables, and computers or game consoles, plus a **teen center** with computers, video games, a dance floor, and a music system. The two-story playrooms on *Golden* and *Grand* have a large, fenced-in outside deck dedicated to kids only and featuring a teen section with a hot tub and private sunbathing area. The rest of the Grand-class ships have a great fenced-in outdoor play space for toddlers, and the *Coral, Island, Diamond,* and *Sapphire Princess* have a small swimming pool for adults adjacent to the outdoor Kids' Deck, allowing parents to relax while their kids play.

Traditional kids' activities include arts and crafts, scavenger hunts, game tournaments, spelling bees, movies and videos, coloring contests, pizza and ice-cream parties, karaoke, dancing, tours of the galley or behind the scenes at the theater, hula parties (complete with grass skirts!), and teen versions of *The Dating Game.*

Learning activities may include **environmental education programs** developed by the California Science Center, which teach about oceans and marine life through printed materials and specially created films. The kids' equivalent of an onboard guest lecturer program is also offered occasionally, allowing children to go stargazing with an astronomer, learn drawing skills from an animator, and so on.

Children must be at least 6 months of age to sail. Kids must be at least age 3 to register for the youth programs, but kids under 3 can still use the youth centers if accompanied and supervised by a parent.

When kids are registered in the youth program, their parents are given pagers so that they can be contacted if their children need them. Parents may also rent walkie-talkies through the purser's desk if they want two-way communication with their kids. Two **parent "date nights"** let adults have a calm evening while kids dine with counselors in a separate restaurant. Teens have their own group night in one of the main dining rooms, complete with photographs and an after-dinner show. Younger kids can then be taken straight to group babysitting in the children's center (available nightly 10pm–1am for kids ages 3–12; $5 per hour, per child). Princess does not provide private in-cabin babysitting.

On days in port, Princess offers children's center activities straight through from 8am to 5pm (on sea days, the center closes for lunch), allowing parents to explore the port while their kids do their own thing. On Princess's private Bahamas beach, Princess Cays, kids can be checked in at a play area supervised by the shipboard youth staff (for details on Princess Cays, see "The Cruise Lines' Private Islands" in chapter 10). In Alaska, kids ages 6 to 12 and teens ages 13 to 17 can participate in the **Junior Ranger and Teen Explorer program,** a joint effort between Princess and the National Parks Service that uses interactive projects to teach kids about Glacier Bay's natural and cultural history.

ENTERTAINMENT

Princess has some of the better entertainment at sea, with variety acts on the ships' main stages ranging from Vegas-style song-and-dance revues and cabaret singers to ventriloquists, acrobats, aerialists, stand-up comics, and musical soloists. The Sun-class ships have entertainment in two showrooms, while the Grand-, Diamond-, and Coral-class vessels offer three shows nightly in their main theater and two smaller venues, plus quieter music in a few lounges, including the popular piano bars. At several other venues, including the Wheelhouse Bar and the atrium, you'll find pianists, guitarists, or string quartets providing live background music, and out by the pool, a deck band plays at various times during the day. For those who would rather participate, there are regular karaoke nights and a **passenger talent show.** The ships' **casinos** are among the most comfortable at sea, very large and well laid out.

SERVICE

Overall, service is efficient and passengers rarely have to wait in lines, even in the busy Horizon Court buffet restaurants. As is true generally of staff aboard all the mainstream lines, you can expect them to be friendly, efficient, and happy to help. Cabin steward service is the most consistent, with dining service only slightly behind. Suite guests get extra service goodies, including complimentary Internet access, dry cleaning, laundry, and shoe polishing; a complimentary corsage and boutonniere on formal

Getting Off Princess Ships

Fleetwide, Princess now offers a program it calls **Silent Disembarkation.** Rather than wait around for their color-code to be called, as on most other lines, Princess guests now receive a note the night before telling them the exact time they'll be debarking, and in which public room they should wait. When the time comes, a member of the ship's staff escorts them to the gangway. Simple, efficient, and guess what? It works. Princess gets major kudos for finding a way around one of cruise travel's more annoying processes.

nights; en suite afternoon tea; expedited embarkation and debarkation; and other perks.

Through the line's **Captain's Circle loyalty program,** cruisers who have sailed with Princess before are issued specially colored onboard keycards and door nameplates (gold after taking one to five cruises, platinum after five cruises or 50 cruise days, and elite after 15 cruises or 150 cruise days) so that staffers will know to be extra helpful. Platinum Captain's Circle members also get expedited embarkation and credit toward free Internet access, while Elite members receive free laundry and dry-cleaning services, a complimentary wine-tasting class, 10% off in the onboard gift shops, and more.

Gratuities for all service personnel are automatically added to all guest shipboard accounts at the rate of $10.50 per day, or $11 per person per day for guests occupying suites and minisuites. You can make adjustments (up or down) by visiting or calling the purser's desk at any time. Passengers who wish to tip more traditionally—dispensing cash in person—can also make arrangements for this through the desk.

All of the Princess vessels provide laundry services, and also have **self-service laundromats.**

The Grand Class: Grand • Golden • Star • Caribbean • Crown • Emerald • Ruby Princess

The Verdict

These huge, well-equipped vessels are very easy to navigate, never feel as crowded as you'd expect, and are amazingly intimate for their size.

Grand Princess *(photo: Princess Cruises)*

Specifications

Typical Per Diems: $85–$145

Size (in tons)		Caribbean/Crown/Emerald/Ruby	1,200
Grand/Golden/Star	109,000	Passenger/Crew Ratio	
Caribbean/Crown/Emerald/Ruby	113,000	Grand/Golden/Star	2.4 to 1
Passengers (double occ.)		Caribbean/Crown/Emerald/Ruby	2.6 to 1
Grand/Golden/Star	2,600	Year Launched	
Caribbean	3,100	Grand	1998
Crown/Emerald/Ruby	3,070	Golden	2001
Passenger/Space Ratio		Star	2002
Grand/Golden/Star	41.9	Caribbean	2004
Caribbean/Crown/Emerald/Ruby	36.8	Crown	2006
Total Cabins/Veranda Cabins		Emerald	2007
Grand/Golden/Star	1,300/710	Ruby	2008
Caribbean	1,557/881	Last Major Upgrade	
Crown/Emerald/Ruby	1,538/1,102	Grand/Star	2008
Crew		Golden/Caribbean	2009
Grand/Golden/Star	1,100	Crown/Emerald/Ruby	N/A

Frommer's Ratings (Scale of 1–5)

★★★★ ½

Cabin Comfort & Amenities	5	Dining Options	4.5
Appearance & Upkeep	4.5	Gym, Spa & Sports Facilities	4.5
Public Comfort/Space	5	Children's Facilities	4
Decor	4	Enjoyment Factor	4.5

Sailing Regions, Seasons & Home Ports

Caribbean	**Caribbean,** from San Juan (Nov–Apr), from New York (May–Oct). **Canada/New England,** from New York (Sept–Oct).
Crown	**Caribbean,** from Fort Lauderdale (Nov–Apr). **Canada/New England,** from New York & Quebec City (Sept–Oct).
Emerald	**Caribbean,** from Fort Lauderdale (Sept–Apr).
Golden	**Hawaii,** from Los Angeles (Jan–Apr & Sept–Dec).
Grand	**Caribbean,** from Fort Lauderdale (Jan–Apr).
Ruby	**Caribbean,** from Fort Lauderdale (Nov–Apr).
Star	**Caribbean,** from Fort Lauderdale (Mar–Apr).

Princess's signature vessels, the Grand-class ships, were so ahead of their time when they debuted in 1998 (when *Grand Princess* was briefly the largest cruise ship in the world) that the design of even recent sisters such as *Crown* and *Emerald Princess* isn't significantly changed. They look like nothing else at sea, with their 18 decks soaring up to space-age discos hovering at their very stern, stretching from port to starboard. Though the vessels give an impression of immensity from the outside, inside they're extremely well laid out, very easy to navigate, and surprisingly cozy. In fact, their public areas never feel as crowded as you'd think they would with almost 4,000 people aboard, including guests and crew. The cozy carries over to public rooms like the clubby and dimly lit Explorer's Lounge and Wheelhouse Bar, whose traditional accents recall a grander era of sea travel. In the elegant three-story atriums, classical string quartets perform on formal nights and during embarkation.

Caribbean Princess, Crown Princess, Emerald Princess, and *Ruby Princess* are slightly larger versions of the original Grand-class concept, with a similar layout but one extra deck, plus a cafe serving Caribbean dishes, an international cafe, a wine and seafood bar, a "piazza-style" atrium with a street-cafe vibe, and a steak and seafood restaurant. *Ruby Princess,* the latest of the series, added some newness to the onboard experience: a British pub lunch on sea days (no charge) and a range of cheeses to go with the wine and seafood snacks available in Vines.

CABINS Though staterooms on these vessels are divided into some 35 categories, there are actually fewer than 10 configurations. For the most part, the category differences reflect location—such as midships versus aft. Cabins are richly decorated in light hues and earth tones, and all have safes, hair dryers, minifridges, and TVs. Storage is adequate with more closet shelves than drawer space. Cabin balconies are tiered so that they get more sunlight, but this also means your neighbors above can look down at you.

A standard outside cabin without a balcony, such as categories F and FF, ranges from 165 to 210 square feet, while insides, such as category JJ, measure 160 square feet. Balcony cabins range from 165 to 257 square feet, including the balcony. At 324 square feet, including the balcony, the 180 minisuites on each vessel are ultracomfortable, with a roomy sitting area with a full-size pullout couch, two televisions, a minifridge, a large bathroom with full tub and shower, generous closet and drawer space, and terry robes. When coauthor Heidi sailed with her young sons on the *Caribbean Princess,* she had two cribs set up in the living area and there was still plenty of space for playing. Storage was so plentiful that even the kids' copious gear didn't fill it all.

Two Grand Suites measure 782 square feet and feature all the above amenities plus a bathroom with a large whirlpool tub and multidirectional shower, and a separate toilet compartment. There are two 607-square-foot family suites that can sleep up to eight, with two bathrooms. Minibars in the suites are stocked once on a complimentary basis with soda, bottled water, beer, and liquor. Suite guests are also on the receiving end of a slew of perks highlighted in the "Service" section above.

Lifeboats partially or completely obstruct the views from most cabins on Emerald Deck. More than 600 cabins can accommodate a third passenger in an upper berth. Each ship has 28 wheelchair-accessible cabins.

PUBLIC AREAS These are huge ships with a not-so-huge feeling. Because of their smart layout, six dining venues, expansive outdoor deck space, multiple sports facilities, four pools, and nine hot tubs, passengers are dispersed rather than concentrated into one or two main areas. Even sailing with a full load of passengers (as many as 3,100 on *Grand, Golden,* and *Star* if all additional berths in every cabin are filled, and almost 3,800 on *Caribbean, Crown, Emerald,* and *Ruby*), you'll wonder where everyone is.

Coupled with this smart layout is Princess's pleasing-if-plain contemporary decor. Public areas are done up in tasteful caramel-colored wood tones and color schemes of warm blue, teal, and rust, with some brassy details and touches of marble.

While the decor is soothing, the entertainment is pretty hot. Three main entertainment venues include a well-equipped two-story theater for big Vegas-style musical revues; a second one-level show lounge for smaller-scale entertainment such as hypnotists and singers; and the travel-themed Explorer's Lounge, decorated with vaguely

Islamic tile motifs, African and Asian art pieces, primitivist exotic paintings, and a dark, woodsy atmosphere. It's a venue for bands, comedians, or karaoke nightly. There's also the clubby, old-world Wheelhouse Bar, offering laid-back pre- and post-dinner dancing and jazz in an elegant setting, as well as a woodsy sports bar and a wine bar selling caviar by the ounce and wine, champagne, and iced vodka by the glass. For gamblers, each ship has a sprawling casino.

Skywalkers is a multilevel disco/observation lounge, sequestered 150 feet above the ship's stern like a high-tech treehouse, a unique spot with floor-to-ceiling windows and two impressive views: forward for a look over the ship itself, or back toward the sea and the giant vessel's very impressive wake. It's well positioned away from any cabins (so the noise won't keep anyone up) and is our favorite disco at sea. Check out the view at sunset or read a book during the day.

For kids, the indoor/outdoor Fun Zone kids' play area has tons of games, toys, computers, and an outdoor, fenced-in play area equipped with a fleet of tricycles and mini-basketball setup. It's an awesome place to let your little ones run free while you sit on the sidelines and relax. A kiddie pool is located nearby. A separate teen center has several computers, plus video games, a dance floor, and a sound system. On *Grand* and *Golden,* there's also a teens-only sunbathing area with deck chairs and a hot tub, as well as a truly amazing arcade.

Each ship also has a large Internet center (moderate pricing, slow speed), and an attractive wedding chapel where the captain himself performs about six or seven bona fide, legal marriages on almost every cruise.

DINING OPTIONS   Each ship has three pleasant, one-story main dining rooms, laid out on slightly tiered levels. By way of some strategically placed waist-high dividers, they feel cozy, although the ceilings are a tad on the low side. The 24-hour **Horizon Court** casual restaurant serves buffet-style breakfasts and lunches and is designed to feel much cozier than it actually is. With clusters of buffet stations serving stir-fry, beef, turkey, pork, and lots of fruit, salads, cheeses, and more, lines are kept to a minimum and you're hardly aware of the space's enormity. This restaurant turns into a sit-down bistro from 11pm to 4am, with the same dinner menu each night. If you like the idea of New York strip sirloin at midnight, this is the place to go.

For a more intimate yet still casual meal, there are two alternative, reservations-required restaurants. **Sabatini's** specializes in Italian cuisine, featuring an eight-course menu emphasizing seafood. Service is first rate and the food is tasty. The second venue is the **Sterling Steakhouse,** where you can choose your favorite cut of beef and have it cooked to order. *Caribbean, Crown, Emerald,* and *Ruby* also have the **Café Caribe,** a themed buffet carved out of the Horizon Court, serving Caribbean specialties such as jerk chicken, grilled Caribbean rock lobster, whole roast suckling pig, Guiana pepper pots and curries, and paella-style prawns. Musicians play Caribbean music, and guests can order their meal cooked to taste at the cafe's open kitchen. There's no cover charge here. On *Caribbean, Crown, Star, Emerald,* and *Ruby,* the **International Café** serves food 24 hours a day—pastries in the morning; tapas, panini, and the like later; and fondue, gelato, and fresh-baked cookies 'round the clock (with some items at extra charge). *Ruby, Crown,* and *Emerald* also serve a no-charge pub-style lunch on sea days with traditional pub fare including fish and chips, bangers and mash, and cottage pie. Additionally, suite guests can enjoy complimentary breakfast in Sabatini's with complimentary breakfast cocktails and the full breakfast menu, plus specialty items such as brioche French toast and freshly made Belgian waffles.

POOL, FITNESS, SPA & SPORTS FACILITIES   The Grand-class ships have around 1¾ acres of open deck space, so it's not hard to find a quiet place to soak in the sun. On *Grand, Golden,* and *Star,* our favorite spot on a hot, humid day is portside aft on the deck overlooking the swimming pool, where the tail fin vent blows cool air. It's like having an outdoor air-conditioner. In 2006, Princess introduced a different kind of wonderful at a space called the Sanctuary, which is now installed on all the Grand-class ships. Three-quarters canopied and dotted with lounge chairs, trees, and private cabanas, it's a perfect onboard chill-out space, staffed with "serenity stewards" who make sure things stay quiet. Light meals, massages, and beverages are available. Admission carries a $10 fee for half-day use, a measure intended to limit use to those who really want some peace and quiet.

The ships each have four great swimming pools. On *Grand, Golden,* and *Star,* one has a retractable roof for inclement weather. Another aft, under the disco, feels miles from the rest of the ship, while outside the spa, a resistance pool allows you to swim steadily against a current. The fourth pool is for kids. Other recreational offerings include a Sports Deck with a jogging track and a 300-square-foot outdoor LED movie screen for watching movies under the stars (and kids' movies during the day). You can reserve deck chairs for the evening feature films, and, yes, there's popcorn (free) and Raisinettes (for a price). It's great fun, and the sound and picture are awesome.

Spa, gym, and salon facilities are located in a large, almost separate part of each ship, surrounding the lap pool set among tiered, amphitheater-style wooden benches. As is the case fleetwide with Princess, the oceanview gym is surprisingly small for ships of this size, although there's an unusually large aerobics floor.

The Diamond Class: Diamond Princess • Sapphire Princess

The Verdict

Diamond and *Sapphire* are two of the best megaships ever, with beautiful proportions, airy outdoor spaces, and clubby, intimate public areas.

Diamond Princess *(photo: Princess Cruises)*

Specifications   Typical Per Diems: $90–$195

Size (in tons)	116,000	Crew	1,100
Passengers (double occ.)	2,670	Passenger/Crew Ratio	2.4 to 1
Passenger/Space Ratio	42.3	Year Launched	2004
Total Cabins/Veranda Cabins	1,337/748	Last Major Upgrade	N/A

Frommer's Ratings (Scale of 1–5)   ★★★★½

Cabin Comfort & Amenities	4.5	Dining Options	4
Appearance & Upkeep	5	Gym, Spa & Sports Facilities	4.5
Public Comfort/Space	5	Children's Facilities	5
Decor	4.5	Enjoyment Factor	5

Sailing Regions, Seasons & Home Ports

Diamond	**Alaska,** from Vancouver and Anchorage/Whittier (May–Sept).
Sapphire	**Mexican Riviera,** from Los Angeles (Nov–Apr). **Hawaii,** from Los Angeles (Oct–Mar). **Alaska,** from Seattle (May–Sept).

Built in Nagasaki, Japan, *Diamond* and *Sapphire* are Princess's best ships ever, with a design that's more sleek, graceful, and streamlined than the line's more visible Grand-class ships, while still embodying the idea of "big ship choice with small ship feel." Inside, the nearly identical vessels have comfortable cabins; woodsy lounges with hints of seagoing history; understated central atrium lobbies; relaxing indoor/outdoor "Conservatory" pool areas; and large Asian-themed spas. Outside, in the stern, four decks descend in curved, horseshoelike tiers, creating a multilevel resort area with two pools, two hot tubs, two bars, and magnificent views of the ship's wake. One of our favorite things about these ships is that the Promenade Deck wraps around the bow, just below the open top deck, affording a view straight out to where you're going. When we sailed, we walked up there late one moonless night and made a discovery: With the whistling wind drowning out the ship's hum and no light coming from above, behind, or to the sides, the starry sky and dark sea merge and you feel as if you're all alone, flying into outer space.

The only thing that keeps these vessels from a five-star rating is their relative dearth of dining options: Even though there are eight restaurants in all, five of them have the same basic menu (though a steakhouse and Italian trattoria do liven up your options). That said, Princess has significantly improved its cuisine in recent years, so what you do get is choice. At press time, *Diamond* was slated for a late-2010 makeover that will add Princess's Movies Under the Stars outdoor movie screen and adults-only Sanctuary option. *Sapphire* will get the same treatment in 2011.

CABINS   Though cabins on *Diamond* and *Sapphire* are a bit bigger than those on the Grand- and Coral-class ships, they still stick close to the Princess family look, with upholstery and walls done in easy-on-the-eyes earth tones and off whites, all trimmed in butterscotch wood. All have safes, hair dryers, minifridges, and TVs. Standard inside (168 sq. ft.) and outside cabins (183–275 sq. ft.) are smaller than those aboard the newer Holland America and Carnival ships, but are still comfortable and stylish, and more than 70% of outside cabins have verandas. Balconies are tiered, ensuring direct sunlight for those on Decks 8 and 9 (where most of the popular minisuites are located), but also ensuring voyeurism, as folks standing on the balconies above can look right down on you. Standard cabin bathrooms have smallish shower stalls and adequate counter space.

Minisuites (354 sq. ft.) provide substantially more space without jumping into the cost stratosphere. All have those big, less-than-private balconies and sizable sitting areas with sofa beds and two televisions, one facing the sitting area and the other the bed (cheaper and less bothersome, the line told us, than installing a Lazy Susan to swivel a single TV). They're ideal for families with children. Bathrooms have bathtubs and more counter space than standard cabins. Storage space in both standard outsides and minisuites is more than adequate, with a large shelved closet and open-sided clothes rack facing a small dressing alcove by the bathroom door. The 16 full suites have curtained-off sitting and sleeping areas, very large balconies, a complimentary stocked minibar, robes, a walk-in closet, and separate whirlpool tubs and showers in the bathroom. Suite guests are also on the receiving end of numerous perks high-lighted in the "Service" section, above.

Twenty-seven cabins on each ship are wheelchair accessible.

PUBLIC AREAS   These ships are huge—a fact you'll learn the first time you have to walk from one end to the other to retrieve something you forgot in your cabin. On the other hand, when you're sitting in one of their cozy lounges or bars, you might well think you're on a 40,000-ton ship rather than one three times that size. It's an appealing combination, giving passengers a large ship's range of options in a more personal, human-scaled package. You don't feel like you're lost in the crowd.

Most public rooms on these ships are on Decks 6 and 7. Toward the bow, the two-deck Princess Theater is the main show space, with tiers of upholstered theater seats (with little cocktail tables that fold out of their armrests, airline-style) and a pair of opera boxes to either side of the large stage. It's a very minimalist room, and a very appealing one, putting the emphasis on the stage rather than distracting with fanciful decor. Just outside the entrance is the clubby Churchill's, a classically decorated cigar bar with TVs for sports. You'll also find a multipurpose entertainment lounge called Club Fusion, used principally for games (think bingo and talent shows) and evening music. Down a spiral staircase in the back of the room, you'll find one of our favorite spaces, the very small, cozy Wake View Bar, a classy nook full of dark wood, leather chairs, and paintings depicting turn-of-the-20th-century tobacconists. TVs are tuned to sports (though the sound is often off), and six portholes overlook the namesake wake. Few people seem to venture down here, so let's keep it to ourselves, okay?

At midships are two of Princess's signature lounge spaces: the English-adventurer-themed Explorer's Lounge, a secondary show lounge for comedians, impressionists, and other small-scale entertainment; and the ocean-liner-themed Wheelhouse Bar, the prime space aboard for elegant music, with a jazz combo playing in the evenings. Decor matches the name for both rooms, with Egyptian art, jungle-pattern carpeting, clubby furniture, and faux Moorish screens in Explorer's, and leather couches, dark wood, brass candlestick sconces, and paintings of old P&O liners in Wheelhouse. There's dancing here, but the "I love the nightlife, I like to boogie" crowd is more likely to be up in the top-deck disco, the highest point of the ship, with a balcony looking back over the stern if you want to head out for air or romance.

Explorer's jungle theme carries over into the ships' casinos, with their tree-trunk pillars and leafy ceilings. Next door, the three-story atrium is admirably restrained, with lots of creamy marble and wood, understated grillwork art fronting the atrium elevators, and musicians performing throughout the day. Opening off the space is the relaxing library and the charmingly old-fashioned writing room, along with several shops, a coffee bar, and Crooners, a Rat Pack–themed bar serving 56 different martini recipes in two sizes: the standard Sinatra and the supersize (and misspelled) Deano. Clusters of low-slung wicker-frame chairs along the windows give a '50s-rumpus-room effect. Very slinky.

On Deck 7, the Internet Café is notable not only for being large and exceedingly stylish (among the most attractive at sea), but also for being a cafe in more than just name: A bar toward the back dispenses gourmet coffee for a few bucks, along with free croissants and sweet rolls. Passengers who bring their laptops can connect wirelessly here, as well as in the atrium. Four computer terminals are also located in the atrium's library, and computer classes are generally held in the wedding chapel, just across from the Wheelhouse Bar.

For kids, *Diamond's* and *Sapphire's* Fun Zone centers are divided into four separate and sizable rooms, segregating kids by age. Younger tots get a climbing maze, flower-backed chairs, toys, computers, and a great, cushiony amphitheater for watching movies. Teens get a sort of Austin Powers–looking room, brightly colored and looking much like a normal adult bar. "That was on purpose," one Princess exec told us. "What teen wants to be treated like a kid?"

DINING OPTIONS   Passengers opting for traditional dining take their meals in the 518-seat **International Dining Room,** with its simple but elegant wood-panel walls and classical paintings, or in the smaller **Vivaldi Restaurant,** with its 18th-century European decor. Passengers on the anytime-dining program can eat in any of four smaller themed dining rooms, all with the same menus, but with one specialty dish themed to that room.

Guests wanting to gorge long and hard should make a reservation at **Sabatini's,** the extra-cost Italian trattoria, which serves eight-course, 2½-hour meals. Meat lovers can make a reservation at the **Sterling Steakhouse.** For ultracasual dining, head to the **Horizon Court** buffet.

POOL, FITNESS, SPA & SPORTS FACILITIES   Like most megaships, *Diamond* and *Sapphire* have two pools at midships: a partying main pool out in the sun and a secondary "Conservatory" space with a large pool, two hot tubs, a balcony (which does double duty as sunning space and as a venue for the line's pottery-making classes), and a retractable roof for bad weather. Our favorite outdoor spaces are in the stern, where four decks descend in curved, horseshoelike tiers, creating a multilevel resort with two pools, two hot tubs, two bars, and a magnificent view of the ship's wake.

Another pool, this one an adults-only resistance pool for swimming laps in place, is set in a cleft just outside the large, well-appointed spa. The spa is totally minimalist in its elegant Asian theme, with a great suite of steam rooms and stone lounging chairs for guests to use before or after their treatment. Next door, the gym is one of the few sour notes on board—well stocked (and with little TVs on all the aerobics machines), but still inadequately small considering the number of people aboard. When we sailed, it got crowded often. A large aerobics studio is attached, offering spinning, yoga, and other aerobics and fitness classes (mostly for $10 a class).

Out on Deck 16, at the top of a very quietly marked stairway and almost completely shielded from wind and view, is a small miniature-golf course. More serious golfers can play illusory courses at a virtual-reality center farther forward, near a nicely designed, covered and netted sports court suitable for basketball and volleyball.

The Coral Class: Coral Princess • Island Princess

The Verdict

Beautiful, spacious, and at the same time surprisingly intimate, *Coral* and *Island* look beautiful inside and out, with a nice range of entertainment options and venues, and great onboard learning experiences.

Coral Princess *(photo: Matt Hannafin)*

Specifications

Typical Per Diems: $110–$190

Size (in tons)	91,627	Crew	981
Passengers (double occ.)	1,970	Passenger/Crew Ratio	2 to 1
Passenger/Space Ratio	46.5	Year Launched	2003
Total Cabins/Veranda Cabins	987/727	Last Major Upgrade	N/A

Frommer's Ratings (Scale of 1–5)

★★★★ ½

Cabin Comfort & Amenities	4.5	Dining Options	4
Appearance & Upkeep	5	Gym, Spa & Sports Facilities	4
Public Comfort/Space	5	Children's Facilities	4
Decor	4.5	Enjoyment Factor	4.5

Sailing Regions, Seasons & Home Ports

Coral	**Panama Canal,** from Fort Lauderdale & Los Angeles (Sept–May). **Alaska,** from Vancouver and Anchorage/Whittier (May–Sept).
Island	**Panama Canal,** from Fort Lauderdale & Los Angeles (Sept–May). **Alaska,** from Vancouver and Anchorage/Whittier (May–Sept).

Coral Princess and *Island Princess* are two of the loveliest cruise vessels out there, further refining Princess's vision of mega-size ships with an intimate feel. Outside, there are balconies on some 83% of their outside cabins, but their tiered design is a vast improvement over the typical megaship "wall of balconies" look, contributing to a clean and flowing profile. Up top, the ships' futuristic-looking but purely decorative jet-engine funnels give you the impression the ships are going to fly right out of the water and into orbit.

Built to *j-u-u-u-ust* be able to squeeze through the Panama Canal (with approximately 2 ft. of space on each side), these ships are extremely spacious and well laid out, and never feel crowded even when full. Though they're a fifth larger than the line's older Sun-class ships, they carry only 20 more passengers apiece based on double occupancy, meaning more room for you. Understated interiors are both classic and modern, with Internet centers and Times Square–style news tickers right around the corner from woodsy, almost Edwardian lounges. Our favorite spaces: the clubby Wheelhouse Bar for a before-dinner drink; the bar at the New Orleans–themed Bayou Restaurant for jazz until around midnight; the peaceful, Balinese-style solarium, where your book will have to be damn good to keep you from dozing off; and the Universe Lounge for everything from cooking classes and lectures to full-blown production performances.

CABINS   Decor sticks to Princess's fleetwide standard, with upholstery and walls done in easy-on-the-eyes earth tones and off whites, all trimmed in butterscotch wood. All have safes, hair dryers, minifridges, and TVs. Inside and standard outside cabins are serviceable if smallish at 160 and 168 square feet, respectively. Most private balconies are set up in descending tiers—a positive for soaking up the sun, a negative for total privacy. Standard cabin bathrooms have smallish shower stalls and adequate counter space.

Minisuites (323 sq. ft.) provide substantially more space without jumping into the cost stratosphere, and have larger balconies and sizable sitting areas with sofa beds and two televisions, one facing the sitting area and the other the bed—an odd touch since there's no partition, but what the hell. Bathrooms have bathtubs and more counter space than in standard cabins. Storage space in both standard outside cabins and mini-suites is more than adequate, with a large shelved closet and open-sided clothes rack facing a small dressing alcove by the bathroom door. Sixteen full suites have curtained-off sitting and sleeping areas, very large balconies, complimentary stocked minibars, robes, whirlpool tubs and separate showers in the bathroom, and a walk-in closet. Suite guests get additional perks highlighted in the "Service" section above.

Twenty cabins on each ship are wheelchair accessible.

PUBLIC AREAS Layout is one of the areas in which these vessels really shine, with decks and public areas arranged so it's always easy to find your way around. Most indoor public spaces are on Decks 6 and 7, starting with the large Princess Theater in the bow. Unlike the ornately decorated, two- and three-deck theaters on many new ships, this is a classic sloping one-level space, decorated with no theme whatsoever. You get a good view from every one of the comfortable theater seats, which have lit-tle flip-up tables in their arms to hold drinks or, when the room is used for lectures or other enrichment activities, your notebook. Farther aft, the Explorer's Lounge is a smaller-scale show lounge for comedians, karaoke, game shows, and dancing, deco-rated to evoke the romantic European explorers of the 19th century, with vaguely Islamic tile motifs, African and Asian art pieces, primitivist exotic paintings on the walls, and a dark, woodsy atmosphere. Important sports events are broadcast here on multiple large screens.

In the stern, the Universe Lounge is an innovative multipurpose space, hosting TV-style cooking demonstrations (with a full kitchen onstage), computer classes (with hookups for 50 computers around the room), lectures, and full-blown production performances on three low interconnected stages, which revolve and rise and segment and contort and do more things than you think a stage could—it's a regular three-ring circus. Shows are tailored to utilize all these options, with much of the action taking place at ground level for a true floor-show feel.

Some standout bars and lounges include the maritime-themed Wheelhouse Bar, an intimate spot decorated in classic dark woods, with heavy leather and corduroy arm-chairs and love seats, faux marble pillars, domed ceiling lights, and small end-table lamps. In the evening, a small band performs smooth jazz and pop numbers for danc-ing, and in some afternoons, the ships' string quartets perform classical repertoire. At one entrance to the lounge, a small museum displays memorabilia from P&O history. Nearby, the low-key four-deck atrium is surrounded by the ships' shops, Internet cen-ter, news ticker, and several other rooms. Churchill's cigar lounge is a cozy room with big windows, a humidor under a portrait of the room's namesake, and armchairs and sofas seating just 10 people. Crooners is a Rat Pack–themed piano bar with a Vegas/martini vibe. A real live crooner performs at the piano each evening.

One level down, the ship's library and card room are both exceptionally large and comfortable, though the layout—with entrances both from the atrium and from the midships elevators/stair tower—means that people often use the rooms as a passage-way, adding more bustle than we'd like in a library. Themed casinos (London on *Coral,* Paris on *Island*) and a wedding chapel round out the adult public room spaces.

At the stern on Deck 12, there's the bright and very kid-scaled Fun Zone and Pel-ican's Playhouse children's center and smallish Off Limits teen center, with computers and a dance floor. Outside is a children's play area and the small Pelican Pool. The ships' bright pottery studio is hidden away back here as well, giving it the feel of a playroom for grown-ups.

DINING OPTIONS To accommodate Princess's Personal Choice concept, two similar dining rooms—the **Provence** and the **Bordeaux**—are dedicated to traditional fixed-seating dining and to anytime Personal Choice dining, respectively. Both single-level rooms are understated and spacious, with lots of elbowroom (except, that is, in the unusually narrow armchairs at some tables).

There are two specialty restaurants aboard: **Sabatini's** ($20 per person) for eight-course Italian extravaganzas and the **Bayou Cafe and Steakhouse** ($15 per person), a New Orleans–themed restaurant with a subdued, woodsy ambience, faux brick walls, lantern lighting, and New Orleans murals on the walls. Dinners here include a barbe-cued alligator ribs appetizer and main courses like seafood gumbo, fried catfish, grilled jumbo prawns, and chicken-and-chorizo jambalaya. Steak options include New York strip and porterhouse. A jazz trio plays during dinner, then continues on until midnight for patrons of the attached bar. Tables are sprinkled with Mardi Gras beads for extra atmosphere.

The ships' 24-hour **Horizon Court** buffet restaurants are comfortable enough, though the circular layout of the food stations—and no clear path through them—often leads to light chaos. Overlooking the main pool, the **Grill** serves burgers, hot dogs, and the like in the afternoon, with excellent pizza available one deck down (just forward of the pool) and ice cream and fresh juices available aftward at the solarium's ice-cream bar and juice bar. Inside, at the bottom of the atrium, **La Patisserie** is a pleasant lounge/cafe serving regular coffee free and specialty coffees at extra cost, with cookies and sweets free for the taking. As the room is almost at sea level, it's a great spot from which to watch the waves go by, and it's worth spending at least a minute here as your ship goes through the Panama Canal, with the canal walls literally only a couple of feet away. It's a startlingly weird experience.

POOL, FITNESS, SPA & SPORTS FACILITIES The ships' main pool areas are spacious but surprisingly plain, with a main pool and three large hot tubs surrounded by sunning areas. A steel-drum duo performs on a tiny, low-key stage at one end during the day. Moving toward the stern, the solarium (aka the Lotus Pool) is a much more interesting area, decorated with a Balinese motif that gives a sense of tranquillity—though if there are lots of kids aboard, that tranquillity probably won't last. The stylish wooden deck chairs here (and the more traditional "Royal Teak" ones on the wraparound Promenade Deck) are much classier than the white plastic loungers around the main pool. A sliding-glass roof protects the area during inclement weather. Up on the Sports Deck, there's a wading pool for adults. Both ships also offer Princess's Movies Under the Stars outdoor movie screens and adults-only Sanctuary relaxation areas.

Fitness facilities include a surprisingly small though reasonably equipped gym, plus a relatively large separate aerobics room. Up on the top decks, there's a basket-ball/volleyball court, a computerized golf simulator, and a 9-hole miniature-golf course. Though the latter is in the open air, you have to enter through a windowless wooden door that makes it look permanently closed. It's not; just go on in.

In the stern on Deck 14, the Balinese-themed Lotus Spa offers the usual massage, mud, and beauty treatments, plus a thermal suite (a unisex room with various heat treatments) and a lovely seaview salon. For what it's worth—because the spa is run by Steiner (the company that runs almost all cruise ship spas) and personnel change regularly—we had one of our best cruise ship massages on *Coral Princess,* an almost painful deep-tissue sports massage that left us feeling completely loose and refreshed.

Sea Princess

The Verdict

A remnant from another century, this older Princess ship has a relaxed, comfortable atmosphere without too much flash.

Sea Princess *(photo: Princess Cruises)*

Specifications

Typical Per Diems: $100–$190

Size (in tons)	77,000	Crew	900
Passengers (double occ.)	1,950	Passenger/Crew Ratio	2.2 to 1
Passenger/Space Ratio	39.5	Year Launched	1998
Total Cabins/Veranda Cabins	975/410	Last Major Upgrade	2009

Frommer's Ratings (Scale of 1–5)

★★★★

Cabin Comfort & Amenities	4	Dining Options	4
Appearance & Upkeep	4	Gym, Spa & Sports Facilities	4
Public Comfort/Space	5	Children's Facilities	4
Decor	5	Enjoyment Factor	4

Sailing Regions, Seasons & Home Ports

Sea Princess	**Caribbean,** from Barbados (Jan–Apr). **Panama Canal,** from Barbados (Apr). **Alaska,** from San Francisco (May–Sept). **Hawaii,** from San Francisco (Sept).

Here's the scoop on *Sea Princess:* She's just like all the other Princess ships, only less so. Being among the line's oldest vessels (along with her sister ships *Dawn Princess* and *Sun Princess,* which aren't currently sailing from North America), she's among the vessels that led the way toward the design Princess has used ever since: a bit plain Jane: comfortable, quiet, un-flashy, and (so far) aging gracefully. Light color schemes predominate, with lots of beiges, and their layout is very easy to navigate. By the end of the first day, you'll know where everything is.

CABINS   Though cabins are divided into some 28 categories, there are actually fewer than 10 configurations—for the most part, the category differences reflect location (midships vs. aft, and so on), and thus price. More than 400 cabins boast private balconies, though they're small at about 3x8^{1}/2 feet. And that leads to our main point: The staterooms on Sea Princess are cramped. Standard outside cabins, such as categories BC and BD, are 178 square feet *including* their balconies, while Carnival's standards, by comparison, are nearly 186 square feet without balconies. On this ship, what little balcony space you gain is deducted from your room. Inside cabins clock in at 135 to 148 square feet. All cabins have minifridges, safes, TVs, and hair dryers, and 300 will accommodate third passengers in upper berths.

Six suites sprawl out over 678 square feet of space and include robes to use while aboard and minibars stocked once on a complimentary basis with soda, bottled water, beer, and liquor. Suite guests also get a slew of perks highlighted in the "Service" section (p. 226). The 32 minisuites (365 sq. ft.) are really nice, with a separate bedroom area divided from the sitting area by a curtain. Each has a pullout sofa, a chair and desk, a minifridge, two TVs, a walk-in closet, and a whirlpool tub and shower in a separate room from the toilet and sink.

Nineteen cabins are wheelchair accessible.

PUBLIC AREAS *Sea Princess* has a decidedly unglitzy decor that relies on lavish amounts of wood, glass, marble, and collections of original paintings, statues, and lithographs. The one-story showroom offers good lighting and sound and unobstructed views from every seat, and several spaces in the back are reserved for wheelchair users. The smaller Vista Lounge also presents entertainment, with good sight lines and comfortable cabaret-style seating. The elegant, nautical-motif Wheelhouse Bar is done in warm, dark-wood tones and features small bands, sometimes with a vocalist; it's the perfect spot for pre- or post-dinner drinks.

There's a dark and sensuous disco; a bright, spacious casino; a wine bar selling caviar by the ounce and wine, champagne, and iced vodka by the glass; and lots of little lounges for an intimate rendezvous.

DINING OPTIONS *Sea Princess's* two dining rooms have an intimate feel, their expanse broken up by dividers topped with frosted glass. There are also two alternative dining venues. The sit-down pizzeria (no extra charge) on Dolphin Deck is open approximately 11am to 2:30pm and 7pm to 1am for casual dining, with tables seating two, four, and six. Sorry, no takeout or delivery. The **Sterling Steakhouse** ($15 per person) is set out of the wind just outside the **Horizon Court**, overlooking the main pool, and is open from 6 to 10pm. On Alaska sailings, the steakhouse is moved inside adjacent to the 24-hour Horizon Court buffet restaurant, which is an ultracasual option for all meals, including sit-down bistro-style dinners from 11pm to 4am.

POOL, FITNESS, SPA & SPORTS FACILITIES *Sea's* pool deck is well laid out, with three adult pools (one of them in the stern), one kids' wading pool, and hot tubs scattered around the Riviera Deck, along with a 300-square-foot LED movie screen for showing feature films, sports events, and other entertainment. Three spacious decks are open for sunbathing.

The ship's gym is appealing, and though it's on the small side for a vessel of this size, it's actually roomier than the ones on the much larger Grand-class ships. Aerobics, stretching, and meditation classes are held in the spacious aerobics room, and the nearby spas offer the usual massages, mud treatments, and facials. The teak Promenade Deck provides space for joggers, walkers, and shuffleboard players, and a computerized golf center called Princess Links simulates the trickiest holes at some of the world's best golf courses.

12 Royal Caribbean International

1050 Caribbean Way, Miami, FL 33132. ✆ 800/327-6700 or 305/539-6000. Fax 800/722-5329. www.royalcaribbean.com.

THE LINE IN A NUTSHELL Royal Caribbean has basically been *the* innovator in the mainstream sector of the cruise business over the past decade, transforming the architectural look and layout of big cruise ships and also rewriting the book on what's possible at sea: rock climbing, ice skating, boxing, surfing on deck, ziplining . . . what's next? The line's fleet includes the 10 biggest cruise ships ever built, and while sheer size alone doesn't justify choosing these ships, the fact that Royal Caribbean puts the extra space to good use does justify it. These big ships really do deliver the goods in terms of variety, comfort, design, and amenities. **Sails to:** Caribbean, Panama Canal, Alaska, The Bahamas, Bermuda, Mexican Riviera, Hawaii, Canada/New England (plus Europe, transatlantic, Asia, South America, Australia/New Zealand, Dubai/United Arab Emirates).

THE EXPERIENCE Royal Caribbean prides itself on being ultra-innovative and cutting edge, pushing the envelope with each new class of ship it builds. If there's something that's never been done at sea before, Royal Caribbean will figure out how to do it. The newest ships, sisters *Oasis* and *Allure of the Seas,* give new meaning to the phrase *over the top,* carrying a whopping 5,400 passengers apiece and designed with citylike neighborhoods and an incredible new plan that opens up the center of the ship to sunlight and fresh air. The supersize megacruisers were preceded by the three Freedom-class ships, which introduced a surfing simulator, full-size boxing ring, and "sprayground" kids' aqua park to the cruise world. All of these fun, active, and glamorous megaships provide a great experience for a wide range of people, whether your idea of a good time is riding a wave or relaxing in the Solarium pool. There are huge children's centers for the kids and elegant jazz clubs, kick-back sports bars, and flashy entertainment for adults. Decor-wise, these ships are a shade or three toned down from the Carnival brood: Rather than trying to overwhelm the senses, many of their public areas are understated and classy.

Pros

- **Unparalleled innovation:** For the past decade, Royal Caribbean has been the leader in redesigning the cruise ship for tomorrow's world, but it totally knocked the ball out of the park with the new Oasis-class ships, which changed the whole paradigm for big-ship design.
- **Activity central:** With rock-climbing walls, surfing machines, ziplines, water parks, basketball courts, miniature golf, ice skating, and bungee trampolines among the many diversions, these ships are tops in the adrenaline department.
- **Pretty public areas:** Lounges, restaurants, and outdoor pool decks are well designed, spacious, glamorous, and just plain inviting.
- **Great solariums:** Solariums nearly fleetwide (but especially on the Oasis-class ships) are relaxing oases far away from the maddening crowd.

Cons

- **Too big?** Size, of course, is in the eye of the beholder, but some folks just can't get around the idea that traveling with 5,400 fellow shipmates is a bit much. On the plus-size plus side, these ships are so well designed that passengers tend to disperse widely—so often, you'd never guess so many people are aboard.
- **Small cabins on the older ships:** At just about 120 to 160 square feet, most cabins aboard the line's pre-1999 vessels are downright tiny.

ROYAL CARIBBEAN: SUPERSIZE ME, WITH A SIDE OF CLASS

Royal Caribbean International (RCI) was the first company to launch a fleet specializing exclusively in Caribbean ports of call—hence the company name. In the late 1980s, it expanded its horizons beyond the Caribbean (hence the "International") and

Compared with the other mainstream lines, here's how RCI rates:

	Poor	Fair	Good	Excellent	Outstanding
Enjoyment Factor					✓
Dining				✓	
Activities					✓
Children's Program				✓*	
Entertainment					✓
Service				✓	
Worth the Money					✓

Read this as "Outstanding" for the Oasis-class ships, whose facilities and programs are among the best in the business.

now offers cruises in every major cruising region. It's the line that launched the mega-ship trend (with 1988's 73,192-ton *Sovereign of the Seas*), as well as the super-mega-ship trend (with 1999's 3,114-passenger *Voyager of the Seas*), the super-duper-megaship trend (with the 3,634-passenger *Freedom of the Seas* in 2006), and the double-super-duper-megaship trend (with the 5,400-passenger *Oasis* and *Allure of the Seas,* which debuted in 2009 and 2010, respectively). Beyond sheer size though, the line's ships have been incredibly innovative, challenging traditional notions of cruise ship activities as well as the basic architectural form that a cruise ship can take. *Voyager* launched the idea of ice-skating rinks, interior boulevards, and rock-climbing walls in 1999, and barely more than a decade later, these features seem almost standard. Who would have thought? *Oasis* and *Allure* doubled the innovation by being the first cruise ships designed with a split superstructure, meaning the top eight decks are split lengthwise by a long canyon, in which sits a huge open-air garden and a boardwalk-like entertainment zone. Besides letting light and air into the center of the ships, the effect makes the vessels feel more 3-D overall—like you're walking around a city rather than just shuffling around on unconnected horizontal decks. Architecture aside, the ships also introduced a number of advances in entertainment, infrastructure (new digital signage, for instance), and activities, at least some of which will soon be rolling out to the line's older vessels.

PASSENGER PROFILE

You'll find folks from all walks of life on a Royal Caribbean cruise: passengers in their 20s through 60s and older, mostly couples (including a good number of honeymoon-ers), some singles traveling with friends, and also lots and lots of families. Overall, passengers are energetic, social, and looking for a good time, no matter what their age. While the majority of passengers come from somewhere in North America, the line also attracts a lot of foreigners, including many Asians and Latin Americans.

Over the past years, the line has been making a push for younger, hipper, more active passengers via ad campaigns that portray the ships as a combination of hyper-active urban health club, chic restaurant district, and adventure-travel magic potion—which is a bit of a stretch, though the line's newer ships give that ideal a good shot. RCI's ships are active, yes, but don't expect the Shackleton expedition (or the Four Seasons, for that matter).

RCI's shorter 3- and 4-night cruises tend to attract a more party-oriented crowd, as is the case with most short cruises.

DINING

Overall, the food is hit and miss. One dinner will be very tasty—like a Thai chicken dish and the Tuscan white-bean soup that our coauthor Heidi enjoyed on a recent cruise—and another will be disappointing. As aboard big ships at other lines, serving thousands of passengers a day doesn't always translate into a memorable dining experience. As far as dining times, Royal Caribbean has just started offering an alternative to the fixed early- and late-seating dinners in traditional main dining rooms. And just as with all the other mainstream lines, there are also many casual and specialty dining spots.

TRADITIONAL   In keeping with the flexible dining setup at the likes of Princess and NCL, Royal Caribbean's new My Time Dining reservation system means you can eat in the main restaurant whenever it is convenient for you between 6 and 9:30pm if you make a reservation with a maitre d' stationed outside the restaurant several hours a day. Flexible dining is typically allowed on one level of the main restaurants, while diners also have the more traditional two seatings on a different level, with typical entrees such as poached Alaskan salmon, oven-roasted crispy duck served with a rhubarb sauce, sirloin steak marinated with Italian herbs and served over a chunky tomato stew, shrimp scampi, and often an Asian dish. At lunch and dinner, there's always a **light and healthy option** such as herb-crusted baked cod with steamed red-skinned potatoes and vegetables, or a pasta tossed with smoked turkey, portobello mushrooms, and red-pepper pesto; as well as a **vegetarian option** such as vegetable strudel served in a puff pastry with black-bean salsa.

SPECIALTY   Unlike lines such as NCL, Royal Caribbean hasn't generally gone overboard with alternative, extra-cost specialty restaurants, though that paradigm is changing with the new Oasis-class ships. The Voyager-class ships each have one intimate, reservations-only Italian restaurant called **Portofino** ($20 per person), while the Radiance- and Freedom-class ships and *Mariner* and *Navigator of the Seas* have Portofino and the **Chops Grill** steakhouse ($25 per person). *Oasis* and *Allure* each have five specialty restaurants (see ship reviews for details). Specialty restaurants are being installed on the line's older ships as they're renovated.

CASUAL   Fleetwide, an open-seating casual dinner is served every night from 6:30 to 9:30pm in the buffet-style **Windjammer Café.** Meals follow the general theme of dinners in the main restaurants (Italian, Caribbean, and so on), and the room is made a bit more inviting through dimmed lighting and the addition of tablecloths. Long open hours mitigate the crowds on the bigger ships, but on a recent cruise aboard *Rhapsody,* the place was a madhouse at lunchtime and we literally couldn't find a seat inside or out. You can also eat breakfast and lunch in the Windjammer—and most passengers do. Different stations have salads, soups, sandwiches, burgers, pasta daily specials, meats, desserts, and so on. The Oasis-class ships (and others, as they're renovated) have additional stations serving different regional cuisine, including Asian, Mediterranean, and Latin.

RCI's Oasis-, Freedom-, and Voyager-class ships and the older *Monarch* and *Majesty* also have one of the most distinctive casual-dining spots at sea: an honest-to-God **Johnny Rockets diner** with red vinyl booths and chrome accents, serving burgers, milkshakes, and other diner staples. There's a nominal $4.95-per-person service charge, and sodas and shakes are a la carte; but that doesn't stop lines from forming here during prime lunch and dinner times. The Oasis-class ships add a slew of other casual eateries as well, including a seafood shack, an indoor/outdoor restaurant in their open-air Central Park neighborhood, a pizzeria, and a health-conscious bistro in the Solarium.

SNACKS & EXTRAS   Oasis-, Freedom-, and Voyager-class ships have an extensive coffee shop on the indoor promenade (serving a variety of pastries, sandwiches, and pizza), plus several self-serve soft ice-cream stations and free nacho-and-hot-dog-type snacks in the sports bars. The line's other ships have similar choices, with decent pizza served in the afternoon and late night for those suffering from post-partying munchies, and ice cream and toppings available throughout the day from a station in the buffet. The ships all have Latté-tudes coffee shops serving gourmet java, cookies, and other baked goods (all priced a la carte). *Freedom, Independence, Liberty, Mariner, Monarch,* and *Navigator* also have a **Ben & Jerry's** ice-cream shop serving cones and sundaes at extra cost, while *Oasis* and *Allure* have a 50's-style ice cream parlor (also extra cost) as part of their Boardwalk neighborhood. There are no midnight buffets in the traditional sense on any of the ships, but something is always open for those with the late-night munchies, from the pizza counter to the buffet and 24-hour room service.

A decent **kids' menu** features the usual options: burgers, hot dogs, fries, fish sticks, chicken tenders, spaghetti, and pizza, plus lots of desserts.

Room service is available 24 hours a day from a fairly routine, limited menu, though the rub is that now you'll be charged $4.95 per order between midnight and 5am (don't be surprised if this becomes an industry trend).

ACTIVITIES

Royal Caribbean's ships have the greatest variety of activities and sports facilities at sea, bar none. Fleetwide, you'll find **rock-climbing walls** (with multiple climbing tracks and training available), plus lots of typical cruise fare: spa and beauty demonstrations, art auctions, wine tastings, salsa and ballroom dance lessons, bingo, oddball crafts/ hospitality classes (such as napkin folding), "horse race" gambling, and outrageous poolside games such as a men's sexy legs contest, designed to draw big laughs. Sports facilities vary by ship: All the Oasis-, Freedom-, and Voyager-class ships have **ice-skating rinks,** combo basketball/volleyball courts, rock walls, and miniature-golf courses. The Oasis class bumps things up a notch with a zipline that zooms you across the ship's central canyon, an aqua theater (a pool with a movable floor for synchronized swimming and high-dive shows), and two FlowRider surfing simulators (each of the Freedom-class ships also has one of these). If shopping can be considered an activity, Royal Caribbean has an impressive selection of boutiques clustered somewhere near each ship's atrium.

For those whose goal is to not gain 5 pounds at the buffet, **gyms** are well equipped fleetwide, with specialized fitness classes such as yoga and cardio-kickboxing for $10 per person. **Onboard spas** offer the usual range of massages, facials, and other beauty treatments like teeth whitening, but here's a piece of advice: If you want a treatment, sign up immediately after boarding, as these are big ships and a lot of people will be competing with you for desirable time slots. If you're flexible, you can often find more openings and special discounts on port days and off times.

CHILDREN'S PROGRAM

Year-round and fleetwide, Royal Caribbean offers its **Adventure Ocean** supervised kids' programs for children ages 3 to 17, divided into Aquanauts (ages 3–5), Explorers (6–8), Voyagers (9–11), Navigators (12–14), and older teens (15–17). All youth staffmembers have college degrees in education, recreation, or a related field. Each ship has a large children's playroom and facilities for teens, with complimentary supervised activities on sea and port days. In general, the scope of the kids' facilities on the Oasis-, Freedom-, Voyager-, and Radiance-class ships far exceeds that on the older vessels, with huge playrooms, and a large, sequestered outdoor deck with ship-shaped play equipment.

Kids' activities fleetwide include movies, talent shows, karaoke, pizza and ice-cream parties, bingo, scavenger hunts, game shows, volleyball, face painting, and beach parties. **Internet access** is available to Adventure Ocean kids at half-price (25¢ vs. 50¢ per minute for adults). Several programs also mix learning with play. The **Adventure Science** program entertains kids with fun yet educational scientific experiments like volcano making and projects that vaguely touch on meteorology and fossils; **Adventure Art,** offered in partnership with Crayola, focuses on art projects made with the company's crayons, modeling clay, glitter, glue, markers, and paint. **Adventure Theatre** exposes kids to theater arts via vocal and physical exercises, and activities that foster creativity. There are also activities geared to the whole family, including Mom and Dad.

For younger kids (ages 6 months–3 years), RCI has partnered with Fisher-Price on a program of **supervised play dates** in which babies (6–18 months) and toddlers (19 months–3 years) are invited to daily 45-minute play sessions with their parents in a designated lounge. Offered on all but embarkation day, the interactive dates incorporate music, storytelling, and a variety of Fisher-Price toys to explore physical development, problem-solving skills, cause and effect, and other lessons. In ship cabins, Fisher-Price TV has programming for kids and you can also borrow Fisher-Price toys for kids to play with in your cabin. (By the way, if you don't feel like schlepping your own stuff, you can now preorder organic baby food and Huggies-brand diapers, wipes, and creams for delivery into your cabin when you arrive. Go to Royal Caribbean's Shop Gifts & Gear section at www.royalcaribbean.com.) There's also a morning Stroll & Roll for parents who want to push their infant in a stroller around the ship's jogging track.

For teens, each ship has a **teen center,** a disco, and a video arcade. The Freedom-class ships, *Mariner, Navigator,* and *Monarch of the Seas,* have three teen-only areas, including a dedicated teen Sun Deck. Teen programming hours are daily 9am to 5pm and 7pm to 2am.

Kids' facilities and activities on the **Oasis-class ships** outshine any others in the fleet, and rank among the best in the cruise biz, with highlights including one of the very few **nurseries** at sea (accepting kids btw. 6 months and 3 years), plus nine different play spaces and a huge water park out on deck (also on the Freedom-class ships).

Radiance-class ships and *Voyager, Adventure,* and *Explorer* also have a water slide and a kids' pool.

Slumber-party-style **group babysitting** for children ages 3 and up is available in the kids' playroom nightly between 10pm and 1am. The hourly charge is $6 per child (kids must be at least 3 years old and potty-trained). Private, in-cabin babysitting for kids ages 1 year and up is provided by off-duty crewmembers from 8am to 2am, and must be booked at least 24 hours in advance through the purser's desk; a new Fisher-Price partnership means the babysitter will arrive with Fisher-Price and Mattel toys and games, and play with your child. Upon the parents' return, the sitter gives them a log of what they did together. The cost: $10 per hour for up to two siblings; $15 per hour for a maximum of three. As for the few hours of adult time to enjoy dinner, drinks, entertainment, a workout, and/or spa treatment: priceless.

Alternatively, a revamped **Adventure Ocean dinner program** is a kind of "get out of parenting free" card for adults, inviting kids to have dinner with youth staff in the Windjammer Café, the Solarium, or Johnny Rockets diner (depending on the ship) from 6 to 7pm, then take part in an activities session until 10pm. This is offered on 3 nights of a 7-night cruise and once or twice on shorter cruises. A complete child's menu is provided. At midday on sea days, the new Lunch and Play program invites kids ages 3 to 11 to eat with counselors between noon and 2pm and enjoy movies, cartoons, and playtime (it's $7.95 per kid). New interactive kids' menus (parents, bring your own crayons, though—on our last cruises, the dining staff didn't have any) have just been introduced, with more healthy choices. Other new stuff includes a kids' section in the ships' libraries and, for the suites, a Mattel board game menu, including Pictionary, Balderdash, and UNO Flash.

Infants must be at least 6 months old to sail. Note that transatlantic, transpacific, Hawaii, and some South American cruises require infants to be at least 12 months old.

ENTERTAINMENT

Royal Caribbean has always done a good job with its show, music, and guest performers, but over the past couple of years it's upped its game so much that it now ranks among the very best cruise lines for entertainment. Its biggest ships, *Oasis* and *Allure of the Seas,* both feature honest-to-god Broadway productions—***Hairspray!*** on *Oasis* and **Chicago: The Musical** on *Allure.* Real shows, with words and everything! That's rare enough in the cruise biz to be revolutionary, but it seems to be working. Just before this book went to press, Royal Caribbean announced that it would be expanding the idea to *Liberty of the Seas* in early 2011, though it hadn't yet named the show that will be featured. *Liberty* and sister-ship *Freedom of the Seas* will also be presenting a second musical on each sailing, this one a kid-friendly show targeted at families. Royal Caribbean is very good at moving ideas that work fleetwide, so we might see major entertainment advances across its fleet over the next couple of years.

Besides its big theater shows, RCI also offers passenger talent shows, **ballroom dancing competitions,** karaoke, sock hops, and occasional **"name" groups and soloists,** such as the Platters, the Drifters, the Coasters, John Davidson, and Marty Allen. The newer the ship, the larger and more sophisticated the stage, sound, and lighting equipment, with some boasting a wall of video monitors to augment live performances.

Aside from its showrooms and huge glitzy casinos, Royal Caribbean is big on signature spaces, with each ship offering the nautical, woodsy **Schooner Bar** as well as the **Viking Crown Lounge,** an observation-cum-nightclub set high on a top deck and boasting panoramic views of the sea and ship in all directions. The Latin-themed **Bolero's bar** (aboard *Oasis, Allure, Freedom, Liberty, Independence, Navigator, Mariner, Monarch,* and *Majesty*) serves a mean mojito and has Latin music into the night. Atrium bars also feature live music, often classical trios.

SERVICE

In general, dining, bar, and cabin service are surprisingly good considering the sheer volume of passengers with which crewmembers must deal. At dinner on a recent cruise, we found that even when staff was rushed, our water glasses were always filled, wine orders were delivered promptly, and our servers always found time for a little friendly chitchat—though on this same cruise at lunchtime, crewmembers seemed tired, grumpy, and struggling to keep up with demand (which was really high at lunch). Generally, however, the crew is efficient and friendly, from a crewman polishing the brass to the guest service staff, which was superpatient and very helpful on our recent *Rhapsody* cruise. These folks work long, hard days, though, and on ships this size (and especially on those operating quick-turnaround 3- and 4-night cruises), it's possible to run into some crewmembers who look like they need a vacation.

Guests on Royal Caribbean have the option of **tipping** traditionally—giving tips as deserved to crewmembers on a one-to-one basis—or adding a prepaid gratuity to their onboard accounts ($10 per day is suggested), to be divided among service staff later. Guests enrolled in the line's flexible My Time Dining program are required to prepay their gratuities.

Laundry and dry-cleaning services are available on all the ships, but none have self-service laundromats.

The Oasis Class: Oasis of the Seas • Allure of the Seas

Oasis of the Seas *(photo: RCCL)*

The Verdict

Oasis and *Allure of the Seas* are the future, the ultimate extension (so far) of the old "city at sea" chestnut with which big ships have been tagged for more than 4 decades. They're the biggest cruise ships ever, by far, but they've also got heart, and a design that opens up that heart to the air, sky, and sea in a way no other big ships have ever done before. If this is the new face of mainstream, then mainstream's got it good.

Specifications   Typical Per Diems: $135–$180

Size (in tons)	225,282	Passenger/Crew Ratio	2.3 to 1
Passengers (double occ.)	5,400	Year Launched	
Passenger/Space Ratio	41.7	*Oasis*	2009
Total Cabins/Veranda Cabins	2,706/1,956	*Allure*	2010
Crew	2,394	Last Major Upgrade	N/A

Frommer's Ratings (Scale of 1–5)   ★★★★★

Cabin Comfort & Amenities	4.5	Dining Options	5
Appearance & Upkeep	5	Gym, Spa & Sports Facilities	5
Public Comfort/Space	5	Children's Facilities	5
Decor	4.5	Enjoyment Factor	5

Sailing Regions, Seasons & Home Ports

Allure	**Caribbean,** from Fort Lauderdale (year-round).
Oasis	**Caribbean,** from Fort Lauderdale (year-round).

Welcome to the future. When *Oasis of the Seas* launched in 2009 (after taking some $1.4 billion and 9 to 10 million working hours to design and build), we spent a few days walking among her entertainment neighborhoods, sports decks, and innovative staterooms. We then came to the conclusion that the ship would prove to be a true game-changer—a vessel that will be for future cruise ships what, say, *The Matrix* was for modern action movies: the model on which the face of the new is built.

We don't say that just because of her size, and we don't say that because of the many flashy amenities and attractions. No, what we think will prove to be the single most influential feature of the ship is the way she's laid out. In large part, that's a function of the revolutionary split-superstructure design, in which the ship's nine upper decks (that is, everything above the hull) are split lengthwise into two separate, parallel port and starboard structures, with a 19-meter-wide open-air gap between them and structural supports joining them forward and at midships. To accommodate this kind of arrangement, the ship had to be designed with another revolutionary feature, albeit a prosaic one: extra width. *Oasis* measures some 27 feet wider than Royal Caribbean's huge Freedom-class ships and probably double the width of traditional vessels such as Holland America's Statendam class.

The effect of these design changes is remarkable, transforming the onboard vibe from that of two dimensions—the horizontal plane of most ships' decks being generally unconnected to the decks above and below—to three, and adding a feeling of light and air that's completely new in the cruise ship world. To explain what it's like, we'd like you to close your eyes and first picture yourself walking around an average public deck on any other megaship you've sailed. You get off the elevator and walk past the photo shop, then through the casino and past a couple of lounges, then maybe you get to the atrium, where you can see up a few decks. If you keep going, you'll be in the theater, or maybe a restaurant. All along the way, you've only been able to see a short distance in any direction, and only in the atrium have you been able to look up or down—and even there, your view is limited by the relative narrowness of the space. To have any sense of the rest of the ship, or of the world around the ship, you're required to navigate elevators and stairways, giving you a fragmented, piece-by-piece impression.

Now here's what it's like walking around *Oasis*—on, say, Deck 8, whose central section is taken up with Central Park, a 21,000-square-foot, open-air tropical garden lined with alfresco restaurants, sculpture, and seating nooks. From the park's pathways, you can see all the way up to Deck 18, as well as scope the balconies of hundreds of cabins that face inward toward the park, looking for all the world like luxury apartments in a city streetscape. Walk all the way through the park to Dazzles nightclub near the center of Decks 8 and 9 and take a look through its huge, two-story window. Looking down, you can see the open-air Boardwalk entertainment neighborhood and adjoining Aqua Theater at the ship's stern, with the open ocean beyond. Looking up, you can see people flying by on the zipline, which runs from starboard to port on Deck 16, above the Boardwalk's cheery carousel and below the sunny sky.

There are literally thousands of these open, airy, encompassing views from public and private spaces throughout the ship, and they're made even better by architecture that favors curving lines to lead the eye from one visual to another.

That's the big picture. Now follow us below for a tour of what Royal Caribbean has done with all that space, light, and air.

Note: Since twin sister *Allure of the Seas* didn't launch until after this book went to press, this review only deals with *Oasis. Allure* will, by all reports, be essentially identical.

CABINS One of the more remarkable things about the Oasis ships is that their split-superstructure design allows staterooms to have views inward as well as outward. This means that staterooms that would otherwise have been windowless interior cabins can now sport balconies looking out over either the greenery of Central Park or the nighttime excitement of Boardwalk. So you have to decide: oceanview or people-watching view? The 254 balcony staterooms and 70 window-view staterooms that flank Central Park are by far the most serene of the interior-view staterooms, with pleasant greenery below and a shifting skyscape above. The 225 balcony cabins and eight window cabins that flank the Boardwalk entertainment space are much more boisterous, akin to having a hotel room in Times Square or Disney World. There are also 18 window-view cabins facing the interior Royal Promenade, but they seem more of an afterthought, and their bay-window views of the "street" below seem almost claustrophobic by comparison.

Standard interior staterooms, without windows of any kind, are still available onboard, and run 149 square feet. Standard oceanview cabins come in at 179 square feet, while window cabins overlooking Boardwalk and Central Park (all on low decks, just above those areas) measure between 191 and 199 square feet. Superior oceanview, Central Park view, and Boardwalk view staterooms with balconies measure 182 square feet, plus between 50 and 80 square feet of outdoor space, depending on category. Family cabins (available either as insides, with windows, or with balconies) are a sizable 260 to 271 square feet and sleep six, with two convertible twin beds, a sleeper sofa for two, two Pullman beds, a sitting area, and (on balcony cabins) 82 square feet of outside space.

All these staterooms have a flatscreen interactive TV (through which you can book shore excursions, and so on), a vanity, hair dryer, sitting area, and minifridge. Bathrooms are pleasant and functional, with sizable shower stalls (with a little footrest for leg-shaving), plenty of shelf space, and towels with little fabric loops that make them easier to hang. Sink counters are fairly small, however, and seem to be set slightly lower than usual—a strange sensation for tall people. Cabin closets have retractable clothing and shoe shelves and self-closing sliding doors: just flick the door toward closed and the mechanism will finish the job for you. There's also additional storage space under the bed.

Amazingly, there are 13 different categories of suites on the Oasis-class ships, starting at the low end with the 287-square-foot Junior Suites, which have a sitting area with table and sofa, a bathroom with tub, and an 80-square-foot balcony. Undoubtedly, though, the one plus ultra of Oasis-class accommodations are the 27 Loft Suites, an entirely new concept in onboard living, clustered at the very top of the ship near the Viking Crown Lounge. Double-height and with double-height, superwide windows to match, they have a downstairs with a sitting area, chaise longue, sleeper sofa, flatscreen TV, two baths (one with a superlarge shower for two), and a balcony with sweeping sea (and sometimes ship-and-sea) views. At the top of the stairs, the loft bedroom floats like a dream behind transparent glass panels that afford open views through the main floor-to-ceiling windows. Loft options start with the "basic" Crown Loft Suite (545 sq. ft., plus 114-sq.-ft. balcony). Larger Sky Loft Suites (722 sq. ft., balcony 410 sq. ft.) and Royal Loft Suites (1,524 sq. ft., balcony 843 sq. ft.) pack in additional living, sleeping, and playing space, with superlarge balconies that have whirlpools and dining areas. All suites, loft or not, offer perks like priority check-in, a dedicated suite attendant, coffee and tea service, bathrobes for onboard use, and additional bathroom amenities.

A total of 46 staterooms aboard each ship are wheelchair accessible.

PUBLIC AREAS   Public areas aboard *Oasis* and *Allure* are generally clustered into four main themed "neighborhoods," with a handful of other bars, lounges, and entertainment rooms scattered around the periphery.

Our favorite neighborhood aboard these ships—and one of our very favorites on *any* ship—is **Central Park,** the 21,000-square-foot, open-air tropical garden that sits in the gap between the ships' split superstructure. Taking up the better part of Deck 8, it has a remarkably upscale, bucolic, adult atmosphere, with a wide, tiled pathway undulating through the garden, rising and falling in gentle slopes, flanked by cute red benches and surrounded by garden beds, seating nooks, a Sculpture Garden, and a number of restaurants and other venues. Gorgeous when the ships were brand new, the Central Park spaces on *Oasis* and *Allure* have an aspect unique in the cruise business, in that they'll actually get better over time. Right now, the parks each contain about 12,000 individual trees, plants, vines, and flowers, all contained within 2,200 individually sized aluminum modules which are in turn housed within 46 large planter beds. While the number of plants won't change significantly, their maturity will: Black and green bamboo and Cuban laurel trees will eventually grow to more than two and a half decks high, vines will be trained along a winding pergola, and the vines and plants of two immense Living Walls that flank the center of the park to port and starboard will burst with flowers.

Throughout the park, plants are a mix of coastal and highland subtropical species selected for their ability to survive and thrive both in Central Park's microclimate and in the geographical areas in which *Oasis* and *Allure* will sail. An interpretive garden includes regional Caribbean cash crops such as coffee plants, a cocoa tree, tiny dwarf pineapples, ginger, sugar cane, dwarf banana trees, and tapioca plants, each of them ID'd with plaques that explain their origin and agricultural or medicinal use. Other plants around the park include ground orchids, flax lilies, flamingo flowers, and bird's nest ferns, all tended by several full-time horticulturists who, in addition to their regular duties, conduct tours, give talks on plant care, and are generally around to answer questions.

Entering from the stern, you first pass the Rising Tide bar, which connects to the Royal Promenade below like a very slow elevator—so slow that you have time to buy a drink as you travel. Paths lead to either side of the glass enclosure that shelters the bar from weather, and restaurants sit to either side (see "Dining," below, for descriptions). Moving forward, we pass the Trellis Bar, which our friend Art dubbed the best bar on board during our sailing—and y'know, we agree. Seating just 17 people, it's entirely open-air, the bar itself topped by a glass-topped, vine-looped trellis, the seating either barside or at a handful of high tables. Planter boxes full of greenery surround the space on one side, and one of the five-deck-high Living Walls rises at the other.

Continuing our walk forward, we next pass one of the two enormous Crystal Canopy skylights that let natural light pass through to the Royal Promenade below. Beyond that is the park's central square, which is actually round. Designed to be a sort of communal meeting spot, it's the kind of place where you'd expect to see a busker performing if this were an on-land park. (And it wouldn't surprise us if Royal

Caribbean stations some buskers here, too, to complete the effect.) The park's forward end houses three shops: a Coach shop selling high-end bags; a portrait studio that can take your formal picture in a variety of locations around the park; and Art Actually, a gallery where passengers can buy prints and other edition works by artists represented in the ship's collection, and also attend various art-themed events. The Vintages wine bar sits across from these three shops, with wines by the glass as well as various wine-tasting events.

The **Royal Promenade,** a Main Street–like horizontal atrium first introduced aboard Royal's Voyager-class ships in 1999, sits three levels below Central Park, and is connected via the two enormous (and aforementioned) Crystal Canopy skylights (which let in natural light) and the Rising Tide Bar. The general idea of the Royal Promenade has always been that it forms a focal point for the ship—an area that guests can meander while heading from one enticement to another, a natural meeting spot, a port of last resort when you just can't decide where else to go—basically an all-purpose space with a number of pleasant drinking spots, shops, cafes, and clubs along its length. It's also an entertainment spot: Each night, a parade of costumed characters and stilt-walkers wanders through, and there are also places for bands to set up and perform. Our bet is that the Royal Promenade on these ships will prove less central than aboard the Freedom- and Voyager-class ships, if only because it has com-petition from the wonderful, open-air Central Park and the fun Boardwalk. Here's a thought, though: It'll be a damn good place to go on a rainy night, when Central Park and Boardwalk get just a little too soggy.

Aboard *Oasis* and *Allure,* the Royal Promenade is almost twice as wide as the com-parable space on RCI's Voyager- and Freedom-class ships, creating a much more open boulevard feel. It's also substantially more subdued design-wise, resembling any num-ber of currently fashionable, mixed-use shopping/entertainment/residential districts in any number of American cities, and has a mezzanine level full of bar/lounges and additional seating.

At street level, entering from the forward end of the ship, you'll pass first a gourmet coffee island and a couple of clubs: Bolero's, a Latin-themed bar that's been a staple aboard Royal Caribbean ships for years, and the On-Air Club, another semistaple that here has been expanded into a full-service sports bar, with a multiband, Times Square–style news ticker outside. Moving forward, we hit the first of the boulevard's shops, of which there are seven, ranging from the usual logo-wear shop to a sports-wear boutique, jewelry store, duty-free shop, camera store, and more. Drinking spots along the way include the Globe and Atlas Pub, serving beer and such in an English pub atmosphere; the Champagne Bar for you-know-what; and the quieter Schooner Bar, perched on the Promenade's mezzanine level. There are also a number of casual dining spots (see "Dining," below) as well as the cute little Cupcake Cupboard, serv-ing a range of fancy, cream-heavy cupcakes at extra cost. Toward the stern end of the promenade, the oval Rising Tide bar shuttles continually up and down between the promenade and Central Park. It has seating for 32 guests, who can get on or off at either venue and make the approximately 10-minute ascent or descent while ordering a quick drink—but no rush; you can stay on for multiple laps if you'd like.

Along with Central Park, the other open-air neighborhood aboard is **Boardwalk.** Stretching for almost a third of the ship's length on Deck 6, Boardwalk is a family-oriented entertainment zone that balances the altogether more adult-oriented atmos-phere of Central Park. Most guests enter Boardwalk via a wide hall that opens from the ship's aft stair/elevator tower, and is lined with stainless-steel funhouse mirrors and old-timey sideshow advertisements to set the carnival mood. Just beyond, flanked by the Boardwalk Donut Shop (free donuts!) or Ice Cream Parlor (extra cost) is a traditional carousel full of intricate, hand-carved wooden animals. The first traditional carousel at sea, it's also the first one ever created that can compensate for a ship's pitch and roll—which, honestly, isn't much of a problem aboard these amazingly stable ships. Beyond the carousel are five shops: Pets at Sea, where kids can create their own stuffed animals; the Smile Portrait Studio for carnival-style photos; Pinwheels, selling kids' clothes; Candy Beach, selling both vat candy by the pound and classics like Clark Bars, Skybars, Tootsie Rolls, and the like; and Star Pier, selling clothing and gadgets for teens and tweens.

Throughout the Boardwalk space, various permanent and temporary amusements keep things lively. Near the carousel is a classic photo booth where you and your closest can mug to your heart's content. The space also hosts a daily Family Festival with face-painting and games oriented to the whole family. Three restaurants are great casual eateries (see "Dining," below) and the AquaTheater in the very stern is a venue for swimming during the day and aquatic performances at night (see "Pool, Fitness, Spa & Sports Facilities," below).

Traditional entertainment spaces are clustered at Deck 4's **Entertainment Place,** which features a jazz club, comedy club, and disco, as well as the ship's huge casino; its Studio B ice rink, for open skating and elaborate ice shows; and the middle level of its three-deck main theater, home to production shows and featured guest performers. Note that some shows at various venues require timed (but free) tickets, which you can book through your cabin's interactive TV. Other random public rooms scattered around the ship include the lovely Viking Crown Lounge, perched at the very top of the ship on Deck 17; Dazzles Nightclub, a very deco-style space at the center of Decks 9 and 10; a library on Deck 11; and a card room and chapel on Deck 14.

For kids, *Oasis* and *Allure*'s Youth Zone children's center is one of the best in the business, stretching over an amazing 28,700 square feet, with a central boulevard connecting 10 different areas: an open, all-ages gym and activities area; the Adventure Ocean Theater, where kids can put on shows; Imagination Studio, an art-oriented space created in collaboration with Crayola, and concentrating on destination-oriented art projects; the Workshop, for activities like jewelry-making and scrapbooking; the Adventure Science Lab, where kids can make DNA strands out of licorice, learn about volcanoes and dinosaurs, and so on (the kids even get cute little lab coats and goggles!); the Kid's Arcade for video games; and three play spaces segmented by age group. Lastly, there's the Royal Babies & Royal Tots nursery, a real rarity in the cruise biz. Open daily, the nursery provides child-care drop-off options both day and evening, charging $8 per hour and catering to kids between 6 months and 3 years. Teen spaces are located one deck above, adjacent to the Sports Deck, and comprise a teen disco, an outdoor deck, a large arcade, and a living-room-style lounge with computer stations and activities like Scratch DJ classes. On one of the top decks, the H2O Zone water park is full of water-spouting sculptures, sprayers, and water cannons.

DINING OPTIONS   Like RCI's Freedom- and Voyager-class ships, both *Oasis* and *Allure* have a gorgeous three-level dining room, able to seat more than 3,000 guests at a time. What distinguishes these ships from their fleetmates, though, is the number of specialty restaurants and casual dining spots on board. Central Park, for instance, has two casual restaurants and two fine-dining establishments. On the casual side,

Giovanni's Table ($15 per person at dinner, $10 at lunch) is a family-style Italian restaurant serving pizzas, pastas, and various rustic dishes, while the **Park Cafe** (free) is sort of an adjunct to the traditional buffet restaurant upstairs, serving made-to-order salads, panini sandwiches, soups, and the like. On the fancy side, **Chops Grill** is a Chicago-style steakhouse serving both inside and out on its alfresco patio ($25 per person), while 150 Central Park is the fanciest restaurant on board, serving six- to eight-course menus with wine pairings ($35 per person). Unlike any other restaurant we know of aboard a mainstream megaship, **150 Central Park** has a menu and ambience overseen not by executives in the main office or by an absentee celebrity chef, but solely by its resident chef, the young Keriann Von Raesfeld, 2008 winner of the World Association of Chefs Societies' "Best Young Cook in the World" award. Both Chops and 150 Central Park are open for dinner only.

Boardwalk has three casual dining spots. The **Seafood Shack** is a theme park version of a ratty old boardwalk restaurant, serving a menu of seafood and oversize desserts. It's open for lunch ($7.95 cover charge) and dinner ($9.95). Across the way, Johnny Rockets is the '50s-style diner that's been a staple aboard Royal Caribbean's Voyager- and Freedom-class ships for the past decade. Where those diners were wedged into an indoor/outdoor space on one of the ships' top decks, here the locale is more thematically appropriate, with most seating on a huge, checkered outdoor patio. It's open for all three meals, with breakfast running $3.95 per person and lunch and dinner costing $4.95. Between the two restaurants, the Boardwalk Bar serves snacks, sandwiches, and salads in addition to drinks.

Down in the Royal Promenade, Sorrento's Pizza serves its namesake, which is no rival to good land-based pizzerias, but will do in a late-night pinch—and of course, it has the benefit of being free. Across on the promenade's port side, Cafe Promenade acts as yet another snack and light-meal alternative to the more traditional buffet restaurant. There's also a 24-hour coffee, pastry, and sandwich stand called the **Mondo Cafe.**

Other dining spots on board include the Solarium Bistro, serving health-conscious food at lunch and dinner and dancing under the stars at night (breakfast and lunch buffet free, dinner $20 per person); the **Wipe-Out Cafe** near the ships' surfing simulators, serving pizza, hamburgers, sandwiches, and fresh salads (free); the spa's **Vitality Café,** serving healthy snacks, sandwiches, wraps, fruit, and smoothies; and **Izumi,** serving sushi and other Asian favorites in a casual, light-filled space with seating for only 76 patrons. All items at Vitality and Izumi are priced on an a la carte basis.

POOL, FITNESS, SPA & SPORTS FACILITIES With *Oasis* and *Allure,* Royal Caribbean overturned the "traditional" layout of cruise ship pool, sports, and spa facilities, which for decades meant a Pool Deck in the middle, butting up against the buffet restaurant, with the ship's gym, spa, and other sports options located on the deck above the pool, toward the bow. On these ships, everything has been moved around, and with good effect.

Unlike any other Pool Deck at sea, the ones aboard *Oasis* and *Allure* are split into four sections—forward, aft, port, and starboard—with the deep canyon that houses Central Park splitting them lengthwise and a large structural bridge quartering them at midships. In total, the deck holds three large pools: the main pool, a sports pool, and the beach pool, where the seating area slopes right into the water, letting guests wade in or just park their lounge chairs in the shallow end and dangle their toes and fingers. Several whirlpools and a number of private cabanas flank each pool, while a pair of deck bars are located at the center of the deck. In the central pool deck's sternmost starboard section, the H2O Zone is a water park for kids, dominated by a giant, colorful octopus sculpture with water-spraying tentacles, plus a number of other sprayers and water cannons, plus separate wading and current pools and a dedicated infant and toddler pool. Across the canyon, the sports pool hosts water basketball, water badminton, and water polo in the afternoons, and is dedicated to lap swimming in the morning.

Behind the pool zone is where Royal Caribbean keeps some of its best toys—some mainstays, some relatively recent, some totally new. As has been the case on its ships for decades now, there's a miniature golf course and a large basketball court, while an elevated platform across the back of the deck holds two FlowRider Surfing Simulators (see description in the Freedom-class review, below) and the launch pad for the only ziplines at sea, which allow guests to fly across the chasm that houses Boardwalk, a full nine stories below. The ride takes all of about 7 seconds, but folks seem to like it.

The ship's gym and spa have been moved from the top-deck bow position they hold on most other megaships down to a forward position on Deck 6. The enormous fitness center is outfitted with cycles, treadmills, weight machines, and all the usual (plus the still unusual but rapidly popularizing Kinesis wall, a system of cantilevered pulleys and weights that, in the right hands, can provide a total body workout), and offers spinning, kickboxing, Pilates, and yoga classes. For us, though, the most charming part of the fitness center is the stairway that leads down one deck, providing direct access to the ship's nearly ½-mile jogging track, which is in open air along its long port and starboard stretches and ducks between walls when it snakes through the ship near the bow. It's by far the longest on any cruise ship and nearly twice as long as a standard Olympic-size track. At the tranquil Vitality at Sea spa, guests can begin their experience by unwinding in the calming relaxation rooms, then partake from a large menu of treatments or visit the Thermal Suite, with its heated tile loungers, saunas, and steam rooms. There's also a dedicated kids' and teens' spa.

Moving the spa and gym down allowed Royal Caribbean to repurpose the ships' valuable top-deck real estate to the very best Solariums at sea, each a two-deck-high wonder that manages to be both covered and open-air simultaneously, owing to a curved canopy with open strips to let in the air. A riverlike water feature separates seating into various "islands" in the space's main level, which also has a small pool and two whirlpools. Additional lounging space is available on the mezzanine level, and the Solarium Bistro on the main level (see "Dining") serves casual spa cuisine by day and transforms into an intimate restaurant at evening and a dance club at night. To both port and starboard, between the Solarium and the main Pool Deck, two cantilevered whirlpools sit within domed, semi-open bubbles jutting out over the sides of the ship, 136 feet above the ocean.

At the stern end of the Boardwalk neighborhood, twin six-deck-high rock-climbing walls flank the AquaTheater, which spreads across the entire stern. Its focus is the largest and deepest freshwater pool at sea, a 51-by-22-foot kidney-shaped body whose depth can be adjusted for various uses, up to a maximum of 18 feet. (According to its designers, this single pool holds as much water as all the pools on one of Royal's Freedom-class ships combined.) During the day, passengers can swim or take scuba lessons here, or lounge in the tiered amphitheater of deck chairs that surround it. At night, those deck chairs are replaced with theater seating and the pool goes pro, with performances that mix synchronized swimming, acrobatics, aerialism, high diving from a pair of 30-foot platforms, trapeze artistry, and water ballet. To either side of the pool, a pair of giant screens project what's going on beneath the scenes, via underwater cameras. When no shows are scheduled in the evening, a choreographed fountain show (a la Vegas's Bellagio) has water jets shooting sprays up to 65 feet high, all synched to a program of music and light.

The Freedom Class: Freedom • Liberty • Independence of the Seas

Freedom of the Seas *(photo: RCCL)*

The Verdict

Supersize versions of the already supersize Voyager-class ships, *Freedom, Liberty,* and *Independence of the Seas* offer everything those ships do and more, though they come very close to being too commercial for their own good.

Specifications

Typical Per Diems: $80–$125

Size (in tons)	160,000	Year Launched	
Passengers (double occ.)	3,634	*Freedom*	2006
Passenger/Space Ratio	44	*Liberty*	2007
Total Cabins/Veranda Cabins	1,815/844	*Independence*	2008
Crew	1,360	Last Major Upgrade	N/A
Passenger/Crew Ratio	2.7 to 1		

Frommer's Ratings (Scale of 1–5)

★★★★½

Cabin Comfort & Amenities	4	Dining Options	4.5
Appearance & Upkeep	5	Gym, Spa & Sports Facilities	5
Public Comfort/Space	4.5	Children's Facilities	5
Decor	4	Enjoyment Factor	5

Sailing Regions, Seasons & Home Ports

Freedom	**Caribbean,** from Port Canaveral (year-round).
Independence	Not currently sailing from North America.
Liberty	**Caribbean,** from Miami (Jan–Mar 2011), from Fort Lauderdale (Nov 2011–Apr 2012).

The second-largest class of cruise ships in the world, after Royal's own Oasis class, these three vessels are, at essence, just larger versions of Royal Caribbean's popular 142,000-ton, 3,114-passenger Voyager-class ships (see below), which introduced the line's now-brandwide "active vacation" image with their rock-climbing walls, ice-skating rinks, and full-size basketball courts; the Freedom ships also sport some new stuff, namely a kids' water park and a surfing simulator. Extremely well designed, the Freedom vessels disperse their large complement of passengers among many interesting public areas—including the four-story, boulevard-like interior Royal Promenade, which runs more than a football field's length down the center of each ship and is lined with bars, shops, and entertainment lounges. The promenade, with its strollable, urban feel, makes the Freedom vessels a great compromise for couples who can't decide between a tropical cruise and a city vacation. They really do feel like "cities at sea."

The Freedom ships carry at least 500 more passengers (and more if all berths are full) and have a nearly identical layout and ambience to the Voyager ships, but stretched out and with a few new eye-catching activities and entertainment features. But those extras come with a price: the Freedom ships' Royal Promenade, for instance, is more dominated by shops and corporate cobranding arrangements (a Ben & Jerry's ice-cream parlor, a sportswear shop with a dedicated New Balance section, and so on), giving it a feel that's as much mall as theme park. When crowds are low—say, during the early dinner seating, or late at night—it can still be a lot of fun to sit at the "sidewalk" cafe or bar and catch a drink, but when things are hopping, you'd be forgiven for thinking your car was parked outside, in lot D.

Just as this book went to press, Royal Caribbean announced a series of upgrades to *Liberty* and *Freedom of the Seas*. In 2011, the ships will offer nurseries for babies and tots ages 6 through 36 months; big video screens by their main pools; new digital signage to help you get around; and specialty cupcake shops. Entertainment will also get a boost, with *Liberty* presenting two major musical-theater shows—one big-name musical that hadn't been ID'd yet, and another targeted to families with kids. *Freedom* will run the family show only.

CABINS   Standard outside cabins are a livable if not overlarge 161 square feet, though standard insides seem small at 152 square feet. All cabins come with Internet dataports, minifridges, flat-panel TVs, safes, pleasant pastel color schemes, regular hair dryers, and supercomfortable beds. Bathrooms are on the cramped side, with little storage space, few amenities (soap and shampoo only), and only a thin sliver of counter. The cylindrical shower stalls, though definitely tight for large-size people, have RCI's standard sliding doors that keep in the water and warmth.

Of the 1,815 cabins, 1,084 have ocean views and 844 have verandas. Suites range from the affordable junior suites (with sitting area and balcony) to a handful of family suites (with two bedrooms, two bathrooms, and a living area with sofa bed) up to the huge Presidential Suite with its four bedrooms, four bathrooms, and 810-square-foot balcony.

For those who want an "urban" (aka voyeuristic) experience, the 168 atrium cabins on the second, third, and fourth levels of the four-story Royal Promenade have windows facing the action below, with curtains and soundproofing to keep most of the light and noise out, when you want downtime.

Thirty-two cabins are wheelchair accessible.

PUBLIC AREAS   These ships have more than 3 miles of public corridors apiece, and it can feel like a real hike if your cabin is on one end of the ship and you have to get to the other. Running 445 feet down the center of Deck 5 is the bustling, four-story Royal Promenade, designed to resemble Memphis's Beale Street or New Orleans's Bourbon Street. Like those famous thoroughfares, it's lined with shops, bars, and cafes, and has evening musical performances by the ships' various musical groups, including their big bands. Other promenade attractions include a Ben & Jerry's ice-cream parlor, a coffee bar, a casual pizza-and-snacks restaurant, an English-style pub with evening entertainment, a champagne bar, a wine bar with tastings (see "Public

Areas" section in the Voyager-class review below for a detailed description), a small bookstore, several shops, and, for our money, the best thing on the whole strip: a men's barbershop giving old-timey professional shaves spiced with a helping of New Age spa frippery. The half-hour Express Shave includes hot towels, deep-cleansing exfoliation, a superclose shave, and did we mention hot towels? *N-i-i-i-ice.* Only downside? They use safety razors instead of straight. Wimps.

Down on Decks 3 and 4, the two-level disco is entered through a theme-park-like "secret passage." There also is a huge multistory theater, a casino with more than 300 slot machines, a Latin-themed bar with live music, and the nautically themed Schooner Bar. One deck down, excellent ice shows as well as game shows and fashion shows are held throughout each cruise at the Center Ice Rink, which has a sliding floor to cover the ice during nonskate events. Other public rooms include a library, an Internet center, a sprawling kids' area with huge oceanview playroom, a living-room-style teen center, a jumbo arcade, a top-deck jazz club and cocktail lounge, a card room, and a wedding chapel. There's also a "peek-a-boo" bridge that allows guests to watch the crew steering the ship.

DINING OPTIONS   The ships' three-level main dining rooms are, like those on RCI's Voyager-class ships, among the most stunning and classy aboard any of today's megaships, with a design that follows a generally classical theme. Each level—linked by a large open area and grand staircase at its center—is considered a separate restaurant, though service and menus are consistent throughout. A pianist or piano trio entertains from a platform in the aft end of the room and a huge crystal chandelier hangs overhead, both setting an elegant mood.

Two alternative restaurants occupy spots immediately to port and starboard at the entrance to the buffet restaurant: **Portofino,** serving Italian meals in a cozy setting, and **Chops Grille,** a woodsy room for manly steaks. Portofino has a $20 per person cover charge; for Chops, it's $25 per person. Out in the buffet, a section called **Jade** serves Japanese, Chinese, Indian, and Thai dishes.

Another casual spot for lunch, dinner, and late-night snacks is the popular **Johnny Rockets,** a 1950s-style diner set out on deck and serving burgers, shakes, fries, and the like, with veggie burgers to satisfy non-meat-eaters. There's a nominal $4.95 per-person service charge, and sodas and shakes are a la carte.

POOL, FITNESS, SPA & SPORTS FACILITIES   Sticking with their active image, Royal Caribbean has outfitted the Freedom ships with several features sure to entertain both actual athletes and weekend warriors, as well as their active kids. The biggest hoo-ha is each ship's FlowRider surfing simulator—similar to swim-in-place lap pools with their recycling currents, except that this one has a stream that flows up an inclined, wedge-shaped surface 40 feet long and 32 feet wide. At the bottom are powerful jets that pump 30,000 gallons per minute up the slope, creating a wavelike flow on which boarders can ride—at least in theory. Located in the stern of each ship's sports court, spanning Decks 12 and 13, the ride is adjoined by bleachers for gawkers and fans, creating a bonding atmosphere where those who aren't inclined to flow can wager on those who are. We had our money on the kid with the puka beads and board shorts, who did manage to get to his knees before falling off and being swept up and *bam!* into the padded back bumper—just like everybody else. It's sports as a metaphor for life: Eventually, you fall down and get swept away by the currents, only here you can get back in line and try again. Participants must sign up for free group sessions and go through a quick introduction, after which they and the other members of their group take turns riding the wave, in either traditional stand-up surfing or less-balance-demanding bodyboarding. A soft, flexible surface absorbs the impact when you fall—which you will.

A free-standing "surf shack" bar near the FlowRider provides drinks. Also nearby are Royal Caribbean's signature rock-climbing wall (the biggest one at sea, naturally), a miniature-golf course, a golf simulator, a jogging track, and a full-size basketball court.

In the ship's gym, an honest-to-God 20×20-foot boxing ring takes the place of the large hot tub that greets guests on the Voyager ships. The ring is part of what the line bills as the largest fitness center at sea, with an enormous number of aerobics and weight machines plus workouts (for a fee) that are rare even in shore-side gyms. Options include Fight Klub boxing training (one-on-one training sessions using speed bags, jump ropes, heavy bags, and padded punching mitts), personal training with Pilates instructors, onboard yoga and a class on the beach at Labadee (Royal Caribbean's private resort in Haiti), Boot Camp X-Treme Training, and linked treadmill workouts. Stretch and fitness tips are located at intervals along the onboard running track, and a program of mapped running/jogging routes is available in the ports of call.

On deck, the kid-friendly H2O Zone Water Park takes up almost half the Pool Deck, with water cannons, jets, buckets, and sprays hidden among colorful cartoon statues, some controlled by motion sensors, others by the kids themselves. The area also includes two wading pools (one geared to toddlers) and two hot tubs, a great place for Mom and Dad to soak while the kiddies are having a ball. Farther forward, the main pool area has two pools (one traditional, one "sports") and two large hot tubs at port and starboard, extending 12 feet over the edge of the ship and some 112 feet above the sea. Extremely popular, they get socially crowded—but, of course, with hot tubs, that's the point.

While crowds tend to disperse around the ships' public areas, things can get very crowded on sunny days out on the main Pool and Sports decks. Guests seeking something more peaceful can sometimes find it in the adjacent, adults-only Solarium, where a second swimming pool is bisected by a little bridge.

The Voyager Class: Voyager • Explorer • Adventure • Navigator • Mariner of the Seas

The Verdict

Sports club meets Vegas meets theme park meets cruise ship, these enormous vessels are real winners if you like your vacations larger than life. As we overheard one little boy say to his father, "This doesn't look like a ship, daddy. It looks like a city!"

Explorer of the Seas *(photo: Matt Hannafin)*

Specifications

Typical Per Diems: $75–$115

Size (in tons)	142,000	Year Launched	
Passengers (double occ.)	3,114	*Voyager*	1999
Passenger/Space Ratio	45.6	*Explorer*	2000
Total Cabins/Veranda Cabins	1,557/757	*Adventure*	2001
Crew	1,176	*Navigator*	2002
Passenger/Crew Ratio	2.7 to 1	*Mariner*	2003
Last Major Upgrade	N/A		

Frommer's Ratings (Scale of 1–5)

★★★★ ½

Cabin Comfort & Amenities	4	Dining Options	4.5
Appearance & Upkeep	4	Gym, Spa & Sports Facilities	5
Public Comfort/Space	5	Children's Facilities	5
Decor	4	Enjoyment Factor	5

Sailing Regions, Seasons & Home Ports

Adventure	**Caribbean,** from San Juan (Dec–Apr).
Explorer	**Caribbean** (Nov–Mar), **Bermuda** (Apr–Nov), and **Canada/New England** (Sept–Oct), all from Cape Liberty, NJ.
Mariner	**Mexican Riviera,** from Los Angeles (Jan 2011). **Caribbean,** from Galveston (Nov 2011–Apr 2012).
Navigator	**Caribbean,** from Fort Lauderdale (Jan–Apr).
Voyager	**Caribbean,** from Galveston (Jan–Apr 2011), from New Orleans (Nov 2011–Apr 2012).

Truly groundbreaking when they were first launched, the Voyager-class ships are still among the largest and most activity-rich passenger ships at sea, boasting a full-size ice-skating rink; an outdoor in-line skating track; a 1950s-style diner sitting right out on deck; a 9-hole miniature-golf course and golf simulator; regulation-size basketball, paddleball, and volleyball courts; huge two-level gyms and spas; and the rock-climbing walls that have become one of Royal Caribbean's most distinguishing features. And did we mention they also have monumentally gorgeous, three-story dining rooms, florist shops, and a "peek-a-boo" bridge on Deck 11 that allows guests to watch the crew steering the ship?

Great for people-watching, the four-story, boulevard-like Royal Promenade runs more than a football field's length down the center of each ship and is lined with bars, shops, and entertainment lounges and anchored at each end by huge twin atria. Voyeurs will be glad to know that three decks of inside cabins have views from bay windows of the "street scene" below.

Though each ship carries 3,114 guests at double occupancy (because many state-rooms have third and fourth berths, total capacity for each vessel can reach as high as 3,838), remarkably, the ships rarely feel as crowded as you'd expect. On our last three sailings, we found many public rooms nearly empty during the day and didn't have to wait in line much at all the entire week, even though more than 3,200 passengers were aboard. As we heard one woman comment to her companion, "I know there are 3,000 people on this ship, but where are they all?" Kudos go to the crew for efficiency, and also to Royal Caribbean for a design that features enough appealing public areas to diffuse crowds comfortably, plus a layout that encourages traffic to flow in several different directions. This keeps crowding down and also means you don't tend to find yourself in the same spots day after day—it's entirely possible to be aboard for 6 days, turn a corner, and find yourself in a room you've never seen before. That said, when meeting up with family and friends around the ship, make sure you decide exactly where and when you're rendezvousing or chances are you won't see them for days!

One thing that deserves mention about ships this large is that even though ongoing maintenance is standard (replacing stained upholstery or carpeting, for instance), it's tough keeping up with the demands of constant use by thousands of passengers, especially on the ship's soft goods. On one sailing aboard the *Voyager,* for instance, we noticed some work that hadn't yet been addressed (a torn curtain in the dining room and soiled fabric on some chairs).

CABINS Though not huge (at 160 sq. ft. for insides and 173 sq. ft. for standard ocean views, including balcony), Voyager-class cabins are comfortable, with Internet dataports, minifridges, safes, TVs, pleasant pastel color schemes, and hair dryers. Bathrooms are on the cramped side, with little storage space, few amenities (soap and shampoo only), and only a thin sliver of counter. The cylindrical shower stalls, though definitely tight for large-size people, have good sliding doors that keep in the water and warmth.

Of the 1,557 cabins, 939 have ocean views and 757 have verandas. There's a single huge Penthouse Suite, 10 Owner's Suites, and four Royal Family Suites that accommodate a total of eight people with two bedrooms, plus a living room with sofa bed and a pair of bathrooms. Smaller and cheaper family cabins sleep six, some on sofa beds. For voyeurs, the 138 atrium cabins on the second, third, and fourth levels of the four-story Royal Promenade have windows facing the action below, with curtains and soundproofing to keep most of the light and noise out when you want downtime.

Twenty-six cabins are wheelchair accessible.

PUBLIC AREAS Each ship has about 3 miles of public corridors, and it can feel like a real hike if your cabin is on one end of the ship and you have to get to the other. Running down the center of each ship is the bustling, four-story Royal Promenade; lined with shops, bars, and cafes, it's the center of onboard life. Other promenade attractions include an elegant champagne bar; a comfy English/Irish bar with "sidewalk" seating; a Ben & Jerry's ice-cream bar; shops; and a bright cafe that serves pizza, cookies, pastries, and coffee 24 hours a day. *Voyager, Explorer,* and *Adventure* also have a large sports bar that gets big, raucous crowds when games are broadcast (and puts out free hot dogs and nachos to keep them there), and an arcade stocked with classic 1980s video games. On *Navigator* and *Mariner,* those were scrapped in favor of Vintages Wine Bar, created in collaboration with the Mondavi, Beringer Blass, and Niebaum-Coppola wineries. Full of wood and leather, with terra-cotta floors, attractive vineyard-themed lithographs, and a 600-bottle "cellar," the bars showcase more than 60 vintages. Prices are reasonable and guests can taste any variety before ordering. Classes in wine appreciation are held here throughout the week, and passengers can also stage their own tastings by ordering any of 13 special "wine flight" tasting menus, with selections grouped by taste profile, varietal, or region—for example, merlots, Australian wines, and so on.

In total, there are some 30 places aboard each ship to grab a drink, including the Viking Crown complex on the top deck, with its elegant jazz club and golf-themed

19th Hole bar; the dark, romantic, nautically themed Schooner Bar; and the clubby cigar bar, tucked away behind a dark door and hosting blackjack games on formal evenings. Aboard each ship, the futuristic or Gothic-dungeon-themed disco is entered through a theme-park-like "secret passage," while the huge three-story showrooms occupy the opposite end of the kitsch spectrum: beautifully designed, with simple, elegant color schemes and truly lovely stage curtains—the one on *Adventure* decorated with peacock designs, the one on *Explorer* depicting a chorus of women standing under golden boughs amid a rain of leaves. Excellent ice shows as well as game shows and fashion shows are held throughout each cruise at the Center Ice Rink, which has a sliding floor to cover the ice during nonskate events. Open skating for passengers is scheduled throughout the week.

Each ship has a two-story library-cum-computer-room with about 18 computer stations and Web cams that allow you to send your picture as an electronic postcard. There are also sprawling kids' areas with huge oceanview playrooms, teen discos, and jumbo arcades.

The best spots for chilling out with a book during days at sea include the seaview Seven of Hearts card room and Cloud Nine Lounge on Deck 14. Those really wanting to get away from people can retreat up the curving stairway to the Skylight Chapel on Deck 15, which gets almost no traffic and is even free of piped-in music. (It also lacks windows.)

DINING OPTIONS   The three-level main dining rooms on these ships are among the most stunning on any of today's megaships, with designs that follow a general European theme. Each level—linked by a large open area and grand staircase at its center—is considered a separate restaurant, though service and menus are consistent throughout. A pianist or piano trio entertains from a platform in the aft end of the room and a huge crystal chandelier hangs overhead, both setting an elegant mood.

For a dining alternative, the oceanview Portofino restaurant serves Italian meals in a cozy setting (and at an additional $20-per-person charge), but be sure to reserve a table as soon as you get aboard, as they book up fast.

The pleasant, spacious Island Grill and Windjammer casual buffet restaurants are joined into one large space, but have separate lines and stations to keep things moving. On *Navigator* and *Mariner,* this area also incorporates the Asian-themed Jade buffet. There's no outdoor seating per se, but the ship's main pool area is on the same deck, just outside the restaurants' entrances.

Another casual option for lunch, dinner, and late-night snacks is the popular Johnny Rockets, a 1950s-style diner set out on deck and serving burgers, shakes, fries, and the like, with veggie burgers to satisfy non-meat-eaters. The international waitstaff is cute enough in their '50s-style soda-jerk clothes, but we could do without the cutesy lip-sync-and-dance routines to songs such as "YMCA" and "Respect." There's a $4.95-per-person service charge and sodas and shakes are a la carte.

POOL, FITNESS, SPA & SPORTS FACILITIES   Each ship has a large, well-equipped oceanview gym, though the arrangement of machines and the many pillars throughout can make them feel tight when full. Each has a large indoor whirlpool and a huge aerobics studio (among the biggest on any ship), and their two-level spa complexes are among the largest and best equipped at sea, with peaceful waiting areas where New Agey tropical-birdsong music induces total relaxation—until you get your bill.

While crowds tend to disperse around the ships' public areas, on sunny days things can get tight out on the main pool decks, where deck chairs are squeezed into every level of the multistoried, amphitheater-like decks. The vibe can be electric (or at least loud) when the pool band starts playing. Guests seeking something more peaceful can usually find it in the adjacent Solarium, with a second swimming pool and two enormous whirlpool tubs under a sliding roof. Behind the Johnny Rockets diner, *Voyager, Adventure,* and *Explorer* have a kids' pool area with a water slide, wading pool, hot tub for adults, and dozens of adorable half-size deck chairs for the kids. On *Navigator* and *Mariner,* the area is reserved for teens, with deck chairs for sunbathing and an outdoor dance floor with sound and light systems. Deck 13 is the hub of sports action, with the much-touted rock-climbing wall, skating track, miniature-golf course, and basketball court. Appointments must be made to use the more popular facilities (especially the wall), but this is a good thing as it cuts down on lines.

The Radiance Class: Radiance • Brilliance • Serenade • Jewel of the Seas

Radiance of the Seas *(photo: RCCL)*

The Verdict

With their classic nautical profiles and interior decor, these are Royal Caribbean's most elegantly traditional ships, though they also offer a lot of the fun and games of RCI's larger vessels, including rock climbing and miniature golf.

Specifications

Typical Per Diems: $85–$140

Size (in tons)	90,090	Year Launched	
Passengers (double occ.)	2,100	*Radiance*	2001
Passenger/Space Ratio	42.9	*Brilliance*	2002
Total Cabins/Veranda Cabins	1,050/577	*Serenade*	2003
Crew	857	*Jewel*	2004
Passenger/Crew Ratio	2.5 to 1	Last Major Upgrade	N/A

Frommer's Ratings (Scale of 1–5)

★★★★ ½

Cabin Comfort & Amenities	4	Dining Options	4.5
Appearance & Upkeep	5	Gym, Spa & Sports Facilities	5
Public Comfort/Space	5	Children's Facilities	4
Decor	5	Enjoyment Factor	5

Sailing Regions, Seasons & Home Ports

Brilliance	Not currently sailing from North America.
Jewel	**Caribbean & Panama Canal,** from Fort Lauderdale (Jan–Apr 2011). **Canada/ New England,** from Boston (Sept–Oct 2011). **Caribbean,** from Tampa (Nov 2011– Apr 2012).
Radiance	**Caribbean,** from Tampa (Jan–Apr 2011). **Alaska,** from Vancouver and Anchorage/ Seward (May–Sept 2011). **Hawaii,** Honolulu to Vancouver (Apr 2012).
Serenade	**Caribbean,** from San Juan (year-round).

These ships are just plain handsome, with some of the adventure features of their larger Oasis-, Freedom-, and Voyager-class siblings, but a sleeker seagoing profile outside and a more nautical look and feel inside—and acres of windows to bring the two together. These ships are of more manageable size, too. When you first board, you'll see one of Royal Caribbean's typical wiry modern art sculptures filling the bright, nine-story atrium, but venture a little farther and you'll see that the ships have a much more traditional interior, with dark-wood paneling, caramel-brown leathers, and deep-sea-blue fabrics and carpeting. Some 110,000 square feet of glass covers about half of their sleek exteriors, affording wide-open views from the Viking Crown Lounge, Singapore Sling's piano bar, Crown & Anchor Lounge, Sky Bar, Windjammer Café, and Champagne Bar. The same goes for the atrium, which is an uninterrupted wall of glass from Decks 5 through 10 portside, and has four banks of glass elevators. All this transparency comes in handy in scenic destinations such as Alaska.

CABINS Cabins are fairly spacious, with the smallest inside ones measuring 165 square feet and some 75% of outside staterooms measuring at least 180 square feet, some with 40-square-foot verandas. The rest have jumbo-size portholes. Decor is appealing, done in attractive navy blues and copper tones. All cabins have minifridges, hair dryers, interactive televisions (for buying shore excursions, checking your onboard account, and looking up stock quotes), small sitting areas with minicouches, lots of drawer space, roomy closets, bedside reading lights, and TVs. Vanity/desks have pullout trays to accommodate laptops, plus modem jacks to connect them to the Internet. Bathrooms are small, with Royal Caribbean's typical hold-your-breath-and-step-in shower stalls, but they do have lots of storage space.

All but a handful of suites are located on Deck 10. The best, the Royal Suite, measures 1,001 square feet and has a separate bedroom, living room with baby grand piano, dining table, bar, entertainment center, and 215-square-foot balcony. Six Owner's Suites are about half that size, with 57-square-foot balconies, a separate living room, a bar, and a walk-in closet; and the 35 Grand Suites are one step below at 358 to 384 square feet, with sitting areas and 106-square-foot balconies. Three 586-square-foot Royal Family Suites have 140-square-foot balconies and two bathrooms and can accommodate six people in two separate bedrooms (one with third and fourth berths, and another two on a pullout couch in the living room). Suite guests are treated to complimentary in-cabin butler service in addition to cabin stewards, and there's also a Concierge Club on Deck 10, where suite guests can request services and grab a newspaper.

One snag on the balcony front: On each ship, Cabin Decks 7 through 10 are narrower than those on the rest of the ship, resulting in cabin balconies on Deck 10 (many of them suites) being shaded by the overhanging deck above. Meanwhile, cabin balconies on the aft and forward ends of Deck 7, being indented, look out onto the top of Deck 6 instead of directly out onto the sea. Balconies on cabin nos. 7652 to 7670 and nos. 7152 to 7170, also aft on Deck 7, are not completely private because the dividers between them don't go all the way to the edge of the space. Keep your clothes on; your neighbors can look right over at you.

Fifteen cabins on each ship can accommodate wheelchair users.

PUBLIC AREAS Our favorite space aboard is the cluster of five intimate, wood-and-leather lounges on Deck 6, which recall the decor of classic yachts, university clubs, and cigar lounges. Expect low lighting, inlaid wood flooring, cozy couches, and Oriental-style area rugs. The best of these rooms is the romantic piano bar and lounge that stretches across each ship's stern, with a bank of floor-to-ceiling windows. For amazing views, don't miss having a cocktail here on a moonlit night. Adjacent is a lovely colonial-style Billiard Club boasting herringbone wood floors, redwood veneer paneling, and a pair of ultra-high-tech gyroscopic pool tables. No excuse for missing shots: The tables compensate for the ship's movements, staying remarkably level.

The main theaters are refreshingly different from most in the cruise biz, with a cool ambience, warm wood tones, and seats in deep-sea blues and greens. Artful handmade curtains, indirect lighting, and fiber optics all come together to create a quiet, ethereal look. But guys, watch those protruding armrests: It's very easy to snag your pants pockets on them.

Other public areas include the attractive Casino Royale, with more than 200 slot machines and dozens of gaming tables; a baseball-themed sports bar with interactive games on the bar top; the nautically themed Schooner Bar; a 24-hour Internet center; a specialty-coffee bar with several Internet stations; a small library; a conference-center complex with a small movie theater; and, high up on Deck 13, Royal Caribbean's signature Viking Crown Lounge, which is divided between a quiet lounge and a large disco with a rotating bar. Even the ships' high-style public bathrooms are impressive, with their marble floors and counters and funky portholelike mirrors.

The huge kids' area on Deck 12 includes a sprawling playroom divided into several areas, with a video arcade and an outdoor pool with water slide. Teens have their own nightclub, with a DJ booth, music videos, and a soda bar.

DINING OPTIONS   The two-story main dining rooms on all four ships are glamorous and elegant, like something out of a 1930s movie set. Four willowy, silk-covered columns dominate the vaulted main floor, and a wide double staircase connects the two decks dramatically—all that's missing are Cary Grant and Deborah Kerr. On *Serenade*, painter Frank Troia's huge, Impressionist *Gala Suite* amplifies the mood, depicting formally dressed couples dancing amid floating globes of light.

The nautically decorated **Windjammer Café** takes self-serve buffet dining to new levels, with 11 food stations (nine inside and two outside) set up as islands to keep the lines down and the crowds diffused. It really works. If you prefer taking your meals while reclining, there's a small strip of cozy tables with oversize rattan chairs and thick cushions between the indoor and outdoor seating areas.

The cozy, 90-seat **Chops Grille** is an oceanview spot with dark woods, rich upholsteries, and high-backed booths that bring home the meat-and-potatoes mood. You can watch your steak being cooked in the open kitchen. Adjacent is the 130-seat **Portofino,** an oceanview Italian restaurant. Expect more refined and gracious service than in the main dining room, plus a more leisurely pace (and a cost: Portofino charges a $20 per person cover charge; for Chops, it's $25 per person). Up on the Sport Deck, the **Seaview Café** is a casual lunch and dinner eatery with checkered floors, rattan chairs, and lots of light, and it serves quick meals such as fish and chips, popcorn shrimp, and burgers.

At a counter in the Solarium freshly made pizza is served by the slice, and a coffee shop serves cappuccino and pastries.

POOL, FITNESS, SPA & SPORTS FACILITIES   The Radiance vessels have tons of recreation outlets and acres of space to flop on a deck chair and sunbathe. At the main pool, passengers pack in like sardines on sunny days at sea, and deck chairs can be scarce during the prime hours before and after lunch—par for the cruise ship course. On *Radiance,* the Pool Deck is presided over by a 12-foot-high cedar totem pole carved for the ship by Alaska Native artist Nathan Jackson of Ketchikan.

Much more relaxing are the ships' large, lush Solariums, with their exotic eastern motifs. Tropical foliage and waterfalls impart an Asian-spa mood, and stone reliefs, regional woodcarvings, and statues drive home the mood. The area's adjacent (and popular) pizza counter adds a little pandemonium to the otherwise serene scene (as can kids, if they happen to find the place), but overall this is a great spot to settle in for a lazy afternoon at sea. The padded wooden chaise longues are heavenly. The adjacent spa has 13 treatment rooms and a special steam-room complex with heated tiled lounges and showers that simulate tropical rain and fog.

The Sports Deck has a 9-hole miniature-golf course and golf simulators, a jogging track, a rock-climbing wall attached to the funnel, and a combo basketball, volleyball, and paddle-tennis court. The sprawling oceanview gym has a huge aerobics floor and dozens of exercise machines, including sea-facing treadmills and elliptical stair-steppers.

The Vision Class: Legend • Enchantment • Grandeur • Rhapsody • Splendor • Vision of the Seas

Rhapsody of the Seas *(photo: RCCL)*

The Verdict

These ships are glitzy and exciting without going overboard, though they're on the frumpy side compared to their newer fleetmates.

Specifications

Typical Per Diems: $70–$175

Size (in tons)		*Grandeur*	975/212
Legend/Splendor	69,130	*Enchantment*	1,126/248
Grandeur	74,140	*Rhapsody/Vision*	1,000/229
Enchantment	80,700	Crew	
Rhapsody/Vision	78,491	*Legend/Splendor*	720
Passengers (double occ.)		*Grandeur*	760
Legend/Splendor	1,804	*Enchantment*	840
Grandeur	1,950	*Rhapsody/Vision*	765
Enchantment	2,252	Passenger/Crew Ratio	2.5 to 1
Rhapsody/Vision	2,000	*Enchantment*	2.7 to 1
Passenger/Space Ratio		Year Launched	
Legend/Splendor	38.3	*Legend*	1995
Grandeur	38	*Splendor/Grandeur*	1996
Enchantment	35.8	*Enchantment/Rhapsody*	1997
Rhapsody/Vision	39.2	*Vision*	1998
Total Cabins/Veranda Cabins		Last Major Upgrade	
Legend/Splendor	902/231	*Enchantment*	2005

Frommer's Ratings (Scale of 1–5)

★★★½

Cabin Comfort & Amenities	3	Dining Options	3
Appearance & Upkeep	4	Gym, Spa & Sports Facilities	4
Public Comfort/Space	4	Children's Facilities	4
Decor	3.5	Enjoyment Factor	4

Sailing Regions, Seasons & Home Ports

Enchantment	**Caribbean** (Jan–Aug, Oct–Nov), **The Bahamas** (Jan–Apr, Nov–Dec), **Bermuda** (May–Nov), and **Canada/New England** (Aug–Oct), all from Baltimore.
Grandeur	**Caribbean,** from Colon, Panama (Jan–Apr).
Legend	Not currently sailing from North America.
Rhapsody	**Hawaii,** Honolulu to Vancouver (Apr), Vancouver to Honolulu (Sept). **Alaska,** from Seattle (May–Sept).
Splendor	Not currently sailing from North America.
Vision	Not currently sailing from North America.

It's a funny thing with cruise ships. One year they're the newest, hottest, biggest thing on water, and just a few cycles around the sun later, you look at them and think, "How quaint. How '90s." Still, they afford a decent cruise experience, but things have changed so fast in the cruise biz that even the best ships from the late–20th century can seem dated. That's sort of the story with RCI's Vision-class vessels, which offer an open, light-filled feel and many of the same amenities as aboard the line's newer, larger ships; and to us, their relatively smaller size is a big plus. You won't feel overwhelmed or lost on these ships.

All the ships have been kept up-to-date (they were even retrofitted with rock-climbing walls after those proved so popular on the Voyager ships), but *Enchantment of the Seas* is by far the most modernized of the bunch. In mid-2005, RCI revisited a trend common in the mid-'90s, literally sawing the ship in half like a magician's assistant, inserting a new 73-foot midsection, and then welding it all back together. As a result, *Enchantment* offers a lot more than her Vision-class sisters. On the much-enlarged Pool Deck, there's an additional stage and midships bar for adults and an "interactive splash deck" with water jets that kids can control to spray each other or create their own water ballet. Additions to the nearby Sports Deck include four bungee trampolines where guests can bounce up to 35 feet above the deck, doing somersaults in midair. Passengers with disabilities aren't left out, with new accessibility features including pool and Jacuzzi lifts, access to the Splash Deck, a lift to the bungee trampoline area, and improved thresholds and ramps throughout the vessel. Below-deck changes include the addition of a Latin-themed bar, an expanded casino, a larger shopping area, and a new coffee bar serving Seattle's Best coffee and Ben & Jerry's ice cream—features currently available aboard RCI's newer vessels. No word yet on whether *Enchantment's* sister ships will get a similar refurbishment anytime soon.

Generally, when these ships are sailing full, things can feel crowded. On a recent *Rhapsody* sailing with just under 2,300 passengers, lunchtime in both restaurants was not a pretty sight. Getting on and off the ship in port can also be a hassle with so many people to move.

Splendor is sailing in Europe and South America at least through mid-2010.

CABINS   To be polite, cabins are "compact," with insides measuring 138 to 174 square feet and outsides measuring between 154 and 237 square feet—larger than the staterooms on the line's older *Majesty* and *Monarch,* but smaller than those on the Oasis-, Freedom-, and Voyager-class ships and on many competitors' vessels. All cabins come with TVs, safes, and an impressive amount of storage space. Bathrooms are not the largest you'll ever see, with shower stalls that are a tight squeeze for anyone thicker than a supermodel. Expect an unmemorable decor with blond furniture and wood trim; on a recent *Legend* cruise, there were quite a few spots where the paint was peeling, and on a recent *Splendor* sailing, the bathroom mirror was held together with a wide piece of electrical tape. Overall, the cabins have seen better days. On the bright side, carpeting and bedding are in good shape, and the duvets and supercomfy bedding make sleeping a dream.

For something big, check out the 1,140-square-foot Royal Suites, which have a baby grand piano and huge marble bathroom with double sinks, a big whirlpool bathtub, and a glass-enclosed shower for two. For something in between, check the roomy, 190-square-foot category-D1 cabins, with private verandas, minifridges, small sitting areas with pull-out couches, and tons of storage space. All told, about a quarter of each ship's cabins have private verandas, and about a third can accommodate third and fourth passengers.

Each vessel has between 14 and 17 staterooms equipped for wheelchair users.

PUBLIC AREAS   Throughout each vessel, warm woods and brass, gurgling fountains, green foliage, glass, crystal, and buttery leathers highlight the public areas, whose ambience ranges from classic to glitzy to a bit dated. The bright, wide open, and easy-to-navigate Promenade and Mariner decks are home to most public rooms, their corridors converging at a seven-story atrium where glass elevators take passengers from Deck 4 all the way up to the glass-walled Viking Crown Lounge on Deck 11. Full musical revues are staged in glittery two-story showrooms, where columns obstruct views from some balcony seats. The ship's casinos are Vegas-style flashy, with hundreds of gambling stations so densely packed that it's sometimes difficult to move and always difficult to hear. Other nice spots include the Schooner piano bar (a great place for a pre-dinner drink or late-night unwinding, with a nautical wood-and-rope decor) and the Champagne Terrace at the foot of the atrium, where you can sip a glass of fine wine or bubbly while swaying to the two- or three-person band playing there.

In contrast to its showcase spaces, each ship also contains many hideaway refuges, including an array of cocktail bars, a card room and a library, though not a very well-stocked one. A couple of thousand original artworks aboard each ship (including the good, the bad, and the weird) add humanity and warmth.

For kids, there's a decent playroom stocked with toys, books, and games, and nearby is a roomy teen center and a small video-game arcade.

DINING OPTIONS   The large dining rooms aboard these vessels span two decks connected with a grand staircase and flanked with 20-foot walls of glass. The rooms are of their era, with lots of stainless steel, mirrors, dramatic chandeliers, and a slight feel of a banquet hall. At lunchtime on our recent *Rhapsody* cruise, the whole operation seemed disorganized—there was a long wait for tables and waiters seemed hassled to keep up. There's also a large indoor/outdoor buffet restaurant serving breakfast, lunch, and dinner. Again, on a recent *Rhapsody* sailing, the Windjammer buffet was a chaotic sea of humanity during lunchtime; it was hard to find a seat and crew seemed to struggle a bit keeping things tidy and bins filled. A small snack counter where pizza, sandwiches, and various salads are served can be a welcome respite from the frenetic Windjammer buffet at lunchtime.

POOL, FITNESS, SPA & SPORTS FACILITIES   The Steiner-managed spas on these ships offer a wide selection of treatments as well as the standard steam rooms and saunas. Adjacent Solariums have a pool, lounge chairs, floor-to-ceiling windows, and a retractable glass ceiling for inclement weather. Designed after Roman, Egyptian, or Moorish models, these bright, spacious areas are a peaceful place to lounge before or after a spa treatment, or any time at all (well, except during lunch and pre-dinner hours, when the snack bar in the corner attracts a following which takes away from the serenity of the space). Gyms are surprisingly small and cramped considering the ships' size.

Each ship has a higher-than-expected amount of open deck space. The outdoor pool on the Sun Deck has the usual blaring rah-rah music during the day, along with silly contests of the belly-flop variety. A rock-climbing wall, minigolf course (on the *Legend* and *Splendor*), jogging track, shuffleboard, and Ping-Pong round out the on-deck options.

Monarch of the Seas • Majesty of the Seas

The Verdict

This pair sure ain't spring chickens, but they are a bargain, sailing inexpensive 3- and 4-night cruises on the U.S. East and West Coasts.

Majesty of the Seas *(photo: RCCL)*

Specifications

Typical Per Diems: $55–$165

Size (in tons)	73,941	Year Launched	
Passengers (double occ.)	2,390	*Monarch*	1991
Passenger/Space Ratio	30.9	*Majesty*	1992
Total Cabins/Veranda Cabins	1,177/62	Last Major Upgrade	
Crew	825	*Monarch*	2003
Passenger/Crew Ratio	2.9 to 1	*Majesty*	2007

Frommer's Ratings (Scale of 1–5)

★★★

Cabin Comfort & Amenities	3	Dining Options	3
Appearance & Upkeep	4	Gym, Spa & Sports Facilities	3
Public Comfort/Space	3	Children's Facilities	4
Decor	3.5	Enjoyment Factor	3.5

Sailing Regions, Seasons & Home Ports

| Majesty | **The Bahamas,** from Miami (year-round). |
| Monarch | **The Bahamas,** from Port Canaveral (year-round). |

Along with their predecessor *Sovereign of the Seas* (which now sails for Spain's Pullman-tar Cruises), *Monarch* and *Majesty of the Seas* were once among the largest cruise ships in the world, but today they're literally less than half the size of their largest fleetmates. A decade and a half of hard use has given them their share of bumps and bruises, and even though recent makeovers have hammered out some of the dents and updated their look, expect well-worn and comfortable rather than sophisticated.

CABINS   Standard staterooms are very snug at only 120 square feet, bathrooms are similarly cramped, and closet space is limited—but then, how much space do you need on the kind of short itineraries these ships offer? More than 100 cabins have upper and lower berths to accommodate four, albeit very tightly. Overall, cabin decor is spartan and uninspired, with pastel fabrics and blond woods, and like other ships of their generation, relatively few have balconies. All cabins have TVs and safes. Soundproofing in these cabins isn't the greatest; in some you can hear every word your neighbors say.

Four to six cabins on each ship can accommodate wheelchair users.

PUBLIC AREAS   A dramatic five-story atrium is the focal point of each ship, separating the public areas (which are mostly clustered in the stern) from the cabins forward, an arrangement that minimizes bleed-through noise and also gives the impression that these ships are smaller than they are. Shops, the ship's salon, the Internet center, the library, several information desks, and a champagne bar are all clustered around the atrium at various levels. Elsewhere, you'll find a sprawling casino, a cinema, the popular Schooner piano bar, and (as on all pre-*Voyager* RCI ships) the Viking Crown Lounge, perched on the topmost deck some 150 feet above sea level and with amazing panoramic views. It's a great place for a pre-dinner drink and after-dinner dancing. Down on Decks 5 and 7, the two-story main show lounge is roomy and well planned, with lots of cocktail-table-and-chair clusters for two and a huge stage.

As part of their makeovers in recent years, both ships have been fitted with a Boleros Latin Lounge, featuring Latin music, a dueling-piano-players act, and drinks from Brazil, Cuba, and Central America. The ships' children's centers were also expanded and three teens-only hangouts added: the Living Room coffee bar, a disco called Fuel, and a private outdoor Sun Deck with a dance floor.

DINING OPTIONS   Each ship has a pair of one-story dining rooms, plus a large indoor/outdoor buffet restaurant on Deck 11 serving breakfast, lunch, and dinner. *Monarch*'s buffet also has an Asian option (for an extra charge), and *Majesty*'s has multiple self-service islands with regional dishes from Asia, Latin America, the Mediterranean, the U.S., and elsewhere, plus a cooked-to-order pasta station, a carving station, a deli, and a soup-and-salad bar. You can also nosh at a dedicated pizzeria or grab a specialty coffee or a Ben & Jerry's ice cream from the Latté-tudes coffee shop. *Majesty* also features a '50s-style Johnny Rockets diner serving burgers and shakes (with a $4.95 cover charge).

POOL, FITNESS, SPA & SPORTS FACILITIES   The deck layout and two good-size swimming pools seem plenty spacious when they're empty, but the number of passengers who typically sail these short itineraries almost guarantees that they'll fill up, becoming a wall-to-wall carpet of people. That said, there are many patches of more isolated deck space all over each ship, from the quiet slices on the tiered aft decks to two levels of far-forward deck space.

The Sports Deck, up high in the stern, has Ping-Pong tables and a basketball court. The half-moon-shaped gym on Deck 10 is fairly spacious, with a wall of windows facing aft. Treadmills, stationary bikes, step machines, and free weights line the perimeter of the room, facing the sea, and the inner part of the room serves as the aerobics space. A smallish spa is adjacent.

Both ships sport Royal Caribbean's signature rock-climbing walls.

7

The Ultraluxury Lines

If you've got taste, tend to avoid the mass market, and have lots and lots of money, then these are the cruise lines for you. Most people attracted to these types of cruises are wealthy, relatively or actually sophisticated, and social. They're well traveled if not necessarily adventurous, tend to stick to five-star experiences, and don't blink at paying top dollar to be pampered—which is exactly what they get here.

On these ships, elbowroom is abundant and service is very personal, with staff getting to know your likes and dislikes early on. The onboard atmosphere is much like a private club, with guests trading tales over drinks or over delicious French, Italian, Mediterranean, and Asian meals that often rival what's served in respected shore-side restaurants. It might not quite be up to the three-star Michelin level, but it's absolutely the best you'll find at sea, served in high style by gracious waiters who know their jobs. A full dinner can, of course, be served in your cabin, course-by-course if you like.

Entertainment and organized activities are both more dignified than on other ships and more limited. Guests tend to amuse themselves, enjoying cocktails and conversation in a piano bar, listening to singers or musicians, and attending lectures just for the fun of it. Itineraries tend to shun the big megaship ports in favor of yachting destinations like St. Barts, Bequia, and Jost Van Dyke.

As a rule, ships in the luxury market are smaller than those in the mainstream, which lets them visit smaller ports and aids the staff in providing truly personalized service. The smallest vessels (the two SeaDream yachts, plus Seabourn's *Pride, Legend,* and *Spirit*) carry only 100 to 200 passengers, while the largest would barely be midsize by mainstream standards, carrying only 700 to 1,000 passengers apiece. Several new ships have spiced up the luxury market in the past couple of years, with Silversea adding two (one an expedition vessel and the other a 540-passenger palace) and Seabourn adding three sisters carrying 450 passengers apiece. All the luxe lines in this chapter have also spent millions refurbishing their older ships, making sure they can compete with the demand for "new new new" in today's marketplace.

While the high-end lines have not been immune to the economic marketplace and have adjusted their individual pricing policies and programs to meet the times, they'll still cost lots more than your typical mainstream cruise. Expect to pay at least $2,000 per person for a week in the Caribbean, and easily twice that or more if you opt for a large suite or cruise during the busiest times of the year. Balancing the high fares is the fact that all the lines in this chapter include a lot of extras in their rates. For instance, all except Crystal provide **free unlimited wine, liquor, and beverages,** along with gratuities and a stocked minibar. Regent goes a step further and includes most **shore excursions** in its rates, too. Many of these lines include other nice little perks, from luscious chocolates on your pillow on formal nights (Silversea) to cotton logo PJ's (SeaDream) and high-end bathroom amenities from names such as Bulgari, Bronnley, Molton Brown, and Ferragamo.

Frommer's Ratings at a Glance: The Ultraluxury Lines

1 = poor   2 = fair   3 = good   4 = excellent   5 = outstanding

	Enjoyment Factor	Dining	Activities	Children's Program	Entertainment	Service	Worth the Money
Crystal	5	5	5	4	4	4	5
Regent Seven Seas	5	4	3	2	3	4	5
Seabourn	5	5	2	N/A*	2	5	4
SeaDream	5	4	3	N/A*	3	5	5
Silversea	5	5	3	N/A*	2	5	4

Note: Cruise lines have been graded on a curve that compares them only with the other lines in the ultraluxury category. See "How to Read the Ratings," in chapter 5, for a detailed explanation of the ratings methodology.

* An N/A rating for children's programs indicates that line has no such program.

These ships are not geared to children, although aboard Crystal, the kid-friendliest of the lot, you might see 100 or more during holidays or school vacation months. Babysitting can often be arranged privately with an off-duty crewmember.

DRESS CODES   Though these are still the lines on which you'll see the most tuxedos and long gowns at sea, all of the luxe operators have in recent years relaxed their dress codes, going along with the overall travel industry trend toward a more casual environment. Regent is a perfect example: In 2009, the line went to an "elegant casual" policy, with the only formal nights being on longer cruises. It's entirely possible now for a couple to travel on any of the luxe ships with nothing spiffier than a dark suit and elegant cocktail dress.

1 Crystal Cruises

2049 Century Park E., Ste. 1400, Los Angeles, CA 90067. © **888/799-4625** or 310/785-9300. Fax 310/785-0011. www.crystalcruises.com.

THE LINE IN A NUTSHELL   Stylish and upbeat, Crystal provides top-shelf service and cuisine on ships large enough to have lots of outdoor deck space, generous fitness facilities, tons of activities, multiple restaurants, and more than half a dozen bars and entertainment venues. **Sails to:** Caribbean, Panama Canal, Mexican Riviera, Hawaii, Canada/New England (plus Europe [Baltic and Mediterranean], Africa, Asia, Australia/New Zealand, South Pacific, South America, transatlantic, the Middle East, and a world cruise—in short, just about anywhere you can cruise).

THE EXPERIENCE   Crystal has the only truly upscale large ships in the industry. Carrying 922 to 1,070 passengers, they aren't huge, but they're big enough to offer much more than their high-end peers. You won't feel hemmed in and you likely won't be twiddling your thumbs from lack of stimulation. Service is excellent and the line's Asian cuisine is tops. Unlike Seabourn's small ships, which tend to be more calm and staid, Crystal's sociable California ethic and large passenger capacity tend to keep things mingled, chatty, and more active. No question, these vessels have a vitality and energy that the smaller Seabourn, Regent, SeaDream, and Silversea ships definitely do not.

Compared with the other ultraluxury lines, here's how Crystal rates:

	Poor	Fair	Good	Excellent	Outstanding
Enjoyment Factor					✓
Dining					✓
Activities					✓
Children's Program				✓	
Entertainment				✓	
Service				✓	
Worth the Money					✓

Pros

- **Four or five restaurants:** In addition to the formal dining room, there are three alternative restaurants (including two on each ship with cuisine by famed chef Nobu Matsuhisa), plus a poolside grill, an indoor cafe, and a casual restaurant that puts on great themed luncheon buffets.
- **Best Asian food at sea:** The ships' reservations-only Asian restaurants (all run by the famous Nobu Matsuhisa) serve up utterly delicious Japanese food, including sushi. The sushi bar is first-come, first-served, no reservations. At least once per cruise, an Asian-themed buffet lunch consists of an awesome spread.
- **Fitness choices:** There is a nice-size gym, along with paddle-tennis courts, shuffleboard, Ping-Pong, a jogging circuit, golf-driving nets, and a putting green. The line also features "Tour de Spin" indoor cycling classes and state-of-the-art kinesis cable resistance equipment. Also, the 360-degree Promenade Deck, complimentary yoga, Walk-on-Water program, and Nordic Walking Poles keep folks busy.
- **Enrichment programs:** No other line has as many, with four or five impressive lecturers as well as complimentary computer training classes on every cruise, plus dozens of themed sailings focused on food and wine, art, film, jazz, wellness, and other subjects. Complimentary Yamaha keyboard and Berlitz language classes help to keep the noggin stimulated.

Cons

- **Least all-inclusive of the luxe lines:** Only nonalcoholic drinks are included in the rates, not tips, booze, and so on.
- **Cabin size:** Accommodations (especially on *Symphony*) are smaller than those aboard Silversea, Seabourn, and Regent.

Crystal: Sparkling & Spacious

Established in 1990, Crystal Cruises has gained recognition for its unique and award-winning place in the high-stakes, super-upscale cruise market. Its ships are the largest true luxury vessels in the category, and while not quite as generous as some other lines in the stateroom department (rooms are smaller than those on Regent, Silversea, and Seabourn) and the freebies department (Crystal doesn't include complimentary champagne, liquor, and wine in the rates, though cruise fares tend to be less expensive than the other lines that do), they provide a truly refined cruise for discerning guests who appreciate really good service and top-notch cuisine. No doubt about it, Crystal is one of our favorite lines.

The line is the North American division of Japan's largest container shipping enterprise, Nippon Yusen Kaisha (NYK). Despite these origins, a guest aboard Crystal could conceivably spend an entire week at sea and not even be aware that the ship is Japanese-owned-and-funded. More than anything else, Crystal is international, with a strong emphasis on European service. The Japanese exposure is subtler, and you'll feel it pretty much only in the excellent Asian cuisine and tasty sake served in the alternative Japanese restaurants and at the Asian-themed buffets. A Japanese activities director is on board to attend to the handful of Japanese passengers you'll see on many cruises.

Passenger Profile

Like other high-end lines, Crystal draws a lot of repeaters. On most cruises, more than 50% hail from affluent regions of California, and many are Crystal fans who have sailed with the line numerous times. There's commonly a small contingent of guests (about 15% of the mix) from the United Kingdom, Australia, Japan, Hong Kong, Mexico, Europe, South America, and other places. Most are well-heeled couples ages 55 and over. A good number step up to Crystal from lines such as Princess and Holland America.

Many Crystal guests place great emphasis on the social scene before, during, and after mealtimes, and many enjoy dressing up (sometimes way up) for dinner. Although the scene is way less formal than in the line's early days, you'll see no shortage of diamonds and gold Rolexes, and it's obvious that women on board have devoted much care and attention to their wardrobes and accessories. The onboard jewelry and clothing boutiques also do a brisk business, and a guest forking over $50,000 for a diamond-encrusted watch isn't uncommon. On formal nights—two or three of which occur during every 10- or 12-day cruise—most men wear tuxes and many women wear floor-length gowns, although your classic black cocktail dress is just fine. As on all ships, dress codes are much more relaxed during the day.

Though not a kid-centric line compared to the mainstream lines, of the high-end ships, Crystal is the most accommodating for families with kids. Each ship has a dedicated playroom called Fantasia, a teen club, and supervised activities are held for kids ages 3 and up when demand warrants it. During holidays and the summer months of July and August, 100 or so kids on board is not that unusual. Junior activities directors are on board during these cruises to organize dedicated programming for children.

Dining

Service by the team of ultraprofessional, gracious, European waiters is excellent. In the main dining room—and to a somewhat lesser degree in the alternative restaurants—table settings are lavish and include heavy leaded crystal, Frette linens, and Villeroy & Boch as well as Wedgwood china. Even in the Lido restaurant, waiters are at hand to serve your salad from the buffet line, prepare your coffee, and then carry your tray to wherever you want to sit.

TRADITIONAL   Dinner is served in two seatings in the main dining room; at lunch and breakfast, there is open seating. Cuisine selections include dishes such as *coq au vin* (braised chicken in burgundy-wine sauce with glazed onions and mushrooms over a bed of linguine); Black Angus beef tenderloin with burgundy-wine gravy; oven-baked quail with porcini-mushroom-and-bread stuffing; and seared sea scallops served with a light lobster beurre blanc over a bed of risotto. Simple items are always available as well. At lunch and dinner, there's a **light, low-cholesterol selection** such as grilled fresh halibut served with steamed vegetables and herbed potatoes, as well as an entree salad—for example, a mixed salad with grilled herb-marinated chicken breast, lamb, or filet mignon. **Vegetarian selections,** such as spinach and ricotta cannelloni or a brochette of Mediterranean vegetables, are also featured, as are **kosher foods** and **low-carb choices. Sugar-free, gluten-free,** and **low-fat options** are now part of all menus, too, even at buffets. Virtually any special diet can be accommodated.

In a kind of homage to the California wine industry, Crystal has one of the most sophisticated inventories of **California wines** on the high seas, as well as a reserve list of more than two dozen rare wines and an extensive selection of French wines. In 2004, the line also created its own proprietary label called **C Wines:** six chardonnays, cabernet sauvignons (smooth and yummy to the palette), and merlots made in limited production with grapes from the Napa and Sonoma valleys, Arroyo Seco, and the Santa Lucia Highlands. All are available on board by the glass or the bottle.

SPECIALTY   The line's Asian dining spots are the best at sea. Master chef **Nobuyuki "Nobu" Matsuhisa,** known for his restaurants in New York, Miami, L.A., London, Paris, and other cities, partnered with Crystal to create menus for both ships' Pan-Asian restaurant **Silk Road** and the **Sushi Bar.** Dishes feature Nobu's eclectic blend of Japanese cuisine with Peruvian and European influences. In the Sushi Bar, sample the salmon tartare with sevruga caviar or the yellowtail sashimi with jalapeño; in Silk Road, choices include lobster with truffle *yuzu* sauce and chicken with teriyaki balsamic. While Nobu himself makes occasional appearances, chef Toshiaki Tamba, personally trained by Nobu, oversees the restaurants. The Sushi Bar is a great spot for appetizers before a full meal elsewhere on the ship.

Aboard both ships, famed restaurateur Piero Selvaggio showcases the cuisine of his award-winning Santa Monica and Las Vegas Valentino restaurants at the Italian **Valentino at Prego.** The best dishes we sampled on a recent *Symphony* cruise were the king crabmeat salad with fresh pear and aged balsamic, and the linguine with lobster tail, zucchini, and spicy tomato sauce. The recent refurbishment aboard *Symphony* did away with the Venetian "barber" poles in favor of a calmer cream and burgundy decor. The only sour note: On a recent cruise we could hear someone jogging on the track on the deck above during dinner.

Reservations are required for each of the specialty restaurants, which are complimentary aside from a suggested $7 gratuity. It's an amazing price for such great dining experiences.

CASUAL   Excellent **themed luncheon buffets**—Asian, Mediterranean, Western barbecue, or South American/Cuban, for instance—are generously spread out at lunchtime by the pool, and an extraspecial **gala buffet** is put on once per cruise in the lobby/atrium. No expense or effort is spared to produce elaborate food fests, with heaps of jumbo shrimp, sushi, Greek salads, shish kabobs, beef satay, stir-fry dishes, gourmet cheeses, and more.

While you can have breakfast in the **Lido Café,** the **Bistro Café** serves a late continental breakfast from 9:30 to 11:30am and is open between 11:30am and 6pm for complimentary grazing at the buffet-style spread of cheeses, cold cuts, fruit, cookies, and pastries; on a recent cruise, coauthor Heidi had an absolutely delicious Portuguese custard here and she still talks about it. Nonalcoholic specialty drinks, such as hazelnut latte and fruit shakes, are complimentary here. The Bistro tends to be a real social hub and people-watching spot.

For something casual poolside, the **Trident Grill** serves lunches daily between 11:30am and 6pm for those who'd like something simple and easy (beef, chicken, and salmon burgers; wraps and tuna melts; pizza, hot dogs, and fries; fruit; and a special of the day). You can place your order at the counter and either have a seat at the adjacent tables or head back to your deck chair and let a waiter bring your lunch. You don't even have to change out of your bathing suit. The grill also operates several evenings per cruise between 6 and 9pm, providing an open-air ambience with table service, with dishes such as grilled shrimp, Cobb salad, and gourmet pizza.

SNACKS & EXTRAS For **afternoon tea**—with live music, of course—it's the ultrachic **Palm Court,** forward on one of the uppermost decks. A sprawling space with floor-to-ceiling windows and pale-blue-and-white furniture in leather and rattan, the area has a light, ethereal ambience. Pre-dinner and midnight hot and cold canapés in the lounges include delicious foie gras, caviar, and marinated salmon.

There is, of course, **24-hour room service,** as well as free unlimited nonalcoholic drinks everywhere aboard, from cappuccino to soda and bottled water.

Activities

Crystal has an interesting selection of activities, most of which are part of the ships' **Creative Learning Institute.** The extensive program features an array of expert speakers, plus alliances with well-known organizations, schools, and brands—Yamaha for music classes, Berlitz for language classes, the Cleveland Clinic for health topics, and the Tai Chi Cultural Center, to name a few—to provide an even greater authority to the classes. You can count on several **enrichment lectures** throughout each cruise, such as a historian presenting a slide show and speaking about the Panama Canal and how it was built, a former ambassador or two speaking about regional politics, or a scientist talking about conservation. Most speakers are not celebrities, but well-known personalities do occasionally show up. Guests have included political commentators James Carville and Mary Matalin, songwriter Neil Sedaka, business consultant Ken Blanchard, former press secretary Marlin Fitzwater, medical expert Dr. Art Ulene, biographer Chris Ogden, publisher Steve Forbes, chef Andre Soltner, TV personality Monty Hall, journalist Jane Bryant Quinn, and singer Clint Holmes.

In addition to each cruise's guest lecturers, some of Crystal's sailings have Experiences of Discovery, themed programs with activities built around them. More than a dozen annual Wine & Food Festival cruises feature a respected wine expert who conducts at least two complimentary tastings, plus guest chefs conducting cooking demonstrations for guests and then presenting the results of those lessons at dinner. There are also music-themed cruises from time to time, featuring big bands, ballroom dancing, jazz singers, and film and theater presentations. Other cruises have experts conducting seminars on finance issues, language, and art appreciation, the latter with speakers from the famous auction house Sotheby's. Mind, Body & Spirit cruises focus on health and wellness, while golf cruises allow guests to play at some of the world's most exclusive courses.

Guest teachers give swing, tango, and jive dance lessons on some cruises. Group lessons are complimentary, and private lessons can sometimes be arranged with the instructors for about $50 per hour per couple. Other activities include bridge and paddle-tennis competitions; game-show-style contests; trivia games; midafternoon dance music with the resident dance trio or quartet; interesting arts and crafts such as glass etching; and even guest fashion shows. Commonly, a **golf expert** sails on board, too, conducting complimentary group golf lessons by the driving nets several times per cruise (again, private lessons can be arranged; prices start at $50 per hr.). A variety of free aerobics classes are held in the fitness center, along with Pilates and yoga (private personal trainers are available for a fee).

The line's **Computer University @ Sea** gives some free courses on all cruises, with topics such as basic computing, understanding the Internet, website design, and creating spreadsheets using Excel. Private lessons are also available for $50 an hour. Internet centers, which have the best support staffs of any cruise liner we've been on, have about 30 workstations apiece, featuring Dell PCs; however, you must buy Internet time in 2-hour $50 installments—not convenient if you just need a few minutes to send e-mail toward the end of the cruise. There are now Wi-Fi hotspots for those who want to work on their own laptops, along with onboard cellphone service via a satellite link, at prices in the same range as your provider's regular roaming charges.

With all this activity, on past sailings we've always run out of days before actually getting to do everything.

Children's Program

Crystal is a sophisticated cruise line that focuses its attention on adults but, more than any other line in the luxury end of the market, it also does its part to cater to the little people. Each ship has a bright **children's playroom,** primarily used during holiday and summer cruises (mostly in Europe or Alaska), when some 100 kids may be aboard. Both ships also have another room with PlayStations, computers, and arcade machines for older kids and teens, with counselors on hand to supervise activities such as scavenger hunts, arts and crafts, karaoke, and games that take place during several hours in both the morning and afternoon, for three age groups between 3 and 17. There are kiddie books and videos in the library for guests to take back to their staterooms, and a children's menu in the main dining room, as well as kid favorites at the poolside Trident Grill.

For children as young as 6 months, **in-cabin babysitting** can be arranged privately through the concierge at an hourly rate of $10 for one child, $15 for two kids, and $20 for three kids. Cribs, highchairs, and booster seats are available. As for food, if you notify the line ahead of time, it'll special order jars of baby food at no charge, or the chef will puree organic food for your baby. Note that children ages 11 and under pay 50% of the lowest adult fare when accompanied by two full-fare guests.

The minimum age for sailing is 6 months.

Entertainment

Onboard entertainment is well produced. Shows in the horseshoe-shaped, rather plain **Galaxy Lounge** include everything from classical concertos by accomplished pianists to comedy to tired Broadway-style medleys, ventriloquists, and magic acts. The bright spot on a recent cruise was definitely the a cappella group that roamed the ship. A young, talented, and handsome foursome performed both impromptu and scheduled concerts in the atrium and other entertainment lounges, and also ran a few of the karaoke nights. A cappella singers are typically featured on longer cruises of 10-plus nights. From time to time, there's a celebrity entertainer aboard, such as the Tommy Dorsey Orchestra, Maureen McGovern, Tommy Tune, or Marvin Hamlisch.

After dinner each night, a second large, attractive lounge is the venue for **ballroom-style dancing** to a live band, with a clutch of gentleman hosts aboard each sailing to provide dance (and dinner) partners for single ladies. Both ships have spacious **casinos** and rooms for dancing, in either *Serenity*'s dedicated nightclub or *Symphony*'s Starlight lounge. A pianist in the dark, paneled, and romantic **Avenue Saloon**—our favorite room on board—plays standards, show tunes, and pop hits before and after dinner. On both ships, you can also enjoy cigars (from Monte Cristo to Davidoff) in the **Connoisseur Club**, recent-release movies several times a day in the theater (where lectures and religious services are also held), and a varied and full menu of movies on the in-cabin TVs.

Service

The hallmark of a high-end cruise such as Crystal is its service, so the line's staff is better trained and more attentive than those aboard most other cruise lines. Dining room and restaurant staffs hail from Italy, Portugal, and other European countries, and have trained in the grand restaurants of Europe and North America; the stewardess who tidies your stateroom is likely to be from Scandinavia, Hungary, or elsewhere in the E.U. Everyone, from the dining/bar staff to those at the information and concierge desks in the lobby, is endlessly good natured and very helpful. Guests in Penthouse Suites are treated to the services of male butlers. As far as tipping goes, most passengers charge gratuities to their onboard accounts, though you can pay in cash if you wish.

All guests get complimentary unlimited nonalcoholic drinks everywhere aboard, from cappuccino to soda and bottled water.

In addition to laundry and dry-cleaning services, complimentary **self-serve laundry rooms** are available.

Crystal Serenity

The Verdict

Crystal Serenity is Crystal's best, largest, and newest ship, offering an ultra-elegant cruise with a huge array of onboard choices, from dining to activities and public spaces.

Crystal Serenity *(photo: Crystal Cruises)*

Specifications   Typical Per Diems: $460–$780

Size (in tons)	68,870	Crew	655
Passengers (double occ.)	1,070	Passenger/Crew Ratio	1.6 to 1
Passenger/Space Ratio	64.1	Year Launched	2003
Total Cabins/Veranda Cabins	535/465	Last Major Upgrade	2008

Frommer's Ratings (Scale of 1–5)   ★★★★½

Cabin Comfort & Amenities	4.5	Dining Options	5
Appearance & Upkeep	5	Gym, Spa & Sports Facilities	5
Public Comfort/Space	4.5	Children's Facilities	3.5
Decor	4.5	Enjoyment Factor	5

Sailing Regions, Seasons & Home Ports

Serenity	**Caribbean,** from Miami (winter).

The largest truly ultraluxe vessel afloat, *Serenity* is 38% bigger than the older *Symphony*, but carries only 15% more guests. She's one of the most spacious ships out there, from her beautifully designed public rooms to the expansive Pool Deck. There's simply no crowding at any time. With many refurbishments and improvements made in late 2008, this ship continues to shine.

CABINS   Standard staterooms on this ship are somewhat bigger than those on *Symphony*, and the bathrooms and balconies are larger. The majority of standard cabins (categories A and B) are 226 square feet, not including balconies; even with this increase, cabin size is not Crystal's strong suit when compared to the line's luxury peers. There are 100 suites in three different categories, with the largest running 1,345 square feet. The 2008 refurbishment added eight more Penthouses by eliminating 16 Deluxe Staterooms.

Most of the standard cabins, called Deluxe Staterooms, have a veranda, while 70 rooms have a large picture window. All feature a seating area, complimentary soft drinks and water, TV and DVD, a small fridge, a computer dataport, Egyptian cotton sheets and feather bed toppers, and a pillow menu. Choose from "regular" king- and standard-size pillows or four specialty options, which include round, foam-filled neck pillows for neck or lumbar support. Besides all of this, Penthouse Staterooms toss in butler service and free beer, while the Penthouse Suites also throw in complimentary liquor and wine setup at embarkation, a flatscreen TV, a separate bedroom area with a vanity, a Jacuzzi tub, a bidet, and a walk-in closet. If you're going straight to the top, the ship's Crystal Penthouses are incredibly spacious abodes, with a separate living room, a dining area, a CD player, three TVs (one in the bathroom, if that floats your boat!), a cordless phone, a library, a pantry, and, believe it or not, a small gym.

Decor-wise, wood accents and furniture in the staterooms are on the medium to dark side, creating an elegant atmosphere offsetting the more colorful curtains, wall coverings, upholstery, and bedcovers. The feel is soothing. As aboard *Symphony*, the bathrooms are nicely laid out, but still on the small side for a ship of such high quality. You'll find plenty of drawer and closet space for a cruise of up to about 2 weeks.

Only a handful of cabins have a third berth available, and none offers four berths. Eight rooms are designated as wheelchair accessible.

PUBLIC AREAS   Public rooms on the *Serenity* are all so appealing that it's difficult to pick a favorite. The ship has such a quiet, elegant atmosphere throughout that you won't even find glitz in the casino. Color schemes are muted and calming, with lots of blues, greens, reds, golds, and grays. As aboard *Symphony*, one of the most popular lounges is dark and cozy **Avenue Saloon,** with its wonderful round bar and plenty of table seating. The two show lounges, **Galaxy Lounge** and **Stardust Club,** have great sightlines and comfy seating, both theater- and table-style. The lobby bar has been redesigned, making the whole area more enjoyable for daytime or evening drinks.

The ship has a good **library** that's well stocked with books, DVDs, and CDs that can be checked out only when the librarian is on duty. Two large rooms are dedicated to the line's learning programs: one for computer instruction and the other for classes offered in partnership with well-known institutions, such as piano instruction by Yamaha, language immersion by Berlitz, art classes conducted by the Parsons School of Design, and wellness programs run by the Cleveland Clinic and the Tai Chi Cultural Center. The casino features a gorgeous gold, purple, and magenta color palette.

DINING OPTIONS   Fine dining has been a trademark of Crystal's since the line began sailing in 1990, and the *Serenity* carries on the tradition with her two impressive alternative, open-seating specialty restaurants, both of which require reservations (and a suggested $7 cover charge). In **Prego,** the surroundings make you feel as if you're really in a fine Italian restaurant ashore, with meat, pasta, and fish dishes served a la carte or through a tasting menu with items selected by Piero Selvaggio, proprietor of the Valentino restaurants in Santa Monica and Las Vegas (the table-side prep of the carpaccio is worth the price of entry). On the Asian side of things, famed chef Nobu Matsuhisa oversees the menus in **Silk Road,** an ultrastylish space designed in a sea of ethereal shades of mint green and white, with seating at tables or at the sushi bar (go early for a sushi snack, have a drink, and then go to late-seating dinner). Just forward of Silk Road, the **Vintage Room** is an intimate, boardroom-style wine cellar that hosts special wine-and champagne-themed dinners and other events. In the ship's formal restaurant, the **Crystal Dining Room,** there are two seatings at assigned tables each evening. The lovely decor is a rich blend of dark woods with blue-and-mauve chairs. The latest dining spot on board is **Tastes,** a casual eatery serving breakfast, lunch, and dinner under a retractable roof near the Neptune Pool. It has a completely separate menu from the other dining areas and is a great dinner alternative when you don't feel like dressing up.

Other dining outlets include the Bistro Café, open for a variety of snacks and beverages all day long; the poolside Trident Grill; and the Lido Café, which serves buffet-style breakfast and lunch, with some made-to-order specialties such as omelets and pastas.

The 24-hour room-service menu is quite extensive. During dining hours, guests can also order from the Crystal Dining Room menu for in-cabin delivery.

POOL, FITNESS, SPA & SPORTS FACILITIES   There are two reasonably sized pools, one of which features a sliding glass roof. Indoors, the stunning **Crystal Spa** was designed according to feng shui principles, putting you right into relaxation mode. The complex includes a quiet room with very comfortable seating and great aft-facing views for those relaxing moments before or after a spa treatment. The changing rooms are stocked with lotions, shampoos, hair dryers, clocks, and bottles of water, while the steam rooms have large picture windows for great views while you roast. A wide range of treatments includes a handful geared to men, such as a pro-collagen shave, frangipani hair conditioning, and aroma stone therapy massage. There's also a spacious salon and a gym with a separate weight room, aerobics studio, two full-size paddle-tennis courts, table tennis, golf driving nets, and a putting green.

Crystal Symphony

The Verdict

A gracious, floating pleasure palace, small enough to feel intimate and personal, yet large enough for a whole range of entertainment, dining, and fitness diversions.

Crystal Symphony *(photo: Crystal Cruises)*

Specifications

Typical Per Diems: $375–$740

Size (in tons)	51,044	Crew	545
Passengers (double occ.)	922	Passenger/Crew Ratio	1.7 to 1
Passenger/Space Ratio	55.4	Year Launched	1995
Total Cabins/Veranda Cabins	461/279	Last Major Upgrade	2009

Frommer's Ratings (Scale of 1–5)   ★★★★ ½

Cabin Comfort & Amenities	4	Dining Options	5
Appearance & Upkeep	5	Gym, Spa & Sports Facilities	5
Public Comfort/Space	4.5	Children's Facilities	3.5
Decor	4	Enjoyment Factor	5

Sailing Regions, Seasons & Home Ports

Symphony	**Panama Canal,** from Miami, Caldera (Costa Rica) & Los Angeles (winter, fall), from San Francisco (fall). **Mexican Riviera,** from Los Angeles (winter, spring). **Alaska,** from San Francisco (summer). **New England/Canada,** from New York & Montreal (fall).

The *Symphony* is one of the most spacious vessels we've ever been on, though her staterooms are not impressively large (they're pleasant, but smallish); but her public spaces are so open, generous, and sweeping compared to the smaller Regent, Seabourn, SeaDream, and Silversea ships, Crystal's luxury peers. You'll never feel hemmed in, even when the ship is sailing full. In late 2009, she had a major overhaul, to the tune of $25 million, resulting in a redone Lido Deck, elimination of one pool in favor of more deck space, and the addition of a huge whirlpool as well as new and gorgeous deck furniture throughout both areas. The Lido Café was redone to be more efficient in buffet food service. Many changes were made to the three penthouse categories, including new color palettes across the board and new electronics and bathroom fixtures at the top level.

CABINS   Though the majority of *Symphony*'s cabins are smaller than those aboard competing luxe lines Silversea, Regent, and Seabourn, they're still quite comfortable and were completely redone in late 2006. Cabins are decorated in shades of mauve, burgundy, rose, and light wood tones and accented with Murano glass bedside lamps, Rubelli fabrics, and leather headboards. Starting at 202 square feet (plus 48-sq.-ft. verandas on many), their one fault is their size. They're about 30% smaller than the standard staterooms on the Silversea, Regent, and Seabourn ships; booking a room with a balcony is a good idea for the additional space and light it provides. Otherwise, rooms are well designed. Standard amenities include a 20-inch LCD flatscreen TV, VCR, LED reading lights, and a stocked minibar; bottled water and sodas are free, but booze isn't. The single closet with a sliding door isn't overly large and it may be a challenge getting all of your stuff in there if you're on a long cruise of 2 weeks or more. The small bathrooms were redesigned and now feel a bit more spacious; each has both a shower and bathtub (a short little one in the lower category cabins) and a pair of trendy but splash-making oval glass sinks over granite countertops. Egyptian cotton sheets, feather bed toppers, and a choice of pillows make sleeping a dream.

Deck 10 holds the ship's penthouses, the best of which measure more than 750 square feet, with nearly 200-square-foot balconies, full-fledged oceanview Jacuzzis in their living rooms, dark-wood furniture, and sofas upholstered in silk and satin, plus Oriental rugs and entertainment centers. A butler is part of the package. Decor changes were made to all three categories in late 2009, including two flatscreen TVs, plusher bedding, two lighter fabric color palettes and, in the completely redesigned Crystal Penthouses, expanded living space, new audio/visual electronics, floor-to-ceiling dining area windows, and spiffier bathroom fixtures, including Philippe Starck bathtubs.

Cabins without verandas have large rectangular windows. The category E cabins located midships on Decks 7 and 8 have views obstructed by lifeboats. There are no inside cabins.

Five cabins are wheelchair accessible.

PUBLIC AREAS   The spacious atrium and main lobby area is a central meeting point and elegant shops wrap around the second tier. The adjacent **Bistro** coffee and snack cafe is open to the atrium and is the place to see and be seen; it's the ship's social heart. Overall, the *Symphony*'s decor incorporates everything from standard cruise ship marble, glass, chrome, and mirrors, to old-world dark-wood paneling and funky touches like aluminum.

Aside from the several bar/entertainment lounges, a roaming staff wanders the public areas throughout the day and much of the night, offering to bring drinks to wherever you happen to be sitting. The dark **Avenue Saloon,** where polished mahogany, well-maintained leather upholstery, and a live pianist draw passengers in, is one of the prime before- and after-dinner cocktail spots and our personal favorite, by far. There are also two large entertainment lounges, including the **Starlite Club** that's used for lectures by day and dancing by night (though if you're there for a lecture, avoid seating in the back of the room; the noise from passersby looking at mug shots in the adjacent photo gallery is a distraction). The hub has a dramatic round bar and walls of sparkling Swarovski crystals. You'll find a large theater for movies and slide lectures, and a hushed library outfitted with comfortably upholstered chairs and a worthy collection of books, periodicals, and videos. The revamped **Casino** now features a dramatic black-and-silver color scheme, while next door a nightclub, called **Luxe,** attracts attention with its polished aluminum Philippe Starck bar stools and glass Bisazza mosaics. The cozy little spot hosts karaoke a couple of times per cruise.

If learning is more your speed, there's a 25-seat classroom and an adjacent Internet center, both with brand-new Dell computers. The **Connoisseur's Club** cigar lounge (Monte Cristo, anyone?) is attractive with wood tones and dark leather furniture.

For young kids, *Symphony* has a cute playroom, Fantasia, with a tiered movie-viewing nook; for teens, there's a teen center/video arcade.

DINING OPTIONS   Designed with curved walls and low, vaulted ceilings, the ship's main dining room is elegant and spacious, with dark wall paneling. Tables are not too close together, and there are well over 20 tables for two, mostly along the side or near the oceanview windows (try and sit along the outer portions, since the raised center section can get a bit noisy).

The ship's two themed, reservations-only alternative restaurants—the Italian **Prego** and Nobu's **Silk Road** and the **Sushi Bar**—are right up there with the best at sea. The **Vintage Room,** an intimate boardroom-style wine cellar, was added to host special wine- and champagne-themed dinners and other events.

A casual indoor/outdoor buffet restaurant is open for breakfast and lunch, and the poolside **Trident Grill** serves ultracasual lunches, as well as dinners, several evenings per cruise. **Bistro Café** is going for an earthy European ambience and it's open from 9:30am to 6pm for continental breakfast, snacks, specialty coffees, and more.

POOL, FITNESS, SPA & SPORTS FACILITIES   *Symphony* provides a lot of outdoor activities and spacious areas in which to do them. During the extensive redesign and refurbishment in late 2009, the smaller Neptune Pool was replaced with an expansive, comfortable, conversational seating area, also allowing for more alfresco dining. This area and the large Seahorse pool area now feature crisp white deck furniture accented with gorgeous citrus-hued cushions and throw pillows. The oversize sofas and loungers along the sides of the ship are particularly attractive and comfy. There's also now a huge whirlpool near Seahorse pool. Seahorse pool is refreshingly oversize, stretching almost 40 feet across. The gym and aerobics area are positioned for a view over the sea, with plenty of space for the line's complimentary yoga, Pilates, and aerobics classes (and personal training sessions, too, for a fee). The Steiner-managed spa and salon has a quiet oceanview waiting room to create an atmosphere of peace and relaxation. On deck, there's a pair of golf driving nets, a putting green, a large paddle-tennis court, Ping-Pong tables, and a broad, uninterrupted teak Promenade Deck for walkers and joggers. Our favorite hideaway is a chaise longue along the lovely tiered aft decks facing the ship's wake.

2 Regent Seven Seas Cruises

1000 Corporate Dr., Ste. 500, Fort Lauderdale, FL 33334. ℂ **800/285-1835**. Fax 402/501-5599. www.rssc.com.

THE LINE IN A NUTSHELL   Operating a fleet of stylish and extremely comfortable midsize vessels, Regent Seven Seas Cruises (RSSC) provides a casually elegant, luxurious cruise experience. Its service is as good as it gets, and its cuisine is near the top. And, having spent over $100 million on refurbishment in the last few years, the line has kept its three ships up-to-date, comparing favorably to the younger ships in the category. **Sails to:** Caribbean, Alaska, Bermuda, Panama Canal (plus Europe, Asia, Australia/New Zealand, Africa/India, world cruises, Antarctica, South America).

THE EXPERIENCE   If you insist on luxury but like to keep it quietly elegant, Regent might be your cruise line of choice. Its ships are spacious and understated, with a relaxed onboard vibe that tends to be less stuffy than Seabourn and Silversea. As aboard all the luxury ships (with the exception of Crystal's vessels), entertainment and activities are a relatively low priority, with guests left to enjoy their vacations at their own pace. In keeping with the industry trend toward more casual attire, Regent's code is now "elegant casual," with formal nights now held only on longer cruises. Service is friendly and absolutely spot on, and cuisine is some of the best at sea, in both the formal dining rooms and, especially, the alternative restaurants. Even if what tickles your fancy isn't on the menu, the chef will prepare it for you. Passengers tend to be unpretentiously wealthy. When we've sailed, our social circle included an economist with an international banking institution, an environmental lobbyist, and a man who starts banks—all of them aboard to enjoy a quiet, relaxed vacation.

Pros

- **Great dining:** Cuisine is superb, and the main dining room and alternative restaurants operate on an open-seating basis, the latter by reservation. The steak restaurant, now on all three ships, is the best at sea.
- **Special offers:** In 2009, Regent revamped its pricing policies, offering great airfare deals, free and unlimited shore excursions, plus alcoholic and nonalcoholic beverages and tips included in the fare.
- **Lots of private verandas:** *Seven Seas Navigator* has them in 90% of her staterooms and *Mariner* and *Voyager* have them in every single one.
- **Amazing bathrooms on *Navigator* and *Voyager*:** Bigger and better than those on Seabourn and Crystal, these cabin bathrooms all have separate shower stalls and bathtubs long enough for normal-size humans.

- **You know where they're going to be:** Whereas many luxury ships hopscotch from cruise region to cruise region, never staying long in any one place, the three Regent ships sometimes spend full seasons in the Caribbean and Alaska, as well as the Mediterranean.

Cons

- **Not-quite-private balconies:** Walls separating the balconies aboard *Voyager* and *Navigator* don't extend to the edge of the ship's rail, making it possible to lean out and see what your neighbors are up to.
- *Navigator* **vibration:** Even with the technical improvements made in late 2009, the ship can vibrate a lot, even in relatively calm waters. Try for midships rooms if possible.

Regent: Low-Key, All-Inclusive Elegance

There's been a lot of change at this line over the past few years. First, it went through a name change—from **Radisson Seven Seas Cruises** to Regent—to satisfy the desire of its owners to link the line's operations to those of its Regent Hotels group. Then, less than 2 years later, those same owners sold the line lock, stock, and barrel to the Apollo Management investment firm, which created and is now the majority share-holder in Prestige Cruise Holdings, operating Regent and Oceania Cruises and hold-ing a 50% stake in NCL. As a result, there have been some changes at the line. Some improvements to amenities, decor, and technology were implemented in the wake of the Regent rebranding, and in 2007 the line poured another $20 million into further refurbishments, adding Wi-Fi computer access, onboard cellphone service, improved bed linens, new espresso bars in the Internet centers, and other upgrades. A further $105 million was committed for changes to *Seven Seas Voyager* in 2008, *Seven Seas Mariner* in 2009, and *Seven Seas Navigator* in the beginning of 2010. For example, various public rooms have been redesigned with new, highly upgraded furnishings and materials; Regent has replaced its Indochine alternative restaurants with upscale steak-houses; the Pool Grill has been redone; and *Voyager* now has an extended coffee and snack area similar to the very popular Coffee Connection on *Mariner.* The changes on *Navigator* bring this older ship up to speed with the rest of the fleet.

In late 2009, the line revamped its pricing policy in a way that's made it the most all-inclusive of the luxury lines. Fares now include round-trip air from 23 U.S. and Canadian cities, free unlimited shore excursions (not all excursions in all ports are free, but most are), staff gratuities, alcoholic and nonalcoholic beverages, stocked minibars in staterooms, and more.

Compared with the other ultraluxury lines, here's how Regent rates:

	Poor	Fair	Good	Excellent	Outstanding
Enjoyment Factor					✓
Dining				✓	
Activities			✓		
Children's Program		✓			
Entertainment			✓		
Service				✓	
Worth the Money					✓

Passenger Profile

RSSC appeals primarily to well-traveled and well-heeled passengers in their 50s and 60s (Regent says the average age is 58), but younger guests, honeymooners, and older cruisers pepper the mix as well. Many passengers are frequent cruisers who have also sailed on Silversea, Seabourn, and Crystal, or are taking a step up from Holland America, Celebrity, Princess, or one of the other mainstream lines. Though they have sophisticated tastes and can do without a lot of inane shipboard activities, they also appreciate the line's less formal ambience. On our recent cruises, casual nights in the main dining room saw some guests dressed in polo shirts and jackets and others in nice T-shirts with khakis and sneakers. You're also likely to find some women with full makeup, coifed hairdos, coordinated jewelry, shoes, and handbags, and many men sporting businessman bling. A kids' program on summer sailings and some holiday sailings attracts some **families,** but the limited number of third berths in suites tends to keep those numbers down as does the lack of kids' facilities.

Dining

Superb menus are designed for a sophisticated palate, and the overall cuisine is some of the best in the cruise industry. Each ship has an extensive wine list, with vintages from France, California, Italy, Germany, South Africa, and Chile.

TRADITIONAL   In the main restaurants, elaborate and elegant meals are served in open seatings by a mostly European staff. Appetizers may include baked escargots in garlic-herb butter, beef carpaccio, and an eggplant-tomato-mozzarella roll; and main entrees include such enticing dishes as grilled venison medallions and mushroom fricassee, Chinese tangerine shrimp, and grilled grouper filet with pink grapefruit. Each dinner menu also has a **vegetarian option** such as a forest mushroom quiche, and a **light and healthy choice** such as broiled whole Dover sole. When you've had enough of fancy, several standards called **simplicity dishes** are also available daily: pasta with tomato sauce, filet mignon, grilled chicken breast, or salmon filet. **Special diets** (kosher, halal, low-fat, low-salt, and so on) can be accommodated at all meals, but for very stringent regimes, such as glatt kosher, you must make arrangements before your cruise. Breakfasts include made-to-order omelets, as well as a typical selection of hot and cold breakfast foods. Lunch entrees include soups, salads, sandwiches, and entrees like Indian lamb patties with mint-coriander-lentil chutney, pan-seared chicken breast, and a fisherman's platter of fried jumbo prawns, scallops, and filets. For those looking for simpler and/or healthier recipes, Compass Rose and La Veranda now serve Canyon Ranch Spa Cuisine.

SPECIALTY   *Mariner* and *Voyager* each have three alternate choices. The 110-seat **Signatures** restaurants are directed by chefs from Paris's famed **Le Cordon Bleu** cooking school, serving very elegant French cuisine. The new **Prime 7 steakhouse** serves prime aged steaks and chops along with fresh seafood and poultry entrees. Appetizers include avant-garde choices such as a trio of steak tartare and foie gras sliders with rhubarb chutney, as well as traditional items such as oysters Rockefeller and a jumbo lump crab cake. **La Veranda** serves Mediterranean and North African dishes in the evening, providing a casually elegant option.

Seven Seas Navigator has two alternative choices: La Veranda, similar to the two larger ships, as well as Prime 7. Both have been added during the 2010 refurbishment. All alternative venues are intimate spaces with tables for two or four. Make reservations early in the cruise to guarantee yourself a table. Booked passengers can make specialty-dining reservations online up to 75 days before their cruise (naturally, once final payment has been made).

CASUAL   All three vessels have casual buffet restaurants. And now, all three ships have extensive poolside hot and cold buffets, salad bars and grills, along with ice-cream and milkshake bars.

SNACKS & EXTRAS   Hot hors d'oeuvres are served in the lounges before dinner, and if you take advantage of the 24-hour room service, a steward will come in and lay out a white tablecloth along with silverware and china, whether you've ordered a full-course dinner, a personal pizza, or just a plate of fruit. Specialty coffees, soft drinks, mineral water, and most alcoholic beverages are complimentary at all times, and **high tea** is served each afternoon.

Activities

Days not spent exploring the ports are basically unstructured, with a variety of activities thrown in for those who aren't pursuing their own relaxation. During the day, there may be ballroom dance classes, wine tastings, art auctions, bingo, computer classes, bridge (with instructors sailing on all cruises), and **lectures** by visiting writers, anthropologists, naturalists, and retired diplomats, often speaking on a topic relevant to the region you're sailing—for example, Colonial America on New England/Canada cruises, Incan culture on South America cruises, and so on.

Themed **Spotlight Cruises** may cover food and wine, photography, chocolate, music, the arts, and so on. On **Le Cordon Bleu cooking cruises,** for instance, chefs trained in the Le Cordon Bleu cooking method hold three onboard workshops, a special chef's dinner, and a market visit in port to see how the chef chooses the best local ingredients. Participation costs $499 per person. On **Art Experience** cruises, Regent teams with noted museums to offer art-related shore excursions and onboard lectures.

Active passengers can work out in the ships' gyms, run on the tracks, or whack some balls into a golf net, then take a massage at the ships' spas, run by the Canyon Ranch SpaClub. Besides the usual wide range of services, it also offers company specialties such as the Euphoric Coffee Scrub, the Ohana Circulation Polish, and the Organic Mermaid's Purse Wrap.

Children's Program

These ships are geared to mature adults, but summer sailings and select holiday cruises have a **Club Mariner** kids' program in which counselors supervise activities such as games, crafts projects, and movies for three age groups (ages 5–9, 10–13, and 14–17). For the younger kids, counselors are on hand for games, crafts projects, movies, and "food fun," while teens help the counselor select the activities they prefer. On non–summer/holiday cruises, an ad-hoc kids' program is put together if enough kids are aboard to warrant it. The minimum age for children to sail aboard is 1 year, and the line reserves the right to limit the number of children age 3 and under on any cruise. **Babysitting** may be available for $25 an hour if a female crewmember is willing to perform the service outside of her regular-duty hours.

Entertainment

As on most luxe ships, entertainment is not the highest of priorities, and many guests are content to spend their evenings exploring the cocktail circuit, visiting the casino, singing along in the piano bar, or dancing to the ships' elegant musical groups. In the production show area, Regent used to be known for lackluster performances, but lately quality has improved, demonstrating what some imagination and talent will do—along with a larger budget. Recent shows include *Thoroughly Modern Broadway,* a mix of musical theater numbers from the 1960s through 1980s; the Beatles tribute *Here, There and Everywhere;* the outstanding *Beyond Imagination,* which mixes opera and classical song with sea songs, folk tunes, and pseudo-classical modern hits; the wonderful *On a Classical Note,* with music by Mozart, Verdi, Rossini, Puccini, Gilbert and Sullivan, and Bizet; and *Oh What a Night,* with hits by the Four Seasons, Billy Joel, Simon and Garfunkel, Ray Charles, Neil Diamond, and others. Prediction: Regent will soon be known for excellent evening entertainment along with Crystal Cruises.

Occasional sailings provide **themed entertainment**—small-group and big-band jazz, for instance, or performances by a chamber group. Check with the line or your travel agent for a schedule of upcoming themed cruises.

Service

Service by the mostly European and Filipino staff is a major plus. You rarely if ever hear the word *no,* and because the crew-to-passenger ratio is quite high, you rarely have to wait when someone else gets served first. Stewardesses care for your cabin ably and unobtrusively, **room service** is speedy and efficient, and restaurant waitstaff is supremely gracious and professional, with an intimate knowledge of the menu. Bar staff will often remember your drink order after the first day.

The ships all have complimentary **self-serve laundries** in addition to standard laundry and dry-cleaning services. **Cellphone service** is available (with passengers charged a roaming fee by their carrier), and **shipwide Wi-Fi** allows laptop users to connect to the Web from all public areas and most suites. Also, we know of no other line besides Regent that allows guests to use the ship's Internet system to type documents and then paste/append them to an e-mail, getting charged only for transmission time.

Gratuities are included in the cruise rates, but many guests still end up leaving more at the end of their trip.

Seven Seas Mariner • Seven Seas Voyager

The Verdict

The 700-passenger, all-suite *Mariner* and *Voyager* are Regent's largest ships, boasting balconies on every single stateroom, plus extra pampering.

Seven Seas Voyager *(photo: Regent)*

Specifications

Typical Per Diems: $495+

Size (in tons)		Crew	490
Mariner	50,000	Passenger/Crew Ratio	1.6 to 1
Voyager	46,000	Year Launched	
Passengers (double occ.)	708	*Mariner*	2001
Passenger/Space Ratio		*Voyager*	2003
Mariner	71.4	Last Major Upgrade	
Voyager	65.7	*Mariner*	2009
Total Cabins/Veranda Cabins	354/354	*Voyager*	2008

Frommer's Ratings (Scale of 1–5)

★★★★ ½

Cabin Comfort & Amenities	5	Dining Options	4.5
Appearance & Upkeep	5	Gym, Spa & Sports Facilities	3.5
Public Comfort/Space	5	Children's Facilities	N/A
Decor	4.5	Enjoyment Factor	4.5

Sailing Regions, Seasons & Home Ports

Mariner	Caribbean, from Fort Lauderdale (winter).
Voyager	N/A (sailing internationally in 2011).

Introduced in 2001, the all-suite *Seven Seas Mariner* was designed to be exceedingly spacious, and was the first vessel built by any line to have a private balcony off every single stateroom. Sister ship *Seven Seas Voyager,* which entered service 2 years later, continued this theme and has improvements in some areas where we found *Mariner* lacking, particularly public-room warmth and bathroom layout. In addition, *Voyager* was designed with an efficient one-corridor approach, making for extremely smooth traffic flow in the public areas.

CABINS   Deluxe Suites represent the vast majority of the available accommodations aboard *Mariner* and *Voyager.* On *Mariner,* they measure 252 square feet, plus a 49-square-foot balcony; on *Voyager,* they've been enlarged to 306 square feet, with a 50-square-foot balcony. Even beyond size, *Voyager's* standard accommodations are superior, with a warmer feel and more over-the-top marble bathrooms, each with separate shower/bathtub facilities. Conversely, *Mariner's* top-end suites are somewhat larger than *Voyager's,* from the forward-facing, 1,204-square-foot Master Suites (with two balconies, including one enormous 721-sq.-ft. expanse) down to the 359-square-foot Horizon Suites, located in the stern and opening onto expansive views of the ship's wake from their oversize balconies. (*Voyager's* Master Suites have only one balcony, measuring a comparatively tiny 183 sq. ft.)

All staterooms are designed with blond woods and rich fabrics and feature king-size beds convertible to twins, cotton bathrobes, a hair dryer, flatscreen TV with DVD player (with movies available from the ships' DVD libraries), stocked refrigerator, safe, and a large walk-in closet. Refurbishments in 2006, 2007, and 2008–09 upgraded cabin upholstery, mattresses, bed linens and duvets, towels, and bathroom amenities, and added slippers and bathrobes for guest use while aboard. Balconies overall are a little less than private—walls separating them do not extend to the edge of the ship's rail, making it possible to lean out and see what your neighbor is up to. Top-level accommodations, from Penthouses up to Master Suites, come with butler service and iPods with Bose speakers.

Six suites on *Mariner* and four on *Voyager* are wheelchair-friendly.

PUBLIC AREAS   Both ships have beautifully laid-out, two-deck theaters with terrific sightlines from virtually every seat, plus an Observation Lounge sitting high up on the top deck and featuring a semicircular bar, plush chairs and sofas, and a 180-degree view of the sea. It's a particularly attractive room at night. Lower down, each ship also boasts a well-stocked library, a cigar lounge, a card and conference room (popular with bridge players), and a computer center. A very nice feature here is that guests are charged only for transmission time, meaning you can compose a document in Word or another program free of charge, then open your e-mail and paste it in, and incur a cost only while you're in active e-mail mode. Wi-Fi access throughout the ships lets laptop users surf from all public areas and most suites, and cellphone access is also available via a satellite system. *Mariner* also has a dedicated disco, which seems underutilized and mostly patronized by the officers. On *Voyager,* the Voyager Lounge serves as the disco at night and as a piano lounge before dinner.

DINING OPTIONS *Mariner* and *Voyager* each have four restaurants, with the main dining room, the Compass Rose, serving all three meals in single open seatings. Casual breakfasts and lunches are available in the indoor/outdoor La Veranda Restaurant, up near the top of the ship on Deck 11.

Two reservations-only (but no-charge) restaurants are open for dinner only. Signatures features world-ranging and primarily French upscale cuisine prepared in classic French style by chefs trained at Paris's famous Le Cordon Bleu School. The new Prime 7 steakhouses serve prime aged steaks and chops along with fresh seafood and poultry entrees. Appetizers include avant-garde choices such as a trio of steak tartare and foie gras sliders with rhubarb chutney as well as traditional items such as oysters Rockefeller and a jumbo lump crab cake. Additionally, in the evening, half of La Veranda is turned into an excellent candlelit, white-tablecloth Mediterranean Bistro with a combination of waiter and self-service dining. Grilled food is available poolside, and might just be the best pool food at sea. Room service runs 24 hours, and guests can even have the Compass Rose dinner menu served course by course in their suites during dinner hours.

POOL, FITNESS, SPA & SPORTS FACILITIES Each ship's one pool and three hot tubs are located on Deck 11. Deck chairs are set up around the roomy pool area, as well as on the forward half of the deck above, where you'll also find a paddle-tennis court, golf driving nets, shuffleboard courts, and an uninterrupted jogging track. Sunbathing doesn't seem to be the biggest priority for Regent guests, so deck chairs are usually readily available, even on sea days in warm cruising areas.

Each ship's somewhat spartanly decorated Canyon Ranch SpaClub is located in an attractive but rather small space. A similarly smallish oceanview gym and separate aerobics area are located in the same area, as well as a salon.

Seven Seas Navigator

The Verdict

Warm and appealing, the 490-passenger *Navigator* is an ideal size for an ultraluxe cruise: small enough to be intimate and large enough to have plenty of elbowroom, more than a few entertainment outlets, and some of the best cabin bathrooms at sea.

Seven Seas Navigator *(photo: Regent)*

Specifications

Typical Per Diems: $750+

Size (in tons)	28,550	Crew	345
Passengers (double occ.)	490	Passenger/Crew Ratio	1.4 to 1
Passenger/Space Ratio	58.3	Year Launched	1999
Total Cabins/Veranda Cabins	245/216	Last Major Upgrade	2010

Frommer's Ratings (Scale of 1–5)

★★★★

Cabin Comfort & Amenities	5	Dining Options	4
Appearance & Upkeep	4.5	Gym, Spa & Sports Facilities	4
Public Comfort/Space	4.5	Children's Facilities	N/A
Decor	4.5	Enjoyment Factor	4.5

Sailing Regions, Seasons & Home Ports

Navigator	**Caribbean,** from Fort Lauderdale (winter, spring). **Alaska,** from Vancouver & Seward (summer). **New England/Canada,** from New York & Montreal (fall).

Navigator has well-laid-out cabins and public rooms, and if you've been on the Silversea ships, you'll notice a similar layout (especially in the Star Lounge and Galileo Lounge), as the interiors were all designed by the same architects and built at the same yard, Italy's Mariotti. While *Navigator's* interior is very attractive, outside she looks a little bit top-heavy, a consequence of her odd provenance: Her hull was originally built to be a Russian spy ship. When Regent purchased the uncompleted vessel, they redesigned her superstructure with additional decks.

In early 2010, *Navigator* underwent a $35-million refurbishment program. While the usual range of furniture and carpeting changes were made, the line also changed her Italian restaurant to a great steakhouse, redid the casual spot to be very similar to La Veranda which is on *Mariner* and *Voyager,* and seriously upgraded the pool grill menu.

CABINS   *Navigator* is an all-suite, all-outside-cabin ship, so there's not a bad room in the house. Each elegant suite is done up in shades of deep gold, beige, and burnt orange, with caramel-toned wood furniture and a swath of butterscotch suede just above the beds. Nearly 90% of them have private balconies, with only suites on the two lowest passenger decks having bay windows instead. Of these, the only ones with obstructed views are those on the port side of Deck 6 looking out onto the promenade. And for those who do not want balconies, the ship's design creates a trade-off for more inside space. The standard suites are a roomy 301 square feet; the 18 top suites range from 448 to 1,067 square feet, plus 47- to 200-square-foot balconies. Every suite has a sitting area with a couch, terry robes, a pair of chairs, desk, vanity table and stool (with an outlet above for a hair dryer or curling iron), flatscreen TV with DVD player (and movies available from an onboard library), minibar stocked with two complimentary bottles of wine or spirits, private safe, and wide walk-in closet with a tall built-in dresser. The marble bathrooms that come standard in all suites are absolutely huge, with a separate shower stall, a long tub, and lots of counter space. Along with those on *Seven Seas Voyager* and Silversea's *Silver Whisper,* they're the best bathrooms at sea today. Butler service comes to those in categories C and above; these rooms also get a docking station for iPods and constantly replenished fine champagne.

Four suites are wheelchair accessible.

PUBLIC AREAS   Full of autumn hues and deep blues, *Navigator's* attractive decor is a marriage of classic and modern design, with contemporary wooden furniture, chairs upholstered in buttery leather, walls covered in suede, and touches of stainless steel, along with silk brocade draperies, dark-wood paneling, burled veneer, and marble. The ship has lots of intimate spaces, so you'll never feel overwhelmed the way you sometimes do on larger ships.

Most of the public rooms are on Decks 6 and 7, just aft of the three-story atrium and main elevator bank (whose exposed wiring and mechanics could have been better disguised). The well-stocked library has nine new Dell touch-screen computers with e-mail and Internet access, while Wi-Fi hotspots enable laptop users to surf from virtually any area of the ship. The cozy Navigator Lounge, paneled in mahogany and cherrywood, is a popular place for a variety of coffee items during the day and for pre-dinner cocktails, which means it can get tight in there during rush hour. Next door is the Connoisseur Club cigar lounge, a somewhat cold and often underutilized wood-paneled room with umber leather chairs. Down the hall is the roomier Stars Lounge, with a long, curved, black-granite bar and clusters of oversize ocean-blue armchairs around a small dance floor. A live music duo croons pop numbers here nightly. The attractive dark-paneled casino with its striking mural is bound to attract your eye, even if you don't gamble.

Galileo's Lounge, surrounded by windows on three sides and featuring a new burgundy, gold, and lavender color scheme, is our favorite spot in the evening, when a pianist is on hand and the golden room glows magically under soft light. On warm nights, the doors to the outside deck are thrown open and dancers spill out from the small dance floor, creating a truly romantic, dreamy scene. By day, Galileo's is a quiet venue for continental breakfast, high tea, seminars, and meetings, and is also a perfect perch from which to view the seascape via new and very comfy deck furniture.

The stage of the twinkling, two-story Seven Seas Lounge is large enough for the kind of sizable, Vegas-style song-and-dance revues typical of much larger ships—a rarity in the luxe market. While sightlines are good from the tiered rows of banquettes on the first level, views from the sides of the balcony are severely obstructed.

As part of the refurbishment in 2010, the forwardly placed Vista Lounge has been replaced with fitness facilities.

DINING OPTIONS   There are three restaurants: the redecorated Compass Rose (the main dining room); La Veranda for casual dining, day or night; and the newly added Prime 7 (similar to *Voyager* and *Navigator*). Compass Rose, a pleasant, wide-open room done in warm caramel-colored woods, has open seating at all meals. La Veranda, quite casual and buffet-style for breakfast and lunch, is a much more nicely decorated space than the old Portofino restaurant and provides a Mediterranean-inspired menu for dinner (part buffet, part waiter service). Adjacent to La Veranda is now the 52-seat Prime C, which may just be the best steakhouse at sea, along with the two on the line's other ships. One of our favorite dishes is the Alaskan king crab legs (a lot of them per meal) and the tender filet mignon for main courses; for appetizers, it's the three-steak tartare and jumbo lump crab cake. Good luck having room for dessert. There's also an enhanced casual barbecue grill on the Pool Deck for burgers, panini, fries, salads, coffees, and desserts (ice and milkshakes!) at lunchtime. A Coffee Corner is part of Navigator Lounge on Deck 6, with complimentary deluxe coffees available (from a machine) 24 hours a day.

POOL, FITNESS, SPA & SPORTS FACILITIES   The oceanview gym is bright and roomy for a ship of this size, and a separate aerobics room has impressively grueling classes, such as circuit training and step. A pair of golf nets and two Ping-Pong tables are available for guest use, but they're situated high on Deck 12 in an ash-plagued nook just behind the smokestacks, and are accessible only by a hard-to-find set of interior crew stairs. The whole area looks like an afterthought. At the pool area, a wide set of stairs joins a balcony with deck chairs to the large pool and pair of hot tubs on the deck below. The ship's spa/salon is now run by the famed Canyon Ranch SpaClub.

3 Seabourn

6100 Blue Lagoon Dr., Ste. 400, Miami, FL 33126. ℂ 800/929-9391 or 305/463-3070. www.seabourn.com.

THE LINE IN A NUTSHELL   Genteel and refined, these small megayachts are intimate, quiet, and very comfortable, lavishing guests with personal attention and very fine cuisine. **Sails to:** Caribbean, Central America, New England/Canada, Panama Canal (plus Africa, Asia, Mediterranean, Middle East).

THE EXPERIENCE   Strictly upper-crust Seabourn caters to guests who are well mannered and prefer their fellow vacationers to be the same. Generally, they aren't into pool games and deck parties, preferring a good book and cocktail chatter, or a taste of the line's special complimentary goodies, such as free mini-massages on deck and soothing eucalyptus-oil baths drawn in suites upon request.

Due to the ships' small sizes, guests mingle easily and enjoy mellow pursuits such as trivia games and presentations by guest lecturers. An extremely high passenger/crew ratio and a high standard of training ensure that service is both personal and top-notch. Staff members greet you by name from the moment you check in, and your wish is their command.

Pros

- **Top-shelf service:** Staff seems to know what you need before you ask.
- **Lots of price-inclusiveness:** Unlimited wines and spirits are included, as are gratuities, and there's also one free shore excursion per cruise, usually a special treat not found in other lines' shore excursion brochures.
- **Nontouristy ports of call:** These small ships are able to visit smaller, less touristy ports that bigger ships can't access.
- **Excellent dining:** Even the breakfast buffets are exceptional, and on select itineraries they even bring the luxury ashore, setting up a refined Champagne and Caviar in the Surf lunch on the beach.

Cons

- **Limited activities and nightlife:** There's not a whole lot going on aboard ship, but most guests like it that way.
- **Older vessels getting older:** When compared to its newer ships (and those of its competitors), Seabourn's *Spirit, Legend,* and *Pride* lack luster—though to be fair, recent renovations have spiffed up cabins and many public areas. This criticism obviously doesn't apply to the brand-new *Odyssey* and *Sojourn.*

Compared with the other ultraluxury lines, here's how Seabourn rates:

	Poor	Fair	Good	Excellent	Outstanding
Enjoyment Factor					✓
Dining					✓
Activities		✓			
Children's Program	N/A*				
Entertainment		✓			
Service				✓	
Worth the Money			✓		

* Seabourn has no children's program.

Seabourn: The Caviar of Cruise Ships

Seabourn was established in 1987 when luxury-cruise patriarch Warren Titus and Norwegian shipping mogul Atle Brynestad commissioned a trio of ultra-upscale 10,000-ton vessels from a north German shipyard. They sold the line to industry giant Carnival Corporation in 1991 and eventually transferred the ships' registries from Oslo to The Bahamas, but the ships' captains are still Norwegian, their decor is very Scandinavian, and you may still find your suite minibar stocked with bottles of Norwegian Ringnes Pilsener.

Today, the Yachts of Seabourn (as the line officially calls itself) operates its original three vessels plus two larger newcomers, and focuses on doting, personalized service, fine food and wine, and the ability to venture into exotic harbors where megaships can't go.

Passenger Profile

Seabourn's guests are well-traveled, mature adults mostly in their 50s, 60s, and 70s and used to the five-star treatment. Many are current or former executives, lawyers, investment bankers, and so on, and have a lot of zeros on their bank balance. The majority of passengers are couples, but there's usually a handful of singles as well, usually widows or widowers. Though most passengers are American and British, guests from Germany, Switzerland, Australia, and elsewhere sometimes spice up the mix. Families with children are a rarity, and only occasionally appear during the holidays and summers. These ships do not cater to kids at all, and Seabourn passengers prefer it that way.

Dining

Seabourn's cuisine remains one of the line's strong points.

TRADITIONAL   Aboard both the older and newer ships, the main restaurant serves dinner in a single open seating for all guests, who can sit where and with whom they want, and wander in anytime between about 7 and 10pm. Dinner service is high style, with waiters dramatically lifting silver lids off dishes in unison and almost running at a trot through the elaborate, multicourse meals. Service is attentive and unobtrusive, and the waitstaff is programmed to please. Celebrity restaurateur **Charlie Palmer,** of New York's Aureole and Astra fame, is behind the ships' menus, and the ships' chefs are trained at Palmer's shore-side restaurants.

Appetizers may include such dishes as citrus-marinated fluke, iced Russian Malossol caviar, sautéed *escallope* of foie gras, and eggplant relish and hummus. Five entrees change nightly and may include such dishes as pink-roasted rack of veal, rosemary-grilled double-cut lamb chops, roast prime rib, pan-fried sea bass, whole pan-fried Dover sole, scallops wrapped in smoked bacon, and, of course, lobster. **Vegetarian entrees** might include toasted angel-hair pasta with black trumpet mushrooms and a stew of braised artichokes, with white beans, thyme roasted tomatoes, and diced saffron potatoes. A number of **classics** are always on the menu (think baked filet of salmon, grilled New York sirloin, filet mignon, and Caesar salad), as are a number of **lighter-choice** options. If nothing on the menu appeals to you, just ask for something you'd prefer and the galley will do its best to whip it up. Decadent **desserts** include the likes of three-chocolate crème brûlée and hot Grand Marnier soufflé, plus ice creams, sorbets, frozen yogurt, and a selection of international cheeses.

Formal nights (one per weeklong cruise) are very formal, with virtually every gentleman aboard wearing a tuxedo and ladies dressed in sequins and gowns. On other nights, things have relaxed somewhat as Seabourn focuses on attracting a younger crowd (younger as in 40- and 50-somethings), so ties are not required. Regardless, passengers always look very pulled together.

Complimentary wines (about 18 vintages on any given cruise, including champagne) are served not only at lunch and dinner, but basically any time and place you want them. Ditto for spirits and soft drinks. An extensive list of extra-cost vintages is also available, including a collection called **Vintage Seabourn.** For $225, guests can choose three bottles from a list of six premium whites and six premium reds, or you can choose six bottles from a larger menu for $450.

Formal restaurants also serve traditional **breakfast** and **lunch** daily.

SPECIALTY   All Seabourn ships have a specialty option called **Restaurant 2,** which features multicourse tasting menus for up to 72 guests per night (reservations suggested). A pair of chefs prepares an array of small plates typically served two to a course during the five- to six-course meals. Expect such dishes as artichoke salad, cured and roasted duck breast, crispy sea bass, and barbecue-glazed short ribs. Your meal might end with something like a "sweet coffee sandwich" with sea-salt caramel ice cream and hazelnut foam. The ambience is more casual here than at the Restaurant, with a "jackets but no ties" rule for men on formal nights. Aboard *Legend, Spirit,* and *Pride,* the Restaurant 2 experience is presented at the indoor/outdoor Veranda Café (see "Casual" below). Aboard *Odyssey* and *Sojourn,* it's a dedicated space done up in high style.

On *Legend, Pride,* and *Spirit,* the outdoor Sky Bar on Deck 8 is transformed into the **Sky Grill** dining alternative a couple of nights per cruise, weather permitting. It serves freshly grilled seafood and sizzling steak dinners for about 40 guests, by reservation only.

All specialty dining aboard Seabourn is included in the cruise fare.

CASUAL   The indoor/outdoor casual restaurants on all five Seabourn ships offer a combination buffet and table-service menu at breakfast and lunch. At breakfast, omelets are made to your specifications, and there's also an impressive fresh fruit selection along with the usual breakfast spread. At lunch, you'll find salads, sandwich makings, fresh pasta, and maybe jumbo shrimp, smoked salmon, and smoked oysters, plus hot sliced roast beef, duck, and ham on the carving board. On *Odyssey* and *Sojourn,* a casual restaurant, the **Colonnade,** has an open kitchen and themed evening meals in addition to breakfast and lunch.

One night on each warm-weather itinerary has a **festive buffet dinner** served by the pool.

SNACKS & EXTRAS   Daily afternoon **tea service** includes a slew of exotic teas, freshly loose brewed to order. **Room service** is available 24 hours a day on all ships. During normal lunch or dinner hours, your private multicourse meal can mirror the dining room service, right down to the silver, crystal, and porcelain. Don't expect the same level of service you get in the restaurants, but do expect a very cushy, lazy way of "ordering in" one night, with meals served course by course. Outside of mealtimes, the room-service menu is more limited, though you can order treats such as gourmet pizza (topped with garlic rock shrimp, cherry tomatoes, and a basil-and-goat-cheese crumble) and crudités served with *tzatziki* dip, along with the more humdrum burgers, salads, sandwiches, pastas, and so on. In-cabin breakfasts are popular, and you can have your eggs prepared any way you like them.

In the Caribbean, Seabourn's ships have a once-per-cruise **Champagne and Caviar in the Surf beach barbecue** at places like Prickly Pear Island (British Virgin Islands), Mayreau (Grenadines), and Hunting Caye (in Belize's barrier islands). In the morning, crewmembers go ashore and set up a grill, shaded beach chairs, a full bar, and tables with fine china and silver service. Guests step from the landing boats onto a red carpet laid across the sand and find galley staff preparing steaks, jumbo shrimp, grilled local seafood, and other meats, plus a huge selection of antipasti, salads, soup, breads, and desserts. Pastas are prepared to order at a flambé trolley. If you want to swim, you won't miss much: At some point, a uniformed waiter will wade out waist-deep to serve you iced champagne and caviar from a custom life-ring or surfboard.

Activities

The small size of Seabourn's ships contributes to a generally sociable atmosphere, but otherwise the line keeps things quiet, completely eschewing the kind of in-your-face, "rah-rah" activities you find on many mainstream ships. Public announcements are few, and, for the most part, passengers are left alone to enjoy conversation and pursue their personal peace. Such organized activities as there are may include trivia contests, galley tours, computer classes, **wine tastings,** bridge tournaments, exercise classes, and makeover demonstrations. Many cruises feature noted **guest lecturers,** who might be well-known chefs, scientists, historians, authors, diplomats, wine connoisseurs, and TV directors. **Recent-release movies** are available for viewing in cabins, and movies are sometimes shown out on deck as well, with popcorn.

All Seabourn ships have retractable **watersports marinas** that unfold from their stern, allowing passengers direct access to the sea for water-skiing, windsurfing, sailing, snorkeling, banana-boat riding, kayaking, and swimming. It's used, weather and sea conditions permitting, on special "marina days" when at anchor, and during beach parties ashore on select cruises.

Children's Program

Seabourn is an adult line, and has no special programs, menus, or playrooms for kids. If you do bring a kid aboard (minimum age 1 year, please), you may be able to arrange for an available crewmember to provide babysitting service.

Entertainment

Due to the ships' small size, there are no elaborate, splashy production shows such as you sometimes find on the larger luxe ships of Regent and Crystal. Instead, a variety of smaller entertainment is offered each night, with dancing and cabaret in the main lounge (the former accompanied by a band, the latter often featuring comedians, puppeteers, and so on), dancing to a duo before and after dinner in the **Club,** and a late-night DJ for dancing. There's quiet guitar or piano music in the observation lounge, and gambling at each ship's small **casino.**

Service

Seabourn's staff is one of its most valuable assets, with service that's friendly, courteous, discreet, and highly competent. Most of the staff is European, and most have gained experience at fine European hotels. The cabin staff is all female. All **gratuities** are included in the rates.

Each ship has a small business center with computers for e-mail and Internet access. **Wi-Fi** connections are also available everywhere aboard for people who bring their own laptops.

Laundry and **dry cleaning** are available, and there are also complimentary self-service laundry rooms.

Seabourn Odyssey • Sojourn • Quest (Preview)

The Verdict

Seabourn's biggest ships ever, these two new-bies use their extra space to great advantage, most notably with wonderful public spaces (especially the dining spots), a superhigh passenger/space ratio, and balconies off virtually every suite.

Seabourn Odyssey *(photo: Seabourn Cruise Line)*

Specifications

Typical Per Diems: $350–$495+

Size (in tons)	32,000	Passenger/Crew Ratio	1.4 to 1
Passengers (double occ.)	450	Year Launched	
Passenger/Space Ratio	71	*Odyssey*	2009
Total Cabins/Veranda Cabins	225/199	*Sojourn*	2010
Crew	330	*Quest*	2011
Last Major Upgrade	N/A		

Frommer's Ratings (Scale of 1–5)

★★★★★

Cabin Comfort & Amenities	5	Dining Options	5
Appearance & Upkeep	5	Gym, Spa & Sports Facilities	4.5
Public Comfort/Space	5	Children's Facilities	N/A
Decor	5	Enjoyment Factor	5

Sailing Regions, Seasons & Home Ports

Seabourn Odyssey	**Panama Canal,** from Fort Lauderdale (winter).
Seabourn Quest	**Caribbean,** from Fort Lauderdale (winter).
Seabourn Sojourn	**New England/Canada,** from New York & Québec City (fall).

Until 2009, Seabourn hadn't had a new vessel in 17 years (since the launch of *Seabourn Legend* in 1992) and no one thought it ever would have one again—mostly because it was presumed that Carnival Corporation, the line's owner, would consider it more economical to put money into bigger ships. To everyone's pleasant surprise, we were wrong. And to everyone's even pleasanter surprise, the ships turned out to be fantastic: spacious, luxurious, with just the right mix of new features and old favorites that longtime Seabourn guests have come to expect.

Because *Sojourn* debuted in summer 2010, just as this book was going to press (and since *Quest* isn't due to launch until summer 2011), all details in this review refer to *Odyssey*—but no worries: The ships are essentially identical.

CABINS   The ship's 225 suites are all outside, and 199 of them have private balconies. All are done in a softly muted color palette with fashionable furniture that doesn't clutter up the room or distract by being over-the-top plush. About 85% of all rooms fit into the Seabourn Suite (295–300 sq. ft.) and Veranda Suite (295–300 sq. ft., plus a 65-sq.-ft. balcony) categories. All of these staterooms have separate bedroom and living room areas, queen-size or twin beds, walk-in closets, flatscreen TVs with music and movie channels, a fully stocked (and complimentary) bar and refrigerator, a writing desk (with personalized stationery being a nice, if sort of frilly, touch), a separate tub and shower in the bathroom, robes, slippers, hair dryers, and more. Both the walk-in closets and the drawers are plenty spacious and the push-to-open-and-close mechanism for the drawers is excellent.

At the higher end, accommodations run from the Penthouse Suites (436 sq. ft. and larger, plus 98-sq.-ft. balconies) all the way up to the Wintergarden Suites (914 sq. ft., plus two balconies totaling 183 sq. ft.) and the forward placed Signature Suites (907 sq. ft., plus 353-sq.-ft. balcony). Passengers who book the Wintergarden or Signature Suites but still need more legroom can book the suites next door as well, and the two can be connected to make one enormous space. All of these suites come with added amenities when compared to the standard suites, including (based on category) separate dining areas, an extra TV, a butler pantry, whirlpool tubs, a guest bath, an extra closet, an extra bedroom, a glass-enclosed solarium with a tub and day bed, and even an extra bar. The Wintergarden Suites, placed as they are midships, have a curved balcony that allows 180 degree viewing forward and aft.

Seven suites are wheelchair accessible.

PUBLIC AREAS   *Odyssey* and *Sojourn* are much more than proportionately larger vessels compared to Seabourn's earlier ships. The company has done a sensational job of using the extra tonnage while also increasing the passenger-space ratio, and it has done this while remaining faithful to many of the design and decor features that made the three smaller ships so popular and so highly rated. The Club is one popular room that has gotten bigger. There's still the back bar area, sort of set apart from the rest of the room and the stage by glass barriers, while the rest of the room has the stage, the dance floor, and lots of seating. The aft area outside the Club has a pool, whirlpool, and a smattering of seating. It's one of the ship's many great daytime escapes. Seabourn Square is a new addition that's a big hit with passengers. Essentially serving the purpose of a concierge area (such as you'd see at a small luxury hotel), it has four central desks where staffers take care of all administration needs, including those traditionally covered by the purser's desk (of which there's none on board). Grouped around are various sitting areas for the library, the Internet area (with its eight computers), and a neat little European-style cafe serving snacks and beverages.

The main entertainment lounge is the place for the small production shows staged by four talented performers. This is the only room on board that's not quite up to snuff, or at least to the fine snuff that's otherwise the standard here. Pillars hinder sight lines and the assorted seating types are less than really comfy. Another evening (and day) area is the Observation Bar way up on Deck 10, which has a 270-degree view over the bow. It's a wonderfully quiet room during the day and a fun conversation/dancing/meeting place in the evening, when a piano player is on hand for live pre/post-dinner music. Other public rooms such as the casino, card room, and shops are no larger than they need to be.

DINING OPTIONS   The stunningly attractive Restaurant is done primarily in white with silver highlights. It seats 450, meaning there are enough seats here for every guest on board to dine at the same time. The central two-story section is our preferred dining spot as it offers a greater feeling of space and is a bit quieter, but the tables for two and four along the windows are also very appealing, especially depending on what time of the year one cruises. The billowing white curtain dividers add intimacy to the overall space.

Restaurant 2, open in the evening for specially combined pairing menus, is done in black and red with really comfy chairs. The casual restaurant, the Colonnade, is one of the most beautiful casual spots we've seen. There are 138 seats inside and 124 seats outside, making it big enough so that guests can really linger, enjoying breakfasts and lunches that combine great buffets with custom-made items. At the Chef's Table setup, chefs also make a limited number of items as guests look on. (Our favorite meal on board was when the chef put two beautiful crab cakes on a delightfully decorated plate and we then combined them with great grilled shrimps and salad items from the buffet.) At night this room has a variety of themed dinners. Those who want to dine outside during the day can get burgers, franks, chicken, and so on at the poolside Patio Grill, plus pizza from noon to 3pm, panini, and more. All specialty dining is complimentary, but reservations are recommended for dinner in either Restaurant 2 or the Colonnade.

POOL, FITNESS, SPA & SPORTS FACILITIES   This is an area where Seabourn has really put *Odyssey* and *Sojourn*'s extra space to great use. The pool area on Deck 8 is very spacious (much more so than on the line's smaller ships) and is a wonderful location for relaxing and enjoying the outside world. The nicely sized pool is surrounded by two large whirlpools. Above the pool area, on Deck 9, is additional space full of deck chairs. One surprising note: While the chairs were comfortable, there were no cushions. Way up at the top of the ship and forwardly placed is the Sun Terrace, probably the quietest place to relax and enjoy the view and the rays. Perhaps the most overlooked pool area is the aft section of the ship behind the Club, which has a small pool plus two whirlpools, lounge chairs, and tables. It's quiet and the views over the ship's wake are mesmerizing.

Seabourn is justifiably proud of its two-deck spa and gym area, called simply the Spa at Seabourn. Run by Steiner Leisure (as are most other ship spas), it's a series of rooms ranging from gym to spa, salon to private villas, spa pool to "kinesis wall" (a new kind of modular strength-training system that requires some explanation from one of the gym's trainers). Overall, it's 11,400 square feet and designed with an indoor/outdoor look and feel. The gym is much larger than aboard the line's smaller ships, with 19 pieces of training equipment as well as eight high-tech treadmills. Those who want a retreat within a retreat can rent out either of two spa villas for specialized treatments of up to 4 hours (or longer based on special arrangements). Each villa can accommodate up to four guests for private massages including stone therapy, facials, bathing rituals, and more. The regular spa and salon are no slouches either when it comes to offering exotic treatments, including the Seabourn 24 Karat Gold Facial, the Elemis Tri-Enzyme Resurfacing Facial, SkinCeuticals Gel Peel Treatment, Bamboo Massage, Thai Herbal Poultice Massage, Fire and Ice Manicures, and Pedicures and many, many more, all of them in the not-so-cheap category.

Seabourn Spirit • Seabourn Legend

The Verdict

Though a bit dated, these smallish mega-yachts are almost a throwback to a more intimate and refined, less frenetic, and definitely less glitzy style of cruising.

Seabourn Spirit *(photo: Seabourn Cruise Line)*

Specifications

Typical Per Diems: $500+

Size (in tons)	10,000	Passenger/Crew Ratio	1.5 to 1
Passengers (double occ.)	208	Year Launched	
Passenger/Space Ratio	48.1	*Spirit*	1989
Total Cabins/Veranda Cabins	100/6	*Legend*	1992
Crew	157	Last Major Upgrade	2008

Frommer's Ratings (Scale of 1–5)

★★★★

Cabin Comfort & Amenities	4	Dining Options	3.5
Appearance & Upkeep	4	Gym, Spa & Sports Facilities	3
Public Comfort/Space	5	Children's Facilities	N/A
Decor	3	Enjoyment Factor	4

Sailing Regions, Seasons & Home Ports

Seabourn Legend	**Caribbean,** From Fort Lauderdale and St. Thomas (winter).
Seabourn Spirit	**Central America,** from Fort Lauderdale (winter 2011). **Caribbean,** from Fort Lauderdale & St. Thomas (winter 2012).

While the newer *Odyssey* and *Sojourn* outshine Seabourn's original ships in pretty much every way, these are still superfine vessels that carry just 208 passengers each, so you'll never feel lost in the crowd. In fact, you'll feel like you practically own the place. Choose to be as social or as private as you wish, with no rowdiness or loud music and no one exhorting you to get involved. While you're on board, the ship is your floating boutique hotel or your private yacht.

A third sister, *Seabourn Pride,* doesn't currently visit any of the regions covered in this book.

CABINS Just about everything in these ships' 277-square-foot standard suites has the feel of an upscale Scandinavian hotel, including ice-blue or champagne color schemes, lots of bleached oak or birch-wood trim, and mirrors and spot lighting to keep things bright. Only the Owner's Suites have proper balconies, though 36 regular suites on Decks 5 and 6 have French balconies with sliding doors and a few inches of decking—not nearly enough to fit a chair, but they do allow sunlight to pour into the cabin and afford a great view up and down the length of the ship. You can sit on the sofa or in a chair and read while sunning yourself out of the wind and out of view. You can also sleep with the doors wide open and the sounds and smells of the ocean pouring in—unless, of course, the officers on the bridge decide to lock up: If seas get even a little choppy or the wind picks up, a flick of a switch locks your door automatically and there's not a thing you can do about it. (Remember, these ships are small, so you're not that far above the waterline. The cruise line likes to avoid waves and sea spray messing up its lovely decor.)

The best features of the suites are their bathrooms and spacious walk-in closets (which contrast with a fairly minimal amount of drawer space). White marble bathrooms usually include both a tub and a shower (though 10 to 14 suites on each ship have showers only), and lots of shelf, counter, and cabinet space. Molton Brown bath products plus designer soaps by Chanel, Bijan, Hermès, and Bronnley are provided for guests along with a world atlas, terry bathrobes, slippers, and umbrellas to use on board.

The coffee table in the sitting area can be pulled up to become a dining table, and the minibar is stocked on embarkation day with a chilled bottle of champagne and two bottles of complimentary liquor or wine of your choice (a request form comes with your cruise documents). Unlimited bottled water, beer, and soft drinks are restocked throughout the cruise. Ice is replenished twice daily (more often on request), and bar setups are in each room. Each cabin has a desk, hair dryer, safe, radio/CD player (music CDs and audio books are available for borrowing), and flatscreen TVs and DVD players. Fresh fruit and a flower complete the suite scene.

The two Classic Suites measure 400 square feet, and a pair of Owner's Suites on each ship measure 530 and 575 square feet and have verandas, dining areas, and guest powder rooms. Their dark-wood furnishings make the overall feeling more like a hotel room than a ship's suite, but, as is true of any cabins positioned near the bow of relatively small ships, they can be somewhat uncomfortable in rough seas. Owner's Suites 05 and 06 have obstructed views.

Some suites are marketed as 554-square-foot Double Suites, and that's exactly what they are: two 277-square-foot suites connected by an interior door, with one suite converted into a lounge.

There are four wheelchair-accessible suites on each ship.

PUBLIC AREAS Step onto most ships today, and you'll oooh and ahhh at the decor. Not so here, where a minimalist Scandinavian design aesthetic is in play. For the most part, public rooms are spare and almost ordinary looking. Art and ornamentation are conspicuous by their absence.

The forward-facing observation lounge on Sky Deck is the most attractive public room, a quiet venue for reading or cards, the spot for afternoon tea (during which a pianist provides background music), and a good place for a drink before dinner. A chart and compass on the wall outside will help you pinpoint the ship's current position, and a computerized wall map lets you track future cruises.

The Club piano bar in the stern has great views during daylight hours, is packed before dinner, and sometimes has after-dinner entertainment such as a Name That Tune game or a cabaret show. Hors d'oeuvres are served here before and after dinner. A tiny, cramped casino is adjacent, with a couple of blackjack tables, a roulette wheel, and about 10 slots. The downstairs show lounge is a dark, tiered, all-purpose space for lectures, the captain's cocktail party, and featured entertainers such as singers, comedians, and pianists.

One of the best places for a romantic, moonlit moment is the isolated patch of deck far forward in the bow on Deck 5, where a lone hot tub also resides.

DINING OPTIONS The formal Restaurant, located on the lowest deck, is a large, low-ceilinged room with elegant candlelit tables. It's open for breakfast, lunch, and dinner, and officers, cruise staff, and sometimes guest lecturers host tables at dinnertime. If you're not in the mood for the formal dining room, the Veranda Café serves a combination buffet and full-service breakfast and lunch. Come evening, the cafe becomes the casual specialty Restaurant 2, serving multicourse tasting menus (reservations suggested).

Guests who don't want to change out of their swimsuits can get burgers, chicken, hot dogs, grilled items, and a special of the day (maybe pizza with pineapple topping, or fresh ingredients for tacos) at the pleasant Sky Bar, overlooking the Lido Deck. On sunny days, themed lunches are often served here, and in the evening a menu with steak-and-seafood is offered to guests by reservation. Occasionally, the tables and chairs may be pushed back later at night for entertainment and dancing.

POOL, FITNESS, SPA & SPORTS FACILITIES The outdoor pool, which gets little use, is awkwardly situated in a shadowy location aft of the open Deck 7, between the twin engine uptakes and flanked by lifeboats hanging from both sides. A pair of whirlpools is better situated just forward of the pool. A third hot tub is perched far forward on Deck 5. It's wonderfully isolated and a perfect spot (as is the whole patch of deck here) from which to watch a port come into sight or fade away.

A retractable, wood-planked watersports marina opens out from the stern of each ship so that passengers can hop into sea kayaks or go windsurfing, water-skiing, or snorkeling right from the vessel. An attached steel mesh net creates a protected saltwater pool when the marina is in use.

Located forward of the Lido Deck, the gym and Steiner-managed spa are surprisingly roomy for ships this small, and renovations have incorporated modern gym equipment. There are also two saunas, massage rooms, and a salon. Yoga, Pilates, and aerobics classes are held in a lounge or on deck.

4 SeaDream Yacht Club

601 Brickell Key Dr., Ste. 1050, Miami, FL 33131. ℂ **800/707-4911** or 305/631-6100. Fax 305/631-6110. www.seadream.com.

THE LINE IN A NUTSHELL We're unequivocally in love with this kind of ship experience. SeaDream's pair of intimate cruise-ships-turned-yachting-vessels delivers an upscale yet casual vacation without the regimentation of traditional cruise itineraries and activities. **Also sails to:** Caribbean (plus Europe).

THE EXPERIENCE SeaDream was created for independent-minded travelers craving high-end service and food sans formality and rigid schedules. Step aboard one of these 112-passenger yachts and you're boarding a floating club of mostly like-minded travelers who cringe at the thought of sailing en masse to the Nassaus of the world. It's an intimate group that wants to feel like it inhabits an exclusive and remote seaside hamlet on some hard-to-reach, difficult-to-spell island, where the food is good, the masseuses are on hand, and the drinks are flowing. On a SeaDream cruise, everything is included in the cruise fare and you'll never be pestered to pay for drinks or tip the crew. There also aren't art auctions, roving photographers, or "special" restaurants vying for your money, but instead cool adult toys such as WaveRunners, appealing Caribbean ports off the megaship drag, and pampering service that includes complimentary orders of jumbo shrimp served to you in the hot tub (or wherever) whenever the desire strikes. The line's flexible itineraries and fluid daily schedules should appeal to landlubbers used to exclusive resort vacations.

Pros

- **Cool tech stuff:** These ships were built in the mid-1980s, but they've been outfitted for the 21st century. Every cabin is equipped with a flatscreen TV, Internet access, and CD and DVD players; and jet skis and MP3 players are available for passenger use.
- **Late-night departures from key ports:** Instead of leaving port around cocktail hour—just when things begin to get interesting—the ships will stay late or even overnight in places such as St. Barts to allow passengers a night of carousing on terra firma.

- **Flexible itineraries:** Captains have the authority to duck inclement weather by visiting a different port or to extend a stay off an island because of perfect snorkeling conditions.
- **Free booze and tips:** Unlimited wines and spirits as well as tips are included in the rates.

Cons

- **Rough seas:** While the intimacy of these ships can be a selling point, their size can be a detriment: They bob like buoys in even mildly rough waters, and the diesel engines sometimes produce a shimmying sensation.
- **Limited entertainment:** A piano player and guitarist are the sum total of the ship's entertainment. Mostly it's socializing with other passengers over cocktails at the Top of the Yacht bar (who's complaining?).

SeaDream: Your Yacht Awaits

In fall 2001, Norwegian entrepreneur Atle Brynestad, who founded Seabourn in 1987 and chaired the company for a decade, bought out Carnival Corporation's stake in Seabourn's *Sea Goddess I* and *Sea Goddess II.* He then worked with former Seabourn and Cunard president and CEO Larry Pimentel to form the SeaDream Yacht Club, reintroducing the ships as twin yachts. *SeaDream II* was redesigned and refitted at a Bremerhaven, Germany, shipyard and was unveiled in Miami in February 2002. Her sister ship debuted 2 months later, following her own refurbishment. In early 2009, Pimentel resigned from the company due to fundamental disagreements with management over the direction of the company, and Bob Lepisto, who has been with SeaDream since the beginning, was appointed president, and founder and owner Atle Brynestad was named CEO.

The mantra from management is that these vessels are not cruise ships. They are yachts and have been painstakingly renovated to invoke the ambience of your best friend's private vessel, on the theory that cruising is about what happens inside the vessel, and yachting is about what happens outside. Toward this end, deck space has been expanded and refurbished with such touches as queen-size sun beds. The Main Salon is cozy, with fabrics and art handpicked by Linn Brynestad, the owner's spouse. The dress code steers clear of the traditional tux-and-sequins dress-up night by favoring "yacht casual" wear. Some men wear jackets, but never ties. Itineraries are designed so that ships stay overnight once or twice a week so that passengers can enjoy the local nightlife if they wish. Plus, because SeaDream's ports of call tend to be the less commercialized ones that

Compared with the other ultraluxury lines, here's how SeaDream rates:

	Poor	Fair	Good	Excellent	Outstanding
Enjoyment Factor					✓
Dining				✓	
Activities			✓		
Children's Program	N/A*				
Entertainment			✓		
Service					✓
Worth the Money					✓

* SeaDream has no children's program.

are generally off the megaship main drag, you'll rarely be meandering around a port town with thousands of others (thank goodness). If the ships are anchoring offshore, their size generally enables them to get close enough so that the tender ride between ship and shore is short. And given how few passengers the ships carry, you'll never have to queue up to be shuttled back and forth—it's practically on demand.

With many crewmembers having migrated to SeaDream from the *Goddess* days, meticulous attention to detail and personalized service are still the ships' greatest assets.

Passenger Profile

Most passengers are in their 40s and 50s, with the line reporting an average age of 47. About 70% are American (with British, Canadians, and other Europeans making up most of the remainder), and are not veteran cruisers. They're the kind who have refined tastes and want top-notch service and gourmet food, but are secure enough to dispense with a stuffy atmosphere. When coauthor Heidi sailed aboard the *SeaDream I* in the Caribbean, the mix included a fun-loving, middle-aged doctor and his wife from Texas; a 30-something couple-next-door from Pennsylvania, who ran a successful baking business and liked to swig beer from the bottle; a retired travel executive who was clearly used to the good life; a restaurant owner; and a group of well-dressed, hard-drinking friends celebrating a 40th birthday. Many passengers have chartered their own small yachts for a vacation or actually own one. Passengers were friendly and mingled easily, and by day three, alliances had been made and clusters of new friends were enjoying drinks by the pool and dining together in the open-seating restaurants.

The SeaDream yacht experience is most similar to a cruise with Windstar, whose intimate, motorized sailing ships provide casually elegant, yachty jaunts for mostly 40- and 50-somethings to similarly great places in the Caribbean and Europe—though not with SeaDream's all-inclusive price tag. The SeaDream experience is less highbrow and way more playful than Seabourn, whose three 208-passenger ships attract an older, more sober clientele.

A big chunk of the line's business comes from full charters of the ships, often by large (rich) families. Smaller groups can sometimes take advantage of a deal that offers one free cabin for every four booked, up to a maximum of 25 cabins. Groups of 50 are a significant presence on ships this size, so when booking, inquire whether there will be any large groups aboard, to avoid the "in crowd/out crowd" vibe.

Dining

TRADITIONAL Dining is a high point of the SeaDream experience; it's roughly on a par with Windstar's cuisine, and just under Silversea and Seabourn. Daily five-course dinners in the **Dining Salon** include five entrees that change nightly, with a **healthy selection** always among them. Expect delicious dishes such as a hot and tangy prawn and fruit salad; sautéed sea scallops with cauliflower crème, herb lettuce, and potato crisps; and yellowfin tuna steak on roast zucchini and tomato compote. You'll also find a **vegetarian option** and a la carte items such as linguine with pesto and rosemary-marinated lamb chops. The kitchen will prepare **special requests** provided the ingredients are on board. **Local specialties,** such as fresh fish from markets in various ports, are likely to be incorporated into the menu. Open-seating dining is from 7:30 to 9:30pm, and table arrangements include everything from the nine-seat captain's table to cozier places for two (though during the evening rush, it's not easy to snag one). Generally, you'll be seated with other guests unless you don't want to, and by the second or third day of the cruise, many passengers prefer to sit at larger tables with new friends.

There are no formal evenings. Jackets are not required; some men wear them, but many just stick to collared shirts. On Heidi's cruise, passengers' interpretation of the **informal dress code** ranged from a classic navy blue sport jacket to Bermuda shorts and a T-shirt—the latter frowned upon by the ship's manager, but generally overlooked. It's not easy to tell someone who paid several thousand dollars for his cruise to go back to his cabin to change clothes.

Guests can venture "out" for dinner by requesting a spot in advance at one of several private alcoves on Deck 6, or even on the bridge. These special dining opportunities may not be advertised heavily on board—you'll have to ask for them.

CASUAL   The partially covered, open-sided **Topside Restaurant** on Deck 5 serves breakfast and lunch daily, with guests choosing from a buffet or menu.

SNACKS & EXTRAS   Room service is available 24 hours a day for those who don't want to pause their DVD player. You'll also find mini-sandwiches, wraps, pastries, and other snacks throughout the day in the Topside Restaurant's buffet area or at the pool. One afternoon on Heidi's cruise, waiters circulated by the pool at happy hour with trays of bloody marys and homemade mini-pizzas. For a real treat, you can ask for a generous (and complimentary) jumbo shrimp cocktail whenever the mood strikes; on our last cruise, the craving struck while we were soaking in the hot tub. Caviar is available, though it's no longer complimentary (except on special occasions); a 1-ounce portion goes for $32.

Dining highlights from the old *Sea Goddess* cruises are carried over here, including lavish **beach barbecues,** called the Champagne and Caviar Splash, on Jost Van Dyke and Virgin Gorda (see "Activities," below, for more details). A buffet lunch, served on tables with linen and china, includes grilled shrimp and chicken, pork ribs, and plenty of side dishes.

The line's **open-bar policy** means that unlimited alcoholic beverages are served throughout the vessels, though cabin minifridges are stocked only with complimentary beer and soft drinks. If you want wine and spirits for your minifridge, you'll have to pay. Advance requests for favorite libations are encouraged. Each ship's wine cellar includes some 3,500 bottles, of which an excellent selection is complimentary.

Activities

If hanging out can be considered an activity, you can do it well on a SeaDream cruise. Who can complain about summoning a waiter from the hot tub for a jumbo shrimp cocktail and a piña colada? The SeaDream experience is about being outdoors. The ship's main social hubs are not the indoor entertainment lounge or library, but out on deck at the Top of the Yacht Bar, Pool Deck, and sunbathing areas, where there are chaise longues, a pair of hammocks, and the line's much-touted ultrafirm **Balinese sun beds.** Upon request, you can even sleep on them under the stars with duvets and pillows. There's also a **golf simulator** up top, and below, a **retractable marina for watersports** and swimming, which operates a couple of hours a day in ports where the ship anchors, which is virtually everywhere in the Caribbean, but fewer ports in Europe. Cabins have DVD players and you can borrow a portable **MP3 player** from the reception desk (there are about 25, and they're preprogrammed with a wide selection of music). The ships carry along **mountain bikes** for use in port.

For those who consider a **massage** a beloved pastime—like we do—the ship's well-equipped spa and gym are very impressive for ships so small. Staffs of eight Thai women run the spas, which feature traditional therapies such as Swedish massage, along with Asian ones. Heidi sampled an excellent Thai massage during which the therapist used her arms and legs, as well as hands, to execute a variety of stretching moves. The adjacent oceanview gym has up-to-date equipment and daily classes such as tai chi and yoga.

One of the highlights of Caribbean cruises is an ultrapopular holdover from the *Sea Goddess* days, the lavish **Champagne and Caviar Splash beach party** thrown on Jost Van Dyke or Virgin Gorda. Guests are tendered ashore by Zodiac inflatable boats to a quiet beach, where chaise longues are set up on the sand and a nice buffet lunch is served in a rustic pavilion. The main event that gets the cameras clicking is when the manager and his assistants wade into the surf with their uniforms on and serve champagne and caviar from a floating surfboard. It appeals to the inner frat boy in all of us, and passengers of all types just loved the whole ritual on a recent cruise. The entire ship was happily treading through the water to partake of a glass (or two or three) of bubbly and a dollop of caviar, reveling in the frivolity of it. The buffet lunch is served on long tables (with linens and china). A pair of kayaks and snorkeling equipment was also provided, though few people had the energy to bother. Nearby, a local vendor was renting paddleboats, windsurfers, and other watercraft.

Children's Activities

Though the only actual restriction is that children under age 1 are prohibited, these ships are by no means kid-friendly. There are no babysitting services or child-related activities. Teens, though, may enjoy these cruises' emphasis on watersports and unstructured activities. Keep in mind, the standard Yacht Club staterooms can accommodate only three people; the third person/child sleeps on the couch (which doesn't pull out) and generally pays half of the full per-person rate. If you've got a larger family, you'll have to spring for two staterooms. The rate for a child up to age 12 is $100 per day and $200 per day for children ages 13 and older; in both cases, it is assumed that they'll be sharing a stateroom with two adults.

Entertainment

Evening entertainment is mostly of the socializing-over-drinks variety—and that's how passengers seem to like it. This isn't generally a musical-loving cabaret crowd. Typically, a **pianist** plays after dinner in the Main Salon lounge, while a **guitarist** serenades diners at the entrance to the restaurant and sometimes afterward up on deck at the **Top of the Yacht bar,** the liveliest spot to hang out before and after dinner. Occasionally, **local bands** are brought on for the night, and there is a **tiny casino** area with two poker tables and a handful of slots. Weather permitting, on 1 night per cruise, a large **movie** screen is set up on deck so that passengers can watch a flick under the stars (with popcorn, of course).

Service

Given the small number of guests and large number of crew, everyone is quick to satisfy whims and commit your name to memory. Make sure that your first drink is your favorite; you may find fresh ones reappearing automatically throughout the evening. The dining room waitstaff is courteous and knowledgeable, though a bit harried; even though dining is open seating, most passengers tend to eat about the same time each evening. As aboard the Silversea ships, cabin bathrooms are stocked with Bulgari amenities and guests all get a complimentary set of frumpy (but comfortable) Sea-Dream pajamas. **Laundry, dry cleaning,** and **pressing** are available, but there is no self-service laundry.

SeaDream I • SeaDream II

The Verdict

The service, cuisine, and intimacy of the SeaDream yachts are an even better package than their old incarnation as the *Sea Goddess* ships. Their flexible itineraries and laid-back atmosphere are designed to pry landlubbers from their resorts and out to sea.

SeaDream II *(photo: SeaDream Yacht Club)*

Specifications

Typical Per Diems: $470+

Size (in tons)	4,260	Passenger/Crew Ratio	1.2 to 1
Passengers (double occ.)	112	Year Launched	
Passenger/Space Ratio	38.7	*SeaDream I*	1984
Total Cabins/Veranda Cabins	55/0	*SeaDream II*	1985
Crew	95	Last Major Upgrade	2007/2008

Frommer's Ratings (Scale of 1–5)

★★★★½

Cabin Comfort & Amenities	5	Dining Options	3.5
Appearance & Upkeep	4	Gym, Spa & Sports Facilities	4
Public Comfort/Space	4.5	Children's Facilities	N/A
Decor	4	Enjoyment Factor	5

Sailing Regions, Seasons & Home Ports

SeaDream I	**Caribbean,** from St. Thomas, San Juan & St. Martin (winter).
SeaDream II	**Caribbean,** from St. Thomas, San Juan, St. Martin & Barbados (winter).

If you like a high-quality, sophisticated cruise experience without the formality of the other luxe lines or the crowds of the bigger ships, SeaDream is the answer to your prayers. These former *Sea Goddess* ships, which started sailing in 1984, have occupied their yachty luxe niche for more than a quarter-century, and they're still a great way to explore the Caribbean and Europe.

CABINS   All of the 54 one-room, 195-square-foot, oceanview suites are virtually identical, with the bedroom area positioned alongside the cabin's large window (or portholes in the case of Deck 2 suites) and the sitting area inside—the exact opposite of most ship cabin layouts. During a May 2007 dry dock, the suites on *SeaDream I* were refreshed with new furniture upholstery, curtains, and bedspreads; same deal in 2008 for *SeaDream II*. The standard cabins are a bit bigger than Windstar's, and about 100 square feet smaller than those of Seabourn, Silversea, and Regent. None have balconies. Soundproofing between cabins is good and engine noise minimal, as all cabins are located forward and amidships.

Built in the mid-1980s, these ships have a lot more real wood incorporated into the cabins than you'll see on today's newer ships that sport veneers and synthetics at every turn. Wood cabinetry and moldings are complemented by blue-and-white fabrics to create an appealing nautical look with a modern twist. Each suite has a small sitting area with a couch (that can accommodate a third adult or a child) and an entertainment center that includes a flatscreen TV with CD/DVD player (and wired for Internet access). The amount of storage space is plentiful. A minifridge is stocked with sodas and beer (booze from any of the bars and restaurants is included in the rates, but oddly enough, if you want liquor for your minibar, you'll have to pay for it). Bathrooms are compact, as you would expect on ships of this size, but feature huge marble showers with glass doors and a generous supply of Bulgari toiletries. Each cabin comes with a hair dryer and extrathick bathrobes, and all guests are given a set of personalized cotton pajamas with the SeaDream logo to take home. Unlike Silversea and Seabourn, the 24-hour room-service menu is limited to salads and sandwiches, and you cannot order from the restaurant menus.

There are 16 staterooms that are connectable to form eight 390-square-foot Commodore Club Staterooms. The 450-square-foot Owner's Suite has a bedroom, living room, dining area, main bathroom with bathtub and separate oceanview shower, and a guest bathroom. Both ships also have a new, 375-square-foot Admiral suite with a similar layout and amenities.

These ships are not recommended for passengers requiring the use of a wheelchair. Doorways leading to staterooms are not wide enough, many thresholds in public areas are several inches high, and tenders that shuttle passengers from ship to shore in many ports cannot accommodate wheelchairs. Though there are elevators, they don't reach all decks.

PUBLIC AREAS The SeaDream yachts retain much of *Sea Goddess*'s former sophisticated decor, but with periodic face-lifts that keep carpeting and furniture spruced up. Stained wood floors, Oriental carpets, and striking exotic floral arrangements are appealing. The Main Salon and its small but popular alcove bar is the place for the weekly captain's cocktail party, plus other group events. One deck above is the Piano Bar, and next door is the ship's small casino, a gift shop, and an attractive library furnished with comfy chairs and stocked with everything from books on military history to Oprah Book Club favorites.

By far, the favorite place to socialize is the Top of the Yacht bar amidships on Deck 6, which has been designed with teak decking, rattan furniture, and contrasting blue-striped cushions. The bar area is partially covered and has alcove seating. On this deck, you'll also find a flotilla of queen-size sun beds for reading, sunbathing, or napping; they're slightly elevated at the stern of the ship to allow for uninterrupted ocean viewing. For those who might want to sleep on deck one night, management will allow it and outfit beds with blankets. There's a large collection of original artwork by exclusively Scandinavian artists, placed throughout the ship and commissioned or otherwise chosen by Linn Brynestad.

DINING OPTIONS Dinners are served indoors in the simple but elegant Dining Salon on Deck 2. On 1 or 2 nights during the trip, a festive dinner is served in the open-sided, teak-floored Topside Restaurant on Deck 5, and some special meals are served on the beach during port calls. (See "Dining," above, for details.)

POOL, FITNESS, SPA & SPORTS FACILITIES Because yachting is all about being outdoors, there are great open spaces on the SeaDream ships. Stake an early claim to one of the sun beds because they're prime real estate. Eight of them are aftward on Deck 6, and more are forward, near the golf simulator. Aft on Deck 3 is the attractive pool area, with comfortable lounge chairs and umbrellas, tables, a bar, and, not too far away, a hot tub. It's the place where social passengers gather when the ship departs a port to enjoy the view. A covered deck above has more chairs.

Toward the bow on Deck 4 are the salon and an impressively well-designed and well-equipped spa and gym, with four treadmills with flatscreen TVs, an elliptical machine, two stationary bikes, and free weights (and lowish ceilings if you're on the tall side). Classes include aerobics, yoga, and tai chi. The uninterrupted ocean views add a calming diversion while you're burning calories. The teak-lined spa, the Asian Spa and Wellness Center, has three treatment rooms and features the usual decadent (and pricey) suspects, including wraps, facials, and massages, plus more exotic options such as hot-lava-rock massages, a spice-and-yogurt scrub, and a cucumber-and-aloe wrap. You can prebook treatments online at www.seadreamspa.com.

5 Silversea Cruises

110 E. Broward Blvd., Fort Lauderdale, FL 33301. ℂ 800/722-9955. Fax 954/522-4499. www.silversea.com.

THE LINE IN A NUTSHELL It doesn't get better than Silversea if you're looking for a total luxury experience at sea. From exquisite service and cuisine to such niceties as free-flowing Drappier champagne and Ferragamo and Bulgari bath products in the marble cabin bathrooms, the line's six ships offer the best of everything. **Sails to:** Alaska, Caribbean, New England/Canada, Panama Canal (plus Europe, Asia, Middle East, South America, Australia/New Zealand, Africa, transatlantic, world cruise).

THE EXPERIENCE Fine-tuned and genteel, a Silversea cruise caters to guests who are used to the good life, and nothing seems to have been overlooked. The food and service are among the best at sea, and the decor is warm and inviting. Tables are set with Christofle silver and Schott Zwiesel crystal. These are luxe vessels for a luxe crowd that spends a lot of time comparing travel dossiers for their next big trip. If you want the VIP treatment 24-7, this is your cruise line.

Pros

- **Doting service:** Gracious and ultraprofessional, the Silversea crew knows how to please well-traveled guests with high expectations.
- **Excellent cuisine:** Rivaling the best restaurants ashore, cuisine is as exquisite as it gets at sea. Each ship has two alternative venues for dinner, buffets are bountiful, and the room-service menu is extensive.

Compared with the other ultraluxury lines, here's how Silversea rates:

	Poor	Fair	Good	Excellent	Outstanding
Enjoyment Factor					✓
Dining					✓
Activities			✓		
Children's Program	N/A*				
Entertainment		✓			
Service					✓
Worth the Money				✓	

* Silversea has no children's program.

- **Large staterooms and great bathrooms:** Most of the line's suites are larger than Seabourn's and Crystal's, and the huge marble bathrooms are among the best at sea.
- **Free booze and tips:** An impressive selection of wines and spirits is included in the rates, as are gratuities.

Cons

- **Stuffy crowd:** Of course, not every guest fits that bill, but expect a good portion of the crowd on any cruise to be . . . reserved.

Silversea: The Crown Jewels

Silversea Cruises was conceived in the early 1990s by the Lefebvre family of Italy, former owners of Sitmar Cruises, a legendary Italian line that was merged into P&O/Princess in the late 1980s. Created to cater to discerning travelers looking for a superluxurious cruise experience, the line's four ships were built and outfitted at shipyards in Italy and no expense was spared in their design.

The new line joined Seabourn right at the top of the heap when it introduced the 296-passenger *Silver Cloud* and *Silver Wind* in 1994 and 1995—and, in fact, features such as stateroom balconies and a two-level show lounge actually gave them the edge. With the introduction of the larger, even more impressive *Silver Shadow* and *Silver Whisper* in 2000 and 2001, that bar was raised even higher, with larger staterooms and huge marble bathrooms, dimly lit and romantic cigar lounges, and more entertainment lounges—all in all, the absolute height of style, paired with itineraries that spanned the globe. A concerted effort has been made to play up the line's Italian connections. The ships have specialty Italian restaurants; Italian-made bath amenities come from Ferragamo and Bulgari; high-end Italian clothes and accessories are in the boutiques.

In late 2009, Silversea took delivery of *Silver Spirit,* its new 36,000-ton, 540-passenger ship, built at Italian shipyard Fincantieri. The line also purchased an expedition ship (formerly Society Expedition's *World Discoverer*), and relaunched her in mid-2008 as *HSH Prince Albert II* in tribute to Prince Albert of Monaco, who in 2006 journeyed to the North Pole to draw attention to the effects of global warming on the Arctic regions. The ship currently sails in the Arctic, Antarctica, and the tropical coast of South America.

For the purposes of this review, references are made to the line's five mainstream vessels, not the expedition one.

Passenger Profile

While Silversea's typical passenger mix tends to be older, shorter cruises and Caribbean sailings often skew the mix a tad younger, adding at least a handful of 30- and 40-something couples to the pot. Typically, about 50% of passengers are American and the rest are mostly from Europe, with some from Australia, South America, and the Far East in the mix. Overall, they're well traveled, well heeled, well dressed, well accessorized, and well into their 50s, 60s, and 70s. Most guests are couples, though singles and small groups of friends traveling together are usually part of the scene, too. Many have cruised with Silversea before.

Dining

Foodies should consider Silversea for the food alone. The cuisine is well prepared and presented, and creative chefs continually come up with a wide variety of dishes. Many ingredients are imported from Italy (the pasta, cheese, and Parma ham, aka prosciutto, for instance) and many of the baked goods—including the excellent focaccia and flat breads—are made right on board. Each ship has a formal open-seating dining room and two or more alternative choices. There are plenty of tables for two in all restaurants, though in the main dining room, you may have to wait at the peak of the dining hours.

TRADITIONAL   While the cuisine in the elegant main dining room (straightforwardly called the **Restaurant**) is not as impressive as that of the more intimate, casual **La Terrazza** (see below), it still serves delicious meals, with entrees such as a duet of king prawn and halibut with wild-rice cakes, crispy roasted duck, and penne pasta with spicy tomato, olive, caper, and anchovy sauce. The wine list is excellent, and a pair of complimentary wines is suggested at each meal from more than 40 choices; if you'd like something other than the featured ones, ask and ye shall find. You can also choose one of the wines not included on the complimentary list—a $745 1990 Château Margaux, anyone?

SPECIALTY   Two specialty restaurants serve dinner on each ship, both by reservation. Open most evenings for dinner, **La Terrazza** is an intimate spot serving Italian cuisine. Start with a plate of antipasto—fresh parmigiano, prosciutto, olives, sun-dried tomatoes, and marinated eggplant—before moving on to delicious dishes such as a mushroom tart or buffalo mozzarella with fresh tomato and basil; gnocchi filled with Gorgonzola; and a juicy pork loin. Featured desserts, such as a delicious *millefoglie* (or mille-feuille: puff pastry with cream filling), are paired with a tray of Italian-made biscotti.

The **second alternative restaurant** provides a new twist on cruise dining, offering **menus that pair food with wine**—and not the other way around. Developed in consultation with master sommeliers trained in the member boutique lodgings and restaurants of Relais & Châteaux–Relais Gourmands, the wine menus reflect regions of the world known for their rich viticultural heritage, including France, Italy, northern California, South Africa, Australia, and New Zealand. Sommeliers describe the origin and craft of each vintage, then present dishes created especially to bring out the wine's full richness. Guests enjoy a different wine with each course, with the extra charge for dinner varying in accordance with the wines presented. On a recent cruise, it was $200 per person, and frequented mostly by European passengers.

See the *Silver Spirit* review, below, for that ship's additional alternative restaurants.

CASUAL   Burgers, sandwiches, and salads are served poolside at lunchtime, in addition to service in the **Restaurant** and the buffet-style **Terrace Cafe** (which is transformed into La Terrazza in the evenings). Once per cruise, passengers are also invited into the galley for the traditional **galley brunch,** which features more than 100 delectable dishes, from stone crab claws to pickled herring, Hungarian goulash, rabbit a la Provençal, and German bratwurst. A red carpet is rolled out, literally, through the galley, and the chef is on hand to chat with guests about the feast.

SNACKS & EXTRAS   The line's **24-hour room-service menu** includes such mouthwatering choices as a snack-size portion of crabmeat served with lime mayonnaise and guacamole, and delicious thin-crust gourmet pizzas. Plus, if you'd rather dine in, you can order off the Restaurant's menu (during its lunchtime and dinnertime operating hours) and have your meal served course by course on a table set with linens and china in your suite. There's an elegant, white-gloved tea service in one of the lounges on most days.

Activities

Aside from trivia games, card tournaments, stretch and aerobics classes, and bridge tours, Silversea tries to focus on more cerebral pursuits. **Wine-tasting seminars** are excellent. The line's **enrichment lectures** are varied and interesting; at least one guest speaker is featured on every sailing, and speakers have ranged from explorers and adventurers to authors and journalists. **Culinary-themed cruises,** offered in partnership with Relais & Châteaux, are hosted by Relais Gourmands chefs and feature demos and tastings.

Other pursuits include language classes, **golf instruction** and driving nets, and computer classes. *Silver Shadow* and *Silver Whisper* also have special golf cruises that feature PGA golf pros, golfing excursions, and the latest video teaching technology.

Lighter activities include a dip in the pool or two hot tubs; shopping in the boutiques (which include H. Stern, where you'll find high-end gold, diamond, and gemstone pieces); and surfing in the Internet center. Passengers who travel with their laptops can take advantage of Wi-Fi throughout the ships. **Onboard cellphone service** is also an option. Overall, though, these ships are low-key (don't expect music on the Pool Deck, for instance) and guests are left to their own devices when it comes to keeping busy—just the way most like it. Reading, dozing, and sipping cool drinks seem to keep most of them happily occupied.

The spa beckons with its flower-strewn copper foot bowls, warm massage stones, and other treatments. To avoid waiting in line on the first day of the cruise to make your appointments, you can now book your treatments via the line's website up to 48 hours before your cruise. You can also prebook **shore excursions** online up to the week before sailing.

When ready for bed, guests can choose from the new pillow menu which offers eight different kinds, from the popular 25% down/75% feather soft pillow to the Buckwheat Pillow for relieving body aches and pains, or even the Body Pillow for head-to-toe comfort with its 100% silk charmeuse pillow case.

Children's Program

These ships are not geared to children and there are no facilities for them, although every so often, one or two are on board. Babysitting may be arranged with an available crewmember (no guarantee); otherwise, no activities or services are provided specifically for children. The minimum age for sailing is 12 months.

Entertainment

For evening entertainment, the ships each have a small casino; a combo entertaining in the nightclub adjacent to the show lounge; a pianist in another lounge; and dozens of in-cabin movies, including oldies and current films. On warm-weather cruises, there are movies shown on deck by the pool and dancing under the stars at the weekly barbecue buffet on deck. There are also small-scale song-and-dance revues in the two-level show lounges, plus magic acts, singers, instrumentalists, jugglers, and sometimes performances by local folkloric groups. Popular **themed cruises** from time to time feature classical musicians, guest chefs, and renowned wine experts conducting demonstrations and talks. The pace is calm, and that's the way most Silversea guests like it; most are perfectly content to spend their after-dinner hours with cocktails and conversation. Occasionally, depending on the crowd, the **Panorama Lounge** (on *Shadow* and *Whisper*) or the **Bar** (on all ships) attracts a contingent of revelers who dance and drink into the wee hours.

Service

All suites include the services of a butler who will unpack your bags, draw your bath, make spa or dinner reservations, put together an in-suite cocktail party for you and the maharajah, or arrange a private car at the next port. Butlers will now also clean luggage with a bio- and eco-friendly cleaner (safe even on fine leather).

The gracious staff knows how to please. Staff members are friendly and oftentimes remember your name, but are never obtrusive or pushy. Waitstaff and stewards are as discreet as the guests are, and chances are you'll never hear the word *no*. The room-service menu is extensive and at dinnertime you can also order from the Restaurant's menu and have it served in your suite, course by course. Unlimited wines, Drappier champagne, spirits, and soft drinks are included in the rates, as are gratuities. Hot and cold canapés are served in the lounges before dinner, and fine chocolates are left on suite pillows on formal evenings. **Laundry** and **dry cleaning** are available. There are also **self-service laundry** rooms.

Silver Spirit

The Verdict

The new Silversea ship takes the line to a whole new level. She's the largest ship in the fleet and carries the most passengers. But she is the most innovative and most filled with facilities, offering the line's loyal followers another terrific option.

Silver Spirit *(photo: Silversea Cruises)*

Specifications

Typical Per Diems: $415+

Size (in tons)	36,000	Crew	376
Passengers (double occ.)	540	Passenger/Crew Ratio	1.4 to 1
Passenger/Space Ratio	67	Year Launched	2009
Total Cabins/Veranda Cabins	270/258	Last Major Upgrade	N/A

Frommer's Ratings (Scale of 1–5)

★★★★

Cabin Comfort & Amenities	5	Dining Options	5
Appearance & Upkeep	5	Gym & Spa Facilities	4.5
Public Comfort/Space	4.5	Children's Facilities	N/A
Decor	4.5	Enjoyment Factor	5

Sailing Regions, Seasons & Home Ports

Silver Spirit	**Caribbean,** from Fort Lauderdale (fall 2011, winter 2012).

Silver Spirit, the line's first new ship in nearly a decade, takes Silversea to a whole new level. At 36,000 tons, the ship is 27% bigger than *Shadow* and *Whisper* and twice the tonnage of *Wind* and *Cloud.* While the space ratio has dropped a bit from 74 to 67, it's a negligible change; at that high a ratio, the ship is at the very top portion of the cruise apex. Silversea has taken advantage of this space—new dining options, a range of amenities not found on its other ships, a greater percentage of verandas, a vastly expanded spa and casino, and new lounges. As for any worries about service levels being different, with 376 crewmembers, the ratio of guest to crew is 1.4 to 1, virtually identical to the rest of the fleet.

CABINS Of the 270 outside suites, 258 have private verandas (about 95%). All suites have butlers who provide a wide range of services, from packing and unpacking, to getting one's luggage cleaned, making spa and restaurant reservations, and helping to choose one of the eight options from the Pillow Butler—and, of course, providing endless amounts of Drappier champagne.

The suites range in size from 312 square feet for the 12 insides to 1,292 square feet for the two Owner's Suites (this includes a veranda measuring 190 square feet). These two suites can also be combined with the room next door, adding another bedroom and veranda totaling 190 square feet. Grand Suites and Silver Suites (a total of 32) are either 990 or 742 square feet (including veranda). Grand and Owner's suites have their own libraries.

The rest of the rooms are all the same, with location and deck determining whether they are in the Midships Veranda Suite or Veranda Suite category, measuring 376 square feet (including veranda). All of them have a considerable amount of closet and drawer space as well as plenty of horizontal counters for miscellaneous items. If there's a weakness, it's that there are not enough 110V electrical outlets.

All suites, regardless of category, can be personalized via a series of scents created by renowned Italian perfumer Laura Tonatto. They have sitting areas, twin or queen-size beds, marbled bathrooms and vanities, full-size bathtubs, separate showers, walk-in closets, personal safes, vanity tables with hair dryers, writing desks, and direct-dial phones. One of the best design features on this or any of the new ships is the way the TVs are placed behind the mirrors; when they are not on, they are hidden from view, creating a very classy, uninterrupted feeling. There are even iPod docking stations.

Luxury touches abound, from duvets to a choice of Ferragamo or Bulgari bathroom amenities, stocked refrigerators, personalized stationery, complimentary movie channels, and, naturally, fresh fruit and flowers.

PUBLIC AREAS Italian architect Giacomo Mortola has used the *Spirit*'s larger space to present a 1930s Art Deco–inspired series of public rooms with a touch of old-world, Victorian elegance thrown in as well. Many of the rooms would be right at home on the classic ocean liners of the past, or in the Chrysler Building or Empire State Building, or the many classic hotels of Europe. One of the most popular rooms is the Bar, located right next to the reception area; it's an ideal meeting, drinking, and relaxing spot anytime of day or night. In keeping with the line's heritage, it serves Italian coffees, of course. The Bar is a dividing line of sorts; the forward portion of each deck has suites, the aft portions have the restaurants, lounges, spa, casino and the rest. It helps to create a vertical world and makes sure that there are no long walks from the front to back of the ship. The only exception is the Observation Lounge, on Deck 11, which is forward, offering views ahead. By contrast, the Panorama Lounge on Deck 9 covers where the ship has been with views out over the aft of the ship (outside seating is available). The casino and boutiques are much expanded compared to earlier ships, providing ample opportunity for on-board spending.

DINING OPTIONS Dining is, of course, a highlight of any Silversea cruise, and, with the larger tonnage of *Silver Spirit* comes an expanded range of options. The four venues, found on all Silversea ships, include the Restaurant for breakfast, lunch or dinner, served in elegant surroundings with the widest range of menu options, all put together under the auspices of Relais & Châteaux; La Terrazza for indoor or alfresco dining with breakfast and lunch buffets (a much improved setup compared to earlier ships) and authentic Italian cuisine at night; Le Champagne for a six-course epicurean experience in an intimate atmosphere; and the Pool Grill for both lunch and dinner, with a wider than normal range of options including a hot-rock dinner for the evenings. Two new restaurants fill out the menu. The intimate Seishin Restaurant has a range of Asian fusion menu items, from Kobe beef and spider lobster to caviar and lots of sushi choices (per-person degustation menu cost is $40). In the evening, there's the Stars Supper Club where live music, dancing, and nightclub-style entertainment complement the innovative menus and provide a relaxed feeling; the small bar is a great place to just hang out before and after evening meals in other restaurants. And, if this range isn't enough, there's 24-hour room service with an extensive menu, with lunch and dinner offered from the Restaurant menus, served course by course if so desired.

POOL, FITNESS, SPA & SPORTS FACILITIES   Compared to earlier Silversea ships, the spa run by Steiner is absolutely massive; it's 8,300 square feet, indoors/outdoors with separate relaxing areas, and has nine treatment rooms with floor-to-ceiling windows, a salon, workout area, gym, whirlpool, sauna, and steam rooms (although not much in the way of luxe amenities). The changing rooms are coed, which some passengers may find uncomfortable. The pool area is bigger than on other Silversea ships and has lots of wicker furniture with comfy cushions for lounging around. For those not-so-fitness-or-pool-area-inclined, the aft sitting areas on Decks 7 and 9 are sure to please.

Silver Shadow • Silver Whisper

The Verdict

These handsome, well-run ships are perfect for those looking for a small-ship experience with superb dining and service.

Silver Shadow *(photo: Silversea Cruises)*

Specifications

Typical Per Diems: $455+

Size (in tons)	28,258	Passenger/Crew Ratio	1.3 to 1
Passengers (double occ.)	388	Year Launched:	
Passenger/Space Ratio	74	*Silver Shadow*	2000
Total Cabins/Veranda Cabins	194/157	*Silver Whisper*	2001
Crew	295	Last Major Upgrade	2007

Frommer's Ratings (Scale of 1–5)

★★★★★

Cabin Comfort & Amenities	5	Dining Options	5
Appearance & Upkeep	4.5	Gym, Spa & Sports Facilities	4
Public Comfort/Space	5	Children's Facilities	N/A
Decor	5	Enjoyment Factor	5

Sailing Regions, Seasons & Home Ports

Silver Shadow	**Alaska,** from Seward & Vancouver (summer).
Silver Whisper	**Caribbean,** from Fort Lauderdale & Barbados (winter, spring 2011), from New York (fall 2011). **New England/Canada,** from New York & Montreal (fall 2011).

With the introduction of *Silver Shadow* and *Silver Whisper,* Silversea set the bar very high for the rest of the small-ship ultraluxe lines. They're small enough to be intimate, but large enough to offer a classy, two-story show lounge, a dark and romantic cigar lounge, three dining venues, an impressive spa and gym, and some really great suites, in addition to the fine service and cuisine provided fleetwide.

CABINS   The suites aboard *Silver Shadow* leave nothing to be desired. With a chilled bottle of Drappier bubbly at your side, just settle down in the comfy sitting area and bask in the ambient luxury. Private balconies are attached to three-quarters of the plush staterooms, which measure a roomy 287 square feet or more. They're done up in an ultrapleasant color scheme focused on rich blues and soft golds, along with coppery-brown wood tones. Each suite has a walk-in closet, minibar, DVD player, sitting area, lighted dressing table with hair dryer, writing desk, and wonderful marble-covered bathrooms stocked with Ferragamo or Bulgari toiletries (the stewardess comes around at the beginning of the cruise to ask your preference, though you can change your mind at any time). The separate shower stall and long bathtub, along with double sinks, make these among the best loos at sea. All beds have feather-down pillows and duvets, and Egyptian cotton linens. The largest of the four two-bedroom Grand Suites are really something else, measuring 1,435 square feet with three bathrooms, a pair of walk-in closets, an entertainment center, two verandas, and a living room and dining area. All suites have flatscreen TVs and plush mattresses and bedding.

PUBLIC AREAS   The low-key main lobby area, where the purser's desk resides, branches out into a pair of attractive, four-deck-high staircases, with shiplike railings, and corridors done in a mix of Wedgwood blue and golden peach fabrics and carpeting, along with warm caramel wood tones. The impressive **two-story show lounge** has tiered seating and lots of cozy clusters of chairs; the **Bar,** just outside the show lounge's first level, can be a social hub, with a long bar, dance floor, and plenty of seating. The **Observation Lounge,** high on Deck 10 overlooking the bow, is a great place to relax, read, and watch the scenery unfold through floor-to-ceiling windows. You'll find a radar screen, astronomical maps, binoculars, and reference books, and, during the day, a self-service coffee, tea, and juice bar. On Deck 8 at the stern, the windowed **Panorama Lounge** also affords great sea views and lots of comfortable seating. By day, enjoy a continental breakfast or high tea here, while by night the lounge becomes an intimate nightspot, with a pianist serenading dancers. The Connoisseurs Corner is a dark, cozy, and plush spot for cocktails—even nonsmokers can't help but be drawn to the ambience, while cigar lovers should enjoy the walk-in humidor. There's also a small casino and attached bar, a card room with felt-topped tables, a boutique, and a pool bar.

DINING OPTIONS   In the **Restaurant,** the main dining room, a live trio plays romantic oldies on some nights, and guests are invited to take a spin around the small dance floor. There are plenty of tables for two, though during popular times you may have a short wait. Breakfast, lunch, and dinner are served here in high style, while a more casual buffet-style breakfast and lunch are served in the indoor/outdoor **La Terrazza.** Service is doting even in the casual restaurant, with waiters rushing to carry plates to your table, serve drinks, and clear things off just moments after you finish. A special pasta dish is made to order by a chef for guests who do lunch in La Terrazza. Come evening, it has a wonderful Italian menu that focuses on different Italian regions throughout the cruise; reservations are required. A third dining spot has special wine-pairing menus (see "Dining," above) in an intimate setting on Deck 7 next to the Terrace Cafe.

POOL, FITNESS, SPA & SPORTS FACILITIES   A combination of old-style wooden deck chairs and brand-new aluminum and blue canvas deck chairs line the open decks. Unfortunately, jolting grass-green Astroturf covers the entirety of Decks 9 and 10 (a teak-colored synthetic flooring would have been a better choice). There are plenty of places to retire with a good book or take an afternoon snooze, either near the pool and hot tubs on Deck 8 (which is teak, by the way), or at the stern on that deck. There's also a golf driving cage and shuffleboard.

The spa, gym, and salon occupy much of Deck 10, and are spacious for a ship of this size. There's a separate workout room with exercise machines, plus a separate aerobics room.

Silver Cloud • Silver Wind

The Verdict

Big enough to have a two-story show lounge and several other entertainment outlets, and cozy enough that you'll feel like you practically have the vessel to yourself, these ships are an absolute dream.

Silver Cloud *(photo: Silversea Cruises)*

Specifications

Typical Per Diems: $400+

Size (in tons)		Passenger/Crew Ratio	1.4 to 1
Silver Wind	17,400	Year Launched	
Silver Cloud	16,800	*Silver Cloud*	1994
Passengers (double occ.)	296	*Silver Wind*	1995
Passenger/Space Ratio	57	Last Major Upgrade	
Total Cabins/Veranda Cabins	148/11	*Silver Cloud*	2009
Crew	212	*Silver Wind*	2008

Frommer's Ratings (Scale of 1–5)

★★★★

Cabin Comfort & Amenities	4	Dining Options	4.5
Appearance & Upkeep	4	Gym & Spa Facilities	4
Public Comfort/Space	4	Children's Facilities	N/A
Decor	4.5	Enjoyment Factor	5

Sailing Regions, Seasons & Home Ports

Silver Cloud	**Caribbean,** from Fort Lauderdale & Barbados (winter, spring 2011). **Panama Canal,** from Fort Lauderdale & San Diego (winter, spring 2011).
Silver Wind	N/A (sailing internationally in 2011).

Superintimate and large enough to have multiple entertainment venues, two restaurants, and lots of outdoor deck space, sister ships *Silver Cloud* and *Silver Wind* were built in the mid-1990s, just in time to get in on must-have ship fashions such as balconies. *Silver Cloud* had a major makeover in 2009 (which sister *Silver Wind* got in late 2008), which created a larger spa and gym, a new observation lounge, and eight new suites, in addition to renovating all of the suite bathrooms and sprucing up cabins, public rooms, and corridors to bring their decor in line with Silversea's newest ship, *Silver Spirit.*

CABINS   Like their fleetmates, *Silver Wind* and *Silver Cloud* are all-suite ships, with balconies on more than three-quarters of the staterooms. All standard 240-square-foot suites have sitting areas, roomy walk-in closets, bathtubs, vanities, new flatscreen TVs and DVD players, stocked minibars, Ferragamo or Bulgari toiletries, plush mattresses and bedding, as well as new furniture, carpeting, drapes, and bathroom fixtures and finishings. The top of the lot, the 1,314-square-foot Grand Suites, have two bedrooms, two living rooms, three televisions, two bathrooms, and a full-size Jacuzzi tub. Color schemes revolve around creamy beige fabrics and golden brown wood. *Silver Cloud* has swirled peachy-gray marble that covers bathrooms from head to toe, and though indulgent enough, the bathrooms on these ships don't hold a flame to the larger, simply decadent loos on the line's newer fleetmates. Goose-down pillows ensure a good night's rest. A face-lift in May 2009 saw the addition of four new Medallion suites on Deck 8 and four new suites on Deck 7. The *Silver Wind* face-lift saw the addition of four new Medallion suites on Deck 8, and four new suites on Deck 7.

PUBLIC AREAS   Public areas inside and out are spacious and open. High tea is served by day in the windowed Panorama Lounge, which at night hosts piano entertainment. Magic and other acts are performed in the attractive two-story show lounge, and, on most nights, a dance band plays oldies or a DJ spins in the intimate and dimly lit adjacent bar. There's a small casino, too, plus boutiques where you can spend your winnings, including an H. Stern fine jewelry shop with the requisite gold-and-diamond-studded watches.

DINING OPTIONS   The formal, open-seating dining room, called the Restaurant, is delicately decorated in pale pink and gold, and elegant candlelit tables are set with heavy crystal glasses, chunky Christofle silverware, and doily-covered silver show plates. The indoor/outdoor La Terrazza cafe, where buffet-style breakfast and lunch are served, is transformed into a nightly spot for more casual evening dining, featuring a scrumptious Italian menu.

POOL, FITNESS, SPA & SPORTS FACILITIES   The *Silver Cloud* oceanview gym occupies a roomy space by itself on Deck 9 (where an observation lounge used to be) on the far-forward part of the deck (oddly, it's not attached to the ship's interior, so one must go out on deck to enter). On *Silver Wind,* a new, two-floor glass elevator connects Decks 8 and 9; there is an observation lounge at the bow of Deck 9, plus just behind it is a new spa with five treatment rooms, a salon, and fitness center (similar to the layout on *Shadow* and *Whisper*). Both ships have a pool and two hot tubs.

8

Small Ships, Sailing Ships & Adventure Cruises

Aside from the fact that they both sail in water, mainstream cruise ships and the small ships in this chapter have hardly anything in common. Whereas big ships allow you to see a region while immersed in a resortlike onboard atmosphere, small ships allow you to see it from the waterline, without distraction from anything that's not an inherent part of the locale—no glitzy interiors, no big shows or loud music, no casinos, no spas, and no crowds either, as the majority of these ships carry fewer than 100 passengers. Whether sailing through Alaska's coastal wilderness, along the Erie Canal or the Columbia River, or between tiny islands in the Caribbean or the Sea of Cortez, you're part of a destination from the minute you wake up until the minute you fall asleep, and for the most part, you're left alone to form your own opinions.

Of the lines reviewed in this chapter, most operate small, motorized **coastal and river cruisers** that are like floating B&Bs, with a main public lounge, a dining room, and little else besides cabins and open decks. A few of these lines also operate slightly larger ships with deep drafts that are suitable for longer open-sea cruises. Five of the lines we review—Star Clippers, Windstar, Sea Cloud, Island Windjammers, and the independently owned Maine Windjammers—operate honest-to-God **sailing ships,** the first three with a yachtlike vibe (luxury-yacht-like in the case of Sea Cloud, and fairly luxe for Windstar), the latter two more like summer camp for adults.

Beyond these physical distinctions, the experience provided by all these lines breaks down into two main subcategories: **soft-adventure cruises,** which are generally arranged around activities like hiking, kayaking, tide-pooling, and snorkeling, plus visits to out-of-the-way ports; and **port-to-port cruises,** which mix days in port with days spent visiting great natural sites.

We absolutely love the small-ship experience—in fact, it's our favorite way to sail— but there are a few caveats: (1) **Stay away if you're not a self-starter,** since these ships have few or no organized activities; (2) **stay away if you're weak in the stomach,** as

---

The Scoop on Small-Ship Tonnage

When reading the reviews in this chapter, bear in mind that small-ship lines often measure their ships' **gross register tonnage** or GRTs (a measure of internal space, not actual weight) differently than the large lines do. There's not even a definite standard within the small-ship market, so to compare ship sizes it's best to just look at the number of passengers aboard. Also note that where GRTs measures are nonstandard, **passenger/space measurements** are impossible to calculate accurately.

Frommer's Ratings at a Glance: The Small-Ship Lines

1 = poor   2 = fair   3 = good   4 = excellent   5 = outstanding

	Enjoyment Factor	Dining	Activities	Children's Program	Entertainment	Service	Worth the Money
American Cruise Lines	4	4	2	N/A	3	4	4
American Safari Cruises	5	4	4	N/A	2	5	4
Blount Small Ship Adventures	4	3	4	N/A	2	3	3
Cruise West	4	3	4	N/A	2	4	4
Island Windjammers	5	4	3	N/A	2	4	5
Lindblad Expeditions	5	3	5	N/A	3	4	4
Maine Windjammers*	5	3	3	N/A	2	3	5
Sea Cloud Cruises	5	5	3	N/A	3	5	4
Star Clippers	5	4	4	N/A	3	4	5
Windstar	5	4	3	N/A	3	5	5

Note: Cruise lines have been graded on a curve that compares them only with the other lines in the Small Ships, Sailing Ships & Adventure Cruises category. See chapter 5 for the ratings methodology. None of the lines and vessels in this chapter offers a children's program.

* Because the Maine schooners are all owner-operated, programs vary significantly. These ratings should be taken only as a general indication of fleetwide quality.

these ships tend to pitch and roll more in rough seas than the megaships do; (3) **families beware**—these are not ships for kids; (4) **wheelchair users beware, too,** as only the four American Cruise Lines ships and Cruise West's *Spirit of '98* and *Spirit of Oceanus* are fully or even partially accessible; and (5) **stay away if you're looking for a bargain**—'cause with only a few exceptions (such as the Island and Maine Windjammers), small-ship cruises are among the more expensive cruise options—though on the plus side, the onboard costs of these trips tend to be less, and sometimes include excursions.

A NOTE ON LINE/SHIP RATINGS   Because the small-ship experience is so completely different from the megaship experience, we've had to adjust our ratings. For instance, because all but a tiny fraction of these ships have just one dining room for all meals, we can't judge them by the same standard we use for ships with 5 or 10 different restaurants. So, we've set the default **Dining Options** rating for these ships at 3, or "good," with points deducted if a restaurant is particularly uncomfortable or ugly, and points added for any options above and beyond. Similarly, we've changed the "Gym, Spa & Sports Facilities" rating to **Adventure & Fitness Options** to reflect the fact that on small ships the focus is on what's outside, not inside. Options covered in this category might include kayaks, trips by inflatable launch, bow-landing capability, and frequent hiking, tide-pooling, and/or snorkeling trips.

DRESS CODES   The word is *casual*. Depending on the region sailed, polo shirts, khakis or shorts, and a fleece pullover and Gore-Tex shell will pretty much take care of you all week. On warm-weather cruises, consider bringing a pair of aqua-socks or rubber sandals, as you may be going ashore in rubber landing craft and have to step out into the surf.

1 American Cruise Lines

741 Boston Post Rd., Ste. 200, Guilford, CT 06437. ℭ **800/814-6880**. www.americancruiselines.com.

THE LINE IN A NUTSHELL   Part cruise, part historical tour, part Rotary Club meeting, Connecticut-based American Cruise Lines operates five U.S.-flagged vessels that offer a congenial ambience, an emphasis on American history and culture, and (a rarity for small ships) some cabins with balconies. Life on board is comfortable, reserved, and so hassle-free that many passengers don't even lock their cabin doors. If you want to bring a guest on board for dinner one night when in port, simply tell the cruise director. If you decide not to go on a shore excursion you signed up for, don't worry: If you don't show up, you don't get billed. **Sails to:** eastern U.S. coastal cruises from Maine to Florida, Pacific Northwest.

THE EXPERIENCE   Take some great East Coast destinations, throw in some very comfortable small ships, add a few enrichment lectures and complimentary cocktails and a boatload of uniformly older passengers, and you end up with American Cruise Lines. Operating along the Eastern seaboard and in the Pacific Northwest, the company's five ships are designed to poke into the smallest and most scenic ports, docking among sailboats at marinas or within a few blocks of museums, shops, and historic districts. Itineraries are port-intensive, with the ship underway for only a few hours in the morning or afternoon, usually arriving at the evening's port before dinnertime and spending the night at dock.

While the company is neither a luxury cruise line nor an adventure cruise line, it falls into a pleasant niche that succeeds in large part because of its ships. The line's four East Coast vessels are far younger and roomier than the competition's, boasting the largest cabins in the small-ship market (save for those aboard Cruise West's *Spirit of Oceanus*), many of which have balconies. This appeals to passengers who want the comforts of a shrunken cruise ship and will gladly pay for the extra space. The line's West Coast ship, *Queen of the West,* is an old-fashioned paddle-wheeler. On all vessels, east and west, guest lecturers provide some enrichment, helping passengers learn about their destination, and chefs from the Culinary Institute of America prepare good regional selections.

Pros

- **America the beautiful:** From Florida's Okeechobee Swamp to Maine's rocky coast and out to Oregon's Columbia Gorge, ACL ships sail wonderful coastal and river itineraries off limits to larger, foreign-flagged ships, and they spend every night in port.
- **Roomy rooms with a view:** Cabins in the line's East Coast ships are the largest by far in the small-ship category, and almost half of them feature balconies—a first for this type of coastal ship.
- **Have a drink:** The company tries for an upscale feel, and complimentary drinks go a long way in making the cruise seem a bit more luxurious.
- **Totally smoke-free:** ACL is the only line in this book that's 100% smoke-free on all of its ships. Smoking is prohibited everywhere inside and even on all outside decks.

- **Hassles? Not here:** ACL works hard to keep things straightforward, relaxed, and sensible, even to the point of letting passengers invite friends on board for dinner. Everything that seems like it should be simple at other companies, but isn't, is here.

Cons

- **A bit too staid:** In the end, the ships can be just a little too quiet.
- **Limited activities:** While the ships are comfortable, there isn't much choice in activities.

AMERICAN CRUISE LINES: HASSLE-FREE AMERICANA

If only every company got a second chance. Originally formed in the late 1970s, American Cruise Lines operated more or less successfully until new ownership drove it into the ground in the late 1980s. Jump forward to 2000, and the original owner decides to jump back into the business. Rather than reinventing the wheel, he uses the same name, the same basic ship design, similar itineraries, and even the same logo. This time around, the formula seems to be working well and the company has grown quickly. Since its reincarnation, it's launched four ships built right in its own shipyard on the Chesapeake Bay. In 2009, it added a fifth vessel to its fleet by purchasing the paddle-wheeler *Queen of the West* from defunct Majestic America Line, and at press time was preparing to sail her on nearly year-round cruises on the Pacific Northwest's Columbia and Snake rivers.

For several years, ACL has also been in the process of launching a sister company called **Pearl Seas Cruises,** dedicated to oceangoing itineraries in the Caribbean, Nova Scotia, and Newfoundland. However, long delays in construction of its first ship, the 210-passenger *Pearl Mist,* have repeatedly pushed back the line's debut. At this point, we're unwilling to speculate as to when (or whether) the line will begin operations.

PASSENGER PROFILE

Make no mistake about it: American Cruise Line passengers are older, and then some. The company's cozy, low-impact, American style of cruising suits them perfectly, and the fact that each ACL ship has an elevator linking all the decks (a rarity in the small-ship world) is a big draw. Hailing from all over the country, passengers generally appreciate changing for cocktail hour, with about half the men wearing a jacket and/or tie. They are also the types who readily wear the provided name tags for the entire week and don't mind visiting four historic homes in one cruise.

In port, slightly less than half of them tend to explore the towns independently, combing antiques shops or just strolling along Main Street. Well educated and usually comfortably heeled, they are eager to learn about the region and enthusiastically

Compared with the other small-ship lines, here's how ACL rates:

	Poor	Fair	Good	Excellent	Outstanding
Enjoyment Factor				✓	
Dining				✓	
Activities		✓			
Children's Program	N/A				
Entertainment			✓		
Service				✓	
Worth the Money				✓	

attend the nightly lecture. With diverse cruising backgrounds (from luxe Seabourn to mainstream Princess), they do not necessarily expect five-star service, but they do want comfy, spacious cabins along with the conveniences and camaraderie of a small ship. A very high percentage consists of repeaters, who collect the line's various itineraries like game pieces.

DINING

On the line's four East Coast ships, a pleasant but uninspiring dining room is situated on the lowest deck all the way at the stern, surrounded on three sides by windows that afford a good view of the passing scenery. On *Queen of the West,* the single dining room is on the lowest passenger deck, near the waterline.

The usually straightforward, unfancy meals can be surprisingly good. **Seafood** frequently appears on the menu, including local specialties like Maryland crab cakes on Chesapeake Bay cruises or lobster in Maine, along with seasonal flavors such as butternut squash or apple pie. In order to minimize waste, waiters tell you at breakfast what's for lunch and dinner, and you choose what you're going to eat for the rest of the day—although at the last minute, plenty of passengers change their minds. A choice of two entrees is available nightly, along with three appetizers.

Lunch options might include a ham sandwich on a baguette with apples and melted brie or pork loin with goat cheese and onion. While there is no official vegetarian choice, tasty salads often appear on the menu, and special requests can always be accommodated if you let the line know in advance.

SNACKS & EXTRAS Fresh-baked cookies appear at 10am, and everyone gathers in the main lounge at 5:30pm for complimentary drinks at the daily **cocktail hour.** By 9pm, just as the lecture is finishing, trays of **root beer floats and ice-cream sundaes** appear, no matter that it's only 2 hours after dinner.

Aboard *Queen of the West,* continental breakfast, casual lunch fare, and snacks are available in the Calliope Bar & Grill, a bright, indoor/outdoor space that resembles an old-time ice-cream parlor.

The ships do not provide room service.

ACTIVITIES

Forget art auctions or poolside games; you won't even find low-impact activities such as dance lessons aboard these sedate ships. In the main lounge, passengers might read or play a quiet board game, and you're almost sure to find at least one game of bridge in the two smaller lounges. Most passengers seem content to just sit on deck and chat. **Guest lecturers** speak most evenings, and spend days pointing out passing sights. On one night, a local musician might be brought on board for a concert, or bingo could be slotted in place of the nightly lecture. Besides an occasional documentary film shown in the lounge, a tour of the ship's bridge, or a once-per-week teatime, there really aren't any other organized activities, though some summer itineraries may feature **kite flying** from the stern on one afternoon. In port, about half the passengers choose the reasonably priced **shore excursions,** which are usually bus tours to museums, areas of natural beauty, or historic homes. Active excursions simply aren't offered, which is just fine for this crowd.

CHILDREN'S PROGRAM

This is a cruise line for older adults, so children are extremely rare. A few families may sail on the summer New England itineraries, but the ships have no kids' programs or activities.

ENTERTAINMENT

Entertainment is limited to nightly lectures, the occasional entertainer brought aboard for an evening to sing regional songs, and a satellite TV set up in the corner of the main lounge, tuned to football. This is a line for self-starters.

SERVICE

Because of the Passenger Vessel Services Act (which requires ships to be U.S.-flagged and U.S.-staffed if they want to sail all-U.S. itineraries), ACL's crews are all fresh-faced, college-age American kids who've decided to try an unusual summer job. Mostly enthusiastic and genuine, they try hard and are eager to please, even if the finer points of service don't come naturally: Being addressed by your waiter as "Sweetie" every once in awhile only adds to the charm. A maitre d' keeps a watchful eye over the restaurant operations to make sure his staff is on the right track.

Tipping can be charged to your onboard account, with a relatively steep recommended amount of $17.85 per person, per day.

American Glory • American Spirit • American Star • Independence (Preview)

American Spirit *(photo: ACL)*

The Verdict

Simple but comfortable, these ships were built to nestle into small coves and ports along the East Coast, and their large cabins, numerous balconies, and multiple lounges have really raised the standard for the U.S. coastal fleet.

Specifications

Typical Per Diems: $615+

Size (in tons)		Crew	
Glory	86*	*Glory*	18
Spirit/Star	97*	*Spirit/Star*	26
Independence	1,200	*Independence*	27
Passengers (double occ.)		Passenger/Crew Ratio	
Glory	49	*Glory*	2.7 to 1
Spirit/Star	100	*Spirit/Star/Independence*	3.8 to 1
Independence	102	Year Launched	
Passenger/Space Ratio	N/A*	*American Glory*	2002
Total Cabins/Veranda Cabins		*American Spirit*	2005
Glory	27/14	*American Star*	2007
Spirit/Star	48/27	*Independence*	2010
Independence	52/40	Last Major Refurbishment	N/A

See note on p. 317 regarding small-ship tonnage and passenger/space measurements.

Frommer's Ratings (Scale of 1–5)   ★★★½

Cabin Comfort & Amenities	5	Dining Options	3
Appearance & Upkeep	4	Adventure & Fitness Options	2
Public Comfort/Space	4	Children's Facilities	N/A
Decor	3	Enjoyment Factor	4

Sailing Regions, Seasons & Home Ports

Glory	**Great Rivers of Florida,** from Jacksonville, FL (winter, spring). **U.S. South & Atlantic Islands,** from Charleston and Jacksonville, FL (spring). **Chesapeake Bay,** from Baltimore (spring, summer, fall). **New England Islands,** from Providence, RI (summer). **Grand New England,** from Providence and Bangor, ME (summer). **Hudson River,** from New York (fall).
Independence	**U.S. South & Atlantic Islands,** from Charleston and Jacksonville, FL (spring, fall, winter). **Chesapeake Bay,** from Baltimore (spring, fall). **New England Islands,** from Providence, RI (spring). **Maine Coast,** from Portland (summer). **Hudson River,** from New York (fall).
Spirit	**U.S. South & Atlantic Islands,** from Charleston and Jacksonville, FL (winter, spring). **Philadelphia & the Potomac,** from Philadelphia and Washington, D.C. (spring). **Maine Coast,** from Portland (summer). **Chesapeake Bay,** from Baltimore (summer, fall).
Star	**U.S. South & Atlantic Islands,** from Charleston and Jacksonville, FL (winter, spring). **Chesapeake Bay,** from Baltimore (summer, fall). **New England Islands,** from Providence, RI (summer). **Hudson River,** from New York (fall).

American Cruise Lines' four East Coast vessels were all built at the line's own shipyard in Salisbury, Maryland. While they're a bit boxy on the outside, they're refreshingly large and comfortable inside, with a decor that's simple and pleasant, if a bit dull. Numerous floor-to-ceiling windows surround the main lounge, and everywhere there are large windows for viewing the passing scenery. Except for their varying sizes (the older *Glory* is about half the size of the still-small *Spirit, Star,* and *Independence*), the ships are virtually identical, right down to the carpet patterns and furniture.

The ships' shallow drafts allow passage up small rivers straight into the heart of town, where port facilities might look like they were designed for a kayak rather than a cruise ship—in one port, we actually sent the ship's mooring lines to a tree in a park rather than to the usual iron bollards. This attitude of keeping things simple extends on board as well. Forget electronic ID cards to get you on or off the ship; here, the crew just recognizes everyone. Rather than waiting for scheduled sailing times, the ships often just sail when everyone is back aboard. A small boat hung from the stern can be used to tender passengers ashore in the very rare ports where the ship doesn't dock. It's also occasionally used for bird-watching excursions.

Because the itineraries always hug the coast, there are rarely any waves or motion to speak of, so these cruises are popular with those who worry about seasickness. The unstabilized *Glory, Spirit,* and *Star* still bounce around when they get hit with any waves, but the newest vessel, *Independence,* corrects that problem with the addition of Rolls-Royce stabilizers, making the ship able to sail waters the other ships can't, at least comfortably. Since *Independence* was due to be introduced in summer 2010, after this book goes to press, all details in this review describe *Glory, Spirit,* and *Star* unless otherwise noted.

CABINS   If there is one thing that really differentiates American Cruise Lines from other coastal competitors, it's the cabins. Rather than the closet-size boxes usually found on similar-size American ships, these cabins average 225 square feet—bigger than most standard megaship cabins, and nearly twice the size of those of the main regional competitor, Blount Small Ship Adventures. Cabins are comfortable, clean, and pleasant—not to mention bright, thanks to large picture windows that actually slide open and to the narrow but serviceable balconies (you get one or the other). As in the public areas, though, their decor isn't exactly stylish. Each cabin comes with a large writing desk, decent storage space, bedside tables, a hair dryer, and a satellite TV that gets about 20 channels. Bathrooms are very roomy, with excellent water pressure. Cabins on the older *Glory* are a touch smaller than those on *Spirit, Star,* and *Independence,* especially on the forward end of the lowest deck, where the curvature of the bow reduces square footage.

Each ship has several cabins for solo passengers (a real rarity these days) as well as at least one that's wheelchair accessible. Each ship also has an elevator, giving wheelchair-using passengers access to the entire ship.

PUBLIC AREAS Three public lounges and plenty of open deck space give passengers a good amount of elbowroom. The main lounge is located forward, directly underneath the bridge, and has tall windows on three sides, which provide great views. As the spot for the nightly cocktail hour and the evening lecture, it is the ship's social hub and a good place for board games or chatting with shipmates during the day. The two smaller, cabin-size lounges by the central stairwell allow smaller groups the opportunity to mingle before dinner or play bridge at any time without being bothered by others. All three lounges are decorated in the same simple, muted colors and functional, unpretentious furniture, all of it attractive without being exciting. Just forward of the main lounge is a small deck with a few chairs and tables, allowing you to imbibe outdoors while watching the sunset.

The top deck of each ship is covered in an AstroTurf–like material and there are sports awnings, plastic-webbed sun lounges, and tables and chairs. On warm, sunny days, this deck is a great spot for reading and chatting, with the shoreline often within view.

DINING OPTIONS Each ship's single dining room is situated on the lowest deck all the way at the stern, with windows on three sides. Breakfast usually runs from 7:30 to 9am, preceded by early-risers' coffee and muffins set out in the main lounge at 6:30am. Lunch is timed to start shortly after the shore excursion returns, usually around 12:30pm. A 5:30pm cocktail hour precedes the 6:30pm dinner.

ADVENTURE & FITNESS OPTIONS Exercise equipment is limited to a single exercise bike and a Stairmaster. Most passengers get their exercise by going ashore independently and walking through the towns.

Queen of the West

The Verdict

Currently the only old-style paddle-wheeler with overnight cruises in the United States, *Queen of the West* combines the charm and history of the classic river vessels with some of the comforts and amenities of a newer ship.

Queen of the West *(photo: American Cruise Lines)*

Specifications   Typical Per Diems: $615+

Size (in tons)	1,308	Crew	37
Passengers (double occ.)	120	Passenger/Crew Ratio	2.7 to 1
Passenger/Space Ratio	9.6	Year Launched	1995
Total Cabins/Veranda Cabins	65/40	Last Major Upgrade	2010

Frommer's Ratings (Scale of 1–5)   ★★★★

Cabin Comfort & Amenities	4	Dining Options	4
Appearance & Upkeep	4	Adventure & Fitness Options	3
Public Comfort/Space	4	Children's Facilities	2
Decor	5	Enjoyment Factor	5

Sailing Regions, Seasons & Home Ports

Queen of the West	Columbia & Snake Rivers, from Portland, OR, and Clarkston, WA (spring, summer, fall).

Treading the line between modern and old-fashioned, *Queen of the West* feels authentically antique while being more spacious than you may think when you see it from shore. Its public rooms evoke a bygone era, and the long bow-landing ramp allows the vessel to cozy up to shore so passengers can walk easily on and off, even in secluded spots that lack docking facilities.

Built for American West Steamboat Company in 1995, the vessel was taken over by now-defunct Majestic America Line as part of its scheme to rule the North American river-cruise market. Instead, it collapsed spectacularly just a few years later, leaving most of its fleet in limbo and, among other things, depriving the United States of any overnight cruise presence on its greatest river, the Mississippi. *Queen of the West,* always intended for sailing the Pacific Northwest, was scooped up in 2009 by American Cruise Lines as part of its gradual expansion. At press time, the vessel was scheduled to be refurbished, reconfigured to have fewer (and larger) cabins, and launched in August 2010 on spring, summer, and fall cruises on the Columbia and Snake rivers. All details in this review are based on the vessel's time in service with American West and Majestic America, plus what's known about American Cruise Lines' plans for her.

CABINS   At 155 to 390 square feet, *Queen of the West*'s cabins are smaller than the extralarge digs on American Cruise Lines' East Coast ships, though the vast majority of them have private balconies. Each is outfitted with a large picture window, satellite TV with DVD player, and a writing desk, and decor runs to "cozy bedroom" aesthetic, with dark-wood tones, flowery bedspreads, and lace curtains. All cabins open onto interior public corridors, as on larger cruise ships.

Two cabins are wheelchair accessible.

PUBLIC AREAS   In keeping with the ship's 19th-century aesthetic, *Queen of the West*'s public areas are done up in pressed-metal ceilings, chandeliers, balloon-back chairs, and other period touches. Our favorite room is definitely the Paddlewheel Lounge, where you can sip a cocktail to the thrum of the huge propulsion wheel, visible through the room-wide window at the back. Snacks and drinks are served here before dinner, and there's entertainment at night. The vessel also has an old-fashioned, one-level show lounge with a dance floor and a small bandstand/stage.

DINING OPTIONS Breakfast, lunch, and dinner are all served in the ship's main dining room.

ADVENTURE & FITNESS OPTIONS None. Most passengers get their exercise by going ashore and walking the port towns.

2 Mini-Review: American Safari Cruises

3826 18th Ave. W., Seattle, WA 98119. ℂ **888/862-8881.** Fax 206/283-9322. www.AmericanSafariCruises.com.

THE LINE IN A NUTSHELL American Safari Cruises offers one of the most luxurious and yet adventurous experiences in the small-ship market—and also one of the most expensive. **Sails to:** Alaska and British Columbia, Sea of Cortez/Baja, U.S./Canada coastal/river cruises, Hawaii.

THE EXPERIENCE Unlike the competition's mostly basic vessels, American Safari's three ships—12-passenger *Safari Spirit* ✹✹✹✹, 22-passenger *Safari Quest* ✹✹✹✹, and 36-passenger *Safari Explorer* ✹✹✹✹—are honest-to-God yachts that bathe passengers in plush comfort, with homey lounges, hot tubs, and large cabins. Everything except gratuities is included in the pricey base price, including alcoholic beverages and shore and water activities. The always-casual onboard vibe is in keeping with mostly middle-aged passengers who tend to be wealthy granola types looking to bond with nature without sacrificing luxury. Some charter an entire vessel for a family reunion. Days might be spent kayaking in the wilderness (kayaks and inflatable launches are carried on board), fishing right off the side of the yachts, and meeting families living in remote pockets to exchange stories and buy their fresh sea catch. Expedition leaders accompany passengers on off-vessel exploration, and in Alaska, you might take out a Zodiac boat or kayak to investigate shoreline black bears or river otters, or to navigate fjords packed with ice floes and lolling seals. Expeditions include trips to cannery towns with boardwalks, Tlingit villages, and tiny hamlets.

Cabins are comfortable and have TV/DVDs. The newer *Explorer* and the *Spirit* have the largest cabins and are considered the most luxurious of the fleet. The best accommodations on the *Spirit* are the Admiral's Cabins and the Commodore Suites on the *Explorer,* all of which have large picture windows, a small sitting area, plus other features such as a cedar-lined sauna, bathrobes, slippers, memory-foam mattresses, heated tile bathroom floors, and iPod docking stations. Some have a small step-out balcony with a sliding glass door (two cabins have balconies on *Spirit* and *Explorer,* and four cabins on *Quest*). The main lounge is the social center of each ship, a place for guests to relax, listen to an informal lecture by the ship's naturalist, play a game of cards or Scrabble, or watch a movie from the ship's library on the big-screen TV. There's a hot tub on deck and a couple of fitness machines for those who want to work

Sailing Regions, Seasons & Home Ports

Safari Explorer	**Columbia/Snake Rivers,** from Portland, OR, and Lewiston, ID (spring). **Alaska,** from Juneau (summer). **Hawaii,** from Maui & the Big Island (fall, winter, spring).
Safari Quest	**Alaska,** from Juneau (summer). **Columbia/Snake Rivers,** from Portland, OR, and Lewiston, ID (fall).
Safari Spirit	**Alaska,** from Juneau (summer). **Pacific Northwest/British Columbia,** from Friday Harbor, WA (fall). **Baja/Sea of Cortez,** from La Paz (winter & spring).

out. For dining, there's a choice of entrees and all meals are served family-style on a burnished mahogany table in a casual room on *Spirit,* and at a cluster of tables on *Quest* and *Explorer,* usually when the ship is at anchor.

American Safari's typical per diems are $950+.

3 Mini-Review: Blount Small Ship Adventures (formerly ACCL)

461 Water St., Warren, RI 02885. ℂ **800/556-7450** or 401/247-0955. Fax 401/247-2350. www.accl-smallships.com.

THE LINE IN A NUTSHELL   A family-owned New England line, Blount Small Ship Adventures (formerly American Canadian Caribbean Line/ACCL) operates tiny, no-frills ships that attract a well-traveled, extremely casual, and down-to-earth older crowd. It's a "what you see is what you get" experience: friendly, homespun, and visiting places few other ships do. For 2011, Blount will sail the Mississippi River system for the first time, becoming one of only two lines (along with Cruise West) to operate "sleep aboard" overnight cruise vessels in the region. **Sails to:** U.S./Canada river/coastal cruises, Intracoastal Waterway, Caribbean, Central America.

THE EXPERIENCE   The line began as ACCL in 1966 when late Rhode Island shipbuilder Luther Blount realized there was a demand for small-ship sailing on the rivers, canals, and coasts of New England and Canada. Over the years, his company's vessels have gone well beyond their regional home. Today, many of the line's almost universally older passengers (average age around 72) have sailed with the line before, and appreciate its casualness, its lack of glitz and gimmicks, its early-to-bed lifestyle, and its "just us folks" features such as a BYOB policy. (It's a real money saver for passengers, who can stock up in port and keep their bottles in the bar area, labeled with their cabin number. Tonic and soda are free.)

Built in 1997 and 1998, the line's three vessels—the 100-passenger twins **Grande Caribe** ✴✴✴ and **Grande Mariner** ✴✴✴ and the older, 84-passenger **Niagara Prince** ✴✴✴—are as basic as cruise ships come, with tiny, spartan cabins; no-fuss decor; minuscule head-style cabin bathrooms; and only two public rooms (a lounge and a dining room). But no one expects luxury on these cruises. Instead, Blount cruises are all about the real life of the regions they visit, with most activities oriented toward exploring ports and natural areas. Some 85% to 90% of cruises sail in domestic waters, concentrating on visits to historically rich, colonial ports and natural areas that are rich with plants and wildlife. These ships can go where few others can because of innovative exploratory features built into them: a shallow draft and retractable wheelhouse, which allow them to sail through shallow canals and under low bridges; bow ramps that enable them to pull right up to pristine, dockless beaches; and a platform in the stern for swimming and launching the ships' glass-bottom boats.

Onboard activities and entertainment are usually limited to occasional informal lectures, a few printed quizzes, cooking demonstrations, card playing, and movies from the ship's video collection. Meals are well prepared and all-American, but limited and not terribly inspiring. The daily menu, with selections for all three meals, is posted every morning on the blackboard in the dining room. There's only one entree per meal, so anyone wanting an alternative must notify the kitchen before 10am. Owing to the average passenger age, the ship line's cooks try to keep things low in salt and fat. Service by the staff of young Americans (many from Blount's home state of Rhode Island) is casual and friendly.

These ships won't appeal to the vast majority of young couples, singles, honeymooners, and families. Children under age 14 are prohibited, and the line offers no children's facilities or activities, nor any particularly active activities. Very tall people should also stay away, as ceilings on all Blount ships are set at not much more than 6 feet 4 inches.

Blount is one of the less expensive of the small-ship lines, with typical per diems at $290–$305.

Sailing Regions, Seasons & Home Ports

Grande Caribe	**Central America,** from Belize City (winter). **Antebellum South,** from Charleston & Jacksonville, FL (spring). **Chesapeake Bay,** from Baltimore (summer). **Maine Coast,** from Portland (summer). **New England Islands,** from Warren, RI (summer). **Erie Canal/Saguenay River,** from New York & Montreal (fall).
Grande Mariner	**Caribbean,** from St. Thomas, St. Maarten & Caicos Nassau (winter). **Antebellum South,** from Jacksonville, FL (spring). **Great Lakes,** from Chicago, Toronto, New York & Warren, RI (spring, summer). **Erie Canal/Saguenay River,** from New York & Montreal (fall).
Niagara Prince	**Mississippi River System,** from New Orleans, Chattanooga, Nashville & Chicago (spring, summer). **Great Lakes,** from Chicago (summer, fall). **Lake Champlain,** from New York & Burlington, VT (fall).

4 Cruise West

2301 5th Ave., Ste. 401, Seattle, WA 98121. ⓒ 888/851-8133 or 206/441-8687. Fax 206/441-4757. www.cruise west.com.

THE LINE IN A NUTSHELL   Family-owned Cruise West has been the preeminent small-ship line in Alaska for decades, but over the past decade it's also branched out to more far-flung destinations. Most of its itineraries are port-to-port and geared to older, well-traveled, intellectually curious passengers. It also offers a handful of more expeditionary sailings on the deep-water *Spirit of Oceanus,* which in 2010 sailed a nearly yearlong world cruise. **Sails to:** Alaska, Central America/Caribbean, Sea of Cortez/Baja, U.S./Canada river/coastal cruises (plus South Pacific, East Indies, Asia, Europe, Galapagos, Antarctica, world cruise).

THE EXPERIENCE   Like all small ships, Cruise West's nine vessels can navigate tight waterways, visit tiny ports, and scoot up close to shore for wildlife-watching. The majority of the cruises are casual, relaxed, port-to-port trips in which passengers watch nature from the deck rather than trekking out into it. On most cruises, a quick excursion by inflatable launch is as active as it gets. At sea, the lack of organized activities leaves you free to scan for wildlife, peruse the natural sights, talk to the other guests, or read. In port—whether one of the large, popular ports or a less visited one—the line provides a good slate of shore excursions oriented mostly to nature and history.

Cruise West also has some more outdoors-oriented and exploratory cruises, and has lately jumped whole hog into far-flung international voyages, operating cruises in the South Pacific and Asia and (in 2010) sailing one of the most amazing world cruises ever, an 11-month circumnavigation aboard *Spirit of Oceanus.* Just as this book was going to press, we also learned that CW is going to be offering cruises on the **Mississippi River** system beginning in spring 2011.

Pros

- **The staff:** The line's friendly, enthusiastic staffs are a big plus, making guests feel right at home.
- **Comfort and old-fashioned style:** Two of the line's ships—the oceangoing *Spirit of Oceanus* and the old-fashioned coastal steamer *Spirit of '98*—have snazzier surroundings than most of their small-ship competitors.

Cons

- **Limited adventure:** Most Cruise West trips are geared to older passengers, so don't book if you're looking for an active, adventurous cruise.

CRUISE WEST: ALASKA'S SMALL-SHIP LEADER & THEN SOME

Cruise West is the legacy of Chuck West, a man who arrived in Alaska after serving as a pilot in World War II, liked what he saw, and decided to share it with others. After offering the first flightseeing tours above the Arctic Circle, he went on to found Alaska's first hotel chain and first motorcoach sightseeing line. In the mid-1980s, he started experimenting with cruises, and the rest is history. Chuck West died in October 2005, but his company—now the largest small-ship line in America—is still run by his son Dick, and it's still growing: In 2006, Cruise West acquired two U.S.-flagged coastal ships from now-defunct Clipper Cruise Line, allowing it to expand its reach to the U.S. East Coast, the Great Lakes, and the Caribbean. And between 2007 and 2010, it expanded to the far reaches of the world, with itineraries in Antarctica, the Galapagos, Europe, and Asia. These itineraries are generally offered aboard *Spirit of Oceanus* and a number of chartered vessels. The line is also trying to improve its onboard program, introducing an improved onboard enrichment program, a new food-and-wine program, and a new category of cabins with eco-friendly amenities.

PASSENGER PROFILE

Passengers with Cruise West tend to be in the higher end of the 50-to-75-plus age demographic, financially stable, well educated, and intellectually curious. Many have sailed with the mainstream lines, but come to Cruise West because they want a more relaxed, small-scale, dress-down atmosphere. On recent cruises, our fellow passengers have included vacationing State Department employees, several teachers, a retired bank president, a magazine art director, and a pair of behavioral psychologists. On one cruise a few years back, the passenger list included a group of 30-odd Yale University alumni, including one 80-something lady from New Haven who was set on doing every active shore excursion she could—hiking, kayaking, the lot. Ditto for a 40-ish

Compared with the other small-ship lines, here's how Cruise West rates:

	Poor	Fair	Good	Excellent	Outstanding
Enjoyment Factor				✓	
Dining			✓		
Activities				✓	
Children's Program	N/A				
Entertainment		✓			
Service				✓	
Worth the Money				✓	

couple from Pennsylvania on a 2003 Alaska cruise, who were hell-bent on sampling the delicacy known as halibut cheeks.

DINING

Breakfast, lunch, and dinner are served at set times at one unassigned seating. An early-riser's buffet is set out in the lounge before the set breakfast time, but if you're a late riser, you'll miss breakfast entirely, as no room service is available. At all meals, the fare is home-style American—not overly fancy, but varied enough. Chefs make a point of stocking up on fresh seafood while in port. **Vegetarian options** aren't particularly notable, but are offered at every meal, as are **heart-healthy entrees** and **staple favorites** such as steak, chicken, and fish. With advance notice, the galley can accommodate other special diets (kosher, low-salt, low-fat). Aboard all ships, a buffet-style lunch and/or dinner may be served on the top deck in good weather. *Spirit of Oceanus* has a buffet with outdoor seating, where breakfast and lunch are served daily.

A new dining program introduced in 2009 focuses on the synergy between food and wine. All Cruise West ships now highlight Pacific Northwest cuisine and pair menu items with bottles selected by line chairman Dick West. Additionally, in affiliation with the U.S. Sommelier Association, onboard servers participate in a certificate course to ensure improved service. As an added plus, alfresco dining is enjoyed aboard *Spirit of Oceanus, Spirit of Yorktown, Spirit of Endeavour,* and *Spirit of '98,* weather permitting. Menu items include fresh grilled favorites, salads, and a carving or taco bar.

SNACKS & EXTRAS   A late-afternoon snack is provided every day to tide passengers over until dinner, and the chef will occasionally whip up a batch of cookies. Pretzels, nuts, and other crunchy snack foods are usually left out in the lounge/bar, where there's also a 24-hour coffee/tea/cocoa station.

ACTIVITIES

As with most small ships, Cruise West vessels don't have much in the way of onboard diversions. What activities there are may include **post-dinner discussions** of the port or region to be visited the next day, **afternoon talks** by expert guests while at sea, and perhaps a tour of the bridge or galley. Onboard fitness options are limited to walking around the open decks (except aboard *Oceanus,* which has a small gym). Along with a full slate of extra-cost excursions, one **complimentary shore excursion** is offered at each port. Sometimes they're very worthwhile—as at the Alaska Native town of Metlakatla, where passengers are treated to a wonderful performance by a Native music and dance troupe, or on the California wine country cruises, which include luncheons and tours at various wineries. Other times, though, they're just short bus trips.

Occasionally, expedition leaders will take passengers for a spin in the ships' inflatable **Zodiac boats,** getting close to shore.

At least one and sometimes two **"expedition leader" naturalists** accompany each trip to answer passengers' questions about flora, fauna, geology, and history. As part of the line's new Compass enrichment program, experts in diverse fields will serve as **guest lecturers,** speaking on the scientific, cultural, and historic aspects of their cruise destination. In tandem with onboard naturalists, they'll also lead guests on an expanded roster of excursions by inflatable Zodiac boats (on select itineraries).

Cruise West Goes South, Sails the Mighty Mississip

Just as this book was going to press, we learned that Cruise West will be offering Mississippi River cruises beginning in spring 2011. This will de facto make them the dominant cruise operation on the river, since the 2008 collapse of Majestic America Line (a successor company to Delta Queen Steamboats) left America's greatest river without any overnight cruise service at all.

Between mid-March and mid-May 2011, the 102-passenger *Spirit of Adventure* will be offering a total of eight sailings on two different 7-night itineraries, operating between New Orleans, Memphis, and Nashville, then will move north to offer a series of Great Lakes/St. Lawrence Seaway cruises in summer (mostly btw. Quebec City and Chicago) and Hudson River cruises from New York in fall. Competitor Blount Small Ship Adventures (p. 327) will have a no-frills small ship on similar routes in 2011, and a number of day-cruise operators (two with an "overnight in hotels along the way" option, see p. 324 and 379) provide a third alternative.

CHILDREN'S PROGRAM
No children's program is available.

ENTERTAINMENT
As is standard on small-ship lines, entertainment is almost nonexistent, and what you do get will be catch-as-catch-can. One evening, the crew might put on a **talent show** featuring skits, music, magic, and whatever else they can drum up. Passengers sometimes get involved. Another evening, during dinner, passengers might be given the task of creating art from whatever is on their tables, with the winning table getting a bottle of wine for the effort. Some cruises also bring **local musicians and dancers** aboard to perform. *Pacific Explorer, Spirit of Endeavour, Spirit of '98,* and *Spirit of Oceanus* have TV/VCRs in their cabins and a shelf of videos in the lounge for passengers to take at will. *Spirit of Oceanus, Spirit of '98, Spirit of Glacier Bay,* and *Spirit of Yorktown* all have pianos in their lounges for passenger use.

SERVICE
The line strives for a family feeling, employing young, energetic crews composed mostly of American college students. Crewmembers do double and triple duty, waiting tables at breakfast, making beds and cleaning cabins, polishing the handrails, and unloading baggage at the end of the trip. They may not be consummate pros, but they do go out of their way to learn your name and give personal service. Passengers tend to find them adorable. Crews aboard *Spirit of Oceanus* and *Pacific Explorer* are international. Laundry service is available only on *Spirit of Oceanus* and *Pacific Explorer.*

The line's Explorer Class cabins (formerly AAA cabins)—introduced in 2009 aboard *Spirit of '98, Spirit of Endeavour,* and *Spirit of Yorktown*—feature **eco-friendly amenities,** including bamboo fiber linens and towels, cotton waffle-weave bathrobes, water-conserving adjustable-stream shower heads, and hypoallergenic down duvets.

Tipping is traditional, at your discretion.

Spirit of Oceanus

The Verdict

Spirit of Oceanus is one of the most luxurious small ships in the market, an ocean cruiser able to sail far-flung itineraries in style and comfort. Her cabins are downright huge.

Spirit of Oceanus *(photo: Cruise West)*

Specifications   Typical Per Diems: $429–$615

Size (in tons)	4,500	Crew	59
Passengers (double occ.)	114	Passenger/Crew Ratio	2 to 1
Passenger/Space Ratio	39.5	Year Launched	1991
Total Cabins/Veranda Cabins	57/12	Last Major Upgrade	2001

Frommer's Ratings (Scale of 1–5)   ✮✮✮✮✮

Cabin Comfort & Amenities	5	Dining Options	5
Appearance & Upkeep	4	Adventure & Fitness Options	5
Public Comfort/Space	5	Children's Facilities	N/A
Decor	5	Enjoyment Factor	5

Sailing Regions, Seasons & Home Ports

Oceanus	**U.S. Eastern Seaboard,** from Halifax, N.S. (fall). **Central America & Panama Canal,** from Palm Beach, FL (fall).

Her name says it all. Unlike all the other Cruise West ships, *Spirit of Oceanus* was built for sailing in open (rather than coastal) waters, allowing the line to offer more wide-ranging itineraries. The ship was launched in 1991 as *Renaissance V,* one of the original vessels of now-defunct Renaissance Cruises. She sailed briefly for the Asian line Star Cruises before Cruise West bought and refurbished her in 2001. Today, she's the line's largest and most luxurious ship, with more public rooms, a small gym, an elevator, and a hot tub on the top deck. Her decor is more private yacht than cruise ship, with corridors and cabins done in glossy wood-look paneling studded with gleaming brasswork, and the cabins are absolutely massive.

CABINS   All 57 staterooms are outside cabins with picture windows or (in a few cases) large portholes, and range in size from 215 to 353 square feet, which ranks them among the largest in the small-ship world. Each has a couch, TV/VCR, minifridge, marble-topped vanity, walk-in closet or wardrobe, hair dryer, and comfortably sized bathroom. Decor is a far cry from the usual off-white walls and modular furnishings of most small ships. Instead, walls are paneled in dark, polished wood tones, with rich carpeting that helps to create a yachtlike look. There are 12 staterooms on the Sun and Sports decks with private teak balconies, but the cabins themselves are actually smaller than those without balconies—what you gain in outside space, you lose on the inside.

Spirit of Oceanus is one of the few small ships with an elevator—a boon to folks with mobility problems—but no cabins are designed specifically for wheelchair users.

PUBLIC AREAS Public rooms include the main Oceanus Lounge—the place for frequent lectures and slide presentations by the ship's large staff of naturalists and historians—and the smaller Oceanus Club, a combo bar and reading room with a baby grand piano that gets infrequent use. Corner nooks in the club are stocked with games, a small book and video library, and the ship's one public computer (for e-mail only).

DINING All meals are served in single open seatings in the pleasantly decorated Pacifica Restaurant. Passengers can also take breakfast and lunch at the partially covered outdoor buffet on the Sun Deck—a very pleasant perch in most weather, affording great views.

ADVENTURE & FITNESS OPTIONS There's a small gym with free weights, a step machine, an exercise bike, and two treadmills. A hot tub is outside, just behind the Bistro buffet. Destination-specific activities—excursions by inflatable boat, hikes, and so on—are often built into the price of the trip on this vessel.

Spirit of '98

The Verdict

Built as a replica of a 19th-century coastal steamer, *Spirit of '98* is one of the most distinctive small ships you'll ever see.

Spirit of '98 *(photo: Cruise West)*

Specifications
Typical Per Diems: $420+

Size (in tons)	96*	Crew	23
Passengers (double occ.)	96	Passenger/Crew Ratio	4.2 to 1
Passenger/Space Ratio	N/A*	Year Launched	1984
Total Cabins/Veranda Cabins	49/0	Last Major Upgrade	1995

See note on p. 317 regarding small-ship tonnage and passenger/space measurements.

Frommer's Ratings (Scale of 1–5)
★★★★

Cabin Comfort & Amenities	4	Dining Options	4
Appearance & Upkeep	4	Adventure & Fitness Options	2
Public Comfort/Space	4	Children's Facilities	N/A
Decor	4	Enjoyment Factor	5

Sailing Regions, Seasons & Home Ports

Spirit of '98	**Columbia & Snake Rivers,** from Portland, OR (spring, summer, fall).

Spirit of '98 is a time machine. Built in 1984 as a replica of a 19th-century steamship and extensively refurbished in 1995, she carries her Victorian flavor so well that some of the people we've met on board think the ship really is 100 years old. If you want to get a look at her, rent Kevin Costner's movie *Wyatt Earp;* the ending was filmed on board.

CABINS Cabins are comfortable and of varying size, ranging from tight 8-square-foot singles to extralarge 228-square-foot deluxe staterooms. All continue the Victorian

In Central America with the *Pacific Explorer*

In addition to the ships profiled here, Cruise West also operates the 100-passenger *Pacific Explorer*, launched in 1995 as the *Temptress Explorer* of Costa Rica's Temptress Adventures Cruises. Sailing for Cruise West since 1998, the vessel offers 6- and 9-night Costa Rica and Panama cruises, with prices for 9-nighters starting around $3,999. *Pacific Explorer* cruises tend to be more active than most other Cruise West itineraries, with guided hikes, kayaking, and snorkeling excursions built into the rates.

---

motif (except in their bathrooms), and feature TV/VCR combos. Deluxe cabins have a minifridge, a seating area, and a trundle bed to accommodate a third passenger. One 550-square-foot Owner's Suite provides a spacious living room with a meeting area, a large bathroom with whirlpool tub, a king-size bed, a stocked bar with refrigerator, TV/VCR, stereo, and enough windows to take in all of Alaska at one sitting.

Cabin 309, located on the Upper Deck, is fully wheelchair accessible, and there's an elevator connecting most passenger decks, though it doesn't go up to the open Sun Deck. Two cabins are for solo passengers.

PUBLIC AREAS The Grand Salon is the ship's bar/lounge, with a suitably plinky-sounding player piano, a 24-hour tea/coffee station, and a small library of books and videos. The room continues the ship's 19th-century design theme with decorative ceiling tiles, balloon-back chairs, ruffled draperies, and plenty of polished woodwork and brass. Just aft of the dining room, a small bar called Soapy's Parlour (after legendary Skagway con man Soapy Smith) is used only at mealtimes, making it a good, quiet reading spot at other times. Out in the air, passengers congregate in the large bow area, on the open Sun Deck (where the staff sometimes sets up a bar on nice days), and at the railing in front of the bridge, which is open except when the ship is passing through rough water.

DINING OPTIONS The Klondike Dining Room is beautifully decorated and large enough to seat all guests in booths and at round center tables.

ADVENTURE & FITNESS OPTIONS The Upper Deck circles the ship, giving walkers a place to exercise. Inflatable launches allow off-vessel exploration.

Spirit of Endeavour • Spirit of Adventure • Spirit of Yorktown

The Verdict

Low on frills and style, but high on coziness and comfort, these ships all make a nice home base for a week of coastal cruising.

Spirit of Endeavour *(photo: Matt Hannafin)*

Specifications

Typical Per Diems: $295–$490

Size (in tons)		Crew	
Endeavour	1,471	*Endeavour*	28
Adventure	1,471	*Adventure*	32
Yorktown	2,354	*Yorktown*	40
Passengers (double occ.)		Passenger/Crew Ratio	
Endeavour	102	*Endeavour*	3.6 to 1
Adventure	102	*Adventure*	3.2 to 1
Yorktown	138	*Yorktown*	3.5 to 1
Passenger/Space Ratio		Year Launched	
Endeavour	14.7	*Endeavor*	1983
Adventure	14.7	*Adventure*	1984
Yorktown	17	*Yorktown*	1988
Total Cabins/Veranda Cabins		Last Major Refurbishment	
Endeavour	51/0	*Endeavour*	1999
Adventure	51/0	*Adventure*	N/A
Yorktown	69/0	*Yorktown*	N/A

Frommer's Ratings (Scale of 1–5)

★★★½

Cabin Comfort & Amenities	3	Dining Options	3
Appearance & Upkeep	4	Adventure & Fitness Options	2
Public Comfort/Space	3	Children's Facilities	N/A
Decor	3	Enjoyment Factor	5

Sailing Regions, Seasons & Home Ports

Adventure	**Mississippi River,** from New Orleans, Memphis & Nashville (winter, spring).
Endeavour	**Alaska,** from Juneau (summer). **British Columbia & Pacific Northwest,** from Seattle (spring, fall).
Yorktown	**Alaska,** from Juneau (summer).

When discussing these ships, we always come back to the impression that someone took one of the older Holland America vessels and shrank it to one-fiftieth its normal size. Though not boasting the many bright public rooms of those large ships, these four-deck vessels have similar clean styling, with cozy cabins and lounges. All three formerly sailed for now-defunct Clipper Cruise Line, under the names *Newport Clipper, Nantucket Clipper,* and *Yorktown Clipper,* respectively. *Spirit of Yorktown* is a slightly larger version of what's otherwise the same design, with more cabins.

CABINS Although generally smallish (beginning at 93 sq. ft.), cabins are pleasantly styled, with blond-wood writing desks, chairs, and bed frames and a goodly amount of closet space, plus additional storage space under the beds. Beds are either permanently fixed into an L position (better for tall people) or set parallel to one another and abutted by the wall and headboard. Some cabins have twin beds that can be pushed together to make a double, and some contain upper berths to accommodate a third person. All three ships have three or four extra-large cabins measuring 163 to 204 square feet. Cabin bathrooms are compact, with toilets wedged between the shower and sink area. Bathrooms have showers only.

All cabins have picture windows, except for a handful of forward cabins on the Main Deck, which have portholes. All cabins on the Promenade/Upper Deck and a handful at the stern on the Lounge Deck open to outside decks rather than onto an interior corridor—our favorite kind of arrangement on a small ship.

There are no cabins suitable for travelers with disabilities, and no elevators between decks.

PUBLIC AREAS   Each ship has four decks and only two indoor public areas: the dining room and the Observation Lounge. The pleasant lounge has big windows, a bar, a small library, and enough space to comfortably seat everyone on board for lectures and meetings. It's the main hub of onboard activity. The lounge on *Yorktown* also has a piano for passenger use.

DINING OPTIONS   All three ships have a single large dining room down by the waterline, with windows on both sides. This was the spot from which we sighted our first bear on our last trip, midway through our main dinner course. The captain obliged by making a U-turn, then cut his engines and let the ship drift within easy view for almost 30 minutes. Dessert was served afterwards.

Snacks are served in the lounge throughout the day, along with coffee, tea, and other drinks.

ADVENTURE & FITNESS OPTIONS   The only onboard fitness options are walking or jogging around the deck. When the ship is anchored in calm, warm waters, you can sometimes go swimming and snorkeling right off it, courtesy of a small platform that's lowered into the water. Inflatable launches allow off-vessel exploration.

Spirit of Discovery • Spirit of Columbia • Spirit of Alaska

Spirit of Alaska *(photo: Cruise West)*

The Verdict

Utilitarian small ships that have been in service since the '70s, these three provide Cruise West's usual intimate cruise experience, but the word of the day is *spartan*.

Specifications

Typical Per Diems: $380–$465

Size (in tons)		Crew	21
Discovery	94*	Passenger/Crew Ratio	
Columbia/Alaska	97*	*Discovery*	4 to 1
Passengers (double occ.)		*Columbia/Alaska*	3.7 to 1
Discovery	84	Year Launched	
Columbia/Alaska	78	*Discovery*	1976
Passenger/Space Ratio	N/A*	*Columbia*	1979
Total Cabins/Veranda Cabins		*Alaska*	1980
Discovery	43/0	Last Major Upgrade	
Columbia/Alaska	39/0	*Discovery*	1992
		Columbia/Alaska	1995

* See note on p. 317 regarding small-ship tonnage and passenger/space measurements.

Frommer's Ratings (Scale of 1–5)

★★★½

Cabin Comfort & Amenities	3	Dining Options	3
Appearance & Upkeep	4	Adventure & Fitness Options	2
Public Comfort/Space	3	Children's Facilities	N/A
Decor	3	Enjoyment Factor	5

Sailing Regions, Seasons & Home Ports

Spirit of Alaska	**Alaska,** from Juneau (summer).
Spirit of Columbia	**Alaska/Prince William Sound,** from Whittier (summer).
Spirit of Discovery	**Alaska,** from Juneau (summer). **Columbia & Snake Rivers,** from Portland, OR (fall).

Though of slightly dissimilar sizes and passenger capacities, these three vessels are extremely similar, all providing the friendly Cruise West experience, though in a somewhat plainer package than their fleetmates. Though they're older ships, all have been kept in good condition. *Alaska* and *Columbia* were originally built by Captain Luther Blount for his American Canadian Caribbean Line, and therefore share a problem common to all Blount vessels: They're not good choices for very tall people, as ceilings throughout are set at little more than 6 feet 4 inches, and many beds are too short for those 6 feet 2 inches or taller. On the other hand, both have Blount's patented bow ramp, which, in combination with their shallow draft, allows the ships to basically beach themselves, debarking passengers right onto shore in places that lack docks.

CABINS   Cabins aboard all three ships are very snug (btw. 80 and 128 sq. ft.), but they're comfortable, with light, B&B-ish decor and lower twin or double beds. (Aboard *Discovery,* one category has upper and lower bunks, and deluxe cabins have queen-size beds.) Storage space is ample, and most Bridge and Lounge deck cabins have picture windows. None of the cabins accommodates wheelchairs.

PUBLIC AREAS   All three ships have a lounge with a bar, a 24-hour tea/coffee station, and a book and video library. Lounges are a little too small to accommodate all passengers comfortably when the ships are full.

DINING OPTIONS   All meals are served in a single dining room.

ADVENTURE & FITNESS OPTIONS   Inflatable launches allow off-vessel exploration.

5 InnerSea Discoveries (Preview)

3826 18th Ave. W, Seattle, WA 98119. (℃ **877/901-1009.** www.innerseadiscoveries.com.

THE LINE IN A NUTSHELL   Once upon a time, there was a great little small-ship line called Glacier Bay Tours and Cruises, aka Glacier Bay Cruiseline. Owned by an Alaska Native corporation, it specialized in extremely casual, off-the-grid cruises in Southeast Alaska, spending most of the time kayaking and hiking in wilderness areas and only occasionally visiting port—and then usually such small, out-of-the-way ports that it was like touching down on the moon. That line went belly up in 2006, leaving a gap in the Alaska cruise market that was only partially filled by the much pricier Lindblad Expeditions and several small niche operators.

Sailing Regions, Seasons & Home Ports

Wilderness Adventurer	**Alaska,** from Juneau and Ketchikan (summer).
Wilderness Discoverer	**Alaska,** from Juneau and Ketchikan (summer).

Now, though, that gap seems ready to be filled. Up in Seattle, the folks who own high-end American Safari Cruises were at press time about to start up a brand-new small-ship line offering adventure cruises at a fairly reasonable price point, and employing the excellent Glacier Bay Cruiseline vessels *Wilderness Adventurer* and *Wilderness Discoverer.* The line's cruises will focus on wilderness hiking, snorkeling, inflatable boat and kayak excursions, beachcombing, and whale-watching, with optional activities like caving, glacier walks, river rafting, stand-up paddle-boarding, fishing, and overnight backpacking and kayaking. Essentially, the Glacier Bay experience is being re-created under a new name, with somewhat more comfort onboard and, we hope, more success. The brand is expected to debut in May 2011.

THE EXPERIENCE   Since InnerSea Discoveries had not yet debuted at press time, we'll just clue you in to what we do know. As to its nearly identical vessels, the 156-foot, 72-guest *Wilderness Adventurer* and 169-foot, 88-guest *Wilderness Discoverer* were built originally by and for American Canadian Caribbean Line (now Blount Small Ship Adventures), and have all the exploratory features that line always builds into its vessels, principally an incredibly shallow draft that allows them to access shallow waters. There's also a dry-launch platform in the stern so that passengers can board their kayaks right from the ship. Prior to their introduction by InnerSeas, both vessels will undergo extensive refurbishment, duding up what were very spartan interiors during the ships' days with ACCL and Glacier Bay. Cabins, which before were the most basic of boxes, will all be modernized, with simple but appealing decor, Tempur-Pedic memory foam mattresses, and iPod docks. Unfortunately, nothing can be done to improve the existing cabin bathrooms, which are minuscule "head-style" units, in which the toilet is essentially in the shower stall.

The main public lounge will be redone with a lodge/pub feel to encourage socializing in the evening. The bar will have a dozen microbrews in addition to wine and liquor. Hot tubs, saunas, exercise equipment, and yoga classes will jazz up the formerly nonexistent menu of onboard feel-good features. Each vessel will carry a fleet of stable sea kayaks, fishing poles and tackle, binoculars, and daypacks for guest use, and be fitted with an underwater hydrophone so guests can listen to whale-song. Naturalists will lead excursions and give lectures onboard, and other guests will occasionally board to provide their insider's perspective on Alaska living. Cruises will sail in Alaska's Inside Passage, operating between Juneau and Ketchikan, and visit natural areas like Prince of Wales Island, Sea Otter Sound, Baranof and Kuiu Islands, Frederick Sound, Admiralty Island (known for its bear population), and Endicott Arm.

We have high hopes for this new brand, having sailed *Wilderness Adventurer* twice during her time with Glacier Bay Cruiseline—and it'd be fair to say that those trips spoiled us for a lot of other cruise experiences, truly going where other cruise lines didn't, wouldn't, or couldn't. On our Alaska trip, we stuck so resolutely to the wilderness that we literally saw more whales and bears than people during the course of the week. Try saying that about a megaship cruise.

Per-person prices are expected to run between $2,500 to $3,000 per week. Typical per diems are $255–$340.

A note on passenger capacity: During their inaugural 2011 season, *Adventurer* and *Discoverer* will be sailing with a maximum of 49 guests per sailing, but a company spokesperson tells us they anticipate going to full capacity during their 2012 season at least aboard *Discoverer.*

6 Mini-Review: Island Windjammers

165 Shaw Dr., Acworth, GA 30102. (C) **877/772-4549.** Fax 877/766-6502. www.islandwindjammers.com.

THE LINE IN A NUTSHELL   Remember Windjammer Barefoot Cruises? A decade ago, they were the self-styled pirates of the cruise business, with weeklong (and longer) cruises on a fleet of old-fashioned tall ships, plus one shady-looking cargo/passenger vessel that kept them all supplied. The vessels prowled the Caribbean like privateers, scooping up passengers at different island ports and taking off on itineraries that were only kinda-sorta thought out ahead of time. The line lived on the edge, keeping its ships just about legal and its crews just about paid while accumulating a loyal cohort of repeat guests drawn by its outsider image and promise of unstructured, few-holds-barred fun. And it *was* fun—terrific fun, and we miss it, because in 2007 the line finally fell off the ethical and financial tightrope it'd been walking, and collapsed with a reverberating kaboom.

Flash forward to 2009, and all those Windjammer fans—some of whom sailed with the line dozens of times, year after year—were still out there, many still saddened that no similar cruise operation had sprung up to take Windjammer's place. Enter Island Windjammers, a start-up created by former crew and passengers of Windjammer Barefoot. In November 2009, the line began offering weekly 6-night cruises from Grenada aboard the 101-foot, 12-passenger brigantine schooner *Diamant.* Everything old is new again! If a bit more mature and less, shall we say, illegal. Though the line is starting small, it hopes to add larger ships as it matures. We wish them good luck, because the Caribbean cruise biz desperately needs this kind of small, casual option to balance out the megaship bigwigs.

THE EXPERIENCE   *Diamant* was built in 1978 and is more akin to the small windjammers that sail the Maine coast (p. 346) than to the big vessels of Windjammer Barefoot. The vessel is tight and simple, with six air-conditioned cabins with portholes and private bathrooms, a combo lounge/dining room, an outdoor dining area, and lots of open deck space. Oh, and there's this: She's *gorgeous,* with a beautiful profile, lovely detailing, and shiny woodwork throughout. Cruises sail among the Grenadine Islands (an absolutely ideal locale for this type of ship), visiting Carriacou, Mayreau, Tobago Cays, Union Island, Palm Island, and Bequia. Though the line consciously tries to emulate the ultracasual Windjammer Barefoot vibe and does whip up the iconic rum swizzles in the evening, it shies away from the heavy drinking and risqué party atmosphere that sometimes sent Windjammer ships over the edge.

Rates for *Diamant*'s cruises start at $1,599 per person (or $265 per day), including all meals, beer, wine, soft drinks, port taxes, and crew gratuities.

Sailing Regions, Seasons & Home Ports

Diamant	**Eastern Caribbean/Grenadines,** from Grenada (year-round).

7 Lindblad Expeditions

96 Morton St., New York, NY 10014. ✆ **800/397-3348** or 212/765-7740. Fax 212/265-3770. www.expeditions.com.

THE LINE IN A NUTSHELL   Lindblad Expeditions is the most adventure- and learning-oriented of the small-ship lines, offering itineraries that stay far away from the big ports, concentrating instead on wilderness and wildlife. **Sails to:** Alaska, Columbia and Snake rivers, Sea of Cortez/Baja, Central America (plus Europe, Arctic Norway, Antarctica, South America, Galapagos, Nile River, Mediterranean, and New Zealand).

THE EXPERIENCE   Want to trade in casinos and gold by the inch for 6:30am wakeup calls and shipboard forums on climate change? Then look no further than Lindblad Expeditions, which for the past few years has been operating cruises in partnership with the National Geographic Society, offering a more international, professional product than any of its small-ship competitors. The company attracts passengers who want to see, learn, and do as much as possible: You may find yourself kayaking along Alaska's intertidal zone, hiking deep into old growth forest near running salmon streams, or simply admiring the scenery while the ship's captain adjusts the itinerary to follow breaching whales. Some activities even start before breakfast. Throughout it all, flexibility and spontaneity are key, and high-caliber expedition leaders and guest scientists and photographers work hard to make the experience fresh and exciting. Significantly, they ensure that you come away having learned a lot, and just as importantly, having had lots of fun, too.

Pros

- **Great expedition feeling:** Lindblad's programs have innovative, flexible itineraries, outstanding lecturers/guides, a casual but professional atmosphere, and a friendly, accommodating staff.
- **Alliance with National Geographic:** Beyond providing top-notch lecturers and photographers aboard ship, Lindblad's relationship with the National Geographic Society means its ships are sometimes actively engaged in scientific research, with passengers right in the thick of things.
- **Family fun:** Lindblad's Alaska and Costa Rica itineraries are great for kids, making it one of the few family-friendly expedition companies.
- **Built-in shore excursions:** Lindblad programs its shore excursions as an integral part of its cruises, with all costs included in the cruise fare. And they'd better be, because these trips are . . .

Cons

- **Very expensive:** Lindblad's fares are among the highest in the small-ship market and in the industry.

LINDBLAD: LEARNING CRUISES FOR THE WELL HEELED

In 1958, adventure travel pioneer Lars-Eric Lindblad formed Lindblad Travel and began offering the first tours to remote regions of the world such as Antarctica and the Galapagos. Lars-Eric came to be considered one of the fathers of eco-tourism, and in 1979, his son Sven followed in his father's footsteps by forming what is today called Lindblad Expeditions. From the beginning, the line has specialized in providing environmentally sensitive adventure/educational cruises to remote places in the world, with visits to a few large ports thrown in for good measure. Today, it still strives to go

Compared with the other small-ship lines, here's how Lindblad rates:

	Poor	Fair	Good	Excellent	Outstanding
Enjoyment Factor					✓
Dining			✓		
Activities					✓
Children's Program			✓*		
Entertainment			✓		
Service				✓	
Worth the Money				✓	

* The line sometimes offers family cruises in Costa Rica. Children's programs are not otherwise available.

as far off the beaten path as possible and is keen to keep its heritage and spirit of adventure alive while providing a very comfortable, well-organized experience.

In 2004, the company strengthened its already outstanding academic and enrichment program through its association with the National Geographic Society. Today, all Lindblad-owned ships have been renamed to include the National Geographic moniker; the society and company work together to develop new technology for shipboard use; and National Geographic writers and photographers accompany many sailings. The two organizations have also joined forces to create a fund promoting conservation, reflecting their motto of "Inspiring people to explore and care about the planet."

The line's two Alaska ships, the identical, 62-passenger *National Geographic Sea Bird* and *National Geographic Sea Lion,* are more jeeps than sports cars, with small cabins and basic public areas. Though many of the amenities and services of big ship cruising—TVs, room service, minibars, and so on—are absent, Lindblad has outfitted the ships with more tools than a Swiss Army knife, including underwater video cameras, video microscopes, kayaks, inflatable Zodiac landing boats, and a hydrophone to eavesdrop on marine mammals. Particularly fun is an **underwater "bow cam"** that allows you to glimpse dolphins swimming in the bow wave or watch schools of fish below you while the ship is anchored. Despite the two ships' basic facilities, they are attractively furnished, well maintained, and have wireless Internet and a small spa/wellness program.

In addition to Alaska, these ships also sail Washington's and Oregon's Columbia and Snake rivers, the Pacific Coast of Central America and Panama, and Mexico's Baja Peninsula. The larger, completely rebuilt *National Geographic Explorer* hosts many of the line's most exploratory sailings and, in the Galapagos, Lindblad operates two vessels year-round: the 48-passenger *National Geographic Islander* and the 96-passenger *National Geographic Endeavour.*

PASSENGER PROFILE

Lindblad tends to attract well-traveled, well-heeled, and well-educated professionals who are looking for an active, casual, up-close experience of their destinations, packed with wildlife, culture, and history. They're the granola crowd with money, and they're fiercely loyal to the company and willing to pay an often substantial premium to sail. While most of them are in the 55-plus age range, a surprising number are younger, active couples. Lindblad actively encourages children and families to go on its trips, strongly believing that most kids would love to go kayaking near glaciers or snorkeling with sea lions. Single travelers are also welcome, and the line has a cabin-share program so that singles can sail without paying double for a double-occupancy room.

In general, passengers must be active and fit due to the lack of elevators, the necessity of climbing in and out of Zodiacs, and kayaking and other activities.

DINING

Lindblad believes in serving **local and organic foods** wherever possible, and has several partnerships to source environmentally sustainable food. A fleetwide policy even prohibits the use of shrimp onboard due to the harmful by-catch when harvesting. The food may not be gourmet, but it is fresh and tasty and often reflects the culture and tastes of the region, along with such standard entrees as filet mignon, glazed shallots with red-wine sauce and giant scallops, and pasta primavera with spinach fettuccine. Dinners are served in single open seatings, and lecturers and other staff members dine with passengers, providing opportunities to, say, have a conversation about humpback whale migration over dinner. **Vegetarian options** are available at every meal, and other **special diets** (low-fat, low-salt, kosher, and so forth) can be accommodated with advance notice. Weather permitting, *National Geographic Sea Bird* and *National Geographic Sea Lion* offer **deck barbecues,** as well as **beach barbecues** in Mexico's Sea of Cortez, featuring such local dishes as grilled local seafood, handmade tortillas, tomatillo salsa, and a selection of Baja wines. Guests eat their fish tortillas by tiki torchlight, then sip their wine by a shore-side bonfire, soaking in some of that fabled "sense of place." A similar barbecue is held for the Central America sailings.

SNACKS & EXTRAS   Appetizers served in the late afternoon include items such as fruit and cheese platters, and baked brie with pecans and brown sugar. Occasional extras, such as hot chocolate with schnapps served on the bow in front of a glacier, make for unexpected and welcome treats.

ACTIVITIES

Lindblad cruises are part summer camp and part college seminar, with days typically spent off-ship aboard Zodiac boats or kayaks, and/or on land excursions. While on board, passengers entertain themselves with the usual small-ship activities: wildlife-watching, reading, and conversation. Five **naturalists** (the most carried by any of the small-ship lines) and a video chronicler, plus historians and undersea specialists where appropriate, present numerous **lectures and slide shows** throughout each cruise and also lead guest exploration onshore.

Many voyages also feature guest scientists, photographers, and lecturers from the **National Geographic Society.** Amateur photographers will be especially delighted with the many **photography-themed sailings,** where you can learn from and interact with some of the very best wildlife photographers in the world.

CHILDREN'S PROGRAM

Though Lindblad is primarily an adult line, families and younger couples make up a good portion of passengers on Alaska, Central America, and Galapagos sailings. Staffmembers on these sailings have taken a family-travel course designed by Lindblad in conjunction with the National Geographic Education department.

ENTERTAINMENT

Each evening, the onboard naturalists lead discussions recapping the day's events, and, after dinner, **documentary and feature films** are occasionally screened in the main lounge. Naturalists take advantage of their toys, like the video microscope that allows

Lindblad Central America Cruises

Lindblad also operates the *National Geographic Sea Lion* in Central America. The vessel sails from Central American home ports during the winter, visiting Costa Rica and Panama and putting the emphasis on the region's jungle and marine life. Panama cruises also incorporate the history of the Canal. Prices start around $4,660 per person for weeklong Central America sailings.

you to get more up close and personal with plankton than you ever imagined, or the hydrophone that's dropped over the side to let passengers listen to whales singing. In some regions, local musicians may come aboard to entertain. Books on nature and wildlife are available from each ship's small library.

SERVICE

Dining room staff and room stewards are affable and efficient, and seem to enjoy their work. As on other small ships, there's no room service unless you're ill and unable to make it to the dining room, and no laundry service.

Tipping is traditional, with $15 to $20 per day suggested.

National Geographic Sea Bird • National Geographic Sea Lion

National Geographic Sea Lion *(photo: Lindblad Expeditions)*

The Verdict

Fairly utilitarian expedition vessels, *Sea Bird* and *Sea Lion* are designed to get you out into the wilderness, with naturalists on board to teach you something about it, too.

Specifications

Typical Per Diems: $805+

Size (in tons)	100*	Passenger/Crew Ratio	2.6 to 1
Passengers (double occ.)	62	Year Launched	
Passenger/Space Ratio	N/A*	*Sea Lion*	1981
Total Cabins/Veranda Cabins	31/0	*Sea Bird*	1982
Crew	24	Last Refurbishment/Upgrade	2005

* See note on p. 317 regarding small-ship tonnage and passenger/space measurements.

Frommer's Ratings (Scale of 1–5)

★★★½

Cabin Comfort & Amenities	3	Dining Options	3
Appearance & Upkeep	4	Adventure & Fitness Options	4
Public Comfort/Space	3	Children's Facilities	N/A
Decor	3	Enjoyment Factor	5

Sailing Regions, Seasons & Home Ports

Sea Bird	**Alaska,** from Juneau and Sitka (summer). **Columbia & Snake Rivers,** from Portland, OR (fall). **Baja/Sea of Cortez,** from La Paz (winter).
Sea Lion	**Alaska,** from Juneau and Sitka (summer). **Columbia & Snake Rivers,** from Portland, OR (fall). **Baja/Sea of Cortez,** from La Paz (winter). **Central America,** from San Jose, Costa Rica, and Colon, Panama (winter).

The shallow-draft *National Geographic Sea Lion* and *National Geographic Sea Bird* are identical twins, right down to their decor schemes and furniture. Not fancy, with just two public rooms and utilitarian cabins, they're very similar to several other small ships in this chapter, including the Blount ships and Cruise West's *Spirit of Alaska*. As a matter of fact, *Spirit of Alaska* and the two Lindblad ships all sailed at one time for the now-defunct Exploration Cruise Lines. Make no mistake: The enrichment program and the overall experience are the main draws here, and not the ships themselves.

CABINS   Postage-stamp cabins running 95 to 110 square feet are tight and functional rather than fancy. Each has twin or double beds, an adequate closet and drawers under the bed for extra storage, and a sink and mirror in the main room (none have televisions or minifridges). Behind a folding door lies a tiny bathroom with a head-style shower (toilet opposite the shower nozzle). All cabins have picture windows, and most have doors that open directly onto the deck, thrusting you into nature from the moment you wake up. The lowest priced cabins are more traditionally arranged.

Cabins can only be locked from the inside; none have an outside lock. A few cabins can squeeze a third person, and none are wheelchair accessible.

PUBLIC AREAS   Public space is limited to an observation lounge that serves as the nerve center for activities, plus open areas on the Sun Deck and in the bow. In the lounge, you'll find a bar and a library of atlases and books on the culture, geology, history, plants, and wildlife of the sailing region. The bridge is open to passengers, and effectively becomes another public room as passengers chat with the captain or his officers.

DINING OPTIONS   A single dining room hosts all meals in an open seating, and within a few days, you probably will have dined and met with all the passengers and naturalists aboard. Breakfast is a buffet, lunch is often family style, and dinner is traditional, with waiter service.

ADVENTURE & FITNESS OPTIONS   Each cruise involves frequent hikes in wilderness areas, accessed via Zodiac landing boats, and you'll get the opportunity to kayak whenever the weather is right. You can also walk around the Upper Deck for exercise, partake in morning stretch classes (picture yoga on deck with the Alaskan mountains as a backdrop), or use the two exercise bikes and one elliptical trainer on board. A tiny spa (a former cabin, actually) provides a wellness program and body treatments including massages.

8 The Maine Windjammers

See individual ship reviews for contact information.

THE LINE IN A NUTSHELL   Actually, it's not a line. Unlike every other review in this book, this one discusses a collection of owner-operated vessels—classic schooners that in some cases date back as far as 1871—all taking sail-powered summer trips along the gorgeous mid-Maine coast. It's the most natural cruise you'll ever take. **Sails to:** Mid-Maine coast.

THE EXPERIENCE Let's take a poll: How many of you harried, PDA-toting, 21st-century types dream of going quietly offline for awhile, back to some kind of ideal summertime memory—you in a sailboat on the open water, cozy bunks and kerosene lamps at night, stars in the sky, and quiet all around? Aboard Maine's fleet of old-time schooners, that's exactly what you get, on mostly 3- to 6-night cruises that cost from about $400 to $1,100. With no engines on most vessels, little electricity, and only the most basic accommodations, these ships remind passengers that days don't all have to be rushed and multitasked. Days are filled with sailing and walks around quaint Maine towns, and evenings are pure serenity.

Pros

- **Off-the-grid experience:** You can hardly get more "away" than on these ships, and since they rely almost exclusively on sail power (and what goes over the side is policed quite rigidly), they're an environmentally friendly way to cruise, too.
- **Relaxation in the pure sense of the word:** Passengers on these ships have no obligations and nothing to distract them from just sitting back and enjoying the ride. The experience is casual all the way, and you and the crew will bond in no time.
- **Classic ships:** Some of the association's member vessels date from as far back as 1871, and fully half the fleet's ships have been designated National Historic Landmarks.
- **Gorgeous scenery:** The Penobscot Bay region is one of the most picturesque sailing grounds anywhere, made all the more gorgeous by other schooners off in the distance. It's a perfect match of vessel and destination, picking up where New England's great 19th-century whaling ships and cargo schooners left off.

Cons

- **Rustic accommodations:** Cabins are almost universally tiny, most with only rudimentary furniture and lighting. This is actually a plus for many passengers, who come seeking just that kind of experience.
- **Few private facilities:** Only nine cabins in the whole fleet have private toilets (known as "heads" in the windjammer world). Generally, ships have two or more shared toilets and showers.
- **Few activities:** Again, it's why many people sign up, so if you need a lot of organized stimulation, look elsewhere. (On the other hand, many of the schooners have cruises themed on seamanship, photography, watercolor painting, knitting, and bird-watching.)

MAINE WINDJAMMIN': A CURE FOR THE 50-HOUR WORK WEEK

It all began in the 1930s, decades after steamships had supplanted the schooners and other sail craft that had been the mainstay of commerce and transportation for centuries. In Maine, formerly one of the top boatbuilding regions of the country, the boats that had escaped the scrapyard were in danger of simply rotting away from despair and disuse. In 1936, though, Maine artist Frank Swift began offering pleasure cruises on one of the old vessels, confident that people would be glad to escape the bustle of modern life for a few days of relaxation and simple pleasures. As Swift later recalled of his first trip, "We had only three lady passengers from Boston. The next

Compared with the other small-ship lines, here's how the schooners rate:

	Poor	Fair	Good	Excellent	Outstanding
Enjoyment Factor					✓
Dining			✓*		
Activities			✓*		
Children's Program	N/A*				
Entertainment		✓*			
Service			✓*		
Worth the Money					✓*

* Because the Maine schooners are all owner-operated, programs vary significantly. These ratings should be taken as only a general indication of fleetwide quality. Ratings for "activities" and "entertainment" should be read in the spirit of these cruises, which are entirely outdoors oriented, with few organized activities. There's also very little of what you'd traditionally call "service." If you want a drink, you bring it aboard yourself, and there's no cabin service unless something goes drastically wrong. Meals are often prepared by the same people who trim the sails. There are no real children's programs aboard any of these ships.

time, I believe, we took off without any passengers." But Swift didn't give up, and soon his trips were in such demand that over the next 3 decades, he not only grew his fleet, but also lured other captains into the business. By 1977, there were so many schooners operating in coastal Maine that several decided to pool their advertising and marketing dollars and form the **Maine Windjammer Association** (© **800/807-WIND** [807-9463]; www.sailmainecoast.com). Today, the association includes 12 member vessels, all of which are included in this review. You can request information for all member ships from the association and get basic info through its website, but bookings must be made directly with the captain of each schooner. Phone numbers and Web addresses for each are listed below. Other schooners discussed here operate independently; see individual ship reviews for contact information.

PASSENGER PROFILE

The Maine windjammers attract passengers in their 30s and those in their 90s, and everything in between. Many are returnees who sail a particular schooner every year, often coordinating with friends they've met on previous trips. Some are sailors themselves who enjoy helping out or taking a turn at the wheel. Most folks know the kind of experience they're signing on for, but first-timers often aren't quite prepared for just how rustic it can be. Bob Tassi, owner/captain of the schooner *Timberwind,* told us, "Initially, a lot of passengers experience some sense of shock, especially if they're not sailors and don't understand what a boat is . . . but then suddenly by Wednesday they almost transform. . . . Very few go away unhappy."

DINING

Meals on all the schooners are prepared on woodstoves in rustic galleys and served out on deck, picnic-style. In inclement weather, all passengers pack into the galley for meals. Expect traditional **New England staples** such as fresh seafood, chowder, roasts, Irish soda bread, and homemade ice cream. The cooks can accommodate **vegetarian** and some other **special diets,** but be sure to mention your needs when you book.

Sailing Regions, Seasons & Home Ports

Entire fleet	2- to 6-night Maine coastal cruises: The whole fleet sails from Rockland, Rockport, and Camden, Maine, late May through mid-October.

Photos courtesy of the Maine Windjammer Association and Maine Adventure Sails.

Dinner is served soon after the ship drops anchor for the night, and chances are that other schooners will be anchored not far away. You'll hear their passengers off across the water, singing folk songs or saluting you with blasts from their tiny brass signal cannons. A few passengers or crew may even brave the frigid Maine water and swim over for a visit.

All the ships are **BYOB,** with coolers and ice provided if you've got beer to keep chilled. During the day, snacks are usually available in the galley. Once per cruise, most of the ships debark passengers onto a quiet, rocky beach for a traditional **lobster bake,** sometimes with champagne.

ACTIVITIES

An exact opposite of the typical cruise experience, the Maine schooners sail during the day and anchor in protected coves every night. In the evenings or mornings, they'll often run a small boat to shore and allow passengers to explore small **fishing towns** and **uninhabited islands.** You can also see the sights at your port of embarkation because all the schooners encourage guests to arrive a day before sailing and spend the night on board, at the dock.

Most guests participate in the work of sailing: hauling the sails, raising the center-board, or hand-cranking the anchor from the bay's floor (the latter not for sissies). Otherwise, days aboard are totally unstructured, leaving guests free to talk ship with the captain, take a turn at the wheel, climb the rigging for a watchman's view, or just read or stare out over the water, looking for seals, porpoises, puffins, and the occasional whale. An easy intimacy develops fast, and because the mid-Maine coast is a cruising paradise, passengers can expect to encounter any number of other schooners, sloops, and other sail craft. Often, two or more ships will take on one another in an impromptu race.

CHILDREN'S PROGRAM

Many of the Maine windjammers have restrictions on young children sailing aboard (see individual reviews below). Others accept kids as young as age 5, but there are no formal programs to keep them entertained. On one of our recent trips, a Texas couple was aboard with their 6-year-old daughter, who spent the week playing with the captain's young son. The schooner became a whole world to explore, the week an opportunity to use the imagination most kids cede to TV and video games.

ENTERTAINMENT

There is none to speak of, though many of the schooner captains and crew are musicians who may break out their instruments in the evening. Guests who play are encouraged to bring acoustic instruments.

SERVICE

Don't expect much. Crew aboard these ships are *really* crew—the folks who haul the sails and swab the decks. In their spare time, they do the dishes, clean the shared restrooms, and mend what needs mending. The first mate might also be the cook (and, often, the spouse of the captain). For the most part, you're on your own.

American Eagle

Launched in 1930, *American Eagle* was a fishing schooner for 53 years before being refurbished for passenger sailing. She's a gorgeous, immaculately maintained vessel, with a sleek profile and gleaming, polished woodwork. Named a National Historic Landmark in 1991, she's the only schooner in the area certified to sail internationally, enabling her to make an annual cruise to Canada.

Ambience: Quiet. There's often a cribbage game in the galley, and in the evening Captain John Foss reads Maine stories and poems appropriate to the day's sights. Guests spend an hour a day onshore, minimum. **Cabins:** Cabins have hot and cold running water, reading lights, and some heat in the spring and fall. **Bathrooms/Showers:** Two shared heads below deck, each with a wash sink. One shower in the midships compartment. **Size:** 92 ft. **Passengers:** 26 (min. age 12). **Contact:** Captain John Foss, P.O. Box 482, Rockland, ME 04841. ✆ **800/648-4544**.

Angelique

Launched in 1980 for passenger sailing, she's the only non-schooner in the fleet, rigged instead as a gaff topsail ketch with dark-red sails that really make her stand out.

Ambience: Quiet, with no organized activities. There's music if someone brings aboard an instrument and isn't shy. (There's also a piano in the deckhouse salon.) Guests can go ashore both morning and evening if time allows. **Cabins:** Cabins have upper and lower bunks or double beds. All have running water and reading lights. **Bathrooms/Showers:** Three shared heads below deck, and three showers. **Size:** 95 ft. **Passengers:** 29 (min. age 12). **Contact:** Yankee Packet Company, P.O. Box 736, Camden, ME 04843. ✆ **800/282-9989**; www.sailangelique.com.

Grace Bailey

Launched in 1882, *Grace Bailey* came to Maine for cargo work in 1910. Designated a National Historic Landmark in 1990, she has won and placed multiple times in the Windjammer Association's annual Great Schooner Race.

Ambience: Quiet, with no predetermined activities. There's music if any musicians are aboard (there's a piano in the after-cabin lounge). Guests can often go ashore in the mornings, with hiking time also allowed during the lobster bake on longer sailings. **Cabins:** Rustic cabins with upper and lower bunks, a water basin, and battery-powered lights. **Bathrooms/Showers:** Three shared heads below deck. One hot/cold freshwater shower. **Size:** 80 ft. **Passengers:** 29 (min. age 16, but younger teens can be accommodated with supervision). **Contact:** Maine Windjammer Cruises, P.O. Box 617, Camden, ME 04843. ℰ **800/736-7981;** www.mainewindjammercruises.com.

Heritage

Built by her captains on a 19th-century model, *Heritage* was launched in 1983 for the windjammer trade and is an exceptionally spiffy vessel, with clean lines and a lovely profile.

Ambience: Flexible to whatever the group on board is interested in: singing, story-telling, games, and/or quiet. Guests are able to go ashore several times a week, as time permits. **Cabins:** Cabins have hot and cold running water and 12-volt cellphone charging outlets. Two cabins have private heads—talk about luxury! **Bathrooms/Showers:** Three shared heads. One hot/cold freshwater shower. **Size:** 95 ft. **Passengers:** 30 (min. age 12, but returning guests may bring younger children). **Contact:** Schooner Heritage, P.O. Box 482, Rockland, ME 04841. ℰ **800/648-4544;** www.schoonerheritage.com.

Isaac H. Evans

Launched in 1886, the *Evans* spent 85 years working Delaware Bay as an oyster schooner before switching to passenger sailing in Maine. Designated a National Historic Landmark, she was for a number of years the only Maine schooner exclusively owned and operated by a woman, but now Capt. Brenda has gotten married and is a co-captain with her husband Brian.

Ambience: Varies, with games, music, and activities programmed if passengers want them. Guests are able to go ashore at least once per day, sometimes twice. Some sailings are themed on photography, hiking, knitting, and so on. **Cabins:** Cabins have hot and cold running water, electric reading lights, windows for light and ventilation, and more than the average number of extras (soap, lotion, shampoo, and so on). Six cabins have double beds; the rest have upper and lower berths. **Bathrooms/Showers:** Two shared heads. One enclosed shower with water heated by the galley's woodstove. **Size:** 65 ft. **Passengers:** 22 (min. age 6, though younger children are sometimes okay). **Contact:** Captains Brenda and Brian Thomas, P.O. Box 791, Rockland, ME 04841. ℭ **877/238-1325;** www.isaacevans.com.

J & E Riggin

Launched in 1927, *Riggin* worked as an oyster dredger before being rebuilt for passenger sailing in 1977. Known for speed, she won the first and only oyster schooner race ever held on the Delaware Bay, and has won the Great Schooner Race several times. She was named a National Historic Landmark in 1991.

Ambience: Days are quiet, while nights usually have music, games, and storytelling. Guests can usually go ashore in the mornings for an hour or two. Co-captain Anne Mahle is known for her cooking, and has published a cookbook of the dishes served on board. **Cabins:** All cabins have quilts, reading lights, a porthole, and a sink with cold running water and handmade soap. **Bathrooms/Showers:** Two shared heads and one hot/cold shower, all on deck. **Size:** 89 ft. **Passengers:** 24 (min. age 12, but summer family cruises take kids as young as age 6). **Contact:** Captains Jon Finger and Anne Mahle, 136 Holmes St., Rockland, ME 04841. ℭ **800/869-0604;** www.riggin.com.

Lewis R. French

Built in Maine in 1871, the *French* is the oldest schooner in the fleet (along with *Stephen Taber*) and the only Maine-built 19th-century schooner still in existence. She operated as a cargo schooner until 1971, after which she was converted for passengers and named to the National Register.

Ambience: There are no planned events, leaving guests to provide their own atmosphere. Guests can go ashore almost every day for an hour or two. Smoking is not allowed on board, nor are cellphones, TVs, or loud radios. **Cabins:** Cabins have cold running water and a window for ventilation. **Bathrooms/Showers:** Two shared heads and one hot/cold freshwater shower, all on deck. **Size:** 64 ft. **Passengers:** 22 (min. age 16). **Contact:** Captains Garth Wells and Jenny Tobin, P.O. Box 992, Camden, ME 04843. ✆ **800/469-4635;** www.schoonerfrench.com.

Mary Day

Launched in 1962, *Mary Day* was the first schooner built specifically as a windjammer and the first coastal schooner built in Maine since 1930.

Ambience: Games and music are encouraged aboard *Mary Day*, with Captain Barry King often playing guitar. Guests are able to go ashore every day for an hour or more, and the weekly lobster bake allows for 3 hours ashore on a remote beach. **Cabins:** Cabins have cold running water, reading lights, skylights and windows, and unusually high headroom (9 ft. in most). **Bathrooms/Showers:** Two heads and two hot/cold showers, all on deck. **Size:** 90 ft. **Passengers:** 30 (min. age 15). **Contact:** Schooner Mary Day, P.O. Box 798, Camden, ME 04843. ✆ **800/992-2218;** www.schoonermaryday.com.

Mercantile

Launched in 1916, *Mercantile* hauled cargo before windjammer pioneer Frank Swift converted her for passengers in 1942. She was named a National Historic Landmark in 1990.

Ambience: Onboard experience is tailored to the passengers aboard, with music and games if anyone's interested. When possible, guests can go ashore in the mornings, and on longer sailings, extra hiking time is available during the lobster bake. **Cabins:** Rustic cabins with bunks, a water basin, and battery-powered lights. **Bathrooms/Showers:** Two heads below deck and a third in the galley/dining area. One hot/cold freshwater shower. **Size:** 78 ft. **Passengers:** 29 (min. age 16, but younger teens can be accommodated). **Contact:** Maine Windjammer Cruises, P.O. Box 617, Camden, ME 04843. ✆ **800/736-7981;** www.mainewindjammercruises.com.

Mistress

The smallest ship in the windjammer fleet, *Mistress* was launched in 1960 as a blend of traditional schooner and private yacht. A local blacksmith did all the ironwork, and much of the hardware was secured from an old-time ship's chandlery in Nova Scotia.

Ambience: Onboard experience is tailored to the passengers, with music, games, and time ashore based on interest. Lobster bakes are included on 4- and 5-day cruises, with time for hiking. **Cabins:** Each of the three private cabins has its own head, sink, and private companionway from the deck. Two have double beds; the third has upper and lower bunks. **Bathrooms/Showers:** Three private heads. One sun shower for impromptu wash-ups during warm weather, plus stops at friendly B&Bs and inns, where passengers may use the showers. **Size:** 46 ft. **Passengers:** 6 (min. age 16 unless booking whole boat). **Contact:** Maine Windjammer Cruises, P.O. Box 617, Camden, ME 04843. ℭ **800/736-7981;** www.mainewindjammercruises.com.

Nathaniel Bowditch

Built in East Boothbay, Maine, and launched in 1922 as a private racing yacht, *Bowditch* won class honors in the Bermuda Cup in the 1920s and during World War II was used by the Coast Guard for submarine surveillance. She fished the North Atlantic in the postwar years and was rebuilt for the passenger trade in the early 1970s.

Ambience: Music is encouraged, and games and puzzles are kept in the galley for passenger use. Guests are able to go ashore most days. Quiet time is encouraged after 8pm. **Cabins:** Rustic cabins with either double or single beds, barrel water, and reading lights. Some cabins have skylights. **Bathrooms/Showers:** Three shared heads below deck. One hot/cold shower on deck, with a privacy curtain set up while the ship is at anchor. **Size:** 82 ft. **Passengers:** 24 (min. age 14, but designated family sailings accept kids as young as age 5). **Contact:** Captain Owen and Cathie Dorr, 4 Gay St. Place, Rockland, ME 04841. ℭ **800/288-4098;** www.windjammervacation.com.

Stephen Taber

Like the *Lewis R. French, Stephen Taber* was built way back in 1871, and is the oldest sailing vessel in continuous service in the U.S. She hauled lumber, stone, and produce up and down the Eastern seaboard for a full century, and is now listed on the National Register.

Ambience: The *Taber* is known as a fun vessel, and a day's sail often ends with music and stories. Guests are able to go ashore once or twice daily, weather permitting. Operated by the same family for over a quarter-century, the *Taber* is known for her food (former captain Ellen Barnes, mother of the current captain, has published many family recipes in the cookbook *A Taste of the Taber*) and draws a huge number of repeat passengers—upward of 70% on most sailings. **Cabins:** Cabins have running water, lights, windows, and enough headroom to stand and dress. **Bathrooms/Showers:** Two shared heads and one hot-water shower, all on deck. **Size:** 68 ft. **Passengers:** 22 (min. age 14). **Contact:** Captain Noah Barnes and Jane Barnes, Windjammer Wharf, P.O. Box 1050, Rockland, ME 04841. ✆ **800/999-7352;** www.mainewindjammers.com.

Timberwind

Built in Portland, Maine, in 1931, *Timberwind* spent the first 38 years of her life stationed 18 miles off Portland Head, taking pilots to meet large ships that had to be navigated into port. She was converted for passenger sailing in 1969, designated a National Historic Landmark in 1992, and today is one of the most rustic vessels in the fleet, affording a real back-in-time experience.

Ambience: Quiet, with days spent sailing and guests able to go ashore most days for 1 to 3 hours. Music lovers might be particularly interested in this vessel because her owner, Captain Bob Tassi, was a Nashville studio engineer before chucking it all to become a schooner man. Evenings frequently find him on guitar, and a framed portrait of Frank Sinatra adds an incongruous grace note to the rustic galley. **Cabins:** Tiny varnished-wood cabins have small electric lights, barrel water, and an enamel wash basin. Beds are either bunks or doubles. **Bathrooms/Showers:** Two shared heads below deck. One on-deck shower with privacy curtain. **Length:** 70 ft. **Passengers:** 20 (min. age 5). **Contact:** Schooner Timberwind, P.O. Box 247, Rockport, ME 04856. ✆ **800/759-9250;** www.schoonertimberwind.com.

Victory Chimes

Launched in 1900, *Victory Chimes* is the largest U.S.-flagged commercial sailing vessel and the only classic three-masted schooner still operating. Because of the size, her onboard feel is less cozy than the other vessels in the fleet—more ship than sailboat. Her image adorns the back of the Maine State Quarter, minted in 2003.

Ambience: There are no scheduled activities, though music and games often break out. Guests can go ashore in the morning and evening every day for an hour or two. **Cabins:** Cabins have bunk beds, portholes, 110-volt outlets, reading lights, and sinks with hot and cold running water. Most have upper and lower berths. There are also three single cabins, one cabin with twin beds, one that sleeps four, and four cabins with double beds and private toilets. **Bathrooms/Showers:** Three shared heads (two on deck, one below). Two showers. **Size:** 132 ft. **Passengers:** 40 (min. age 10). **Contact:** Victory Chimes, P.O. Box 1401, Rockland, ME 07841. © 800/745-5651; www.victorychimes.com.

9 Mini-Review: Sea Cloud Cruises

32–40 N. Dean St., Englewood, NJ 07631. © 888/732-2568 or 201/227-9404. Fax 201/227-9424. www.seacloud.com.

THE LINE IN A NUTSHELL   Germany-based Sea Cloud Cruises caters to a well-traveled clientele looking for a deliciously exotic, five-star sailing adventure, and an international one too: Typical Caribbean cruises draw about 30% American passengers, 30% German, 20% British, and the rest from elsewhere in Europe. A trip aboard one of the line's sailing ships—the 2,532-ton, 64-passenger *Sea Cloud* ✰✰✰✰✰, or the 3,849-ton, 94-passenger replica *Sea Cloud II* ✰✰✰✰✰, or the up-and-coming 138-passenger *Sea Cloud Hussar*—will spoil small-ship lovers forever. **Sails to:** Caribbean (plus Europe).

THE EXPERIENCE   In 1931, Wall Street tycoon **E. F. Hutton** commissioned construction of the four-masted sailing ship *Hussar* from the Krupp family shipyard in Kiel, Germany. Outfitting of her interior was left to Hutton's wife, heiress and businesswoman **Marjorie Merriweather Post,** who spent 2 years on the task, eventually drafting a full-scale diagram showing every detail of her design, down to the placement of antiques. After the couple's divorce, Post renamed the vessel *Sea Cloud* and sailed her to Leningrad, where second husband Joseph E. Davies was serving as U.S. ambassador. World War II saw the vessel commissioned to the U.S. Navy, which removed her masts and used her as a floating weather station. After the war, the vessel passed through numerous hands: first back to Post, then to Dominican dictator Rafael Leonidas Trujillo Montinas, then to a number of American owners before she was purchased by German economist and seaman Hartmut Paschberg. A lover of great ships, Paschberg and a group of Hamburg investors put up the money for an 8-month overhaul that restored *Sea Cloud*'s original grandeur, full of marble, gold, and

Sailing Regions, Seasons & Home Ports

Sea Cloud	Not currently sailing in the Caribbean.
Sea Cloud II	**Caribbean,** from Barbados, Curaçao, Puerto Limon (Costa Rica), Havana (Cuba), and Santo Domingo (winter).

mahogany detailing. Today, the line is owned by the Hansa Treuhand Group based in Hamburg, Germany. The ship has cabins for 64 passengers, the luckiest (and richest) of whom can stay in Post's own museum-like suite, with its Louis XIV–style bed and nightstands, marble fireplace and bathroom, chandeliers, and intricate moldings. The other original suites are similarly if less sumptuously furnished. Standard cabins are comfortable, but lack the suites' time-machine quality. Still, everyone aboard gets to enjoy **a taste of the past** in the main restaurant, with its dark-wood paneling, brass trimmings, and nautical paintings.

The larger, three-masted *Sea Cloud II* is a modern reinterpretation of the classics, built in 2001. Her elegant lounge has rich mahogany woodwork, ornate ceiling moldings, leather club couches, and overstuffed bucket chairs, and she has several opulent suites, one with burled wood paneling and a canopy bed. On both ships, standard cabins are very comfortable and designed with true yachting elegance. Those on *II* have small sitting areas, and all cabins have TV/VCRs, telephones, safes, hair dryers, bathrobes, and bathrooms with showers and marble sinks. At press time, the 138-passenger *Sea Cloud Hussar* was under construction and slated for an early 2011 debut; the three-masted, fully rigged sailing ship is expected to be even more extraordinary than her sisters.

The dining room on each ship accommodates all guests in a single, open seating, and fine wines and beer are complimentary at lunch and dinner. Breakfast and some lunches are provided **buffet-style,** while the more **formal dinners** are served on elegant candlelit tables set with white linens, china, and silver. Most men wear jackets nightly, though the 2 formal nights on each cruise are not black-tie affairs—jackets and ties work just fine. Most cruises also feature a **barbecue night** out on deck.

These being small sailing ships, organized activities are few; it's the ships themselves that entertain, and watching the crew work the rigging, as well as visits to less touristed ports such as Les Saintes, Dominica, Bequia, Tobago, and St. Barts. Usually only 1 day of each cruise is spent at sea. Outside decks of both ships are covered with lines, winches, cleats, brass compasses, wooden deck chairs, and other ship accouterments, providing a wonderfully nostalgic and nautical setting. **Sailing lectures** are given on every cruise, though passengers are not allowed to handle the sails. *Cloud II* also has a library, a small gym, a sauna, and a swimming platform. Evenings may consist of **piano music** and mingling over cocktails. Other activities may include talks by resident **guest lecturers;** local **musicians** who come aboard for a few hours; and **"open houses,"** during which guests enjoy champagne and caviar on the Main Deck before touring each other's cabins (with the residents' permission, of course).

Weeklong *Sea Cloud* cruises in the Caribbean run from $4,375 to $9,025. Sailings aboard *Sea Cloud II* run from $4,195 to $7,565. Typical per diems for each ship are $615–$1,185. Sea Cloud sometimes charters its ships to other entities.

10 Star Clippers

7200 NW 19th St., #206, Miami, FL 33126. ℂ **800/442-0551** or 305/442-0550. Fax 305/442-1611. www.star clippers.com.

THE LINE IN A NUTSHELL   It's easy to fall in love with the Star Clippers experience—it's simply intoxicating. With the sails and rigging of a classic clipper ship and some of the cushy amenities of modern megaships, a cruise on these beauties spells adventure and comfort. **Sails to:** Caribbean (plus Costa Rica and Europe).

THE EXPERIENCE   The more ships we've sailed on, the more Star Clippers stock goes up. Few other lines combine the best of two worlds in such an appealing package. On the one hand, the ships have comfortable, almost cushy public rooms and cabins. On the other, they espouse an unstructured, let-your-hair-down, hands-on ethic—you can climb the masts (with a harness, of course), help raise the sails, crawl into the bow netting, or chat with the captain on the open-air bridge.

On board, ducking under booms, stepping over coils of rope, leaning against railings just feet above the sea, and watching sailors work the winches are constant reminders that you're on a real working ship. Furthermore, listening to the captain's or cruise director's daily talk about the next port of call, the history of sailing, or some other nautical subject, you'll feel like you're exploring some of the Caribbean's more remote stretches in a ship that really belongs there—an exotic ship for an exotic locale. In a sea of look-alike megaships, *Royal Clipper* stands out, recalling a romantic, swashbuckling era of ship travel.

Pros

- **Hands-on experience:** You never have to lift a finger if you don't want to, but if you do, you're free to help out.
- **Comfortable amenities:** Pools, a piano bar and deck bar, a bright and pleasant dining room serving tasty food, and a wood-paneled library balance out the swashbuckling spirit. ***Bonus:*** *Royal Clipper* has a gym and a small spa.
- **Rich in atmosphere:** On these ships, the ambience is a real treat.
- **Offbeat itineraries:** Itineraries take passengers to remote places such as the Grenadines and French West Indies.

Cons

- We're still trying to think of something . . .

STAR CLIPPERS: COMFY ADVENTURE

Clipper ships—full-sailed, built for speed, and undeniably romantic—reigned for only a brief time on the high seas before being driven out by steam engines and iron (and then steel) hulls. During their heyday, however, these vessels, including famous names such as *Cutty Sark, Ariel,* and *Flying Cloud,* engendered more romantic myths than any before or since, and helped open the Pacific coast of California during the gold rush of 1849, carrying much-needed supplies around the tip of South America from Boston and New York.

By the early 1990s, despite the nostalgia and sense of reverence surrounding every aspect of the clippers' maritime history, nothing that could be technically classified as a clipper ship had been built since *Cutty Sark* in 1869. Enter Mikael Krafft, a Swedish-born industrialist and real estate developer with a passion for ship design and deep,

deep pockets, who invested vast amounts of personal energy and more than $80 million to build *Star Flyer* and *Star Clipper* at a Belgian shipyard in 1991 and 1992.

To construct these 170-passenger twins, Krafft procured the original drawings and specifications of Scottish-born Donald McKay, a leading naval architect of 19th-century clipper-ship technology, and employed his own team of naval architects to solve such engineering problems as adapting the square-rigged, four-masted clipper design to modern materials and construction. In mid-2000, Krafft went a step further, launching the 227-passenger *Royal Clipper,* a five-masted, fully rigged sailing ship inspired by the famed *Preussen,* a German clipper built in 1902. *Royal Clipper* now claims the title of the largest clipper ship in the world, and it's a stunning sight.

Overall, the experience is quite casual, and salty enough to make you feel like a fisherman keeling off the coast of Maine, without the physical hardship of actually being one. As Krafft put it during one sailing, "If you want a typical cruise, you're in the wrong place."

All the Star Clippers vessels are at once traditional and radical. They're the tallest and among the fastest clipper ships ever built, and are so beautiful that even at full stop they seem to soar. As opposed to ships such as Windstar's *Wind Surf,* a bulkier cruise vessel that just happens to have sails, Star Clippers' ships do generally rely on sails alone about 25% to 50% of the time; the rest of the time, the sails are used with the engines. Each ship performs superlatively—*Royal Clipper* was designed to make up to 20 knots under sail (14 max under engine alone), and on a recent cruise, she easily hit 15 knots one afternoon. During most cruises, however, the crew tries to keep passengers comfortable and decks relatively horizontal, so the vessels are kept to speeds of 9 to 14 knots with a combination of sail and engine power.

A couple of years ago, Star Clippers announced its intention to build a new five-masted ship. Planned as the most expensive sailing ship ever built, the 7,400-gross-ton, 296-passenger barque is being modeled on *France II,* the largest sailing ship when she was launched in 1912 at 5,633 gross tons. The plan is for the ship to have 37 sails, measure 518 feet long, and have an Ice Class C hull so she can sail anywhere in the world. Though 48% larger than the *Royal Clipper,* she will only carry 30% more passengers. We hope it happens!

PASSENGER PROFILE

With no more than 227 passengers aboard, each Star Clippers cruise seems like a triumph of individuality and intimacy. The line's unusual niche appeals to passengers who might recoil at the lethargy and/or sometimes forced enthusiasm of cruises

Compared with the other small-ship lines, here's how Star Clippers rates:

	Poor	Fair	Good	Excellent	Outstanding
Enjoyment Factor					✓
Dining				✓	
Activities				✓	
Children's Program	N/A				
Entertainment			✓		
Service				✓	
Worth the Money					✓

aboard larger, more typical vessels. Overall, the company reports that a whopping 60% of passengers, on average, are repeaters back for another Star Clippers cruise.

While you're likely to find a handful of 30-something honeymoon-type couples and an extended-family group or two, the majority of passengers are well-traveled couples in their 50s to 60s who are active and intellectually curious professionals (such as executives, lawyers, and doctors) who appreciate a casual yet sophisticated ambience and enjoy mixing with fellow passengers. During the day, polo shirts, shorts, and sandals are standard issue; and for dinner, many passengers simply change into cleaner and better-pressed versions of the same, with perhaps a switch from shorts to slacks for most men. However, men in jackets and women in stylish dresses aren't uncommon on the night of the captain's cocktail party.

With a nearly even mix of North Americans and Europeans (most often from Germany, Austria, Switzerland, France, and the U.K.) on a typical Caribbean cruise, the international onboard flavor is as intriguing as the ship herself. Announcements are made in English, German, and French.

DINING

Star Clippers' cuisine has evolved and improved over the years as the line has poured more time and effort into it, with an enhanced menu that includes four well-presented entree choices at each evening meal. All meals are open seating, with tables for four, six, and eight in the restaurant; the dress code is always casual (though some guests don jackets on the night of the captain's cocktail party). Breakfast and lunch are served buffet-style and are the best meals of the day. The continental cuisine reflects the line's large European clientele and is dominated at breakfast and lunch by cheeses (such as brie, French goat cheese, and smoked Gouda), as well as marinated fish and meats. Breakfasts also include a hot-and-cold buffet spread and an omelet station, where a staff member will make your eggs the way you like them. Late-afternoon snacks served at the Tropical Bar include such munchies as crudités, cheeses, and chicken wings.

Dinners consist of appetizers, soup, salad, dessert, and a choice of five entrees: seafood (such as lobster and shrimp with rice pilaf), meat (beef curry, for example), vegetarian, a chef's special, and a light dish. Dinner choices such as fusilli in a tomato sauce, grilled Norwegian salmon, and herb-crusted rack of lamb are tasty, but tend toward the bland side. Most dinners are sit-down (as opposed to the occasional buffet spread up on deck), and service can feel a bit rushed and frenetic during the dinner rush. Breakfast and lunch don't get as crowded because passengers tend to eat at staggered times. Waiters and bartenders are efficient and friendly, and, depending on the cruise director, often dress in costume for several themed nights each week.

A worthwhile selection of wines is available on board, with a heavy emphasis on medium-priced French, German, and California selections.

SNACKS & EXTRAS   Coffee and tea are available from a 24-hour coffee station in the piano bar. At happy hour each day are complimentary canapés to go along with the daily drink special. At about 11:30pm each night, a cheese board, fruit, or another snack is set out by the piano bar for late-night noshing. Passengers staying in the 14 suites and Owner's Suites get 24-hour room service.

ACTIVITIES

If you want action, shopping, and dozens of organized tours, you won't find much of what you're looking for on these ships and itineraries—in fact, their absence is a big part of the line's allure. For the most part, enjoying the experience of being on a sailing ship and socializing with fellow passengers and crewmembers is the main activity, as it is on almost any ship of this size. Plus, the ships are generally in port every single day, so boredom is not an issue.

The friendliness starts at the get-go, with smiling waitstaff offering guests complimentary fruit drinks as they board. Throughout the cruise, the captain gives at least one **informal talk** on maritime themes, and, at least once a day, the cruise director speaks about the upcoming ports and shipboard events. Within reason, passengers can lend a hand with deck duties, observe the mechanics of navigation, **climb the masts** (at designated times and with a safety harness), and have a token try at handling the wheel when circumstances and calm weather permit. Each ship maintains an **open-bridge policy,** allowing passengers to wander up to the humble-looking navigation center at any hour of the day or night (you may have to ask to actually go into the chart room, though).

Other activities may include a brief engine-room tour, morning exercise classes on deck, excursions via tender to photograph the ship under sail, in-cabin movies, and hanging out by one of the pools. Of course, sunbathing is a sport in itself. Best spot for it? In the bowsprit netting, hanging out over the water. It's sunny, it's a thrill in itself, and it's the perfect place from which to spot dolphins in the sea just feet below you, dancing in the bow's wake. Massages are available, too, at a reasonable $75 an hour.

Port activities are a big part of these cruises. Sailing from one island to another and often arriving at the day's port of call sometime after 9am (but usually before 11am, and usually after a brisk early-morning sail), the ships either dock alongside the shore right in town or anchor offshore and shuttle passengers back and forth by tender. On many landings, you'll have to walk a few feet in shallow water between the tender and the beach.

Activities in port revolve around beaches and watersports, and all are complimentary. That's partly because owner Mikael Krafft is an avid scuba diver and partly because itineraries focus on waters teeming with marine life; each ship allows (for an extra charge) the option of PADI-approved **scuba diving.** Certified divers will find all the equipment they'll need on board. Even noncertified/inexperienced divers can pay a fee for scuba lessons that will grant them resort certification and allow them to make a number of relatively simple dives (on every sailing, there's a certified diver on the watersports staff). There's also snorkeling (complimentary equipment is distributed at the start of the cruise), water-skiing, windsurfing, sailing, and banana-boat rides offered by the ship's watersports team in all ports. The ships carry along Zodiac motorboats for this purpose, and *Royal Clipper* has a retractable marina at her stern for easy access to the water. Because there are few passengers on board and everything is so laid-back, no sign-up sheets are needed for these activities; guests merely hang out by the gangway or on the beach until it's their turn.

The ships tend to depart from their ports early so that they can be under full sail during sunset. Trust us on this one: Position yourself at the ships' rail or dawdle over a drink at the deck bar to watch the sun melt into the horizon behind the silhouetted ships' masts and ropes. It's something you won't forget.

CHILDREN'S PROGRAM

An experience aboard a sailing ship can be wonderfully educational and adventurous, especially for self-reliant children who are at least 10 years old. That said, this is not generally a line for young kids (though the line has no age restrictions, there are no supervised activities and no babysitting unless a well-intentioned crewmember agrees to volunteer his or her off-duty hours). The exception is during holiday seasons such as Christmas, when families are accommodated and some children's activities are organized by the watersports staff, including treasure hunts, beach games, and arts and crafts.

ENTERTAINMENT

Some sort of featured entertainment takes place each night after dinner by the Tropical Bar, which is the main hub of activity. There's a crew talent show one night that's always a big hit with passengers; other nights may have a trivia contest, dance games, or a performance by local entertainers (such as a steel-drum band) who come on board for the evening. A keyboard player is also on hand to sing pop songs before and after dinner, which may or may not fit in with the ships' otherwise rustic ambience. Most nights, disco music is put on the sound system and a section of the deck serves as an impromptu dance floor, with the action usually quieting down by about midnight (if not earlier). Sometimes films are shown up on deck against a sail.

You can borrow DVDs from the library or watch the movies that are shown each day on cabin TVs in English, German, and French if you feel like vegetating. Besides that, it's just you, the sea, and conversation with your fellow passengers.

SERVICE

Service is congenial, low-key, unpretentious, cheerful, and reasonably attentive. During busy times, expect efficient but sometimes distracted service in the dining rooms; and during your time on deck, realize that you'll have to fetch your own bar drinks and whatever else you may need. *Royal Clipper* has a second bar on the Top Deck adjacent to the pools, so you're never more than a 30-second walk from a cool drink.

The crew is international, hailing from Poland, Belgium, Ukraine, Russia, Germany, Romania, Indonesia, India, the Philippines, and elsewhere, and their presence creates a wonderful international flavor on board. Crewmembers are friendly and usually good-natured toward passengers who want to help with the sails, tie knots, and keep the deck shipshape.

Officers, the cruise director, and the watersports team may dine with passengers during the week, and if you'd like to have dinner with the captain, just go up to the bridge one day and ask; he may oblige you (it depends on the captain). Unlike a lot of other small-ship lines, Star Clippers has a nurse aboard all sailings (though don't be surprised when you see her busing tables in the restaurant or doing floral arrangements, too). **Laundry service** is available and so is dry cleaning.

Tipping is traditional, at your discretion.

Royal Clipper

The Verdict

This stunning, fully rigged, five-masted, square-sail clipper is a sight to behold, and the interior amenities, from marble bathrooms to an Edwardian-style three-level dining room, are the company's most plush.

Royal Clipper *(photo: Star Clippers)*

Specifications

Size (in tons)	5,000	Crew	106
Passengers (double occ.)	227	Passenger/Crew Ratio	2.2 to 1
Passenger/Space Ratio	22	Year Launched	2000
Total Cabins/Veranda Cabins	114/14	Last Refurbishment/Upgrade	2007

Frommer's Ratings (Scale of 1–5)

❋❋❋❋

Cabin Comfort & Amenities	4	Dining Options	4.5
Appearance & Upkeep	5	Adventure & Fitness Options	4
Public Comfort/Space	4	Children's Facilities	N/A
Decor	3	Enjoyment Factor	5

Sailing Regions, Seasons & Home Ports

Royal Clipper	**Caribbean,** from Barbados (winter, spring).

Star Clippers' biggest and poshest ship to date—and at 439 feet in length, one of the largest sailing ships ever built—the 5,000-ton, 227-passenger *Royal Clipper* boasts more luxurious amenities than the line's older ships, including marble bathrooms, roomier cabins, a small gym and spa, and three pools. In fact, the ship definitely gives the somewhat-tired-looking, 15-plus-year-old Windstar ships a run for their money in the amenities department, while still having a more rustic ambience. With five masts flying 42 sails that together stretch to 56,000 square feet, *Royal Clipper* is powerful, too, able to achieve 20 knots under sail power only, and 14 knots under engine power. (Still, as on *Star Clipper,* the sails are more for show, and typically the engines are also in use 60%–80% of the time, especially at night.) Engines or not, for true sailors and wannabes, the web of ropes and cables stretched between *Royal Clipper's* sails, masts, and deck—along with the winches, *Titanic*-style ventilators, brass bells, wooden barrels, and chunky anchor chains cluttering the deck—are constant and beautiful reminders that you're on a real ship. The same goes for the creaking, rolling, and pitching.

The bottom line: This ship is a big winner for those who like the good life, but in a gloriously different way than any mainstream megaship could ever provide.

CABINS   The ship's 114 cabins are lovely and roomy, done up in a nautical motif with navy blue and gold fabrics and dark-wood paneling. All but six are outside cabins measuring 148 square feet (the suites are larger) with portholes, and are some 20 to 30 feet larger than cabins aboard *Star Clipper* and *Star Flyer;* they're equivalent in size to the standard cabins on many Royal Caribbean and Norwegian Cruise Line ships, though they're about 40 square feet smaller than Windstar cabins. Bathrooms are marble in all except the six inside cabins, and all have brass and chrome fittings and plenty of elbowroom, as well as brass lighting fixtures, vanity/desks, hair dryers, safes, telephones, and TVs with DVD players. One problem: There are no full-length closets in the cabins—but then again, who's bringing an evening gown?

Some 22 cabins on the Main and Clipper decks have a pull-down third berth, but unfortunately it's only about 2 feet above the beds, so even when folded up, it juts out enough so that you can't sit up in bed without bumping your head.

Six tight 113-square-foot inside cabins on the Clipper Deck (category 6) and four outside cabins in the narrow forward section of the bow on the Commodore Deck (category 5) tend to be the best cabin bargains, if you're looking to save a buck. (See chapter 2, "Booking Your Cruise & Getting the Best Price," for more information about cabin categories.)

The 14 255-square-foot Deluxe Suites located forward on the Main Deck are exquisite, with private balconies, sitting areas, minibars, and whirlpool tubs. The Main Deck also has two Owner's Suites measuring 355 square feet; they're connectable, so you could conceivably book them together to create a 710-square-foot suite. Each boasts a pair of double beds, a sitting area, a minibar, and—count 'em—two marble bathrooms. Neither suite has a balcony. Suite guests get 24-hour butler service.

There are no standard-room connecting cabins, nor any wheelchair-accessible cabins.

PUBLIC AREAS *Royal Clipper* is like no other small sailing ship we've ever set foot on, with a three-level atrium and frilly multilevel dining room that are more like what you'd find on a much larger ship. Like the cabins, the decor of the ship's main lounge, library, and corridors follows a strong nautical thread, with navy blue and gold upholstery and carpeting complementing dark-wood paneling.

The open-air Tropical Bar, with its long marble and wood bar, is the hub of evening entertainment and pre-dinner hors d'oeuvres and drinks, while the more elegant piano lounge just inside hosts the weekly captain's cocktail party. (The ceiling of the piano bar is the glass bottom of the main swimming pool, so shave those legs, girls!) A clubby library is adjacent to the Tropical Bar aft on the Main Deck, and far forward on this deck is an observation lounge where you'll find two computers with e-mail and Internet capability (don't expect to see many people here—everyone's out on deck).

On the lowest deck, under the waterline and adjacent to the gym, is the little Captain Nemo Lounge, where an underwater spotlight allows you to see fishy creatures swim past the portholes while at anchor (though we never saw anyone using it when we were on the ship).

DINING OPTIONS The dining room is plush in its deep-red velveteen upholstery and dark paneling, and is spread out over three levels. With its brilliant blue sea-scene murals, white moldings and fluted columns, frilly ironwork railings and staircase, and dark-red upholstery, it's vaguely reminiscent of a room on an early-20th-century ocean liner—and feels somewhat out of place on an otherwise rustic ship. The buffet table is in the center on the lowest level, with seating fanning out and up. Breakfast and lunch are buffet-style and dinner is sit-down. You may notice that the low overhang from the staircase makes maneuvering around the buffet table in the dining room a bit tricky.

ADVENTURE & FITNESS OPTIONS Considering her size, *Royal Clipper* has amazing recreational facilities, with three pools, a gym, and a small spa. The spa boils down to two small massage rooms divided by a partition, plus a room with a hot tub and a small steam room. The treatments are expertly doled out at about $75 an hour.

The ship also has a retractable watersports marina at her stern for easy access to kayaking, sailing, and swimming.

Star Clipper • Star Flyer

The Verdict

With the sails and rigging of a classic clipper ship and the creature comforts of a modern mega, this pair of 170-passenger beauties provide a wonderfully rustic and cozy way to do the Caribbean.

Star Clipper *(photo: Star Clippers)*

Specifications

Typical Per Diems: $275+

Size (in Tons)	2,298	Passenger/Crew Ratio	2.5 to 1
Passengers (double occ.)	170	Year Launched	
Passenger/Space Ratio	13.5	*Star Clipper*	1992
Total Cabins/Veranda Cabins	85/0	*Star Flyer*	1991
Crew	72	Last Refurbishment/Upgrade	N/A

Frommer's Ratings (Scale of 1–5)

★★★½

Cabin Comfort & Amenities	3	Dining Options	3.5
Appearance & Upkeep	4	Adventure & Fitness Options	3
Public Comfort/Space	3	Children's Facilities	N/A
Decor	3	Enjoyment Factor	5

Sailing Regions, Seasons & Home Ports

Star Clipper	**Panama Canal,** from Barbados and Balboa (winter). **Caribbean,** from St. Maarten (winter, spring).
Star Flyer	**Central America,** from Puerto Caldera, Costa Rica, and Barbados (winter, spring).

Life aboard these tall ships means hanging out up on deck, and that's where most passengers spend their days. It's a beautiful sight to take in the sea and next port of call through the ships' riggings, a throwback to a simpler age. There's plenty of passenger space, including the many little nooks between the winches, ropes, and other pieces of equipment that appealingly clutter the decks of these good-looking working ships. Even with a full load, the ships rarely feel too crowded, except at dinner. Much of the sail-trimming activity occurs amidships and near the bow, so if you're looking to avoid all bustle, take yourself off to the stern.

CABINS Cabins are compact at 118 to 130 square feet for outsides, but feel roomy for ships of this size, and were designed with a pleasant nautical motif—blue fabrics and carpeting, portholes, brass-toned lighting fixtures, and a dark-wood trim framing the off-white furniture and walls. The majority of cabins have portholes, two twin beds that can be converted into a double, a small desk/vanity with stool, and an upholstered seat in the corner. Storage space is more than adequate for a 7-night casual cruise in a warm climate, with both a slim floor-to-ceiling closet and a double-width closet of shelves; there's also storage space below the beds, a desk, a nightstand, and a chair. Each cabin has a telephone, hair dryer, and safe, and all but the six smallest 97-square-foot windowless inside cabins have a color TV and DVD player.

Standard bathrooms are very small but functional, with marble walls, a nice mirrored storage cabinet that actually stays closed, and a narrow shower divided from the rest of the bathroom by only a curtain; surprisingly, the rest of the bathroom stays dry when the shower is being used. The sink is fitted with water-saving (but annoying) push valves that release water only when they're pressed.

The eight Deluxe Cabins measure about 150 square feet, open right out onto the main deck, and have minibars and whirlpool bathtubs. Because of their location near the Tropical Bar, though, noise can be a problem, especially if there are late-night revelers at the bar. Take note: The ship's generator tends to drone on through the night; cabins near the stern on lower decks get the most of this noise, though it sometimes filters throughout the lowest deck. Note that four cabins share walls with the dining room, and cabin no. 311 and no. 310 actually open right into the dining room itself (so be sure you're dressed before peeking outside to see what's on the menu).

Note that the only difference between the cabins in categories 2 and 3 is a quieter location and a few square feet of space.

None of the units is a suite except for one carefully guarded (and oddly configured) Owner's Suite in the aft of the Clipper Deck, which is available to the public only when it's not being set aside for special purposes or occupied by the owner himself (which happens quite often). There are also no connecting cabins, and no cabins designed for wheelchair accessibility. Lacking an elevator, these ships are not recommended for passengers with mobility problems.

PUBLIC AREAS The handful of public rooms include the dining room; a comfy piano bar; the outside Tropical Bar (sheltered from the sun and rain by a canopy); and a cozy, paneled library with a decorative, nonfunctioning fireplace, a good stock of titles, and a computer with e-mail and Internet access. Debit cards for sending and receiving messages can be purchased from the purser.

The roomy yet cozy piano bar has comfy banquette seating and is a romantic place for a drink. That area and the outdoor Tropical Bar are the ships' hubs of activity.

Throughout, the interior decor is pleasant but unmemorable, mostly white with touches of brass and mahogany or teak trim—not as upscale looking as *Royal Clipper,* but cozy, appealing, well designed, and shipshape.

DINING OPTIONS All meals are served in the single dining room, which has mahogany trim and a series of thin steel columns that pierce the center of many of the dining tables—mildly annoying, but necessary from an engineering standpoint. The booths along the sides, seating six, are awkward when couples who don't know each other are forever getting up and down to let their tablemates in and out. With tables only for six and eight, and no assigned seating, each evening you can dine with a different set of friends, or maybe make some new ones. The *Royal Clipper*'s roomier dining-room layout avoids this problem.

ADVENTURE & FITNESS OPTIONS The ships' two small pools are meant more for dipping than swimming. Both have glass portholes, the one amidships peering from its depths into the piano bar. The pool near the stern tends to be more languid and is thus the favorite of sunbathers, whereas the one amidships is more active, with more noise and splashing, and central to the action. At both, the ship's billowing and moving sails occasionally block the sun's rays, although this happens amidships much more frequently than it does at the stern.

While there's no gym of any sort, aerobics and stretch classes are frequently held on deck between the library and the Tropical Bar. You can sign up for a massage (at $75 an hour) that's doled out in an empty cabin or in a semiprivate area of the Top Deck.

11 Windstar Cruises

2101 4th Ave., Ste. 210, Seattle, WA 98121. ℂ 877/827-7245 or 206/292-9606. Fax 206/340-0975. www.windstar cruises.com.

THE LINE IN A NUTSHELL   Windstar walks a tightrope between luxury line and sailing-ship line, with an always-casual onboard vibe, beyond-the-norm itineraries, and first-class service and cuisine.

THE EXPERIENCE   You say you want a cruise that visits interesting ports; has active options like watersports; has superfriendly yet efficient, on-the-nose service; provides excellent cuisine; has sailing trips with a romantic vibe; and still doesn't cost an arm and a leg? You pretty much only have one option: Windstar.

This is no barefoot, rigging-pulling, paper-plates-in-lap kind of cruise, but a refined yet down-to-earth, yachtlike experience for a sophisticated, well-traveled crowd of folks who wouldn't be comfortable on a big ship full of tourists. On board, stained teak, brass details, and lots of navy blue fabrics and carpeting lend a traditional nautical ambience, and though the ships' tall masts and white sails cut a traditional profile, they're also state of the art, controlled by a computer so that they can be furled or unfurled at the touch of a button. Despite the ships' relatively large size (*Wind Surf* is one of the world's largest sailing ships, if not the largest), they're able to travel at upward of 12 knots under sail power alone, though usually the sails are up more as a fuel-saving aid to the diesel engines.

Pros

- **Sails:** While you won't get a full-on sailing experience here like you do with the Maine Windjammer ships or (sometimes) Star Clippers and Sea Cloud, you do get the ambience, plus the good karma of knowing the sails help save fuel.
- **Service:** Windstar employs mostly Indonesian and Filipino staff, many of whom have worked for the company for years. They're extremely professional and friendly as can be.
- **Cuisine:** Few small ships can match Windstar for the quality and ambience of its dining experience, with meals served in open-seating restaurants where guests can usually get a table for two.
- **Informal and unregimented days:** Beyond "don't wear shorts in the dining rooms," there's no real dress code here, and most men don't even bother with sport jackets at dinner. Similarly, there are zero "rah-rah" activities, keeping days loose and languid. Just explore onshore (the itineraries visit a port almost every day) or kick back and relax aboard ship without a lot of distractions.

Cons

- **Limited activities and entertainment:** This is intentional, but if you need lots of organized hoopla to keep you happy, you won't find much here.
- **No verandas:** If they're important to you, you're out of luck.

WINDSTAR: CASUAL ELEGANCE UNDER SAIL

Thank goodness there's a company like Windstar in the frequently homogenous cruise industry. It's an individual. It's got personality. Its operations are friendly and almost old-fashioned, small-scale and full of employees who've been with the line for years. Reportedly, many repeat passengers check to make sure their favorite cabin steward, waiter, captain, or host/hostess will be aboard before they'll book a particular sailing.

The line got its start in 1984, founded by a consortium of two shipowners and Jean Claude Potier, a former U.S. head of the legendary French Line. From the start, it was all about the sails—and specifically about a new cruise ship design by the Finnish shipbuilding company Wartsila. Dubbed the Windcruiser, the concept combined 19th-century sailing-ship technology with modern engineering to create a kind of vessel never seen before in the cruise ship world: huge by sailing-ship standards, with at least 21,489 square feet of computer-controlled staysails that furl and unfurl at the touch of a button and can work on their own or in concert with a diesel-electric engine. The concept worked then, and it works now: As you see a Windstar ship approaching port, with its long, graceful hull and masts the height of 20-story buildings, you'll forget all about the giant megaships moored nearby and think, "Now that's a ship."

PASSENGER PROFILE

People who expect high-caliber service and very high-quality cuisine, but dislike the formality of most of the luxe ships (as well as the mass mentality of the megaships) are thrilled with Windstar. Most passengers are couples in their late 30s to early 60s, with the average around 50. Overall, an amazing 60% to 70% of passengers are repeaters, back for their annual or semiannual dose of Windstar. There is also usually a handful of honeymoon couples aboard any given sailing—a good choice on their part, as Windstar ranks high on our list of most romantic cruise lines. The line gets very few families with young kids—rarely more than six or seven on any sailing, and usually only during school holiday periods. Children who do sail are usually in the 10-plus age range.

Overall, Windstar's sophisticated and well-traveled passengers are more down to earth than guests on the luxury lines, but not as nature- and learning-focused as guests on most of the other small-ship lines. Most want something different from the regular cruise experience, eschew the "bigger is better" philosophy of conventional cruising, and want their vacation to focus more on the ports than on onboard activities.

Compared with the other adventure lines, here's how Windstar rates:

	Poor	Fair	Good	Excellent	Outstanding
Enjoyment Factor					✓
Dining				✓	
Activities			✓		
Children's Program	N/A				
Entertainment			✓		
Service					✓
Worth the Money					✓

These cruises are for those who are seeking a romantic escape and like to visit ports not often touched by regular cruise ships.

Windstar caters to corporate groups, too, with about 25% of its annual cruises booked as full charters or hosting affinity groups.

DINING

Windstar's cuisine is tops in the small-ship category and is a high point of the cruise, served in two or three always-casual restaurants.

TRADITIONAL   Dinner is served primarily in each ship's spacious, nautically appointed main restaurant, though the vibe here is less formal and regimented than aboard most larger ships. At dinner, the line's **no-jackets-required** policy for men means guests do the "casual elegance" thing—pants or casual dresses for women, and trousers and nice collared shirts for men—and its open-seating policy means you can show up when you want (within a 2-hr. window) and dine with whomever you want. Restaurants aboard all three ships are set up with an unusual number of tables for two, and there's rarely a wait—proof that Windstar is serious about its romantic image.

Overall, Windstar's cuisine tends toward the straightforward, but with surprising twists and regional touches. Appetizers may include golden fried brie served with cranberry sauce and crispy parsley, or a sweet shrimp and crab salad. Among the main courses, there may be a grilled local fish served with a roast-corn salsa and sweet plantains, sautéed jumbo prawns served with garlic spinach and spaghetti, or an herb-and-peppercorn-coated prime rib of beef. Desserts such as an apple tart with raspberry coulis and chocolate crème brûlée are beyond tempting. A selection of exotic fine cheeses (many bought fresh in local markets) is served table side from a cheese cart, and petits fours are served with coffee after dinner. The restaurant's **wine list** features many boutique labels from California, Australia, New Zealand, Spain, France, and South Africa.

Vegetarian dishes and **healthy choices** are available for breakfast, lunch, and dinner; fat and calorie content is listed on the menu. The light choices may be Atlantic salmon with couscous and fresh vegetables, or a Thai country-style chicken with veggies and Asian rice. The vegetarian options may include a fresh garden stew or a savory polenta with Italian salsa.

ALTERNATIVE   Windstar's largest ship, *Wind Surf,* offers alternative dining at the casual, 128-seat **Degrees,** an intimate space with an understated fantasy-garden motif and a rotating menu reflecting the fresh and seasonal preparations of Mediterranean cooking. Reservations are required, but there's no additional fee. The *Surf* also has alfresco dining at a new seafood bar called **Le Marché,** also accommodating 30 guests a night. Aboard all three ships, **Candles** is an intimate poolside grill serving steaks and skewers for about 30 guests a night; reservations are required.

CASUAL   Breakfast and lunch are available at the buffet-style **Veranda Cafe,** which provides a generous spread, as well as a specialty omelet station at breakfast and a grill choice at lunch. Waiters will bring the latter to your table, so there's no waiting. You can also opt for a simple continental breakfast at the stern-side **Compass Rose Bar.**

The once-a-week evening **barbecues** on the Pool Decks of the *Star* and *Spirit* are wonderful parties under the stars, with an ample and beautifully designed buffet, tables set with linens, and a band for more ambience. On *Wind Surf,* there's a **gala**

buffet dinner once per cruise in the main lounge, which is transformed into a third dining room for the evening, with a culinary theme matching your cruise region. All three ships also have weekly barbecue lunches on deck.

Burgers, pizza, hot dogs, and the like are available from a grill in the afternoons.

SNACKS & EXTRAS Speedy **room service** delivers continental breakfast; a menu of about a dozen sandwiches, salads, seafood, and steaks from 11am to 10pm; and a dozen more snack items (from popcorn and chips and salsa to a cheese platter or beef consommé) 24 hours a day. During restaurant hours, you can have items from the restaurant's menu served course by course in your cabin, speedy and hot.

ACTIVITIES

Because Windstar's itineraries emphasize days in port over days at sea (most cruises hit a port every day or spend just 1 day at sea per week), its ships have few organized activities, leaving days relaxed and unregimented—the way guests prefer it. The handful of scheduled diversions usually include casino gaming lessons, walk-a-mile and stretch classes on deck, and an occasional vegetable-carving or food-decorating demonstration. A **watersports platform** can be lowered from the stern to allow kayaking, sailing, water-skiing, windsurfing, and ski tubing when the ship anchors offshore. Up top, the Pool Deck has a small pool and hot tub, deck chairs, and an open-air bar. Other open areas, especially on the larger *Wind Surf,* have quiet spots for reading.

In port, the company's shore excursions tend to be more creative than usual, and the onboard hosts or hostesses (aka cruise directors, who sometimes double as shore excursion managers and jacks-of-all-trades) are usually very knowledgeable about the ports and are able to point passengers toward good spots for swimming, places of cultural or historical interest, or a nice meal. Brief orientation talks are held before port visits.

The ships all maintain an open-bridge policy, so at most times you're free to walk right in and chat with the captain and officers on duty. There's an extensive collection of DVDs and CDs that passengers can borrow for use in their cabins. Guests may also check out fully loaded **Apple iPod Nanos** free of charge from the reception desk, using them either with headphones or in conjunction with the Bose SoundDock speakers in each cabin. There are also docking stations and headphones in *Surf*'s **Yacht Club Internet cafe lounge.** All three ships provide Internet connectivity—*Wind Surf* from eight computers in the Yacht Club, *Star* and *Spirit* via two computers in their libraries. All three vessels are also rigged for **bow-to-stern Wi-Fi service,** and wireless laptops are rentable at the front desk if you don't want to lug your own.

CHILDREN'S PROGRAM

Because children sail infrequently with Windstar, no activities are planned for them. Kids who do sail are generally ages 10 and up, but there are rarely more than six or seven on any sailing, and those only during school breaks. The ships' DVD libraries stock some children's films. The minimum age for children to sail is 2 years.

ENTERTAINMENT

For the most part, passengers entertain themselves, though each ship does carry a number of musicians who provide tunes for evening dancing and background music. Most evenings, passengers either retire to their cabins, head for the modest **casino** with its table games and slots, or go up to the **Compass Rose Bar** (and also the indoor/outdoor **Terrace Bar** on the *Surf*) for a nightcap under the stars. Sometimes after 10 or 11pm, disco/pop music is played in the lounge if guests are in a dancing mood, and once per cruise, the ship's Indonesian and Filipino crewmembers put on a **crew show** featuring traditional and contemporary music and dance. It's always a crowd pleaser.

SERVICE

Windstar is a class operation, and its level of service is no exception. The staffmembers smile hello and often learn passengers' names within the first hours of sailing. Dining staff is efficient and first-rate as well, but not in that ultraprofessional, five-star-hotel, Seabourn-esque kind of way. That's not what Windstar is all about. As for **tipping,** Windstar automatically adds gratuities of $12 per person, per day to passengers' onboard accounts.

Wind Surf

The Verdict

An enlarged version of *Wind Star* and *Wind Spirit,* the 312-passenger *Wind Surf* is a sleek, sexy, supersmooth sailing ship with a large spa and lots of suites, along with an intimate, yachtlike ambience.

Wind Surf *(photo: Windstar Cruises)*

Specifications

Typical Per Diems: $230+

Size (in tons)	14,745	Crew	191
Passengers (double occ.)	312	Passenger/Crew Ratio	1.6 to 1
Passenger/Space Ratio	48	Year Launched	1990
Total Cabins/Veranda Cabins	156/0	Last Refurbishment/Upgrade	2010

Frommer's Ratings (Scale of 1–5)

★★★★

Cabin Comfort & Amenities	4	Dining Options	3.5
Appearance & Upkeep	3.5	Adventure & Fitness Options	5
Public Comfort/Space	4	Children's Facilities	N/A
Decor	4	Enjoyment Factor	4.5

Sailing Regions, Seasons & Home Ports

Wind Surf	**Caribbean,** from Barbados and St. Martin (winter).

Wind Surf is the pumped-up big sister of Windstar's smaller original vessels, the *Wind Star* and *Wind Spirit.* Built at French shipyard Societe Nouvelle des Ateliers et Chantiers du Havre, she originally sailed for Club Med Cruises (as *Club Med I*) until purchased by Windstar in 1997.

Despite a passenger capacity more than double that of her sister ships, *Wind Surf* maintains the feel of a private yacht, but also something more: Unlike almost any ship today, she mimics the size and flavor of some older, more intimate ocean liners, with a real seagoing feel that's rare among today's breed of cruise ships. In essence, *Wind Surf* is in a class by herself, offering one of the few cruise experiences that really bridges the gap between casual-luxe and adventure, at prices starting lower than $2,000 per week.

CABINS   Decor is nearly identical in all cabins and suites, with white walls, varnished wood detailing, patterned upholstery and bedding, and understated carpets. Amenities include flatscreen TVs, DVD/CD players, Bose SoundDocks (usable with preloaded Apple iPod Nanos that you can check out from the reception desk), minifridges, terry-cloth bathrobes, L'Occitane toiletries, large desks with granite tops, and full-length mirrors. At 188 square feet, the standard cabins are as large as some of the largest mainstream megaship cabins, and storage space is adequate, though not overly generous. Refurbished bathrooms sport a contemporary look, with open glass shelves, granite countertops, white porcelain sinks, new custom shower heads, new shower curtains, and an illuminated magnifying mirror. Fortunately, the lovely teak bathroom floors remain intact.

Thirty suites on Deck 3 (created by combining two regular staterooms) have a single large space divided into a comfortable sitting area and a bedroom, with a thick curtain to separate them as needed. They have his-and-hers bathrooms (each with shower and toilet) and two flat-panel TVs and DVD players. No cabins or suites have balconies or even picture windows. Instead, chunky portholes add to the ship's nautical ambience. Go with it. We loved 'em.

Each of the two 500-square-foot plush suites on the Bridge Deck has a living and dining area, a separate bedroom, a walk-in closet, and a marble bathroom with a tub and separate shower. Posh perks for these suites include unpacking service, an invitation to dine with the captain, laundry and pressing service, evening appetizers, complimentary bottled water in the suite, chilled champagne upon arrival, and extra L'Occitane bath amenities.

Wind Surf has two elevators (unlike the other Windstar ships, which have none), but no cabins tailored for wheelchairs. The vessel is not recommended for people with serious mobility problems.

PUBLIC AREAS   All around, *Wind Surf* is the roomiest of the three Windstar ships, with an airy layout and a passenger-space ratio to match that of the luxe Seabourn ships.

The vessel's main public room is her nautically decorated **main lounge,** bright and airy with well-spaced tables for four spread around a decent-size dance floor and bandstand. Passengers gather here in the evening for cocktails, music, and port talks, as well as gambling in the adjoining casino. Aft, the **Compass Rose Bar** is the most popular spot aboard, with indoor/outdoor seating, a view over the wake, and music in the evenings. A second small stern lounge, the tiny, adorable **Terrace Bar,** is decorated with classic wood paneling and thick leather couches and bar stools, and has additional seating and tables just outside, on deck. In the evening, it's the spot for Cigars Under the Stars sessions.

Midships on Main Deck, just aft of the lounge, the former library has been transformed into the **Yacht Club,** the ship's new social hub and Internet cafe, with an espresso bar, eight computers, and Wi-Fi access for your laptop. A large flatscreen TV anchors a cluster of comfy couches and chairs, and there's a library of books, CDs, and

DVDs available for checkout. Nearby are four card tables and the ship's one shop, next to the main reception desk.

DINING OPTIONS   *Wind Surf* has multiple dining spots: the **Restaurant** on the Main Deck, a casual alternative venue on the Star Deck, and the buffet-style **Veranda** restaurant, also on the Star Deck. The Restaurant has 34 tables for two, making it easy for couples to enjoy a romantic dinner alone. Dinners are open seating, served in a 2-hour window between 7:30 and 9:30pm. Dinner in the cozy alternative venue, named **Degrees,** is by reservation only and features a menu reflecting the fresh and seasonal preparations of Mediterranean cooking. For dining under the stars, two alfresco Top Deck eateries include **Candles** for steaks and skewers, and **Le Marché,** for seafood.

As on the other Windstar ships, a combo buffet and a la carte breakfast and lunch are served in the glass-enclosed Veranda, which also has outdoor seating. Guests can also get grilled lobster, shrimp, ribs, hamburgers, hot dogs, sausages, veggie burgers, and vegetables from the **Grill,** right outside the Veranda's doors.

POOL, FITNESS, SPA & SPORTS FACILITIES   *Wind Surf* has the most elaborate fitness and spa facilities in the Windstar fleet, outclassing most facilities on other similar-size ships. At the spa, therapists dole out a variety of massages and other treatments in rooms that may look suspiciously familiar: They were created out of regular cabins when Windstar expanded the spa. Various spa packages geared to both men and women can be purchased in advance through your travel agent, with appointment times made once you're on board. Poolside spa services are also available.

The ship's glass-walled gym is located on the Top Deck and is surprisingly well stocked for a vessel this size, with four treadmills, four bikes, several step machines and elliptical trainers, a full Cybex weight circuit, dumbbells, a ballet bar, and a rowing machine that uses water resistance. Up on deck, you'll find a schedule of yoga, Pilates, Body Blitz, and self-defense classes for $11 a pop, plus free aerobics, stretching, and abdominals classes.

There are two pools on board: one on the Top Deck, beneath the sails, and another in the stern, alongside two hot tubs. Adjacent to the pools are recently installed Balinese sun beds. For joggers, a full-circuit teak promenade wraps around the Bridge Deck. The flying bridge is strung with two-person hammocks, providing a prime relaxation opportunity under the ships' billowing sails.

Wind Spirit • Wind Star

The Verdict

Two of the most romantic, cozy-yet-roomy small ships out there, these vessels look chic and have just the right combination of creature comforts and first-class cuisine, along with a casual, laid-back, unstructured atmosphere.

Wind Spirit *(photo: Windstar Cruises)*

Specifications   Typical Per Diems: $230–$320+

Size (in tons)	5,350	Passenger/Crew Ratio	1.6 to 1
Passengers (double occ.)	148	Year Launched	
Passenger/Space Ratio	36	*Wind Spirit*	1988
Total Cabins/Veranda Cabins	74/0	*Wind Star*	1986
Crew	94	Last Refurbishment/Upgrade	2010

Frommer's Ratings (Scale of 1–5)   ★★★½

Cabin Comfort & Amenities	4	Dining Options	3.5
Appearance & Upkeep	3.5	Adventure & Fitness Options	2
Public Comfort/Space	4	Children's Facilities	N/A
Decor	4	Enjoyment Factor	4.5

Sailing Regions, Seasons & Home Ports

| **Wind Spirit** | **Caribbean,** from St. Martin (winter) |
| **Wind Star** | **Panana Canal,** from St. Martin (fall) |

These are great ships, combining high-tech design with the lines of a gracious private yacht, from their soaring masts to their needle-sharp bowsprits. They're the kind of lived-in, well-sailed vessels that a certain type of passenger latches on to forever and keeps coming back to year after year. In 2010, both ships received a refurbishment that spruced up their interiors and amenities.

CABINS   All cabins are nearly identical at 188 square feet, with a burgundy and navy color scheme, a flatscreen TV, a DVD/CD player, Bose SoundDocks (usable with Apple iPod Nanos that you can check out from the reception desk), a minibar, a pair of large round portholes with brass fittings, a compact closet, bathrobes, L'Occitane toiletries, and fresh fruit. Like the ships' main public rooms, cabins have wood accents and trim, and are attractive and well constructed. Their square footage exceeds that of most small ships and matches the size of the largest standard cabins on the mainstream ships. Teak-decked bathrooms, rather large for ships this size, are better laid out than those aboard many luxury vessels, and contain a hair dryer and compact but adequate storage space. Another hair dryer (one with enough power to actually dry hair) is stowed out in the main cabin. Both ships have one Owner's Cabin that has a little more breathing room, at 220 square feet.

   Although all the cabins are comfortable, cabins amidships are more stable in rough seas—a rule of thumb aboard all ships. Note that the ships' engines, when running at full speed, can be a bit noisy.

   This line is not recommended for passengers with serious disabilities or those who are wheelchair bound. There are no elevators on board, no wheelchair-accessible cabins, and many raised doorsills.

PUBLIC AREAS   There aren't a lot of public areas on these small ships, but they're more than adequate, as passengers spend most of their time in port. The four main rooms include two restaurants, a library, and a vaguely nautical-looking **bar/lounge** with cozy, partitioned-off nooks and clusters of comfy, caramel-colored leather chairs surrounding a wooden dance floor. This is where passengers congregate for port talks, pre- and post-dinner drinks, dancing, and performances by local musicians and dancers. A second bar is out on the Pool Deck and also attracts passengers before and after dinner for drinks and sometimes cigar smoking under the stars.

The small wood-paneled **library** manages to be both nautical and collegiate at the same time. Guests can read, play cards, or check out one of the hundreds of DVDs and CDs for use in their cabins. You can surf the Internet and send e-mail in the library; there's also Wi-Fi for laptop users.

DINING OPTIONS   The elegant, dimly lit **main restaurant** is styled with teak trim and paneling, rope-wrapped pillars, navy blue carpeting and fabrics, and other nautical touches. It's the main dinner venue, though a new second spot is **Candles,** an intimate poolside grill serving steaks and skewers for about 30 guests a night. The **Veranda** breakfast and lunch restaurant is a sunny, window-lined room with tables extending outdoors onto a covered deck. You have to go outside on deck to enter the restaurant, so if it's raining, you'll get wet.

POOL, FITNESS, SPA & SPORTS FACILITIES   Each ship has a tiny swimming pool and an adjacent hot tub in the stern. Deck chairs around the pool can get filled during sunny days, but there's always space available on the crescent-shaped slice of deck above, outside the Veranda restaurant, and in a nice patch of deck forward of the bridge. The flying bridge is strung with two-person hammocks, providing a prime relaxation opportunity under the ships' billowing sails.

The ships' small gyms provide elliptical trainers, recumbent bikes, a ballet bar, free weights, and a flatscreen TV—not bad for ships this size. Deck 4 has an unobstructed wraparound deck for walkers. Massages, facials, and a few other treatments are available out of a single massage room next to the hair salon on Deck 1 (or poolside). Don't fault it just on size, though: One of the best massages we've ever had at sea was aboard *Wind Spirit.*

12 Niche Cruise Roundup

We admit it: We're guilty of focusing on the two dozen or so cruise lines that dominate the current seagoing market, from the big mainstream lines to the handful of relatively "major players" in the small-ship market. There's some logic to that—after all, those companies together probably carry 98% of all travelers taking their vacations at sea—but it leaves out some wonderful niche operations, most of them operating only one ship and carrying fewer than 25 passengers. In this section, we try to expiate our guilt by giving props to 15 of the more interesting, super-small-ship lines in the North American market.

Arabella

Sailing Regions: New England, Chesapeake, Caribbean
Contact: Atlantic Star Lines, 1 Christie's Landing, Newport, RI 02840. ✆ **800/ 395-1343.** www.cruisearabella.com.

Launched in 2001, the 160-foot, three-masted staysail schooner *Arabella* is a sleekly modern tall ship that carries 40 passengers in yachtlike comfort, with a

Arabella *(Photo: Classic Cruises of Newport)*

hot tub on deck, kayaks and snorkel gear for off-vessel fun, and cozy cabins with port-holes. She sails New England cruises from June through September, Chesapeake Bay cruises in fall, and Caribbean cruises from December through May. New England cruises visit ports such as Newport, Nantucket, and Martha's Vineyard, as well as sail-ing along the Maine coast. In the Caribbean, she has several different itineraries, one visiting the U.S. and British Virgin Islands (to ports such as Tortola, Norman Island, Coopers Island, Virgin Gorda, and Jost Van Dyke), one featuring the Spanish Virgin Islands (visiting Vieques and Culebra, plus St. John, Tortola, and Jost Van Dyke), and one concentrating on St. Barts, St. Kitts, and Nevis. Rates for weeklong cruises range from about $1,150 to $2,550 per person.

Baja Expeditions

Sailing Regions: Baja/Sea of Cortez
Contact: 3096 Palm St., San Diego, CA 92104. ℂ **800/843-6967** or 858/581-3311. www.bajaex.com.

Founded in 1974, Baja Expeditions takes environmentally conscious small-ship cruises in Mexico's Sea of Cortez, focused on education and preservation. Frequent anchorages

Don Jose *(Photo: Baja Expeditions)*

allow for swimming, snorkeling, kayaking, and hiking. Departures run from January through July aboard the 16-passenger *Don Jose,* built especially for the line in 1978. Rates for 7-night cruises start at around $1,700 per person.

Bluewater Adventures

Sailing Regions: British Columbia, Alaska
Contact: 3-252 E. First St., North Van-couver, BC, Canada. ℂ **888/877-1770** or 604/980-3800. www.bluewater adventures.ca.

Also founded in 1974, this Vancou-ver-based company offers 7- to 11-night Alaska Inside Passage sailings as

Island Roamer *(Photo: Bluewater Adventures)*

well as a slew of 7- to 9-night British Columbia cruises. They visit the wildlife-rich Queen Charlotte Islands, the coastal Great Bear Rainforest (home to black bears, griz-zlies, and the white spirit bear), northern Vancouver Island (great for orca sightings), and Canada's Gulf Islands (home to Canada's Gulf Islands National Park), and they sail along BC's north coast (home to the port of Prince Rupert and the Khutzeyma-teen grizzly bear sanctuary). Sailings adhere to a casual, low-impact, eco-tourism ethic, focusing on wildlife watching, nature and culture hikes, visits to Native village sites, kayaking, and excursions by inflatable launch. BC cruises are aboard the 68-foot,

16-passenger sailing ketches *Island Odyssey* and *Island Roamer*—rare sailing ships in a generally motor-driven cruise region. Alaska sailings are aboard *Island Odyssey* and the 12-passenger, 65-foot motor yacht *Snow Goose*. Weeklong trips are priced from about $4,000 per person.

The Boat Company

Mist Cove *(Photo: The Boat Company)*

Sailing Regions: Alaska
Contact: 18819 3rd Ave. NE, Ste. 200, Poulsbo, WA 98370-0258. ℂ **877/ 647-8268** or 360/697-4242. www. theboatcompany.com.

The Boat Company is a true rarity: a not-for-profit cruise line, whose revenues after operating expenses all get channeled back into conservation efforts in Southeast Alaska. Founded in 1980, the company offers cruises aboard two small vessels: the 20-passenger *Liseron,* a restored, wooden-hulled former Navy minesweeper built in 1952, and the 24-passenger *Mist Cove,* a metal-hulled re-creation of *Liseron* built by the company in 2000. All trips are focused completely on nature, sailing among the islands and coastal wilderness of the Tongass National Forest and steering well clear of the usual cruise stops. Fishing is a big draw on these boats, which are licensed to allow passengers to fish from the skiffs they carry on board. Other activities include nature hikes, kayaking, and excursions by inflatable launch. Only the embarkation and debarkation ports and dates are set; the rest of each trip is flexible, based on the interests of the guests sailing that week. Several cruises each summer are designated as family cruises—a rarity in the small-ship world. Weeklong trips are priced from about $4,900 per person, with discounted rates available for kids.

Discovery Voyages

Discovery *(Photo: Discovery Voyages)*

Sailing Regions: Alaska
Contact: P.O. Box 688, Whittier, AK 99693. ℂ **800/324-7602** or 907/ 653-1957. http://discoveryvoyages.com.

This one-ship operation takes cruises in Prince William Sound aboard the 65-foot, 12-passenger M/V *Discovery,* a former Presbyterian mission vessel specifically designed for service in coastal Alaska, and now dedicated to casual passenger cruising. Cruises are themed on whale-watching, birding, hiking and kayaking, photography, and general "adventure," but all concentrate on quiet natural destinations. All cruises have their carbon load offset through Vermont-based Native Energy, among whose renewable energy programs is the conversion of some remote

Alaska Native villages to wind-powered electricity. Per-person rates for weeklong voyages run from around $4,200 on up, and include pre- and post-trip hotel stays and all onboard beverages.

Duen Sailing Adventures

Sailing Regions: British Columbia, Alaska
Contact: 1168 Damelart Way, Brentwood Bay, BC, Canada V8M 1R3. ℭ **888/922-8822** or 250/652-8227. www.duenadventures. com.

Operating the eight-passenger, gaff-rigged ketch *Duen* (built in Norway in 1939, and spiffed up for passenger cruising btw. 1990 and 1994), Duen Sailing Adventures provides an intimate sailing experience—both in the small number of passengers and in the tiny, woody cabins and shared bathrooms, a fairly standard arrangement aboard this kind of vessel. Cruises sail in the summer months only and focus on British Columbia's natural and cultural history, with activities like forest hikes, tide-pooling, whale- and bear-watching, visits to Native sites, and stops at hot springs. In spring and fall, the ship offers coastal youth sailing certification programs. Fares for 8-night cruises run around $4,350 per person.

Duen *(Photo: Duen Sailing Adventures)*

Maple Leaf Adventures

Sailing Regions: British Columbia, Alaska
Contact: P.O. Box 8845, Stn. Central, Victoria, BC, Canada V8W 3Z1. ℭ **888/599-5323** or 250/386-7245. www.mapleleafadventures.com.

This BC-based (and BC-oriented) company has been in business since 1986, offering nature and cultural history cruises aboard the restored, 92-foot, tall ship *Maple Leaf*, a one-time pleasure yacht (built in 1904) that spent 6 decades as a fishing vessel before being reconverted back to passenger use.
The vessel carries just eight passengers in small but supremely nautical-looking cabins,

Maple Leaf *(photo: Kevin J. Smith/Maple Leaf Adventures)*

full of gleaming woodwork. The three bathrooms aboard are all shared, as is common on relatively small sailing ships. *Maple Leaf* carries two inflatable launches for daily off-vessel exploration, as well as kayaks for use while the ship is at anchor, and an expert coastal naturalist sails with each trip to help guests learn about the region's natural history and wildlife. In BC, the line offers 5- to 9-night cruises in Gulf Islands National Park, the Great Bear Rainforest, and the Queen Charlotte Islands. There are also a couple of 11-night Alaska Supervoyages in summer, between Prince Rupert, BC, and Sitka. Rates for weeklong sailings start around $2,550.

Mothership Adventures

Sailing Regions: British Columbia
Contact: P.O. Box 30, Heriot Bay, BC, Canada V0P 1H0. *(C)* **888/833-8887** or 250/202-3229. www.mothershipadventures.com.

This small, one-ship, family-run company is centered around the 68-foot, 12-passenger *Columbia III*, a classic wooden working boat built in 1956 for service as a hospital ship with the

Columbia III *(Photo: Mothership Adventures)*

Columbia Coast Mission, which provided medical and social care to coastal BC's remote settlements and logging camps from 1905 to 1969. Refurbished for passenger use in the early 1990s, *Columbia III* won first place in Victoria's Northwest Classic Boat Show in 2003. Cabins are small but nicely appointed, with either bunk-style or "together" beds. The boat's three bathrooms are shared, and the dining room doubles as a lounge. In May and June, the ship sails 3- to 5-night cruises in the Discovery Islands, the Canadian Inside Passage, and the Broughton Archipelago, with all sailings carrying a theme (kayaking, coastal history, photography, First Nations culture, or watercolor painting, for instance). June through September, the focus shifts to 3- to 9-night trips focused on sea kayaking, paddling the same regions plus the Great Bear Rainforest. On typical days, passengers leave the vessel by kayak right after breakfast and paddle amid the islands and fjords all morning before stopping ashore for a picnic lunch and hike or tide-pooling excursion. Per-person rates start at around $1,600 for 4-night trips and $2,300 for 6-night trips.

Northwest Navigation Company

Sailing Regions: Pacific Northwest, British Columbia, Alaska
Contact: P.O. Box 1431, Bellingham, WA 98227. *(C)* **877/670-7863** or 360/201-8184. http://northwestnavigation.com.

David B *(Photo: Northwest Navigation Co.)*

Built in 1929, the classic *David B* served for decades as a tow boat, pulling a string of sailed fishing craft from Alaska's Libby, McNeil and Libby Co. cannery into salmon fishing grounds. Converted to passenger use in the late 1990s, the classic little vessel now offers cruises for just six passengers. The majority of the trips are in Washington's San Juan Islands with 2-night getaway cruises and 3-night kayaking cruises, all round-trip from Bellingham, Washington, May to June and August to October. The vessel also takes a handful of longer cruises in the Canadian Inside Passage (btw. Bellingham and Ketchikan) and Alaska cruises that focus on natural areas, quiet anchorages like Wood Spit and No Name Cove, and small communities like Petersburg. Per-person rates for 3-night kayaking cruises are $1,400; per-person rates for 6-night Alaska voyages are around $4,200.

Pacific Catalyst

Sailing Regions: Alaska, Pacific Northwest, British Columbia
Contact: P.O. Box 3117, Friday Harbor, WA 98250. ✆ **800/378-1708** or 360/378-7123. www.pacificcatalyst.com.

The wooden, 75-foot, 12-passenger *Pacific Catalyst* was built in 1932 as a research vessel for the University of

Pacific Catalyst *(Photo: Pacific Catalyst)*

Washington, and her maiden voyage was up the Inside Passage and across the Gulf of Alaska. Today, the ship is a wonderful bit of history, still operating her original Washington Diesel engine and offering trips that eschew port visits entirely and focus instead on natural areas, with days spent hiking, sea kayaking, and observing both the wilderness and wildlife. From late April to late August, the company has several different 6-night Alaska sailings, all of them concentrating on natural areas rather than ports. One cruise spends 4 whole days in Misty Fjords National Monument—a unique option. A pair of 10-night cruises in Canada's Inside Passage bracket the ship's Alaska season in April and August, and in September she sails 2- to 5-night cruises among Washington's San Juan Islands, round-trip from Friday Harbor. Rates for 6-night Alaska cruises start at around $3,900 per person. Rates for 5-night San Juan Island cruises start at $1,600 per person.

St. Lawrence Cruise Lines

Sailing Regions: Eastern Canada
Contact: 253 Ontario St., Ste. 200, Kingston, Ontario, Canada K7L 2Z4. ✆ **800/267-7868** or 613/549-8091. www.stlawrencecruiselines.com.

Sailing Canada's St. Lawrence River, Thousand Islands region, and Ottawa

Canadian Empress *(Photo: St. Lawrence Cruise Lines)*

River since 1981, the 66-passenger *Canadian Empress* was designed after turn-of-the-century river vessels, her decor pegged to what you would have seen around 1908 and her shallow draft allowing her to maneuver in close to shore. The vessel offers 2- and 3-night Thousand Islands cruises round-trip from Kingston, Ontario; 3-night Heritage Waterways cruises on the St. Lawrence and Thousand Islands, between Kingston and Montreal; 5-night one-way cruises on the St. Lawrence and Ottawa rivers between Kingston and Ottawa; and 6-night one-way cruises between Kingston and Quebec City, all from May to October. Prices for 3-night cruises start at around $1,100 per person. Prices for 6-night cruises start at around $2,150.

Sea Wolf Adventures

Sailing Regions: Alaska, British Columbia
Contact: P.O Box 312, Gustavus, AK 99826. *(C)* **907/957-1438.** www.sea wolfadventures.net.

The 97-foot *Sea Wolf* was built as the Navy minesweeper USS *Observer* in 1941 and protected San Francisco Bay

Sea Wolf *(Photo: Sea Wolf Adventures)*

until 1947, after which she was sold into private hands and converted into a private yacht. Refitted as a charter vessel in the 1980s, she now offers nature-oriented Alaska cruises for just 12 passengers, who can explore via the ship's skiff or her six two-person kayaks, or view the scenery through wraparound windows in the enclosed, heated aft viewing/dining deck, covered side decks, cozy main salon, or open topside areas. Cabins are woody and nautical, with bunk-style beds and private bathrooms. Wheelchair travelers take note: *Sea Wolf* is a great rarity in the small ship world, with wide 32-inch decks, three wheelchair-accessible staterooms, lifts between all passenger decks, and a crew that's used to having guests with disabilities aboard. *Sea Wolf's* 5-night Alaska itineraries (May–Aug) are spent entirely in Glacier Bay, hiking, kayaking, whale-watching, and glacier-viewing. The company also offers a handful of 9-night sailings in British Columbia's Great Bear Rainforest and two annual 10-night Glacier Bay cruises. The 5-night Alaska trips are priced at around $3,000 per person.

Vermont Discovery Cruises

Sailing Regions: Lake Champlain, Vermont
Contact: 348 Flynn St., Burlington, VT 05401. *(C)* **802/863-3350.** www. vermontdiscoverycruises.com.

Vermont Discovery is the first overnight cruise service to operate on Vermont's Lake Champlain since

Moonlight Lady *(Photo: Vermont Discovery Cruises)*

1932. Launched in 2002, the 16-passenger *Moonlight Lady* was brought to the Champlain region in summer 2008, where she began offering 1- to 6-night cruises on the lake, the St. Lawrence River, and the Chambly Canal, from May to mid-October. The experience emulates lake cruises of the early–20th century, concentrating on pure relaxation: taking in the lake views, bike riding, wildlife-watching, and visiting small lakeside towns (and, in some cases, major cities like Montreal). Shore excursions allow access to regional theaters, museums, gardens, festivals, and villages. Though very basic, *Moonlight Lady* is cute as a bug with her spiffy blue-and-white paint job, cozy cabins (each with a tiny bathroom), open kitchen and pilot house, and both open and enclosed viewing areas. Cruises cost $199 per person, per night, and range from 1 to 6 nights.

Wanderbird Expeditions

Wanderbird *(Photo: Wanderbird Expeditions)*

Sailing Regions: Maine Coast, Canada/Newfoundland, Caribbean, Alaska
Contact: P.O. Box 272, Belfast, ME 04915. ✆ **866/732-2473.** www.wanderbirdcruises.com.

The 12-passenger *Wanderbird* is a 90-foot, Dutch-built trawler that fished the North Sea from 1963 until 1990 and is now based in Maine, where she's one of the weirder vessels among that coast's more characteristic schooners and sloops. On the outside, she could almost pass for a working research or fishing vessel, if she weren't so spic and span (and if you discount the sails, which provide auxiliary power). On the inside, she's woody, homey, and yachtlike. The cruises mix total relaxation (few planned activities) with nature observation and exploration, whale- and bird-watching, wildlife photography, and unusual touches like listening to and recording whale songs. The ship also carries two small boats and several kayaks for off-vessel exploration. Unlike most of Maine's coastal fleet, *Wanderbird* tends to wander: At this writing, she was in the midst of her first Caribbean seasons, sailing among the Virgin Islands. Summers usually find her taking 6-night coastal cruises, but in summer 2011, she will go sailing beyond the state to Newfoundland, Labrador, and Greenland. In summer 2012, the vessel will tentatively sail in Alaska. The 5-night cruises tend to run from $1,100 to $1,600 per person.

Westwind Tugboat Adventures

Sailing Regions: British Columbia
Contact: P.O Box 48131 RPO, Queensborough, New Westminister, BC, Canada V3M 0A7. ⒸⒻ **888/ 599-8847.** www.tugboatcruise.com.

Here's a really unusual one: a cruise line that operates a classic tugboat and has a serious jones for fishing. Built in 1941, the wooden tug *Parry* has been con-

Parry *(Photo: Westwind Tugboat Adventures)*

verted for passenger sailing, carrying 12 guests in comfortable two-berth cabins. Inside, the boat is suitably woody, with a feel that makes you expect a grizzled captain in a pea coat to come walking through the door at any moment, pipe in hand. Cruises concentrate on the Great Bear Rainforest and different portions of the Canadian Inside Passage (May–Oct), and include activities like sea kayaking, fishing, whale-watching, forest hikes, clam digging, and beach barbecues. Rates for 5-night cruises run around $4,900 to $5,100 per person.

Part 3

The Ports

With tips on the best tours and advice on things you can see and do on your own in 21 ports of call, plus information on the ports of embarkation.

The Ports of Embarkation

At one time, cruises from the U.S. left only from the corners of the country—from Florida to the Caribbean, from New York and Boston to Canada's Maritimes and Bermuda, from Vancouver (not in the U.S., but real close) to Alaska, and from L.A. and San Diego to the Mexican Riviera. That's already a lot of options, but the question remained: Why stop there? Both coasts are full of cities with excellent port facilities, and cruise ships are, after all, ships, not trains on rails. They can sail from anywhere, as long as the water's deep enough.

That realization began dawning on the cruise industry around the turn of the millennium, and today, cities like Seattle, Galveston, Houston, Baltimore, and even Bayonne, New Jersey, host cruise ships for all or part of each year.

In this chapter, we give you all the info on what to see and do in each of the 17 major U.S. and Canadian embarkation ports. Cruise lines generally offer **pre- and post-cruise hotel packages** for passengers wanting to extend their vacations or add in some decompression time between ship and home, but in case you want to make your own arrangements, we also include some distinctive hotel and restaurant choices. **Hotel prices** listed here are standard rack rates for double rooms unless stated otherwise, and represent examples of what you'll pay during cruise season—summer months for ports that serve Alaska, for instance. Hotel prices may vary considerably in ports that serve year-round cruise destinations like the Caribbean. For more extensive information on any of these cities, check the relevant Frommer's city, state, or regional guide.

PORTS NOT COVERED IN THIS CHAPTER San Juan (Puerto Rico) and **Honolulu (Hawaii)** are major ports of call as well as ports of embarkation, and therefore appear in chapters 10 and 14, respectively. **Québec City** occasionally acts as a home port for Canada/New England cruises, but because it's more often a port of call, it's discussed in chapter 15. Three other ports—**Norfolk,** Virginia, **Jacksonville,** Florida, and **Mobile,** Alabama—also act as home ports, but to only one or two ships apiece.

DRIVING TO THE PORT All the ports in this chapter have **secure parking** for passengers who drive to their ships. We include parking prices in all the reviews. Your cruise line and/or travel agent will also provide info.

FLYING TO THE PORT If flying to the port of embarkation, you can take a taxi or purchase transfers ahead of time from the cruise line to get you from the airport to the cruise port. We include **taxi prices** in all these reviews, so compare them against your cruise line's **transfer prices** to see which you prefer. While cruise line transfers allow you to fall into the cruise line's warm embrace immediately (and meet some of your fellow passengers before you board), you'll often have to wait awhile for the bus to load up and go. A taxi is speedier.

Choosing a Chain

In addition to the hotels listed in this chapter, the following big motel and hotel chains are represented in most of the port cities.

- **Best Western** ✆ 800/780-7234; www.bestwestern.com
- **Clarion** ✆ 877/424-6423; www.clarionhotel.com
- **Comfort Inn** ✆ 800/424-6423; www.comfortinn.com
- **Comfort Suites** ✆ 800/424-6423; www.comfortsuites.com
- **Courtyard by Marriott** ✆ 888/236-2427; www.courtyard.com
- **Days Inn** ✆ 800/329-7466; www.daysinn.com
- **Doubletree** ✆ 800/222-8733; www.doubletree.com
- **Econo Lodge** ✆ 800/424-6423; www.econolodge.com
- **Holiday Inn** ✆ 888/465-4329; www.holiday-inn.com
- **Howard Johnson** ✆ 800/466-4656; www.hojo.com
- **Motel 6** ✆ 800/466-8356; www.motel6.com
- **Quality Inn** ✆ 800/424-6423; www.qualityinn.com
- **Red Roof Inns** ✆ 800/733-7663; www.redroof.com

1 Anchorage, Alaska

Anchorage, Alaska's largest city, stands between the Chugach Mountains and the waters of upper Cook Inlet. Started as a tent camp for workers building the Alaska Railroad in 1914, it remained a sleepy railroad town until World War II, when the opening of a couple of military bases livened things up a bit. Even so, Anchorage did not start becoming a city in earnest until the 1950s, when the Cold War (and Alaska's proximity to the old "Evil Empire") spurred a huge investment in infrastructure.

Today, Anchorage enjoys the distinction of being incorrectly perceived as the state capital by just about everybody in the Lower 48, simply because it seems so obvious that it should be. (Trivial Pursuit answer: Juneau is the real capital; see chapter 11.) It also boasts good restaurants, worthwhile museums, shops, a few small historic attractions, and the must-do **Tony Knowles Coastal Trail** in and around its walkable if not thrillingly attractive 8×20-block downtown. Outside town, the world-class **Alaska Native Heritage Center** is a 26-acre celebration of Alaska's five major Native groups. And always, of course, there is wilderness—so close that moose regularly annoy the city's gardeners, and bears sometimes amble through town.

Plan to spend at least a half-day or full day here. If you have time, plan another half-day at the Native Heritage Center or a day trip about 50 miles south along the incredibly scenic inlet known as **Turnagain Arm.**

Note: If you're ending your cruise in Anchorage, you'll probably arrive via the port towns of **Seward** or **Whittier.** The reason is speed: From the south, cruising around the Kenai Peninsula to get to Anchorage would add another day to itineraries, so the vast majority of ships dock instead in southerly Seward (about 125 miles from Anchorage, on the southeast coast of the Kenai) or Whittier (in the northwestern waters of Prince William Sound, about 60 miles southeast of Anchorage), and then shuttle passengers to the city by bus or train. A few ships, mostly small but occasionally large, dock in Anchorage proper.

GETTING TO ANCHORAGE & THE PORT

If arriving by plane before the cruise, you'll land at the **Ted Stevens Anchorage International Airport** (© **907/266-2526;** www.dot.state.ak.us/anc), located within city limits, a 10- to 15-minute drive from downtown. **Taxis** cost about $25 for the trip. By car, there is only one road into Anchorage from the rest of the world: the Glenn Highway. The other road into town, the Seward Highway, leads up from the Kenai Peninsula.

GETTING AROUND   Most **car rental** companies operate at the airport. **Taxis** are available in town at a rate of $2 per mile, plus a $2 initial fee. Anchorage's $1.75-per-ride People Mover **bus system** is an effective way of getting to and from the top attractions and activities. Day passes are an excellent deal at $4, allowing unlimited rides.

BEST CRUISE LINE SHORE EXCURSIONS

Shore excursions in Anchorage often carry restrictions based on whether (and when) you're sailing from Seward or Whittier and whether you're staying over in Anchorage proper.

Prince William Sound Kayaking ($99, 3½ hr.): Departing from Whittier, this tour takes you to one of Prince William Sound's deep-water fjords for a guided paddle around gorgeous waterfalls and rock formations.

Resurrection River Float Trip ($115, 3 hr.): Board an eight-person piloted raft for a relaxing 8-mile float down the Resurrection River, starting from a spot near the base of Exit Glacier. The trip is whitewater-free.

EXPLORING ANCHORAGE ON YOUR OWN

Anchorage's downtown area is pleasant, but don't expect an old-fashioned Alaskan town: Most of its buildings were leveled in the big 1964 earthquake, which at a magnitude of 9.2 was more powerful than the magnitude-8.8 quake that tore apart Chile in early 2010. Today, downtown Anchorage is thoroughly modern, albeit in an Alaskan way, with stretches of touristy shops interspersed with government buildings, shops for locals, a few seedy sections, and occasional dashes of homespun public art. Check out Bob Patterson's *History of Anchorage* **mural** at 7th Avenue and F Street, which depicts exactly that. At 4th Avenue and E Street, the 1936 **Old City Hall** has an interesting display of city history in its lobby, including dioramas of the early streetscape. Recent development around the big new Dena'ina Civic and Convention Center (which sits btw. F and G sts. and 7th and 8th aves.) promises to liven up its part of the downtown core.

Our pick for number-one downtown activity is taking a walk along the **Tony Knowles Coastal Trail,** which allows for gorgeous views over the waters of Knik Arm. The trail runs through downtown and the arm for about 11 miles, from the western end of 2nd Avenue to Kincaid Park. You can hop on at several points, including via **Elderberry Park,** at the western end of 5th Avenue, where you'll also find the **Oscar Anderson House** museum (© **907/274-2336**). Built in 1915 for Swedish butcher Anderson and his family, it's a quaint dwelling surrounded by a lovely little garden, with a tour that provides a glimpse into the city's short history. Furnishings include a working 1909 player piano. It's open Monday to Friday noon to 5pm. Admission is $3.

The **Anchorage Museum at Rasmuson Center,** 121 W. 7th Ave., between A and C streets (© **907/343-4326;** www.anchoragemuseum.org), is the state's largest museum, with a large permanent collection and interesting touring and temporary exhibits. At press time, a major expansion was near completion, which added display space and a planetarium, brought more than 600 Alaska Native artifacts from the Smithsonian Institution in Washington, and created a 2-acre public park for outdoor exhibits and recreation. On the museum's second floor, the large Alaska Gallery presents an informative and enjoyable walk through the history and some of the anthropology of the state and its Native peoples. The art galleries present Alaskan works from yesterday and today, along with photos of pre-quake Anchorage and Alaskan pop-culture artifacts. For kids, the newly expanded museum provides a new home for an old Anchorage favorite: the **Imaginarium,** a kids-oriented, hands-on science museum with a strong Alaska theme. More than 80 exhibits include live animal touch tanks, simulated earthquakes and auroras, a space that uses bubbles to demonstrate scientific principles, and interactive exhibits for infants and toddlers. The museum's restaurant, Muse, is operated by the excellent Marx Brothers Café (see below) and serves some of the best lunches downtown. The museum is open daily from 9am to 6pm (Thurs 9pm). Admission is $10 adults, $2 suggested donation for kids ages 17 and under. A $27 combo ticket will also get you a free shuttle and admission to . . .

. . . the 26-acre **Alaska Native Heritage Center,** 8800 Heritage Center Dr. (© **800/315-6608;** www.alaskanative.net), located about 15 minutes from downtown Anchorage. Opened in 1999, the center introduces visitors to the lives and cultures of the state's five major Alaska Native groupings: the Southeast's Tlingit, Eyak, Haida, and Tsimshian tribes; the Athabascans of the interior; the Inupiat and St. Lawrence Island Yupiks of the far north; the Aleuts and Alutiiqs of the Aleutian Islands; and the Yup'ik and Cup'ik tribes of the extreme west. The central Welcome House holds a small museum displaying some remarkable Native carvings and masks; a workshop where Native craftspeople demonstrate their techniques; a theater presenting a rotating series of films on Native culture; and a rotunda where storytelling, dance, and music performances are presented throughout the day. Outside, spaced along a walking trail around a small lake, are five traditional dwellings representing the five Native cultures and regions. Native staffers are on hand at each to provide information about the dwellings. Though the center is offered as a shore excursion by most ships, it's worth going on your own if you're interested in Native culture, because the tours don't give you enough time to experience all the place has to offer. The center is open daily 9am to 5pm. Admission is $25 adults, $17 kids ages 7 to 16. A free shuttle leaves regularly from the Anchorage Museum, the Anchorage Visitor Center at 4th Avenue and F Street, and several other sites. Times are posted at all pickup points, or call for information (© **907/330-8000**).

About 8 miles from downtown, the **Alaska Zoo,** 4731 O'Malley Rd. (© **907/346-2133;** www.alaskazoo.org), has gravel paths meandering through the woods past natural flora and local wildlife such as polar and brown bears, seals and otters, musk oxen, Dall sheep, moose, caribou, and waterfowl—most of which you may see on your cruise, but not this close up. There are also elephants, Siberian tigers, yaks, and Bactrian camels, which you won't see from the ship unless you're having flashbacks. The zoo is open daily 10am to 5pm. Admission is $12 adults, $6 kids ages 3 to 17. To get here, take either the old or the new Seward Highway south to O'Malley Road, turn left, and travel for about 1½ miles.

Downtown Anchorage

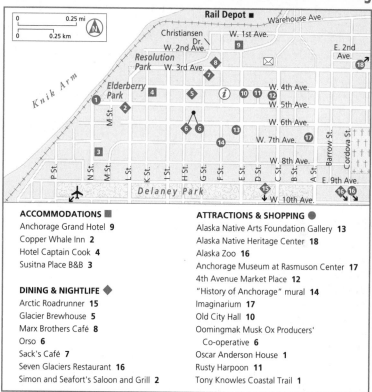

ACCOMMODATIONS ■
Anchorage Grand Hotel **9**
Copper Whale Inn **2**
Hotel Captain Cook **4**
Susitna Place B&B **3**

DINING & NIGHTLIFE ◆
Arctic Roadrunner **15**
Glacier Brewhouse **5**
Marx Brothers Café **8**
Orso **6**
Sack's Café **7**
Seven Glaciers Restaurant **16**
Simon and Seafort's Saloon and Grill **2**

ATTRACTIONS & SHOPPING ●
Alaska Native Arts Foundation Gallery **13**
Alaska Native Heritage Center **18**
Alaska Zoo **16**
Anchorage Museum at Rasmuson Center **17**
4th Avenue Market Place **12**
"History of Anchorage" mural **14**
Imaginarium **17**
Old City Hall **10**
Oomingmak Musk Ox Producers'
  Co-operative **6**
Oscar Anderson House **1**
Rusty Harpoon **11**
Tony Knowles Coastal Trail **1**

ATTRACTIONS IN SEWARD & WHITTIER

Most people pass through Seward and Whittier without a second glance on their way to Anchorage or the Interior, but if you have time, there are a few interesting sights to see in these two port towns. In Seward, the spectacular **Alaska SeaLife Center,** right on the waterfront at Mile 0 of the Seward Highway (© **800/224-2525;** www. alaskasealife.org), allows scientists and visitors (the latter through windows) to study the sea lions, porpoises, sea otters, harbor seals, fish, and other forms of marine life that abound in the area, as well as the umpteen species of local seabirds. The center is open Monday to Thursday 9am to 6:30pm, Friday to Sunday 8am to 6:30pm. Admission costs $20 adults, $15 kids ages 12 to 17, $10 kids ages 4 to 11.

As for Whittier, the most amazing thing about the town is that almost the entire population lives in a single 14-story concrete building known as **Begich Towers.** It was built during the 1940s, when Whittier's strategic location on the Alaska Railroad and at the head of a deep Prince William Sound fjord made it a key port in the defense of Alaska, and after awhile everybody in town just migrated here to make things easier. Eventually, businesses opened in the towers as well, including a small grocery store and a medical clinic. Kids don't even have to go outside to get to school in winter—a tunnel leads right from the tower to the school building.

SHOPPING

Many stores in Anchorage carry Native-looking arts and crafts, but most are just touristy knockoffs. Give 'em your back and head for the good stuff instead. The **Oomingmak Musk Ox Producers' Co-operative,** 604 H St., at 6th Avenue (✆ **888/360-9665** or 907/272-9225; www.qiviut.com), is a co-op owned by 200 Alaska Native women in villages across the state. All of their products are knitted from qiviut (*kiv-ee-oot*), the light, warm, silky underhair of the musk ox, which is collected from shedding animals. Each village has its own knitting pattern. Items are expensive—adult caps start at $175, scarves at $245—but considering the rarity and beauty of the work (not to mention qiviut's exceptional warmth), they're really a bargain. The website has a "letters" page with notes sent by the knitters, discussing their work. The **Rusty Harpoon,** 411 W. 4th Ave. (✆ **907/278-9011;** www.rustyharpoongifts.com), also has authentic Native items and less expensive crafts, and the longtime proprietors only buy direct from Native artists they know. Right next door, at 4th Avenue between C and D streets, the **4th Avenue Market Place** has several good shops. Nearby, the **Alaska Native Arts Foundation Gallery,** at 6th Avenue and E Street (✆ **907-258-2623;** www.alaskanativearts.org), is a nonprofit organization promoting the best work of indigenous artists, both traditional and contemporary.

WHERE TO STAY

Rooms can be hard to come by in Anchorage in the summer, so be sure to arrange lodging as far in advance of your trip as possible, whether through your cruise line or on your own. Here are some good options:

The **Hotel Captain Cook,** 4th Avenue and K Street (✆ **800/843-1950;** www.captaincook.com), is Alaska's great, grand hotel, where royalty and rock stars stay. Cruise season rates: from $260 double. The all-suite **Anchorage Grand Hotel,** 505 W. 2nd Ave. (✆ **888/800-0640;** www.anchoragegrand.com), has a superb central location; large, quiet suites with a bedroom, living room, and kitchen; and amenities such as free high-speed Internet. Cruise season rates: from $189 double. The casual **Copper Whale Inn,** 440 L St. (✆ **907/258-7999;** www.copperwhale.com), takes up a pair of clapboard houses overlooking Elderberry Park right on the coastal trail downtown, with charming rooms of every shape and size. Cruise season rates: from $210 double (rooms with shared bathroom from $185 double).

A few blocks from downtown, the little **Susitna Place B&B,** 727 N St. (✆ **907/274-3344;** www.susitnaplace.com), doesn't look like much from the back-door entrance, but once you get inside, you realize the house actually sits on a high bluff facing Cook Inlet and Mount Susitna, and has amazing views. Nine rooms are available, four of them with a shared bathroom. Cruise season rates: from $135 double (rooms with shared bathroom from $105 double).

DINING & NIGHTLIFE

Though hardly a culinary or nightlife capital, Anchorage does have a few good restaurants if you want an evening out before or after your cruise. For a fun, casual experience, the **Glacier Brewhouse,** 737 W. 5th Ave. (✆ **907/274-BREW** [2739]; www.glacierbrewhouse.com), has an ever-changing menu of tasty, eclectic dishes served in a large dining room with lodge decor, where the scent of the wood-fired grill hangs in the air. They brew their own hearty beers behind a glass wall. If it's crowded (and it often is), head for the large bar area, where you can just hover like a vulture until a table opens up. Main courses: $11 to $37. The **Marx Brothers Café,** 627 W. 3rd Ave.

(© **907/278-2133;** www.marxcafe.com), began as a hobby among three friends and has become a standard of excellence in the state. The cuisine is varied and creative, ranging from Asian to Italian, but everyone orders the Caesar salad made at the table. The decor and style are studied casual elegance. Main courses: $36 to $38.

Sack's Cafe, 328 G St. (© **907/274-4022;** www.sackscafe.com), is the most fashionable restaurant in Anchorage, and one of the best, with an ever-changing menu that mixes Alaskan seafood with Italian influences and eclectic touches. Main courses: $19 to $34. **Orso,** 737 W. 5th Ave. (© **907/222-3232;** www.orsoalaska.com), serves superb wood-grilled steaks and locally caught seafood, as well as excellent pastas, all in an ornate dining room. Main courses: $19 to $38. **Simon and Seafort's Saloon and Grill,** 420 L St. (© **907/274-3502;** www.simonandseaforts.com), is one of Anchorage's great dinner houses, with a turn-of-the-20th-century decor, a cheerful atmosphere, and fabulous sunset views of Cook Inlet. Prime rib and seafood are the specialties. Main courses: $16 to $49. Lighter meals are served at the bar. For the best, most original takeout burgers in town, head for **Arctic Roadrunner,** with locations at 2477 Arctic Blvd. at Fireweed Lane (© **907/279-7311**), and 5300 Old Seward Hwy. at International Airport Road (© **907/561-1245**). Try the Kodiak Islander, which has peppers, ham, onion rings, and who knows what else on top.

For a memorable dining experience out of town, the Mount Alyeska Resort's **Seven Glaciers Restaurant** (© **800/880-3880;** www.alyeskaresort.com) has views that match its name. Located 2,300 feet up a tramway on the mountainside, the restaurant serves trendy and beautifully presented dinners in a sumptuous dining room floating above the clouds. Notable menu selections include the cold smoked and grilled Alaskan salmon and the Alaskan king crab. Main courses: $35 to $65. The resort is on Arlberg Avenue in Girdwood, a funky little town 37 miles south of Anchorage along Turnagain Arm.

2 Baltimore, Maryland

Charm City has welcomed visitors since 1729. Founded as a shipping and shipbuilding town and later transformed into a manufacturing center, the city rode the new-economy wave of the '90s with more service industries and nonprofits. Today, tourism plays an ever-increasing role in the local economy, with a combination of historical sites, museums, and a revitalized harbor area drawing visitors and cruise lines, too.

GETTING TO BALTIMORE & THE PORT

All cruise vessels depart from the Port of Baltimore's **South Locust Point Marine Terminal,** 2001 E. McComas St., about 5 miles from the Inner Harbor, where many of the best attractions and hotels are located. Parking at the port costs $15 per day. If you're arriving by plane, you'll likely fly into **Baltimore/Washington International Thurgood Marshall Airport** (© **800/435-9294;** www.bwiairport.com), located 10 miles south of downtown Baltimore, off I-295 (the Baltimore-Washington Pkwy.). Taxis to the Inner Harbor area run about $35. **SuperShuttle** (© **800/258-3826;** www.supershuttle.com) also operates vans every half-hour between the airport and all major downtown hotels for about $22 per person.

GETTING AROUND   If you plan to stay near the Inner Harbor, it's easiest to walk or take **Ed Kane's Water Taxi** (© **800/658-8497;** www.thewatertaxi.com), which charges $10 adults, $5 kids ages 10 and under for an all-day pass. There's also regular metered taxi service to get you to the port. On foot, you only have to know a few streets to get your bearings. The **promenade** around the Inner Harbor will take you to Federal Hill and the American Visionary Art Museum, the Maryland Science Center, Harborplace, the USS *Constellation,* and the National Aquarium. The promenade extends along the water through the Harbor East neighborhood to Fells Point and Canton. It makes for a pretty walk. **Pratt** and **Lombard streets** are the two major east-west arteries just above the Inner Harbor. **Charles Street** is Baltimore's main route north and home to some good restaurants. **St. Paul Street** is the major route south. If you're driving around, expect things to be fairly easy. The streets are on a straight grid, and many are one-way. All the major **car rental** companies have offices at the airport.

BEST CRUISE LINE SHORE EXCURSIONS

Baltimore City Tour ($42, 2½ hr.): Take in Baltimore's historic sites, visiting the Harborplace, Babe Ruth's birthplace, Johns Hopkins University, Baltimore's Washington Monument, Fort McHenry, and the historic ships berthed at the seaport.

EXPLORING BALTIMORE ON YOUR OWN

Baltimore's **Inner Harbor** is the starting point for most visitors. A major cargo port until the 1960s, it's been a destination instead for pleasure boaters and tall ships since the city began revitalizing the area in the late '70s. In addition to **restaurants** and extensive **shopping** (see below), there are a number of historic attractions in the neighborhood. The **Baltimore Visitor Center,** adjacent to Harborplace at 401 Light St., has a short film that introduces you to the city, along with all the usual brochures and maps.

The **USS** *Constellation,* moored at 301 E. Pratt St. (© **410/539-1797;** www. constellation.org), is a stunning, triple-masted sloop of war originally launched in 1854. It's the last Civil War–era vessel afloat. Tour the gun decks, visit the wardrooms, see a cannon demonstration, and learn about the life of an old-time sailor. It's open daily 10am to 5:30pm. Admission is $10 adults, $5 kids ages 6 to 14. More seagoing history is to be had at the **Baltimore Maritime Museum** (© **410/396-3453;** www. baltomaritimemuseum.org). Located at Piers 3 and 5, it's really four museums in one. The Coast Guard Cutter *Taney* survived the bombing of Pearl Harbor, the submarine USS *Torsk* sank the last two Japanese merchant ships of World War II, and the lightship *Chesapeake* spent 40 years anchored near the mouth of the Chesapeake Bay. The "screwpile"-style Seven-Foot Knoll Lighthouse looks more like a New England UFO than a traditional lighthouse. Built in 1856, it marked the entrance to Baltimore's harbor for 133 years before being moved to its current location. The four museum ships are open daily 10am to 5:30pm. Admission to the lighthouse is free. Admission to all four ships (including the *Constellation*) is $18 adults, $7 kids ages 6 to 14. Tickets are available at Pier 3, in front of the National Aquarium, and at the USS *Constellation* Building on Pier 1.

At the nearby **National Aquarium,** 501 E. Pratt St. (© **410/576-3800;** www.aqua. org), visitors can walk into a room surrounded by patrolling sharks, wander among the coral reefs, follow the yearly migration of fish, and visit a rainforest on the roof at one of the best aquariums in the country. Though you walk in front of most of the exhibits, you get to actually walk *inside* the doughnut-shaped Coral Reef and the Open Ocean shark tanks. There's also a Marine Mammal Pavilion that's home to a family of dolphins and an exhibit re-creating an Australian river gorge and a "4-D Immersion" movie theater. The aquarium is open daily 9am to 5pm (Fri 8pm, Sat

6pm). Admission to the aquarium is $25 adults, $20 kids ages 3 to 11 (or $30 adults, $25 kids ages 3 to 11, including the dolphin experience and the movie).

Oh, say, can you see by the dawn's early light? Apparently Francis Scott Key could, back in 1814, when the British attacked star-shaped **Fort McHenry,** which sits on a point in the harbor at the end of East Fort Avenue (© **410/962-4290;** www.nps.gov/fomc). It was the sight of the fort's enormous 15-star flag that showed the fort's 1,000 defenders had held their ground, halting the British offensive and inspiring the U.S. national anthem. After that day, the fort never again came under attack, but it remained an active fort on and off for the next 100 years. Today, it's both a National Park and a National Historic Shrine and still flies its huge flag, which takes about 20 people to manage when it's raised and lowered daily. Stop by at 9:30am or 4:30pm (7:30pm June–Aug) to join in. The fort's buildings display historical and military memorabilia, and you can tour the restored barracks, commander's quarters, guardhouse, and powder magazine. The grounds, fort, and visitor center are open daily 8am to 5pm (8pm in summer). Admission is $7 adults, free for kids ages 15 and under.

The **Walters Art Museum,** 600 N. Charles St. (© **410/547-9000;** www.thewalters.org), with its collections of ancient art, medieval armor, and French 19th-century paintings, has always been one of Baltimore's great attractions. It tells the story of Western civilization through its permanent collection that covers some 55 centuries. It's open Wednesday to Sunday 10am to 5pm. Admission is free.

For something different, visit the **American Visionary Art Museum,** 800 Key Hwy. at the base of historic Federal Hill on the south side of the Inner Harbor (© **410/244-1900;** www.avam.org). You can't miss it: Just look for the multicolored, 55-foot wind-powered sculpture out front. As defined by the museum, visionary art is "art produced by self-taught individuals, usually without formal training, whose works arise from an innate personal vision that revels foremost in the creative act itself." This can range from narrative embroideries by Holocaust survivors to the 10-foot model of the *Lusitania* that dominates a first-floor gallery—made from 193,000 matchsticks. All in all, it's some of the most interesting art you'll ever see. It's open Tuesday to Sunday 10am to 6pm. Admission is $16 adults, $10 kids.

Baseball fans will want to catch a game at **Oriole Park at Camden Yards,** 333 W. Camden St. (© **410/685-9800;** www.theorioles.com). If there's a home game during your visit, do whatever it takes to get a ticket: It's a real Baltimore experience. Games are usually held at 1:35 or 7:35pm, with tickets going for between $18 and $93 for same-day sales.

SHOPPING

The Inner Harbor is Baltimore's prime shopping district, with malls and hundreds of shops. **Harborplace** (© **410/332-4191;** www.harborplace.com) is actually three separate locations with more than 160 stores. Between them, they sell everything from onion rings to diamond rings. The **Light Street Pavilion** has the most food stalls and restaurants, with some souvenir shops. The **Pratt Street Pavilion** has specialty stores, clothing and jewelry shops, and more restaurants. The **Gallery,** a mall connected to the Renaissance Harborplace Hotel, has three floors of shops and a food court on the fourth.

For a more classic taste of the city, head to one of its centuries-old markets. The 200-year-old **Broadway Market,** on South Broadway between Fleet and Lancaster streets in Fells Point, has two large covered buildings staffed by local vendors selling fresh produce, flowers, crafts, and an assortment of ethnic and raw-bar foods, ideal for snacking, a quick lunch, or a picnic. You'll even find an old-fashioned Baltimore tradition: "sweet potatoes," soft white candies powdered with cinnamon. The **Lexington Market,** 400 W. Lexington St. (© 410/685-6169; www.lexingtonmarket.com), claims to be the oldest continuously operating market in the United States, having opened for business in 1782. This Baltimore landmark on downtown's west side houses more than 140 merchants, selling prepared ethnic foods (for eat-in or takeout), fresh seafood, produce, meats, baked goods, sweets, and even freshly grated coconut. It's worth a visit for the aromas, flavors, sounds, and sights, as well as good shopping. Bring cash, as credit cards are not accepted. It's open Monday to Saturday 8:30am to 6pm.

WHERE TO STAY

A number of hotels are located in the Inner Harbor and Fells Point neighborhoods, the latter Baltimore's original seaport and home to the first shipyards. Both are a maximum of 7 miles from the cruise terminal.

The **Hyatt Regency Baltimore,** 300 Light St. (© 800/233-1234; http://baltimore. hyatt.com), was the Inner Harbor's first hotel 20 years ago and still has its best location, just a few steps from everything. Rooms have breathtaking harbor views; the amenities are terrific. Cruise season rates: from $249 double.

The **InterContinental Harbor Court Baltimore,** 550 Light St. (© 800/824-0076; www.harborcourt.com), strives for quiet dignity, refinement, and graciousness, with exquisitely furnished rooms. Cruise season rates: from $240 double.

The **Renaissance Harborplace Hotel,** 202 E. Pratt St. (© 800/468-3571; www. renaissanceharborplace.com), is also located right in the middle of everything, across the street from Harborplace and the Inner Harbor. Rooms are very large, and many have great views. Cruise season rates: from $219 double.

The French Renaissance–style **Radisson Plaza Lord Baltimore,** 20 W. Baltimore St. (© 800/333-3333; www.radisson.com/lordbaltimore), opened in 1928, so if you love grand old hotels with modern conveniences, this is the one for you. The entrance features marble columns, handcarved artwork, brass fixtures, and chandeliers, and the Inner Harbor is only 5 blocks away. Cruise season rates: from $175 double.

In Fells Point (southeast of the Inner Harbor), the **Admiral Fell Inn,** 888 S. Broadway (© 866/583-4162; www.harbormagic.com), is composed of seven buildings built between 1790 and 1920, and blends Victorian and Federal-style architecture. Originally a boardinghouse for sailors, later a YMCA, and then a vinegar-bottling plant, the inn has an antiques-filled lobby and library and guest rooms individually decorated with Federal period furnishings. Cruise season rates: from $179 double.

DINING & NIGHTLIFE

Baltimore used to be very quiet after dark, but not anymore. We suggest heading to the Inner Harbor or Fells Point for some of the town's legendary seafood and an evening out.

Fells Point, the neighborhood where Baltimore began, is one of the city's best areas for seafood, and the benchmark of all the eateries here is **Obrycki's,** 1727 E. Pratt St. (© 410/732-6399; www.baltimorecrabhouse.com). This is the quintessential crab house, where you can crack open steamed crabs in their shells and feast on the tender, succulent meat. There's crab soup, crab cocktail, crab balls, crab cakes, crab imperial, and soft-shell crabs, and the rest of the menu is just as tempting. Main courses: $15

Baltimore

CRUISE TERMINAL 19 ●

ATTRACTIONS & SHOPPING ●

American Visionary Art
  Museum 12
Baltimore Maritime Museum 9
Broadway Market 15
Fort McHenry 16
Harborplace 10
Lexington Market 2
National Aquarium 11
Oriole Park at Camden Yards 4
USS Constellation 9
Walters Art Museum 1

ACCOMMODATIONS ■

Admiral Fell Inn 16
Hyatt Regency Baltimore 6
InterContinental Harbor Court 8
Radisson Plaza Lord Baltimore 3
Renaissance Harborplace Hotel 5

DINING & NIGHTLIFE ◆

Bertha's 16
Black Olive 17
Cat's Eye Pub 16
Nick's Fish House 18
Obrycki's 13
Sabatino's 14
Tír na Nóg 7
Vaccaro's 14

to $30. It's open mid-March through November. At the **Black Olive,** 814 S. Bond St. (© **410/276-7141;** www.theblackolive.com), a Greek taverna just beyond the busier streets of Fells Point, the combination of Greek fare and the freshest seafood is magic. Choose the catch of the day and trust the chef to make it wonderful. Main courses: $27 to $40. Reservations required.

At the festive Harborplace development, try **Tír na Nóg** (© **410/483-8968;** www. tirnanogbaltimore.com), a cosmopolitan Irish pub with great Inner Harbor views, a gorgeous interior, and an urbane menu. For dinner, try the hearty crab soup followed by the roasted trout and Irish bacon with crab butter. Main courses: $14 to $24.

If you're geographically adventurous, **Nick's Fish House,** 2600 Insulator Dr. (© **410/347-4123;** www.nicksfishhouse.com), is a great seafood choice. It's in a very industrial area on the Patapsco River, about 2½ miles south of the Inner Harbor, but the crab cakes are delicious and a good value, the service is friendly and efficient, and the atmosphere is Baltimore–meets–Eastern Shore casual. It's worth going out of your way for this place. Main courses: $13 to $27.

Baltimore's Little Italy is located between the Inner Harbor and historic Fells Point, and has both casual and fancy restaurants. We like **Sabatino's,** 901 Fawn St. (© **410/ 727-9414;** www.sabatinos.com), for pasta and garlicky salad dressing just like Nonna used to make. Main courses: $13 to $30.

To top off a perfect day, drop by **Vaccaro's,** 222 Albemarle St. in Little Italy, near Fells Point (© **410/685-4905;** www.vaccarospastry.com), for Italian desserts, coffee, and cappuccino. There's also a location at the Light Street Pavilion in Harborplace. For something more sudsy and musical, head to Fells Point, where the **Cat's Eye Pub,** 1730 Thames St. (© **410/276-9866;** www.catseyepub.com), has live music every night, from Irish folk to zydeco. **Bertha's,** 734 S. Broadway (© **410/327-5795;** www.berthas.com), has live jazz or blues nearly every night, as well as a large menu heavy on seafood and pub grub.

3 Boston, Massachusetts

Boston is a port of call on many itineraries from New York and is also an embarkation port for a handful of Bermuda and New England/Canada cruises (many of the latter terminating in Montréal). Of all the New England ports, it has perhaps the richest history, dating from its founding in 1630 through the Revolution and beyond. Wend your way through the city's many important historical sites via the Freedom Trail walking tour, which includes the **USS** *Constitution* (aka Old Ironsides) and the **Paul Revere House.** In other neighborhoods, stroll past the beautiful Victorian-era town houses in the stylish Back Bay area, take in the Federal architecture of Beacon Hill, or head across the Charles River to Cambridge for a romp around the classic red-brick campus of **Harvard University,** founded way back in 1636. If you're not much for history, you can focus on pure fun, whether it's shopping (perhaps at **Faneuil Hall Marketplace**) or pub hopping—the beloved *Cheers* bar (at least the exterior used in the opening credits) is on Beacon Street, while a replica of the interior is in Faneuil Hall Marketplace.

GETTING TO BOSTON & THE PORT

Ships dock at the **Black Falcon Cruise Terminal** (© **617/330-1500;** www.massport.com/ports/cruis.html) at 1 Black Falcon Ave., in the Boston Marine Industrial Park on the South Boston Waterfront, also called the Seaport District.

There's nothing at the industrial park except ships and sheds, but the heart of Boston is only a couple of miles away, and tour buses and taxis line up to meet cruise passengers. Parking at the port costs $15 per day. By air, you'll arrive at Boston's **Logan International Airport** (© **800/235-6426;** www.massport.com/logan) in East Boston, 3 miles across the harbor from downtown. A **taxi** to the port costs about $20 for two passengers; the drive takes about 10 to 15 minutes, depending on traffic.

GETTING AROUND   The best way to see the historic heart of Boston is on foot. Alternatively, you can sign up for one of your ship's organized tours or hop on the **Beantown Trolley shuttle** (www.brushhilltours.com/tours/beantown.html), which makes a continuous circuit among Boston's top sites. You can hop on or off at any of them, and then catch the next shuttle when you're ready to move on. Tickets are $32 adults, $11 kids ages 5 to 11, and include a Harbor Cruise from the New England Aquarium or the U.S.S. *Constitution.* You can also grab a **taxi** at the pier and drop about $15 for the 3-plus-mile ride to Boston Common, a good starting point for walking tours. Once in town, spend the day walking or take advantage of Boston's efficient subway system, the **"T"**—short for MBTA (© **800/392-6100** or 617/222-3200; www.mbta.com)—which has stops all over the city. Subway fares are $1.70 to $2, bus fares are $1.25 to $1.50, or you can pay $9 for a 1-day pass that allows unlimited travel on both.

BEST CRUISE LINE SHORE EXCURSIONS

Freedom Trail Walking Tour ($39, 4 hr.): You can easily do this well-marked walk on your own, but it's also a good choice if you'd like a guide to explain the highlights.

Beacon Hill Walking Tour ($49, 3 hr.): A guided walking tour goes from the Back Bay neighborhood past Trinity Church, along Newbury Street with its boutiques and cafes, and through the lush Public Garden, with a stop for a quick beer at the *Cheers* pub, inspiration for the classic TV show. Move on to Boston Common, the narrow streets and brick sidewalks of Beacon Hill, and finally to Quincy Market.

The Path of Paul Revere ($49, 4 hr.): This bus ride follows the route of Paul Revere's famous ride to Lexington. In Concord, drive along Author's Row for views of the homes of Nathaniel Hawthorne, Ralph Waldo Emerson, and Louisa May Alcott. In Lexington, see where 77 Minutemen faced 700 British soldiers in the first engagement of the American Revolution.

Lexington & Concord Tour ($79, 7½ hr.): Outside Boston, the towns of Lexington and Concord witnessed the first battles of the Revolutionary War. The tour includes the Old North Church; Lexington Green, where the first skirmish of the war took place; the North Bridge, where the American militia met the British forces; and Harvard Yard.

EXPLORING BOSTON ON YOUR OWN

Boston's cruise port is in an industrial section of town. The *Institute of Contemporary Art* museum (see below) is within easy walking distance, but downtown and most attractions lie a short distance away by taxi, shuttle, or public transit.

Visitors in town for just a day will probably want to concentrate on the city's famed **Freedom Trail** (www.thefreedomtrail.org), a 2.5-mile route that links 16 historic sites, many of them associated with the American Revolution and the country's early days. The route begins at **Boston Common,** the country's oldest public park (dating to 1640), and cuts across downtown, passing through the busy shopping area around

Downtown Crossing, the Financial District, and the North End, on the way to Charlestown. A line of red paint or red brick on the sidewalk marks the route, markers identify the stops, and plaques point the way from one stop to the next. You can download a map at **www.thefreedomtrail.org/maps/maps.html**.

Many of the stops along the route will be familiar to anyone who studied American history in school. At State and Devonshire streets, a ring of cobblestones on a traffic island marks the spot where, on March 5, 1770, colonists threw snowballs, garbage, rocks, and other debris at a group of redcoats, who responded by firing into the crowd and killing five men. That incident, which became known as the **Boston Massacre,** helped consolidate the spirit of rebellion in the colonies. At Dock Square (Congress and North sts.), **Faneuil Hall** was built in 1742 and was a site for speeches by orators such as Samuel Adams (whose statue stands outside) in the years leading to the Revolution. In later years, abolitionists, temperance advocates, and suffragists also used the hall as a pulpit.

Detour before the North End to wander for a block or two (or more) along the **Rose Fitzgerald Kennedy Greenway** (www.rosekennedygreenway.org), which parallels the downtown waterfront. Where an elevated interstate once loomed, a ribbon of parkland, sculpture, fountains, and greenery now delights Bostonians and visitors of all ages. In the North End, the **Paul Revere House,** 19 North Sq. (© **617/523-2338;** www.paulreverehouse.org), is the home from which Revere set off on April 18, 1775, riding to Lexington to warn the local militias that British troops were on the march. The two-and-a-half-story wood structure is the oldest house in downtown Boston, built around 1680 and bought by Revere in 1770. Inside, 17th- and 18th-century furnishings and artifacts—including the famous Revere silver—re-create the period. It's open daily 9:30am to 5:15pm. Admission is $3.50 adults, $1 kids ages 5 to 17. A few blocks away, the **Old North Church,** 193 Salem St. (www.oldnorth.com), is the place where sexton Robert Newman hung two lanterns from the steeple on the night of Revere's ride, as a signal that British troops were setting out for Lexington in boats, rather than on foot ("One if by land, and two if by sea"). It's open daily 9am to 5pm. Requested donation is at least $1.

At the Charlestown Navy Yard, **USS** *Constitution* (© **617/242-5670;** www. oldironsides.com) is one of the U.S. Navy's six original frigates, constructed between 1794 and 1797 using bolts, spikes, and other fittings from Paul Revere's foundry. As the new nation built its naval and military reputation, the *Constitution* played a key role, battling French privateers and Barbary pirates, repelling the British fleet during the War of 1812, participating in 40 engagements, and capturing 20 vessels. The frigate earned its nickname, Old Ironsides, during a battle on August 19, 1812, when shots from HMS *Guerriere* bounced off its thick oak hull as if it were iron. The ship is still a commissioned vessel of the U.S. Navy, and the active-duty sailors who lead tours wear 1812 dress uniforms. It's open Tuesday to Sunday 10am to 6pm; free guided tours of the vessel are led Tuesday to Sunday year-round. A museum (**www.ussconstitutionmuseum.org**) is adjacent. Admission is by voluntary donation.

Beyond Revolutionary sites, Boston has several wonderful museums. Its **Museum of Fine Arts,** 465 Huntington Ave. (© **617/267-9300;** www.mfa.org), is one of the nation's best, known for its collections of Impressionist paintings (including one of the largest collections of Monets outside of Paris), Asian and Old Kingdom Egyptian collections, classical art, Buddhist temple art, and medieval sculpture and tapestries. It's open daily 10am to 4:45pm (Wed–Fri 9:45pm). Admission is $20 adults, $7.50 for

Boston

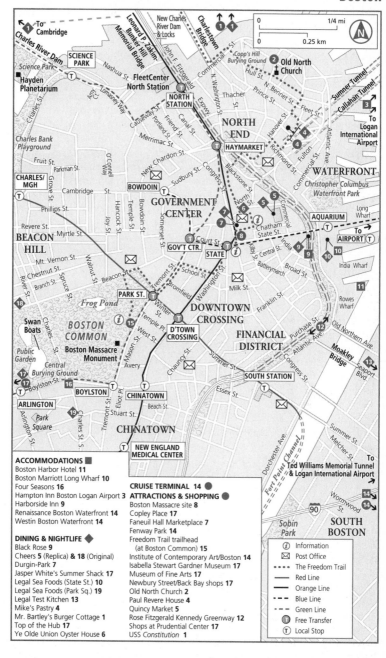

ACCOMMODATIONS ■
Boston Harbor Hotel **11**
Boston Marriott Long Wharf **10**
Four Seasons **16**
Hampton Inn Boston Logan Airport **3**
Harborside Inn **9**
Renaissance Boston Waterfront **14**
Westin Boston Waterfront **14**

DINING & NIGHTLIFE ◆
Black Rose **9**
Cheers **5** (Replica) **& 18** (Original)
Durgin-Park **7**
Jasper White's Summer Shack **17**
Legal Sea Foods (State St.) **10**
Legal Sea Foods (Park Sq.) **19**
Legal Test Kitchen **13**
Mike's Pastry **4**
Mr. Bartley's Burger Cottage **1**
Top of the Hub **17**
Ye Olde Union Oyster House **6**

CRUISE TERMINAL 14 ●
ATTRACTIONS & SHOPPING ●
Boston Massacre site **8**
Copley Place **17**
Faneuil Hall Marketplace **7**
Fenway Park **14**
Freedom Trail trailhead
   (at Boston Common) **15**
Institute of Contemporary Art/Boston **14**
Isabella Stewart Gardner Museum **17**
Museum of Fine Arts **17**
Newbury Street/Back Bay shops **17**
Old North Church **2**
Paul Revere House **4**
Quincy Market **5**
Rose Fitzgerald Kennedy Greenway **12**
Shops at Prudential Center **17**
USS *Constitution* **1**

(i) Information
⊠ Post Office
• • • • The Freedom Trail
—— Red Line
—— Orange Line
– – – Blue Line
– – – Green Line
Ⓣ Free Transfer
Ⓣ Local Stop

kids ages 7 to 17 before 3pm weekdays (free after 3pm and Sat–Sun). The **Isabella Stewart Gardner Museum,** 280 The Fenway (✆ **617/566-1401;** www.gardnermuseum. org), was created by its namesake, who designed her home in the style of a 15th-century Venetian palace and filled it with European, American, and Asian paintings and sculpture, including works by Titian, Botticelli, Raphael, Rembrandt, Matisse, James McNeill Whistler, and John Singer Sargent. It's open Tuesday to Sunday 11am to 5pm. Admission is $12 adults, free for accompanied minors and adults named Isabella. The **Institute of Contemporary Art/Boston,** 100 Northern Ave. (✆ **617/ 478-3100;** www.icaboston.org), mounts rotating exhibits of 20th- and 21st-century paintings, sculpture, photography, and video and performance art at its dramatic waterfront home near the cruise terminal. It's open daily 10am to 5pm (Thurs–Fri 9pm). Admission is $15 adults, free for kids ages 17 and under.

Not far from the MFA and the Gardner is **Fenway Park,** home field of the 2004 and 2007 World Series champions. Game tickets are nearly impossible to get, but tours (✆ **617/226-6666;** www.redsox.com) run every day, year-round. Stops may include the press box, the Red Sox Hall of Fame, and even a walk on the warning track. Check ahead for schedules; no tours on holidays or before day games. Tour tickets are $12 adults, $10 kids ages 3 to 15.

SHOPPING

The top shopping area is Boston's **Back Bay,** with dozens of classy galleries, shops, and boutiques on **Newbury Street,** a world-famous destination. Nearby, the **Shops at Prudential Center** and **Copley Place** (linked by an enclosed walkway across Huntington Ave.) make up a giant retail complex that includes the posh department stores **Neiman Marcus** and **Saks Fifth Avenue.** The adjacent **South End,** though less commercially dense, boasts a number of art galleries and quirky shops. Another popular spot is **Faneuil Hall Marketplace,** bounded by North, Congress, and State streets and Atlantic Avenue (✆ **617/523-1300;** www.faneuilhallmarketplace.com). Amid the national chain outlets at Boston's busiest attraction are shops, boutiques, and push-carts that sell everything from cookies to costume jewelry, sweaters to souvenirs. Street performers do their thing throughout the day.

WHERE TO STAY

You have a lot of choices in Boston's many appealing neighborhoods, from B&Bs to boutique hotels and major chains—but don't expect bargains. Rates are generally on the high side during spring and summer, and are steepest during fall foliage season.

Two hotels are near the cruise port. The **Westin Boston Waterfront,** 435 Summer St. (✆ **800/937-8461;** www.westin.com), at the Boston Convention and Exhibition Center, offers the usual abundant Westin amenities (Heavenly Beds, for example) and lovely water views. Cruise season rates: from $259 double.

The **Renaissance Boston Waterfront Hotel,** 606 Congress St. (✆ **800/468-3571;** www.marriott.com), opened in 2008 adjacent to the Seaport World Trade Center. The spacious, well-appointed guest rooms have the latest in high-tech furnishings and striking harbor views. Cruise season rates: from $199 double.

The **Boston Harbor Hotel,** 70 Rowes Wharf, at the waterfront and Faneuil Hall Marketplace (✆ **800/752-7077;** www.bhh.com), is one of the finest and prettiest choices in town, a 16-story brick building that's within walking distance of downtown and the waterfront attractions. It prides itself on top-notch service. Rooms have wonderful harbor and skyline views. Cruise season rates: from $365 double.

The **Boston Marriott Long Wharf,** 296 State St. (© **800/228-9290;** www.marriottlongwharf.com), affords easy access to downtown and waterfront attractions, and lovely harbor views. The terraced brick exterior of the seven-story, 389-room hotel is one of the most recognizable sights on the waterfront. Cruise season rates: from $279 double.

You get a lot for your money at the **Harborside Inn,** 185 State St. (© **888/723-7565;** www.harborsideinnboston.com), a renovated 1858 warehouse across the street from Faneuil Hall Marketplace and the harbor. The nicely appointed rooms have queen-size beds and contemporary decor. Cruise season rates: from $169 double.

You can't beat the **Four Seasons,** 200 Boylston St. (© **800/819-5053;** www.fourseasons.com), for exquisite service, a beautiful location, elegant guest rooms and public areas, a terrific health club, and wonderful restaurants. If you can afford it, this is unquestionably the place to stay. Each room in the 16-story brick-and-glass building has a great view. Cruise season rates: from $550 double.

The **Hampton Inn Boston Logan Airport,** 230 Lee Burbank Hwy., Revere (© **800/426-7866;** www.hamptoninn.com), is on an ugly commercial-industrial strip, but it's just 1½ miles from the airport and 3 miles from downtown Boston. A free 24-hour shuttle bus serves the 227-room hotel, transporting guests to and from the airport and nearby restaurants. The hotel also has a pool, and the rates include continental breakfast. Cruise season rates: from $143 double.

DINING & NIGHTLIFE

Downtown, people have poured into **Durgin-Park,** 340 Faneuil Hall Marketplace (© **617/227-2038;** www.durgin-park.com), since 1827 for huge portions of delicious food, famously cranky waitresses, and a rowdy atmosphere where CEOs share tables with students. Feast on prime rib the size of a hubcap, lamb chops, fried seafood, and roast turkey. Fresh seafood arrives twice daily. Main courses: $11 to $40. If you want to check out America's oldest restaurant (which also happens to be Boston's best raw bar), visit **Ye Olde Union Oyster House,** 41 Union St. (© **617/227-2750;** www.unionoysterhouse.com). The place opened in 1826 and looks much the same as it did then, with a menu of traditional New England seafood. Daniel Webster and John F. Kennedy were regulars. Main courses: $21 to $30.

In Cambridge, **Jasper White's Summer Shack,** 149 Alewife Brook Pkwy. (© **617/520-9500;** www.summershackrestaurant.com), is a one-of-a-kind 300-seat place with picnic-table-style seating and baby blue leather booths. It serves the chef's signature pan-roasted lobster, plus all kinds of seafood, from clam rolls to steamers (not to mention corn dogs). Go for the food and the experience. Main courses: $6 to $29. (Another location in the Back Bay, at 50 Dalton St., is smaller but not much quieter at busy times, especially before Red Sox games; © **617/867-9955.**) For more mainstream dining, there's **Legal Sea Foods** (www.legalseafoods.com), a family-run chain known for its top-quality seafood. There are 10 locations around Boston and Cambridge, including 255 State St., on the waterfront (© **617/742-6300**); 26 Park Sq., btw. Columbus Ave. and Stuart St. (© **617/426-4444**); and in the Shops at Prudential Center, 800 Boylston St. (© **617/266-6800**). Main courses: $11 to $35. **Legal Test Kitchen,** 225 Northern Ave. (© **617/330-7430**), not far from the cruise port, is a spinoff that serves eclectic international food. In Harvard Square, go to **Mr. Bartley's Burger Cottage,** 1246 Massachusetts Ave. (© **617/354-6559;** www.bartleysburgers.com), famous for its burgers, onion rings, and down-to-earth atmosphere. Most items are $9 to $11.

Boston's Italian-American enclave, the North End, has dozens of restaurants; many are tiny and don't serve dessert or coffee. To satisfy those cravings, hit the *caffès* for coffee and fresh pastry in an atmosphere where lingering is welcome. Check out **Mike's Pastry,** 300 Hanover St. (© **617/742-3050;** www.mikespastry.com), a bakery that's famous for its bustling takeout business and its cannoli.

Boston's bar scene was the inspiration for the TV show *Cheers.* The Bull & Finch Pub, the original bar that inspired the show, is now known as **Cheers Beacon Hill,** 84 Beacon St. (© **617/227-9605;** www.cheersboston.com). Another Cheers, at Quincy Market in Faneuil Hall Marketplace (© **617/227-0150;** www.cheersboston. com), is a replica with an interior modeled after the one in the show. Nearby, the jam-packed **Black Rose,** 160 State St. (© **617/742-2286;** www.irishconnection.com/ blackrose.html), books live Irish music. The breathtaking 52nd-floor view makes the lounge at **Top of the Hub,** in the Prudential Tower, 800 Boylston St. (© **617/536-1775;** www.topofthehub.net), a favorite destination for dessert, drinks, and live jazz.

Nightlife listings can be found in the city's two main newspapers, the *Boston Globe* and *Boston Herald,* or in free publications (available at newspaper boxes around town) such as the weekly *Boston Phoenix* and the biweekly *Improper Bostonian* and *Stuff@Night.*

4 Cape Canaveral & Cocoa Beach, Florida

Known as the Space Coast because of **Kennedy Space Center,** the Cape Canaveral/ Cocoa Beach/Melbourne area boasts 72 miles of beaches, plus fishing, golfing, and surfing. The area is only about an hour east of Orlando's theme parks, which explains why Port Canaveral is one of the busier home ports on the East Coast, offering many 3- and 4-night cruise options (often sold as packages with pre- or post-cruise visits to the Orlando resorts) as well as weeklong itineraries. It also serves as a port of call for some ships sailing southbound from New York and other ports, allowing day-trip access to the Orlando parks.

Outside the port area, Cape Canaveral is . . . well, it's no Miami. Highways, strip malls, chain stores, and tracts of suburban homes predominate from the port area south into Cocoa Beach, home to most of the hotels, restaurants, and beaches discussed here. The central areas of Cocoa Beach are mildly more interesting, with some great '50s and '60s condo and hotel architecture, but stylish they're not. In the other direction, much of the land around the National Aeronautics and Space Administration (NASA) is set aside as the **Canaveral National Seashore** and the **Merritt Island National Wildlife Refuge** (www.nbbd.com/godo/minwr), a prime destination for nature lovers.

GETTING TO CAPE CANAVERAL & THE PORT

Port Canaveral (© **888/767-8226** or 321/783-7831; www.portcanaveral.org) is at the eastern end of the Bennett Causeway, just off S.R. 528 (the Bee Line Expwy.), the direct route from Orlando. From the port, S.R. 528 turns sharply south and becomes S.R. A1A, portions of which are known as Astronaut Boulevard and North Atlantic Avenue. Parking at the port costs $15 a day.

Those flying in will probably land at the **Orlando International Airport** (© **407/ 825-2001;** www.orlandoairports.net), a 45-mile drive from Port Canaveral via S.R. 528, or **Melbourne International Airport** (© **321/723-6227;** www.mlbair.com), a straight drive from I-95 to S.R. 528. If you've booked air and/or transfers through your cruise line, a representative will meet you. Otherwise, **Cocoa Beach Shuttle** (© **888/784-4144** or 321/631-4144; www.cbshuttle.com) has shuttle service between Orlando's airport and Port Canaveral; a one-way trip costs $33 per person or $58 for two people. By taxi, the fare from Orlando to Port Canaveral is a hefty $100-plus; but taxis charge the same rate for up to nine passengers, so if you're traveling with a group, this might be a good option. From the Melbourne Airport, the **Melbourne Airport Shuttle** (© **321/724-1600**) will take you to most local destinations for about $10 to $20 per person.

GETTING AROUND   Having a car is vital here. Most **car rental** companies oper-ate at the Orlando airport. **Space Coast Area Transit** (© **321/633-1878;** www.ride scat.com) operates buses, but routes tend to be circuitous and, therefore, extremely time-consuming. The fare is $1.25.

BEST CRUISE LINE SHORE EXCURSIONS

In addition to the tour below, lines typically offer pre- and post-cruise stays in Orlando, for the theme parks. Disney Cruise Line (of course) is the leader in linking passengers to Orlando, offering 3- and 4-night cruise itineraries specifically designed to dovetail with 4- and 3-night stays at the Disney resorts.

Kennedy Space Center VIP Tour ($67, 8 hr.): Participants on this tour get access to otherwise off-limits areas of the U.S. space center, meet a real astronaut, touch a piece of Mars, and stand inches from the largest rocket ever built.

THE ORLANDO THEME PARKS

All it took was a sprinkle of pixie dust in the 1970s to begin the almost-magical trans-formation of Orlando from a swath of swampland into the most visited tourist desti-nation in the world. Today, it's home to three giants—Walt Disney World, Universal Orlando, and SeaWorld—with 7 of the 10 most popular theme parks in the United States. Many cruises from Port Canaveral are sold as land-sea packages that include park stays, but if you decide to visit Orlando before or after your cruise, it's essential to plan ahead. Otherwise, the number of attractions begging for your time and the hyper-commercial atmosphere can put a serious dent in your psyche, your wallet, and your stamina. Even if you had 2 weeks, it wouldn't be long enough to hit everything, so don't even try. Stay selective, stay sane. That's our motto. Here's some basic info on each of the main parks. If you plan to spend a considerable amount of time here, we suggest picking up a copy of *Frommer's Walt Disney World & Orlando 2011*.

WALT DISNEY WORLD

Walt Disney World is the umbrella above four theme parks: the **Magic Kingdom, Epcot, Hollywood Studios,** and **Animal Kingdom,** which welcome about 50 mil-lion people each year. Besides its theme parks, Disney has two water parks, several entertainment venues, and a number of shopping spots. It's all southwest of Orlando off I-4, west of the Florida Turnpike. For information, vacation brochures, and videos, contact the Walt Disney World Co. (© **407/934-7639;** www.disneyworld.com) at least 6 weeks in advance of your trip.

TICKET PRICES & HOURS   At press time, 1-day, one-park tickets for any one of the four parks were a whopping $79 for adults, $68 for children ages 3 to 9 (plus tax). Discounted multiday, multipark tickets are available; many land-sea cruise packages include these passes. Park hours vary, so call ahead or go to **www.disneyworld.com** to check. Generally, expect hours to be from 9am to 8pm (until 6pm for Animal Kingdom), though the parks may open earlier and close later depending on special events and the economy. Epcot is usually open from 9am to 9pm.

THE MAGIC KINGDOM   The most popular theme park on the planet has some 40 attractions, plus restaurants and shops, in a 107-acre package. Its symbol, **Cinderella Castle,** forms the hub of a wheel whose spokes reach to seven "lands" simulating everything from an Amazonian jungle to Colonial America. If you're traveling with little kids, this is the place to go.

EPCOT   This 260-acre park (the acronym stands for Experimental Prototype Community of Tomorrow) has two sections. **Future World** is centered on Epcot's icon, a giant geosphere that looks like a big golf ball. Major corporations sponsor this section's themed areas, and the focus is on discovery, scientific achievements, and tomorrow's technologies in areas running from energy to undersea exploration. The **World Showcase** is a community of 11 miniaturized nations surrounding a 40-acre lagoon. All of these "countries" have indigenous architecture, landscaping, restaurants, and shops; cultural facets are explored in art exhibits, dance or other live performances, and innovative films. Epcot definitely appeals more to adults than children, even though it has a few thrill rides. If they're a requirement, go elsewhere. *Note:* Hiking through this park will often exhaust even the fittest person—some folks say Epcot really stands for "Every Person Comes Out Tired"—so we recommend splitting your visit over 2 days if possible.

DISNEY'S HOLLYWOOD STUDIOS   You'll probably spy the **Earrfel Tower**—a water tower outfitted with gigantic mouse ears—before you enter this 110-acre park, which Disney bills as "the Hollywood that never was and always will be." You'll find pulse-quickening rides such as the Aerosmith-themed **Rock 'n' Roller Coaster** and the **Twilight Zone Tower of Terror,** movie- and TV-themed shows such as **Jim Henson's Muppet*Vision 3D,** and some wonderful street performers. Adults and kids both love it. Best of all, it can be done comfortably in a day.

ANIMAL KINGDOM   This 500-acre park combines animals, elaborate landscapes, and a handful of rides. Because it's as much a conservation venue as an attraction, it's easy for most of the animals to escape your eyes (unlike at Tampa's Busch Gardens, the state's other major animal park). The thrill rides are better at Busch (though **Expedition Everest** will get your adrenaline pumping), but Animal Kingdom has much better shows, such as *Festival of the Lion King* and *Finding Nemo—the Musical.* The park is good for both adults and children and can be done in a single outing, but if you come on a hot summer day, arrive early or it's unlikely you'll see many of the best animals, which are smart enough to seek shade.

UNIVERSAL ORLANDO

Universal Orlando (© **877/801-9720** or 407/363-8000; www.universalorlando. com) is Disney's number-one competitor in the ongoing "anything you can do, we can do better" theme-park brawl. Although it's a distant second in terms of attendance, it's unquestionably the champion at entertaining teenagers and older members of the thrill-ride crowd, with two major parks—**Universal Studios Florida** and **Islands of Adventure**—plus an entertainment district and several resorts. It's at Universal Boulevard, off I-4.

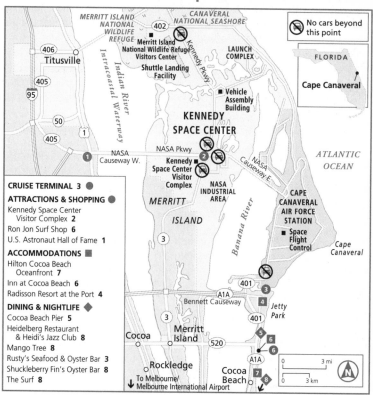

No cars beyond this point

MERRITT ISLAND
NATIONAL
WILDLIFE
REFUGE
Titusville
406
405
95
50
1
405
402
CANAVERAL
NATIONAL SEASHORE
Merritt Island
National Wildlife Refuge
Visitors Center
Shuttle Landing
Facility
Kennedy Pkwy
LAUNCH
COMPLEX
Vehicle
Assembly
Building
KENNEDY
SPACE CENTER
NASA
Causeway W.
NASA Pkwy
Kennedy
Space Center
Visitor
Complex
NASA
INDUSTRIAL
AREA
NASA
Causeway E.
Indian River
Intracoastal Waterway

FLORIDA

Cape Canaveral

ATLANTIC
OCEAN

MERRITT
ISLAND
Banana River
CAPE
CANAVERAL
AIR FORCE
STATION
Space
Flight
Control
Cape
Canaveral

CRUISE TERMINAL 3 ●

ATTRACTIONS & SHOPPING ●
Kennedy Space Center
  Visitor Complex **2**
Ron Jon Surf Shop **6**
U.S. Astronaut Hall of Fame **1**

ACCOMMODATIONS ■
Hilton Cocoa Beach
  Oceanfront **7**
Inn at Cocoa Beach **6**
Radisson Resort at the Port **4**

DINING & NIGHTLIFE ◆
Cocoa Beach Pier **5**
Heidelberg Restaurant
  & Heidi's Jazz Club **8**
Mango Tree **8**
Rusty's Seafood & Oyster Bar **3**
Shuckleberry Fin's Oyster Bar **8**
The Surf **8**

Cocoa
Rockledge
To Melbourne/
Melbourne International Airport

401
A1A
Bennett Causeway
401
520
Merritt
Island
A1A
Cocoa
Beach
Jetty
Park

0   3 mi
0   3 km

TICKET PRICES & HOURS   A 1-day, one-park ticket costs $79 for adults, $69 for children ages 3 to 9 (plus 6.5% tax); a 1-day, 2-park ticket costs $109 for adults, $99 for kids ages 3 to 9. The parks are open 365 days a year, generally from 9am to 6pm, though often later, especially in summer and around holidays. Call to confirm hours before you go.

UNIVERSAL STUDIOS FLORIDA   Even with fast-paced, grown-up rides such as **Revenge of the Mummy** and **Men in Black Alien Attack,** Universal Studios Florida is fun for kids. A talented group of actors portraying a range of characters from Universal films usually roams the park. The newest adventure, *The Wizarding World of Harry Potter,* uses a combination of live action, robotic technology, and filmmaking to take visitors inside Hogwarts, giving the illusion that you're living the story. You can do the park in a day, although you'll be a bit breathless when you get to the finish line.

ISLANDS OF ADVENTURE   This 110-acre theme park is, bar none, *the* Orlando theme park for thrill-ride junkies. With areas themed on Dr. Seuss, Jurassic Park, and Marvel comics, the park successfully combines nostalgia with state-of-the-art technology. Roller coasters roar above pedestrian walkways; water rides slice through the park. The **Amazing Adventures of Spider-Man** is a 3-D track ride that is arguably the best all-around attraction in Orlando; the **Jurassic Park River Adventure** has a 70-foot drop that scared creator Steven Spielberg into jumping ship before going over; and both the **Incredible Hulk Coaster** and **Dueling Dragons** draw raves from coaster crazies. Unless it's the height of high season, the park can be done in a day. It is not, however, a park for families with young kids: 9 of the park's 14 major rides have height restrictions. If, however, you have teens or are an adrenaline junkie, this is definitely the place for you.

SEAWORLD

A 200-acre marine-life park, **SeaWorld** (✆ 800/327-2424 or 407/351-3600; www.seaworld.com) explores the deep in a format that combines conservation awareness with entertainment—basically what Disney is attempting at Animal Kingdom, but SeaWorld got here first, and its message is subtler and a more integrated part of the experience. The park is fun for everyone from small children to adults (who doesn't like dolphins and whales?) and is easily toured in a single day. The pace is much more laid-back than at Universal or Disney, so it makes for a nice break if you're in the area for several days. SeaWorld has a handful of high-tech roller coasters such as **Journey to Atlantis** and **Kraken,** but, all in all, the park can't compete in this category with Disney and Universal. On the other hand, those parks don't let you discover the crushed-velvet texture of a stingray or the song of a sea lion, not to mention the killer whale **Shamu,** the park's star attraction, and the other resident orcas. The park entrance is at the intersection of I-4 and S.R. 528 (Bee Line Expwy.).

Tip: SeaWorld's latest adventure park, **Aquatica,** made its debut in spring 2008. The 59-acre eco-themed water park blends its signature up-close animal encounters with high-energy thrills (including racing tunnels and raft rides, slides, and more) with a plethora of pools, lagoons, winding rivers, and stretches of white sandy beaches. Call for additional information (✆ 888/800-5447; www.aquaticabyseaworld.com).

TICKET PRICES & HOURS A 1-day ticket to SeaWorld costs $79 for visitors ages 10 and over, $69 for children ages 3 to 9 (plus 6.5% tax). The park is usually open from 9am to 6pm, later during summer and holidays. Admission to Aquatica costs $48 for adults, $42 for kids ages 3 to 9. Combination passes for both parks are available.

EXPLORING CAPE CANAVERAL & COCOA BEACH ON YOUR OWN

Port Canaveral probably wouldn't be on the cruise industry's radar if it weren't so close to Orlando, and most passengers shuttle directly from theme park to pier rather than spending any significant time here. Nevertheless, anyone interested in the space program and its history should plan to arrive a day early (or stay a day after) to check out Kennedy Space Center and the Astronaut Hall of Fame. There are also a number of attractive beaches.

KENNEDY SPACE CENTER & THE ASTRONAUT HALL OF FAME

Set amid 150,000 acres of marshy wetlands favored by birds, reptiles, and amphibians, the **Kennedy Space Center (KSC)** (✆ 321/449-4444; www.kennedyspacecenter.com) has been at the center of America's space program since 1969, when astronauts took off from here to the moon. Even if you've never really considered yourself a science or space buff, you can't help being impressed by the achievements represented here. The only public access to the center (Hwy. 405) leads directly to the **Kennedy Space Center Visitor Complex,** which has real NASA rockets, the actual Mercury Mission Control Room from the 1960s, and numerous exhibits and films portraying space exploration from the '50s to the present day. There's a rocket garden displaying now-obsolete Redstone, Atlas, Saturn, and Titan rockets; a daily "Encounter" with a real astronaut; several pricey dining spots; and an obligatory gift shop selling various space memorabilia and souvenirs. Two space-related IMAX movies (one in 3-D) shown on five-and-a-half-story-high screens are informative and entertaining.

While you could spend an entire day at the visitor complex, you must take the included **KSC Tour** or an optional, extra-cost tour to see the actual space center, where rockets and shuttles are prepared and launched. Buses for the included tour operate continuously, leaving every 15 minutes and making stops at the **LC-39 Observation Gantry,** with a dramatic 360-degree view over launchpads where space shuttles blast off, and the impressive **Apollo/Saturn V Center,** which includes artifacts, photos, interactive exhibits, and the 363-foot **Saturn V,** the most powerful rocket ever launched by the United States. At each stop, you can get off, look around, and then take the next bus that comes along. Plan to take the tour early in your visit and be sure to hit the restroom before boarding—there's only one restroom on the tour. Several **optional, extra-cost tours** get you closer to sights like the Space Shuttle launchpads, the massive Vehicle Assembly Building, and the original launch sites of the Mercury, Gemini, and Apollo programs. Optional tours frequently sell out in advance, so call ahead for reservations.

At the Visitor Complex, don't miss the **Astronaut Memorial,** a moving black-granite monument with the names of U.S. astronauts who have died on missions or during training. The 60-ton structure rotates on a track that follows the movement of the sun, causing the names to stand out above a brilliant reflection of the sky.

Near the intersection of routes 1 and 405, across the Indian River to the west of KSC, the **U.S. Astronaut Hall of Fame** has displays, exhibits, and tributes to the heroes of the Mercury, Gemini, and Apollo space programs. Film presentations introduce visitors to the origins of rocketry and to the sheer power of the rockets themselves, while displays of personal memorabilia provide insight into the astronauts' lives. Displays of NASA memorabilia include actual Mission Control terminals (at which you can sit to access interactive information) and, most mind-blowing of all, the actual Apollo 14 command module *Kitty Hawk,* whose plaque bears the inscription "This spacecraft flew to the moon and back January 31 February 9, 1971." Enough said.

But let's get down to brass tacks. The Astronaut Hall of Fame has one main thing that the rest of the KSC Visitor Complex doesn't: the chance to pretend you're an astronaut through various ways, including a **G-force simulator** that spins at high speed to four times the force of gravity; a **Mission to Mars** rover that sends you bumping over the surface of the Red Planet (this one can be skipped if you're short on time); and a **Walk on the Moon** that imitates weightlessness, using harnesses and counterweights. Now the warnings: Simulators are off limits to folks under 48 inches, and if you tend to suffer from motion sickness, you'll probably want to avoid everything except the Walk on the Moon. Also, be sure to allow at least a few minutes between simulations, even if you've got a cast-iron constitution. Trust us on this one.

Kennedy Space Center is accessible via S.R. 405, just off U.S. 1. The Visitor Complex, including the Astronaut Hall of Fame, is open daily, except Christmas and certain launch days, from 9am to 5:30pm. The last bus tour departs at 2:15pm from the Visitor Complex. Regular admission (including all exhibits, Astronaut Encounter, IMAX space films, the KSC tour, and the Astronaut Hall of Fame) is $38 for adults, $28 for kids ages 3 to 11. Parking at the Visitor Complex and Hall of Fame is free, but there is no shuttle between the two. Be sure to pick up maps as you enter each branch, and expect to spend most of the day here to get the full experience: You'll need at least 2 hours to see the Visitor Complex (plus another couple to see the IMAX films), another 2 hours to see the highlights of the included tour (plus another 2 or 3 hr. if you linger at the tour stops or take one of the guided tours), and at least *another* 2 hours to see the Astronaut Hall of Fame.

BEACHES

Though the Cape Canaveral/Cocoa Beach area doesn't have the spectacular beach culture of Miami, it doesn't lack for pleasant coastline, much of which is famous for surfing. The following beaches (or "parks" in the local lingo) are within an easy drive of the port area. Closest to the cruise ship port and actually part of the larger port complex, the clean, nicely landscaped 41/2-acre **Jetty Park,** 400 E. Jetty Rd. (© **321/ 783-7111;** www.portcanaveral.org/recreation/beaches.php#jetty), is the most elaborate of the local beaches, perched at a point from which the whole expanse of the Cape Canaveral/Cocoa Beach coastline stretches away to the south. A snack bar, restrooms, showers, picnic facilities, a children's playground, and fishing are available. Parking costs $10 per car. Follow the signs after entering the port area, near where S.R. 528 and the A1A intersect. A series of beaches are accessible (and generally signposted) off the A1A heading south from the port. The **Cocoa Beach Pier,** on Meade Avenue east of the A1A (© **321/783-7549;** www.cocoabeachpier.com), is a great surfing spot with an open-air bar, volleyball, and a party atmosphere. **Lori Wilson Park,** farther south at 1500 N. Atlantic Ave. (© **321/868-1123;** www.brevardparks.com/visittheparks/ parks/prkbch1.php), is another nicely landscaped area on the order of Jetty Park, with restrooms and showers; a rustic boardwalk with some shaded picnic areas and benches; a nature center; and the Hammock, a .25-mile boardwalk nature trail that winds past ferns, twisted trees, and other *Jurassic Park*–like foliage, while butterflies flutter by and spiders eye them from their webs. Parking is free.

SHOPPING

Let's be unkind: You could shop here, but why bother? Cape Canaveral and Cocoa Beach have mostly the kind of national mall chains that you probably have at home, so save your energy and dollars for the Caribbean. An exception—as much for the experience as for the goods—is the **Ron Jon Surf Shop,** 4151 N. Atlantic Ave./A1A (© **321/799-8888;** www.ronjons.com). Inside, the blue-and-yellow, South Beach–looking Art Deco building has enough au courant beachwear to transform you and a good-size army into surfer dudes. The store also rents beach bikes, body boards, surfboards, kayaks, beach chairs, and other equipment by the hour, day, or week. It's open 24 hours a day, 365 days a year.

WHERE TO STAY

While the area has a wealth of cheap beach hotels, we'll instead concentrate on the few that are really notable.

The **Radisson Resort at the Port,** 8701 Astronaut Blvd./A1A (© **800/333-3333;** www.radisson.com/capecanaveralfl), is only a 5-minute drive from the port and has comfortable rooms. Even more comfy are the two-room suites that are a great option for families, each featuring a bedroom with a Jacuzzi and living room with a sofa bed. Cruise passengers arriving by car can leave their vehicles free in the hotel's lot during their cruise and take the free Radisson shuttle to and from the port. Cruise season rates: from $120 double.

At the other end of the spectrum, the **Inn at Cocoa Beach,** 4300 Ocean Beach Blvd., just off the A1A behind the Ron Jon Surf Shop (© **800/343-5307;** www.the innatcocoabeach.com), is almost entirely couples-oriented, presenting itself as more of a personalized inn than a traditional hotel. Almost all of its 50 romantic B&B-style rooms face the ocean and have rocking chairs on their balconies. The hotel staff includes several parrots and dogs, and guests are treated to daily breakfast, afternoon tea, and evening wine-and-cheese socials. Cruise season rates: from $150 double.

The six-story **Hilton Cocoa Beach Oceanfront,** 2080 N. Atlantic Ave. (© **800/ 445-8667** or 321/799-0003; www.hilton.com), is one of the few upscale beachfront properties here, with rooms that are spacious and comfortable, but weirdly lacking in balconies. Cruise season rates: from $125 double.

DINING & NIGHTLIFE

The **Surf** (formerly Bernard's Surf), 2 S. Atlantic Ave., Cocoa Beach (© **321/783-2401;** www.thesurfbarandgrill.com), was opened by Bernard Fischer in 1948, and its photos testify to the many astronauts who've celebrated their safe return to Earth with the restaurant's steak and fresh seafood. Upstairs, the **Surf Bar & Grill** has a more casual atmosphere. At the same address, **Shuckleberry Fin's Oyster Bar** serves oysters, seafood, and burgers and is even more casual, to the point where dogs are welcome on the patio. Main courses: at the Surf $18 to $30; at the Bar & Grill $11 to $23; at Shuckleberry Fin's, $6 to $13 (bucket of oysters $21).

On the south side of Port Canaveral harbor, **Rusty's Seafood & Oyster Bar,** 628 Glen Cheek Dr. (© **321/783-2033;** www.rustysseafood.com), serves the likes of spicy seafood gumbo, raw or steamed oysters, burgers and sandwiches, and pasta, and it has views of fishing boats and cruise ships heading in and out of the port. Main courses: $10 to $24.

The **Mango Tree,** 118 N. Atlantic Ave./A1A, between North First and North Second streets (© **321/799-0513;** www.themangotreerestaurant.com), is the most beautiful and sophisticated restaurant in Cocoa Beach, serving gourmet seafood, pasta, chicken, and Continental dishes in a plantation-home atmosphere, amid grounds lush with tropical foliage. Main courses: $16 to $38.

In downtown Cocoa Beach, the **Heidelberg Restaurant,** 7 N. Orlando Ave./A1A, at the Minuteman Causeway (© **321/783-6806**), serves German and Continental dinners, such as beef stroganoff, goulash, roast duck, sauerbraten, and grilled loin pork chops. Main courses: $20 to $33. The adjoining **Heidi's Jazz Club** (© **321/783-4559;** www.heidisjazzclub.com) has music nightly except Mondays, with a jam session Sundays from 7 to 11pm. See the website for a schedule of performances.

The **Cocoa Beach Pier,** 401 Meade Ave., off the A1A, and a half-mile north of S.R. 520 (© **321/783-7549;** www.cocoabeachpier.com), juts 800 feet over the Atlantic Ocean, providing a casual beer-and-fruity-drinks atmosphere, an open-air tiki bar with live music most nights, an ice-cream shop, sit-down seafood restaurants, and an arcade, plus beach-equipment rentals and volleyball right next door on the sand.

5 Charleston, South Carolina

In the closing pages of *Gone With the Wind,* Rhett tells Scarlett that he's going back home to Charleston, where he can find "the calm dignity life can have when it's lived by gentle folks, the genial grace of days that are gone." In spite of all the changes and upheavals over the years, Rhett's endorsement of Charleston still holds true, sans slavery and petticoats. Near-fanatical preservationists have assured that, architecturally at least, the Old South lives on here, and they've even managed to hold on to some of that famous graciousness, too. It's one of the best-preserved cities in the South, boasting 73 pre-Revolutionary buildings and more than 600 built before the 1840s. With cobblestone streets and horse-drawn carriages, stately old homes, and the scent of jasmine and wisteria in the air, it's a nice little time machine of a place, totally conscious of its history but gratifyingly averse to becoming an Old South theme park.

GETTING TO CHARLESTON & THE PORT

The **Port of Charleston**'s cruise ship terminal (© **843/958-8298**; www.port-of-charleston.com) is at 196 Concord St., at the foot of Market Street, smack in the heart of the historic district. Parking at the port is $15 per day. People arrive by plane at **Charleston International Airport** (© **843/767-7009**; www.chs-airport.com), located in North Charleston, 12 miles from the terminal. If you've made arrangements for transfers through your cruise line, a representative will meet your arriving flight and direct you to shuttle buses. **Taxis** are available to downtown for about $27.

GETTING AROUND   You can easily walk around the historic district right from the cruise docks. Narrated horse-drawn **carriage tours** are available at Market Street from several operators. **Palmetto Carriage Tours** (© **843/723-8145**; www.carriage tour.com) uses mule teams and takes off from the red barn behind the Rainbow Market. Tickets are available at 40 N. Market St. From there, exit out back and through the parking lot to the barn. A 1-hour tour costs $20 for adults.

BEST CRUISE LINE SHORE EXCURSIONS

Historic Charleston Carriage Tour ($39, 1¼ hr.): As hokey as carriage tours may seem, this is actually a nice way to see historic Charleston. The leisurely ride just seems to match the pace of the place. You'll pass carefully restored 18th- and 19th-century homes and buildings as your guide gives some historical perspective.

Boone Hall Plantation ($79, 3 hr.): See the historic Boone Hall Plantation, with its *Gone With the Wind* ambience. You can tour the lovely Georgian plantation house as well as the slave quarters, built from brick made on the plantation in the 1800s.

Historic Homes Walking Tour ($59, 2½ hr.): A narrated walking tour of Charleston's historic district, visiting the Nathaniel Russell House and the Edmondston-Alston House (see below) and passing the Old Exchange Building, St. Michael's Episcopal Church, Rainbow Row (the longest set of contiguous Georgian facades in the entire country), Catfish Row (a setting in *Porgy and Bess*), and the Calhoun Mansion.

Civil War History & H.L. Hunley Submarine ($89, 3 hr.): After touring Charleston's historic district, this tour visits the Warren Lasch Conservation Center, where the world's first "successful" submarine now resides in a conservation tank. Its moment in history was February 17, 1864, when it used a spar torpedo to sink the union warship *Housatonic* just outside Charleston Harbor. Its "success" is questionable—it sank immediately after the explosion, killing all the crew, and wasn't found again for 131 years—but its history is fascinating.

EXPLORING CHARLESTON ON YOUR OWN

Charleston's streets are laid out in an easy-to-follow grid. The main north-south thoroughfares are King, Meeting, and East Bay streets. Tradd, Broad, Queen, and Calhoun

Charleston

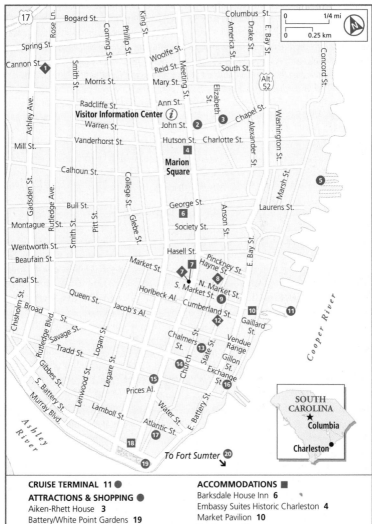

CRUISE TERMINAL 11 ●

ATTRACTIONS & SHOPPING ●
Aiken-Rhett House **3**
Battery/White Point Gardens **19**
Charleston Museum **2**
Edmondston-Alston House **17**
Fort Sumter **20**
Fort Sumter Visitor Education Center **5**
Heyward-Washington House **14**
Joseph Manigault House **2**
Nathaniel Russell House **15**
Old City Market **9**
Old Exchange & Provost Dungeon **16**
Old Slave Mart Museum **13**

ACCOMMODATIONS ■
Barksdale House Inn **6**
Embassy Suites Historic Charleston **4**
Market Pavilion **10**
Planters Inn **7**
Two Meeting Street Inn **18**

DINING & NIGHTLIFE ◆
Anson **8**
A. W. Shucks **12**
Hominy Grill **1**
Hyman's Seafood Co. **7**

streets cross the city from east to west. South of Broad Street, East Bay becomes East Battery. The cruise terminal is located in the **Downtown** neighborhood, which extends north from Broad Street to Marion Square at the intersection of Calhoun and Meeting streets. You can't miss the **Old City Market** here (see "Shopping," below); it shoots straight at the terminal like an arrow. Meeting Street, Church Street, and all the other streets east to the waterfront are full of gorgeous homes and shady gardens, plus many of the historical attractions.

Not far from the City Market, the **Old Exchange & Provost Dungeon,** 122 E. Bay St. (© **843/727-2165;** www.oldexchange.com), served as a prison during the American Revolution, then in 1873 became Charleston's City Hall. Its large collection of antique chairs was donated in 1921 by the local Daughters of the American Revolution, and its dungeon (which you tour with a costumed docent) displays the only visible chunk of Charleston's original city wall, the Half-Moon Bastion. We could do without its hokey animatronic displays, though. It's open daily 9am to 5pm. Admission is $8 adults, $4 kids ages 7 to 12.

One block to the north, the **Old Slave Mart Museum,** 6 Chalmers St. (© **843/ 958-6467;** www.nps.gov/history/nr/travel/charleston/osm.htm), is the only surviving slave market in South Carolina, dating from 1859. Its collection of artifacts, letters, oral histories, and video documents provides visitors with a sense of the real people involved in the domestic slave trade—buyers, traders, and slaves. It's open Monday to Saturday 9am to 5pm. Admission is $7.

The **Nathaniel Russell House,** 51 Meeting St. (© **843/724-8481;** www.historic charleston.org/experience/nrh), is one of the finest examples of Federal architecture you'll ever see. Built in 1808, it's noted for a "free flying" staircase, spiraling unsupported for three floors. The staircase's elliptical shape is repeated throughout the house. The interiors are ornate with period furnishings, especially the elegant music room with its golden harp and neoclassical-style sofa. You can also visit the **Aiken-Rhett House,** 48 Elizabeth St. (© **843/723-1159;** www.historiccharleston.org/ experience/arh), built by merchant John Robinson in 1818, and then expanded by Governor and Mrs. William Aiken in the 1830s and 1850s. Like other Charlestonians of their time, the Aikens furnished their home with crystal and bronze chandeliers, classical sculpture, and paintings purchased on trips to Europe. Today, many of those objects are still in the rooms for which the Aikens bought them. Original outbuildings include the kitchens, slave quarters, stables, privies, and cattle sheds. Both of these historic homes are open Monday to Saturday 10am to 5pm, Sunday 2 to 5pm. Admission to each house is $10, or $16 for a combo ticket to both.

The **Charleston Museum,** 360 Meeting St. (© **843/722-2996;** www.charleston museum.org), was founded in 1773, making it the first and oldest museum in America. The collections preserve and interpret the social and natural history of Charleston and the South Carolina coastal region, with early crafts, historic relics, and a series of hands-on exhibits for children. It's open Monday to Saturday 9am to 5pm, Sunday 1 to 5pm. Admission is $10 adults, $5 kids ages 3 to 12. A $16 combination ticket also gets you admission to the **Joseph Manigault House,** 350 Meeting St. (across from the museum), a three-story Federal-style town house built in 1803 for its namesake, a French Huguenot plantation owner and politician. Many rooms have been restored to their original colors, with period furniture. Outbuildings such as the kitchen, slave quarters, stable, and privy are part of the experience. A $22 combo ticket also includes the museum's **Heyward-Washington House,** 87 Church St., built in 1772 by Daniel

Heyward, the "rice king" of Charleston. It was also the home of Thomas Heyward, Jr., a signer of the Declaration of Independence. President George Washington bedded down here in 1791. Many of the fine period pieces in the house are the work of Thomas Elfe, one of America's most famous cabinetmakers. Both houses are open Monday to Saturday 10am to 5pm, Sunday 1 to 5pm. Admission to either house alone is $10 adults, $5 kids ages 3 to 12.

At the southernmost point of the historic area stands the **Battery** (aka the White Point Gardens), where the Cooper and Ashley rivers converge. It has a landscaped park shaded by palmettos and live oaks, with walkways lined with monuments and other war relics. Virtually every home around here is of historic or architectural interest, including the **Edmondston-Alston House,** 21 E. Battery (© **843/722-7171;** www.middletonplace.org/default.asp?catID=4515), an 1825 house originally built in Federal style and later modified to a Greek Revival style. Inside are heirloom furnishings, silver pieces, and paintings. Robert E. Lee once found refuge here when his hotel uptown caught fire. Guided tours are held Monday 1 to 4:30pm, Tuesday to Saturday 10am to 4:30pm, Sunday 1:30 to 4:30pm. Admission is $10. The house is a property of the Middleton Place Foundation, which also operates the Middleton Place estate, 14 miles northwest of town.

Head back toward the cruise terminal along the seawall on East Battery and Murray Boulevard to absorb Charleston's riverfront ambience and catch the distant view of **Fort Sumter** (© **843/883-3123;** www.nps.gov/fosu), where the first shot of the Civil War was fired on April 12, 1861. Confederate forces launched a 34-hour bombardment of the fort, leading Union forces to surrender and the government in Washington to declare war. Amazingly, Confederate troops held onto Sumter for nearly 4 years, but by the end, continual bombardment from Union forces had reduced it to a heap of rubble. You can visit the fort with **Fort Sumter Tours/SpiritLine Cruises** (© **800/789-3678;** www.spiritlinecruises.com), which runs ferries from town to the fort. You can buy tickets at Liberty Square's Fort Sumter Visitor Education Center, near the foot of Calhoun Street. The 2¼-hour tour consists of approximately 1 hour at Fort Sumter plus a 30-minute harbor cruise in each direction. Park rangers are on hand at the fort to answer questions, and you can explore gun emplacements and visit a small museum filled with artifacts related to the siege. Ferry tickets cost $16; tours are offered two or three times a day, usually at 9:30am, noon, and 2:30pm, though there are seasonal variations. Call or check the website to confirm times.

SHOPPING

Located within sight of the cruise ship docks, the **Old City Market** comprises four open-sided buildings that run from East Bay Street up to Meeting Street. The market originally sold foodstuffs, including meat, fish, and local produce, but today it's packed with vendors hawking local art, food, books, clothing, and souvenirs. One standout item here: **sea-grass baskets** woven by Gullah women, descendents of coastal slaves who maintain a distinct culture on South Carolina's islands.

King Street is known for its shopping, with antiques at the south end of the street, clothes and jewelry along the main stretch, and housewares and interior decor along North King (aka Upper King).

If you fall for the period furniture you see in the historic houses, you can buy reproductions online from the **Historic Charleston Foundation** (www.historiccharleston. org), which operates the Nathaniel Russell House, the Aiken-Rhett House, and several other historic properties.

WHERE TO STAY

There are quite a few distinctive accommodations in Charleston within walking distance of the cruise pier.

The **Embassy Suites Historic Charleston,** 337 Meeting St. (© **843/723-6900;** www.embassysuites.com), is close to the visitor center, on Marion Square in the original home of the 19th-century Citadel Military College. It's listed on the National Register of Historic Places and has British West Indies colonial plantation decor and two-room suites. Cruise season rates: from $309 double.

Close to the dock, the **Market Pavilion,** 225 E. Bay St. (© **877/440-2250;** www.marketpavilion.com), has opulent old-Charleston-style guest rooms with old-world decor, plaster crown moldings, mahogany touches, and four-poster beds. There's also the wonderful rooftop Pavilion Bar and the excellent Grill 225 restaurant. Cruise season rates: from $400 double.

Barksdale House Inn, 27 George St. (© **888/577-4980;** www.barksdalehouse.com), is a neat, tidy, and well-proportioned Italianate building about ¼ mile north of the City Market, constructed as an inn in 1778 and later altered and enlarged. Many bedrooms have four-poster beds and working fireplaces—as if you need more heat in often-sweltering Charleston. Cruise season rates: from $149 double.

The **Planters Inn,** 112 N. Market St. (© **800/845-7082;** www.plantersinn.com), next to the City Market, is an opulent yet tasteful and cozy enclave of Colonial charm, and one of the finest small luxury hotels in the South. The spacious rooms have hardwood floors, marble bathrooms, and 18th-century decor. Afternoon tea is served in the lobby. The Peninsula Grill's setting has a 19th-century charm unlike any other restaurant in Charleston. The menu changes frequently, with main courses in the $25-to-$39 range. Cruise season rates: from $240 double.

Two Meeting Street Inn, 2 Meeting St. (© **843/723-7322;** www.twomeetingstreet.com), has the most enviable location in the city, right across from the Battery, looking over the confluence of the Charles and Ashley rivers. The house was built in 1892 as a wedding gift from a prosperous father to his daughter. Inside, the proportions are as lavish and gracious as the Gilded Age could provide. Cruise season rates: from $229 double.

DINING & NIGHTLIFE

Foodies flock to Charleston for refined Low Country cookery as well as an array of French and international specialties. Among the best is **Anson,** 12 Anson St., in the City Market area (© **843/577-0551;** www.ansonrestaurant.com), which blends the grace notes of a big New York restaurant with Low Country charm and cuisine. Its setting is a century-old, brick-sided ice warehouse, and the decor is full of Corinthian pilasters salvaged from demolished Colonial houses, with enough Victorian rococo for anyone's taste. Main courses: $19 to $31.

Nearby, **Hyman's Seafood Co.,** 215 Meeting St. (© **843/723-6000;** www.hymanseafood.com), occupies a location that's been in the same family since 1890, originating as a dry-goods business. Inside, multiple dining rooms and a takeout deli serve seafood platters and individual dishes, po' boy sandwiches, and more. Main courses: $10 to $37.

A. W. Shucks, 70 State St. (© **843/723-1151;** www.a-w-shucks.com), is a hearty, casual oyster bar in a restored warehouse next to City Market, around the corner from

East Bay Street. Menu highlights are oysters and clams on the half shell, tasty seafood chowders, deviled crab, and a wide beer selection. Main courses: $12 to $24.

Farther from the market area, **Hominy Grill,** 207 Rutledge Ave. (© **843/937-0930;** www.hominygrill.com), serves simply and beautifully prepared dishes inspired by the kitchens of the Low Country. It has gained a devoted family following that comes here to feast on such specialties as oven-fried chicken with spicy peach gravy. From the market, head north on Meeting Street, turn left on Calhoun, and walk 7 blocks west to Rutledge. Breakfast, lunch, and dinner are served Monday through Friday and brunch Saturday and Sunday. Main courses: $7 to $17.

6 Fort Lauderdale, Florida

Broward County's Port Everglades is the second-busiest cruise port in the world, drawing more than 3.5 million cruise passengers a year. It boasts the deepest harbor on the Eastern seaboard south of Norfolk, 12 ultramodern cruise ship terminals, and an easy access route to the Fort Lauderdale–Hollywood International Airport, less than a 10-minute drive away.

GETTING TO FORT LAUDERDALE & THE PORT

Port Everglades (© **954/523-3404;** www.broward.org/port) is about 23 miles north of Miami within the city boundaries of Fort Lauderdale, Hollywood, and Dania Beach. Parking at the port costs $12 a day. If you're coming by air, you'll land at the **Fort Lauderdale–Hollywood International Airport** (© **954/359-6100;** www.broward.org/airport), whose location less than 2 miles (5 min. by bus or taxi) from Port Everglades makes this the easiest airport-to-ship trip in Florida. If you've booked air or transfers through the cruise line, a representative will take you to your shuttle after landing. If you haven't, taking a **taxi** to the port costs about $12.

GETTING AROUND   For a taxi, call **Yellow Cab** (© **954/565-5400**). Rates start at $4.50 for the first mile and are $2.40 for each additional mile. **Broward County Transit** (© **954/357-8400;** www.broward.org/bct) runs bus service throughout the county; 1-day passes are $3.50. **Water Taxi** (© **954/467-6677;** www.watertaxi.com) sails between Oakland Park Boulevard and Southeast 17th Street along the Intracoastal Waterway, and west along the New River into downtown Fort Lauderdale. All-day passes are $15, and you can hop on and off at will. If you want to take the water taxi to South Beach in Miami, it's $33.

BEST CRUISE LINE SHORE EXCURSIONS

Everglades Airboat Ride ($45, 2½ hr.): The Seminole Indians called it Pahay Okee, the "grassy water," and on this 30-minute airboat ride, you'll get to see some of the area's indigenous wildlife, including water birds and American alligators.

EXPLORING FORT LAUDERDALE ON YOUR OWN

Fort Lauderdale Beach, a 5-mile strip along S.R. A1A, gained fame in the 1950s as a spring-break playground, popularized by the movie *Where the Boys Are,* but today the scene is a lot more affluent and family-oriented. In addition to the beaches (see below), there are a few other attractions that might float your boat.

The **Museum of Discovery & Science,** 401 SW Second St. (© **954/467-6637;** www.mods.org), is an excellent interactive science museum with an IMAX theater. The exhibit Florida Ecoscapes is particularly interesting, with a living coral reef, bees, bats, frogs, turtles, and alligators. It's open Monday to Saturday 10am to 5pm, Sunday noon to 6pm. Admission to the exhibits is $11 adults, $9 kids ages 2 to 12; for the exhibits and film, it's $16 adults, $12 kids ages 2 to 12. The **Museum of Art,** 1 E. Las Olas Blvd. (✆ **954/525-5500;** www.moafl.org), is a truly terrific, small museum whose permanent collection of 20th-century European and American art includes works by Picasso, Calder, Warhol, Mapplethorpe, Dalí, Frank Stella, and William Glackens. African, South Pacific, pre-Columbian, Native American, and Cuban art are also on display. It's open Tuesday to Saturday 11am to 5pm (Thurs 8pm), Sunday noon to 5pm. Admission is $10 adults, $7 kids ages 6 to 17, but may vary for special exhibitions.

Stranahan House, 335 SE Sixth Ave. (✆ **954/524-4736;** www.stranahanhouse.org), is Fort Lauderdale's oldest standing structure and a prime example of classic Florida Frontier architecture. Built in 1901 by the "father of Fort Lauderdale," Frank Stranahan, it's been a post office, town hall, and general store, and now serves as a worthwhile little museum of South Florida pioneer life. Tours are held daily at 1, 2, and 3pm. Admission is $12 adults, $7 kids.

In the walk-through, screened-in aviary at **Butterfly World,** Tradewinds Park South, 3600 W. Sample Rd., Coconut Creek, west of the Florida Turnpike (✆ **954/977-4400;** www.butterflyworld.com), visitors can watch newly hatched butterflies emerge from cocoons and flutter around as they learn to fly. There are more than 150 species in residence. It's open Monday to Saturday 9am to 5pm, Sunday 11am to 5pm. Admission is $25 adults, $20 kids ages 3 to 11.

BEACHES

Backed by an endless row of hotels and popular with visitors and locals alike, the **Fort Lauderdale Beach Promenade** is set along A1A, also known as Fort Lauderdale Beach Boulevard, between SE 17th Street and Sunrise Boulevard. The fabled strip from *Where the Boys Are* is Ocean Boulevard, between Las Olas and Sunrise boulevards. On weekends, parking spots at the oceanside meters are difficult to find. **Fort Lauderdale Beach** at the Howard Johnson is another perennial local favorite. A jetty bounds the beach on the south side, making it rather private, although the water gets a little choppy. High school and college students share this area with an older crowd. One of the main beach entrances is at 4660 N. Ocean Dr. in Lauderdale-by-the-Sea.

SHOPPING

If you're looking for unusual boutiques and art galleries, head to quaint **Las Olas Boulevard,** located west of A1A and a block east of Federal Highway/U.S. 1 (off SE 8th St.), where hundreds of shops have alluring window decorations like kitchen utensils posing as modern-art sculptures. **Las Olas Riverfront,** at SW First Avenue and Las Olas Boulevard (✆ **954/522-6556;** www.riverfrontfl.com), is a huge retail complex with restaurants, clothing stores, arcades, and a multiplex movie theater.

The **Swap Shop,** 3291 W. Sunrise Blvd. (✆ **954/791-7927;** www.floridaswapshop.com), is one of the world's largest flea markets. In addition to endless acres of vendors, there's a mini-amusement-park and a 15-screen drive-in movie theater. It's open daily. About 10 miles outside town, **Sawgrass Mills,** 12801 W. Sunrise Blvd., at Flamingo Road (✆ **954/846-2300;** www.sawgrassmillsmall.com), is one of the premier outlet malls in the country, with more than 300 shops, kiosks, a 24-screen movie theater, and many restaurants and bars.

Fort Lauderdale

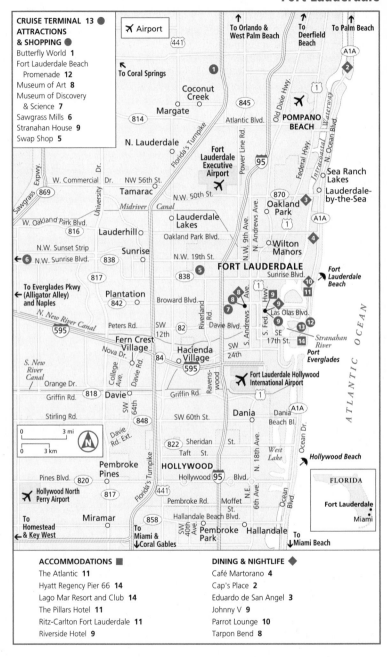

CRUISE TERMINAL 13 ●

ATTRACTIONS & SHOPPING ●

Butterfly World **1**
Fort Lauderdale Beach Promenade **12**
Museum of Art **8**
Museum of Discovery & Science **7**
Sawgrass Mills **6**
Stranahan House **9**
Swap Shop **5**

✈ Airport

To Coral Springs

To Orlando & West Palm Beach

To Deerfield Beach

To Palm Beach

A1A

Coconut Creek
Margate
N. Lauderdale
Tamarac
Lauderhill
Sunrise
Plantation
Fern Crest Village
Davie
Pembroke Pines
Miramar

To Everglades Pkwy (Alligator Alley) and Naples

Fort Lauderdale Executive Airport

Atlantic Blvd.
POMPANO BEACH
Sea Ranch Lakes
Lauderdale-by-the-Sea
Oakland Park
Wilton Manors
FORT LAUDERDALE
Sunrise Blvd.
Fort Lauderdale Beach
Las Olas Blvd.
Stranahan River
Port Everglades

Hacienda Village
Broward Blvd.
Peters Rd.
Davie Blvd.

Fort Lauderdale Hollywood International Airport

Griffin Rd.
Stirling Rd.
Dania
Dania Beach Bl.
Sheridan St.
Taft St.
HOLLYWOOD
Hollywood Blvd.
Hollywood Beach

West Lake

ATLANTIC OCEAN

0   3 mi
0   3 km

To Homestead & Key West

To Miami & Coral Gables

Pembroke Rd.
Moffet St.
Hallandale Beach Blvd.
Pembroke Park
Hallandale

To Miami Beach

FLORIDA
Fort Lauderdale
Miami

ACCOMMODATIONS ■

The Atlantic **11**
Hyatt Regency Pier 66 **14**
Lago Mar Resort and Club **14**
The Pillars Hotel **11**
Ritz-Carlton Fort Lauderdale **11**
Riverside Hotel **9**

DINING & NIGHTLIFE ◆

Café Martorano **4**
Cap's Place **2**
Eduardo de San Angel **3**
Johnny V **9**
Parrot Lounge **10**
Tarpon Bend **8**

WHERE TO STAY

Fort Lauderdale Beach has a hotel or motel on nearly every block, and the selection ranges from run-down to luxurious.

The **Hyatt Regency Pier 66,** located close to the port at 2301 SE 17th St. Causeway (✆ **800/233-1234** or 954/525-6666; www.pier66.hyatt.com), is a circular landmark whose large rooms are decorated with a retro-modern look. Its famous revolving rooftop bar, the Piertop Lounge, is often filled with cruise ship patrons. A $25-million refurbishment has transformed the lobby, lawn, and remaining guest rooms with a retro-modern decor. Cruise season rates: from $179 double.

Open since 1936, the **Riverside Hotel,** 620 E. Las Olas Blvd. (✆ **800/325-3280;** www.riversidehotel.com), is a charming six-story lodging set on the sleepy and scenic New River, capturing the essence of Old Florida. Guest rooms, outfitted in Mexican tile and wicker furnishings, are spacious and well maintained. Try for one of the ground-floor units, which have higher ceilings and more space. Cruise season rates: from $239 double.

Located on its own little island between Lake Mayan and the Atlantic, the **Lago Mar Resort and Club,** 1700 S. Ocean Lane (✆ **800/524-6627** or 954/523-6511; www.lagomar.com), is an utterly inviting, casually elegant, yet family-friendly slice of Old Florida. Rooms and suites have Mediterranean or Key West influences, and guests have access to the broadest and best strip of beach in the entire city, not to mention a wonderful bougainvillea-lined, 9,000-square-foot swimming lagoon. A new six-story wing of one- and two-bedroom oceanfront suites with balconies and big, luxurious bathrooms includes a deck of native tropical landscaping and a 5,000-square-foot saltwater lagoon. Cruise season rates: from $205 double.

The **Pillars Hotel,** 111 N. Birch Rd. (✆ **800/800-7666;** www.pillarshotel.com), is the quintessential Fort Lauderdale retreat, its two-story, 23-room structure done up in British colonial/Caribbean style, with luxurious rooms, lush landscaping, and white-tablecloth room service. This is the best hotel of its size in the region. Cruise season rates: from $265 double.

The **Atlantic,** 601 N. Fort Lauderdale Beach Blvd. (✆ **877/567-8020** or 954/567-8020; www.atlantichotelfl.com), sits on a stunning white-sand beach and has decor that's a study in minimal modernity—soothing, comfortable, and stylish. Cruise season rates: from $219 double.

The **Ritz-Carlton Fort Lauderdale,** 1 N. Fort Lauderdale Beach Blvd. (✆ **800/325-3589** or 954/465-2300; www.ritzcarlton.com/fortlauderdale), elevates the Fort Lauderdale Beach strip to an entirely new level of luxury. The 183 rooms all have views of the Atlantic or the Intracoastal Waterway. Cruise season rates: from $299 double.

DINING & NIGHTLIFE

Las Olas Boulevard is the hub for restaurants in Fort Lauderdale. Look here for **Johnny V,** 625 E. Las Olas Blvd. (✆ **954/761-7920;** www.johnnyvlasolas.com), the domain of chef Johnny Vincenz, who cooks up Caribbean-influenced new-Floridian cuisine (think smoked-pheasant nachos or sage-grilled Florida dolphin with lobster pan gravy served atop rock-shrimp plantain stuffing with cranberry-mango chutney) for the famous and not-so-famous. Main courses: $25 to $42.

For something more classic, **Cap's Place,** 2765 NE 28th Court (✆ **954/941-0418;** www.capsplace.com), is a famous old-time seafood joint, serving good food at reasonable prices. The restaurant is on a peninsula; you get a ferry ride over (see its website for directions). Mahimahi and snapper are popular and, like the other meat and pasta dishes here, can be prepared any way you want. Main courses: $14 to $30. At **Tarpon Bend,** 200 SW Second St. (© **954/523-3233;** www.tarponbend.com), fishermen still bring the fish to the back door. The oysters from the raw bar are shucked to order, and the steamed clambake (with half a Maine lobster, clams, potatoes, mussels, and corn on the cob) is scrumptious and served in its own pot. Main courses: $10 to $20.

Head north for ethnic cuisine. **Café Martorano,** 3343 E. Oakland Park Blvd. (© **954/561-2554;** www.cafemartorano.com), is like a big, fat, Italian wedding, where eating, drinking, and dancing are paramount. The menu changes daily, and because reservations aren't accepted, the wait can be up to 2 hours for a table. Main courses: $15 to $45. A little farther north, **Eduardo de San Angel,** 2822 E. Commercial Blvd. (© **954/772-4731;** www.eduardodesanangel.com), serves gourmet Mexican cuisine in a room that resembles an intimate hacienda, adorned with fresh flowers and candlelight. Main courses: $24 to $36. Closed Sunday.

For pre-cruise imbibing, the **Parrot Lounge,** 911 Sunrise Lane (© **954/563-1493;** www.parrotlounge.com), is Fort Lauderdale's most famous dive bar, a local's and out-of-towner's choice for an evening of beer and bonding.

7 Galveston, Texas

Some 50 miles south of Houston, Galveston is on a 30-mile-long barrier island averaging only 2 miles wide. Ships departing from here can reach the open sea in about 30 minutes, compared to several hours of lag time from the Port of Houston. The city's main attractions are the downtown historic district; the Strand, with its Victorian commercial buildings and houses; and the beaches, which draw crowds of Houstonians and other Texans during the summer.

At the end of the 19th century, Galveston was the largest city in Texas and the third-busiest port in the country. But then, on September 8, 1900, a massive storm came ashore, carrying with it 140-mph winds and a 20-foot surge that washed completely over the island. Houses were smashed into matchwood, and more than 6,000 islanders—a sixth of the island's population—were drowned. Those who remained went to work to prevent a recurrence of the disaster, raising the city's ground level by up to 17 feet and erecting a stout seawall that now stretches along 10 miles of shoreline, with several jetties of large granite blocks projecting out into the water. These defenses helped a bit on September 13, 2008, when **Hurricane Ike** came ashore, but the powerful storm seemed to know just where to hit, in effect outflanking the seawall to the east and pushing water into the bay, which then flooded Galveston's most vulnerable, low-lying areas. At press time, a year and a half after the storm, most of the storm damage has been repaired and the areas most visited by tourists are mostly back to normal, but many residents had left town for good, and full reconstruction of the island could still take some time.

GETTING TO GALVESTON & THE PORT

The **Texas Cruise Ship Terminal** at the Port of Galveston (© **409/766-6113;** www.portofgalveston.com) is at Harborside Drive and 25th Street, on Galveston

Island. Parking at the port costs $45 for cruises of 3 nights, $50 for 4 nights, and $70 for 7 nights. The lots are a half-mile from the terminal, but shuttle buses are available.

If you're flying in, you'll land at one of two Houston airports: **William P. Hobby Airport** (south of downtown Houston, and about 31 miles, or a 45-min. drive, from the terminal) or the larger **George Bush Intercontinental Airport** (north of downtown Houston, and about 54 miles, or an 80-min. drive, from the terminal). Information on both is available at **www.fly2houston.com**. Because it's a long way from both airports to the cruise ship terminal (and because taxi prices are correspondingly high), it's a good idea to arrange transfers through your cruise line. **Airport Shuttle America** (© 281/530-4000 or 713/270-4200; www.airportshuttleamerica.net) also transports cruise ship passengers from either airport to Galveston. From Hobby Airport, the fare is $30 per person; from Bush, it's $35. **Taxis** cost about $65 from Hobby Airport and $105 from Bush.

GETTING AROUND   Within walking distance of the port's two terminals is the historic **Strand District,** Galveston's revitalized downtown, with shops, art galleries, museums, and eateries lining its quaint brick streets. Most of Galveston's hotels, motels, and restaurants are located along the seawall from where Broadway meets the shore all the way west past 60th Street. At present, service on the **Galveston Island Rail Trolley** (© 409/797-3900; www.islandtransit.net) remains suspended owing to heavy damage to the line from Hurricane Ike. No date has been set for its return to operation.

BEST CRUISE LINE SHORE EXCURSIONS

City Tour ($50, 3½ hr.): For guests with late-departing flights, this bus tour passes through Galveston's scenic and historic Strand District. It then travels to Houston, touring the downtown theater and museum districts; Hermann Park, home to the Houston Zoo; and River Oaks, Houston's most prestigious residential neighborhood, before ending at Bush airport.

EXPLORING GALVESTON ON YOUR OWN

If you've got only a few hours before you have to board your cruise, focus on the Strand National Historic Landmark District, the heart of Galveston in the late 1800s and early 1900s, and the East End Historic District, both located north of Broadway.

The **Strand District** is the restored commercial district that runs from 19th to 25th streets between Church Street and the harbor piers. When cotton was king, the Strand was dubbed the Wall Street of the Southwest. Today, its three- and four-story Victorian iron-fronts (so named because of their ironwork facades) are full of shops and dining spots. Near the cruise dock, at Pier 21, the **Texas Seaport Museum** (© 409/ 763-1877; www.tsm-elissa.org) is centered around the three-masted, iron-hulled sailing ship *Elissa,* built in 1877 in Aberdeen, Scotland, and still fully functional today. You can also browse a computer database listing the names of 133,000 immigrants who first entered the U.S. through Galveston in the 19th and early–20th centuries. The museum is open daily 10am to 5pm. Admission is $8 adults, $5 children ages 6 to 18.

The **East End Historic District** is the old silk-stocking neighborhood that runs from 9th to 19th streets between Broadway and Church Street. It has many lovely houses that have been completely restored. The **Galveston Historical Foundation** (www.galvestonhistory.org) has regular tours of several properties, including ornate

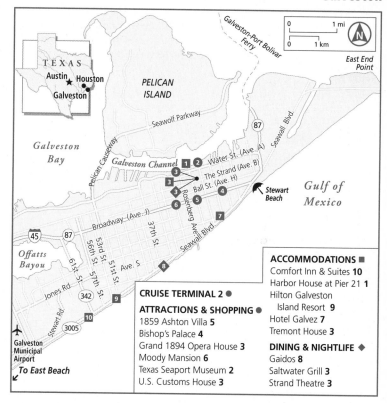

CRUISE TERMINAL 2 ●

ATTRACTIONS & SHOPPING ●
1859 Ashton Villa **5**
Bishop's Palace **4**
Grand 1894 Opera House **3**
Moody Mansion **6**
Texas Seaport Museum **2**
U.S. Customs House **3**

ACCOMMODATIONS ■
Comfort Inn & Suites **10**
Harbor House at Pier 21 **1**
Hilton Galveston
 Island Resort **9**
Hotel Galvez **7**
Tremont House **3**

DINING & NIGHTLIFE ◆
Gaidos **8**
Saltwater Grill **3**
Strand Theatre **3**

Victorian **Bishop's Palace,** 1402 Broadway (© **409/762-2475;** www.galveston.com/
bishopspalace), Galveston's grandest and best-known historic building, built between
1887 and 1893. It's open Monday to Saturday 11am to 4pm, Sunday noon to 4pm.
Admission is $10 adults, $7 kids ages 6 to 18. Others among its properties, including
Galveston's first great Broadway mansion, the **1859 Ashton Villa,** 2328 Broadway
(© **409/762-3933**), sustained heavy storm damage in 2008 and are still closed to visitors. Other mansions-turned-museums include the **Moody Mansion,** 2618 Broadway (© **409/762-7668;** www.moodymansion.org), whose ornately furnished rooms
depict the home life of the wealthy Moody family, who built the house in 1895. It's
open daily 11am to 3pm. Admission is $7 adults, $3.50 children.

Elsewhere in town, Postoffice Street is a restored historic district with more than 25
buildings, including the **Grand 1894 Opera House,** still in operation (see below),
and the **U.S. Customs House,** now home of the Galveston Historical Foundation.

BEACHES

The beaches are another of Galveston's most popular attractions, with light-tan sand and
warm waters much of the year. **East Beach** and **Stewart Beach,** operated by the city,
have pavilions with dressing rooms, showers, and restrooms, ideal for day-trippers.

Stewart Beach is at the end of Broadway, while East Beach is about a mile farther east. All of the beaches are free, and are looking spiffy following a multimillion-dollar post-Ike reconstruction. Another activity popular with visitors and locals alike is walking, skating, or riding a bike atop the **seawall,** which extends 10 miles along the shoreline.

SHOPPING

Galveston has more than 20 art galleries on the Strand, Pier 21, and in the Postoffice Street Entertainment District. The Strand is also known for its quaint antiques, art, and memorabilia shops.

WHERE TO STAY

The **Tremont House,** 2300 Ship's Mechanic Row (ⓒ **800/WYNDHAM** [996-3426] or 409/763-0300; www.wyndham.com), is a 117-room gem in the heart of the Strand neighborhood. A replica of the original hotel built in 1839, which stood nearby, this Tremont occupies the Leon & H. Blum Building built in 1879, and has been designed to re-create the atmosphere of its 19th-century namesake. Cruise season rates: from $110 double.

Harbor House at Pier 21, No. 28–Pier 21 (ⓒ **800/874-3721** or 409/763-3321; www.harborhousepier21.com), is a 42-unit hotel built on a pier and overlooking the harbor. It has modern styling and is very close to the Strand District and many restaurants. Cruise season rates: from $119 double.

Hotel Galvez, 2024 Seawall Blvd. (ⓒ **800/WYNDHAM** [996-3426] or 409/765-7721; www.wyndham.com), Galveston's historic grand hotel, is located on the shore facing the seawall and one of the municipal beaches. It has 231 units and is on the trolley line leading to the Strand District. Cruise season rates: from $169 double.

Other properties on Seawall Boulevard include the 149-unit **Hilton Galveston Island Resort,** 5400 Seawall Blvd. (ⓒ **800/HILTONS** [445-8667] or 409/744-5000; www.galvestonhilton.com), with cruise season rates from $135 double; and the 100-unit **Comfort Inn & Suites,** 6302 Seawall Blvd. (ⓒ **800/221-2222;** www.comfortinn.com), with cruise season rates from $135 double.

DINING & NIGHTLIFE

Seafood is what people come to Galveston for, and there's quite a variety. **Gaidos,** 3800 Seawall Blvd. (ⓒ **409/762-9625;** www.gaidosofgalveston.com), is a Galveston favorite that's been owned and operated by the Gaido family for four generations, with fresh seafood and attentive service. The soups and side dishes are mostly traditional Southern and Gulf Coast recipes that are comfort food for longtime customers; the stuffed snapper is to die for. Main courses: $15 to $33. **Saltwater Grill,** 2017 Postoffice St. (ⓒ **409/762-3474**), set in an old building near the Strand, prints a daily menu that usually includes some inventive seafood pastas, a fish dish with an Asian bent, gumbo or bouillabaisse, and a few non-seafood options. Main courses: $14 to $29.

There are enough bars and restaurants along the seawall and in the historic Strand and Postoffice Street districts to pleasantly while away an evening. For concerts, musicals, and plays, check out the 200-seat **Strand Theatre,** 2317 Ship's Mechanic Row (ⓒ **877/787-2639;** www.strandtheatregalveston.org), in the heart of the historic district, or the elegant **Grand 1894 Opera House,** 2020 Postoffice St. (ⓒ **800/821-1894;** www.thegrand.com), for Broadway productions, orchestral performances, country music, and more.

8 Los Angeles, California

Los Angeles isn't a city or even a county; it's a whole planet unto itself, its nation-states linked by dozens of superhighways that turn into slow-motion performance art at rush hour. The place is just as sunny, smoggy, rich, poor, sybaritic, hard-boiled, movie-happy, New Agey, and unreal as the movies make it seem, and so obsessively cataloged by those same movies that you'll be experiencing déjà vu every other minute of your visit, spotting places you've seen on the silver screen. We had an argument with a friend once about which U.S. city would be most recognizable to anybody, anywhere in the world. We said New York, she said L.A., and while we still stick with our opinion, our friend wasn't too far off the mark.

Now here's the downside to L.A.'s abundance: Unless you stay for several weeks, you won't have a hope in hell of getting a real handle on the place. It's just too big, too diverse, and takes a much bigger guidebook to cover (one like *Frommer's Los Angeles*, for instance . . . hint, hint).

GETTING TO LOS ANGELES & THE PORT

There are two major cruise centers in L.A.: the **World Cruise Center,** off Harbor Boulevard in San Pedro (© 310/732-7678; www.portoflosangeles.org), and Carnival Corporation's **Long Beach Cruise Terminal,** 10 miles west at 231 Windsor Way, Long Beach (www.sanpedro.com/spcom/crusshp2.htm). The World Cruise Center is the busier of the two, hosting most of the cruise lines that sail to or from L.A. The Long Beach terminal is pretty much all Carnival ships, all the time, though Princess ships also dock here on occasion. Parking is $12 per day at the World Cruise Center, $15 per day at Long Beach.

Most visitors fly into **Los Angeles International Airport** (© 310/646-5252; www.lawa.org/welcomelax.aspx), better known as LAX. This behemoth is situated oceanside, between Marina del Rey and Manhattan Beach, about 18 miles north of the World Cruise Center. You may also opt to fly into **Long Beach Municipal Airport,** 4100 Donald Douglas Dr. (© 562/570-2600; www.lgb.org), if you're heading right to the port and don't intend to stay on after your arrival.

GETTING AROUND   Even though L.A. does have a public-transportation infrastructure, getting around without a car is still like trying to see Mars without a spacesuit. All the major **car rental** companies are represented at the airports, but if you want to look like a star on the freeways, you can rent a Porsche, BMW, Mercedes, or Bentley at **Budget Beverly Hills Car Collection,** 9815 Wilshire Blvd. (© 800/227-7117 or 310/274-9174; www.budgetbeverlyhills.com). For even more spiff, **Beverly Hills Rent-A-Car,** 9732 Little Santa Monica Blvd., Beverly Hills (© 800/479-5996 or 310/337-1400; www.bhrentacar.com), rents cars from Lamborghini, Maserati, Ferrari, and Rolls, plus classic Caddies and muscle cars from the '50s, '60s, and '70s. Those with more eco-conscience can also choose from among four different hybrids or a Smart car. Both companies offer airport pickup service and complimentary delivery to local hotels.

BEST CRUISE LINE SHORE EXCURSIONS

Universal Studios on Your Own ($39, 7 hr.): A bus ride takes you to huge Universal Studios, where you board the Glamour Tram for a backstage look at the movie biz (see below).

EXPLORING LOS ANGELES ON YOUR OWN

Los Angeles is a very confusing city in that its "downtown" isn't considered the center of the city. In fact, there really *is* no center—just a whole bunch of neighborhoods and independently incorporated communities that run into one another and spread out as far as the eye can see. The best way to grasp the geography is to break it into six regions, roughly west to east: **Santa Monica** and the beach communities, **L.A.'s Westside** and **Beverly Hills, Hollywood** and **West Hollywood, downtown,** the **San Fernando Valley,** and **Pasadena** and environs. You'll probably concentrate your visit in the city's western districts, because that's where the majority of tourist attractions, restaurants, and shops are. Despite such downtown attractions as the Disney Concert Hall and the Staples Center (a major sports and entertainment arena), most short-stay visitors never make it that far east.

There are so many things to see and do in this town that most *residents* never see and do them all, so in this section we'll be concentrating on the quintessential L.A. experience—to wit: taking a big swan dive into pop culture and swimming around.

Begin your adventure on Hollywood Boulevard at the **Hollywood Walk of Fame,** between Gower and La Brea (and also Vine St. btw. Yucca and Sunset Blvd.). Currently more than 2,200 past and present celebrities have bronze medallions on the world's most famous sidewalk, each one set in the center of a terrazzo star. You'll need to Google some of the more obscure names (who's Blanche Thebom again?), but you'll be surprised by how many will pop your brain buttons. A complete list of stars and their addresses is available online at **www.hollywoodchamber.net**. This part of Hollywood is a funky mix of tourist shops, businesses catering to the local rocker and biker subcultures, and **Scientologists,** who own a lot of the local real estate.

At the corner of Hollywood Boulevard and Highland Street, the massive 8¾-acre **Hollywood & Highland** entertainment complex (© **323/464-6412;** www. hollywoodandhighland.com) has all the top-end merchants as well as studio broadcast facilities, restaurants, nightclubs, cinemas, the Lucky Strike Lanes "upscale bowling alley/lounge," a hotel (see "Where to Stay," later in this section), and the **Kodak Theatre,** home of the Academy Awards. The mall's other centerpiece is the open-air **Babylon Court,** designed after a set from the 1916 film *Intolerance,* with giant elephant-topped pillars and a colossal arch that frames the **Hollywood sign** in the distance. (Trivia: The sign, perched at the top of Mount Lee, started as an advertisement for the Hollywoodland housing development. It was only later that it lost the "land" and was adopted as the symbol of the movie industry.)

Between Highland and La Brea Avenue is the famed **Grauman's Chinese Theatre,** 6925 Hollywood Blvd. (© **323/464-8111;** www.manntheatres.com/chinese), one of the world's great movie palaces, opened in 1927 by impresario Sid Grauman. Visitors by the millions flock to the theater for its famous entry court, where stars such as Gary Cooper, Elizabeth Taylor, Ginger Rogers, and more than 160 others set their signatures and handprints/footprints in concrete.

From Hollywood, you're in an ideal position to set off on a drive along **Sunset Boulevard**—the street, the myth, the legend. This is a must for first-time visitors because you'll see a cross-section of everything that is L.A.: legendary clubs, studios, hotels, and zip codes that you'll instantly recognize from movies and television. The 45-minute drive takes you from Hollywood's seedy/starry streets to flamboyant **West Hollywood,** past glittering **Beverly Hills,** through **Brentwood** (O.J.'s old neighborhood), into the secluded enclave of **Pacific Palisades,** and finally to the sea. From

Los Angeles

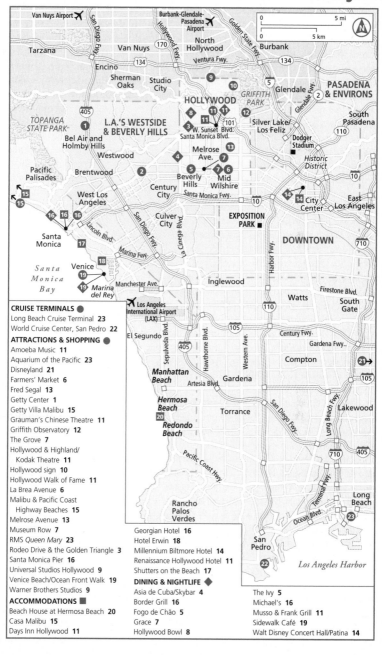

there, you can head north to Malibu's fabled beaches (land of *Baywatch*) or head south along the coast to the funkier beach town of **Santa Monica.** Park at the **Santa Monica Pier** and head south on foot toward **Venice Beach** along the carnival-like **Ocean Front Walk.** You haven't visited L.A. properly until you've toured the area on the right kind of wheels (in-line skates), taken in the human carnival around you, noshed on boardwalk food, watched a few street performers, and bought some cheap sunglasses or ethnic garb—all the while enjoying the blue sea, the wide beach, and the world's vainest weight lifters, who pump themselves up at an outdoor gym right in the heart of things.

Venice is street theater, but for theater of the big-budget kind, you'll want to tour one of the movie studios. **Warner Brothers Studios,** 3400 Riverside Dr., Burbank (© 818/972-8687; www.wbstudiotour.com), has the most comprehensive tour, taking visitors on a 2¼-hour drive and walk around the studio's faux streets. After a brief introductory film, you'll pile into glorified golf carts and cruise past parking spaces marked with stars' names, then walk through active film and television sets, where you'll get a glimpse of how the biz really works. Sometimes you can also visit working sets to watch actors filming. Reservations are recommended, and children ages 7 and under are not admitted. Bring valid photo ID. Tours are $48 per person, departing every 30 minutes on weekdays only (8:20am–4pm, with extended hours in spring and summer).

In nearby Griffith Park, the bronze domes of **Griffith Observatory,** 2800 E. Observatory Rd. (© 213/473-0800; www.griffithobservatory.org), have been Hollywood Hills landmarks since 1935. The observatory features 60 space-related exhibits and a 300-seat planetarium that hosts hourly screenings of a narrated half-hour projection show. Outside, the grounds allow unparalleled city views. The Observatory is open Tuesday to Friday noon to 10pm, Saturday and Sunday 10am to 10pm. Observatory admission is free, but the planetarium show costs $7 adults/youths ages 13 and over, $3 kids ages 5 to 12.

The "other" studio tour is at **Universal Studios Hollywood,** Hollywood Freeway (Universal Center Dr. or Lankershim Blvd. exits), Universal City, in the San Fernando Valley (© 800/864-8377 or 818/622-3801; www.universalstudioshollywood.com), but this isn't just a working studio; it's also one of the world's largest amusement parks. The main attraction continues tobe the Studio Tour, a 1-hour guided tram ride around the company's 420 acres, passing stars' dressing rooms and visiting famous back-lot sets. The rest of the experience is thrill rides themed on blockbusters such as *The Mummy, Jurassic Park,* and *Shrek.* Basic 1-day admission is $69, though other options are available. Hours vary, with the park generally opening at 9 or 10am and closing anytime between 5 and 9pm. Check before you go.

Just outside the gate is **Universal CityWalk** (© 818/622-4455; www.citywalk hollywood.com), a 3-block-long pedestrian promenade crammed with flashy name-brand stores, themed nightclubs, theme restaurants (the Hard Rock Cafe and others), a 3-D IMAX theater, an 18-screen cinema, NASCAR virtual racing, and more, More, MORE! Getting in is free, but after that you're on your own. It's generally open daily from 11am to 9pm (Fri–Sat 11pm).

Now, lest we forget, **Disneyland** is also not so far away, at 1313 Harbor Blvd. in Anaheim, an hour south of downtown L.A. on I-5 (© 714/781-4565; www. disneyland.com). The complex is divided into several themed "lands," ranging from the archetypal Main Street U.S.A. to Adventureland, inspired by Asia, Africa, and

Culture? You Want Culture?

If you have any energy left after being a shameless L.A. tourist, pay a visit to the **Getty Center,** 1200 Getty Center Dr. (© **310/440-7300;** www.getty. edu), the Richard Meier–designed cultural cornerstone that displays J. Paul Getty's enormous collection of art, ranging from antiquities to Impressionist paintings, contemporary photography, and graphic arts. Admission is free, but you have to pay $15 and make a reservation to park your car, which is *so* L.A. For more culture, there's also **Museum Row,** a stretch of Wilshire Boulevard just east of Beverly Hills that's home to about a dozen different institutions, from the **Los Angeles County Museum of Art,** 5905 Wilshire Blvd. (© **323/857-6000;** www.lacma.org), to the **La Brea Tar Pits** and **George C. Page Museum of La Brea Discoveries,** 5801 Wilshire Blvd. (© **323/ 934-7243;** www.tarpits.org).

Up in Malibu, a mile north of Sunset Boulevard, the **Getty Villa Malibu,** 17985 Pacific Coast Hwy. (© **310/440-7300;** www.getty.edu), is the former residence of oil tycoon J. Paul Getty, built in 1974 and modeled after a 1st-century Roman country house. The museum holds a permanent collection of more than 1,200 Greek, Roman, and Etruscan artifacts dating from 6,500 B.C. to A.D. 400, augmented by various temporary exhibitions. In addition to art, the place has dazzling ocean views. It's open Wednesday to Monday 10am to 5pm. Admission is free, but advance, timed tickets are required (see website). Parking is $15.

South America. For our money, no ride in the park (or in its Florida cousin, for that matter) has ever topped **It's a Small World,** a slow-moving indoor river ride in which creepy dolls of all the world's children sing their saccharine song through hinged mouths. When it was built in the '50s, could Walt Disney have known that he was creating a preview of every bad acid trip that happened in the '60s? It's a classic. Disneyland Park is open daily 9am to 9pm. Disney's California Adventure Park is open daily 10am to 7pm. One-day admission to either park is $72 kids ages 10 and up, $62 kids ages 3 to 9. A pass that covers both parks is $97 kids ages 10 and up, $87 kids ages 3 to 9. Multiday passes are also available, as are resort accommodations.

For cruise travelers with a sense of history, one of the most vital attractions in all L.A. has to be the **RMS *Queen Mary,*** 1126 Queen's Hwy. in Long Beach, at the end of I-710 (© **562/435-3511;** www.queenmary.com). One of the greatest ocean liners ever, it's now moored permanently in Long Beach, in the same complex that holds Carnival's Long Beach terminal. Though most of its original furnishings are long gone, it's still the only surviving example of this particular kind of 20th-century elegance, from the staterooms' tropical-hardwood paneling to the incredible deco artwork and miles of Bakelite handrails. Stroll the teakwood decks and, with just a little imagination, you're back in 1936. It's open daily 10am to 5pm. Admission is $25 adults, $13 kids ages 5 to 11. The *Queen Mary* also functions as a hotel, with rates starting around $120 double. Several onboard restaurants serve brunches and dinners at various rates, and packages include special exhibits, guided tours, and the Soviet submarine moored next door.

Just across the harbor is the huge **Aquarium of the Pacific,** 100 Aquarium Way, off Shoreline Drive (© **562/590-3100;** www.aquariumofpacific.org), featuring re-creations of three Pacific habitats, from the warm tropics to the frigid Bering Sea. More than 12,000 creatures inhabit its three-story tanks, from sharks and sea lions to delicate sea horses and moon jellies. It's open daily 9am to 6pm. Admission is $24 adults, $12 kids ages 3 to 11.

BEACHES

Los Angeles County's 72-mile coastline sports more than 30 miles of beaches, most of which are operated by the **Department of Beaches & Harbors,** 13837 Fiji Way, Marina del Rey (© **310/305-9503;** www.beaches.co.la.ca.us). Parking costs between $2 and $14. Call for recorded **surf conditions** and coastal weather forecasts (© **310/457-9701**). The following are the best beaches in L.A., listed from north to south.

Jampacked on warm weekends, **Zuma Beach County Park** is L.A. County's largest beach park, located off the Pacific Coast Highway, a mile past Kanan Dume Road. Although it can't claim to be the most scenic beach in the Southland, Zuma has the most comprehensive facilities: plenty of restrooms, lifeguards, playgrounds, volleyball courts, and snack bars. The southern stretch, toward Point Dume, is **Westward Beach,** separated from the noisy highway by sandstone cliffs.

Not just a pretty white-sand beach, but an estuary and wetlands area as well, **Malibu Lagoon State Beach** is the historic home of the Chumash Indians. The entrance is on the Pacific Coast Highway south of Cross Creek Road. Marine life and shorebirds teem where the creek empties into the sea, and the waves are always mild.

Highway noise prevents solitude at short, narrow **Topanga State Park,** located where Topanga Canyon Boulevard emerges from the mountains. Why go? Ask the surfers who wait in line to catch Topanga's excellent right point breaks. There are restrooms and lifeguard services here, and across the street you'll find one of the best fresh-fish restaurants around. The popular **Will Rogers State Beach,** comprising 3 miles along the Pacific Coast Highway, between Sunset Boulevard and the Santa Monica border, has friendly waves, competitive volleyball games, restrooms, lifeguards, and a snack hut in season.

Santa Monica State Beach, on either side of the Santa Monica Pier, is popular for its white sands and accessibility. A paved path runs along here, allowing you to walk, bike, or skate to Venice. To the south, the wide and friendly **Manhattan Beach** was once a hangout for the Beach Boys. Today, it's lined with beautiful oceanview homes and has some of the best surfing around, plus restrooms, lifeguards, and volleyball courts. Not far away are the wide **Hermosa Beach** and **Redondo Beach.**

SHOPPING

Rodeo Drive and the Golden Triangle, between Santa Monica Boulevard, Wilshire Boulevard, and Canon Drive in Beverly Hills, is the city's (and one of the world's) most famous shopping districts, so chichi and pricey that it's almost like a theme park, with the theme being *money.* Couture shops from high fashion's old guard are located along these hallowed blocks, along with plenty of newer high-end labels. Come and gawk. Crossing Wilshire a bit east of Rodeo, the blocks of **La Brea Avenue** north of Wilshire make up L.A.'s artiest shopping strip, home to lots of great urban antiques stores dealing in Art Deco, Arts and Crafts, 1950s moderne, and the like. You'll also find vintage clothiers, furniture galleries, and other warehouse-size stores, as well as some of the city's hippest restaurants.

In Hollywood, scruffy but fun **Melrose Avenue** has many secondhand and avant-garde clothing shops as well as good restaurants and almost-guaranteed celebrity sightings. The original **Fred Segal** complex—breezy, ultrahip boutiques linked like departments of a single-story fashion maze—is at 8100 Melrose Ave. (© **323/655-3734**). Shops include the latest apparel for men, women, and toddlers, plus lingerie, shoes, hats, luggage, cosmetics, workout/loungewear, and a cafe. Fred Segal also affords major star-spotting potential. A few blocks to the north, **Amoeba Music,** 6400 Sunset Blvd. (© **323/245-6400;** www.amoebamusic.com), may be the best record store in the world, with a huge selection of new and used CDs, vinyl discs, and videos.

A few blocks to the south, **West Third Street** between Fairfax and Robertson is a trendy strip with some Melrose Avenue émigrés, along with terrific up-and-comers, cafes, and the like. *Fun* is more the catchword here than *funky,* and the shops are a bit more refined than those along Melrose. It's all anchored on the east end by the **Farmers' Market,** 6333 W. Third St. (© **323/933-9211;** www.farmersmarketla.com), a sprawling marketplace with food and produce stalls, a gourmet market, and a wine bar. The original market was just a bunch of Depression-era farmers setting up stands to sell produce, but eventually permanent buildings grew up, including the trademark shingled 10-story clock tower. The **Grove,** 189 The Grove Dr. (© **888/315-8883** or 323/900-8080; www.thegrovela.com), is a huge retail complex at the market's eastern end, with all the usual high-end mall stores and architectural styles ranging from Art Deco to Italian Renaissance.

Santa Monica, location of several of our recommended hotels, is also a great place for shopping. **Main Street,** stretching from Pico Boulevard to Rose Avenue, between Fourth Street and Neilson Way, is an excellent area for strolling, crammed with a combination of mall standards and upscale, left-of-center boutiques. You can also find plenty of casually hip cafes and restaurants. The primary strip connecting Santa Monica and Venice, Main Street has a relaxed, beach-community vibe that sets it apart from similar strips. The **Third Street Promenade,** a pedestrian-only stretch of Third between Broadway and Wilshire Boulevard, is packed with chain stores and boutiques as well as dozens of restaurants and three multiscreen cinemas. It's one of the most popular shopping areas in the city, bustling well into the evening.

WHERE TO STAY

If surf and sand compose the Southern California image in your mind's eye, book a hotel along Santa Monica Bay, on the city's west side, stretching from Redondo Beach in the south to Malibu in the northwest. The more southerly properties are an easy drive to or from the cruise terminals, and all of them are a fairly easy drive to Beverly Hills shops and the Hollywood attractions.

The **Beach House at Hermosa Beach,** 1300 The Strand, Hermosa Beach (© **888/895-4559;** www.beach-house.com), sports a Cape Cod style that suits the on-the-sand location. It's luxurious and romantic, with 96 beautifully designed and outfitted split-level studio suites. Cruise season rates: from $239 double.

The **Hotel Erwin,** 1697 Pacific Ave., Venice (© **800/786-7789;** www.jdvhotels.com/hotels/erwin), is a haven of hipness and kitschiness, located just off the Venice boardwalk. The spacious rooms are brightened with beachy colors. Many units have at least partial ocean views, and the view from the open-air rooftop cocktail lounge can't be beat. Cruise season rates: from $219 double.

Shutters on the Beach, 1 Pico Blvd., Santa Monica (© **800/334-9000;** www. shuttersonthebeach.com), is a Cape Cod–style luxury hotel that sits directly on the beach, a block from Santa Monica Pier. Each unit has a beachview balcony. Try to get one of the beach-cottage rooms overlooking the sand—these are more desirable and no more expensive than those in the hotel's towers. Cruise season rates: from $455 double.

The eight-story, Art Deco **Georgian Hotel,** 1415 Ocean Ave. (© **800/538-8147;** www.georgianhotel.com), boasts luxury, loads of historic charm, and a terrific ocean-view location, just across from Santa Monica's beach and pier. Established in 1933, the place was popular among Hollywood's golden-age elite, who enjoyed its veranda lounge and beautifully designed guest rooms. Cruise season rates: from $255 double.

Casa Malibu, sitting on its own private beach at 22752 Pacific Coast Hwy., Malibu (© **800/831-0858;** casamalibu@earthlink.net), is a leftover jewel from Malibu's golden age and it doesn't try to play the sleek resort game. Instead, the modest, low-rise inn sports a traditional California-beach-cottage look that's cozy and timeless, with 21 comfortable, charming units. More than half have ocean views, but even those facing the courtyard are quiet and provide easy beach access via wooden stairs. Cruise season rates: from $169 double.

If you don't care to stay by the beach, here are some choices for different personality/family types:

For Oscar-winner wannabes, the **Renaissance Hollywood Hotel,** 1755 N. Highland Ave. (© **800/769-4774;** www.renaissancehollywood.com), is part of the Hollywood & Highland complex (see "Exploring Los Angeles on Your Own," earlier in this section). On Oscar night, it's the headquarters for a frenzy of participants and paparazzi, but the rest of the year it's just a centrally located hotel with a nice respect for its location—think guest rooms outfitted like swinging '50s bachelor pads, with wood-paneled headboards and Technicolor furniture. Cruise season rates: from $239 double.

While it's east of the prime Sunset Strip action, the **Days Inn Hollywood,** 7023 Sunset Blvd., between Highland and La Brea (© **800/329-7466;** www.daysinn hollywood.com), is safe and convenient, and extras such as free underground parking and continental breakfast make it an especially good value for travelers on a budget. Some rooms have microwaves, fridges, and coffeemakers. Cruise season rates: from $79 double.

In downtown L.A., the historic **Millennium Biltmore Hotel,** 506 S. Grand Ave. (© **800/245-8673;** www.thebiltmore.com), opened in 1923 and has hosted presidents, kings, and Hollywood celebrities, all of them drawn by its old-world charm, grand lobby, and warmly elegant rooms. The Gallery Bar and Cognac Room is one of the best places in town for a cocktail, and Sai Sai is among the best Japanese restaurants in downtown L.A. Cruise season rates: from $159 double.

DINING & NIGHTLIFE

For a dinner that channels the ghost of Old Hollywood, head to **Musso & Frank Grill,** 6667 Hollywood Blvd., Hollywood (© **323/467-7788**). This comfortable, dark-paneled room, virtually unchanged since 1919, begs you to order up one of

L.A.'s best martinis and some chops or the legendary chicken potpie. Then, listen to the longtime waitstaff spin historical yarns about the days when Orson Welles held court here and Faulkner, Fitzgerald, and Hemingway all popped in for a drink between writing screenplays. Main courses: $13 to $35. You'll always find living celebrities, on the other hand, frequenting the Sunset Strip hot spots, including the Mondrian hotel and its chic Chino-Latin restaurant, **Asia de Cuba,** 8440 Sunset Blvd., West Hollywood (© **323/848-6000;** www.mondrianhotel.com). Main courses: $22 to $79. Celebrity dieters can be glimpsed bypassing the eats for the A-list-only **Skybar** on the other side of the pool.

The **Ivy,** 113 N. Robertson Blvd., West Hollywood (© **310/274-8303**), a perennial power spot, attracts L.A.'s more conservative celebs. Main courses: $23 to $38. Nearby, **Grace,** 7360 Beverly Blvd., West Hollywood (© **323/934-4400;** www.grace restaurant.net), provides a flawless dining experience, from the service to the new American cuisine, the wine, and the decor. Executive chef and co-owner Neal Fraser is a culinary scion of Wolfgang Puck, Thomas Keller, and Joachim Splichal, and has put together a menu that makes for one of the best splurges in the city. Main courses: $25 to $30. Just to the west, **Fogo de Chão,** 133 N. La Cienega Blvd., Beverly Hills (© **310/289-7755;** www.fogodechao.com), is an enormous Brazilian-style *churrasco* steakhouse—the kind where everything except alcohol is covered by one flat rate and waiters circulate continuously, bringing cuts of slow-roasted meats and endless side dishes until you tell them to stop. FYI, the name is pronounced "Fogo dee *Shown.*" Fixed-price menu: $57.

Many great restaurants are clustered around the Santa Monica area. For some of the best California cuisine in town, head to chef/owner Michael McCarty's eponymous **Michael's,** 1147 Third St., Santa Monica (© **310/451-0843;** www.michaelssanta monica.com). Main courses: $34 to $45. The **Border Grill,** 1445 Fourth St., Santa Monica (© **310/451-1655;** www.bordergrill.com), fills the ticket if you're craving a taste from south of that border. Main courses: $17 to $30. From here, you can head to Venice's Ocean Front Walk for some primo people-watching. The **Sidewalk Café,** 1401 Ocean Front Walk, Venice (© **310/399-5547;** www.thesidewalkcafe.com), allows unobstructed views of parading skaters, bikers, skateboarders, musclemen, break dancers, street performers, sword swallowers, and other participants in the daily carnival. You can also get your dinner here, if you think you won't be distracted. Main courses: $8 to $15.

Bar none, the most classic L.A. thing you can do after the sun goes down is take a picnic dinner to the **Hollywood Bowl,** 2301 N. Highland Ave., Hollywood (© **323/ 850-2000;** www.hollywoodbowl.org). In addition to being the summer home of the Los Angeles Philharmonic, the Bowl hosts visiting performers ranging from chamber-music quartets to jazz greats to folk humorists. The imposing white band shell always elicits appreciative gasps from first-time Bowl-goers. Don't forget your bottle of wine. If you prefer your entertainment with a roof, the **Walt Disney Concert Hall,** at First Street and Grand Avenue, downtown (© **213/972-7211;** www.disneyhall.com), should fit the bill. The strikingly beautiful hall, designed by Frank Gehry, has a dazzling 2,273-seat auditorium, plus a cafe, bookstore, gift shop, and Joachim Splichal's flagship restaurant, **Patina** (© **213/972-3331;** www.patinagroup.com/patina). Main courses: $36–$55. The concert hall is open to the public for viewing, but to witness it in full glory, attend a concert by the world-class Philharmonic.

9 Miami, Florida

Miami is the most Latin city in the U.S., with a hot-hot-hot club scene, sparkling beaches, crystal-clear waters, and more palm fronds, glittering hotels, and red sports cars than anywhere outside Monte Carlo and Rio. On top of all that, it's also the spiritual and actual home of the U.S. cruise biz, the place where cruising as we know it today was birthed in the late 1960s. Today, it's still the country's top port, with more than four million passengers passing through annually, and more supersize ships berthing here than anywhere else.

GETTING TO MIAMI & THE PORT

The **Port of Miami** is at 1015 N. America Way on Dodge Island (© **305/371-7678;** www.miamidade.gov/portofmiami), reached via a four-lane bridge from Miami's downtown district. Parking lots right at street level face the cruise terminals, and charge $20 per day. **Miami International Airport** (© **305/876-7000;** www.miami-airport.com) is about 8 miles west of downtown Miami and the port (about a 15-min. drive). If you've arranged air transportation and/or transfers through your cruise line, a representative will meet you and direct you to shuttle buses to the port. **Taxis** are also available at a flat fare of $24. Blue taxis serve only the immediate area around the airport; yellow taxis serve all other destinations, including the port.

GETTING AROUND   **Taxis** start at $2.50 for the first ¼ mile and cost $2.40 for each additional mile; travel to some destinations is on a flat fare basis. Almost two dozen taxi companies serve Miami–Dade County, including **Yellow Cab** (© **305/444-4444;** www.ycab.com) and, on Miami Beach, **Central Cab** (© **305/532-5555;** www.centralcab.com). There's also the **Metromover** (© **305/770-3131;** www.miami dade.gov/transit/mover.asp), a 4⅓-mile elevated line that circles downtown, stopping near important attractions and shopping (including Bayfront Park and Bayside Marketplace). It's fun if you've got time to kill. It runs daily from about 5am to midnight; there are 21 stations, each spaced about 2 blocks apart; and service is free.

BEST CRUISE LINE SHORE EXCURSIONS

Everglades Airboat Ride ($69, 4 hr.): The Seminole Indians called the Everglades Pahay Okee, the "grassy water," and on this 40-minute airboat ride, you'll get to see some of the area's indigenous wildlife, including water birds and American alligators.

EXPLORING MIAMI ON YOUR OWN

A sizzling multicultural mecca, Miami offers the best in cutting-edge restaurants, entertainment, shopping, beaches, and the whole range of hotels, from luxury to boutique, kitschy to charming. Miami's best attraction is actually a neighborhood, the **South Beach Art Deco District,** located at the southern end of Miami Beach below 20th Street. It's filled with outrageous and fanciful 1920s and 1930s architecture, plus outrageous and fanciful 21st-century people. This treasure-trove, usually just called "the Beach" or "SoBe," features more than 900 pastel-painted buildings in the Art Deco, streamline moderne, and Spanish Mediterranean Revival styles. The district stretches from 6th to 23rd streets, and from the Atlantic Ocean to Lennox Court. Ocean Drive boasts many of the premier Art Deco hotels.

Also in South Beach, the **Bass Museum of Art,** 2121 Park Ave. (© **305/673-7530;** www.bassmuseum.org), is Miami's most progressive art museum, with an expanded building designed by Arata Isozaki; a permanent collection of European paintings from the 15th through the early–20th century (including Dutch and Flemish old masters); and collections of textiles, period furnishings, objets d'art, ecclesiastical artifacts, and sculpture. Rotating exhibits include pop art, fashion, and photography. It's open Wednesday to Sunday noon to 5pm. Admission is $8 adults, $6 seniors and students.

The adjoining **Coral Gables** and **Coconut Grove** neighborhoods are fun to visit for both their architecture and ambience. In Coral Gables, the Old World meets the New as curving boulevards, sidewalks, plazas, fountains, and arched entrances evoke Seville. Today, the area is an epicurean's Eden, boasting some of Miami's most renowned eateries as well as the University of Miami and the half-mile-long **Miracle Mile,** a 5-block retail mecca (see "Shopping," below). Coconut Grove, South Florida's oldest settlement, remains a village surrounded by the urban sprawl of Miami. It dates back to the early 1800s, when Bahamian seamen first sought to salvage treasure from the wrecked vessels stranded along the Florida Reef. People come here mostly to shop, drink, dine, or simply walk around and explore.

Just minutes from the Port of Miami in Key Biscayne, the **Miami Seaquarium,** 4400 Rickenbacker Causeway (© **305/361-5705;** www.miamiseaquarium.com), is a delight, featuring eight different marine mammal shows (dolphins and killer whales a specialty) and the opportunity to see endangered manatees, sea lions, tropical-theme aquariums, and a shark feeding. It's open daily 9:30am to 6pm. Admission is $38 adults, $28 kids ages 3 to 9.

BEACHES

A 300-foot-wide sand beach runs for about 10 miles from south of **Miami Beach** to clothing-optional **Haulover Beach Park** in the north. Although most of this stretch is lined with a solid wall of hotels, beach access is plentiful, and you are free to frolic along the entire strip. A wooden boardwalk runs along the hotel side from 21st to 46th streets—about 1½ miles. You'll find lots of public beaches here, wide and well maintained, with lifeguards, toilet facilities, concession stands, and metered parking (bring lots of quarters). Lifeguard-protected public beaches include **21st Street,** at the beginning of the boardwalk; **35th Street,** popular with an older crowd; **46th Street,** next to the Fontainebleau Hilton; **53rd Street,** a narrower, more sedate beach; **64th Street,** one of the quietest strips around; and **72nd Street,** a local old-timers' spot. On the southern tip of the beach is family-favorite **South Pointe Park,** where you can watch the cruise ships. **Lummus Park,** in the center of the Art Deco District, is the best place for people-watching and model-spotting. The stretch between 11th and 13th streets is popular with Miami's large gay community. The area from 1st to 15th streets is popular with seniors.

In Key Biscayne, **Crandon Park,** 4000 Crandon Blvd. (© **305/361-5421;** www.miamidade.gov/parks/parks/crandon_beach.asp), is one of metropolitan Miami's finest white-sand beaches, stretching for some 3½ miles. There are lifeguards here, and you can rent a cabana with a shower and chairs for $38 per day. On Saturday and Sunday, the beach can be especially crowded.

SHOPPING

Most cruise ship passengers shop right near the Port of Miami at **Bayside Marketplace,** 401 Biscayne Blvd. (© **305/577-3344;** www.baysidemarketplace.com), a mall with 150 specialty shops, street performers, live music, and some 30 eateries, including a Hard Rock Cafe and others serving everything from Cuban dishes to crepes. Many restaurants have outdoor seating right along the bay for picturesque views of the yachts harbored here. The mall can be reached via regular shuttle service from the port or by walking over the Port Bridge.

Bal Harbour Shops, 9700 Collins Ave. (© **305/866-0311;** www.balharbour shops.com), is a high-fashion, big-money mecca, with big-name stores including Chanel, Prada, Armani, Neiman Marcus, Saks Fifth Avenue, and dozens of others.

In South Beach, **Lincoln Road,** an 8-block pedestrian mall, runs between Washington Avenue and Alton Road, near the northern tier of the Art Deco District. It's filled with popular chains such as Victoria's Secret and Banana Republic, interior-design stores, art galleries, and clothing boutiques, as well as coffeehouses, restaurants, and cafes. Despite the recent influx of commercial anchor stores, Lincoln Road still manages to maintain its funky, arty flair, attracting an eclectic, colorful crowd. Or try **Espanola Way,** a small pedestrian road with a European feel that starts at 15th Street and Collins.

Coconut Grove, centered on the intersection of Main Highway and Grand Avenue, is the heart of the city's boutique district and features two open-air shopping-and-entertainment complexes: **CocoWalk,** 3015 Grand Ave. (© **305/444-0777;** www.cocowalk.net), and the much less cool **Streets of Mayfair,** 2911 Grand Ave. (© **305/448-1700**).

In Coral Gables, **Miracle Mile,** actually a half-mile stretch of SW 22nd Street between Douglas and Le Jeune roads (aka 37th and 42nd aves.), has more than 150 shops. The **Village of Merrick Park,** 358 San Lorenzo Ave. at SW 42nd Ave. (© **305/529-0200;** www.villageofmerrickpark.com), gives the Bal Harbour Shops a run for their money with high-end stores such as Jimmy Choo, Neiman Marcus, and Nordstrom, plus both casual and upscale eateries.

WHERE TO STAY

Two hotels are right across the bay from the cruise ship piers, near Bayside Marketplace: the 34-story **Hotel InterContinental Miami,** 100 Chopin Plaza (© **800/327-3005;** www.intercontinental.com/miami), with rates from $270 double; and the **Marriott Biscayne Bay,** 1633 N. Bayshore (© **800/228-9290;** www.marriott.com/miami), with rates from $159 double. Thanks to Miami's good highway network, though, you can stay virtually anywhere in Greater Miami and still be within 10 to 20 minutes of your ship.

SOUTH BEACH   Two blocks from the beach, the Art Deco, comfy-chic **Hotel Astor,** 956 Washington Ave. (© **800/270-4981;** www.hotelastor.com), was originally built in 1936, but you'd never know that from the sleek and near-minimal modern interiors it sports today. Cruise season rates: from $298 double.

The **Catalina Hotel & Beach Club,** 1732 Collins Ave. (© **305/674-1160;** www.catalinahotel.com), is one of the newer boutique hotels on South Beach, with a retro *Mod Squad* decor, rooms glazed in white with hints of bright colors. It has a happening bar and lounge scene and a happy hour that really is: From 7 to 8pm nightly, mixed well drinks are free at all four of its bars. Cruise season rates: from $229 double. The **Hotel,** 801 Collins Ave., at 8th Street (© **305/531-2222;** www.thehotelof southbeach.com), is a deco gem with a stylishly whimsical interior designed by haute couturier Todd Oldham. Cruise season rates: from $335 double.

It's hard to find a hotel on South Beach with both good value and excellent service, but the **Crest Hotel Suites,** 1670 James Ave. (© **800/531-3880;** www.cresthotel.com), delivers. It's one of Miami's best bargains and coolest hotels, retaining its original 1939 Art Deco architecture, but with a thoroughly modern interior. Cruise season rates: from $115 double.

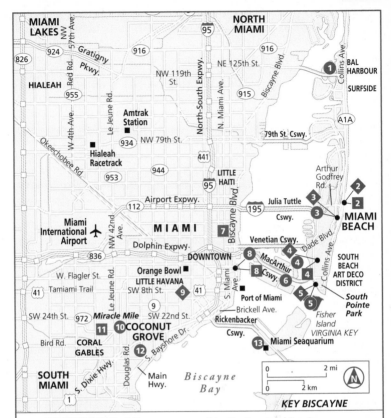

CRUISE TERMINAL 6 ●

ATTRACTIONS & SHOPPING ●
Bal Harbour Shops **1**
Bass Museum of Art **3**
Bayside Marketplace **8**
CocoWalk **12**
Lincoln Road pedestrian mall **4**
Miami Seaquarium **13**
Miracle Mile **10**
South Beach Art Deco District **4**
Streets of Mayfair **12**
Village of Merrick Park **12**

ACCOMMODATIONS ■
Biltmore Hotel **11**
Catalina Hotel & Beach Club **4**
Crest Hotel Suites **4**

Eden Roc Resort and Spa **2**
Fontainebleau Hotel and Resort **2**
Hotel Astor **4**
Hotel InterContinental Miami **8**
Marriott Biscayne Bay **7**

DINING & NIGHTLIFE ◆
Barton G. The Restaurant **2**
The Forge **4**
Joe's Stone Crab **5**
Larios on the Beach **4**
Lincoln Road pedestrian mall **4**
Little Havana **9**
Nobu **3**
Prime One Twelve **5**
Skybar **4**
Spris **4**
Sushi Samba **4**
Van Dyke Cafe **4**

MIAMI BEACH   The **Eden Roc Resort and Spa,** 4525 Collins Ave. (© **800/ 327-8337** or 305/531-0000; www.edenrocresort.com), was a Rat Pack hangout in the '50s, but a $110-million renovation a few years back completely transformed the place, adding a 283-room oceanfront tower, five pools, two restaurants, and a spa. Cruise season rates: from $349 double.

Speaking of face-lifts, the historic Art Deco landmark **Fontainebleau Hotel and Resort,** 4441 Collins Ave. (© **800/548-8886** or 305/538-2000; www.fontainebleau. com), which appeared in movies like *Scarface* and *Goldfinger,* got the mother of all face-lifts a couple of years ago, reopening with a 40,000-square-foot spa and 11 restaurants and lounges run by celebrity chefs from New York and London. Choose from the main property or the modern, brand-new all-suite hotel tower, where rooms are plush and posh. Cruise season rates: from $347 double.

CORAL GABLES   The famous **Biltmore Hotel,** 1200 Anastasia Ave. (© **305/445- 1926;** www.biltmorehotel.com), opened its doors in 1926, and its list of famous and infamous guests has included Al Capone and the duke and duchess of Windsor. The place is a national landmark, with the largest hotel pool in the continental United States as well as a 300-foot bell tower modeled after the Cathedral of Seville. Cruise season rates: from $300 double. Even if you're not staying here, you can take a free tour on Sundays at 1:30, 2:30, and 3:30pm, conducted by the Dade Heritage Trust.

DINING & NIGHTLIFE

Count on **South Beach** as your dining and nightlife spot, with dozens of first-rate restaurants and cafes. With very few exceptions, the places on **Ocean Drive** are crowded with tourists and priced accordingly. You'll do better to venture a little farther into the pedestrian-friendly streets just west. The **Lincoln Road** pedestrian-mall area is so packed with places offering great food and atmosphere that it would take a full guidebook to list them all. We recommend strolling and browsing. A couple of standout outdoor cafes are: **Spris,** a pizzeria at 731 Lincoln Rd. (© **305/673-2020;** www.spris.cc), with main courses at $10 to $15; and the **Van Dyke Cafe,** 846 Lincoln Rd. (© **305/534-3600;** www.thevandykecafe.com), with main courses at $9 to $16. **Sushi Samba,** 600 Lincoln Rd. (© **305/673-5337;** www.sushisamba.com), features a fusion of Brazilian, Peruvian, and Japanese cuisine. Main courses: $9 to $29; sushi: priced by the piece. **Nobu,** at the Shore Club, 1901 Collins Ave. (© **305/ 695-3232;** www.noburestaurants.com/miamibeach/index.html), is, of course, legendary for its nouvelle Japanese cuisine. Main courses: $21 to $80; *omakase* "chef's choice" menu: from $70.

Even if Gloria Estefan weren't co-owner of **Larios on the Beach,** 820 Ocean Dr. (© **305/532-9577;** www.bongoscubancafe.com), the crowds would still flock to this bistro, which serves old-fashioned Cuban dishes such as *masitas de puerco* (fried pork chunks). Main courses: $14 to $38. For a steakhouse vibe, try **Prime One Twelve,** at the Browns Hotel, 112 Ocean Dr., South Beach (© **305/532-8112;** www.prime112. com), which has a sleek ambience, a bustling bar, and arguably the best beef in the entire city. A powerhouse crowd gathers here for lunch and dinner, and reservations are more rare than the yellowfin tuna tartare appetizer. Main courses: $30 to $68.

At the legendary **Joe's Stone Crab,** 11 Washington Ave., Miami Beach, between South Point Drive and 1st Street (© **305/673-0365;** www.joesstonecrab.com), about a ton of stone crab claws is served at lunch and dinner daily during stone crab season (mid-Oct to mid-May) and at dinner only in summer (mid-May to early Aug,

Wed–Sun only). Because the place doesn't take reservations, the wait for a table can be up to 2 hours. Crab prices vary depending on the market rate, but figure about $30 per order.

After dark, look for the klieg lights to direct you to South Beach's hot nightspots. While the blocks of Washington Avenue, Collins Avenue, and Ocean Drive are the main nightlife thoroughfares, you'll have better luck spotting a celebrity in a more off-the-beaten-path eatery such as: **Barton G. The Restaurant,** 1427 W. Ave., Miami Beach (© **305/672-8881;** www.bartong.com/restaurant), with main courses at $18 to $50); or the **Forge,** 432 41st St., Miami Beach (© **305/538-8533;** www.theforge.com), an ornately decorated rococo-style venue with a fine wine selection and main courses at $15 to $55. Also popular are the hotel bars, such as the Shore Club's hot, hauter-than-thou celeb magnet **Skybar,** 1901 Collins Ave. (© **786/276-6772;** www.shoreclub.com).

For a change of pace from the fast-paced glitz of South Beach or the serene luxury of Coral Gables, head for **Little Havana,** where pre-Castro Cubans commingle with young artists who have begun to set up performance spaces in the area. It's just west of downtown Miami on SW 8th Street. In addition to authentic Cuban cuisine, the cafe Cubano culture is alive and well.

10 Montréal, Québec

A good number of New England/Canada cruises sail northbound or southbound between Boston or New York and the beautiful city of Montréal, an island on the St. Lawrence River southwest of Québec City.

One of the most European cities in North America, Montréal has a strong French heritage dating from 1835, when explorer Jacques Cartier arrived here believing the wide St. Lawrence River was the route to the Orient. As with Québec City, a few hours upriver, it was the fur and timber trade that eventually put Montréal on the map. British and French forces battled for rights to the region in 1759. Britain won, but the French influences on language, food, and overall culture remained. Today, the legacies of both cultures survive in force. French speakers still make up about 70% of the city's population, but many locals grow up speaking both French and English. (*Note:* Provincial law requires that signs be French-only, so information here includes both the French names and English translations to help you get your bearings.)

It's the city's tenacious French connection that gives Montréal its special character. It's a cosmopolitan city full of historic neighborhoods and thriving restaurants, and it's even good-looking below the ground: A mazelike **Underground City** was born in the 1960s with the idea of keeping Montréalers warm during the frigid winters. Head down and you'll find a controlled climate where it's eternally spring, with over 20 miles of tunnels, 900-plus retailers, 350-plus restaurants and food court eateries, and 13 cinemas—not to mention waterfalls, fountains, and trees with hanging vines.

Note: At press time, the exchange rate between U.S. and Canadian dollars was essentially one-to-one, though it's fluctuated by as much as 20¢ over the past couple of years. Prices in this section are in Canadian dollars.

GETTING TO MONTREAL & THE PORT

Cruise ships call at the **Iberville Cruise Terminal** at the Port of Montréal on rue de la Commune. For more information, contact the **Montréal Port Authority** (© **514/283-7011;** www.port-montreal.com). If you're flying in, you'll come through **Aéroport**

International Pierre-Elliot-Trudeau de Montréal (airport code YUL; ℂ **800/465-1213** or 514/394-7377; www.admtl.com), more commonly known as Montréal-Trudeau Airport. The public **747 Express Bus** (**www.stm.info/English/bus/GEOMET/A-GEO747.htm**) travels between the airport and several downtown locations for $7 one-way for adults. **Taxis** between the airport and downtown Montréal cost a flat rate of C$38 plus tip and take less than 30 minutes if traffic isn't tangled.

GETTING AROUND   Ships dock in the **Vieux-Port (Old Port)** district. One block inland, this area is simply called **Vieux-Montréal (Old Montréal).** With atmospherically teeny streets, pedestrian promenades, and wide green spaces by the water, these neighborhoods are easiest to explore by foot. The **Métro** (subway) system is fast and efficient, and single rides cost C$2.75. The closest stop to Vieux-Port is Place d'Armes, about a 10-minute walk from the water. Note that accessibility is sometimes difficult for people with mobility problems, as many stops require the use of escalators and stairs. Plenty of **taxis** queue up at the cruise terminal, if you'd rather go that route for sightseeing, although drivers do not serve as guides. Rates are metered, with an initial C$3.30 charge and another C$1.60 per kilometer thereafter.

BEST CRUISE LINE SHORE EXCURSIONS

Montréal Highlights ($50, 2½ hr.): Because Montréal is generally a port of embarkation only, the cruise lines usually offer just a basic city tour on the day passengers debark, and it typically ends at the airport. This bus tour of Montréal's most famed attractions includes a visit to Mont Royal, which towers above the city, plus a drive through the major shopping districts, and finally to Old Montréal to get a look at the remarkable concentration of 17th-, 18th-, and 19th-century buildings.

EXPLORING MONTRÉAL ON YOUR OWN

If you have only a few hours before your cruise departs, a stroll around **Vieux-Montréal (Old Montréal)** is a must. The city was born here in 1642, when the colony of Ville-Marie was founded by the soldiers of Paul de Chomedey, by the river at Pointe-à-Callière. Today, especially in summer, activity centers around **Place Jacques-Cartier,** a scenic plaza that borders the riverfront. Cafe tables line narrow terraces and flower sellers, artists, street performers, and strolling locals and tourists congregate. Head any direction off of the plaza to see the restored 18th- and 19th-century buildings that have been adapted for use as shops, boutique hotels, galleries, restaurants, and apartments. In the evening, many of the finer buildings here are illuminated.

Among the most worthwhile sites in walking distance is **Pointe-à-Callière,** the **Montréal Museum of Archaeology and History,** 350 Place Royale, at rue de la Commune (ℂ **514/872-9150;** www.pacmuseum.qc.ca). A 16-minute multimedia show in an auditorium that stands above actual exposed ruins of the old city provides a terrific introduction to the city. There's also a self-guided tour through a subterranean complex. It's open Tuesday to Friday 10am to 5pm, Saturday and Sunday 11am to 5pm (daily in summer). Admission is C$14 adults, C$6 kids ages 6 to 12.

Gothic-Revival **Basilique Notre-Dame (Notre-Dame Basilica),** 110 rue Notre-Dame ouest (ℂ **514/842-2925;** www.basiliquenddm.org), built between 1824 and 1829, has a stunning interior of sculpted wood, gold leaf, and stained glass. It's open Monday to Friday 8am to 4:30pm, Saturday 8am to 4pm, Sunday 12:30 to 4pm. Admission is C$5 adults, C$4 kids ages 7 to 17. The 18th-century **Musée du Château Ramezay (Château Ramezay Museum),** 280 rue Notre-Dame est (ℂ **514/861-3708;** www.chateauramezay.qc.ca), is another must. Formerly the governor's home,

Montréal

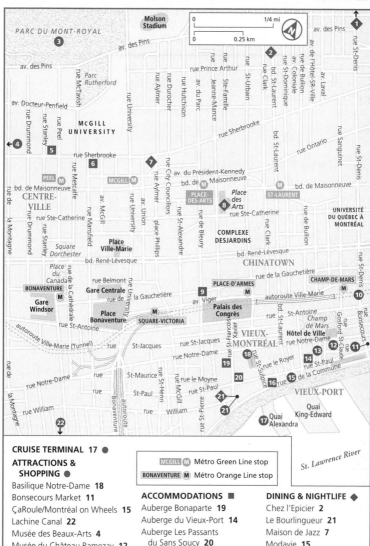

CRUISE TERMINAL 17 ●

ATTRACTIONS & SHOPPING ●

Basilique Notre-Dame **18**
Bonsecours Market **11**
ÇaRoule/Montréal on Wheels **15**
Lachine Canal **22**
Musée des Beaux-Arts **4**
Musée du Château Ramezay **12**
Parc du Mont-Royal **3**
Place Jacques-Cartier **13**
Pointe-à-Callière **21**
Rue Sherbrooke **4**
Rue St-Denis **10**
Rue St-Paul **20**

MCGILL Ⓜ Métro Green Line stop
BONAVENTURE Ⓜ Métro Orange Line stop

ACCOMMODATIONS ■
Auberge Bonaparte **19**
Auberge du Vieux-Port **14**
Auberge Les Passants
  du Sans Soucy **20**
Hôtel Le Dauphin **9**
Hôtel Le Germain **6**
Hôtel Nelligan **16**
Sofitel Montréal Golden Mile **5**

DINING & NIGHTLIFE ◆
Chez l'Epicier **2**
Le Bourlingueur **21**
Maison de Jazz **7**
Modavie **15**
Rue Crescent **4**
Toqué! **8**
Vitrine culturelle
  de Montréal **1**

it's now a history museum with exhibits on Montréal and Québec. It's open Tuesday to Sunday 10am to 4:30pm. Admission is C$9 adults, C$4.50 kids ages 5 to 17.

If you're in the mood for a stroll, head to the **Lachine Canal,** which starts right at the Old Port. The canal was opened for recreational use in 1997 after much renovation and is lined with 19th-century industrial buildings, many converted into high-end apartments. Paths on either side are good for walking or biking. Bike rentals are available for C$8/hour or C$25/day at **ÇaRoule/Montréal on Wheels** (© 514/866-0633; www.caroulemontreal.com) at 27 rue de la Commune est, the waterfront road. For something woodsier, head to **Parc du Mont-Royal (Mount Royal Park)** (www.lemontroyal.qc.ca/en). The city of Montréal (which translates as "Royal Mountain") is named for it, and it's well used by locals. Paths lead all through the park to a top view of the city and the St. Lawrence River.

If you're staying for a few days, explore Montréal's other neighborhoods. **Rue St-Denis** is the thumping central artery of Francophone Montréal, running from the Latin Quarter downtown north into the **Plateau Mont-Royal** residential neighborhood. Thick with bistros, offbeat shops, and lively nightspots, it is to Montréal what boulevard St-Germain is to Paris; if you want to know what the youth and young adults of Montréal are all about, spend an evening here.

SHOPPING

In Vieux-Montréal, **Rue St-Paul** (St-Paul St.) and the narrow cobblestone streets off of it have art galleries, high-end clothing boutiques, and interesting jewelry shops. They sometimes sit elbow to elbow with T-shirt shops and souvenir stands in this most heavily touristed area of the city. A prominent icon of the port skyline, the silver-domed **Bonsecours Market,** 350 rue St-Paul est, was built in the mid-1800s and is lined with small galleries and lively cafes with terraces.

In downtown Montréal, **Rue Sherbrooke** is the major shopping street for international and domestic designers, luxury items such as furs and jewelry, and art galleries. The Holt Renfrew department store is on Sherbrooke, and the blocks near the **Musée des Beaux-Arts** (Museum of Fine Arts) are thick with antiques shops. Farther from the port, in the Plâteau Mont-Royal neighborhood north of downtown, **Rue St-Denis** has strings of shops filled with fun, funky items, especially near the rue Rachel cross street.

Some of the best shopping in Montréal is in city museums. Tops among them are the boutiques in **Pointe-à-Callière,** in Vieux-Montréal, which sell toys and home items such as maple spoons made by Québec artist Tom Littledeer, and the **Musée des Beaux-Arts,** which has more arts and crafts.

WHERE TO STAY

Accommodations in Montréal range from soaring glass skyscraper lodgings and grand boulevard hotels to converted row houses. There's a large number of stylish inns and boutique hotels close to the port in Vieux-Montréal.

In Vieux-Montréal, the plush **Hôtel Nelligan,** 106 rue St-Paul ouest (© 877/788-2040 or 514/788-2040; www.hotelnelligan.com), has a great full-service restaurant **(Versa),** goose-down duvets on the beds, and a rooftop terrace. Rates: from C$235 double. Romantic, upscale **Auberge du Vieux-Port,** 97 rue de la Commune est (© 888/660-7678 or 514/876-0081; www.aubergeduvieuxport.com), is right on the waterfront and has bedrooms with exposed brick and stone walls and a small, sophisticated wine bar off the lobby, often with live jazz on the weekends. Rates: from

C$185 double. The cozy **Auberge Les Passants du Sans Soucy,** 171 rue St-Paul ouest (© **514/842-2634;** www.lesanssoucy.com), built in a former fur warehouse from 1723, is a more upscale and stylish B&B than most of its peers and is within a block of nearly a dozen good places to eat. Rates: from C$120 double. If Sans Soucy is booked up, around the corner is **Auberge Bonaparte,** 447 rue St-François-Xavier (© **514/844-1448;** www.bonaparte.com), a graceful, urban inn with 31 units. Generous breakfasts, included in the cost of the room, are served in the stately **Bonaparte** restaurant. Rates: from C$145 double.

For a more urban downtown experience, the **Sofitel Montréal Golden Mile,** 1155 rue Sherbrooke ouest (© **514/285-9000;** www.sofitel.com), is part of the French hotel chain and matches its luxury rivals in every detail. Its **Renoir** restaurant is good, and there's a 24-hour gym. Rates: from C$189 double. **Hôtel Le Germain,** 2050 rue Mansfield (© **877/333-2050** or 514/849-2050; www.hotelgermain.com), with 101 units, offers a magical mix of Asian minimalism and Western comforts and is home to **Laurie Raphaël Montréal,** an offshoot of Québec City's most esteemed restaurant. Rates: from C$230 double. A good budget option, the **Hôtel Le Dauphin,** 1025 rue de Bleury (© **888/784-3888** or 514/788-3888; www.hotelsdauphin.ca), is simple and clean. Each unit is equipped with a computer terminal and free Internet access, and the hotel is centrally located at the edge of both Vieux-Montréal and downtown. Rates: from C$154 double.

DINING & NIGHTLIFE

You could never leave Vieux-Montréal and still eat well for a week. If stylish, innovative French food is your main goal, then get a reservation at **Toqué!,** 900 Place Jean-Paul-Riopelle (© **514/499-2084;** www.restaurant-toque.com), which is in a league of its own. Main courses: C$40 to C$45; tasting menus: from C$92. **Chez l'Epicier,** 331 rue St-Paul est (© **514/878-2232;** www.chezlepicier.com), is a crisp little eatery that functions as both a high-end delicatessen with takeout food and a fashionable restaurant with Asian ingredients. Main courses: C$28 to C$36; tasting menu: C$85. For good value, **Le Bourlingueur,** 363 rue St-François-Xavier (© **514/845-3646;** www.lebourlingueur.ca), is a bistro well short of chic, but features roast pork with apple sauce, *choucroute garnie* (sauerkraut with meat), seafood dishes, and four-course *(table d'hôte)* meals at low prices—C$16 to C$19. The Vieux-Montréal restaurant **Modavie,** 1 rue St-Paul ouest (© **514/287-9582;** www.modavie.com), offers live jazz along with dinner, nightly from 7 until about 10pm. Main courses: C$16 to C$34.

For a true Montréal experience, look for *poutine,* french fries doused with gravy and cheese curds—a Québécois comfort food that's available both as fast food and on fancier menus.

Discount tickets for cultural events are sold at **Vitrine culturelle de Montréal** ("cultural window of Montréal"; © **866/924-5538** or 514/285-4545; http://vitrine. cyberpresse.ca), in downtown's Place des Arts at 145 rue Sainte-Catherine ouest. For an evening of jazz, one of the city's best-known treats, the **Maison de Jazz,** 2060 rue Aylmer (© **514/842-8656;** www.houseofjazz.ca), has live music every night beginning around 8pm in a room decorated in mock Art Nouveau style. It's downtown, charges a C$5 cover price for shows, and serves dishes from a menu of Southern-style favorites. For a more spontaneous night out, head to **Rue Crescent,** one of Montréal's major nightlife districts. The area's center is rue Crescent between rue Sherbrooke and boulevard René-Lévesque, on the northwest edge of the downtown skyscrapers. Here you'll find restaurants with outdoor cafes and bars, clubs of all styles, and a party atmosphere that never fades.

11 New Orleans, Louisiana

Despite popular perception, New Orleans was not, in fact, washed from the face of the earth by Hurricane Katrina in 2005 and by the bungled disaster relief that followed. Yes, the city got whacked bad, but you can do a lot of cleanup in 5 years, and the city has. The **French Quarter,** the oldest and most historic part of the city, actually saw no flooding at all during the storm, and survived almost completely intact. Other neighborhoods where tourists typically go—the **Garden District,** for instance, with its beautiful ornate homes—today look about the same as they did before the storm. Things were much worse, though, out beyond the tourist areas, and recovery there is still ongoing. Psychologically, the whole city is still in recovery mode, but day-to-day life, business, and tourism are all in full swing. The Big Easy may not be quite as easy at it once was, but give it time.

GETTING TO NEW ORLEANS & THE PORT

Cruise ships depart from the **Erato Street Cruise Terminal** and the **Julia Street Wharf,** located adjacent to each other on the east bank of the Mississippi, south of the French Quarter. Both are operated by the **Port of New Orleans** (© 504/522-2551; www.portno.com). Parking is available at both terminals, at a cost of $14 per day. The port is also planning construction of an additional cruise terminal on the **Poland Avenue Wharf,** in the Bywater area just east of the French Quarter. If you're flying in, you'll probably land at **Louis Armstrong International Airport** (© 504/464-0831; www.flymsy.com), about 17 miles from the cruise terminal. A **taxi** costs about $35 for two people to the terminal or downtown.

GETTING AROUND Taxis are plentiful. If you're not near a taxi stand, call **United Cabs** (© 504/522-9771; www.unitedcabs.com) and a car will come in 10 minutes. Rates are $2.50 to start, plus $1.60 per mile (20¢ per ⅛-mile) thereafter, with a $1 surcharge for additional passengers. The famous **St. Charles streetcar** (www.norta.com/stcharles) from the French Quarter to the Garden District was out of service for more than 2 years after Hurricane Katrina, but is now back up and running, with a main boarding point at the intersection of Carondelet and Canal streets. The fare is $1.25 each way.

From Jackson Square (at Decatur St.), you can ride a horse-drawn carriage through the French Quarter. **Royal Carriages** (© 504/943-8820; www.neworleanscarriages.com) gives private half-hour rides for up to four passengers for $75 a pop, daily from 8:30am to midnight.

BEST CRUISE LINE SHORE EXCURSIONS

City Tour ($40, 5 hr.): Offered post-cruise, this bus tour takes in St. Charles Avenue, the Superdome, the Loyola and Tulane University campuses, Audubon Park and City Park, the Garden District, and the French Quarter, where you get 2 hours to poke around before transferring to the airport.

EXPLORING NEW ORLEANS ON YOUR OWN

Comprising about 90 square blocks, the **French Quarter** (also known as the Vieux Carré, or "Old Square") was laid out by the French engineer Adrien de Pauger in

1718, and a strict preservation policy pre-Katrina (and high ground and good luck during and after the storm) has kept it looking much as it always has. Its major public area is **Jackson Square** (bounded by Chartres, Decatur, St. Peter, and St. Ann sts.), where musicians, artists, fortunetellers, jugglers, and those silver-painted "living statue" guys gather to sell their wares or entertain for change. The quarter's main drag, however, is **Bourbon Street,** a lively strip with rowdy bars and music clubs. Many of the quarter's best attractions are covered under "Dining & Nightlife"(see below), but here are some of its more historic highlights.

Incorporating seven historic buildings connected by a brick courtyard, the **Historic New Orleans Collection,** 533 Royal St., between St. Louis and Toulouse streets (© 504/523-4662; www.hnoc.org), evokes the New Orleans of 200 years ago. The oldest building in the complex escaped the tragic fire of 1794. The others hold exhibitions about Louisiana's culture and history. The collection is open Tuesday to Saturday 9:30 am to 4:30pm (Royal Street Complex also Sun 10:30am–4:30pm). Admission is free; guided tours $5 per person.

Founded in 1950, the **New Orleans Pharmacy Museum,** 514 Chartres St., at St. Louis Street (© 504/565-8027; www.pharmacymuseum.org), is just what the name says. In 1823, the first licensed pharmacist in the United States, Louis J. Dufilho, Jr., opened an apothecary shop here. Today, you'll find old medicine bottles, voodoo potions, and suppository molds, as well as the old glass cosmetics counter and a jar of leeches, in case you feel the need to bleed. It's open Tuesday to Saturday 11am to 5pm. Admission is $5 adults, $4 students and seniors.

Constructed from 1795 through 1799 as the Spanish government seat in New Orleans, the **Cabildo,** 701 Chartres St., at Jackson Square (© 800/568-6968 or 504/568-6968; http://lsm.crt.state.la.us/cabex.htm), was the site of the signing of the Louisiana Purchase transfer. The building is now the center of the Louisiana State Museum's facilities in the French Quarter, with an exhibition that traces the history of Louisiana from exploration through Reconstruction, covering all aspects of life, including antebellum music, mourning and burial customs, immigrants, and the changing roles of women in the South. Also part of the Louisiana State Museum on Jackson Square, the **Presbytère,** 751 Chartres St. (© 800/568-6968 or 504/568-6968; http://lsm.crt.state.la.us/presbex.htm), was planned as housing for clergy, but is now a Mardi Gras museum that traces the history of the annual event, with everything from elaborate Mardi Gras Indian costumes to Rex Queen jewelry from the turn of the 20th century on display. A re-creation of a float allows you to pretend you're throwing beads to a crowd on a screen in front of you. Both the Cabildo and Presbytère are open Tuesday to Sunday 10am to 4:30pm. Admission is $6 adults, $5 students and seniors.

In the Warehouse District, just west of the Quarter, the **National WWII Museum,** 945 Magazine St. (© 504/527-6012; www.ddaymuseum.org), was the creation of historian Stephen Ambrose, telling the story of all U.S. amphibious assaults worldwide on that fateful day. Many of the artifacts on display emphasize personal stories, including audio exhibits that tell the experiences of soldiers and civilians alike. It's open daily 9am to 5pm. Admission is $16.

Aside from the Quarter, the one other neighborhood that absolutely deserves your attention is the **Garden District,** one of the city's most picturesque areas. It's mostly residential, but what residences! Bounded by St. Charles Avenue and Magazine Street between Jackson and Louisiana avenues, the whole district was originally the site of a plantation, and the land was eventually subdivided and developed as a residential neighborhood for wealthy Americans. Throughout the mid–19th century, developers built the Victorian, Italianate, and Greek Revival homes that still line the streets. Take the **St. Charles streetcar** from the French Quarter for the full effect (see "Getting Around," above).

And then, of course, there are the dead: Because New Orleans has always been prone to flooding, bodies have been interred aboveground since its earliest days, sometimes in very elaborate tombs that are definitely worth a visit. **St. Louis Cemetery No. 1,** on Basin Street between Conti and St. Louis streets, at the top of the French Quarter, is the oldest extant cemetery (1789) and the most iconic. The acid-dropping scene from *Easy Rider* was shot here, prompting the city to declare that no film would ever, ever, ever be shot again in one of its cemeteries. In the Garden District, **Lafayette Cemetery No. 1,** 1427 Sixth St. (right across the street from Commander's Palace Restaurant), is another old cemetery that's been beautifully restored.

SHOPPING

Despite what you may think while taking your first walk down **Bourbon Street,** there's more to New Orleans shopping than cheap T-shirts, alligator snow globes, and other souvenir items—although there are plenty of those, too, along with an absolutely mind-boggling selection of **hot sauces.**

On Decatur Street across from Jackson Square, the **French Market** (www.french market.org) has shops selling candy, cookware, fashion, crafts, toys, New Orleans memorabilia, and candles. There's a lot of kitsch, but some good buys are mixed in, and it's always fun to stroll through and grab a few beignets at **Café du Monde** (see "Dining & Nightlife," below). The French Market is open daily from 9am to 6pm; Café du Monde is open 24 hours.

From Camp Street down to the river on Julia Street, you'll find many of the city's best **contemporary art galleries.**

Magazine Street is the Garden District's premier shopping street, with many antiques stores, art galleries, boutiques, and crafts shops among the 19th-century brick storefronts and cottages.

WHERE TO STAY

In the Garden District, the **McKendrick-Breaux House,** 1474 Magazine St. (© **888/ 570-1700** or 504/586-1700; www.mckendrick-breaux.com), was built at the end of the Civil War by a wealthy plumber and Scottish immigrant. Today, it's one of the best guesthouses for value. It's been completely restored to its original charming state, and each room is furnished with antiques, family collectibles, and fresh flowers. Cruise season rates: from $145 double.

In the French Quarter, the **Hotel Villa Convento,** 616 Ursulines St., between Royal and Chartres (© **504/522-1793;** www.villaconvento.com), is incredibly New Orleans, occupying an 1830s Creole town house that, they say, was the original House of the Rising Sun bordello. Inside, the decor is guesthouse cozy, with some rooms opening onto the tropical patio and others to the street. Many have balconies. Cruise season rates: from $105 double.

At the other end of the spectrum, the Quarter's **Omni Royal Orleans,** 621 St. Louis St., between Royal and Chartres streets (© **800/843-6664** or 504/529-5333; www.omnihotels.com), is an elegant hotel whose lobby is a small sea of marble, and

New Orleans: The French Quarter

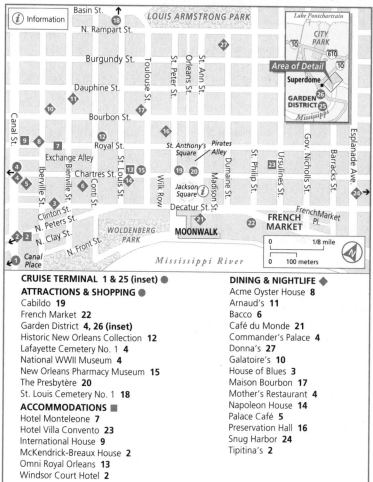

CRUISE TERMINAL 1 & 25 (inset) ●

ATTRACTIONS & SHOPPING ●
Cabildo **19**
French Market **22**
Garden District **4, 26** (inset)
Historic New Orleans Collection **12**
Lafayette Cemetery No. 1 **4**
National WWII Museum **4**
New Orleans Pharmacy Museum **15**
The Presbytère **20**
St. Louis Cemetery No. 1 **18**

ACCOMMODATIONS ■
Hotel Monteleone **7**
Hotel Villa Convento **23**
International House **9**
McKendrick-Breaux House **2**
Omni Royal Orleans **13**
Windsor Court Hotel **2**

DINING & NIGHTLIFE ◆
Acme Oyster House **8**
Arnaud's **11**
Bacco **6**
Café du Monde **21**
Commander's Palace **4**
Donna's **27**
Galatoire's **10**
House of Blues **3**
Maison Bourbon **17**
Mother's Restaurant **4**
Napoleon House **14**
Palace Café **5**
Preservation Hall **16**
Snug Harbor **24**
Tipitina's **2**

whose units are sizable and elegant, full of muted tones and plush furniture. Windows allow views out over the Quarter. Cruise season rates: from $279 double.

In the Central Business District, just outside the French Quarter and close to the cruise ship terminal, the **International House,** 221 Camp St., just west of Canal (© **800/633-5770** or 504/553-9550; www.ihhotel.com), is a modern, minimalist hotel housed in an old Beaux Arts bank building. Units are simple, with high ceilings, ceiling fans, modern bathrooms, dataports, Wi-Fi, and photos and knickknacks that remind you that you're in New Orleans. It's all corridors, dark and chic. Cruise season rates: from $159 double.

Also in the Central Business District, the **Windsor Court Hotel,** 300 Gravier St. (© **888/596-0955** or 504/523-6000; www.windsorcourthotel.com), is consistently named to lists of America's top hotels, so feel free to hold it to a high standard. Accommodations are exceptionally spacious and classy, with large bay windows or a private balcony overlooking the river or the city. Downstairs, two corridors display original 17th-, 18th-, and 19th-century art. A plush reading area with international newspapers is on the second floor. Cruise season rates: from $260 double.

About 7 blocks from the cruise ship terminal is the atmospheric **Hotel Monteleone,** 214 Royal St., between Iberville and Bienville streets (© **800/535-9595** or 504/523-3341; www.hotelmonteleone.com), the oldest hotel in the city and the largest one in the French Quarter, and it boasts an exceptionally helpful staff. Decor and floor layouts are slightly different in each of the units, so ask to see a few different ones. Cruise season rates: from $189 double.

DINING & NIGHTLIFE

New Orleans has always essentially been one giant restaurant and nightlife spot with rich foods such a specialty that the city perennially finds itself on the "fattest cities" lists. After dinner, be sure to head out to the clubs—this is, after all, the city that gave birth to jazz. Many of the best restaurants and clubs are in the French Quarter.

For oysters, head to the **Acme Oyster House,** 724 Iberville St. (© **504/522-5973;** www.acmeoyster.com). It's the quarter's oldest oyster bar, a noisy, crowded place where you can shoot your freshly shucked half-shell oysters at the bar or order them in a po' boy sandwich. A dozen will cost you $11; po' boys are $8 to $13.

In business since 1918 and still mighty fine, the legendary **Arnaud's,** 813 Bienville St. (© **504/523-5433;** www.arnauds.com), is set in three interconnected, once-private houses from the 1700s. The restaurant's three Belle Epoque dining rooms are lush with Edwardian embellishments. Especially delicious menu items include the signature appetizer, shrimp Arnaud (boiled shrimp topped with a spicy rémoulade sauce), as well as the crabmeat Ravigotte, the charbroiled oysters, the snapper Pontchartrain, the filet mignon, and the classic bananas Foster dessert. Dinner main courses: $24 to $40.

Bacco, 310 Chartres St., between Bienville and Conti streets (© **504/522-2426;** www.bacco.com), a great New Orleans bistro, has an elegant setting of pink faux-marble floors and Venetian chandeliers. At night, it's romantic and candlelit, while at lunchtime, it's more affordable and casual. The menu changes regularly, but always features rich, arresting Italian and Creole creations, many with fresh local seafood. Dinner main courses: $18 to $35.

Galatoire's, 209 Bourbon St., at Iberville Street (© **504/525-2021;** www.galatoires.com), feels like a bistro in turn-of-the-20th-century Paris, and is one of the city's most venerable restaurants, run by the same family since 1905 and served by waiters who've been here for decades. Don't come expecting cutting-edge cuisine. Do come expecting a nice piece of perfectly prepared fish—perhaps the red snapper or redfish topped with sautéed crabmeat meunière. Tradition rules. Dinner main courses: $17 to $39.

Not far outside the Quarter, **Mother's Restaurant,** 401 Poydras St., at Tchoupitoulas Street (© **504/523-9656;** www.mothersrestaurant.net), has long lines and zero atmosphere, but damn, those po' boys! Customers have been flocking here since 1938 for homemade biscuits and red-bean omelets at breakfast, po' boys at lunch, and softshell crabs and jambalaya at dinner. Everything is between $5 and $23.

Napoleon House, 500 Chartres St., at St. Louis Street (© **504/524-9752;** www.napoleonhouse.com), would allegedly have been the home of the lieutenant himself if some locals' wild plan to bring him here to live out his exile had panned out. Instead, it's now a restaurant and bar serving large portions of traditional New Orleans food (po' boys, jambalaya, muffuletta), plus wild-card items like pita and hummus. Sandwiches: $6 to $8.

Right on the border of the French Quarter, the open kitchen at **Palace Café,** 605 Canal St., between Royal and Chartres streets (© **504/523-1661;** www.palacecafe. com), serves contemporary Creole food with a big emphasis on seafood: catfish pecan meunière, andouille-crusted fish of the day, and lots more. Don't miss the white-chocolate bread pudding. Dinner main courses: $17 to $34.

Outside the quarter, at the corner of Washington Avenue and Coliseum Street in the Garden District, **Commander's Palace,** 1403 Washington Ave. (© **504/899-8221;** www.commanderspalace.com), sustained serious Katrina damage and required a major renovation, but now it's back, and it still reigns as one of the finest dining choices not only in New Orleans, but also in the whole United States. The cuisine is haute Creole. Try anything with Gulf fish, or the Mississippi quail, or . . . oh hell, just try anything. Dinner main courses: $26 to $42.

For a snack anytime of the day or night, visit **Café du Monde,** 800 Decatur St., right on the river (© **504/581-2914;** www.cafedumonde.com). It's basically a 24-hour coffee shop that specializes in beignets, which are square doughnuts served hot and drowned in powdered sugar. It's a great spot for people-watching, but if you don't want to wait for a table, you can always get a bag of beignets to go. Grab lots of napkins, too. Moist towelettes would also help, or maybe just a big wet towel.

Life in the Big Easy has always been conducive to all manner of nighttime entertainment, usually raucous, and that spirit helped combat the city's case of post-Katrina stress syndrome. Do what most people do: Start at one end of **Bourbon Street** (say, around Iberville St.), walk down to the other end, and then turn around and do it again. Along the way, you'll hear rock, R&B, blues, and jazz pouring out of dozens of bars; be beckoned by numerous strip clubs; and see one tiny little storefront stall after another sporting hand-lettered signs that say OUR BEER IS CHEAPER THAN NEXT DOOR. It's a scene. Bacchanalian? Sorta. Will you spend time in purgatory for it? Not likely, and it's loads of fun. Grab yourself a big cheap beer or one of the famous rum-based Hurricanes and join the party.

Most of the places in this section have a cover charge that varies depending on who's performing; some are free.

The famous **Preservation Hall,** 726 St. Peter St., just off Bourbon (© **504/522-2841;** www.preservationhall.com), is a deliberately shabby little hall with very few places to sit and no air-conditioning. Still, crowds show up nearly every night to hear older and younger jazzmen and jazzwomen playing classic jazz amplified by nothing but passion. Admission is $10.

Close by, **Maison Bourbon,** 641 Bourbon St. (© **504/522-8818**), presents authentic and often fantastic Dixieland and traditional jazz. Stepping into the brick-walled room, or even just peering in from the street, takes you away from the mayhem outside. There's a one-drink minimum.

If you're looking to get away from the Bourbon Street scene, head up to **Donna's,** 800 N. Rampart St., at the top of St. Ann Street (© **504/596-6914;** www.donnasbar andgrill.com), which specializes in real brass-band jazz—the sound that made New Orleans famous. The cover varies, but is always reasonable.

One block beyond Esplanade, on the periphery of the French Quarter, the jazz bistro **Snug Harbor,** 626 Frenchman St. (© **504/949-0696;** www.snugjazz.com), is a classic spot to hear modern jazz in a cozy setting. Sometimes R&B combos and blues are added to the program. There's a full dinner menu in the restaurant, but only appetizers are served in the club.

Other nightlife options include the nostalgia-laden bar and concert hall **Tipitina's,** way out in Uptown at 501 Napoleon Ave. (© **504/891-8477;** www.tipitinas.com), where jazz, blues, and Dixieland pour out the doors nightly; and **House of Blues,** 225 Decatur St. (© **504/529-2583;** www.hob.com/venues/clubvenues/neworleans), one of the city's largest live-music venues, with several bars and a restaurant on-site.

12 New York City, New York

What can you say that hasn't already been said about the capital of the world? New York is just *it:* the biggest, loudest, and most historic city in the U.S., with a population that includes people from every country, race, religion, and social predilection on the face of the earth. It's the melting pot done up in concrete, steel, and glass, with a few patches of green that stand out like moss on a chessboard. And it even looks like a chessboard: From the near-perfect grid of Manhattan's streets and the vertical lines of the skyscrapers to its direct, no-nonsense speaking style, New York is a city of straight lines. And why not? A straight line is, after all, the fastest way to get to the point.

GETTING TO NEW YORK CITY & THE PORT

New York is served by three different cruise ports: one in Manhattan, one in Brooklyn, and another in Bayonne, New Jersey, just across the Hudson.

Manhattan's historic if utilitarian **New York Cruise Terminal** (© **212/246-5450;** www.nycruiseterminal.com) is stretched out between the Hudson River and the West Side Highway, between 46th and 54th streets (enter via the vehicle ramp at 55th St.). It's frequently congested on turnaround days when ships debark and embark, though improvements in the works promise to reduce roadway congestion and improve passenger circulation. Parking is available for $30 a day. Just across the highway, near the corner of 46th Street, **H&H Bagels** (© **212/765-7200;** www.hhbagels.net) sells the best bagels in New York, hands down, and it's open 24 hours a day. One block inland, at 11th Avenue and 46th Street, is the **Landmark Tavern** (© **212/247-2562;** www.thelandmarktavern.org), one of the most beautiful and historic bars in New York. When it opened in 1868, it was on the waterfront—meaning everything between it and your ship is landfill created over the past century or so.

Down in the old blue-collar neighborhood of Red Hook, the **Brooklyn Cruise Terminal** (© **718/246-2794;** www.nycruiseterminal.com) is just across New York Harbor from Lower Manhattan and Governors Island, former site of the country's largest Coast Guard base. The port is easily accessible to locals driving by car, as well as to visitors flying into Kennedy, LaGuardia, and Newark airports. While Red Hook itself is industrial and gritty (if slowly gentrifying), it's just minutes from picturesque Colonial-era Brooklyn Heights and the great expanse of the **Brooklyn Bridge.** Parking at the port is $23 per day.

In Bayonne, New Jersey, the **Cape Liberty Cruise Port** (© **201/823-3737;** www. cruiseliberty.com) opened in 2004 as a home port for Royal Caribbean and Celebrity vessels. We know: Sailing from Bayonne doesn't sound as romantic as sailing from Manhattan, but Cape Liberty does have the advantage of being less congested. And where else can you get a view of the Statue of Liberty's butt? Parking is $19 per day.

If you're coming in by plane, you'll fly into one of three New York–area airports. **John F. Kennedy International Airport (JFK)** is in southern Queens, about 15 miles southeast of Midtown Manhattan. **LaGuardia Airport (LGA)** is in northern Queens, about 8 miles northeast of Midtown Manhattan. **Newark Liberty International Airport (EWR)** is in Essex and Union counties, New Jersey, about 16 miles southwest of Midtown Manhattan. For information on all three, go to the Port Authority of New York & New Jersey website at **www.panynj.gov.** Kennedy and Newark are the larger airports and accommodate both domestic and international flights. If you've arranged air transportation and/or transfers through your cruise line, a representative will direct you to shuttle buses that take you to whichever port your ship is sailing from. **Yellow taxis** are usually lined up in great numbers at the airports and can take you to any port or your hotel, though the fare will be stiff. From JFK to Manhattan, yellow taxis charge a flat fee of $45 per carload, plus tolls and tip. From Newark to Manhattan, a taxi will run you between $50 and $70, depending on where you're going. From LaGuardia, the fare to Manhattan will be between $20 and $30. Taxi surcharges apply at peak hours and at night. **Super Shuttle** (© **212/258-3826;** www.supershuttle.com) is a cheaper shared-van alternative, costing $13 per guest from LaGuardia, $17 per guest from JFK or Newark Liberty to midtown Manhattan.

GETTING AROUND   The beauty of New York City is that it's so walkable and so relatively compact, with the island of Manhattan measuring only about 2 miles wide by 13 miles long—and most visitors stick to its lower half anyway. Most of its streets (north of Greenwich Village, at least) follow an unvarying grid pattern, so it's next to impossible to lose your way—avenues run north-south, streets run east-west. The Manhattan cruise terminal is close to the heart of Midtown, about a mile west of Times Square.

If you don't care to walk everywhere, don't hesitate to take the **subway** or **bus.** Most subway lines in Manhattan run north-south, while buses run both north-south and east-west, with routes marked (usually) at each bus stop. The per-ride fare is $2.25, for which you can go anywhere in the city. The system works on stored-fare **Metro-Card** passes, which are available in any denomination at any subway station. If you'll be riding a lot, you can also get a **1-day Fun Pass** that's good for unlimited rides from first use until 3am the following day. It costs $8.25. If you'll be in town longer, a 7-night pass costs $27. Buses accept both MetroCards and coins, but not paper money. **Subway** maps are available at the stations. **Bus maps** are usually available aboard the buses. Route, schedule, and fare info can also be found at **www.mta.info**.

You can also hail one of the city's ubiquitous **yellow cabs.** The meter starts at $2.50 and increases 40¢ every ⅕-mile or 90 seconds, whichever comes first. For an overview of town, you can join one of the red double-decker **Gray Line tour buses** (© **800/669-0051** or 212/445-0848; www.coachusa.com/newyorksightseeing) at the Circle Line terminal, just a few steps south of the Manhattan cruise ship piers. A 48-hour hop-on/hop-off pass is $54 for adults, $44 for kids, but there's a steep discount if you buy tickets online, in advance.

New York City

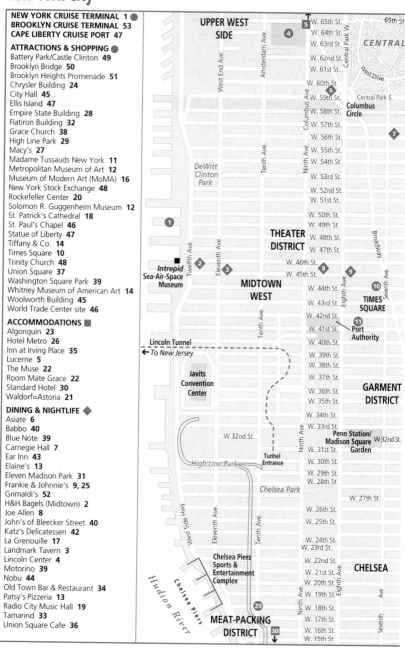

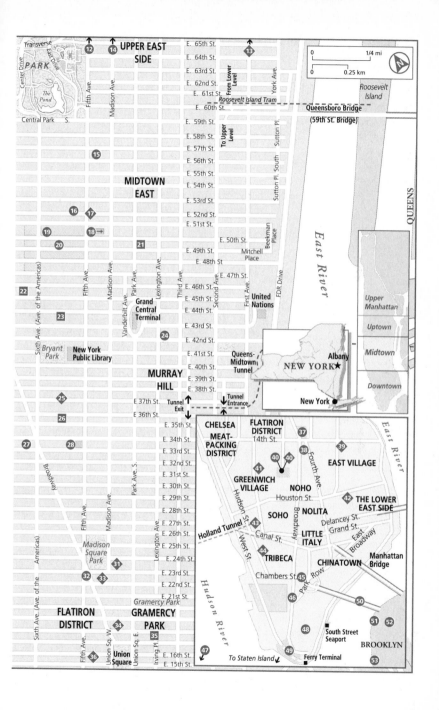

BEST CRUISE LINE SHORE EXCURSIONS

Because New York is mostly a port of embarkation, the cruise lines generally offer only a few tour choices, including several **bus tours** ($59–$109, 4–8 hr.). If you've got a day or two in town, though, don't bother: You can see more (and better) on your own.

EXPLORING NEW YORK CITY ON YOUR OWN

There's much more to see and do in New York than we have space for here, so we'll concentrate on some highlights—some big touristy ones, as well as some personal favorites.

MIDTOWN   Let's triangulate from **Times Square.** Once the center of New York's entertainment industry, the whole area around 42nd Street and Broadway fell into deep, dark, sleazy blight starting in the 1960s and running right up to the early 1990s. Back then, you couldn't walk through without being offered heroin, switchblades, or porn—or all three, if you were really lucky. Now, it's a corporate America theme park, overseen by the eight-story **NASDAQ** video screen (the world's largest) at 43rd Street and Broadway, nestled in among acres of other high-tech signage. Even at midnight, the whole area is bright as noon and packed with visitors, musicians, and street artists—but not many New Yorkers. The fact is, it's a total tourist trap, but it sure is a sight to behold.

At 44th Street, ABC's *Good Morning America* has set up a street-facing studio, while **MTV** has done the same across Broadway at 45th Street, drawing busloads of fans. A couple of blocks away, the former porn-peddler's paradise of **42nd Street** between Seventh and Eighth avenues has been rebuilt into a family-oriented entertainment mecca. In addition to a spate of beautifully renovated theaters—including the **New Victory,** the **New Amsterdam,** and the Selwyn (aka the **American Airlines Theatre**)—the neon-bright block is chock-full of retail shops and amusements, including two huge movie-theater complexes and **Madame Tussauds New York,** 234 W. 42nd St. (© **800/246-8872;** www.nycwax.com), a six-floor, new-world version of London's famous wax museum. It's open daily 10am to 8pm (Fri–Sat 10pm). Admission is $36 adults, $33 seniors, $28 kids ages 4 to 12.

Just a few blocks east, running from 48th to 50th streets between Fifth and Sixth avenues, the Art Deco buildings of **Rockefeller Center** (© **212/632-3975;** www. rockefellercenter.com) make you feel like you're standing in a classic 1930s movie. For a dramatic approach, start at Fifth Avenue between 49th and 50th streets, where a promenade leads to the Lower Plaza, home to the famous ice-skating rink in winter and alfresco dining in summer. All around, the flags of United Nations member countries flap in the breeze. In December and early January, this is also home to the city's official Christmas tree. **St. Patrick's Cathedral** (© **212/753-2261;** www.saintpatricks cathedral.org/homepage/home.html), one of the city's most imposing churches, is on the other side of Fifth Avenue, at 50th Street. Three blocks away, the **Museum of Modern Art,** 11 W. 53rd St., between Fifth and Sixth avenues (© **212/708-9400;** www.moma.org), is one of the world's great modern art museums. It's open daily (except Tues) 10:30am to 5:30pm (Fri 8pm). Admission is $20 adults, $16 seniors, free for kids ages 16 and under.

From Midtown, you have two main choices: Head uptown or head downtown.

UPTOWN   To the north, starting at 59th Street, is **Central Park** (www.central parknyc.org). Laid out between 1859 and 1870 on a design by Frederick Law Olmsted and Calvert Vaux, the park's 843 acres are New York's greatest marvel, simply by virtue of their continued existence amid some of the world's priciest real estate. Highlights include the Wollman Memorial Ice Rink, the Bethesda Fountain, the Sheep Meadow (a huge sunbathing spot in summer), and the old carousel with its 58 handcarved horses. West of the park, the **Upper West Side** is one of the city's most beautiful residential neighborhoods, its most scenic stretch running from 59th Street north to about 89th Street, between Central Park West and Riverside Drive. On the park's eastern edge, along Fifth Avenue between 82nd and 104th streets, is **Museum Mile,** home to the **Metropolitan Museum of Art,** at 82nd Street (© **212/535-7710;** www.met museum.org), and eight other museums. The Met is one of the country's largest and best museums, with a collection of more than two million works spanning the globe and the ages. It's open daily (except Mon) 9:30am to 5:30pm (Fri–Sat 9pm). Admission is $20 adults, $15 seniors, free for children ages 12 and under. Other museums in the area include the **Solomon R. Guggenheim Museum,** at Fifth Avenue and 88th Street (© **212/423-3500;** www.guggenheim.org), with its landmark seashell design by Frank Lloyd Wright, its collection spanning the late–19th century to the present, and a rotating series of near building-wide temporary exhibitions. It's open daily (except Thurs) 10am to 5:45pm (Sat 7:45pm). Admission is $18 adults, $15 seniors, free for children ages 12 and under. Not on the Mile but nearby, the **Whitney Museum of American Art,** 945 Madison Ave. (© **212/570-3600;** www.whitney. org), is dedicated to American art of the 20th and 21st centuries, with more than 18,000 works in its permanent collection, including works by Edward Hopper, Jackson Pollock, Willem De Kooning, and Louise Nevelson. It's open Wednesday through Sunday 11am to 6pm (Fri 1–9pm). Admission is $18 adults, $12 students/seniors, free for children ages 18 and under.

DOWNTOWN & BROOKLYN   Heading downtown from the Times Square area will take you eventually to New York's most historic districts, where the original colony of New Amsterdam got its start. From the corner of Broadway and 42nd Street, look east. That tall building with the gleaming stainless-steel spire is the **Chrysler Building,** the city's most beautiful skyscraper. Walk toward it, and stop when you get to Fifth Avenue. Look south from here and start walking toward that other big spire ahead of you, the **Empire State Building** (© **877/NYCVIEW** [692-8439]; www.esbnyc.com), which sits at the corner of Fifth Avenue and 34th Street. Following the 2001 destruction of the World Trade Center, it's once again the tallest building in Manhattan. Lines to get up to the 86th-floor observatory can be horrible at the concourse-level ticket booth, so be prepared to wait—or consider purchasing advance tickets online. The observatory is open daily 8am to 2am. Admission is $20 adults/youths ages 13 and over, $18 seniors, $14 kids ages 6 to 12. You can also shell out $45 for an express ticket that lets you bypass the lines. At the observatory, you can walk out on the windy deck and look through coin-operated viewers (bring quarters) over what, on a clear day, can be as much as an 80-mile visible radius.

Back on the street, head downtown on Fifth Avenue. Where it crosses Broadway at 23rd Street, you'll see the famous **Flatiron Building** from 1902, looking like the prow of a ship. Walk south along Broadway past **Union Square,** site of protest rallies from the 1870s through today. At Broadway and 10th, **Grace Church** was designed by James Renwick, Jr., who later designed St. Patrick's Cathedral. At Waverly Place, turn right and go 1 block to **Washington Square Park,** a landmark typically full of musicians and other street performers. Meander through (and maybe take a side trip west into the warren of narrow, cozy streets that make up **Greenwich Village**), then walk south on LaGuardia Place past Houston Street and into **SoHo.** Once the city's main arts neighborhood, it's now a center for fashion and design. (Give your credit cards to a designated driver.)

Après shopping, walk east to Broadway and catch the downtown R train at either Prince or Canal streets. Get off at Court Street/Borough Hall and exit at the rear of the platform. Ta da! You're in **Brooklyn,** the Borough of Kings. Walk west on Montague Street. This is the heart of **Brooklyn Heights,** once a Colonial-era village and now a protected historic district. Wander off on some of the tree-lined side streets to see beautiful 19th-century homes. At the end of Montague, the **Brooklyn Heights Promenade** offers the most spectacular Manhattan view there is, bar none. To the right, that gorgeous span between the two islands is the **Brooklyn Bridge,** completed in 1883. When built, it was the largest suspension bridge in the world, its two stone towers dwarfing every other structure in the city. Though newer bridges around the city are larger, none are as graceful or beautiful.

The best way to see the bridge is to walk it, and that's what you're going to do next. Walk to the end of the Promenade, up the ramp, past Cranberry Street and the playground, and go through the alley to Middagh Street. Take that about 3 blocks, crossing Cadman Plaza West into the park, where it curves around to the left and eventually runs under an overpass. There, look for the stone stairway on your left up to the **Brooklyn Bridge footpath.** The bridge is about 1¼ miles long, with historical plaques on its two towers and the magnificence of New York all around.

Back in Manhattan, the bridge lets you off facing **City Hall** and its surrounding park. On the far side, the 1910 **Woolworth Building** was the tallest building in the world until the Chrysler Building beat it out in 1929, and it remains one of New York's most beautiful. Farther down Broadway, at Fulton Street, **St. Paul's Chapel** is New York's oldest church, built in 1766. George Washington prayed here on Inauguration Day 1789, and in 2001 it served as a refuge for 9/11 rescue workers. Thousands of small memorials left by mourners are preserved inside, along with other displays. The **World Trade Center site,** with its constant bustle of super-slow-motion rebuilding, is just behind the church's graveyard.

Walk south to narrow little **Wall Street.** On the corner, **Trinity Church** was founded in 1697, with the present structure dating from 1846. Its small cemetery holds the graves of Alexander Hamilton and other great New Yorkers. One block down Wall is the unprepossessing entrance to the **New York Stock Exchange.** Go to the corner on Broad Street for the more ceremonial view. Next door, a statue of George Washington marks the entrance to **Federal Hall,** a reminder that the first seat of U.S. government was at this location, from 1789 to 1790. In true New York fashion, it was demolished in 1812 to make room for something newer.

At the very tip of Manhattan, **Battery Park** and the streets around are where the Dutch first settled New Amsterdam in 1625. The park's centerpiece, **Castle Clinton,** began as a fort during the War of 1812 and later served as New York's immigration facility, welcoming eight million new Americans between 1855 and 1890. You can see its more famous successor, **Ellis Island,** from the waterside, adjacent to the **Statue of Liberty.** Ferries (© **877/523-9849;** www.statuecruises.com) sail to both between 9am and 3pm. Crown Access tickets let you take in the view from Liberty's crown, but you have to be able to climb 354 steps for the privilege. Otherwise, you'll want a Pedestal/Museum ticket. (Access to the pedestal and museum are also included in Crown Access tickets.) Prices for both are $12 adults, $10 seniors, $5 kids ages 4 to 12, with $3 extra for Crown Access. You'll have to get there early and be prepared to wait in line. You can also buy ferry tickets in advance, online.

If you still have time, one of New York's newest and most cutting-edge attractions sits far on the West Side, starting in the trendy Meatpacking District. We're talking about **High Line Park** (© 212/500-6035; www.thehighline.org), a once abandoned elevated rail line that was built for freight use between 1929 and 1934, then abandoned in 1980—at which point Mother Nature began planting its rail beds with wind-blown seeds. By the late 1990s, it was essentially a long, narrow wilderness, forgotten by all except the few who climbed its supports and braved its barbed-wire barricades. A preservation movement spent years lobbying for its reuse, and in 2006, plans were finally drawn up to turn the High Line into a major new public park, running from Gansevoort Street in the Meatpacking District to 34th Street, between 10th and 11th Avenues. Enter at either end and you'll be on a 1.5-mile path of smooth concrete planks dotted with benches and a few photogenic sections of track, and surrounded by beds of grasses, trees, and other greenery that mimic the line's environment during its years of disuse. The park is open daily from 7am to 10pm. The High Line Art program brings in artists to create site-specific pieces in the park and vicinity—appropriate since **Chelsea,** the neighborhood through which most of the park runs, is also the city's gallery district.

SHOPPING

Almost every block in New York City has some interesting shop on it, from up-up-upmarket boutiques to funky little joints. Here's a quick read: Downtown, along Canal, Mott, Mulberry, and Elizabeth streets, **Chinatown** is chock-full of shops selling fish and herbal cures—fun for their bustle, exotica, and sometimes downright weirdness. Dispersed among them—especially along **Canal Street**—you'll find a mind-boggling collection of knockoff sunglasses and watches, cheap backpacks, discount leather goods, and exotic souvenirs. A cleaned-up distillation of it all can be found at the **Pearl River** Chinese emporium (www.pearlriver.com), a few blocks north of Canal at 477 Broadway. Going north, **SoHo,** stretching from Broadway east to Sullivan Street, and from Houston down to Broome Street, is still the epicenter of cutting-edge fashion. Going up even farther, **East Ninth Street** between First and Second avenues is lined with a smart collection of boutiques that sell original fashions of excellent quality for women.

At Herald Square (where 34th St., Sixth Ave., and Broadway converge), you'll find **Macy's,** the self-proclaimed world's biggest department store. Enter if only to see the classic wooden escalators that have been running since 1902. At **Times Square,** you can step into the giant **Toys "R" Us** flagship on Broadway and 44th Street, complete with a 60-foot Ferris wheel. West 47th Street between Fifth and Sixth avenues is the city's famous **Diamond District,** with more than 2,600 retail and wholesale diamond and jewelry businesses. **Tiffany & Co.** reigns at Fifth Avenue and 57th Street, with other big-name, big-ticket designers radiating out from the crossroads, including **Versace, Chanel, Dior,** and **Cartier.** You'll also find big-name jewelers in the area, as well as chichi department stores such as **Bergdorf Goodman, Henri Bendel,** and **Saks Fifth Avenue,** all of which help this stretch of Fifth Avenue maintain its ritzy cachet.

New York's Best Pizza

There's nothing more New York than pizza, and even though there are roughly a zillion pizzerias in the naked city (more than 40 of them named Ray's, amazingly enough), we're suckers for the real old-school joints: classic, cool, and delicious.

Up at 116th Street in Spanish Harlem, **Patsy's Pizzeria,** 2287 First Ave. (© 212/534-9783), is our favorite. Open since 1933, it celebrated its 75th anniversary by rolling prices back to what they were on opening day: 60¢ for a pizza, 40¢ for mussels, 10¢ for a soda, and so on. That was a 1-day deal, but it gives you an idea of what kind of place this is: totally traditional, totally historic, friendly, and did we mention delicious? Its pies are fashioned with a slightly sweet sauce, a thin and perfectly baked crust, fresh mozzarella melted evenly across the top, fresh basil, and a variety of optional toppings. *Absolutely do not* just get a slice from the takeout window. Instead, go in, sit down, and have a pie made for you fresh, served by the consistently friendly staff. Down in Brooklyn, **Grimaldi's,** 19 Old Fulton St. (© 718/858-4300; www.grimaldis.com), was founded by Patsy's nephew in 1990, right in the shadow of the Brooklyn Bridge. Its pizza is on a par with Patsy's, but its ambience is less old-time restaurant and more everyday joint—albeit with a big line of tourists outside waiting to get in. Back in Manhattan, **John's of Bleecker Street,** 278 Bleecker St. (© 212/243-1680; www.johnsbrickovenpizza.com), is known for its great crust—not too chewy, not too crispy—with full-spread mozzarella, fresh sauce, and generous toppings. Its interior is woody and lived-in, with a tile floor, walls with murals, and booths and tables covered with decades of carved initials.

Lest we live completely in the past and ignore the spate of artisanal pizzerias that have bloomed around New York over the past decade, let's give a shout-out to **Motorino,** 349 E. 12th St. (© 212/777-2644; www.motorinopizza.com), which serves consistently excellent Neapolitan-style pizza cooked in a handcrafted brick oven from Naples—and they're super-friendly, too.

A large pie at any of these places will run you between $12 and $18, without extra toppings. Eat up: It gets no better than this.

WHERE TO STAY

There are tons of choices all over town, with rates for standard rooms easily running more than $300, $400, or $500. That said, there are often special promotional rates on weekends, when business travelers have all left town.

Classic New York hotels have a tendency to charge robber-baron prices. Not so the **Waldorf=Astoria,** 301 Park Ave. (© **800/925-3673;** www.waldorfastoria.com), a bastion of old-school Art Deco elegance with more than 1,000 airy rooms with high ceilings and traditional decor, all at a classy Park Avenue location. Cruise season rates: from $299 double. The **Algonquin,** 59 W. 44th St. (© **888/304-2047** or 212/840-6800; www.algonquinhotel.com), is another legendary New York spot, its restaurant once hosting the Algonquin Round Table, a daily luncheon where Dorothy Parker, Robert Benchley, Alexander Woollcott, and other luminaries set the tone for the 1920s literary scene. The hotel makes the most of this association, its small but comfortable rooms stocked with the latest issue of *The New Yorker* and its publike Blue Bar home to a rotating collection of Hirschfeld drawings. Cruise season rates: from $259 double.

With artistic interiors and great service, the **Muse,** 130 W. 46th St. (② **877/692-6873** or 212/485-2400; www.themusehotel.com), is a little jewel of the Theater District, with its beautiful contemporary decor, good-size rooms with featherbeds, and sumptuous bathrooms. Cruise season rates: from $325 double. One block south, the **Room Mate Grace,** 125 W. 45th St. (② **212/354-2323;** www.room-matehotels.com), is another of the best moderately priced Midtown options, its rooms designed with a modern, minimalist aesthetic, plus niceties like a lobby swimming pool with a swim-up bar. Cruise season rates: from $215 double. A little farther south, the **Hotel Metro,** 45 W. 35th St. (② **800/356-3870;** www.hotelmetronyc.com), is a Midtown gem that's a surprisingly good deal. Cruise season rates: from $255 double.

In the fashionable Meatpacking District, literally straddling the new High Line Park (see above), the **Standard Hotel,** 848 Washington St., at 13th Street (② **212/645-4646;** www.standardhotels.com/new-york-city), is über-chic, with streamlined modern rooms angled to maximize views of the city, the park, and the Hudson River just 1 block away. Cruise season rates: from $293 double.

Nestled into the residential Upper West Side, the **Lucerne,** 201 W. 79th St. (② **800/492-8122** or 212/875-1000; www.thelucernehotel.com), occupies a landmark 1904 building with a magnificent terra-cotta exterior, and is only a few blocks from the American Museum of Natural History. Inside, its rooms are done in a classic style, with a real New York feel. Cruise season rates: from $225 double. Even more New York is the 12-room **Inn at Irving Place,** 56 Irving Place, at East 17th Street (② **800/685-1447** or 212/533-4600; www.innatirving.com). An absolute jewel of a place, it was created from two joined brownstone town houses built in 1834. Outside, only the address on the door gives away its location; inside, it's all 19th century, from the period furnishings and Persian rugs to the old-style New York grace, dignity, and charm. Cruise season rates: from $395 double.

DINING & NIGHTLIFE

You can get any type of cuisine imaginable in this foodie city, from steakhouse and seafood to Chinese and Japanese to Korean, Indian, Thai, Portuguese, Argentinean, German, French, Ethiopian, Tibetan, Burmese . . . you get the picture.

In the lobby of the ornate, Art Deco MetLife building, **Eleven Madison Park,** 11 Madison Ave. (② **212/889-0905;** www.elevenmadisonpark.com), serves hearty, French-infused country cuisine in a magnificent, high-ceilinged setting. Three-course prix-fixe dinner: $95. To get even more French, visit **La Grenouille,** 3 E. 52nd St. (② **212/752-1495;** www.la-grenouille.com), which serves the classics with elegant perfection. Three-course prix-fixe dinner: $95. In the "best views" category, **Asiate,** 80 Columbus Circle, at 60th Street (② **212/805-8881;** www.mandarinoriental.com/newyork), in the Mandarin Oriental Hotel, might steal the show, perched 34 floors above Central Park. The Japanese/French fare is divine. Three-course prix-fixe dinner: $85. If it's Italian you're craving, go downtown to **Babbo,** 110 Waverly Place (② **212/777-0303;** www.babbonyc.com), where Food Network chef Mario Batali has created the ideal setting for his exciting northern Italian cooking. Main courses: $19 to $29. For Japanese, try **Nobu,** 105 Hudson St., in TriBeCa (© **212/219-0500;** www.myriadrestaurantgroup.com/nobu), whose namesake also happens to have a hand in the specialty restaurants on Crystal Cruises' ships. Main courses: $28 to $42.

In the Theater District, **Joe Allen,** 326 W. 46th St. (© **212/581-6464;** www.joe allenrestaurant.com), is the ultimate Broadway pub—and the meatloaf is marvelous. Main courses: $18 to $30. For a steakhouse experience, **Frankie & Johnnie's,** 269 W. 45th St. (© **212/997-9494;** www.frankieandjohnnies.com), is a Theater District legend, in business since 1926. The steaks (especially the house sirloin) are extraordinary and the service is old school. A second location, at 32 W. 37th St. (© **212/997-8940**), is in a two-story former town house that was once home to legendary actor John Barrymore. Main courses: $25 to $40.

Heading downtown, the **Union Square Cafe,** 21 E. 16th St. (© **212/243-4020;** www.unionsquarecafe.com), is a perennial favorite, serving new American cuisine in a cheerful setting. Main courses: $27 to $38. Carrying the flame of the old Jewish Lower East Side, **Katz's Delicatessen,** 205 E. Houston St. (© **212/254-2246;** www. katzdeli.com), is the choice among those who know their kreplach, knishes, and pastramis. The all-beef wieners are legendary in a town known for its hot dogs. For those keeping score, this is the place where Meg Ryan had her fake orgasm in *When Harry Met Sally.* Main courses: $5 to $19.

For Indian food, Sixth Street between First and Second avenues is an **entire block of inexpensive Indian eats** and over-the-top decor. Just walk down the street and see which of the sidewalk solicitors seems most persuasive. For something fancier, head up to **Tamarind,** 41–43 E. 22nd St. (© **212/674-7400;** www.tamarinde22.com), one of the best Indian restaurants in Manhattan, serving innovative and flavorful variations on the old standards. Main courses: $16 to $33.

When it comes to nightlife in New York City, where to start? There's **Broadway** for world-class shows (and the **TKTS** booth in Times Square for cheapish last-minute seats: www.tdf.org/tkts); **Carnegie Hall** (www.carnegiehall.org) and **Lincoln Center** (www.lincolncenter.org) for symphonies, opera, and ballet; **Radio City Music Hall** (www.radiocity.com) for concerts and shows; and the **Blue Note,** at 131 W. Third St. (www.bluenote.net), for jazz. The list goes on. Or you could just barhop. Assuming you have only a day or two to sample the Big Apple, downtown has the most interesting bars, such as trendoid lounges in **TriBeCa** and **SoHo,** where a cosmo goes for the price of a small car. We prefer old-time downtown pubs such as the **Ear Inn,** 326 Spring St. at Greenwich (© **212/226-9060;** www.earinn.com), whose two-story brick home dates to 1817; or the **Old Town Bar & Restaurant,** 45 E. 18th St. between Broadway and Park Avenue (© **212/529-6732;** www.oldtownbar.com), which opened in 1892 and boasts a great old mahogany bar and fantastic burgers. If you want a more Woody Allen experience, head up to the Upper East Side, where Second and Third avenues between 72nd and 96th streets have no shortage of bars and restaurants where comfortably well-off uptown intellectuals feel at home. A scene in Allen's quintessential *Manhattan* was actually filmed at **Elaine's,** 1703 Second Ave. at 88th Street (© **212/534-8103**), a legendary Upper East Side eatery.

For listings of currents shows, plays, and live music, check out local publications such as *Time Out New York* (www.timeoutny.com), the *Village Voice* (www.villagevoice.com), *The New Yorker* (www.newyorker.com), and *New York* magazine (www.nymag.com).

13 San Diego, California

San Diego was the first European settlement on the west coast of America, and though it spent a lot of years being looked down on as a conservative, slow-growth Navy town, it has come to life over the past couple of decades. Today, the city in the bottom-left corner of the U.S. boasts a growing and diverse population, revitalized neighborhoods, a strong connection with its Hispanic heritage (Mexico, remember, is just 16 miles to the south), a benign climate, and fabulous beaches. With 70 miles of sandy coast-line—plus pretty, sheltering Mission Bay—you can choose from a whole slew of watersports, while miles of paved pathways make for great biking and skating.

San Diego's **downtown** sits at the edge of San Diego Bay, a large natural harbor with flat Coronado on one side and peninsular Point Loma on the other. Splendid **Balboa Park,** at the eastern edge of downtown, is one of the finest urban oases in the country, home to 15 museums as well as gardens, theaters, and recreational facilities. North from Point Loma is **Mission Bay,** a lagoon that was carved out of an estuary in the 1940s, and now serves as a watersports mecca. A series of communities are found along the beach-lined coast: Ocean Beach, Mission Beach, Pacific Beach, La Jolla, and, just outside San Diego's city limits, Del Mar.

GETTING TO SAN DIEGO & THE PORT

San Diego's **B Street Cruise Ship Terminal** is at 1140 N. Harbor Dr., right in the heart of downtown (✆ **800/854-2757** or 619/686-6200; www.sandiegocruise port.com). No parking is available at the terminal, but there are several options nearby, including: **Five Star Parking,** 900 W. Broadway (✆ **619/233-2000;** www. fivestarparking.com), which is right across the street from the pier and charges $15 per day; and **Park & Go,** 2535 Pacific Hwy. (✆ **619/525-9885;** www.parkandgosd. com), which charges $10 per day and offers a free shuttle to the pier (a distance of about a dozen blocks).

If you're arriving by air, you'll probably touch down at the **San Diego International Airport** (✆ **619/231-2100;** www.san.org), also called Lindbergh Field. It's just northwest of downtown, along the bay and close to the piers. Metered **taxis** cost about $9.50 to the port.

GETTING AROUND   Those staying for a short time in the downtown area will be able to cover the close-in attractions (including Balboa Park and Old Town) on foot or by using the city buses and trolleys. You can also try the narrated **Old Town Trolley Tours** (✆ **619/298-8687;** www.historictours.com/sandiego), which make a big loop around town, past all the major attractions. A complete loop takes about 90 min-utes, and you can hop off at any point, then reboard later. (Trolleys come by about every 30 min.) Rates are $34 for adults and $17 for children, but you can get them cheaper by buying online ahead of time.

For attractions, accommodations, and beaches in the greater city, having your own wheels is a big advantage. Major **car rental** agencies are based at the airport. Taxis are also available, though after dark they don't cruise the streets looking for passengers (except in the Gaslamp Quarter). If you need one, call ahead. Among the local com-panies are **Orange Cab** (✆ **619/291-3333**), **San Diego Cab** (✆ **619/226-8294**), and **Yellow Cab** (✆ **619/234-6161**). The **Coronado Cab Company** (✆ **619/435-6211**) serves Coronado. Rates are $2.40 for the first ¹⁄₁₀-mile and $2.60 for each addi-tional mile.

BEST CRUISE LINE SHORE EXCURSIONS

SeaWorld ($89, 7 hr.): San Diego's SeaWorld Adventure Park is one of the largest and best marine-life parks in the world. While this tour is about $20 more than the park's admission price, it's a viable option if you don't want to worry about arranging your own transportation.

EXPLORING SAN DIEGO ON YOUR OWN

Unless you head to the beaches, you'll probably spend most of your time in **downtown** and **Old Town.** The business, shopping, dining, and entertainment heart of the city, the downtown area encompasses the Embarcadero (waterfront), the Gaslamp Quarter, Horton Plaza (see "Shopping," below), the Convention Center, San Diego's Little Italy, and other areas. A **Visitor Information Center** (© **619/236-1212**) is right across the street from the cruise terminal at the corner of Harbor Drive and West Broadway.

Right on the waterfront, just north of the cruise terminal, is the **Maritime Museum of San Diego,** 1492 N. Harbor Dr. (© **619/234-9153;** www.sdmaritime.org), which comprises a flotilla of ships. The full-rigged merchant vessel *Star of India* dates from 1863 and is the world's oldest ship that still goes to sea. The gleaming white, steam-powered ferry *Berkeley* (1898) once ran the route between San Francisco and Oakland, and worked round-the-clock to carry people to safety following the 1906 San Francisco earthquake. Among the other vessels are the HMS *Surprise,* a replica of an 18th-century Royal Navy frigate used in the film *Master and Commander;* a Cold War–era Soviet submarine; the sleek *Medea* (1904), one of the last remaining large steam yachts; and *Californian* (1984), the official tall ship of the State of California. You can board and explore each vessel and also check out the collection of maritime artifacts and themed exhibits. The museum is open daily 9am to 8pm. Admission is $14 adults, $11 seniors, $8 kids ages 6 to 17, free for kids ages 5 and under.

Along the same stretch of the harbor, the **San Diego Aircraft Carrier Museum,** 910 Harbor Dr., at Navy Pier (© **619/544-9600;** www.midway.org), is actually the aircraft carrier *Midway,* commissioned in 1945 and a veteran of Vietnam and Gulf War I. In all, more than 225,000 men served aboard the vessel. A self-guided audio tour takes visitors to several levels of the ship, telling the story of life on board. The highlight is climbing up the superstructure to the bridge and gazing down on the 1,001-foot-long flight deck, with various aircraft poised for duty. What really brings the experience to life is the occasional graffiti and other reminders left behind by the crew. The museum is open daily 10am to 5pm. Admission is $18 adults, $15 seniors and students, $10 kids ages 6 to 17; free for kids ages 5 and under.

Visitors looking for something less nautical can head across Harbor Drive to the Santa Fe Depot and check out one of the city's cultural landmarks, the **Museum of Contemporary Art San Diego Downtown,** 1100 Kettner Blvd. (© **858/454-3541;** www.mcasd.org). This new museum space was built originally in 1915 as the baggage building for the historic train station; repurposed in 2007, it now features permanent, commissioned pieces by artists such as Richard Serra and Jenny Holzer, as well as exhibitions of world-class contemporary art. Across the street is MCASD's original downtown annex (1001 Kettner Blvd.), which has a great little gift shop. The museum is open daily (except Wed) 11am to 5pm. Admission is $10 adults, $5 seniors, free for anyone ages 25 and under.

San Diego

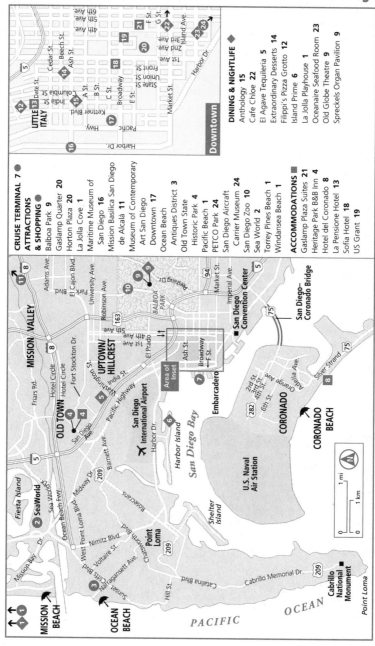

Downtown

CRUISE TERMINAL 7 ●

ATTRACTIONS & SHOPPING ●

Balboa Park **9**
Gaslamp Quarter **20**
Horton Plaza **20**
La Jolla Cove **1**
Maritime Museum of San Diego **16**
Mission Basílica San Diego de Alcalá **11**
Museum of Contemporary Art San Diego Downtown **17**
Ocean Beach Antiques District **3**
Old Town State Historic Park **4**
Pacific Beach **1**
PETCO Park **24**
San Diego Aircraft Carrier Museum **24**
San Diego Zoo **10**
Sea World **2**
Torrey Pines Beach **1**
Windansea Beach **1**

ACCOMMODATIONS ■

Gaslamp Plaza Suites **21**
Heritage Park B&B Inn **4**
Hotel del Coronado **8**
La Pensione Hotel **13**
Sofia Hotel **18**
US Grant **19**

DINING & NIGHTLIFE ◆

Anthology **15**
Cafe Chloe **22**
El Agave Tequileria **5**
Extraordinary Desserts **14**
Filippi's Pizza Grotto **12**
Island Prime **6**
La Jolla Playhouse **1**
Oceanaire Seafood Room **23**
Old Globe Theatre **9**
Spreckels Organ Pavilion **9**

A National Historic District covering 17 city blocks, San Diego's **Gaslamp Quarter** (**www.gaslamp.org**) has many Victorian-style commercial buildings built between the Civil War and World War I. As the center of a massive redevelopment that kicked off in the mid-1980s with the opening of the Horton Plaza shopping complex, the once-seedy area is now packed with trendy boutiques, restaurants, and nightspots. Lit by electric versions of old gas lamps, the Gaslamp Quarter lies between Fourth Avenue to the west, Sixth Avenue to the east, Broadway to the north, and L Street and the waterfront to the south. It makes for good walking and shopping during the day, but the real action here is at night. Immediately southeast of the Gaslamp Quarter is **PETCO Park** (**http://sandiego.padres.mlb.com/sd/ballpark/index.jsp**), stylish home of the San Diego Padres since 2004.

At the northeast edge of downtown lies **Balboa Park,** one of San Diego's true treasures, sitting on a 1,200-acre square that contains the San Diego Zoo, more than a dozen museums, a classic carousel, wonderful gardens, and splendid architecture. Stop by the **Balboa Park Visitor Center,** located in the House of Hospitality (© **619/ 239-0512;** www.balboapark.org), to learn about free walking and museum tours, or to pick up a brochure about the gardens. The park was established in 1868 in the heart of the city, fringed by the early communities of Hillcrest and Golden Hill to the north and east. Tree plantings started in the late–19th century, while the initial buildings were created to host the 1915 to 1916 Panama–California International Exposition; another expo in 1935 and 1936 brought additional developments. The park is divided by Highway 163 into two distinct sections. The narrow western wing has largely grassy, open areas that parallel Sixth Avenue. It's a good place for picnics, strolling, and sunning. The main portion of the park, east of Highway 163, contains all of the park's 15 museums (many of them in the beautiful Spanish Colonial Revival buildings that line **El Prado,** the park's east-west pedestrian thoroughfare) and is bordered by Park Boulevard.

This is also where you'll find the world-famous **San Diego Zoo,** 2920 Zoo Dr. (© **619/231-1515;** www.sandiegozoo.org), operated by the Zoological Society of San Diego. Founded in 1916 with a handful of animals originally brought here for that same Panama–California Exposition, the zoo now has more than 4,000 creatures in residence, including four giant pandas from the People's Republic of China, wild Przewalski horses from Mongolia, Buerger's tree kangaroos from New Guinea, lowland gorillas from Africa, and giant tortoises from the Galapagos, as well as more than 700,000 plants. One of the zoo's newest attractions is Elephant Odyssey, featuring a herd of Asian elephants, as well as life-size replicas of prehistoric animals that once roamed Southern California. The park's Children's Zoo features a nursery with baby animals and a petting area where kids can cuddle up to sheep, goats, and the like. The zoo is open daily 9am to 6pm. Admission is $37 for adults/youths ages 12 and over, $27 for children ages 3 to 11; the price includes a guided bus tour and aerial tram ride.

Northwest of the park, heading toward Mission Bay, is San Diego's **Old Town** (**www.oldtownsandiegoguide.com**), where the first European settlement of California took place. It's the Williamsburg of the West, allowing you to go back to a time of one-room schoolhouses and village greens, when many of the people who lived, worked, and played here spoke Spanish. At **Old Town State Historic Park,** on San Diego Avenue and Twiggs Street (© **619/220-5422;** www.parks.ca.gov), you don't have to look hard or very far to see the past. Dedicated to re-creating the early life of the city from 1821 to 1872, this is where San Diego's Mexican heritage shines brightest. Seven of the park's 20 structures are original, including homes made of adobe; the rest are reconstructed. The park's headquarters is at the **Robinson-Rose House,** 4002 Wallace St., where you can pick up a map and peruse a model of Old Town as it looked in 1872. Among the park's attractions are **La Casa de Estudillo,** which depicts the living conditions of a wealthy family in 1872; and **Seeley Stables,** named after A. L. Seeley, who ran the stagecoach and mail service in these parts from 1867 to 1871. On Wednesdays, from 10am to 2pm, costumed park volunteers re-enact life in the 1800s with cooking and crafts demonstrations, a working blacksmith, and parlor singing. Free 1-hour walking tours leave daily at 11am and 2pm from the Robinson-Rose House. The Old Town State Historic Park visitor center and museums are open daily 10am to 5pm. Admission is free.

Not far from Old Town lies the vast suburban sprawl of **Mission Valley.** Until I-8 was built in the 1950s, it was little more than cow pastures with a couple of dirt roads, but shopping malls, motels, a golf course, condos, car dealerships, and a massive sports stadium fill the expanse today, following the San Diego River upstream to the **Mission Basilica San Diego de Alcalá,** 10818 San Diego Mission Rd. (© 619/281-8449; www.missionsandiego.com). Established in 1769 above Old Town, this was the first link in a chain of 21 missions founded by Spanish missionary Junípero Serra. It was moved to its present location in 1774 for agricultural reasons, and to separate Native American converts from the fortified compound that included the original building. The mission was burned by Indians a year after it was built, and when Father Serra rebuilt it, he used 5- to 7-foot-thick adobe walls and clay tile roofs—making it less likely to burn again, and in the process inspiring a bevy of 20th-century California architects. It's still an active Catholic parish, with Mass daily. The visitor center museum is open daily 9am to 4:45pm. Admission is $3.

Head back west toward the water to experience **Mission Bay,** where someone probably took the photos for the postcards you'll send home. Mission Bay is a watery playground perfect for water-skiing, sailing, and windsurfing. The adjacent communities of Ocean Beach, Mission Beach, and Pacific Beach are known for their wide stretches of sand, active nightlife, and casual dining. This is the place to stay if you want to walk barefoot on the sand or are traveling with beach-loving children, and it's also home to **SeaWorld,** 500 Sea World Dr. (© 800/257-4268; www.seaworld.com), one of the big draws for many visitors to San Diego. Owned by Anheuser-Busch, the 189-acre aquatic theme park has performing animals (from dogs to dolphins), thrill rides, and marine enclosures featuring penguins, sharks, and manatees. Several successive 4-ton black-and-white killer whales have held the role of **Shamu,** the park's mascot, performing in two shows: *Believe* and *Shamu Rocks,* a nighttime production incorporating concert lighting and contemporary music. There's also a passel of *Sesame Street*–related attractions, including a "4-D" interactive movie experience. SeaWorld is open daily 10am to 6pm. Admission costs $69 adults/youths ages 10 and over, $59 kids ages 3 to 9. Discount packages are available that combine SeaWorld with admission to the San Diego Zoo (see above).

BEACHES

San Diego County is blessed with 70 miles of sandy coastline and more than 30 individual beaches that cater equally to surfers, snorkelers, swimmers, sailors, divers, walkers, volleyball players, and sunbathers. Here are some of the best, moving south to north.

Lovely, wide, and sparkling, **Coronado Beach** is conducive to strolling and lingering, especially in the late afternoon. Waves are gentle here, so the beach draws many Coronado families. South of Mission Bay is **Ocean Beach,** a hot spot for surfers, though the water can be rough for swimming. Above Mission Beach, there's always action at **Pacific Beach,** particularly along Ocean Front Walk, a paved boardwalk similar to L.A.'s funky Venice Beach promenade. Surfing is popular year-round here, in marked sections, and the beach is well staffed with lifeguards. Just north, **Windansea Beach** is legendary among California's surfer elite and remains one of San Diego's prettiest strands. Reached by way of Bonair Street (at Neptune Place), it has no facilities and isn't really ideal for swimming. Come to surf, watch surfers, and soak up the party atmosphere. Up in La Jolla, the calm, protected waters of **La Jolla Cove** (part of the San Diego–La Jolla Underwater Park Ecological Reserve) attract snorkelers and scuba divers, along with a fair share of families to its small beach. The park's "look but don't touch" policy protects the colorful garibaldi, California's state fish, plus other marine life, including abalone, octopus, and lobster. The Underwater Park stretches from here to the northern end of Torrey Pines State Reserve, at the southern end of which you'll find **Torrey Pines Beach** (www.torreypine.org), a fabulous underused shoreline, accessed by a pay parking lot ($10 per car; $9 seniors) at the entrance to the park. It's rarely crowded, though be aware that at high tide most of the sand gets a soaking. In almost any weather, it's a great beach for walking.

SHOPPING

Downtown, **Horton Plaza,** 324 Horton Plaza (© **619/239-8180;** www.westfield. com/hortonplaza), is the Disneyland of shopping malls and the heart of the revitalized city center, bounded by G Street, Broadway, and First and Fourth avenues. Covering 6½ city blocks, the multilevel mall has more than 180 retail establishments, including major department store chains, clothing and shoe stores, bookshops, and fun stores for kids, plus a variety of restaurants and short-order eateries; there's a 14-screen cinema and a performing arts venue as well. It's almost as much an attraction as SeaWorld or the San Diego Zoo, transcending its genre with a conglomeration of rambling paths, bridges, towers, piazzas, sculptures, fountains, and live greenery.

North of downtown, compact **Hillcrest** is the hub of San Diego's gay and lesbian community. You'll find swank shops selling chic home furnishings, and places selling used books, vintage clothing, trinkets, and memorabilia. You'll also see some chain stores, bakeries, cafes, and an array of modestly priced, globe-hopping dining spots. For antiques, head for the **Ocean Beach Antiques District,** along the 4800 block of Newport Avenue. Situated just a few blocks from the beach, this has the city's largest concentration of antiques dealers.

WHERE TO STAY

The following lodgings run the gamut of styles, as well as locations, from Coronado and downtown to La Jolla.

The **Hotel del Coronado,** 1500 Orange Ave., Coronado (© **800/468-3533;** www.hoteldel.com), is the last of California's stately seaside hotels. Opened in 1888 and the subject of meticulous restoration, this Victorian masterpiece had some of the first electric lights in existence, and its early days are well chronicled in displays throughout the property. Cruise season rates: from $315 double. For something just as historic, but much more homey, check out the **Heritage Park Bed & Breakfast**

Inn, 2470 Heritage Park Row, San Diego (℗ **800/995-2470;** www.heritagepark inn.com). This exquisite 1889 Queen Anne mansion is artfully set within a cluster of restored Victorian buildings saved from the wrecking ball; it's just 1 short block from the shops, restaurants, and attractions of Old Town. Cruise season rates: from $125 double.

The 11-story **Gaslamp Plaza Suites,** 520 E St. (℗ **800/874-8770;** www.gaslamp plaza.com), is a comfortable landmark (dating from 1913, when it was San Diego's first skyscraper) with super-friendly rates, located smack-dab in the heart of the trendy Gaslamp Quarter. Cruise season rates: from $83 double. In downtown's Little Italy neighborhood, **La Pensione Hotel,** 606 W. Date St. (℗ **800/232-4683;** www. lapensionehotel.com), feels like a small European hotel and has tidy lodgings at bargain prices. There's an abundance of great dining spots in the surrounding blocks, and you'll be perfectly situated to explore the rest of town by car or trolley. Cruise season rates: from $83 double.

The Gothic Revival **Sofia Hotel,** 150 W. Broadway (℗ **800/826-0009;** www.the sofiahotel.com), was once one of the city's luxury properties, built in 1926 as the Pickwick. Centrally located on the edge of the Gaslamp Quarter and within walking distance of the Embarcadero, the 211-unit hotel now has a comfortably chic design scheme and an excellent American-style bistro, Currant. Cruise season rates: from $169 double.

The **US Grant,** 326 Broadway (℗ **800/237-5029;** www.usgrant.net), is one of San Diego's most historic properties, originally built in 1910 by the son of Ulysses S. Grant. It sits at the northern edge of the Gaslamp Quarter in all its impressive Beaux Arts beauty, and guest rooms have 9-foot ceilings, ornate decor, and Native American artwork (the hotel is owned by the Sycuan Band of the Kumeyaay Nation, which was given sovereignty in 1875 by President Grant). Cruise season rates: from $180 double.

DINING & NIGHTLIFE

You're *s-o-o-o-o-o* close to Mexico, you might as well have Mexican food, no? The best place in San Diego is, naturally, in Old Town, at **El Agave Tequileria,** 2304 San Diego Ave. (℗ **619/220-0692;** www.elagave.com). Rather than the "combination plate" fare that's common on this side of the border, this place presents a memorable selection of freshly prepared recipes from Veracruz, Chiapas, Puebla, and Mexico City, along with an impressive choice of boutique and artisan tequilas. Main courses: $16 to $32.

If you want to know what San Diego tastes like, you can find out at **Market,** 3702 Via de la Valle (℗ **858/523-0007;** www.marketdelmar.com), where native son Carl Schroeder creates a daily menu from the best ingredients bought from local ranches, farms, and seafood purveyors. Main courses: $28 to $35.

For seafood, try **Island Prime,** 880 Harbor Island Dr. (℗ **619/298-6802;** www. cohnrestaurants.com), and enjoy over-the-water dining, a patio with a fireplace, and a menu by chef Deborah Scott that rivals the spectacular bay and skyline views. Main courses: $30 to $49. The Gaslamp Quarter's **Oceanaire Seafood Room,** 400 J St. (℗ **619/858-2277;** www.theoceanaire.com), is another great spot to sample the ocean's bounty. Have your catch of the day simply broiled or grilled, or enjoy a more elaborate preparation; there's an oyster bar, too. Main courses: $20 to $55.

Creative, whimsical touches abound at **Cafe Chloe,** 721 Ninth Ave. (© **619/232-3242;** www.cafechloe.com), a French bistro in downtown's East Village serving breakfast, lunch, and dinner. There is a children's play area, as well as retail space and a patio built for two. Main courses: $15 to $23. For gigantic portions of family-style Italian fare, head to Little Italy and **Filippi's Pizza Grotto,** 1747 India St. (© **619/232-5094;** www.realcheesepizza.com), where a salad for one is enough for three, and an order of lasagna must weigh a pound. Filippi's has locations all over the area, including Pacific Beach, Mission Gorge, and Escondido. Main courses: $6 to $15.

Considering dinner and a show? **Anthology,** 1337 India St. (© **619/595-0300;** www.anthologysd.com), has you covered. This Little Italy supper club is architecturally striking and features a modern American cuisine created by award-winning chef Bradley Ogden. The music onstage is as compelling as the food, ranging from jazz and blues to world music and rock. Main courses: $18 to $28. Be sure to save some room for extraordinary desserts at the nearby **Extraordinary Desserts,** 1430 Union St. (© **619/294-7001;** www.extraordinarydesserts.com). Also set in a fabulously modern space, this longtime local favorite is open late on weekends. There's another location a block from the western edge of Balboa Park, at 2929 Fifth Ave. (© **619/294-2132**). Desserts: $2 to $9.

Wherever you choose to dine, finish your evening in the **Gaslamp Quarter,** which always promises a lively after-dark scene with its restaurants, bars, clubs, theaters, and music venues. Another great option is attending a concert in **Balboa Park.** Free year-round organ concerts are held on Sundays from 2 to 3pm at the **Spreckels Organ Pavilion,** south of El Prado between Park Boulevard and the Cabrillo Freeway (© **619/702-8138;** www.sosorgan.com). The music runs the gamut from classical to contemporary. Or consider taking in a play—San Diego has a well-deserved reputation as a theater hotbed. The city's two leading operations are the **Old Globe Theatre** in Balboa Park (© **619/234-5623;** www.theoldglobe.org) and **La Jolla Playhouse,** located on the campus of the University of California, San Diego (© **858/550-1010;** www.lajollaplayhouse.org). Both have produced Tony Award winners, and between them have sent nearly 50 productions to Broadway, including the musicals *Jersey Boys* and *The Full Monty.* The Globe is also known for its summer Shakespeare Festival, which runs June through September.

14 San Francisco, California

San Francisco is America's most romantic European-style city, full of Victorian architecture, stunning bay vistas, swank boutiques, clanky cable cars, and walkable beaches, all tightly tucked into about 7 square miles. With its strong liberalism, and a hugely influential gay population, it's one of those cities that's constantly renewing itself while also retaining its cultural and historic character. For visitors, it's a place to just dive into and enjoy. Feel the cool blast of salty air as you walk across the Golden Gate Bridge. Browse the secondhand shops along the historic hippie zone of Haight Street. Take in a meal at any of a zillion great restaurants. Watch in amazement as cable car conductors manhandle their arcane levers and switches. Walk along the beach, skate through Golden Gate Park, tour a Victorian mansion, explore Alcatraz Island, and stuff yourself with dim sum in Chinatown. San Francisco is a cool, progressive Disneyland full of good-looking liberals, great architecture and design, and high rents. And that's why we love it.

GETTING TO SAN FRANCISCO & THE PORT

Ships dock at the **Port of San Francisco** piers along the Embarcadero (© **415/274-0400;** www.sfgov.org/site/port_page.asp?id=31686), within walking distance of Fisherman's Wharf. Parking is $12 per day at **City Park,** 80 Francisco St. (© **415/398-4162;** www.cityparksf.com), and **Ace Parking,** 55 Francisco St. (© **415/398-0208;** www.aceparking.com), both located within a couple of blocks of the piers. From the piers, Union Square, Powell Street, Market Street, and the center of downtown can be reached by **taxi.**

If you're flying in, you'll land at one of the Bay Area's two major airports. **San Francisco International Airport** (© **650/821-8211;** www.flysfo.com) is 14 miles directly south of downtown on U.S. 101. Travel time to downtown during commuter rush hour is about 40 minutes; at other times, it's about 20 to 25 minutes. **BART (Bay Area Rapid Transit)** (© **415/989-2278;** www.bart.gov) runs from the airport to downtown, avoiding gnarly traffic and costing a heck of a lot less than taxis and shuttles—about $8 per person to the Embarcadero. Just jump on the airport's free shuttle bus to the International terminal and the BART station. Trains leave approximately every 20 minutes. A **taxi** from the airport to downtown costs about $45, plus tip. **SuperShuttle** (© **415/558-8500;** www.supershuttle.com) takes you anywhere in the city, charging $17 to the cruise pier.

Oakland International Airport (© **510/563-3300;** www.oaklandairport.com), about 5 miles south of downtown Oakland, is a popular alternative to flying directly into San Francisco, and is also accessible on the BART system (see above). A **taxi** to downtown San Francisco costs approximately $55, plus tip. **Bayporter Express** (© **877/467-1800** in the Bay Area, or 415/467-1800 elsewhere; www.bayporter.com) is a shuttle service that charges $32 for the first person and $15 for each additional person for the ride from the Oakland Airport to downtown San Francisco.

GETTING AROUND   You can walk to many attractions from the cruise terminal, including the Embarcadero and sights in the Fisherman's Wharf area, such as Ghirardelli Square (once home to the world-famous chocolate factory), the Cannery, the National Maritime Museum, the Museum of the City of San Francisco, and the ferry to Alcatraz. Otherwise, you have lots of transportation options. The San Francisco Municipal Railway, better known as **Muni** (© **415/673-6864;** www.sfmuni.com), operates the city's buses, streetcars, and the iconic **cable cars.** The three cable car lines are concentrated in the downtown area. The most scenic and exciting is the **Powell–Hyde line,** which follows a zigzag route from the corner of Powell and Market streets, over both Nob Hill and Russian Hill, to a turntable at gaslit Victorian Square in front of Aquatic Park (the closet point to the port, near the intersection of Beach and Hyde sts.). The Powell–Mason line starts at the same intersection and climbs Nob Hill before descending to Bay Street, just 3 blocks from Fisherman's Wharf. The third is the California Street line. Rides cost $5 each way.

Buses reach almost every corner of San Francisco and beyond—they even travel over the bridges to Marin County and Oakland. Overhead electric cables power some buses; others use gas engines. All are numbered and display their destinations on the front. Many buses travel along Market Street or pass near Union Square. A bus ride costs $2 for adults. If you plan to use public transportation extensively, you might want to pick up the inexpensive **Muni Street & Transit Map,** sold at the cable car ticket booths at Powell and Market streets and Hyde and Beach streets, as well as in many shops around town.

This isn't New York, so don't expect a **taxi** to appear whenever you need one—or ever, for that matter. You can often find cabs at the major hotels and downtown during rush hour, but otherwise you'd do better calling ahead to **Veteran's Cab** (© 415/ 552-1300), **Luxor Cabs** (© 415/282-4141), or **Yellow Cab** (© 415/333-3333). Rates are $3.10 for the first ⅕-mile and 45¢ each ⅕-mile thereafter.

BEST CRUISE LINE SHORE EXCURSIONS

Sausalito & Muir Woods ($54, 5 hr.): After a stop in charming Sausalito for bay views and browsing at the town's boutiques, art galleries, and crafts shops, your bus heads to 550-acre Muir Woods, home to a grove of ancient coastal redwoods. You'll have 1½ hours to hike the area's trails on your own before heading back.

Alcatraz & Sausalito by Bus & Ferry ($99, 5½ hr.): This tour begins with a short drive along the Embarcadero to Fisherman's Wharf, where you board the ferry to Alcatraz Island. When you get to Alcatraz, a park ranger will explain the prison's history before you go inside for a private audio tour—and view cells previously inhabited by prison inmates. Afterward, you travel back to Fisherman's Wharf by ferry and board your bus for a drive over the Golden Gate Bridge. In Sausalito, you're free to walk around town and shop.

EXPLORING SAN FRANCISCO ON YOUR OWN

Just north of the cruise docks, **Fisherman's Wharf** (© 415/674-7503; www. fishermanswharf.org) is almost the definition of "tourist trap," a long coastal shopping mall that stretches from Ghirardelli Square at the west end to Pier 39 at the east. If you like this kind of thing—shops, restaurants, street performers, and the like, few of which have anything intrinsically to do with San Francisco—then linger a bit. For decades, the most interesting thing about the place was the enormous, 1,000-strong colony of **sea lions** that hung out on the west (left) side of Pier 39, but at press time they'd almost all packed up and moved on, to the bafflement of scientists and the horror of the wharf's PR people. Take a look. Maybe they've come back.

From here, follow the smell of fresh-baked bread to **Boudin at the Wharf,** 160 Jefferson St., between Taylor and Mason streets (© 415/928-1849; www.boudin bakery.com). Once just a bakery, it's now a half-block-long celebration of bread, with a demonstration bakery, museum, gourmet marketplace, and cafe/espresso bar/ restaurant. You can the 3,000 daily loaves being baked through a 30-foot observation window along Jefferson Street or from a catwalk suspended directly over the bakery, then grab a takeout snack from the cafe, and head out to see the city.

From nearby Pier 41, ferries depart throughout the day bound for **Alcatraz Island** (www.nps.gov/alcatraz), the former military post and maximum-security prison that once housed Al Capone, Machine Gun Kelly, and the famous Birdman, Robert Stroud. Now administered by the National Park Service, "the Rock" offers self-guided tours, ranger-led talks about its famous "escape-proof" prison, and nature trails that lead to spectacular San Francisco views and glimpses of the island's abundant wildlife. Ferries are run by **Alcatraz Cruises** (© 415/981-7625; www.alcatrazcruises.com). Tickets are $26 adults, $16 kids, with headset tour. Make your reservation as far in advance as possible, and bring a jacket—it gets cold out there.

Whether traveling to the Rock or not, your next stop should be the intersection of Hyde and Beach, where you can hop the **Powell–Hyde cable car.** Sit or stand near

San Francisco

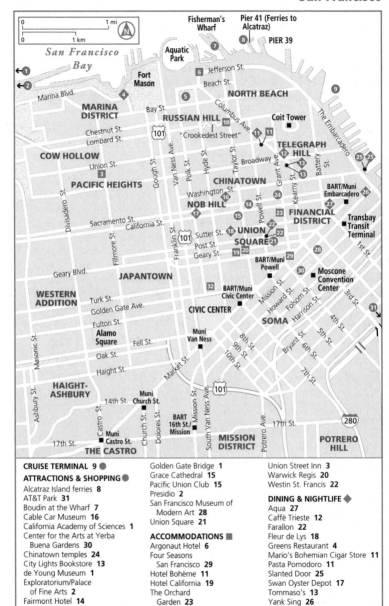

CRUISE TERMINAL 9 ●

ATTRACTIONS & SHOPPING ●

Alcatraz Island ferries **8**
AT&T Park **31**
Boudin at the Wharf **7**
Cable Car Museum **16**
California Academy of Sciences **1**
Center for the Arts at Yerba
   Buena Gardens **30**
Chinatown temples **24**
City Lights Bookstore **13**
de Young Museum **1**
Exploratorium/Palace
   of Fine Arts **2**
Fairmont Hotel **14**
Ferry Building Marketplace **25**
Fisherman's Wharf **7**
Ghirardelli Square **5**

Golden Gate Bridge **1**
Grace Cathedral **15**
Pacific Union Club **15**
Presidio **2**
San Francisco Museum of
   Modern Art **28**
Union Square **21**

ACCOMMODATIONS ■

Argonaut Hotel **6**
Four Seasons
   San Francisco **29**
Hotel Bohème **11**
Hotel California **19**
The Orchard
   Garden **23**
Phoenix Hotel **32**
Ritz-Carlton **23**
San Remo Hotel **10**

Union Street Inn **3**
Warwick Regis **20**
Westin St. Francis **22**

DINING & NIGHTLIFE ◆

Aqua **27**
Caffè Trieste **12**
Farallon **22**
Fleur de Lys **18**
Greens Restaurant **4**
Mario's Bohemian Cigar Store **11**
Pasta Pomodoro **11**
Slanted Door **25**
Swan Oyster Depot **17**
Tommaso's **13**
Yank Sing **26**

the back, on the left-hand side if possible; that way, you get the view down snakelike Lombard Street as well as the spectacular bay view from the top of **Nob Hill.** When the cable cars started running in 1873, Nob Hill became the most desirable residential area in the city, chockablock with mansions. Only two survived the earthquake and fire of 1906: the Flood Mansion, which serves today as the **Pacific Union Club,** 1000 California St., at Mason Street, and the **Fairmont Hotel,** 950 Mason St., which was under construction when the earthquake struck and is worth a visit for its spectacular lobby. **Grace Cathedral,** on California Street between Taylor and Jones streets, is notable, among other things, for its stained-glass windows, depicting Thurgood Marshall, Jane Addams, Robert Frost, John Glenn, and Albert Einstein—representations of divinely inspired human endeavor in law, social work, letters, exploration, and science.

Just northeast of Nob Hill, San Francisco's **Chinatown** gives you a taste of that Asian cruise you couldn't afford this year. The first Chinese immigrants came to San Francisco in the early 1800s to work as servants, and today the city boasts one of the largest Chinese communities in the U.S. Cheesy camera and luggage stores cater to the tourists, but skip those and head for the vegetable and herb markets, restaurants, and shops that draw Chinese shoppers. The gateway at Grant Avenue and Bush Street marks the entry to Chinatown. On Waverly Place, a street where the Chinese celebratory colors of red, yellow, and green are much in evidence, you'll find three **Chinese temples:** Jeng Sen (Buddhist and Taoist) at no. 146, Tien Hou (Buddhist) at no. 125, and Norras (Buddhist) at no. 109. If you enter, do it quietly so you do not disturb those in prayer. A block west of Grant Avenue, **Stockton Street,** from 1000 to 1200, is the community's main shopping drag, lined with grocers, fishmongers, tea sellers, herbalists, noodle parlors, and restaurants. Here, too, is the **Buddhist Kon Chow Temple,** at no. 855, above the Chinatown post office. About a quarter-mile away, the **Cable Car Museum,** 1201 Mason St. (© **415/474-1887**), is the powerhouse, repair shop, and storage place for San Francisco's cable cars. Built in 1887, the building underwent an $18-million reconstruction to restore its original gaslight-era look, adding an amazing spectators' gallery and a museum of San Francisco transit history. The museum is open daily 10am to 5pm. Admission is free.

South of Chinatown and Nob Hill, **Union Square** is the commercial hub of the city, site of most major hotels and department stores. Life is more interesting, though, on the other side of the tracks—or Market Street, as the case may be. There, the neighborhood known as **SoMa** ("South of Market," running btw. Market, the Embarcadero, and Hwy. 101) was transformed from a district of old warehouses, industrial spaces, and underground clubs into the hub of "dot-com-dom" in the late '90s, and is now the city's cultural and multimedia center. The **San Francisco Museum of Modern Art,** 151 Third St. (© **415/357-4000;** www.sfmoma.org), holds more than 23,000 works, including paintings and sculptures by Henri Matisse, Jackson Pollock, Willem de Kooning, Richard Serra, Diego Rivera, Georgia O'Keeffe, and Paul Klee. It's open daily (except Wed) 11am to 5:45pm (Thurs 8:45pm). Admission is $15 adults, $9 students and seniors, free for kids age 12 and under.

The **Center for the Arts at Yerba Buena Gardens,** 701 Mission St. (© **415/978-2787;** www.ybca.org), is San Francisco's official cultural facility, presenting music, theater, dance, and visual arts. Cutting-edge computer art, multimedia shows, traditional exhibitions, and performances occupy the center's high-tech galleries. The 5-acre gardens are a great place to relax in the grass on a sunny day; they feature dramatic outdoor sculpture in memory of Martin Luther King, Jr. Between May and October, the gardens host a series of free concerts, festivals, and community events. The galleries are open Thursday and Friday 2 to 8pm, Saturday noon to 8pm, and Sunday noon to 6pm. Admission is $7adults, $5 seniors, students, and teachers. At Third and King streets on SoMa's waterfront, you'll find the home of the **San Francisco Giants** (© 415/972-2000; www.sfgiants.com). Its corporate name has changed three times in less than a decade because of big-money mergers, and it's now called AT&T Park— a god-awful name for a very pretty ballpark, with its unobstructed bay vistas and bobbing boats beyond the outfield. Tickets are hard to come by, but you can try to track them down through **www.tickets.com**, **www.stubhub.com**, or **sfbay.craigslist.org**.

Southwest of SoMa, few of San Francisco's neighborhoods are as varied as **Haight-Ashbury**, which gained everlasting fame as a capital of '60s hippie culture. Walk along Haight Street today and you'll encounter a weird mix of aging Deadheads, neo-flower-children, homeless people, throngs of tourists, and the kind of clean-cut yuppies who can afford the steep rents of Upper Haight, on the eastern border of **Golden Gate Park**. Funky-trendy shops, clubs, and cafes still line the commercial district, and if someone offers you a bud, he's not talking about beer. To the south, **Castro Street**, between Market and 18th streets, is the center of the city's gay community as well as a lovely neighborhood teeming with shops, restaurants, bars, and cafes.

Within Golden Gate Park, 2 blocks from the park entrance at Eighth Avenue and Fulton, the **de Young Museum**, 50 Hagiwara Tea Garden Dr. (© 415/750-3600; www.famsf.org), is one of San Francisco's oldest museums, founded in 1895. Its vast holdings include one of the finest collections of American paintings in the United States, from Colonial times through the 20th century, as well as decorative arts and crafts; Western and non-Western textiles; and arts from Africa, Oceania, and the Americas. Its 144-foot tower slowly spirals from the ground floor and culminates with an observation floor providing panoramic views of the entire Bay Area. Surrounding sculpture gardens and lush, grassy expanses are perfect for picnicking. The museum is open Tuesday to Sunday 9:30am to 5:15pm (Fri 8:45pm). Admission is $10 adults, $7 seniors, $6 kids ages 13 to 17.

Across from the de Young, the **California Academy of Sciences**, 55 Music Concourse Dr. (© 415/379-8000; www.calacademy.org), was recently completely revamped and reopened as a true homage to Mother Nature. The 412,000-square-foot, mazelike learning center houses an aquarium, a natural history museum, a planetarium, and a four-story rainforest. A 90-foot glass dome puts many of the animals—from as far away as the Philippine coral reefs to as nearby as the northern California coast—front and center. The center is open Monday to Saturday 9:30am to 5pm, Sunday 11am to 5pm. Admission is $25 adults, $20 seniors/youths ages 12 to 17, and $15 for kids ages 4 to 11.

Back up north along San Francisco Bay, the famous **Golden Gate Bridge** connects the City by the Bay with Marin County and the redwoods to the north. Completed in 1937, it's often regarded as the world's most beautiful bridge. If at all possible, take a walk across, accessing the walkway from the parking lots on each side of the span.

The bridge is at the west end of the huge **Presidio** (**www.nps.gov/prsf/index.htm**). Once an Army base, it's now an urban national park full of historic buildings, parkland, and a national cemetery. Near the east end of the park, the **Exploratorium**, 3601 Lyon St. (© 415/561-0360; www.exploratorium.edu), is a must for families with kids—though be warned that you'll be there for most of the day. Designed for hands-on learning, the museum has more than 650 interactive exhibits exploring all facets of science; kids can touch a tornado, shape an electrical current, and finger-paint on a computer. It's located at the gorgeous **Palace of Fine Arts,** the only remaining building from the 1915 Pan-Pacific Exhibition. The Exploratorium is open Tuesday to Sunday 10am to 5pm. Admission is $15 adults, $12 seniors/students/youths ages 13 to 17, $10 kids ages 4 to 12.

SHOPPING

San Francisco's most congested and popular shopping mecca is centered on **Union Square** and bordered by Bush, Taylor, Market, and Montgomery streets. Most of the big department stores and many high-end specialty shops are here. Be sure to venture to Grant Avenue, Post and Sutter streets, and Maiden Lane. This area is a hub for public transportation; all Market Street buses and several others run here, as do the Powell–Hyde and Powell–Mason cable car lines. When you pass through the gate to **Chinatown** on Grant Avenue, say goodbye to the world of fashion and hello to a swarm of cheap tourist shops selling everything from linen and jade to plastic toys and $2 slippers. The real gems, however, are tucked away on side streets and in small, one-person shops selling Chinese herbs, art, and jewelry.

Union Street, from Fillmore Street to Van Ness Avenue, caters to the upper-middle-class crowd. It's a great place to stroll, window-shop the plethora of boutiques, try the cafes and restaurants, and watch the beautiful people parade by. Take bus no. 22, 41, or 45. Some of the best shopping in town is packed into the 5 blocks of **Fillmore Street** from Jackson to Sutter in Pacific Heights. It's the perfect place to grab a bite and peruse the high-priced boutiques, crafts shops, and incredible housewares stores.

The shops in the 6 blocks of **Upper Haight Street** between Central Avenue and Stanyan Street reflect the area's clientele, selling everything from incense and European and American street styles to furniture and antique clothes. If your shopping tastes are humble, the tourist-oriented malls along Jefferson Street in the **Fisherman's Wharf** area include hundreds of shops, restaurants, and attractions. If your tastes run more literary, head to **City Lights Bookstore,** 261 Columbus Ave., at Broadway on the east edge of Chinatown (© **415/362-8193;** www.citylights.com). Founded by Beat poet Lawrence Ferlinghetti in 1953, the three-level shop specializes in world literature, the arts, and progressive politics.

At the foot of Market Street, along the Embarcadero, the magnificent **Ferry Building Marketplace** (© **415/693-0996;** www.ferrybuildingmarketplace.com) is a former transportation hub dating to 1898. Long underused after bridges and cars supplanted ferry use, it was transformed between 1999 and 2003 into a mixed-use space with a 660-foot sky-lit central nave holding a world-class gourmet marketplace. You can browse, sample, nosh, and caffeinate at dozens of specialty shops, then savor the bayfront views from tables set up both indoors and out.

WHERE TO STAY

Looking like a federal building outside and a mansion within, the **Ritz-Carlton,** 600 Stockton St., in Nob Hill (© **800/241-3333** or 415/296-7465; www.ritzcarlton.com), is the best bet for those with more traditional tastes and a hankering for every possible amenity. Cruise season rates: from $269 double. The **Four Seasons San Francisco,** 757 Market St., SoMa (© **800/819-5053** or 415/633-3000; www.four seasons.com/sanfrancisco), provides understated luxury, great service, and oversize rooms with custom-made mattresses. Cruise season rates: from $325 double. The **Westin St. Francis,** 335 Powell St., Union Square (✆ 800/WESTIN-1 [937-8461] or 415/397-7000; www.westin.com), is a favorite with VIPs for its luxurious rooms—and with kids because they get complimentary goodies, such as coloring books, at check-in. Cruise season rates: from $170 double. Also in Union Square are two great boutique hotels, the **Warwick Regis,** 490 Geary St. (✆ 800/827-3447 or 415/928-7900; http://warwicksf.com), with rates from $94 double, and the **Hotel California,** 580 Geary St. (✆ 800/227-4223 or 415/441-2700; www.hotelca.com/sanfrancisco), with rates from $169 double.

At Fisherman's Wharf, the **Argonaut Hotel,** 495 Jefferson St. at Hyde St. (✆ 866/415-0704 or 415/563-0800; www.argonauthotel.com), is a boutique gem with rooms done up in a nautical motif, full of blues, whites, reds, and yellows. Try to book a "view" room, which overlooks the wharf, the bay, and, in some cases, Alcatraz and the Golden Gate Bridge. The four-story timber-and-brick landmark building was originally built in 1908 as a warehouse, used at one point by William Randolph Hearst to store treasures that eventually ended up at Hearst Castle in San Simeon. Cruise season rates: from $245 double.

If Al Gore were to build a hotel, it might well look like the **Orchard Garden,** 466 Bush St., at Grant (✆ 888/717-2881 or 415/399-9807; www.theorchardgardenhotel.com). Built to U.S. Green Building Council (USGBC) standards, it has an in-room recycling system, cleans up with citrus-based cleaning products, and uses a keycard system that turns your room's power off each time you leave. Good karma! It's comfortable, too, with super-quiet rooms decorated in natural wood tones and light colors, and outfitted with Egyptian cotton linens and real feather down pillows. Cruise season rates: from $169 double.

The **Hotel Bohème,** 444 Columbus Ave. (✆ 415/433-9111; www.hotelboheme.com), is a second-floor boutique hotel with 15 small rooms that are reminiscent of a home in upscale Nob Hill, with gauze-draped canopies, ornate parasols shading the ceiling lights, and walls dramatically colored with lavender, sage green, black, and pumpkin. The staff is ultrahospitable, and bonuses include sherry in the lobby each afternoon. Cruise season rates: from $174 double.

Attention to detail, comfortable rooms, and a location along a prime stretch of Union Street make the tiny, six-unit **Union Street Inn,** 2229 Union St. (✆ 415/346-0424; www.unionstreetinn.com), an excellent way to experience true San Francisco–style living. Cruise season rates: from $199 double. The **Phoenix Hotel,** 601 Eddy St. (✆ 800/248-9466 or 415/776-1380; www.thephoenixhotel.com), is a favorite with the music and movie set (Sinéad O'Connor, David Bowie, and Keanu Reeves have all slept here); it's also one of the only moderately priced hotels in San Francisco with an outdoor pool. Cruise season rates: from $129 double.

At the small, adorable **San Remo Hotel,** 2237 Mason St. (✆ 800/352-REMO [352-7366] or 415/776-8688; www.sanremohotel.com), the rooms may be small and the bathrooms shared, but the North Beach location (within walking distance of Fisherman's Wharf), friendly staff, and low prices can't be beat. Cruise season rates: from $75 double.

DINING & NIGHTLIFE

Fleur de Lys, 777 Sutter St., Union Square (✆ 415/673-7779; www.fleurdelyssf.com), serves formal French cuisine in a romantic dining room. Three-course menu:

$72. Whimsical **Farallon,** 450 Post St., Union Square (© **415/956-6969;** www. farallonrestaurant.com), offers high-priced seafood amid an orgy of oceanic artwork, from jellyfish lamps to sea urchin chandeliers. Main courses: $25 to $34. San Francisco's finest seafood restaurant might be **Aqua,** 252 California St. (© **415/956-9662;** www.aqua-sf.com), which dazzles customers with artfully composed and delicately decadent dishes like Alaskan black cod wrapped in smoked bacon with tomato-and-date chutney. Main courses: $29 to $40.

For a totally classic San Francisco dining experience, stop by the **Swan Oyster Depot,** 1517 Polk St. (© **415/673-1101**). Opened in 1912, this tiny hole in the wall is little more than a narrow fish market that decided to slap down 20 or so bar stools, all jammed cheek-by-jowl along a long marble bar. The menu is limited to fresh crab, shrimp, oyster, clam cocktails, a few types of smoked fish, Maine lobster, and Boston-style clam chowder, all exceedingly fresh. *Note:* Don't let the lunchtime line dissuade you—it moves fast. Clams and oysters on the half shell: $10 per half-dozen (cash only). Closed Sunday.

North Beach, San Francisco's Italian quarter, stretches from Montgomery and Jackson to Bay Street. It's one of the best places in the city to grab a coffee, pull up a cafe chair, and do some serious people-watching. Nightlife is equally happening; restaurants, bars, and clubs along Columbus and Grant avenues attract folks from all over the Bay Area, who fight for a parking place and romp through the festive neighborhood. Gourmands and everyday diners alike squeeze into **Tommaso's,** 1042 Kearny St. (© **415/398-9696;** www.tommasosnorthbeach.com), for killer pizza and a no-frills Italian cafe atmosphere. Main courses: $14 to $22; pizzas: $16 to $26. **Pasta Pomodoro,** 655 Union St. (© **415/399-0300;** www.pastapomodoro.com), serves heaping plates of fresh pasta at penny-pinching prices. It has several other locations around town as well. Main courses: $9 to $16. Among the area's coffeehouses, we love the authentic atmosphere at **Mario's Bohemian Cigar Store,** 566 Columbus Ave. (© **415/362-0536**), and **Caffè Trieste,** 601 Vallejo St. (© **415/392-6739;** www.caffe trieste.com).

For the best dim sum in the downtown area, go to cavernous **Yank Sing,** 101 Spear St. (© **415/957-9300;** www.yanksing.com). Confident, experienced servers take the nervousness out of novices—they're good at guessing your gastric threshold as they stop by your table with shrimp balls, pork buns, *congee* (porridge), spareribs, stuffed crab claws, and other palate pleasers. Most items: $3.50 to $10 for two to six pieces. At the Ferry Building (see "Shopping," above), the **Slanted Door,** 1 Ferry Plaza (© **415/861-8032;** www.slanteddoor.com), is one of the most popular restaurants in the city, serving incredibly fresh and flavorful Vietnamese dishes, along with tea from an eclectic collection. Main courses: $11 to $36.

Greens Restaurant, Building A, Fort Mason Center, Marina/Pacific Heights (© **415/771-6222;** www.greensrestaurant.com), serves inventive vegetarian cuisine in an old waterfront warehouse, with a view of the bay and the Golden Gate Bridge. Main courses: $17 to $23.

At night, dozens of piano bars and top-notch lounges augment San Francisco's lively dance-club culture, and skyscraper lounges afford dazzling city views. The city's arts scene is also extraordinary: The opera is justifiably world renowned, the ballet is on its toes, and theaters are high in both quantity and quality. In short, there's always something going on, so get out there. For up-to-date nightlife information, turn to the *San Francisco Weekly* and the *San Francisco Bay Guardian,* both of which run comprehensive listings. They're available free at bars and restaurants and from street-corner boxes all around the city. *Where,* a free tourist-oriented monthly, also lists programs and performance times; it's available in most of the city's finer hotels. As for bars and lounges, there are hundreds of 'em throughout San Francisco. **Chestnut** and **Union Street** bars attract a post-collegiate crowd, **Upper Haight** caters to eclectic neighborhood cocktailers, and **Lower Haight** draws snowboarder types. Tourists mix with theatergoers and thirsty businesspeople in **downtown** pubs, while the **Castro** caters to gay locals and visitors.

15 Seattle, Washington

There's an argument to be made that the Pacific Northwest is *the* place to be in the U.S. right now. It's got money (thank you, Microsoft and Intel), it's got a slew of new residents, it's an early adopter of green technologies and lifestyles, and as a result of all this, it's geekily hip. That goes double for Seattle, the Northwest's biggest city, which over the past decade has been spiffed up with new sports stadiums, a new and architecturally avant-garde library, a new opera house and symphony hall, and countless new hotels, restaurants, and shops. It's very much a water-oriented city, set between Puget Sound and Lake Washington, with Lake Union in the center. Practically everywhere you look, the views are of sailboats, cargo ships, ferries, windsurfers, and anglers. The only drawback is the rain, which falls (or threatens to) an average of 226 days a year. But look on the bright side: All that moisture is good for your complexion.

After decades in the shadow of nearby Vancouver, British Columbia, Seattle finally emerged a few years back as a major port of embarkation for Alaska-bound ships, which operate from here throughout the summer.

GETTING TO SEATTLE & THE PORT

Cruise ships dock at Pier 66, the **Bell Street Terminal,** right in downtown Seattle near Pike Place Market, or at the **Terminal 91** cruise facility, located at 2001 W. Garfield St. at the north end of the downtown waterfront. Parking is $17 per day at the Bell Street Terminal, $21 per day at Terminal 91. See **www.portseattle.org/seaport/cruise/** for maps and other information. If you're arriving by air, you'll fly into the **Seattle-Tacoma International Airport** (© **800/544-1965;** www.portseattle.org/seatac/), often referred to as **Sea-Tac,** situated about 14 miles south of Seattle and connected to the city by I-5. **Light rail service** (www.soundtransit.org) connects the airport and downtown for just $2.50 per person. A **taxi** downtown will cost you around $45.

GETTING AROUND   You can walk or take public transportation around downtown Seattle, but if you want a **rental car,** nearly every major company has an outlet at Sea-Tac. **Seattle Metro** (© **206/553-3000;** http://metro.kingcounty.gov) provides free bus transportation within the downtown area (from Battery St. to S. Jackson St. north-south and from 6th Ave. to the waterfront east-west) between the hours of 6am and 7pm. The company also operates a waterfront service using old-fashioned streetcars, some in the ride-free area, some outside. The most it will cost you is $2.75 one-way. On weekends and holidays, you can also get a 1-day unlimited-ride pass for $4.50 at various locations (see website for details). Visitors to the Space Needle can use the **Seattle Center Monorail** (© **206/905-2600;** www.seattlemonorail.com) from downtown, 1¼ miles away, for $2 one-way.

BEST CRUISE LINE SHORE EXCURSIONS

Shore excursions in Seattle are usually pretty sparse. Often your choices are limited to a **bus tour** ($49; 3½ hr.) that includes the Space Needle, Pioneer Square, and shopping time at Pike Place Market.

EXPLORING SEATTLE ON YOUR OWN

The **Seattle Waterfront,** along Alaskan Way from Yesler Way North to Bay Street and Myrtle Edwards Park, is the city's single most popular attraction, and much like San Francisco's Fisherman's Wharf area, which is both good and bad. Yes, it's very touristy, with tacky gift shops, saltwater taffy, T-shirts galore, and lots of overpriced restaurants, but it's also home to the Seattle Aquarium, the Pike Place Market and its many vendors (see "Shopping," below), and a whole lot of scenery.

Located at Pier 59, the **Seattle Aquarium,** 1483 Alaskan Way (© **206/386-4300;** www.seattleaquarium.org), has well-designed exhibits dealing with the water worlds of the Puget Sound region. The underwater dome is the aquarium's largest and most amazing exhibit, a round undersea room (accessible via a short tunnel) where visitors are surrounded by a fish-filled 400,000-gallon tank. The aquarium is open daily 9:30am to 5pm. Admission is $17 adults/youths ages 13 and over, $11 kids ages 4 to 12, plus extra for special exhibits.

At Pier 57, the **Bay Pavilion** (www.pier57seattle.com) has a vintage carousel and a video arcade nestled among shops and restaurants. At Piers 55 and 56, boats leave for 1½-hour harbor cruises, as well as trips to **Tillicum Village,** a faux Northwest Native longhouse built for the 1962 Seattle World's Fair, located at Blake Island State Marine Park, across Puget Sound. It's a beautiful spot. **Tillicum Village Tours** (© **800/426-1205** or 206/933-8600; www.tillicumvillage.com) bundles a cruise on Puget Sound with a lunch or dinner of alder-smoked salmon and a performance of traditional masked dances. The 4-hour tour costs $80 adults, $30 kids. At **Pier 54,** you'll find companies offering sea-kayak tours, sport-fishing trips, jet-boat tours, and bicycle rentals.

The **Seattle Art Museum,** 1300 First Ave. (at University St.) (© **206/654-3100;** www.seattleartmuseum.org), is a repository for everything from old masters and Andy Warhol to African masks and one of the nation's premier collections of Northwest Coast Indian art. It reopened in 2007 after an expansion that added 70% more gallery space. Its entrance is unmistakable, fronted by Jonathan Borofsky's giant, kinetic *Hammering Man* sculpture. The museum is open Wednesday to Sunday 10am to 5pm (Thurs–Fri 9pm). Admission is $15 adults, $12 seniors, $9 students/youths ages 13 to 17, free for kids 12 and under. One mile northwest along the waterfront, the museum's **Olympic Sculpture Park,** 2901 Western Ave. at Broad Street, is a 9-acre outdoor site, opened in 2007, where world-class sculpture (by the likes of Richard Serra, Alexander Calder, Mark Di Suvero, and Tony Smith) sits amid lawns planted with native ground cover, all with wide views of the Olympic Mountains and Puget Sound. It's a stunning spot, and admission is free.

To the west, **Seattle Center** was the epicenter of the 1962 World's Fair and is still home to the fair's futuristic **Space Needle,** 203 Sixth Ave. N. (© **206/905-2100;** www.spaceneedle.com), a 607-foot tower that's become the quintessential symbol of

Seattle

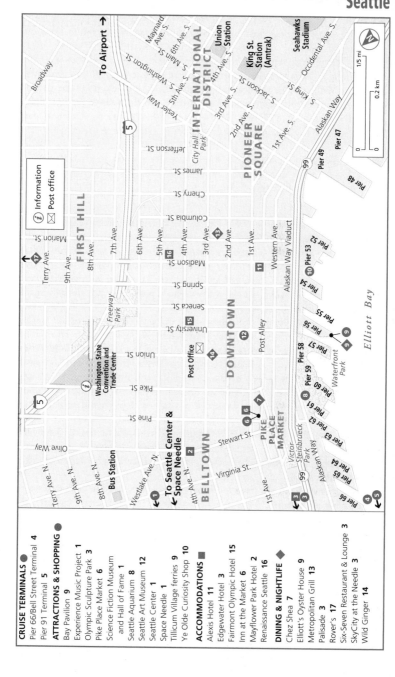

CRUISE TERMINALS ●
Pier 66/Bell Street Terminal **4**
Pier 91 Terminal **5**

ATTRACTIONS & SHOPPING ●
Bay Pavilion **9**
Experience Music Project **1**
Olympic Sculpture Park **3**
Pike Place Market **6**
Science Fiction Museum
  and Hall of Fame **1**
Seattle Aquarium **8**
Seattle Art Museum **12**
Seattle Center **1**
Space Needle **1**
Tillicum Village ferries **9**
Ye Olde Curiosity Shop **10**

ACCOMMODATIONS ■
Alexis Hotel **11**
Edgewater Hotel **3**
Fairmont Olympic Hotel **15**
Inn at the Market **6**
Mayflower Park Hotel **2**
Renaissance Seattle **16**

DINING & NIGHTLIFE ◆
Chez Shea **9**
Elliott's Oyster House **9**
Metropolitan Grill **13**
Palisade **3**
Rover's **17**
Six-Seven Restaurant & Lounge **3**
SkyCity at the Needle **3**
Wild Ginger **14**

Seattle. At 518 feet above ground level, the views from its observation deck are stunning. High-powered telescopes let you zoom in on distant sights, and there's a lounge and two very expensive restaurants inside. It's open Monday to Thursday 10am to 9:30pm, Friday and Saturday 9:30am to 10:30pm, Sunday 9:30am to 9:30pm. Admission is $17 adults/youths ages 14 and over, $15 seniors, $9 kids ages 4 to 13. Next door, the Frank Gehry–designed building that looks like it's in the process of melting is home to the **Experience Music Project** and the **Science Fiction Museum and Hall of Fame** (© 877/367-7361; www.empsfm.org). Inside, the music part of the building has displays, interactive music rooms, performance spaces, galleries, and research facilities dedicated to all phases of American popular music, while the Sci-Fi Museum holds artifacts spanning the history of science fiction, in print, film, and TV. Both places are open daily 10am to 5pm. Admission is $15 adults, $12 seniors/kids ages 5 to 17, free for kids ages 4 and under.

SHOPPING

Inland from the waterfront, between Pike and Pine streets at First Avenue, the historic **Pike Place Market** (© 206/682-7453; www.pikeplacemarket.org) was originally a farmers' market and is now a National Historic District, home to more than 200 local craftspeople and artists who sell their creations here throughout the year. It's one of the city's great destinations for both locals and visitors, loaded with excellent restaurants and shops and plenty of street performers. At press time, the market was in the midst of an extensive 4-year renovation designed to shore up its century-old buildings and modernize their systems. Some areas of the market and some shops may be closed temporarily during different phases of construction.

To the east, **Ye Olde Curiosity Shop,** 1001 Alaskan Way (© 206/682-5844; www.yeoldecuriosityshop.com), is a cross between a souvenir store and *Ripley's Believe It or Not.* It's weird! It's tacky! It's always packed! See Siamese-twin calves, a natural mummy, the Lord's Prayer on a grain of rice, a narwhal tusk, shrunken heads, and a 67-pound snail. The collection of oddities was started by Joe Standley in 1899. Oh, and they sell a lot of wacky stuff, too.

The corner of **Pine Street** and **Fifth Avenue** is ground zero for upscale Seattle shopping, home to two major department stores (**Nordstrom** and **Macy's**) and two upscale urban shopping malls (**Westlake Center** and **Pacific Place**). Other boutiques fan out to the east and south.

South of downtown, the historic **Pioneer Square** area has the city's greatest concentration of art galleries (some of which specialize in Native-American art), along with the country's largest concentration of **Victorian-Romanesque architecture,** and a lot of bars (see "Dining & Nightlife," below).

WHERE TO STAY

In an enviable location halfway between Pike Place Market and Pioneer Square and only 2 blocks from the waterfront, the **Alexis Hotel,** 1007 First Ave., at Madison Street (© 866/356-8894 or 206/624-4844; www.alexishotel.com), part of the Kimpton group of boutique hotels, is a sparkling gem with a pleasant mix of classic styling and a friendly staff. Cruise season rates: from $225 double. The **Fairmont Olympic Hotel,** 411 University St. (© 888/363–5022 or 206/621-1700; www.fairmont.com/seattle), is one of the bigger, and absolutely one of the most elegant, hotels in Seattle, reminiscent of an Italian Renaissance palace. Cruise season rates: from $229 double.

The **Edgewater Hotel,** 2411 Alaskan Way, at Pier 67 (© **800/624-0670;** www. edgewaterhotel.com), may look like a mountain lodge, but it's actually right on the water, built on Pier 67 over the waters of Elliott Bay, right downtown. Rooms have rustic lodgepole-pine furniture; the lobby affords gorgeous sunset views. Cruise season rates: from $249 double.

Renaissance Seattle, 515 Madison St. (© **800/546-9184;** www.renaissancehotels. com), has larger-than-average rooms, many with views of either Puget Sound or the Cascade Range. Cruise season rates: from $170 double. If shopping or sipping martinis is your thing, stay at the **Mayflower Park Hotel,** 405 Olive Way (© **800/426-5100;** www.mayflowerpark.com), built in 1927, connected to the upscale shops of Westlake Center, and flanked by Nordstrom and Macy's. The hotel's Oliver's Lounge also serves Seattle's best martinis. Cruise season rates: from $149 double. The **Inn at the Market,** 86 Pine St. (© **800/446-4484** or 206/443-3600; www.innatthemarket.com), meanwhile, is situated right at Pike Place Market, providing an understated European atmosphere, spacious accommodations, proximity to restaurants and shopping, and views of Elliott Bay from its rooftop deck. Cruise season rates: from $245 double.

DINING & NIGHTLIFE

In a quiet corner of Pike Place Market, **Chez Shea,** 94 Pike St. (© **206/467-9990;** www.chezshea.com), has candlelit tables, subdued lighting, views of ferries crossing the bay, and superb meals. It all adds up to the perfect combination for a romantic dinner. Main courses: $23 to $35. Closed on Monday.

If you're feeling above it all, pick a restaurant to match. **SkyCity at the Needle,** in the Space Needle at 400 Broad St. (© **800/937-9582** or 206/905-2100; www.space needle.com/restaurant), has the best views in Seattle. Simply prepared steaks and seafood make up the bulk of the menu. Main courses: $34 to $59. At **Rover's,** 2808 E. Madison St. (© **206/325-7442;** www.rovers-seattle.com), chef Thierry Rautureau combines his love of local ingredients with classic French training to produce a distinctive take on Northwest cuisine. Main courses: $16 to $27; five-course tasting menu: $99. Closed on Monday.

For waterfront dining, head to the Edgewater Hotel's **Six-Seven Restaurant & Lounge,** 2411 Alaskan Way, at Pier 67 (© **206/269-4575;** www.edgewaterhotel. com), which provides superb food, very cool decor, a great little deck, and one of the best views from any restaurant in the city. Main courses: $16 to $39. Another waterfront option, **Palisade,** Elliott Bay Marina, 2601 W. Marina Place (© **206/285-1000;** www.palisaderestaurant.com), has a 180-degree view that takes in Elliott Bay, downtown, and West Seattle. Never mind that it also has great food and some of the most memorable decor of any Seattle restaurant. Main courses: $19 to $59. For the best selection of oysters, head to **Elliott's Oyster House,** 1201 Alaskan Way, Pier 56 (© **206/623-4340;** www.elliottsoysterhouse.com), where the oyster bar can have as many as 20 varieties of oysters. Main courses: $15 to $40.

Wild Ginger, 1401 Third Ave. (© **206/623-4450;** www.wildginger.net), is a long-time Seattle favorite, serving Pan-Asian specialties in a stylish and usually very busy setting. Pull up a comfortable stool around the large satay grill and watch the cooks grill little skewers of anything from chicken to scallops to pork to lamb. Main courses:

$13 to $30. For steaks, go to **Metropolitan Grill,** 820 Second Ave. (© **206/624-3287;** www.themetropolitangrill.com), which serves corn-fed, aged beef grilled over mesquite charcoal. Main courses: $20 to $70.

Much of Seattle's evening entertainment scene is clustered in the **Seattle Center** and **Pioneer Square** areas, the former hosting theater, opera, and classical-music performances, the latter a bar-and-nightclub district. Seattle Center is home of the Space Needle and several performance halls for the Seattle Opera and the Seattle Symphony. Pioneer Square, centered around the corner of First Avenue and Yesler Way, is known for its restored 1890s buildings, tree-lined streets, and cobblestone plazas, plus a plethora of restaurants and bars.

16 Tampa, Florida

Tampa was a sleepy port until Cuban immigrants founded **Ybor City**'s cigar industry in the 1880s. A few years later, Henry B. Plant built a railroad to carry tourists into town and constructed his garish Tampa Bay Hotel (now the Henry B. Plant Museum). During the Spanish-American War, Teddy Roosevelt trained his Rough Riders here and walked the Ybor City streets with Cuban revolutionary José Marti. A land boom in the 1920s gave the city its charming, Victorian-style **Hyde Park** suburb (now a gentrified area, just across the Hillsborough River from downtown), and the go-go 1980s and 1990s brought skyscrapers, a convention center, a performing-arts center, and lots of shopping and dining options to the **downtown** area.

On the western shore of Tampa Bay, **St. Petersburg** is the picturesque and pleasant flip side of Tampa's busy business, industrial, and shipping life. Originally conceived and built primarily for tourists and wintering snowbirds, it's got a nice downtown area, some quality museums, and a few good restaurants.

GETTING TO TAMPA & THE PORT

The Port of Tampa's three **cruise terminals** (© **813/905-7678;** www.tampaport.com) are set along deep-water Ybor Channel, amid a complicated network of channels and harbors near historic Ybor City. Access is via Channelside Drive. Parking at any of the terminals is $14 per day.

If you're coming by air, you'll probably land at **Tampa International Airport** (© **813/870-8700;** www.tampaairport.com), 5 miles west of downtown Tampa. If you haven't arranged transfers with your cruise line, the port is an easy 30-minute **taxi** ride away; the set fare is $25 per car for up to four people.

GETTING AROUND   Taxis in Tampa do not normally cruise the streets for fares; instead, they line up at public loading places, such as the airport, cruise terminal, and major hotels. **Yellow Cab** (© **813/253-0121;** www.yellowcaboftampa.com) and **United Cab** (© **813/253-2424;** www.unitedtaxicab.com) charge $2 for the first ⅕ of a mile and 45¢ for each ⅕ mile thereafter. All major **car rental** companies have counters at the airport. For transit between downtown and Ybor City, there's the 2⅖-mile **TECO Line Street Car System** (© **813/254-4278;** www.tecolinestreetcar.org), whose old-fashioned (but new-built) streetcars are powered by overhead power lines. The cars run every 30 minutes; one-way fares are $2.50.

BEST CRUISE LINE SHORE EXCURSIONS

Tampa City Tour ($42, 4 hr.): This tour visits Ybor City and the Ybor State Museum, and passes the University of Tampa and Hyde Park on the way to the airport.

BUSCH GARDENS

Admission prices are high, but **Busch Gardens Africa,** 3000 E. Busch Blvd., at McKinley Drive/North 40th Street (© **888/800-5447;** www.buschgardens.com), remains Tampa Bay's most popular attraction, an Africa-themed miniworld full of thrill rides, games, live entertainment, shops, restaurants, and habitats that are home to more than 2,000 animals.

The park has eight areas, each with its own theme, animals, live entertainment, thrill rides, kiddie attractions, dining, and shopping. A Skyride cable car soars over the park, offering a bird's-eye view of it all. Turn left after the main gate and head to **Morocco,** a walled city with exotic architecture, crafts demonstrations, a sultan's tent with snake charmers, and an exhibit with alligators and turtles. The Moorish-style Moroccan Palace Theater features an ice show that many families consider to be the park's best entertainment for both adults and children. You can also attend a song-and-dance show in the Marrakesh Theater. Overlooking it all is the Crown Colony Restaurant, the park's largest dining spot.

After watching the snake charmers, walk east past Anheuser-Busch's fabled Clydesdale horses to **Egypt,** where you can visit King Tut's tomb with its replicas of the real treasures and listen to comedian Martin Short narrate Akbar's Adventure Tours, a wacky simulator that "transports" one and all across Egypt via camel, biplane, and mine car. The whole room moves on this ride, which lasts only 5 minutes—much less time than the usual wait to get inside. Youngsters can dig for their own ancient treasures in a sand area. Adults and kids 54 inches or taller can ride Montu, the tallest and longest inverted roller coaster in the world, with seven upside-down loops. Your feet dangle loose on Montu, so make sure your shoes are tied tightly and your lunch has had time to digest.

From Egypt, walk to the **Edge of Africa,** the most unique of the park's eight areas, and home to most of the large animals. Go immediately to the Expedition Africa Gift Shop and try to get on one of the park's zoologist-led wildlife tours.

Next stop is **Nairobi,** the most beautiful part of the park, where you can see gorillas and chimpanzees in their lush rainforest habitat in the Myombe Reserve. Nairobi also has a baby-animal nursery, a petting zoo, turtle and reptile displays, an exhibit of sadly bored-looking elephants, and Curiosity Caverns, where bats, reptiles, and small mammals that are active in the dark are kept in cages (it's the most traditional zoolike area here). The entry to Rhino Rally, the park's safari adventure, is at the western end of Nairobi.

Now head to the **Congo,** where the highlights are the rare white Bengal tigers that live on Claw Island. The Congo is also home to Kumba, the largest and fastest roller coaster in the southeastern United States (54-in. minimum height for riders), and the Congo River Rapids, where you're turned loose in round boats that float down the swiftly flowing "river" (42-in. minimum)—you will get drenched (and refreshed on a hot day). Bumper cars and kiddie rides can be found here, too.

From the Congo, walk south into **Stanleyville,** a prototype African village, with a shopping bazaar, orangutans living on an island, and the Stanleyville Theater, featuring shows for children. Two more water rides here are the Tanganyika Tidal Wave (48-in. minimum height for riders), where you'll come to a very damp end, and the Stanley Falls Flume (an aquatic version of a roller coaster). Also, the picnic-style Stanleyville Smokehouse serves ribs and chicken—some of the best chow in the park.

Up next is **Land of the Dragons,** the most entertaining area for small children. They can spend the day enjoying a variety of entertainment in a fairy-tale setting, plus just-for-kids rides. The area is dominated by Dumphrey, a whimsical dragon that interacts with visitors and guides children around a three-story treehouse with winding stairways, tall towers, stepping stones, illuminated water geysers, and an echo chamber.

The next stop is **Bird Gardens,** the park's original core, offering rich foliage, lagoons, and a free-flight aviary for hundreds of exotic birds, including golden and American bald eagles. Be sure to see the Florida flamingos and Australian koalas while you're here.

If your stomach can take another hair-raising ride, try **Gwazi** (48-in. minimum for riders), an adrenaline-pumping attraction in which a pair of old-fashioned wooden roller coasters (named the Lion and the Tiger) start simultaneously and whiz within a few feet of each other six times as they roar along at 50 mph and rise to 90 feet. If you want to experience the park's fifth roller coaster, head to **Timbuktu** and climb aboard the **Scorpion,** a high-speed number with a 60-foot drop and 360-degree loop (42-in. height minimum). Or if you're really crazy, check out the floorless **SheiKra,** where for 200 feet up and 90 degrees straight down, you can view the world—from a floorless perspective. For visual amusement, there's *Pirates 4-D,* an animated "4-D" special effects movie and theater production starring comedic actor Leslie Nielsen. **Jungala** is a 4-acre attraction in the Congo area that features exotic creatures, animal interactions, multistory family play areas, rides, and live entertainment.

One-day, one-park admission is $75 adults and $65 kids ages 3 to 9. Parking is $12. Various combo tickets are also available, as is a 6-hour "zookeeper-for-a-day" program (tack $250 onto your admission) and other interactive options. Park hours vary, but generally it opens around 9:30 or 10am and closes between 7 and 9pm. See the website for the calendar of hours and events. To get here, take I-275 northeast of downtown to Busch Boulevard (exit 33), and go east 2 miles to the entrance on 40th Street (McKinley Ave.).

EXPLORING THE REST OF TAMPA ON YOUR OWN

Tampa is best explored by car, as only the commercial district can be covered on foot. If you want to go to the beach, you'll have to head to neighboring St. Petersburg. **Ybor City,** Tampa's historic Latin enclave and one of only three National Historic Districts in Florida, lies only a mile or so from the cruise ship docks. Once known as the cigar capital of the world, Ybor provides a charming slice of the past with its Spanish architecture, antique street lamps, wrought-iron balconies, ornate grillwork, and renovated cigar factories. Stroll along Seventh Avenue, the main artery (closed to traffic at night), where you'll find cigar shops, boutiques, nightclubs, and the famous 100-year-old Columbia Restaurant (see "Dining & Nightlife," below). The **Ybor City Museum State Park,** 1818 Ninth Ave., between 18th and 19th streets (© **813/247-6323;** www.ybormuseum.org), is primarily devoted to the area's cigar history, with a collection of cigar labels, cigar memorabilia, and works by local artisans. It's open daily 9am to 5pm. Admission is $4 and walking tours of Ybor City cost $8.

With 13 silver minarets and distinctive Moorish architecture, the stunning **Henry B. Plant Museum,** 401 W. Kennedy Blvd. (© **813/254-1891;** www.plantmuseum.com), is the focal point of the Tampa skyline. This national historic landmark, built in 1891 as the Tampa Bay Hotel, is filled with European and Oriental furnishings and decorative arts from the original hotel collection. It's open Tuesday to Saturday 10am

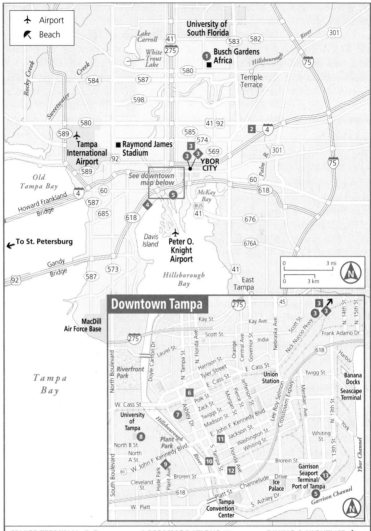

Downtown Tampa

CRUISE TERMINAL 5 ●

ATTRACTIONS & SHOPPING ●

Busch Gardens Africa **1**
Henry B. Plant Museum **8**
Tampa Museum of Art **7**
Ybor cigar shops **3**
Ybor City Museum State Park **3**

ACCOMMODATIONS ■

Hilton Garden Inn **3**
Hyatt Regency Tampa **12**
Seminole Hard Rock Hotel
  & Casino **2**
Tampa Marriott Waterside
  Hotel & Marina **11**
Vinoy Renaissance Resort
  & Golf Club **6**

DINING & NIGHTLIFE ◆

Bern's Steak House **4**
Centro Ybor **3**
Channelside Bay Plaza **13**
Columbia Restaurant **3**
Mise en Place **9**
Restaurant BT **4**

to 5pm, Sunday noon to 5pm. Admission is $10 adults, $7 seniors/students, $5 kids ages 4 to 12.

The permanent collection of the **Tampa Museum of Art,** 600 N. Ashley Dr. (© **813/274-8732;** www.tampamuseum.com), is especially strong in ancient Greek, Etruscan, and Roman artifacts, as well as 20th-century art. It's all housed in a new 66,000-square-foot facility in downtown Tampa's Curtis Hixon Waterfront Park. Its ultramodern, boxy aluminum exterior houses seven galleries with translucent ceilings. The museum is open Monday to Friday 11am to 7pm (Thurs 9pm), Saturday and Sunday 11am to 5pm.

BEACHES

You have to start at **St. Petersburg,** across the bay, for a north-to-south string of inter-connected white sandy shores. Most beaches have restrooms, refreshment stands, and picnic areas. You can park either on the street at a meter (usually 25¢ for each half-hour) or at one of the four major parking lots situated, from north to south, at: **Sand Key Park,** in Clearwater, beside Gulf Boulevard (also known as Rte. 699), just south of the Clearwater Pass Bridge; **Redington Shores Beach Park,** beside Gulf Boulevard at 182nd Street; **Treasure Island Park,** on Gulf Boulevard just north of 108th Avenue; and **St. Pete Beach Park,** beside Gulf Boulevard at 46th Street.

SHOPPING

The most distinctive shopping here is in Ybor City. The area is no longer the major producer of hand-rolled cigars it once was, but you can still watch artisans making sto-gies at the **Gonzalez y Martinez Cigar Factory/Columbia Cigar Store,** 2103 Seventh Ave., in the Columbia Restaurant building (© **813/247-2469**). Rollers are on duty Monday through Saturday. You can also stock up on fine domestic and imported cigars at **El Sol,** 1728 E. Seventh Ave. (© **813/248-5905;** www.elsolcigars.com), the city's oldest cigar store; **La Harencia De Cuba,** 1817 E. Seventh Ave. (© **813/248-9620;** www.ramirezcigars.com); and the **King Corona Cigar Factory,** 1523 E. Seventh Ave. (© **813/241-9109;** http://kingcoronacigars.com).

WHERE TO STAY

All of the hotels listed in this section are in downtown Tampa or Ybor City.

The modern, four-story **Hilton Garden Inn,** 1700 E. Ninth Ave. (© **800/445-8667;** www.hiltongardeninn.com), is primarily oriented to business travelers, but it's just 2 blocks north of the heart of Ybor City's dining and entertainment district. Cruise season rates: from $101 double. The **Hyatt Regency Tampa,** Two Tampa City Center at 211 N. Tampa St. (© **800/233-1234;** http://tamparegency.hyatt.com), sits in Tampa's commercial center and also caters mostly to the corporate crowd. Cruise season rates: from $109 double. The **Tampa Marriott Waterside Hotel & Marina,** 700 S. Florida Ave. (© **800/228-9290;** www.marriott.com), has a lot of rooms with balconies overlooking the bay or city (the best views are high up on the south side). Cruise season rates: from $159 double.

If the slots on the ship aren't enough for you, the 500-room **Seminole Hard Rock Hotel & Casino,** 5223 Orient Rd. (© **866/502-7529;** www.seminolehardrock tampa.com), has a 130,000-square-foot casino plus several other grand features—stay here if you're looking for lots of excitement. Cruise season rates: from $189 double.

For a special experience farther from the cruise docks, the **Vinoy Renaissance Resort & Golf Club,** 501 Fifth Ave. NE at Beach Drive, St. Petersburg (℗ **888/ 303-4430;** www.marriott.com), is the grande dame of the region's hotels. Built as the Vinoy Park in 1925, this elegant Spanish-style establishment was restored meticulously in the 1990s. Many rooms have lovely views of Tampa Bay. Accommodations in the newer wing (the Tower) are slightly larger than those in the hotel's original core. Cruise season rates: from $169 double.

DINING & NIGHTLIFE

Nightfall transforms **Ybor City,** Tampa's century-old Latin Quarter, into a hotbed of Cuban food, music, poetry readings, and after-midnight coffee and dessert. The nearly 100-year-old **Columbia Restaurant,** 2117 Seventh Ave. E. (℗ **813/248-4961;** www.columbiarestaurant.com), occupies an attractive tile-sheathed building that fills an entire city block between 21st and 22nd streets, about a mile from the cruise docks. The aura is pre-Castro Cuba, and the simpler your dish is, the better it's likely to be. Filet mignon and roasted pork, as well as the black beans, yellow rice, and plantains are flavorful and well prepared. Catch a flamenco show on the dance floor Monday through Saturday. Main courses: $15 to $30. After dinner, all you have to do is stroll along Seventh Avenue East, between 15th and 20th streets, and you'll hear music blaring out of the clubs that change names and characters frequently. Just follow your ears into the one that sounds best to you. With all of the sidewalk seating, it's easy to judge what the clientele is like, too. At **Centro Ybor,** a shopping/entertainment complex between Seventh and Eighth avenues and 15th and 17th streets (℗ **813/242-4660;** www.centroybor.com), you'll find a multiscreen cineplex, several restaurants, a comedy club, a large open-air bar, and a bunch of typical mall-type stores. The Ybor City Chamber of Commerce has its **Cigar Museum & Visitor Center** here, too, on Eighth Avenue next to Centro Español.

Although Ybor City is better known, Tampa's trendiest dining scene is actually along South Howard Avenue, between West Kennedy Boulevard and the bay in affluent Hyde Park. That's where you'll find **Mise en Place,** 442 W. Kennedy Blvd., opposite the University of Tampa (℗ **813/254-5373;** www.miseonline.com), run by chef Marty Blitz and his wife, Maryann, the culinary darlings of Tampa since 1986. They present the freshest of ingredients for a creative, eclectic menu that changes weekly. Main courses: $19 to $36. Hyde Park is also the home of **Bern's Steak House,** 1208 S. Howard Ave. (℗ **813/251-2421;** www.bernssteakhouse.com), whose steaks are close to perfect. You order according to thickness and weight. Main courses: $21 to $233. Close by, **Restaurant BT,** 1633 W. Snow Ave. (℗ **813/258-1916;** www. restaurantbt.com), deserves every bit of the massive hype it's received lately, serving French-Vietnamese fare that's as gorgeous as it is delicious, and the place has a sophisticated, stylish ambience to boot. Main courses: $17 to $29.

Within steps of the cruise ship piers, the shopping, dining, and entertainment complex known as **Channelside Bay Plaza,** 615 Channelside Dr. (℗ **813/223-4250;** www.channelsidebayplaza.com), continues to grow. Worthwhile eateries here include Stumps Supper Club and Tinatapas.

17 Vancouver, British Columbia

Situated in the extreme southwestern corner of British Columbia, Vancouver is probably one of the "newest" cities you'll ever visit, and it's certainly one of the most cosmopolitan. New glass-and-steel high-rises create a distinctive skyline, and a medley of foreign tongues testify to the city's international character. There's a youthfulness, too, a certain Pacific chic that consists of equal parts movie-biz buzz (the city has been a setting for so many movies that it's sometimes called Hollywood North) and pure wonderment over living in such a beautiful, vibrant place. It's everything a midsize city should be: both majestic and intimate, bustling and laid-back, sophisticated and free-spirited, and with a wealth of natural beauty all around—from the wide waters of Burrard Inlet to the deep green woods of Stanley Park to the snow-capped mountains in the north. Rich Native culture, a thriving Asian community, numerous summertime festivals, and a great arts scene fill out the picture. What's more, Vancouverites are just so blatantly *nice.* Maybe it's all that fresh air. Who knows, but it makes us want to move here every time we visit.

Though Seattle has usurped some of Vancouver's cruise steam over the past several years, Vancouver is still the major southern embarkation port for Alaska cruises, and it's occasionally a port of call as well.

Note: At press time, the exchange rate between U.S. and Canadian dollars was essentially one-to-one, though it's fluctuated by as much as 20¢ over the past couple of years. Prices in this section are in Canadian dollars.

GETTING TO VANCOUVER & THE PORT

Most cruise ships dock at **Canada Place,** at the end of Burrard Street (© **604/775-7200;** www.canadaplace.ca). The pier terminal is a city landmark designed to resemble a sailing ship setting off to sea. Next door is the new Convention Center, with its 6-acre green roof. Both buildings are at the edge of the downtown district and just a quick stroll from the **Gastown** area, with its cafes, art galleries, and souvenir shops (see below), and from **Robson Street,** a destination for trendy fashions. Hotels, restaurants, and shops are all located right near the terminal. Most visitors arrive in Vancouver by plane, touching down at **Vancouver International Airport** (© **604/207-7077;** www.yvr.ca), 8 miles south of downtown. The average **taxi** fare from the airport to downtown is between C$28 and C$32. Another option is the **Canada Line** train (**www.translink.ca/en/Rider-Info/Canada-Line**), built as part of the run-up to the 2010 Vancouver Winter Olympics. It takes you from the airport to downtown Vancouver's Waterfront Station in only 26 minutes, and the fare is C$8.75.

GETTING AROUND You can easily walk the downtown area of Vancouver, but if you want transportation, you've got a few options. **Car rental** agencies with local branches include Avis, Budget, Hertz Canada, and Thrifty, and **taxis** are always found around the major hotels and tourist sites. For public transportation, the **Translink system** (© **604/953-3333;** www.translink.bc.ca) includes electric buses, ferries, and the magnetic-rail SkyTrain. Fares are based on a zone system: A one-zone fare is C$2.50, two-zone is C$3.75, and three-zone is C$5. You can also get a 1-day all-zone pass for C$9.

BEST CRUISE LINE SHORE EXCURSIONS

We don't recommend taking the limited (and touristy) shore excursions offered here. You'll do a lot better just seeing the city on your own.

EXPLORING VANCOUVER ON YOUR OWN

Within easy walking distance of the pier, **Gastown**—situated between the waterfront and Hastings Street, from Cambie Street to Columbia—is Vancouver's oldest neighborhood. It retains its Victorian flavor of low, shoulder-to-shoulder buildings, ornate

Vancouver

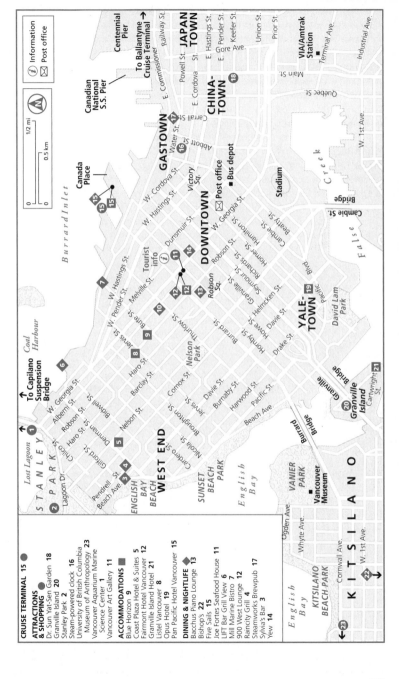

CRUISE TERMINAL 15 ●

ATTRACTIONS & SHOPPING ●
Dr. Sun Yat-Sen Garden **18**
Granville Island **20**
Stanley Park **2**
Steam-powered clock **16**
University of British Columbia
  Museum of Anthropology **23**
Vancouver Aquarium Marine
  Science Center **1**
Vancouver Art Gallery **11**

ACCOMMODATIONS ■
Blue Horizon **9**
Coast Plaza Hotel & Suites **5**
Fairmont Hotel Vancouver **12**
Granville Island Hotel **21**
Listel Vancouver **8**
Opus Hotel **19**
Pan Pacific Hotel Vancouver **15**

DINING & NIGHTLIFE ◆
Bacchus Piano Lounge **13**
Bishop's **22**
Five Sails **15**
Joe Fortes Seafood House **11**
LIFT Bar Grill View **6**
Mill Marine Bistro **7**
900 West Lounge **12**
Raincity Grill **4**
Steamworks Brewpub **17**
Sylvia's Bar **3**
Yew **14**

485

streetlights, and cobblestone squares, now leavened by expensive condos and high-end boutiques. The area was named for "Gassy" Jack Deighton, who in 1867 built a saloon in Maple Tree Square (at the intersection of Water, Alexander, and Carrall sts.) to serve the area's loggers and trappers. The Gastown of today has a touch of bohemia, with street musicians, galleries, boutiques, and antiques and art shops, plus lots of touristy stuff, and even more restaurants, clubs, and cafes. At the corner of Water and Cambie streets, a **steam-powered clock** draws its power from an underground steam system that heats many of downtown's buildings. It hoots the Westminster chimes every 15 minutes as steam vents from its top.

Adjoining Gastown, Vancouver's historic **Chinatown**—bordered by East Pender and Keefer streets between Carrall Street and Gore Avenue—is one of the largest in North America. Even though the vast majority of Vancouver's large Asian population has moved out, many return here to shop, keeping the area vital and lively. It's filled with bright-red low-rise buildings, photogenic Chinese gates, food, and open-air markets selling Chinese wares. Chinatown's biggest draw is the **Dr. Sun Yat-Sen Garden,** 578 Carrall St. (✆ **604/689-7133;** www.vancouverchinesegarden.com), a perfectly traditional Chinese garden based on the yin-yang principle, in which harmony is achieved by placing contrasting elements in juxtaposition: soft moving water against solid stone, smooth swaying bamboo around gnarled immovable rocks, dark pebbles against light pebbles, and so on. It's one of only a few classical Chinese gardens in North America (along with ones in Portland, Oregon, and Staten Island, New York, and another under development in Seattle), and was created by master artisans from Suzhou, the garden city of China. The garden is open Tuesday to Sunday 10am to 4:30pm. Admission is C$12 adults, C$10 seniors, C$9 students. Immediately next door, separated from the garden by only a classical footbridge and koi pond, the public **Dr. Sun Yat-Sen Park** is less meditative, but beautiful in its own right, with walking paths winding among Chinese trees and foliage. Admission is free.

Downtown, the **Vancouver Art Gallery,** 750 Hornby St. (✆ **604/662-4719;** www.vanartgallery.bc.ca), is housed in a grand neoclassical building originally used as a courthouse. Its collection of more than 8,000 works is heavy on regional work (including a large collection by British Columbia native Emily Carr) and related works by other Canadian and international artists. There are also frequent large-scale temporary exhibitions, many of them in a very contemporary vein that contrasts nicely with the old-style museum building. The gallery is open daily 10am to 5pm (Tues 9pm). Admission is C$20 adults, C$10 seniors, C$9 students.

Only about a mile from the heart of downtown Vancouver, northwest of the cruise ship terminal, **Stanley Park** (http://vancouver.ca/parks/parks/stanley) is one of Vancouver's great gems. Its 1,000 acres comprise rose gardens, totem poles, a yacht club, a water park for kids, miles of wooded hiking trails, and great views all around. For an overview, rent a bike from Spokes, 1798 W Georgia St. at Denman (✆ **604/688-5141;** www.vancouverbikerental.com), and ride the 11km (6.5-mile) **biking and walking trail** that circles the park's perimeter, letting on to amazing views and passing many of the park's best sights. Rentals are available from about C$7 per hour (C$20 half-day).

Within Stanley Park, the outstanding **Vancouver Aquarium Marine Science Center** (✆ **604/659-3474;** www.vanaqua.org) is one of North America's largest and best, with an excellent display on the Pacific Northwest, plus sea otters, beluga whales, sea lions, and Pacific white-sided dolphins. The center is open daily 9:30am to 5pm. Admission is C$22 adults, C$17 seniors/kids ages 13 to 18, C$14 kids ages 4 to 12.

If you're up for a 20-minute drive west of downtown, the **University of British Columbia's Museum of Anthropology,** 6393 NW Marine Dr. (© **604/822-5087;** www.moa.ubc.ca), isn't just any old museum. In 1976, architect Arthur Erickson re-created a classic Native post-and-beam structure out of modern concrete and glass to house one of the world's finest collections of West Coast Native art. You enter through doors that resemble a huge, carved, bent-cedar box. Artifacts from potlatch ceremonies flank the ramp leading to the Great Hall's collection of totem poles and Haida artwork, including masterpieces by sculptor Bill Reid; other artwork and sculpture are found outdoors. The museum is open daily 10am to 5pm (Tues 9pm). Admission is C$14 adults, C$12 students/seniors, free for kids ages 6 and under.

SHOPPING

About 1½ miles southwest of the cruise docks, **Granville Island** (www.granville island.com) is a former industrial site with warehouses and factories that now house galleries, museums, restaurants, theaters, shops, a small brewery, and a few remaining industrial businesses to keep the place real. You could easily spend a full day here, browsing for crafts, grabbing picnic fixin's from the incredible **Public Market** (one of the best gourmet food markets we've ever seen, anywhere), strolling along the waterfront, and watching the street performers, then stay into the evening to enjoy a great dinner and catch a comedy show or theater performance. If you have a few thousand bucks to drop (or are willing to pretend you do), stop in to **Eagle Spirit Gallery,** 1803 Maritime Mews (© **604/801-5205;** www.eaglespiritgallery.com), which specializes in original, museum-quality Northwest Coast Native and Inuit art, including hand-carved masks, argillite stone carvings, and paintings. (Several other Native art galleries are clustered on Water St. in Gastown, near the cruise docks.) To get to Granville Island, walk or take a taxi south on Burrard Street from the cruise docks. At some point, make a left 1 block to Hornby Street and then continue south all the way to the end. There, you'll find a dock for the **Aquabus** (© **604/689-5858;** www.the aquabus.com), a cute little ferry that will deposit you right by the Public Market. The one-way fare is C$3 adults, C$1.50 kids.

Downtown, not far inland from the cruise docks, **Robson Street** is chockablock with big international chain stores, high-fashion boutiques, coffeehouses, and bistros. In Gastown, **Water Street** may be a little too heavy on the knickknack shops, but it also boasts galleries of First Nations art, funky retro boutiques, and antiques shops.

WHERE TO STAY

Virtually all of Vancouver's downtown hotels are within walking distance of shops, restaurants, and attractions.

The **Fairmont Hotel Vancouver,** 900 W. Georgia St. (© **800/257-7544** or 604/684-3131; www.fairmont.com/hotelvancouver), is the grande dame of Vancouver's hotels. Designed on a generous scale, with a copper roof, marble interiors, and massive proportions, the hotel is all luxury and spaciousness, with marble bathrooms and mahogany furnishings in the guest rooms. If you enjoy picturing yourself in a 1930s movie, this is the place for you. Cruise season rates: from C$217 double.

The **Pan Pacific Hotel Vancouver,** Suite 300–999 Canada Place (© **800/937-1515;** www.panpacific.com), sits right atop Canada Place, home of the cruise terminal and a convention center. All of the guest rooms are modern, spacious, and comfortably furnished. Try to book a harborside room so you can enjoy the view. Cruise season rates: from C$275 double.

Right at the western end of the Robson Street shopping and restaurant strip are three worthwhile hotels. The **Listel Vancouver,** 1300 Robson St. (© **800/663-5491;** www.listel-vancouver.com), has subtly luxurious rooms and public areas adorned with quality contemporary art. In the evenings, you can hear live jazz at O'Doul's, the hotel's street-level restaurant and bar. Cruise season rates: from C$159 double. Just down Robson, the **Blue Horizon,** 1225 Robson St. (© **800/663-1333** or 604/688-1411; www.bluehorizonhotel.com), provides large rooms with comfortable if not adventurous decor, offset with some of the best views in the downtown and west end (above the 12th floor). Cruise season rates: C$159 double.

In trendy Yaletown, the seven-story **Opus Hotel,** 322 Davie St. (© **866/642-6787** or 604/642-6787; www.opushotel.com), is Vancouver's most stylish. Expect superstylish decor and artwork, lots of natural light, lots of amenities, and guest international DJs performing in the superhip lobby lounge. Cruise season rates: from C$200 double.

On Granville Island, the **Granville Island Hotel,** 1253 Johnston St. (© **800/663-1840** or 604/683-7373; www.granvilleislandhotel.com), has a beautiful waterfront setting, pleasantly decorated rooms (some with balconies), and a lovely dining patio outside. Cruise season rates: from C$235 double.

Just a few blocks from English Bay and busy Denman Street, the **Coast Plaza Hotel & Suites,** 1763 Comox St. (© **800/716-6199** or 604/688-7711; www.coast hotels.com/hotels/canada/bc/vancouver/coast_plaza/overview), has unremarkable decor, but a great location and amazing views from its upper floors. Cruise season rates: from C$190 double.

DINING & NIGHTLIFE

The **Five Sails,** in the Pan Pacific Hotel, Suite 410–999 Canada Place (© **604/844-2855;** www.fivesails.ca), combines truly top-notch food and a killer view of Coal Harbour, the Lions Gate Bridge, and the mountains. Cuisine is an eclectic mix of Thai, Mongolian, Japanese, Vietnamese, and nouvelle influences. Main courses: C$32 to C$52.

For a more hip and casual view of Coal Harbour, Stanley Park, and the North Shore mountains, there's **LIFT Bar Grill View,** 333 Menchions Mews (© **604/689-5438;** www.liftbarandgrill.com), which serves small dishes to be shared, as well as regular a la carte dishes. Sample fare includes such delights as venison with a chocolate-cherry demiglace, jumbo wild prawns with seared foie gras, and Thai curry duck confit. Main courses: C$22 to C$39.

Joe Fortes Seafood House, 777 Thurlow St. (© **604/669-1940;** www.joefortes.ca), is a two-story, dark-wood restaurant with an immensely popular bar. The roof garden is pure Vancouver, and pan-roasted oysters are a menu staple. Main courses: C$16 to C$58.

At **Bishop's,** 2183 W. Fourth Ave. (© **604/738-2025;** www.bishopsonline.com), owner John Bishop makes every customer feel special, and the candlelight, white linens, and soft jazz don't hurt, either. The food is even better: a mix of "contemporary home cooking" like roasted duck breast with sun-dried Okanagan Valley fruits and candied ginger glace. Main courses: C$36 to C$40; reservations required.

Just off English Bay Beach in the West End, **Raincity Grill,** 1193 Denman St. (© **604/685-7337;** www.raincitygrill.com), was one of the first restaurants in the city to concentrate on local produce and sustainable practices. Main courses: C$17 to C$36.

Vancouver has an enormous range of after-dinner spots. For a wine bar, choose the classic **900 West Lounge** at the Fairmont, 900 W. Georgia St. (© **604/684-3131**; www.fairmont.com), or the superstylish **Yew** at the Four Seasons, 791 W. Georgia St. (© **604/689-9333**; www.fourseasons.com). For a dark, woodsy piano lounge, head to the **Bacchus Piano Lounge** at the Wedgewood Hotel, 845 Hornby St. (© **604/689-7777**; www.wedgewoodhotel.com). Two Vancouver bars offer unmatched water views: to the south, **Sylvia's Bar** at the Sylvia Hotel, 1154 Gilford St. (© **604/681-9321**; www.sylviahotel.com), a woodsy, cozy spot with views of English Bay (and its famous sunsets) through big picture windows; and to the north, the **Mill Marine Bistro,** 1199 W. Cordova St. (© **604/687-6455**; www.millbistro.ca), Vancouver's largest outdoor dining and drinking spot, with wonderful views of Coal Harbour and North Vancouver mountains. In Gastown, near the cruise docks, the huge **Steamworks Brewpub,** 375 Water St. (© **604/689-2739**; www.steamworks.com), has different themed rooms for different tastes, from pub to wine bar to oyster bar.

10

The Caribbean, The Bahamas & the Panama Canal

The Caribbean is the classic cruise destination, tailored to people who want nice white-sand beaches, tiki bars serving tropical drinks, some hot island music, and sun, sun, sun—plus throngs of other cruise passengers enjoying it all with you. Culture and history also have their place in this region. In general, western Caribbean itineraries provide opportunities for visiting the ruins of Maya cities and temple sites on the mainland, while eastern Caribbean itineraries are more likely to offer reminders (albeit faint ones) of British, French, Spanish, and Dutch colonial history. Panama Canal itineraries mix the lore of that massive construction effort with rich Central American culture. And, of course, there's all that gorgeous Caribbean scenery, from the lush jungles of Dominica to the arid moonscape of Aruba.

The Caribbean islands each provide slightly different versions of sun and fun, so depending on your likes and dislikes, you'll appreciate some more than others. Some—especially St. Thomas and Nassau—are much more touristy and commercial than others, but they'll appeal to shoppers with their large variety of bustling stores. Others—Virgin Gorda, St. John, and Jost Van Dyke, for instance—are quieter and more natural and will appeal to those who'd rather walk along a calm beach or take a drive down a lonely, winding road amid lush tropical foliage. Ports such as St. Barts and Virgin Gorda have a low-key yachting-port atmosphere,

while Key West and Cozumel are all about whooping it up. In general, all the Caribbean islands are getting more business by bigger and bigger ships, and more of them. It's harder than ever to find the unspoiled, uncrowded corners of the Caribbean, though they still exist if you know where to look.

HOME PORTS FOR THIS REGION
Though the majority of Caribbean cruises still leave from the traditional Florida ports of **Miami, Fort Lauderdale, Port Canaveral,** and to a lesser extent **Tampa,** you can also sail from Galveston, Texas; New Orleans, Louisiana; Charleston, South Carolina; Norfolk, Virginia; Jacksonville, Florida; and even New York, Baltimore, and Philadelphia. Some Caribbean islands commonly serve as home ports, especially Puerto Rico's capital, **San Juan,** but also St. Thomas, Barbados, and others. The upside to these is that you'll start your cruise in the midst of the islands, and probably be able to visit more ports over the course of your trip. The downside is that except for San Juan, it can be more complicated and expensive to fly to these ports than to one of the mainland embarkation points.

LANGUAGE & CURRENCY
Both vary by island, though English is spoken widely in all the port towns and the U.S. dollar is commonly accepted everywhere. All prices in this chapter are quoted in U.S. dollars, though we include information on local currency in the individual reviews.

CALLING FROM THE U.S. & CANADA Most of the islands in this chapter are part of the North American Numbering Plan, meaning you call them just as you would another state or territory on the mainland, adding a "1" before the area code and local number. Where that is not the case (as with Mexico, Belize, the French islands, and so forth), we include dialing information in the port review.

SHOPPING TIPS You'll find it all here, from cheesy tourist souvenirs to jewelry (lots and lots of jewelry), perfume (ditto), and electronics, with some quality indigenous art available, too, if you look hard enough. Prices vary by port. Some—such as the U.S. Virgin Islands, St. Barts, St. Martin, and Aruba—are pretty pricey, while Cozumel and the ports of Jamaica are cheaper. **Duty-free merchandise** can save you as little as 5% to as much as 50%, so if there are particular goods you're thinking of buying, it pays to check prices at your local discount retailer before you leave home so you'll know whether you're really getting a bargain. Many ports have particularly good deals on **liquor,** though keep in mind you'll pay tax when coming back into the U.S. if you buy more than your legal limit (see section 5, "Tipping, Customs & Other End-of-Cruise Concerns," in chapter 3 for more information).

When shopping, be aware that some items sold may not be allowed by U.S. Customs. You might be eyeing that gorgeous piece of **black-coral jewelry,** for instance, but laws prohibiting the trade in endangered species make it illegal to bring many products made from coral and other marine animals back to the United States. (Remember, corals aren't rocks, they're living animals—a single branch of coral contains thousands of tiny marine invertebrates called polyps.) **Sea turtles,** too, are highly endangered, and sea horses and conch (yes, the ones you eat in restaurants), while not yet globally protected by law, are currently threatened with extinction. The shopkeeper selling items made from these creatures probably won't tell you they're questionable from a Customs standpoint, but the Customs agent sure will, and may fine you or, at the very least, confiscate the item if he catches you with it. Better to buy a cheap underwater camera and take pictures of these beauties on a snorkeling expedition—you get the memories, the evidence, a little exercise, and good karma to boot.

Cuban cigars are also prohibited by U.S. Customs. You'll see them all over the islands, but be aware that, *legally* speaking, you have to smoke 'em before you head for home.

1 The Cruise Lines' Private Islands

Ideally, a Caribbean cruise should be like acting out a Jimmy Buffett song—lots of eating, drinking, and hanging out on deserted beaches. If only it were that easy. As ships get bigger and cruise line fleets grow, some Caribbean ports feel like being at home in your SUV: all primped up and no place to go. Our recent experiences in St. Thomas, San Juan, Cozumel, and Nassau were more about traffic jams and crowded shopping malls than frosty margaritas on windswept beaches. With easily 15,000-plus passengers pouring off as many as 8 to 10 ships on an average day, it's goodbye to a relaxing beach paradise, and hello to queues, crowds, gridlock, and pushy solicitors.

The antithesis to all of this Caribbean madness, of course, is the cruise line private island, where only one ship or two ships at a time stop for the day. It seems as if these islands were invented solely to preserve the sanity of the cruise passenger. The mission is simple: provide passengers with a sane, surefire, hassle-free means to enjoy a classic day of sun and fun. All the mainstream lines (except Carnival) have private islands (or parts of islands) that are included as a port of call on many of their Caribbean and Bahamas itineraries. While few have any true Caribbean culture, they do allow cruisers a guaranteed beach day with all the trimmings and a more private experience than enjoyed at most ports' public beaches. Note that aside from Disney's Castaway Cay, none of the islands has a large dock, so passengers are ferried ashore by tender.

CELEBRITY CRUISES   See "Royal Caribbean & Celebrity Cruises," below.

COSTA CRUISES   Passengers on Costa's eastern Caribbean itineraries spend 1 day at **Catalina Island,** off the coast of the Dominican Republic. This relaxing patch of paradise has a long beach fringed by palm trees, with activities such as volleyball, beach Olympics, and snorkeling. The area adjacent to the tender dock is the busiest spot, as is to be expected, but if you walk down the beach a bit, you'll get a quieter, more private experience (though the coastline gets a little rocky when you get farther away from the dock). Costa provides cruisers with floating beach mats free of charge (most lines charge for them), so you can find your quiet nirvana by paddling out to sea. A local island vendor rents jet skis and offers banana-boat rides, the ship's spa staff sets up a cabana to do massages on the beach, and locals roam around offering them, too. (For a fraction of the cost on ship, a local woman gave our coauthor Heidi a great foot and shoulder massage.) Locals also sell coconuts for a couple of bucks apiece, first hacking off the end and plunking in a straw or two so you can drink the milk. After you're finished, take the coconut back and they'll whack the thing to pieces with a machete and scrape out the tender coconut meat for you to eat. Music and barbecues round out the day, and there's also a strip of shops hawking jewelry, beachwear, and other souvenirs. *Note:* On some itineraries, passengers must pay to hang out here for the day.

DISNEY CRUISE LINE   A port of call on all *Disney Magic* and *Disney Wonder* cruises, 1,000-acre, 3×2-mile **Castaway Cay** is an "out island" of The Bahamas. It's rimmed with idyllic, clear Bahamian waters and fine sandy beaches. Guests can swim and snorkel, rent bikes and boats, get their hair braided, shop, send postcards, have a massage, or just lounge in a hammock or on the beach. Barbecue burgers, ribs, fish, and chicken are available at Cookie's Bar-B-Q, and several bars are scattered around near the beaches.

The island's best quality is its accessibility. Unlike other private islands that require ships to anchor offshore and shuttle passengers back and forth on tenders, Castaway Cay's dock allows guests of *Magic* and *Wonder* to just step right off the ship and walk or take a shuttle tram to the island's attractions. Families can head to their own beach, lined with lounge chairs and pastel-colored umbrellas, where they can swim, explore a 12-acre snorkeling course, climb around on the offshore water-play structures, or rent a kayak, paddle boat, banana boat, sailboat, or other beach equipment. There's even a barnacle-encrusted, 175-foot *Flying Dutchman* ghost ship anchored offshore just for fun (it's an actual prop from Disney's *Pirates of the Caribbean: Dead Man's Chest,* which was filmed in Freeport). Teens have a beach of their own, where they can play volleyball, soccer, or tetherball or hit a new hangout spot called **Hide Out;** go on a Wild Side bike, snorkel, and kayak adventure; or design, build, and race their own boats. Parents who want some quiet time can drop preteens at Scuttle's Cove, a supervised children's center for ages 3 to 12, with activities including arts and crafts, music and theater, and scavenger hunts. An excavation site here allows kids to go on their own archaeological dig and make plaster molds of what they find—including a 35-foot reproduction of a whale skeleton. The new **Pelican Plunge** floating platform has two slides and other water features, and there's the **Spring-a-Leak** water park on shore as well with jets and geysers.

Meanwhile, Mom and Dad can walk, bike, or hop the shuttle to quiet, secluded Serenity Bay, a mile-long stretch of beach in the northwest part of the island, at the end of an old airstrip decorated with vintage prop planes for a 1940s feel. You can enjoy massages here in private cabanas open to a sea view on one side (sign up for your appointment at the onboard spa on the first day of your cruise to ensure a spot), and the Castaway Air Bar serves up drinks. Heidi sampled a piña colada and a deep-tissue massage at Serenity Bay while her kids were back in the nursery aboard the *Wonder,* and she gives it a giant thumbs-up.

Adult- and child-size bicycles can be rented for $6 per hour and there's a bike/walking path that lets you stretch those hamstrings, but don't go looking for scenery or wildlife—at best, you'll see the occasional bird or leaping lizard. Parasailing can be enjoyed for $79 (45 min., airborne 5–7 min.; ages 8 and over). All-terrain strollers with canopies and beach wheelchairs are available free of charge.

HOLLAND AMERICA LINE   Located on the 2,400-acre Bahamian island of Little San Salvador, 65-acre **Half Moon Cay** is a port of call on most of HAL's Caribbean and Panama Canal cruises. The sand here is ultrasoft, so go ahead and lie right down in it or flop on one of the many beach chairs or under a blue canvas sun shade (though you'll have to rent it; they're in limited supply).

Families will appreciate the water park at one end of the 2-mile beach (closest to the tender pier), where there are water slides on the sand for young children, as well as a couple for teens. Just offshore in the shallow turquoise sea, a cluster of floating toy animals—including a crocodile, shark, and octopus—are tethered to the sea floor and perfect for climbing. Other highlights of the beach area include massage huts as well as 15 air-conditioned, beachfront cabanas available for rent (the regular ones accommodate four people and start at $249 a day, while a superdeluxe cabana for up to 25 people has a private bar, hot tub, water slide, and a steeper price tag). A couple of hundred bucks will buy you butler service and an open bar. Away from the main beach area and accessible via a short tram ride, shore-excursion opportunities include horseback riding (1½ hr., including a scenic trail ride and a gallop through the surf), a visit to a 150×75-foot water pen where you can pet and feed tame stingrays, and a bicycle tour of part of the island. You can also sign up for windsurfing, snorkeling, kayaking, scuba diving, deep-sea fishing, parasailing, sailboarding, or aqua-cycling. Half Moon Cay has lunch facilities, several bars, a playground, and even nature trails through a wild bird preserve at a remote part of the island.

NORWEGIAN CRUISE LINE   NCL's private island, **Great Stirrup Cay,** is a stretch of palm-studded beachfront 120 miles east of Fort Lauderdale in the Berry Island chain of The Bahamas, and was the very first private resort developed by a cruise line in the Caribbean. At press time, a $20-million face-lift was in the works for the island, alleviating some of the crowding with a significant expansion of the cramped, rocky beach area. The renovation will add additional dining facilities, private beachside cabanas, a new kids' area, a straw market, and new beach volleyball courts.

Music is either broadcast or performed live, several bars dispense plenty of frosty tropical dinks, there's a generous barbecue-style lunch spread, and hammocks are strung between palms. For more active folks, several new island highlights include WaveRunner rentals, a floating water park, kayak tours through man-made rivers within the island, an eco-cruise, and a stingray encounter experience. Passengers can also ride paddle boats, sail Sunfish, go snorkeling or parasailing, or do nothing more

The Gulf of Mexico & the Caribbean

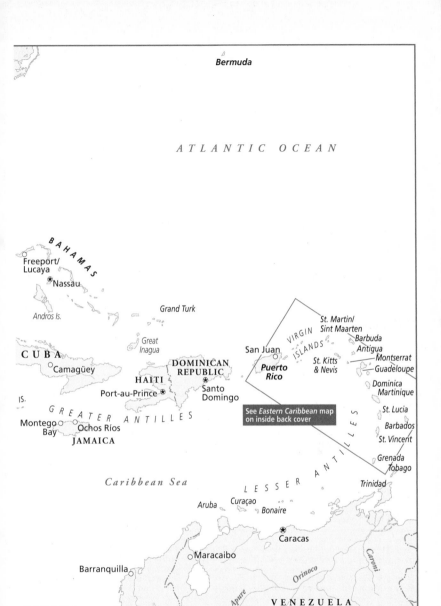

Bermuda

ATLANTIC OCEAN

BAHAMAS

Freeport/
Lucaya

Nassau

Andros Is.

Grand Turk

*Great
Inagua*

CUBA

Camagüey

DOMINICAN
REPUBLIC

HAITI

Port-au-Prince

Santo
Domingo

San Juan

*Puerto
Rico*

VIRGIN
ISLANDS

St. Martin/
Sint Maarten

Barbuda
Antigua

St. Kitts
& Nevis

Montserrat
Guadeloupe

Dominica
Martinique

IS.

GREATER ANTILLES

Montego
Bay

Ochos Ríos

JAMAICA

See *Eastern Caribbean* map
on inside back cover

St. Lucia

Barbados

St. Vincent

Grenada

Tobago

LESSER ANTILLES

Caribbean Sea

Trinidad

Aruba

Curaçao

Bonaire

Caracas

Maracaibo

Barranquilla

Caroni

Orinoco

VENEZUELA

Apure

PANAMA

Colon

Panama
City

San Cristóbal

Cauca

Magdalena

*Gulf of
Panama*

Medellín

COLOMBIA

Uraricuera

BRAZIL

than sunbathe all day long. For kids, there are volleyball tournaments and organized activities in the new play area.

PRINCESS CRUISES   Most of Princess's eastern and western Caribbean itineraries stop at **Princess Cays,** a 40-acre beachfront strip off the southwestern coast of Eleuthera in The Bahamas, which is basically cut off from the rest of the island. The half-mile of shoreline allows passengers to swim, snorkel, and make use of Princess's fleet of Hobie Cats, Sunfish, banana boats, kayaks, seaboards, aqua-bikes and pedal boats. (If you want to rent watersports equipment, be sure to book while aboard ship or even online, before your cruise, to ensure that you get what you want.) There's also a beach barbecue, three bars, and live music. Those who want to get away from it all can head for the several dozen tree-shaded hammocks at the far end of the beach. For kids, there's a supervised play area with a sandbox and a pirate-ship-themed playground. The Princess shop sells T-shirts and other clothing, plus souvenirs of the mug-and-key-chain variety, and local vendors set up stands around the island to hawk conch shells, shell anklets, straw bags, and other crafts, as well as to do hair braiding.

ROYAL CARIBBEAN & CELEBRITY CRUISES   Many ships of sister lines Royal Caribbean and Celebrity stop for a day at one or another of the lines' two private beach resorts, CocoCay and Labadee. Both have organized children's activities such as beach parties, volleyball, seashell collecting, and sand-castle building.

At **CocoCay** (aka Little Stirrup Cay), an otherwise uninhabited 140-acre landfall in The Bahamas' Berry Islands, you'll enjoy lots of beaches, hammocks, food, drink, and watersports, plus such activities as limbo contests, water-balloon tosses, relay races, and volleyball tournaments. Kids, both big and small, will like the aqua-park with a floating trampoline, water slides, and a sunken airplane and schooner for snorkelers. The newest gimmick: Kids ages 3 to 8 can now hop in battery-operated mini-race-cars for what the line bills as a "special driving adventure" on the Fisher-Price Power Wheels Track. For something quieter, head for Wanderer's Beach; it's a longer walk from the tender pier than the other beaches, so it's usually less crowded and quieter. With calm surf and ultrasoft sand, it's perfect for families with young children.

Labadee, an isolated, sun-flooded, 270-acre peninsula along Haiti's north coast, was largely unaffected by the horrendous earthquake that devastated the majority of the country in early 2010. It's a completely tourist-oriented and sequestered area, so even if you had been in Labadee just after the quake, you'd never know it was attached to the rest of devastated, poverty-stricken Haiti. In the spirit of keeping locals employed, especially in the time of such great tragedy, Royal Caribbean decided to maintain Labadee as a port of call in the immediate wake of the quake.

A rarity among the cruise lines' private islands, Labadee does give visitors a real glimpse of island culture. At the straightforwardly named Folkloric Show, a large, colorfully costumed troupe performs Haiti's distinctly African brand of dancing, drumming, and song; bands at the various bars and restaurants play the kind of acoustic guitar, banjo, and percussion "mento" music that was a precursor to reggae and other Caribbean styles. Five beaches spread around the peninsula are progressively less crowded the farther you walk from the dock, where enormous tenders make the short ride to and from the ship. For children, there's the pirate-themed Splash Bash area with water sprinklers, fountains, and spilling buckets. There are also floating trampolines, inflatable iceberg-shaped slides, and water seesaws. Kayaking and parasailing are enjoyed from a dock nearby. The latest rage is a 2,800-foot-long zipline called Dragon's

Breath that takes you over the water of Dragon's Tail Beach. At the center of the peninsula, the Haitian Market and Artisans' Market are the port's low points, full of cheesy Africanesque statues and carvings, with touts trying to lure you in with "Sir, let me just show you something over here." Steer clear unless you're desperate for a souvenir. When we were here last, a painter near the dock had much more interesting work for sale.

2 Antigua

Though it's the largest of the British Leeward Islands, Antigua (pronounced An-*tee*-gah) is still only 23km (14 miles) long and 18km (11 miles) wide, and affords a much more laid-back experience than some of the glitzier Caribbean islands. Nice, relaxing beaches are close to port, and **St. John's,** the island's capital and main town, is sleepy and undemanding, full of cobblestone sidewalks and weather-beaten wooden houses. Close to port, you can shop lazily in historic, restored warehouses, while away from St. John's, the rolling, rustic island boasts important historic sites. **Nelson's Dockyard,** for example, was once Britain's main naval station in the Lesser Antilles, and is now a well-maintained national park.

COMING ASHORE   Most cruise ships dock at **Heritage Quay** (pronounced *Key*) or the **Nevis Pier in St. John's,** the island's only town of any size on Antigua's western coast, or, if both are occupied, the commercial pier at **Deepwater Harbour,** about 1 mile from town. The three piers have a total capacity of six ships. From the piers, you can either walk or take a short taxi ride into town. A handful of smaller vessels drop anchor at **Falmouth Harbour,** on the English Harbour main road in Falmouth, on the south side of the island. This anchorage is also used for overflow if the St. John's piers are all occupied. A handful of smaller vessels drop anchor at **English Harbour,** on the south coast.

GETTING AROUND   Most of the major attractions here are beyond walking distance. **Taxis** meet every cruise ship. Although meters are nonexistent, rates are fixed by the government and posted at the taxi stand at the end of Heritage Quay's pedestrian mall. Drivers often double as tour guides for about $25 per hour for up to four people, with a 2-hour minimum. Tip between 10% and 15% for all rides. **Water taxis** are also available, usually prearranged by the cruise lines or tour operators. Privately operated **buses** are cheaper (about $1.50 to almost anywhere on the island), but service is erratic and you'll need exact change. Avis, Budget, Hertz, and National all provide **rental cars** on the island, but driving is on the left, signage is inadequate, and you have to buy a $20 temporary driving permit.

LANGUAGE & CURRENCY   The language is **English,** often spoken with a musical West Indian lilt. The **Eastern Caribbean dollar** (EC$2.65 = US$1; EC$1 = US37¢) is Antigua's official currency, but the U.S. dollar is readily accepted.

Best Cruise Line Shore Excursions

Nelson's Dockyard National Park Tour ($60, 3 hr.): The tour begins with a drive through the capital of St. John's and stops at Antigua's national park before heading to Nelson's Dockyard for a guided tour of the admiral's house, sailmaker's loft, officers' quarters, and an 18th-century inn. A short drive brings you to the Blockhouse Ruins, Indian Creek, and the St. James Club and Shirley Heights—the latter sitting atop a rugged cliff with spectacular views.

Helicopter to Montserrat Volcano ($265, 2 hr.): In December 1997, the Soufrière Hills Volcano on the neighboring island of Montserrat blew its top, spewing lava and ash over a huge area and burying large swaths of the island, including the former capital, Plymouth. This trip takes you over both the volcano and the charbroiled highlights of Montserrat's exclusion zone, the area declared off limits to ground transportation.

Off-Road 4×4 Jeep Safari Adventure ($78, 3 hr.): Tour the island's only remaining rainforest via a four-wheel-drive vehicle, and stop at the ruins of forts, sugar mills, and plantation houses. The excursion includes beach time.

Bird Island Catamaran Sail ($84, 5 hr.): Sail along the reef-protected north coast of Antigua into the sheltered bay of Bird Island, a designated national park that is perfect for beginning snorkelers. If you want some exercise, venture up the trail for a fantastic view of the Atlantic from 100-foot cliffs.

On Your Own: Within Walking Distance

In addition to shopping (see below), St. John's has a few attractions that can be easily reached on foot. The **Museum of Antigua and Barbuda,** at the intersection of Market and Long streets (📞 **268/462-1469;** www.antiguamuseums.org), traces the history of the nation from its geological birth to the present day. Housed in a neoclassic former courthouse built in 1750, its exhibits include pre-Columbian tools and artifacts, a replica of an Arawak wattle-and-daub hut, African-Caribbean pottery, and sections dedicated to the island's naval, sugar, and slavery eras. It's open Monday through Friday from 8:30am to 3 or 4pm, Saturday from 10am to 2pm. Tickets are $3. A couple of blocks uphill from the museum, bordered by Church, Long, and Newgate streets, **St. John's Anglican Cathedral** dominates St. John's skyline with its 21m (69-ft.) aluminum-capped twin spires. The original building, a simple wooden structure built in 1681, was replaced in 1720 by a brick building, which was destroyed during an 1843 earthquake. Upon completion in 1847, the present baroque structure was not universally appreciated: Ecclesiastical architects criticized it as being like "a pagan temple with two dumpy pepper-pot towers." The cavernous interior is entirely encased in pitch pine, a construction method intended to secure the building from hurricanes and earthquakes.

On Your Own: Beyond the Port Area

One of the major historical attractions of the eastern Caribbean, **Nelson's Dockyard National Park** (📞 **268/481-5021;** www.antiguamuseums.org/nelsonsdockyard.htm) lies 18km (11 miles) southeast of St. John's, alongside one of the world's best-protected natural harbors. English ships used the site as a refuge from hurricanes as early as 1671, and the dockyard played a major role during the 18th century, an era of privateers, pirates, and great sea battles. Admiral Nelson's headquarters from 1784 to 1787, the restored dockyard today remains the only Georgian naval base still in use. At its heart, the **Dockyard Museum** (www.antiguamuseums.org/dockyardmuseum.htm), housed in a former naval officers' house built in 1855, traces the history of the site from its beginnings as a British Navy stronghold to its development as a national park and yachting center. Nautical memorabilia make up much of the display.

Uphill and east of the dockyard, the **Dow's Hill Interpretation Center** (📞 **268/ 481-5045**) features an entertaining 15-minute multimedia overview of Antiguan history and an observation platform that affords a 360-degree view of the park. Farther uphill, Palladian arches mark the **Blockhouse,** a military fortification built in 1787 with officers' quarters and a powder magazine. For an eagle's-eye view of English Harbour, continue to the hill's summit, to the **Shirley Heights Lookout.** Fortified to defend the precious cargo in the harbor below, Fort Shirley's barracks, arched walkways, batteries, and powder magazines are scattered around the hilltop. The lookout, with its view of the French island of Guadeloupe, was the main signal station used to warn of approaching hostile ships.

The grounds of the national park, which represent 10% of Antigua's total land area, are well worth exploring. Bordered on one side by sandy beaches, the park is blanketed in cactus, tamarind, cinnamon, and turpentine trees, as well as mangroves that shelter African cattle egrets. An array of **nature trails,** which take anywhere from 30 minutes to 5 hours to walk, meander through the vegetation and provide vistas of the coast. One trail climbs to **Fort Berkeley,** built in 1704 to protect the harbor's entrance. Admission, which is $5 for adults and free for children ages 11 and under, covers the dockyard, the Dockyard Museum, Dow's Hill Interpretation Center, the Blockhouse, Shirley Heights, and the rest of the park. The complex is open daily from 9am to 5pm. It's within walking distance of cruise ships that dock at English Harbour. Free guided tours of the dockyard last 15 to 20 minutes; tipping is discretionary.

If you've worked up an appetite, the dockyard's rustic **Admiral's Inn** (© 268/460-1027) serves lunches that usually include pumpkin soup and main courses such as local red snapper, grilled steak, and lobster. Built in 1788, the restored brick building originally stored barrels of pitch, turpentine, and lead used to repair ships. Lunch prices start at $12.

To see what's billed as the only operational 18th-century sugar mill in the Caribbean, visit **Betty's Hope,** not far from Pares village on the island's east side (© 268/462-1469; www.antiguamuseums.org/BettysHopeHome.htm). On-site are twin mills, the remnants of a boiling house, and a small visitor center, which opens its doors Monday through Saturday from 8:30am to 4pm. Gardeners should be able to spot goldenseal bushes, neem trees, and wild tamarinds on the rolling hills. Serene cows saunter lazily on the grounds.

Not far from Betty's Hope, on the extreme eastern tip of the island, **Devil's Bridge** is one of Antigua's most picturesque natural wonders. Over the centuries, powerful Atlantic breakers, gathering strength over the course of their 4,830km (3,000-mile) run from Africa, have carved out a natural arch in the limestone coastline and created blowholes through which the surf spurts skyward at high tide.

Another option for nature lovers is **Wallings Conservation Area,** Antigua's largest remaining tract of tropical rainforest. Located in the southwest, this lush wilderness area provides three hiking trails and numerous opportunities to spot wildlife (including many Caribbean birds) and rich vegetation. If you've spent your day at Nelson's Dockyard National Park, pass through the area on the way back to your ship via the circular Fig Tree Drive. Although plagued with potholes, this is the island's most scenic drive. It winds through the tropical forest, passing fishing villages, frisky goats, and old sugar mills along the way.

Beaches

Antiguans claim that the island is home to 365 beaches, one for each day of the year. True or not, all of them are public, and quite a few are spectacular. Closest to St. John's, **Fort James Beach,** only 5 minutes and a $7 cab fare from the cruise dock, is popular with both locals and tourists. There is volleyball and cricket daily, plus umbrellas and beach chairs available for rent. For a change of pace, hike up the hill to explore the authentically derelict ruins of Fort James, which once protected St. John's harbor. A bit farther north, a $12 cab ride from the dock, the half-mile beach at **Dickenson Bay** is bustling with numerous hotels, restaurants, and watersports vendors. The water is calm, and chairs and umbrellas are available for rent. If you crave complete peace and quiet, head to Antigua's most beautiful beach, at **Half Moon Bay,** isolated at the island's southeast extreme. Waves at the beach's center are great for bodysurfing, while the quieter eastern side is better for children and snorkeling. A restaurant and bar are near the parking lot.

Antigua's **dive sites** include reefs, wall drops, caves, and shipwrecks. To arrange a dive, contact **Dive Antigua,** at the north end of Dickenson Bay (© **268/462-3483**). A two-tank dive costs $90. Reef snorkeling is $40.

Shopping

To your right as you leave the docks, **Redcliffe Quay** is Antigua's most interesting shopping complex. Most of the sugar, coffee, and tobacco produced on the island in years past was stored in the warehouses here, and slave auctions were common before the island abolished slavery in 1834. Today, the restored buildings house an array of boutiques and restaurants. For more local color, turn right (south) once you've reached Market Street and walk 5 blocks to the **Public Market,** which is a good place to sample locally produced fruits and vegetables or to pick up some Antiguan pottery or baskets. Other shopping districts include **Heritage Quay,** right at the dock (home to some 40 duty-free shops), and **St. Mary's Street.**

3 Aruba

Situated only 32km (20 miles) north of Venezuela, arid Aruba has unwaveringly sunny skies, warm temperatures, and cooling breezes, along with some of the best beaches in the Caribbean, scuba diving, snorkeling, windsurfing, and all the other watersports you'd expect. Away from the beach, Aruba is full of cactus, iguanas, donkeys, and strange boulder formations. Contrasting sharply with the southern shoreline's beaches, the north coast has craggy limestone cliffs, sand dunes, and crashing breakers. Focused on shopping? The concentration of stores and malls in **Oranjestad,** the island's capital, is as impressive as any in the Caribbean. In between purchases, try your luck at one of the island's dozen casinos; two are just steps away from your ship. Aruba is still part of the Netherlands, so there's a Dutch influence, which adds a nice European flavor. Though it has a few small museums, and some centuries-old indigenous rock glyphs and paintings, nobody comes to Aruba for culture or history.

COMING ASHORE   Cruise ships arrive at the **Port of Oranjestad.** The three modern terminals have tourist information booths, phones, ATMs, and a handful of shops. The terminals can accommodate three megaships and two smaller ships; one of the three terminals is a container berth a short walk from the main terminal. From the pier, it's a 5-minute walk to the shopping districts of downtown Oranjestad and a 10-minute drive to the beaches.

GETTING AROUND   You'll need transportation to get to most of the beaches. **Taxis** line up at the dock to take you wherever you want to go. Fares are fixed, and every driver has a copy of the official rate schedule (it's generally $8–$12 to the beach resorts). Excellent roads connect major tourist attractions, and all the major **car rental** companies accept valid U.S. or Canadian driver's licenses. Avis, Budget, Dollar, Hertz, and National all have offices here. Good daily **bus service** costs $2.30 round-trip

between the beach hotels and Oranjestad. The bus terminal is across the street from the cruise terminal on L. G. Smith Boulevard. Be sure to have exact change ready.

LANGUAGE & CURRENCY   The official languages are **Dutch** and **Papiamentu,** but nearly everybody speaks **English.** Spanish is also widely spoken. The **Aruba guilder** (AG), also known as the florin, is the official currency (1.80 AG = US$1; 1 AG = US55¢), but U.S. dollars are just as widely accepted.

Best Cruise Line Shore Excursions

In addition to the tours described here, cruise lines typically offer about a dozen snorkeling, diving, sailing, and other water-oriented tours.

Island Bike Adventure ($58, 3½ hr.): Explore Aruba's wild northeast coast by mountain bike, pedaling 16km (10 miles) and visiting the Baby Natural Bridge (cut by the sea and wind), the Bushiribana Gold Mine, the Alto Vista Chapel, and the California Lighthouse.

Arikok National Park Hike & Beach ($52, 3½ hr.): Travel about 30 minutes by bus to Aruba's east end, where a park ranger will lead you on a hike through the desertlike environment, full of divi-divi trees, iguanas, cacti, and (if you can spot 'em) wild donkeys. After your hike, you can cool off with a swim or go snorkeling at Baby Beach.

Off-Road Land Rover Adventure ($115, 7½ hr.): Take off into Aruba's backcountry in an SUV, with you behind the wheel and in radio contact with your guide. You'll visit attractions such as the Baby Natural Bridge, an ostrich farm, and the Bushiribana Gold Mine.

Atlantis Submarine Adventure ($99, 1½ hr.): Cruise 45m (148 ft.) below the sea in a submarine. During the gentle descent, you'll pass by scuba divers, coral reefs, shipwrecks, and hundreds of curious sergeant majors, damselfish, parrotfish, and angelfish.

On Your Own: Within Walking Distance

Aruba's capital has a sunny Caribbean demeanor, with Dutch colonial buildings painted in vivid colors. The main thoroughfare, **L. G. Smith Boulevard,** runs along the waterfront and is crowded with marinas, shopping malls, restaurants, and bars. The harbor is packed with fishing boats and schooners docked next to stalls, where vendors hawk fruits, vegetables, and fish. Two casinos—the elegant, 24-hour **Crystal Casino,** at the Aruba Renaissance Beach Resort, L. G. Smith Blvd. 82 (ⓒ **297/58-36000**), and the less assuming **Seaport Casino,** L. G. Smith Blvd. 9 (ⓒ **297/58-36000**)—are just steps from the dock.

For a dash of culture, head to one of the town's small museums, which are open on weekdays only. Squeezed between St. Franciscus Roman Catholic Church and the parish rectory is the small **Archaeological Museum of Aruba,** J. E. Irausquinplein 2A (ⓒ **297/58-28979**), whose exhibits highlight the island's Amerindian heritage, with pottery vessels, shell and stone tools, burial urns, and skulls and bones on display. It's open Tuesday through Friday from 10am to 5pm, Saturday and Sunday 10am to 2pm. Admission is free.

To defend the island against pirates, the Dutch erected **Fort Zoutman** in 1796, and added a tower in 1867. Since 1992, the complex has housed the modest **Museo Historico Arubano,** Zoutmanstraat 4 (ⓒ **297/582-6099**), which displays island history from the colonial period till now, prehistoric Amerindian artifacts, and relics from the Dutch colonial period. Admission is $6. The small **Numismatic Museum of Aruba,** Westraat z/n (ⓒ **297/965-6969**), has meticulous, homemade exhibits telling the history of the world through coins. Dedicated numismatists can spend the better part of the morning perusing the 35,000 different specimens from more than 400 countries. It's open only weekdays till 4pm (Fri till 1pm) and Saturday mornings. Admission is free, though donations are appreciated.

On Your Own: Touring by Rental Jeep

The best way to see Aruba's desertlike terrain is to rent a four-wheel-drive vehicle. Be careful of the increasingly popular ATVs that share the road and often at high speeds. Car rental companies have maps highlighting the best routes to reach the attractions. Here's one popular option:

Following the system of roads that traces the perimeter of the island, start clockwise from Oranjestad. Drive past the hotel strip, toward the island's northwesternmost point. Here, the **California Lighthouse** affords sweeping 360-degree views of spectacular scenery—gentle sand dunes, rocky coral shoreline, and turbulent waves. The pictur-esque lighthouse gets its name from the *California,* a passenger ship that sank off the nearby coast in 1916. From here on, your adventure will take you into the island's moonlike terrain, past heaps of giant boulders and barren rocky coastline. The well-maintained road that links the hotel strip with Oranjestad deteriorates abruptly into a band of rubble, and the calm, turquoise sea turns rough and rowdy.

By the time you reach the **Alto Vista Chapel,** about 8km (5 miles) from the light-house, you'll probably be coated with red dust; it should contrast nicely with the quaint pale-yellow church, built by native Indians and Spanish settlers in 1750, before the island had its own priest. It was the island's first chapel.

Farther along the northern coast, you'll approach the hulking ruins of the **Bushiribana Gold Smelter.** Built in 1872, its massive stone walls are remnants of Aruba's 19th-century gold-mining heritage. Climb the multitiered interior for impres-sive sea views. Too bad the walls have been marred with artless graffiti. Too bad, too, that the nearby Natural Bridge, a limestone arch above the sea, once the most pho-tographed attraction in Aruba, collapsed in 2005. You can still see the **Baby Natural Bridge,** though, in the same area, its span carved out by centuries of pounding surf.

Next, head toward the center of the island and the bizarre **Ayó and Casibari rock formations.** Looking like something out of *The Flintstones,* the gargantuan Ayó rocks served Aruba's early inhabitants as a dwelling or religious site. The reddish-brown pet-roglyphs on the boulders suggest mystical significance. If you have children, or just like animals, stop by the **Donkey Sanctuary** (*©* **297/965-6986;** www.aruban donkey.org), a half-mile from the Ayó Rock Formation, where dozens of these feral yet gentle animals are corralled, fed, and cared for. The staff will eagerly share their knowledge with you about the history and ecology of Aruba's donkeys, many of which still roam the countryside. It's open Monday to Friday from 9am to 12:30pm, Satur-day and Sunday 10am to 3pm.

Farther east, back along the northern coast, **Arikok National Park,** Aruba's show-case ecological preserve, sprawls over roughly 20% of the island. Its premier attraction is a series of caves that punctuate the cliff sides of the area's mesas. The most popular, **Fontein Cave,** has brownish-red drawings left by Amerindians and graffiti etched by early European settlers. Nearby **Quadirkiri Cave** boasts two large chambers with roof openings that allow sunlight in, making flashlights unnecessary. Hundreds of small bats use the 30m-long (98-ft.) tunnel to reach their nests deeper in the cave. You'll need a flashlight (rentable at the entrance) to explore the 90m (295-ft.) passageway of **Baranca Sunu,** another cave in the area commonly known as the Tunnel of Love because of its heart-shaped entrance. (At press time, the Tunnel of Love was closed indefinitely by the Park Rangers in order to protect and replenish the bat population.)

Heading southeast toward Aruba's behemoth oil refinery, you'll eventually come to **Baby Beach,** at the island's easternmost point. Like a great big bathtub, this shallow bowl of warm turquoise water is protected by an almost complete circle of rock—it's a great place for a dip after a sweaty day behind the wheel. Just try to ignore the giant oil refinery visible in the distance.

Beaches

All of Aruba's beaches are public, but chairs and shade huts are hotel property. If you use them, expect to be charged. Shade huts located at beaches with no hotels are free of charge, such as Baby Beach, Arashi, and Malmok. **Palm Beach,** home of Aruba's glam-orous high-rise hotels, is great for swimming, sunbathing, sailing, people-watching, fishing, and snorkeling. It has two piers and numerous watersports operators, and can get crowded. Separated from Palm Beach by a limestone outcrop, **Eagle Beach** stretches as far as the eye can see. The sugar-white sand and gentle surf are ideal for swimming, and though the nearby hotels offer watersports and beach activities, the ambience is relaxed and quiet. A couple of bars punctuate the expansive strand, and shaded picnic areas are provided for the public. Well-protected **Baby Beach** (see above) is a prime destination for families with young children.

The island's best **snorkeling sites** are around Malmok Beach (also a great **windsurfing** spot) and Boca Catalina, where the water is calm and shallow and marine life is plentiful. **Dive sites** stretch along the entire southern coast, but most divers head for the German freighter *Antilla,* which was scuttled during World War II off the island's northwestern tip, near Palm Beach. The island's largest watersports operators, **Pelican Adventures** (© 297/586-3271; www.pelican-aruba.com) and **Red Sail Sports** (© 877/733-7245 or 297/586-1603; www.redsailaruba.com), offer sailing, windsurfing, and water-skiing in addition to one- and two-tank dives ($55 and $80, respectively) and snorkeling trips ($45 for 2½ hr., $65 for 4½ hr., champagne brunch sometimes included).

Shopping

Because the island is part of the Netherlands, Dutch goods such as Delft porcelain, chocolate, and cheese are especially good buys. Items from Indonesia, another former Dutch colony, are reasonably priced, too. Skin- and hair-care products made from locally produced aloe are also popular and practical. If you're looking for big-ticket items, shops have the usual array of watches, cameras, gold and diamond jewelry, Cuban cigars, premium liquor, porcelain, French and American fragrances, and designer shoes, bags, and clothing; the 3.3% duty and lack of sales tax make for some decent prices.

Caya G. F. Betico Croes (aka Main St.) is the city's major shopping street, running roughly parallel to the waterfront several blocks inland. **Renaissance Mall,** right downtown, is the number-one high-end shopping area, while **Renaissance Marketplace,** across the street, is a distant second. Combined, they have more than 100 stores, 10 restaurants and cafes, two casinos, and a movie theater. Just down the road, **Royal Plaza Mall** is chock-full of popular restaurants and less upscale boutiques. Two new malls across from the high-rise hotel area have sprung up and are gaining popularity. **Paeo Herencia (Aruba's Pride)** is a two-level mall with boutiques and restaurants around a central plaza with a fountain. The **Village** was mostly vacant at press time, but because it's in the bustling resort zone, it will no doubt fill with plenty of places to spend your cash.

4 The Bahamas: Nassau & Freeport

Nassau and **Freeport** are among the busiest cruise ports on the Caribbean circuit, even though technically The Bahamas aren't in the Caribbean at all—they're in the Atlantic, north of the Caribbean and less than 161km (100 miles) from Miami. Though holdovers from Great Britain's long colonial occupation linger in some architecture and culture, the vibe here isn't all that much different from parts of Florida, and the ports are totally tourist-oriented, with more shopping than the Mall of America, all surrounded by beaches and casinos.

LANGUAGE & CURRENCY   **English** is the official language of The Bahamas. Its legal tender is the **Bahamian dollar** (B$), whose value is always the same as that of the U.S. dollar. Both currencies are accepted everywhere on the islands.

Nassau

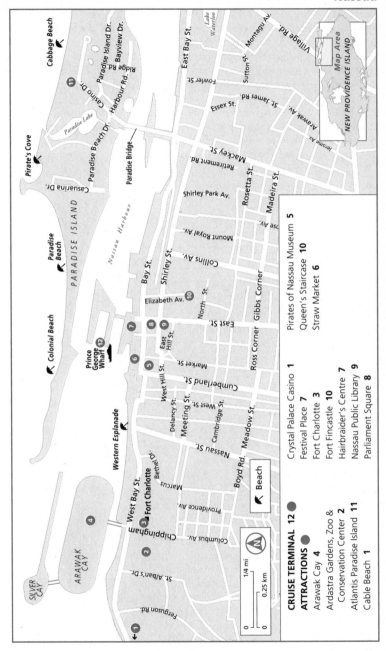

CRUISE TERMINAL 12 ●

ATTRACTIONS ●

Arawak Cay **4**
Ardastra Gardens, Zoo &
  Conservation Center **2**
Atlantis Paradise Island **11**
Cable Beach **1**

Crystal Palace Casino **1**
Festival Place **7**
Fort Charlotte **3**
Fort Fincastle **10**
Hairbraider's Centre **7**
Nassau Public Library **9**
Parliament Square **8**

Pirates of Nassau Museum **5**
Queen's Staircase **10**
Straw Market **6**

Map Area

NEW PROVIDENCE ISLAND

Nassau

Nassau is the cultural, social, political, and economic center of The Bahamas. With its beaches, shopping, resorts, casinos, historic landmarks, and water and land activities, it's also the island chain's most visited destination—one million travelers a year make their way to the town, and Nassau is one of the world's busiest cruise ship ports. The Nassau/Paradise Island area comprises two separate islands. Nassau is on the northeastern shore of 34km (21-mile) New Providence Island, while tiny Paradise Island is linked to New Providence by bridges, and protects the Nassau harbor for a 5km (3-mile) stretch. It was here that the white-sand beaches of the Atlantis Hotel and Ocean Club served as locations for James Bond in *Casino Royale.*

COMING ASHORE   The cruise ship docks at **Prince George Wharf** are in the center of town at Rawson Square, in the middle of Nassau's shopping frenzy. The main docks and channel entrance can accommodate at least six large cruise ships, including the *Oasis of the Seas* class.

GETTING AROUND   Walk. The major attractions and stores are pretty concentrated, and if you're really fit, you can even trek over to Cable Beach or Paradise Island. Otherwise, you'll have no problem finding taxis—they'll find you (it'll be about $15 to Cable Beach). There's no good reason to rent a car here.

Best Cruise Line Shore Excursions

In addition to the excursions below, cruise lines typically offer a variety of snorkeling, diving, and boat tours. Avoid the city bus tours, which are dull, dull, dull.

Harbor Cruise & Atlantis Resort ($69, 2½ hr.): A tour boat with a local guide shows you the sights (such as they are) from the water. It then drops you at the fanciful Atlantis Resort for a brief tour that includes a visit to Predator Lagoon, home to sharks, barracuda, and other toothy fish.

Ardastra Gardens & City Tour ($55, 2½ hr.): It's a short ride to Ardastra, home to The Bahamas' largest collection of endangered land animals. In a tropical setting of brilliant bougainvillea, hibiscus, and other exotic plants, see the world's only trained flamingo show. Feed beautiful South Pacific lory parrots by hand. Take a narrated city tour to some of the historical monuments of The Bahamas, such as Fort Fincastle. Admire the Queen's staircase, honoring Queen Victoria's reign.

Dolphin Swim at Blue Lagoon ($180, 3½ hr.): Begin with a 30-minute scenic catamaran ride to the dolphin facility at Blue Lagoon Island. Meet the dolphins and participate in an educational lecture before the interactive program begins. Pet, kiss, hug, and feed the dolphins in small groups.

On Your Own: Within Walking Distance

As you exit from the cruise ship wharf into the main port area, you'll have no choice but to pass through **Festival Place,** a barnlike hall full of little shops and stalls selling arts and crafts, T-shirts, hot sauces, and other touristy items. Outside, hawkers will encourage you to have your hair braided at the **Hairbraider's Centre.** This government-sponsored open-air pavilion attracts braiding experts from all over the island.

Shopping is *the* thing here, but there are a few other sights of interest. Just across Bay Street from Rawson Square (inland from the wharf) are the flamingo-pink government buildings of **Parliament Square,** constructed in 1815. The House of Assembly, old colonial Secretary's Office, and Supreme Court flank a statue of Queen Victoria, while a bust on the north side of the square honors Sir Milo B. Butler, the first governor-general of The Bahamas. One block inland, the pink, octagonal **Nassau Public Library** was built as a prison in 1798, and today its collections of books, historical prints, colonial documents, and Arawak Indian artifacts are kept in what were once cells. It's one of the city's oldest buildings.

Slaves carved the **Queen's Staircase** out of a solid limestone cliff in 1793, originally designed as an escape route for soldiers; each step now represents a year in Queen Victoria's 65-year reign. Lush plants and a waterfall stand guard over the staircase, which is a few blocks up from the library on East Street and leads to **Fort Fincastle,** on Elizabeth Avenue, built in 1793 by Lord Dunmore, the royal governor. An elevator climbs a 38m-high (125-ft.) water tower, where you can look down on the arrowhead-shaped fort. If you're inclined to walk around on your own here, keep in mind that in December 2009, there was an armed robbery of a group of 11 cruise passengers at the Queen's Staircase, which is a bit isolated, relatively speaking. There was no police presence at the staircase that day, which there sometimes is, and so at gun point, the group was brazenly robbed of money and personal items. You may feel safer on one of the ship's guided tours.

At the corny **Pirates of Nassau Museum,** at King and George streets (© 242/356-3759; www.pirates-of-nassau.com), Captain Teach and his fearsome crew guide you through the age of piracy in the lawless Nassau of 1716. Hours are Monday through Saturday from 9am to 6pm, Sunday from 9am to noon. Admission is a steep $12 for adults and $6 for kids ages 4 to 17.

On Your Own: Beyond the Port Area

About a mile west of downtown Nassau, just off West Bay Street, **Fort Charlotte** is the largest fort in The Bahamas, covering more than 41 hilltop hectares (100 acres) and with impressive views of Paradise Island, Nassau, and the harbor. The complex, constructed in 1788, features a moat, dungeons, underground passageways, and 42 cannons. Nearby, parading pink flamingos are the main attraction at the lush, 2-hectare (5-acre) **Ardastra Gardens, Zoo & Conservation Center,** on Chippingham Road (© 242/323-5806; www.ardastra.com). The graceful birds obey the drillmaster's orders daily at 10:30am, 2:10, and 4:10pm. Other exotic wildlife—parrots, boa constrictors, honey bears, macaws, and capuchin monkeys—are less talented but still fascinating in their own right. Meandering paths show off the garden's exotic fruit trees, coconut palms, ackee and mango trees, bougainvillea, and hibiscus blossoms. Admission is $15 for adults, $7.50 for children ages 4 to 12.

If you're in the mood for some conch, head for **Arawak Cay,** a small man-made island across West Bay Street from Ardastra Gardens and Fort Charlotte. Join the locals in sampling conch with hot sauce, and wash it down with a cocktail made from coconut water and gin. Farther to the west, the 3,252-sq.-m (35,000-sq.-ft.) **Crystal Palace Casino,** West Bay Street, Cable Beach (© 800/222-7466 or 242/327-6200), is the only casino on New Providence Island. It's open from 3:30pm to 4:30am.

On Paradise Island, the towering, fancifully designed megaresort known as **Atlantis Paradise Island** (© 242/363-3000; www.atlantis.com) is the largest gaming and entertainment complex in the Caribbean, its casino boasting nearly 1,000 slot machines and 78 gaming tables, all tied together with a Lost City of Atlantis theme. Though only paying hotel guests can use Atlantis's beaches, water slides, and pools, cruise passengers in for the day can visit the casino, eat at the restaurants, and sign up for the Discover Atlantis tour. The guided excursion, which includes round-trip ferry transport between the ship and property, includes a walk through the resort's sprawling

11-million-gallon lagoon system that boasts more than 200 sea species and 50,000 individual creatures. You'll also tour the **Dig,** a fantastic world of faux Atlantis ruins flooded by the sea. The interconnected passageways, boulevards, and chambers, now inhabited by piranhas, hammerhead sharks, stingrays, and morays, are visible through huge glass windows. It is purported to be the largest man-made marine habitat in the world. To see this part of the resort, you must sign up for the guided Discovery Tour. Tickets, available at the resort's guest services desks, cost $35 adults, $25 kids ages 4 to 12. Another tour, sometimes available to a handful of cruise lines, gives access to the resort's beaches and restaurants.

Beaches
On New Providence Island, sun worshipers make the 8km (5-mile) pilgrimage to 6.5km (4-mile) **Cable Beach,** which has various watersports and easy access to shops, a casino, bars, and restaurants. Not on the same level but more convenient for cruise ship passengers, the **Western Esplanade** sweeps westward from the Hilton British Colonial hotel, with changing facilities, restrooms, and a snack bar.

Paradise Beach, on Paradise Island, is a ferry ride away from Prince George Wharf. The price of admission ($3 for adults, $1 for children) includes use of a shower and locker. An extra $10 deposit is required for towels. Paradise Island has a number of smaller beaches as well, including **Pirate's Cove Beach** and **Cabbage Beach,** the latter often filling up with guests of the nearby resorts.

Shopping
In 1992, The Bahamas abolished import duties on 11 luxury-goods categories, including china, crystal, fine linens, jewelry, leather goods, photographic equipment, watches, and fragrances. Even so, you can end up spending more on an item here than at home. True bargains are rare.

The principal shopping area is **Bay Street** and the adjacent blocks, almost the first things you see when leaving your ship. Here, you'll find dozens of duty-free luxury-goods stores, plus hundreds of others selling T-shirts, tourist gimcracks, duty-free booze and cigars, and recordings of Junkanoo music. The crowded aisles of the **Straw Market,** a few blocks west of the docks, display all manner of straw hats, handbags, dolls, place mats, and other items, but be aware that most aren't of the best quality, nor even made locally—much of it is imported from Asia. Welcome to the global market. If you want really beautiful handmade straw work, walk a few blocks to the **Plait Lady,** at Victoria and Bay streets, where the merchandise is vastly superior to what's peddled in the Straw Market—and it's 100% Bahamian-made.

Freeport/Lucaya
Freeport/Lucaya, on Grand Bahama Island, is the second-most-popular destination in The Bahamas. Technically, Freeport is the landlocked section of town, while adjacent Lucaya hugs the waterfront. Originally two separate developments, they've grown together over the years, and though they have none of Nassau's colonial charm, they do have plenty of sun, surf, golf, tennis, and watersports. Gambling and shopping were big business here for awhile, but three hurricanes in 2 years have quelled the frenzy, leaving the port with a calmer, quieter feel.

COMING ASHORE   Ships dock at **Lucayan Harbor,** a dreary port in the middle of nowhere, with a small straw market, shopping area, and hair braiders camped out in the middle of an industrial zone. The docks can accommodate three larger ships, or several smaller ones. You're better served by taking a $24 taxi ride to the **Port Lucaya Marketplace,** where you'll find most of the action. Closer to the pier, but not as bustling, is the **International Bazaar,** which will cost you $16 in cab fare.

GETTING AROUND   Once you get to Freeport by **taxi,** you can explore the center of town on foot. Taxis can also take you to far-flung attractions. The government sets taxi rates, which start at $4 and increase 40¢ for each additional .5km (¼ mile), plus $3 extra per passenger.

Best Cruise Line Shore Excursions

Dolphin Encounter ($118, 3½ hr.): Pat a dolphin on the nose! On this excursion, you can watch, touch, and photograph Flipper, or at least one of his relatives. It's organized by UNEXSO Dolphin Encounter (at Sanctuary Bay).

Kayak Nature Tour ($90, 6 hr.): Visit a protected island creek, kayak through a mangrove forest, explore the island's caves, and take a guided nature walk into Lucayan National Park. The excursion includes lunch and beach time.

On Your Own: Beyond the Port Area

Nothing of note is within walking distance of the port. You must take a cab over to Freeport/Lucaya for all attractions.

A couple of miles east of downtown Freeport on East Settlers Way, the 40-hectare (100-acre) **Rand Nature Centre** (© 242/352-5438; www.geographia.com/grand bahama/rand.htm) serves as the regional headquarters of The Bahamas National Trust. Pineland nature trails meander past native flora and wild birds, including the Bahama parrot. Other highlights include native animal displays (don't miss the boa constrictors), an education center, and a gift shop. It's open Monday through Friday from 9am to 4pm. Admission is $5.

One of the island's top attractions, the 5-hectare (12-acre) **Garden of the Groves,** at Midshipman Road and Magellan Drive in Freeport (© 242/373-5668;), was once the private meditation garden of Freeport's founder, Wallace Groves. It has waterfalls, flowering shrubs, some 10,000 trees, tropical birds, Bahamian raccoons, Vietnamese potbellied pigs, and West African pygmy goats (and a playground). The Garden is open daily from 9am to 5pm. Admission is $15 for adults, $10 for kids.

If you'd like a taste of The Bahamas the way they used to be, head for the **Star Club,** on Bayshore Road, on the island's west end (© 242/346-6207). It's open on Sundays only from 4 to 11pm. Built in the 1940s, the Star was Grand Bahama's first hotel, and over the years it's hosted many famous guests. You can order Bahamian chicken in the bag, burgers, fish and chips, "fresh sexy" ceviche conch salad, or conch fritters. But don't come for the food; come for the good times, the island music, and to mix with the locals. Lunch costs $8. Next door, **Austin's Calypso Bar** is a colorful old dive if ever there was one.

Another well-known spot is **Billy Joe's,** a stand on Lucayan Beach (© 242/373-1300, ext. 5803). Though the developers of the Westin and the Sheraton hotels bought the property where the stand sits, the famous Billy Joe's was spared, so like the old days, patrons can still go barefoot on the white sand while sampling the chef's "fresh, sexy conch." His conch salad is hailed as the island's best; he'll also grill or "crack" the conch for you. There are also fish and chips, fresh snapper or grouper, and the island's best cheeseburgers, according to many patrons.

Bahamas Golf Excursions

Our Lucaya Beach & Golf Resort, Royal Palm Way, Lucaya (© **866/870-7148** or 242/373-2003; www.ourlucaya.com), has two 18-hole, par-72 courses. The Lucayan course, designed by Dick Wilson, features well-protected elevated greens, fairways lined with tropical foliage, and doglegs. The links-style Reef course, designed by Robert Trent Jones, Jr., has water hazards on 13 of 18 holes. Greens fees are $155 for 18 holes, including cart. Club rentals are $50.

Beaches

Grand Bahama Island has miles of white-sand beaches. **Xanadu Beach,** immediately east of Freeport at the Xanadu Beach Resort, is the closest to the cruise pier, but two of the island's best are **Taíno Beach** and **Lucayan Beach,** both on the Lucaya oceanfront. Of the two, Lucayan Beach is easier to reach and closer to the Port Lucaya Marketplace, and has beach-chair rentals, watersports, and restaurants. A 20-minute ride east of Lucaya, **Gold Rock Beach** may be the island's best if total isolation is your thing. Hidden away in Lucayan National Park, it has barbecue pits, picnic tables, and a spectacular low tide. **Barbary Beach,** slightly closer to Lucaya, is great for seashell hunters, and white spider lilies in the area bloom spectacularly in May and June.

Shopping

The **International Bazaar,** at East Mall Drive and East Sunrise Highway, is pure 1960s Bahamian kitsch, and though relentlessly cheerful, it's rather long in the tooth. Each area of the 4-hectare (10-acre), 100-shop complex attempts to capture the ambience of a different region of the globe. Buses marked INTERNATIONAL BAZAAR deliver passengers to the center's much-photographed Torii Gate, a Japanese symbol of welcome.

The **Port Lucaya Marketplace,** on Seahorse Road, across the street from the Lucayan Beach, is a large shopping-and-dining complex that in recent years has eclipsed the International Bazaar. This is definitely where the shopping/dining action is now. Many of the restaurants and shops overlook a 50-slip marina next to **UNEXSO Dive Shop** (© 242/373-1244; www.unexso.com), where you should stop if you're in need of a wet suit, snorkel, mask, fins, underwater camera, or more prosaic items such as swimsuits, sunglasses, and hats.

Next door to the marketplace, the **Straw Market** sells items with a Bahamian touch—baskets, hats, handbags, and place mats. Quality varies, so look around before buying.

5 Barbados

No port of call in the southern Caribbean can compete with Barbados when it comes to natural beauty, attractions, and especially its seemingly endless stretches of pink and white sandy beaches—among the best in the entire Caribbean Basin. Originally operated on a plantation economy that made its British colonial aristocracy rich, the island is the most easterly in the Caribbean, floating in the mid-Atlantic like a great coral reef. Topography varies from rolling hills and savage waves on the eastern (Atlantic) coast to densely populated flatlands, rows of hotels and apartments, and sheltered beaches in the southwest. The people in Barbados are called Bajans, and you'll see this term used everywhere.

COMING ASHORE About a mile from the capital **Bridgetown,** the island's modern cruise ship terminal provides car rentals, taxi services, sightseeing tours, and there's a tourist information office, plus shops, bars, restaurants, an Internet cafe, a post office, and scads of vendors. The main terminal has docking capacity for five cruise ships. A sixth vessel can tie up at a nearby commercial pier, a 5-minute shuttle ride from the terminal.

GETTING AROUND You'll probably need transportation to get to the beaches, though you can walk into Bridgetown in about 15 minutes via a scenic park that runs along the shoreline between the port and city center. You'll find **taxis** just outside the cruise terminal. They're not metered, but their rates are fixed by the government (settle on the price before getting in). Recently opened, a **shuttle service** also takes visitors to key attractions.

LANGUAGE & CURRENCY **English** is spoken with an island lilt. The **Barbados dollar** (Bds$) is the official currency (Bds$1.95 = US$1; Bds$1 = US49¢), but U.S. dollars are commonly accepted.

Best Cruise Line Shore Excursions

It's not easy to get around Barbados quickly and conveniently, so a shore excursion is a good idea here.

Mount Gay Rum Distillery & Banks Beer Tour ($55, 3½ hr.): Talk about getting in the spirit. This excursion takes you for a tour and tipple at Barbados's number-one rum distillery; then it heads over to the Banks Brewery for the yeasty side of things.

Rainforest Hike & Cave Adventure ($80, 4 hr.): A guide leads your group through one of Barbados's rainforest gullies, then down into a natural cave.

Harrison's Cave & Tropical Rainforest Hike ($80, 4 hr.): Most cruise lines offer a tour to Harrison's Cave in the center of the island (see "On Your Own: Beyond the Port Area," below, for details), coupled with a 45-minute guided hike through the rainforest.

On Your Own: Beyond the Port Area

For the purposes of argument, let's consider Bridgetown "beyond walking distance," but for those who like a bit of a stroll, it's a pleasant walk into town, where you can take in the waterfront parks and classic Caribbean architecture. For the truly hearty hiker, a first-class beach can be found about a half-kilometer down the road once you cross over the charming bridge in town. Look for the entrance at an outdoor eatery called Taboo.

Most visitors spend their time exploring the island's beauty. All cruise ship excursions visit **Harrison's Cave,** Welchman Hall, St. Thomas (℡ **246/438-6640;** www.harrisonscave.com), Barbados's newly renovated top tourist attraction. Here, you can see a beautiful underground world from aboard an electric tram and trailer. Tours run daily from 8:45am to 3:45pm. Admission is $30 adults and $15 children age 12 and under. If you'd like to go on your own, the taxi ride takes about 30 minutes and costs at least $50 round-trip. About 1.6km (1 mile) away is the **Flower Forest,** Richmond Plantation, St. Joseph (℡ **246/433-8152;** www.barbados.org/flowfrst.htm), a former sugar plantation that's now a junglelike botanical garden, with paths winding among huge tropical flowers and plants. It's open daily from 9am to 5pm. Admission is $7 adults, $3.50 children.

Welchman Hall Gully (www.welchmanhallgullybarbados.com), St. Thomas (Hwy. 2 from Bridgetown), is a lush tropical garden owned by the Barbados National Trust. It's 13km (8 miles) from the port (reachable by bus) and features some plants that were here when English settlers landed in 1627, plus later imports like cocoa bushes, exotic orchids, and breadfruit trees that are supposedly descendants of the seedlings brought ashore by Captain Bligh, of *Bounty* fame. Many of the plants are labeled; occasionally you'll spot a wild green monkey. The gardens are open daily from 9am to 4:30pm. Admission is $10 adults, $5 children age 12 and under.

The **Sunbury Plantation House,** 25 minutes from Bridgetown along Highway 5 (© 246/423-6270; www.barbadosgreathouse.com), is the only plantation great house on Barbados whose rooms are all open for viewing. The 300-year-old house is steeped in history, with mahogany antiques, old prints, and a collection of horse-drawn carriages. It's open daily from 9am to 5pm. Admission is $9. Signs along the highway will guide you in, right before Six Cross Roads.

Beaches

Beaches on the island's western Gold Coast are far preferable (and closer) than those on the surf-pounded Atlantic side, which are dangerous for swimming. All Barbados beaches are open to the public, even those in front of the big resort hotels and private homes. You'll need a good pair of walking shoes or a taxi to get to them, but the baby-powder sand between your toes makes the trip well worth it.

ON THE GOLD COAST **Payne's Bay,** with access from Mannie's Suga Suga restaurant (© 246/419-4511), is a good beach for watersports, especially snorkeling. There's also a parking area here. This beach can get rather crowded, but the beautiful bay makes it worth it. Directly south of Payne's Bay, at Fresh Water Bay, is a trio of fine beaches: **Brighton Beach, Brandon's Beach,** and **Paradise Beach.** Farther north, **Church Point** can get crowded, but it's one of the most scenic bays in Barbados, and the swimming is ideal. Retreat under some shade trees when you've had enough sun. You can also order drinks at the Colony Club Resort's beach terrace.

Snorkelers in particular seek out the glassy blue waters by **Mullins Beach.** There are some shady areas, and you can park on the main road. Just north of here is another good stretch, **Heywoods Beach.**

ON THE SOUTH COAST Just outside Bridgetown, **Carlisle Bay Beach** is popular with locals and is a great snorkeling spot. Farther south, near Rockley, **Accra Beach** is the biggest on the south coast, and very popular with both locals and visitors. **Sandy Beach,** reached from the parking lot on the Worthing main road, has tranquil waters opening onto a lagoon. This is a family favorite, with lots of screaming and yelling, especially on weekends. Food and drink are sold here. Windsurfers are particularly fond of the trade winds that sweep across wide **Casuarina Beach,** even on the hottest summer days. Access is from Maxwell Coast Road, across the property of the Casuarina Beach Hotel. **Silver Sands Beach** is to the east of the town of Oistins, near the very southernmost point of Barbados, directly east of South Point Lighthouse. This white sandy beach is a favorite with many Bajans, who probably want to keep it a secret from as many visitors as possible. (Tough luck, Bajans!) Windsurfing is good here.

ON THE SOUTHEAST COAST The southeast coast is known for its big waves, especially at **Crane Beach,** a white sandy stretch backed by cliffs and palms, which often appears in travel-magazine articles about Barbados. The waters here allow excellent bodysurfing—but this is real ocean swimming, not just a dip in the calm Caribbean, so be careful. This one will cost you about $20 in taxi fare from the cruise pier, each way.

Shopping

The shopping-mall-size cruise terminal contains retail stores, duty-free shops, and a plethora of vendors selling arts and crafts, jewelry, liquor, china, crystal, electronics, perfume, leather goods, and great local hot sauce, as well as yummy Punch de Crème (you can get a free sample before buying), a creamy rum drink. Among Barbados handicrafts, you'll find lots of black-coral jewelry, but beware—because black coral is endangered, it's illegal to bring it back to the United States. We suggest looking, but not buying. Local clay potters turn out some really interesting products, some based on centuries-old designs.

6 Belize

Situated on the northeastern tip of Central America, bordering Mexico on the north, Guatemala to the west and south, and the Caribbean to the east, Belize combines Central American and Caribbean cultures. It's home to ancient Maya ruins and a 298km (185-mile) coral reef that runs the entire length of the country—the largest in the Western Hemisphere and the second largest in the world—and supports a tremendous number of patch reefs, shoals, and more than 1,000 islands called cayes (pronounced *keys*), the largest and most populous being **Ambergris Caye.** (Both Ambergris Caye and Caye Caulker are popular with visitors, but require a flight from Belize City. However, smaller lines such as Windstar may just skip Belize City completely and anchor offshore from the cayes and other parts of the mainland, such as southern Dangriga and Placencia.) Unlike many other Caribbean countries, Belize is serious in its dedication to conservation: One-fifth of its total landmass is dedicated as nature reserves, and 7,770 sq. km (2,973 sq. miles) of its waters are protected as well.

Belize City is the economic center of the country. Choosing which natural or manmade wonder to explore will be the most stressful thing you do in this very laid-back, diverse, stable, and English-speaking nation. Its population ranges from Creoles, Garifuna (Black Carib Indians), and mestizos (a mix of Spanish and Indian) to Spanish, Maya, English, Lebanese, and Chinese peoples and Eastern Indians. The country has the highest concentration of Maya sites among all Central American nations.

COMING ASHORE   Shallow waters mean ships must anchor offshore and tender passengers in—a 20- to 30-minute trip. You arrive at a multimillion-dollar pier called the **Fort Street Tourism Village,** which has four main terminals with shops, restaurants, and tourist information. The port can accommodate four cruise ships on a given day; each is assigned to a separate terminal.

GETTING AROUND   Taxis are available at the pier, in town, and in resort areas, and are easily recognized by their green license plates. Although the taxis have no meters, the drivers do charge somewhat standard rates, but it's always important to settle your fare before hiring a taxi. Aside from the local shopping, most other attractions are about an hour away.

LANGUAGE & CURRENCY   English is the official language of Belize, although Spanish, Creole, Garifuna, and Mayan are spoken throughout the country as well. The **Belize dollar** (BZ) has a fixed exchange rate of BZ$2 = US$1 (BZ$1 = US50¢). Most establishments, as well as taxis and vendors on the street, take U.S. dollars. In especially touristy areas, just be sure to ask if the price quoted is in U.S. or Belize dollars. Unless otherwise specified, prices in this section are given in U.S. dollars.

CALLING FROM THE U.S.   To make a call from the U.S. to Belize, dial the international access code **(011),** the country code **(501),** and then the number of the establishment.

Best Cruise Line Shore Excursions

Lamanai ($96, 7 hr.): Lamanai is one of the largest ceremonial centers in Belize. In the original Mayan language, its name means "submerged crocodile," and various crocodile carvings are seen throughout the site. After a 45-minute drive, you'll board a riverboat and head up the New River. Along the way, through the mangroves, your guide will point out crocodiles basking in the sun, a variety of birds (including jaçanas and hawks), delicate waterlilies, and other exotic flowers such as black orchids. You'll pass local fisherman and, surprisingly, Mennonite farms—Mennonites from Canada and Mexico began arriving in Belize in 1958 in search of land and a more isolated and simple life, and today their community numbers around 7,000. Landing at the Lamanai grounds, you'll have lunch and then tour the series of temples. There are more than 700 structures, most of them still buried beneath mounds of earth. For a view above the thick jungle, you can climb some of the temples—look in the trees for toucans and spider monkeys playing or napping. You won't mistake the roar of the howler monkey.

Xunantunich ($90, 7 hr.): This site, also called Maiden of the Rock, is near the Guatemalan border overlooking the Mopan River; it was a major ceremonial center during the classic Maya period. After crossing the river by hand-cranked ferry, you can explore six major plazas surrounded by more than 25 temples and palaces, including El Castillo (the castle), largest of the temples. Be sure to climb to the top—it's well worth it for the amazing panoramic view. There's also a visitor center with old excavation photos, a scale model, and a few exhibits and souvenir shops. Afterward, you'll head to San Ignacio to eat lunch and enjoy a marimba band.

Hol Chan Marine Reserve & Shark Ray Alley ($100, 7½ hr.): You'll head north for an hour-long speedboat ride to Hol Chan (Mayan for "little channel"), 6.4km (4 miles) southeast of San Pedro on Ambergris Caye; snorkel the reef for about an hour; and then head off to the Shark Ray Alley dive site, about 5 minutes away, where you'll see and pet dozens of southern stingrays and nurse sharks.

Cave Tubing & Jungle Trek ($109, 6¼ hr.): On arriving at Jaguar Paw, you take a 45-minute hike down a jungle trail where your guide will point out various plants and trees used by the ancient Maya for medicinal purposes. When you get to the cave, your guide will hand out flashlights and inner tubes and set you afloat, propelled by the current, through the cave system. On several occasions, you'll emerge into the sunlight before entering another cave. The float lasts about 2 hours, after which you'll have lunch. Bring a change of clothes. Minimum age: 12.

Two-Tank Scuba Dive at Turneffe Atoll ($169, 6 hr.): After a 50-minute boat ride, you arrive at Turneffe Atoll for dives at two different sites (with depths of 50–70 ft.) among reef fish and growths of sponge and coral.

On Your Own: Within Walking Distance

Belize City is the hub of the country, but doesn't boast the country's major attractions. The historic **harbor district** right around the pier is small and quaint. You'll find a few restaurants here, and the **Baron Bliss Park and Lighthouse** is just a short stroll away. After sailing from Portugal, the eponymous baron arrived sick with food poisoning and remained aboard his yacht for 2 months while local fisherman and administrators treated him kindly and taught him about Belize. He died soon after, but not before changing his will and leaving $2 million to Belize in a trust fund. That money made possible the building of the Bliss Institute Library and Museum and a number of health clinics and markets around the country, as well as helping with the Belize City water system. The baron is considered Belize's greatest benefactor, and Baron Bliss Day, a national holiday, is celebrated on March 9.

Outside the immediate port area, much of the rest of the city is run-down and poor, with narrow, crowded streets and many old colonial structures in need of repair. However, because tourism is an important industry in Belize, the country is making an effort to spruce up the city and reduce crime, instituting a squad of tourism police to patrol popular tourist areas. Its officers are dressed in brown uniforms.

On Your Own: Beyond the Port Area

See "Best Cruise Line Shore Excursions," above, for a discussion of the Maya ruins. Animal enthusiasts might want to visit the **Community Baboon Sanctuary,** about 48km (30 miles) west of Belize City off the Northern Highway in the Belize District (© 501/220-2181; www.howlermonkeys.org), which offers a guided tour through forest trails for $5. Through a grass-roots effort, the villagers and landowners are committed to preserving the habitat necessary to ensure a healthy population of black howler monkeys (known locally as baboons). Those more interested in birding can tour the **Crooked Tree Wildlife Sanctuary,** about 8km (5 miles) farther up the Northern Highway (© 501/614-5658). The sanctuary provides a habitat for more than 360 species of birds. A visit to the **Belize Zoo,** along the Western Highway (© 501/220-8004; www.belizezoo.org), is a worthwhile venture. First created as a haven for injured animals that couldn't be returned to the wild, the zoo now houses an impressive array of large cats, primates, reptiles, and birds in large, airy enclosures. It's open daily from 8am to 5pm. Admission is $8 adults, $4 children.

Back in Belize City, if you want to do some gambling, the small **Princess Hotel-Casino** is 2km (1¼ miles) from the cruise pier on Newtown Barricks Road (© 501/223-2670); it's about 10 minutes and $6 by taxi from the pier.

Beaches

Compared to many other parts of the Caribbean, the beaches of Belize are neither the biggest nor the widest, but they are relaxing, with very clear water. Areas with the best beach sunbathing are in the cayes, including Ambergris Caye, Caye Caulker, and Tobacco Caye, and on the mainland to the south in Dangriga and Placencia. There are no beaches near Belize City.

Shopping

In general, the best buys in Belize are wooden and slate carvings, Maya calendars, pottery, ceramics, and furniture made by the Mennonites. At the pier, the **Tourism Village** has shops specializing in local souvenirs such as mahogany bowls, jewelry, clothes, assorted carvings, and artwork. A local favorite is **Marie Sharp's hot sauces and jams.** They're served everywhere and can be purchased to take home.

7 British Virgin Islands: Tortola & Virgin Gorda

With small bays and hidden coves that were once havens for pirates (Norman Island is said to have been the prototype for Robert Louis Stevenson's *Treasure Island*), the British Virgin Islands (BVIs) are among the world's loveliest cruising regions. Among its 60-some islands, only **Tortola, Virgin Gorda,** and **Jost Van Dyke** (plus Anegada, 16 miles to the north) are of significant size. The English officially annexed the islands in 1672, and today they're a British territory, with their own elected government and a population of about 21,000. Tortola attracts the megaships, while Virgin Gorda and Jost Van Dyke attract the small ships of the Seabourn, SeaDream, Windstar, and Star Clippers fleets.

LANGUAGE & CURRENCY   English is spoken here, and the **U.S. dollar** is the legal currency (much to the surprise of arriving Brits).

Tortola

Situated on the island's south shore, the once-sleepy village and colonial capital of **Road Town** became a bustling center after the 70-acre Wickhams Cay marina brought in a massive yacht-chartering business. The rest of the southern coast is characterized by rugged mountain peaks. On the northern coast are beautiful bays with white sandy beaches, banana trees, mangoes, and clusters of palms.

If your ship isn't scheduled to visit Virgin Gorda, but you want to, just catch a boat, ferry, or launch here and you'll be on the island in no time, because it's only a 12-mile trip.

COMING ASHORE   Many ships dock right in **Road Town Harbour** or anchor offshore and tender in passengers to Road Town, **West End** ferry terminal or **Soper's Hole.**

GETTING AROUND   You can walk around Road Town. Open-air and van-style **taxis** meet every arriving cruise ship and carry passengers to the beaches and other attractions. It's more economical to travel with at least three people, which can bring down the per-head price to go to the beach from $24 to $8.

Best Cruise Line Shore Excursions

Town & Country Excursion ($36, 3½ hr.): Tour the island in an open-air minibus, visiting the Botanic Gardens, Cane Garden Bay, Bomba's Surfside Shack at Cappoon's Bay, and Soper's Hole.

Tortola Snorkeling Adventure ($60, 3 hr.): Cross the Sir Frances Drake Channel by boat to Norman Island, one of the BVI's prime snorkel sites, full of coral formations, colorful fish, and a group of caves at Treasure Point, where pirate treasure is reputedly hidden.

Forest Walk & Beach Tour ($46, 4½ hr.): Safari buses take you to Tortola's interior for a 1-mile hike through the Sage Mountain rainforest to the highest point in the Virgin Islands, then head down the Ridge Road for a brief stop at the Botanic Gardens. Minimum age: 12.

Wreck of the *Rhone* Two-Tank Certified Dive ($155, 4 hr.): A guided dive takes you to a British ship sunk in an 1867 hurricane, its bow lying almost fully intact in 80 feet of water. All divers must be certified and have dived within the past 2 years.

The Baths at Virgin Gorda ($75, 5 hr.): If your ship doesn't stop in Virgin Gorda, you can still go from Tortola, taking a 45-minute cruise across the Drake Channel and then spending a couple of hours swimming around at the Baths, a veritable bouquet of seaside boulders formed by volcanic activity (see description under Virgin Gorda, below).

On Your Own: Within Walking Distance

Besides the handful of shops on Main and Upper Main streets in Road Town, there's also the **Botanic Gardens** (*C* 284/494-4557) right in the middle of town, across from the police station. It has a wide variety of flowers and plants, including a section on medicinal plants. It's open daily from 8:30am to 4:30pm. Admission is $3.

On Your Own: Beyond the Port Area

On Tortola, you have mainly the natural landscape to observe. The big attraction is **Sage Mountain National Park** (www.bvinationalparkstrust.org/toparks.html), its peak rising to 1,716 feet, the highest point in the BVIs and USVIs. The park was established in 1964 to protect those remnants of Tortola's original forests not burned or cleared during its plantation era. You'll find a lush forest of mango, papaya, breadfruit, coconut, birch berry, mountain guava, and guava berry trees, many labeled for identification. This is a great place to enjoy a picnic while overlooking neighboring islets and cays. Any taxi driver can take you to the mountain. Before going, stop at the Wickhams Cay tourist office, near the pier, and pick up a brochure with a map and an outline of the park's trails. The two main hikes are the Rain Forest Trail and the Mahogany Forest Trail.

Beaches

Most of the beaches are a 20-minute taxi ride from the cruise dock. Figure on about $20 per person one-way (some will charge less, as little as about $6 per person if you've got a group), but discuss it with the driver before setting out. You can also ask him to pick you up at a designated time.

The finest beach is at **Cane Garden Bay** on the island's northwest coast, across the mountains from Road Town but worth the trip. **Rhymer's** (*C* 284/495-4639) serves a good if not inexpensive lunch of the conch, whelk, and barbecue-spareribs variety (main courses: $15 and up). Surfers like **Apple Bay,** also on the northwest side, while next-door **Cappoon's Bay** is known more for **Bomba's Surfside Shack** (*C* 284/495-4148), the oldest, most memorable bar on Tortola, covered with Day-Glo graffiti and ladies' undergarments and laced with wire and rejected odds and ends of plywood, driftwood, and abandoned rubber tires. Lunch is about $10, and beer and Painkillers, that classic Caribbean rum specialty, are dispensed till the cows come home. At the extreme west end of the island, **Smuggler's Cove** is a wide crescent of white sand wrapped around calm, sky-blue water.

Shopping

Shopping on Tortola is a minor activity compared to other Caribbean ports. Only British goods are imported without duty, and they are the best buys, especially English china. You'll also find West Indian art, terra-cotta pottery, wicker and rattan home furnishings, Mexican glassware, dhurrie rugs, baskets, and ceramics.

Most stores are on Main Street in Road Town. The **Pusser's Company Store,** Main Street, Road Town (*C* 284/494-2467; www.pussers.com), has a selection of classic travel and adventure clothing, along with Pusser's famous rum, which was served aboard British Navy ships for over 300 years.

A Slice of Paradise: Jost Van Dyke

Covering only 10 sq. km (4 sq. miles), mountainous Jost Van Dyke is an off-beat treat, visited mostly by private yachts and a few small cruise ships, which all anchor offshore. They often throw afternoon beach parties on the sands at White Bay, with the crew lugging ashore a picnic lunch for a leisurely afternoon of eating, drinking, and swimming. If your ship stays late, don't miss a trip to **Foxy's** (✆ **284/495-9258;** www.foxysbar.com), a well-known watering hole at the far end of Great Harbour and popular with the yachting set as well as locals. It's your classic island beach bar, with music pounding and drinks flowing into the wee hours.

Virgin Gorda

Instead of visiting Tortola, some small cruise ships put in at lovely Virgin Gorda, famous for its boulder-strewn beach known as the **Baths.** The third-largest island in the colony, it got its name ("Fat Virgin") from Christopher Columbus, who thought the mountain framing it looked like a protruding stomach. Megaships that stop at Tortola usually provide a 4½-hour excursion to Virgin Gorda for about $70.

COMING ASHORE Virgin Gorda doesn't have a pier to suit any of the large ships. Most vessels anchor in Gorda Sound and tender passengers to a pier at **Spanish Town,** which can accommodate smaller cruise ships. Ferries from Tortola also berth here.

GETTING AROUND Taxis are available at the pier and will take visitors to the Baths and area beaches for about $6 per person each way. Entry fee to the Baths is $3 per person. For a tour of the island, contact Andy Flax of the **Virgin Gorda Tours Association** (c/o the Fischer's Cove Beach Hotel; ✆ **284/495-5252**). It costs about $60 per couple, and you'll be picked up at the dock if you give at least 24-hours notice.

Best Cruise Line Shore Excursions

Island Tour & the Baths ($80, 4 hr.): Most Virgin Gorda tours are variations on this theme: touring the island by open-air bus, stopping at its highest point for a snapshot, taking in the village of Spanish Town, then stopping at Copper Mine National Park, where Amerindian and later European miners once dug for copper. The ruins you see today are what's left of a British operation from 1860. Tours end at the Baths, where you'll have time for swimming, snorkeling, and exploring among the boulders.

On Your Own: Within Walking Distance

The **Virgin Gorda Yacht Harbour** at St. Thomas Bay has several restaurants and shops.

On Your Own: Beyond the Port Area

You might consider cabbing up to glamorous **Little Dix Bay Resort** (✆ **284/495-5555;** www.littledixbay.com), established by Laurance Rockefeller in 1965, to enjoy a lunch buffet at an outdoor pavilion that shows off Virgin Gorda's beautiful hills, bays, and sky (best to call first to make reservations). Aside from this, most people head for the Baths, which really is a spectacular site (see "Beaches," below).

Beaches

The major reason why cruise ships come to Virgin Gorda is to visit the **Baths,** where geologists believe ice-age eruptions caused house-size boulders to topple onto one another to form the saltwater grottoes we see today. The pools around the Baths are excellent for swimming and snorkeling (equipment can be rented on the beach), and a crawl between and among the boulders, which in places are very cavelike, is more than a little bit fun. A cafe sits just above the beach for a quick snack or a cool drink. There's a $3 entry fee to the Baths if you are not visiting with a tour.

Devil's Bay, a great beach just south of the Baths, is usually less crowded. Just north of the Baths is **Spring Bay,** one of the island's best beaches, with white sand, clear water, and good snorkeling. Nearby is the **Crawl,** a natural pool formed by rocks, great for novice snorkelers; a marked path leads here from Spring Bay. **Trunk Bay,** just to the north, is a wide sand beach that can be reached via a rough path from Spring Bay.

Devil's Bay National Park can be reached by a trail from the Baths. The walk to the secluded coral-sand beach takes about 15 minutes through a natural setting of boulders and dry coastal vegetation.

Shopping

The only notable shopping here is right at the Yacht Harbour complex, where you'll find a few dive shops, boutiques, and handicrafts shops.

8 Cozumel & the Yucatán Peninsula

The island of Cozumel, just off Mexico's Yucatán coast, is one of the busiest cruise ports you'll ever see, with up to 16 ships visiting every day during high season, counting those that anchor offshore and ferry in passengers. All that activity can make the port town of **San Miguel** seem more like Times Square than the sleepy, refreshingly gritty town it once was, and the pace of transformation doesn't seem to be slowing down, despite the major thrashing from Hurricane Wilma in 2005. A superfast cleanup and rebuilding effort had such success that ships began returning to the port only a month after the storm hit, and things have been moving apace ever since. By the time you read this, Wilma's damage should be completely erased.

The bustling shops, bars, and restaurants of San Miguel have their draw, but for us the major allure of Cozumel remains its proximity to the ancient Maya ruins such as **Tulum** and **Chichén Itzá,** on the mainland of the Yucatán Peninsula. To see the ruins from here, you must take the 45-minute ferry ride between Cozumel and **Playa del Carmen,** on the mainland, though a few cruise ships call directly at Playa, anchoring offshore. Many ships en route to Cozumel pause in Playa del Carmen to drop off passengers who have signed up for ruins tours. After the tours, passengers take a ferry back to the ship in Cozumel (or, if the tour is by plane, get dropped off at the airport in Cozumel, near downtown). If your ship is not stopping at Playa, bear in mind that the ferry ride back and forth from Cozumel will take almost 2 hours total (note, the swells can be rough for those prone to sea sickness); if you're more interested in relaxing, you may want to hang out on the island.

In recent years, a handful of other Yucatán ports have come onto the scene, including **Calica,** just south of Playa, where there's little more than a pier; **Progreso,** on the Gulf coast of the Yucatán, making it the closest to Chichén Itzá, as well as the city of Mérida; and **Costa Maya,** about 161km (100 miles) south near the sleepy fishing village of Mahajual.

LANGUAGE & CURRENCY **Spanish** is the tongue of the land, although **English** is spoken in most places that cater to tourists. The Mexican currency is the **nuevo peso (new peso).** Its symbol is the "$" sign, but it's hardly the equivalent of the U.S. dollar—the exchange rate is 13 pesos = US$1 (1 peso = about US7¢). The main tourist stores gladly accept U.S. dollars.

CALLING FROM THE U.S. You need to dial the international access code **(011)** and the country code **(52)** before the numbers listed below.

Maya Ruins & Other Mainland Attractions

Because all of the sites listed here are quite far from the cruise piers, most cruise passengers visit them as part of **shore excursions.** Admission to the sites is included in the excursion prices, which typically run from $75 to $100 (by bus) to $200-plus by plane for Chichén Itzá, around $75 for a bus to Tulum or Cobá. Chichén Itzá and Cobá are all-day excursions. Visits to smaller Tulum are often paired with a visit to the Xel-Ha Eco Park, making it a full-day trek ($125 on up). Guests are usually served free and refreshingly cold Mexican beer on the bus ride back after exploring the ruins.

CHICHÉN ITZÁ The largest and most fabled of the Yucatán ruins, Chichén Itzá (meaning "Mouth of the Well of the Itza Family") was founded in A.D. 445 by the Maya and later inhabited by the Toltecs of central Mexico. At its height, the city had about 50,000 residents, but it was mysteriously abandoned only 2 centuries after its founding. After lying dormant for 2 more centuries, the site was resettled and enjoyed prosperity again until the early–13th century, when it was once more relinquished to the surrounding jungle. The area covers 18 sq. km (7 sq. miles), so you can see only a fraction of it on a day trip, which typically includes a flight from Playa del Carmen, since it's a 3-hour drive each way. Following are some of the area's highlights:

The best known of Chichén Itzá's ruins is the magnificent **El Castillo pyramid** (also called the Pyramid of Kukulkán), which was built with the Maya calendar in mind. The four stairways leading up to the central platform each have 91 steps, making a total of 364; when you add the top central platform, you get the 365 days of the solar year. On either side of each stairway are nine terraces, for a total of 18 on each face of the pyramid, equaling the number of months in the Maya solar calendar. Decorating these terraces are 52 panels that represent the 52-year cycle when both the solar and religious calendars would become realigned. The pyramid's alignment is such that on the **spring** or **fall equinox,** light striking the pyramid gives the illusion of a snake slithering down the steps to join its gigantic stone head mounted at the base.

Northwest of El Castillo is Chichén's main **Ball Court (Juego de Pelota),** the largest and best preserved of such Maya ruins anywhere. Carved on both walls of the ball court are scenes of Maya figures dressed as ball players and decked out in heavy protective padding. The carved scene also shows a headless player kneeling with blood shooting from his neck; another player holding the head looks on. Here's the way it worked: Players on two teams tried to knock a hard rubber ball through one of the two stone rings placed high on either wall, using only their elbows, knees, and hips. According to legend, the losing players paid for defeat with their lives. Some experts, however, say the victors were the only appropriate sacrifices for the gods. Note the lack of bleacher seating: As the games were played as a ritual, for the entertainment of the gods, only a single judge looked on.

Temples are set at both ends of the ball court. The **North Temple** has sculptured pillars and more sculptures inside, as well as badly ruined murals. The acoustics of the

Cozumel & the Yucatán Ports

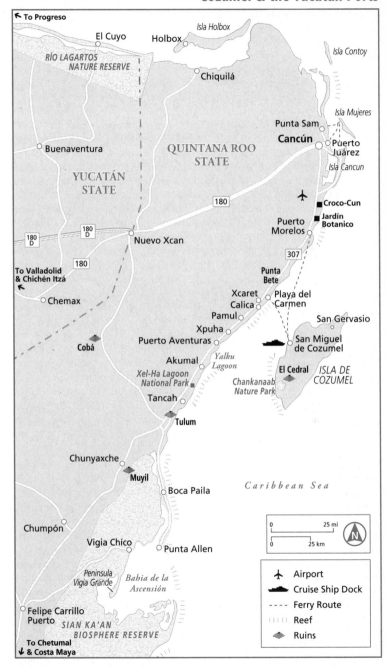

To Progreso

Isla Holbox

El Cuyo

Holbox

Isla Contoy

RÍO LAGARTOS
NATURE RESERVE

Chiquilá

Isla Mujeres

Punta Sam

Cancún

Buenaventura

QUINTANA ROO
STATE

Puerto
Juárez

Isla Cancun

YUCATÁN
STATE

180

Croco-Cun

Jardín
Botanico

180
D

180
D

Puerto
Morelos

180
D

Nuevo Xcan

307

180

To Valladolid
& Chichén Itzá

Punta
Bete

Chemax

Xcaret
Calica

Playa del
Carmen

Pamul

San Gervasio

Xpuha

Cobá

Puerto Aventuras

San Miguel
de Cozumel

Akumal

Yalku
Lagoon

Xel-Ha Lagoon
National Park

El Cedral

ISLA DE
COZUMEL

Chankanaab
Nature Park

Tancah

Tulum

Chunyaxche

Muyil

Caribbean Sea

Boca Paila

Chumpón

0   25 mi

0   25 km

N

Vigía Chíco

Punta Allen

Peninsula
Vigia Grande

Bahia de la
Ascensión

✈ Airport

Cruise Ship Dock

Felipe Carrillo
Puerto

SIAN KA'AN
BIOSPHERE RESERVE

- - - - Ferry Route

Reef

To Chetumal
& Costa Maya

Ruins

ball court are so good that from the North Temple, a person speaking can be heard clearly at the opposite end, about 136m (450 ft.) away. Near the southeastern corner of the main ball court is the **Temple of the Jaguars,** a small temple with serpent columns and carved panels showing warriors and jaguars. Up the steps and inside the temple, a mural chronicles a battle in a Maya village. To the right of the ball court is the **Temple of the Skulls (Tzompantli),** decorated with rows of skulls carved into the stone platform. When a sacrificial victim's head was cut off, it was impaled on a pole and displayed in a tidy row with the others.

Follow the dirt road (actually an ancient *sacbé,* or causeway, made from a white, compacted, claylike soil that made the way visible at night) that heads north from the Platform of Venus. After about 5 minutes, you'll come to the **Sacred Cenote,** a great natural well that may have given Chichén Itzá its name. This well was used for ceremonial purposes, not for drinking water. According to legend, sacrificial victims adorned with gold and other riches were drowned in this pool to honor the rain god Chaac. In the early–20th century, American consul and Harvard professor Edward Thompson bought the ruins of Chichén Itzá and explored the cenote with dredges and divers, unearthing (and exporting) a fortune in gold and jade.

Due east of El Castillo is one of the most impressive structures at Chichén: the **Temple of the Warriors,** named for the carvings of warriors marching along its walls. It's also called the Group of the Thousand Columns for the rows of broken square pillars that flank it. A figure of Chaac-Mool sits at the top of the temple, surrounded by impressive columns carved in relief to look like enormous feathered serpents. According to scholars, the high priest would tear out a sacrificial victim's heart here, and then throw the body down the steps, where another priest would strip off its skin. The high priest would then dress himself in the skin, cross to a nearby platform, and dance. Lovely, eh?

South of the temple is another group of columns (these ones round) that were once an important **market,** controlling the trade in salt on the Yucatán. South of the market, a cluster of interesting ruins include the **Observatory (El Caracol),** a complex building with a circular tower through whose slits astronomers could observe the cardinal directions and the approach of the all-important spring and autumn equinoxes; the **Edifice of the Nuns (Edificio de las Monjas),** which was named for its resemblance to a European convent; and the **Church (La Iglesia),** one of the oldest buildings at Chichén and named for its beautiful decorations. Its ceiling, with a Maya false arch, is a stone replica of the thatched ceiling in a typical Maya home of the period.

TULUM About 130km (80 miles) south of Cancún and about a 30-minute drive from Playa del Carmen, the small walled city of Tulum is the single-most-visited Maya ruin due to its proximity to the ports. It was the only Maya city built on the coast and the only one inhabited when the Spanish conquistadors arrived in the 1500s. From its dramatic perch atop seaside cliffs, you can see wonderful panoramic views of the Caribbean. Though nowhere near as large and impressive as Chichén Itzá, Tulum shares a similar prominent feature: a ruin topped with a **temple to Kukulkán,** the primary Maya/Olmec god. Other important structures include the **Temple of the Frescoes,** the **Temple of the Descending God,** the **House of Columns,** and the **House of the Cenote,** which is a well. There's also a sliver of silky beach amid the site, so bring your bathing suit for a quick refreshing dip. New visitor facilities include a well-stocked bookstore and a soon-to-open museum.

COBÁ A 35-minute drive northwest of Tulum puts you at Cobá, site of one of the most important city-states in the Maya empire. Cobá flourished from A.D. 300 to

1000, with its population numbering perhaps 40,000. Excavation work began in 1972, but archaeologists estimate that only a small percentage of this dead city has yet been uncovered. The site lies on four lakes. Its 81 primitive acres provide excellent opportunities for exploration by hikers. Cobá's pyramid, **Nohoch Mul,** is the tallest in the Yucatán.

XCARET ECOLOGICAL PARK   About 6.5km (4 miles) south of Playa del Carmen on the coast, Xcaret (pronounced Ish-car-*et*) (© **998/881-2400;** www.xcaret. com) is a 100-hectare (247-acre) ecological theme park with small Maya ruins scattered about the lushly landscaped acres. Visitors can put on life jackets and snorkeling gear and ride the currents through more than a kilometer of well-lit underground caves, or don a Sea-Trek helmet and walk across the ocean floor. (You can also swim with dolphins, though this is not included in the cost of excursions.) The park has a botanical garden, an aquarium, a sea-turtle breeding and release facility, a dive shop, a rotating observation tower, a Maya village, and two theaters with worthwhile cultural shows. Excursions run about $90 on up and take up a full day from Cozumel.

XEL-HA ECO PARK   Farther south of Xcaret, Xel-Ha (pronounced Shell-*Ha*) (© **998/883-0470;**) features a sprawling natural lagoon filled with sparkling blue-green water and surrounded by lush foliage. The use of inner tubes and life vests is included in the admission price, and you can spend a great couple of hours wending your way from one end of the snaking body of calm water to the other, accompanied by schools of tropical fish—or you can just chill on a beach chair and grab lunch from one of the restaurants. Xel-Ha has dolphins, too, and snorkeling gear, snuba (a combination of snorkeling and scuba), and sea-trekking are also available at additional cost. Alternatively, you can take a trail walk with a knowledgeable, eco-minded guide who will identify local plants and take you to sacred cenote sinkholes where ancient Mayas made offerings to the gods. Full-day excursions start at about $125 on up from Cozumel.

Cozumel

The ancient Mayas, who lived here for 12 centuries, would be shocked by the two-million-plus cruise passengers who now visit Cozumel each year, and by the fast-food, raucous-bar, and power-shopping character of San Miguel. Outside town, though, development hasn't destroyed the island's natural beauty, and there are still acres of low-lying scrub forest containing protected plant and animal species. Offshore, the government has set aside 32km (20 miles) of coral reefs as an underwater national park, including the stunning **Palancar Reef,** the world's second-largest natural coral formation.

COMING ASHORE   There are three main piers in Cozumel, all within about 3 miles of the tourist hub San Miguel. The pier at **Punta Langosta** is right in the center of town, which puts you just steps from the shops, restaurants, and cafes across the street. **Puerto Maya** pier is about 5km (3 miles) south of town and the busy **International Pier** is in between the two. On busy days when all three piers are full, ships anchor offshore. Both Puerto Maya and the International Pier are a $10 taxi ride from town.

GETTING AROUND   The town of San Miguel is so small that you can walk anywhere you want to go. For pedestrians, the classic grid layout makes it easy to get around, though note that all odd-numbered streets are on the south side of the pier and all even-numbered streets are heading north. Essentially, there's only one major road on the island—it starts at the northern tip, hugs the western shoreline, then loops around the southern tip and returns through the middle of the island to the capital.

Taxis are available at the piers; the average fare from San Miguel to most major resorts and beaches is about $25. More distant island rides cost $25 and up. It's customary to overcharge cruise ship passengers, so settle on a fare before getting in. **Motor scooters** and **mopeds** are also a popular means of getting around (though be careful!), and can be rented from (among others) **Auto Rent** (© 987/872-3532), in the Hotel El Cid La Ceiba, right next to the International Pier. The cost is about $35 per day, including helmet; insurance is an extra $6.

Best Cruise Line Shore Excursions

See "Maya Ruins & Other Mainland Attractions," above, for details on the big mainland excursions. In addition to the tours below, the cruise lines each offer over 50 to 75 different tours, from snorkeling to diving, hikes, party-boats, tours by Segway, dolphin encounters, and tons more.

Tropical 4×4 Safari Tour ($90, 5 hr.): Hop in a four-seat jeep, draw straws to see who gets to drive, and explore the natural side of Cozumel. Much of the roller-coaster-like route is off-road, and the jeeps travel in a convoy, stopping eventually at a lovely secluded beach for swimming, snorkeling, and a picnic lunch. Similar tours are also offered via ATV, Dune Buggy, and Jungle Buggy.

Discover Mexico theme park ($50, 2 hr.): One of Cozumel's newest attractions, this indoor/outdoor cultural park takes visitors through simulations of Mexico's archaeological sites, colonial buildings, and museum-style exhibits. Walk among scale models of Mexico's most famous monuments and sites.

Maya Frontier Horseback Riding ($85, 4 hr.): Worthwhile horseback-riding tours allow a chance to see Cozumel's landscape, but although they tout visits to Maya ruins, don't get your hopes up—there's little more than a few refrigerator-size rocks here and there on Cozumel. A bus transports riders to a ranch, where the ride begins.

Harley-Davidson Custom Sportster Island Tour ($300, 5 hr.): Tour the island on the seat of a way cool bike, with stops for taking photos, eating lunch, and swimming. Riders must be at least 23 years old and passengers, 18 years.

On Your Own: Within Walking Distance

Avenida Rafael Melgar, the principal street along the waterfront, traces the western shore of the island, site of the best resorts and beaches. Most of the shops and restaurants are along this street. The things to do here are basically shop and drink, and boy oh boy, are there a lot of choices!

Carlos 'n Charlie's, Av. Rafael Melgar 551 (© **987/869-1647;** www.carlosand charlies.com), is Mexico's equivalent of the Hard Rock Cafe, but much wilder. Though it moved a few years ago from its old beer-slopped digs into a more sterile Houlihan's-style space right across from the Punta Langosta pier, it's still got deafening music, with tourists dancing and gulping down yard-long glasses of beer. Many a cruise passenger has stumbled back from this place clutching a souvenir glass as if it were the Holy Grail—dubious proof of a visit to Mexico. There also is actually a **Hard Rock Cozumel,** at Av. Rafael Melgar 2A (© **987/872-5271;** www.hardrock.com), which serves the hard stuff as well as burgers and grilled beef or chicken fajitas. Another party spot is **Fat Tuesday,** at the end of the International Pier (© **987/ 872-5130**), where 16-ounce margaritas cost $7 a pop and 24-ounce versions a few bucks more.

If that's not your scene, you can drop into the small **Museo de la Isla de Cozumel,** on Avenida Rafael Melgar between calles 4 and 6 North (✆ **987/872-1475**). Once Cozumel's first luxury hotel, it now displays exhibits that take you from pre-Hispanic times through the colonial era to the present. Admission is $3.

On Your Own: Beyond the Port Area

About a $10 taxi ride from the center of San Miguel is the **Chankanaab Nature Park** (www.cozumelparks.com), Carretera Sur, Km 9 (no phone), where a saltwater lagoon, offshore reefs, and underwater caves have been turned into an archaeological park, botanical garden, and wildlife sanctuary. More than 10 countries have contributed seedlings and cuttings. Some 60 species of marine life occupy the lagoon, including sea turtles and captive dolphins (swim with them for $150 for 1 hr., minimum age 6). Reproductions of Maya dwellings are scattered throughout the park. There's also a wide white-sand beach with thatch umbrellas and a changing area with lockers and showers. Both scuba divers and snorkelers enjoy examining the sunken ship offshore; there are four dive shops here. Admission is $19 adults and $10 children ages 3 to 11. The 10-minute taxi ride from the downtown tender and ferry pier (Muelle Fiscal) costs about $15.

The few Maya ruins on Cozumel—**San Gervasio** (north of San Miguel), once a ceremonial center and capital, and **El Cedral** (to the south), site of a Maya arch and a few small ruins covered in heavy growth—are very, very minor compared to those on the mainland, and worth visiting only if you happen to be in the neighborhood (visiting Playa San Francisco, say, which lies about 3.2km/2 miles from El Cedral).

Beaches

Cozumel's best powdery white-sand beach, **Playa San Francisco,** stretches for some 5km (3 miles) along the southwestern shoreline. You can rent equipment for watersports here, or have lunch at one of the many palapa restaurants and bars on the shoreline. There's no admission to the beach, and it's about a $15 taxi ride south of San Miguel's downtown pier. If you land at the International Pier, you're practically at the beach already.

Playa Mia (formerly called Playa del Sol) is a fine beach about a mile south of Playa San Francisco, but because it has a big reputation, it's likely to be wall to wall with your fellow cruisers. It's also built up with bars, restaurants, watersports rentals, a miniature zoo, a small playground, underwater re-creations of all the major Maya ruins, and more, and there's a $12 entrance fee.

Playa Bonita (sometimes called Punta Chiqueros) is one of the least crowded beaches; it lies on the east (windward) side of the island and is difficult to reach unless you rent a vehicle or throw yourself at the mercy of a taxi driver. It sits in a moon-shaped cove sheltered from the Caribbean Sea by an offshore reef. Waves are only moderate, the sand is powdery, and the water is clear.

If you don't want to go far, two hotel beaches are a stone's throw north of the International Pier (facing the water, they're on the right). Both welcome day visitors to use their small beach, cabanas, pools, and changing facilities. **El Cid La Ceiba** charges a hefty $75 per person for the day, while the **Park Royale** charges $60, which includes all drinks, snacks, and lunch.

Shopping

Wall-to-wall shops along the waterfront in San Miguel, starting right across the street from the Punta Langosta pier and stretching in every direction, sell the usual tourist goods, Mexican crafts, and especially **silver jewelry,** which is big business here. The latter is generally sold by weight. Because of the influx of cruise ship passengers, prices are relatively high, but you can and should bargain. The International Pier and Puerto Maya have on-pier gift shops.

Playa del Carmen

Some cruise ships spend a day at Cozumel and then anchor offshore at Playa del Carmen for another day, but most ferry passengers to Playa from Cozumel for tours to Tulum and Chichén Itzá, then head on to spend the day docked at Cozumel. Despite the ongoing threat of hurricanes, Playa Del Carmen continues to grow like crazy, catering to an endless parade of tourists who pass their time on the beach, perched at an outdoor bar, or wandering through the laid-back yet colorful scene for which Mexico is famous. Go snorkeling, enjoy the beach, and then stroll by the many shops on Avenida 5.

COMING ASHORE   Some cruise ships anchor offshore or at the pier of Cozumel, then send passengers over to Playa del Carmen by tender. Others dock at the **Puerto Calica Cruise Pier** (which doubles as a dock for cement freighters), 13km (8 miles) south of Playa del Carmen. Taxis meet each arriving ship here, and drivers transport visitors into the center of Playa del Carmen—which is a good thing, as there's nothing to do at Calica besides making a phone call or buying a soda.

GETTING AROUND   The ferry dock is right in town, near the beach and most major shops. You probably won't need them, but **taxis** are available to take you anywhere. If you'd like to drive your own vehicle for the day, Avis, Budget, Hertz, and National all have **car rental** offices right next to the ferry pier.

Best Cruise Line Shore Excursions

Most visitors head for the Maya ruins or one of the local water parks as soon as they reach shore (see "Best Cruise Line Shore Excursions" in the "Cozumel" section, above).

On Your Own: Within Walking Distance

From the ferry docks, you can walk to the center of Playa del Carmen, to the beach, and to the small but ever-expanding shopping district with its trendy boutiques and hip restaurants. **Señor Frog's,** right at the ferry pier (© 984/873-0930), is another of those "all the beer and shots you can stomach" places, like **Carlos 'n Charlie's** (© 984/803-3498), which sits just up the street. For all attractions beyond town, see "Maya Ruins & Other Mainland Attractions," earlier in this chapter.

Shopping

From the tender pier, you are funneled like cattle right into the **Paseo del Carmen Shopping Mall.** Most shops are along Avenida 5, which runs parallel to the coast and has a pedestrian-only stretch not far from the dock. The **Rincon del Sol** plaza is a tree-filled courtyard between calles 4 and 6, built in the colonial Mexican style. It has the best collection of handicrafts shops in the area, some with better-quality items than the junky souvenirs peddled elsewhere.

Costa Maya

Costa Maya is near the sleepy fishing village of Mahajual, just over 161km (100 miles) south of Playa del Carmen and not too far from the Mexico/Belize border. Don't confuse Costa Maya with Riviera Maya, which stretches between Cancún and Tulum. Technically, Costa Maya is the region between Punta Herrero and Xcalak, near the border with Belize. Millions of dollars have been invested in a pier that opened just a few years ago; there's also a lavish oceanfront shopping-and-restaurant complex that caters exclusively to the needs of cruise ship passengers (there are no hotels in the area). The Maya ruins of nearby Kohunlich and Chacchoben are popular attractions, along with silky white beaches and diving and snorkeling at the Chincorro, Mexico's largest coral atoll.

COMING ASHORE   Costa Maya is a self-contained port stop, and you're dropped off right at the purpose-built facilities.

GETTING AROUND   **Taxis** line up just outside the pier, and are the only way of getting to sites beyond walking distance. Because of this, prices are steep and non-negotiable.

9 Curaçao

Welcome to Curaçao (pronounced Coo-ra-*sow*), the largest and most populous of the Netherlands Antilles, just 56km (35 miles) north of the Venezuelan coast. Because much of the island's surface is arid, Dutch settlers in the 17th century developed it into a trading post rather than trying to farm it; a huge oil-processing operation here in the early–20th century resulted in a large population influx and today's curious mixture of bloodlines, including African, Dutch, Venezuelan, and Pakistani. Today, the island still retains a Dutch flavor, especially in **Willemstad,** whose harbor is bordered by rows of picture-postcard, pastel-colored, gabled Dutch colonial houses. While these structures give the town a storybook appearance, the rest of the island looks like the American Southwest, its desertlike landscape dotted with three-pronged cacti, spiny-leafed aloes, and divi-divi trees bent by trade winds.

COMING ASHORE   As you sail into the harbor of Willemstad, be sure to look for the quaint **Queen Emma floating pontoon bridge,** which swings aside to open the narrow channel. Two megaships at a time can dock near the bridge at **Rif Otrobanda,** which leads to the duty-free shopping sector and the famous Floating Market in downtown Willemstad. Adjacent to the megapier, the Rif Fort Renaissance hotel has integrated shops, restaurants, and a casino into this historic landmark. A few smaller cruise ships may dock inside the entrance channel at the **St. Annabay Wharves.**

GETTING AROUND   From the pier, it's a 5- to 10-minute walk to the center of town, or you can take a **taxi** from the stand. The town itself is easy to navigate on foot. Most of it can be explored in 2 or 3 hours, leaving plenty of time for beaches or watersports. Taxi drivers waiting at the cruise dock will take you to any of the beaches. To be on the safe side, arrange to have your driver pick you up at a certain time and take you back to the cruise dock. Up to four passengers can share the price of an island tour by taxi, which costs about $40 per hour.

LANGUAGE & CURRENCY   **Dutch, Spanish,** and **English** are spoken on Curaçao, along with the local tongue, **Papiamentu.** The official currency is the **Netherlands Antilles guilder** (ANG) (1.80 ANG = US$1; 1 ANG = US54¢). Most places accept U.S. dollars for purchases.

Best Cruise Line Shore Excursions

Many excursions aren't really worth the price here—you can easily see the town on your own and hop a taxi to the few attractions on the island outside of Willemstad.

Spanish Water Kayaking & Snorkeling ($75, 3½ hr.): At Jan Sofat, you'll board kayaks for a paddle through the Spanish Water Lagoon, heading for Barbara Beach. Swim and relax before paddling back.

Exploring Curaçao's Jewish Heritage ($55, 3½ hr.): Jews have lived on Curaçao since the mid–17th century. On this tour, participants visit the Mikve Emmanuel Israel synagogue (the Western Hemisphere's oldest) as well as Beth Haim Cemetery (consecrated in 1659) and Landhouse Bloemhof, with its collections of art and artifacts from Curaçao's Jewish past.

On Your Own: Within Walking Distance

Willemstad is the major attraction here, and you can see it on foot. After years of restoration, the town's historic center and the island's natural harbor, Schottegat, have been inscribed on UNESCO's World Heritage list. Be sure to watch the **Queen Emma pontoon bridge** in action. It's motorized, and a man actually drives it to the side of the harbor every so often to allow ships and boats to pass through the channel—it's the coolest thing to see. In the **Brionplein** square at the Otrabanda end of the bridge, a statue commemorates Curaçao-born Pedro Luis Brion, who fought for the independence of Venezuela and Colombia as an admiral under Simón Bolívar. **Fort Amsterdam,** site of the Governor's Palace and the 1769 Dutch Reformed church, has the task of guarding the waterfront. The church still has a British cannonball embedded in it. A corner of the fort stands at the intersection of Breedestraat and Handelskade, the starting point for a plunge into the island's major shopping district.

A few minutes' walk from the pontoon bridge, at the north end of Handelskade, is the **Floating Market,** where scores of fishing boats arrive from Venezuela, Colombia, and neighboring West Indian islands, tying up alongside the canal to sell tropical fruits, vegetables, and handicrafts.

Between the I. H. (Sha) Capriles Kade and Fort Amsterdam, at the corner of Columbusstraat and Hanchi di Snoa, is the **Mikve Israel-Emanuel Synagogue.** Dating from 1651, the Jewish congregation here is the oldest in the New World. The sand that blankets the floor symbolizes the Jews' years of wandering in the desert. Next door, the **Jewish Cultural Historical Museum,** Hanchi Snoa 29 (© **599/9-461-1633;** www.snoa.com), is housed in two buildings dating from 1728. Entry is through the synagogue; open weekdays from 9am to 4:30pm. Admission is $5.

The sleepy **Curaçao Museum,** Van Leeuwenhoekstraat (© **599/9-462-3873;** www.curacaomuseum.an), is housed in a restored 1853 building constructed by the Royal Dutch Army as a military hospital. Today, it displays paintings, objets d'art, and antique furniture, as well as a large collection from the Caiquetio tribes. It's open Monday to Friday from 8:30am to 4:30pm, Sunday 10am to 4pm. Admission is $5. The **Museum Kurá Hulanda,** Kipstraat 9 (© **599/9-434-7765;** www.jurahulanda.com/museum) is one of the most unusual and riveting museums in the Caribbean. With an anthropological focus on the predominant cultures of Curaçao, it presents a chronicle of the origins of man, from the West African empire to Mesopotamian relics and Antillean art. Housed in once dilapidated 19th-century buildings, the exhibits display the dismal history of slave trading, a major part of the island's past. It's open Tuesday to Saturday from 10am to 5pm. Admission is $9 adults, $6 seniors and children ages 11 and under.

On Your Own: Beyond the Port Area

Cacti, bromeliads, rare orchids, iguanas, donkeys, wild goats, and many species of birds thrive in the **Christoffel National Park** (© **599/9-864-0363;** www.christoffelpark.org), about a 30-minute taxi or car ride from the capital near the northwestern tip of Curaçao. The park rises from flat, arid countryside to 369m (1,211-ft.) **St. Christoffelberg,** the tallest point in the Dutch Leewards. Along the way are ancient Arawak paintings and the **Piedra di Monton,** a rock heap piled by African slaves who cleared this former plantation. According to legend, slaves could climb to the top of the rock pile, jump off, and fly back home across the Atlantic to Africa. If they had ever tasted a grain of salt, however, they would crash to their deaths. The park has 32km (20 miles) of one-way trail-like roads. The shortest is about 8km (5 miles) long, but takes 40 minutes to drive because of its rough terrain. One of several hiking trails goes to the top of St. Christoffelberg. It takes about 1½ hours to walk to the summit (come early in the morning before it gets hot; trails open at 7:30am). Admission is $10.

The **Curaçao Sea Aquarium,** off Bhpor Kibra (© **599/9-461-6666;** www.curacao-sea-aquarium.com), displays more than 400 species of fish, crabs, anemones, and other invertebrates, sponges, and coral. It's open daily from 8am to 5pm. Admission is $19. It also has an Animal Encounter experience and various **dolphin swims,** starting at $149 (© **599/9-465-8900;** www.dolphin-academy.com). Nonswimmers can enjoy the impressive dolphin show and invertebrate touch tank.

Stalactites are mirrored in a mystical underground lake in **Hato Caves,** F. D. Rosseveltweg (© **599/9-868-0379**). Long ago, geological forces uplifted this limestone terrace, originally a coral reef. The limestone formations were created over thousands of years by water seeping through the coral. After crossing the lake, you enter two caverns known as the Cathedral and La Ventana ("The Window"), where you'll see samples of ancient Indian petroglyphs. Local guides take visitors through every hour starting at 10am. Admission is $8.

Beaches

Curaçao has some 38 beaches, but in general, they aren't as good as others in the region. The **Curaçao Sea Aquarium** has the island's only full-facility, white-sand, palm-shaded beach, but you'll have to pay the full aquarium admission to get in (see "On Your Own: Beyond the Port Area," above). The rest of the beaches here are public.

Blauwbaai (Blue Bay), just north of town, is the largest and most frequented beach on Curaçao; with a $6 entry fee, there's enough white sand for everybody. Along with showers and changing facilities, there are plenty of shady places to retreat from the noonday sun. At the top of the island, **Westpunt** is known for its gigantic cliffs and the Sunday divers who plunge off them. **Knip Bay** and **Playa Abao,** just south of Westpunt, have lovely turquoise waters.

Shopping

Curaçao is a shopper's paradise, with more than 100 stores lining Heerenstraat, Breedestraat, and other streets in the 5-block district called the **Punda.** Many shops occupy the town's old Dutch houses.

The island is famous for its 2.2kg (5-lb.) "wheelers" of Gouda and Edam cheese. Also look for good buys on French perfumes, Dutch blue Delft souvenirs, finely woven Italian silks, Japanese and German cameras, jewelry, silver, Swiss watches, linens, leather goods, and liquor, along with island-made rum and liqueurs, especially Curaçao liqueur, with its distinctive blue color. Some stores have good buys on intricate lacework imported from regions between Portugal and China. If you're a street shopper and want something colorful, consider a carving or flamboyant painting from Haiti or the Dominican Republic; both are hawked by street vendors at main plazas.

10 Dominica

First things first. It's pronounced Dome-i-*nee*-ka, not Doe-*min*-i-ka. And it has nothing to do with the Dominican Republic. The Commonwealth of Dominica is an independent country, and English, not Spanish, is the official language. The only Spanish commonly understood in Dominica is *mal encaminado a Santo Domingo* ("accidentally sent to the Dominican Republic"), the phrase stamped on many letters that arrive here only after an erroneous detour.

Dominica is the lushest and most mountainous island in the eastern Caribbean, a 47×26km (29×16-mile) swath of land with 365 crystal-clear rivers (one for every day of the year), dramatic waterfalls, volcanic lakes, and gargantuan foliage, all accessible via river trips or hikes along undemanding jungle trails. Dominica served as a backdrop for the second and third *Pirates of the Caribbean* movies, and many of the locations in the film are easily recognized. The island's people, primarily descendants of the West African slaves, are another great natural resource. Don't be surprised when you're greeted with a smile and an "okay," the island's equivalent of "hi." Unfortunately, in the capital Roseau, tourism is a still-developing industry; but the town has a feel of authenticity lacking in other, more developed island towns. The island is also notable for its population of some 3,000 Carib Indians, the last remaining descendants of the people who dominated the region when Europeans arrived.

COMING ASHORE   Dominica has three cruise ship ports, each handling one ship at a time. The most frequented is the cruise ship berth in the heart of **Roseau,** the country's capital and largest town. The **Woodbridge Bay** port is about a mile north of Roseau, and the other is the Cabrits cruise berth, near the northwestern town of **Portsmouth,** with a tourist welcome center and quick access to Fort Shirley and Cabrits National Park.

GETTING AROUND   Taxis and **public minivans** are designated by license plates that begin with the letters *H, HA,* or *HB.* Also look for a round decal on the front of the car and the pink-and-green badges that signify the driver is a certified tourism operator. Fleets of both await cruise ship passengers at the Roseau and Portsmouth docks. Drivers are generally knowledgeable about attractions and local history, and the standard sightseeing rate averages $25 per site per person. The vehicles are unmetered, and while prices are technically set by the government, you should negotiate a price in advance and make sure you and the driver are talking about the same currency.

LANGUAGE & CURRENCY   **English** is Dominica's official language. The **Eastern Caribbean dollar** (EC$2.65 = US$1; EC$1 = US37¢) is its official currency, but U.S. dollars are accepted almost everywhere.

Best Cruise Line Shore Excursions

Trafalgar Falls & Sulfur Springs ($62, 5 hr.): Travel to the island's interior and visit two of Dominica's most stunning wonders: beautiful Trafalgar Falls and a thermal sulfur spring; then drive to Morne Bruce for a panoramic view of Roseau and learn about local flora and fauna at the Botanical Gardens. Proceed to a lookout point for a majestic view of Trafalgar Falls. After another drive, you take a 15-minute walk along a relatively easy trail to the thermal sulfur springs that are so hot, you can actually boil an egg in them.

Carib Indian Territory & Emerald Pool ($100, 5 hr.): The tour stops at the Emerald Pool before heading to a rugged portion of Dominica's northeastern coast, where the 1,327-hectare (3,278-acre) Carib Territory is home to the world's last surviving Carib Indians. The Caribs today live like most other rural islanders—growing bananas and coconuts, fishing, and operating small shops—but their sturdy baskets of dyed and woven larouma reeds and wooden canoes carved from the trunks of massive gommier trees are evidence of their links to the past. Kalinago Barana Aute, the Carib Cultural Village by the Sea, honors the diversity, history, and heritage of the Kalinago people. Lunch is included.

River Tubing & Emerald Pool Adventure ($82, 4 hr.): A 40-minute drive takes you into the Layou Valley, where tubing guides take you down the river lined with tall, overhanging cliffs and lush vegetation. A longer version of this tour also visits the Emerald Pool.

Dominica by Jeep & Swimming at the Titou Gorge ($90, 3½ hr.): A jeep convoy heads up Morne Bruce for a picturesque view, stopping at the Botanical Gardens and the Wotten Waven Sulphur Springs before arriving at the volcanic Titou Gorge. Here, sheer 6m (20-ft.) black walls, rock outcrops, caves, and a thundering waterfall provide an exhilarating swimming experience. Scenes from *Pirates of the Caribbean* were filmed here.

Whale- & Dolphin-Watching ($72, 3½ hr.): Dominica has been hailed by some marine biologists as one of the most reliable spots to see sperm whales. Board a motorized vessel and cruise to a point approximately 13km (8 miles) offshore. As you search for marine mammals, your guide provides a running commentary on marine life found off Dominica. Whales and dolphins are usually spotted on the surface or located with an underwater hydrophone. The deep waters surrounding Dominica are a natural breeding ground for sperm whales.

On Your Own: Within Walking Distance

IN ROSEAU   As you come ashore, you'll see the **Dominica Museum** (℅ 767/ 448-8923), which faces the bayfront. Housed in an old market building dating from 1810, the museum's permanent exhibit provides a clear and interesting overview of the island's geology, history, archaeology, economy, and culture. The displays on pre-Columbian peoples, the slave trade, and the Fighting Maroons—slaves who resisted their white owners and established their own communities—are particularly informative. It's open Monday to Friday from 9am to 4pm, Saturday 9am to noon (and Sun when a ship is in port). Admission is $2.

It took more than 100 years to build the **Roseau Cathedral of Our Lady of Fair Heaven,** on Virgin Lane. Made of cut volcanic stone in the Gothic-Romanesque Revival style, it was finally completed in 1916. The original funds to build it were raised from levies on French planters; Caribs erected the first wooden ceiling frame, and convicts on Devil's Island built the pulpit.

On the eastern edge of Roseau, the **Botanical Gardens** lie at the base of Morne Bruce, the mountain overlooking the town. The gardens were established at the end of the 19th century to encourage crop diversification and to provide farmers with correctly propagated seedlings. London's Kew Gardens provided exotic plants collected from every corner of the tropical world, and experiments to discover what could grow in Dominica revealed that everything does.

IN PORTSMOUTH   The cruise ship dock at Portsmouth leads directly to 104-hectare (260-acre) **Cabrits National Park,** with its stunning mountain scenery, tropical deciduous forest and swampland, volcanic-sand beaches, and coral reefs. Also in the park is the 18th-century **Fort Shirley,** comprising more than 50 major structures and one of the most impressive and historic military complexes in the West Indies. Admission is $5.

On Your Own: Beyond the Port Areas

Approximately 15 to 20 minutes by car from Roseau, **Trafalgar Falls** is actually two separate falls referred to as "the mother and the father falls." The cascading white torrents dazzle in the sunlight before pummeling the black-lava boulders below. The surrounding foliage is in countless shades of green. To reach the lookout to the natural pool at the base of the falls, you'll have to step gingerly along slippery rocks, so don't attempt the climb if it makes you nervous.

Hard-core masochists have an easy choice—the forced march through the **Valley of Desolation** to **Boiling Lake.** Experienced guides say this 6-hour hike is like spending hours on a maximally resistant Stairmaster. So why would any sane person endure this hell? To breathe in the harsh, sulfuric fumes that have killed all but the hardiest vegetation? Because the idea of baking a potato in the steam rising from the earth is irresistible? Maybe to feel the thrill that comes with the risk of breaking through the thin crust separating you from hot lava? Or could it be the final destination, the wide cauldron of bubbling, slate-blue water of unknown depth? Don't even think about taking a dip in this flooded fumarole: The water temperature is about 190°F (88°C). Can we sign you up?

Other beautiful natural areas of the island are discussed in "Best Cruise Line Shore Excursions," above.

Beaches

If your sole focus is beaches, you'll likely find Dominica disappointing. Much of the seacoast is rocky, and many beaches have dark, volcanic sand. There are golden-sand beaches as well, but all are on the northern coast, quite far from Roseau, and include Hampstead Beach, Hodges Beach, L'Anse Noire, and Woodford Hill Bay. Watch out for the strong currents.

Shopping

In addition to the usual duty-free items, Dominica sells handicrafts and art not obtainable anywhere else, most notably **Carib Indian baskets** made of dyed larouma reeds and balizier (heliconia) leaves, their designs handed down from generation to generation. More than souvenirs, these baskets are a real link to the pre-Columbian Caribbean, and some of the most "authentic" items you can buy in the whole Caribbean. You can buy Carib crafts directly from the craftspeople in the Carib Territory or at various outlets in Roseau. Prices are ridiculously reasonable.

In Roseau, the cobbled **Old Market Square** is a bustling market directly behind the Dominica Museum, selling mostly handicrafts and souvenirs. At **Tropicrafts,** at the corner of Queen Mary Street and Turkey Lane, you can watch local women weave grass mats with varied and complex designs. The large store also stocks Carib baskets, locally made soaps and toiletries, rums, jellies, condiments, woodcarvings, and masks made from the trunks of giant fougère ferns.

11 Grand Cayman

Grand Cayman is the largest of the Cayman Islands and it's the top of an underwater mountain, whose side—known as the Cayman Wall—plummets straight down for

150m (490 ft.) before becoming a steep slope that falls away for 1,800m (5,900 ft.) to the ocean floor. Scuba divers love the place. Onshore, though the terrain is flat, rel-atively unattractive, and full of scrubland and swamps, Grand Cayman and its sister islands (Cayman Brac and Little Cayman) nevertheless boast more than their share of upscale, expensive private homes and condos, owned by millionaire expatriates from all over who come because of the tiny nation's lenient tax and banking laws. (Enron, the poster child of shady business dealings, reportedly had more than 690 different subsidiaries here to help avoid paying U.S. taxes.) Grand Cayman, a British Colony, is also popular because of its laid-back civility—so civil that ships aren't allowed to visit on Sunday. **George Town** is the colony's capital and its commercial hub, and many hotels line the sands of the nation's most famous sunspot, **Seven-Mile Beach.**

COMING ASHORE   Up to nine cruise ships can anchor off **George Town** and ferry passengers to a pier at the cruise terminal on Harbour Drive, right in the midst of George Town's shopping district. The tender ride is short, but it can be choppy. A unique feature of this port is that some tour and dive operators have their own water shuttles that go out to greet the ships and take booked passengers directly to their activities, eliminating the ride to shore via boat.

GETTING AROUND   **Taxis** line up at the pier to meet cruise ship passengers. Fares are fixed; typical one-way fares range from $10 to $20. **Motor scooters** and **bicycles** are another way to get around. **Island Scooter Rental** (© 345/949-2046), at Bernard Drive in Industrial Park, has shuttle service to and from George Town and rents scooters for $55 a day. A public **bus service** has recently started, with inexpen-sive service to local attractions for about $1.50 to $2 one-way.

LANGUAGE & CURRENCY   **English** is the official language of the islands. The legal tender is the **Cayman Islands dollar** (CI80¢ = US$1; CI$1 = US$1.20), but U.S. dollars are commonly accepted. Be sure to note which currency is used on price tags before making a purchase.

Best Cruise Line Shore Excursions

Cruise lines typically offer about 30 shore excursions here, most of the swimming, snorkeling, sailing, submarine, and glass-bottom-boat variety.

Stingray City ($45–$60, 2–3 hr.): The waters off Grand Cayman are home to Stingray City, one of the world's most unusual underwater attractions. Set in very shal-low waters of North Sound, about 2 miles east of the island's northwestern tip, the site was discovered in the mid-1980s when local fishermen noticed that scores of stingrays showed up to feed on the offal dumped overboard. Today, anywhere from 30 to 100 relatively tame stingrays swarm around the hundreds of visiting snorkelers like so many aquatic basset hounds, eager for handouts. The guides bring buckets of squid and show you the correct way to feed the stingrays, which sort of suck the food right out of your hand. Stingrays are terribly gentle creatures, and love to have their bellies rubbed, but never try to grab one by the tail—their barbed stingers are indeed poison-ous, and although rarely a genuine threat to one's life, they can inflict a lot of pain. Be sure to bring your waterproof camera for this one.

Atlantis **Submarine Expedition** ($95, 1½ hr., including 45-min. dive): Board a 48-passenger submarine and descend to 100 feet through coral canyons, while an auto-matic fish feeder draws swarms of colorful marine creatures.

Cayman Cycling ($72, 3 hr.): Pick up your touring mountain bike at the Spanish Bay Reef Resort and ride along the rugged coastline of Boatswain Bay and the palm-covered country lanes of the Cobalt Coast. On the final leg, participants can visit the Turtle Farm and the post office in Hell before returning to the Spanish Bay.

On Your Own: Within Walking Distance

In George Town, the small **Cayman Islands National Museum,** Harbour Drive (© **345/949-8368;** www.museum.ky), is housed in a veranda-fronted building that once served as the island's courthouse. Today, the formal exhibits include Caymanian artifacts collected by Ira Thompson beginning in the 1930s, and the museum comprises a gift shop, theater, cafe, and more than 2,000 items portraying the natural, social, and cultural history of the Caymans. Hours are Monday through Friday from 9am to 5pm, Saturday from 10am to 2pm. Admission is $4 adults, $2 seniors and students.

The **National Gallery of the Cayman Islands,** Harbour Place, South Church Street (© **345/945-8111;** www.nationalgallery.org.ky), is an educational nonprofit organization that supports the growth of the Cayman Islands arts scene; it has an average of eight exhibitions each year of both local and international art. It's open Monday to Friday 9am to 5pm, Saturday 11am to 4pm. Admission is free (donations appreciated).

On Your Own: Beyond the Port Area

For years, one of Grand Cayman's most popular attractions has been the **Cayman Turtle Farm** (© **345/949-3894;** www.boatswainsbeach.ky), the only green-sea-turtle farm of its kind in the world. Once a multitude of turtles lived in the waters surrounding the Cayman Islands, but today these creatures are an endangered species. The turtle farm's purpose is twofold: to replenish the waters with hatchlings and yearling turtles and, at the other end of the spectrum, to provide the local market with edible turtle meat. You can peer into about 100 circular concrete tanks containing turtles ranging in size from 6 ounces to 600 pounds, or sample turtle dishes at a snack bar and restaurant. The turtle farm is now part of a 9.2-hectare (23-acre) marine park called **Boatswain's Beach** (pronounced *Boe*-suns), which will also include a snorkeling lagoon, a predator tank full of sharks and moray eels, a separate tank for dolphin swims, an aviary, a nature trail, and other mostly marine-oriented displays. Many, but not all, of the exhibits are completed. Admission to the entire park is $45 adults and $25 children ages 4 to 12. Admission for the Turtle Farm only is $30 for adults and $20 for kids ages 4 to 12.

The nearby town of **Hell** is mostly notable for its name (and the T-shirts bearing it), but there are also some unusual rock formations from which the town got its name. If you mail your postcards from here, guess what the postmark says.

Beaches

Lined with condominiums and plush resorts, **Seven-Mile Beach** begins north of George Town, an easy taxi ride from the cruise dock. It has sparkling white sands with a backdrop of casuarina trees, and is known for its array of watersports and translucent aquamarine waters. The average water temperature is a balmy 80°F (27°C).

Shopping

There's duty-free shopping here for silver, china, crystal, Irish linens, and British woolen goods, but we've found most prices to be similar to those in the U.S. You'll also find cigar shops and international chains. Don't succumb and purchase turtle or black-coral products. You'll see them everywhere, but it's illegal to bring them back into the U.S. and most other Western nations.

12 Grand Turk

Welcome to the Caribbean's newest cruise port. Just 11km (6¾ miles) long and about 2km (1¼ miles) wide, with 3,700 residents, Grand Turk has long been known as one of the top five diving destinations in the world. The reason? Just a few hundred yards from shore, the shallow continental shelf suddenly plunges 2,135m (7,000 ft.) straight down, with healthy coral reefs and great visibility making conditions absolutely perfect. The whole western shore of the island is a protected underwater park. Above water, things are practically perfect too, with an average temperature of 83°F (28°C) and an amazing 350 days of sunshine a year. It can reach the 90s (30s Celsius) in the summer, but the surprisingly strong trade winds keep things comfy.

Though ships had visited the island in the past, it really wasn't equipped to handle a massive influx of passengers until the Grand Turk Cruise Center opened in February 2006, its deepwater pier accommodating even the largest megaships. Carnival was the prime mover behind the project, leasing 15 hectares (37 acres) from the government and developing less than half of them, building a transportation center, restaurant, shopping area, crafts stalls, fountains, and a duty-free building. The cruise center welcomes all ships, not just Carnival lines.

About 5km (3 miles) from the pier is charming downtown **Cockburn Town,** a sleepy half-mile stretch that also happens to be the administrative capital of the Turks and Caicos Islands. Along its streets, Bermudan-influenced colonial buildings sit beside simple gift shops, guesthouses, and a couple of laid-back bars; all are near miles of public powder-white beaches. Islanders describe the ambience here as how the rest of the Caribbean was 25 years ago. A bit neglected over the years, Grand Turk received a $7-million boost from Carnival for infrastructure improvements, ranging from pedestrian crossings to the creation of ready-made tourist attractions based on the island's substantive history.

So far, Grand Turk retains its air of quaintness, but developers are moving in. This is one port you should make a special effort to visit as soon as possible.

COMING ASHORE   Located on the south side of Grand Turk, the **Grand Turk Cruise Center** may seem to arriving passengers like one of the cruise lines' private islands, with its carefully placed landscaping between the dock and the beach. Its advantages, of course, are that (a) it's part of a real country, and (b) passengers don't have to tender ashore because the cruise pier can accommodate the largest ships. However, in the event that two ships are at the pier, a third must then drift (ships may not anchor) and tender passengers ashore, usually no more than a 10-minute ride. At the cruise center, you can get visitor info, rent a car, eat, drink, shop, or catch a taxi or water taxi into Cockburn Town, about 5km (3 miles) away.

GETTING AROUND   **Taxi** fares from the port to Cockburn Town run about $15, but get a quote from the driver before you commit. There's no public transportation on the island, but one shore excursion offered by the cruise lines is a **bus loop** and you can hop off and on at will (see below). **Car rental** desks are found at the cruise terminal, but if you want a car, be sure to book ahead, as supplies are limited. Also be prepared to drive on the left side of the road, as the Turks and Caicos are one British colony.

LANGUAGE & CURRENCY   **English** is spoken everywhere. The official currency is the **U.S. dollar,** but there's local currency called the TCI crown (equivalent in value to the dollar) and a quarter, either of which is a nice souvenir.

Best Cruise Line Shore Excursions

In addition to the excursions listed here, **whale-watching** is added to ships' offerings on an ad-hoc basis. It has to be the right season and the right weather. Atlantic humpback whales travel down Turk's Passage trench on the western side of the island every year, heading for their breeding grounds south of Grand Turk, where they take care of their calves from January to April. Otherwise, the thing to do in Grand Turk is to get underwater.

Scuba Diving ($100–$135, 4 hr.): You won't get better conditions anywhere in the Caribbean than Grand Turk, with its tranquil, crystal-clear waters and protected reef. Experienced divers will be wowed by the manta rays, whale sharks, and sea turtles, and the beautiful colors of the third-largest coral reef in the world. Even a first-timer can get to the reefs via a resort course, with intensive one-on-one instruction followed by a half-hour of diving.

Snorkeling ($90, 3 hr.): If you're not up for scuba, you can at least go snorkeling to see the beauty of Grand Turk's undersea world. Snorkeling cruises departing from the cruise terminal visit two sites, typically Horseshoe Reef (with depths averaging 1.8–3.7m/6–12 ft.) and a reef off Round Cay, one of Grand Turk's best dive locations.

Hop-On, Hop-Off Island Tour ($45, 2–3 hr.): Air-conditioned buses loop around the island whenever there's a ship in port, letting booked excursioners see things at their leisure. A wristband allows entry to various tourist spots along the route, including Cockburn Town's Millennium Clock Tower and restored 1800s prison; Lighthouse Park, with its namesake light built in 1852 and two nature trails; the Turks and Caicos National Museum, which has some information on John Glenn's splashdown off Grand Turk in 1962; and the Philatelic Bureau. Anyone who's ever collected stamps will know that Turks and Caicos is well known for its beautiful stamps, created almost solely for collectors. Stops are approximately every half-mile along the route, with many close to island attractions. Buses arrive at each stop approximately every 15 minutes.

On Your Own: Within Walking Distance

Passengers could easily spend their whole day just hanging out at the cruise center, whose biggest structure by far is the two-story, 1,579-sq.-m (17,000-sq.-ft.) **Margaritaville Cafe,** the largest stand-alone Jimmy Buffett franchise in the Caribbean. Wastin' away again? Behind the restaurant is a giant amoeba-shaped swimming pool with a swim-up bar, slide, cabanas, and infinity-edge view. It's open to the public and, because it's only 1m (3¼ ft.) deep, it makes a great place to hang out with the younger kids.

On Your Own: Beyond the Port Area

Cockburn Town's **historic district** is centered along Duke and Front streets, with houses built of wood and limestone standing along the waterfront. Historic government buildings surround a small plaza where cannons and a bronze plaque mark the spot where Christopher Columbus allegedly first set foot in the New World, on October 14, 1492. Columbus's logbook notes landfall at a bean-shaped island, but there's no absolute proof that said bean was Grand Turk.

Also on Front Street is the **Turks and Caicos National Museum** (② **649/ 946-2160;** www.tcmuseum.org). Housed in 180-year-old Guinep House, the museum has wreckage from a Spanish caravel that sank offshore in shallow water sometime before 1513, plus exhibits on the island's natural history, salt industries, plantation economy, and pre-Columbian inhabitants. It's open Monday to Saturday 9am to 1pm. Admission is $5.

Just behind Cockburn Town's historic waterfront is the town's **saltwater pond,** and in the middle of that is an island once used to quarantine sick sailors. Today, it's a favorite of birders who come to see some of Grand Turk's 190 bird species, including the flamingos, pelicans, and herons that feed in the pond's shallow waters.

Beaches

The cruise terminal's powder-white-sand beach is just steps from the pier, and you'll find lounge chairs and hammocks, as well as the bartending staff that comes by to take your drink orders. For about $20 a day, you can rent a clamshell shade with room for two lounge chairs. You can also sample the underwater view that makes Grand Turk famous by going snorkeling, with equipment available for rent or purchase.

On the island's southwest coast, below Cockburn Town, **Governor's Beach** is one of the few blue-flagged beaches in the Caribbean, which means it passes stringent tests for water quality, cleanliness, and lifeguard availability. It's also reputed to have the best snorkeling on the island. Right next door is **Waterloo,** the governor's mansion, a pretty structure with the curved stucco architecture characteristic of Bermudan buildings.

Shopping

Grand Turk isn't particularly known for its arts and crafts, though you will find shops at the cruise center and at the island's various attractions and museums, plus a couple along Duke Street, which borders the western beach in the downtown area.

13 Grenada

Once a British crown colony, the now-independent nation of Grenada (Gre-*nay*-dah) produces more spices than any other country in the world, including clove, cinnamon, mace, cocoa, tonka beans, ginger, and a fifth of the world's nutmeg—thus its nickname, the Spice Island. **St. George's,** the country's capital, is one of the most colorful ports in the West Indies, nearly landlocked in the deep crater of a long-dead volcano, full of charming Georgian colonial buildings, and flanked by old forts. The island's coast is white and sandy, while its interior is a jungle of palms, oleander, bougainvillea, and other tropical foliage, crisscrossed by roads and trails.

Grenada was one of the hardest-hit Caribbean islands during 2004's devastating hurricane season. Almost every building sustained some level of damage, but you can't keep a good island down. Known for its lushness and most extravagant fertility (results of a gentle climate and volcanic soil), Grenada started springing back almost immediately, its coastal greenery growing rapidly and its rainforests filling out slowly. You should, however, expect to see some reminders of the destruction, such as old churches with no roofs or windows.

COMING ASHORE Two ships at a time can dock at the modern **Melville Street Cruise Terminal,** plus one more at the main quay. Up to four vessels can anchor in the picturesque St. George's harbor and send passengers on a short tender ride to the pier. Passengers exit the cruise terminal through the Esplanade shopping mall onto the Carenage (St. George's main street).

GETTING AROUND Taxi fares are set by the government. A one-way taxi to Grand Anse (one of the Caribbean's best beaches) is about $12 to $15 for up to four passengers. You can also tap most taxi drivers to serve as a guide for a day's sightseeing, for about $25 per hour. **Water taxis** also head from the cruise ship welcome center to Grand Anse; the round-trip fare is about $6.

LANGUAGE & CURRENCY   **English** is commonly spoken on this island, and the official currency is the **Eastern Caribbean dollar** (EC$2.65 = US$1; EC$1 = US37¢), though dollars are widely accepted. Always determine which dollars—Eastern Caribbean or U.S.—you're talking about when discussing a price.

Best Cruise Line Shore Excursions

Because of Grenada's lush landscape, we recommend spending at least a few hours touring its interior, one of the most scenic in the West Indies.

Hike to Seven Sisters Waterfalls ($80, 4 hr.): After a 40-minute hike along a muddy path in the lush Grand Etang rainforest, passengers are free to take a swim in the natural pools or hop off the edge of the cascading waterfalls. It's gorgeous and lots of fun. Don't forget to wear your bathing suit and maybe a pair of Teva-type sandals.

Island Tour, Grand Etang Lake & Fort Frederick ($55, 4 hr.): This is a great way to experience Grenada's lush, cool, dripping-wet tropical interior. You travel by bus past the red-tiled roofs of St. George's en route to the Grand Etang Lake, within an extinct volcanic crater some 530m (1,740 ft.) above sea level. A profusion of floating plants hugging the edges gives it more the appearance of an emerald wetland than a crystal blue lake. On the way, you drive through rainforests and stop at a spice estate. Some tours include a visit to Annandale Falls and Fort Frederick.

On Your Own: Within Walking Distance

In St. George's, you can visit the **Grenada National Museum,** at the corner of Young and Monckton streets (© **473/440-3725**), set in the foundations of an old French army barracks and prison built in 1704. Small but interesting, it houses ancient petroglyphs and other archaeological finds, a rum still, Joséphine Bonaparte's bathtub from her girlhood in Martinique, and various Grenada memorabilia. It's open Monday to Friday from 9am to 4:30pm, Saturday 10am to 1pm. Admission is $2.50 adults and $1 kids.

If you're up for a good hike, walk from the cruise terminal around the historic Carenage and head up to **Fort George,** built in 1705 by the French and originally called Fort Royal. While the fort ruins and the 200- to 300-year-old cannons are worth a peek, it's the 360-degree panoramic views of the entire harbor area that are most spectacular. Look for the bronze plaque commemorating the assassination of the prime minister and several citizens during the unrest in 1983, which resulted in U.S. intervention. You can pick up a rudimentary walking-tour map from the cruise terminal to help you find interesting sights along the way. **Church Street,** which leads right to the fort, has lots of quaint 18th- and 19th-century architecture, as well as several 19th-century cathedrals and the island's Houses of Parliament.

On Your Own: Beyond the Port Area

You can take a taxi up Richmond Hill to **Fort Frederick,** which the French began in 1779. The British retook the island in 1783 and completed the fort in 1791. From its battlements, you'll have a panoramic view of the harbor and the yacht marina.

Don't miss the mountains northeast of St. George's. If you don't have much time, 15m (49-ft.) **Annandale Falls** is just a 15-minute drive away, on the outskirts of the **Grand Etang Forest Reserve.** The overall beauty is almost Tahitian. You can swim and picnic while surrounded by liana vines, elephant ears, and other tropical flora and spices. If you've got more time and want a less crowded spot, the even better **Seven Sisters Waterfalls** are farther into Grand Etang, an approximately 30-minute drive, and then a mile hike along a muddy trail. It's well worth the trip—you'll really get a feel for the power and beauty of the tropical forest here. The falls themselves are lovely, and you can climb to the top and jump off into the pool below.

If you have time, head to **Levera National Park,** in the north of the island, for hikes through a mangrove swamp and a bird sanctuary. Just to the south, the 1912 **Morne Fendue Plantation House,** at St. Patrick's (© **473/442-9330;** www.mornefendue plantation.com), gives you a chance to enjoy old-time island recipes while dining like an upper-class family in the 1920s. It serves a fixed-price ($20) lunch Monday through Saturday from noon to 4pm; call for reservations.

Beaches

Grenada's **Grand Anse Beach,** with its 3km (2 miles) of wide sugar-white sands, is one of the best in the Caribbean, boasting calm waters and a great view of St. George's. There are several restaurants beachside, and you can also join a banana-boat ride or rent a Sunfish sailboat.

Shopping

Grenada is no grand Caribbean merchandise mart, so if you're cruising on to such islands as Aruba, St. Martin, or St. Thomas, you might want to postpone serious purchases until then. On the other hand, you can find some fine local handicrafts, gifts, and art here. The best buy is, of course, fresh **spices** and related items. **Nutmeg products** are especially popular. The Grenadians use every part of the nutmeg: They make the outer fruit into a tasty liqueur and a rich jam, and ground the orange membrane around the nut into a different spice called mace. You'll also see the outer shells used as gravel to cover trails and parking lots.

14 Jamaica

A favorite of North American honeymooners, Jamaica is the third-largest of the Caribbean islands after Cuba and Hispaniola, with dense jungle in its interior, mountains rising as high as 2,220m (7,282 ft.), and many beautiful white-sand beaches along its northern coast, where the cruise ships dock. Most head for **Ocho Rios,** although more and more are opting to call at the city of **Montego Bay** ("Mo Bay"), 108km (67 miles) to the west. These ports have comparable attractions, shore excursions, and shopping possibilities.

One of the most densely populated nations in the Caribbean, with a vivid sense of its own identity, Jamaica has a history rooted in the plantation economy and some of the most impassioned politics in the Western Hemisphere, resulting in a sometimes-turbulent day-to-day reality. You've probably heard, for instance, that the island's vendors and hawkers can be pushy and the locals not always the most welcoming to tourists. While there's some truth to this, we've had nothing but positive experiences, so keep an open mind. The island is also the birthplace of Robert Nesta Marley, who was born in 1945 to a 50-year-old British naval officer and his 18-year-old Jamaican wife. With its themes of love, freedom, and global unity, Bob Marley's reggae music has inspired generations of musicians and music lovers. In 1981, Bob Marley died of cancer and was laid to rest in a mausoleum in Nine Mile, the town of his birth.

LANGUAGE & CURRENCY The official language is **English,** but most Jamaicans speak a richly nuanced patois. The unit of currency is the **Jamaican dollar** (J$87 = US$1; J$1 = US1¢). Visitors can pay in U.S. dollars, but should always find out if a price is being quoted in Jamaican or U.S. dollars—though it'll probably be obvious by the huge difference.

Shore Excursions from Both Ports

Because there's little besides shopping near the docks at either Ocho Rios or Montego Bay, most passengers sign up for shore excursions. The following are usually offered from both ports.

Dunn's River Falls Tour ($80, four tours from Ocho Rios; $110, seven tours from Mo Bay): These falls cascade 180m (590 ft.) to the beach and are the most visited attraction in Jamaica, which means they're hopelessly overcrowded when a lot of cruise ships are in port. Tourists are allowed to climb the falls, and it's a ball to slip and slide your way up with hundreds of others, forming a human chain of sorts. Wear a bathing suit under your clothes, and don't forget your waterproof camera and your aqua-socks. (If you do forget, most cruise lines will rent you aqua-socks for an extra $5.) The prettiest part of the falls, known as the Laughing Waters, was used in the James Bond classics *Dr. No* and *Live and Let Die.* This tour usually visits other local attractions as well, with time allocated for shopping.

River Tubing Safari ($80, 3½ hr.): This is one of the best excursions we've ever taken. After a scenic van ride deep into the pristine jungles, the group of 20 or so passengers and a couple of guides sit back into big black inner tubes (they have wooden boards covering the bottom so your butt doesn't get scraped on the rocks) and glide a few miles downriver, passing gorgeous, towering bamboo trees and other lush foliage. It's sometimes peaceful and sometimes exhilarating—especially when you hit the rapids! If you're docking in Ocho Rios, this tour is usually on the White River; if in Montego Bay, it's on the Great River. *Note:* We find this trip much more interesting than the popular **Martha Brae River Rafting,** which takes you down the river on two-seat bamboo rafts. The cost is about the same.

Horseback-Riding Excursion ($92, 3 hr.): Riders will love this trip: After a 45-minute ride from the stables through fields, you'll gallop along the beach and take your horse bareback into the surf for a thrilling ride.

Ocho Rios

Once a small banana and fishing port, Ocho Rios is now Jamaica's cruise ship capital, welcoming a couple of ships every day during high season. Though the area has some of the Caribbean's most fabled resorts, and Dunn's River Falls is just a 5-minute taxi ride away, the town itself is not much to see, despite a few outdoor local markets within walking distance. Don't expect to shop in the markets without a lot of hassle and pushy hawking of merchandise—some of which is likely to be "ganja" (the wacky weed). In recent years, an army of blue-uniformed "resort patrol" officers on bikes has been helping to keep order.

COMING ASHORE Most cruise ships dock at the **Ocho Rios Cruise Terminal,** near Dunn's River Falls and adjacent to Island Village and several shopping and eating spots. The normal docking area has space for three ships; megaships occasionally use the adjacent industrial pier, which is a short walk from the terminal. Additional vessels must anchor and tender passengers for the short 15- to 20-minute trip to the terminal.

GETTING AROUND It's about a 5-minute walk to the shopping area, but otherwise **taxis** are your best means of getting around on your own. They'll be waiting for you at the pier. Those licensed by the government display *JTB* decals, indicating they're official Jamaica Tourist Board taxis. Fixed rates are posted.

Best Cruise Line Shore Excursions

In addition to the excursions from both Jamaican ports (see "Shore Excursions from Both Ports," above), tours to several nearby attractions are also offered from Ocho Rios.

Prospect Plantation & Dunn's River Falls ($82, 4 hr.): About 5km (3 miles) east of town, Prospect Plantation provides a taste of Jamaica's colonial days (sans slavery), with a tractor-drawn jitney driving through fields of seasonal crops such as bananas, sugar cane, coffee, pineapple, and papaya. The trip includes a stop at Dunn's River Falls (see above).

Coyaba River Garden & Dunn's River Falls ($60, 3½ hr.): About 1.6km (1 mile) from town, Coyaba River Garden and Museum was built on the grounds of the former Shaw Park plantation. The museum displays artifacts from the Arawak, Spanish, and English settlements in the area, while the gardens are filled with native flora, a cut-stone courtyard, and fountains. Like many of the other tours in Ocho Rios, it hits Dunn's River Falls on the way back.

Mountain Biking to Chukka Cove ($68, 4 hr.): A minivan takes you into the mountains above St. Ann, where you hop on a bike to ride along back roads, through meadows and woodlands, to picturesque Chukka Cove, where you can take a swim.

Dolphin Cove ($45–$95, 2 hr.): Various excursions to this beachfront site allow you to look at the resident dolphins, or even touch or swim with them. For $10 more, you can add on 1½ hours at (you guessed it) Dunn's River Falls.

On Your Own: Within Walking Distance

Adjacent to the cruise pier, **Island Village** (www.islandjamaica.com) is a 1.6-hectare (4-acre) entertainment-and-shopping complex developed by Island Records' Chris Blackwell. Attractions include the ReggaeXplosion museum, a museum of Jamaican art, a casino, an outdoor concert venue and indoor theater, a beach with watersports, shopping (lots of it), and a branch of Jimmy Buffett's Margaritaville.

On Your Own: Beyond the Port Area

South of Ocho Rios, **Fern Gully** was originally a riverbed. Today, the main A3 road winds through a rainforest filled with wild ferns, hardwood trees, and lianas. For the botanist, there are hundreds of varieties of ferns; for the less plant-minded, roadside stands sell fruits and vegetables, woodcarving souvenirs, and basketwork. The road runs for about 6.4km (4 miles).

The 1817 **Brimmer Hall Estate,** Port Maria, St. Mary's (© **876/994-2309**), 34km (21 miles) east of Ocho Rios, is a working plantation where you're driven around in a tractor-drawn jitney to see the tropical fruit trees and coffee plants. Knowledgeable guides tell you about the processes necessary to produce the fine fruits of the island. Afterward, you can relax beside the pool and sample a wide variety of drinks, including an interesting one called Wow! The Plantation Tour Eating House serves typical Jamaican dishes for lunch. Tours run weekdays if there are enough people, so call ahead. Admission is $18. In the same general area, toward the coast, at Grants Pen above Oracabessa, **Firefly** (© **876/725-0920**) was the home of Sir Noël Coward and his longtime companion, Graham Payn, who, as executor of Coward's estate, donated it to the Jamaica National Heritage Trust. The house has been restored to its condition on the day Sir Noël died in 1973. It's open Monday through Saturday from 9am to 5pm. Admission is $10.

Beaches

The **Sunset Jamaica Grande Resort,** on Main Street (© **876/974-2201**), has two beaches, shared by hotel guests and cruise ship passengers. The beaches, situated at the North and South Towers, can sometimes get jampacked. You might also want to check out the big **James Bond Beach,** in Oracabessa, about 20 minutes from town. Nearby is Goldeneye, home of Ian Fleming, author of the James Bond series.

Shopping

Shopping in Ocho Rios is not as good as in Montego Bay and other ports, but if your money is burning a hole in your pocket, you can wander around the **Ocho Rios Craft Park,** opposite the **Ocean Village Shopping Centre** off Main Street. Some 150 stalls stock hats, handbags, place mats, woodcarvings, and paintings, plus the usual T-shirts and jewelry. The **Island Plaza** shopping complex, right in the heart of town, has paintings by local artists, local handmade crafts (be prepared to do some bargaining), carvings, ceramics, and even kitchenware. At all of these places, prepare yourself for aggressive selling and fierce haggling. Every vendor asks too much for an item at first; it allows leeway to negotiate the price. (Note that some so-called duty-free prices are indeed lower than stateside, but then the Jamaican government hits you with a 16.5% General Consumption Tax, so figure it in when shopping.)

Montego Bay

Montego Bay has better beaches, shopping, and restaurants than Ocho Rios, as well as some of the best golf courses in the Caribbean. Like Ocho Rios, Mo Bay also has its crime, traffic, and annoyances, but there's much more to see and do here, at least nearby. (There's little of interest in the town itself except shopping.) Getting from place to place is one of the major difficulties, however. Whatever you want to visit seems to be in yet another direction. Shore excursions and taxis are the way to go.

COMING ASHORE   Montego Bay has a modern, expanded cruise dock for three to four ships, with a large terminal and the usual duty-free stores, refreshments, phones, tourist information, and taxi/bus stands.

GETTING AROUND   If you don't book a shore excursion, **taxis** are the way to get around. They'll be waiting for you at the pier. Those licensed by the government display *JTB* decals, indicating they're official Jamaica Tourist Board taxis. Fixed rates are posted.

Best Cruise Line Shore Excursions

In addition to the excursions from both Jamaica ports (see "Shore Excursions from Both Ports," above), Mo Bay provides tours to several interesting plantations and great houses.

Rose Hall Great House ($50, 3 hr.): This is the most famous plantation home in Jamaica. Built about 2 centuries ago by John Palmer, it gained notoriety from the doings of "Infamous Annie" Palmer, wife of the builder's grandnephew, who supposedly dabbled in witchcraft and took slaves as lovers, killing them when they bored her. Annie was also said to have murdered several of her husbands while they slept, and

Montego Bay Golf Excursions

Montego Bay provides a number of excellent golf opportunities. Various cruise lines offer organized excursions, but you can also arrange play ahead of time on your own, and then taxi to the course.

- **Tryall Club** (☏ **876/956-5660**; www.tryallclub.com), 19km (12 miles) from Montego Bay, is an excellent, regal 18-hole, par-72 course that's often been the site of major golf tournaments, including the Jamaica Classic Annual and the Johnnie Walker Tournament. Greens fees are about $145, plus $30 for a cart.

- **Rose Hall Resort & Country Club,** at Rose Hall (☏ **876/953-2650**; www. rosehallresort.com), has a noted 18-hole, par-71 course with an unusual and challenging seaside and mountain layout, designed by Robert Von Hagge. The 90m-high (295-ft.) 13th tee affords a rare panoramic view of the sea, and the 15th green is next to a 12m-high (39-ft.) waterfall, once featured in a James Bond movie. Amenities include a fully stocked pro shop, a clubhouse, and a professional staff. Greens fees are $159.

- **Half Moon Resort,** at Rose Hall (☏ **876/953-2211**; www.halfmoongolf. com), features an 18-hole, par-72 championship course designed by Robert Trent Jones, Sr. Greens fees are about $150, plus $25 for a mandatory caddy.

eventually suffered the same fate herself. For what it's worth, many Jamaicans insist the house is haunted.

Greenwood Great House ($42, 3½ hr.): More interesting to some than Rose Hall, this Georgian-style building was the residence of Richard Barrett, a first cousin of Elizabeth Barrett Browning. On display is the family's library, along with portraits, antiques, and period musical instruments.

Croydon Plantation Tour ($65, 6 hr.): A guided tour of this mountain estate includes a .5km (⅓-mile) walk over gently sloping terrain, with many great views. Stops are made for refreshments and seasonal fresh fruits, and at the end you get a traditional Jamaican-style lunch.

On Your Own: Beyond the Port Area

There are no real attractions within walking distance. If you're not taking a shore excursion, consider a visit to **Rocklands Wildlife Station,** Anchovy, St. James (☏ **876/952-2009**). Lisa Salmon, known as the "Bird Lady of Anchovy," established this sanctuary, which is perfect for nature lovers and bird-watchers. You can feed small doves and finches from your hand, and might even coax a Jamaican doctor bird to perch on your finger and drink syrup. Rocklands is about 1.2km (¾ mile) outside Anchovy on the road from Montego Bay. Admission is $15.

Beaches

Doctors Cave Beach (☏ **876/952-2566**) on Gloucester Avenue across from the Doctors Cave Beach Hotel (☏ **876/952-4355**; www.doctorscave.com), helped to

New Port in Town

Set between Montego Bay (20-min. drive) and Ocho Rios (30 min.), Falmouth is the newest Jamaican port to serve the cruise biz (there's also the less-used Port Antonio on the eastern end of the island). The capital of the parish of Trelawny, Falmouth has the largest collection of intact colonial Georgian architecture in the Caribbean. In its early years, it was one of the busiest ports in Jamaica, hosting up to 30 tall ships on any given day to exchange European goods for rum and sugar. By late 2010, Falmouth will once again be on the map as a port of call for Royal Caribbean's Oasis-class ships, with a terminal and shops designed to complement the local Georgian architecture. Falmouth and nearby attractions are about a 32km (20-mile) drive from Montego Bay and 72km (45 miles) from Ocho Rios.

launch Mo Bay as a resort in the 1940s. Dressing rooms, chairs, umbrellas, and rafts are available.

One of the premier beaches of Jamaica, **Aquasol Theme Park** (formerly Walter Fletcher Beach) is in the heart of Mo Bay. It's noted for tranquil waters, so it's a particular favorite for families with children. Changing rooms are available, and lifeguards are on duty. Nearby, the **Pork Pit,** 27 Gloucester Ave. (© **876/952-1046**), is the best place for the famous Jamaican jerk pork and jerk chicken. Many beachgoers come over here for a big lunch. Picnic tables encircle the building, and everything is open air and informal. Order half a pound of jerk meat with a baked yam or baked potato and a bottle of Red Stripe beer. Prices are very reasonable; lunch will cost $10.

On the main road, 18km (11 miles) east of Montego Bay, the .75km (½-mile) **Rose Hall Beach Club** has a secure and secluded, white sandy beach with crystal-clear water; a full restaurant, along with two beach bars and a covered pavilion; an open-air dance area; showers, restrooms, and changing facilities; plus beach volleyball courts, various beach games, live music, and a full watersports activities program.

Note: All of these beaches charge admission, which runs about $5 to $10 for adults.

Shopping

The main shopping areas are at: **Montego Freeport,** within easy walking distance of the pier; **City Centre,** with most of the duty-free shops, aside from those at the large hotels; and **Holiday Village Shopping Centre,** across from the Holiday Inn on Rose Hall Road, heading toward Ocho Rios.

The **Old Fort Craft Market,** a shopping complex with nearly 200 vendors licensed by the Jamaica Tourist Board, fronts Howard Cooke Boulevard up from Gloucester Avenue in the heart of Montego Bay, on the site of Fort Montego. With a varied assortment of handicrafts, this is browsing country. You'll see wall hangings, hand-woven straw items, and handcarved wood sculptures, and you can also get your hair braided. Vendors can be extremely aggressive, so be prepared for some major hassles, as well as serious negotiation. Persistent bargaining on your part will lead to substantial discounts.

You can find the best selection of handmade Jamaican souvenirs at the **Crafts Market,** near Harbour Street in downtown Montego Bay. Straw hats and bags, wooden platters, straw baskets, musical instruments, beads, carved objects, and toys are all sold here. That "jipijapa" hat will come in handy if you'll be out in the intense island sun.

15 Key West

Located at the end of the Florida Keys, Key West is America's southernmost city and has the vibe of a colorful Caribbean outpost with a dash of New Orleans high life. It's a fun-loving, heavy-drinking town with a lot of history, more than a little touristy goofiness, a thousand Hemingway look-alikes, and a large gay community. It's a regular melting pot. It's also, as many tour guides like to point out, the Pulitzer Prize–winner capital of the U.S., with more winners per capita than anywhere else. Because most attractions are in good proximity to the cruise docks, there's little sense in taking an excursion here unless you have mobility problems. Wander around touristy Mallory Square and Duval Street, check out some of the theme bars, and then take a walk down some of the quieter side streets, maybe visiting Truman's Little White House or the Hemingway Home & Museum. Or, you might want to spend your day playing golf, diving, or snorkeling. Several "raw bars" near the dock area serve seafood, including oysters and clams, although the king here is conch—grilled, ground into burgers, made into chowder, fried in batter as fritters, or served raw in a conch salad (though beware, some of the quickie conch vendors near the docks are pretty skimpy with the conch . . . can we say dough balls?). If you have more of a sweet tooth than anything else, be sure to sample the decadent frozen, chocolate-dipped, Key lime pie on a stick that you can pick up at several places in town.

COMING ASHORE   Ships dock at **Mallory Square** (Old Town's tourist central), at the nearby Hilton Resort's **Pier B,** and at the U.S. Navy base's **"Outer Mole" pier.** All are on the Gulf side of the island. Passengers arriving at the Navy pier must take an official shuttle bus for the short distance to and from Mallory Square, as individuals are not permitted to transit the base on their own. Additional ships can anchor for the short tender ride to shore.

GETTING AROUND   The island is only 4 miles long and 2 miles wide, so getting around is easy. The most popular attractions are within walking distance of Mallory Square. The farthest is Hemingway Home, about a mile down Duval. Many passengers opt for one of the island's tram tours, which are sold as shore excursions, but are also available on a walk-up basis. The **Conch Tour Train** (© 305/294-5161; www.conchtourtrain.com) is a narrated 90-minute tour with commentary on 100 local sites. The depot is at Mallory Square, and trains depart every 30 minutes ($29 adults, $14 children ages 4–12). The trip has only one stop where passengers can get on and off (at the Historic Seaport). If you want more flexibility, try the **Old Town Trolley** (© 305/296-6688; www.trolleytours.com), which allows you to hop on and off its trains to explore on your own. Prices are the same as the Conch Train, and pickup stops are signposted around town. If you want wheels of your own, **bicycles** and **motor scooters** are a good bet here and are widely available, with daily rates hovering around $15 and $40, respectively.

LANGUAGE & CURRENCY   The official language is **English.** The unit of currency is the **U.S. dollar.**

Best Cruise Line Shore Excursions

In addition to the Conch Tour Train described above, most cruise lines offer walking tours and sometimes bike tours for those who like the services of a guide. But this is really a port to explore on your own.

Key West Catamaran Sail & Snorkel Tour ($45, 3 hr.): The popular *Fury* catamarans take passengers to a reef for some snorkeling, and then finish the trip back to shore with music, booze, and a good time.

On Your Own: Within Walking Distance

All attractions in Key West are within walking distance, though the Hemingway Home and Nancy Forrester's Secret Garden are at least 20 minutes from Mallory Square.

Bars—large, packed theme bars, usually with someone playing guitar and singing the hits in one corner—are a big draw in Key West. **Captain Tony's Saloon,** 428 Greene St. (② **305/294-1838;** www.capttonyssaloon.com), is the oldest active bar in Florida, and is both heavily patronized by cruise ship passengers and tacky as hell. The 1851 building was the original Sloppy Joe's, a rough-and-tumble fishermen's saloon. Hemingway drank here from 1933 to 1937; Jimmy Buffett got his start here before opening his own bar and going on to fame and fortune. The current **Sloppy Joe's,** 201 Duval St. (② **305/294-5717;** www.sloppyjoes.com), is the most touristy bar in Key West, visited by almost all cruise ship passengers—even those who don't normally go to bars. It aggressively plays up its association with Hemingway, with pictures of Hemingway lookalike contest winners plastered all over the walls. Hit **Jimmy Buffett's Margaritaville,** 500 Duval St. (② **305/296-3070;**), if you've got a hankering for a cheeseburger from paradise or want to waste away again on margaritas—this is your place. Much less commercial is the open-air **Hog's Breath Saloon,** 400 Front St. (② **305/296-4222;** www.hogsbreath.com), near the cruise docks. Raucous and loud, it's populated by visiting fishermen and bikers alike, all of them with a drink in hand. Meanwhile, the local sailors and fishermen head over to **Finnegan's Wake,** 320 Grinnell St. (② **305/293-0222;** www.keywestirish.com), a truly authentic Irish pub with an extensive and creative food menu.

Wherever you end up, try some of the favorite local beer, Hog's Breath, or some of the favorite local rum, Key West Gold (even though it's a cheat—it isn't actually made on the island). Most places recommended sell fast food to go with their drinks.

There's a bar at the **Harry S. Truman Little White House,** 111 Front St. (② **305/294-9911;** www.trumanlittlewhitehouse.com), too, in the back room where Truman and his friends played poker—though visitors can't drink there. The house, formerly the home of the Navy base commander, served as Truman's vacation home during his presidency and today remains just as he left it, decorated in late-1940s style. By the time the guides finish their well-organized 1-hour tour, you'll feel as if you've gone back in time. Tours run daily every 15 minutes from 9:30am till 4pm. Admission is $14 adults, $5 kids.

Deep-Sea Fishing in Key West

As Hemingway, an avid fisherman, would attest, the waters off the Florida Keys are some of the world's finest fishing grounds. You can follow in Papa's wake aboard the 40-foot *Linda D IV* and *Linda D V* (② **800/299-9798** or 305/296-9798; www.charterboatlindad.com), which offer the best deep-sea fishing here. Full-day charters for up to six people cost $950; a half-day charter is $600. Full-day shared charters are $225 per person; a half-day is $160. Make arrangements as far in advance as possible.

Key West

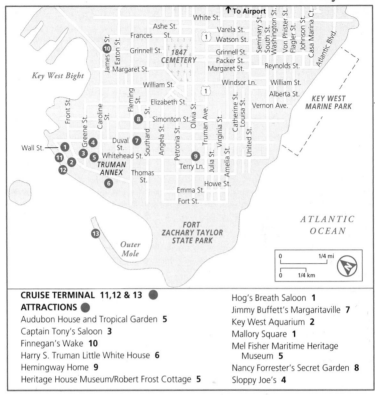

To Airport

White St.

Ashe St.

Frances St.

Varela St.

Watson St.

Grinnell St. 1847 CEMETERY

Grinnell St.

Packer St.

Margaret St.

Margaret St.

Reynolds St.

Key West Bight

William St.

Windsor Ln.

William St.

Alberta St.

Elizabeth St.

Vernon Ave.

KEY WEST MARINE PARK

Simonton St.

Duval St.

Whitehead St.

TRUMAN ANNEX

Wall St.

Thomas St.

Terry Ln.

Howe St.

Emma St.

Fort St.

FORT ZACHARY TAYLOR STATE PARK

ATLANTIC OCEAN

Outer Mole

| 0 | 1/4 mi |
| 0 | 1/4 km |

CRUISE TERMINAL 11,12 & 13 ●	Hog's Breath Saloon **1**
ATTRACTIONS ●	Jimmy Buffett's Margaritaville **7**
Audubon House and Tropical Garden **5**	Key West Aquarium **2**
Captain Tony's Saloon **3**	Mallory Square **1**
Finnegan's Wake **10**	Mel Fisher Maritime Heritage
Harry S. Truman Little White House **6**	Museum **5**
Hemingway Home **9**	Nancy Forrester's Secret Garden **8**
Heritage House Museum/Robert Frost Cottage **5**	Sloppy Joe's **4**

The **Hemingway Home,** 907 Whitehead St. (© **305/294-1136;** www.hemingway home.com), provides a similar if less formal look back at the island's old days. "Papa" lived here with his second wife, Pauline, completing *For Whom the Bell Tolls* and *A Farewell to Arms* in the studio annex out back. Hemingway had some 60 polydactyl (many-toed) cats, whose descendants still live on the grounds. It's open daily from 9am to 5pm. Admission is $12 adults, $6 kids.

The **Audubon House and Tropical Garden,** 205 Whitehead St., at Greene Street (© **877/294-2470** or 305/294-2116; www.audubonhouse.com), is dedicated to the 1832 Key West sojourn of the famous naturalist John James Audubon. The ornithologist didn't live in this three-story building, but it's filled with his engravings. The main reason to visit is to see how wealthy sailors lived in Key West in the 19th century, and to admire the lush tropical gardens surrounding the house. It's open daily from 9:30am to 5pm. Admission is $10 adults, $5 kids ages 6 to 12.

The **Key West Heritage House Museum and Robert Frost Cottage,** 410 Caroline St. (© **305/296-3573;** www.heritagehousemuseum.org), was the home of Jessie Porter Newton, the grande dame of Key West. Today, it's filled with mementos of the illustrious guests who partook of her hospitality, including Tennessee Williams, Gloria Swanson, and Robert Frost, who stayed in a cottage out back. It's open daily from

10am to 4pm. Self-guided tours are $6. Guided tours are $9 for adults, $3 for children ages 12 to 16.

On the waterfront at Mallory Square, the **Key West Aquarium,** 1 Whitehead St. (© **800/868-7482;** www.keywestaquarium.com), in operation since 1932, was the first tourist attraction built in the Florida Keys. The aquarium's special feature is a touch tank where you can feel a sea urchin, a sea star, or a conch, the town's mascot and symbol. It's open daily from 10am to 6pm. Admission is $12 adults, $5 kids ages 4 to 12.

Near the docks, the **Mel Fisher Maritime Heritage Museum,** 200 Greene St. (© **305/294-2633;** www.melfisher.org), contains some of the more than $400 million in gold jewelry, doubloons, and other artifacts that the late treasure hunter Mel Fisher plucked from the Spanish galleon *Nuestra Señora de Atocha,* which sank off the Keys in 1622. Educational exhibits explain salvage operations and the history of the Spanish and piracy in the islands. Open hours are Monday to Friday 8:30am to 5pm, Saturday and Sunday 9:30am to 5pm. Admission is $12 adults, $6 children.

Nancy Forrester's Secret Garden, 1 Free School Lane, off Simonton between Southard and Fleming streets (© **305/294-0015;** www.nfsgarden.com), is the most lavish and verdant garden in town, with some 150 species of palms and thousands of orchids, climbing vines, and ground covers. It's open daily 10am to 5pm. Admission is $6.

Beaches

Beaches are not too compelling here, but the best and closest to the cruise docks is **Fort Zachary Taylor State Beach** (www.fortzacharytaylor.com), a 12-minute walk away. To get here, go through the gates leading into the Truman Annex (site of the Little White House).

Shopping

Within a 12-block radius of **Mallory Square,** you'll see mostly tawdry, overpriced tourist merchandise, but if you're in the market for some Key West kitsch, you'll find flamingo snow globes, floppy straw hats, seashell ashtrays, and the like. At Mallory itself, shops sell seashells from the seashore—actually, from around the world, including some you'd hardly believe are real. They also sell wine-bottle holders shaped like lobsters, but what the hell. As you move farther along **Duval Street** from Mallory, you'll notice that the shops get more and more stylish. Could it be a coincidence that this part of town is the center of Key West's gay community? We don't think so.

16 Martinique

Fairy-tale romance and horrific disaster: Who could resist such an enticing combination? Martinique was the birthplace and childhood home of Empress Joséphine, sweetheart and wife of Napoleon; as if that weren't enough to entice you, consider the epic tragedy that befell St. Pierre one fair day in 1902 when it was a bustling cosmopolitan capital one minute, then a devastated volcanic graveyard of 30,000 souls the next. Love and death make quite a one-two punch, but they're just the hook. Look a bit deeper to appreciate Martinique's subtler attractions—quaint seaside villages, colonial ruins dating from when France and England vied for the island, and captivatingly beautiful rainforests and beaches. In 1946, Martinique became an overseas department of France, which it remains today.

COMING ASHORE Most cruise ships dock in the heart of Fort-de-France, at the **Pointe Simon Cruise Dock,** which has quays for two mid- to large-size vessels. Because Martinique is a popular port of call, one megaship, or two smaller vessels, may also wind up docking at the **Tourelles Passenger Terminal** at the main harbor, a 5-minute cab ride from Fort-de-France. When all cruise piers are full, additional ships can dock across from the Tourelles terminal at a commercial pier, about a 5-minute shuttle ride from Tourelles.

GETTING AROUND Travel by **taxi** is convenient, but expensive. Most cabs are metered; you'll find them waiting at the cruise pier. To cross the bay to La Pagerie (Empress Joséphine's birthplace) and the resort area of Pointe du Bout, take one of the blue **ferries** that sail from east of the cruise dock in Fort-de-France at least once per hour. Round-trip tickets cost about $8 per person. Avis, Budget, and Hertz all have **rental cars,** too.

LANGUAGE & CURRENCY **French** is Martinique's official language, but you can get by with **English** at most restaurants and tourist sights. Martinique is an overseas region of France, so the **euro** (€) is the official currency (.85€ = US$1; 1€ = US$1.20). U.S. dollars are commonly accepted in tourist areas.

CALLING FROM THE U.S. When calling Martinique from the U.S., dial the international access code **(011)** and the country code **(596)** before the numbers listed in this section. The numbers listed here already begin with 596, but an effort by the French telephone authorities to standardize procedures requires that you dial those three digits twice.

Best Cruise Line Shore Excursions

Rainforest & Plantations 4WD Safari ($105, 4–5 hr.): Take your off-road vehicle through tropical forests and sugar cane plantations (stopping to sample the crop) to a banana plantation and a distillery, where you'll do short tours.

Martinique Snorkeling ($64, 3 hr.): Across the bay from Fort-de-France, the reef at Anse Dufour has excellent snorkeling for experts and novices. The reef is filled with marine animals, including French grunts, blackbar soldierfish, and silversides. Snorkeling equipment is provided, along with professional instruction, supervision, and transportation.

On Your Own: Within Walking Distance

Fort-de-France is a bustling town of 100,000 residents, full of ochre buildings, ornate wrought-iron balconies, cascading flowers, and tall palm trees. The town's narrow streets, cluttered with boutiques and cafes, climb from the bowl of the sea to the surrounding hills, forming a great urban amphitheater. There's plenty here to keep you busy.

At the eastern end of downtown, **La Savane** is a broad formal park with palms, mangoes, and manicured lawns, perfect for a promenade or rest in the shade. Its most famous feature is the **Statue of Empress Joséphine,** carved in 1858 by Vital Dubray. Expect her to be headless: Napoleon's Little Creole was unceremoniously decapitated in 1995 in commemoration of her role in reinstating slavery on the island in the early 1800s. Across the street, **Bibliothèque Schoelcher (Schoelcher Library)** (© 596/70-26-67) is one of Fort-de-France's great Belle Epoque buildings. Named in honor of Victor Schoelcher, one of France's most influential abolitionists, this elaborate structure, designed by French architect Henri Pick, was first displayed at the 1889

Paris Exposition. Four years later, it was dismantled and shipped across the Atlantic. Today, it houses Schoelcher's books as well as an impressive archive of colonization, slavery, and emancipation documents. Admission is free; closed Sunday.

Another Henri Pick masterpiece, **St. Louis Cathedral,** on rue Victor Schoelcher at rue Blénac, was built in 1895. A contemporary of Gustave Eiffel (of Eiffel Tower fame), Pick used massive iron beams to support the walls, ceiling, and spire. A grand example of Industrial Revolution architecture, it's been likened to a Catholic railway station. The organ, stained-glass windows, and ornamented interior walls are well worth a look and can be viewed every morning except on Saturday.

Built in 1640, **Fort St. Louis,** boulevard Alfassa, dominates the rocky promontory east of La Savane. A noteworthy example of 17th- and 18th-century military architecture, it first was used to defend Fort-de-France in 1674 against Dutch invaders. Today, the bastion remains the French navy's headquarters in the Caribbean and is open to visitors only on special occasions.

The best of Fort-de-France's many museums, the **Musée Départemental d'Archéologie Précolombienne Préhistoire,** 9 rue de la Liberté (© **596/71-57-05**), traces 2,000 years of Martinique's pre-Columbian past with more than 1,000 relics from the Arawak and Carib cultures. Admission is about $5 for adults; closed Sunday.

You can expect to find great food all over town if you want to stop for lunch. More than any other island in the French West Indies, Martinique gives French and Creole cuisine equal billing.

On Your Own: Beyond the Port Area

Martinique is much too large to tackle in a single day. You'll have to make some tough choices about which of its many museums, plantations, floral parks, and natural wonders to visit. Here are two suggested itineraries for the day.

NORTH OF FORT-DE-FRANCE Martinique's Carib name, Madiana, means "island of flowers." To see what the Caribs were talking about, stroll through the **Jardin de Balata** (© **596/64-48-73;** www.jardindebalata.fr). Located about 8km (5 miles) north of town, this lush, Edenic garden showcases 200 species of plants, trees, and tropical flowers, as well as resident hummingbirds, frogs, and lizards. It's open daily 9am to 5pm. Admission is about $8.

Yes, it's hot outside, but things could be worse. One of Martinique's must-see attractions, the village of **St. Pierre** on the northwest coast was the cultural and economic capital of the island until 8am on May 8, 1902, when the **Mount Pelée** volcano exploded in fire and lava. Three minutes later, all but two of St. Pierre's 30,000 inhabitants had been incinerated, buried in ash and lava, or asphyxiated by poisonous gas. The town once hailed as the Paris of the Antilles became the Pompeii of the Caribbean, and today it's no more than a sleepy fishing village, home to fewer than 5,000. Ruins of a church, theater, and other buildings punctuate the town, memorials to St. Pierre's former glory. The one-room **Musée Volcanologique,** rue Victor Hugo (© **596/78-15-16**), traces the story of the cataclysm through pictures and relics excavated from the debris. Admission is about $2. In lieu of walking from one ruin to another, you can hop on the Cyparis Express trolley from here for an hour-long tour (tickets about $12). The trolley is named in honor of Cyparis, a prisoner locked behind thick cell walls, who was one of the survivors of the eruption. He later toured with P. T. Barnum's circus, showing off his burn scars.

Martinique Golf Excursions

When Robert Trent Jones, Sr., designed **Golf de la Martinique** (𝄞 596/68-32-81; www.golfmartinique.com) in 1976, he chose a picturesque, historic site: the seaside hills neighboring La Pagerie, the birthplace of Empress Joséphine. Just 32km (20 miles) from Fort-de-France, this good, tough, 18-hole, 6,640-yard, par-71 course features emerald hills, swaying palms, constant vistas of the turquoise sea, and, thankfully, year-round trade winds that help keep things cool. The par-5 12th hole, with a dogleg to the right, is the most difficult hole. The fairway here is narrow, the green is long, and the wind, especially between December and April, is tricky. The 15th and 16th require shots over sea inlets. Facilities include a pro shop, a golf academy, a bar, a restaurant, and tennis courts. English-speaking pros are at your service. Greens fees and cart rental run about $65 for 18 holes. A set of clubs is another $25. Some cruise lines offer organized excursions to the club.

Part sugar-plantation ruins, part tropical paradise, **Habitation Céron** (𝄞 596/52-94-53) is the most evocative of Martinique's historical agricultural sites. This sprawling 17th-century estate, 15 minutes north of St. Pierre, is almost as wild and tranquil as the surrounding rainforest, but its verdigris cisterns, moss-covered stone buildings, and archaic, still functioning water mill are all haunted with the ghosts of a time when sugar was king, slaves toiled in the heat, and French colonists lived in languid comfort. Admission is about $9.

A few miles south of St. Pierre, **Le Carbet** is where Columbus landed in 1502, the first French settlers arrived in 1635, and the French painter Paul Gauguin lived for 5 months in 1887. The unassuming **Musée Paul Gauguin,** Anse Turin (𝄞 596/78-22-66), sits not far from the hut once occupied by the painter. It has no original paintings, but you will see biographical texts and whiny, self-pitying letters he wrote to his wife back in France. Admission is about $5.

SOUTH OF FORT-DE-FRANCE   Marie Josèphe Rose Tascher de la Pagerie was born in 1763 in the quaint little village of **Trois Ilets,** across the bay from Fort-de-France. As Joséphine, she became the wife of Napoleon Bonaparte in 1796 and empress of France in 1804. A small museum, the **Musée de la Pagerie** (𝄞 596/68-34-55), sits in the former estate kitchen building, where Joséphine gossiped with her slaves. Displays include the bed that she slept in until she departed for France at age 16; portraits of her and of Napoleon; invitations to Parisian balls; and several letters, including a passionate missive from lovelorn Napoleon. Admission costs about $7; closed Monday.

You'll have passed through a number of quaint coastal villages by this time, but none sweeter than **Ste. Luce.** Absurdly picturesque with its blindingly white stucco walls, red-tile roofs, turquoise sea, and multicolored fishing boats, this town is pure sun-drenched maritime serenity. Swim or snorkel off the small, pleasant beach; meditate on horizon-dominating Diamond Rock (a former British citadel); or check out the village boutiques and cafes. For an unhurried taste of French island life, it's as good a place as any to spend the day.

Beaches

Serious beach bunnies hop south of Fort-de-France to **Grand Anse des Salines,** widely regarded as Martinique's nicest strand. At the island's extreme southern tip, about an hour from the capital by car, it has coconut palm trees, views of Diamond Rock, and white sand that seems to go on for miles. Beachside stands provide refreshments. To get to the island's main **gay beach,** turn right at the entrance to Grand Anse des Salines and drive to the far end of the parking lot, near the sign for Petite Anse des Salines. Follow the path through the woods and then veer left till you find the quiet section with the good-looking guys.

Conveniently across the bay from Fort-de-France, **Pointe du Bout** is Martinique's most lavish resort area. Aside from a marina and a variety of watersports, the area has some modest man-made, white-sand beaches. The sandy, natural beaches at nearby **Anse Mitan** and **Anses d'Arlet** are popular with both swimmers and snorkelers.

Beaches north of Fort-de-France have mostly gray (they like to call it silver) volcanic sand. The best of the bunch is **Anse Turin,** just to the side of the main Caribbean coastal road, between St. Pierre and Le Carbet. Extremely popular with locals and shaded by palms, it's where Gauguin swam when he called the island home.

Martinique has no legal nudist beaches, but toplessness is as common here as anywhere in France. As a rule, public beaches lack changing cabins or showers, but hotel lockers and changing cabanas can be used by nonguests for a charge.

Shopping

Martinique has a good selection of French luxury items—perfumes, fashionable clothing, luggage, crystal, and dinnerware—at prices that can be as much as 30% to 40% lower than those in the United States. Unfortunately, because some luxury goods, including jewelry, are subject to a hefty value-added tax, the savings are ultimately less compelling. Paying in dollar-denominated traveler's checks or credit cards is sometimes good for a 20% discount.

The main shopping district in Fort-de-France is bound by rue Ernest Deproge (on the waterfront), La Savane, rue Lamartine, and rue de la République, with **rue Victor Hugo** being the single most important stretch. Local goods, such as the excellent island rum, Creole jewelry, madras fabric, folk paintings, and handwoven baskets and straw hats, are good buys and representative of the island. The **open-air market** in La Savane, at rue de la Liberté and rue Ernest Deproge, has the best selection of these items.

17 Nevis

Off the beaten tourist track, south of St. Martin and north of Guadeloupe, Nevis is the junior partner in the combined Federation of St. Kitts and Nevis, which gained self-government from Britain in 1967 and became a totally independent nation in 1983. Though smaller than St. Kitts and lacking a major historical site like that island's Brimstone Hill Fortress, Nevis is nevertheless the more appealing and upbeat of the two islands. Columbus first sighted the island in 1493, naming it Las Nieves, Spanish for "snows," because its 970m (3,182-ft.) mountain reminded him of the Pyrenees. Settled by the British in 1628, Nevis became a prosperous sugar-growing island as well as the most popular spa island of the 18th century, when people flocked in from other West Indian islands to visit its hot mineral springs. Nevis's two most famous historical residents were Admiral Horatio Nelson, who married a local woman here in 1787, and Alexander Hamilton, who was born here and went on to find fame as a drafter of the American Federalist Papers, as George Washington's treasury secretary, and as Aaron Burr's unfortunate dueling partner. Today, the island's capital city, **Charlestown,** has a lovely mixture of port-town exuberance and small-town charm, and the popular **Pinney's Beach** is just a knockout.

COMING ASHORE   Only small ships can dock at the **Charlestown Port,** right in the center of Charlestown. Larger vessels must anchor off the coast of **Pinney's Beach.** The small cruise terminal has restrooms and a bar, but the main street is just a few steps away and is where you'll find eats, shops, and taxis.

GETTING AROUND   The entirety of Charlestown is accessible on foot, but if you want to visit Pinney's Beach or elsewhere on the island, you can get a **taxi** from Charlestown. The cost to Pinney's is about $7. Taxis also give island tours; just negotiate a price with your driver.

LANGUAGE & CURRENCY   **English** is the language of both St. Kitts and Nevis. The local currency is the **Eastern Caribbean dollar** (EC$2.65 = US$1; EC$1 = US37¢), though most shops and restaurants quote prices in U.S. dollars. Always determine which currency locals are talking about before making a purchase.

Best Cruise Line Shore Excursions

Some of the small-ship lines offer a day at Pinney's Beach as part of their regular visit, along with hiking and snorkeling options, but Nevis is so small and easy to negotiate on your own that excursions are neither necessary nor advised.

On Your Own: Within Walking Distance

If your ship docks in Charlestown, you're at dead center of a perfect walking-tour opportunity. Charlestown is a lovely little place, laid back in somewhat the same manner as St. John, but with some of the rural character of sister island St. Kitts.

If you head left from the docks and walk a little ways (around .4km/¼-mile) along Main Street, you'll come to the **Museum of Nevis History at the Birthplace of Alexander Hamilton** (℗ 869/469-5786; www.nevis-nhcs.org/nevishistory.html), where the road curves just before the turnoff to Island Road. It's a rustic little two-level house set right on the coastline. On the first floor is the small **Museum of Nevis History** and gift shop (admission $5; Mon–Fri 9am–4pm, Sat 9am–noon).

Backtracking along Main Street, you'll pass several serviceable if unremarkable shops. Keep walking through the center of town, saying hi to the occasional passing mama goat and kids, and then turn left onto Government Road. One block up on the left, you'll find the **Jews' Burial Ground,** with graves from 1684 to 1768. When we were there, the dead were being entertained with reggae music drifting over from a shop across the street, while a breeze stirred the few trees on the property. All in all, not a bad resting spot.

Amble back to Main Street, turn left, and continue on past the Grove Park Cricket Ground, bearing left when the road forks. Head up the hill (where you'll see several buildings standing alone on the hill to your right) and then turn at the first right, which will bring you back behind those buildings, the first of which is the inaccessible Government House and the second of which is the **Nelson Museum** (℗ 869/469-5786; www.nevis-nhcs.org/nelsonmuseum.html). A very small, very homemade, and very appealing kind of place, it traces the history of Admiral Horatio Nelson's career enforcing England's Navigation Acts in the Caribbean, and also houses artifacts from Nevis's Carib, Arawak, and Aceramic peoples. The timeline of Nelson's Caribbean career is portrayed in ship models, ceramic and bronze Nelson figures, paintings of his battles and other scenes, a scrap from the Union Jack (under which the admiral was standing when he was shot), and more memorabilia. The museum is open Monday to Friday 9am to 4pm (Sat–Sun for a group by request). Admission is $5.

Once back outside, amble slowly off in the same direction you were going (right from the gate). Keep bearing right and you'll eventually be back on Main Street, in plenty of time to do a little shopping or stop at one of the local bars or restaurants.

On Your Own: Beyond the Port Area

The 3.2-hectare (8-acre) **Botanical Garden of Nevis** (© **869/469-3399;** www. botanicalgardennevis.com) is located 5km (3 miles) south of Charlestown on the Montpelier Estate. There are several gardens, including a tropical rainforest conservatory, a rose and vine garden, a cactus garden, a tropical fruit garden, and an orchid garden. Fountains, ponds, and re-creations of Maya sculptures dot the grounds. It's open Monday to Saturday 10am to 4pm, Sunday 11am to 2pm. Admission is $16.

The island of Nevis is essentially one big cone, sloping upward on all sides to Nevis Peak in the center. Hiking even halfway up the mountain is a strenuous climb, but pays off with spectacular views and sightings of monkeys, birds, and rare plants. Under no circumstances should you hike this mountain alone; not only is it unsafe, but you'll also miss out on your guide's explanations of the surroundings. The **Peak Haven Village Experience,** Zetland Village, Gingerland (© **869/665-6926;** www. peakhavennevis.com), offers various tours and guided walks to an old sugar mill and village huts. Admission is $12 per person. Stay and have lunch atop Nevis Peak on an outdoor dining deck at the **Coal Pot Restaurant.** Lunch is about $17.

Beaches

The name to know on Nevis is **Pinney's Beach,** located north of Charlestown. It's a lovely spot for swimming, snorkeling, beachcombing, or just sitting back and watching the pelicans dive-bomb into the surf. It's home to the gorgeous Four Seasons resort and, as a counterpoint to conspicuous luxury, the rickety **Sunshine's Bar and Grill,** which sits right on the beach and bills itself as "Home of the Killer Bee." **Oualie Beach,** just north of Pinney's, isn't as popular as its sister to the south, but is no less pristine. Visitors here are protected from rough waves by reefs far out into the bay, so the water is usually safe for small children. Behind the beach sits Oualie Beach Resort, with a restaurant, bar, and live, open-air music for all beachgoers.

Shopping

Nevis is no shopping hub. A few uninteresting gift shops dot Main Street. The **Nevis Philatelic Bureau,** at the Head Post Office, on Market Street next to the public market, 1 block south and 1 block east of the docks (© **869/469-5535**), has a range of Nevis stamps for collectors.

18 The Panama Canal

The Panama Canal is an awesome feat of engineering and human effort. Construction began in 1880 and wasn't completed until 1914, at the expense of thousands of lives, and the vast majority of the original structure and equipment is still in use. Transiting the Canal, which links the Atlantic Ocean with the Pacific, is a thrill for anyone even vaguely interested in engineering or history.

Passing completely through the Canal takes about 8 hours from start to finish, and is a fascinating procedure—the route is about 80km (50 miles) long and includes passage through three main locks, which, through gravity alone, raise ships over Central America and down again on the other side. Between the locks, ships pass through artificially created lakes such as the massive Gatun Lake, 26m (85 ft.) above sea level. It often costs ships about $100,000 to pass through, with fees based on each ship's weight. Your ship will line up in the morning, mostly with cargo ships, to await its turn through the Canal. While you're transiting, there will be a running narration of history and facts about the Canal by an expert who's brought on board for the day.

The Canal is so vital to the cruise industry that it has spawned its own word, *panamax*, meaning the maximum size a ship can be and still make it through. Panamax ships, it should be noted, make for a tight fit: Sometimes there are only a couple of feet between the hull and the sides of the lock. Sitting in a lower-deck lounge and watching the walls go by less than an arm's length outside the windows is really, really disorienting. That tight-fit experience may soon be a thing of the past, though. In late 2006, Panamanian voters approved a plan to widen and modernize the Panama Canal, digging a new, 60% wider channel that will parallel the existing canal along its narrowest sections on either side of Gatun Lake. Once complete (somewhere around 2014), it will effectively double the Canal's capacity and give cruise lines much greater flexibility in planning the deployment and itineraries of their largest, post-panamax ships.

Cruises that include a **Canal crossing** are generally 10 to 14 nights long, with popular routes running between Florida and Acapulco; they visit a handful of Caribbean and Mexican ports and a few ports in Central America along the way, including Panama's San Blas Islands, Costa Rica's Puerto Caldera, and Guatemala's Puerto Quetzal. Many ships also do a **partial crossing** of the Canal, sailing into Gatun Lake from the Caribbean side, docking to let passengers off for excursions, and then sailing back out again.

Colón

In compliance with a treaty signed between the United States and Panama in 1977, Canal operations passed from U.S. to Panamanian hands at the stroke of midnight on December 31, 1999. Not only did the transition go smoothly, but the changeover also spurred government agencies and private developers in Panama to expand the Canal Zone's tourism infrastructure. This meant not simply trying to attract as many ships as possible, but also developing new attractions at the Canal's Atlantic entrance to lure cruise passengers off their ships and into Panama's interior on shore excursions and for pre- and post-cruise stays. Even ships not transiting the Canal are being wooed, with a long-term goal of making the city of Colón a home port for cruise ships sailing to the southern Caribbean.

The linchpin project in the new developments is **Colón 2000,** a $45-million private port development that opened in October 2000 in Colón, near the Canal's Caribbean entrance, and that is capable of handling any size cruise vessel—even the 100,000-plus-ton ships that are too large to pass through the Canal. Colón 2000's developer, Corporación de Costas Tropicales, has created a tour company, **Adventuras 2000** (www.colon2000.com), which offers a series of shore excursions highlighting Panama's history, culture, and diverse natural attractions (see "Best Cruise Line Shore Excursions," below). The project has opened many new jobs to locals, who are being trained as bilingual tour guides, drivers, and so on.

Colón 2000's glass-and-marble terminal building has a large lounge, an Internet cafe, a huge duty-free shopping mall (part of the Colón Free Zone, the second-largest tax-free zone in the world), restaurants, and crafts shops. Unfortunately, the town surrounding the splashy new development remains poverty stricken and extremely unsafe, so tourists absolutely should not wander around town. With all the activity in the Colón Free Zone and the organized tours offered by ships, there's enough to keep any cruise ship passenger occupied there.

Another new development in Colón, the **Cristobal Cruise Terminal (Pier 6),** has piers for two ships of any size, along with a duty-free shopping area, restaurants, and telephones.

Best Cruise Line Shore Excursions

The following excursions represent a sampling of those offered from Colón.

Emberá Indian Village Tour ($120, 3 hr.): Today, Panama's Emberá Indians live much as they did in the early–16th century, when their first tourist—Vasco Nunez de Balboa, who "discovered" the Pacific Ocean—came through. You'll travel by dugout canoe up the Chagres River, visit the Emberá village, witness a performance of traditional dance, and (surprise, surprise) have an opportunity to purchase handicrafts.

Kayak in the Panama Canal ($132, 9 hr.): From Colón, you'll travel to Sol Melina, where you'll spend about an hour kayaking amid the plant life, mammals, and birds. You'll then head by bus to the Gatun Locks for a look at the Canal's workings.

Panama City Tour ($95, 5½ hr.): Visit the ruins of Old Panama, founded in 1519 by Pedro Arias Davila and destroyed in 1671 by the pirate Sir Henry Morgan; head to colonial Panama, built to replace the original capital; and then visit the Miraflores Locks for a look at the Canal.

Monkey Watch ($88, 5½ hr.): After a 30-minute ride at high speed through the heart of the Panama Canal, the boat will slow down and enter the labyrinth of jungle-covered islands of Gatun Lake. Wildlife is plentiful in this protected area: You'll likely encounter capuchin monkeys, three-toed sloths, howler monkeys, toucans, turtles, butterflies, crocodiles, and more.

Panama City

If you're not in the mood to shop in the Duty-Free Zone, take a tour of Panama City. It's sophisticated with a modern downtown area—with the heart of Latin America's banking industry—and still has Spanish colonial remnants in Casco Antiguo. If you want to discover Panamanian city life, this is the place to go—not Colón.

Visit the **Amador Causeway (Calzada de Amador),** where you can take in views of the city skyline and Bridge of the Americas. When you want to stop for food, go to **Café Barko** on the Flamingo Island section of the Causeway, which specializes in Panamanian cuisine and seafood. You won't be disappointed.

One of the best things about Panama City is its proximity to the rainforests. **Metropolitan Nature Park** is the only rainforest within a capital city in the Americas. Observe toucans, woodpeckers and parrots within their natural habitat. **Soberania Rainforest** is just 25km (16 miles) out of Panama City and is abundant with wildlife, including 500 different bird species. You'll see monkeys, sloths, crocodiles, and other animals that you'll never find in your own backyard.

Exploring the rainforest is a must if you're in Central America, but do it with a guide, as you don't want to risk getting lost in unfamiliar terrain. If you don't go with one of the tours from the cruise ship, then go with **Advantage Tours Panama** (www.advantagepanama.com). Many of the bilingual guides have science degrees and are armed with knowledge about the local wildlife and environment; if possible, request Guido Berguido—he's amazing. The half-day Metropolitan Rainforest tour starts at $64.

Ports Along the Canal Route

The **San Blas Islands** are a beautiful archipelago and home to the Kuna Indians, whose women are well known for their colorful, hand-embroidered stitching. If you get a chance to go ashore, the tiny women, dressed in their traditional *molas* (bright, intricately appliquéd blouses), sell all manner of this textile art in square blocks and strips, all of which are known as *molas* and make great pillow covers or wall hangings. They cost about $10 each, but don't try to bargain too much—these gals will only go so low before standing firm. When your ship anchors offshore at the islands, be prepared for throngs of Kunas to emerge from the far-off distance, paddling (or, in a few cases, motoring) their dugout canoes up to the ship, where they will spend the entire day calling for money or anything else ship passengers toss overboard. The Kunas seem to enjoy diving overboard to retrieve coins thrown, but it's a sad sight, too, watching entire families so needy, and it makes you feel damn guilty for rolling in on that fancy cruise ship.

In Costa Rica, many ships call at **Puerto Caldera,** on the Pacific side, or **Puerto Limón,** on the Atlantic side. While there's nothing to see from either cargo port, both are great jumping-off points for tours from ships of the country's lush, beautiful rainforests, which are alive with some 850 species of birds, 200 species of mammals, 9,000 species of flowering plants, and about 35,000 species of insects. After a scenic bus ride, tours will take you on a nature walk through the jungle or on a mild white-water rafting trip.

In Guatemala, most Panama Canal–bound ships call at **Puerto Quetzal,** on the Pacific coast; a few may call at **Santo Tomas,** on the Caribbean side. Both are used as gateways to Guatemala's spectacular Maya ruins at Tikal. They're the country's most famous attractions, and are considered the most spectacular yet discovered, with more than 3,000 temples, pyramids, and other buildings of the ancient civilization—some of them dating as far back as A.D. 300—nestled in a thick, surreal jungle setting. Excursions here are neither cheap nor easy—a 10-hour tour involves buses, walking, and a 1-hour flight, and costs about $500—but the journey is well worth the effort. Excursions to the less spectacular Maya sites in Honduras are also offered from Puerto Quetzal, as are several overland tours of Guatemala's interior.

19 Puerto Rico

San Juan, the capital of Puerto Rico, has the busiest ocean terminal in the West Indies and is one of the cruise trade's most important ports. While cruise groups, by their sheer size, can overwhelm many ports of call, San Juan absorbs them with ease. The San Juan metropolitan area, home to about a third of Puerto Rico's 3.8 million people, is one of the largest and most sophisticated urban centers in the Caribbean, with all the amenities of a modern major city: great shopping, interesting neighborhoods, beautiful people, excellent restaurants, glamorous bars and nightclubs, and fine museums. **Old San Juan** is the prime haunt for cruise passengers because it's the most beautiful, historic part of town and because the docks are right at its foot. The neighborhood's hilly cobblestone streets are lined with brightly painted colonial town houses, colonial churches, intimate parks, and sun-drenched plazas. Like the pyramids of Egypt and the Great Wall of China, Old San Juan's Spanish colonial forts and city walls are United Nations World Heritage Sites, and this neighborhood is our top pick for spending your day here.

COMING ASHORE Almost all cruise ships dock at historic **Old San Juan,** but during periods of heavy volume, you may get stuck at one of the much less convenient cargo piers across the water from the Old Town, requiring a taxi ride. Over the next few years, plans call for more docks and attractions to the east of the current piers.

GETTING AROUND Old San Juan is eminently walkable, if hilly. **Taxis** operated by the Tourist Transportation Division are available at the piers. They're metered in San Juan, but the fare structure between major tourism zones is standardized. The set rates from the cruise ship piers are $8 to Old San Juan, $12 to Condado, and $20 to Isla Verde. The minimum fare is $3. After 10pm, there's a night charge (add $1 to the meter reading). Call **Metro Taxi** (© 787/725-2870) or **Borican Taxi** (© 787/843-6000) for a cab.

LANGUAGE & CURRENCY **Spanish** is the native tongue, but most people on the island also speak **English** (both are official languages here). The farther you venture

San Juan as a Port of Embarkation

Puerto Rico is the number-one port of embarkation in the Caribbean, with more than 1.2 million visitors embarking on 700 cruises every year from here. Most cruise lines sell pre- and post-cruise packages that include hotel stays.

GETTING TO SAN JUAN & THE PORT **Luis Muñoz Marín International Airport** (© 787/791-1014) is on the city's east side, about 7½ miles from the port. Taxi fares from the airport are fixed at $12 to Isla Verde, $18 to Condado and Ocean Park, and $22 to Old San Juan and the cruise ships. The ride to the port takes at least 30 minutes—longer if traffic is heavy, and it often is.

ACCOMMODATIONS Following are some hotels that are commonly part of cruise line packages, plus a couple of others. Rates are per room based on double occupancy.

- **Sheraton Old San Juan Hotel & Casino,** 100 Brumbaugh St. (© 800/325-3535 or 787/721-5100; www.sheratonoldsanjuan.com), on the waterfront across the street from the cruise ship docks. Rates start at $260.
- **Hotel El Convento,** 100 Calle del Cristo (© 800/468-2779 or 787/723-9020; www.elconvento.com), a former Carmelite convent, with large rooms, many with views of the Old Town. Rates start at $160.
- **El Condado Plaza Hotel & Casino,** 999 Ashford Ave. (© 866/317-8934 or 787/721-1000; www.condadoplaza.com), in Condado, the original high-rise, high-glamour section of modern San Juan, to the east of Old Town. Rates start at $240.
- **San Juan Marriott Resort & Stellaris Casino,** 1309 Ashford Ave., also in Condado (© 800/464-5005 or 787/722-7000; www.marriott.com). Rates start at $275.

from San Juan, the more likely it is you'll have to practice your Spanish. Because Puerto Rico is part of the United States, the **U.S. dollar** is the currency of the realm.

Best Cruise Line Shore Excursions

Unless you want a guide to offer historical perspective ($35, 2½ hr.), don't bother with organized tours of Old San Juan—it's easy enough to get around on your own. On the other hand, if you explore somewhere farther afield, an organized tour is a good idea.

El Yunque Rainforest ($45, 4–5 hr.): Get acquainted with one of Puerto Rico's premier natural wonders. After arriving at Baño Grande, a natural swimming hole, hike a half-hour along the Camimitillo trail and see parrot nests, giant ferns, orchids, and palms. Listen for the song of Puerto Rico's national symbol, the tiny coquí tree frog. After a short stop at an interpretive station, proceed to Yohakú observation tower and Coca waterfall.

Rainforest Horseback Adventure ($100, 3½ hr.): Once you get to the ranch, you'll meet your horse, briefly learn the ropes, and then ride down a beautiful beach. Take a quick swim during the refreshment stop.

City Tour & Bacardi Rum Distillery ($40, 4 hr.): After a tour of the old city, with a stop at the San Cristóbal fort, you'll travel to the Bacardi distillery to learn about the Puerto Rican sugar and rum industries, watch giant fermenting tanks transform sugar cane into rum, learn how to pronounce the product's name (Baa-carrrr-*di!*), and then get a taste for yourself.

WALKING TOUR   **OLD SAN JUAN**

The streets are narrow and teeming with traffic, but strolling through Old San Juan is like walking through 5 centuries of history. More than 400 Spanish colonial buildings from the 16th and 17th centuries, many featuring intricate wrought-iron balconies with lush hanging plants, have been lovingly restored here. The streets' blue paving stones were originally used as ballasts by ships crossing the ocean from Spain. Although Old San Juan is a National Historic Zone, it's as vibrant today as it's ever been. Block after block, you'll find shops, cafes, museums, plazas, people, and pigeons. The crowds thin out by late afternoon, so linger around to experience Old San Juan's more sedate charms.

Begin your adventure near the post office, amid the taxis, buses, and urban hubbub of:

❶ Plaza de la Marina

The plaza is a small park that overlooks San Juan Bay, which was one of the New World's most important harbors for trading and military protection. Walking west from the plaza, you'll come to San Juan's showcase promenade, El Paseo de Princesa. This renovated 19th-century walkway traces the ancient city walls past heroic statues, gurgling fountains, and landscaped gardens.

Proceed along the Paseo to:

❷ La Princesa

This gray-and-white building on the right served as one of the Caribbean's most notorious prisons for centuries. Today, it houses contemporary Puerto Rican art exhibits and the offices of the Puerto Rico Tourism Company.

Continue walking westward to the fountain near the sea's edge. Turn right and follow the promenade as it skirts the base of the:

❸ City Wall (La Muralla)

The wall was completed in the 1700s and once formed part of the New World's most impregnable defenses against enemy invaders and pirates. Marvel at the immensity, antiquity, and engineering genius of the wall, which on average is 40 feet high and 20 feet thick.

Follow the promenade until you reach the:

❹ San Juan Gate

The gate stands at Calle San Juan and Recinto del Oeste. Turn right through the portal. The gate was built in 1635 and served as the main entrance into San Juan. Today, it's the only remaining passage through the wall into the city.

Walk up the tree-lined San Juan Street to the:

❺ Catedral de San Juan

If you'd like to retrace the steps of the colonial visitors of Old San Juan, stop by the cathedral and make an offering as a thank-you for a safe journey.

The original thatched-roof wooden cathedral, built in the early 1520s, was destroyed by a hurricane in 1529. Reconstruction in 1540 added a circular staircase and vaulted Gothic ceilings, but most of the current church was built in the 1800s. Look for the tomb of Ponce de León and the wax-encased mummy of St. Pio, a Roman martyr (153 Calle del Cristo; free admission; daily 8am–5pm).

Across the street is:

❻ El Convento

The New World's first Carmelite convent, El Convento opened in 1651 with 30-foot walls designed to withstand hurricanes and enemy attacks. The building remained a convent for 250 years, but fell on hard times early in the 20th century and served as a dance hall and flophouse. Today, the beautifully restored building is the Hotel El Convento, possibly Puerto Rico's most elegant hotel (see "San Juan as a Port of Embarkation," above).

Walking away from Cathedral Plaza, head west down Las Monjas to the wrought-iron gates of:

❼ La Fortaleza

Also known as Santa Catalina Palace, La Fortaleza is the residence of Puerto Rico's governor. Although it initially served military purposes, it's now the oldest executive mansion in continuous use in the Western Hemisphere (built in 1540). English-language tours are given on weekdays, every hour from 9am to 5pm.

Now retrace your steps along Calle Recinto del Oeste, downhill to Caleta de San Juan. The colonial house at no. 51, on the northeast corner, is the:

❽ Felisa Rincón de Gautier Museum

This is the former home of one of San Juan's most popular mayors. An organizer of the city's women and other dispossessed people, Fela, as her many admirers called her, swept into power in 1946 and led the city for 22 years.

Walking back to Calle Recinto del Oeste, turn right and proceed 1 block to Caleta de las Monjas. Fork left to a panoramic view and a modern statue marking the center of:

❾ Plazuela de la Rogativa

According to local legend, the British, while besieging San Juan in 1797, misidentified the flaming torches of a *rogativa,* or religious procession, as Spanish reinforcements. Frightened by the display, the would-be invaders hastily retreated. Statues in this plaza memorialize the event.

Continue west, parallel to the city wall, passing through a pair of urn-topped gateposts. The road will fork. Bear to the right and continue climbing the steep cobblestone-covered ramp to its top. Walk west across the field toward the neoclassical gateway leading to the:

❿ Castillo San Felipe del Morro ("El Morro")

The big draw in Old San Juan, this castle had a strategic position that was the envy of the Caribbean for several centuries. It's where Spanish Puerto Rico defended itself against the navies of Great Britain, France, and Holland, as well as hundreds of pirate ships. First built in 1539, and

Old San Juan Walking Tour

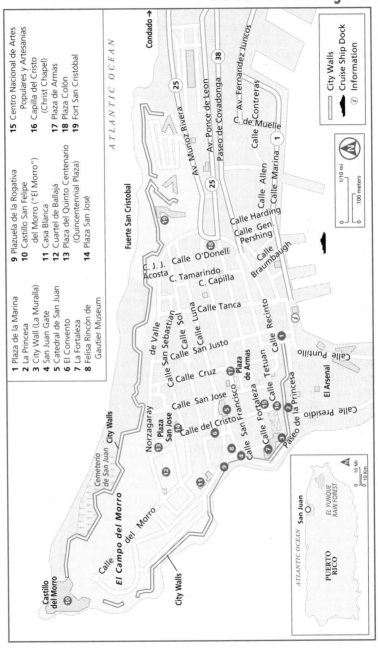

1 Plaza de la Marina
2 La Princesa
3 City Wall (La Muralla)
4 San Juan Gate
5 Catedral de San Juan
6 El Convento
7 La Fortaleza
8 Felisa Rincón de Gautier Museum

9 Plazuela de la Rogativa
10 Castillo San Felipe del Morro ("El Morro")
11 Casa Blanca
12 Cuartel de Ballajá
13 Plaza del Quinto Centenario (Quincentennial Plaza)
14 Plaza San José

15 Centro Nacional de Artes Populares y Artesanías
16 Capilla del Cristo (Christ Chapel)
17 Plaza de Armas
18 Plaza Colón
19 Fort San Cristóbal

City Walls
Cruise Ship Dock
Information

ATLANTIC OCEAN

Condado →

1/10 mi
100 meters

PUERTO RICO

ATLANTIC OCEAN

San Juan

EL YUNQUE RAIN FOREST

10 Mi
10 Km

substantially enhanced in 1787, the fortress was part of a comprehensive defense network. The six-level complex rises 140 feet above the sea on a rocky promontory. You can spend the better part of the morning exploring its labyrinth of dungeons, barracks, towers, ramps, and tunnels on your own. Check out the small, air-conditioned military museum and the gift shop. Both El Morro and San Cristóbal (see no. 19, below) are managed by the U.S. National Park Service, with continuous video presentations and guided tours in English (admission $3; San Cristóbal daily 9am–6pm, El Morro daily 9am–5pm).

Retrace your steps through the treeless field to Calle del Morro; then walk uphill to the small plaza at the top of the street. On the right is:

⓫ Casa Blanca

Though it was his family home, Juan Ponce de León, the conquistador and Puerto Rico's first governor, never actually lived here. While the structure was being built, he was off looking for the Fountain of Youth, ironically dying from battle wounds along the way, in 1521. The city's oldest fort, Casa Blanca, was San Juan's only defense against attacks until La Fortaleza was completed in 1533. Today, it has a small museum (1 Calle de San Sebastián; ℂ **787/724-4102;** admission $3; Mon–Sat) illustrating Indian life and 16th- and 17th-century colonial family life. The garden and fountains in back are a tranquil respite from the streets.

Exit through the front entrance and walk downhill, retracing your steps for a half-block; then head toward the massive tangerine-colored building on your right, the:

⓬ Cuartel de Ballajá

These former military barracks once housed 1,000 Spanish soldiers and their families. Built between 1854 and 1864, the complex is the last and largest military building erected by Spain in the Western Hemisphere. Today, the building's second floor is home to the **Museo de las Américas (Museum of the Americas)** (Cuartel de Ballajá; ℂ **787/724-5052;** admission $3; Tues–Fri 10am–4pm, Sat–Sun 11am–5pm), which showcases Caribbean as well as North, Central, and South American cultures. The popular art exhibits focus on housing and furniture styles, handicrafts, tools, musical instruments, toys, clothing, and religious objects. The carved wooden saints (santos) are especially interesting.

Exit through the barracks' eastern door, where you'll immediately spot the dramatic and modern:

⓭ Plaza del Quinto Centenario (Quincentennial Plaza)

This plaza is dominated by a large, totem-pole-like column that commemorates the 500th anniversary of Columbus's arrival.

Now walk a short block southeast to the borders of:

⓮ Plaza San José

This plaza features a statue of Juan Ponce de León cast from an English cannon captured during a 1797 naval battle. Three sites around this square are worth visiting. Built in 1532, the **Iglesia de San José** is where Ponce de León's descendants worshiped, and features beautiful artwork. Check out the exterior while the church interior is under restoration. Next door is the **Galería Nacional,** part of the Instituto de Cultura Puertorriquena (admission $3). Four rooms tell the history of art in Puerto Rico, beginning with religious works from early colonial times to modern art. The **Museo Pablo Casals** (ℂ **787/723-9185;** admission $1; Tues–Sat 9:30am–4:30pm) honors the Spanish-born cellist who adopted Puerto Rico as his home; it displays his cello, his piano, and original manuscripts of his music. The **Museo de Nuestra Raíz Africana (Museum of Our African Roots)** (ℂ **787/724-4294;** admission $3; Wed–Sun 8am–4:30pm) traces the slave experience and focuses on African contributions to local music, dance, clothing, art, cuisine, religion, and language. Placards are in Spanish.

Now walk 2 blocks south along Calle del Cristo, through one of the Caribbean's most attractive shopping districts. After passing Calle Fortaleza, look on your left for the:

⑮ Centro Nacional de Artes Populares y Artesanias

Operated by the Institute of Puerto Rican Culture, this center, at 253 Calle del Cristo (℃ **787/722-0621;** admission $3; Mon–Sat 9am–5pm), displays a collection of the island's folk arts and crafts.

Continue to the southernmost tip of Calle del Cristo (just a few steps away) to the wrought-iron gates that surround a chapel no bigger than a newspaper kiosk, the:

⑯ Capilla del Cristo (Christ Chapel)

Legend has it that in 1753, a young rider lost control of his horse in a race down Calle del Cristo during the feast of St. John the Baptist and plunged over the steep precipice at the street's end. A person who witnessed the tragedy promised to build a chapel if the young man's life were saved. Records maintain that the horseman died, but lore contends otherwise. In another version of the story, the horseman, after himself praying to God while falling over the cliff, survived to build the chapel. The delicate silver altar here can be seen through glass doors (free admission; Mon, Wed, and Fri).

Retrace your steps about a block north along the Calle del Cristo; then turn right on Calle Fortaleza. A block later, take a left onto Calle San José and proceed another block to the capital's liveliest square, the:

⑰ Plaza de Armas

This broad, open plaza has lots of pigeons, several old men playing dominos, office workers and shoppers basking in the sun, and a 19th-century statue representing the four seasons. Originally used for military drills, the plaza now hosts folk dances and concerts on weekends. The neoclassical **Intendencia** (which houses offices of the U.S. State Department) and the **Alcadía** (San Juan's city hall) flank the square.

Walk east along the plaza's northern border, Calle San Francisco, for 4 blocks until you reach another square:

⑱ Plaza Colón

This park is notable for its **statue of Cristóbal Colón (Christopher Columbus).** Bronze plaques at the monument's base commemorate episodes in the explorer's life.

Finally, walk to the plaza's northeast corner, where Calle San Francisco meets Boulevard del Valle. Turn left and follow the signs to:

⑲ Fort San Cristóbal

Built in 1634 (and expanded in the 1770s), this fortress rises more than 150 feet above the sea. A complex maze of tunnels and moats connects the central fort with wave after wave of outlying posts. Don't miss the Garita del Diablo (Devil's Sentry Box), a lonely post at the edge of the sea where, legend has it, the devil himself snatched away solitary sentinels. (The fort is uphill from Plaza Colón on Calle Norzagaray; ℃ **787/729-6960;** admission $3; ticket stubs from El Morro are good for admission here, too.)

Casinos

Most large hotels have casinos, which are one of San Juan's biggest draws. They're generally open daily from noon to 4am, but some never close. The **Casino at the Ritz-Carlton,** Avenue of the Governors, Isla Verde (℃ **800/241-3333** or 787/253-1700; www.ritzcarlton.com/en/Properties/SanJuan/Casino), is the largest in Puerto Rico. Combining elegant 1940s decor with tropical fabrics and patterns, it's one of the plushest entertainment complexes in the Caribbean. The **InterContinental San Juan,** 5961 Isla Verde Ave. (℃ **800/496-7621** or 787/791-6100), is another elegant

Puerto Rico Golf Excursions

Puerto Rico is a golfer's dream, but you'll need to sign up for a ship excursion or rent a car to reach the major courses from San Juan.

- Situated on about 400 hectares (1,000 acres) and with 72 holes, **Hyatt Dorado Beach Resort & Country Club** (℃ **800/554-9288** or 787/796-8916; www.hyatt.com), about 30 miles west of San Juan, offers the greatest concentration of golf in the Caribbean. Greens fees, including cart, are $195 for play before 1pm and $105 after 1:30pm. Club rentals are $55. All four 18-hole courses at the **Hyatt Regency Cerromar** and **Dorado Beach** properties here were designed by Robert Trent Jones, Sr. Jack Nicklaus ranks the 4th hole at the Dorado Beach East course as 1.

- **Doral Resort at Palmas del Mar** (℃ **787/285-2221**; www.palmas countryclub.com), 45 miles east of San Juan, has two courses: the par-71 Palm course, designed by Gary Player, and the newer 18-hole Flamboyan course, designed by Rees Jones. Greens fees for 18 holes are $150 at the Palm, $180 at the Flamboyan, including cart (clubs are $40).

- **Wyndham Rio Mar Beach Resort & Spa** (℃ **877/636-0636** or 787/888-6000; www.wyndhamriomar.com), 20 miles from San Juan in Rio Grande, also has two 18-hole courses, one designed by Tom and George Fazio, the other by Greg Norman. Greens fees, including cart, are $190 ($130 for play after noon).

place to rendezvous. One of its Murano glass chandeliers is, they say, "longer than a bowling alley." Most convenient for cruise ship passengers, the **Sheraton Old San Juan Hotel & Casino,** 100 Brumbaugh St. (℃ **800/325-3535** or 787/721-5100; www.sheratonoldsanjuan.co), is directly across from Pier 3 and often bustling.

Beaches

Puerto Rico is ringed by hundreds of miles of sandy beaches, and you won't have to leave San Juan to play in the surf. Perhaps the most famous beach in the Caribbean, **Condado Beach,** at the western end of Ashford Avenue, is the backyard playground of Condado's resort hotels. A favorite of families, it can get pretty crowded in winter. The beaches of **Isla Verde,** behind the hotels and condominiums along Isla Verde Avenue, are less rocky and are excellent for people-watching. Both have white sand, palm trees, ocean breezes, beautiful bodies, and plenty of bars and eateries. Snorkeling gear and other watersports equipment can be rented.

Shopping

San Juan has some great bargains—prices here are often even lower than those in St. Thomas—and U.S. citizens pay no duty on items bought in Puerto Rico. The streets of the Old Town, especially **Calle San Francisco** and **Calle del Cristo,** are a major shopping area. Local handicrafts can be good buys, including *santos* (handcarved wooden religious figures), needlework, straw work, hammocks, loose-fitting guayabera shirts, papier-mâché masks, and paintings and sculptures by local artists.

20 Roatán, Honduras

Roatán, the largest of Honduras's Bay Islands, is also the most visited destination in the country. It has been on the cruise map for a number of years, but only recently graduated to the major leagues, with lines like Carnival, Princess, HAL, Norwegian, Costa, and Royal Caribbean scheduling calls at its port. Measuring almost 40 miles in length and with a total landmass of 127 sq. km (49 sq. miles), the island has a mountainous backbone and is totally surrounded by the world's second largest barrier reef, which allows for superb diving as well as excellent fishing, and it has great beaches. An added bonus is that the beaches and towns are much less crowded than in places like Cozumel, and the place is still charmingly rough around the edges, though English seems as widely spoken as Spanish. Both in its shore waters and interior, Roatán is a prime ecotourism destination, with wildlife reserves, marine mammal encounters, reef diving, and other watersports. At the western tip of the island, **West Bay** has Roatán's best beach, while the community of **West End** (just 5 min. away) is full of bars, souvenir shops, and restaurants—from Thai and Italian spots to countless Honduran restaurants serving traditional local foods like *sopa de gallina* (chicken broth seasoned with basil and spearmint) and *platos tipico* (tortillas with beef and rice and beans). Most cruise passengers head here or take a shore excursion.

COMING ASHORE   Ships dock in **Coxen Hole,** the island's largest community (named after the 17th-century pirate John Coxen, and also known as **Roatán City**). In early 2010, the new $62-million Mahogany Bay Cruise Center opened there. Partly funded by Carnival Corporation, the facility sits on 20 acres of waterfront property and includes a two-berth cruise terminal that can accommodate up to 8,000 passengers daily. A funky chair-lift system takes cruise passengers from the terminal to Mahogany Beach, a private island with a white-sand beach, volleyball court, and lots of watersports.

GETTING AROUND   You'll find plenty of **taxis** lined up right at the cruise dock to take you around the island. Unfortunately, some taxis try to rip off customers with outlandish fares on days when ships are in port, so be sure to settle on a price before getting in. A daily rate for an island tour should cost about $100 (for the whole taxi, not per person), while the average trip between the pier and West End or West Bay should cost between $7.50 and $10 per person. **Water taxis** are a good way to get between West End and West Bay. It's about a 10-minute ride and costs $2. Look for the dock near Foster's Bar in West End. The return trip from West Bay has two easily identifiable pickup spots. **Bicycle rentals** are available at **Captain Van's** (© **504/ 403-8751;** www.captainvans.com) in West End for $9 per day.

LANGUAGE & CURRENCY   **Spanish** is the main language in Honduras, but most people on the Bay Islands speak English as well. The native languages of Lenca, Miskitu, and Garifuna are also spoken in some regions. Honduras's currency is the **Honduran lempira** (18 HNL = US$1; 1 HNL = US 5¢), but U.S. dollars are widely accepted as well throughout the Bay Islands. Some establishments may charge an additional fee for processing credit cards. All prices in this section are in U.S. dollars.

CALLING FROM THE U.S.   To place a call to Honduras, you need only dial **011** before the numbers listed in this section.

Best Cruise Line Shore Excursions

Coral Cay Snorkel Adventure ($56, 5½ hr.): Take a 15-minute bus ride to the Coral Cay Marine & Nature Park, where certified snorkel guides will lead you through the marine park's labyrinthine coral reefs, home to tropical fish, brain coral, sea fans, and other marine life—maybe even sea turtles and nurse sharks.

Certified Dolphin Dive ($120, 2hr.): Take a short ride to Anthony's Key Resort and the Roatán Institute for Marine Sciences, where you'll head out by boat with a dive guide, dolphin behaviorist, and videographer. You'll spend 45 minutes observing, photographing, and playing with the dolphins in the open ocean, in a one-tank dive at depths of up to 18m (60 ft.) over a white-sand bottom, adjacent to a shallow reef wall. Divers need a certification card to participate. Nondivers also can take part in a dolphin swim here ($75, 2½ hr.).

Garifuna Experience & Mangrove Tunnel ($75, 4 hr.): A 30-minute bus ride takes you to Roatán's northeast shore to experience the culture of the Garifuna people, descendants of slaves who settled here in 1797. The tour includes a dance performance, crafts and cooking demonstrations, and a little dose of history; it also includes a visit to a stilt village and a 30-minute boat ride through canals with the intertwined boughs of mangrove trees as roofing overhead.

Pirates, Birds & Monkeys at Gumbalimba Park ($55, 3 hr.): Gumbalimba Park (www.gumbalimbapark.com) is a one-stop shop for all things Roatán: a tropical bird and animal sanctuary with resident macaws and capuchin monkeys; hiking trails through a botanical garden full of orchids and heliconia; a beach destination and watersports center; with a restaurant and "pirates' cave" thrown in for good measure. This tour basically gives you access to all of that, to explore at your leisure. By the time you read this, cruise lines will probably also have resumed **zipline canopy tours** at the site. At this writing, they were underplaying them after a snapped cable caused the death of a cruise passenger in March 2008.

On Your Own: Within Walking Distance

The area around the Coxen Hole piers holds few attractions, just lots of tourist shops. Carnival's new Mahogany Bay will have a welcome center, shops, restaurants, and bars just off the docks.

On Your Own: Beyond the Port Area

West End is the most popular village on the island, with restaurants, bars, shopping, and proximity to West Bay.

If you want something a little different, head to the village of French Harbour, about 25 minutes from Coxen Hole on the south side of the island. On the outskirts, in French Key, **Sherman Arch's Iguana Farm** (© 504/445-7743) is home to between 2,500 and 3,000 iguanas of four different species. You can take a tour, feed and pet the lizards, and greet the resident yellow-necked parrots and macaws that live on the property. Getting there is easy: Take a taxi along the road leading east from French Harbour toward the Fantasy Island Hotel. You'll see a clearly marked sign showing the detour toward the farm. It's open daily 8am to 4pm. Admission is $8.

Beaches

The best beaches on the island are **Half Moon Bay** and **West Bay.** Half Moon Bay is a small beach right at the entrance to West End, and is bordered by a fossilized, raised coral. The reef passes right along the mouth of Half Moon Bay, an easy swim from shore. West Bay is about 5 minutes from West End. Scattered with resorts, this beach is blessed with powdery white sands and the reef is an easy swim from the shore. Boat transfers are available from West End, and you can rent kayaks along the beach.

Shopping

The best place to find souvenirs on the island is in West Bay, whose single lane dirt road has a variety of shops selling Honduran-made goods, including Lenca pottery that is unique to the country.

21 St. Barts

Chic, sophisticated St. Barts (or, technically, St. Barthélemy, a name no one ever uses) is internationally renowned as one of the ritziest refuges in the Caribbean. Rivaled only by Mustique or Anguilla, it's the preferred island retreat of the rich and famous, attracting the likes of Tom Cruise, Harrison Ford, and Mikhail Baryshnikov. Yet despite all the hoopla, St. Barts retains its charm, serenity, natural beauty, and incredibly French flavor. In contrast to most Caribbean islands, where descendants of African slaves form the majority, St. Barts's 8,000 year-round residents are primarily of French ancestry. **Gustavia,** the main port (whose name hearkens back to the 19th century, when Sweden controlled the island), is full of French restaurants and semi-chic, semibohemian nightspots. Many of the small luxe ships that call here stay into the evening so passengers can enjoy a night out. Away from town, the island is full of dramatic hills and pristine white-sand beaches.

COMING ASHORE   Cruise ships anchor off **Gustavia,** the main town, and ferry passengers to the dollhouse-size harbor and town via tenders.

GETTING AROUND   Taxis congregate at Gustavia's harbor to take cruise passengers to the beaches. Rates are set by the government but taxis are not metered. For **car rentals,** Budget, Avis, Hertz, and National all have offices here. If you want some stylin' Euro-fun, rent a Suzuki Samurai, a MINI Cooper, or a bright-lime-green Smart Car, the hippest toys on the island, for a ride up and down the picturesque, hilly local roads.

LANGUAGE & CURRENCY   **French** is the official language, but virtually everyone speaks **English** as well. St. Barts is part of the French overseas region of Guadeloupe, so the **euro** (€) is the official currency (.85€ = US$1; 1€ = US$1.20). U.S. dollars are commonly accepted.

CALLING FROM THE U.S.   When calling St. Barts from the United States, dial the international access code **(011)** and the country code **(590)** before the numbers listed here, which also begin with 590. That's right: If you want to make a connection, you have to dial 590 twice. It's just one of those oddities that makes the world go 'round.

Best Cruise Line Shore Excursions

Jet-Set Boat & Beach Excursion ($200, 4 hr.): Circumnavigate St. Barts in a 40-foot cruiser; then tender ashore at St. Jean Beach to swim, snorkel, and have drinks from the open bar.

St. Barts on Horseback ($55, 2 hr.): Travel to northern St. Barts for a relaxed, guided ride through the island's outback.

On Your Own: Within Walking Distance

For a taste of the island's celebrity vibe, make a beeline to **Le Select,** rue de la France at rue du Général de Gaulle (© **590/27-86-87**), the epicenter of Gustavia's afternoon social life for more than 60 years. This cafe's tables rest in a tree-shaded garden a block from the harbor. A full bar is available, along with simple meals. The classic, funky ambience inspired Jimmy Buffett's "Cheeseburger in Paradise," and a mix of salty locals and chic tourists typically make up the clientele.

Aside from hanging out, shopping, and eating, cruise passengers sticking close to port can also visit Gustavia's modest points of interest. **St. Bartholomew's Church,** on rue Samuel Fahlberg, dates from 1855 and has limestone and volcanic stone walls, as well as imported pitch-pine pews. Across from the dock, on the opposite side of the harbor, the **Municipal Museum,** on rue Duquesne (© **590/29-71-55**), is an unfocused but respectable introduction to the history, sociology, ethnology, economy, and ecology of the island. The most interesting items include Amerindian artifacts, rustic farm furnishings, and clothing used by early French settlers. It's open Monday to Saturday (closed Wed and Sat afternoon). Admission is about $3. Walking around the harbor takes a pleasant 20 minutes.

On Your Own: Beyond the Port Area

Visiting the tiny fishing village of **Corossol** is a vibrant way to experience the St. Barts of the past. About 10 minutes by taxi from the dock, this quaint, totally unchic hamlet was once home to traditional folk who still lived off the sea. Until not too long ago, you could still spot women in traditional 17th-century bonnets. That generation has all but died off, but Corossol is still a charming destination.

On the town's waterfront, just to the left of the road from Gustavia, the **Inter Oceans Museum** (© **590/27-62-97**) catalogs thousands of shells, corals, sand dollars, sea horses, sea urchins, and fish from around the world, all displayed in an endearingly homemade style (literally homemade—the museum is an extension of the owner's house). Don't miss the collection of sand from beaches around the world: A cocktail umbrella is planted in each specimen. Admission is about $4, but be sure to call first as the owner is old and ailing. Stop by **Le Regal** (© **590/27-85-26**) afterward and have a beer or a bite with the locals.

Beaches

The 22 beaches of St. Barts are first-rate. Few are ever crowded, even during the peak season, and all are public, free, and easily accessible by taxi from the cruise pier (make arrangements with your driver to be picked up at a specific time). St. Barts is a French island, so toplessness is common at all beaches. As you drive along, keep an eye out for small signs indicating beach access.

Shell Beach, so named for the mounds of tiny pink shells that litter the beach, is just a short walk from the harbor in Gustavia and is the most convenient place to soak up the sun if your time is limited. The water isn't always calm and there is a tiny dropoff, making it necessary to supervise children. **Do Brazil** (© **590/29-06-66;** www.dobrazil.com), a lively fusion restaurant right on the beach, is an ideal spot for lunch or watching the sunset. You can also grab a sandwich to go at **Zen Beach Bar** (© **590/27-19-39**).

If you're looking for an active beach strand, with restaurants and watersports, **Grand Cul de Sac** fits the bill, with waters that are shallow, warm, and protected. An even busier and equally social beach, **St. Jean** is actually two beaches divided by a rock promontory. Protected by a coral reef, the calm waters here attract families and watersports enthusiasts, including windsurfers, and there are numerous eating, drinking, shopping, and people-watching opportunities. Because it's near the airstrip, you have the added fun (or stress) of watching small planes take off and land. The short taxi ride will cost you about $40 each way, so bring friends to defray the cost.

Gouverneur, on the south-central coast, is quiet and relatively remote. Its idyllic setting and unspoiled beauty make it a favorite with locals. Farther east, in a wild and rustic area that was once the site of salt ponds, **Saline** is reached by a 3-minute hike over a sand dune. Most famous for its adult environment and nude bathers, it also boasts great bodysurfing waves.

Shopping

A duty-free port, St. Barts is a good place to buy liquor, perfume, and other French luxury items. Good buys on apparel, crystal, porcelain, and watches can also be found, especially during April, the biggest sale month. Moisturizer mavens can stock up on the island's own cosmetic line, Ligne St. Barth.

Shops are concentrated in Gustavia and St. Jean, where the quality-to-schlock ratio is as high as anywhere in the Caribbean. Most shops and offices close for a long lunch, usually from 1 to 3pm, but then stay open until 7pm.

22 St. Kitts

Somewhat off the beaten tourist track, south of St. Martin and north of Guadeloupe, St. Kitts forms the larger half of the combined Federation of St. Kitts and Nevis, two islands separated by only about 3.2km (2 miles) of ocean. St. Kitts—or St. Christopher, a name hardly anyone uses—is by far the more populous of the two islands, with some 35,000 people. St. Kitts is almost ridiculously lush and fertile, dotted with rainforests and waterfalls and boasting some lovely beaches along its southeast coastline; it's also extremely poor, still dependent on the same sugar cane crop that brought riches to its English plantation owners (and hot misery to its slaves) back in colonial days. Cane fields climb the slopes of its volcanic mountain range, and you'll see ruins of old mills and plantation houses as you drive around the island. **Basseterre,** the capital city, is full of old-time colonial architecture, but it's a small-scale place with little to offer visitors beyond a pleasant walk around. The island's most impressive landmark, **Brimstone Hill Fortress,** is about 15km (9⅓ miles) west of town.

COMING ASHORE   **Port Zante** has undergone a rebuilding and expansion, with a modern pier long enough to accommodate two large ships at one time (including the Oasis class and *QM2*). Additional vessels may dock at nearby commercial **Birdrock Deepwater Port,** about 3km (2 miles) from downtown Basseterre.

GETTING AROUND   You can walk around Basseterre, but you'll need **taxis** to get anywhere else. They greet cruise passengers (loudly) at the docks and also around the Circus, a public square near the docks at the intersection of Bank and Fort streets. Taxis aren't metered, so you must agree on the price before heading out; a 3-hour tour of the island will cost you about $60. Always ask if the rates quoted are in U.S. dollars or Eastern Caribbean dollars.

LANGUAGE & CURRENCY   **English** is the language of both St. Kitts and Nevis. The local currency is the **Eastern Caribbean dollar** (EC$2.65 = US$1; EC$1 = US37¢). Many shops and restaurants quote prices in U.S. dollars; always determine which currency locals are talking about before making a purchase.

Best Cruise Line Shore Excursions

Brimstone Hill Fortress & Gardens ($50, 3 hr.): Among the largest and best-preserved forts in the Caribbean, **Brimstone Hill** (www.brimstonehillfortress.org) dates from 1690, when the British fortified the hill to help recapture Fort Charles, situated below, from the French. Today, it's the centerpiece of a national park crisscrossed by nature trails, with a population of green vervet monkeys to keep things lively. Perched on the upper slopes of a tall, steep hill, it's a photographer's paradise, with views of mountains, fields, and the Caribbean Sea. Tours typically include a visit to the beautiful **Romney Gardens,** set amid the ruins of a sugar estate between Basseterre and the fort. You can check out the lush hillside gardens or shop at **Caribelle Batik** (© **869/ 465-6253**), one of the island's most popular boutiques, where artisans demonstrate their Indonesian-style hand-printing amid rack after rack of brightly colored clothes. It's open daily 8:30am to 4pm (Sat–Sun till 1pm).

Mount Liamuiga Volcano Hike ($110, 7 hr.): This dormant volcano, in the northwest area of the island, has long been known as "Mount Misery." On this excursion, you'll hike about 240m (800 ft.) to the summit, traveling along narrow trails and through the island's rainforest. It takes about 3 hours to reach the top. Refreshments are provided before the hike back down. This is a great trip if you're in shape.

Mountain Biking & Beach Tour ($78, 4 hr.): From the pier, you'll ride through Basseterre, and then out through sugar cane fields and up 450m (1,476-ft.) Olivees Mountain for views and refreshments. After the ride down, you'll stop at Friar's Bay for a swim and snack. It's a nice way to see this lush island.

Sail & Snorkel Catamaran Trip ($95, 3½ hr.): A sailing catamaran takes you to secluded Smitten's Bay for snorkeling among diverse reef fish and coral formations. Complimentary snacks are served aboard the boat on your return trip.

On Your Own: Within Walking Distance

The capital city of Basseterre, where the docks are located, has typical British colonial architecture and some quaint buildings and a few shops. Drop by the **marketplace,** where country people bring baskets brimming with mangos, guavas, soursop, mammee apples, and wild strawberries and cherries just picked in the fields. Tropical flowers abound. The town is built around a so-called **Circus,** the town's round square. A tall green Victorian clock stands in the center of the Circus. After Brimstone Hill Fortress, **Berkeley Memorial Clock** is the most photographed landmark of St. Kitts. In the old days, wealthy plantation owners and their families used to promenade here. **St. George's Anglican Church,** on Cayon Street (walk straight up Church St. or Fort St. from the dock), is the oldest church in town and is worth a look. **Independence Square,** a stone's throw from the docks along Bank Street, is pretty, with its central fountain and old church, but there's no good reason to linger unless it's to sit in the shade and toss back a bottle of Ting, the local grapefruit-based soda.

On Your Own: Beyond the Port Area

All of the good out-of-town sites on St. Kitts are covered under "Best Cruise Line Shore Excursions," above.

Beaches

The narrow peninsula in the southeast contains the island's salt ponds and also boasts the best white-sand beaches (approach via the winding, hilly road for a dramatic and gorgeous view); beaches in the north are made of gray volcanic sand. You'll find the best swimming at **Conaree Beach,** 5km (3 miles) from Basseterre; **Frigate Bay,** with its talcum-powder-fine sand; and the twin beaches of **Banana Bay** and **Cockleshell Bay,** at the southeast corner of the island, where you can have a bite at the nearby restaurant and where you might just be greeted by the resident pig, Wilbur. If you're lucky, the green vervet monkeys may come down from the hillside behind the beach to say hello as well. Food and drink are available. (**Beware:** The monkeys have been known to steal drinks from unsuspecting tourists.) All beaches, even those that border hotels, are free and open to the public. You must, however, usually pay a fee to use a hotel's beach facilities.

Shopping

Basseterre is not a shopping town, though you will find local specialties in a handful of shops, ranging from paintings to pottery, jewelry, jams, teas, and handmade batik fabrics. The most popular shop with visitors is probably **Caribelle Batik,** which is a stop on many shore excursions (see above).

23 St. Lucia

With a turbulent history shared by many of its Caribbean neighbors, St. Lucia (pronounced *Loo*-sha) changed hands often during the colonial period, being British seven times and French seven times. Today, though, it's an independent state that's become one of the most popular destinations in the Caribbean, with some of the finest resorts. The heaviest development is concentrated in the northwest, between the capital of Castries and the northern end of the island, where there's a string of white-sand beaches. The interior boasts relatively unspoiled green-mantled mountains and gentle valleys, as well as the volcanic **Mount Soufrière.** Two dramatic peaks—the **Pitons**—rise along the southwest coast.

Castries, the capital, has grown up around an extinct volcanic crater that's now a large harbor surrounded by hills. Because of fires that devastated many of its older structures, the town today has touches of modernity, with glass-and-concrete buildings, although there's still an old-fashioned Saturday-morning market on Jeremie Street. The country women dress in traditional cotton headdresses to sell their luscious fruits and vegetables, while weather-beaten men sit close by playing *warrie* (a fast game played with pebbles on a carved board) or dominoes using tiles the color of cherries.

COMING ASHORE Most cruise ships arrive at the fairly new pier at **Pointe Seraphine,** within walking distance of the center of Castries and boasting St. Lucia's best shopping right on-site. Two mid- to large-size cruise ships can be accommodated. With the rapid increase in cruise tourism, the limited capacity at Pointe Seraphine may necessitate docking at **Port Castries,** an industrial terminal on the other side of the colorful harbor. There's a shopping terminal here called La Place Carenage. Some smaller lines, such as Star Clippers and Seabourn, visit other sites around the island, anchoring off **Rodney Bay** to the north or **Soufrière** to the south and carrying passengers ashore by tender.

GETTING AROUND There is an official **taxi** association servicing both Pointe Seraphine and La Place Carenage, with standard fares posted. You can hire a taxi to go to Soufrière, too. Many taxi drivers offer 3- to 4-hour tours, with a stop at the beach, for about $150 for four people. From Castries, the fare to Marigot Bay should be about $35. Be sure to find out whether you're talking U.S. or Easter Caribbean dollars before agreeing on a price.

LANGUAGE & CURRENCY **English** is the official language. The official currency is the **Eastern Caribbean dollar** (EC$2.65 = US$1; EC$1 = US37¢), though shops and restaurants commonly take the U.S. dollar as well. Be sure you know which currency locals are talking about before making a purchase.

Best Cruise Line Shore Excursions

Because of the difficult terrain, shore excursions are the best means of seeing this beautiful island in a day or less. In addition to the sampling below, most ships typically offer bus tours (many visiting the island's banana plantations) and snorkeling cruises.

Pigeon Island Sea Kayaking ($75, 3 hr.): After transferring to Rodney Bay, you'll make the roughly 30-minute paddle out to the island, where you'll have time to swim, kayak some more, or make the steep climb up to Fort Rodney. From the summit, you'll have great views of the Pitons; sometimes you'll even be able to see Martinique.

Rainforest Bicycle Tour ($60, 4½ hr.): After being dropped off by bus in the middle of the forest, you'll ride past banana plantations and the Errard Falls waterfall, stopping to sample various fruits that grow along the roadside. Some time for swimming at the falls is usually included.

Soody Nature Hike & Mineral Waterfall ($65, 7 hr.): Drive along the west coast through fishing villages, banana plantations, and the edge of the rainforest before arriving at Soufrière, location of the Pitons and the Diamond Botanical Gardens. A guided 1-hour hike through the volcanic forest introduces you to the island's flora and fauna, ending up at a therapeutic sulfuric waterfall where you can take a dip to cure whatever ails you. Lunch at a Creole restaurant is included.

Beach Snorkel ($70, 3½ hr.): Snorkeling is spectacular around St. Lucia. This trip departs the Castries harbor by boat, traveling an hour en route to the island's marine reserve, which has a special area for snorkeling. There's also a supersize 7-hour ($97) version of this trip that includes a buffet lunch.

Caribbean Pirates Extravaganza ($95, 4 hr.): The 42m (138-ft.) brig *Unicorn* was featured in several *Pirates of the Caribbean* movies and was also used in the filming of the TV miniseries, *Roots.* Swashbucklers and wenches alike can board this beauty and set sail to Pigeon Island, in search of buried treasure, or just a patch of sand and a relaxing swim.

On Your Own: Within Walking Distance

The principal streets of Castries are **William Peter Boulevard** and **Bridge Street.** Don't miss a walk through town: People are very friendly, and **Jeremie Street** is chock-ablock with variety stores of the most authentic local kind, selling everything from spices to housewares. A Roman Catholic cathedral stands on **Columbus Square,** which has a few restored buildings. Take a gander at the enormous 400-year-old "rain" tree, also called a "no-name" tree, that grows in the square. The nearby **Government House** is a late-Victorian structure.

Beyond Government House lies **Morne Fortune,** which means "Hill of Good Luck." Actually, no one's had much luck here, certainly not the French and British soldiers who battled for **Fort Charlotte.** The fort switched between the two sides many times. You can visit the 18th-century barracks, complete with a military cemetery, a small museum, the Old Powder Magazine, and the Four Apostles Battery—four grim muzzle-loading cannons. The view of the harbor of Castries is panoramic from this point. You can also see north to Pigeon Island or south to the Pitons. To reach Morne Fortune, head east on Bridge Street.

Castries has a very colorful **Central Market,** right near the dock, that's also worth a visit. The airplane-hangar-size emporium sells local food, trinkets, and produce. Buy some banana ketchup or local cinnamon sticks to take home.

On Your Own: Beyond the Port Area

St. Lucia's first national park, the 18-hectare (44-acre) **Pigeon Island National Land-mark** (www.slunatrust.org), was originally an island, but is now joined to the north-west shore of the mainland by an environmentally unfriendly causeway. It's about 30 minutes by taxi from Castries. The park, an ideal spot for picnics and nature walks, is covered with lemon grass, which spread from original plantings made by British light opera singer Josset, who leased the island for 30 years and grew the grass to provide thatch for her cottage's roof. The island's **Interpretation Centre** contains artifacts and a multimedia display of local history, covering everything from the Amerindian set-tlers of A.D. 1000 to 1782's Battle of Saints, when Admiral Rodney's fleet set out from Pigeon Island and defeated the French Admiral De Grasse. Right below the interpre-tation center is the cozy **Captain's Cellar Pub,** located in what was formerly a soldiers' mess. From the tables outside, you get amazing scenes of the crashing surf on the Atlantic coast, just a few steps away. From here, you can walk up the winding and moderately steep path to a **lookout,** from which you get a wonderful view that stretches all the way to Martinique. Two white-sand beaches lie on the island's west coast. Island admission is $7.50.

La Soufrière, a fishing port and St. Lucia's second-largest settlement, is dominated by Petit Piton and Gros Piton, collectively known as the **Pitons,** two of the dramatic pointed peaks that rise right from the sea to 738m and 786m (2,421 ft. and 2,579 ft.), respectively. Formed by lava and once actively volcanic, these mountains are now cloaked in green vegetation, with waves crashing around their bases. Their sheer rise from the water makes them such visible landmarks that they've become the symbol of St. Lucia. Near the town lies the famous "drive-in" volcano, **La Soufrière,** a rocky lunar landscape of bubbling mud and craters seething with fuming sulfur. You can lit-erally drive into an old crater and walk between the sulfur springs and pools of hiss-ing steam. The fumes are said to have medicinal properties. A local guide is usually waiting nearby; if you do hire a guide, agree—and then doubly agree—on what the fee will be. Nearby are the **Diamond Mineral Baths,** also called Botanical Gardens. They were originally constructed in 1784 by order of Louis XVI, whose doctors told him that these waters were similar in mineral content to the waters at Aix-les-Bains. The baths were built to help French soldiers who had been fighting in the West Indies recuperate from wounds and disease. Regular admission is $13 but for an extra $10, you can bathe and benefit from the recuperative effects of the baths yourself. They're open daily from 10am to 5pm (Sun till 3pm).

Beaches

If you don't take a shore excursion, you might want to spend your time on one of St. Lucia's famous beaches, all of which are open to the public, even those at hotel prop-erties (though you must pay to use a hotel's beach equipment). Taxis can take you to any of the island's beaches, but we recommend that you stick to the calmer shores along the western coast, because the rough surf on the windward Atlantic side makes swimming potentially dangerous.

Leading beaches include **Pigeon Island,** off the northern shore, with white sand and picnic facilities; **Vigie Beach,** north of the Castries harbor, with fine sand; **Marigot Beach,** south of the Castries harbor, framed on three sides by steep emerald hills and skirted by palm trees; and **Reduit Beach,** between Choc Bay and Pigeon Point, with fine brown sand. Just north of Soufrière is a beach connoisseur's delight, **Anse Chastanet** (© **758/459-7000**), boasting an expanse of white sand at the foothills of lush mountains. This is a fantastic spot for snorkeling, with spectacular coral reefs starting only a little way offshore, providing shelter for thousands of fish and other sea creatures. **Choc Bay** is a long stretch of sand and palm trees on the northwestern coast, convenient to Castries, with tranquil waters especially appealing for families with small children. You'll find miles of white sand at the beach at **Vieux Fort,** at the southern end of the island. Reefs protect the crystal-clear waters here, rendering them tranquil and ideal for swimming. At the southern end of the windward side of the island is **Anse des Sables,** which opens onto a shallow bay swept by trade winds, great for windsurfing.

Shopping

You'll find some good but not remarkable buys on bone china, jewelry, perfume, watches, liquor, and crystal. Souvenir items include designer bags and mats, local pottery, and straw hats—again, nothing remarkable. *Tip:* If your cruise is also calling in St. Thomas, let the local vendors know; it may make them more amenable to bargaining.

Built for cruise ship passengers, **Pointe Seraphine** has the best collection of shops on the island. You must present your cruise pass when making purchases here.

24 St. Martin/Sint Maarten

Who can resist a two-for-one deal? That's what you get on St. Martin, a 96-sq.-km (37-sq.-mile) island that's been shared by France (with 52 sq. km/20 sq. miles of it) and the Netherlands (with 44 sq. km/17 sq. miles) for more than 350 years. Although the border between the two sides is virtually imperceptible—a monument along the road marks the change in administration—each side retains elements of its own heritage. The French side, with some of the best beaches and restaurants in the Caribbean, emphasizes quiet elegance. French fashions and luxury items fill the shops, and the fragrance of croissants mixes with the spicy aromas of West Indian cooking. The Dutch side, officially known as Sint Maarten, reflects Holland's anything-goes philosophy: Development is much more widespread, flashy casinos pepper the landscape, and strip malls make the larger towns look as much like Anaheim as Amsterdam. The 100% duty-free shopping has turned both sides of the island into a bargain hunter's paradise.

COMING ASHORE   Cruise ships usually dock on the Dutch side, at **Dr. A. C. Wathey Pier,** about 1.6km (1 mile) southeast of Philipsburg. The majority of passengers are then tendered to the smaller Captain Hodge Pier at the center of town, but others choose to walk the distance on a newly developed boardwalk or take taxis. The pier can accommodate up to four vessels; any more than that may anchor in **Great Bay,** a superquick ride by tender from the Captain Hodge Pier, where a terminal has shops, food outlets, ATMs, and an Internet cafe. Smaller vessels sometimes dock on the French side of the island, at **Marina Port la Royale,** adjacent to the heart of Marigot.

GETTING AROUND   Taxis on both sides of the island are unmetered. Agree on a rate and currency before getting in. Dutch law requires that drivers list government-regulated fares based on two passengers. Shorter rides, including the route between Marigot and Philipsburg, average around $15; longer trips can climb to $20-plus. Privately owned and operated **minivans,** with signs to indicate their destination, can be hailed anywhere on the street. Fares are usually about $1.50. **Rental cars** are a great way to see both sides of the island. Avis, Budget, and Hertz all have offices here. **Water taxis** are also a popular way to get around.

LANGUAGE & CURRENCY   Surprise, surprise: The official language on the Dutch side is **Dutch,** and the official language on the French side is **French.** Most people on both sides also speak **English.** The legal tender in Dutch Sint Maarten is the **Netherlands Antilles guilder** (1.80 ANG = US$1; 1 ANG = US55¢), and the official currency on the French side is the **euro** (.85€ = US$1; 1€ = US$1.20). Most prices are also quoted in U.S. dollars, which are widely accepted on both sides.

CALLING FROM THE U.S.   When calling Dutch Sint Maarten from the United States, simply dial the international access number **(011)** before the numbers listed here. Calling French St. Martin requires more of an effort: Dial **011** and then **590** before the numbers listed. Yes, 590 already appears in the numbers in this section, but those three digits must be dialed twice to make a connection.

Best Cruise Line Shore Excursions

America's Cup Sailing Regatta ($90, 3 hr.): Get a taste of nautical exhilaration by competing in a race aboard an America's Cup–winning sailboat. This extremely popular hands-on excursion lets you grind winches, trim sails, and duck under booms—after you've been trained by professionals, of course. Alternatively, sit back and watch others do all the work.

Pinel Island Shore Snorkel & Beach Tour ($40, 3½ hr.): After a scenic bus ride to the French town of Cul de Sac, along the northeast coast, hop on a tender to the small offshore island of Ilet Pinel for some of St. Martin's best snorkeling.

Hidden Forest Hike ($84, 5 hr.): Take a 45-minute drive to Loterie Farm, where you'll do a 2-hour hike through the tropical forest, eventually emerging at Pic Paradise, the island's highest point. Along the way, your guide will point out a secret freshwater spring and the island's famous guava berry trees. Return to the farm for a complimentary rum or fruit punch and a typical Caribbean farmhouse lunch.

Butterfly Farm & Marigot ($45, 3½ hr.): After a scenic drive through both the French and Dutch sides of the island, walk through a surrealistic enclosed garden with pools, waterfalls, and hundreds of exquisitely beautiful and exotic butterflies from around the world. Amusing guides identify species, describe courtship and mating rituals, and give tips on attracting butterflies to your garden at home. Afterward, absorb the Creole charm and French atmosphere of Marigot.

On Your Own: Within Walking Distance

Shopping, sunbathing, and gambling are the pastimes that interest most cruise passengers who hit this island, but folks with a taste for culture and history can make a day of it here as well.

ON THE DUTCH SIDE   Directly in front of the Philipsburg town pier, on Wathey Square, the **Courthouse** combines northern European sobriety with Caribbean brightness. Originally built in 1793 of freestone and wood, this venerable old building has suffered numerous hurricanes, but has been restored after each tempest and continues to house government offices. East of the Courthouse, down a little shopping alley, the tiny **Sint Maarten Museum,** 7 Front St. (© **599/542-4917;** www.speetjens.com/museum), features modest, cluttered exhibits that focus on the island's history and geology. The second-floor gallery is open Monday to Friday from 10am to 4pm. Admission is $1.

   Fort Amsterdam is the Dutch side's most important historic colonial site. Since 1631, it has looked out over Great Bay from the hill west of Philipsburg. The fort was the Netherlands' first military outpost in the Caribbean. The Spanish captured it 2 years later, making it their most significant bastion east of Puerto Rico. Peter Stuyvesant, who later became governor of New Amsterdam (now New York), lost his leg to a cannonball while trying to reclaim the fort for Holland. The site affords grand views of the bay, but ruins of the walls and a couple of rusty cannons are all that remain of the original fort.

Gambling is also big here, with several casinos clustered along Front Street in the heart of Philipsburg. All of them are open early enough to snag cruise passengers.

ON THE FRENCH SIDE   **Fort St. Louis** is Marigot's answer to Fort Amsterdam. Built in 1767 to protect the waterfront warehouses that stored the French colony's agricultural riches, the cannons of this bastion frequently fired on hostile British raiders from Anguilla. After restorations and modification in the 19th century, the fort was eventually abandoned. In addition to the fort's cannons, crumbling walls, and French tricolor flag flapping in the breeze, the short climb up the hill flanking Marigot Bay's north end affords splendid vistas. As a respite from the sun, duck into Marigot's **Museum of Saint Martin** (*C* **590/29-22-84**), next to the tourism office and adjacent to the marina. Much more thorough and scholarly than its Philipsburg counterpart, this institution boasts a first-rate collection of Ciboney, Arawak, and Carib artifacts excavated from the island's Amerindian sites, plus a reproduction of a 1,500-year-old burial mound. Another display details the history of the plantation and slavery era, while early-20th-century photographs trace the island's modern development. It's open Monday to Friday 10am to 4pm, Saturday 10am to 2pm. Admission is about $5.

Beaches

St. Martin has more than 30 beautiful white-sand beaches—some social, some serene. The busier ones boast bars, restaurants, watersports, and hotels, where changing facilities are usually available for a small fee. Toplessness is ubiquitous; nudism is common on the French side, and increasingly evident on the Dutch side as well.

ON THE DUTCH SIDE   **Great Bay Beach** is your best bet if you want to stay in Philipsburg. This mile-long stretch is convenient and has calm water, but it lacks the tranquillity and cleanliness of the more remote beaches.

Just west of the airport, on the west side of the island, **Maho Beach** boasts a casino, shade palms, and a popular beachside bar and grill. It's a good snorkeling spot, too. Farther west, **Mullet Beach** borders the island's golf course. Shaded by palm trees and crowded on weekends, it's popular with swimmers and snorkelers. On-site vendors rent an array of watersports equipment. **Dawn Beach,** on the east coast, is the best snorkeling site on the island. Rent equipment from Busby's Beach Bar, which is right on the sand.

ON THE FRENCH SIDE   Far and away the island's most visited strand, **Orient Beach,** on the northeast coast, fancies itself the St. Tropez of the Caribbean. Hedonism is the name of the game here: plenty of food, drink, music, and flesh (a naturist resort occupies the beach's southern tip, but nudism isn't confined to any one area). Watersports abound. South of Orient Beach, the waveless waters of **Coconut Grove** or **Galion Beach** are shallow up to 30m (98 ft.) offshore. Protected by a coral reef, this area is popular with kids and windsurfers.

On the island's west coast, just north of the Dutch border, **Long Bay** is the island's longest beach and another refuge for adults seeking peace and quiet. There are no facilities here, but this wild beach bordering some of the island's grandest mansions is

Sint Maarten Golf Excursions

The **Mullet Bay Golf Course** (© 599/545-2850), on the Dutch side, has an 18-hole course designed by Joseph Lee, which is considered one of the more challenging in the Caribbean, especially the back 9. Mullet Pond and Simpson Bay lagoon provide both beauty and hazards. Greens fees, including carts, are $140 for 18 holes. Club rental is an additional $30 for 18 holes. The course opens daily at 7am.

popular with the rich and (sometimes) famous. The water and sand here are silky. **Friars Beach,** just outside of Marigot, is a quiet sheltered cove at the end of a bumpy road, with gorgeous views of the neighboring island Anguilla on clear days. Beach chairs, umbrellas, and food are available on the beach.

Shopping

St. Martin is a true free port—no duties are paid on any item coming in or going out—and neither side of the island has a sales tax. Shops on the much busier Dutch side are concentrated in Philipsburg, along **Front Street** and the numerous alleys radiating from it. The district is largely nondescript, but you'll find all the usual jewelry/gift/luxury-item shops, as well as some quirky local boutiques. In general, prices in the major stores are nonnegotiable, but at small, family-run shops, you can try your luck with a little polite bargaining. The T-shirt and souvenir epicenter is in the open-air market behind the Courthouse in front of the town pier. **Guavaberry Emporium** (www.guavaberry.com), 8–10 Front St., sells Guavaberry "island folk liqueur," an aged rum with a distinctive fruity, woody, almost bittersweet flavor; it's available only on Sint Maarten.

On the French side, Marigot has a much calmer, more charming, and sophisticated ambience, with waterfront cafes where you can rest your weary feet after shopping. Many stores here close their doors for a 2-hour lunch break starting at noon. The wide selection of European merchandise is skewed toward an upscale audience, but French crystal, perfume, liqueur, jewelry, and fashion can be up to 50% less expensive than in the U.S.

25 U.S. Virgin Islands: St. Thomas & St. John

Ever since Columbus discovered the Virgin Islands during his second voyage to the New World in 1493, they have proven irresistible to foreign powers seeking territory; at one time or another, they've been governed by Denmark, Spain, France, England, Holland, and, since 1917, the United States.

Vacationers discovered **St. Thomas** right after World War II and have been flocking here ever since. Tourism and U.S. government programs have raised the standard of living to one of the highest in the Caribbean, and today the island is one of the busiest and most developed cruise ports in the West Indies, often hosting more than six ships a day during the peak winter season. **Charlotte Amalie** (pronounced Ah-*mahl*-yah), named in 1691 in honor of the wife of Denmark's King Christian V, is the island's capital and has become the Caribbean's major shopping center.

The most tranquil and unspoiled of the U.S. Virgins is **St. John,** the smallest of the lot, more than half of which is preserved as the gorgeous **Virgin Islands National Park.** A rocky coastline, forming crescent-shaped bays and white-sand beaches, rings the whole island, whose miles of serpentine hiking trails lead past the ruins of

18th-century Danish plantations and allow panoramic ocean views. A few ships anchor directly off St. John, but those that dock in St. Thomas usually offer excursions here as well, via ferry.

St. Croix, the largest of the USVIs, gets nowhere near as many visitors as St. Thomas, making for a more tranquil port experience. (A few years back, a spate of robberies and muggings against passengers and crew drove most cruise lines out of St. Croix, though a concerted effort by the island recently to improve conditions has seen some lines returning.) The island's major attraction is Buck Island Reef National Monument, an offshore park full of gorgeous coral reefs.

LANGUAGE & CURRENCY **English** is spoken on all three islands, and the **U.S. dollar** is the official currency. Americans get a break on shopping in the U.S. Virgins, as they can bring home $1,600 worth of merchandise without paying duty, as opposed to $400 from most other Caribbean ports. You can also bring back more liquor from here. See section 5, "Tipping, Customs & Other End-of-Cruise Concerns," in chapter 3, for more **Customs** information.

St. Thomas

With a population of more than 50,000 and a large number of American expatriates and temporary sun-seekers in residence, tiny St. Thomas isn't exactly a tranquil tropical retreat. You won't have any beaches to yourself. Shops, bars, and restaurants (including a lot of fast-food joints) abound here, and most of the locals make their living off the tourist trade.

COMING ASHORE Most cruise ships anchor at **West Indian Dock/Havensight Mall.** Located along the southern end of Charlotte Amalie Harbor, 2½ miles from the town center, it has its own restaurants, bookstores, banks, postal van, and lots of duty-free shops. The dock can accommodate three to four large ships. If Havensight is clogged with cruise ships, you'll dock at the **Crown Bay Cruise Ship Terminal,** to the west of Charlotte Amalie. The two piers can accommodate three ships of varying size, although unlike Havensight, they cannot dock the megaships. If both terminals are at capacity, ships anchor in **Charlotte Amalie Harbor.** From the terminals, some people make the long, hot, 30-minute-plus walk into Charlotte Amalie, but it's not terribly picturesque. A taxi ride into town costs about $6; keep in mind there are often traffic jams, so it could take as much as 30 minutes or longer to get into town on the busiest days.

GETTING AROUND Taxis are the chief means of transport here. They're unmetered, but a guide of point-to-point fares around the island is included in most tourist magazines. A typical fare from Havensight Mall to Magens Bay, for a day at the beach, runs from $10 per person or $7 per person in a shared cab. If you want to hire a taxi and a driver (who just may be a great tour guide) for a day, expect to pay about $35 per person for 2 hours of sightseeing in a shared car, or $50 per hour for two to four people. Less formal, privately owned **taxi vans** make unscheduled stops along major traffic arteries, charging less than a dollar for most rides. If you look like you want to go somewhere, one will likely stop for you. They may or may not have their final destinations written on a cardboard sign displayed on the windshield.

Best Cruise Line Shore Excursions

In addition to the excursions below, a huge number of booze cruises, island tours, and beach/snorkeling tours are offered here. The waters off these islands are rated among the most beautiful in the world.

The U.S. & British Virgin Islands

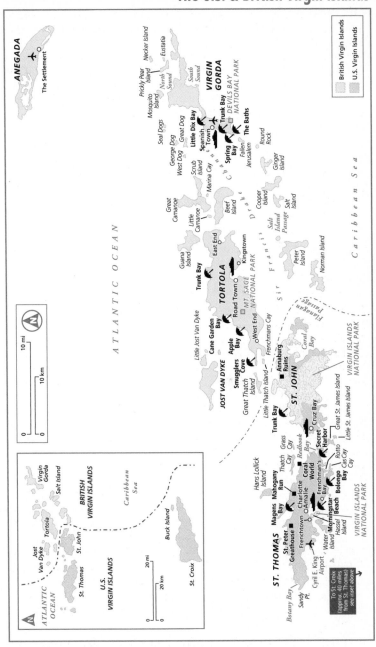

Coral World & Island Drive ($58, 3 hr.): Coral World Underwater Observatory and Marine Park is St. Thomas's number-one attraction. The 3½-acre complex features a three-story underwater observation tower 100 feet offshore, plunging the depths to allow views of tropical fish, coral formations, sharks, and other sea beasts. In the Marine Gardens Aquarium, saltwater tanks display everything from sea horses to sea urchins, and a Touch Pool lets you fondle some of them. Another tank is devoted to sea predators, including circling sharks.

Kayaking the Marine Sanctuary ($80, 3½ hr.): Paddle a kayak from the mouth of the marine sanctuary at Holmberg's Marina and spend nearly an hour among the mangroves while a naturalist explains the ecosystem. This trip includes a free half-hour to go snorkeling or walk along the coral beach at Bovoni Point.

St. John Eco-hike ($70, 4 hr.): Take the ferry to St. John for a walkabout through Virgin Islands National Park. The Lind Point Trail ascends about 250 feet to the Lind Point Overlook for views of St. John, St. Thomas, and the surrounding islands. An expert guide discusses the park's ecosystem and St. John's cultural history while you walk to Honeymoon Beach for a bit of swimming.

Water Island Bike Trip & Beach Adventure ($82, 3½ hr.): After a ferry ride to Water Island, a 5-minute bus ride brings you to the island's highest point, from which you get a nice downhill ride. Your guide will point out various historic sights and wildlife en route to Honeymoon Beach, where you can swim and enjoy a drink.

ON YOUR OWN: WITHIN WALKING DISTANCE

In days of yore, seafarers from all over the globe flocked to the old Danish town of Charlotte Amalie, including pirates and, during the Civil War, Confederate sailors. The old warehouses that once held pirates' loot still stand and, for the most part, contain shops, shops, and more shops. The main streets (called *gades* here in honor of their Danish heritage) are a veritable shopping mall, especially close to the waterfront. Stray farther landward and you'll find pockets of 19th-century houses and the truly charming, brick-and-stone **St. Thomas Synagogue,** built in 1833 by Sephardic Jews high on steep, sloping Crystal Gade. There's a great view from here as well.

Dating from 1672, **Fort Christian,** 32 Raadets Gade, rises from the harbor to dominate the center of town. Named after Danish King Christian V, the structure has been everything from a governor's residence to a jail. Many pirates were hanged in its courtyard.

Seven Arches Museum, on Government Hill (✆ **340/774-9295;** www.sevenarches museum.com), is a 2-centuries-old Danish house completely restored to its original condition and furnished with antiques. You can walk through the yellow ballast arches and visit the great room with a view of the busy harbor. It's open Monday to Friday from 10am to 2pm (Sat–Sun by appointment). Admission is by donation.

The **Paradise Point Tramway** (✆ **340/774-9809;** www.paradisepointtramway. com) is a cable car that afford visitors a dramatic view of Charlotte Amalie Harbor at a peak height of 697 feet. The tramway transports riders from the Havensight area to Paradise Point, where they disembark to visit shops and a popular restaurant and bar. The cost is $21 round-trip.

On Your Own: Beyond the Port Area

The lush **St. Peter Greathouse Estate and Gardens,** at the corner of St. Peter Mountain (Rte. 40) and Barrett Hill roads (✆ **340/774-4999;** www.greathouse-mountain top.com), adorns 11 acres on the volcanic peaks of the island's northern rim. It's the creation of Howard Lawson DeWolfe, a *Mayflower* descendant who, with his wife, Sylvie, bought the estate in 1987 and set about transforming it into a tropical paradise. It's filled with some 200 varieties of plants and trees, including an umbrella plant from Madagascar. There's also a rainforest, an orchid jungle, waterfalls, and reflecting ponds. From a panoramic deck, you can see some 20 of the U.S. Virgin Islands. The house itself is worth a visit, its interior filled with local art. It's open daily from 8am to 4pm. Admission is $12 adults, $8 seniors and kids.

Beaches

St. Thomas has some good beaches, all of which are easily reached by taxi. Arrange for your driver to return and pick you up at a designated time. All the beaches in the U.S. Virgin Islands are public, but some still charge a fee. Mind your belongings, as St. Thomas has pickpockets and thieves who target visitors. If you're going to St. John, you may want to do your sunning there instead (see "Beaches" under "St. John," below), as the beach options there are generally nicer.

Located 3 miles north of Charlotte Amalie, across the mountains on the north side of the island, **Magens Bay Beach** was once hailed as one of the world's most beautiful, but it isn't as well maintained as it should be and is often overcrowded, especially when many cruise ships are in port. Admission is $5. Changing facilities, restrooms, a snack bar, snorkel gear, and float rentals are available. In the northeast, near Coral World, **Coki Beach** is another good, but often crowded spot. Snorkelers come here often. Also on the north side, **Sapphire Beach** is one of the finest on St. Thomas, set against the backdrop of the Doubletree Sapphire Beach Resort & Marina complex, where you can lunch or order drinks. Windsurfers like this beach a lot; you can also rent snorkeling gear and lounge chairs.

On the island's south side, **Morningstar** lies about 2 miles east of Charlotte Amalie at Marriott's Frenchman's Reef Beach Resort. You can wear your most daring swimwear here. Sailboats, snorkeling equipment, and lounge chairs are available for rent. To reach the beach, take the cliff-front elevator at the Marriott. **Bluebeard's Beach Club,** just a little to the east, has a secluded setting. Still farther east, the **Bolongo Bay** lures those who love a serene spread of sand. You can feed hibiscus blossoms to iguanas and rent snorkeling gear and lounge chairs here. There's also a variety of watersports, including parasailing. At the far eastern end, little **Secret Harbor** sits near a collection of condos. With its white sand and coconut palms, it's a veritable cliché of Caribbean charm.

Shopping

Shopping is the number-one activity in Charlotte Amalie, and you'll sometimes find well-known brand names at savings of up to 40% off prices in the U.S.—but you have to plow through a lot of junk to find the bargains. The main goodies are jewelry, watches, cameras, china, and leather, plus the local Cruzan Rum, which is so ridiculously cheap that you'll think it's mismarked.

Many cruise ship passengers shop at the **Havensight Mall,** where the ships dock, but the major shopping is along the harbor of Charlotte Amalie. **Main Street** (or Dronningens Gade, its old Danish name) is the prime shopping area, with nearby **Back Street,** or Vimmelskaft, not too far behind. Many shops are also spread along the **Waterfront Highway** (also called Kyst Vejen) and along the side streets. All the usual Caribbean mega-tourist-shops sell all the usual jewelry, watches, perfume, and gift items, but some more singular boutiques and gift shops are mixed in. At the

Vendors Plaza, on the corner of Veterans Drive and Tolbod Gade, hundreds of street vendors ply their trade beneath oversize parasols. Food vendors set up on sidewalks outside.

St. John

A tiny gem, lush St. John lies about 3 miles east of St. Thomas across Pillsbury Sound. It's the smallest and least populated of the U.S. Virgins, only about 7 miles long and 3 miles wide, with a total land area of some 19 square miles. The island was slated for big development under Danish control, but a slave rebellion and the decline of the sugar cane plantations ended that idea. Since 1956, more than half of St. John's landmass, as well as its shoreline waters, have been set aside as the **Virgin Islands National Park** (www.virgin.islands.national-park.com), and today the island leads the Caribbean in eco- (or "sustainable") tourism. Miles of winding hiking trails lead to panoramic views and the ruins of 18th-century Danish plantations. Mysterious geometric petroglyphs incised into boulders and cliffs can be seen all over the island (ask a guide to point them out if you can't find them). These figures, of unknown age and origin, have never been deciphered. Because St. John is easy to reach from St. Thomas and the beaches are spectacular, many cruise ship passengers spend their entire day here.

COMING ASHORE Cruise ships cannot dock at either of the piers in St. John. Instead, they moor off the coast at **Cruz Bay,** sending in tenders to the National Park Service Dock, the larger of the two piers. Most cruise ships docking at St. Thomas offer shore excursions to St. John's pristine interior and beaches.

GETTING AROUND You'll find shops, bars, and restaurants right by the docks. Otherwise, the most popular way to get around the island is by **surrey-style taxi.** Typical fares from Cruz Bay are $8 to Trunk Bay, $10 to Cinnamon Bay, and $13 to Maho Bay. Taxis wait at the pier. You can also rent open-sided **jeeps;** Avis and Hertz both have offices here. Just remember to drive on the left, even though steering wheels are on the left, too. Go figure.

Best Cruise Line Shore Excursions

St. John Island Tour ($50, 5 hr.): Because most ships tie up in St. Thomas, tours of St. John first require a ferry or tender ride to Cruz Bay in St. John. Then you board open-air safari buses for a tour that includes a stop at the ruins of a working plantation (the Annaberg Ruins), as well as a pause at Trunk Bay or one of the other beaches. The island and sea views from the coastal road are spectacular.

On Your Own: Within Walking Distance

Most cruise passengers dart through **Cruz Bay,** a cute little West Indian village with interesting bars, restaurants, boutiques, and pastel-painted houses. **Wharfside Village,** near the dock, is a complex of courtyards, alleys, and shady patios with a mishmash of boutiques, restaurants, fast-food joints, and bars.

On Your Own: Beyond the Port Area

In November 1954, the wealthy Rockefeller family began acquiring large tracts of land on St. John. It then donated more than 5,000 acres to the Department of the Interior for the creation of **Virgin Islands National Park,** which Congress voted into existence on August 2, 1956. Over the years, the size of the park has grown steadily; it now totals 12,624 acres, including over two-thirds of St. John's landmass, plus submerged land and water adjacent to the island. Stop off first at the **visitor center**

(© 340/776-6201) right on the dock at St. Cruz, where you'll find some exhibits and learn more about what you can see and do in the park. Peddle along more than 20 miles of biking trails; rent your own car, jeep, or Mini-Moke; or take a hike. If you decide to hike, stop at the visitor center first to pick up maps and instructions. The starting points of some trails are within walking distance, while others can be reached by taxi for about $5 to $20. Within the park, try to see the **Annaberg Ruins,** on Leinster Bay Road, where the Danes founded thriving plantations and a sugar mill in 1718. They're situated off North Shore Road, east of Trunk Bay on the north shore.

Beaches

For a true beach lover, missing the great white sweep of Trunk Bay would be like touring Europe and skipping Paris. That said, it's usually overcrowded. The beach has lifeguards and snorkeling gear is rented for exploring the underwater trail near the shore. Snorkelers find good reefs at Cinnamon Bay and Maho Bay, also a great place to spot turtles and schools of parrotfish. Changing rooms and showers are available.

Shopping

Compared to St. Thomas, St. John is a minor shopping destination, but the boutiques and shops at Cruz Bay are interesting and of good quality, though lacking in number. Most are clustered at Mongoose Junction (www.usvi.net/shopping/mongoose), in a woodsy area beside the roadway, about a 5-minute walk from the ferry dock in Cruz Bay.

11

Alaska & British Columbia

It's practically impossible not to be amazed by Alaska. Most of its coastline is wilderness, with snowcapped mountain peaks, enormous glaciers, dense rainforests, deep fjords, and the cycles of geologic time visible all around. Sail the Inside Passage or Prince William Sound and you'll be where the wild things are: humpback and killer whales, grizzly and black bears, dancing porpoises and barking sea lions, adorable sea otters, and bald eagles in the thousands. Visit the towns, and you'll find people who retain the spirit of frontier independence that brought them here in the first place. Add Alaska's history and heritage, with its rich Native culture, its European influences, and its gold-rush and oil-pipeline chutzpah, and you have a destination that is utterly and endlessly fascinating.

The fact that more than a million cruise passengers arrive in Alaska during the average summer has had its impact, of course, turning some towns into veritable tourist malls populated by seasonal vendors hawking imported souvenirs and jewelry—lots and lots of jewelry. Even in the most touristy towns, though, it's easy to get out and experience the real thing. In Skagway, take one of the trails that run off east of town and in 10 minutes you'll never know there are 6,000 other cruisers shopping behind you. In Ketchikan, walk in either direction out of the dockside tourist zone and you're suddenly in residential Alaska, where the real people live. Throughout the state, you'll also find the influence of the state's great **Native peoples,** who continue to make their presence felt in business, art, and politics: the Tlingit (pronounced Klink-*get*), Haida, and Tsimshian in the Southeast; the Athabascans of the interior; the Inupiat and St. Lawrence Island Yupiks of the far north; the Aleuts and Alutiiqs of the Aleutian Islands; and the Yup'ik and Cup'ik tribes of the extreme west.

Cruises in Alaska concentrate mostly on the **Inside Passage,** a series of connecting waterways threaded between the thousands of forested islands that make up the panhandle commonly known as Southeast Alaska, or just **Southeast.** The passage actually begins in British Columbia, though ships bound north from Vancouver or Seattle tend to buzz quickly through BC's long stretch of the passage en route to Alaskan waters, which begin just south of Ketchikan. From there, the region is home to scattered fishing towns, a number of larger towns and cities (including state capital Juneau), and numerous wonders of nature, including Glacier Bay National Park, Tracy Arm fjord, and (mostly for small ships) Misty Fjords National Monument. North of Southeast, ships sailing one-way itineraries between Vancouver/Seattle and Anchorage also visit attractions such as Hubbard Glacier and College Fjord along the **Gulf of Alaska,** which starts just above Glacier Bay.

HOME PORTS FOR THIS REGION

Vancouver, British Columbia, and **Seattle,** Washington, are the main southern termini for Alaska cruises, with ships either sailing round-trip or doing alternating north- and south-bound departures between here and either Seward or Whittier, the two main port towns for **Anchorage.** Some lines also offer long Alaska cruises that sail round-trip from **San Francisco.** Most of the small ships sail from one or another of the ports in Southeast (primarily **Juneau,** but also Ketchikan and Sitka), but sometimes sail from Anchorage and Seattle as well.

LANGUAGE & CURRENCY The language is English and the currency, for the most part, is U.S. dollars. In Vancouver, you'll want to get some Canadian dollars, though both here and in Victoria, many businesses will also accept U.S. currency.

SHOPPING TIPS Shops throughout Alaska are chock-full of knockoff "Native Alaskan" art shipped in from Asia. So, when shopping for the real thing, ask the dealer for details about the artist, and also look for the **Silver Hand sticker,** a state certification that guarantees the item was, in fact, crafted in Alaska by a Native artist. Sky-high prices will also be a tip-off that an item is the real thing. You get what you pay for.

1 Cruising Alaska's Natural Wonders

Most Alaska cruises spend at least 3 days cruising the natural areas of the state's coast, including areas protected as national parks and national monuments. Regulations control access to some of them (most notably Glacier Bay, where only two large cruise ships and several smaller ones are permitted on any given day), while geography controls access to others: Misty Fjords, for instance, gets very narrow just where it gets most interesting, so only small ships can enter.

Glacier Bay

There are about 5,000 glaciers in Alaska, but **Glacier Bay** (www.nps.gov/glba) has the kind of name recognition that other glaciers can only dream about. Mostly, this is due to the fact that, in little more than 200 years, the area has gone from being a solid wall of ice up to 4,000 feet thick to being a 65-mile bay ecosystem full of wildlife, whales, and slowly returning vegetation, with glaciers extending up from its cold waters like fingers. That's a story people just can't resist.

When first noted by European-Americans in 1794, Glacier Bay was just an indentation in the shoreline of Icy Strait, plugged by a glacial cork. A mere 105 years later, the ice had receded some 35 miles, allowing naturalist **John Muir** to penetrate a landscape he described as "a solitude of ice and snow and newborn rocks," the latter not yet smoothed by the elements, and still retaining the heavy scratches left by the retreating glaciers. Today, that ice has retreated even farther, leaving behind a series of inlets headed by 11 tidewater glaciers. Among them, the **Johns Hopkins, Reid, Lamplugh, Margerie,** and **Grand Pacific** are all in the bay's western arm, and are regularly approached by cruise ships. Calving activity (large chunks of ice breaking off) from these glaciers is the big draw (Johns Hopkins has so much that ships can seldom approach closer than 2 miles, though it feels a lot closer), but don't forget to look at the land, which is a kind of living time-lapse photograph of earth's life cycles. Trees grow thick near the bay's head, but as you penetrate farther and farther, you'll see less and less vegetation, and finally none at all. It just hasn't had time to grow back yet.

Glacier Bay was named a national park in 1925, and today each ship that enters takes aboard a park ranger to provide information about glaciers and wildlife (which includes mountain goats, brown bears, and minke, orca, and humpback whales) and

Alaska

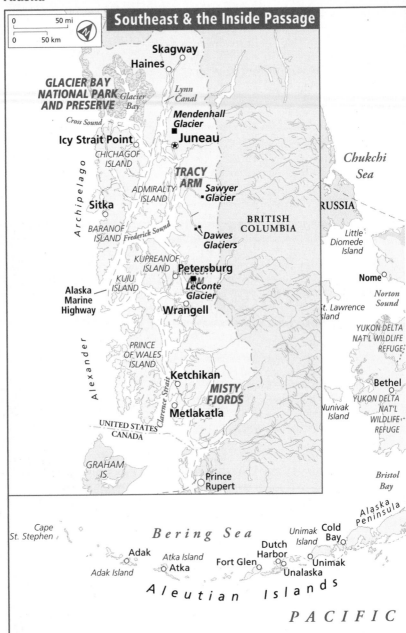

Southeast & the Inside Passage

0   50 mi
0   50 km

Skagway

Haines

GLACIER BAY NATIONAL PARK AND PRESERVE   *Glacier Bay*

Lynn Canal

Cross Sound

Mendenhall Glacier

Icy Strait Point   **Juneau**

CHICHAGOF ISLAND

Chukchi Sea

TRACY ARM   *Sawyer Glacier*

ADMIRALTY ISLAND

Archipelago

Sitka

BARANOF ISLAND   *Frederick Sound*

Dawes Glaciers

BRITISH COLUMBIA

RUSSIA

Little Diomede Island

KUPREANOF ISLAND   **Petersburg**

KUIU ISLAND

Alaska Marine Highway

LeConte Glacier

Wrangell

Nome

Norton Sound

St. Lawrence Island

YUKON DELTA NAT'L WILDLIFE REFUGE

Alexander

PRINCE OF WALES ISLAND

Ketchikan

MISTY FJORDS

Metlakatla

Clarence Strait

UNITED STATES CANADA

Bethel

YUKON DELTA NAT'L WILDLIFE REFUGE

Nunivak Island

GRAHAM IS.

Prince Rupert

Bristol Bay

Cape St. Stephen

Bering Sea

Unimak Island   **Cold Bay**

Dutch Harbor

Adak

Atka Island

Fort Glen

Atka

Unimak

Adak Island

Unalaska

Alaska Peninsula

Aleutian Islands

PACIFIC

586

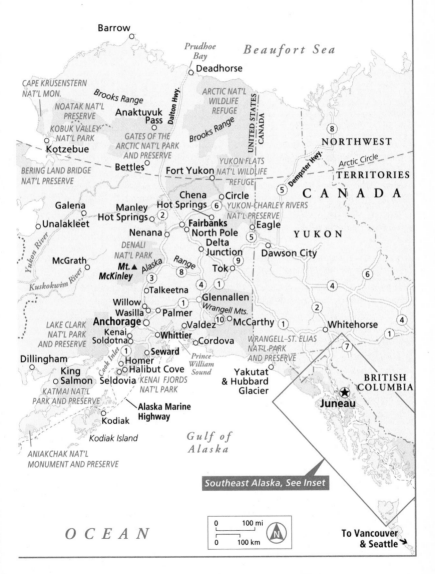

ARCTIC OCEAN

Barrow

Prudhoe Bay

Beaufort Sea

Deadhorse

CAPE KRUSENSTERN NAT'L MON.

Brooks Range

ARCTIC NAT'L WILDLIFE REFUGE

NOATAK NAT'L PRESERVE

Anaktuvuk Pass

KOBUK VALLEY NAT'L PARK

GATES OF THE ARCTIC NAT'L PARK AND PRESERVE

Brooks Range

Dalton Hwy.

UNITED STATES / CANADA

NORTHWEST

Kotzebue

BERING LAND BRIDGE NAT'L PRESERVE

Bettles

Fort Yukon

YUKON FLATS NAT'L WILDLIFE REFUGE

Arctic Circle

Dempster Hwy.

(8)

TERRITORIES

CANADA

Galena

Manley Hot Springs

Chena Hot Springs

Circle

(5)

(6)

YUKON-CHARLEY RIVERS NAT'L PRESERVE

Unalakleet

(2)

Fairbanks

Eagle

YUKON

Nenana

North Pole

(5)

Yukon River

McGrath

DENALI NAT'L PARK

Mt. ▲ McKinley

Alaska

Range

Delta Junction

Dawson City

Tok

(9)

(3)

(8)

(4)

(1)

Kuskokwim River

Talkeetna

(1)

Glennallen

(6)

Willow

Wasilla

Palmer

Wrangell Mts.

(2)

(4)

Anchorage

Valdez

(10)

McCarthy

(1)

Whitehorse

(1)

LAKE CLARK NAT'L PARK AND PRESERVE

Kenai

Soldotna

Whittier

Cordova

WRANGELL–ST. ELIAS NAT'L PARK AND PRESERVE

(7)

Dillingham

Seward

Cook Inlet

(1)

Homer

Halibut Cove

Prince William Sound

Yakutat & Hubbard Glacier

BRITISH COLUMBIA

King Salmon

Seldovia

KENAI FJORDS NAT'L PARK

KATMAI NAT'L PARK AND PRESERVE

Juneau ★

Alaska Marine Highway

Kodiak

Kodiak Island

Gulf of Alaska

ANIAKCHAK NAT'L MONUMENT AND PRESERVE

Southeast Alaska, See Inset

OCEAN

0   100 mi
0   100 km

N

To Vancouver & Seattle ↘

Paved Road
(1) State or Provincial Route
Dirt Road

Glaciers: An Intro to the Ice

Along with whales, glaciers are the big drawing card on Alaska cruises, and with good reason: They're truly awesome. To see one spread between the bulk of massive mountains, flowing down into the sea, is to quite literally see how our world came to be. As the naturalist John Muir wrote while standing near an Alaskan glacier in the late–19th century: "Standing here with facts so fresh and telling and held up so vividly before us . . . one learns that the world, though made, is yet being made; that this is still the morning of creation."

HOW GLACIERS FORM   Glaciers form when snow accumulates over time at high altitudes. Successive snowfalls add more and more weight, compacting the snow underneath into extremely dense **glacial ice.** As the accumulation assumes mass, forming what is known as an **ice field,** gravity takes over and the ice field begins to flow very slowly downhill through the lowest, easiest passage. The glacier's enormous mass sculpts the landscape as it goes, grinding the shale and other rock and pushing rubble and silt ahead and to the sides. This sediment is known as **moraine.** *Terminal moraine* is the accumulation of rubble at the front of a glacier; *lateral moraine* lines the sides of glaciers. A dark area in a glacier's center—seen when two glaciers flow together, pushing their ice and crushed rubble together—is *median moraine.*

TYPES OF GLACIERS   Glaciers come in several different varieties. **Tidewater glaciers** are the kind most often seen on postcards; they spill down out of the mountains and run all the way to the sea. **Piedmont glaciers** are two glaciers that have run together into one. When seen from above, piedmonts resemble a highway interchange, edged by road slush, with the median moraine looking like lane dividers. There are also mountain or **alpine glaciers,** which are confined by surrounding mountain terrain and unable to flow. Other types—such as *hanging glaciers* that spill over rounded hillsides, *valley glaciers* that are confined by valley walls, and *cirque glaciers* that sit in basins and are usually circular (as opposed to river-shaped)—are essentially variants on these three main varieties.

GLACIAL BEHAVIOR   Glaciers are essentially rivers of ice that flow continually downhill. When they reach the sea, the effects of water and gravity cause **calving,** a phenomenon where large chunks of their ice faces break off from the mass and crash into the sea, producing a sound like two 1,000-foot bowling balls colliding. The ice that has calved off floats away as an **iceberg.** Calvings are always a high point on a cruise.

Depending on temperature and the rate of precipitation, glaciers may either **advance** or **retreat.** Think of glaciers as human bodies and snowfall as calories—when the accumulation of snowfall (and resultant glacial ice) is greater than the amount of ice lost to melting and calving, the glacier grows, which is known as *advancing*. When the opposite occurs—when melting and calving outpace new buildup of ice—the glacier is said to be *retreating*. Glaciers can also be in a state of equilibrium, where the amount of snowfall roughly equals the amount of melt-off. Even where this is the case, the glacier is still a slow-moving river, always flowing downhill—it's just that its total length remains the same, with new ice replacing old at a more or less constant rate.

In recent years, **global warming** has begun to have a noticeable effect on Alaska's glaciers. All over the state—and in other northern lands such as Greenland and the Canadian Arctic—temperatures have risen three to five times more than the global average, causing glaciers, sea ice, and permafrost to melt. Juneau's popular Mendenhall Glacier, for instance, is losing about 200 feet of ice per year and will soon retreat fully from Mendenhall Lake, at which point its terminus will be sitting on bare rock—which means fewer of the dramatic calving events visitors enjoy so much. Without dramatic action on climate change, the Mendenhall and other glaciers will slowly retreat farther and farther into the mountains, and eventually disappear forever.

AN ICEBERG BY ANY OTHER NAME   When a glacier calves, the icebergs it forms are classified differently depending on their size, a system that allows one ship's captain to warn another of the relative ice hazard. Very large chunks are officially called **icebergs;** pieces of moderate size (usually 7–15 ft. across) are known as **bergy bits; growlers** are slightly smaller still, at less than 7 feet across, with less than 3 feet showing above water; and **brash ice** consists of any random smaller chunks. And remember the adage: What you're seeing is only the tip—most of the berg is below the water.

By the way, glacial ice isn't blue. It may look blue—and a startling, electric blue at that—but it's really a trick of the light. The ice absorbs all colors of the spectrum *except* blue, which is then reflected away, making the ice itself appear to be blue.

THE VIEW FROM ABOVE   While glaciers are impressive enough from the water, it takes a **glacier flightseeing trip** to really drive home how completely stupendous they are, stretching away into the mountains as far as the eye can see. It's literally like getting a glimpse back into the ice age. The trips are expensive, yes, but definitely worth it. On many trips, your helicopter flightseeing will be combined with time spent down on the glacial ice, where you'll have a chance to walk around on the surface. It's like being on Mars.

Cruisetours—'Cause All Alaska Ain't on Water

Most folks who go to the trouble of getting to a place as far off the beaten path as Alaska try to stick around for awhile once they've arrived. Knowing this, the cruise lines have set up in the land-tour business as well, offering a number of land-based extensions that can be tacked on to your cruise experience, either before or after you sail.

ANCHORAGE–DENALI–FAIRBANKS   The most popular cruisetour is an Anchorage-Denali-Fairbanks package consisting of a 7-night Vancouver-Anchorage cruise, followed by 2 nights in Anchorage and a scenic ride in a private railcar into **Denali National Park** for 2 more nights at one of the cruise line's lodges. A full day in the park allows guests to view the staggeringly beautiful wilderness expanse and its wildlife. If you're lucky, the gods will part the clouds to give you a look at **Mount McKinley,** North America's highest peak at 20,320 feet. From there, you'll go by train to **Fairbanks,** spending 2 more days. Fairbanks itself isn't much to look at, but the activities in outlying areas are fantastic, including paddle-wheel day cruises on the Chena and Tanana rivers, jet-boat rides, and excursions to gold mines and dredges. Passengers typically fly home from Fairbanks. A shorter variation of that itinerary might skip Fairbanks and return to Anchorage for departure. Princess's cruisetours bypass Anchorage on the way north, giving more time in the interior.

YUKON TERRITORY   Tours into Canada's Yukon Territory typically combine a 3- or 4-day cruise between Vancouver and Juneau/Skagway with a land program into the Klondike. En route, passengers travel by rail, riverboat, motorcoach, and possibly air. Tours typically include overnight stops in **Whitehorse,** the territorial capital, and **Dawson City,** a remote, picture-perfect gold-rush

the history of Native peoples and white men in the bay. On large ships, the ranger will speak over the PA system and may also give a presentation about conservation in the show lounge; on small ships, the ranger will often be on deck throughout the day, speaking over the PA and/or just talking with the passengers and answering questions. A strict rationing of permits to the cruise lines means only two ships a day can sail in the park, preventing the place from getting too busy for its own good.

Hubbard Glacier

Hubbard lies at the northern end of **Yakutat Bay** and has two claims to fame: It's the largest tidewater glacier on the North American continent (with Alaska's widest ice face, at about 6 miles across), and it's one of the fastest-moving glaciers in Alaska. In the mid-1980s, it moved so fast that it created a wall across the mouth of **Russell Fjord,** one of the inlets lining Yakutat Bay. That effectively turned the fjord into a lake and trapped hundreds of migratory marine creatures inside. After causing such a hubbub, it receded to its original position several months later. It's still an active mother, calving off a substantial amount of ice.

town, then cross the Alaska border near Beaver Creek, travel to Fairbanks, and from there go through Denali to Anchorage. The tour can be taken in either direction.

CANADIAN ROCKIES   A Canadian Rockies cruisetour allows glimpses of some of the finest mountain scenery on earth. The glacier-carved mountains are astonishingly dramatic and beautiful, and there are hundreds and hundreds of miles of this wonderful wilderness high country. Between them, **Banff National Park** and **Jasper National Park** preserve much of this mountain beauty. Other national and provincial parks make accessible other vast and equally spectacular regions of the Rockies, as well as portions of the nearby Columbia and Selkirk mountain ranges. The beautiful **Lake Louise,** colored deep green from its mineral content, is situated 35 miles north of Banff.

KENAI PENINSULA   The Kenai Peninsula, just across a narrow channel from Anchorage, has long been known as the city's natural playground, packed with opportunities for fishing, hiking, sightseeing, kayaking, and wildlife-watching. Cruisetours to the area are typically 2-night add-ons to a regular Denali-Fairbanks route, though Holland America (one of the leaders in the cruisetour market) offers a dedicated 13-night Kenai-centric trip, with nights spent in Homer, Cooper Landing, and Anchorage either before or after your 7-night cruise.

Other cruisetour options include an add-on to Wrangell–St. Elias National Park, east of Anchorage. There's also an Arctic itinerary that takes you to Prudhoe Bay on Alaska's far northern shore.

Tracy Arm & Endicott Arm

Located about 50 miles due south of Juneau, these long, deep fjords reach back from the Stephens Passage stretch of the Inside Passage into the Coastal Mountain Range, their steep-sided waterways ending in active glaciers—the **North Sawyer** and **South Sawyer Glaciers** in Tracy Arm and **Dawes Glacier** in Endicott. All of them calve constantly, filling the waters with miles of brash ice and bergs that ping and thunk off your ship's hull as you approach the ice faces. The show can be pretty spectacular. Several years ago, we saw South Sawyer calve off a sheet of ice as big as our ship. Granted, we were on one of Cruise West's 100-passenger small ships, but still . . . .

The passage through either fjord is incredibly dramatic, the sheer mountain walls rising a mile straight from the water, cut by cascading waterfalls and tree-covered, snow-topped mountain valleys. Wildlife here might include Sitka black-tailed deer, bald eagles, mountain goats, and harbor seals (which often haul themselves out on ice floes to get some sun). You may also see a black bear. We once looked all day without luck, then, at dinner, our friend Cindy looked up from her plate of salmon and spotted one on shore, eating a salmon of its own.

Misty Fjords National Monument

The 2.3-million-acre, Connecticut-size area of Misty Fjords starts at the Canadian border in the south and runs on the eastern side of the Behm Canal, which has Revillagigedo Island on the other side. (Ketchikan is on the western coast of Revillagigedo.) It's the topography, not the wildlife, that makes a visit here worthwhile, with volcanic cliffs rising up to 3,150 feet and plunging hundreds of feet below the waterline, a reminder that you're sailing in a flooded cleft between mountains. Peace and serenity are the stock in trade of the place, with its namesake mists imparting a storybook, *Lord of the Rings* kind of atmosphere, abetted by dense hemlock and spruce forests, high ridges covered in alpine grass, and the occasional petrified lava flow reaching toward the shoreline.

Only passengers on small ships will see Misty Fjords close up, as its waterway is too narrow in most places for big ships. The bigger ships pass the southern tip of the area, and then veer away northwest to dock at Ketchikan, where shore excursions can take you back into the area by **floatplane.** Some fly in, do a water landing, and then fly out again. Others fly you to an excursion boat for exploration of the monument, and then make the short cruise back to Ketchikan.

Prince William Sound & College Fjord

Located directly south of Anchorage on the bottom side of the Kenai Peninsula, Prince William Sound suffered mightily following the *Exxon Valdez* oil spill in 1989, which killed innumerable marine creatures and birds. Today, following more than 2 decades of cleanup, the area is well on its way to recovery, with whales, harbor seals, eagles, sea lions, sea otters, puffins, and fish all returned to its waters. It's truly one of Alaska's most appealing wilderness areas, surrounded on three sides by the Chugach Mountains and only sparsely populated by humans, most of them congregated in a few isolated towns such as Valdez, Whittier, Cordova, and the Native villages of Tatitlek and Chenega.

College Fjord is in the northern sector of Prince William Sound, roughly midway between Whittier and Valdez. It's not one of the more spectacular Alaska glacier areas, being very much overshadowed by Glacier Bay, Yakutat Bay (for Hubbard Glacier), and others, but it's scenic enough to merit a place on a lot of cruise itineraries, mostly for **Harvard Glacier,** which sits at its head. The fjord was named by members of the 1899 Harriman Expedition, which saddled the glaciers lining College Fjord and neighboring Harriman Fjord with the names of prominent eastern schools—hence Harvard, Vassar, Williams, Yale, and so on. Perhaps the most spectacular of the sound's ice faces is **Columbia Glacier,** whose surface spreads over more than 400 square miles and whose tidewater frontage is nearly 6 miles across. Columbia is receding faster than most of its Alaska counterparts. Scientists say it will retreat more than 20 miles in the next 20 to 50 years, adding another deep fjord to Prince William Sound's collection.

2 Haines

Sitting near the northern end of the Lynn Canal, Haines (pop. 2,500) is a small, laid-back Alaska town, without the kind of self-referential tourist gloss that's so evident in neighboring Skagway. Despite the town's dramatic setting amid the peaks of the Fairweather Mountain Range, few ships come here, partly because of a shortage of large, deepwater docks, partly because of a shortage of large, obvious attractions. If you're sailing on a ship that does come, you'll be experiencing a town that maintains its local vibe well.

Haines was established in 1879 by Presbyterian missionary S. Hall Young and naturalist John Muir as a place to convert the Chilkoot and Chilkat Tlingit tribes to Christianity. They named it for Mrs. F. E. Haines, secretary of the Presbyterian National Committee, who had raised the funds for their explorations. The Tlingits called the place *Dei-Shu,* or "end of the trail," while traders knew it as Chilkoot. The U.S. military arrived in the early part of the 20th century and constructed **Fort William H. Seward,** a very 19th-century-looking group of white clapboard structures arranged around a rectangular parade ground. The fort was decommissioned after World War II, and today its structures have been turned into private homes, B&Bs, and arts and performances spaces, some of them devoted to Native culture (see "On Your Own: Within Walking Distance," below). A re-created Tlingit tribal house sits at the center of the parade ground.

Ships that don't stop in Haines regularly provide excursions to the town from Skagway, traveling by boat. Some combine a quick tour of town with a float or jet-boat ride through the **Chilkat Bald Eagle Preserve** (see below; from Skagway it's $199, 6½ hr.), a **rainforest nature hike** outside town ($149, 6½ hr.), or a **kayaking excursion** in the waters of Chilkoot Lake ($169, 6 hr.).

COMING ASHORE   Ships tie up to the **Port Chilkoot Dock,** directly opposite Fort Seward and a half-mile from downtown. Visitor information is available at the dock.

GETTING AROUND   It's easy to explore Fort Seward and the town on foot, or you can rent a bike at **Sockeye Cycle,** 24 Portage St. in Fort Seward, just uphill from the dock (© **877/292-4154** or 907/766-2869; www.cyclealaska.com). Rentals cost $14 for 2 hours, $25 for 4 hours, or $35 for 8 hours, helmet and lock included. They also offer bike tours of the area.

Best Cruise Line Shore Excursions

Chilkat Bald Eagle Preserve Float Trip ($129, 4 hr.): Head out to the Chilkat Preserve (see below) by bus, then suit up in boots and a life vest for a gentle float by rubber raft down the Chilkat River. An expert guide rows and also provides commentary on the area's natural environment, steering the raft close to shore to spot animal tracks and keeping an eye out for moose, bears, eagles, and wolves. A **jet-boat trip** ($134, 4 hr.) is also provided on a different section of the river, and wildlife sightings are usually reported on these trips.

Chilkoot Lake Bicycle Adventure ($90, 3 hr.): After being driven to your start point, you'll ride 8 miles along the shore of Lutak Inlet, where the river meets the sea. Highlights include some amazing views of the lake, glaciers, waterfalls, and mountains, and a chance at spotting eagles and bears.

Offbeat Haines ($59, 3 hr.): Where else but Haines can you take a tour that includes the world's one and only hammer museum (see below), a visit to an artists' studio out in Mud Bay, a stop at a set created for the Disney film *White Fang,* and a visit to Chilkat State Park, whose hanging Rainbow Glacier has a waterfall pouring from its face?

Remote Coastal Nature Hike ($84, 4 hr.): This 3- to 6-mile hike gets you out into the spruce and hemlock forests, wildflower meadows, and pebbly beaches surrounding Haines, with a naturalist guide to clue you in to what you're seeing. The length of the hike is based on the group's abilities, with two levels accommodating the fit and not-so-fit.

Valley of the Eagles Golf ($89, 3½ hr.): Outside town, along the banks of the Chilkat River, the 9-hole, par-36 Valley of the Eagles Golf Links allow you the rare opportunity of being able to say you golfed in Alaska. The course meanders through typical Alaskan landscape and affords beautiful views of the Chilkat Mountains.

Taste of Haines Tour ($69, 2 hr.): Visit the Haines Brewing Company, the smallest brewery in Alaska, for a sample and a talk with the brewmaster, then head to a local smoked-salmon shop to sample the stuff and learn how it's prepared.

Best of Haines by Classic Car ($64, 1 hr.): Explore Haines in style in a 1930s or 1940s vintage automobile. The entertaining guides share the history of the area, and you'll get an insight into how Hainesians live and make a living.

On Your Own: Within Walking Distance

The **Alaska Indian Arts Cultural Center,** located in the old fort hospital on the south side of the Fort Seward parade grounds (© **907/766-2160;** www.alaskaindianarts. com), has a small gallery selling traditional artwork and prints, plus a carvers' workshop where you may see totem carving in progress. It's open Monday to Friday from 9am to 5pm. Between the fort and the town center, the **American Bald Eagle Foundation and Natural History Museum,** Haines Highway at 2nd Avenue (© **907/766-3094;** www.baldeagles.org), is essentially a huge diorama representing 48,000 acres of the Chilkat Bald Eagle Preserve, with more than 180 stuffed eagles and other animals. The museum is open daily in summer months. Admission is $3. The place has a real folk-art quality that's entirely appropriate for Haines. Ditto for Dave and Carol Pahl's quirkily remarkable **Hammer Museum,** 108 Main St. (© **907/766-2374;** www.hammermuseum.org), with more than 1,500 completely different hammers from all over the world, including whale-blubber hammers, bookbinders' hammers, little hammers used by 1920s nightclub patrons to applaud performers, Tlingit ceremonial hammers, and an Egyptian "dolorite ball" hammer dating to 2500 B.C. Some are displayed in action, wielded by mannequins donated by the Smithsonian Institution. The museum is open May through September from Monday to Friday 10am to 5pm. Admission is $3 adults, free for kids ages 12 and under. Also on Main Street, down near the small-boat harbor, the small **Sheldon Museum and Cultural Center** (© **907/766-2366;** www.sheldonmuseum.org) was established by local shopkeepers Steve and Bess Sheldon around 1925. It has a great collection of Hainesiana: Tlingit artifacts, gold-rush-era weaponry, military memorabilia, and more. It's open mid-May to mid-September from Monday to Saturday 10am to 5pm and Saturday and Sunday 1 to 4pm (extended hours on cruise ship days). Admission is $3 adults, free for kids ages 12 and under.

On Your Own: Beyond the Port Area

Haines is probably the best place on earth to see bald eagles. About 20 miles outside town, the **Chilkat Bald Eagle Preserve** (www.dnr.state.ak.us/parks/units/eagleprv. htm) protects 48,000 acres of river bottom along the Chilkat River. Summer cruisers will miss the biggest eagle season (Oct to mid-Dec, when up to 3,000 eagles gather in the cottonwood trees, waiting to swoop down on late-spawning salmon), but a healthy 200 to 400 are in residence the rest of the year. You'll really need to take a float-trip shore excursion to see the place in the limited time you have here. The water is so gentle that if your raft gets stuck, the guide will just hop out and push. Eagle sightings are practically guaranteed, and occasionally you might spot a moose lurking along the shoreline, too.

Shopping

More than a dozen galleries and shops are located around Fort Seward (mostly concentrating on **Native arts**) and the downtown area.

3 Icy Strait Point

Situated on Chichagof Island about 50 miles west of Juneau and 22 miles southeast of Glacier Bay, **Icy Strait Point** (www.icystraitpoint.com) is a stop on some Princess, Celebrity, and Royal Caribbean cruises. Unlike all the other ports in this chapter, though, it's not a town; rather, it's a self-contained destination owned and managed by Tlingit Indians from the nearby village of Hoonah and designed specifically for cruise passengers. Opened to ships in 2004, the site is centered around a restored 1930s salmon cannery that now houses a museum, a 1930s cannery display, a restaurant, and shops. Principally, though, Icy Strait Point is a destination for shore excursions.

Best Cruise Line Shore Excursions

Tribal Dance & Cultural Legends ($38, 1 hr.): At the Native Heritage Center Theater, near the cannery, a group of Huna Tlingit performs traditional song, dance, and storytelling.

Whale & Marine Mammals Cruise ($149, 2½ hr.): Sail aboard a sightseeing boat through Icy Strait to Point Adolphus, one of Alaska's best whale-watching sites. An onboard naturalist discusses marine life as you scan for humpbacks and orcas, Steller sea lions, and harbor seals.

Remote Wildlife & Brown Bear Search ($119, 2½ hr.): Head toward the Spasski River Valley by bus, then take a short hike on gravel and boardwalk paths to viewing platforms that provide opportunities for viewing bald eagles, land otters, Sitka blacktail deer, and Alaska coastal brown bears—aka grizzlies.

Glacier Bay Flightseeing ($359, 1¾ hr.): Take off in a fixed-wing plane from Hoonah Airport and spend an hour flying above Glacier Bay, including the glaciers, waterfalls, deep crevasses, and new forests of the park, as well as the humpback whale feeding grounds of Point Adolphus.

ZipRider Adventure ($119, 1½ hr.): They claim this is the world's longest zipline, at 5,330 feet. True or not, that's still one damn long line. The tour begins with a narrated drive through Hoonah, after which you and five others are strapped into harnesses and launched down the line, accelerating up to 60mph, 300 feet above the woods.

Icy Strait Point Sport Fishing ($245, 5½ hr.): Board a cabin cruiser for a fishing excursion in Icy Strait, where five species of salmon make for some great angling. (*Note:* A $20 fishing license and $10 king-salmon tag are extra. For an additional charge, your catch can be packed and shipped to your home.)

Halibut Fishing ($259, 3⅓ hr.): Head out into Icy Strait for a little halibut fishing. See above for licensing requirements and fees.

Hoonah Bike Trek ($69, 2 hr.): Take an 8-mile ride through Alaska's largest Tlingit village, home to about 900 residents. Along the way, your guide will discuss the town's history and present-day life.

4 Juneau

Juneau is a great town. Fronted by the busy Gastineau Channel and backed by 3,819-foot Mount Juneau and 3,576-foot Mount Roberts, its location is beyond picture-perfect. But it's the city's quirks we appreciate, like the fact that Juneau is the capital of the state but is completely surrounded by water, forest, and the massive Juneau Icefield, and is therefore unreachable by road. Or the fact that the whole town lies at the base of a landslide zone, and has numerous treeless hillsides to prove it. Or that at one time a bull terrier named Patsy Ann was the official town greeter, trotting down to the docks whenever a ship came in. (Long dead now, she's memorialized with a bronze statue in Marine Park, where the cruise ships dock.) We even appreciate the town's love-hate relationship with the cruise industry, with many lamenting the fact that downtown and the Egan Expressway are completely overrun by visitors and tour buses from late May through September. Democracy thrives on debate, and we can't argue with the locals' concerns: On any given day, four or five cruise ships may be in port, ranging from megaships to microships. That means about 6,000 people are added daily to a population that numbers only 31,000 total—and those are spread out across the greater town's 3,255-square-mile area. It makes for a bit of chaos downtown.

Tourism woes aside, modern Juneau is a product of Alaska's golden past. It was no more than a fishing outpost for local Tlingit Indians until 1880, when gold was discovered in a creek off the Gastineau Channel by Chief Kowee of the Auk Tlingit clan. Kowee passed the information on to German engineer George Pilz in return for 100 warm blankets and a promise of work for his tribe, and agreed to lead prospectors Joe Juneau and Richard Harris to the find. Mines quickly sprang up on both sides of the channel, including the **Alaska-Juneau Mine,** known locally as the A-J, which produced a whopping 3.5 million ounces of gold before it closed in 1944. You can still see its ruins up on the slope of Mount Roberts.

Outside of town, the big attraction is **Mendenhall Glacier.** At 12 miles long and 1½ miles wide, it's the most visited glacier in the world.

COMING ASHORE Both large and small ships dock right in the downtown area, along Marine Way. Occasionally, overcrowding might mean a ship has to anchor in the channel and tender people to shore. A **visitor information center** is in a green building right on the dock, near the base of the Mount Roberts Tram. The **Patsy Ann statue** is near the head of the dock at Marine Park. Pat her head and consider yourself greeted.

GETTING AROUND Most of the in-town sites are within walking distance of the pier, though some of it is uphill. **Alaska Coach Tours** (www.alaskacoachtours.com) also provides narrated 45-minute trolley tours of the downtown area ($19 adults, $12 kids) as well as 2½-hour tours to Mendenhall Glacier ($40 adults, $25 kids). Taxis waiting at the pier can also take you to the Mendenhall and other sights along the Egan Expressway.

Best Cruise Line Shore Excursions

The number of excursions typically offered in Juneau is fairly stupefying, but that's because a lot of mixing and matching is going on: a glacier visit paired with a salmon bake or a horseback trek, a salmon bake paired with a flightseeing adventure, or a half-dozen different helicopter/glacier options. Here are some of the best.

Mendenhall Glacier Helicopter Flightseeing & Glacier Hike ($349–$499, 2½–5½ hr.): This is one of the very best shore excursions we've ever taken. After transferring to the airport by bus, guests board helicopters for a flight that follows the flowing ice of Mendenhall Glacier high into the mountains. While glaciers are impressive enough from the water, this trip gives you an idea of how magnificent they really are. After about 20 minutes of flightseeing, your helicopter will touch down on the glacial ice, where (outfitted in special boots provided by the helicopter company) you'll have a chance to walk around on the surface. Different packages give you more or less time on the glacier. The **Helicopter Glacier Trek** ($399, 4¼ hr.) and **Extended Helicopter Glacier Trek** ($499, 5½ hr.) include 2 or 3 hours respectively of rugged hiking and climbing on the glacier surface. It's one of the most amazing shore excursions we've ever done. Some tours add additional activities, such as the **Glacier Dog-Sled Expedition** that combines a flight over the Juneau Icefield with a landing on either the Norris or Mendenhall glaciers, where you board dog sleds with an Iditarod veteran ($549, 3½ hr.).

Mendenhall Glacier & Salmon Bake ($79, 4 hr.): Three for the price of one: a visit to the Macaulay Salmon Hatchery to learn about rearing or raising salmon; a visit to the Mendenhall, where you can stick to the interpretive center or get closer to the ice on one of several different trails; and an all-you-can-eat salmon bake in a rustic setting, with folk-music entertainment, the ruins of an old mine to explore, and lush rainforest all around. A less expensive option ($45, 3 hr.) visits only the hatchery and glacier.

Bike & Brew Tour ($99, 4½ hr.): This bicycle tour sets off outside town along Fritz Cove Road, allowing views of picturesque Auke Bay and the Mendenhall Glacier. The 11-mile ride ends at the Alaska Brewing Company for a tour and sampling of the wares.

Sled Dog Summer Camp ($159, 2½ hr.): In Sheep Creek Valley, an Iditarod musher and his dogs will show you the ropes of dogsled racing, so you learn how the racers prep and then take a 1½-mile ride on a wheeled dogsled. Back in camp, there's time to visit with the dogs and their puppies.

Mendenhall Glacier Float Trip ($129, 4 hr.): On the shore of Mendenhall Lake, you'll board 10-person rafts. An experienced oarsman will guide you from there out past icebergs and into the Mendenhall River, where you'll encounter moderate rapids and stunning views. Expect a snack of smoked salmon and reindeer sausage somewhere along the way.

Mendenhall Lake Canoe Adventure ($164, 3½ hr.): Board 12-person Native canoes, paddling out onto the lake's water while a guide shares natural history and Native stories about the surrounding scenery and wildlife. You'll pull into shore near roaring Nugget Falls, just a few yards from the glacier face.

Alaska-Gastineau Gold Mine Tour ($69, 3½ hr.): Just south of town, the Alaska-Gastineau mine was once one of the world's richest. Today, you can don a hard hat and venture down a 360-foot mine tunnel, where experienced miners demonstrate hard-rock mining techniques and explain mine operations. Dress warm: It's cold down there.

On Your Own: Within Walking Distance

Juneau's town center is compact and fun to walk around, but if you want to escape the crowd or get an overview (literally), take the **Mount Roberts Tramway** (© 888/461-8726 or 907/463-3412; www.goldbelttours.com) from the docks up to the clear air and overwhelming views at the 1,760-foot tree line. The ride takes only 6 minutes, but it's like entering another world. At the top, there's a reception center with a restaurant/bar, a gift shop (of course), and a theater showing a pretty good film about Tlingit culture, but try not to linger here too long. Instead, head outside to the network of paths that let on to really incredible views as you pass through a fascinating alpine ecosystem. If you're energetic, you can start a 6-mile round-trip to the Mount Roberts summit (at 3,819 ft.), though there are also several shorter loops. Watch your footing up here, especially if the trails are wet or covered in snow—a possibility in the shoulder seasons. Tickets are $27 for adults and $14 for children ages 6 to 12, and allow unlimited rides. Most ships offer the tram as an excursion for the same price, but we suggest waiting till you get to town and buying a ticket on your own, as it's not worth it if you arrive on an overcast day with no visibility.

Heading into town, the faux-notorious and realistically touristy **Red Dog Saloon,** 278 S. Franklin St. (© **907/463-3658;** www.reddogsaloon.com), stands right at the intersection where Egan Drive heads left toward Mendenhall Glacier and Franklin Street continues up into town. Through its swinging doors, you'll find a contrived but still infectious frontier atmosphere, with a sawdust-covered floor, live music, and walls covered with memorabilia and messages from previous visitors. You'll also find current visitors—lots of them—and often live music. Locals and less touristy tourists are more apt to hang out up the street at the **Alaskan Bar,** 167 S. Franklin St. (© **907/ 586-1000;** www.thealaskanhotel.com), a two-story Victorian barroom in an authentic gold-rush hotel. Down Egan, the **Hangar,** 2 Marine Way (© **907/586-5018;** www.hangaronthewharf.com), also serves a good brew, as well as decent pizza.

Continue down Egan and make a right at Whittier to get to the **Alaska State Museum,** 395 Whittier St. (© **907/465-2901;** www.museums.state.ak.us), and its large collection of art and artifacts. Opened as a territorial museum in 1900, it has a wildlife exhibit, artifacts of the city's mining and fisheries heritage, and a first-class collection reflecting the state's Russian history and Native cultures. It's open mid-May to mid-September daily from 8:30am to 5:30pm. Admission is $5, free for children age 18 and under. Not far off, at the intersection of Main and Fourth streets, the fun little **Juneau-Douglas City Museum** (© **907/586-3572;** www.juneau.lib.ak.us/parksrec/ museum) displays artifacts and photographs from the city's pioneer and mining history and Tlingit culture, with special exhibits changing annually. The plaza in front is where the 49-star U.S. flag was first raised in 1959, when Alaska got its statehood before Hawaii. The museum is open daily 9am to 5pm. Admission is $4. About 3 blocks away, at Fifth and Gold streets, the tiny, octagonal **St. Nicholas Russian Orthodox Church** (© **907/586-1023;** www.stnicholasjuneau.org) was built in 1893 by local Tlingits who, under pressure to convert to Christianity, chose the only faith that allowed them to keep their own language.

On Your Own: Beyond the Port Area

About 13 miles from downtown, at the head of Mendenhall Valley, the **Mendenhall Glacier** (© **907/789-0097;** www.fs.fed.us/r10/tongass/districts/mendenhall) glows bluish white, looming above the suburbs like an ice-age monster that missed the general extinction. Mendenhall is a truly impressive sight, but it's also the most easily accessible glacier in Alaska, with great views even from the parking lot, along with a wheelchair-accessible trail that leads to the water's edge. The land near the parking lot shows signs of the glacier's recent passage: little topsoil, stunted vegetation, and, in many places, bare rock that shows the scratch marks of the glacier's movement. It's still moving, too, and fast: Due to global warming, the ice face will recede from Mendenhall Lake onto bare rock sometime in the next dozen or so years, at which point the calving activity that makes glacier-viewing popular will slow significantly—though, on the upside, so will the glacier's retreat. Trails of various lengths depart from the Forest Service visitor center, the easiest being a .5-mile nature trail, the longest being two fairly steep, 3.5-mile trails that approach each side of the glacier. The visitor center itself contains a glacier museum with excellent explanatory models, computerized displays, and ranger talks; admission is $3.

Along the Egan Expressway about 3 miles from downtown, the **Macaulay Salmon Hatchery,** 2697 Channel Dr. (© **877/463-2486** or 907/463-4810; www.dipac.net/visitor.htm), has a visitor center where you can watch the whole process of harvesting and fertilizing salmon eggs. The resultant offspring are later released back into the wild. Admission is $3.25 adults, $1.75 kids. If that doesn't float your boat, try the nearby **Alaskan Brewing Company,** 5429 Shaune Dr. (© **907/780-5866;** www.alaskanbeer.com). Located off Egan at Vanderbilt Hill Road (then right on Anka St. and right again on Shaune Dr.), it gives low-key tours with a sampling of beer at the end, and its logo-wear is also pretty hip. The brewery started small in 1986 when Geoff and Marcy Larson had the idea of bringing a local gold-rush-era brew back to life. It worked, and now Alaskan Amber and several other brews are found everywhere in Alaska and most of the western U.S., and they're mighty tasty, too.

Shopping

The shops near the dock are mostly aimed at tourists, with cheap souvenir stores mixed in with jewelry shops, but there are some good picks, including the **Decker Gallery,** 233 S. Franklin St. (© **907/463-5536**), selling the works of local artist Rie Muñoz. If you're in need of reading material, Juneau is the best port to buy a book, with several decent shops downtown. If you're in need of smoked salmon (and who ain't?), **Taku Smokeries,** 550 S. Franklin St. (© **800/582-5122;** www.takustore.com), will ship it anywhere in the U.S.

5 Ketchikan

Ketchikan sits just north of the Canadian border and, like many border towns, wears its mercantile heart on its sleeve. They call it "Alaska's first city" because it's the first port visited on most northbound cruises, but the way people throng the port area's gift shops, you'd think it was their last chance to use credit cards before Judgment Day. Here's our advice: Walk down the gangway, take three deep breaths, and say to yourself, "I do not need to shop." Instead, walk right past the souvenir stores and head for one of the town's several **totem-pole** parks or take an excursion to **Misty Fjords.** When you get back, you can spend some time poking around the galleries and shops on Creek Street, which are much better than those fronting the pier.

Shopping aside, the town's port area is interesting in that much of it is either landfill or sitting on stilts above the water. The town is also notable for being one of the soggiest in Alaska: The average annual rainfall is about 160 inches (more than 13 ft.), and has topped 200 inches in its most intense years.

COMING ASHORE   Ships dock at a pier just steps from downtown Ketchikan.

GETTING AROUND   Ketchikan's downtown port area is completely flat and walkable. Taxis are available at the pier if you want to go out to Totem Bight Park on your own.

Best Cruise Line Shore Excursions

Misty Fjords Flightseeing ($259–$359, 2–4 hr.): Everyone gets a window seat aboard the floatplanes that run these flightseeing jaunts over mysterious, primordial Misty Fjords National Monument (see p. 592). The less expensive planes tool around, make a water landing so you can step out onto the pontoon, and then return to Ketchikan by air. The more expensive (and better) floatplane transfers you to a tour boat after landing at the monument, allowing you to see more of it from sea level. The boat takes you back to Ketchikan at the end.

Saxman Native Village Tour ($59, 2½ hr.): This Native village, about 2½ miles outside Ketchikan, is home to hundreds of Tlingit, Tsimshian, and Haida, and is a center for the revival of Native arts and culture. The tour includes a storytelling session and a performance by the Cape Fox Dancers at the Beaver Clan House, as well as a guided walk through the grounds to see the totem poles and learn their stories. Craftspeople are sometimes on hand in the working sheds to demonstrate totem-pole carving. A short bus tour of Ketchikan is usually appended to the end of the trip.

Rainforest Wildlife Sanctuary ($79, 3 hr.): After an 8-mile coastal drive, you'll do a .5-mile hike with a naturalist guide, trying to spot eagles, bears, seals, and various birdlife. After, you'll have an opportunity to feed Alaskan reindeer, watch a totem-pole carver at work, and take a tour of a historic sawmill.

Sportfishing ($199, 5 hr.): If catching salmon is your goal, Ketchikan is a good spot to do it. Chartered fishing boats come with tackle, bait, fishing gear, and crew to help you strike king and coho around the end of June, or pink, chum, and silver from July to mid-September. *Note:* A $20 fishing license and $10 king-salmon tag are extra-cost.

Tatoosh Island Sea Kayaking ($149, 4½ hr.): There are typically two kayaking excursions offered in Ketchikan: this one (which requires you to take a van and motorized boat to the islands before starting your 90-min. paddle) and a trip that starts right beside the cruise ship docks. Of the two, the former is far more enjoyable, getting you out into a wilder area rather than just sticking to the busy port waters. The scenery is incredible, and you have a good chance of spotting bald eagles, leaping salmon, and seals, which may be swimming around your boat or just basking on the rocks.

Totem Bight Historical Park & City Tour ($39, 2½ hr.): This tour takes you by bus around Ketchikan and through the Tongass National Forest to Totem Bight State Park, where you'll walk a winding forest trail to an old Indian campsite filled with totem poles.

The Great Alaskan Lumberjack Show ($35, 1½ hr.): Touristy fun: Watch lumberjacks compete in logrolling, speed climbing, tree topping, chainsaw carving, and all the other skills every lumberjack needs. The amphitheater, behind Salmon Landing and just a few hundred yards from the pier, has covered grandstands to keep you from getting soggy. If you don't book this as an excursion, you can still buy tickets at the door for the same price.

On Your Own: Within Walking Distance

Near the pier, the **Southeast Alaska Discovery Center,** 50 Main St. (© **907/228-6220;** www.fs.fed.us/r10/tongass/districts/discoverycenter), houses the best museum in the region for illustrating the interaction of the region's ecology and human society, both Native and white. An auditorium shows a high-tech slide show, and there are also information desks and a good bookstore. It's open May through October from

Monday to Friday 8am to 5pm, Saturday and Sunday 8am to 4pm. Admission to the exhibits is $5 adults, free for kids ages 15 and under.

The centerpiece of downtown Ketchikan is **Creek Street,** a row of quaint wooden houses built on pilings above a busy salmon stream. Today, the narrow, boardwalk street is filled mainly with boutiques, funky shops and restaurants, and galleries specializing in offbeat pieces by local artists, but back in the day it was Ketchikan's notorious and semicondoned red-light district, with more than 30 brothels lining the waterway. That all came to an end in the mid-1950s, and today all that's left is the touristy **Dolly's House museum,** 24 Creek St. (© **907/225-6329**), once the establishment of a madam who worked under the name Dolly Arthur. Like the house's old clientele, you have to pay to get inside. We don't know what the old patrons had to shell out, but today it'll cost you $5. At the end of Creek Street, a **funicular** takes you uphill to the West Coast Cape Fox Lodge, which has nice views. Walk through the lobby and back outside, then follow the signs to the **Married Men's Trail,** allegedly a route taken by local men to reach the "spawning grounds" below. It makes for a nice little hike back into town.

Near its bottom, the Married Men's Trail branches off, left to Creek Street and right to Park Avenue. At Park, an observation deck above the artificial **salmon ladder** lets you watch the determined fish battle the water's current to their spawning grounds at the top of Ketchikan Creek. Walk about ⅓ mile up Park Avenue and make a right at Herring Way to reach the indoor **Totem Heritage Center,** 601 Deermount St. (© **907/225-5900**), built by the city in 1976 to house a fine collection of 33 original 19th-century totem poles, all retrieved from the Tlingit Indian villages of Tongass and Village Islands and the Haida village of Old Kasaan. The Tsimshian people are also represented in some exhibits. The poles have not been restored, and are displayed mostly unpainted, many with the grass and moss still attached from when they were rescued from the elements. Totem poles were never meant to be maintained or repainted—they generally disintegrate after about 70 years, and in traditional usage were constantly replaced—but these were preserved to help keep the culture alive. A high ceiling and muted lighting highlight the spirituality of the art. Well-trained guides are on hand to explain what you're looking at, and there are good interpretive signs, as well as authentic Native crafts for sale. The center is open May through September daily 8am to 5pm. Admission is $5. Across the creek, the **Deer Mountain Tribal Hatchery and Eagle Center,** 1158 Salmon Rd. (© **907/228-5278;** www.kictribe.org), raises and releases young salmon to supplement the natural runs. You can view them in holding pools and learn about their lifecycle, then wander over to the huge outdoor cages, home to injured eagles that were nursed back to health and are unable to return to the wild. The hatchery is open daily 8am to 4:30pm. Admission is $10 adults, $5 for kids ages 2 to 11.

Okay, now you can go shopping.

On Your Own: Beyond the Port Area

About 10 miles outside town, **Totem Bight State Historical Park,** 9883 N. Tongass Hwy. (© **907/247-8574;** www.dnr.state.ak.us/parks/units/totembgh.htm), presents poles and a clan house carved beginning in 1938. Working under the New Deal's Civilian Conservation Corps, Native craftsmen used traditional tools to copy fragments of historic poles that had mostly rotted away, thereby helping to preserve an aspect of Tlingit and Haida culture that had essentially been outlawed until that time.

The setting, purportedly the site of a traditional fishing camp, is a peaceful spot at the end of a short walk through the woods. Admission is free.

Shopping

You'll wonder whether the town should be renamed "Kitschikan" if you spend much time in the many souvenir stores that line Front Street and the rest of the port area, but there are a few decent shops among them. Our favorites are all on **Creek Street,** which has galleries, kitchenware shops (moose-shaped cookie molds!), bookshops, and other appealing places to drop some coin.

6 Sitka

Geographically speaking, Sitka is not on the Inside Passage at all, but rather on the Pacific coast of Baranof Island, sheltered by a fringe of islands at the head of Sitka Sound. Its name, in fact, comes from the Tlingit *Shee Atika,* which means "people on the outside of Shee." Small ships can thread in through narrow Peril Strait, which separates Baranof and Chichagof islands, but the big cruise ships have to sail around Baranof into the open Pacific. This minor inconvenience—and the fact that Sitka lacks docking facilities for megaships, which must send passengers ashore in tenders—means the town has fewer cruise ship visits than Juneau, Ketchikan, and Skagway. Because of this, it retains a more residential feel than similar-size towns in Southeast, and its combination of location, multicultural heritage, a mixed economy, and sheer local pride keep it just plain beautiful to look at. Remarkably, little has changed since the old days: Historic photographs bear an uncanny resemblance to today's city.

Sitka's history is by far Alaska's richest. The powerful and sophisticated Kiksadi Tlingit clan called this part of Baranof Island home for centuries. In 1799, however, they came face to face with European power when Alexander Baranof, manager of the fur-trading Russian-American Company, established a new fort here in order to expand its sea otter hunting operations and territorial claims. Faced with the prospect of subjugation, the Tlingit attacked the Russian's redoubt in 1802 and killed almost everyone inside. Two years later, Baranof returned with reinforcements, forcing the tribe to make way for the new colonial city of Novoarkhangelsk (New Archangel). Today, Sitka preserves the Russian buildings of Alaska's earliest white settlement and, more deeply, the story of the cultural conflict between Alaska Natives and the invaders, and their resistance and ultimate accommodation to the new ways.

COMING ASHORE Most passengers will arrive in Sitka by tender because the harbor is too small to accommodate large ships. Tenders drop you right in the downtown area, where small ships can also dock. Maps are available at the volunteer-staffed visitor information desk in the Crescent Harbor Dock's **Harrigan Centennial Hall,** which also houses the Isabel Miller Museum and the auditorium where the New Archangel Dancers perform (see below). The other docking facility is at the nearby O'Connell Bridge, where maps can be picked up from the information kiosk. Map boards are found near both docking facilities. Proposals have been floated to build a new pier for large ships at the Sawmill Cove Industrial Park, but nothing had been resolved at this writing.

GETTING AROUND Unless you have mobility problems, we recommend walking in this town. You can hoof it to everything there is to see, and it's a beautiful place to explore. The **Visitor Transit Shuttle bus** also makes a circuit of the town's attractions throughout the day whenever large ships are in town, meeting arrivals at the docks and stopping at the Sheldon Jackson Museum, the Historical Park, the Alaska Raptor Center, the Tribal Community House, and downtown. An all-day pass costs $10.

Best Cruise Line Shore Excursions
We advise against shore excursions here. The town is lovely enough by itself, and the various attractions have very good interpretive programs. If, however, you want something organized or want to get out in the wilds, here are a few options.

Fortress of the Bears & Sea Otter Quest ($169, 4¼ hr.): Visit a sanctuary for orphaned brown bears, where you can observe the bears up-close, then cruise in a water-jet-driven tour boat while a naturalist leads the search for sea otters, whales, sea lions, porpoises, harbor seals, brown bears, blacktail deer, bald eagles, and a variety of marine birds. The shorter, cheaper **Sea Otter and Wildlife Quest** ($120, 3 hr.) just does the cruise, skipping the bear sanctuary.

Russian America Tour ($46, 2½ hr.): Tour Sitka on foot and by coach, visiting the Russian Cemetery, Castle Hill, the Russian Blockhouse, Sitka National Historical Park, and St. Michael's Russian Orthodox Cathedral. Later, take in a performance of Russian folk dances by the New Archangel Dancers (see below). The **Russian America & Raptor Center Tour** ($59, 4 hr.) also includes a visit to the Raptor Rehabilitation Center.

Sitka Bike & Hike ($89, 3 hr.): After transferring to Sawmill Creek, you'll ride 4 miles and then hike approximately 1 mile in the Tongass National Forest before being brought back to the docking area.

Sport-fishing ($230, 4 hr.): An experienced captain will guide your fully equipped boat to a good spot for halibut and salmon; the rest is up to you. Your catch can be frozen or smoked and, if you wish, shipped to your home. *Note:* A $20 fishing license and a $10 king-salmon tag are extra-cost.

On Your Own: Within Walking Distance
Essentially, everything in Sitka is within walking distance, though the farthest attraction, the Alaska Raptor Center (see below), might prove too much of a hike for some.

St. Michael's Cathedral, with its striking onion-shaped dome and its ornate gilt interior, is at the intersection of Lincoln and Cathedral streets, forming the focal point of Sitka's downtown. One of the 49th state's most striking and oft-photographed structures, the current church is actually a replica of the 1840s original, which burned to the ground one night in 1966. So revered was the cathedral that Sitkans, whether Russian Orthodox or not, formed a human chain and carried many of its precious icons, paintings, vestments, and jeweled crowns from the flames. St. Michael's was later re-created on the same site, from the same plans, and was rededicated in 1976. It still houses those religious symbols that the citizens worked so hard to rescue from the inferno, and is the official seat of the Russian Orthodox Church in Alaska. The vast majority of the church's congregation is made up of Alaska Native peoples, who were evangelized by the cathedral's designer, Bishop Innocent Veniaminov, in the 19th century. A $2 donation is requested.

Innocent's 1842 home, straightforwardly called the **Russian Bishop's House** (© 907/747-0110; www.nps.gov/sitk), is a fascinating place a few blocks east at Lincoln and Monastery streets. It's operated by the National Park Service, which provides surprisingly enjoyable and informative tours of the bishop's furnished quarters and impressive private chapel. Born in 1797 in a remote Siberian village, Innocent first traveled to Alaska as a missionary in 1824, and was named the territory's first resident bishop in 1840. A giant for his time at 6 feet 3 inches, he was also something of a Renaissance man, accomplished in architecture, carpentry (he built several of the pieces on display), ethnography, clockmaking, and linguistics. During his service, he became fluent in Tlingit and Aleut, and translated liturgical texts and his own spiritual treatises into these languages by adapting the Russian Cyrillic alphabet. Exhibits downstairs trace Sitka's history. The house is open mid-May through September daily 9am to 5pm. Admission is $4.

A little farther down Lincoln, you'll see the campus of Sheldon Jackson College, founded by its namesake Presbyterian missionary in 1878 as a vocational school for young Tlingits. The **Sheldon Jackson Museum** (© 907/747-8981; www.museums. state.ak.us), located on the grounds, contains a fine collection of Native artifacts, including Tlingit, Aleut, Athabascan, Haida, and Tsimshian peoples, as well as the Native peoples of the Arctic. The core of the collection was assembled by Jackson himself on his travels around the territory. The museum is open mid-May through September daily from 9am to 5pm. Admission is $4, free for kids ages 18 and under.

Continue down Lincoln until you come to the **Sitka National Historical Park** (© 907/747-0110; www.nps.gov/sitk). This is where the Tlingit made their stand against Russia in 1804, holding off imperial gunboats and Aleut mercenaries for 6 days before finally melting away one night after taking heavy losses. The land was officially protected starting in 1890, and in 1910 the site was designated a National Historic Park, emphasizing the Native perspective. In the visitor center, exhibits explain the history and the art of totem carving, with 19th-century poles displayed in one hall and new ones created in the on-site Southeast Alaska Indian Cultural Center, which also has windowed workshops devoted to traditional crafts of metal, wood, beads, textiles, and woven grass. The visitor center is open mid-May through September daily 8am to 5pm. Admission is $4, free for kids ages 12 and under. Outside, a **rainforest trail** winds along the coast of the 113-acre park past a collection of towering totems nestled among the spruce and hemlock. The **battle site**—just a grassy area now—is also along the trail, but among the trees and totems, with the sound of the lapping sea and raven's call, you can feel deep down what the Tlingits were fighting for. The park trails are open mid-May through September daily 6am to 10pm.

The **Alaska Raptor Center,** 1000 Raptor Way (© 800/643-9425; www. alaskaraptor.org), located just across Indian River, is just on the border between "within walking distance" and not. A nonprofit venture supported by tour companies, cruise lines, and public donations, the center was opened in 1980 to treat sick or injured birds of prey (primarily eagles), and to provide an educational experience for visitors. Birds that cannot be returned to the wild are sent to zoos or housed here permanently, providing guests the rare experience of standing just a few feet from a huge, unblinking eagle. The flight center allows an exciting view of the eagles training just prior to release. It's open May to September from 8am to 4pm. Admission costs $12 adults, $6 kids ages 12 and under.

Back in the center of town are several worthwhile sites. **Castle Hill,** up the stairs near the intersection of Lincoln and Katlian streets, was where the first U.S. flag was raised on Alaskan soil, after the U.S. and Russia held a transfer ceremony here in 1867. You get a great panoramic view of town from the top. Across the street, the beautiful building behind the big bronze statue is the **Sitka Pioneers Home,** a state retirement home. Next to the Pioneers Home, the **Sheetka'Kwaan Naa Kahidi Building,** 200 Katlian

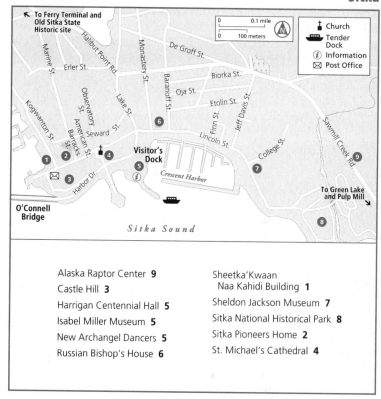

St. (© **888/270-8687;** www.sitkatours.com/dance.html), is a modern version of a traditional Tlingit tribal house. It hosts regular performances of traditional Tlingit dance, often coinciding with cruise ship visits. Show times are posted here and at the Centennial Hall. Behind the stage is the largest handcarved wooden screen in Southeast Alaska, depicting Eagle and Raven, the two principal clans of the Tlingit people. The 30-minute dance performances cost $8 adults, $5 kids.

Next to the Crescent Harbor Dock, the **Isabel Miller Museum** at the Harrigan Centennial Hall (© **907/747-6455;** www.sitka.org/historicalmuseum) outlines the city's history with art, artifacts, and a large diorama of Sitka as it was in 1867. It's open May to September from Sunday to Friday 9am to 5pm, Saturday 11am to 3pm. Admission is $2. Centennial Hall is also the home of the **New Archangel Dancers** (© **907/747-5516;** www.newarchangeldancers.com), an all-woman company that gives 30-minute performances of Russian and Ukrainian traditional dance on most days when cruise ships are in port. Tickets are $8, and must be purchased at least a half-hour before the show. The schedule is posted at the hall.

Shopping

There are some good shops and galleries in Sitka, mostly on Lincoln and Harbor streets, with several shops selling **Russian crafts** clustered in the neighborhood of St.

Michael's Cathedral. The gift shop at the **Sheldon Jackson Museum** is an excellent place to buy authentic Alaska Native arts and crafts.

7 Skagway

Situated at the end of the picturesque Lynn Canal, Skagway served as the jumping-off point for the tidal wave of prospectors who arrived in 1897 for the short but intense **Yukon Gold Rush.** Greed is a great motivator, but not many of these fellas realized the hardships they'd have to endure before they could get close to the gold, hiking some 3,000 vertical feet over 20 miles along either the **White Pass** or the **Chilkoot Pass** through the coastal mountain range to the Canadian border. By itself, that might not have been too bad, but by order of Canada's North West Mounted Police, they had to have at least a year's supply of provisions with them before they could enter the country. Numbed by wind and temperatures that fell at times to 50 below zero—Skagway's Tlingit name, *Skagua,* means "home of the North Wind"—most inched their way up, carrying some of their supplies midway, then returning for more. The process often required as many as 20 trips.

The town, such as it was then, was entirely a product of the gold rush, having been established as a dock and lumber mill by former steamboat captain William Moore and his son in the 1890s, after they realized the nearby pass would be a good entry to Canada if gold were ever discovered there. They were right, but rather than enriching the Moores as intended, the rush simply brought total anarchy to Skagway, with a swarm of opportunists arriving with the prospectors to either service or swindle them—usually both. The most notorious of the Skagway bad men was Jefferson Randolph **"Soapy" Smith,** a con man and thug who knew an open town when he saw it, and effectively took over the place before getting himself shot in a now-mythic gunfight with city surveyor Frank Reid. Reid died in the fight, too, and both were buried in the town's Gold Rush Cemetery—Reid inside, under a granite marker that reads "He gave his life for the honor of Skagway," and Smith under a simple marker in unconsecrated ground. As is the way of things, Smith is the one whose name is all over today's Skagway, part of the town's totally Disneyesque "wild and wonton frontier town" image—about which you'll hear a lot.

Remember the actor Walter Brennan, who played the old coot in every other Hollywood Western from the '30s through the '50s? Well, every single person in Skagway seems to have gone to his acting school. Yes, people do live here (862 of them year-round, according to the 2000 census), but most of the folks you see in the summer are seasonal workers, brought in essentially as actors to man the set. It's some set, with the wide main drag, Broadway, lined end to end with gold-rush-era buildings and protected as a National Historic District. A few that look like real businesses turn out to be displays showing how it was back in frontier days, but most house gift shops—lots and lots of gift shops.

Pieces of history are preserved all around town, from cute touches such as the huge watch painted on the mountainside, advertising long-gone Kirmse's watch repair, to the monumental **White Pass and Yukon Route Railroad,** which opened in 1900 to carry late stampeders into Canada and bring gold out. It's one of the first things you'll see when coming in from the cruise ship piers. The round-trip to the summit of the pass, following a route carved out of the side of the mountain by an American/Canadian engineering team, takes 3 hours from the depot, set right at the foot of town.

COMING ASHORE   Ships dock at the cruise pier, at the foot of Broadway or off Congress or Terminal Way. Though the docks are in sight of downtown, it's about a 20-minute walk, so free shuttle buses are provided.

GETTING AROUND   Skagway is almost hermetically self-contained, like a theme park. The only street you really need to know about is **Broadway,** which runs through the center of town and off which everything branches. **Walking maps** describing the historic buildings and **trail maps** of the surrounding area are available at the Arctic Brotherhood Hall on Broadway between 2nd and 3rd avenues and at the National Historic Park visitor center, located at the railroad depot. Hikes range from 1 to 10 miles, and most involve some good hill walking. The Skagway Streetcar Company also offers tours via historic period limos (see below).

Best Cruise Line Shore Excursions

In addition to the excursions below, there are also trips by boat to the laid-back town of **Haines** (p. 592), which lies about 15 miles southwest on the Lynn Canal.

White Pass & Yukon Route Railway ($125–$399, 3–8½ hr.): The sturdy engines and vintage parlor cars of this famous narrow-gauge railway take you from the town and past waterfalls and still-visible parts of the famous "Trail of '98" to the White Pass Summit, the boundary between Canada and the United States. On a clear day, you'll be able to see all the way down to the harbor, and you might see the occasional hoary marmot or other critter fleeing from the train's racket. Several variations are offered: one an up-and-back trip to the summit ($125, 3 hr.); one that includes a bus ride to the village of Carcross near Lake Bennett, Yukon Territory, where you have lunch at the Caribou Trading Post before boarding the train for the ride back to Skagway ($199, 8 hr.); one that combines the train ride with kayaking at Bernard Lake ($229, 5 hr.); another that adds a helicopter flight over the Juneau Icefield and a 5-mile hike along the upper Skagway River to view Laughton Glacier ($399, 5 hr.); and another that adds a walking tour of the gold-rush-era ghost town of Bennett, along with a "prospector's meal" of gold miner's stew, nugget baked beans, sourdough bread, and apple pie, plus a motorcoach trip back to Skagway via the Klondike Highway ($299, 8½ hr.). Now the caveat to the whole experience: On an overcast day, you won't see a damn thing from the train. If you're on the fence, consider waiting to buy your tickets at the depot when you arrive, if there are seats available. Schedule info is available at **www.wpyr.com**.

Dyea Rainforest Bicycle Tour ($89, 3 hr.): The ghost town of Dyea, about 9 miles west, was established around the same time as Skagway, but was abandoned completely after the gold rush. On this tour, you'll start in Dyea and ride 6 miles back to Skagway through the rainforest, whose coastal tidal flats are home to eagles, salmon, and wildflowers.

Dyea on Horseback ($169, 3½ hr.): A van takes you to Dyea, where you tour the town aboard an even-tempered mount while your guide spins some history.

Sled Dog Musher's Camp ($125, 2¾ hr.): An introduction to the sled-dog life, with a tour of a musher's camp, includes a 20-minute ride through the forest aboard a wheeled sled, and a chance to cuddle husky pups.

Chilkoot Trail Hike & Float Trip ($119, 4½ hr.): From the pier, travel to the historic Dyea ghost town and hike the first 2 miles of the Chilkoot Trail through the rainforest. At the shore of the Taiya River, you'll board 18-foot rafts for a float back to Dyea.

Glacier Point Wilderness Safari ($229, 6½ hr.): A 40-minute trip by fast catamaran takes you through Alaska's deepest fjord, where you can watch for whales and sea lions en route to a remote beach at Glacier Point. After a short wobble by 4-wheel-drive school bus along a rough road, you'll walk a quarter-mile down to the water and board a 31-foot canoe, then paddle out into the waters around Davidson Glacier. This tour is also available from Haines.

Klondike Bicycle Tour ($89, 2½ hr.): After taking a van to the White Pass summit, you'll ride down the Klondike Highway, 15 miles from peak to sea, pausing along the way for photos.

Yukon Golf Odyssey ($179, 8 hr.): After a ride across the White Pass, you'll head into the Yukon to the town of Carcross and its 9-hole, par-36 Meadow Lakes Golf & Country Club course, with four sets of tees on each hole and lengths ranging from 1,800 to 2,800 yards. Golfing in the Yukon! Now there's something to tell your regular partners.

Skagway by Streetcar ($40, 2 hr.): This is as much performance art as historical tour: Guides in period costume relate tales of the boomtown days as you tour the sights both in and outside of town in a 1920s limo. Though theatrical, it's all done in a homey style, as if you're getting a tour from your cousin. The guide is as likely to point out funky oddities as major historical sites. After seeing the Historic District, the Lookout, the Gold Rush Cemetery, and other sights, guests see a little song-and-dance and film presentation about Skagway, and become honorary members of the Arctic Brotherhood. This last part is very, very hokey.

On Your Own: Within Walking Distance

Though Skagway's historic district includes some three dozen buildings from the 1890s and early 1900s, most are either privately owned or leased by the Park Service for use as businesses. Be sure to pick up the "Skagway Walking Tour" map at the Arctic Brotherhood Hall or the National Historic Park visitor center (see "Getting Around," above) and consult it as you wander around. A little knowledge could transform that souvenir shop back into a dry goods store. Everything here is within walking distance, though the Gold Rush Cemetery (see below) might be a bit far for some. If so, skip it; it's not that interesting by itself.

As you're coming into town from the docks, via Broadway, you'll be greeted by a few interesting sights. To the right, that fiendish-looking machine near the tracks is a **rotary snowplow** that was used by the railroad whenever the White Pass tracks got snowed in. The two buildings just behind it, on the corner of 2nd Avenue and Broadway, house the offices of the **National Park Service,** with the **White Pass and Yukon Route** depot right next door. The NPS buildings are worth a stop for information and historical ambience (they once housed the original railroad depot and offices), while the latter merits a stop for its gift shop, which has some nifty railroad souvenirs.

Across the street, at the corner of 2nd Avenue, bartenders at the **Red Onion Saloon** (© **907/983-2414;** www.redonion1898.com) still serve drinks over the same mahogany bar they used back in gold-rush days. Waitresses wear busty dance-hall outfits, as do the double-entendre-flinging docents, who lure visitors to the former bordello upstairs for a tour—$5 for 15 minutes, just like in the old days. If you have less time, you can even get a "quickie" tour for less. It's actually interesting, with rooms re-created to look as they did in the 1890s, and a decent presentation by the guides, too.

On the same block, the **Arctic Brotherhood Hall** is mostly notable for its facade, covered in thousands of pieces of driftwood.

At the other end of town, at 7th Avenue and Spring Street, the 1899 McCabe College building houses the **Skagway Museum** (© **907/983-2420**), a very professional display providing a look at Skagway's history through artifacts, photographs, and historical records. Items on display include a Tlingit canoe and Bering Sea kayaks, as well as a collection of gold-rush supplies and tools and Native American items such as baskets and beadwork. Admission is $2. If you'd like to get out of town for awhile, continue walking about 1½ miles up State Street to the old **Gold Rush Cemetery,** where Frank Reid and Soapy Smith are buried.

Back on Broadway, at 6th Avenue, the *Days of '98 Show* has been playing at the Fraternal Order of Eagles Hall No. 25 (© **907/983-2545;** http://thedaysof98show. eskagway.com) since 1927, which tells you how long Skagway has relied on tourism. A melodrama of the Gay '90s featuring dancing girls, ragtime music, a recitation of Robert Service poetry, and (naturally) actors playing Smith and Reid in their historic shootout, the show is almost always part of a shore excursion, but you can also buy tickets at the door for $18. From the theater, walk down 6th Avenue and make a right to see the historic **Moore Cabin,** built in 1887 by Skagway founder William Moore.

Shopping

Skagway is all about shopping, but we try to avoid it. Most of the shops sell either cheap tourist gimcracks or jewelry. The most characteristic items from town are probably railroad souvenirs from the **White Pass and Yukon Route,** available at the depot. **Heart of Broadway,** 305 Broadway at 9th Avenue (© **907/983-3773**), stocks jewelry and other work by local artists, including salmon-tooth earrings made by Nan Saldi, whose family is in the local fishing business.

8 Victoria, British Columbia

Cruises that start in Seattle or San Francisco typically visit Victoria on the way north to Alaska. Located on Vancouver Island, this lovely little city is the capital of British Columbia, and appropriately so, as it's almost more British than Britain, with gorgeous Victorian architecture and lovely gardens among its main attractions. Take a tour around the island and you'll see beautiful homes, stately government buildings, and views that include the snowcapped mountains of Washington State.

COMING ASHORE Cruise ships dock at the Ogden Point cruise ship terminal on the Strait of Juan de Fuca, about a mile southwest of the **Inner Harbour** and the **Downtown/Old Town** area, where most attractions are located.

GETTING AROUND Cruise lines offer a shuttle to the Inner Harbour, where flower baskets, milling crowds, and street performers liven the scene around the grand Fairmont Empress Resort Hotel, famed setting for English-style high tea.

Note: At press time, the exchange rate between U.S. and Canadian dollars was essentially one-to-one, though it's fluctuated by as much as 20 cents over the past couple of years. Prices in this section are in U.S. dollars.

Best Cruise Line Shore Excursions

Butchart Gardens ($70, 3½ hr.): The world-renowned Butchart Gardens are set in a former quarry (see details below). Expanded trips include high tea at the gardens ($119, 4 hr.) and a **Behind the Scenes Tour** ($169, 4 hr.) that delves into the gardens' history and operations.

Victoria Pub Crawl ($89, 3½ hr.): Visit three of the city's finest pubs and sample its best local brews, all without having to choose a designated driver.

Orca & Wildlife-Watching Adventure ($119, 3 hr.): A catamaran takes you out on the waters off southern Vancouver Island, home to killer whales, seals, porpoises, and myriad birds.

Horse-Drawn Trolley Tour ($49, 1 hr.): A fully narrated tour takes you past James Bay, Beacon Hill Park, and Victoria's Old Town, which includes the Legislative Buildings and the Fairmont Empress Resort Hotel.

On Your Own: Within Walking Distance

It's about a mile from the docks to the central attractions around the Inner Harbour, but let's call that walking distance, for argument's sake. Once you're there, the big attraction is the ivy-covered, grandly Edwardian **Fairmont Empress Resort Hotel,** 721 Government St. (© **250/384-8111;** www.fairmont.com/empress). Built in 1908, the hotel has a grand lobby and is *the* place to go for British-style high tea. Many shore excursions include tea here; but if you plan to go on your own, call 2 weeks before your cruise for reservations, and be sure to follow the dress code: no sleeveless shirts, tank tops, short-shorts, or cutoffs. To the side of the hotel, you'll find the **Miniature World** museum (© **250/385-9731;** www.miniatureworld.com), with quirky displays like big dollhouses, the world's smallest working sawmill, and a model of London in 1670. It's open daily 9am to 5pm (later in summer months). Admission is $13 adults, $10 youths ages 12 to 17, $8 children ages 5 to 11. Nearby, British Columbia's **Legislative Buildings,** 501 Belleville St. (© **250/387-3046;** www.leg.bc.ca), exude typical British government gravitas, their stony bulk surrounded by vast lawns and headed by a statue of the city's namesake, Queen Victoria. Visitors can watch the proceedings from upper galleries, and free tours of the buildings are held every 20 to 30 minutes in summer.

Just to the east sits the **Royal British Columbia Museum,** 675 Belleville St. (© **888/447-7977;** www.royalbcmuseum.bc.ca), its entrance graced by towering totem poles and other large sculptural works by Northwest First Nations artists. Inside, exhibits highlight the natural history of the province and Victoria's recent past, and one demonstrates how archaeologists study ancient cultures, using artifacts from numerous local tribes. It's open daily 10am to 5pm. Admission is $15 adults, $9.50 kids ages 6 to 18. The museum's **National Geographic IMAX Theatre** shows extra-cost movies on various scientific themes and exotic locations. Adjacent to the museum is **Thunderbird Park,** a gorgeous spot full of First Nations totem poles and a ceremonial house.

On Your Own: Beyond the Port Area

Some 13 miles north of downtown Victoria on the Saanich Peninsula, the 130-acre **Butchart Gardens,** 800 Benevenuto Ave., in Brentwood Bay (© **866/652-4422** or 250/652-5256; www.butchartgardens.com), was started as a beautification project by the wife of a quarry owner, and today has world-renowned English, Italian, and Japanese gardens, along with water gardens and rose gardens. There are also restaurants and a gift shop on-site. Open daily 9am to closing (call for hours). Admission (mid-June to Sept) is $28 adults, $14 kids ages 13 to 17, and $3 kids ages 5 to 12 (check website for admission during other seasons). Most cruise passengers visit as part of a shore excursion. Ditto for the Highland-style **Craigdarroch Castle,** 1050 Joan Crescent (© **250/592-5323;** www.craigdarrochcastle.com), which was built in the 1880s as the

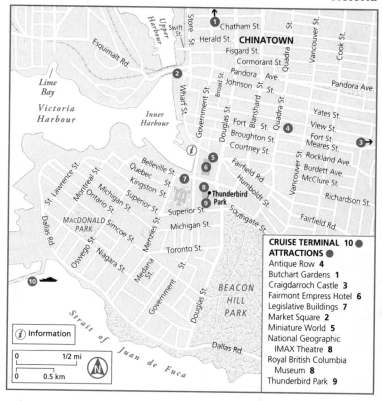

CRUISE TERMINAL **10** ●
ATTRACTIONS ●
Antique Row **4**
Butchart Gardens **1**
Craigdarroch Castle **3**
Fairmont Empress Hotel **6**
Legislative Buildings **7**
Market Square **2**
Miniature World **5**
National Geographic
  IMAX Theatre **8**
Royal British Columbia
  Museum **8**
Thunderbird Park **9**

home of millionaire Scottish coal magnate Robert Dunsmuir. Four stories high and 39 rooms strong, it's topped with stone turrets and furnished in opulent Victorian splendor. It's open daily 10am to 4:30pm (June 15 to Labor Day 9am–7pm). Admission is $14 adults, $9 kids ages 13 to 17, $5 kids ages 6 to 12. Those wishing to visit on their own can make the 40-minute walk up Fort Street from the Inner Harbor, or grab a taxi.

Shopping

At the Inner Harbor, the **Government Street promenade** is a 5-block stretch of souvenir shops sprinkled with the occasional treasure, including shops selling thick Cowichan Indian sweaters. On the eastern edge of downtown, a 3-block stretch on Fort Street between Blanshard and Cook streets is known as **Antique Row,** renowned for quality British collectibles. Farther north in Old Town, a complex of former shipping offices and supply stores has been transformed into **Market Square,** 560 Johnson St., at Wharf and Shore streets (© **250/386-2441;** www.marketsquare.ca), a self-contained shopping, dining, and entertainment area, with 35-plus shops.

12

The Mexican Riviera & Baja

The so-called Mexican Riviera—the stretch of port cities and resorts extending from Mazatlán in the north to Acapulco in the south—is one of the classic cruise destinations, and not just because it's where *The Love Boat* used to sail every week. Blessed with miles of beaches backed by picturesque mountains, and with a climate that practically guarantees perfect beach weather any day of the year, this is the Caribbean for folks who live on the West Coast.

Spanish conquistadors and missionaries came to this coast in the 16th and 17th centuries to find riches, convert the heathen (frequently at sword point), and establish ports for sailing to the Far East. But it wasn't until the mid–20th century that other travelers discovered the region to be almost tailor-made for relaxation. Hollywood stars arrived first, heading south for anonymity and great sport-fishing. Later, the spring-break crowd followed, seeking a place to get lewd and goofy on $1 beers. Today, the region still appeals to them as well as others, offering plenty of family-oriented relaxation and a dash of both history and culture, along with lots of traditional and modern art.

In addition to the Riviera ports, many cruises on those itineraries also stop at **Cabo San Lucas,** at the tip of the Baja Peninsula, a great town that's all about beaches and bars, but also boasts some amazing golf courses and adventure-travel excursions.

HOME PORTS FOR THIS REGION Cruises to this region sail from **San Diego, Los Angeles,** and **San Francisco.**

LANGUAGE & CURRENCY Spanish is the tongue of the land, although **English** is spoken in most places that cater to tourists. The Mexican currency is the **nuevo peso** (new peso). Its symbol is the "$" sign, but it's hardly the equivalent of the U.S. dollar—the exchange rate at press time was 13 pesos to US$1 (1 peso = US7¢). Most tourist stores gladly accept U.S. dollars. *Note:* All prices in this chapter are given in U.S. dollars.

CALLING FROM THE U.S. & CANADA You need to dial the international access code **(011)** and Mexico's country code **(52)** before the numbers listed in this chapter.

1 Acapulco

Why is it we think of the late Ricardo Montalban every time we think of Acapulco? Some kind of mixed 1970s TV metaphor, we suppose, but it still works: The city is a charming star from the old days, when men were men and Latin America meant romance backed by a big string section. The town's temptations are hard to resist, from the nearly year-round sunshine to the men diving off seaside cliffs at sunset. Though most beach resorts are made for relaxing, Acapulco has nonstop 24-hour energy, and its perfectly sculpted bay is an adult playground filled with water-skiers and studs on

The Mexican Riviera

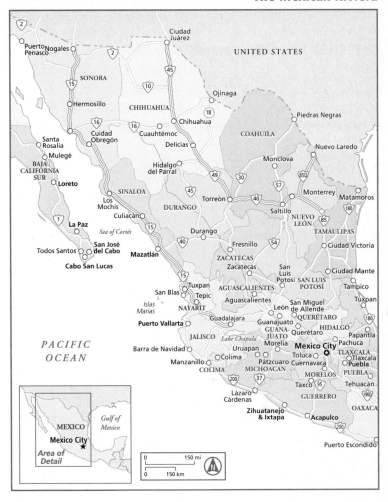

WaveRunners. Back in the days when there were members of a jet set, this was their town, and it's not hard to understand why: The view of Acapulco Bay, framed by mountains and beaches, is just breathtaking.

COMING ASHORE Cruise ships dock west of the Golden Zone hotel strip, a 5-minute walk from Old Acapulco's main plaza, the *zócalo,* right on the Costera (aka Av. Costera Miguel Aleman), the main avenue through the tourist zone, lined with hotels, restaurants, shopping centers, and open-air beach bars. Fort San Diego is just above the docks.

GETTING AROUND **Taxis** are plentiful and inexpensive (only a few dollars) if you're traveling in the downtown area only. Just remember that you should always establish the price with the driver before starting out. The city **buses** are also easy and inexpensive, with covered bus stops all along the Costera, posted with maps that show routes to major sights.

Best Cruise Line Shore Excursions

Acapulco City Highlights & Cliff Divers ($52, 4 hr.): A bus tour travels from one end of Acapulco Bay to the other, taking in the beaches, resort hotels, and La Quebrada, where the world-famous **cliff divers** plunge into the Pacific.

Acapulco Walking Tour ($32, 4 hr.): A walking tour takes in Fort San Diego with its museum of Mexican history and folk art, the old *zócalo* town square, the cathedral, and other local highlights.

Rafting on the Papagayo River ($135, 5½ hr.): Travel to Pueblo Bravo for a trip down the Papagayo River, floating through narrow canyons and Class II rapids.

On Your Own: Within Walking Distance

Acapulco is all about great beaches and watersports (and nightlife, which early-departing cruise passengers will have to put out of their minds), and as with most of the Mexican Riviera ports, the thing to do here is take in the surf and the seaside cafes. The traditional downtown area, with its shady town square, the *zócalo* (also called Plaza Alvarez), is worth a trip, allowing you a glimpse of local life and color. Inexpensive cafes and shops border the plaza, which is shaded by huge mango and rubber trees and cooled by fountains. At its far north end is the **Nuestra Señora de la Soledad** cathedral with its rounded blue tower domes and vaulted roof. From the church, turn east along the side street going off at a right angle (Calle Carranza) to find an arcade with newsstands and more shops. The hill behind the cathedral affords a fantastic view of the town. Just follow the signs for **El Mirador** (lookout point), or take a taxi if it looks like too much of a walk for you.

Near the cruise docks, star-shaped **Fort San Diego** was built in 1616 to defend the bay, and was later rebuilt after a 1776 earthquake leveled the original structure. After years of baking in the Acapulco sun, it was finally refurbished and turned into a museum directed by Mexico's department of archaeological and historic preservation. Today, the fort houses the **Acapulco Historical Museum** (℗ 744/482-3828), whose displays illuminate Acapulco's past, from precolonial times through the conquistador era, the silver trade between Acapulco and China, the Mexican War of Independence, and beyond. A glass floor in several rooms allows visitors to see the remains of the original fort. Admission costs about $2.40; closed Monday.

Just above downtown, on the other side of the narrow Peninsula de las Playas, **La Quebrada** is probably the most recognized Acapulco icon. It's from here that professional high divers plunge each day at 1pm from a ledge on the cliff, diving into the roaring surf of an inlet that's just 20 feet wide and 12 feet deep—but 130 feet down. Many shore excursions include the show as part of a larger city tour, but you can also go on your own, starting behind the cathedral and walking 4 blocks along La Quebrada Street. Admission is about $3.

Beaches

In the old days, the downtown beaches—Manzanillo, Honda, Caleta, and Caletilla—were the focal point of Acapulco. The latter two remain popular with both visitors and locals, but now beaches and resort developments also stretch along the 4-mile shoreline of the bay. Here's a rundown, going from west to east around the bay.

Playa la Angosta is a small, sheltered, often-deserted cove just around the bend from **La Quebrada,** where the cliff divers perform. About 10 minutes south of downtown by taxi, on the Peninsula de las Playas, **Caleta** and **Caletilla** beaches have calm waters and thatched-roof restaurants, with watersports equipment, beach chairs, and umbrellas for rent. From here, brightly painted boats ferry passengers to **Roqueta Island,** a good place to snorkel, sunbathe, hike to a lighthouse, visit a small zoo, or have lunch. The ride across costs about $5 round-trip.

East of the *zócalo,* the major beaches are **Hornos** (near Papagayo Park), **Hornitos, Paraíso, Condesa,** and **Icacos,** followed by the naval base **(La Base)** and **Punta del Guitarrón.** From here, the road climbs to the legendary Las Brisas hotel, then continues to the small, clean bay of **Puerto Marqués,** followed by **Punta Diamante,** about 12 miles from the *zócalo,* fronting the open Pacific and dominated by several resort hotels.

Shopping

Acapulco is not one of the best places to buy Mexican crafts, but it does have a few interesting shops. The best are at the **Mercado Parazal** (often called the Mercado de Artesanías), on Calle Velázquez de León near Cinco de Mayo in the downtown *zócalo* area. When you see Sanborn's department store/drugstore, turn right and walk behind it for several blocks, asking directions if necessary. Here, you'll find stalls of curios from around the country, including silver, embroidered cotton clothing, rugs, pottery, and papier-mâché, as well as on-site artists who paint ceramics with village scenes. The shopkeepers aren't pushy, but they'll test your bargaining mettle. Before buying silver, examine it carefully and look for ".925" stamped on the back. This supposedly signifies that the silver is 92.5% pure, though the less expensive silver called *alpaca* may also bear this stamp.

For resort wear, head to the boutiques crowding the **Costera,** where you'll find prices generally lower than what you'd pay in the United States.

2 Cabo San Lucas

Cabo San Lucas, the rowdier half of the conjoined towns commonly referred to as Los Cabos, is one big bar-and-beach scene perched at the very tip of the Baja Peninsula, with the Pacific Ocean on one side and the mouth of the Sea of Cortez on the other. (Its quieter twin, San Jose del Cabo, is about 21 miles away, down a corridor lined with resorts.) Cabo made hardly a blip on the world's radar until after World War II, when Hollywood celebs and yachters started traveling here for sport-fishing. In 1973, the completion of the Transpeninsular Highway finally linked the town to the rest of North America. By the early 1980s, the Mexican government had realized the area's growth potential and began investing in new highways, a larger airport, golf courses, and modern marine facilities. Today, the town is a playground seemingly built entirely for vacationers' gratification, full of beaches, beach bars, bar bars, crafts shops, restaurants, and did we mention bars? There's almost nothing of cultural or historic significance here (unless you're big on pop sociology), so your choices are to throw yourself into the hedonism or sign up for a nature- or adventure-oriented excursion.

COMING ASHORE   Cabo San Lucas lacks pier facilities for anything but small ships (in the 100-passenger range), so large cruise ships must anchor offshore and ferry passengers in by tender. You step ashore in the **Cabo San Lucas Marina** (in the Cabo San Lucas Bay harbor), which is chockablock with tour operators, information stands, shops, and transportation options.

GETTING AROUND   The tender dock at the marina is a pleasant 10- to 15-minute walk from the town center, around the rim of the Y-shaped harbor. Essentially, everything in town is within a few blocks of the harbor rim. If you keep walking all the way around (at least a 30-min. walk, just because of the harbor's twists and turns), you'll reach the start of the beaches, but the fastest way to access them is by **water taxi,** which costs about $10 per person. You can also catch a regular **car taxi** (about $5 per carload) or a **bicycle taxi** (for which you'll have to negotiate a rate). All are in vast supply right at the dock. Taxis can also take you to the golf courses on the corridor between Cabo San Lucas and San Jose del Cabo; expect to pay between $25 and $40 each way.

Best Cruise Line Shore Excursions

In addition to the excursions listed here, the cruise lines typically offer nearly two dozen other snorkeling, scuba, sailing, and bus tours.

Snorkel Tour by Zodiac ($72, 3 hr.): A two-stop snorkeling trip via inflatable Zodiac boats leaves from the tender pier. The boats pass Lovers Beach (see "Beaches," below) en route to Pelican Rock Cove for your first dive, then on to palm-lined Santa Maria Cove, which is part of a protected marine sanctuary.

Cabo San Lucas Sport-Fishing ($180, 5 hr.): Superb sport-fishing put Cabo San Lucas on the map. After boarding your sport-fishing vessel, you'll take a brief cruise to the fishing grounds, then spend a few hours trolling for marlin and sailfish. The good news: Beer is included. The bad news: Because the cruise ships can't store your catch, fishing for trophy fish is catch and release. Nontrophy fish are kept by the crew. A $10 fishing license is required.

Cabo Zodiac Whale-Watch ($90, 2½ hr.): Every year from January to March, Cabo San Lucas is visited by humpback, gray, and blue whales, and the best, most intimate, and action-packed way to see them is aboard one of these inflatable craft, which seat only 15 people.

Horseback Ride on the Beach ($80, 3 hr.): Mount up for an hour-long ride along Cabo's cactus-lined beaches, followed by a cool drink at a beach hotel and another hour free to swim and work on your tan.

On Your Own: Within Walking Distance

Cabo is small and manageable, spreading out north and west of the harbor and edged by foothills, dramatically jagged rocks, and desert mountains. A wide **walkway** wraps most of the way around the harbor, lined with bars, restaurants, and shops. On the other side of those bars and restaurants, about 650 feet from the water's edge, **Boulevard Marina** is the main artery that curves around the harbor and essentially *is* the town, at least from a short-term visitor's standpoint. Bars and Mexican restaurants serving fresh seafood crowd one another for space, so pick the one that seems to say "you." The most famous of the bunch is the **Cabo Wabo Cantina** (*©* **624/143-1188;** www.cabowabo.com), partly owned by former Van Halen frontman Sammy Hagar. It's right in the center of town, with a big sign on Marina and the main entrance around back on Vicente Guerrero, at Cárdenas. Expect a rock-theme-bar atmosphere, with Van Halen videos and music playing on TV monitors. Unfortunately for cruise passengers, the place doesn't get happening till the evening, after your ship has sailed, but you'll still be able to sip in the atmosphere. Nearby, **El Squid Roe,** on Marina opposite Plaza Bonita (*©* **624/143-0655;** www.elsquidroe.com), is another "Spring Break for Life" kind of bar of the Señor Frog and Carlos 'n Charlie's variety. For an antidote to big bars, drop into **Slim's Elbow Room,** "the World's Smallest Bar," on Marina just in front of the building that houses Cabo Wabo. It's just a little bit bigger than a pool table. That's our kind of place.

On Your Own: Beyond the Port Area

Cruise ship passengers who are in town for just a few hours should stick to downtown Cabo and the beaches, unless they're on a shore excursion and/or want to play **golf,** a sport with which Los Cabos is increasingly associated. Most of the courses are along the corridor between the two towns.

- The 18-hole, 7,100-yard, Nicklaus-designed Ocean Course at the corridor's **Cabo del Sol Resort** (© **800/386-2465;** www.cabodelsol.com) is known for its challenging 3 finishing holes. Tom Weiskopf designed the newer 18-hole Desert Course. Greens fees for both are $99 to $355 (including cart), depending on time and season.

- The 18-hole, 6,945-yard course at **Cabo Real,** by the Me Meliá in the hotel zone (© **877/795-8727** or 624/144-1200; www.caboreal.com), was designed by Robert Trent Jones, Jr., and features holes that sit high on mesas overlooking the Sea of Cortez. Greens fees are $140 to $280, including cart.

- The 18-hole course at **Cabo San Lucas Country Club/Raven Golf Club,** designed by Roy Dye (© **888/328-8501;** www.golfincabo.com), overlooks the juncture of the Pacific Ocean and Sea of Cortez, including the famous Land's End rocks. It includes the longest hole in Mexico, a 607-yard par-5. Greens fees are $80 to $185.

Beaches

When your ship anchors offshore, you'll see the long, curving sweep of **Medano Beach** stretching into the distance to the right of town (on the east side of the bay). It looks to be about a 5-minute walk from the docks, but looks can be deceiving: The Marina's two main arms stand between the tender dock and the sand, so you either have to walk all the way around (about a 30-min. trek) or hop a water taxi or regular taxi (see "Getting Around," above). At practically any point along the stretch, you'll be able to rent WaveRunners, kayaks, windsurfing boards, and snorkeling gear. Restaurant/bars line the sand at intervals, with some quiet stretches in between.

As your ship comes into the bay, you may see a small beach off your port bow, nestled amid the rugged rocks that separate the bay from the Pacific. This is **Lovers Beach,** the most beautiful beach spot in town. It's accessible only by water taxi from the docks and there are no facilities to speak of (just the occasional local selling drinks), but it's totally dreamy, with a real *From Here to Eternity* kind of vibe. At low tide, you can cross through the famous natural arch that connects the two seas here. Swimming is generally safe only on the Sea of Cortez side, facing the bay.

Farther north, along the Pacific Coast, **Playa Solmar** (at the Solmar and Playa Grande resorts) is a magnificent stretch of sand, but don't bother going unless you just want a great view: There's a bad riptide, and swimming is prohibited.

Shopping

You'll find no shortage of shopping opportunities in Cabo, but few surprises either. **Puerto Paraíso** (www.puertoparaiso.com), located on the far west end of the marina, has luxury outlets like Cartier, Hermés, Montblanc, and Fendi, as well as souvenir and clothing stores. Just beyond the tender dock at the harbor, a large, covered **handicrafts**

market has scores of vendors selling pretty much the same merchandise you'll find in town: a mixture of T-shirts, crafts, blankets, trinkets, and tequila. In town, Cabo Wabo (see above) sells its own brand—**Tequila Cabo Wabo**—at its gift shop, while other shops stock every other brand in existence. Shops and crafts marts alternate with jewelry stores and high-end (if not too inspiring) art galleries along Boulevard Marina.

3 Ixtapa/Zihuatanejo

Located side by side about 158 miles northwest of Acapulco, Ixtapa and Zihuatanejo are the odd couple of twin beach resorts. Ixtapa (Eex-*tah*-pah) is a model of modern infrastructure, services, and luxury resorts, while Zihuatanejo (See-wah-tah-*neh*-hoh, or just "Zihua"), only 4 miles to the south, is the quintessential rustic Mexican beach village—and, oddly, the place where cruise ships pull in. The area, with a backdrop of the Sierra Madre mountains and a foreground of Pacific Ocean waters, provides opportunities for enjoying beaches, scuba diving, deep-sea fishing, and golf.

Zihuatanejo spreads out around a beautiful bay, with the downtown area to the north and a beautiful long beach and the Sierra foothills to the east. The heart of town is the Paseo del Pescador, a brick waterfront walkway bordering the Municipal Beach with many shops and calm, casual restaurants. A good highway connects Zihua to **Ixtapa,** where tall hotels line the wide Playa Palmar beach, with lush palm groves and mountains as their backdrop. The main street, Boulevard Ixtapa, is full of small shopping plazas and restaurants, with the Marina Ixtapa at the north end of the beach from the hotel zone boasting excellent restaurants, private yacht slips, and an 18-hole golf course. Unless you want to play golf or explore Ixtapa's more resortlike style, we recommend settling back for a quiet day in Zihua.

COMING ASHORE Ships anchor in sheltered **Zihuatanejo Bay** and tender passengers to the town's municipal pier. The brick-paved Paseo del Pescador adjoins it, with shops and restaurants within easy walking distance.

GETTING AROUND You can walk around Zihuatanejo. **Taxi** fares between Ixtapa and Zihuatanejo run about $6, while fares within either town hover in the $5 range.

Best Cruise Line Shore Excursions

Zihuatanejo Sail & Snorkel ($80, 3 hr.): Climb aboard a trimaran and sail to Manzanillo Beach, one of the best snorkeling spots on the bay, where you'll drop anchor for direct access to the water.

Countryside Tour ($55, 3½ hr.): Leave Zihuatanejo by bus and head into the countryside, where you'll tour a fruit plantation that raises papaya, mango, grapefruit, and coconut; then visit an open-air factory to see bricks and floor tiles made using traditional methods. At Barra de Potosi lagoon, you can stroll the beach and watch local fishermen cast their nets.

On Your Own: Within Walking Distance

In Zihuatanejo, here's what you do: Step off the tender, take a deep breath, let it out, and order a beer or margarita. That's about it. **Paseo del Pescador** is full of nice little bars, shops, and seafood restaurants, and occasionally a musician will stroll by. For a little history, the **Museo de Arqueología de la Costa Grande,** near Guerrero at the east end of Paseo del Pescador (© **755/554-7552**), traces the history of the Acapulco-to-Ixtapa/Zihuatanejo "Costa Grande" region from pre-Hispanic times (when it was known as Cihuatlán) through the colonial era. Most of the museum's pottery and stone artifacts give evidence of extensive trade with far-off cultures and regions, including the Toltec and Teotihuacán near Mexico City, the Olmec on the Pacific and Gulf coasts, and areas known today as the states of Nayarit, Michoacán, and San Luis Potosí. Local indigenous groups gave the Aztec tribute items, including cotton *tilmas* (capes) and *cacao* (chocolate), representations of which can be seen here. Signs are in Spanish, but an accompanying brochure is available in English. Admission is $2; closed Monday.

Beyond the port area, there's only Ixtapa, and for cruise visitors, Ixtapa is mostly about . . .

Beaches

IXTAPA   Ixtapa's main beach, **Playa Palmar,** is a lovely white-sand arc on the edge of the hotel zone, with dramatic rock formations silhouetted in the sea. The surf can be rough, so use caution and don't swim when a red flag is posted. Lovely **Playa Vista Hermosa,** just south of Ixtapa, fronting the Hotel Las Brisas Ixtapa, is framed by striking rock formations and is very attractive for sunbathing, but has heavy surf and strong undertow (use caution if you swim here). **Playa Linda,** about 8 miles north of Ixtapa, is the primary out-of-town beach, with watersports equipment rentals available.

ZIHUATANEJO   At Zihuatanejo's town beach, **Playa Municipal,** the local fishermen pull their colorful boats up onto the sand, making for a fine photo op. The small shops and restaurants lining the waterfront are great for people-watching and absorbing the flavor of daily village life. A cement-and-sand walkway runs from the *malecón* east along the water to **Playa Madera (Wood Beach),** which is good for bodysurfing. To the south is Zihuatanejo's largest and most beautiful beach, **Playa La Ropa,** a mile-long sweep of sand with calm waters and a great view of the sunset. Palm groves edge the shoreline, and some lovely small hotels and restaurants nestle in the hills. A taxi from town costs about $5. The beach's name stems from the sinking of a galleon that was carrying silk clothing *(ropa)* back from the Philippines. When the ship went down, its cargo washed ashore here. **Playa Las Gatas (Cats Beach),** across the bay from Playa La Ropa and Zihuatanejo, has exceptionally clear waters and a man-made reef that makes for calm swimming (good for kids) and good snorkeling. A little dive shop on the beach rents gear; there are also a number of open-air seafood restaurants. Water taxis from the Zihuatanejo town pier can get you here for about $4 round-trip.

Shopping

IXTAPA   Shopping in Ixtapa is not especially memorable: mostly T-shirts and Mexican crafts, plus brand-name sportswear. All of the shops are in the same area on Boulevard Ixtapa, across from the beachside hotels.

ZIHUATANEJO   Zihuatanejo has its share of T-shirt and souvenir shops, but it's also a decent place to buy crafts, folk art, and jewelry. The **artisans' market** on Calle Cinco de Mayo is a good place to start browsing before moving on to specialty shops that spread inland from the waterfront. For a taste of local commerce, visit the **municipal market,** which sprawls over several blocks off Avenida Benito Juárez (about 5 blocks inland from the waterfront). Here, produce, fish, and nut vendors mix with stands selling huarache sandals, hammocks, and baskets.

4 Mazatlán

Almost straight across the Sea of Cortez from Cabo San Lucas, Mazatlán—"The Land of the Deer" in the old Nahuatl language—dates from the beginning of the 19th century, when German immigrants developed it as a shipping port. After a lull of about 160 years, it gained new fame as a sport-fishing capital, then as a destination for American college kids on spring break. Today, families and mature vacationers are flocking here as well, taking advantage of the low prices and 10-plus miles of beaches. For cruise travelers, the points of interest form a huge barbell shape, with the historic **downtown** area at the south end (near where your ship docks), the tourist-oriented **Zona Dorada (Golden Zone)** about 4 miles to the north, and the long, uninteresting curve of Avenida del Mar in between.

COMING ASHORE   Ships dock on the south side of town along a navigational channel, in the midst of substantial commercial shipping. Debarking passengers must take a short tram from the ship to the welcome terminal, where they run a veritable gauntlet of gift and craft shops before popping out into air again on the far side.

GETTING AROUND   The port is about a 15- or 20-minute walk from the center of the old downtown, but you can also take a **taxi.** In fact, we challenge you *not* to—there are so many of them on hand at the pier that you might find yourself sitting in one without ever having that intention. In addition to the green-and-white, fixed-rate **taxis,** you'll also see hundreds of open-sided *pulmonía* cars, which look like a cross between a jeep and a golf cart. Apparently the name (which literally means "pneumonia") stems from an old belief that riding in an open-air car can make you sick. Fares between the port (or Old Mazatlán) and the Zona Dorada average $5 to $10 for either kind of taxi.

Best Cruise Line Shore Excursions

In addition to the tours listed here, cruise lines offer a lot of "mix-and-match" Mazatlán bus tours, taking in highlights of downtown and almost always heading through the Golden Zone for shopping.

Old Mazatlán Walking Tour ($34, 4 hr.): Start at the shore-side Cerro de Neveria, where divers plunge off a cliff into the sea. Then amble through Old Mazatlán's narrow, shady streets, visiting the Teatro Angela Peralta (see "On Your Own: Within Walking Distance," below), stopping at a cafe for refreshments, and then heading to the main plaza and the cathedral. It's not a bad way to get oriented, and you can continue walking on your own around the old market, and then (if you like) grab a taxi out to the Golden Zone.

Sierra Madre Tour ($82, 7½ hr.): Travel by bus into the foothills of the Sierra Madre to the town of Concordia, founded in 1550 and famed for its furniture, handmade pottery, and baroque church. Continue to Copala, a former gold-mining town founded in 1565, where you can wander the narrow, cobbled streets and see the old colonial houses and 16th-century stone church. The tour includes a traditional Mexican lunch and a shopping stop in the Zona Dorada.

Pacifico Brewery Tour ($60, 2½ hr.): Founded in 1900, Pacifico brews one of Mexico's most popular beers. Tour the brewery, have a taste or three, and take in the incredible view of Mazatlán from the rooftop bar/hospitality room.

On Your Own: Within Walking Distance

Though most people will probably take a taxi the short distance to downtown, we're going to consider it "walking distance" both for argument's sake (we walked it easily) and to distinguish it from the more distant Golden Zone.

Downtown Mazatlán is centered around the palm-shaded **Plaza Principal,** also called Plaza Revolución and filled with vendors, pigeons, shoeshine men under Pacífico beer umbrellas, and old gentlemen sitting in the shade. A Victorian-style wrought-iron bandstand sits at its center and the **Cathedral of the Immaculate Conception** hovers over one end. Built in the 1800s, the cathedral has twin, yellow-tiled steeples, while its interior has a vaulted ceiling and more than a dozen chandeliers. It's worth a quick peek. One block behind the cathedral is the covered **Mercado Municipal** (aka Mercado Pino Suarez, or just "the municipal market"). Taking up the whole city block between Juarez and Serdan, it has its share of tourist shops, but is more a place for locals, with stands selling fresh produce, meat, clothing, herbal remedies, and religious mementos. It's a vibrant slice of life, as are all the streets around it.

Backtrack along Juarez a few blocks to reach Mazatlán's **historic district,** a 20-square-block area centered around the pretty little **Plazuela Machado,** which boasts a few sidewalk restaurants and sometimes hosts local cultural events. It's bordered by Frías, Constitución, Carnaval, and Sixto Osuna. On one corner of the square stands the Italian-style **Teatro Angela Peralta** (© **669/982-4447;** www.culturamazatlan. com/tap1.php), built between 1869 and 1881. A center of Mazatlán arts and culture for its first 40 years, the theater fell into disrepair following the Mexican revolution of 1910 and began a period of decay that lasted until the late 1980s, when a group of concerned citizens spearheaded its renewal. Today, the 841-seat theater is a national historic monument and regularly hosts folkloric ballets, contemporary dance, symphony concerts, opera, and jazz performances. Its sumptuous, jewel-box-like interior, with three levels of dark, woody balconies, has been restored to its 19th-century glory. It costs about $1 to tour the building.

The blocks around the theater and Plazuela abound with beautiful old buildings and colorful town houses trimmed with wrought iron and carved stone. Many buildings were restored as part of a downtown beautification program, which aimed to turn the neighborhood into the center of Mazatlán's artistic community. Half a block to the right of the theater's entrance is the **Nidart Galería** (see "Shopping," below). Check out the **town houses** on Libertad between Domínguez and Carnaval and the two lavish **mansions** on Ocampo at Domínguez and at Carnaval. For a rest stop, try the **Café Pacífico** (decorated with historic pictures of Mazatlán) or one of the other cafes on the Plazuela. Those with an interest in Mexican history can walk a couple of blocks down Sixto Osuna to Venustiano Carranza, where you'll find the small **Museo Arqueológico de Mazatlán,** Sixto Osuna 76 (© **669/981-1455**), which displays both pre-Hispanic artifacts and contemporary art. Admission is free; closed Monday.

If you feel like taking a good, tiring walk, head west down Constitución toward the ocean; then turn left and walk along the oceanside walkway on Paseo Clausen. Passing the beach at Olas Altas (the original Mazatlán beach strip), you'll see signs for **Cerro del Vigía** (Lookout Hill). Follow these up the steep hill at the edge of town, bending around the school and then hugging the coast. Below, accessible via several sets of stairs, is **Playa del Centenario,** a lovely stretch of pounding surf with views of the offshore Sea Lion rocks, the El Faro lighthouse (the second-highest in the world, after Gibraltar), and Deer and Wolf islands, just off the Zona Dorada. Frigate birds and pelicans soar overhead, and down below are sea-carved arches and patches of bright-green vegetation. You'd be pounded to death on the rocks if you tried to swim here, but it's a romantic picnic spot. At the point of the lookout, a stair-path leads out to a viewing platform that resembles the prow of a ship and affords some wonderful

Mazatlán Golf

Mazatlán probably affords the best golf value in Mexico, with two notable courses open to the public.

- The 27-hole course at the **El Cid** resorts, just east of the Zona Dorada (*©* **669/913-3333**; www.elcid.com), has 9 holes designed by Lee Trevino as well as 18 designed by Robert Trent Jones, Jr. It's open to the public, though preference is given to hotel guests, and tee times book up quickly. Greens fees are $90 for 18 holes, plus $20 for the caddy.
- The **Estrella del Mar Golf Club,** across the channel from downtown, on Isla de la Piedra (*©* **669/982-3300**; www.estrelladelmar.com), is an 18-hole, 7,004-yard course, also designed by Robert Trent Jones, Jr. Greens fees, including cart, run $75 to $110 depending on the season.

vistas. From here, continue along the coast road right around and back to the cruise docks.

On Your Own: Beyond the Port Area

Four miles from downtown, the **Zona Dorada (Golden Zone)** begins where Avenida del Mar intersects Avenida Rafael Buelna and becomes Avenida Camarón Sábalo, which leads north through the tourist zone. While shops, restaurants, and bars are much more abundant here than downtown, it's very, very, very touristy, and worth the drive only if you're in a beach-party mood.

Beaches

Much as we're not nuts about the Golden Zone, it is the better spot for beaches. At the beginning of the zone, you'll find **Playa Gaviotas** and several other beaches backed by resort hotels. Remember that all beaches in Mexico are public property, so all of these are accessible to visitors. Farther north, **Playa Sábalo** is perhaps the best beach in Mazatlán. The next point jutting into the water is Punta Sábalo, beyond which you'll find a bridge over a channel that flows in and out of a lagoon. Beyond the marina, more beaches stretch all the way to Los Cerritos.

In the downtown area, **Playa Olas Altas** (at the western edge of town) is a thin strip of curving beach backed by several low-key sidewalk bars. It's the closest beach to the docks, but lacks any amenities or any kind of "scene." Around a rocky promontory north of Olas Altas is **Playa Norte,** which has several miles of good sand beach with numerous palapa bars, but busy Avenida del Mar is right there behind you, taking something away from the experience.

Shopping

La Zona Dorada is the biggest area for shopping, with hundreds of shops and stalls selling the usual items for this part of Mexico: jewelry, shell-covered art, T-shirts, and lots of other touristy souvenirs, with a smattering of folk art mixed in, most of dubious quality. **Downtown** is more oriented toward locals, but is much more authentic. Check the historic district around the Teatro Angela Peralta for small galleries and shops, among them the wonderful **Nidart Galería,** av. Libertad 45 at Carnaval

(✆ **669/981-0002;** www.nidart.com), an exhibition space selling works created by local artists on-site, as well as works from around Mexico. This is quality stuff, including clay and leather sculptures and masks, paintings, woodwork, jewelry, and other items, priced much lower than you'd expect.

5 Puerto Vallarta

Looking at the vibrant, bustling Puerto Vallarta of today, it's hard to imagine that only 50 years ago, the only tourists who stopped here landed on a dirt airstrip outside town. Established in the 1850s as a port for processing silver from the Sierra Madre mountains, the place took off as a resort destination only when Hollywood stars began arriving 110 years later. In 1963, John Huston brought Ava Gardner and Richard Burton here to film the Tennessee Williams play *Night of the Iguana,* and Burton's new love, Elizabeth Taylor, came along even though both were married to other people at the time. Paparazzi arrived hot on their heels, and the rest is history.

Downtown, a seaside promenade (or *malecón*) runs north-south beside Paseo Díaz Ordaz, adorned with public art and stretching the length of El Central—the center of town. From the waterfront, cobblestone streets reach a mere half-dozen blocks back into the hills. The areas bordering the **Río Cuale** are the oldest parts of town, and a lovely island in midstream, **Isla Cuale,** is full of shops and lush foliage. Three bridges link the two sections of downtown, the most pleasant being a footbridge that hugs the shoreline. Isla Cuale can be accessed from any of them. The area north of the river is the main tourist zone, while the area immediately to the south is home to a growing number of sidewalk cafes and fine restaurants, plus the town's better beaches.

Many excursions here will take you outside town and up into the foothills of the **Sierra Madre.** Farther up, the Huichol Indians still live in relative isolation, simultaneously protecting their culture from outside influences and making a living off their distinctive beaded artwork, which you'll see around town.

COMING ASHORE   Cruise ships dock at the **Puerto Vallarta Marina,** about 3 miles north of downtown along the busy Avenida Francisco Medina Ascencio. A plethora of crafts and T-shirt shops, along with several small bars and restaurants, are clustered right in the port area; but it's not a destination in itself, so plan to take a taxi into town if you're not doing an excursion. Marina Vallarta, a resort and yacht harbor, is just north of the terminal.

GETTING AROUND   Technically, you can walk into town. We did it, just to see if it's worth doing, and here's the scoop: It's not. Instead, take a shore excursion to get back into the hills, or grab one of the **taxis** that greet ships at the dock, charging about $7. Once you're in the center of town, nearly everything is within walking distance both north and south of the river. And don't worry about getting back to the ship from here; the cabbies will find you.

Best Cruise Line Shore Excursions

Jungle Canopy Adventure ($142, 5 hr.): Ever wanted to be George of the Jungle? At a private reserve in the Sierra Madre, professional guides help you master the techniques of using horizontal traverse cables to travel through the jungle canopy, high up in the trees. Observation platforms give you a breather and a chance to observe the flora and fauna. At the end of your adventure, you rappel down a tree to the forest floor.

Sierra Madre Hiking Expedition ($40, 4 hr.): Head by bus to Rancho Sierra Madre, where a local naturalist leads your 5-mile hike through the forest to a volcanic hot spring, where you can take a dip. Back at the ranch, you're free to wander around to check out the operation or just relax with a drink.

Hideaway at Las Caletas ($92, 7½ hr.): Las Caletas was Oscar-winning director John Huston's hideaway, so basically on this tour you get to live like a celeb, traveling to the cove by motor launch, relaxing on its palm-lined beaches and drinking in its bar, taking a nature hike, or going kayaking or snorkeling. Some of Huston's possessions are still on display.

Swimming with Dolphins ($180, 2–3 hr.): At the Dolphin Adventure Center, you get a half-hour in a saltwater pool with two Pacific bottlenose dolphins. Do we really have to say more? A longer excursion, **Dolphin Trainer for a Day** ($300, 7 hr.), lets you work with dolphin trainers in the water and out.

Swimming with Sea Lions ($105, 2½ hr.): At the Dolphin Adventure Center, you'll get an orientation about sea lion physiology and behavior before entering the water to swim with the big goofballs. The **Snorkel with a Sea Lion at Las Caletas** tour ($160, 7 hr.) takes you an hour north of Puerto Vallarta by boat to Las Caletas, once the hideaway of film director John Huston, where you can interact with sea lions in open water, close to the beach.

On Your Own: Beyond the Port Area

Assuming you don't want to make the hot, dusty 3-mile walk into town, let's call everything here beyond walking distance. Once you do make it to town, though, Puerto Vallarta's cobblestone streets are a pleasure to explore on foot: filled with small shops, rows of windows edged with wrought-iron curls, and vistas of red-tile roofs and the sea. Start with a walk up and down the malecón, taking in the fine collection of public art that stretches from end to end. Across from Carlos O'Brien's restaurant on the north end is Ramiz Barquett's *Nostalgia,* depicting a couple sharing a romantic moment while gazing out to the bay. Farther south is an array of fanciful, almost Dr. Seuss–like chairs by renowned Mexican artist Alejandro Colunga, one topped with a large octopus head, another with giant ears for backrests. Farther south is Sergio Bustamante's *Ladder to Heaven,* depicting children climbing a ladder to nowhere. Closer to the main square, you'll find *Boy on the Seahorse,* which has become a Puerto Vallarta icon.

Near here, the main square is dominated by the **Parish of Nuestra Señora de Guadalupe church,** topped with a curious crown held in place by angels. It's a replica of the one worn by Empress Carlota during her brief time in Mexico as Emperor Maximilian's wife. On its steps, women sell religious mementos; across the narrow street, stalls sell herbs for curing common ailments. Stretching along the north end of the square is the municipal building, which has a large, folkloric **Manuel Lepe mural** inside in its stairwell.

Three blocks south of the church, head east on Libertad, lined with small shops and pretty upper windows, to the **Río Cuale municipal market** by the river (see "Shopping," below); then cross the bridge to **Isla Cuale.** Near the sea end of the island, the small **Museo Río Cuale** has a permanent exhibit of pre-Columbian ceramics, jewelry, and statuary (free admission).

Retrace your steps to the market and Libertad, and follow Calle Miramar to the set of rough stone steps. Follow these past the cafe, then take the steep, narrow, pastel steps up to Calle Zaragoza, pausing on the stairs to catch your breath and also for a nice view of the sea. Once on Zaragoza, go right 1 block to the famous **arched pink bridge** that connected Richard Burton's and Elizabeth Taylor's houses.

Beaches

For years, beaches were Puerto Vallarta's main attraction. Unfortunately, those near the cruise terminal are the worst in the area, with darker sand and seasonal inflows of stones. Stretching south to town, the **hotel zone** is known for broad, smooth beaches, open to the public and accessible primarily through hotel lobbies. Just south of town, the easiest beach to reach is **Playa Los Muertos** (aka Playa Olas Altas or Playa del Sol), just off Calle Olas Altas, south of the Río Cuale. The water can be rough, but the wide beach is home to several palapa restaurants with food, beverages, and beach-chair service. About 6 miles south of town along Highway 200, **Playa Mismaloya,** where *Night of the Iguana* was filmed, boasts clear waters. Entrance to the public beach is just to the left of the Jolla de Mismaloya Resort. There's an *Iguana*-themed restaurant and bar on-site.

Shopping

Puerto Vallarta is one big shopping opportunity, with hundreds of small stores selling everything from fine folk art and modern art to tacky T-shirts, plus tremendous amounts of silver jewelry and sculpture depicting everything from Aztec calendars to Mickey Mouse. The **municipal market** is just north of the Río Cuale, where Calle Libertad and Calle Rodríguez meet. The *mercado* sells clothes, jewelry, serapes, shawls, leather accessories and suitcases, papier-mâché parrots, stuffed frogs and armadillos, and, of course, T-shirts. Be sure to comparison-shop, and definitely bargain before buying. Upstairs, a sort of low-key food court serves inexpensive Mexican meals, giving adventurous diners a cheap, authentic local experience. Exit the market by the corner of Encino and Maramoros and walk across the suspended plank-and-rope bridge to **Río Cuale Island,** where outdoor stalls sell crafts, gifts, folk art, and clothing.

Back in El Centro, head for the corner of Calle Galeana and Calle Morelos (right across from the *Boy on the Seahorse* statue) to find the **Huichol Collection** (© 322/223-2141), the best shop in town for authentic Huichol Indian art. Descendants of the Aztec, the Huichol live in the high sierra north and east of Vallarta. They produce remarkable beadwork and "yarn painting" inspired by visions they experience during hallucinogenic peyote ceremonies. The colors explode from wall hangings, masks, bowls, and animal forms, the latter three made from carved wooden shapes to which incredibly intricate beadwork is added, eventually covering the entire surface. A Huichol artist is often at work in the back of the shop, and explanations in English tell you what you're looking at. Prices can be high for large pieces, but are worth it for the quality.

Some of the more attractive shops are a block or two inland from the *malecón,* centered roughly around the intersection of Calle Corona and Calle Morelos. One block north, near the corner of Calle Aldama, **La Casa del Tequila** (© 322/222-2000) has a tasting room where you can sample a selection of fine tequilas, plus a hacienda-style taco bar with swirling ceiling fans and cane seating.

13

Bermuda

This neat and tidy oasis in the middle of the Atlantic is edged with pink-sand beaches and rocky cliffs—and crawling with Brits in shorts. And not just any shorts, but shorts colored in perky tones of pink, green, or yellow, and paired with sports jackets, ties, and knee-highs. To the casual visitor, Bermuda is a pleasant paradox of sorts, mixing sane and proper with a healthy dose of silly (back to those shorts again). But what really matters to the cruise passenger is that Bermuda is an orderly, beautiful, easy place to visit. Aside from the Caribbean and The Bahamas, the 21-square-mile island nation of Bermuda (which is actually a chain of more than 100 small islands), sitting out in the Atlantic roughly parallel to South Carolina (or Casablanca, if you're measuring from the east), is the other major island cruise destination from the U.S. Eastern seaboard.

Although the Spanish stumbled upon Bermuda in the early–16th century, it was the British who first settled here in 1609, when the ship *Sea Venture,* en route to Virginia's Jamestown colony, was wrecked on the island's reefs. No lives were lost, and the crew and passengers built two new ships and continued on to Virginia; but three crewmembers stayed behind and became the island's first permanent settlers. Bermuda became a crown colony in 1620 and remains one today, retaining a very British character— the island is divided up into parishes, driving is on the left, and horse-drawn carriages trot about—but the sun and the ubiquitous Bermuda shorts serve as proof you're in the islands.

That's not to say things aren't bustling when the ships are in town at King's Wharf, in the West End, where most ships are now docking because they're too large for the piers in Hamilton and St. George's, Bermuda's other two port towns, but a calm and controlled atmosphere reigns as visitors fan out across the island. There are many powdery-soft beaches easily accessible by taxi or motor scooter, and Bermuda has more golf courses per square mile than any other place in the world. For shoppers, Front and Queen streets in Hamilton have dozens of shops and department stores, most specializing in English items, while the interest of history buffs is piqued by the 300-year-old St. Peter's Church, museums, and other sites within walking distance of the pier in St. George's. From King's Wharf, there are also impressive exhibits at the Maritime Museum, which is built into the ruins of Bermuda's oldest fort at the Royal Naval Dockyard.

Unlike most Caribbean itineraries, on which ships visit ports for a day at most, the many Bermuda-bound ships spend several whole days at the island. In recent years, Bermuda has begun allowing bigger ships to visit the island, and as a consequence has developed the King's Wharf complex in the West End as the main cruise ship pier. The ports of Hamilton and St. George are still used by small and midsize ships.

Bermuda

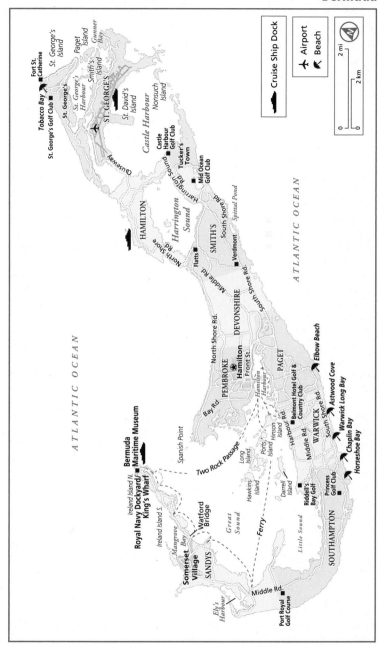

HOME PORTS FOR THIS REGION
New York/New Jersey and Boston are the main hubs for Bermuda cruises, with ships sailing round-trip on mostly 7-night itineraries. A few ships also sail to Bermuda round-trip from Baltimore, Norfolk, Charlotte, and Philadelphia. A few more itineraries include Bermuda on transatlantic crossings in spring and fall, or visit the island as part of longer itineraries that also include Caribbean ports.

LANGUAGE & CURRENCY The official language is **English.** The currency is the **Bermuda dollar** (BD$), which is pegged to the U.S. dollar on an equal basis—BD$1 equals US$1. There's no need to exchange any U.S. money for Bermudian currency.

SHOPPING TIPS While St. George's and the West End Dockyard both have souvenir shops, Hamilton is the center of Bermuda's shopping universe. Here, it's all about English (and some Irish) goodies such as porcelain, crystal, wool clothing, cashmere sweaters, and linens, and it's within walking distance, right outside of the terminal. Don't expect great deals, though—prices in Bermuda are generally on the high side.

1 Attractions Around Bermuda

Because Bermuda is relatively small and easy to get around, and because ships typically spend several days at its ports, you can access the following sights and excursions no matter where you're docked. Depending on traffic, St. George's and Hamilton are about a 20- to 30-minute taxi ride apart, as are Hamilton and King's Wharf (Hamilton is roughly in the middle). It takes about an hour to drive from one end of Bermuda to the other. **Taxis** are metered and relatively inexpensive, starting at $6.40 and going up $2 for each additional mile, with a variety of surcharges. Roads around the island are well maintained, but narrow and winding. The **bus** (go to the "Transport" section of www.gov.bm) and **ferry** (www.seaexpress.bm) systems are also userfriendly. Many folks go the **scooter** or **moped** route; rentals are available for $50 to $60 per day at all three ports.

In Flatts Village, about halfway between Hamilton and St. George's, is the **Bermuda Aquarium, Museum & Zoo** (© **441/293-2727;** www.bamz.org). There are interactive displays, huge aquariums, and seal feedings throughout the day. It's open daily from 9am to 5pm (last admission at 4pm); admission is $10 for adults and $5 for seniors and children ages 6 to 12.

The throngs head to the **beaches,** and for good reason. Many are powdery soft and some even pinkish (from crushed shells, corals, and other sea life); they're easily accessible by taxi or motor scooter from Hamilton and St. George's, and most are free. **Horseshoe Bay,** in Southampton Parish, is our top pick. Though you won't have it to yourself because it's so popular with other tourists, the horseshoe-shaped beach has scenic rocky cliffs at its edges and a vast soft plane of sand in the middle. It's perfect for little kids, as the sand is so silky smooth that it won't irritate delicate little faces. Horseshoe Bay is free and has a snack bar, restrooms, and showers. Lifeguards are on duty here between May and October.

Other beach options include **Warwick Long Bay** (Warwick Parish); **Tobacco Bay Beach** (St. George's Parish), where the water is very calm and the beach is tiny; and **Elbow Beach** (in Paget Parish).

The more adventurous can hop on a scooter and beach-hop among the many unnamed slivers of silky sand tucked into the jagged coastline. If you're itching to see more than Hamilton, and beaches aren't your bag, another great option is hopping on a local ferry (there are terminals in Hamilton and King's Wharf adjacent to the cruise docks). For just a few bucks, you can either ride just for the view of Bermuda's colorful harbors and coastline, or travel between King's Wharf and Hamilton.

It's a treat to climb the 185 steps of the **Gibbs Hill Lighthouse** (Lighthouse Rd., Southampton; halfway btw. King's Wharf and Hamilton; www.bermudalighthouse.com), the oldest cast-iron lighthouse in the world. At the top, you'll be rewarded with a panoramic view of Bermuda and its coast. In the base, there's a tearoom serving snacks. It's open daily 9am to 5pm.

The **Bermuda Railway Trail** has about 29km (18 miles) of trails divided into easy-to-explore sections. It was created along the course of the old Bermuda Railway, which stretched a total of 34km (22 miles) and served the island from 1931 to 1948, until the automobile was introduced. Armed with a copy of the *Bermuda Railway Trail Map and Guide,* available at the various visitor centers in and right outside the cruise terminals, you can set out on your own expedition via foot or bicycle (most of the moped/scooter rental agencies have bicycles as well). Most of the trail winds along a car-free route, and there is a section of trail in St. George's and near Hamilton.

Best Cruise Line Shore Excursions

There's a lot you can do independently, from beach hopping to shopping and walking and tram-style tours; however, if you crave a guide to narrate the highlights, or want to do something active such as snorkel or bike ride, the ships' organized tours are your best bet. The sampling of tours below are generally available from King's Wharf, Hamilton, and St. George's.

Railway Trail Cruise & Bike Tour ($75, 3 hr.): Take a scenic coastal cruise to the rural West End, where you'll hop on a 21-speed bike. Pedal along the path where the original Bermuda Railway once ran on narrow-gauge tracks. The tracks are gone, but a trail remains behind. This excursion is a great opportunity to get views of the ocean and the island's lush gardens and bird life. The flat route covers 8km to 13km (5–8 miles).

Snorkeling Trip ($75, 3 hr.): Board a boat and motor out to a snorkeling spot near the West End as the captain talks to passengers about Bermuda history and customs. Then, after an hour or so of snorkeling, the fun begins: The music is turned on, the dancing starts, and the bar opens as the boat heads back to port.

Coral Reef Glass-Bottom Boat Cruise ($50, 2 hr.): See the coral reefs and colorful fish living in Bermuda's waters; then view one of Bermuda's famous shipwrecks and enjoy a rum swizzle from a fully stocked bar.

Golf Excursion ($75+, half-day): Excursions include tee times for 18 holes at challenging courses such as Mid Ocean Golf Club, among the best in the world; Riddell's Bay Golf & Country Club, a veritable golfing institution built in 1922; Port Royal Golf Course; and St. George's Golf Club, designed by Robert Trent Jones, Jr. A taxi to and from the courses may be extra-cost and club rental is about $30 extra, but carts are included. The golf excursions are often sold directly through an onboard golf pro who organizes lessons on the ship, too.

2 King's Wharf

Now Bermuda's main port, historic King's Wharf in the West End is the only one of the country's three ports with the facilities to handle today's megaships (such as Royal Caribbean's 3,114-passenger Voyager-class vessels). It's located in the extreme northwest of Bermuda on Ireland Island in Sandys Parish, one of Bermuda's six main islands. The wharf is part of the historic **Royal Naval Dockyard** fortress complex, built by the British in the early 1800s as protection from potential attacks by America.

COMING ASHORE   Ships tie up at a newly refurbished pier within walking distance of the Bermuda Maritime Museum (see below).

GETTING AROUND   You can walk to the main attraction here, the Royal Naval Dockyard military fortress and its Maritime Museum (see below), or if you're beach-bound or heading for a day of golf, **taxis** line up at the docks and a ferry terminal nearby. (See section 1, "Attractions Around Bermuda," above.)

On Your Own: Within Walking Distance

Just steps from the ships is the **Royal Naval Dockyard,** a sprawling, 6-acre 19th-century fortress constructed with convict labor. It was used by the British Navy until 1951 as a strategic dockyard. Today, it's a major tourist attraction whose centerpiece is the **Bermuda Maritime Museum** (✆ **441/234-1418;** www.bmm.bm), the most important and extensive museum on the island. Exhibits are housed in six large halls within the complex, and the displays all relate to Bermuda's long connection with the sea, from Spanish exploration to 20th-century ocean liners. You can have a look at maps, ship models, and such artifacts as gold bars, pottery, jewelry, and silver coins recovered from 16th- and 17th-century shipwrecks such as the *Sea Venture*. Open daily from 9:30am to 5pm (last admission at 3pm); admission is $10 adults and children ages 13 and over, $8 seniors. The Royal Naval Dockyard complex also includes restaurants, shops, an art gallery, and a crafts market. Nearby is a **marina** where you can sign up for parasailing or rent a boat.

3 Hamilton

Hamilton was once known as the Show Window of the British Empire. It has been the capital of Bermuda since 1815, when it replaced St. George's. Today, it's the economic hub of the island.

COMING ASHORE   Only medium and small ships (such as Regent's *Seven Seas Navigator*) dock in Hamilton. Ships tie up at piers smack-dab in the middle of town. The terminal funnels guests into the main shopping drag on Front Street.

GETTING AROUND   You can walk to all of the shops and department stores in town, or take a walking tour for a more historic perspective. Walking-tour maps are available in the terminal. If you're beach-bound or heading for a day of golf or some other attraction, there are **taxis** lined up outside the terminal. For old-timey town tours, **horse-drawn carriages** wait outside the terminal.

On Your Own: Within Walking Distance

A walking tour is a great option. Pick up a map in the cruise terminal and you're on your leisurely way to visiting sights that range from a 200-year-old post office to exhibits in the Bermuda Historical Society Museum. If a relaxing lunch on the waterfront sounds appealing, stroll on over to the waterside **Poinciana Terrace at the Waterloo House,** on Pitts Bay Road (© 441/295-4480), an elegant property within walking distance of the ship docks. Lunch is served on the outdoor patio overlooking the colorful and idyllic harbor. If it's on the menu, the fish chowder, laced with rum and sherry peppers, is a local favorite and a great choice. Lunch costs around $30.

Consider a visit to the **Bermuda Underwater Exploration Institute** (© 441/292-7219; www.buei.org); it's adjacent to the Hamilton docks near the roundabout on East Broadway. There are two floors of interactive exhibits about the ocean, plus the highlight: a capsule that simulates a 3,600m (11,800-ft.) dive below the ocean's surface (it accommodates 21 people at a time). Open 9am to 5pm Monday through Friday, 10am to 5pm Saturday and Sunday (last admission is 3pm); admission is $13 for adults and $6 for kids ages 7 to 16.

4 St. George's

Quaint and historic, St. George's was the second English town established in the New World, after Jamestown in Virginia. King's Square, also called Market Square or the King's Parade, is the center of life here. But because most ships are too big to dock here, this charming little town is visited only by those taking a tour or willing to use a bus, ferry, or taxi to reach it (which does help keep the number of visitors down).

COMING ASHORE   Cruise ships tie up at the edge of the small town, though as the ships going to Bermuda get increasingly larger, few ships dock at St George's these days. Still, you can easily visit the historic town via taxi or bus from Hamilton and King's Wharf.

GETTING AROUND   You can walk to a handful of historic attractions (see below), or if you're beach-bound or heading for a day of golf or some other attraction, you'll be able to find a **taxi** at the dock.

On Your Own: Within Walking Distance

A great option is grabbing a free walking-tour map from the tourism office in King's Square, just steps from your ship. Sights on the tour include **Ordnance Island,** a tiny piece of land that juts into the harbor just in front of the dock, where a replica of *Deliverance*—the vessel that carried the shipwrecked *Sea Venture* passengers on to Virginia—stands. Don't miss a quick stop at **St. Peter's Church,** on Duke of York Street, believed to be the oldest Anglican place of worship in the Western Hemisphere; some headstones in the cemetery date back 300 years, and the present church was built in 1713. The oldest stone building in Bermuda, the **Old State House,** built about 1620, sits at the top of King Street and was once the home of the Bermuda Parliament. At the intersection of Featherbed Alley and Duke of Kent Street, **St. George's Historical Society Museum** houses a collection of Bermudian historic artifacts and cedar furniture.

A mile or so from King's Square in St. George's (many walk it, some hop in taxis), overlooking the beach where the shipwrecked crew of the *Sea Venture* came ashore in 1609, is Fort St. Catherine, which you'll want to see. Completed in 1614, and reconstructed several times after, it was named for the patron saint of wheelwrights and carpenters. The fortress houses a museum, with several worthwhile exhibits. Admission costs $5 for adults and $2 for kids.

14

Hawaii

Honeymooners flock here for a reason: The place is gorgeous and culturally vibrant. Even *The Brady Bunch* schlepped Alice and the six kids to Hawaii (you didn't see them going to Disney World, did you?). However, it's not all about surfer boys and hula girls. The diverse landscape on this cluster of islands in the Pacific ranges from fuming volcanoes to crashing surf, serene beaches, and lush jungles. In a place where the weather really is perfect all the time, it's no surprise that the locals are so mellow. Learn to surf, go to a luau, snooze on the sand, float in warm water surrounded by rainbow-colored tropical fish, enjoy the local coffee, or check out the native Hawaiian culture, of which the locals are fiercely proud. The past survives alongside the modern world in a vibrant arts scene, which includes traditional Polynesian dance and music, as well as painting, sculpture, and crafts. You'll also likely get a glimpse of age-old customs such as outrigger canoe races, the most popular sport in all of Hawaii, and, of course, the ubiquitous ukulele playing.

Norwegian Cruise Line (NCL) has one year-round ship that cruises among the islands round-trip from Honolulu. Thanks to some intense lobbying in Congress a few years back, NCL's Hawaii vessel sails under the U.S. flag, which means the ship can concentrate solely on the islands and doesn't have to throw in a call

to a foreign port (a requirement for foreign-flagged vessels). In isolated Hawaii, this is a real advantage and no other competing line currently has it (see NCL review on p. 192 for details).

Aside from NCL's cruises, other ships typically stop in the islands in April, May, September, and October. The four main ports here are **Oahu,** where you'll find the famous Waikiki Beach; **Maui,** home of the historic town of Lahaina; **Kauai,** the most natural and undeveloped of the four; and Kona and Hilo on the **Big Island,** home of the state's famous volcanoes, including Mauna Kea and the still-active Kilauea.

HOME PORTS FOR THIS REGION
Honolulu, on Oahu, is the main hub for inter-island cruises. Foreign-flagged vessels generally sail from the mainland—from ports such as **Ensenada** (Mexico), **San Diego, Seattle,** and/or **Vancouver**—hitting the Hawaiian Islands as they cruise between seasons in the Caribbean and Alaska.

LANGUAGE & CURRENCY While **English** is the official language, it is infused with a few native **Hawaiian** words, including the customary greeting, *aloha.* (Contrary to what you may believe, "Book 'em, Danno" is not actually a native phrase.) The **U.S. dollar** is the official currency.

1 Oahu

Oahu is a relatively small island, measuring 26 miles long and some 44 miles across at its widest, totaling 597 square miles of land, with 112 miles of coastline. Everyone ventures to Oahu seeking a different experience. Some talk about wanting to find the "real" Hawaii, some are looking for heart-pounding adventure, some yearn for the relaxing and healing powers of the islands, and others are drawn by Hawaii's aloha spirit, where kindness and friendliness prevail.

All kinds of memorable experiences can be yours here. Imagine yourself sitting in a kayak watching the brilliant colors of dawn etched across the sky; sipping a mai tai while taking in sweeping views of the south shore and the Waianae Mountains; battling a magnificent game fish on a high-tech sport-fishing boat; or listening to melodic voices chant the stories of a proud people and a proud culture that was overthrown little more than a century ago. By far the most social of the islands, Oahu has some of the best shopping and most fashionable promenade strips, as well as beautiful beaches with all the classic ingredients: tall palms, white sand, gentle surf, and plenty of sunshine. **Waikiki Beach** offers the best of both worlds. Its trendy eateries, high-end hotels, and ritzy shops collide with a stunning beachfront. It's like Rodeo Drive meets South Beach, only better.

COMING ASHORE Ships dock at the Port of Honolulu, alongside the festive, well-appointed **Aloha Tower Marketplace** in Honolulu. Half shopping center, half cruise pier and promenade, this waterfront two-level mall centers around a five-story tower built in the 1920s. It's a landmark focal point that can easily be spotted around town. There is docking space for three ships, including one at the new $25-million Pier 2 cruise terminal.

GETTING AROUND Aloha Tower is a convenient jumping-off point for walking tours of the downtown historic sites, and it's just a short taxi ride to nearby beaches, shopping, and museums. **Taxis** queue up at the information booth near the adjacent parking area; a ride to Ala Moana Beach costs about $10 for up to five people. If you miss out, call **City Taxi** (🕾 **808/524-2121;** www.citytaxihonolulu.com) or hop on the San Francisco–style open-air trolley called **Waikiki Trolley** (🕾 **800/824-8804** or 808/593-2822; www.waikikitrolley.com), which runs to Ala Moana shopping center, Ala Moana Beach, and downtown. **TheBus** (🕾 **808/848-5555;** www.thebus.org) leaves every 30 minutes or so from in front of the Maritime Center and stops at several locations. You can also pick up a **rental car** at the nearby airport, but with so many other transportation options, it's unnecessary (and the one-way road system can be confusing).

Best Cruise Line Shore Excursions

Pearl Harbor and USS *Missouri* ($75 adults, $60 children, 6½ hr.): For those old enough to remember World War II and those who can't forget 9/11, a tour of Pearl Harbor and the USS *Missouri* is a deeply moving experience.

Grand Circle Island Tour ($105 adults, $80 children, 7 hr.): Given the island's immense natural beauty, a drive around Oahu is time well spent (make sure to bring your camera with you on the bus!). Views from inside Diamond Head Crater, an extinct volcano, rival those of the breathtaking carved shoreline at Hanauma Bay or the sweeping coastal vistas from Pali Lookout. Lunch is included.

On Your Own: Within Walking Distance

A short walk up Richards Street, across Nimitz Highway, brings you into downtown Honolulu. If you go right on South King Street, you'll come to a statue of **King Kamehameha I,** the famed Hawaiian ruler. Across the street, at the corner of South

King and Richards streets, stands **Iolani Palace** (© 808/522-0832; www.
iolanipalace.org), America's only royal residence, where Hawaii's last monarch ruled
until 1893. The building of this Italian Renaissance palace, which had electricity
before both the White House and Buckingham Palace, nearly bankrupted the kingdom. The palace is open Monday to Saturday from 9am to 5pm. Admission for the
self-guided gallery tours is $6 adults and $3 children ages 5 to 12; if you would like
the 45-minute audio tours (a self-guided tour with a prerecorded audio hookup), the
fee is $13 adults and $5 children ages 5 to 12. We recommend the docent-guided
tours, Tuesday to Saturday only, which leave every 15 minutes from 9 to 11:15am and
costs $20 adults and $5 children ages 5 to 12 (kids ages 4 and under admitted only in
the gallery).

One block up King Street, **Kawaiahao Church,** 957 Punchbowl St. (© 808/
522-1333), was the first stone church built on Oahu and is home to a royal burial
ground. If you're lucky enough to be there on Sunday, there's a service in Hawaiian
(with divine singing) at 9am. Admission is free (though donations are happily
accepted). Next door is the **Mission House Museum,** 553 S. King St. (© 808/531-
0481; www.missionhouses.org), a cute old mission house open for tours Tuesday
through Saturday. Guided tours take place at 11am, 1, and 2:45pm. Admission is $10
adults, $8 seniors, $6 kids (6 years to college-age), free for kids ages 5 and under; tickets must be purchased in advance.

Walk 5 blocks west from the museum along South King Street and you'll come to
America's oldest **Chinatown.** Selling everything from flower leis to exotic fruits and
vegetables, this crowded market area is a haggler's dream.

On Your Own: Beyond the Port Area

Just north of Lunalilo Freeway at the end of Puowaina Drive is **Punchbowl Crater,**
which houses the **National Memorial Cemetery of the Pacific** (© 808/532-3720;
www.interment.net/data/us/hi/oahu/natmem/index.htm). This natural landscape feature, called "hill of sacrifice" by early Hawaiians, now serves as a burial ground for
3,500 victims of war. Admission is free.

To really learn about the history of Hawaii and its people, drop in at the **Bishop
Museum,** 1525 Bernice St. (© 808/847-3511; www.bishopmuseum.org). Created in
1889, and now the State Museum of Natural and Cultural History, this Victorian
building houses an extensive collection of artifacts from ancient Polynesians, Hawaiian royalty, turn-of-the-20th-century immigrants, and more. Daily cultural and science shows and tours enrich the experience and cover topics from volcanoes to
astronomy and ancient explorers.

At **Pearl Harbor** (© 808/422-0561), you can't miss the **USS *Arizona* Memorial**
(© 808/422-2771 for recorded info or 808/422-2771; www.nps.gov/usar), built
right above the shallow water where the ship was sunk on December 7, 1941, or the
battleship **USS *Missouri*** (© 877/MIGHTYMO [644-4896] or 808/423-2263;
www.ussmissouri.com), on the decks of which Japan surrendered to the Allies on September 2, 1945. The USS *Arizona* visitor center is open daily from 7am to 5pm, with
timed programs to the memorial from 8am to 3pm. Admission is free. The USS *Missouri* is open daily from 9am to 5pm. Tickets are $29 adults, $10 children ages 4 to
12, plus additional fees for guided tours. What you may not notice, but should, is the
USS *Bowfin* Submarine Museum and Park (© 808/423-1341; www.bowfin.org).

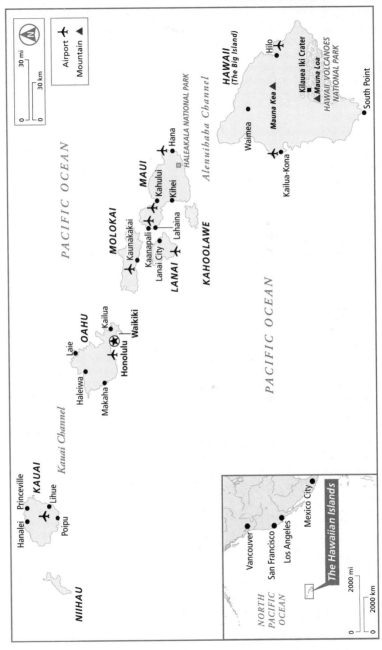

The Hawaiian Islands

Airport ✈ **Mountain** ▲

PACIFIC OCEAN

NIIHAU

KAUAI

Hanalei Princeville
Lihue
Poipu

Kauai Channel

OAHU

Laie
Kailua
Haleiwa
Honolulu Waikiki
Makaha

MOLOKAI

Kaunakakai

LANAI

Kaanapali
Lanai City

MAUI

Kahului
Kihei
Lahaina
Hana

HALEAKALA NATIONAL PARK

KAHOOLAWE

Alenuihaha Channel

PACIFIC OCEAN

HAWAII
(The Big Island)

Hilo
Kilauea Iki Crater
Mauna Kea ▲
Mauna Loa ▲
HAWAII VOLCANOES NATIONAL PARK
Waimea
Kailua-Kona
South Point

The Hawaiian Islands

NORTH PACIFIC OCEAN

Vancouver
San Francisco
Los Angeles
Mexico City

635

This National Historic Landmark provides a rare glimpse into the thrill and danger of life aboard a submarine. The self-guided audio tour is narrated by the vessel's last captain, who takes you through the cramped quarters where men slept nose to nose with torpedoes, bathed in minuscule showers, and took turns dining in the tiny galley. This tour is not recommended for people with claustrophobia or those who have difficulty going up or down ladders. The museum is open daily from 7am to 5pm. Admission is $10 adults, $7 seniors, $4 kids ages 4 to 12.

Beaches

Nearby **Ala Moana Beach Park,** on Ala Moana Park Drive, has white sand and calm warm water—it's perfect for families. Like most beaches in Hawaii, it's free and uncrowded, especially on weekdays. It has a paved walkway and grassy areas where you can lounge or picnic under a tree. A taxi ride to here costs about $10 from the port, or you can catch a bus from the Maritime Center for $2.25 or so. For more information, call or access the website (© **808/848-5555;** www.thebus.org). Buses also allow access to all the beaches below.

A few miles south is the famous **Waikiki Beach.** One-way taxi fare will run about $20. This beach is popular with locals, who will often occupy the cement picnic tables under open-air shelters and play chess or just watch the action. While surprisingly small, it is favored for surfing, suntanning, or just people-watching. Restrooms, showers, and beach rentals are all found at the far end near Kapiolani Park.

Sandy Beach, on the eastern tip of the island, is a favorite spot for boogie boarding. While the white crashing surf may look appealing, take a moment to read the numerous warning signs, and exercise great care—lifeguards do more beach rescues here than anywhere else. If a red flag is flying, it means the surf is too dangerous to enter. A taxi will cost between $50 and $75 each way; keep in mind that many taxis can accommodate six or eight passengers, so the fare can be shared.

Another popular beach is **Hanauma Bay,** nestled in a volcanic crater just before Sandy Beach. Depending on where your ship docks, taxi fare to Hanauma Bay can cost about $45 to $60. You approach the beach from above and pass through the Marine Education Center, which also provides a motorized tram that takes you down the steep road to the beach and back for $1 round-trip. There's a $5 entrance fee; the beach is closed Tuesday. There is also a shuttle ($2.25 each way) from Waikiki to Hanauma Bay, which runs every half-hour between 9am and 1pm, with stops at city bus stops and several hotels.

Shopping

The majority of stores in **Aloha Tower** cater to tourists and sell uniquely Hawaiian wares. Some fine carved wood and bark cloth can be found at a few shops on the second level. For those who like to indulge in serious window-shopping, head to **Kalakaua Avenue** at Waikiki Beach, where you can find everything from Coach bags to board shorts, all on a bustling strip complete with statues, reflecting pools, street performers, and, at dusk, flaming tiki torches and alfresco dining. To see some of the island's handmade artwork, drop into the **Nohea Gallery,** in the lobby of the Moana Surfrider, A Westin Resort & Spa, 2365 Kalakaua Ave. (© **808/922-3111;** www. moana-surfrider.com).

If You're Embarking in Honolulu . . .

WHERE TO STAY   In the minds of many, Oahu and its most famous city, Honolulu, are synonymous. Honolulu's best-known neighborhood, Waikiki, is actually pretty small, but its spectacular beach and array of resort hotels are the attractions that originally put Hawaii on the tourist map. The choices for accommodations are nearly limitless, ranging from budget to ultraluxury.

For families watching their wallets, there are nearly a dozen **Outrigger and Ohana Hotels** that offer clean and affordable lodging in Waikiki, including **Ohana Waikiki West,** 2330 Kuhio Ave. (© **808/922-5022;** www.ohanahotels. com), 2 blocks from Waikiki Beach. Downside? It's on a very busy part of Kuhio Avenue. But rooms can go as low as $79 per night in the off season. To escape the hustle and bustle, head over to the **Breakers,** 250 Beachwalk (© **808/923-3181;** www.breakers-hawaii.com), for spacious motel-style rooms that surround a tranquil pool and garden; rates start at about $130.

Trendy visitors should check into the **Aston Waikiki Beach Hotel,** 2570 Kalakaua Ave. (© **866/77-HAWAII** [774-2924]; www.astonhotels.com), where New York City chic meets Miami cool. Check out the surfboards adorning the walls of the lobby. Rates for a standard room start as low as $125 double. If it's a Victorian setting you crave, don't miss the **Moana Surfrider,** A Westin Resort & Spa, 2365 Kalakaua Ave. (© **808/922-3111;** www.moana-surfrider. com). Lovingly referred to as the first lady of Waikiki, this grand hotel debuted in 1901 as the first true resort on the island and still retains the same elegance and charm it started with 110 years ago. Rates for a standard room can dip as low as $235 for a double in low season.

WHERE TO DINE   On the second floor of the Aston Waikiki Beach Hotel, **Tiki's Grill and Bar,** 2570 Kalakaua Ave. (© **808/923-TIKI** [923-8454]; www. tikisgrill.com), is a restaurant and open-air tiki bar that overlooks the promenade and beach. The live music plays second fiddle to the sunset views and trendy crowd. The cuisine is good ol' American with a touch of Pacific Rim, apparent in all the fish dishes. Tiki's signature dish is king salmon glazed with lemon grass beurre blanc. Main courses at lunch run $14 to $20 and at dinner about $26 to $42.

Surprisingly popular is the **Cheesecake Factory,** the Royal Hawaiian Shopping Center (© **808/924-5001**). Serving its standard plethora of trendy dishes in heaping portions, the place has alfresco dining and a central location, which means there's usually a wait for a table. Main courses cost $16 to $34.

With an equally long wait, but lower price tag, **Cheeseburger in Paradise,** 2500 Kalakaua Ave. (© **808/923-3731**), delivers exactly that. Served in a basket, with a side of fries, the burgers come in nearly every incarnation, including chili, guacamole, bacon, and "Island Style," with a slice of grilled Maui pineapple. There are also tasty salads and veggie or tofu burgers, with or without cheese. Main courses average $10 to $16.

For a serene outdoor dining experience, try dinner on the **Veranda,** at the Moana Surfrider, A Westin Resort & Spa (see "Where to Stay," above). Dinner is available nightly from 5:30 to 9pm. Afternoon tea is served Monday through Saturday from 1 to 4pm and Sunday from 3 to 4pm.

2 Kauai

Kauai ranks right up there with Bora Bora, Huahine, and Rarotonga on any list of the world's most spectacular islands. All the elements are here: moody rainforests, majestic cliffs, jagged peaks, emerald valleys, palm trees swaying in the breeze, daily rainbows, and some of the most spectacular beaches you'll find anywhere. Soft tropical air, sunrise bird song, essences of ginger and plumeria, golden sunsets, sparkling waterfalls—you don't just go to Kauai, you absorb it with all of your senses. It may get more than its fair share of tropical downpours, but that's what makes it so lush and green—and creates an abundance of rainbows.

Kauai is essentially a single large shield volcano that rises 3 miles above the sea floor. The island lies 90 miles across the open ocean from Oahu, but it seems at least a half-century removed in time. It's often called "the separate kingdom" because it stood alone and resisted King Kamehameha's efforts to unite Hawaii. In the end, a royal kidnapping was required to take the Garden Isle: After King Kamehameha died, his son, Liholiho, ascended the throne. He gained control of Kauai by luring Kauai's king, Kaumualii, aboard the royal yacht and then sailing to Oahu; once there, Kaumualii was forced to marry Kaahumanu, Kamehameha's widow, thereby uniting the islands.

A Kauai rule is that no building may exceed the height of a coconut tree—between three and four stories. As a result, the island itself, not its palatial beach hotels, is the attention grabber. There are no opulent shopping malls here, but what Kauai lacks in glitz, it more than makes up for in sheer natural splendor, with verdant jungles, the endless succession of spectacular beaches, the grandeur of Waimea Canyon, and the drama of the Napali Coast. Many Hollywood movies were filmed here, including *Raiders of the Lost Ark; Six Days, Seven Nights;* and parts of all three *Jurassic Park* films.

COMING ASHORE   About the only fun thing to do at **Nawiliwili Harbor** is pronounce the name (*Nah*-willy-willy). The port can accommodate two ships at a time: one at a pier, and one anchored with a short tender ride. Some of the small local malls have free shuttle buses, but the real attraction is the phenomenal beach that is tucked quietly behind the Anchor Cove shopping mall, less than a mile from the pier.

GETTING AROUND   Taxis from the **Kauai Taxi Company** (② **808/246-9554**) and other companies typically meet cruise ships at the pier. Meters start at $3, plus $3 for each additional mile.

Best Cruise Line Shore Excursions

Jungle Mountain Trek, Wagon & Zipline Adventure ($155 adults, $125 children, 7 hr.): Paddle a kayak through a mangrove forest, soar across a jungle stream on a high-wire zipline, swing from a rope swing, leap off a waterfall, and more on this action-packed all-day adventure. This excursion takes you along jungle trails to some of the most scenic waterfalls and ponds in the area. The beauty of the surrounding mountains is sublime, and the guides do a colorful retelling of ancient folklore while you ride in a tractor-pulled wagon through a green valley surrounded by ridges and peaks that served as inspiration for the folklore. Be sure to wear comfortable walking shoes; bring a swimsuit and a towel, too. Lunch is served on a treehouse platform near a waterfall.

Waimea River & Fern Grotto ($55 adults, $45 children, 3½ hr.): This excursion takes you to some of the most breathtaking and contrasting natural wonders of Kauai. First, visit the jagged red-earth cliffs and canyons of Waimea, the Grand Canyon of the Pacific, with a depth of 2,587 feet. Once you've had enough time to marvel at the view (don't forget a camera!), you're off via riverboat to explore the verdant green valley of Fern Grotto. Break in your shoes before you take this excursion. Lunch is included.

Tubing the Ditch ($140, 3 hr.): Travel to a former sugar cane plantation in Kauai's interior and the headwaters of the Hanamaulu Ditch system, a series of open ditches, tunnels, and flumes that once provided irrigation for the farmlands. There, you'll get an inner tube, be outfitted with helmet lamps, and begin your float trip through the tunnels. Not for the claustrophobic!

On Your Own: Within Walking Distance

A few shopping malls are a short walk from the pier (see "Shopping," below) and a sunny beach is even closer still (see "Beaches," below). Otherwise, you'll need wheels of one sort or another.

On Your Own: Beyond the Port Area

To understand life in a small town built around a sugar plantation, head to **Old Koloa Town.** This tiny collection of small wooden buildings, now turned into shops and restaurants, was the new home for waves of immigrants who came to work on the sugar plantations. In the center of town is a small history center that houses a few artifacts from the turn of the 20th century. Plaques on each building describe the original purpose and history. It's about an hour's drive from the harbor, so this is a good bet only for those who've rented wheels.

A visit to the **Allerton and McBryde Gardens** of the **National Tropical Botanical Garden,** Lawai Road, across the street from Spouting Horn, Poipu (© **808/742-2623;** www.ntbg.org), will leave you breathless as you wander amid the intoxicating array of tropical flowers and fragrances. Take a self-guided tour of McBryde Garden, Monday through Saturday 9am to 4pm ($20 adults, $10 kids ages 6–12); or better yet, the guided tour of Allerton Garden, Monday through Saturday at 9 and 10am, and 1 and 2pm ($45 adults, $20 children ages 10–12), to learn about the many useful and culturally significant plants growing in this green oasis. Trams run Monday through Saturday from 9:30am to 2:30pm.

Beaches

Nestled just behind the Anchor Cove shopping center, less than a mile from the pier, is **Kalapaki Beach.** Used by locals and tourists, this strip of natural beauty seems out of place next to the parking lot and strip mall. Protected by a jetty and patrolled by lifeguards, the beach is safe for swimming and ideal for families with children. Restrooms are available at the nearby restaurants, where you can also change and grab a snack.

Beautiful **Poipu Beach** can be reached by heading south from the port along Highway 50 for about 15 miles. This romantic spot has crystal-blue water, pure white sand, palm trees, and even a patch of grass big enough for a game of Frisbee. At the eastern end is a small beach with lava rocks and moderate surf, while to the west, you'll see a string of small crescent beaches. Watch for rare and endangered Hawaiian monk seals that occasionally haul out and lounge on the sand. While seemingly tame, they are dangerous to approach and protected by law. In addition to lifeguards, there are showers, restrooms, and covered picnic areas. A taxi here costs about $38 each way.

Heading north on Highway 56, up the Coconut Coast to the North Shore is **Kee Beach,** a favorite among locals. At the northern tip is a deep but calm swimming area in summer, though just off to the left (when facing the sea) are some dangerous and very sharp rocks just beyond the surf, so take care before you rush in. There are no lifeguards, so stay in the same swimming area as everyone else. If no one is in the water, it is usually for good reason. A taxi runs about $130 each way; but many cars can carry up to six passengers, so you can share the cost with some of your shipmates.

Shopping

At the **Anchor Cove** shopping center, you can purchase some of the most breathtaking pearl jewelry this side of Asia. For spectacular artwork made out of glass, go north on Kuhio Highway and stop in at **Kela's Glass Gallery,** 4–1354 Kuhio Hwy., Kapaa (© **888/255-3527** or 808/822-4527; www.glass-art.com). Along the Coconut Coast is the **Yellowfish Trading Company,** in the town of Hanalei (© **808/826-1227**), where kitschy Hawaiiana hearkens back to the 1950s. Also in Hanalei are **Lotus Gallery** (© **808/828-9898**), a showstopper for lovers of antiques and designer jewelry, and **Ola's,** by the Hanalei River on the Kuhio Highway (Hwy. 560) after the bridge and before the main part of Hanalei town (© **808/826-6937**), where you will find a unique selection of island crafts, from one-of-a-kind furniture (they'll ship it home for you) to hand-blown glass, exquisite jewelry, and many other fine works. For foodies, check out Kauau Kookie Kompany, Kauai Coffee, and Kauai Tropical Fudge—yum!

3 Maui

Maui, also called the Valley Isle, is just a small dot in the vast Pacific Ocean, but it has the potential to allow visitors unforgettable experiences: floating weightless through rainbows of tropical fish, standing atop a 10,000-foot volcano and watching the sunrise color the sky, listening to the raindrops in a bamboo forest, and sunning on idyllic beaches. The island is also packed with interesting cultural sights and colorful history. Here, you can set foot on the spot where ancient Hawaiian royalty and priests once walked, gathered, and worshipped. Later, at the turn of the 20th century, it became a bustling home to native Hawaiians, immigrants, and missionaries. Cruise ships call on two ports, **Kahului** and **Lahaina.**

Kahului

COMING ASHORE   Coming ashore at the **Port of Kahului,** an industrial port that can accommodate one cruise ship at a time, may leave you less than inspired. Don't bother braving the maze of roads that weave around containers and warehouses—all that lies beyond in the immediate vicinity are strip malls and roads. It's best to hop in a taxi to explore the island or sign up for one of the shore excursions.

GETTING AROUND   **Taxis,** as well as **shuttle buses,** line up in an orderly fashion under large, well-marked signs at the pier. If for some reason you don't see one, try **Sunshine Cabs of Maui** (© **808/879-2220**) or **Islandwide Taxi and Tours** (© **808/ 667-5646**). Rates are $3.50 for the first ⅛ mile, plus $3 for each additional mile.

Best Cruise Line Shore Excursions

Haleakala Crater at Sunrise ($75, 6 hr.): Don't miss this chance to experience the dramatic landscape of a dormant volcano. Haleakala, whose vast crater measures 7½ by 2½ miles and is 3,000 feet deep, last erupted in 1790. As you ascend, the terrain changes from forest to scrub to a seemingly barren wasteland near the top. Surprisingly, it is here among the lava rocks and chilly slopes that some of Hawaii's most rare and endangered species of plants and animals can be found. Bring a sweater, as temperatures at the top can sink as low as 40°F (4°C).

Ocean Center & Iao Valley ($55 adults, $45 children, 3½ hr.): This tour combines a visit to a modern interactive aquarium that displays Hawaii's indigenous marine life with a visit to Iao Valley, a lush state park and sacred site of religious and cultural significance for ancient Hawaiians.

Maui Whale-Watch ($80 adults, $55 children, 3 hr.): Some things have to be seen in person, and a breaching whale is one of them. The beauty and grace of these behemoths as they glide between our world and theirs is not to be missed. And, with such an abundance of whales here (about a third of all Pacific whales migrate here for the winter), your chances of seeing one are good (though not absolute). A guide from the Pacific Whale Foundation shares insights into the animals' behavior as you "listen in" to the mammals' conversation via underwater hydrophones. *Note:* This tour is usually offered from mid-December to April only.

On Your Own: Within Walking Distance

The Kahului harbor functions as a working cargo port in addition to serving cruise ships, and the area around the dock is the residential center of the island—lots of subdivisions, a few shopping centers, and not much else. For the most part, you'll need to take a taxi to see the sights, or take a shore excursion. The exception to that rule is the **Kanaha Wildlife Sanctuary,** Haleakala Highway Extension and Hana Highway (© 808/984-8100), situated within walking distance of the dock, next to Maui's busiest intersection and across from Costco and Kmart in Kahului's new business park. Look for the parking area off Haleakala Highway Extension (behind the mall, across the Hana Hwy. from Cutter Automotive), and you'll find a 50-foot trail that meanders along the shore to a shade shelter and lookout. Look for the sign proclaiming this the permanent home of the endangered black-neck Hawaiian stilt, whose population is now down to about 1,000. Naturalists say this is also a good place to see endangered Hawaiian Koloa ducks, stilt, coots, and other migrating shorebirds.

On Your Own: Beyond the Port Area

Next door to the town of Kahului is **Wailuku,** the county seat, worth a visit for a little antiquing and a visit to the **Bailey House Museum,** 2375–A Main St. (© 808/244-3326; www.mauimuseum.org). Missionary and sugar planter Edward Bailey's 1833 home, an architectural hybrid of stones laid by Hawaiian craftsmen and timbers joined in a display of Yankee ingenuity, is a treasure-trove of Hawaiiana. Inside, you'll find an eclectic collection, from precontact artifacts like scary temple images, dogtooth necklaces, and a rare lei made of tree-snail shells to latter-day relics like Duke Kahanamoku's 1919 redwood surfboard and a koa-wood table given to President Ulysses S. Grant, who refused it because he couldn't accept gifts from foreign countries. There's also a gallery devoted to a few of Bailey's landscapes, painted from 1866 to 1896, which capture on canvas a Maui we can only imagine today. The museum is open Monday to Saturday from 10am to 4pm. Admission is $7 adults, $5 seniors, and $2 children ages 7 to 12.

A couple of miles north of Wailuku, where the little plantation houses stop and the road climbs ever higher, Maui's true nature is revealed. The transition from suburban sprawl to raw nature is so abrupt that most people who drive up into the valley don't realize they're suddenly in a rainforest. The moist, cool air and the shade are a welcome comfort after the hot tropical sun. This is **Iao Valley,** a 6¼-acre state park whose nature, history, and beauty have been enjoyed by millions of people from around the world for more than a century. Iao ("Supreme Light") Valley, 10 miles long and encompassing 4,000 acres, is the eroded volcanic caldera of the West Maui Mountains. The head of the valley is a broad circular amphitheater where four major streams converge into Iao Stream. At the back of the amphitheater is rain-drenched Puu Kukui, the West Maui Mountains' highest point. No other Hawaiian valley lets you go from seacoast to rainforest so easily. This peaceful valley, full of tropical plants, rainbows, waterfalls, swimming holes, and hiking trails, is a place of solitude, reflection, and escape for residents and visitors alike.

The main attraction is the feature known as **Iao Needle,** an erosional remnant consisting of basalt dikes. This phallic rock juts an impressive 2,250 feet above sea level. Youngsters play in **Iao Stream,** a peaceful brook that belies its bloody history. In 1790, King Kamehameha the Great and his men engaged in the battle of Iao Valley to gain control of Maui. When the battle ended, so many bodies blocked Iao Stream that the battle site was named Kepaniwai, or "damming of the waters." An architectural heritage park of Hawaiian, Japanese, Chinese, Filipino, and New England–style houses stands in harmony by Iao Stream at **Kepaniwai Heritage Garden.** This is a good picnic spot, with plenty of tables and benches. You can see ferns, banana trees, and other native and exotic plants in the **Iao Valley Botanic Garden** along the stream.

About 3 miles south of Wailuku lies the tiny, one-street village of Waikapu, which has two attractions that are worth a peek. Relive Maui's past by taking a 40-minute narrated tram ride around fields of pineapple, sugar cane, and papaya trees at **Maui Tropical Plantation,** 1670 Honoapiilani Hwy. (© **800/451-6805** or 808/244-7643; www.mauitropicalplantation.com), a real working plantation that's open daily. A shop sells fresh and dried fruit, and a restaurant serves lunch. Admission is free. The tram tours which run daily from 10am to 3:15pm and leave about every 45 minutes, cost $14 adults, $5 kids ages 3 to 12.

Beaches

About 2 miles from the pier is the long and wide **Kanaha Beach Park.** Because there are no lifeguards here, swimming is at your own risk, though the white sand and sweeping vista make lounging on the sand and dabbling your toes in the water enough of a reward. Kanaha has restrooms, showers, a picnic area, picnic tables, a campsite, and parking. Head up to **Hookipa Beach** to relax and watch windsurfers from around the world sail the waves. While not always safe for swimming, this is the best free windsurfing stunt show in town. The beach has restrooms, showers, picnic tables, barbecue pits, and parking.

Shopping

A stroll along Wailuku's Main and Market streets presents a mixed shopping bag, but usually turns up a treasure or two. For made-in-Hawaii items, you can't beat the **Bailey House Museum Shop,** 2375–A Main St. (© **808/244-3326**), which has a remarkable selection of gift items, from Hawaiian music and books to exquisite woods, traditional Hawaiian games, *pareu* (a colorful wrap worn by Polynesian men and women), and prints by the legendary Hawaii artist Madge Tennent.

Lahaina

COMING ASHORE   One ship at a time can anchor offshore at the **Port of Lahaina.** A 10-minute tender ride takes passengers across the small harbor and alongside a pier right in the middle of town.

GETTING AROUND   Just about everything you might want to do—from sightseeing to shopping, beaching, and diving—can be done within walking distance of the pier. If you want to venture farther, **taxis** are usually waiting at the pier; if not, call **Alii Taxi** (© 808/661-3688) or **Island Taxi** (© 808/667-5656). Rates are $3.50 a mile.

Best Cruise Line Shore Excursions

Maui Tropical Plantation & Iao Gardens ($62, 3½ hr.): A narrated 40-minute tram tour takes you around the beautiful Maui Tropical Plantation. From there, the tour continues on to Maui's most well-known and beautiful valley gorge.

Ulalena, Myth & Magic ($60, 3 hr.): This evening tour takes in a theatrical presentation about the mythic creation of the islands and the voyagers who have found their way here, from the first Polynesians to Captain Cook and on to the present day.

Atlantis **Submarine Adventure** ($105 adults, $70 children, 5 hr.): If you don't scuba dive, this 65-foot, air-conditioned submarine is the perfect way to view the spectacle of marine life nearly 150 feet below the surface.

On Your Own: Within Walking Distance

Lahaina (© 808/667-9193; www.visitlahaina.com) is one of the most vibrant yet historic towns in Hawaii. It's rich in history, plus loaded with great shops, watersports facilities, and restaurants. Stop by the centrally located **Courthouse** to browse the two art galleries, grab a self-guided walking-tour pamphlet, or check out the historical exhibits at the newly opened **Lahaina Heritage Museum** (© 808/661-1959), on the second floor. The museum is open daily 9am to 4pm; admission is free. Just outside the Courthouse, artists are camped under a great banyan tree, the largest you'll likely ever see.

As you meander among the shops and sights, clearly numbered plaques correspond to the walking tour. Head for the two-story **Pioneer Inn,** 658 Wharf St. (© 808/661-3636), which was Maui's first hotel; the bar remains a favorite watering hole. Then check out the nearby **Baldwin Home Museum,** 120 Dickenson St. (© 808/661-3262; www.lahainarestoration.org), where a local missionary and medical doctor, Dwight Baldwin, single-handedly vaccinated and saved almost the entire town from a deadly smallpox outbreak in the mid–19th century. It's open daily from 10am to 4pm. Admission is $3. Stroll farther down Front Street, heading west, and drop in at the **Wo Hing Museum** (© 808/661-5553), once an ancient Chinese fraternal society. It's open Saturday to Thursday 10am to 4pm, Friday 1 to 8pm. Admission is $2. While the museum merits only a quick tour, don't miss the film loop playing in the adjacent cookhouse—you can view footage of Hawaii shot by Thomas Edison nearly 100 years ago.

On Your Own: Beyond the Port Area

In the Lahaina area, for a unique eating experience, try some local fare at **Aloha Mixed Plate,** 1285 Front St. (© 808/661-3322). Nowhere else short of a luau can you try the local favorites such as *kailua* roast pork (a full pig wrapped in palm leaves and cooked in a fire pit with lava rocks for 12 hr.), *lomi lomi* salmon (fresh salmon minced with raw tomatoes and spices), *lau lau* (pork cooked with taro leaves that taste like fresh spinach), and, of course, the Hawaiian staple, *poi* (a locally beloved but flavorless goo made from taro root). The cultural experience is well worth the short taxi ride from nearby Lahaina. Main courses cost $5 to $14.

The **Maui Ocean Center,** 192 Ma'alaea Rd., in Maalaea, about 12 miles southeast of Lahaina (✆ 808/270-7000; www.mauioceancenter.com), invites you to explore Hawaii's native marine life in a safe and enjoyable setting. This modern family-friendly facility is the largest tropical reef aquarium in the Western Hemisphere. It has both indoor and outdoor exhibits where you can go nose to nose with an octopus, watch a turtle swim, and even touch a squishy sea cucumber. The center is open daily 9am to 5pm (July–Aug to 6pm). Admission is $26 adults, $23 seniors, and $19 children ages 3 to 12.

To learn everything you ever wanted to know about whaling, head to the **Whalers Village Museum,** 2435 Kaanapali Pkwy., Kaanapali (✆ 808/661-5992; www.whalersvillage.com). This compact museum houses a prized collection of scrimshaw and lets you step into the world of whaling through an innovative, self-guided audio tour. It's open daily from 10am to 6pm; admission is free. Kaanapali is the resort area just north of Lahaina, about 2 minutes away by taxi.

Beaches

The beach at **Lahaina** is calm, clean, and a great place to watch new surfers take their first lessons on the baby waves. Located between a stone breakwater and the shops at 505 Front St., this beach is known by locals as either "505" or "the break wall." There are restrooms, shops, and restaurants nearby. **Kaanapali Beach,** directly behind **Whalers Village** (see above), is a safe and popular beach stretching about a mile past several resorts. Beach chairs, umbrellas, kayaks, boogie boards, and other rentals are available at **Snorkel Bob's,** 180 Dickenson St., #116 (✆ 808/661-4421; www.snorkelbob.com), which also operates several other locations around the island.

Shopping

Front Street in Lahaina is a shopper's mecca, with clothing boutiques full of aloha (aka Hawaiian) shirts, jewelry stores selling pearls and tourmaline, and the usual assortment of galleries. The best art can be found at the **Lahaina Arts Society** galleries inside the Courthouse, 648 Wharf St. (✆ 808/661-0111; www.lahaina-arts.com). Not far away on Honoapi'ilani Highway is the **Lahaina Cannery Mall** (✆ 808/661-5304; www.lahainacannery.com), which used to be a huge pineapple cannery; it now houses lots of shops carrying locally made handicrafts. **Whalers Village,** 2435 Kaanapali Pkwy. (✆ 808/661-4567; www.whalersvillage.com), and **Shops at Wailea,** 3750 Wailea Alanui Dr. (✆ 808/891-6770; www.shopsatwailea.com), are both shopping centers featuring upscale classics (Louis Vuitton, Tiffany & Co.), as well as more affordable standards, a la Tommy Bahama. They are also home to a number of restaurants.

4 The Big Island

Big surprise—the Big Island is the largest island in the Hawaiian chain (4,028 sq. miles—about the size of Connecticut), the youngest (800,000 years), and the least populated (with 30 people per sq. mile). It has an unmatched diversity of terrain and climate: fiery volcanoes and sparkling waterfalls, black-lava deserts and snowcapped mountain peaks, tropical rainforests and alpine meadows, a glacial lake, and miles of golden, black, and green (!) sand beaches. A 50-mile drive will take you from snowy winter to sultry summer, passing through spring or fall along the way. The island looks like the inside of a barbecue pit on one side, and a lush jungle on the other. In a word, it's bizarre, and takes some people aback because it doesn't fit the tropical stereotype.

Five volcanoes—one still erupting—have created this island, which is growing bigger every day. At its heart is snowcapped **Mauna Kea,** the world's tallest mountain (measured from the ocean floor), complete with its own glacial lake. Mauna Kea's nearest neighbor is **Mauna Loa** ("Long Mountain"), creator of one-sixth of the island; it's the largest volcano on earth, rising 30,000 feet out of the ocean floor (of course, you can see only the 13,677 ft. that are above sea level). Erupting **Kilauea** makes the Big Island bigger every day—and, if you're lucky and your timing is good, you can stand just a few feet away and watch it do its work. In just a week, the Kilauea volcano can produce enough lava to fill the Houston Astrodome.

Hilo

COMING ASHORE   Up to two cruise ships can pull alongside the docks at the **Port of Hilo,** which is not much more than an industrial port, so don't plan on walking into town. An organized shore excursion is your best bet here.

GETTING AROUND   In the unlikely event there are no **taxis** waiting at the pier, you can call **Ace-1** (© **808/935-8303**). Note that because the island is so big, taxi rides can be quite expensive. Taxis are metered and start at $3; the first mile costs $5.60 and each subsequent ⅛ mile is 30¢.

Best Cruise Line Shore Excursions

If the weather is good, you can't go wrong with a scenic helicopter tour over Kilauea volcano; there is also a variety of golf excursions offered on the Big Island. Otherwise, here are some of our favorite options.

Kilauea Volcano ($55 adults, $32 children, 4¾ hr.): Volcanoes National Park is, by far, Hawaii's premier tourist destination and well worth a visit. On your excursion, you'll get a look at the still-active Kilauea (5,000 ft.), walk the extinct Thurston Lava Tube, and check out the exhibits at the National Volcano Observatory. There's no need to worry about dramatic eruptions; for the most part, Hawaii's volcanoes are quite tame.

Kilauea Lava Viewing Hike ($125 adults, $110 children, 6 hr.): Drive 51 miles, climb 4,000 feet up Kilauea, and then descend to sea level to watch lava flowing into the sea. The land here is some of the newest on earth, formed by the cooling lava sometimes only hours before you arrive. It's often so hot that it'll melt the soles of your sneakers if you don't keep moving. This is one hike that's only for the really fit, requiring a 2- to 6-mile trek on rough surfaces. Many folks who start out don't make it and have to head back to the van without seeing what they came to see.

Waipi'o Valley Waterfall, Hike & Swim ($130, 7 hr.): There is no better way to appreciate the natural beauty of this sacred "Valley of the Kings" than by hiking all the way through it to the spectacular waterfall.

On Your Own: Beyond the Port Area

To enjoy the beauty of a formal Japanese garden, head down Banyan Drive to **Queen Liliuokalani Gardens,** right near **Coconut Island.** This picturesque 30-acre park has many bonsai trees, as well as carp ponds, pagodas, and an arched bridge. To truly understand the power and fury of the Pacific Ocean, visit the **Pacific Tsunami Museum,** 130 Kamehameha Ave. (© **808/935-0926;** www.tsunami.org). Be sure to speak with the volunteers on hand, many of whom have lived through the "walls of water" that hit Hilo in 1946 and 1960. It's open Monday to Saturday 9am to 4pm. Admission is $8 adults, $4 kids ages 6 to 17.

To learn more about Hawaii's marine ecosystems, visit the **Mokupapapa Discovery Center,** 308 Kamehameha Ave., Ste. 109, in the South Hata Building (© **808/933-8180;** www.hawaiireef.noaa.gov). This education facility opened in 2003 and is run by the National Marine Sanctuaries and the National Oceanic and Atmospheric Administration. Exhibits include a 2,500-gallon saltwater aquarium, a number of photographs and murals, and several interactive research stations. It's open Tuesday through Saturday 9am to 4pm. Admission is free.

Beaches

At the start of Banyan Drive (about 2 miles from the cruise dock) is **Reeds Bay Park,** a small beach popular with locals. While there are no lifeguards or facilities here, the shallow water is well protected from waves and jagged rocks, making it ideal for swimming.

Near the other end of Banyan Drive is Moku Ola, or **Coconut Island.** Accessible by a walking bridge, this serene destination is also popular with locals who want to stroll the shady perimeter, bathe in the rocky pools, or swim off the small grassy beaches.

About 3 miles from the pier on Kalanianaole Avenue is **Leleiwi Beach Park.** Not a traditional white-sand beach, this one has black-lava rocks that form small tide pools, ideal for snorkeling. Keep an eye out for endangered sea turtles that are attracted to this spot. There are lifeguards here, and facilities include showers, restrooms, and a small marine police station.

Shopping

The best shopping in Hilo can be found along Kamehameha Avenue in the heart of downtown. Stop by **Sig Zane Designs,** 122 Kamehameha Ave. (© **808/935-7077;** www.sigzane.com), for the best in Hawaiian wear; **Basically Books,** 160 Kamehameha Ave. (© **808/961-0144;** www.basicallybooks.com), a sanctuary for lovers of books, maps, and Hawaii-themed gift items; and **Dragon Mama,** 266 Kamehameha Ave. (© **808/934-9081;** www.dragonmama.com), for unique comforters, cushions, futons, meditation pillows, hemp yarns and shirts, antique kimonos and obi, tatami mats sold by the panel, and all manner of comforts in the elegantly spare Japanese esthetic.

Kailua-Kona

COMING ASHORE   Two cruise ships anchor offshore here; a 10-minute tender ride takes passengers to the sleepy pier in Kailua-Kona. There's plenty to do within steps of this modest pier, including beach-hopping, shopping, and more. Taxis line up at the dock to whisk you away, but with so much going on at the pier, there is little reason to leave.

GETTING AROUND   As at the other ports in Hawaii, **taxis** await the arrival of cruise ship passengers, in this case lining up in front of the King Kamehameha Hotel.

If you need to call for one, try **AAA-1 TAXI** (© **808/325-3818**); keep in mind, though, that because the island is so big, long-distance trips can be very pricey. To book a car, contact (© **800/GO-ALAMO** [462-5266]; www.alamo.com) or **Enterprise** (© **800/736-8222;** www.enterprise.com) and someone will pick you up at the pier. To cruise the waterfront and around town, rent a bike for $20 a day at **Hawaiian Pedals** (© **808/329-2294**), in the Kona Inn Shopping Village about a half-mile down on Alii Drive.

Best Cruise Line Shore Excursions

Catamaran Sail & Snorkel ($90 adults, $70 children, 4 hr.): Head out on a catamaran to Pawai Bay and enjoy a morning of cruising, music, snacking, and snorkeling. The bay is loaded with multicolored fish, rays, and lava-encrusted coral reefs. In winter, there's a great chance you'll see whales or spinner dolphins breaching and cavorting.

Big Island Helicopter Spectacular ($435, 4½ hr.): There is no better way to see the Big Island's beauty and volcanic fury than from a helicopter. On this journey, you soar over the tropical valleys and waterfalls of the Kohala Mountains, the rainforest of the Hamakua Coast, and the spectacular lava flows of Hawaii Volcanoes National Park.

On Your Own: Within Walking Distance

There is plenty to see and do right near the pier. Just head down the seawall and enjoy the breathtaking ocean view on one side, and the endless stream of shops and galleries along the opposite side of the street. Be sure to stop in at **Hulihee Palace,** 75–5718 Alii Dr. (© **808/329-1877;** www.daughtersofhawaii.com), a two-story New England–style palace. Built in 1838 as a summer residence for Hawaii's royalty, it was, at the time, the largest and most elegant home on the island. Today, it's a well-run and well-preserved museum run by the Daughters of Hawaii organization. It's open Wednesday to Saturday 10am to 3pm. Admission is $6. Across the street is **Mokuaikaua Church** (© **808/329-1589**), the oldest Christian church in Hawaii (open daily; admission free).

On Your Own: Beyond the Port Area

St. Benedict's Catholic Church, on Highway 19 (© **808/328-2227**), is more commonly known as the Painted Church because of the colorful murals and frescoes that cover its walls and ceilings. It was painted by Father John Velge, the church's first priest, in an attempt to enlighten and educate the members of his congregation, who were predominantly illiterate. Admission is free.

Ancient **Hawaiian petroglyphs** can be seen near the **Kings' Shops** at the Waikoloa Beach Resort, just off Waikoloa Beach Drive about 30 miles north on Highway 19 (© **808/886-8811**). Free tours meet at the food court in the Kings' Shops on Sunday at 10:30am (you must register in advance). You can also tour the ancient markings on your own at any time. Follow the signs to the petroglyphs; then take the small path that leads to a craggy trail through a lava field once used by Hawaiian travelers.

Nonguests are welcome to visit **Hilton Waikoloa Village,** 425 Waikoloa Beach Dr. (© **808/886-1234;** www.hiltonwaikoloavillage.com), and enjoy its spectacularly landscaped grounds and walkways that meander past enormous statues, dramatic waterfalls, sweeping coastal vistas, and $7 million worth of artwork. If you like Atlantis on Paradise Island in The Bahamas, you'll love this resort. Enjoy any of the nine restaurants, all reached via air-conditioned tram or open-air mahogany boats that run from one end of the property to the other. For a steep $80, families can use the pools and man-made beach as well (call first to make sure of availability on the day you're in port).

Beaches

At the Kailua-Kona pier, you're practically standing on the beach at the **King Kamehameha Hotel.** Because all beaches are public in Hawaii, this small and sweet waterfront resort is yours to enjoy. For a fee, you can rent watersports gear, a lounge chair, or an umbrella. For those who prefer to swim without all the trappings, there is a minuscule scrap of beach just on the other side of the parking lot. Here, the calm water makes for great paddling, swimming laps, or just floating your cares away.

The best beach for snorkeling (especially for beginners) is **Kahaluu Beach Park,** about 5 miles down Alii Drive from the pier. The salt-and-pepper-colored beach is convenient to restrooms, a snack truck, and sheltered picnic tables. Although shallow, the water can become rough in the winter.

Beautiful **Hapuna Beach State Park,** past the Hilton Waikoloa Village and Mauna Lani Resort, is about 35 miles up the Kohala Coast from the pier. Follow the highway signs and turn left toward the ocean off Highway 19. You'll be greeted by a large white-sand beach. The area is serene and well maintained, and has a food pavilion, restrooms, and showers.

Shopping

There is ample shopping on Alii Drive, which starts at the Kailua Pier and extends southward along a nearly endless strip of small shopping galleries with similar names and equally similar wares. **Kailua Village Artists Gallery,** a co-op of four dozen island artists and a few guest artists, displays watercolors, paintings, prints, hand-blown and blasted glass, and photography at the Outrigger Keauhou Beach Resort, 78–6740 Alii Dr. (© **808/324-7060**). Books, pottery, and an attractive assortment of greeting cards are among the lower-priced items. Other places to browse close to the pier are **Eclectic Craftsman** in the Kona Marketplace, 75–5729 Alii Dr. (© **808/334-0562**), for beautifully carved wood. Farther down, inside Waterfront Row, marvel at the marine-life sculptures made from wood, stone, and metal at **Wyland Gallery,** 75–5770 Alii Dr. (© **808/334-0037**).

15

New England & Eastern Canada

Back in the year 1614, the first successful American colony, at Jamestown, Virginia, was only 7 years old, and exploration of North America had just begun. No one yet knew just how vast the continent was, but Europe's great powers had already begun fighting for its bounty. To the north, the lands known as Northern Virginia caught the imagination of Jamestown founder John Smith, who mounted an expedition along the coasts of what are now Massachusetts and Maine. Returning to England with stories of the region's natural wealth, he argued strongly for its colonization and renamed it New England, a name that King James I made official in 1620. A few years later, James's son, Charles I, sent a party of Scots to colonize the land even farther north, in what are now the Canadian Maritimes. And so it came to pass that, just as England has Scotland on its northern border, New England's nearest neighbor is beautiful Nova Scotia—the "New Scotland."

The legacies left by the English, Scottish, French, and other settlers who immigrated to these parts have lent ports along the New England/Canada coast their unique character, whether it's the Puritan ethics of stubborn independence and thriftiness that define many New Englanders, or the French culture and language that thrive in the Providence of Québec. On a cruise in this region, you'll see lots of **historical sites,** from Boston's Paul Revere House to Québec City's 17th-century Notre-Dame des Victoires Church to the Halifax Maritime Museum's *Titanic* exhibit. But you'll also get a dose of the region's inimitable character: fishing boats piled with netting, Victorian mansions built by wealthy ship owners, lighthouses atop windswept bluffs, and the cold, hard beauty of the north Atlantic sea.

The classic time to cruise here is in autumn, when a brilliant sea of **fall foliage** blankets the region. You can also cruise these waters in the spring and summer, aboard either big 3,000-passenger megaships or smaller vessels carrying less than a tenth that load. Depending on the size of the ship and the length of the cruise, itineraries may include passing through **Nantucket Sound,** around **Cape Cod,** or into the **Bay of Fundy** or **Gulf of St. Lawrence.** Some ships traverse the St. Lawrence Seaway or the smaller Saguenay River.

HOME PORTS FOR THIS REGION
New York, Boston, Montréal, and **Québec City** are the main hubs for these cruises.

LANGUAGE & CURRENCY English and dollars. Virtually all businesses in Canadian ports such as Halifax and Saint John accept U.S. dollars; however, if you're spending time pre- or post-cruise in Montréal or Québec, you'll want to pick up some Canadian dollars, which at press time we valued at C$1 = US$1. Exchange rates fluctuate, however, so prices may not be exactly the same when you arrive in port. Prices in this chapter are in U.S. dollars, unless noted.

SHOPPING TIPS You don't go on a New England/Canada cruise for the shopping, though there are a few choice spots. Of course, New York, Boston, and Montréal, being major cities, have lots of shopping opportunities.

1 Bar Harbor, Maine

Bar Harbor is situated on the mid-Maine coast, overlooking Frenchman's Bay from its perch on the eastern shore of Mount Desert Island—its name an anglicization of Isles des Monts-Deserts ("bare mountains"), the name French explorer Samuel de Champlain gave the island in 1604. In its 19th-century heyday, Bar Harbor was one of the premier resort areas on the East Coast, attracting Astors, Vanderbilts, Rockefellers, and other wealthy families looking for rustic summer getaways. Today, it's a humbler place, with no shortage of T-shirt shops and ice-cream parlors, but is no less popular with tourists.

Bar Harbor's biggest pull is its proximity to the lush **Acadia National Park,** which got its start in 1901 when millionaire George B. Dorr formed a preservation group and began buying up land, eventually turning over thousands of acres to the federal government. The park today covers most of the 12×16-mile island and a few neighboring islands, with some 35,000 acres of lake-dotted fir and spruce forests and surrounded by offshore waters that are great for whale-watching. Winding amid its acreage is a 57-mile network of carriage roads created by John D. Rockefeller, Jr., as well as 120 miles of hiking trails—all of them motor-free, open for walking and bicycling only.

COMING ASHORE While small ships less than 200 feet long can pull alongside the Town Pier, most ships must anchor offshore and send guests to the Harbor Place pier via tenders. The ride to the pier takes only about 10 minutes. The two piers are next to each other in the downtown waterfront area.

GETTING AROUND Once in town, you can walk along the waterfront and to many shops, restaurants, and a few attractions (see below in "On Your Own: Within Walking Distance"), but to see Acadia, your best bet is signing up for one of your ship's shore excursions or renting a bicycle from a local dealer. Try **Bar Harbor Bicycle Shop,** 141 Cottage St. (© **207/288-3886;** www.barharborbike.com), or **Acadia Bike,** 48 Cottage St. (© **800/526-8615;** www.acadiabike.com). Rates are $16 for a half-day, $22 for a full day. If you want a taxi and there aren't any waiting, try **At Your Service Taxi Cab Co.** (© **207/288-9222;** www.atyourservicetaxi.com), which also offers guided tours of the park. Check out www.barharborinfo.com for useful sightseeing info.

Best Cruise Line Shore Excursions

Best of the Park and the Town ($59, 2½ hr.): Traverse the 27-mile Park Loop Road of Acadia National Park via bus, taking in spectacular coastal, mountain, and forest scenery. Pass by grand Victorian mansions from the turn of the century and stop for photos at the summit of Cadillac Mountain and Thunder Hole, where the right tidal conditions can send flumes of ocean spray high into the air.

A Walk in the Park ($45, 3 hr.): A naturalist guide leads a 2-mile hike along Acadia's trails and provides insight into the park's ecosystem, geology, natural history, and legends. The tour also includes a drive to the top of Cadillac Mountain for a 360-degree view of Mount Desert Island.

New England & Eastern Canada

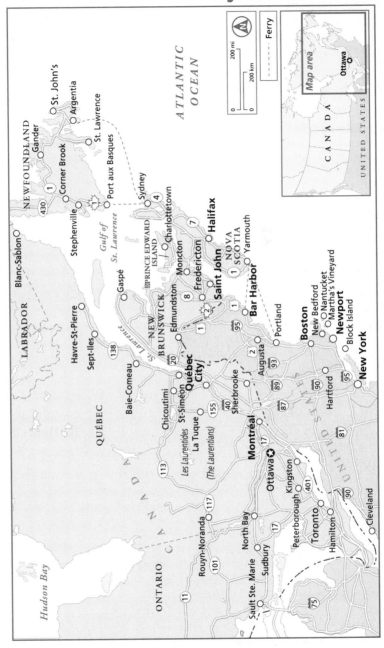

ATLANTIC OCEAN

Ferry

200 mi
200 km
0
0

Map area
Ottawa

CANADA
UNITED STATES

St. John's
Argentina
St. Lawrence
NEWFOUNDLAND
Gander
Corner Brook
1
Port aux Basques
430
Stephenville
Sydney
4
Gulf of St. Lawrence
Charlottetown
PRINCE EDWARD ISLAND
Moncton
Halifax
7
Fredericton
NOVA SCOTIA
Saint John
Yarmouth
1
8
Bar Harbor
Blanc-Sablon
Gaspé
Portland
Boston
New Bedford
LABRADOR
Havre-St-Pierre
NEW BRUNSWICK
Edmundston
1
2
95
1
Nantucket
Martha's Vineyard
Newport
Block Island
New York
Sept-Îles
138
St. Lawrence
2
Augusta
93
QUÉBEC
Baie-Comeau
20
Québec City
Sherbrooke
89
90
Hartford
95
Chicoutimi
St-Siméon
155
40
87
Les Laurentides
La Tuque
(The Laurentians)
Montréal
17
81
113
Ottawa
Kingston
401
117
Peterborough
Toronto
Hudson Bay
Rouyn-Noranda
North Bay
101
17
Hamilton
Cleveland
90
UNITED STATES
ONTARIO
Sudbury
11
Sault Ste. Marie
75

651

Acadia Carriage Ride ($75, 3 hr.): The 15-person horse-drawn carriages provide a chance to experience John D. Rockefeller's carriage paths in the way he intended. Approximately 1 hour is spent in the carriage itself. The tour also includes a drive to the top of Cadillac Mountain for the view.

Biking in Acadia ($50, 2½ hr.): Jump on a 24-speed mountain bike and follow the guide through the park's hard-packed gravel carriage trails that crisscross some of the most scenic areas of the park. The guide makes stops to discuss the island's history and lore.

Frenchman Bay Kayak Adventure ($70, 3 hr.): This scenic paddle passes oceanfront mansions not visible from the road and provides great views of Cadillac Mountain. You also have opportunities to spot harbor seals, porpoises, and seabirds such as the storm petrel, shearwater, and northern gannet.

Whale-Watching ($62, 3½ hr.): This excursion allows visitors to view the humpbacks, finbacks, minkes, and dolphins that gather in the waters off the island between April and October.

On Your Own: Within Walking Distance

If for some reason you're allergic to beautiful forests and want to stay in town, you can check out the great views of the area from the foot of Main Street at grassy **Agamont Park,** which overlooks the town pier and Frenchman Bay. From here, set off past the Bar Harbor Inn on the **Shore Path,** a wide, winding trail that follows the shoreline for about a half-mile along a public right of way. The pathway has views of many elegant summer homes (some converted to inns) and of the **Porcupines,** a cluster of spruce-studded islands just offshore. So named because they look like a group of porcupines migrating southward, the islands' distinctive shape—gently sloped facing north, with abrupt cliffs facing south—is the result of ancient pressure from a southward-moving glacier.

For a glimpse of the area's past life, stroll on over to the **Abbe Museum,** 26 Mount Desert St. (© **207/288-3519;** www.abbemuseum.org), a sprawling 17,000-square-foot gallery housing a top-rate collection of Native American artifacts. Open hours vary; call ahead. Admission is $6 adults; $2 for kids ages 2 to 15. Around the corner is the **Bar Harbor Historical Society,** 33 Ledgelawn Ave. (© **207/288-0000;** www. barharborhistorical.org), set in a handsome former convent dating to 1918. Its collection comprises exhibits on old-time Mount Desert Island hotels and estates, photos of most of the 200 estate homes burned during the great fire of 1947, and a collection of milk bottles from the more than 40 dairy farms that were once active on the island. It's open from June to October Monday to Saturday 1 to 4pm. Admission is free.

Somewhere during your stay, try some fresh **Maine lobster**—served boiled, baked, broiled, in rolls, and any other number of ways—at one of the many restaurants along the waterfront area. The fresh lobster bisque served at many local restaurants will warm you up nicely on cool autumn days.

On Your Own: Beyond the Port Area

You don't want to come to Bar Harbor without getting a taste of the most famous attraction: **Acadia National Park** (www.nps.gov/acad). Sign up for a guided hike or drive along the 27-mile Park Loop Road, which wends around 1,530-foot-high Cadillac Mountain, the highest point on the Atlantic coast. If you luck out and there's no fog, expect awesome views of natural sights like Thunder Hole, where ocean surf dramatically crashes against granite cliffs. Perhaps the best way to really experience nature here is bicycling a stretch of the 55-mile car-free carriage trails that wind through the park (rent a bike in town or sign up for one of your ship's biking excursions). Horse-drawn carriage rides are another popular way to tour. No matter what your transport, there's a great chance you'll spot some wildlife, from beavers, foxes, eagles, hawks, and peregrine falcons to the occasional moose.

SHOPPING   You don't come here for the shopping (unless lobster potholders are your thing), though a handful of interesting shops on **Main Street** sell locally made and/or inspired handicrafts and gifts. At **Island Artisans,** 99 Main St. (℃ 207/ 288-4214; www.islandartisans.com), you can browse for local handicrafts such as tiles, sweet-grass baskets, pottery, jewelry, and soaps. Down the street is the **Bar Harbor Hemporium,** 116 Main St. (℃ 207/288-3014; www.barharborhemp.com), an interesting store dedicated to promoting clothing, paper, and other products made from hemp, an environmentally friendly, fibrous plant that's usually known for other reasons entirely.

2 Halifax, Nova Scotia

Perched midway up the Nova Scotia coast, Halifax is the top port of call for big ships on the New England and Eastern Canada circuit, owing to the city's natural deep-water port and its especially pleasing harborside setting and tree-lined streets. Its history goes back to the days of the Micmac Indians, who called Nova Scotia Chebuctook ("Great Long Harbor"). In 1605, the French staked their claim and renamed it Acadia ("Peaceful Land"). By 1621, the British had a foothold and renamed the land Nova Scotia ("New Scotland"), and in 1749 Edward Cornwallis founded Halifax, naming it for George Montagu Dunk, second earl of Halifax. Halifax eventually became a thriving shipbuilding and trading center as well as a military hub for the Royal Army and Navy. Even into the 20th century, it had strong military ties, serving as an important supply and convoy harbor in both World War I and World War II. In recent years, it's evolved into a vital commercial and financial hub, as well as home to a number of colleges and universities.

COMING ASHORE   All ships dock right in town, with Halifax's attractions just steps away. Typically, two ships are in port at one time, though occasionally as many as four or five ships may be tied up. Be sure you're awake when your ship docks so you can go out on deck to hear the Halifax town crier and members of the 78th Highlander Regiment, who greet all ships with an exciting program of bagpipe and drum music.

GETTING AROUND   Halifax is exceedingly walkable (there are free walking-tour maps available at the terminal), but there are also plenty of **taxis** at the docks if you're inclined to head for the hills. For some useful info on sightseeing, visit www.Destinationhalifax.com.

Best Cruise Line Shore Excursions

Highlander Experience ($100, 3 hr.): Those who want an up-close-and-personal experience of 19th-century Halifax military life can sign up for this excursion offered at the Halifax Citadel, where participants are immersed in the duties and traditions of the Victorian Army and the Scottish Highlanders.

The Small Ports of New England & Eastern Canada

Aside from the major ports listed in this chapter, there are a number of smaller ports that small-ship lines such as American Cruise Line (p. 319), Blount Small Ship Adventures (p. 327), and Cruise West (p. 328) include on their itineraries. Big ships may also visit some of these ports, on occasion.

Block Island, Rhode Island (www.blockislandchamber.com): The Nature Conservancy has called Block Island one of the "last great places in the Western Hemisphere," an 11-square-mile Yankee gem. It has more than 300 freshwater ponds set amidst rolling green hills that end in dramatic 250-foot bluffs that look like the cliffs of western Ireland. A full third of the island is set aside as a wildlife refuge, accessible via 30-plus miles of hiking trails and cliffside bike paths. Down at the shore, the island is ringed by some 17 miles of beach.

Nantucket, Massachusetts (www.nantucketchamber.org): Just 30 miles off the coast of Cape Cod, Nantucket Island is classic New England, and was the world's top whaling hub before New Bedford stole the show. Today, it's vastly popular with summer tourists, but still manages to maintain a low-key attitude. Its main town, also named Nantucket, is all cobblestone streets and historic buildings, with a yacht-filled harbor, while out around the residential island, you'll find tranquil hamlets, rolling moors, heaths, cranberry bogs, and miles of exquisite public beaches, including jetties near Nantucket Town and Surfside on the Atlantic coast.

Martha's Vineyard, Massachusetts (www.mvy.com): New England's largest island, Martha's Vineyard boasts handsome old towns, lighthouses, white picket fences, and charming ice-cream shops . . . plus lots of summer visitors. You'll find great beaches (though many are private), as well as dramatic cliffs and meadows that make for great long walks and bicycle rides. The most genteel of the island's six towns is **Edgartown,** full of regal sea captains' houses and manicured gardens.

Fall River, Massachusetts (www.fallriverchamber.com/visitor): In the northern reaches of Narragansett Bay, about 20 miles north of Newport, Fall River allows visitors a chance to visit **Battleship Cove** (www.battleshipcove.org), a collection of preserved American warships including the USS *Massachusetts,*

Treasures of the *Titanic* ($50, 3 hr.): When the fabled liner *Titanic* sank on April 15, 1912, three ships from Halifax had the grim job of recovering victims from the icy waters 500 miles southeast. In all, only 335 bodies were found, of which 150 were later laid to rest in three Halifax cemeteries. This tour includes all aspects of Halifax's connection to the tragedy, including the historic pier from which the ships were dispatched to pick up victims; the church where memorial services were held; the temporary morgue sites that housed the bodies of such wealthy victims as John Jacob Astor; the cemeteries where rows upon rows of identical gravestones mark the final resting place of 150 victims; and the Maritime Museum of the Atlantic, which houses submarine *Lionfish,* and other veterans of World War II. At the town's Marine Museum, you'll find artifacts from the *Titanic,* while at the Lizzie Borden Museum, you can get the down-and-dirty details on that famous unsolved murder mystery.

New Bedford, Massachusetts (www.newbedford.com): In the 19th century, New Bedford was the whaling capital of the world. Today, it remains a major deep-sea fishing port, and boasts a beautifully restored waterfront area. The town's **Whaling Museum (www.whalingmuseum.org)** displays ship replicas, whale skeletons and paintings, glasswork, and scrimshaw, which is carved whalebone or whale ivory.

Portland, Maine (www.visitportland.com): Maine's largest city is set on a peninsula in scenic Casco Bay. The top attractions include the Portland Headlight (the oldest American lighthouse in continuous use) and the lovely Old Port neighborhood, a revitalized warehouse district that now boasts boutiques, restaurants, and entertainment along its cobblestone streets. Nearby Freeport is a town-size outlet center anchored by *très* Maine **L.L.Bean (www. llbean.com).**

Sydney, Cape Breton Island, Nova Scotia (www.cbisland.com): Nova Scotia's northernmost landmass, Cape Breton Island was principally settled by Highland Scots, and today that influence remains in the island's Scottish-style folk music. The island's scenic highlight is **Cape Breton Highlands National Park (www.pc.gc.ca/pn-np/ns/cbreton/index)** on the northwestern coast, and its spectacular highlands, dramatic cliffs, and ocean scenery are accessible via the 185-mile roadway known as the Cabot Trail.

Charlottetown, Prince Edward Island (www.walkandseacharlottetown. com): In Canada's smallest province, you can visit historic sites such as the house of Lucy Maud Montgomery, who wrote *Anne of Green Gables,* which describes the innocence and beauty of life on the island at the turn of the 19th century. You can also opt for a drive along one of the island's scenic highways that wend past sandstone cliffs, rocky coves, lovely beaches, and fishing villages.

an excellent permanent exhibit on the disaster, featuring the world's largest collection of wooden artifacts—including a post from the famous Grand Staircase and one of the few intact *Titanic* deck chairs in the world.

Pub Crawl ($85, 2½ hr.): Led by a kilted guide and a bagpiper, this tour visits several of Halifax's favorite old-English-style pubs, with libations and music included.

Peggy's Cove ($58, 3½ hr.): For a glimpse of Nova Scotia's more rugged side, head about 45 minutes south to the tiny fishing village of Peggy's Cove, in a picturesque setting on the eastern shore of St. Margarets Bay. Settled by six families in 1811, the village hasn't grown much since, but what it lacks in population it makes up for in scenic beauty, sitting on solid rock just above the crashing surf. A guide leads a walking tour along the craggy coastline, with its bold glacier-formed outcroppings of granite rubbed smooth by eons of crashing waves, and past the town's impressive lighthouse, one of the most photographed spots in Canada.

City and Harbor Duck Tour ($50, 1 hr.): Drive around to see the city highlights in an amphibious vehicle, then plunge into the harbor for views not possible from land.

Lunenburg Getaway ($80, 6 hr.): Just southwest of Halifax, Lunenburg is Nova Scotia's main fishing port, with an Old Town that's been restored to its original colonial character. Tours include a 45-minute walking tour with free time to explore the town's shops and cafes.

On Your Own: Within Walking Distance

Right at the cruise docks, **Pier 21** (⟨℗⟩ **902/425-7770;** www.pier21.ca) was Halifax's version of Ellis Island, where between 1928 and 1971 more than a million immigrants entered Canada. Opened as a museum in 1999, it provides an interactive experience that re-creates 43 years of immigrant life through displays, films, and sound clips. It's open from May through October daily 9:30am to 5:30pm. Admission is $8.50 adults, $5 kids ages 7 to 16.

To the north, **Alexander Keith's Nova Scotia Brewery,** 1496 Lower Water St. (⟨℗⟩ **902/455-1474;** www.keiths.ca), offers one of the best brewery tours we've ever taken. Unlike the typical walk-through of a modern plant with a few historical exhibits, Keith's has restored significant portions of its plant to the way they looked when Keith established his business in 1820. Costumed actors take you through grain storehouses, historic brewing displays, and residential rooms en route to the 19th-century barroom for a sip (or two, or three) of Keith's brew. It's entertaining and fun, it's historical (Keith's is, after all, the oldest brewery in North America), and there's music to boot. Hour-long tours run from June through October on Monday to Saturday, every half-hour from noon until 8pm (Sun noon–5pm). Admission $16.

A few blocks north, the **Maritime Museum of the Atlantic,** 1675 Lower Water St. (⟨℗⟩ **902/424-7490;** http://museum.gov.ns.ca/mma), provides a window into the lives of Halifax's sailors and shipbuilders, its galleries displaying some 24,000 artifacts, 20,000 photos, and even whole vessels. Exhibits include an impressive collection of *Titanic* artifacts, and there's also a fascinating exhibit on the incredible explosion that leveled much of the city in 1917 when a French munitions ship collided with a Norwegian steamer. It's open May through October Monday to Saturday 9:30am to 5:30pm (Sun 1–5:30pm). Admission is $8.75 adults, $4.75 kids ages 6 to 17.

Up at downtown's highest point, about 9 blocks uphill from the waterfront, the star-shaped **Halifax Citadel** (⟨℗⟩ **902/426-5080;** www.pc.gc.ca/lhn-nhs/ns/halifax/index_e.asp) was built by the British between 1820 and 1856, mostly to guard against attack by the United States. The U.S. never did strike (it picked on Mexico instead), but the ever-vigilant British still maintained a garrison here until 1906, after which it was manned by Canadian forces. Restored now to its mid-19th-century appearance, it's one of the most visited National Historic Sites in Canada, with costumed animators portraying a regiment of Scottish soldiers and their families. Visitors can see displays of weapons and uniforms, view audiovisual presentations and demonstrations by soldiers' wives, take an hour-long guided tour, enjoy panoramic views from its ramparts, and watch maneuvers and bagpipe concerts on the central parade ground. At noon each day, one of the fort's cannons is fired ceremoniously. Boom! It's open from early May through October daily 9am to 5pm. Admission is $12 adults, $5.80 kids. To get here, head up Carmichael Street from Grand Parade Square/Barrington Street toward the old **Town Clock,** gifted to the city by Edward, Duke of Kent, who commanded a garrison here in 1800. A staircase at the foot of the clock, on Brunswick Street, will take you to the Citadel's main entrance.

South of the Citadel, Halifax's famous 17-acre **Public Gardens** (www.halifaxpublic gardens.ca) make a beautiful spot to relax after a long walking tour. Created through the merger of the old Nova Scotia Horticultural Society Garden (laid out in 1837) and an adjacent public park opened in 1866, they're the oldest formal Victorian gardens in North America, and look much as they have since the 1870s. The best place to enter is via the ornate, Scottish-made wrought-iron gates at the corner of Spring Garden Road and South Park Street. Inside, winding gravel paths meander among the trees and flowerbeds, with exotic plants from around the world, commemorative statuary and fountains, and, at the park's center, a red-roofed gazebo built in 1887 to celebrate Queen Victoria's Golden Jubilee.

On Your Own: Beyond the Port Area

For information on **Peggy's Cove,** see "Best Cruise Line Shore Excursions," above. Nearer to Halifax is the **Fairview Cemetery,** where 120 *Titanic* victims were buried in 1912. At least one of your ship's organized excursions will generally include a stop here, with the guide explaining Halifax's role in the ocean disaster.

Shopping

Locally made maritime handicrafts such as hooked rugs, pottery, wood items, quilt work, and hand-knit woolens are big in Halifax. Because of the city's Scottish roots, you'll also find plenty of tartans and gifts made of pewter. There is no shortage of shops in and around the waterfront, including the **Historic Properties (© 902/ 422-3077;** www.historicproperties.ca), a group of warehouses dating back to 1800, which have been converted into a shopping, dining, and entertainment complex. It's situated a little north of the Maritime Museum, with cobblestone streets leading between buildings that once held goods seized by privateers who plundered enemy vessels for the British Crown. Outside, street musicians and painters add a touch of the artistic; inside, you'll find fashionable shops, gifts, pubs, and lunch spots.

3 Newport, Rhode Island

Sitting on the southern tip of Aquidneck Island in Narragansett Bay and connected to the mainland by three bridges, Newport is practically synonymous with the term "idle rich." In the late–19th century, it was *the* place for America's wealthy aristocrats to spend their summers. From the Vanderbilts to the Astors, all the Gilded Age millionaires had summer mansions (or, as they called them, "cottages") here, each grander than the next, with an aesthetic that's half-château, half-Versailles, and 100% over-the-top opulence.

It's not difficult to understand how this picture-postcard seaside setting drew the elite. During the Colonial period, Newport rivaled Boston and New York as a center of New World trade, and during the Civil War, it became home to the U.S. Naval Academy. After the war, the town began to draw wealthy industrialists, railroad tycoons, coal magnates, and financiers, who began to build the town's reputation as the center of the U.S. sailing universe. In 1854, the New York Yacht Club held its first annual regatta off Newport, and from 1930 to 1983, the club held the great America's Cup race here in "the City by the Sea"—stopping only after the cup was snatched by the Australian sloop *Australia II* following a 132-year American reign. Despite the fact that U.S. boats won the cup back in 1987, 1988, and 1992, the race has never yet returned to Newport's waters, but the city continues to be a major sailing center, hosting more than 40 races each summer and fall.

Today, Newport has a beautiful sea, rocky coastline, and a bustling town that's all cobblestone streets, shady trees, cute cafes, and historical homes. Much of the hubbub is along the waterfront and its parallel streets: America's Cup Avenue and Thames Street, with the pronunciation of the latter Americanized from the British "tems" to "thaymz" after the Revolution. Though millions of people visit every year, Newport has managed to retain much of its small-town charm and hasn't been overtaken by T-shirt shops and fast-food outlets.

COMING ASHORE   Ships both large and small are visiting Newport these days, all of them anchoring just a short distance offshore and shuttling passengers to the tender pier, just a block from the Newport Visitors Information Center at 23 America's Cup Ave. An information kiosk is also often set up on the pier. You'll find all of Newport's most popular sights, including its famed mansions, within a short walk or drive of the downtown area. For useful info, also check out www.gonewport.com.

GETTING AROUND   From the tender pier, you can walk around the historic town or hop on the **Yellow Line (Rte. 67) RIPTA trolley (✆ 401/781-9400;** www. ripta.com), which visits the mansions, Bellevue Avenue shopping, the Cliff Walk, Rough Point, and other highlights. It'll cost you $5 for an all-day hop-on/hop-off pass, and you board it at the Visitor Information Center (see above). If you want a taxi to drop you off at the mansions, try **Cozy Cab (✆ 401/846-2500).** Another great way to get around town and out to the mansions is by bicycle. One of several rental shops is **Scooters of Newport,** 476 Thames St. (✆ **401/619-0573),** just a 10-minute walk from the tender pier. Bike rentals are $15 for 2 hours or $25 per day; they also rent these cute little three-wheel "scoot coupes" that are ideal for sightseeing and go for $50 an hour (and $35 for each additional hour).

Best Cruise Line Shore Excursions

Colonial Newport Walking Tour ($30, 1½ hr.): An expert guide takes you through a 10-block area of Colonial Newport, noted for nearly 200 restored 18th- and 19th-century Colonial and Victorian homes and landmarks. You'll walk along the city's quaint and shady streets where no buses are allowed, and hear how tobacco heiress Doris Duke and many other residents led the fight to rescue this once-neglected area. Stroll by the superb 1726 Trinity Church, architect Peter Harrison's Brick Market, the Touro Synagogue (the oldest in the country), the Quaker Meeting House, and the Old Colony House.

Guided Cliff Walk Tour ($38, 1½ hr.): You can walk Newport's famous Cliff Walk (see below) on your own, but you can also choose a narrated tour.

The Vanderbilt's Newport ($65, 3½ hr.): This tour combines visits to two of Newport's grandest mansions: Cornelius Vanderbilt II's the Breakers and William K. Vanderbilt's Marble House. Another mansion tour, typically called **Grand Mansions of Newport** ($54, 3 hr.), visits the Elms or Rosecliff, the latter built in 1902 by architect Stanford White on the model of Versailles' Grand Trianon.

America's Cup Sailing Experience ($125, 2 hr.): Though Newport is not currently home to the America's Cup (as it was for more than 50 years), you can sail a 46-foot America's Cup yacht as part of this excursion, which sails past sites like the lighthouses, Newport Bridge, and some of Newport's lavish estates.

On Your Own: Within Walking Distance

This is a place for walking, if there ever was one. If you're reasonably fit, the famed mansions on Bellevue and Ocean avenues are within 1 to 4 miles of the tender pier, or you can take the trolley or a taxi (see "Getting Around," above).

Ten of Newport's grandest 19th-century mansions are operated by the **Preservation Society of Newport County** (© **401/847-1000;** www.newportmansions.org), which offers several **ticket packages** that combine admission to different houses. Admission to the Breakers, the most famous of the mansions, is $18. Admission to any of the others (except Hunter House) is $12. A combo ticket that includes five mansions (choose from the Breakers, Château-sur-Mer, the Elms, Marble House, Rosecliff, Green Animals, Kingscote, Chepstow, and Isaac Bell House) is $31.

The **Breakers,** 44 Ochre Point Ave., east of Bellevue Avenue (© **401/847-1000**), is a 70-room Italian Renaissance–style palace built for Cornelius Vanderbilt II in 1895. Perched above the sea, it was designed by Richard Morris Hunt, the Beaux Arts master who also designed the Metropolitan Museum of Art in New York City. Highlights include the gilded 2,400-square-foot dining room (lit by 12-ft. chandeliers) and the great hall, which was designed to resemble an open-air Italian courtyard—right down to the 45-foot sky-blue ceiling.

While none of the other Newport mansions are quite as grand as the Breakers, several come close. **Marble House** was built between 1888 and 1892 for Cornelius Vanderbilt's younger brother William, making it the earliest of all the Newport mansions. Some $7 million worth of marble was used in its construction. The **Elms** was built for Pennsylvania coal baron Edward Julius Berwind in 1901, its stately design inspired by the Château d'Asnieres, a mid-18th-century home outside Paris. **Rosecliff** was built in 1902 for Nevada silver heiress Theresa Fair Oelrichs, designed by architect Stanford White after the Grand Trianon at Versailles. All the mansions are located off Bellevue Avenue, and tours run throughout the day.

A few other mansions are privately held and open to the public at certain times, including the 60-room **Belcourt Castle,** 657 Bellevue Ave. (© **401/846-0669;** www.belcourtcastle.com). Built from the inherited fortunes of August Belmont, the Rothschild Banking representative in America, its current owners, the Tinney family, still reside here, opening their home to tours. Admission is $15.

The 3.5-mile **Cliff Walk** meanders between Newport's rocky coastline and many of the town's Gilded Age estates, providing a better view of their exteriors than you get from the street. Traversing its length, high above the crashing surf, is more than a stroll but less than an arduous hike. For the full 3.5-mile length, walk about a mile from the pier to the path's start at the intersection of Memorial Boulevard and Eustis Avenue. For a shorter walk, end at the Forty Steps (an access point btw. the path and the street), which is at the end of Narragansett Avenue, off Bellevue. If you want to do the entire Cliff Walk, but don't want to walk all the way back to the pier when you've reached the end, consider taking the trolley back. You can grab it on Bellevue, just 1½ blocks from the walk. Keep in mind that there are some mildly rugged sections to negotiate, no facilities, and no phones. A number of mansions, such as the Breakers,

Rosecliff, Astors' Beechwood, Marble House, and Rough Point, are just on the other side of the walk; others are a few blocks inland from the path.

Just a few blocks from the pier, Newport's **Historic Hill** section contains one of the most impressive concentrations of original 18th- and 19th-century Colonial, Federal, and Victorian houses in America, many of them designated National Historic Sites. Spring Street, the hill's main drag, is an architectural treasure-trove dominated by the 1725 **Trinity Church,** at the corner of Church Street. Said to have been influenced by the work of the legendary British architect Christopher Wren, it certainly reflects that inspiration in its belfry and distinctive spire, which can be seen from all over downtown. Not far away, **Touro Synagogue,** 85 Touro St. (*©* **401/847-4794;** www. tourosynagogue.org), is the country's oldest continually operating synagogue, dedicated in 1763. It's sometimes open for tours and donations are accepted for admission. All around Historic Hill, you'll find homes marked with signs that read NRF, denoting that they're among the 83 **18th-century houses** that were restored by tobacco heiress Doris Duke's Newport Restoration Foundation between 1968 and 1984. All are now owned and maintained by the foundation and rented privately. Historic Hill rises from America's Cup Avenue, along the waterfront, and runs inland to Bellevue Avenue. Walking tour maps are available in the "Preservation" section of **www.newportrestoration.com.**

Other Newport attractions include the Gothic **St. Mary's Church,** 12 William St. (www.stmarynewport.org), where John F. Kennedy and Jacqueline Bouvier married, and the **International Tennis Hall of Fame,** 194 Bellevue Ave. (*©* **800/457-1144;** www.tennisfame.com), one of the few places in North America where you can play on a grass court. It's open daily from 9:30am to 5pm. Museum admission is $11 adults, free for children ages 16 and under. To play on the grass courts, visitors must call (*©* **401/846-0642**) and reserve in advance. Prices for play start at $90 per hour for two players.

Shopping

Lower Thames Street provides some quirky shopping opportunities, including stores that sell vintage clothing, salvaged architectural components, books, and sailing gear. **Spring Street** is noted for its antiques shops and purveyors of crafts, jewelry, and folk art. Spring intersects with **Franklin Street,** which harbors even more antiques shops in its short length. **Bellevue Avenue** also has a collection of resort-type boutiques—shopping in the true Newport style.

4 Québec City, Québec

Perched on a cliff top overlooking the St. Lawrence River, Québec City remains the soul of New France, an enormous territory that once included all of eastern Canada, the eastern U.S., the Great Lakes, and Louisiana, stretching from Hudson Bay in the north to Florida in the south. In 1608, the French explorer Samuel de Champlain was the first European to claim Québec City, and soon after established a fur-trading post. It was the first significant settlement in Canada, and today it is the capital of Québec, a politically prickly province almost as large as Alaska. The old city, a tumble of colorful metallic-roof houses clustered around the dominating Château Frontenac, is a haunting evocation of a coastal town in the motherland of France, as romantic as any on that continent. Because of its history, beauty, and unique stature as the only walled city north of Mexico, the historic district of Québec was named a UNESCO World Heritage Site in 1985—one of only three areas so designated in North America.

The city is split into two sections. The **Lower Town** (or **Basse-Ville**) is where the port is, while the **Upper Town (Haute-Ville),** the city's oldest section, dates back nearly 400 years and is still surrounded by its old stone walls.

Though some 95% of Québec's 167,000 citizens speak French, most people who work in hotels, restaurants, and shops also speak English.

COMING ASHORE The cruise docks at the **Port of Québec,** which includes a bustling commercial shipping operation, are within walking distance of the historic **Lower Town,** just outside the walled city. The **Upper Town** can be reached via a steep walk up the hill or the **funicular** (see below). For lots of useful info on sightseeing, visit www.quebecregion.com.

GETTING AROUND Virtually no place of interest is beyond walking distance, so the best way to explore is definitely on your own two feet. Although there are streets and stairs between the Upper and Lower Towns, there is also a **funicular (www. funiculaire-quebec.com),** which has long operated along an inclined 210-foot track between the Quartier Petit-Champlain and the Terrasse Dufferin, up top. The upper station is near the front of the Château Frontenac, the majestic hotel that towers over the city, and Place d'Armes, a central square; the lower station is actually inside the Maison Louis-Jolliet, a small building with a big FUNICULAIRE sign at 16 rue du Petit-Champlain. It runs year-round daily and wheelchairs are accommodated. The one-way fare is about C$2 (US$2).

Your best bet for getting a **taxi** is by finding a stand—such as the ones on the Place d'Armes and in front of the Hôtel-de-Ville (City Hall). Restaurant managers and hotel bell captains will also summon one if you ask. Fares are somewhat expensive given the short distances of most rides. To call a cab, try **Taxi Coop (© 418/525-5191)** or **Taxi Québec (© 418/525-8123).**

Best Cruise Line Shore Excursions

City Walking Tour ($55, 3 hr.): If you're up for it, the best way to discover Québec's historical side is by walking through the city's narrow cobblestone streets with a knowledgeable guide leading the way. Stroll along the first shopping street in North America, Le Petit Quartier Champlain, in the Lower Town. In the Upper Town, 3 centuries of history come to life in sites such as la Place d'Armes, la Terrasse Dufferin, Place de l'Hôtel de Ville, and le Musée des Ursulines. Some tours ($54) add a stop for high tea at the Fairmont Château Frontenac Hotel, Québec City's best-known landmark.

City Highlights by Bus ($40, 2½ hr.): Explore the narrow streets and stately residences that have hardly changed in more than 3 centuries. Enjoy panoramic views of the St. Lawrence River from the oldest part of town, drive through the Grande Allée neighborhood for a peek at the Victorian-era homes, and then on to the Château Frontenac landmark hotel, where there's time to explore. Finally, drive on to the Plain of Abraham, where the battle between the French and British armies eventually sealed the fate of the French colony.

Biking to Montmorency Falls ($85, 4 hr.): Peddle a mountain bike some 8 miles to Montmorency Falls, which plummet down a 272-foot cliff into the St. Lawrence River. Along the way, you'll pass the Québec Yacht Harbor and cross the St. Charles

River to Domaine Maizerets, then ride along the St. Lawrence River for views of Québec's skyline and the Island of Orleans.

On Your Own: Within Walking Distance

Spend a day strolling Québec City's hilly cobblestone streets, taking in their 17th- and 18th-century buildings, cafes, shops, and homes. Québec's Lower Town contains the restored Quartier Petit-Champlain, including pedestrian-only **rue du Petit-Champlain**, and **Place Royale**, home to the small **Notre-Dame-des-Victoires church**, the city's oldest, dating from 1688. Petit-Champlain is undeniably touristy, but not unpleasantly so, with several pleasant cafes and shops. Restored Place Royale is perhaps the most attractive of the city's many squares, upper or lower. Also in Lower Town, the impressive **Museum of Civilization,** 85 rue Dalhousie (© **866/710-8031** or 418/643-2158; www.mcq.org), is an excellent interactive museum with rotating exhibits representing historical, current, and controversial subjects. It's open Tuesday to Sunday from 10am to 5pm. Admission is $12 adults, $4 children ages 12 to 16.

The highlight of the Upper Town is the gorgeous **Fairmont Château Frontenac hotel,** rue St-Louis (© **866/540-4460** or 418/692-3861; www.fairmont.com/frontenac), a beauty set high above the St. Lawrence River. Colonial governors used to reside on the site, and in later years, the likes of Winston Churchill and Queen Elizabeth II stayed at the hotel, a turreted gem with slanted copper roofs, erected in 1883. Just walking around this amazing hotel is a treat, but do yourself a favor and linger for a drink to savor the aura. Also, 50-minute guided tours are available. Call for information (© **418/691-2166**).

Other popular attractions in the Upper Town include the outdoor **Parc-de-l'Artillerie,** 2 rue d'Auteuil (© **418/648-4205;** www.pc.gc.ca/artillerie), a fortification whose walls were erected by the French in the 17th and 18th centuries (admission $3.90), and the **Basilica of Notre-Dame,** 20 rue Buade (© **418/694-0665**), the oldest Christian parish in the Americas north of Mexico.

On a sloped hill just to the south of the Château Frontenac is the **Citadel,** 1 Côte de la Citadelle (© **418/694-2815;** www.lacitadelle.qc.ca), a partially star-shaped fortress begun by the French in the 18th century and augmented by the English well into the 19th century. Admission is $10. At the eastern edge of the Citadel, the **Terrasse Dufferin** is a pedestrian promenade that attracts crowds in all seasons for its magnificent views of the river and the land to the south, ferries gliding back and forth, and cruise ships and Great Lakes freighters putting in at the harbor below.

Shopping

Côte de la Montagne, which leads from the Upper Town to the Lower Town as an alternative to the funicular, has a few stores with more tourist-geared items and some crafts and folk art. The Lower Town itself, particularly the **Quartier Petit-Champlain,** just off Place Royale and encompassing the tiny streets of rue du Petit-Champlain, boulevard Champlain, and rue Sous-le-Fort (opposite the funicular entrance), has many shops selling clothing, souvenirs, gifts, household items, and collectibles. On the other side of the old city, a few blocks past Parliament down Grande-Allée, **avenue Cartier** has shops and restaurants of some variety, with items from clothing and ceramics to housewares and gourmet foods. The 4- to 5-block area attracts crowds of generally youngish locals, and the hubbub revs up on summer nights and weekends. The area remains outside the tourist orbit.

Dealers in **antiques** have gravitated to the cute **rue St-Paul** in the Lower Town, where they find everything from brass beds and Québec country furniture to knick-knacks, paddywhacks, and 1950s U.S. kitsch. To get there, follow rue St-Pierre from the Place Royale, and then head west on rue St-Paul.

5 Saint John, New Brunswick

New Brunswick's largest city, Saint John, sits along a sizable commercial harbor on the Bay of Fundy, at the mouth of the St. John River. Like Halifax, it was an important shipbuilding hub around the turn of the 19th century, and today its deep-water harbor can accommodate the world's largest cruise liners.

Don't expect a picture-postcard-perfect place overflowing with gardens and neat homes. Instead, Saint John is a predominantly industrial city, with large shipping terminals, oil storage facilities, and paper mills serving as the backdrop to the waterfront area. If you make an effort to look, though, you'll see that its downtown buildings boast some wonderfully elaborate Victorian flourishes, while a handful of impressive mansions lord over the side streets, their interiors a forest of intricate woodcarving—appropriate for the timber barons who built them.

The first Europeans to settle here were the French, when Samuel de Champlain led an exploration party into the Bay of Fundy and founded the first French settlement in North America in 1604. A hundred years later, the British were on the scene, capturing Saint John, which, in 1785, became Canada's first incorporated city.

COMING ASHORE   Ships dock right at the **Pugsley Cruise Terminal,** in the industrial heart of the city, just steps from downtown.

GETTING AROUND   If you haven't signed up for an organized tour, you can walk right into town or opt for a 1-hour city-highlights tour on the vintage bus-style trolleys or horse-drawn trolleys that meet the ship. **Taxis** queue up at the docks and work on set rates, depending on where you're going. If you need to call a taxi, try **Coastal Taxi (© 506/635-1144)** or **Diamond Taxi (© 506/648-8888)**. For helpful sightseeing info, visit www.tourismsaintjohn.net.

Best Cruise Line Shore Excursions

Historical Walking Tour ($35, 2 hr.): See the restored historic district known as Trinity Royal and the bustling City Market that survives from the late 1800s. A bus takes groups to the farthest destination, the Loyalist Burial Ground, where the walk starts. Gravestones there date as far back as 1784. Sights along the way include the beautiful brick town houses along Germain Street; the historic commercial buildings of Prince William Street, whose elaborate facades are decorated with gargoyles, pediments, and Ionic columns; the Market Slip, where thousands of American Colonists who remained loyal to the British Crown landed in 1783; and King's Square, designed in 1848 in the shape of the Union Jack to show loyalty to England.

Reversing Falls Rapids by Jetboat ($110, 3 hr.): Reversing Falls Rapids is a much-photographed spot where the Bay of Fundy meets the St. John River, and strong tidal conditions cause harbor currents to reverse. This large tidal swing means some 2 billion gallons of water surge into the bay twice a day—that's 2 *billion.* Near Fallsview Park, an underwater ledge 36 feet down causes a boiling series of rapids and whirlpools, and the rising tide slows the river current to a stop for about 20 minutes. The tour begins with an orientation drive through Saint John, stopping at the Old

City Market (open since 1876). You then head to Fallsview Park, don life jackets and rain gear, and board your high-speed jet boat for a ride over and around the rapids. You can take a 20-minute jet-boat ride (referred to as the Thrill Ride) independently for just $38 per person by contacting **Reversing Falls Jet Boat Rides** (© **506/ 634-8987;** www.jetboatrides.com). For the same price, you can also do a guided 1-hour boat tour of the reversing falls in a regular old boat, ideal for families with small kids or anyone who doesn't need to be "thrilled" by the fast boats (you can walk there from the pier and it's cheaper than signing up for the ship's tours!). Our coauthor Heidi did this on her last cruise and loved it.

Moosehead Beer Tasting & Saint John Highlights Tour ($60, 3 hr.): Heads up, beer lovers: This is your chance to sample Canadian beers and enjoy a famous local Irish pub, O'Leary's. Also included is a drive around the Saint John area, with time at the Old City Market, and a visit to the famous Reversing Falls.

On Your Own: Within Walking Distance

Start your visit by wandering around near the waterfront, taking note of the gargoyles and sculpted heads that adorn the brick and stone 19th-century buildings. The Saint John visitor information board publishes several **self-guided walking tours** that will give you a great overview of the city. Text and maps are available for download in the "Day Trips & Guided Tours" section of www.tourismsaintjohn.com.

Of the handful of museums in Saint John, the important one to visit is the **New Brunswick Museum,** 1 Market Sq. (© **506/643-2300;** www.nbm-mnb.ca). Established in 1842, it's the oldest continuously operating museum in Canada. Exhibits include a marine mammals gallery whose focal point is "Delilah," the full skeletal remains of a 40-foot North Atlantic right whale that beached off Grand Manan in 1992. Other displays include local and Canadian art, the best collection of Loyalist artifacts on the North American continent, and the largest collection of ships' portraiture in Canada. Don't miss a peek at the cool tidal tube in the lobby. It's connected to the harbor, and water in the tube rises and falls with the tide. The museum is open mid-May through October Monday to Saturday 9am to 5pm (Sun noon–5pm). Admission is $6 adults, $3.25 children.

If the weather is disagreeable when you arrive, you can head indoors to Saint John's elaborate network of underground and overhead pedestrian walkways, dubbed **the Inside Connection.** Passages link the city's downtown malls and shops, two major hotels, the provincial museum, the city library, the city market, a sports arena, and an aquatics center. Another indoor option is the **Old City Market,** 47 Charlotte St. (© **506/658-2820**), a spacious, bustling marketplace crammed with vendors hawking cheeses, flowers, baked goods, meat, fresh seafood, and fresh produce. The market was built in 1876, and it has been a center of commerce for the city ever since. A number of vendors offer meals to go, and there's a bright seating area in an enclosed terrace on the market's south side.

On Your Own: Beyond the Port Area

If you don't sign on to one of the ship's shore excursions, you can walk to the **Reversing Falls Rapids** via the **Harbour Passage,** an interconnected system of walking and biking trails that wind along the waterfront from Market Square to the Reversing Falls, a distance of just under 3 miles. To immerse yourself in an even more natural side of New Brunswick, book an excursion or take a taxi to **Irving Nature Park,** Sand

Cove Road (© **506/653-7367**), situated along the coast across the St. John River, less than 3 miles southwest of town. The park consists of 243 hectares (600 acres) of dramatic coastal scenery and as many as 240 species of birds have been spotted here. Soft wood-chipped trails and marsh boardwalks provide access to a lovely forest and wild, salty seascapes.

Shopping

You'll find art galleries, antiques shops, souvenir shops, and boutiques within a 10-minute walk of the cruise terminal, clustered around **Market Square, Brunswick Square, King Street,** and **Prince William Street.**

16

U.S. River Cruise Routes

In addition to sailing in Alaska, the Caribbean, New England/Canada, Central America, and Baja's Sea of Cortez, many of the small ships reviewed in chapter 8 also offer cruises on America's great rivers, visiting historic towns and sailing through countryside that can take your breath away. This is your chance to experience some real 18th- and 19th-century-era Americana on waterways from the Hudson River and Erie Canal to the Mississippi and the great rivers of the Pacific Northwest. As these rivers cover a good chunk of the continental United States, and because each ship makes different stops along the way, we've limited ourselves to giving you a sort of "virtual float" along each river, with a sampling of the highlights seen on many regional cruises.

1 The Columbia & Snake Rivers, Pacific Northwest

The Columbia and Snake River system is one of America's most important river systems, second to the Mississippi–Missouri in the size of the area it drains. The Columbia River flows 1,200 miles from the Canadian Rockies in southeast British Columbia into Washington, and then forms the border with Oregon on its way to the Pacific. The 1,000-mile Snake River starts in Yellowstone National Park and flows through Idaho into eastern Washington, where it meets the Columbia River.

The two rivers have served as the primary artery for east-west travel in the Pacific Northwest, used first by the Nez Perce Indians and later by Western explorers, fur traders, settlers, military expeditions, and missionaries. Settlers came in increasing numbers in the few years prior to the 1846 Oregon Treaty, and in 1859 Oregon became the 33rd state. Washington, once part of Oregon, was organized as a separate territory in 1853, and became the 42nd state in 1889.

Today, the Columbia–Snake corridor provides a fascinating trip into more varied landscapes than along any North American river. Beginning at the Pacific Ocean breakers, the river mouth near Astoria, Oregon, begins as a broad bay, narrows upriver to a more natural stream, and then squeezes dramatically through the deep **Columbia Gorge** (www.fs.fed.us/r6/columbia/forest). Thickly forested slopes rise to high flanking cliffs, while melting snow cascades into pencil-thin waterfalls. The river's surface is turbulent and the winds strong, but a series of dams built beginning in the Great Depression tame the flow into a series of separate pools. **Navigation locks** lift boats and barges, while parallel fish ladders provide a bypass for salmon heading upstream to spawn, as well as for the young ones heading in the other direction, toward the Pacific.

Beyond the gorge, the land becomes drier, and with the right soil and an ideal climate, **vineyards** have burgeoned in Washington and Oregon to create the second-largest wine-producing region in the U.S. after that of California. **Wildlife** is abundant, as hundreds of thousands of birds come to roost and nest, especially in the **Umatilla National Wildlife Refuge** (www.fws.gov/umatilla). By the time your ship reaches the Snake River, the land on either side shows few signs of habitation, instead rising from the waterline in layers of basalt laid down millions of years ago, forming multicolored buttes and mesas.

Portland, Oregon, a city of just over a half-million souls (with another 1.5 million in its metropolitan area), is the embarkation city for nearly all Columbia–Snake cruises, boarding from docks on the Willamette River, which fronts downtown and meets the Columbia a little over 8 miles to the north. Portland has kept its local culture better than most midsize cities, maintaining a walkable downtown, preventing major expressways from slicing through its heart, and nurturing local businesses, including the dozens of microbreweries for which it's become famous. Known as the Rose City, Portland boasts 250 parks, gardens, and greenways, and since 1907 has celebrated the annual **Portland Rose Festival** (www.rosefestival.org) for several weeks each June, with an extravagant floral parade, music, car and boat races, and visits by U.S. Navy ships.

The city's core is **Pioneer Courthouse Square** (www.pioneercourthousesquare. org), whose modern architecture still manages to convey an old-time-city-square feel. It's surrounded by stores, offices, restaurants, and hotels, and hosts some 300 concerts and other events each year. A half-mile to the northwest, in the city's Old Town neighborhood, the **Saturday Market** (www.saturdaymarket.org) is a big draw for its open-air art, handicrafts, clothing, and jewelry stalls. Nearby, the **Lan Su Chinese Garden** (www.lansugarden.org) is one of only a few classical scholars' gardens in North America, taking up a walled block in Chinatown. Stepping through the gate feels like walking into an entirely different world, with pavilions, bridges, walkways, hundreds of native Chinese plant species, and a teahouse arranged around a central reflecting pond. About 10 blocks southwest, **Powell's Books** (www.powells.com) is the world's largest independent bookstore, with new and used books shelved together in a warren of rooms spread over three floors and a whole city block. It's a true Portland treasure.

High up and to the west of downtown, Washington Park's terraced **International Rose Test Garden** (www.rosegardenstore.org) displays some 550 varieties of roses, usually at their blooming peak during June and July and again in September and October. Just up the hill, the park's 5½-acre **Japanese Garden** (www.japanesegarden. com) is one of the finest of its type outside Japan, with walking paths leading among streams, ponds, Japanese flora, and five distinct gardens representing classical Japanese styles. The views of 11,245-foot **Mount Hood** from both the Japanese and Rose gardens are spectacular on a clear day, but the mountain becomes invisible when it's overcast. Mount Hood is part of a line of regional volcano-formed mountains that also include Mount St. Helens and Seattle's Mount Rainier.

Upon leaving Portland, some cruises sail overnight downriver to where the widening Columbia meets the Pacific Ocean and call at **Astoria, Oregon,** tying up at a pier adjacent to the Columbia Bar lightship *Columbia* and Coast Guard cutter *Steadfast,* both of which are open for visitors. (Other cruises visit Astoria on the return trip.) The **Columbia River Maritime Museum** (www.crmm.org) is part of the pier complex, exhibiting the history of Columbia River trade in ship models, drawings, and photographs. Don't miss the 20-minute walk up Coxcomb Hill to the 125-foot **Astoria Column,** which dominates the landscape from its 600-foot elevation. Erected in 1926 to mark the location of the first permanent American settlement west of the Rockies, it was designed by New York architect Electus D. Litchfield after Trajan's Column in Rome. Italian artist Attilio Pusterla created a bas-relief mural that scrolls around the column to depict the history of the town. The views here are extraordinary, both from the top of the column and from the property around it.

From Astoria, organized excursions head downriver to **Fort Clatsop** (www.nps. gov/lewi/planyourvisit/fortclatsop.htm), where Lewis and Clark spent 4 wet winter months in 1805 and 1806. A historically accurate re-creation of their fort is on-site. Another stop, the popular seaside resort of **Cannon Beach,** has a spectacular beach with impressive rock formations, plus a shopping district full of weathered-cedar buildings housing craft-type boutiques.

Also on the downriver side of Portland, **Longview, Washington,** gives access to **Mount St. Helens** (www.fs.fed.us/gpnf/mshnvm), the site of the May 18, 1980, volcanic eruption that in minutes reduced the mountain's height by about 1,000 feet. The drive uphill winds through increasingly scarred hillsides covered in lava, ash, mud, and 150 square miles of destroyed forest to an interpretive center overlooking the cloud-enshrouded mountaintop and deep into a valley wasteland.

Many cruises skip the downriver jaunt from Portland and head east after reaching the Columbia River. **Bonneville Dam** (www.nwp.usace.army.mil/op/b), dedicated by President Franklin Delano Roosevelt in 1937, signaled the first major WPA undertaking by the U.S. Army Corps of Engineers to create a safe passage through the Cascade Rapids. The dam created 48-mile-long Lake Bonneville, and its hydroelectric plants generate enough power to light 40,000 homes. The visitor center screens a slide film showing the dam under construction and describing how the salmon fish ladders work. From the dam's visitor center, buses take folks to **Multnomah Falls,** the highest falls in Oregon and the second-tallest year-round waterfall in the U.S., its waters dropping 620 feet from mountain to basin.

Upriver, the **Columbia Gorge Discovery Center** (www.gorgediscovery.org) exhibits the area's history and geology, revealing how the Columbia Gorge was formed by violent volcanic upheavals and raging floods, as well as the building of the Columbia River Scenic Highway. An exhibit illustrates how Lewis and Clark equipped their expedition.

At the **Dalles Lock & Dam,** an excursion crosses the river to the **Maryhill Museum of Art** (www.maryhillmuseum.org), set high above the river in Washington. A Midwestern Quaker pacifist named Samuel Hill, son-in-law of James J. Hill of the Great Northern Railroad, established the museum in the late 1920s. It now exhibits Russian Orthodox icons, Rodin sculptures, a collection of 250 chess sets, Queen Marie of Romania's royal regalia, miniature fashion costumes on stage sets, and Native American clothing, baskets, and weapons. Just 4 miles east of the museum, just off Washington Scenic Route 14, is a full-scale **replica of Stonehenge** built by Sam Hill as a monument to Klickitat County soldiers who lost their lives in World War I.

Stops in **Pendleton, Oregon,** may include a visit to the grounds of the annual September **Pendleton Round-Up** (www.pendletonroundup.com) for a presentation of rodeo riding, country music, flintlock rifle firing, and other activities. In town, **Pendleton Underground** (www.pendletonundergroundtours.org) is an odd tour centered around a huge warren of tunnels dug by Chinese laborers in the 19th century. The Chinese lived and ran businesses here entirely underground, while some areas of the complex were used as bars, opium dens, and, later, Prohibition-era speakeasies. Elsewhere in town, the **Tamástslikt Cultural Institute** (www.tamastslikt.com) presents a variety of Native American traditions, including dancing, drumming, and storytelling. Exhibits include horse regalia, war bonnets, bows, and demonstrations of saddle making. Nearby, the **Fort Walla Walla Museum** (www.fortwallawallamuseum.org) exhibits a collection of carefully restored and re-created historic buildings that include a schoolhouse, doctor's office, railroad station, and houses arranged in a closed compound. Other buildings house farm equipment and a fire engine once drawn by a 33-mule team.

Finally, after passing through four **Snake River locks and dams,** your ship reaches the end of deep-water navigation at the border towns of **Lewiston, Idaho,** and Clarkston, Washington, 465 miles upriver from the Pacific Ocean. From here, an all-day **jet boat ride** heads into **Hells Canyon, Idaho** (www.hellscanyonvisitor.com), a National Recreation Area. The Snake River starts out sluggish, but soon becomes a fast-flowing stream of twisting rapids with 20-mph currents. The high bluffs and mountains on either side increase in height, creating a canyon 7,900 feet deep—1,900 feet deeper than the Grand Canyon. Passengers are likely to see bighorn sheep standing still on rocky ledges, mule deer down by the water, eagles and osprey overhead, and Nez Perce Indian petroglyphs depicting bighorn sheep inscribed on the flat rock surfaces.

LINES SAILING THESE ROUTES   **Cruise West** (p. 328), **Lindblad Expeditions** (p. 340), **American Safari Cruises** (p. 326), and **American Cruise Lines** (p. 319) offer cruises here in the spring and/or fall.

2 The Hudson River, Erie Canal & Great Lakes

Inland cruises in the U.S. Northeast sail waterways such as the Hudson River, the Erie Canal, the St. Lawrence Seaway, and the Great Lakes, mixing and matching among these waterways to create itineraries of 1 week to 12 days. Most ships sail from New York City, Chicago, and Providence or Warren, Rhode Island. The description below imagines a trip from New York.

Up the Hudson

The navigable portion of the **Hudson River** (www.hudsonriver.com) extends through New York for about 150 miles, from Manhattan to Albany and Troy. The river is considered to be an estuary, as tidal effects reach the base of the canal locks above Albany, and saltwater content extends about 60 miles northward from Manhattan and even farther during long periods of dry weather. On a cruise, one gets superb water-level views of the Hudson Valley, the towering New Jersey Palisades, the rugged Hudson Highlands, sprawling country estates, and the mighty fortress at West Point.

Leaving from **Manhattan**'s west side, ships skirt the majestic skyline and pass under the two-level George Washington Bridge. Rising on the New Jersey side is **Palisades Interstate Park** (www.njpalisades.org), an especially beautiful scene during fall foliage season. Fishermen will be out in force on weekends, as it's once again safe to eat the catch (though everyday consumption is not recommended). After passing Yonkers, the Hudson widens into the Tappan Zee, passing under the **Tappan Zee Bridge,** which carries the New York State Thruway north to Albany and west to Buffalo.

Looking carefully, one may glimpse **Washington Irving's house** in the Hudson Valley town of Sunnyside; Tarrytown's Victorian Gothic **Lyndhurst Castle,** owned by the National Trust for Historic Preservation; and **Philipsburg Manor,** a 17th-century Dutch farming complex in the town of Sleepy Hollow. From the decks, you get a long-range view north to the Hudson Highlands, and at Ossining, the stone walls of

Sing Sing Prison parallel the river. Information on all these attractions can be found at **www.hudsonvalley.org**.

As your ship approaches Bear Mountain State Park on the left and the Bear Mountain Bridge, a flag rises above the trees marking the rustic **Bear Mountain Inn** (www.visitbearmountain.com), built in 1915. The river becomes noticeably narrower, and the channel under the Bear Mountain suspension bridge deepens dramatically to over 300 feet as the surrounding land rises steeply.

On the cliff tops opposite, the grounds of the United States Military Academy at **West Point** (www.usma.edu) begin, marked first by officers' houses, then the Hotel Thayer, and finally the gray-stone fortress-style buildings. At the base of the cliff, a launch docked near West Shore Line station brings cadets and officers across the Hudson to Garrison station for trains to New York. The colorful cluster of wooden Victorian buildings across the street from the Garrison depot served as the setting for Dolly's return to Yonkers in the film *Hello, Dolly!* Most cruises stop at West Point for tours of the academy and historic Hudson Valley homes.

Rising beside the river are the grassy grounds and yellow Federal-style buildings of **Boscobel** (www.boscobel.org), a museum of early American furniture and decorative arts. Nearby, the 18th- and 19th-century river town of **Cold Spring** is full of restaurants (including the historic **Hudson House Inn,** open since 1832; www.hudson houseinn.com), antiques shops, and collectibles stores. If you come back on your own, it also makes a good base for hiking the Hudson Highlands.

North of Cold Spring is **Bannerman's Island** (www.bannermancastle.org), on which you'll find a mock 19th-century Scottish-style castle and estate built as a munitions warehouse and country retreat. They were destroyed in a huge fire in 1974, leaving behind the stabilized ruins one sees today.

At **Poughkeepsie,** nearby sites include **Franklin Roosevelt's Hyde Park house** (www.nps.gov/hofr/hofrhome.html), with Eleanor's cottage a short distance away; and the **Culinary Institute of America** (www.ciachef.edu), one of the leading U.S. cooking schools.

The Hudson passes numerous **lighthouses** and small river towns en route to Albany, the New York state capital, dominated by Nelson Rockefeller's 98-acre, Internationalist-style **Empire State Plaza,** with its glass-and-marble office towers; reflecting pools; and huge, egg-shaped arts and conference center known as the Egg (www.theegg.org). Not all cruises come this far, and those that do (the Blount Small Ship Adventures ships) simply pass by to begin their trek through the Erie Canal.

Into the Erie Canal

The Erie Canal's highlights are the **Waterford Flight** of five locks (which lift ships a total of 150 ft.), old factory towns such as Amsterdam and Little Falls, and the 22-mile Oneida Lake crossing. From Syracuse to Buffalo, ships pass through **Montezuma National Wildlife Refuge** (www.fws.gov/r5mnwr) for possible sightings of bald eagles and Canada geese, past restored canal towns such as Fairport and Pittsford, and through the original canal's small locks and stone-arched aqueducts. Turning into the Oswego Canal, the vast expanse of **Lake Ontario** is ahead, and soon one is threading among the beautiful **Thousand Islands** (www.thousandislands.com). Ships typically stop at Clayton's **Antique Boat Museum** (www.abm.org) and **Upper Canada Village** (www.uppercanadavillage.com), whose houses, churches, and public and farm buildings span 100 years of Canadian architecture and small-town life. Small ships share the **St. Lawrence Seaway** with huge lake carriers and pass through locks to Montréal for a stop and a landing at Bay of Eternity in the dramatic **Saguenay fjord.** From here, ships often return upriver to debark at **Québec City** (see chapter 15).

The Great Lakes

Until the mid-1960s, the **Great Lakes** were popular summer cruising grounds for Canadian- and U.S.-flagged ships, some of which dated from before World War I. When these ships went out of service, the industry died until American Canadian Caribbean Line (now known as Blount Small Ship Adventures) started offering cruises here again in the late 1990s. It's a great idea, but the lakes are large bodies of water, and small, shallow-draft coastal cruisers like these can get bounced around during summer storms. A charter operation called the **Great Lakes Cruise Company** (www.greatlakescruising.com) offers some cruises on larger vessels such as the 100-passenger *Clelia II,* a sister-ship to Cruise West's *Spirit of Oceanus.*

Great Lakes itineraries are varied and may begin in any number of ports, such as Toronto, Windsor/Detroit, or Chicago. The following ports-of-call sampling will give you some idea of what there is to be seen.

Cruises originating at Toronto will pass from Lake Ontario through the **Welland Canal** locks to Lake Erie, and an excursion will run to **Niagara Falls** (www.tourism niagara.com), including a wet boat trip on the *Maid of the Mist* to the base of the falls.

As you pass into Lake Huron, you'll see **Tobermory** (www.tobermory.org), a fishing port settled by Scots in the early–19th century and the center for a resort region in the beautiful island-studded Georgian Bay. Michigan's **Mackinac Island** (www.mackinacisland.org) is entirely car-free and a popular summer resort. Its centerpiece, the venerable **Grand Hotel** (www.grandhotel.com), is one of the great hotels of North America, built in the 1890s and still maintaining its high standards. **Sault Ste. Marie,** strategically placed between Lake Huron and Lake Superior, is the site of the **Soo Locks,** through which some ships pass if they sail into Lake Superior. The scenic **Algoma Central rail excursion** (www.agawacanyontourtrain.com) from the Soo Locks into the North Country's Agawa Canyon is highly recommended.

Large cities featured on all cruises in this region include **Detroit** for the incredible **Henry Ford Museum and Greenfield Village** (www.thehenryford.org); **Milwaukee** for its German heritage and art museum; and **Chicago** for its outstanding architecture, lakefront skyline, museums, neighborhoods, and the Chicago River.

LINES SAILING THESE ROUTES   American Cruise Lines (p. 319) and **Cruise West** (p. 328) offer Hudson River cruises that sail round-trip from New York City. **Blount Small Ship Adventures** (p. 327) uses the Hudson to reach the Erie Canal for the passage across New York State to the Great Lakes and St. Lawrence Valley. **Blount** and **Cruise West** also offer Great Lakes cruises from Chicago. The **Great Lakes Cruise Company** (www.greatlakescruising.com) arranges cruises on the lakes. **St. Lawrence Cruise Lines** (p. 378) cruises the St. Lawrence and the Thousand Islands region between Kingston and Québec City, Montréal, and Ottawa.

3 The Mississippi River System

The **Mississippi River system** (www.nps.gov/miss) consists of some 50 rivers and tributaries, seven of which—the Atchafalaya, Arkansas, Ohio, Tennessee, Cumberland, Missouri, and Illinois—are navigable for considerable distances. Known as the Western Rivers because they formed part of the original American West, their drainage basin covers an area of 1,245,000 square miles (a full 41% of the contiguous

48 states) and includes all or parts of 31 states and two Canadian provinces. The Lower Mississippi is defined as the 954 miles between the mouth of the river just in from the Gulf of Mexico and the junction with the Ohio River. **New Orleans** (see chapter 9) has historically been the principal embarkation port and terminus for most Lower Mississippi River cruises, though cruises also depart from Memphis and Nashville, and several niche operators berth at other, smaller cities.

Mississippi River cruising was basically on hold for 2009 and 2010 following the 2008 collapse of Majestic America Line, which had basically bought up every river cruise operation in America, said "We're king of the world!" and then went bankrupt, taking middle-America river cruising with it. At press time, we learned that small-ship operators Cruise West and Blount Small Ship Adventures (formerly ACCL) were planning to scoop up some underserved business by positioning one ship apiece on the river for 2011, a development that cheered us substantially. The river is also served by a few very small river-ship companies (see box, p. 673), most of which offer day cruises only, though the *Spirit of Peoria* and riverboat *Twilight* do multiday cruises with passengers sleeping in riverside hotels at night.

The Lower Mississippi

Sailing from New Orleans, the heavily commercial Mississippi gives way to rural, mostly flat southern Louisiana. The river, however, remains a remarkable commercial artery used by the world's most impressive tow ships. As many as 30 to 40 barges loaded with grain, salt, lime, coal, rocks, petroleum products, and other materials may be strapped together to form a solid flotilla that can equal the carrying capacity of 1,800 to 2,400 tractor trailers. All along the route, you'll see the kind of levees Hurricane Katrina made infamous, built to prevent high water from flooding the adjoining farmlands and towns—if they work. Some levees are high enough to block the view inland except from the highest decks, through in other places the long-range vistas remain.

It's the **Antebellum South** (or the present-day interpretation of it) that lower river cruisers come to see. The rural plantation homes and the stately mansions clustered in towns and cities exhibit rich examples of American architecture, some rebuilt after the Civil War, others that have undergone considerable restoration after periods of neglect.

Laura Plantation, Louisiana (www.lauraplantation.com), was originally French-owned, but during its most significant period, it was owned by a Creole family. The main house, built around 1805, has a raised brick basement story with the upper floors executed in Federal style. Six slave quarters and a collection of outbuildings show the development of the sugar-cane industry that lasted into the 20th century.

Oak Alley, Louisiana (www.oakalleyplantation.com), built in 1837–39, features a quintessential double line of live oaks, which stretches from the river landing to the main Greek Revival–style house. The 1840 white-pillared Greek Revival **Houmas House** (www.houmashouse.com) lies at the end of a double line of equally old oak trees, and was once the largest slave-holding plantation in the South.

Baton Rouge, Louisiana, offers the nation's tallest state capitol building, a 34-story Art Deco masterpiece constructed on the orders of legendary governor Huey P. Long. Nearby, the most enlightening experience takes place at the Louisiana State University's **Rural Life Museum** (http://rurallife.lsu.edu). It's arranged so that you'll feel as if you've stepped out the back door of the "Big House" to see how the rest of the working antebellum plantation is going about its daily life.

Niche Operators on the Mighty Mississip

In addition to the new overnight cruises being offered by Cruise West and Blount Small Ship Adventures, a few small, niche operations also offer day cruises, evening cruises, and even a few pseudo-overnight cruises, in which accommodations at a shoreside hotel are sandwiched between days on the river. Here's a rundown of a few of the better ones. Due to their brevity, day cruises typically cost between $15 and $30. Overnights range from about $100 to $300.

- *Spirit of Peoria* (www.spiritofpeoria.com): The traditional-style boat was built in Paducah, Kentucky, in 1988 by Walker Boat Yard, and is solely propelled by its large stern paddle wheel. She offers day, overnight, and 2-, and 4-night cruises, with overnight accommodations at shoreside lodges. She sails from Illinois and Missouri.
- **Riverboat** *Twilight* (www.riverboattwilight.com): Built in Jennings, Louisiana, and launched in 1987, this diesel-driven paddle-wheeler offers an overnight riverboat cruise from Le Claire to Dubuque, Iowa, with evening accommodations ashore.
- *Belle of Louisville* (www.belleoflouisville.org): Built in 1914 in Pittsburgh, the *Belle of Louisville* is a National Historic Landmark vessel that operates day sightseeing and dinner cruises along the Ohio River, from downtown Louisville, Kentucky.
- *Natchez* (www.steamboatnatchez.com): The steamboat *Natchez* is another traditional classic, also operating under old-fashioned steam power. She offers day cruises from New Orleans, boarding at the foot of Toulouse Street in the French Quarter.
- *Creole Queen* (www.creolequeen.com): Also sailing day cruises from New Orleans, *Creole Queen* is a traditional-style paddle-wheeler powered by very untraditional diesel engines. She was built in 1983 in Moss Point, Mississippi.

St. Francisville, Louisiana, boasts 140 structures listed on the National Register of Historic Places, including the Georgian Revival courthouse, Romanesque Revival Bank of Commerce & Trust, and French colonial, antebellum, neoclassical, gingerbread Victorian, and "dog trot" houses. The latter get their name from their design, with a long open corridor through which a dog could trot, if he had a mind to.

Natchez, Mississippi, has 200 historic homes among more than 500 antebellum structures, and about three dozen are open to the public. Your ship will probably offer a tour. In **Vicksburg,** Mississippi, the **National Military Park** (www.nps.gov/vick) is the principal destination. An organized tour details the story of the Civil War city, which suffered through a 42-day siege by Union troops. Its surrender to Ulysses S. Grant on July 4, 1863, coupled with the fall of Port Hudson, Louisiana, divided the South and gave the North control of the Mississippi.

Memphis, Tennessee, a city that bills itself as Home of the Blues and Birthplace of Rock 'n' Roll, is usually an embarkation or debarkation port for river cruises. Small ships dock at Mud Island River Park, a recreation and museum center, and a Main Street trolley gives access to the Beale Street Entertainment District and the **National Civil Rights Museum** (www.civilrightsmuseum.org) where Martin Luther King, Jr., was shot on April 4, 1968. Outside the city, **Graceland** (www.elvis.com), Elvis Presley's jazzed up Georgian-style home, draws the largest crowds north of New Orleans.

The Upper Mississippi

Some river aficionados consider cruises between St. Louis and St. Paul to be the most interesting because of the combination of flanking high bluffs, pleasant farmlands, locking operations, and the intriguing small Victorian-era towns that the ships visit. In fall, the foliage in Wisconsin rivals that of New England.

The upper Midwest's first inhabitants were the Native Sioux and Algonquin peoples, then came the French fur trappers and traders, prospectors to tap the rich lead deposits, entrepreneurs to invest in lumbering, and pioneering Anglo farmers to clear the land for agriculture. Ensuing manufacturing, trade, and transportation in the stretch between St. Paul and St. Louis created numerous river towns and cities of considerable if relatively short-lived importance, such as Cape Girardeau, Missouri; Burlington, Fort Madison, and Dubuque, Iowa; Galena, Illinois; LaCrosse, Wisconsin; and Winona, Wabasha, and Red Wing, Minnesota.

The Upper Mississippi officially begins at Mile 0, Cairo Point, Illinois (where the Ohio River converges), and ends 839 miles to the north at Minneapolis/St. Paul, Minnesota. Locking through is an interesting procedure, and on a 7-day Upper Mississippi cruise you'll be doing this an average of four times a day. Some locks are set up as tourist attractions, with observation towers and parks alongside. It's like a scene out of a history book, with passengers lining the ship's rails exchanging pleasantries with people on shore while the boat sinks or rises in the chamber.

St. Louis, Missouri, historically "The Gateway to the West," is a major embarking and debarking port and worth a night or two before or after the cruise. Eero Saarinen's 630-foot **Gateway Arch** (www.nps.gov/jeff), completed in 1965, has given the city a much-needed icon as well as a monument of considerable beauty, especially when the stainless steel skin reflects the sun. The **Museum of Westward Expansion,** located below the arch, provides an overview of the Lewis and Clark Expedition. The Romanesque train shed at the venerable **St. Louis Union Station** (www.stlouis unionstation.com), about a dozen blocks west of the arch, is now a vast shopping and restaurant mall.

Hannibal, Missouri, opens the world of Mark Twain with a complex of museums and the cave that Tom Sawyer and Becky Thatcher explored.

St. Paul, Minnesota, is the beginning or end of an Upper Mississippi cruise. The city retains a compact center where most of the great civic architecture is located, such as the Beaux Arts–style Minnesota State Capitol Building (1905); the riverfront **Minnesota Museum of American Art** (www.mmaa.org); and the top city attraction, the **James J. Hill House** (www.mnhs.org/places/sites/jjhh), an elaborate Romanesque mansion built in 1891 for the Great Northern Railway baron.

The Ohio River

Some river aficionados consider the scenic **Ohio** (www.ohioriverfdn.org) to be the most interesting Midwestern waterway because of its variety: its high bluffs, attractive agricultural landscapes, the way it twists below Pittsburgh, its small rivers towns and rust belt cities with their active and abandoned industries, its wide variety of graceful bridges, the occasional cross-river ferries, and the impressive arrivals and departures at Pittsburgh and Cincinnati. Most cruises do not cover the entire Ohio River in one go, but include substantial portions such as the stretches between Cincinnati and Pittsburgh, or Cincinnati and Louisville to St. Louis or Memphis. Trips that travel the Cumberland and Tennessee rivers also include short stretches of the Lower Ohio en route to or from Memphis or St. Louis.

Most towns where boats call put out a warm welcome, showing visitors how the river affected their roles in the development of Midwestern culture, manufacturing, and transportation.

The Ohio River, Mile 0, begins at the western Pennsylvanian junction of the Monongahela and Allegheny rivers at **Fort Point,** the very tip of the pie that forms downtown Pittsburgh. From here, it's 982 twisting river miles to Cairo Point, where the Ohio joins the Mississippi (see above), en route forming the borders of West Virginia, Ohio, Kentucky, Indiana, and Illinois.

The Ohio provides more water than the Upper Mississippi and itself is fed by the two Pittsburgh rivers, and by others such as the Kanawha, Big Sandy, Licking, Kentucky, Green, Wabash, Cumberland, and Tennessee. Eighteen locks and dams provide safe navigation, some replacing others that are now submerged in a constant effort to improve river commerce.

Architecturally rich downtown **Pittsburgh** is known as the Golden Triangle. It's clean and clear, with a compact center that's easy to navigate on foot. There's plenty to do if you're staying over before or after your cruise, including a visit to **Station Square** (www.stationsquare.com), the former Pittsburgh and Lake Erie Station and now a restaurant and shop complex; a ride on the scenic **Monongahela or Duquesne Inclines,** the last two of the 19 funicular railways that once connected the town with the residential hills; a visit to the **Carnegie Museum of Art** and the **Carnegie Museum of Natural History;** or a stop at the **Andy Warhol Museum,** just across the 7th Street Bridge from downtown (www.carnegiemuseums.org for all three). The **Frick Art and Historical Center** (www.frickart.org), former home of industrialist Henry Clay Frick, is about 20 minutes east of downtown.

Leaving Pittsburgh, the 172 miles to Marietta, Ohio, are among the loveliest rural stretches of river in the country. High banks define the stream, and where the woods part, farming fields spill right down to the water. **Marietta** is a quintessential Victorian riverfront community that still exudes its historical importance, and boats dock here adjacent to a lovely city park. The **Ohio River Museum** (www.ohiohistory.org/places/ohriver), minutes on foot from the landing, displays steamboat history in models, photographs, an excellent film, and the *W. P. Snyder, Jr.,* the last of the steam-powered stern-wheel towboats.

Maysville, Kentucky, derived its importance from firing bricks and manufacturing wrought-iron fences, gates, and ornamental street furnishings such as clocks, lampposts, benches, and signs. The town's prosperity is revealed in a 24-block, 160-building historic district that is on the National Register of Historic Places, featuring brick streets and Romanesque, Georgian, and Victorian styles, all walkable from the steamboat landing.

The graceful 1931 suspension bridge spanning the river near **Ripley,** Ohio, was the prototype for San Francisco's Golden Gate Bridge. Once an important stop on the Underground Railroad, Ripley also served as the setting for Eliza's escape in Harriet Beecher Stowe's *Uncle Tom's Cabin.*

Arriving at **Cincinnati,** Ohio, boats dock at the Public Landing opposite the Great American Ballpark and just upriver from the **Roebling Suspension Bridge,** once the world's longest suspension bridge and the 1868 prototype for Roebling's masterpiece, New York's Brooklyn Bridge. Just up from the landing, the downtown area is anchored by Fountain Square and the 1931 Art Deco **Carew Tower,** which has a great view from the 48th floor. **Mt. Adams,** a short taxi ride up one of Cincinnati's seven hills, combines a trendy residential neighborhood, restaurants, a wonderful Ohio River overlook, and leafy Eden Park, where the **Cincinnati Art Museum** is located (www.cincinnatiartmuseum.org).

You'll likely hit several towns and cities below Cincinnati. **Madison,** Indiana, is a repository of 19th-century residential architecture. **Louisville,** Kentucky (www. gotolouisville.com), is the home of the **Louisville Slugger Museum** (www.slugger museum.org) and the 1914 steamboat *Belle of Louisville* (see "Niche Cruise Operators on the Mighty Mississip," p. 673), the city's icon and the oldest river steamer in the U.S. An excursion will take you out to Bluegrass Country and **Churchill Downs** (www.churchilldowns.com), home of the annual Kentucky Derby. **Henderson,** Kentucky (www.hendersonky.org), boasts the WPA-constructed **John James Audubon Museum** (http://parks.ky.gov/findparks/recparks/au/), dedicated to the wildlife of the area and housing the largest collection of Audubon memorabilia, including original drawings, paintings, and watercolors, and a complete collection of his publications. Finally, **Paducah,** Kentucky, located at the junction of the Tennessee and Ohio rivers, is a barge and tow repair center and home to the **Museum of the American Quilters' Society** (www.quiltmuseum.org), a nonprofit organization dedicated to the art, history, and heritage of hand-sewn and machine-made quilts.

Casting off from Paducah, your boat has just 47 miles to go to the meeting of the waters of the Ohio and Mississippi at Cairo Point. Depending on the itinerary, you'll make a hard right for an upriver sail to St. Louis or go gently left downriver to Memphis.

LINES SAILING THESE ROUTES   **Cruise West** (p. 328) is the major player here, along with **Blount Small Ship Adventures** (p. 327). There are also a few niche operators (p. 673) offering quirky options.

Index